MW00784779

Handicapping by Example

Also by William L. Quirin

Thoroughbred Handicapping
Winning at the Races

Handicapping by Example

William L. Quirin, Ph.D.

WILLIAM MORROW AND COMPANY, INC.
New York

Copyright © 1986 by Quirin Research Corp—William L. Quirin

The author is grateful for permission to reprint from the following:

Grateful acknowledgment is given for permission to reproduce the numerous past performance tables and race results charts copyright © 1984 and 1985 by *Daily Racing Form*, Inc. Reprinted with permission of the copyright owner.

Excerpts from articles copyright © 1984 and 1985 by *The Thoroughbred Record*. Reprinted with permission of the copyright owner.

From "Horses to Watch" column by Mark Berner copyright © 1986 by Newsday, Inc. Reprinted by permission. A copy of Mark Berner's selections for the ninth race at Aqueduct as they appeared in *Newsday* on February 7, 1985, copyright © 1985 by Newsday, Inc. Reprinted by permission.

All rights reserved. No part of this book may be reproduced or utilized in any form or by any means, electronic or mechanical, including photocopying, recording or by any information storage and retrieval system, without permission in writing from the Publisher. Inquiries should be addressed to Permissions Department, William Morrow and Company, Inc., 105 Madison Ave., New York, N.Y. 10016.

Library of Congress Cataloging-in-Publication Data

Quirin, William L.
Handicapping by example.

1. Horse race betting. I. Title.
SF331.Q559 1986 798.4'01 86-12428
ISBN 0-688-05929-5

Printed in the United States of America

2 3 4 5 6 7 8 9 10

BOOK DESIGN BY BERNARD SCHLEIFER

To my children,
Kristin, Daniel, and James Patrick

Contents

PART II: THE SURFACE UNDERFOOT

PART III: THE HORSE ITSELF

PART IV:
ADVANCED TOPICS IN SPEED HANDICAPPING

Introduction

My second book, *Thoroughbred Handicapping—State of the Art,* looked at the art of handicapping and discussed the modern theories of the pastime. It followed *Winning at the Races: Computer Discoveries in Thoroughbred Handicapping,* which presented the statistical proof of much of that theory and helped usher in the scientific-computer era of handicapping. This book was written to complete the trilogy, to complement its predecessors by demonstrating how the theory is applied. There is no better way to learn handicapping than by observing the logic others apply to a variety of situations.

This book consists of a collection of forty-one chapters, each of which is designed to make a specific point or discuss a special situation. Typically, each does so by analyzing one or two example races. We have attempted to organize each chapter according to the major theme of each, although there is very little continuity from one chapter to the next. However, we have chosen our example races very carefully, demanding that each contribute more than its main point. The reader will find several handicapping hints in each chapter.

Almost half of the chapters in the book focus on special situations to which standard handicapping principles do not fully or directly apply. Most books on handicapping have little, if anything, to say about such topics as maiden races, first-time starters, two-year-olds, state-bred races, starter handicaps, restricted and classified allowance races, races at seven furlongs, or over soft grass, races taken off the grass, races in the slop, European form, to mention just a few. We hope that this book fills that void.

The reader may complain that a large number of our example races happen to be stake races, and that this may present a distorted view of handicapping principles in general. We were aware of this potential pitfall and have tried to avoid it. We feel that for the most part, the analyses we have applied to stakes races work equally as well with ordinary allowance and claiming races. We also feel that making examples of horses the reader might know will help drive the point home and firmly implant it in his or her memory.

We have not selected our example races solely on the basis of having played the winner, although many did add to our coffers. Obviously it is far easier to remember the winners, and the logic that produced them, when looking for examples to include in a book. However, we found several of our examples after the fact, some by searching through stacks of old *Racing Forms* looking for races that demonstrated a specific point. In a few cases, which have been duly noted, the logic behind our selection failed to produce a winner, yet the race nevertheless provided the necessary instructional value to warrant its use.

We had originally intended to subtitle this book *A Handicapper's Thesaurus,* a thesaurus being a dictionary-like book that lists synonyms for a volume of words. So, too, many aspects of a horse's recent past performances can be interpreted in more than one way, and in this variety lies the fascination and challenge of handicapping. Throughout this book we have attempted to point out dual interpretations whenever possible, thereby encouraging the reader to do the same in his or her own handicapping. An inquisitive mind is a handicapper's most valued possession.

No book on handicapping can be written in isolation, nor can it represent solely its author's original thoughts on the subject. In this respect I would like to thank the following people for the contributions they might have made, either directly or indirectly: My right-hand man, Anton Hemm. Longtime friends Phil Zipse, Glenn Magnell, Gary Tobey, Tom Pappas, and Mike Romagnola. My colleagues Jim Quinn, Scott McMannis, Ron Cox, Paul Mellos, Steve Roman, and Marv Small. My friends at *Newsday,* John Pricci, Mark Berner, Paul Moran and Ed McNamara. Two gentlemen, Tom Ainslie and Howard Rowe, for their roles in laying the groundwork the rest of us have built upon. Greg Wohlleber, for his assistance with the grass-sire statistics. And finally, a moment of thought in memory of Johnny Hemm, Anton's father, whose presence is missed.

Handicapping by Example

Chapter 1

Woody Has an Alydar

THE *Daily Racing Form* is much more than a collection of statistics describing the recent performances of the day's entrants. It is a daily newspaper that is meant to be read from cover to cover. Instead, many use its pages to secure their seats in the grandstand. Others cast their *Form* to the winds as they leave the track rather than take it home for further study, thereby losing all chance of gaining some insight into the success or failure of their day's selections.

In addition to the past performances, the *Form* contains daily columns and reports from its correspondents at various tracks—stories about recent and upcoming stakes events across the country, weekly reports from the major European racing centers, workout tabs, and reports from the leading sales auctions. A thorough reading of its pages often provides the serious player with useful information about stakes performers on other circuits or in other countries—horses that may someday race on his or her local circuit—about horses working well in the morning, horses that have been injured or are recovering from injury, or horses that recently have changed hands. The *Form*'s result charts supplement the player's personal impressions of what may have transpired during the running of the day's races.

The *Daily Racing Form* is not the only source of supplemental information available to those willing to look for it. Two excellent weekly magazines, *The Thoroughbred Record* and *The Bloodhorse*, offer their readers reports from the country's major racing centers as well as many features of particular interest to breeders. Correspondents to these magazines work side by side with their peers from the *Racing Form* and local newspapers.

The following was part of Steven Crist's (*The New York Times*) report to *The Thoroughbred Record* concerning the happenings on Jockey Club Gold Cup day at Belmont on October 20, 1984:

> "Stephens, who snapped a month without a winner in New York with Herat's triumph, popped out what is rumored to be his second-best two-year-old October 21. Stephan's Odyssey, yet another Danzig, overcame trouble to win his debut in 1:12 flat on a dead track. Stephens is still taking his time with an attractive Alydar colt who may be his Derby horse."

The 1984 season seemed a subpar one for two-year-old colts. Even the crop's eventual champion, Chief's Crown, had a difficult time convincing skeptics that he measured up to previous years' champions. Consequently, any word from the talent-laden Stephens barn was worth noting. The venerable conditioner had saddled Conquistador Cielo, Caveat, and Swale to capture the 1982, 1983, and 1984 Belmont Stakes, and reporters were curious as to who was regarded their most likely successor among Stephens's well-bred juveniles.

Early in the summer Herat was touted as the heir apparent. But the son of Northern Dancer proved to be lacking in heart, if not talent, and Stephens watchers looked elsewhere. A couple of weeks after Crist's article appeared, Stephan's Odyssey ran a disappointing fourth in his first allowance test. If the 1985 Belmont winner was in Stephens's barn, perhaps it was that Alydar colt. But as Crist had reported, Stephens was taking his time. It was not until Thanksgiving Day that a son of Alydar, trained by Stephens, appeared in the entries.

Favored at 8–5 in a relatively weak field despite a modest workout line, Midway Circle gave his Hall Of Fame conditioner little to be thankful for, fading to fifth in the stretch, beaten almost five lengths (in good time) by Medieval Market, who had been victimized by the sensational Bold Smoocher in his debut. Perhaps there would be no Belmont winner in 1985!

The plot thickened ten days later when a second Alydar colt from the Stephens barn appeared in the entries.

And surprisingly, despite a sharper workout line, Take Control attracted less support at the pari-mutuel windows than did his stablemate. Allowed to start at almost 7–1, he easily handled the 6–5 favorite, Buckner, but succumbed to the impressive late rush of the heavily bet first-starter Proud Truth.

Although we have skirted the issue thus far, and will discuss it

6 AQUEDUCT 6 FURLONGS

6 FURLONGS. (1.08⅘) MAIDEN SPECIAL WEIGHT. Purse $20,000. 2-year-olds. Weights, 118 lbs.

Coupled—How About Now and Mount Guard; Prince Valdez and Favorite Holme.

Medieval Market — Dk. b. or br. c. 2, by Medieval Man—Hawaiian Love Star, by Hawaii
Br.—Crescent S Farms (Fla)
Own.—Live Oak Plantation — Tr.—Kelly Patrick J — 113 5
Lifetime 1 0 0 1 $2,400 — 1984 1 M 0 1 $2,400
11Nov84- 4Aqu fst 6f :22 :45⅘ 1:10⅘ Md Sp Wt 5 1 1hd 22 28 313¾ Ward W A5 113 12.20 74-25 BoldSmoocher11813Buckner118¾MedievalMarket113nk Weakened 13
LATEST WORKOUTS Nov 18 Bel tr.t 5f fst 1:03⅕ b — Nov 8 Bel tr.t 5f fst 1:01⅗ h — ●Nov 3 Bel tr.t 5f fst 1:00 h — Oct 22 Bel 5f fst 1:05⅖ b

Action Eddie — Dk. b. or br. c. 2, by Baldski—Queens Wig, by Bald Eagle
Br.—Cashman E C (Fla)
Own.—Sabarese T M — Tr.—Parisella John — 118
Lifetime 2 0 1 0 $4,180 — 1984 2 M 1 0 $4,180 — Turf 2 0 1 0 $4,180
20Oct84- 1Bel fm 1 1/16 (T):47⅘ 1:11⅘ 1:43⅘ To Market 7 1 11½ 52½ 612 614¾ Bailey J D 115 3.60 69-12 Danger's Hour 1151 Quintile 1153¾ For Certain Doc 1171¼ Tired 7
20Oct84-Run in divisions
5Oct84- 4Bel fm 1 1/16 (T):48⅘ 1:13 1:45⅘ Md Sp Wt 1 4 41½ 31½ 33½ 22½ Skinner K 118 *1.10 72-21 Quintile 1182½ Action Eddie 118nc Abundant 1187¾ Bore in, out 8
LATEST WORKOUTS Nov 10 Bel tr.t 4f fst :48 h — Nov 3 Bel 5f fst 1:02⅗ b — Oct 14 Bel tr.t 6f fst 1:14⅗ h — Oct 3 Bel tr.t 5f fst 1:02 h

Testimonial — Ch. c. 2, by Broadway Forli—Satirical Review, by Reviewer
Br.—Harbor View Farm (Ky)
Own.—Harbor View Farm — Tr.—Martin Frank — 118
Lifetime 6 0 2 1 $10,080 — 1984 6 M 2 1 $10,080
5Nov84- 6Aqu my 1 :46⅘ 1:12⅘ 1:39⅘ Md Sp Wt. 10 2 2hd 1hd 45 69¾ Cruguet J b 118 *.90e 60-25 Numeric 118hd Recognized 1182¾ Cool Joe 1184 Tired 11
15Oct84- 5Bel fst 7f :23⅘ :47⅘ 1:26⅘ Md Sp Wt 6 2 42 45 24 25 Cruguet J 118 *1.70 65-27 He's Home Free 1185 Testimonial 1183 I'mAKnockout1182¼ Wide 8
2Sep84- 4Bel fst 7f :22⅘ :46⅕ 1:24⅘ Md Sp Wt 10 3 32½ 21½ 33 55¼ Maple E 118 6.60 73-17 (DH)SentorBrdy1181(DH)Hberdsher1181¾EsternScrt118no Weakened 14
25Aug84- 6Sar fst 6f :22⅕ :45⅗ 1:10⅗ Md Sp Wt 5 6 69 69 48½ 37¾ Cordero A Jr 118 5.00 79-18 Herat 1187¼ Another Reef 118½ Testimonial 118¾ Wide 11
8Aug84- 4Sar fst 7f :22⅘ :46⅗ 1:25 Md Sp Wt 6 3 74½ 44½ 58 610¾ Cordero A Jr 118 *1.00 66-16 RhomnRule1183½CoyoteDncer1183½FbulousMove1181¼ Weakened 13
20Jly84- 6Bel fst 5f :22⅘ :46⅘ :59⅘ Md Sp Wt 8 8 56 36½ 35 22¾ Cordero A Jr 118 6.30 86-18 FullofSpice1182¾Testimonil1182½ConfirmedPtriot1181¾ Off poorly 8
LATEST WORKOUTS ●Nov 18 Bel tr.t 4f fst :48⅘ b — Nov 12 Bel tr.t 3f my :37⅘ b (d) — Oct 31 Bel tr.t 5f fst 1:01 h — Oct 25 Bel tr.t 4f gd :47⅘ h

How About Now — Ch. c. 2, by For The Moment—Naskranaut, by Naskra
Br.—Johnson & Whitney (NY)
Own.—Cobble View St — Tr.—Johnson Philip G — 118
Lifetime 1 0 0 0 — 1984 1 M 0 0
11Nov84- 2Aqu fst 6f :22⅘ :46⅘ 1:13⅘ Md Sp Wt 6 9 1011 1013 1012 1013¼ Samyn J L 118 15.10 61-25 Romancer 1182 (D)Easton 1181¼ Uene 113nk Bore out st. 11
11Nov84-Placed ninth through disqualification
LATEST WORKOUTS Nov 19 Bel tr.t 4f fst :49⅘ b — Nov 10 Bel tr.t 3f fst :36 h — Nov 7 Bel tr.t 6f fst 1:15⅕ b — Nov 2 Bel tr.t 5f fst 1:02 b

Bold Renegade — B. c. 2, by Majestic Light—Deep Dish Pie, by George Lewis
Br.—Jones W L& Farish (Ky)
Own.—Singer C — Tr.—Tesher Howard M — 118
Lifetime 0 0 0 0 — 1984 0 M 0 0
LATEST WORKOUTS Nov 19 Aqu 5f fst 1:02⅘ b — Nov 14 Aqu 5f fst 1:03 b — Nov 8 Aqu 6f fst 1:16⅘ b — Nov 4 Aqu 4f fst :48⅗ h

Need the Cash — B. c. 2, by Mickey McGuire—Legal Loan, by Correlation
Br.—Southwind Farm (Miss)
Own.—Ordway P — Tr.—Casse Mark — 118
Lifetime 1 0 0 1 $1,100 — 1984 1 M 0 1 $1,100
18Oct84- 3Kee fst 6f :22 :44⅘ 1:10⅘ Md Sp Wt 5 4 21½ 21½ 22 33¾ Melancon L 120 38.20 85-19 Spectacular Rumor 1203¼ TwinkleTwinkle120nkNeedtheCash1201 9
LATEST WORKOUTS Nov 19 Bel 5f fst 1:01⅘ hg — Nov 7 Bel 5f fst 1:01⅕ h

Midway Circle — Ch. c. 2, by Alydar—Friendly Circle, by Round Table
Br.—Nuckols Breeder (Ky)
Own.—Jayeff Stable — Tr.—Stephens Woodford C — 118
Lifetime 0 0 0 0 — 1984 0 M 0 0
LATEST WORKOUTS Nov 21 Bel 3f fst :36⅘ b — ●Nov 17 Bel 6f fst 1:15 h — Nov 14 Bel 4f fst :48⅖ hg — Nov 10 Bel 7f fst 1:28⅘ b

Taylor Road — Dk. b. or br. c. 2, by Proudest Roman—Berkshire Lass, by Greton
Br.—Ridgewood Farm (Ky)
Own.—Dennehy S — Tr.—Ludwig Jack D — 118
Lifetime 0 0 0 0 — 1984 0 M 0 0
LATEST WORKOUTS Nov 15 Bel 6f fst 1:15⅘ hg — Nov 9 Bel tr.t 6f fst 1:16 b — Nov 3 Bel tr.t 4f fst :50 b — ●Oct 28 Bel tr.t 4f gd :49 h

Dual Honor — Dk. b. or br. c. 2, by Seattle Slew—L'Extravagante, by Le Fabuleux
Br.—Allen Joseph & Jones Jr (Ky)
Own.—Tayhill Stable — Tr.—Zito Nicholas P — 113 5
Lifetime 0 0 0 0 — 1984 0 M 0 0
LATEST WORKOUTS Nov 18 Bel 4f fst :48⅕ hg — Nov 14 Bel 5f fst 1:01⅗ h — Nov 9 Bel 4f fst :48⅗ h — Oct 31 Bel 4f fst :51 b

Prince Valdez — Ch. c. 2, by Valdez—Grigia, by Grey Dawn II
Br.—Free W F (NY)
Own.—Free W F — Tr.—Hernandez Ramon M — 118
Lifetime 0 0 0 0 — 1984 0 M 0 0
LATEST WORKOUTS Nov 18 Bel tr.t 4f fst :52 b — Nov 10 Bel 3f fst :36⅘ hg — Nov 3 Bel 3f fst :37 hg — Oct 18 Bel 3f fst :37 hg

The Ol One Two — Ch. c. 2, by An Act—Comical Pasttime, by Funny Fellow
Br.—Sedlacek Sue (NY)
Own.—Sedlacek W — Tr.—Sedlacek Woodrow — 118
Lifetime 2 0 0 1 $2,640 — 1984 2 M 0 1 $2,640
12Nov84- 6Aqu gd 1 :47 1:13⅘ 1:40⅘ (S)Md Sp Wt 3 8 93½ 74½ 87 78½ Gomez E R 118 3.10e 54-25 Classi Valentine 118½ To Catch AKing1183¼Mr.G.J.G.1182¼ Outrun 14
26Oct84- 6Aqu sly 7f :22⅘ :46⅘ 1:25⅘ (S)Md Sp Wt 8 3 65 54 44 32½ Gomez E R 118 23.70 70-22 OnwrdFrmpton118¾RomoVlntin1181½ThOlOnTwo1183 Raced wide 11
LATEST WORKOUTS Nov 7 Aqu 4f fst :48⅕ h — Oct 14 Aqu 5f fst 1:01⅗ h — Oct 7 Aqu 5f fst 1:02⅕ h — Oct 1 Aqu 4f fst :50⅕ b

Brink — Ch. c. 2, by Cox's Ridge—Brilliant Gold, by Your Alibhai
Br.—Roach B & T (Ky)
Own.—Peace J H — Tr.—Nieminski Richard — 118
Lifetime 0 0 0 0 — 1984 0 M 0 0
LATEST WORKOUTS Nov 16 Bel tr.t 4f fst :48⅕ h — Nov 15 Bel 4f fst :49⅗ b — ●Nov 8 Bel 5f fst 1:00⅗ hg — Oct 31 Bel tr.t 4f fst :49⅗ b

Truth Be Told — B. c. 2, by In Reality—Amalie, by Bold and Brave
Br.—Carrion Jaime S (Fla)
Own.—Firestone B R — Tr.—Watters Sidney Jr — 118
Lifetime 1 0 0 0 — 1984 1 M 0 0
11Nov84- 4Aqu fst 6f :22 :45⅘ 1:10⅘ Md Sp Wt 8 5 3nk 46 412 615½ Davis R G 118 9.60 72-25 Bold Smoocher 11813 Buckner 118¾ Medieval Market 113nk Tired 13
LATEST WORKOUTS Nov 20 Bel 4f fst :50 b — Nov 9 Bel 4f fst :48⅖ hg — Nov 6 Bel 5f sly 1:03 b — Oct 31 Bel 4f fst :48 h

Mount Guard — B. c. 2, by Naskra—Dangerous Gunner, by Ack Ack
Br.—Johnson Karen & Kathy (Ky)
Own.—Johnson Kathy M — Tr.—Johnson Philip G — 118
Lifetime 0 0 0 0 — 1984 0 M 0 0
LATEST WORKOUTS Nov 18 Bel tr.t 6f fst 1:16 b — Nov 13 Bel tr.t 6f fst 1:16 b — Nov 8 Bel 4f fst :48⅕ hg — Nov 1 Bel tr.t 6f fst 1:17⅘ b

Also Eligible (Not in Post Position Order):

Weight In Gold — Ch. c. 2, by Alydar—Great Verdict, by Le Fabuleux
Br.—Hexter Mr-Mrs P L (Ky)
Own.—Hexter Mrs P L — Tr.—Freeman Willard C — 118
Lifetime 2 0 0 0 — 1984 2 M 0 0
11Nov84- 4Aqu fst 6f :22 :45⅘ 1:10⅘ Md Sp Wt 1 2 61½ 713 816 717½ Migliore R 118 13.20 70-25 Bold Smoocher11813Buckner118¾MedievalMarket113nk No factor 13
21Oct84- 6Bel fst 6f :22⅘ :46⅘ 1:12 Md Sp Wt 10 11 31½ 54 813 914½ Bailey J D 118 16.40 68-21 Stphn'sOdyssy1181½RollingMnstrl1185¾DmscusSm1182 Off slowly 11
LATEST WORKOUTS Nov 20 Bel 4f fst :49⅕ h — Nov 8 Bel 4f fst :48 hg — Oct 31 Bel 6f fst 1:17⅕ b — Oct 20 Bel 3f fst :38 hg

Cool Joe — B. c. 2, by Cold Reception—Abbey R, by Dancing Count
Br.—Moscarelli V (Md)
Own.—Moscarelli Susan — Tr.—Jerkens H Allen — 118
Lifetime 1 0 0 1 $2,280 — 1984 1 M 0 1 $2,280
5Nov84- 6Aqu my 1 :46⅘ 1:12⅘ 1:39⅘ Md Sp Wt 11 3 3nk 2hd 31 32¾ Bailey J D 118 9.50 67-25 Numeric 118hd Recognized 1182¾ Cool Joe 1184 Weakened 11
LATEST WORKOUTS Nov 17 Bel 4f fst :48 h — Nov 13 Bel 4f fst :49⅕ b — Nov 4 Bel 4f fst :51 hg — Oct 31 Bel tr.t 5f fst 1:03⅘ b

King's Joy — Ch. c. 2, by Screen King—Sharis Joy, by Escardru
Br.—Weinsier R (Ky)
Own.—Weinsier R — Tr.—Barrera Luis — 113 5
Lifetime 1 0 0 0 — 1984 1 M 0 0
11Nov84- 4Aqu fst 6f :22 :45⅘ 1:10⅘ Md Sp Wt 10 7 75½ 69 513 514¾ Thibeau R J 118 29.20 73-25 Bold Smoocher11813Buckner118¾MedievalMarket113nk No factor 13
LATEST WORKOUTS Nov 18 Bel tr.t 4f fst :49⅘ b — Nov 9 Bel tr.t 4f fst :49 b — ●Nov 4 Bel tr.t 5f fst 1:01⅘ h — Oct 22 Bel tr.t 4f fst :48 h

SIXTH RACE **6 FURLONGS. (1.08⅕) MAIDEN SPECIAL WEIGHT. Purse $20,000. 2-year-olds. Weights, 118 lbs.**

Aqueduct

NOVEMBER 22, 1984

Value of race $20,000; value to winner $12,000; second $4,400; third $2,400; fourth $1,200. Mutuel pool $122,385, OTB pool $97,218. Exacta Pool $230,906. OTB Exacta Pool $147,140.

Last Raced	Horse	Eqt.A.Wt	PP	St	¼	½	Str	Fin	Jockey	Odds $1
11Nov84 ^{4}Aqu^{3}	Medieval Market	2 113	1	3	$1^{1\frac{1}{2}}$	$1^{1\frac{1}{2}}$	1^{3}	$1^{2\frac{1}{2}}$	Ward W A^{5}	6.40
11Nov84 ^{4}Aqu^{7}	Weight In Gold	2 118	14	1	5^{2}	5^{2}	4^{1}	$2^{\frac{1}{2}}$	McCarron G	42.40
11Nov84 ^{4}Aqu^{6}	Truth Be Told	2 118	12	2	2^{hd}	3^{1}	$3^{\frac{1}{2}}$	$3^{1\frac{1}{4}}$	Davis R G	22.10
	Brink	2 118	11	12	8^{hd}	8^{1}	6^{3}	$4^{\frac{1}{2}}$	Cruguet J	16.30
	Midway Circle	2 118	7	6	$4^{1\frac{1}{2}}$	2^{2}	2^{hd}	5^{nk}	Maple E	1.60
5Nov84 ^{6}Aqu^{6}	Testimonial	b 2 118	3	8	6^{1}	6^{3}	$5^{\frac{1}{2}}$	$6^{6\frac{3}{4}}$	Velasquez J	5.60
20Oct84 ^{1}Bel^{6}	Action Eddie	2 118	2	10	7^{2}	7^{2}	7^{1}	7^{nk}	Skinner K	9.30
11Nov84 ^{2}Aqu^{9}	How About Now	2 118	4	14	11^{1}	11^{3}	9^{hd}	8no	Cordero A Jr	a-27.80
	Taylor Road	2 118	8	9	12^{2}	12^{4}	10^{hd}	$9^{\frac{1}{2}}$	Lovato F Jr	45.50
	Mount Guard	2 118	13	5	$9^{\frac{1}{2}}$	$9^{\frac{1}{2}}$	8^{1}	$10^{2\frac{1}{4}}$	Samyn J L	a-27.80
12Nov84 ^{6}Aqu^{7}	The Ol One Two	2 118	10	7	10^{hd}	10^{5}	11^{4}	$11^{6\frac{1}{2}}$	Gomez E R	f-25.70
18Oct84 ^{3}Kee^{3}	Need the Cash	2 118	6	4	$3^{\frac{1}{2}}$	4^{1}	12^{5}	$12^{3\frac{1}{2}}$	Migliore R	3.90
	Prince Valdez	2 118	9	11	13^{2}	14	14	13no	Miranda J	f-25.70
	Bold Renegade	2 118	5	13	14	13^{2}	13^{1}	14	Hernandez R	31.80

a-Coupled: How About Now and Mount Guard.
f—Mutuel field.

OFF AT 1:28 Start good, Won driving. Time, :22⅘, :46⅗, 1:12⅘ Track fast.

$2 Mutuel Prices:

2-(A)-MEDIEVAL MARKET	14.80	8.80	5.20
11-(O)-WEIGHT IN GOLD		30.80	21.60
10-(M)-TRUTH BE TOLD			11.00

$2 EXACTA 2-11 PAID $457.60.

Dk. b. or br. c, by Medieval Man—Hawaiian Love Star, by Hawaii. Trainer Kelly Patrick J. Bred by Crescent S Farms (Fla).

MEDIEVAL MARKET controlling pace under clever rating, maintained safe margin to the end, fully extended. WEIGHT IN GOLD, racing well removed from rail entire way had needed response outfinishing TRUTH BE TOLD. The latter, well up throughout, maintained daylight over other BRINK raced wide. MIDWAY CIRCLE flattened out. TESTIMONIAL finishing without wip, never threatened. ACTION EDDIE lacked response. HOW ABOUT NOW began slowly. TAYLOR ROAD and MOUNT GUARD were outrun. THE OL ONE TWO showed little. NEED THE CASH was finished early. PRINCE VALDEZ showed nothing.

more thoroughly in another chapter, the question must be raised: Were either of these colts worth betting in their first start? Indeed, when is a first-starter worth betting? The answer is deceptively simple: The horse must be attracting enough support at the betting windows to suggest stable confidence, yet nevertheless remain a value bet.

Four factors contribute to my estimation of when a well-bet first-starter represents value. Most significant is the trainer and how well he does with first-starters. Then there is the horse's inexperience, which can easily cost it the race. Third, there is the number of opponents who seem likely to run solid races, including heavily bet first-time starters from leading barns. Finally, there is the ever-present possibility that a seemingly hapless rival may have matured overnight and is now ready to run a dramatically improved race. I tend to add one point for the inexperience factor (except with certain trainers) and one point for the surprise factor to the number of solid opponents identified, arriving at an odds figure below which I will not bet a first-time starter. Obviously not many favorites qualify.

6 AQUEDUCT 6 FURLONGS AQUEDUCT START FINISH

6 FURLONGS. (1.08⅕) MAIDEN SPECIAL WEIGHT. Purse $20,000. 2-year-olds. Weight, 118 lbs.

Coupled—Proud Truth and Helmsman.

Mamluk B. c. 2, by Le Fabuleux—Sunny Dame, by Damascus
Br.—Live Oak Stud (Fla)
Own.—Live Oak Plantation Tr.—Kelly Patrick J 118 Lifetime 0 0 0 0 1984 0 M 0 0
LATEST WORKOUTS Nov 29 Bel 3f my :38⅘ b Nov 21 Bel 4f fst :48⅕ hg

Truth Be Told B. c. 2, by In Reality—Amalie, by Bold and Brave
Br.—Carrion Jaime S (Fla)
Own.—Firestone B R Tr.—Watters Sidney Jr 118 Lifetime 2 0 0 1 $2,400 1984 2 M 0 1 $2,400
22Nov84- 6Aqu fst 6f :22⅘ :46⅗ 1:12⅘ Md Sp Wt 12 2 21½ 33½ 33 33 Davis R G 118 22.10 74-29 MedievlMrket1132½WeightInGold118½TruthBTold1181½ Weakened 14
11Nov84- 4Aqu fst 6f :22 :45⅘ 1:10⅘ Md Sp Wt 8 5 3nk 46 412 615½ Davis R G 118 9.60 72-25 Bold Smoocher 11813 Buckner 118¾ Medieval Market 113nk Tired 13
LATEST WORKOUTS Nov 30 Bel 4f fst :52 b Nov 20 Bel 4f fst :50 b Nov 9 Bel 4f fst :48⅘ hg Nov 6 Bel 5f sly 1:03 b

Proud Truth Ch. c. 2, by Graustark—Wake Robin, by Summer Tan
Br.—Galbreath Mrs J W (NY)
Own.—Darby Dan Farm Tr.—Veitch John M 118 Lifetime 0 0 0 0 1984 0 M 0 0
LATEST WORKOUTS Nov 27 Bel 5f fst 1:03⅘ b Nov 24 Bel 4f fst :52⅘ b Nov 18 Bel 6f fst 1:14⅘ h Nov 14 Bel 5f fst 1:01⅘ hg

Turn'n Together B. c. 2, by Apalachee—Lightning Smoke, by Lightning Orphan
Br.—Cooper R M Jr (Ky)
Own.—Mar-Rich Stable Tr.—Kronovich Joseph A 118 Lifetime 0 0 0 0 1984 0 M 0 0
LATEST WORKOUTS ●Nov 26 Bel 3f fst :36 hg Nov 23 Bel 5f fst 1:03⅘ b Nov 17 Bel 4f fst :49⅕ h Nov 13 Bel 4f fst :51 b

Strike Up B. c. 2, by Tilt Up—Devon Lane, by Bold Favorite
Br.—Shaw J B (Ky)
Own.—Cobble View Stable Tr.—Johnson Philip G 118 Lifetime 4 0 2 0 $9,000 1984 4 M 2 0 $9,000
23Nov84- 5Med fst 6f :22⅘ :46⅘ 1:14⅕ Md Sp Wt 1 3 1½ 21 35 68¾ Samyn J L 118 *.60 62-26 Centennial Lane 1183 Slady's Ruller 118no HasWritten1184½ Tired 8
12Oct84- 7Bel fst 6f :22⅘ :46⅕ 1:12⅘ Md Sp Wt 6 3 2hd 2½ 1hd 55¼ Alvarado R Jr 118 *.80 75-22 BroadwayTommy1184ConsulGeneral118½[D]Tahuhh118nk Bothered 11
12Oct84-Placed fourth through disqualification
24Aug84- 4Sar my 5f :22⅕ :45⅘ :57⅘ Md Sp Wt 6 1 11 11 1hd 21¼ Venezia M 118 *.80e 99-09 Boutinierre 1181¼ Strike Up 1185½ Medieval Love 1182 Gamely 11
15Aug84- 4Sar fst 5f :22 :45⅘ :58⅘ Md Sp Wt 8 1 1½ 1hd 1hd 2½ Venezia M 118 *1.60 96-14 Twin Rocket 118½ Strike Up 1188 Nordance 1181½ Gamely 10
LATEST WORKOUTS ●Nov 21 Bel tr.t 3f fst :35 h Nov 16 Bel tr.t 5f fst 1:01⅘ h ●Nov 7 Bel tr.t 4f fst :47⅘ h ●Nov 2 Bel tr.t 3f fst :35 h

Buckner B. c. 2, by Riva Ridge—Chinook, by Bold Ruler
Br.—Beltz Gail P & Hancock (Ky)
Own.—Petters L J Tr.—Kelly Thomas J 118 Lifetime 2 0 2 0 $8,360 1984 2 M 2 0 $8,360
11Nov84- 4Aqu fst 6f :22 :45⅘ 1:10⅘ Md Sp Wt 13 6 5½ 34 39½ 213 Bailey J D 118 *.70 75-25 Bold Smoocher 11813 Buckner 118¾ MedievalMarket113nk Rallied 13
31Oct84- 4Aqu fst 6f :22⅘ :46⅕ 1:11 Md Sp Wt 6 11 96½ 53 21½ 21½ Maple S 118 15.50 84-19 Solgne 1181½ Buckner 1183¾ See The Way 1181½ Poor start 11
LATEST WORKOUTS Nov 30 Bel 4f fst :51 b Nov 26 Bel tr.t 5f fst 1:05 b Nov 20 Bel tr.t 4f fst :51 b ●Nov 8 Bel 3f fst :36 h

Helmsman Ch. c. 2, by Roberto—Candalita, by Olympia
Br.—Galbreath J W (Ky)
Own.—Darby Dan Farm Tr.—Veitch John M 118 Lifetime 0 0 0 0 1984 0 M 0 0
LATEST WORKOUTS Nov 30 Bel 4f fst :49⅘ b Nov 23 Bel 4f fst :52 b Nov 18 Bel 6f fst 1:16 b Nov 14 Bel 5f fst 1:03 hg

Take Control Dk. b. or br. c. 2, by Alydar—Let's Be Gay, by Bagdad
Br.—Nuckols Bros (Ky)
Own.—Reineman R L Tr.—Stephens Woodford C 118 Lifetime 0 0 0 0 1984 0 M 0 0
LATEST WORKOUTS Nov 23 Bel 4f fst :49⅘ b ●Nov 19 Bel 4f fst :47⅘ h ●Nov 15 Bel 6f fst 1:15⅘ h ●Nov 11 Bel 4f fst :47⅘ hg

To Catch A King Ro. c. 2, by Al Hattab—What A Lucky Lady, by What Luck
Br.—Dryman & Leonard (NY)
Own.—Warfield C I Tr.—DiMauro Stephen L 118 Lifetime 3 0 1 1 $8,210 1984 3 M 1 1 $8,210
12Nov84- 6Aqu gd 1 :47 1:13⅘ 1:40⅘ [S]Md Sp Wt 8 5 83½ 64 41 2½ Cordero A Jr 118 6.20 62-25 Classi Valentine 118½ToCatchAKing1183½Mr.G.J.G.1182½ Game try 14
18Oct84- 4Bel fst 1 :46⅘ 1:12⅕ 1:39⅘ [S]Md Sp Wt 9 2 2½ 2hd 2½ 33 Cordero A Jr 118 5.40 63-24 RoyalBoch1181½RomeoVlentine1181½ToCtchAKing1185 Weakened 12
7Oct84- 4Bel fst 6f :22⅘ :47 1:12⅘ [S]Md Sp Wt 7 6 54 55 59½ 816½ Cordero A Jr 118 15.60 63-25 Huddle Up 1185½ Ruler Champ 118nk Red Attack 1189¾ Very wide 13
LATEST WORKOUTS Nov 28 Bel tr.t 4f fst :50⅘ b Nov 23 Bel tr.t 5f fst 1:03⅘ b Nov 9 Bel 5f fst 1:01⅘ hg Nov 4 Bel 5f fst 1:03 b

Wednesday Golf B. c. 2, by Honest Pleasure—Dr Mary Lou, by Dr Fager
Br.—Tartan Farms (Fla)
Own.—Tartan Stable Tr.—Nerud Jan H 113^5 Lifetime 3 0 0 0 1984 3 M 0 0
13Sep84- 4Bel fst 6f :22⅘ :46⅕ 1:12 Md Sp Wt 14 9 1013 1418 1418 1315½ Espinosa R E7 111 62.60 67-21 Script Ohio 118¾ Cullendale 1181½ Mighty Courageous1181½ Wide 14
25Aug84- 6Sar fst 6f :22⅕ :45⅘ 1:10⅘ Md Sp Wt 11 7 915 1024 924 926½ Miranda J 118 49.00 61-18 Herat 1187½ Another Reef 118½ Testimonial 118¾ Outrun 11
30Jly84- 4Bel fst 5½f :22⅘ :46 1:04⅘ Md Sp Wt 9 9 1029 1030 1033 1034½ Venezia M 118 22.50 57-19 Tiffany Ice 1187¾ Varick 1182½ Coyote Dancer 118nk Bore out st. 10
LATEST WORKOUTS Nov 27 Bel tr.t 4f fst :54 b Nov 21 Bel tr.t 4f fst :53 b Nov 14 Bel tr.t 4f fst :53 b Nov 9 Bel tr.t 4f fst :50⅘ b

Careless Bid B. c. 2, by Tanthem—Careless Moment, by Baffle
Br.—Hughes C Jr (Ky)
Own.—Four Fifths Stable Tr.—Dunham Bob G 118 Lifetime 2 0 0 0 1984 2 M 0 0
15Nov84- 4Aqu fst 7f :22⅘ :46⅕ 1:24⅘ Md Sp Wt 12 2 31 84 1223 1331 Venezia M 118 41.70 47-29 Recognized 1187½ Rolling Minstrel 1181½ Slewmobile 113½ Tired 13
2Nov84- 9Aqu fst 6f :23⅘ :48⅘ 1:14⅕ Md Sp Wt 6 10 117¾ 1221 1223 1233¾ Venezia M 118 7.50 36-35 Paths Of Glory 118¾ Yes Sirree 118¾ Verification 118¾ Far back 12
LATEST WORKOUTS Nov 29 Aqu 4f sly :51 b (d) ●Nov 24 Aqu 4f fst :48⅘ h ●Nov 9 Aqu 5f fst 1:01⅘ hg Oct 30 Aqu 5f gd 1:03⅘ b (d)

In the Midway Circle race, for example, three horses looked dangerous: Medieval Market and Truth Be Told, both coming out of the Bold Smoocher race, and the well-backed Kentucky shipper Need The Cash, mandating odds of at least 5–1 on most first-time starters, although perhaps just 4–1 on a Stephens horse. The obvious play among the three experienced colts was Medieval Market, who had been the only horse to challenge Bold Smoocher on November 11, yet nevertheless was able to maintain his place position until deep stretch.

The Take Control race proved more interesting, due in large part to the public's going overboard on Buckner. Yes, the horse had run second twice, the last time behind Bold Smoocher. And true, he had beaten the subsequent winner, Medieval Market, on that occasion.

SIXTH RACE **6 FURLONGS. (1.08⅕) MAIDEN SPECIAL WEIGHT. Purse $20,000. 2-year-olds. Weight, 118 lbs.**

Aqueduct

DECEMBER 2, 1984

Value of race $20,000; value to winner $12,000; second $4,400; third $2,400; fourth $1,200. Mutuel pool $134,226, OTB pool $95,348. Exacta Pool $253,084. OTB Exacta Pool $169,915.

Last Raced	Horse	Eqt.A.Wt	PP	St	¼	½	Str	Fin	Jockey	Odds $1
	Proud Truth	2 118	2	7	8^{hd}	7^{4}	3^{2}	$1^{2\frac{3}{4}}$	Velasquez J	a-2.10
	Take Control	2 118	7	1	4^{1}	$3^{\frac{1}{2}}$	1^{1}	$2^{1\frac{1}{2}}$	McCarron G	6.90
11Nov84 ^{4}Aqu^{2}	Buckner	b 2 118	5	3	2^{hd}	1^{hd}	2^{hd}	3^{3}	Bailey J D	1.30
	Turn'n Together	2 118	3	6	$5^{\frac{1}{2}}$	5^{1}	6^{5}	4^{1}	Samyn J L	43.30
22Nov84 ^{6}Aqu^{3}	Truth Be Told	2 118	1	5	3^{hd}	4^{4}	4^{1}	5^{3}	Davis R G	6.70
23Nov84 ^{5}Med^{6}	Strike Up	2 118	4	4	$1^{\frac{1}{2}}$	2^{hd}	5^{2}	6^{5}	Alvarado R Jr	12.30
	Helmsman	2 118	6	10	7^{hd}	8^{2}	7^{2}	7^{1}	Maple E	a-2.10
15Nov84 ^{4}Aqu^{13}	Careless Bid	2 118	10	2	6^{2}	6^{1}	8^{4}	8^{2}	Venezia M	44.70
13Sep84 ^{4}Bel^{13}	Wednesday Golf	2 113	9	9	10	9^{2}	9	9	Ward W A^{5}	49.40
12Nov84 ^{6}Aqu^{2}	To Catch A King	2 118	8	8	9^{hd}	10	—	—	Antley C W	14.20

To Catch A King, Lost rider.
a-Coupled: Proud Truth and Helmsman.

OFF AT 2:58. Start good, Won handily. Time, :22⅘, :47, 1:12⅖ Track fast.

$2 Mutuel Prices:				
	1-(C)-PROUD TRUTH (a-entry)	6.20	4.20	2.60
	7-(H)-TAKE CONTROL		8.00	3.00
	6-(F)-BUCKNER			2.20
	$2 EXACTA 1-7 PAID $43.40.			

Ch. c, by Graustark—Wake Robin, by Summer Tan. Trainer Veitch John M. Bred by Galbreath Mrs J W (NY).

PROUD TRUTH, unable to keep up during opening stages, angled out at top of the stretch and unleashing powerful burst of speed when tapped left handed, ran by leaders en-route to a handy victory. TAKE CONTROL, disposing of early contenders assuming clear lead during drive, was no match when winner loomed while safely holding others at bay. BUCKNER used vying for command gave way. TURN'N TOGETHER had no excuse. TRUTH BE TOLD flattened out. STRIKE UP faded. HELMSMAN raced greenly. CARELESS BID raced wide. WEDNESDAY GOLF showed little. TO CATCH A KING'S rider bailed out in upper stretch when his mount suffered apparent heart attack.

The fact remained, however, that five horses had finished within two and a half lengths of one another in that race. Buckner looked the part of a solid contender, yet by no means the only contender, and certainly was not worth a wager at 6–5.

If Take Control was the Alydar colt Crist wrote about, then indeed he was worth a wager at 6–1. But if he was that Alydar, why wasn't he supported with the same enthusiasm that greeted Midway Circle on his first appearance at the races? In fact, in the presence of both Buckner and Take Control, the betting action on Proud Truth was truly impressive, especially in light of the absence of sharp workouts. Obviously somebody knew that Proud Truth was not the ordinary maiden. Was he the one to bet? Were his odds also too low? Perhaps the value bet in this race would have been an exacta box of the two first-starters, leaving out the underlaid favorite. The Proud Truth-Take Control exacta did, in fact, return a juicy $43.40!

A major point of this chapter concerns follow-up play on the two Alydar colts. One of the first fruits of my handicapping research was the realization that well-bet horses that lose their debut, while displaying some signs of ability, are good bets in their second and possibly even third starts. The results of this study were documented in *Winning at the Races*. The bottom line was that based on the large number of cases studied, approximately 30 percent of these horses return winners, producing a return on investment of approximately 36 percent.

Before either Alydar colt returned to the races, there were two significant developments. First, Proud Truth was an impressive winner of a seven-furlong allowance event at Calder, despite breaking from the dreaded one-post and wheeling at the start of the race. If Proud Truth was a legitimate Classics prospect, as he appeared to be, could Take Control be far behind?

Second, an article by Crist that appeared in the December 26 issue of *The Thoroughbred Record* identified Midway Circle as Stephens's top prospect:

> "He [Stephans] still thinks he may have a better young prospect (than Stephan's Odyssey, who had just won the Hollywood Futurity) in Midway Circle, an Alydar colt out of the Round Table mare Friendly Circle, who disappointed in his lone start at Aqueduct on Thanksgiving Day."

Both Alydar colts appeared to be logical candidates for improvement in their second starts, making them routine selections in maiden races, as I tend to play them, and system plays, according to the methodology just discussed.

This chapter does not have the typical ending expected in books about handicapping. The two Alydar colts went to Gulfstream Park with the rest of the Stephens entourage and proved to be real money burners rather than world beaters, as updates of their past performances show.

Midway Circle — Ch. c. 3, by Alydar—Friendly Circle, by Round Table
Own.—Jayeff Stable — Br.—Nuckols Breeder (Ky) — Tr.—Stephens Woodford C — 122
Lifetime 3 0 0 1 $1,430 — 1985 2 M 0 1 $1,430 — 1984 1 M 0 0

26Jan85- 3GP fst 6f :21⅘ :45⅘ 1:11⅘ Md Sp Wt 7 6 5^{8} 5^{9} 5^{11} $6^{15\frac{1}{2}}$ Maple E 122 2.30 66-19 Geiger Counter $122^{4\frac{1}{2}}$ Our Colors $122^{5\frac{1}{2}}$ Beveled 122^{1} Outrun 12
8Jan85- 3GP fst 6f :22 :45⅗ 1:10⅕ Md Sp Wt 3 7 5^{5} 5^{5} $3^{4\frac{1}{2}}$ 3^{8} Maple E 122 *1.40 80-16 Flyer Escape 122^{7} Benny Q 122^{1}MidwayCircle122^{nk} Checked str 11
22Nov84- 6Aqu fst 6f :22⅘ :46⅗ 1:12⅘ Md Sp Wt 7 6 4^{2} $2^{1\frac{1}{2}}$ 2^{3} $5^{4\frac{3}{4}}$ Maple E 118 *1.60 72-29 Medieval Market $113^{2\frac{1}{2}}$WeightInGold$118^{\frac{1}{2}}$TruthBeTold$118^{1\frac{1}{2}}$ Tired 14
LATEST WORKOUTS Feb 28 Hia 4f fst :49⅘ b — Feb 23 Hia 5f fst 1:01⅘ b — Feb 19 Hia 3f fst :38 b — Feb 6 Hia 4f fst :48 h

Take Control — Dk. b. or br. c. 3, by Alydar—Let's Be Gay, by Bagdad
Own.—R L Reineman Stables Inc — Br.—Nuckols Bros (Ky) — Tr.—Stephens Woodford C — 122
Lifetime 4 0 2 1 $8,360 — 1985 3 M 1 1 $3,960 — 1984 1 M 1 0 $4,400

11Feb85- 7GP fst $1\frac{1}{16}$:47⅘ 1:13⅕ 1:47 Md Sp Wt 3 4 3^{3} 3^{2} $5^{9\frac{1}{2}}$ 6^{17} Brumfield D 122 *.90 49-26 Faultless One 122^{hd} Northern Cool 122^{5} He's SoPretty122^{3} Tired 10
2Feb85- 3GP fst $1\frac{1}{16}$:47⅘ 1:12⅕ 1:46⅘ Md Sp Wt 10 2 2^{4} $2^{2\frac{1}{2}}$ 2^{hd} 2^{nk} Maple E 122 *1.10 67-22 Sound Proof 122^{nk} Take Control$122^{1\frac{1}{2}}$YesSirree122^{nk} Just missed 12
16Jan85- 6GP fst 6f :22 :45⅘ 1:11⅘ Md Sp Wt 8 2 2^{hd} $3^{\frac{1}{2}}$ 4^{2} 3^{hd} Maple E 122 *.80 80-20 FoxyGreene122^{no}LunchAPegsus122^{hd}TkeControl122^{hd} Weakened 12
20Dec84- 6Aqu fst 6f :22⅘ :47 1:12⅘ Md Sp Wt 7 1 $4^{\frac{3}{4}}$ 3^{nk} 1^{1} $2^{2\frac{3}{4}}$ McCarron G 118 6.90 76-24 Proud Truth $118^{2\frac{3}{4}}$ Take Control $118^{1\frac{1}{2}}$ Buckner 118^{3} 2nd best 10
LATEST WORKOUTS Feb 28 Hia 4f fst :49⅘ b — Feb 23 Hia 5f fst 1:01⅘ b — Feb 19 Hia 5f fst 1:02 b — ●Feb 9 Hia 4f fst :47⅕ h

This leads us to three significant points:

(1) The real value in system or angle play comes not from the favorites it selects but from the longer priced horses it uncovers. Neither Midway Circle nor Take Control was worth

playing in their second starts because their odds were too low. In one case, the big reputation and publicity, and in the other, a second-place finish in New York to a rising star, mitigated against the possibility of getting a fair price the second time out on either horse.

(2) There comes a time when the player must abandon ship, and give up on a promising young horse. If the horse doesn't win after three tries, it might be that it simply doesn't have the ability (Midway Circle) or the heart (Take Control) advertised. Actually, the same can be said of any horse a player might be following. If it doesn't win the first time, give it a second chance if one seems warranted—and possibly even a third try, but no more.

(3) Regardless of how these two colts performed, follow-up play on well-bet first-starters who show some ability in their debut, or have a legitimate excuse for a dull performance in their first start, will prove profitable over an extended period of time.

Midway Circle's third start offered a different twist—the colt wasn't favored. Instead, Geiger Counter, a first-starter from the Leroy Jolley barn, was favored at 4–5. Considering that Midway Circle might have needed his first race in Florida, after a six-week hiatus, and that the well-regarded colt was checked sharply in that race, this was indeed the time to bet him. Or was it? That a first-starter was being bet so heavily into the teeth of expected strong play on Midway Circle said reams for the reputation Geiger Counter must have had on the backstretch prior to making his debut. Indeed, the Mr. Prospector colt lived up to his advance notices, easily winning in excellent time.

Midway Circle did finally break his maiden on June 17 at Belmont, in his eighth start. He did so with a flourish, winning off by seventeen lengths at seven furlongs over a drying-out surface. When he was entered back against allowance rivals on June 26 at the same distance, handicappers faced a standard dilemma: Was Midway Circle just another horse that took advantage of an off track and/or a weak field to crush maiden rivals, looking far more imposing in the process that he actually was? With most recent maiden graduates this would have been the logical conclusion, one that in many cases would point to an upcoming race featuring a false favorite and hopefully a good betting opportunity wagering against the horse. But Midway Circle was different. Had the well-regarded colt finally put it all together? Was he about to live up to his reputed potential? Or was his maiden victory merely an illusion? Either of these interpretations was tenable. Which the handicapper chooses to believe often depends on the odds. Midway Circle went to the gate an enticing 5–1 on June 26. He ran third to a colt named Purple Mountain, who had recently contested the Jersey Derby and Belmont Stakes against the best of his generation, and indeed ran credibly in the former.

Midway Circle Ch. c. 3, by Alydar—Friendly Circle, by Round Table
Br.—Nuckols Breeder (Ky)
Own.—Jayeff Stable Tr.—Stephens Woodford C
122 Lifetime 8 1 2 1 $23,870 | 1985 7 1 2 1 $23,870 | 1984 1 M 0 0 | Turf 2 0 0 0

17Jun85- 6Bel	gd	7f	:22⅘	:45⅘	1:23⅕	Md Sp Wt	5	1	1hd	14	18	117	Maple E	122	*.90	86-18	MidwayCircle12217ChngeTheLock1224LordIrishII117½	Ridden out	6
5Jun85- 6Bel	sly	7f	:22⅕	:45⅗	1:22⅘	3+ Md Sp Wt	2	5	31	21	24	211½	Bailey J D	b 114	2.20	76-17	Sportive 11411½ Midway Circle 1147¾RaiseTheDues1146½	2nd best	8
24May85- 6Bel	gd	1⅜	T:48⅗	1:39⅗	2:18	3+ Md Sp Wt	5	1	11½	2hd	1419	1429¾	Maple E	b 113	6.10	37-32	Mellow Native1136JuniorTerrace1041Singleminded113hd	Stopped	14
16May85- 4Bel	fm	1$\frac{1}{16}$	T:46	1:10⅘	1:42⅘	3+ Md Sp Wt	7	2	31½	32	43½	84¾	Maple E	b 113	*2.10	78-13	Duomo1241JuniorTerrace106½ExplosiveDncer113nk	Factor to str.	11
21Apr85- 6Aqu	fst	7f	:22⅘	:45⅘	1:24⅘	Md Sp Wt	1	8	21	2½	2hd	2nk	Maple E	b 122	3.60	79-21	ArcticGroom122nkMdwyCrcl1221½GrndHorzon's122nk	Just missed	9
26Jan85- 3GP	fst	6f	:21⅘	:45⅗	1:11⅘	Md Sp Wt	7	6	59	59	511	615½	Maple E	122	2.30	66-19	Geiger Counter 1224½ Our Colors 1225½ Beveled 1221	Outrun	12
8Jan85- 3GP	fst	6f	:22	:45⅗	1:10⅕	Md Sp Wt	3	7	56	55	34½	38	Maple E	122	*1.40	80-16	Flyer Escape 1227 Benny Q. 1221MidwayCircle122nk	Checked str.	11
22Nov84- 6Aqu	fst	6f	:22⅘	:46⅘	1:12⅘	Md Sp Wt	7	6	42	21½	23	54¾	Maple E	118	*1.60	72-29	Medieval Market 1132½WeightInGold118½TruthBeTold1181½	Tired	14

LATEST WORKOUTS Jun 24 Bel 4f fst :48⅕ b ●Jun 13 Bel 5f fst :59⅘ h ●Jun 1 Bel 4f gd :48 h May 23 Bel 3f fst :36⅕ b

Most horses are greeted with only moderate enthusiasm, if that, when making their racing debuts. Some of these manage to run well, and indeed a few find their way to the winner's circle. But the vast majority finish "up the track."

One profile worth watching for belongs to the lightly regarded first-timer with nondescript workouts (at best) that shows some life in its debut—specifically, early speed for the first half mile. My interpretation is that the horse has been brought up to its first race short of condition and has performed quite well. It is quite reasonable to expect improvement in its second start, provided considerably more support shows at the betting windows.

A recent case in point was the three-year-old filly Triomphe's Glory.

Triomphe's Glory Ch. f. 3, by Nasty And Bold—Tuckahoe Glory, by Explodent
Br.—Triomphe Farm (NY)
Own.—Pokoik L Tr.—Galluscio Dominick
121 Lifetime 1 0 0 0 | 1985 1 M 0 0

20Dec85- 3Aqu	fst	6f	⊡:23	:47⅘	1:14⅕	ⒻⓈMd Sp Wt	4	5	2½	2hd	32½	56¾	Davis R G	117	38.60	66-27	Hit TheBell1173¾TheZimmermanNote117nkAnchorgram117¾	Tired	12

LATEST WORKOUTS Jan 14 Aqu ⊡ 4f fst :50⅘ b Dec 17 Aqu ⊡ 4f fst :50⅘ b Dec 12 Aqu ⊡ 5f gd 1:03⅘ b Dec 8 Aqu ⊡ 4f fst :51⅕ bg

As her breeder I knew she was blessed with sharp speed, yet her preparations for her debut race on December 20, 1985, consisted of a series of relatively slow breezes at three, four, and five furlongs. Nevertheless, she showed early speed in her first race and held fairly well through the stretch. I was convinced she was short that day and believe the 38–1 odds confirmed the fact that trainer Dominick Galluscio used that race as a conditioner.

Her second start would be the true test, and that came four weeks later, on January 17, in a full field of twelve maiden fillies, half of which were starting for the first time. With ten minutes to post time, Triomphe's Glory was 12–1, but she took all the late action at the track, dropping ultimately to 9–2. To my surprise, Galluscio used this race to experiment. After breaking on top, jockey Robbie Davis rated Triomphe's Glory a few lengths behind three dueling leaders, then sat chilly as two other fillies moved past her on the turn. Once straightened away in the stretch, he asked Triomphe's Glory for her run, and the filly responded. Unfortunately, Gift Of Reason, who moved to the leaders on the turn, got through on the rail and drove clear by four lengths. Triomphe's Glory's run was good only for the place award.

You may have noticed that Triomphe's Glory worked only once during those four weeks between her first two starts. This should not be taken as a reflection on the filly's soundness but should be accepted as part of the winter racing scene. Horses cannot be worked as often, or as vigorously, during the winter months as during the rest of the year. Weather conditions simply do not allow it. In addition, Galluscio faced the uncertainty of not knowing when he would be able to race his filly again. Maiden races for New York-breds always have an overabundance of entrants. A full field of twenty, including also-eligibles, is guaranteed, but countless others fail to make that list. Those horses, including the also-eligibles, that fail to draw into the race must "wait until next week," but they earn what are termed "stars." These give them preference next time over horses that have recently raced. Needless to say, it is difficult to train a horse for a specific race under such uncertain circumstances.

Chapter 2

When to Bet a First-Time Starter

HOW TO DEAL WITH first-time starters ranks among the player's primary concerns when handicapping maiden races. A high percentage of these races, especially those for two-year-olds, are won by first-starters. For example, during the 1984 season in New York, exactly half (118 of 236) of the two-year-old maiden races went to first-time starters. Although this figure is probably abnormally high, it makes our point quite emphatically: First-time starters cannot be ignored.

On the other hand most horses, including the vast majority of eventual stakes winners, lose their debuts due to inexperience and/or lack of maturity at that point in their careers. When, then, should a first-starter be taken seriously as a potential bet? Obviously heavy play at the track is a positive sign, yet no serious player wants to take 6–5 on a horse that lacks established form. However, one gets an uneasy feeling betting against such a horse, not knowing what kind of runner it may be—especially if the trainer is known to crack down with his first-starters. And therein lies the key—knowing the trainer. And with it often comes the answer to our final question: When does a first-time starter represent a value bet?

A race I witnessed from the dining room at Arlington Park during my 1983 visit to that midwestern oval demonstrates quite clearly the various aspects of this problem. The race was the fifth on Friday, August 12, a maiden-claiming contest for Illinois-bred juveniles.

After taking a quick glance at the past performances, most players probably would have given more thought to the luncheon menu than to the fine points of the *Racing Form*. Most of the entrants with

5th Arlington

5½ FURLONGS. (1.03) MAIDEN. CLAIMING. Purse $5,900. 2-year-olds, Illinois conceived, registered and/or foaled. Weight, 118 lbs. Claiming price $25,000; for each $2,500 to $20,000 allowed 1 lb.

Coupled—Fitz's First and Misty's Blackjack; Bobs Pleasure and Catch Me Son; He's A Rake and Costmemoney.

Charming Rouque

Gr. c. 2, by Sr. Diplomat—Merrie Lassie, by Gunflint
Br.—Katz H (Ill) 1983 1 M 0 0
Own.—Mabar Farm 118 Tr.—DiVito James P $25,000
Lifetime 1 0 0 0

26Jly83-4AP 5½f :22^4 :47^1 1:07^{2}ft 25 118 10^{12}10^{15}10^{10} 88¾ Monat A M^5 [S]Mdn 70-24 HighAlexndr,DndyKnight,Irishism 12
Jly 22 AP 4f ft :50 bg Jly 15 AP 5f ft 1:02^1 bg Jun 24 AP 4f ft :49^3 b Jun 17 AP 3f ft :36^2 h

Alpha Delt Swinger

Dk. b. or br. c. 2, by Myriad—Rare Swinger, by Gummo
Br.—Irish Acres Farm (Ill) 1983 4 M 0 0 $335
Own.—Beauregard & King 118 Tr.—Sonnier J Bert $25,000
Lifetime 4 0 0 0 $335

26Jly83-4AP 5½f :22^4 :47^1 1:07^{2}ft 32 118 4^2 43¼ 3^3 66¼ Louviere G P^6 [S]Mdn 72-24 HighAlexndr,DndyKnight,Irishism 12
12Jly83-3AP 5f :22^4 :47^3 1:00^{1}ft 46 118 31½ 33½ 4^6 5^{12} Diaz J L^9 [S]Mdn 73-28 FrindlyBob,DndyKnght,CndnBordr 11
29Jun83-5AP 5f :23 :46^4 :59^{3}sy 25 118 64¼ 65¼ 5^{13} 6^{22} Hirdes R J Jr^5 [S]Mdn 66-34 Pick 'N Win,R.FleetPrince,Irishism 8
17Jun83-5AP 5f :22^4 :46^1 :58^{2}ft 32 118 42½ 4^5 5^{11} 6^{18} Lee M A^7 [S]Mdn 76-26 All Fired Up, Pick 'N Win,Irishism 10
Aug 2 AP 3f ft :36 h Jly 24 AP 3f ft :39 b Jun 24 AP 4f ft :49^4 hg Jun 14 AP 4f ft :48^3 hg

Gabblin Mountain

B. g. 2, by Dependable—Honky Tonk Angel, by Turn-to
Br.—Rosen E K (Ill) 1983 0 M 0 0
Own.—Darjean & Russell 118 Tr.—Darjean Paul $25,000
Lifetime 0 0 0 0

Aug 6 AP 5f ft 1:04 bg Aug 2 AP 5f ft 1:04^4 b Jly 27 AP 4f ft :50 b Jly 22 AP 4f ft :51^2 b

Night or Day

Ch. c. 2, by Nightly's Pleasure—Little Tin Little, by Tin Top
Br.—Schwartz Maxine Dalton (Ill) 1983 0 M 0 0
Own.—Schwartz Maxine 116 Tr.—Bigelow Carl $20,000
Lifetime 0 0 0 0

Aug 11 AP 3f ft :37 b Aug 3 AP 4f ft :48^2 hg Jly 28 AP 4f ft :49 bg Jly 22 AP 4f ft :49 bg

I Am Shazam

B. c. 2, by Sweet Larum—Blacks Barrie, by Cloyce
Br.—McClarney J L (Ill) 1983 2 M 0 0
Own.—Carnes Peggy 116 Tr.—Arnett James G $20,000
Lifetime 2 0 0 0

26Jly83-4AP 5½f :22^4 :47^1 1:07^{2}ft 96 118 11^{14}12^{18}12^{13}11^{12} Brown D^{12} [S]Mdn 66-24 HighAlexndr,DndyKnight,Irishism 12
12Jly83-3AP 5f :22^4 :47^3 1:00^{1}ft 17 118 7^5 11^{16}11^{13} 8^{17} Lopez R D^1 [S]Mdn 68-28 FrindlyBob,DndyKnght,CndnBordr 11
Aug 5 AP 5f ft 1:03^4 b Jly 23 AP 5f ft 1:03^3 b Jly 11 AP 3f ft :38 b Jly 6 AP 4f ft :48 bg

Elderberry

Ch. g. 2, by Ambetella—Inagarden, by Farm to Market
Br.—Vanier H L & Hornbeck L (Ill) 1983 3 M 0 0
Own.—Vanier Nancy, Victor &Frank 116 Tr.—Vanier Harvey L $20,000
Lifetime 3 0 0 0

5Aug83-5AP 5½f :22^4 :47^1 1:07^{2}ft 31 118 6½ 9^{13} 8^{13} 8^{14} Spencer S A^3 [S]Mdn 64-32 Irishism, DandyKnight,GreekValue 12
12Jly83-3AP 5f :22^4 :47^3 1:00^{1}ft 9 118 2^{hd} 43½ 8^{13}11^{21} Spencer S A^3 [S]Mdn 64-28 FrindlyBob,DndyKnght,CndnBordr 11
29Jun83-5AP 5f :23 :46^4 :59^{3}sy 5¾ 118 31½ 43½ 8^{17} 8^{27} Spencer S A^6 [S]Mdn 61-34 Pick 'N Win,R.FleetPrince,Irishism 8
●Jly 30 AP 5f gd 1:01 h Jly 23 AP 5f ft 1:03^1 b Jly 18 AP 5f ft 1:02^1 b Jun 28 AP 3f sy :37^4 b

Point Guard

Dk. b. or br. g. 2, by Dependable—Epinour, by Troy Our Boy
Br.—Wiebe J H (Ill) 1983 1 M 0 0
Own.—Wiebe J H 118 Tr.—Adwell Paul T $25,000
Lifetime 1 0 0 0

26Jly83-4AP 5½f :22^4 :47^1 1:07^{2}ft 7 118 3^1 3^3 8^7 10^{12} Meier R^3 [S]Mdn 66-24 HighAlexndr,DndyKnight,Irishism 12
Aug 5 AP 4f ft :49^2 b Jly 21 AP 4f sy :52 b Jly 13 AP 4f ft :50 bg Jly 7 AP 4f ft :50^2 bg

Fitz's First
B. g. 2, by Fitzhugh—Come on Jadena, by Mike's Red
Br.—Luperi R D (Ill) 1983 0 M 0 0
Own.—Luperi R D 118 Tr.—Cowan Jon M $25,000
Lifetime 0 0 0 0
Aug 6 AP 3f ft :364 hg Jly 27 AP 5f ft 1:03 b

Bobs Pleasure
B. g. 2, by Lucky Pleasure—Jeralin, by Dead Ahead
Br.—Cashman E C (Ill) 1983 0 M 0 0
Own.—Reich H R 118 Tr.—Hazelton Richard P $25,000
Lifetime 0 0 0 0
Aug 2 AP 6f ft 1:17 b Jly 26 AP 4f ft :49 bg Jly 20 AP 4f sy :50 bg Jly 6 AP 4f ft :51 b

He's A Rake
B. g. 2, by The Reprobate—Pitia, by Argos
Br.—Hondo Ranch (Ill) 1983 1 M 0 0
Own.—Hondo Ranch 1135 Tr.—Kirby Frank J $25,000
Lifetime 1 0 0 0
26Jly83-4AP 5½f :224 :471 1:072ft 51 118 64¼ 53¼ 53½ 77 Langlinais E10 ⓈMdn 71-24 HighAlexndr,DndyKnight,Irishism 12
Aug 10 AP 5f ft 1:03 b Aug 2 AP 5f ft 1:01 bg Jly 16 AP 5f ft 1:032 b Jly 10 AP 5f ft 1:03 bg

Raging Battle
Ch. g. 2, by Crimson Battle—Bally Dear, by Ballydonnell
Br.—Gardiner Kimberly A (Ill) 1983 5 M 0 0 $971
Own.—Bar-Cin Stables 118 Tr.—Vinci Charles J $25,000
Lifetime 5 0 0 0 $971
5Aug83-5AP 5½f :224 :471 1:072ft 42 118 94½ 79 611 711 Evans R D9 ⓈMdn 67-32 Irishism, DandyKnight,GreekValue 12
26Jly83-4AP 5½f :224 :471 1:072ft 37 118 75¼ 67¼ 65½ 56 Evans R D2 ⓈMdn 72-24 HighAlexndr,DndyKnight,Irishism 12
12Jly83-3AP 5f :224 :473 1:001ft 89 118 97½ 78 57½ 412 Meier R7 ⓈMdn 73-28 FrindlyBob,DndyKnght,CndnBordr 11
29Jun83-5AP 5f :23 :464 :593sy 55 1135 75¾ 77¾ 616 726 Patin K C7 ⓈMdn 62-34 Pick 'N Win,R.FleetPrince,Irishism 8
17Jun83-5AP 5f :224 :461 :582ft 15 118 1015 1020 1020 826 Evans R D10 ⓈMdn 68-26 All Fired Up, Pick 'N Win,Irishism 10
Aug 2 AP 4f ft :482 b Jly 23 AP 4f ft :534 b Jly 10 AP 3f ft :364 b

Also Eligible (Not in Post Position Order):

Catch Me Son
B. c. 2, by Son Ange—Rezy Catch, by Mr. Crazy
Br.—Snowden Hal Jr (Ill) 1983 2 M 0 0
Own.—Snowden H Jr 116 Tr.—Hazelton Richard P $20,000
Lifetime 2 0 0 0
28Jly83-3AP 5½f :223 :47 1:08 ft 21 116 51¾ 78 913 911 Louviere G P1 M18000 64-28 ExitTime,Recupere'sPrty,CheMuz 12
28Jly83—Had to check along rail early on turn
9Apr83-3Kee 4½f :223 :461 :522sy 34 118 8 815 823 922 Brown D10 Mdn 71-07 DeltaTrace,Wyndom,PublicMence 10
Jly 26 AP 4f ft :502 b Jly 23 AP 3f ft :383 bg

racing experience had performed poorly in state-bred maiden special company—all but one at long odds. Although they were dropping into the claiming ranks for the first time, there was little to recommend any of them, few hints of any ability whatsoever. The list of potential bets quickly narrowed down to four horses:

BOB'S PLEASURE

This first-starter was the betting favorite at 2–1. Our contention here, though, is that even in a field this weak, odds that low are unacceptable on first-starters, especially in maiden-claiming contests. A young horse's inexperience alone may defeat it. Rivals with poor form may suddenly "put it all together" and run surprisingly well. Other first-starters may have some ability and run well in their debuts. Many things can go wrong in races of this type, and odds of 2–1 simply don't account for all of them. Further, if a first-starting two-year-old is so well liked by its connections and is backed so heavily in its debut, why enter it in a claiming race and risk losing it on a claim? Why not first get a line on the horse's ability in maiden-special company?

GABBLIN MOUNTAIN

Were it not for local knowledge of trainer methodology, this horse would have been dismissed along with the other first-starters. But according to Scott McMannis, my host at Arlington, trainer Paul Darjean was more than capable with first-starters, having won with five of seventeen during the current and previous seasons combined, often at good prices. Consequently, Gabblin Mountain had to be respected.

ALPHA DELT SWINGER

Support for this horse at the windows—second choice at 5–2—came no doubt from what many read as improvement last time out. On that occasion, the horse was racing in third position, only three lengths from the lead, at the stretch call. If the horse hadn't also "shown signs" in its prior start, I might have taken him more seriously. If he had held better to the wire last time, I might have been interested. In any event, at 5–2 he didn't seem to represent a value bet.

POINT GUARD

Point Guard combined two things that I like in a losing debut performance: early speed and betting action. Yet he did so only marginally. I would have preferred just a little more interest at the betting windows. And I would have liked the horse more if he had carried his early speed a little farther.

The choice was clearly defined. At 6–1, Point Guard was once again receiving encouraging support at the betting windows. Somebody liked him. And in a field this weak, he was a sensible selection.

The point of this chapter, however, is that Gabblin Mountain represented the ideal situation for playing first-time starters. His trainer, Paul Darjean, tried—often successfully—with first-starters. But he didn't have the large following that can drive the price down and destroy the value of the bet. Gabblin Mountain opened at 70–1, but the late money that brought his odds down to 17–1 hinted of serious stable intentions.

I don't remember whether I stubbornly adhered to my original conclusion, based on my analysis of the *Form*, that Point Guard was the logical play in this race. Or if, hearing about Gabblin Mountain, I simply decided to pass the race. I suppose the logical decision would have been to play both horses, but I didn't. And while I washed the lunch dishes, Scott McMannis paid a visit to the cashiers window to collect the rewards of a $37.80 mutuel—and hopefully provided a couple of lessons for all of us to remember.

FIFTH RACE
Arlington
AUGUST 12, 1983

5 ½ FURLONGS. (1.03) MAIDEN. CLAIMING. Purse $5,900. 2-year-olds, Illinois conceived, registered and/or foaled. Weight, 118 lbs. Claiming price $25,000; for each $2,500 to $20,000 allowed 1 lb.

Value of race $5,900, value to winner $3,540, second $1,180, third $649, fourth $354, fifth $177. Mutuel pool $111,877.

Last Raced	Horse	Eqt.A.Wt	PP	St	¼	⅜	Str	Fin	Jockey	Cl'g Pr	Odds $1
	Gabblin Mountain	b 2 118	3	6	$1^{1/2}$	1^{2}	$1^{3 1/2}$	$1^{5 1/2}$	Strauss R	25000	17.90
26Jly83 4AP6	Alpha Delt Swinger	b 2 118	2	2	3^{hd}	2^{1}	2^{2}	$2^{1 1/4}$	Diaz J L	25000	2.90
26Jly83 4AP7	He's A Rake	b 2 113	10	10	$7^{1/2}$	6^{3}	4^{2}	$3^{1/2}$	Fuentes D M5	25000	6.80
26Jly83 4AP10	Point Guard	2 118	7	4	$4^{1/2}$	5^{hd}	3^{1}	$4^{4 1/2}$	Meier R	25000	6.10
5Aug83 5AP7	Raging Battle	b 2 118	11	8	8^{4}	8^{3}	6^{2}	$5^{3/4}$	Evans R D	25000	9.60
	Bobs Pleasure	b 2 118	9	9	5^{hd}	$4^{1/2}$	$5^{1/2}$	6no	Louviere G E	25000	b-2.10
26Jly83 4AP11	I Am Shazam	2 116	5	1	10^{hd}	$10^{1/2}$	$8^{2 1/2}$	$7^{1 3/4}$	Lopez R D	20000	48.90
26Jly83 4AP8	Charming Rouque	b 2 118	1	12	12	12	10^{hd}	$8^{1 1/4}$	Monat A M	25000	24.80
5Aug83 5AP8	Elderberry	b 2 116	6	5	9^{hd}	11^{4}	$11^{1/2}$	9^{hd}	Patterson A	20000	17.30
	Night or Day	2 116	4	11	11^{6}	9^{hd}	9^{hd}	10^{2}	Colangelo T	20000	13.30
28Jly83 3AP9	Catch Me Son	2 116	12	7	6^{1}	7^{hd}	12	$11^{2 1/2}$	Fires E	20000	b-2.10
	Fitz's First	b 2 118	8	3	2^{hd}	3^{1}	7^{hd}	12	Clark K D	25000	27.80

b–Coupled: Bobs Pleasure and Catch Me Son.

OFF AT 3:20 Start good. Won driving. Time, :22⅘, :47⅖, 1:00⅖, 1:07⅗ Track fast.

$2 Mutuel Prices:				
	4–GABBLIN MOUNTAIN	37.80	12.40	10.00
	3–ALPHA DELT SWINGER		4.60	3.60
	10–HE'S A RAKE			4.60

B. g, by Dependable—Honky Tónk Angel, by Turn-to. Trainer Darjean Paul. Bred by Rosen E K (Ill).

GABBLIN MOUNTAIN split rivals to take command nearing turn, drew out leaving midstretch and under left-handed urging to wire. ALPHA DELT SWINGER had early speed along rail but unable to menace winner in drive. HE'S A RAKE split rivals on turn, lacked needed rally while wide. POINT GUARD raced evenly between horses. RAGING BATTLE rallied mildly while wide. BOBS PLEASURE passed tired horses. CHARMING ROUQUE rallied belatedly. ELDERBERRY and NIGHT OR DAY showed little. CATCH ME SON gave way while wide. FITZ'S FIRST stopped between horses in upper stretch.

People like Scott McMannis do win at the races. The key to their success can be summarized in two four-letter words: hard work. They calculate superior speed and pace figures and/or keep highly detailed trip and track bias notes of their own making. They also study the trainers on their home circuit. Transport them to another locale and they probably will feel lost and naked, as I did in Chicago that summer, without their figs and trips, not knowing the conditioners whose charges they would be forced to analyze, fully aware of what they didn't know, and what an advantage it was to those who shared that information. Hopefully, though, they would have the common sense to listen to the local expert sitting across the table from them.

Every circuit has its Paul Darjeans, trainers known for their ability to have young horses ready to win at first asking. The serious player is well advised to keep records on such matters. And to realize that, in some sense, a horse "belongs to" its trainer and owner until it has established its form on the racetrack. If they can break a horse's maiden at a big price, that is their unquestioned privilege.

In that vein, the following curious story from the 1985 New York racing season comes to mind. On June 3, Jan Nerud entered his father's two-year-old colt, Roy, in a five-furlong maiden dash. Prior to 1985, the Neruds had been known and respected for giving their well-bred youngsters time to mature before cracking down with them. It was rare for one of their juveniles to win early in the year. Yet Roy came to the races with a reputation for being "the fastest horse since Dr. Fager," John Nerud's Hall of Fame champion of the late 1960s—all of this despite a rather modest-looking workout line. Sent to the post as 8–5 favorite, he could only rally mildly for third money.

Roy B. c. 2, by Fappiano—Adlibber, by Neverbend Lifetime 1985 0 M 0 0
Br.—Carelaine Farm (Fla) 0 0 0 0
Own.—Nerud J A Tr.—Nerud Jan H 118
LATEST WORKOUTS May 31 Bel 4f fst :48⅗ h May 26 Bel 4f fst :48⅗ h May 20 Bel 4f fst :48⅗ h May 15 Bel 3f fst :38 bg

Ten days later, on June 13, Leroy Jolley sent out the heralded Mogambo, already tabbed by Angel Cordero as his Derby horse for 1986. Bet down to 1–2, Mogambo set the pace to the top of the lane, then offered little resistance when challenged by Nerud's first-starter, Ogygian. The latter drew off to win by more than two lengths, returning $56.40 to his scattered backers in the audience that day.

Mogambo Ch. c. 2, by Mr Prospector—Lakeville Miss, by Rainy Lake Lifetime 1985 0 M 0 0
Br.—Brant P M (Ky) 0 0 0 0
Own.—Brant P M Tr.—Jolley Leroy 118
LATEST WORKOUTS Jun 8 Bel 5f fst :59⅗ h May 31 Bel 4f fst :47⅗ hg May 20 Bel 5f fst 1:00⅗ h May 6 Bel 5f fst 1:00 h

Ogygian B. c. 2, by Damascus—Gonfalon, by Francis S Lifetime 1985 0 M 0 0
Br.—Tartan Stable (Fla) 0 0 0 0
Own.—Tartan Stable Tr.—Nerud Jan H 118
LATEST WORKOUTS Jun 10 Bel tr.t 4f fst :49⅗ b Jun 5 Bel 4f fst :49 b May 30 Bel 4f fst :49⅗ b May 25 Bel 4f fst :49⅗ b

After the Mogambo race, rumors circulated that the clockers had confused Roy and Ogygian, and that Roy's reputation really belonged to Ogygian. The two colts reportedly were quite similar in appearance, yet no one went out of their way to correct the impression that had been created about Roy. Subsequent developments seemed to substantiate this theory. Roy broke his maiden by seventeen lengths in his third attempt, then placed gamely in the Sanford at Saratoga despite bucking shins in the race. Ogygian, on the other hand, bucked in June, then followed an impressive allowance victory in September with an even more impressive tally in Belmont's prestigious Futurity Stakes, looking every part a champion. Unfortunately, a second case of bucked shins forced him to the sidelines before he could prove his point in the Champagne and Breeders' Cup. Then a freak accident on the farm kept him from competing in the 1986 classics.

Chapter 3

He Could Be Any Kind

WHEN BOLD SMOOCHER entered the starting gate for the second race at Aqueduct on December 2, 1984, the New York cognescenti had decided that he was the proverbial sure thing. After all, the juvenile colt had just demolished a maiden field by thirteen widening lengths in what proved to be the fastest time for a maiden sprint—or debut performance—this writer can recall in more than fifteen years of making speed figures. His 112 figure was the best any two-year-old had posted in New York that season, and it compared favorably with stakes figures logged by such immortals as Secretariat, Seattle Slew, Alydar, Affirmed, and Spectacular Bid in their juvenile seasons. In common racing parlance, Bold Smoocher looked as if he "could be any kind."

But even if New Yorkers could not be accused of going overboard making this colt 2–5 off that one race, they could be chastised for having short memories. Earlier that same year, three juvenile fillies debuted with performances and speed figures reminiscent of the immortal Ruffian—indeed, within three points of her debut figure. Each lost her second start.

On July 19, an obscurely bred filly named Self Image ran a hole in the wind, defeating a small band of maidens in excellent time (107 figure) as 2–1 second choice. New Yorkers anxiously awaited her appearance at Saratoga, but Self Image did not race again until September 12, in the Astarita Stakes at Belmont. Favored at 6–5 based on that single race and excellent workouts since, Self Image was beaten a length by Mom's Command, a (then) obscure invader from New England whose best previous figure placed her ten lengths behind Self Image. Mom's Command's number for the Astarita was merely 102, suggesting that Self Image had fallen off six lengths from her debut performance.

```
Self Image            B. f. 2, by Caro Bambino—Siranna, by Sailing Along          Lifetime    1984 1 1 0 0   $10,800
                         Br.—Lundy R J Jr (Cal)                              112   1 1 0 0
  Own.—Lundy Sarah A     Tr.—Lundy Sarah A                                          $10,800
19Jly84- 3Bel fst 5½f :22⅗ :45⅗ 1:03⅗  ⒻMd Sp Wt  1 1 2hd 11 14 14½ Maple E  117 2.40 96-15 Self Image 1174½AppealingSam1177¾FrenchGold1171½ Ridden out 7
  LATEST WORKOUTS  ●Sep 8 Bel 5f fst :58⅘ h   Sep 2 Bel 6f fst 1:13 h   Aug 21 Sar 5f fst :58⅘ h   Aug 16 Sar tr.t 3f fst :37⅘ b

Mom's Command         Ch. f. 2, by Top Command—Star Mommy, by Pin Star            Lifetime    1984 3 2 0 0   $29,058
                         Br.—Fuller P (Ky)                                   116   3 2 0 0
  Own.—Fuller P          Tr.—Allard Edward T                                        $29,058
27Aug84- 8Sar fst 6f :22⅕ :45⅘ 1:11   ⒻSpinaway     2 6 31½ 35½ 45 46¼ Fuller A    119 15.30 79-16 Tiltlting1191½SocibleDuck1193½Contrednc1191½ Steadied at start 7
 4Aug84-10Suf fst 6f :22⅕ :45⅘ 1:11⅗  ⒻPriscilla    5 2 2hd 2hd 1hd 1¾  Fuller A    116 3.40  83-21 Mom's Command 116¾ SheerIce1162½MyFriendFran1161½ Driving 8
17Jly84- 8Rkmfst 5f :22⅕ :46⅘ 1:00    ⒻⓈFaneuilMiss 5 11 85 64½ 44 1hd Carrasco B  113 44.70 84-21 Mom's Command113hdCircleFoot113nkMyFriendFran113½ Driving 11
  LATEST WORKOUTS  ●Sep 9 Suf 5f fst :58⅘ h   ●Aug 21 Suf 5f sly 1:01⅕ h   ●Aug 13 Suf 4f fst :47⅘ h   Jly 30 Suf 5f fst 1:01⅘ hg
```

On July 29, Harbor View Farm's well-bred filly Outstandingly duplicated Self Image's performance of ten days earlier, defeating six other maidens by twelve lengths while running to a 107 figure. Interestingly, the same filly, Appealing Sam, finished second to both Self Image and Outstandingly, suggesting that Outstandingly's performance was the better of the two, even though their figures were equal. Outstandingly had defeated Appealing Sam by a larger margin while spotting her the experience gained chasing Self Image. When Appealing Sam came back to blow out a field of Saratoga maidens by six and a half lengths on August 13, both Self Image and Outstandingly grew in stature. They had beaten a runner!

Three days later, on August 16, Outstandingly was entered in the Adirondack Stakes at Saratoga and naturally was favored, at 7–5. Yet she was defeated by Contredance, a Danzig filly who had run last in the Schuylerville Stakes on opening day at Saratoga. While an equipment change helped to explain Contredance's form reversal on August 16, it nevertheless remained true that her maiden voyage had produced a figure of just 101, six lengths slower than Outstandingly's number. In this case, it is interesting to note that Outstandingly ran back (exactly) to her maiden figure—Contredance improved dramatically, as often happens with developing young horses. The figure for the Adirondack was 108, with Contredance edging Outstandingly by three quarters of a length.

```
Outstandingly         B. f. 2, by Exclusive Native—La Mesa, by Round Table        Lifetime    1984 1 1 0 0   $10,800
                         Br.—Harbor View Farm (Ky)                           114   1 1 0 0
  Own.—Harbor View Farm  Tr.—Martin Frank                                           $10,800
29Jly84- 6Bel fst 5½f :22⅗ :45⅗ 1:04⅕  ⒻMd Sp Wt  4 4 11½ 11½ 15 112 Cordero A Jr  117 2.50 94-15 Outstndingly11712AppelingSm1175½AliceB.Tobin117no Ridden out 7
  LATEST WORKOUTS  Aug 12 Sar 5f fst :58⅘ h   Aug 6 Sar 4f fst :47⅕ h   Jly 26 Bel tr.t 4f fst :47⅘ h   Jly 19 Bel tr.t 5f gd 1:00⅘ h

Contredance           B. f. 2, by Danzig—Nimble Folly, by Cyane                   Lifetime    1984 2 1 0 0   $10,800
                         Br.—Derry Meeting Farm (Pa)                         114   2 1 0 0
  Own.—Dekwiatkowski H   Tr.—Stephens Woodford C                                    $10,800
 1Aug84- 8Sar fst 6f :22⅕ :46 1:11⅗    ⒻSchuylrville  4 3 2½ 22½ 68 812½ Maple E  114 *1.60 70-13 WeekendDelight1193Resembling114noWinters'Love1144½ Stopped 8
28Jun84- 6Bel fst 5f :22⅗ :46⅗ :59⅕    ⒻMd Sp Wt      2 2 11 1½ 13½ 14 Maple E    117 *.50  91-19 Contrednce1174FlyThruTheSkis1125ElinHmmings1174 Ridden out 6
  LATEST WORKOUTS  Aug 13 Sar 4f fst :47⅘ h   ●Aug 8 Sar 3f fst :34 h   Jly 30 Bel 3f fst :34⅘ h   Jly 26 Bel 4f fst :47⅘ h
```

Shortly after racing returned to Belmont, another unfashionably bred filly had the clockers shaking their heads in disbelief. Kamikaze Rick destroyed a (weak) maiden field by fourteen easy lengths in the same 107 figure posted by both Self Image and Outstandingly. Was she the second coming of Ruffian? Improvers of the breed gathered early at Aqueduct on October 25 to learn more about this mercurial filly, who had been entered in that day's first contest. They were shocked and disappointed when the heavily favored (at 2–5) Kamikaze Rick was ordered scratched by the track veterinarian on her way to the post. Prerace drug testing found her positive for the illegal drug Butazolidin, on which she had been training.

Nine days later, however, Kamikaze Rick was back in the entries, this time in a minor stakes event at seven furlongs. But when she couldn't match strides with Verbality in the late stages of that event, New York's "figure guys" went down for the third time. Verbality had won the allowance contest from which Kamikaze Rick had been scratched, and the experience gained that day helped her overcome her more highly regarded rival. Verbality's figures prior to their meeting had been 101 and 102. She improved to 104 on this occasion, but Kamikaze Rick fell off a few points to accommodate her.

Kamikaze Rick Ch. f. 2, by Hasty Flyer—Great Light, by Rube The Great Lifetime 1984 1 1 0 0 $10,800
Br.—Mangurian H T Jr (Ky) 114 1 1 0 0
Own.—Flame Creek Stable Tr.—Casse Mark $10,800
3Sep84- 4Bel fst 6f :22⅘ :45⅘ 1:10⅕ ⒻMd Sp Wt 4 2 12 13½ 110 114 Migliore R 117 *1.20 91-14 Kamikaze Rick 11714 Bold But Lovely 1172¾ Affirming117¾ Easily 9
LATEST WORKOUTS Oct 29 Bel 7f sly 1:26⅘ h ●Oct 21 Bel 4f fst :47⅕ hg Oct 15 Bel 5f fst 1:00⅘ h ●Sep 20 Bel 7f fst 1:28⅕ b

Verbality B. f. 2, by Verbatim—One Sum, by One for All Lifetime 1984 2 2 0 0 $22,800
Br.—Wilson C T (Ky) 114 2 2 0 0
Own.—Wilson C T Tr.—Hernandez Ramon M $22,800
25Oct84- 1Aqu gd 6f :23 :46⅘ 1:10⅘ ⒻAlw 20000 3 5 41¾ 21½ 2½ 1¾ Guerra W A 118 *.50 87-21 Verbality 118¾ Plastic Lady 1165½IndianRomance116¾ Ridden out 5
19Sep84- 4Bel fst 5½f :23⅘ :47⅕ 1:05⅘ ⒻMd Sp Wt 6 7 52½ 31½ 11½ 16¾ Guerra W A 117 5.60 87-19 Verbality 1176¾ Miss Tresham 1172¾ Icy Art 1175 Easily 9
LATEST WORKOUTS ●Oct 12 Bel tr.t 3f fst :35⅘ h Oct 1 Bel tr.t 4f fst :50 b Sep 17 Bel tr.t 3f fst :37 b Sep 12 Bel tr.t 5f fst 1:03 b

These three examples underline a simple point: One race does not a career make. When a horse wins its debut by a wide margin in fast time, one thing is certain: The horse will be overbet in its second start. Such an effort tells us very little about the horse except that when given its own way in a field of questionable merit, the horse is capable of running very fast. It reveals nothing about the horse's class, consistency, or courage. It provides no clues as to how that horse will perform when facing a sterner task against more qualified rivals.

Although none of the three fillies discussed was disgraced in her second start, it is also true that none proved (at least to that point) to be the whirlwind expected. Only Outstandingly ran back to her impressive debut figure, and it was she who went on to greater things later that year. She was not seen for two months after the Adirondack, then raced dully as 9–10 favorite against colts in a seven-furlong allowance race at Aqueduct on October 28 over an "off" surface she may not have been able to handle. Two weeks later, she was entered in the Breeders' Cup Mile for juvenile fillies. Those aware of her outstanding figures from the summer would have given her serious consideration in that event. At odds of 21–1, she was indeed the logical play in a weak field. Although she didn't win that roughly run contest, she was declared the winner upon the disqualification of Fran's Valentine, then went on to defeat that rival and others in the rich Hollywood Starlet later that month. Outstandingly was a typical example of a horse that improved dramatically to its peak performance after just one conditioning race following a layoff.

Outstandingly B. f. 2, by Exclusive Native—La Mesa, by Round Table Lifetime 1984 3 1 1 0 $31,470
Own.—Harbor View Farm Br.—Harbor View Farm (Ky) 119 3 1 1 0 $31,470
Tr.—Martin Frank
28Oct84- 3Aqu gd 7f :22⅘ :45⅘ 1:22⅘ Alw 20000 3 3 69½ 57 410 410¾ Guerra W A 114 *.90 77-14 YoungMonarch1223½SunnyCabin1173SenatorBrdy1174½ No factor 7
15Aug84- 8Sar fst 6f :22⅘ :45 1:10⅘ ⒻAdirondack 7 6 65¾ 44 22½ 2¾ Cordero A Jr 114 *1.40 87-21 Contredance 114¾ Outstandingly 1142½ Oriental1144½ Wide,dkd in 7
15Aug84-Grade II
28Jly84- 6Bel fst 5½f :22⅘ :45⅘ 1:04⅕ ⒻMd Sp Wt 4 4 11½ 11½ 15 112 Cordero A Jr 117 2.50 94-15 Outstndingly11712AppelingSm1175½AliceB.Tobin117no Ridden out 7
LATEST WORKOUTS Nov 7 Hol 4f fst :47⅕ h Oct 24 Bel 9f sly 1:52⅘ b (d) ●Oct 18 Bel tr.t 4f fst :47⅘ h Oct 12 Bel tr.t 3f fst :36⅘ b

Back to Bold Smoocher. Many will say that his task was much simpler than that faced by any of the three fillies. He was running in an allowance contest, while they were competing in stakes company. Others will counter that juvenile stakes events during the summer months are little more than glorified allowance races. At that time of the year, especially on the major circuits, allowance events for two-year-olds are few and far between. The more impressive maiden winners immediately go after the stakes prizes, leaving only a few horses available to compete in allowance contests. There is a subtle difference, however. The conditions for most (major) stakes races allow previous stakes winners to come back for more. Not so with "nonwinners of one" allowance races. Bold Smoocher would have to face no stakes winners, not even allowance winners, on December 2. In fact, five of his eight rivals had previously run for a claiming tag.

Indeed, Bold Smoocher's task was simple, and he did defeat his field with relative ease, winning off by nine lengths while earning an impressive 111 speed figure. Nevertheless, he left two questions still unanswered: How would he react to first-rate competition, which he had yet to face? And could he go a distance of ground? Even though he had now won at seven furlongs, his distance capabilities had to be suspect simply because his sire, Bold L. B., never won beyond six furlongs while racing mostly on the midwestern circuits, staying away, for the most part, from New York and Los Angeles.

Bold Smoocher appeared next in the million-dollar Hollywood

2 AQUEDUCT 7 FURLONGS

7 FURLONGS AQUEDUCT

7 FURLONGS. (1.20⅘) ALLOWANCE. Purse $22,000. 2-year-olds which have never won a race other than maiden or claiming. Weight, 122 lbs. Non-winners of a race other than claiming since November 15 allowed 3 lbs. Of such a race since November 1, 5 lbs.

Coupled—Medieval Market and Anconeus.

Creative Spirit

Gr. c. 2, by Fire Dancer—Indian Ghost, by Umbrella Fella
Br.—Chak Phyllis & Price Judith L (Fla)
Tr.—Marcus Alan B
Own.—Wood A
117
Lifetime 10 1 1 1 $11,050 — 1984 10 1 1 1 $11,050 — Turf 3 0 0 0

12Nov84- 5Aqu gd 7f :23 :46 1:25 Clm 75000 4 8 74½ 43 44 43½ Davis R G b 117 16.20 72-25 First One Up 113² Jet Wave 117hd Kilts' Nashua 1131½ Wide 8
2Nov84- 4Aqu fst 7f :23⅗ :47⅘ 1:27⅘ Md 50000 7 1 21 2½ 2½ 1hd Davis R G b 118 *2.20 63-35 Creative Spirit 118hd Koffkoff 1144 Casting For 109⁹ Driving 8
26Oct84- 4Aqu sly 1 :46⅗ 1:11⅘ 1:38⅗ Md 50000 8 2 1½ 1½ 11 2nk Davis R G b 118 7.30 74-22 FeelingGallnt114nk CretiveSpirit1181¾DncinOnPins1147 Just failed 10
19Oct84- 4Bel fst 6f :23 :47⅕ 1:12⅘ Md 50000 11 2 2½ 1hd 24 39¾ Davis R G b 118 3.80 70-21 Kilts' Nashua 1189½CopAPlea114nk CreativeSpirit118hd Weakened 13
11Oct84- 4Bel fst 6½f :22⅘ :46⅗ 1:19⅘ Md 75000 2 3 32 54 55½ 56½ Davis R G b 118 35.60 71-26 Scholastic1141¾FabulousMove1141¾HatchetDncer113hd Early foot 13
28Sep84- 6Bel yl 1⅛ Ⓣ:48 1:14 1:47⅕ Md Sp Wt 7 2 2hd 11 77 1016½ Samyn J L b 118 17.60 44-36 Willingness 1182¾ Roman River 1183 Sound Proof 1181¾ Tired 12
14Sep84- 6Bel fm 1⅛ Ⓣ:48 1:12⅗ 1:45⅕ Md Sp Wt 8 7 64 42 54½ 57½ Cruguet J b 118 12.10 67-23 Magnaminous 118½ Lathom 1182¾ Roman River 1182¾ Off slowly 8
22Aug84- 5Sar fm 1 Ⓣ:47⅘ 1:12⅗ 1:38⅕ Alw 21000 4 4 43½ 88½ 916 1027½ Davis R G b 117 35.60 58-20 WesternChmp117¾NicklBck117nkDon'tFoolWithM1173½ Bore out 10
16Jly84- 6Bel fst 6f :22⅘ :46 1:11⅘ Md Sp Wt 9 11 98½ 109 1215 1220 MacBeth D b 118 77.80 65-24 Nickel Back 1184 Eternal Prince 118no Anconeus 1181 Outrun 13
24May84- 4Bel fst 5f :22⅘ :45⅘ :57⅘ Md Sp Wt 2 5 44½ 35½ 48 513 Davis R G 118 3.20e 86-15 MoonProspector118¾NickelBack1186BetMeDddy1183½ Weakened 8
LATEST WORKOUTS Nov 22 Bel tr.t 4f fst :51 b Nov 10 Bel tr.t 3f fst :38 b Oct 6 Bel tr.t 4f fst :49⅗ b

Stasera

Dk. b. or br. c. 2, by L'Enjoleur—Toute Vitesse, by Restless Wind
Br.—Jean De Castella De Delley & Farish (NY)
Tr.—DiAngelo Joseph T
Own.—Lago Vista Farm
112⁵
Lifetime 7 1 0 4 $8,040 — 1984 7 1 0 4 $8,040

23Nov84- 9Aqu fst 1 :47⅘ 1:13 1:39⅘ ⓈAlw 27000 6 1 1½ 32 1011 1024½ Cordero A Jr 117 14.60 42-29 MyMnJohn117¾Romncer1121¾WinWonSoon117hd Done after 3/4's 10
9Nov84- 8FL fst 6f :22⅘ :47 1:14⅕ ⓈAlw 9900 2 4 1hd 1hd 1hd 37 Hilburn K D 114 *1.00 71-27 Prince Steve 1145 American Ayr 109² Stasera 114² Weakened 8
19Oct84- 1FL fst 6f :23 :47⅗ 1:13⅕ ⓈAlw 9700 5 2 32½ 55½ 32 32 Hiraldo J L 116 *.70e 81-21 Sincere Rullah 122² Razorbill 122hd Stasera 1163 Rallied 7
7Oct84- 2FL fst 5½f :23 :47⅘ 1:07 ⓈMd 15000 12 6 2hd 1hd 1½ 13 Hilburn K D 120 3.00 81-20 Stasera 1203 Poppops Josh 120² Hard RockTate1203½ Drew clear 12
25Sep84- 6FL fst 6f :22⅘ :46⅘ 1:14⅕ ⓈMd Sp Wt 6 1 2hd 2½ 32 314 Cook R W 120 3.20 64-24 Smart Silence 12011 Zactay 1203 Stasera 1203½ Weakened 10
15Sep84- 5FL sly 5½f :23⅕ :48⅕ 1:08⅗ ⓈMd Sp Wt 9 2 11 1½ 1½ 31½ Green B 120 3.20 72-25 American Ayr 117hd Smart Silence 1201½ Stasera 120² Weakened 11
31Aug84- 5FL fst 5½f :22⅘ :48 1:09⅕ ⓈMd Sp Wt 5 4 56½ 64¾ 54 54½ Green B 120 4.40 66-31 RoylContry120¾PoppopsJosh120hdH'sInClovr1202½ Bore out turn 12
LATEST WORKOUTS Nov 21 Bel 4f fst :50 b

Eastern Secret

B. c. 2, by Akureyri—Keep A Secret, by Never Bend
Br.—Mereworth Farm (Ky)
Tr.—Veitch Sylvester E
Own.—Sheikh S M
117
Lifetime 6 1 0 1 $14,760 — 1984 6 1 0 1 $14,760

6Oct84- 8Bel fst 1 :45⅗ 1:10⅗ 1:36⅗ Cowdin 7 8 811 713 718 729½ Lovato F Jr 122 47.50 53-17 Chief's Crown 1226 Bionic Light 12212½ Script Ohio 1221½ Outrun 8
6Oct84-Grade I
22Sep84- 4Bel fst 1 :47⅘ 1:12⅘ 1:38⅘ Md Sp Wt 4 6 53 31½ 11½ 13 Lovato F Jr 118 5.00 73-19 Eastern Secret 1183 Numeric 118² Revelrout 1183¾ Ridden out 14
2Sep84- 4Bel fst 7f :22⅘ :46⅕ 1:24⅘ Md Sp Wt 3 9 1117 109½ 67 31¾ Lovato F Jr 118 24.10 77-17 DH SenatorBrdy1181 DH Hberdsher1181¾EsternSecret118hd Rallied 14
23Aug84- 6Sar sly 7f :22⅘ :46 1:24⅘ Md Sp Wt 9 3 108½ 913 58½ 47¾ Lovato F Jr 118 8.00f 72-22 Coyote Dancer 1184½ Haberdasher 1182¾ Foligno 118¾ Rallied 14
4Aug84- 6Sar fst 6f :22 :45⅗ 1:10⅘ Md Sp Wt 9 10 1214 1217 1011 811¾ Lovato F Jr 118 16.80f 74-13 Desert War 1183½ Herat 1186½ Alex's Game 118hd Outrun 14
22Jun84- 4Bel fst 5½f :22⅕ :46⅕ 1:05⅗ Md Sp Wt 4 8 88¾ 714 716 716½ Cruguet J 118 18.00 71-21 Secretary General 1181 Chief'sCrown1181¼TiffanyIce1189 Outrun 10
LATEST WORKOUTS ●Nov 27 Bel 5f fst 1:01⅖ h Nov 23 Bel 4f fst :49 h Nov 19 Bel 5f fst 1:01 h Nov 15 Bel 5f fst 1:04⅖ b

Keep It Down

Ch. c. 2, by Native Uproar—Tehama, by Cohoes
Br.—Bettersworth J R (Ky)
Tr.—Moschera Gasper S
Own.—Davis A
117
Lifetime 4 2 0 0 $15,428 — 1984 4 2 0 0 $15,428

19Nov84- 5Aqu fst 6f :23 :47⅕ 1:12⅘ Alw 22000 1 2 2hd 1hd 2hd 45¾ MacBeth D 117 *2.00 71-33 El Basco 1175 First One Up 117¾ He's HomeFree117hd Weakened 9
12Nov84- 5Aqu gd 7f :23 :46 1:25 Clm c-75000 6 1 11 1hd 2½ 55½ Kaenel J L 117 *.70 70-25 First One Up 113² Jet Wave 117hd Kilts' Nashua 1131½ Tired 8
25Oct84- 5Aqu gd 7f :23 :46⅗ 1:24⅕ Clm 50000 6 3 1½ 11 14 14¾ Kaenel J L 117 *1.70 80-21 KeepItDown1174¾FirstOneUp1171½SavgeRunner113nk Ridden out 8
29Aug84- 1CD gd 6f :23 :47⅘ 1:13⅘ Md 25000 8 1 12 12 15 18 Espinoza J C 118 *.90 79-23 Keep IT Down 1188 Tim's Tune1185MeetTheWinner118nk Handily 8
LATEST WORKOUTS Nov 18 Bel tr.t 3f fst :36⅗ h ●Nov 4 Aqu 5f fst 1:01⅗ h Oct 22 Aqu 4f fst :49⅗ b Oct 17 Aqu 5f fst 1:00⅕ hg

Medieval Market

Dk. b. or br. c. 2, by Medieval Man—Hawaiian Love Star, by Hawaii
Br.—Crescent S Farms (Fla)
Tr.—Kelly Patrick J
Own.—Live Oak Plantation
117⁵
Lifetime 2 1 0 1 $14,400 — 1984 2 1 0 1 $14,400

22Nov84- 6Aqu fst 6f :22⅘ :46⅗ 1:12⅘ Md Sp Wt 1 3 11½ 11½ 13 12½ Ward W A5 113 6.40 77-29 MedievalMrket1132½WeightInGold118½TruthBeTold1181½ Driving 14
11Nov84- 4Aqu fst 7f :22 :45⅗ 1:10⅗ Md Sp Wt 5 1 1hd 22 28 313¾ Ward W A5 113 12.20 74-25 BoldSmoocher11813Buckner118¾MedievalMarket113nk Weakened 13
LATEST WORKOUTS Nov 18 Bel tr.t 5f fst 1:03⅕ b Nov 8 Bel tr.t 5f fst 1:01⅘ h ●Nov 3 Bel tr.t 5f fst 1:00 h Oct 22 Bel 5f fst 1:05⅖ b

Anconeus

B. c. 2, by Tanthem—Green Body, by Green Ticket
Br.—Classic Lines Partnership (Ky)
Tr.—Kelly Patrick J
Own.—Live Oak Plantation
122
Lifetime 9 1 4 1 $28,460 — 1984 9 1 4 1 $28,460

25Nov84- 6Aqu fst 7f :23⅗ :47⅕ 1:25⅗ Md Sp Wt 7 2 52½ 51½ 1hd 1no Skinner K b 118 5.60 73-25 Anconeus 118no Cool Joe 1183 Slewmobile 1182½ Driving 10
16Nov84- 4Aqu fst 6f :23⅗ :47⅘ 1:13⅘ Md 45000 8 2 52 41½ 21 21½ Skinner K 114 *3.20 73-35 DedPiecePck1141½Anconus1141½ConfirmdPtriot107² Second best 14
27Oct84- 4Aqu my 7f :22⅘ :45⅗ 1:22⅘ Md Sp Wt 9 4 99½ 1013 616 513½ Skinner K 118 7.50 74-16 CreamFraiche1183½Recognized1185½SchoirsTsk1111½ Raced wide 13
2Sep84- 4Bel fst 7f :22⅘ :46⅕ 1:24⅘ Md Sp Wt 9 2 76½ 75½ 1013 1214½ Skinner K 118 6.10 65-17 DH SenatorBrady1181 DH Hberdsher1181¾EsternSecret118hd Tired 14
18Aug84- 6Sar fst 6f :22⅘ :46⅕ 1:11⅘ Md Sp Wt 1 4 46 33½ 33 25½ Skinner K 118 2.70 77-15 LightningLep1185½Anconeus1183½AlertRspons1181 Best of others 8
4Aug84- 4Sar fst 6f :22⅕ :45⅗ 1:11 Md Sp Wt 3 6 78½ 27 27 28 Skinner K 118 5.00 77-13 Vindaloo 1188 Anconeus 1184½ Radar Alarm 118¾ 2nd best 13
26Jly84- 6Bel fst 6f :22⅘ :46⅕ 1:11⅗ Md Sp Wt 6 4 32½ 23 22½ 2¾ Skinner K 118 6.50 83-17 Salem Drive 118¾ Anconeus 1181½ Haberdasher 1184 Gamely 10
16Jly84- 6Bel fst 6f :22⅘ :46 1:11⅘ Md Sp Wt 8 10 109½ 87 64½ 34 Skinner K 118 65.40 81-24 Nickel Back 1184 Eternal Prince 118no Anconeus 1181 Fin. well 13
5Jly84- 6Bel fst 5½f :22⅘ :45⅘ 1:04⅘ Md Sp Wt 9 8 810 711 812 614 Skinner K 118 23.40 79-15 Chief's Crown 1185 Desert War 1182½ Tiger Bidder 1184 Outrun 9
LATEST WORKOUTS Nov 12 Bel 4f sly :49⅗ b Nov 7 Bel tr.t 3f fst :37⅕ b ●Oct 17 Bel 3f fst :34⅘ h Oct 8 Bel 3f fst :36⅖ h

Jet Wave

Dk. b. or br. c. 2, by Tri Jet—Saisonic, by Saidam
Br.—Zellen L (Fla)
Tr.—Cuprill Charles A
Own.—Cuprill C A
117
Lifetime 11 1 2 1 $12,400 — 1984 11 1 2 1 $12,400 — Turf 1 0 0 0

17Nov84- 3Med fst 1 :47 1:13 1:38⅘ Alw 13000 5 6 610 67 612 622½ Vergara O 115 7.80 66-22 Skip Trial 1156 Gourami 11710 Silent Scripture 120nk No speed 6
12Nov84- 5Aqu gd 7f :23 :46 1:25 Clm 75000 8 4 62¾ 31 32 22 Vergara O 117 9.70 74-25 First One Up 113² Jet Wave 117hd Kilts' Nashua 1131½ Gamely 8
28Oct84- 3Aqu gd 7f :22⅕ :45⅗ 1:22⅘ Alw 20000 6 6 79½ 77½ 512 513½ Vergara O 117 25.90 74-14 Young Monarch 1223½SunnyCabin1173SenatorBrady1174½ Outrun 7
20Oct84- 1Bel fm 1⅛ Ⓣ:47⅘ 1:11⅘ 1:43⅘ To Market 4 7 79 77 715 716¾ Cordero A Jr 115 13.80 67-12 Danger's Hour 1151 Quintile 1153¾ For Certain Doc 1171½ Outrun 7
20Oct84-Run in divisions
14Oct84- 6Bel fst 1 :46⅗ 1:12 1:38⅗ Alw 21000 8 8 78 65½ 58 39¾ Cordero A Jr 117 11.90 62-28 Stone White 1128 Julie's Bet1171¾JetWave117½ P'ssed tired ones 8
4Oct84- 6Med fst 6f :22⅘ :46⅗ 1:12⅘ Alw 12000 5 7 78½ 67½ 56 45½ Santiago A 114 7.40 74-20 Kpyormothsht1091½ThJk'sOnY1172½DstntOrbt1141¾ Forced bk. st. 7
11Aug84- 3Sar fst 7f :22⅘ :46 1:24⅘ Alw 20000 6 7 42 3½ 54½ 510 Vergara O 117 34.80 70-15 Mugzy'sRullah1221 DQ TiffanyIce1222¾BoltingHolme1191¾ Bumped 8
11Aug84-Placed fourth through disqualification
2Aug84- 6Sar fst 5½f :22⅘ :46 1:05⅗ Alw 20000 7 6 66 78½ 78½ 77 Mendoza C H 117 25.70 82-19 Gentle Kelly 1141½FelterOnTheQuay1171¾BernaCagney114no Wide 7
21Jly84- 10Suf fst 6f :22⅕ :45⅗ 1:11⅘ Mayflower 3 13 1012 913 715 714½ Mendoza C H 114 20.40 68-23 Doubly Clear 1141½MedievalSecret1175½Don'sChoice1171½ Outrun 13
27May84- 4PR fst 5½f :22⅘ :45⅗ 1:06 Alw 4000 4 5 55½ 45 33 2¾ Ulloa J 114 1.60 89-20 Sound Loud 113¾ Jet Wave 1144½TheGoldenBoy1164¾ Closed well 5
LATEST WORKOUTS Nov 27 Bel 5f fst 1:04⅘ h Nov 8 Bel 5f fst 1:01⅘ h Oct 10 Bel 1 fst 1:43⅖ b ●Oct 2 Bel 3f sly :34⅖ h

Haberdasher

Ch. c. 2, by Gummo—Lady Has A Bonnet, by Candy Spots
Br.—Rose & Wagner (Ky)
Tr.—Sedlacek Sue
Own.—Trevant Stable
110⁷
Lifetime 7 1 1 2 $16,310 — 1984 7 1 1 2 $16,310 — Turf 1 0 0 0

20Oct84- 4Bel fm 1⅛ Ⓣ:47⅕ 1:11 1:41⅘ To Market 8 8 812 815 619 619¾ Davis R G 115 16.30 72-12 Herat 1178 Lightning Leap 1151¾ Willingness 1153½ Never close 8
20Oct84-Run in divisions
6Oct84- 8Lrl fst 1⅛ :46⅘ 1:12⅗ 1:43 Laurel Fty 3 3 42 87½ 1216 1227½ Delgado A b 122 32.20 65-15 MightyAppeling1222½CutlssRelity122hdRhomnRule12210 Faltered 12
6Oct84-Grade I
24Sep84- 7Bel fst 7f :22⅘ :46 1:25 Alw 20000 4 6 76 64 52¾ 3½ Davis R G 119 6.40 76-21 Nickel Back 117½ Stone White 112hd Haberdasher 119¾ Wide 7
2Sep84- 4Bel fst 7f :22⅘ :46⅕ 1:24⅘ Md Sp Wt 14 7 66 44 22½ 11¾ Davis R G 118b 5.80 79-17 DH SentorBrdy1181 DH Hberdsher1181¾EsternSecret118hd Driving 14
2Sep84-Dead heat
23Aug84- 6Sar sly 7f :22⅘ :46 1:24⅘ Md Sp Wt 6 5 21½ 23 23 24½ Davis R G 118 *2.10 76-22 Coyote Dancer 1184½ Haberdasher 1182¾ Foligno 118¾ 2nd best 14
26Jly84- 6Bel fst 6f :22⅘ :46⅕ 1:11⅗ Md Sp Wt 4 7 54 55 46 32 Davis R G 118 5.10 82-17 Salem Drive 118¾ Anconeus 1181½ Haberdasher 1184 Rallied 10
25Jun84- 4Bel fst 5f :22 :45⅗ :58⅕ Md Sp Wt 4 6 69 711 69 65¾ Wilson R 118 20.80 90-16 Don's Choice 1181½ Herat 1181½ Nickel Back 1181 In close st. 8
LATEST WORKOUTS Nov 17 Key 4f fst :52 b Oct 17 Key 4f fst :49⅗ b Oct 3 Key 4f fst :49⅕ b

Warrior In Orbit — Ro. c. 2, by Iron Warrior—Orbiting Queen, by Royal Orbit — Br.—Huber R & Susan (Ky) — Tr.—Terrill William V — 1107
Own.—Verdesanna E
Lifetime 11 2 1 1 $18,910 — 1984 11 2 1 1 $18,910 — Turf 1 0 0 0

15Nov84- 3Aqu fst 6f :23 :47 1:13⅗ Clm 35000 8 8 85½ 66½ 41½ 1hd Blackstun K M7 110 9.80 74-29 WarriorInOrbit110hdUncleDaddy108[D]ShiningTyson112hd Driving 9
4Nov84- 4Aqu fst 6f :23⅗ :47⅘ 1:13⅗ Md 25000 10 9 93¾ 44 34 1¾ Blackstun K M7 111 9.10 74-25 Warrior In Orbit 111¾ Mr. G.J.G. 118½ Cedar Lane 118⁶¾ Driving 12
25Oct84- 2Aqu gd 1 :47 1:12⅗ 1:39⅗ Md 25000 12 12 129½ 1113 108¾ 96 Cordero A Jr b 118 4.30 62-21 Sudden Stroke 118nk Park Lane 114¾ Flippant 118nk Raced wide 14
22Oct84- 6Bel fm 1⅛ Ⓣ:47⅕ 1:11 1:43⅗ Md Sp Wt 8 9 108½ 1014 924 923¾ Graell A b 118 37.30 54-18 Space Rider 1181¾ Lord Ashley 1181½ Round Ridge 1181½ Outrun 11
8Oct84- 4Bel fst 7f :23⅕ :47⅘ 1:28⅗ Md 25000 13 1 63½ 54 33½ 22 Cordero A Jr b 1184 *2.80e 58-28 SvgRunnr118²[DH]WrriorInOrbit118[DH]Inflitionsm113¾ Up for place 14
8Oct84-Dead heat
1Oct84- 4Bel gd 6f :22⅗ :46⅗ 1:12⅗ Md 30000 11 5 78¾ 56 67 76½ Cordero A Jr 114 6.90 73-21 Trophy Hunter116¹ConfirmedPatriot118½CastingFor111¹¾ Outrun 12
20Sep84- 4Bel fst 6f :23⅗ :47⅗ 1:13 Md 25000 7 4 46 33 32½ 32 Thibeau R J b 118 4.60 75-26 NoCompetition118¹TrophyHunter118¹WrriorInOrbit118¹⁷ Evenly 7
13Sep84- 4Med fst 6f :23 :46⅗ 1:12⅗ Md 28000 1 7 87¾ 68½ 59 59¾ Doran K7 109 11.70 69-22 SuperScope118³½RoyalChristopher118²½StelSteel118nk No factor 9
6Sep84- 4Bel fst 7f :23⅕ :47⅕ 1:26⅕ Md 25000 8 8 109 87½ 64½ 54½ Doran K7 111 11.30e 66-17 Instant Recall 118¹ Glenn Brooke 118nk Stark Dancer118¹ Outrun 14
31Aug84- 4Bel fst 6f :23 :46⅗ 1:11 Md 45000 8 7 912 811 712 711½ Doran K7 107 43.90 75-13 Stone White 109¹½ Scholastic 114¹ Jal's InTime118¹½ Raced wide 11

LATEST WORKOUTS Nov 28 Bel 4f fst :51⅕ b — Nov 24 Bel 4f fst :53 b — Nov 11 Bel 4f fst :50 b — Nov 1 Bel tr.t 3f fst :39⅕ b

Trophy Hunter — Ch. g. 2, by Hawaiian Sound or Crew—Desperate Action, by Bold Commander — Br.—Hillbrook Farm (Ky) — Tr.—Jerkens Steven T — 117
Own.—Schwartz B K
Lifetime 5 1 2 0 $12,630 — 1984 5 1 2 0 $12,630 — Turf 1 0 0 0

12Nov84- 7Aqu gd 6f :22⅗ :46 1:10⅗ Alw 22000 6 4 31 22 25 27 Miranda J 117 11.90 81-25 Huddle Up 122⁷ Trophy Hunter 117²¾ Full of Spice117¹½ 2nd best 6
7Oct84- 5Bel fm 1 Ⓣ:46 1:10⅗ 1:37⅗ Alw 22000 2 5 53½ 34 55½ 54¾ Miranda J 117 35.60 71-17 Venidium 117¾ Lightning Leap 117²¾ RadarAlarm117nk Weakened 9
1Oct84- 4Bel gd 6f :22⅗ :46⅗ 1:12⅗ Md 32500 4 2 21½ 21 21½ 11 Miranda J 116 4.70 79-21 Trophy Hunter116¹ConfirmedPatriot118½CastingFor111¹¾ Driving 12
20Sep84- 4Bel fst 6f :23⅗ :47⅗ 1:13 Md 25000 1 6 12½ 11 2hd 21 Miranda J 118 *1.10 76-26 NoCompetition118¹TrophyHunter118¹WrriorInOrbit118¹⁷ Bore in 7
28Jly84- 3Bel gd 5½f :22⅗ :45⅗ 1:04⅗ Md 60000 6 7 45½ 46½ 59 615½ Velez R I 118 11.80 75-14 Sunny Cabin 114³ Fuzzy Jack 114³¾ Appoint 114³½ Wide 9

LATEST WORKOUTS Nov 26 Bel tr.t 4f fst :51⅗ b — Nov 7 Bel tr.t 6f fst 1:18 b — Oct 31 Bel 4f fst :47⅘ h — Oct 17 Bel tr.t 3f fst :38 b

Bold Smoocher — Ro. c. 2, by Bold L B—The Smoocher, by Polynesian — Br.—Jones B C (Ky) — Tr.—Nickerson Victor J — 119
Own.—Paulson A E
Lifetime 1 1 0 0 $12,000 — 1984 1 1 0 0 $12,000

11Nov84- 4Aqu fst 6f :22 :45⅗ 1:10⅗ Md Sp Wt 11 3 2hd 12 18 113 Santagata N 118 10.70 88-25 Bold Smoocher 118¹³ Buckner 118¾ Medieval Market113nk Easily 13

LATEST WORKOUTS Nov 29 Aqu 4f sly :50 b (d) — ●Nov 1 Aqu 5f fst :58⅗ hg — Oct 13 Aqu 4f fst :50 b

First One Up — B. c. 2, by Johnny Appleseed—Clearly Early, by Distinctive — Br.—Weinsier R (Ky) — Tr.—Barrera Luis — 117
Own.—Weinsier R
Lifetime 12 2 3 1 $37,790 — 1984 12 2 3 1 $37,790 — Turf 4 0 1 0 $7,140

26Nov84- 5Aqu fst 1⅛ :50⅗ 1:15⅕ 1:53⅗ Alw 23000 1 1 11 1hd 21½ 34½ Ward W A5 b 112 1.50 62-25 Stack 122³½ Uncle Daddy 110¹½ First One Up 112⁵½ Weakened 6
19Nov84- 5Aqu fst 6f :23 :47⅕ 1:12⅗ Alw 22000 8 3 52½ 31 1hd 25 Migliore R b 117 7.50 72-33 El Basco 117⁵ First One Up 117¾ He's HomeFree117hd Weakaned 9
12Nov84- 5Aqu gd 7f :23 :46 1:25 Clm 70000 7 3 31 2hd 1½ 12 Bailey J D b 113 10.00 76-25 First One Up 113² Jet Wave 117hd Kilts' Nashua 113¹½ Driving 8
25Oct84- 5Aqu gd 7f :23 :46⅗ 1:24⅕ Clm 45000 5 4 52 33 24 24¾ Guerra W A b 117 2.30e 75-21 Keep ItDown117⁴¾FirstOneUp117¹½SavageRunner113nk No match 8
14Oct84- 6Bel fst 1 :46⅗ 1:12 1:38⅗ Alw 21000 6 3 31½ 32 37½ 512½ Bailey J D b 117 9.80e 59-28 Stone White 112⁹ Julie's Bet 117¹½ Jet Wave 117½ Factor, tired 8
30Sep84- 7Bel fm 1 Ⓣ:45⅗ 1:10⅗ 1:36⅗ Donut King 8 6 66 611 814 813½ Guerra W A b 115 17.30 69-27 Western Champ 117½ Don't Fool WithMe117³Jonlan122nk Outrun 10
20Sep84- 8Bel fm 1⅛ Ⓣ:46⅗ 1:11⅗ 1:44 Alw 21000 1 1 11 11 2½ 44½ Guerra W A b 117 3.30 72-24 ForCertinDoc117³½Mgnminous122¾McAtTheTrck117hd Weakened 6
9Sep84- 7Bel fm 1⅛ Ⓣ:47⅗ 1:12 1:45⅗ Alw 21000 4 4 42½ 32½ 21 2nk Guerra W A b 117 12.80 72-24 Don'tFoolWithM117nkFirstOnUp117¹½NicklBck117¹½ Just missed 8
22Aug84- 5Sar fm 1 Ⓣ:47⅗ 1:12⅗ 1:38⅕ Alw 21000 2 3 32½ 32½ 41½ 44½ Guerra W A b 117 13.50 81-20 WestrnChmp117¾NicklBck117nkDon'tFoolWithM117³½ Weakened 10
2Aug84- 6Sar fst 5½f :22⅗ :46 1:05⅗ Alw 20000 6 4 43 68 67½ 56 Guerra W A b 117 13.10 83-19 GentleKelly114¹½FelterOnTheQuy117¹¾BernCgny114no No excuse 7

LATEST WORKOUTS Nov 18 Bel tr.t 3f fst :38⅘ b — Nov 9 Bel tr.t 4f fst :51⅗ b — Nov 4 Bel 4f fst :48⅘ hg — Oct 22 Bel tr.t 4f fst :48 h

Numeric — B. c. 2, by Quadratic—Valmara, by Fleet Nasrullah — Br.—Kirkham R & Ryehill FArm (MD) — Tr.—Stephens Woodford C — 119
Own.—Rhehill Farm
Lifetime 6 1 3 0 $23,720 — 1984 6 1 3 0 $23,720 — Turf 1 0 1 0 $4,180

24Nov84- 8Lrl fst 1⅛ :47 1:12⅗ 1:43⅘ [S]Md uvenile 1 7 64½ 75½ 76½ 67½ McCarron G b 122 3.10 81-17 Bea Quality 122¹½ Joyfull John 122¹ Jay Bryan 122²½ Steadied 9
5Nov84- 6Aqu my 1 :46⅗ 1:12⅗ 1:39⅕ Md Sp Wt 3 8 62¾ 63½ 21 1hd Maple E b 118 2.80 70-25 Numeric 118hd Recognized 118²¾ Cool Joe 118⁴ Driving 11
13Oct84- 9Bel fm 1⅛ Ⓣ:47 1:11⅕ 1:44⅗ Md Sp Wt 10 1 2hd 2hd 2½ 21¾ Maple E b 118 6.70 72-21 ForeverCommand115¹¾Numeric118²RomnRiver118¹½ Lacked rally 12
3Oct84- 9Bel fst 7f :23⅕ :46⅗ 1:25⅕ Md Sp Wt 8 2 22½ 2½ 21 23¾ McCarron G b 118 2.70 72-26 Young Monarch 118³¾ Numeric 118⁵¾ Over Spruce 118¹½ Gamely 10
22Sep84- 4Bel fst 1 :47⅗ 1:12⅗ 1:38⅗ Md Sp Wt 1 1 1½ 1½ 21½ 23 Velasquez J b 118 4.00 70-19 Eastern Secret 118³ Numeric 118² Revelrout 118³¾ Slow start 14
6Sep84- 6Bel fst 6f :22⅗ :46⅗ 1:10⅗ Md Sp Wt 6 8 78 64½ 69 57½ Maple E b 118 2.90 80-17 Another Reef 118¹¾ Brookover 118⁵ As You LikeIt118hd Checked 12

LATEST WORKOUTS Nov 23 Bel 3f fst :36⅘ h — Nov 19 Bel 6f fst 1:15 h — Nov 17 Bel 4f fst :51⅗ b — Nov 13 Bel 5f fst 1:02⅗ b

SECOND RACE
Aqueduct
DECEMBER 2, 1984

7 FURLONGS. (1.20⅕) ALLOWANCE. Purse $22,000. 2-year-olds which have never won a race other than maiden or claiming. Weight, 122 lbs. Non-winners of a race other than claiming since November 15 allowed 3 lbs. Of such a race since November 1, 5 lbs.

Value of race $22,000; value to winner $13,200; second $4,840; third $2,640; fourth $1,320. Mutuel pool $95,148, OTB pool $99,177. Quinella Pool $177,801; OTB Quinella Pool $171,502.

Last Raced	Horse	Eqt.A.Wt	PP	St	¼	½	Str	Fin	Jockey	Odds $1
11Nov84 4Aqu1	Bold Smoocher	2 119	7	3	1½	11½	16	19	Santagata N	.40
12Nov84 7Aqu2	Trophy Hunter	2 117	6	4	61	4½	44	2½	Miranda J	23.80
26Nov84 5Aqu3	First One Up	b 2 117	8	1	2½	21	2½	31½	Bailey J D	9.70
25Nov84 6Aqu1	Anconeus	b 2 122	3	7	3hd	32	31	4hd	Skinner K	21.10
24Nov84 8Lrl6	Numeric	b 2 119	9	2	72	51½	5hd	5¾	Maple E	8.50
17Nov84 3Med6	Jet Wave	2 117	4	8	84	61	63	63	Vergara O	31.00
6Oct84 8Bel7	Eastern Secret	2 117	1	9	9	9	71	72	Lovato F Jr	16.00
20Oct84 4Bel6	Haberdasher	2 110	5	5	5hd	7½	83	86½	Espinosa R E7	11.10
19Nov84 5Aqu4	Keep It Down	2 117	2	6	4hd	82	9	9	Davis R G	14.90

OFF AT 12:56 Start good, Won easily. Time, :23⅕, :46⅕, 1:10⅘, 1:23⅘ Track fast.

$2 Mutuel Prices:			
7-(K)-BOLD SMOOCHER	2.80	2.60	2.60
6-(J)-TROPHY HUNTER		8.60	5.40
8-(L)-FIRST ONE UP			4.00
$2 QUINELLA 6-7 PAID $30.60.			

Ro. c, by Bold L B—The Smoocher, by Polynesian. Trainer Nickerson Victor J. Bred by Jones B C (Ky).

BOLD SMOOCHER showing way leaving chute, increased margin during final quarter-mile without need of encouragement displaying ability. TROPHY HUNTER, finishing without aid of whip and racing well removed from rail was along besting FIRST ONE UP The latter, in near pursuit of winner, weakened from efforts. ANCONEUS saving ground failed to pose serious threat. NUMERIC was wide throughout. JET WAVE lacked speed. EASTERN SECRET never reached contention. HABERDASHER showed little. KEEP IT DOWN was soundly beaten.

Futurity, contested at a flat mile, and was the public's choice. Washed out in the paddock, the colt faded badly in the stretch to finish near the rear of the field. It was later discovered that he had suffered a knee injury that promised to keep him out of the classics the following spring. When (if) he returned to the races, the same two questions would remain unanswered, and another would have been added to the list: Did the injury compromise his ability?

Chapter 4

Stretching Out for the First Time

I HAVE ALWAYS ENJOYED two-year-old racing for a variety of reasons. As a devotee of the sport, I relished the chance to gaze into the future, to observe the following season's classics contenders as young men and draw my own conclusions as to which were most likely to go on as the distances lengthened. As a handicapper, I found that juvenile racing offered at least two distinct situations in which taking a position against conventional handicapping wisdom led to potentially lucrative situations betting against a false favorite.

The first situation deals with two-year-olds that prove successful in the midsummer stakes events. For many of these horses, that experience turns out to be the high point of their racing careers. Most of the top-class barns withhold their better prospects from competition until August or later, increasingly so nowadays, with the Breeders' Cup in November being a prospective goal. When these well-regarded colts graduate from the maiden ranks and move into stakes company, they often find their more experienced stakes-winning rivals a bit the worse for the wear and somewhat lacking in true graded stakes quality. Yet these same horses will be favored because of their established record in "name" stakes events. In many years, the changing of the guard seemed almost inevitable, with every impressive maiden winner looming as a potential play in the next stakes event on the calendar. When colts like Ogygian, Seattle Slew, Spectacular Bid, and Soy Numero Uno came to the fore, the winning payoffs may not have been "big balloons," but the satisfaction of being right about them was quite rewarding.

It is on the second situation, however, that this chapter will focus. In the fall, when two-year-olds are tested over a distance of ground for the first time, many players look to the animal with the distance pedigree and some hint of ability at the shorter distances as the one most likely to succeed. The most popular barometer is some sign of life during the stretch run of a recent sprint, with the obvious conclusion being that the extra distance will bring the animal closer. This is not necessarily so!

I prefer to look at the front end of the sprint—the first couple of furlongs—and back the horse now stretching out that flashed early speed at the shorter distance. If that horse happens to have stout bloodlines, all the better, although they certainly are not a prerequisite for consideration. Indeed, those with sprint bloodlines make the more interesting bets. They're more likely to reproduce that dangerous commodity—early speed—and often surprise at quite attractive odds. Many of these "sprint types" are able to go longer as juveniles than they will as older horses due to their own precocity and/or the slower maturation of the "distance types."

Most sprinters can stay a mile on occasion—it's just a matter of finding a field they can dominate early, affording them the chance to relax on the lead and, in effect, turn the route into a half-mile dash. Juvenile maiden routes often provide opportunities of this kind. They tend to be cluttered with animals that have shown little or no ability at shorter distances, specifically the ability to get into gear quickly. Few horses that tire after showing early speed at the sprint distances are asked to stretch out to a route. Those that do are either out for conditioning purposes—to build up their stamina—or must be considered serious betting possibilities. Knowledge of the trainer's strengths and weaknesses, and his modus operandi, are useful in detecting the difference.

The young "closer" stretching out carries with it certain ambiguities. The horse may prove to be nothing more than a closing sprinter, incapable of going long—the type that will rally mildly, then flatten out at longer distances. Or it may prove to be the perennial closer, always charging in the stretch but seldom, if ever, getting the job done. The latter are among the biggest sucker bets on the racetrack—and sufficient reason to think twice before backing a horse first time at a mile or longer simply because it shows some stretch kick at sprint distances.

The sixth race at Aqueduct on Saturday, November 9, 1985, demonstrates these points in dramatic style. We have confined our analysis to the ten horses in the field that rate comment:

6 **AQUEDUCT** 1 MILE AQUEDUCT

1 MILE. (1.33⅕) MAIDEN SPECIAL WEIGHT. Purse $23,000. 2-year-olds. Weights, 118 lbs.

Highfalutin — B. c. 2, by Honest Pleasure—Bemis Heights, by Herbager — Br.—Ryan Eleanor K (Ky) — Tr.—Kelly Edward I Jr — 118 — Lifetime 5 0 0 1 $2,640 — 1985 5 M 0 1 $2,640
Own.—Jayeff B Stables
24Oct85- 3Aqu fst 7f :23 :46⅘ 1:25 Md 35000 4 7 53 53 43 54 Maple E 118 7.00 72-24 Locksley 118hd Proud And Tall 1183 Tower Of Babel 114¾ Evenly 14
29Sep85- 5Bel fst 6½f :22⅘ :46⅕ 1:18⅘ Md 50000 6 9 96¾108½ 911 712¾ Maple E 118 12.40 70-19 Twentyminuteslate 1181½ Fugie 1183½ Princely Screen1134½ Tired 14
6Sep85- 6Bel fst 6f :23 :46⅘ 1:12⅕ Md Sp Wt 5 9 88½131713191318½ McCarron G 118 11.50e 62-21 Royal Doulton 1182 Blini 118nk Full Realization 1181½ Outrun 14
23Aug85- 5Sar fst 5f :22⅘ :46⅕ :58⅘ Md Sp Wt 6 2 53½ 55 46 39¾ Maple E 118 6.20 86-12 BrveProspct1185½FullRliztion1184¼Highflutin1181½ Saved ground 9
12Aug85- 6Sar fst 5f :22⅘ :46⅘ :59⅘ Md Sp Wt 5 9 99 611 68 77 Maple E 118 5.00 84-17 GlintChief1181½Mjsty'sRod118nkBoldAndSpdy1182½ Broke slowly 9
LATEST WORKOUTS Oct 12 Bel 4f fst :48⅕ b Oct 7 Bel 4f fst :48 h Sep 26 Bel 4f fst :48⅘ h Sep 18 Bel 3f fst :37 b

Scrimshaw — Dk. b. or br. c. 2, by Apalachee—Crimson Lace, by First Landing — Br.—Hancock & Peters Betty M (Ky) — Tr.—Kelly Larry — 118 — Lifetime 1 0 0 0 — 1985 1 M 0 0
Own.—Peters Betty M
26Oct85- 3Aqu fst 6f :23 :47 1:13 Md Sp Wt 2 9 85¼ 74½107½ 76 Vasquez J 118 14.50 70-19 Strong Performance 118hd Bold Screen1181BigCoda118½ In close 10
LATEST WORKOUTS Nov 4 Bel 5f fst 1:02⅘ h Oct 23 Bel 3f fst :36 h Oct 11 Bel 5f fst 1:02⅘ bg Oct 2 Bel tr.t 3f fst :37⅘ b

Stride Of Joy — B. c. 2, by Victory Stride—Estates Asset, by King of the Castle — Br.—Perez R (NY) — Tr.—Callejas Alfredo — 111[7] — Lifetime 1 0 0 0 — 1985 1 M 0 0
Own.—Perez R
14Oct85- 6Bel fst 6f :22⅘ :46⅘ 1:12⅕ Md Sp Wt 4 8 87¼ 910 9171122½ Alvarado R Jr 118 8.40f 58-19 Royal Pennant 118no Arctic Beat 1182 Easterner 1182½ Outrun 11
LATEST WORKOUTS Oct 27 Bel tr.t 5f fst 1:03 b Oct 25 Bel tr.t 4f fst :52⅘ b Oct 10 Bel (T) 4f gd :49⅗ b (d) Oct 3 Bel 7f sly 1:32⅘ b

Sure Turn — B. c. 2, by Best Turn—Sugar And Spice, by Key To The Mint — Br.—Calumet Farm (Ky) — Tr.—Casse Mark — 118 — Lifetime 6 0 1 0 $7,700 — 1985 6 M 1 0 $7,700 — Turf 1 0 0 0
Own.—Calumet Farm
23Oct85- 6Aqu fst 1 :48⅕ 1:12⅘ 1:38⅘ Md Sp Wt 7 8 41½ 31½ 33 43¾ Migliore R 118 3.50[D] 70-17 Fabulous Flight 1181¼ Manila 1182½ Man Up 118hd Bore in 8
23Oct85-Disqualified and placed eighth
29Sep85- 6Bel fst 1 :46⅘ 1:12⅕ 1:38⅘ Md Sp Wt 8 9 911 55 55 22 Migliore R 118 9.00 71-19 Thundering Force 1182 SureTurn1181JackOfClubs1182½ Wide str 13
11Sep85- 6Bel gd 7f :22⅘ :46 1:24⅘ Md Sp Wt 5 2 53¾ 45½ 45 44½ Migliore R 118 6.40 74-16 Dunsany 1181 Fabulous Flight 1181 Grace Ave 1182½ Wide str. 7
28Aug85- 6Bel fm 1 (T):48 1:13 1:40⅕ Md Sp Wt 8 12 106¾111111161121½ Cruguet J 118 *2.40 42-36 Knockiemill 1181½ Casa Basso 118hd Man Up 118no Outrun 12
11Aug85- 6Sar fst 6f :22⅘ :46⅕ 1:11⅘ Md Sp Wt 2 5 89½ 98½ 57 47 Davis R G 118 9.80 75-18 Raja's Revenge1182½JohnnyMcCabe118½BalthazarB 1184 Mild bid 9
3Aug85- 3Sar fst 6f :22⅕ :45⅘ 1:11⅘ Md Sp Wt 2 7 1216122010 12 67½ Davis R G 118 23.70 73-11 RealCourage1182½ProudWorld118hdAraMaco1183½ Raced greenly 13
LATEST WORKOUTS Sep 20 Bel tr.t 3f fst :37 b

Masterful Run — Ch. c. 2, by Master Derby—Running Beauty, by Double Jay — Br.—Golden Chance Farm Inc (Ky) — Tr.—Kelley Walter A — 118 — Lifetime 4 0 0 0 — 1985 4 M 0 0 — Turf 1 0 0 0
Own.—Murrell J R
17Oct85- 6Bel fm 1⅟₁₆ [T]:48⅘ 1:13⅘ 1:46 Md Sp Wt 5 4 43½ 66¾ 718 816 Privitera R 118 32.70 55-22 Gold Alert 1181 Daytime Friend 118¾ J. O. Cross 1182 Tired 8
29Sep85- 6Bel fst 1 :46⅘ 1:12⅕ 1:38⅘ Md Sp Wt 13 5 44½ 65½ 812 916¾ Privitera R b 118 72.70 56-19 Thundering Force 1182 Sure Turn 1181 Jack Of Clubs 1182½ Tired 13
15Sep85- 6Bel fst 6f :22⅘ :45⅗ 1:10⅕ Md Sp Wt 4 6 911 815 815 819½ Privitera R5 113 65.90 72-16 Ketoh 11812 Ara Macao 118nk Blini 1184 Outrun 9
11Aug85- 3Sar fst 6f :21⅘ :45⅗ 1:11⅘ Md Sp Wt 6 5 77½ 811 9131016½ Deegan J C 118 66.60 66-18 Mustin Lake 118hd Storm Cat 118½ Perfect By Far 1184½ Tired 12
LATEST WORKOUTS Nov 7 Bel tr.t 3f fst :35⅗ h ●Nov 1 Bel 6f fst 1:13 h Oct 12 Bel 6f fst 1:15⅕ h Oct 7 Bel tr.t 4f fst :50⅘ b

J. O. Cross — Dk. b. or br. c. 2, by J O Tobin—Shamme, by Sham — Br.—Couturier Mr-Mrs B P (Ky) — Tr.—Nieminski Richard — 118 — Lifetime 5 0 1 1 $7,600 — 1985 5 M 1 1 $7,600 — Turf 1 0 0 1 $2,760
Own.—Peace J H
17Oct85- 6Bel fm 1⅟₁₆ [T]:48⅘ 1:13⅘ 1:46 Md Sp Wt 7 6 66¾ 32 23 31¾ Cruguet J 118 8.70 69-22 Gold Alert 1181 Daytime Friend 118¾ J. O. Cross 1182 Bore in 8
29Sep85- 6Bel fst 1 :46⅘ 1:12⅕ 1:38⅘ Md Sp Wt 3 7 55 75¾ 711 816½ Cruguet J 118 23.50 57-19 Thundering Force 1182 Sure Turn 1181 Jack Of Clubs 1182½ Tired 13
11Sep85- 6Bel gd 7f :22⅘ :46 1:24⅘ Md Sp Wt 4 4 43½ 35½ 59 59¾ Davis R G 118 2.90 68-16 Dunsany 1181 Fabulous Flight 1181 Grace Ave 1182½ Tired 7
21Aug85- 3Sar fst 6f :22⅘ :46⅕ 1:11⅕ Md Sp Wt 12 9 98¾ 712 711 79 Davis R G 118 7.80 75-14 Storm Cat 118nk Damascus Steel 1186 Cultivate 1181½ No factor 12
29Jly85- 3Bel fst 6f :22⅘ :46⅕ 1:11⅘ Md Sp Wt 7 8 812 78½ 44½ 24 Davis R G 118 7.80 79-18 Badger Land 1184 J. O. Cross 1183½ Lord Pacal 118nk Off slowly 8
LATEST WORKOUTS Oct 31 Bel tr.t 4f fst :49⅗ h

Star De Triomphe — B. c. 2, by Star de Naskra—Donna B Quick, by Don B — Br.—Casse & Schmidt (Fla) — Tr.—Armstrong Wendell — 118 — Lifetime 3 0 0 1 $1,500 — 1985 3 M 0 1 $1,500
Own.—Brausen K
20Oct85- 4Bel fst 7f :22⅘ :46⅘ 1:25⅕ Md Sp Wt 5 9 11141115 89½ 711¾ Lovato F Jr 118 36.50 64-29 Out East 1181½ Dance of Life 1183 Jack Of Clubs 118½ No factor 14
3Oct85- 6Bel sly 7f :23 :46⅘ 1:25 Md Sp Wt 2 5 811 917 914 612¼ Maple E 118 11.70 65-19 Navy Admiral 1185½ Fabulous Flight 1184¼ Gold Alert118½ Outrun 11
3May85- 3Hia fst 5f :22⅘ :47⅘ 1:00⅕ Md Sp Wt 9 9 43 32 41½ 31 Tejeira J 118 *2.00 84-20 ImprobblStory1181BnnTnTn118hdStrDTromph118nk Couldn't gain 9
LATEST WORKOUTS ●Nov 3 Bel tr.t 7f fst 1:28⅘ b Oct 27 Bel tr.t 5f fst 1:02 b Oct 18 Bel tr.t 3f fst :36⅘ h Oct 10 Bel tr.t 4f fst :49⅕ b

Baron De Graus — Ch. c. 2, by Caucasus—Graus, by Graustark — Br.—Treasure Hill Farm (Ky) — Tr.—LaBoccetta Frank — 118 — Lifetime 6 0 1 0 $5,060 — 1985 6 M 1 0 $5,060 — Turf 4 0 1 0 $5,060
Own.—Anchel E
21Oct85- 8Bel fm 1⅟₁₆ (T):47⅕ 1:10⅘ 1:42⅘ To Market 3 6 66 67½ 87½ 67¼ Santos J A b 115 19.00 76-19 Christiana Hundred1153½OnMyWaytoA.A.1222¾Loose115nk Outrun 9
7Oct85- 4Bel gd 1 (T):48⅘ 1:15⅘ 1:40⅘ Md Sp Wt 11 2 2hd 3½ 8151023½ Santos J A b 118 *1.90 38-36 Loose 118nk Groomsman 1182½ Unlike Anything 1186½ Gave way 12
20Sep85- 3Bel fm 1⅟₁₆ (T):47⅕ 1:11⅘ 1:43⅘ Md Sp Wt 7 9 66½ 66 25 22¾ Santos J A b 118 7.20 75-15 ChrstnHndrd1182¾BronDGrs1185½ToknOfYoth118¾ Best of others 11
28Aug85- 6Bel fm 1 (T):48 1:13 1:40⅕ Md Sp Wt 9 7 74 74½ 53¾ 51½ Hernandez R b 118 26.30 62-36 Knockiemill 1181½ Casa Basso 118hd Man Up 118no Late bid 12
21Aug85- 6Sar fst 6f :22⅘ :46⅕ 1:11⅘ Md Sp Wt 5 8 108¾ 9161114 913½ Hernandez R b 118 59.50 69-14 Perfect By Far 1182 Manila 118½ Royal Doulton 1182½ Outrun 12
11Aug85- 3Sar fst 6f :21⅘ :45⅗ 1:11⅘ Md Sp Wt 1 10 11141113 813 813¾ Hernandez R 118 43.10 68-18 Mustin Lake 118hd Storm Cat 118½ Perfect ByFar1184½ No factor 12
LATEST WORKOUTS Nov 4 Aqu 5f fst 1:01⅘ h ●Oct 16 Aqu 4f fst :48⅕ h Sep 29 Aqu 5f fst 1:01⅕ h Sep 18 Aqu 4f fst :47⅘ h

Jack Of Clubs — B. c. 2, by Sir Ivor—Colony Club, by Tom Rolfe — Br.—Mellon P (Va) — Tr.—Miller Mack — 118 — Lifetime 3 0 0 2 $5,400 — 1985 3 M 0 2 $5,400
Own.—Rokeby Stables
20Oct85- 4Bel fst 7f :22⅘ :46⅘ 1:25⅕ Md Sp Wt 3 10 87½ 86½ 42½ 34½ Guerra W A 118 3.40e 71-29 Out East 1181½ Dance of Life 1183 Jack Of Clubs 118½ Rallied 14
29Sep85- 6Bel fst 1 :46⅘ 1:12⅕ 1:38⅘ Md Sp Wt 7 4 65½ 42 22½ 33 Vasquez J 118 6.40 70-19 Thundering Force 1182SureTurn1181JackOfClubs1182½ Weakened 13
15Sep85- 6Bel fst 6f :22⅘ :45⅗ 1:10⅕ Md Sp Wt 8 9 811 714 714 516¾ Bailey J D 118 16.00 74-16 Ketoh 11812 Ara Macao 118nk Blini 1184 Broke slowly 9
LATEST WORKOUTS Nov 6 Bel 4f my :48 h Oct 31 Bel 5f fst 1:00 h Oct 26 Bel 4f fst :48⅕ h Oct 15 Bel 3f fst :35 h

Inheriting — B. c. 2, by True Colors—Nativeness, by Native Dancer — Br.—Ocala Stud Farms Inc (Fla) — Tr.—Jacobs Eugene — 118 — Lifetime 2 0 0 0 $1,320 — 1985 2 M 0 0 $1,320 — Turf 1 0 0 0
Own.—Allen Herbert
30Oct85- 6Aqu fst 7f :22⅘ :46⅘ 1:24⅘ Md Sp Wt 5 2 43 42 54¾ 49½ Deegan J C 118 39.80 69-21 Wayar 118nk Man Up 1183 Waseca 1186½ No rally 7
17Oct85- 6Bel fm 1⅟₁₆ [T]:48⅘ 1:13⅘ 1:46 Md Sp Wt 6 8 816 811 818 713½ Santagata N 118 12.10 57-22 Gold Alert 1181 Daytime Friend 118¾ J. O. Cross 1182 Outrun 8
LATEST WORKOUTS Nov 5 Bel 3f sly :37 hg Oct 24 Bel tr.t 1 fst 1:48⅘ h Oct 11 Bel tr.t 4f fst :50⅘ b Oct 7 Bel tr.t 3f fst :39 b

Starry Trail — B. c. 2, by Majestic Light—Scattering, by Ack Ack — Br.—Power A M (Ky) — Tr.—Cantey Joseph B — 118 — Lifetime 3 0 0 0 $2,700 — 1985 3 M 0 0 $2,700
Own.—Asbury T
23Oct85- 6Aqu fst 1 :48⅕ 1:12⅘ 1:38⅘ Md Sp Wt 2 6 85 76 712 610 Maple E 118 11.10 64-17 Fabulous Flight 1181½ Manila 1182½ ManUp118hd Jumped shadow 8
23Oct85-Placed fifth through disqualification
29Sep85- 6Bel fst 1 :46⅘ 1:12⅕ 1:38⅘ Md Sp Wt 1 2 23 2½ 33 45½ Maple E 118 27.40 67-19 Thundering Force 1182 Sure Turn 1181 Jack Of Clubs 1182½ Tired 13
15Sep85- 3Bel fst 6f :22⅘ :46⅕ 1:11 Md Sp Wt 5 5 67 56½ 49½ 411¾ Bailey J D 118 14.20 75-16 Faraway Island 1183½ManInMotion1137½RoyalPennant1181½ Wide 7
LATEST WORKOUTS Nov 2 Bel 6f fst 1:14⅘ h Oct 19 Bel 4f fst :48 h Oct 10 Bel 5f fst 1:03 b Sep 25 Bel tr.t 5f my 1:03⅘ b

Ioskeha — B. c. 2, by Exclusive Native—Salmacis, by Gallant Man — Br.—Tartan Farms (Fla) — Tr.—Nerud Jan H — 118 — Lifetime 2 0 0 0 — 1985 2 M 0 0
Own.—Tartan Stable
26Oct85- 6Aqu fst 6f :23 :46⅘ 1:12⅘ Md Sp Wt 4 2 32 56½ 56 67¾ Venezia M 118 4.90 71-19 Alberta Clipper 1184½ Seattle Sunrise118¾SharpThreat118hd Tired 9
15Sep85- 3Bel fst 6f :22⅘ :46⅕ 1:11 Md Sp Wt 2 2 55 67½ 511 614¾ Venezia M 118 5.00 72-16 FarawayIsland1183½ManInMotion1137½RoyalPennnt1181½ Outrun 7
LATEST WORKOUTS Oct 21 Bel 4f fst :52 b Oct 16 Bel 4f fst :49⅘ b Oct 12 Bel 4f fst :48⅕ b Oct 6 Bel 4f gd :47⅘ h

Princely Screen — Dk. b. or br. g. 2, by Princely Pleasure—Top Screen, by Ambehaving — Br.—Bo-Bett Farm (Fla) — Tr.—Ferriola Peter — 113[5] — Lifetime 3 0 1 1 $4,420 — 1985 3 M 1 1 $4,420
Own.—Baselice Arnold C
7Oct85- 6Bel fst 6f :23 :46⅘ 1:11 Md 50000 2 2 2½ 22 26 29¾ Jones B S5 b 113 *2.10 77-23 Othersideofthtrck1189¾PrinclyScrn1132½AnyProspct1183¾ 2nd best 11
29Sep85- 5Bel fst 6½f :22⅘ :46⅕ 1:18⅘ Md 50000 5 3 31½ 3½ 32½ 35 Jones B S5 113 10.90 78-19 Twentyminuteslte1181½Fugie1183½PrincelyScreen1134½ Lugged in 14
12Sep85- 5Bel fst 6f :22⅘ :45⅘ 1:11⅘ Md 60000 10 5 32 57½ 68 64½ Jones B S5 109 25.60 78-23 Fancy Fiddler 118¾ Twentyminuteslate 114¾ Fugie 116hd Tired 12
LATEST WORKOUTS Nov 8 Aqu 4f fst :50⅘ b Oct 29 Aqu 4f fst :50⅘ b

Saratoga Colony B. c. 2, by Pleasant Colony—Witha Cherry Ontop, by Groton
Br.—Stonewall Farm (Ky) 102 100 118
Own.—Wood C N Tr.—Wright Frank I
Lifetime 2 0 0 0 $1,320 1985 2 M 0 0 $1,320

20Oct85- 4Bel fst 7f :22⅘ :46⅘ 1:25⅕ Md Sp Wt 12 8 5 3 3 2½ 2 hd 4 5 McCarron G b 118 5.30 71-29 Out East 118 1½ Dance of Life 118 3 Jack Of Clubs 118½ Weakened 14
3Oct85- 6Bel sly 7f :23 :46⅗ 1:25 Md Sp Wt 6 11 6 7½ 7 8¼ 5 11 5 11 McCarron G 118 14.00 66-19 Navy Admiral 118 5½ FabulousFlight118 4¼ GoldAlert118½ Off slowly 11
LATEST WORKOUTS Nov 1 Bel 5f fst 1:02⅗ b ●Oct 10 Bel 3f fst :34⅖ h Sep 30 Bel 5f fst 1:01⅗ h Sep 26 Bel 6f fst 1:15 h

Also Eligible (Not in Post Position Order):

Fool Me Not Scot B. c. 2, by Foolish Pleasure—Spruce Pine, by Big Spruce
Br.—Greer Esther (Ky) 118
Own.—Belford A Tr.—Tesher Howard M
Lifetime 3 0 0 0 $570 1985 3 M 0 0 $570

31Oct85- 3Aqu fst 1 :48 1:13⅗ 1:37⅗ Md c-50000 11 14 9 5½ 11 11 8 10 26 10 31½ Migliore R 118 10.50 46-18 Bolshoi Boy 114½ Court Masque118 13½ That'sFirCertain107 3 Wide 14
18Oct85- 1Med fst 6f :22⅘ :46⅕ 1:12⅘ Md 35000 8 10 8 14 10 13 5 7½ 4 2¼ Melendez J D 116 34.70 78-18 La Chem De Fe: 118 1½ NancyTheGolfer118 no MaiTaiArt118¾ Rallied 10
10Oct85- 1Med fst 6f :22⅘ :45⅗ 1:11⅕ Md Sp Wt 10 1 10 35 10 29 10 27 10 31¾ Decarlo C P 7 111 15.90 54-15 Water Canon 118 2 Averno 118 2½ Mr. Joe Lane 118 8 Outrun 10
LATEST WORKOUTS Oct 17 Med 3f fst :37 b Oct 7 Med 4f gd :51 b Oct 1 Med 4f fst :50 b Sep 26 Med 4f fst :49⅘ b

HIGHFALUTIN

This horse was closer to the lead at each call last time, which is potentially a sign of improvement, but in this case an illusion exposed either by the relatively weak pace and speed figures for the race or the drop to $35,000 maiden claiming. There is no reason to anticipate the dramatic improvement needed to make this one a factor against maiden specials, especially from the disadvantageous rail post.

SCRIMSHAW

Apparently had traffic problems in upper stretch in his debut, judging by his loss of ground and position between the second and stretch calls that day. Would be more interested had the colt attracted some attention at the betting windows in his first start.

SURE TURN

With two routes already under his saddle, one would have expected a better finishing kick last time. Close up early against a very slow pace, Sure Turn lost ground through the stretch while having difficulty maintaining a straight course. He has finished ahead of the favorite, though.

J. O. CROSS

The improvement last time should be taken at face value—the horse prefers grass to dirt.

BARON DE GRAUS

Obviously grass-meant from the start of his career, this colt rallied well twice on that surface before falling apart when tactics were changed, then showed nothing in stakes company. His last two efforts might be forgiven if today's race were on grass. But it's on dirt, and this colt has shown nothing on that surface.

JACK OF CLUBS

The obvious favorite, Jack Of Clubs closed ground, then hung, first time at a distance, then rallied behind a pair of decent animals at seven furlongs last time out. Out East came out of that race to win a mile stakes at Aqueduct during Breeders' Cup week, and Dance Of Life returned to break his maiden in a sizzling 1:23. Although competitive in that recent key race, there are danger signs to be observed. Jack Of Clubs is bred for distance on both sides of his pedigree; one might say that he was bred to be slow. Two miles might ultimately prove his best distance, not the one mile he must race today. And although he rallied from well back in his last two races, he hung on the money on both occasions. This may be a professional maiden in the making.

INHERITING

This horse's apparent improvement last time is counterfeit, the direct result of a slow pace.

IOSHEKA

Well supported in his first two starts, although apparent improvement last time once again can be attributed to a slow pace. From a top barn, though, so real improvement would come as no surprise.

PRINCELY SCREEN

No horse in this field shows a figure at or above the 100 par for this type of race. Except Princely Screen, that is, whose recent pace figures were especially quick. Based on those numbers, Princely Screen is clearly the "main speed" in this race and is easily capable of shaking loose early. The horse who beat him last time, Othersideofthetrack, equaled the best maiden figure of the New York season (108) turned in by eventual major stakes winners Ogygian and Ketoh, despite running for a claiming tag in his debut. If able to control the pace, both the rise in class and month's layoff may prove of little consequence.

SARATOGA COLONY

Made a nice move in his second start, as forecast by the betting action that day, in the Out East-Dance Of Life race. Although beaten by Jack Of Clubs on that occasion, Saratoga Colony is better situated in the gate today and will probably get the jump on that rival once again, while continuing to improve. Certainly bred to "go on."

Without Princely Screen, this race nonetheless would have offered an interesting bet—Saratoga Colony to reverse over the favored Jack Of Clubs—with the betting action and "bid, hung" move pointing to a horse that was likely to improve. But the presence of Princely Screen changed the complexion of this race altogether. In light of the pace situation, neither closer figured to catch Princely Screen, unless the latter tripped over his sprint pedigree in the stretch run. Yet each figured to attract more action at the betting windows.

Princely Screen did not stop. Instead, he maintained a safe advantage to the wire despite having to fight off an unexpected challenge for the early lead from rank outsiders Fool Me Not Scot and Stride Of Joy. Jack Of Clubs rallied for second money but could gain

SIXTH RACE **1 MILE. (1.33⅕) MAIDEN SPECIAL WEIGHT. Purse $23,000. 2-year-olds. Weights, 118 lbs.**

Aqueduct

NOVEMBER 9, 1985

Value of race $23,000; value to winner $13,800; second $5,060; third $2,760; fourth $1,380. Mutuel pool $143,232, OTB pool $95,837. Exacata Pool $280,256. OTB Exacta Pool $149,132.

Last Raced	Horse	Eqt.	A.	Wt	PP	St	¼	½	¾	Str	Fin	Jockey	Odds $1
7Oct85 ^{6}Bel^{2}	Princely Screen	b	2	113	12	1	2½	1^{hd}	1^{1½}	1^{2}	1^{2}	Jones B S^{5}	12.40
20Oct85 ^{4}Bel^{3}	Jack Of Clubs		2	118	9	9	11½	9^{2}	4½	2^{hd}	2¾	Guerra W A	2.00
23Oct85 ^{6}Aqu^{8}	Sure Turn		2	118	4	8	10^{hd}	7^{hd}	5^{1½}	3½	3^{hd}	Migliore R	3.80
20Oct85 ^{4}Bel^{4}	Saratoga Colony		2	118	13	4	6^{1}	4^{hd}	2½	4^{2}	4^{2½}	Velasquez J	5.20
26Oct85 ^{3}Aqu^{7}	Scrimshaw		2	118	2	11	9^{1}	10½	8½	7^{6}	5^{1¾}	Vasquez J	6.30
20Oct85 ^{4}Bel^{7}	Star De Triomphe	b	2	118	7	14	7½	5^{1½}	3^{1½}	5^{2}	6no	Lovato F Jr	42.60
24Oct85 ^{3}Aqu^{5}	Highfalutin	b	2	118	1	10	5½	6½	6^{3}	6^{2}	7^{9½}	Skinner K	39.50
30Oct85 ^{6}Aqu^{4}	Inheriting	b	2	118	10	5	14	14	10^{1½}	8^{3}	8^{2¾}	Davis R G	28.00
21Oct85 ^{8}Bel^{6}	Baron De Graus	b	2	118	8	13	13^{3}	12½	12^{2}	9^{1½}	9^{nk}	Santos J A	22.10
26Oct85 ^{6}Aqu^{6}	Ioskeha		2	118	11	2	8^{hd}	8½	11^{hd}	11½	10¾	Venezia M	12.90
17Oct85 ^{6}Bel^{3}	J. O. Cross		2	118	6	12	12^{hd}	11^{hd}	14	12½	11^{2¾}	Cruguet J	17.70
17Oct85 ^{6}Bel^{8}	Masterful Run		2	118	5	6	4^{1}	13^{4}	13^{1½}	14	12¾	Santagata N	f-20.30
14Oct85 ^{6}Bel^{11}	Stride Of Joy		2	111	3	7	3^{2½}	3^{hd}	9½	13^{1½}	13no	Guerra A A^{7}	f-20.30
31Oct85 ^{3}Aqu^{10}	Fool Me Not Scot	b	2	118	14	3	1^{1}	2^{2½}	7^{1½}	10½	14	MacBeth D	f-20.30

f—Mutuel field.

OFF AT 3:05. Start good, Won driving. Time, :23, :46⅕, 1:11⅗, 1:37⅘ Track fast.

$2 Mutuel Prices:			
10-(M)-PRINCELY SCREEN	26.80	7.60	6.40
7-(I)-JACK OF CLUBS		4.00	3.00
3-(D)-SURE TURN			3.00

$2 EXACTA 10-7 PAID $94.60.

Dk. b. or br. g, by Princely Pleasure—Top Screen, by Ambehaving. Trainer Ferriola Peter. Bred by Bo-Bett Farm (Fla).

PRINCELY SCREEN took over after going a half, held a clear lead into stretch and held sway under good handling. JACK OF CLUBS rallied from outside approaching stretch, continued on gamely but wasn't good enough. SURE TURN made a run between horses nearing midstretch but hung. SARATOGA COLONY rallied from outside appproaching stretch but lacked needed late response.SCRIMSHAW failed to be a serious factor. STAR DE TRIOMPHE off slowly, advanced steadily to make a bid along inside leaving the turn but gave way under pressure. HIGHFALUTIN lacked room along inside around turn. BARON DE GRAUS raced very wide. IOSKEHA had no apparent excuse. MASTERFUL RUN showed brief speed. STRIDE OF JOY gave way soon after going a half.

no ground on the winner during the final eighth mile. Saratoga Colony once again bid, but hung.

One conclusion seemed unavoidable following this race: No horse was likely to come out of the race and break its maiden in the near future unless it was dropped into the claiming ranks. Specifically, the three runners-up—Jack Of Clubs, Sure Turn, and Saratoga Colony—appeared to be ideal foils, horses that could be bet against with confidence. In fact, Sure Turn ran second at 7–10 on November 17, then second again on November 28, this time at 8–5. Saratoga Colony faded to fifth at seven furlongs on November 24.

Chapter 5

It Seems They Improve Overnight

THE TWO-YEAR-OLD THOROUGHBRED is capable of dramatic improvement from one race to the next, almost overnight, it often seems, as he matures and absorbs the lessons he is taught during his races and morning workouts.

When John Veitch entered Script Ohio in the Cowdin Stakes at Belmont on October 6, 1984, I took notice. The colt had raced only once, gamely winning a six-furlong maiden test at Belmont almost a month earlier. Why, I asked myself, was Veitch throwing him in against the lions of the division, Chief's Crown and Spectacular Love, in this Grade I event when he had such limited experience? I suspected that Veitch felt the colt had considerable ability and wanted to "go long."

Joe Hirsch's column in the *Daily Racing Form* on the day of the Cowdin helped confirm my suspicions. Entitled "An Upstart in the Cowdin?," it read (in part):

> Perhaps the most interesting aspect, however, will be the performance of Dan Galbreath's Script Ohio. This attractive Roberto colt has only run once, but his victory last month was impressive. Racing on the inside he was challenged through the final furlong and never faltered under pressure, impressing many observers, including trainer John Veitch. "The nature of this Cowdin, and the new distance, leads me to believe he has a chance," Veitch was saying at the barn. "There is a good deal of speed in the race and Script Ohio comes from off the pace. That could be an effective strategy. In addition, I think the mile will prove far better suited to his talents than the six furlongs at

which he made his debut. There is no question he has an ambitious assignment Saturday. He's conceding a good deal of seasoning. But he had a very good mile last Monday (1:41.1) on a dead track and is a very fit young horse."

During the Cowdin, I paid particular attention to Script Ohio's progress. After the colt made a promising run on the turn, only to fade in the stretch, I decided that this was a colt with considerable room for improvement and one that would be a good candidate for the "overnight improvement" angle. I did not like the way Chief's Crown finished out his race, though he won by six lengths, and decided that Script Ohio would upset them all in his next start.

Handicapping Expo '84 was scheduled for October 17–20 at the Meadowlands Hilton, and as things worked out, Script Ohio's next start turned out to be in the $500,000 Young America Stakes at the Meadowlands on October 18. For the author, it was a very fortunate coincidence. When I saw the entries for the Young America the day before the race, I began telling Expo participants about Script Ohio—even before I had a chance to evaluate his opposition. Let's take a look at the rest of the field for this Grade I fixture:

DO IT AGAIN DAN

This colt had already raced ten times in his short career, which suggests that his connections did not consider him to be a top prospect. After two sprint victories at the Meadowlands, "Dan" finished behind Script Ohio in the Cowdin. Script Ohio had room for improvement; this colt did not.

WOLTAN

An obscurely bred colt, Woltan had never raced beyond six furlongs and had tired badly at that distance in his only allowance test. With all the speed in this field, he faced what seemed an insurmountable task.

CUTLASS REALITY

This colt's only attempt at a route distance was encouraging. In the Grade I Laurel Futurity he dueled for the early lead after breaking from a disadvantageous outside post and held gamely in the stretch, coming again for the place. Although not bred to go long, he was

8 MEADOWLANDS

1 1-16 MILES
MEADOWLANDS
START FINISH

1 1/16 MILES. (1.41⅘) 8th Running YOUNG AMERICA (Grade I). Purse $500,000 guaranteed. 2-year-olds. By subscription of $500 each, which shall accompany the nomination, $2,000 to pass the entry box, $3,000 additional to start. Supplementary nominations may be made at time of entry by payment of a fee of $20,000 each which qualified to start. The Meadowlands to add $350,000 with a gross purse of $500,000 guaranteed. Added money and all fees to be divided, 60% to the winner, 20% to second, 11% to third, 6% to fourth and 3% to fifth. Weights, 122 lbs. Non-winners of a Sweepstakes at a mile or over allowed 3 lbs. Fillies allowed 3 lbs. Starters to be named through the entry box by the usual time of closing. This race will not be divided. Horses with the highest total earnings at time of entry will be preferred. Trophies will be presented to the winning Owner, Trainer and Jockey. Closed Saturday, September 15, 1984 with 74 nominations.

Do It Again Dan
Dk. b. or br. c. 2, by Mr Leader—Bimbo Sue, by Our Michael
Br.—Edgehill Farm (Ky)
Tr.—Perlsweig Mark
Own.—Edgehill Farm
119 Lifetime 10 3 2 3 $86,174 1984 10 3 2 3 $86,174
6Oct84- 8Bel fst 1 :45⅗ 1:10⅘ 1:36⅘ Cowdin 8 6 65½ 38 410 419¾ Cordero A Jr b 122 10.80 62-17 Chief's Crown 1226BionicLight12212½ScriptOhio1221½ Raced wide 8
6Oct84-Grade I
22Sep84- 6Med fst 6f :22⅘ :45⅗ 1:11 ⓈComet 2 4 33 2½ 1½ 14 Velasquez J b 112 *1.00 87-18 Do It Again Dan 1124 Vindaloo 1126 I'm A Rutabaga 1125 Driving 5
8Sep84- 3Med fst 6f :22⅘ :45⅘ 1:10⅘ Alw 12000 3 1 34 21 11 1½ Velasquez J b 115 1.80 88-18 Do It Again Dan1151½FutureReality1187½Boutinierre1184½ Driving 5
26Aug84- 8Sar fst 6½f :21⅘ :44⅘ 1:16 Hopeful 6 2 75½ 53½ 54½ 711½ Miller D A Jr b 122 22.30 80-15 Chief's Crown 1223¾ Tiffany Ice1223¾Mugzy'sRullah122½ Brushed 9
26Aug84-Grade I
11Aug84- 9Mth fst 6f :22⅕ :45⅕ 1:10⅘ Sapling 5 4 77¾ 56½ 47½ 35½ Miller D A Jr b 122 5.50 82-12 Doubly Clear 1221 Tiltalating 1194½ Do It Again Dan1221½ Rallied 10
11Aug84-Grade II
3Aug84- 8Sar fst 6f :22⅘ :46 1:10⅕ Sar Spec'l 6 1 55 42 32½ 22¾ Miller D A Jr b 117 7.30 86-19 Chief's Crown 1172¾DoItAgainDan117hdSkyCommand122½ Rallied 6
3Aug84-Grade II
18Jly84- 9Mth sly 5f :22⅘ :45⅘ :58 Md Sp Wt 6 1 2hd 2hd 1½ 12 Miller D A Jr b 118 *.80 96-17 Do It Again Dan 1182FutureReality1138DiamondRich1181 Driving 11
20Jun84- 8Bel fst 5½f :22⅘ :46⅘ 1:05⅘ Juvenile 6 5 54½ 44 43 33½ Davis R G b 113 4.10e 83-18 SkyCommand1152½MoonProspector1151DoItAgainDan1131½ Wide 10
8Jun84- 5Mth fst 5f :22 :45⅘ :58 Md Sp Wt 5 2 22 21½ 22 2nk Vega A b 118 *1.30e 96-19 JonIan118nkDoItAgainDan1187RunningMemories1183 Just missed 10
29May84- 1Mth sly 5f :22⅘ :46⅘ :59⅘ Md Sp Wt 5 6 52¾ 44½ 34½ 32½ Vega A b 118 3.80 86-23 Racy N Regal 113¾ Silver Darling 1181½DoItAgainDan1185 Evenly 5
LATEST WORKOUTS ●Oct 17 Med 3f fst :35 h ●Oct 5 Med 3f fst :35 h Aug 25 Sar 3f fst :36 b

Woltan
Dk. b. or br. c. 2, by Bynoderm—Robadrone, by Drone
Br.—Resk V (Ky)
Tr.—Romero Jorge
Own.—Resk V
119 Lifetime 3 1 0 1 $13,210 1984 3 1 0 1 $13,210
1Sep84- 7Bel fst 6f :22⅘ :45⅘ 1:10⅕ Alw 20000 3 2 1½ 52½ 47 411¼ Martinez L A 122 10.90 80-13 Ziggy's Boy 1172½ Full of Spice 1175¾ DesertWar1193½ Weakened 7
18Aug84- 4Sar fst 6f :22⅘ :46⅕ 1:11⅘ Md Sp Wt 10 3 11½ 12 14 13 Martinez L A 116 7.00 83-15 Woltan 1183 Senator Brady 1183½ Scholastic 118hd Ridden out 10
27Jly84- 4Mth sly 5½f :22⅘ :46 1:05⅘ Md Sp Wt 4 4 1½ 1hd 1hd 32 Palabecino N J 118 66.90 86-21 MtthewT.Prker1182FutureRelity113noWoltn1184 Drifted wide str 9
LATEST WORKOUTS Sep 8 Del 4f fst :48⅘ h Aug 29 Atl 3f fst :36⅘ h

Cutlass Reality
Ch. c. 2, by Cutlass—Landera, by In Reality
Br.—Carrion J S (Fla)
Tr.—Reese Walter C
Own.—Kruckel T
119 Lifetime 6 1 3 0 $77,339 1984 6 1 3 0 $77,339
6Oct84- 8Lrl fst 1 1/16 :46⅘ 1:12⅘ 1:43 Laurel Fty 11 2 2½ 11 31 22½ Perret C b 122 36.40 90-15 MightyAppealing1222½CutlssRelity122hdRhomnRuie12210 Gamely 12
6Oct84-Grade I
15Sep84- 8Key sly 6f :22⅕ :46 1:11⅕ Kindergarten 3 7 64 33 23½ 24½ Perret C b 114 3.70 80-21 Doubly Clear 1214½ Cutlass Reality 1147½ Jon Ian 118¾ 2nd best 7
26Aug84- 8Sar fst 6½f :21⅘ :44⅘ 1:16 Hopeful 5 5 64¾ 74½ 65 48 Perret C b 122 58.80 84-15 Chief'sCrown1223¾TiffnyIce1223¾Mugzy'sRullh122½ Lacked room 9
26Aug84-Grade I
17Aug84- 6Mth fst 5½f :23 :46⅕ 1:04⅘ Md Sp Wt 8 1 11½ 13 12½ 14 Perret C b 118 1.70 91-17 Cutlass Reality1184GranOleOpry1186Elloree'sChoice118hd Driving 8
3Aug84- 8Crc fst 6f :23 :46⅘ 1:15⅕ Md Sp Wt 7 4 41½ 55 45 2½ Velez J A Jr b 116 7.00 74-24 DustyHotLine116½CutlassReality1163FoundationPlan116½ Gaining 9
18Jly84- 6Crc fst 6f :23 :47⅘ 1:14⅕ Md Sp Wt 11 6 3nk 2½ 43½ 55 Hernandez C 116 14.20 75-20 Playing Politics 1163½ Lautaro 116no Water Gate 1161½ Faltered 12
LATEST WORKOUTS ●Oct 13 Med 7f fst 1:26 h ●Oct 3 Med 4f fst :47⅘ h ●Sep 25 Med 1 fst 1:42⅘ b Sep 11 Key 4f fst :49 b

Spend A Buck
B. c. 2, by Buckaroo—Belle De Jour, by Speak John
Br.—Harper & Irish Hill Farm (Ky)
Tr.—Gambolati Cam
Own.—Hunter Farm
122 Lifetime 6 5 1 0 $459,985 1984 6 5 1 0 $459,985
22Sep84- 9AP fst 1 :44⅘ 1:10 1:38 Arl Wa Fty 6 3 21 2hd 1½ 1½ Hussey C 122 2.90 71-24 Spend A Buck 122½ Dusty's Darby 1222½ Viva Maxi 1221¾ All out 7
22Sep84-Grade I
2Sep84-11RD fst 1 1/16 :47⅘ 1:12 1:45⅘ Cradle 6 2 11 14 18 115 Hussey C 120 *1.20 80-18 Spend A Buck 12015 Grand Native 1206 Alex's Game 120nk Easily 13
16Aug84- 7Crc fst 6f :22⅘ :46⅕ 1:12⅘ Alw 15000 1 1 11½ 14 16 19½ Hussey C 112 *.50 87-23 Spend A Buck 1129½ Secret Goal 1129½Mr.Introienne1143 Handily 5
4Aug84- 9Crc fst 5½f :22⅘ :47 1:07 Criterium 4 2 23 22 22½ 22½ Hussey C 116 *.60 87-21 Smile 1142½ Spend A Buck 116hd Cherokee Fast 1164½ Held place 7
4Aug84-Run In Divisions
25Jly84- 8Crc fst 5½f :22⅘ :46⅘ 1:06 Alw 11000 3 1 1½ 11½ 13 14 Hussey C 113 2.40 95-20 SpendABuck1134Mr.Introinn1161½PlyingPolitics1144½ Ridden out 8
14Jly84- 2Crc fst 5½f :23 :47 1:07⅕ Md Sp Wt 6 3 11½ 1hd 12 1nk Hussey C 116 5.50 89-19 SpendABuck116nkHickoryHillFlyer1163SuperbAnswr1163½ Driving 12
LATEST WORKOUTS Oct 15 Med 5f fst :59 h ●Oct 8 Med 5f fst :59 h

Bionic Light
B. c. 2, by Majestic Light—Bionic Babe, by Best Turn
Br.—Dickson Loy (Ky)
Tr.—Cappellucci Robert A
Own.—Dickson L E
119 Lifetime 6 3 1 1 $99,093 1984 6 3 1 1 $99,093
6Oct84- 8Bel fst 1 :45⅗ 1:10⅘ 1:36⅘ Cowdin 2 1 11 22 23 26 Maple S b 122 19.00 76-17 Chif'sCrown1226BionicLight12212½ScriptOho1221½ Best of others 8
6Oct84-Grade I
15Sep84- 5Bel sly 7f :22⅘ :46 1:23⅕ Futurity 7 1 2½ 2½ 24 47 Maple S b 122 6.80 79-18 SpctculrLov1221Chif'sCrown1223½Mugzy'sRullh1222¾ Drifted out 8
15Sep84-Grade I
11Aug84- 9Aks fst 6f :21⅘ :44 1:09⅘ Juvenile 3 4 1½ 13 14 16 Maple S b 116 3.10 89-16 Bionic Light 1166 Doctor Dick 1162 Grand Reward 1122 Easily 10
11Aug84-Grade III
22Jly84-12LaM fst 5½f :22⅕ :46⅕ 1:04⅕ Enchntmt Fty 4 8 41½ 3nk 2nk 33 Hidinger M 118 *.40 89-09 Net Effect 1153 Sounds Sharp 115no BionicLight1184½ Weakened 9
7Jly84- 7LaM fst 5½f :22⅘ :46 1:03⅘ Spec'l Wt 10 2 2hd 11½ 13 16 Hidinger M b 118 *.70 94-11 Bionic Light 1186 Charm 1225 Midnite Thunder 1154 Easily 10
9Jun84- 7LaM fst 5f :22⅕ :44⅕ :57⅘ Md Sp Wt 5 6 3½ 11½ 12½ 12½ Hidinger M b 120 *1.00 94-13 Bionic Light 1202½ Moonshake 1197 Contention 1192 Driving 10
LATEST WORKOUTS Oct 15 Med 4f fst :49⅘ b ●Sep 26 Med 5f fst 1:00 h

Script Ohio
B. c. 2, by Roberto—Grandma Lind, by NEver Bend
Br.—Galbreath D M (Ky)
Tr.—Veitch John M
Own.—Galbreath D M
119 Lifetime 2 1 0 1 $25,152 1984 2 1 0 1 $25,152
6Oct84- 8Bel fst 1 :45⅗ 1:10⅘ 1:36⅘ Cowdin 5 5 55 48 310 318½ Maple E 122 23.50 63-17 Chief's Crown 1226BionicLight12212½ScriptOhio1221½ Evenly late 8
6Oct84-Grade I
13Sep84- 4Bel fst 6f :22⅘ :46⅕ 1:12 Md Sp Wt 8 5 31½ 1hd 11 1¾ Maple E 118 5.80f 82-21 Script Ohio 118¾ Cullendale1181½MightyCourageous1181½ Driving 14
LATEST WORKOUTS Oct 16 Bel 4f fst :48⅘ b Oct 12 Bel 3f fst :38⅕ b Oct 5 Bel 3f fst :35⅕ b ●Oct 1 Bel 1 fst 1:41⅕ b

Dusty's Darby
B. c. 2, by Bob's Dusty—Princess DArby, by Big Darby
Br.—Motch Susan T (Va)
Tr.—Foley Vickie
Own.—English Stable
119 Lifetime 7 3 2 1 $144,882 1984 7 3 2 1 $144,882
22Sep84- 9AP fst 1 :44⅘ 1:10 1:38 Arl Wa Fty 4 5 510 36 32½ 2½ Sibille R 122 10.70 70-24 Spend A Buck 122½ Dusty's Darby 1222½ VivaMaxi1221¾ Game try 7
22Sep84-Grade I
2Sep84- 8AP fst 7f :22 :44 1:24 Arch Ward 5 4 36½ 36 34½ 25 Faul J H 124 5.00 77-29 ProudstHour1245Dusty'sDrby1244½HollywoodHcktt1141¾ 2nd best 6
18Aug84-10EIP sly 6f :23⅘ :49⅘ 1:15⅕ J C Ellis 5 5 65½ 2hd 1½ 15 McDowell M 124 2.20 — — Dusty's Darby 1245 Tajawa 114½ English Falcon 1141 Driving 7
5Aug84- 6EIP fst 6f :22⅘ :46⅘ 1:10⅘ Alw 12800 4 8 73½ 55 55½ 59¾ Encinas R I 119 2.60 81-16 Nail Keg 1197 Mr. Smirnoff 117nk Mouthwash 1102 8
22Jly84- 9FP fst 5½f :22⅕ :46⅕ 1:05⅘ Mstr Fairmnt 1 6 43½ 33½ 21 12 Encinas R I 113 2.00 88-20 Dusty's Darby 1132 Mr. Smirnoff1133DukesRevenge1103½ Driving 6
22Jly84-Run in divisions
8Jly84- 4EIP fst 5f :22⅘ :46⅕ :59 Md p Wt 3 4 32½ 32 11 15 Cooksey P J 120 *.80 96-13 Dusty's Darby 1205 Hidden Persuasion 117½ Toronado Man1202½ 6
20Jun84- 1CD fst 5f :22⅘ :46⅘ :59⅕ Md Sp Wt 10 10 98½ 76¾ 47 36½ Cooksey P J 117 5.50 86-13 Clever Allemont 1172½ Jerry F. 1174 Dusty's Darby 117no 12
LATEST WORKOUTS Oct 9 CD 5f my 1:05 b Sep 14 CD 5f fst 1:03 b Aug 30 CD 4f fst :49 b

Rhoman Rule
B. c. 2, by Stop The Music—Morning Bird, by Swaps
Br.—Ledyard L C (Pa)
Tr.—Penna Angel Jr
Own.—Combs B II
119 Lifetime 4 1 1 1 $43,448 1984 4 1 1 1 $43,448
6Oct84- 8Lrl fst 1 1/16 :46⅘ 1:12⅘ 1:43 Laurel Fty 12 8 84¾ 53 2½ 32½ Hernandez R 122 32.50 90-15 MightyAppealing1222½CutlassReality122hdRhomnRule12210 Wide 12
6Oct84-Grade I
8Sep84- 5Bel fst 7f :22⅘ :45⅘ 1:24 Alw 20000 8 7 75½ 54 35½ 24 Hernandez R 119 12.80 78-17 Herat 1224 Rhoman Rule 1193½ Stonewhite 112¾ Wide 8
8Aug84- 4Sar fst 7f :22⅘ :46⅘ 1:25 Md Sp Wt 11 2 31 2½ 13 13½ Hernandez R 118 3.90f 77-16 RhomnRule1183½CoyoteDncer1183½FbulousMov1181½ Ridden out 13
26Jly84- 6Bel fst 6f :22⅘ :46⅕ 1:11⅘ Md Sp Wt 9 10 85½ 66½ 913 817½ Samyn J L 118 13.40 66-17 Salem Drive 118¾ Anconeus 1181½ Haberdasner1184 Broke slowly 10
LATEST WORKOUTS Oct 17 Bel 3f fst :36⅘ b Oct 14 Bel 5f fst 1:02⅕ b Oct 4 Lrl 3f fst :36 b Oct 1 Bel 6f fst 1:14⅕ h

Tank's Prospect
B. c. 2, by Mr Prospector—Midnight Pumpkin, by Pretense
Br.—Seltzer E A (Ky)
Tr.—Lukas D Wayne
Own.—Klein Mr-Mrs E V
119 Lifetime 3 1 1 0 $14,275 1984 3 1 1 0 $14,275

5Oct84- 6SA fst 6f :22⅘ :45⅘ 1:10⅘ Md Sp Wt 6 7 67¾ 66½ 32 13½ Delahoussaye E 117 4.80 85-16 Tank'sProspect1173½Chieftain'sClass1171¾QualityJet117½ Handily 9
11Jly84- 4Hol fst 6f :22⅘ :46 1:11⅕ Md Sp Wt 6 6 63½ 43½ 43 22½ Valenzuela P A 116 8.20 78-16 Metronomic 1162½ Tank's Prospect 116no Royal Olympia 116¾ 9
1Jly84- 6Hol fst 5½f :22⅘ :45⅕ 1:04⅘ Md Sp Wt 3 8 76½ 68¾ 69½ 56¾ Valenzuela P A 116 13.80 81-16 Lomax 1164 Royal Olympia 116¾ Michadilla 1161½ 8
LATEST WORKOUTS Oct 13 SA 7f fst 1:29⅘ h Sep 30 SA 5f fst 1:01⅖ h Sep 25 SA 5f fst 1:01 h Sep 17 Dmr 5f sly 1:03⅘ h

Wealthy Seamen
Ch. c. 2, by Key to the Mint—Sea Sister, by Sea-Bird
Br.—Evans T M (Ky)
Own.—Buckland Farm Tr.—Campo John P
119 Lifetime 4 1 0 0 $11,400 1984 4 1 0 0 $11,400 Turf 2 1 0 0 $11,400
30Sep84- 7Bel fm 1 ①:45⅘ 1:10⅘ 1:36⅘ Donut King 7 5 56 510 712 711½ Lovato F Jr 115 6.80 71-27 Western Champ 117½ Don't Fool With Me 1173Jonlan122nk Tired 10
29Aug84- 4Bel fm 1 1/16 ①:47 1:11⅘ 1:43⅘ Md Sp Wt 9 3 32 32 3½ 11½ Lovato F Jr 118 5.70 78-14 Wealthy Seamen 1181½ Lathom 118nk No Latch 1183 Driving 11
18Aug84- 6Sar fst 6f :22⅘ :46⅕ 1:11⅘ Md Sp Wt 5 3 69 713 612 616¾ Maple E 118 14.00 67-15 Lightning Leap 1185½ Anconeus 1183½ AlertResponse1181 Outrun 8
4Aug84- 4Sar fst 6f :22⅕ :45⅘ 1:11 Md Sp Wt 11 9 1114 813 514 513¾ Samyn J L 118 29.90 71-13 Vindaloo 1189 Anconeus 1184½ Radar Alarm 118¾ Rallied 13
LATEST WORKOUTS Oct 15 Bel tr.t 4f fst :49⅕ b Oct 9 Med 1 fst 1:41 h ●Sep 19 Bel tr.t 6f fst 1:15⅘ b Sep 14 Bel tr.t 5f fst 1:04 b

Old Main
B. c. 2, by Wajima—Bombycid, by Shantung
Br.—Hackman W M (Va)
Own.—Hackman W M Tr.—Thompson J Willard
119 Lifetime 3 2 0 0 $15,000 1984 3 2 0 0 $15,000 Turf 1 1 0 0 $7,800
24Sep84- 5Med fm 1 ①:48 1:13 1:39⅕ Alw 13000 7 2 21½ 2hd 11 1nk McCauley W H b 117 *1.20 78-17 Old Main 117nk Out Lookin 1144½ Sail On Blue 117hd Driving 8
17Sep84- 7Med fst 6f :23 :46⅘ 1:12⅕ Md Sp Wt 4 3 1hd 1hd 11½ 14½ McCauley W H b 118 6.30 81-23 Old Main 1184½ Skip Trial 1184½ Sly Arrival 118¾ Driving 7
20Jun84- 6Mth fst 5f :22⅘ :46⅕ :58⅘ Md Sp Wt 5 12 108 911 713 48 Melendez J D b 118 35.20 84-15 SilverDrling1183SovereignSong1181WhoTughtWho1184 No threat 12
LATEST WORKOUTS Oct 17 Med 3f fst :38⅘ b ●Oct 12 Med 1 fst 1:41 h Oct 6 Med 1 fst 1:41⅘ h Sep 12 Med 4f fst :48 hg

better situated in the gate tonight and with normal improvement figured to be a serious factor, at least in the early running of the race.

SPEND A BUCK

One of two Chicago invaders, Spend A Buck's victory in the Arlington-Washington Futurity was deceptively impressive, but not overwhelming. Scott McMannis, Chicago's representative at the Expo, reported that Spend A Buck's figure for that race was poor. Yet the colt had been game enough to hold on after chasing a :44.4 half and 1:10 six furlongs. On the other hand, the final quarter time of twenty-eight seconds suggested that there was nothing behind him in that race. Yet with a softer pace, Spend A Buck might have more punch in the stretch. He certainly appeared to have blazing speed.

BIONIC LIGHT

Coming off the strongest race of his career, in which he finished twelve lengths ahead of Script Ohio, Bionic Light was the third component of a potential speed duel in the Young America. Would Bionic Light improve off his showing in the Cowdin? Even if he didn't, could Script Ohio improve enough to make up twelve lengths?

DUSTY'S DARBY

The second Chicago invader was a pronounced closer who so far had been unable to "get up" in major-league competition. His performance at Arlington wasn't as impressive as it might look on paper. Although he made up five and a half lengths in the stretch, the last quarter was "walked" in twenty-eight seconds. If all Dusty's Darby could muster was a final quarter in twenty-seven seconds, he wouldn't be in the picture tonight.

RHOMAN RULE

The second horse coming out of the Laurel Futurity, Rhoman Rule was, according to the Expo consensus, the one most likely to succeed. A Saratoga maiden winner—always worth a few extra points—at seven furlongs, Rhoman Rule then ran a good second to Herat, who had raced unchallenged on the early lead. After a four-week hiatus, he raced widest of all in the Laurel Futurity, losing considerable ground to winner Might Appealing, who was "on the wood" all the way. After a bold challenge in early stretch, Rhoman Rule ran out of gas—as might be expected—and hung in the late stages of the long stretch run. Most likely he needed that race and was now coming back in just twelve days. In good hands, and with the closing style to take advantage of the expected speed duel up front, Rhoman Rule seemed the one to beat for the $300,000 winner's share.

TANK'S PROSPECT

Sent east by trainer Wayne Lukas to earn Breeders' Cup points, while stablemate Saratoga Six did the same on the West Coast, Tank's Prospect was the mystery horse of the race. Never having gone beyond six furlongs, the son of the brilliant sprinter, Mr. Prospector, had to be suspect at tonight's distance, although Lukas obviously would not have shipped him across the country if he had doubts. Even if he proved to like route racing, though, Tank's Prospect could very easily prove short of seasoning for tonight's race.

WEALTHY SEAMAN

Ambitiously placed, this colt was observed eyeing the Meadowlands' grass course on his way to the post.

OLD MAIN

Winner of two straight at the Meadowlands, Old Main had never faced this kind of competition, and his task was made all the more difficult by his unlucky draw of post position.

In addition to deciding whether the three speed horses could be eliminated from further consideration because of the likelihood of a killing speed duel, the handicapper had another problem to face. Horses that had never faced one another were gathering from different parts of the country—two each from New York, Maryland, and Chicago among horses we have identified as solid contenders. Good speed figures obviously would help, but that alone couldn't solve the puzzle. The most recent performances of Script Ohio, Rhoman Rule, and Spend A Buck demanded more than just final-time figures for proper analysis and interpretation.

The audience at the Meadowlands that evening made the betting decision easy. For some inexplicable reason, they made Spend A Buck, with Cordero up, not only the favorite—somebody had to be favored—but a very heavy favorite at even money. Obviously Spend A Buck could not be played in such an underlay situation, and that made it easy to take the stand that speed would kill (itself) in this race. Of the three closers, Dusty's Darby seemed counterfeit, leaving just Rhoman Rule, the logical favorite going at odds of 7–1, and the darkhorse Script Ohio, at 37–1.

EIGHTH RACE
Meadowlands
OCTOBER 18, 1984

$1\frac{1}{16}$ MILES. ($1.41\frac{4}{5}$) 8th Running YOUNG AMERICA (Grade I). Purse $500,000 guaranteed. 2-year-olds. By subscription of $500 each, which shall accompany the nomination, $2,000 to pass the entry box, $3,000 additional to start. Supplementary nominations may be made at time of entry by payment of a fee of $20,000 each which qualified to start. The Meadowlands to add $350,000 with a gross purse of $500,000 guaranteed. Added money and all fees to be divided, 60% to the winner, 20% to second, 11% to third, 6% to fourth and 3% to fifth. Weights, 122 lbs. Non-winners of a Sweepstakes at a mile or over allowed 3 lbs. Fillies allowed 3 lbs. Starters to be named through the entry box by the usual time of closing. This race will not be divided. Horses with the highest total earnings at time of entry will be preferred. Trophies will be presented to the winning Owner, Trainer and Jockey. Closed Saturday, September 15, 1984 with 74 nominations.

Value of race $500,000; value to winner $300,000; second $100,000; third $55,000; fourth $30,000; fifth $15,000. Mutuel pool $220,537. Exacta Pool $237,010.

Last Raced	Horse	Eqt.A.Wt	PP	St	¼	½	¾	Str	Fin	Jockey	Odds $1
6Oct84 ^{8}Bel^{3}	Script Ohio	2 119	6	11	11	9^{2}	8^{2}	$3^{1\frac{1}{2}}$	$1^{\frac{3}{4}}$	Maple E	37.00
22Sep84 ^{9}AP^{1}	Spend A Buck	2 122	4	4	$1^{1\frac{1}{2}}$	$1^{1\frac{1}{2}}$	1^{1}	$1^{\frac{1}{2}}$	2^{nk}	Cordero A Jr	1.00
5Oct84 ^{6}SA^{1}	Tank's Prospect	2 119	9	9	9^{2}	$7^{\frac{1}{2}}$	7^{hd}	$5^{\frac{1}{2}}$	3^{2}	MacBeth D	16.00
6Oct84 ^{8}Lrl^{3}	Rhoman Rule	2 119	8	7	6^{2}	6^{3}	4^{3}	$4^{1\frac{1}{2}}$	$4^{\frac{3}{4}}$	Hernandez R	7.60
6Oct84 ^{8}Bel^{2}	Bionic Light	b 2 119	5	5	$2^{2\frac{1}{2}}$	$2^{1\frac{1}{2}}$	$2^{\frac{1}{2}}$	$2^{2\frac{1}{2}}$	5^{5}	Maple S	8.60
6Oct84 ^{8}Bel^{4}	Do It Again Dan	2 119	1	1	$7^{\frac{1}{2}}$	8^{5}	6^{hd}	7^{4}	6^{1}	Velasquez J	7.10
6Oct84 ^{8}Lrl^{2}	Cutlass Reality	b 2 119	3	2	$3^{1\frac{1}{2}}$	$3^{2\frac{1}{2}}$	$3^{2\frac{1}{2}}$	6^{4}	7^{7}	Perret C	8.40
1Sep84 ^{7}Bel^{4}	Woltan	2 119	2	3	5^{4}	4^{2}	5^{hd}	8^{4}	8^{9}	Martinez L A	181.30
24Sep84 ^{5}Med^{1}	Old Main	b 2 119	11	6	4^{1}	5^{3}	9^{6}	9^{10}	9^{16}	McCauley W H	62.60
22Sep84 ^{9}AP^{2}	Dusty's Darby	2 119	7	10	10	10^{4}	10^{20}	10^{12}	10^{10}	Sibille R	5.80
30Sep84 ^{7}Bel^{7}	Wealthy Seamen	2 119	10	8	$8^{\frac{1}{2}}$	11	11	11	11	Bailey J D	111.10

OFF AT 11:05. Start good, Won driving. Time, :23, :46, $1{:}11\frac{1}{5}$, $1{:}38\frac{1}{5}$, 1:45 Track fast.

$2 Mutuel Prices:				
	6–SCRIPT OHIO	76.00	15.60	10.00
	4–SPEND A BUCK		3.40	2.80
	9–TANK'S PROSPECT			7.60
	$2 EXACTA 6–4 PAID $282.00.			

B. c, by Roberto—Grandma Lind, by NEver Bend. Trainer Veitch John M. Bred by Galbreath D M (Ky).

SCRIPT OHIO bobbled soon after the start after clipping a rivals heels, he recovered to race far back for a half, moved with a rush on the extreme outside on the second turn, continued well wide while rallying and wore down SPEND A BUCK. The latter set the pace while kept off the inside, responded willingly when challenged by BIONIC LIGHT entering the stretch and held on gamely despite jumping the marks left on the track by the starting gate. TANK'S PROSPECT unhurried early, advanced inside after a half, moved between rivals after entering the second turn, came outside for the drive and finished well after drifting to the inside in midstretch. RHOMAN RULE commenced a bid after a half, drifted out to bump OLD MAIN near the three furlong marker, moved to a striking position on the outside approaching the stretch but lacked a solid closing bid. BIONIC LIGHT closest to the pace, engaged SPEND A BUCK from the outside entering the stretch but weakened late. DO IT AGAIN DAN steadied momentarily entering the second turn when lacking room, recovered, moved between rivals entering the stretch but could not threaten. CUTLASS REALITY within striking distance from the start, made a bid from the inside after five furlongs but tired in the drive. WOLTAN well placed for five furlongs, tired. OLD MAIN a forward factor, faded after being bumped by RHOMAN RULE with three furlongs remaining. DUSTY'S DARBY was wide. WEALTHY SEAMEN was outrun.

After clipping heels and stumbling at the start, falling several lengths behind his field, Script Ohio began an explosive move going to the turn and charged past Spend A Buck, who had set all the pace, in deep stretch. Rhoman Rule, who seemed to race rank and not handle the turns well, rallied mildly to finish fourth.

As a postscript, we include the following quote from John Veitch, as reported in the October 24 issue of *The Thoroughbred Record:*

> This wasn't an overwhelming field. This is a nice, sensible horse—well balanced and athletic—but I'm not about to say he's the best horse who ever looked through a bridle.

I'm glad I read this after the fact! Although Veitch simply may have been taking a fun shot at Buddy "Spectacular Bid is the greatest horse that ever looked through a bridle" Delp (Spectacular Bid won the 1978 Young America in a three-horse photo) his comment, if taken seriously, might have undermined my logic for liking Script Ohio in the first place.

Chapter 6

As the Ranks Thin Out

MAIDEN RACES usually provide the quickest handicapping study. As a rule, first-time starters are poor risks because of their inexperience. The confirmed maiden, the horse that has tried but failed on numerous occasions, is seldom worth considering. The best bet in these races is the lightly raced horse that ran well (second or third) last time out. But everyone is aware of this, and getting a decent price is usually difficult.

Maiden races come in two varieties: maiden-special events and maiden-claiming contests. The former provide the schooling grounds for well-regarded young horses beginning their careers. In the latter, the contestants race for a claiming tag, as in normal claiming contests. The gap between the typical maiden-special event and top-of-the-line maiden claiming is usually significant. And that is precisely the point of this chapter. With two notable exceptions, as a rule, the typical maiden-claiming horse, as a rule, cannot compete at the maiden-special level. And the maiden-special horse, no matter how dismal its form, often holds a surprise class edge when banished to the claiming ranks for the first time.

For starters, let's take a look at the field for the last race at Belmont on June 27, 1984, a maiden-claiming sprint.

Favored at 3–2 was Movie Queen, who was coming off a game front-running effort in top-rung maiden-claiming company. Generally, odds as low as 3–2 are hard to take in maiden-claiming company. Movie Queen, however, might have been worth serious consideration at the odds had she been returning at the same claiming level as her previous race. Instead, she was being devalued more than 50 percent, which is always a suspicious sign after a sharp race.

9 BELMONT

6 FURLONGS

6 FURLONGS. (1.08⅖) MAIDEN CLAIMING. Purse $9,500. Fillies and Mares, 3-year-old and upward. Weight, 3-year-olds, 114 lbs. Older, 122 lbs. Claiming price $35,000; for each $2,500 to $30,000 allowed 2 lbs.

Sweet Missy G.

B. f. 3, by Winged T—Missy G, by Knightly Manner
$35,000 Br.—Gargano P (Ky) Tr.—DeStasio Richard T — 114
Own.—Gargano P
Lifetime 4 0 0 1 $2,400 — 1983 4 M 0 1 $2,400

26Oct83- 9Aqu fst 1 :48 1:13⅘ 1:40⅗ Ⓕ Md 25000 2 10 8 5½ 7 5¾ 5 6 4 2½ Migliore R 117 3.60 62-21 Tula's Present 113hd Tiki Taylor 117½ Halcyon Cove 1171¾ Rallied 12
27Sep83- 5Med fst 6f :22⅗ :46 1:12⅕ Ⓕ Md 40000 1 8 8 9½ 6 8 4 9 3 5½ Migliore R 118 12.20 76-14 Undulant 118no Dean's List 1165½ Sweet Missy G.118no Mild rally 9
29Aug83- 9Bel my 1 :47 1:11⅗ 1:37⅘ Ⓕ Md Sp Wt 7 7 8 7 8 13 8 15 8 16 Migliore R 117 13.30 60-15 Distaff Magic 117no MiaNordica1173LandoftheBrave112hd Outrun 8
11Jly83- 3Bel fst 5½f :23 :46⅘ 1:06⅗ Ⓕ Md 40000 4 5 5 6 4 6½ 4 7 4 4¾ MacBeth D 117 3.30 77-21 Our Aunt Edith 113nk Iron Franco 112½ Carina1174 Saved ground 8
LATEST WORKOUTS Jun 18 Bel tr.t 6f fst 1:16⅕ b Jun 11 Bel tr.t 5f fst 1:02⅘ b Jun 4 Bel tr.t 4f fst :51 b

War Doll

Dk. b. or br. f. 3, by Wardlaw—Clandy's Doll, by Clandestine
$35,000 Br.—D T S Thoroughbreds (Fla) Tr.—Schaeffer Stephen — 114
Own.—Abe N Akab Stable
Lifetime 4 0 0 2 $2,580 — 1983 4 M 0 2 $2,580

8Dec83- 3Med fst 6f :22⅗ :46⅘ 1:13⅕ Ⓕ Md 25000 1 1 1 4 1 2 1 ½ 3 8 Messina R5 b 113 2.70 69-21 Ticree 1134 Apple Brown Betty 1114 War Doll 1131 Weakened 7
30Nov83- 5Med fst 6f :22⅗ :46⅘ 1:12⅘ Ⓕ Md 32000 1 6 4 2 3 3 3 5 5 9½ Hernandez R b 118 5.00 72-21 Tears N Kisses 1186 Shot Above 113nk HeavenlyReward116½ Tired 8
14Nov83- 3Med fst 6f :22⅗ :46⅘ 1:14 Ⓕ Md 32000 3 1 1 1 1 1 2hd 4 5¾ Santagata N b 118 *1.30 67-23 Phil's Family 1182 Lamister 1161½ J. C. Hon 1182½ Weakened 7
27Oct83- 1Med fst 6f :22⅗ :47⅕ 1:14⅖ Ⓕ Md 32000 9 2 1 2 2 1 2 2½ 3 7 Hernandez R 118 *1.80 64-20 Pam's Button 118no Canninvade 1137 War Doll 1182 Weakened 9
LATEST WORKOUTS Jun 25 Bel tr.t 4f sly :49⅖ h (d) Jun 19 Bel tr.t 6f sly 1:14⅕ h (d) Jun 12 Bel tr.t 7f fst 1:28⅘ h ● Jun 5 Bel tr.t 5f fst 1:01 h

Daddy's Slugger

Ch. f. 3, by Southern Slugger—Bay Tot, by Baybrook
$30,000 Br.—Southern Mist Farm Inc (Ky) Tr.—Horn Philip J Jr — 110
Own.—Manheimer M
Lifetime 5 0 1 0 $3,380 — 1984 4 M 1 0 $3,380 — 1983 1 M 0 0

19Apr84- 4Aqu fst 6f :22⅗ :47⅘ 1:13⅘ Ⓕ Md 25000 12 7 6 6 3 3 2 2 4 6½ McCarron G 121 *2.00 65-26 Holley Springs 1175 Front Lawn 117nk Hotliner 1211½ Bid, hung 12
13Apr84- 4Aqu fst 6f ⊡:23⅗ :47⅘ 1:14⅕ Ⓕ Md 25000 12 1 3 1 2 1½ 2 1½ 2 ¾ McCarron G 121 2.80 72-22 Full Time Wife 121¾ Daddy's Slugger 1211¾ErinTerry1211 Gamely 12
26Jan84- 2Aqu my 6f ⊡:22⅗ :46 1:12⅗ Ⓕ Md 45000 2 6 2hd 3½ 4 2½ 5 4¾ McCarron G 117 *3.00 77-10 Snakey 116nk FullTimeWife121¾LadyLitchfield121no Att. bear out 12
9Jan84- 4Aqu fst 6f ⊡:23 :47⅘ 1:14⅕ Ⓕ Md 45000 4 4 2 2½ 3 1½ 2 3 4 3½ McCarron G 117 5.00 70-25 PirofQueens1172½HevenlySplsh117¾SleekProspct121nk Weakened 11
28Dec83- 4Aqu gd 6f ⊡:23 :47⅘ 1:14⅗ Ⓕ Md 45000 2 11 10 9½ 7 11 7 8 5 4¾ McCarron G 114 13.40 65-25 A Real Find 1171½ FullTimeWife1172½SweetMiranda1171 Late bid 11
LATEST WORKOUTS Jun 22 Bel tr.t 6f fst 1:15⅘ b Jun 17 Bel 6f fst 1:19 b Jun 12 Bel 5f fst 1:04 b Jun 8 Bel 4f fst :50 b

Fabulous Ack

B. f. 3, by Ack Ack—Fabulous View, by Le Fabuleux
$35,000 Br.—Hancock III & Peters (Ky) Tr.—Suss-Kolyer R — 114
Own.—DeMatteis F
Lifetime 4 0 0 0 — 1984 4 M 0 0 — 1983 0 M 0 0 — Turf 1 0 0 0

8Jun84- 3Bel fm 1 Ⓣ:47 1:10⅘ 1:35 3+ Ⓕ Md Sp Wt 11 3 4 2 4 4½ 7 17 10 31¾ Samyn J L 114 14.30 58-14 Double Jeux 12214½ Stormy Lass 114¾ Flora Scent 114½ Tired 11
5May84- 1Aqu gd 7f :23 :46⅘ 1:26⅕ Ⓕ Md Sp Wt 2 3 4 3 7 7¾ 7 9 6 12 Davis R G 121 16.60 58-16 Boldara 1213 Handsewn 116nk Elbarita 1211½ Fin. early 8
14Apr84- 4Aqu sly 6f ⊡:23 :48 1:14 Ⓕ Md Sp Wt 10 2 1hd 4 3½ 9 12 10 12¾ Davis R G b 121 7.50 61-15 PreciousRoslie1161½Tempestously1212Chieftin'sNtive121no Tired 11
2Apr84- 6Aqu fst 6f ⊡:22⅗ :46⅘ 1:12⅘ Ⓕ Md Sp Wt 4 2 4 2 7 10 7 14 8 16¾ Davis R G 121 8.40 64-17 Lassie's Lady 121¾ Hidden Point 1213½ Em An Aye 1214 Tired 10
LATEST WORKOUTS Jun 24 Bel 4f fst :49 h Jun 20 Bel 5f fst 1:06 b Jun 14 Bel 3f fst :36⅘ h Jun 2 Bel 5f sly 1:02⅘ b

She Speaks Well

B. f. 3, by Elocutionist—Thak You Note, by Creme Dela Creme
$35,000 Br.—Pin Oak Farm (Ky) Tr.—Smith David — 114
Own.—Cohn Madeline
Lifetime 0 0 0 0 — 1984 0 M 0 0 — 1983 0 M 0 0
LATEST WORKOUTS Jun 21 Aqu 5f fst 1:01⅘ h Jun 15 Aqu 3f gd :37 bg(d) May 15 Aqu 4f fst :48⅘ b

Movie Queen

Dk. b. or br. f. 3, by Red Wing Bold—Queens Way, by High Echelon
$35,000 Br.—Hekimian L J (Fla) Tr.—Derderian Russell G — 114
Own.—Wachs Michael
Lifetime 8 0 4 0 $8,680 — 1984 7 M 4 0 $8,680 — 1983 1 M 0 0

4Jun84- 3Bel fst 6f :23 :46⅘ 1:12 3+ Ⓕ Md 75000 3 1 1 1 1 1½ 2hd 2 3 Maple E b 114 3.20 79-19 So Fun 1143 Movie Queen 114½ Austerlitz Station 1103 Game try 8
11May84- 8Suf fst 6f :22⅕ :45⅘ 1:12⅘ 3+ Ⓕ Md Sp Wt 5 1 1 2½ 1 2 2hd 2 1½ Gambardella C b 116 1.70 76-20 Sea Trip 1111½ Movie Queen 1162¾ Shoulda Dance 1161½ 2nd best 8
27Apr84- 4Suf fst 6f :22⅗ :46⅘ 1:14 3+ Ⓕ Md Sp Wt 6 1 2½ 2hd 2 2 2 1½ Gambardella C b 114 *1.20 69-29 CoolCs1151½MovieQueen1141SomethingPreppi1144½ Second best 7
13Apr84- 8Suf fst 6f :22⅗ :47⅕ 1:14⅘ 3+ Ⓕ Md Sp Wt 10 2 4 3 3 2½ 4 ¾ 2no Gambardella C b 114 *1.10 67-30 Charmful 114no Movie Queen1142¾ShouldaDance114¾ Just missed 10
4Apr84-10Suf fst 6f :23 :45⅘ 1:10⅘ Md Sp Wt 3 7 5 1¾ 3 7 3 9 4 7½ Gambardella C b 115 5.90 79-19 Imprevu 1205 Convict 1201¾ Super Excited 120¾ Came out 10
23Jan84- 3Aqu fst 6f ⊡:23⅕ :47⅕ 1:13 Ⓕ Md 70000 11 6 5 2½ 3 3 3 4½ 4 6 Skinner K b 117 87.70 73-21 Pricey 1174 Zuppa Inglesa 116nk HeavenlySplash1171½ Weakened 12
9Jan84- 4Aqu fst 6f ⊡:23 :47⅘ 1:14⅕ Ⓕ Md 50000 8 9 6 9 7 11 9 16 9 18½ Skinner K b 121 123.70 54-25 PairofQueens1172½HeavenlySplsh117¾SleekProspect121nk Outrun 11
28Dec83- 4Aqu gd 6f ⊡:23 :47⅘ 1:14⅗ Ⓕ Md 50000 11 6 7 6¾ 11 10 11 17 11 18¾ Migliore R b 117 41.30 51-25 A Real Find 1171½ Full Time Wife1172½SweetMiranda1171 Outrun 11
LATEST WORKOUTS Jun 22 Aqu 4f fst :51 b

The It Girl

Ch. f. 3, by Believe It—Short Cake, by Fleet Nasrullah
$35,000 Br.—Sturgill H & C (Ky) Tr.—Turner William H Jr — 114
Own.—Ritzenberg M
Lifetime 5 0 0 1 $2,530 — 1984 5 M 0 1 $2,530 — 1983 0 M 0 0 — Turf 1 0 0 0 $110

14Jun84- 2Bel fst 7f :22⅗ :46 1:26 3+ Md 30000 7 2 2 4 3 8 2 6 3 ¾ Murphy D J 108 13.70 71-23 New York Blues 114½OutAtSecond117nkTheItGirl1081½ Weakened 11
20May84- 2Bel fst 6f :23⅕ :47⅕ 1:13⅘ 3+ Ⓕ Md 35000 7 1 3 1½ 2 1½ 3 3 4 4 Maple E 113 10.70 71-18 SilentMickey1131½OhMyLrk113hdMs.SemprFidlis1202¾ Weakened 10
9May84- 1Bel fst 6f :23⅗ :47⅕ 1:11⅕ 3+ Ⓕ Md 50000 1 1 2 1½ 4 5 4 12 4 18½ Maple E 113 5.10 67-21 Ruthie's Lassie 11312½ Love Lyric 1091½ ZuppaInglesa1134¾ Tired 6
21Apr84- 6GP fst 1⅟₁₆ :48⅕ 1:13⅕ 1:46⅘ Ⓕ Md Sp Wt 8 6 5 4½ 7 11 8 21 6 26¾ Hernandez C 121 19.20 41-20 Fast Stage 121½ Honey Bee Kind 12111 TootsieBabe11413 Outrun 8
6Apr84- 5GP fm *1⅟₁₆ Ⓣ 1:44⅘ Ⓕ Md Sp Wt 1 8 8 12 8 11 8 14 8 15½ Gonzalez M A 121 27.50 66-14 Battere 1213½ Restless Wendy 1211 Valdance 1211½ Outrun 10
LATEST WORKOUTS Jun 23 Bel 4f fst :50⅘ b Jun 3 Bel 3f sly :36 h May 5 Bel 4f my :48 h

Come On Cotton

B. f. 3, by Anticipating—Cotton, by Isendu
$30,000 Br.—Pollinger Helen M (Md) Tr.—Sedlacek Sue — 105[5]
Own.—Tresvant Stable
Lifetime 4 0 0 0 — 1984 4 M 0 0 — 1983 0 M 0 0

18Jun84- 2Bel fst 6f :22⅗ :46⅘ 1:12 3+ Ⓕ Md 45000 5 7 11 8½ 12 14 12 16 12 17¾ Lopez V5 105 14.90f 64-20 Accostage 1095 Lady Litchfield 114nk Gentle Ram 1096 Outrun 13
4Jun84- 3Bel fst 6f :23 :46⅘ 1:12 3+ Ⓕ Md 70000 5 3 4 1½ 7 5½ 8 11 8 23¾ Lopez V5 105 19.00 58-19 So Fun 1143 Movie Queen 114½ Austerlitz Station 1103 Tired 8
21Apr84- 4Aqu fst 7f :24⅕ :49⅕ 1:28⅕ Ⓕ Md Sp Wt 7 2 2 1½ 4 1 12 14 13 21½ Lopez V5 116 49.30 39-30 Sunset Strait121nkGuideBoat1213½Spring'sPromise1212¾ Checked 13
14Apr84- 4Aqu sly 6f ⊡:23 :48 1:14 Ⓕ Md Sp Wt 6 10 10 9¾ 11 11 5 8 6 7½ Lopez V5 116 48.30 66-15 PreciousRoslie1161½Tmpstously1212Chiftin'sNtiv121no No factor 11

Paddy's Gift

Dk. b. or br. f. 3, by Native Royalty—Anniversary Gift, by Chieftain
$35,000 Br.—Salmon Mrs W J (Ky) Tr.—Nesky Kenneth A — 114
Own.—Salmon Mrs W J
Lifetime 10 0 2 1 $13,100 — 1984 6 M 1 0 $5,320 — 1983 4 M 1 1 $7,780

11Jun84- 6Bel fst 1 :47⅕ 1:13⅘ 1:40⅕ Ⓕ Md Sp Wt 2 10 7 5½ 9 9½ 9 17 10 20½ Bailey J D b 121 28.40 44-19 Solo Energy 121¾ Carol Jane 121¾ Bartlett North121nk Slow start 11
30May84- 6Bel sly 1⅟₁₆ :46⅘ 1:11⅘ 1:44⅘ Ⓕ Md Sp Wt 2 6 3 4½ 4 7 4 12 4 18½ Davis R G b 121 5.90 61-20 Basie 1213 Fiesta 12110½ Solo Energy 1214¾ Tired 7
12Apr84- 6Aqu fst 6f ⊡:22⅗ :46 1:12 Ⓕ Md Sp Wt 6 6 7 7½ 6 8½ 6 12 5 8½ Velasquez J b 121 31.70 75-19 EmAnAye1212JollyVictory1212½RoyalBckground1143 Raced wide 12
23Feb84- 6Aqu fst 6f ⊡:23 :47⅘ 1:13⅘ Ⓕ Md Sp Wt 1 8 6 2¾ 7 5½ 6 7½ 6 8½ Cordero A Jr b 121 6.80 65-22 Cinder Lass 1213½ Evergreen Miss1211¾ExplicitGal1212 No factor 12
5Feb84- 4Aqu sly 6f ⊡:23 :48⅘ 1:14⅘ Ⓕ Md Sp Wt 7 2 2 1 3 2 1½ 2 1 Cordero A Jr b 121 *1.60 69-25 Shipboard Fling 1211 Paddy's Gift 121noNoNoAnnie1215½ Gamely 10
18Jan84- 6Aqu fst 6f ⊡:24 :48⅘ 1:16 Ⓕ Md Sp Wt 9 8 — — 5 5 6 4½ Davis R G b 121 3.90 60-35 Hope Chest 121¾ Land of the Brave121¾RoyalOffense116nk Snow 11
30Dec83- 5Aqu fst 6f ⊡:23⅕ :48 1:14⅗ Ⓕ Md Sp Wt 6 2 2½ 2hd 1 1½ 2hd Velasquez J b 117 3.90 71-26 Corn Acupa 117hd Paddy's Gift 117¾ Guide Boat 117hd Just failed 12
11Dec83- 5Aqu fst 6f ⊡:23 :47⅘ 1:13⅘ Ⓕ Md Sp Wt 12 3 3 2½ 2 3 5 7 10 13½ McHargue D G 117 4.20 61-27 FairRibbons1174½Montage1171½RoyalBckground117½ Early speed 12
16Nov83- 4Aqu gd 7f :22⅗ :45⅘ 1:24⅘ Ⓕ Md Sp Wt 11 4 5 3½ 3 3 3 5 3 6¾ Velasquez J 117 6.00 72-19 FullSong1173½LdyLitchfild1173½Pddy'sGift117nk Lacked response 13
3Nov83- 4Aqu fst 6f :23 :46⅘ 1:12⅘ Ⓕ Md Sp Wt 4 11 8 6½ 5 8 5 7½ 4 8½ Velasquez J 117 10.80 70-23 Sourest Rind 1173¾ Accostage 1171½ Sorbet 1173 Off slowly 11
LATEST WORKOUTS ● Jun 23 Aqu 3f fst :35⅕ h Jun 9 Aqu 4f fst :48⅘ h May 21 Aqu 5f sly 1:01 h (d) ● May 16 Aqu 3f fst :35⅕ h

Temple Goddess

B. f. 3, by Naskra—Thoughts of Love, by Prince John
$35,000 Br.—Evans E P (Va) Tr.—Skiffington Thomas — 109[5]
Own.—Epstein Adele
Lifetime 0 0 0 0 — 1984 0 M 0 0 — 1983 0 M 0 0
LATEST WORKOUTS Jun 26 Bel 3f fst :38⅕ b Jun 20 Bel 6f fst 1:19 b Jun 14 Bel 5f fst 1:03⅕ bg Jun 9 Bel 5f fst 1:02 h

Ann's Gypsy Queen

Dk. b. or br. f. 3, by A Gypsy Says—Pirotta, by Coliseo
$30,000 Br.—Villareal L (NMex) Tr.—Sciacca Gary J — 110
Own.—Bannister M H Jr
Lifetime 3 0 0 0 — 1984 1 M 0 0 — 1983 2 M 0 0

20May84- 2Bel fst 6f :23⅕ :47⅕ 1:13⅘ 3+ Ⓕ Md 30000 5 9 10 9 10 14 10 15 9 13¾ Migliore R b 111 41.10 62-18 Silent Mickey1131½OhMyLark113hdMs.SemperFidelis1202¾ Outrun 10
21Dec83- 4Aqu fst 6f ⊡:23⅕ :48⅘ 1:15⅘ Ⓕ Md 35000 4 7 9 16 9 20 9 20 10 28½ Hernandez R 117 59.30 38-28 Miss Puckett 1175½ Tiki Taylor 1172½ Tall Tell 1172¾ Outrun 10
9Dec83- 2Aqu fst 6f ⊡:23 :47 1:13⅘ Ⓕ Md 45000 1 11 12 25 12 23 12 16 12 19¾ Vega H7 106 32.00 57-19 Elaborately 110no Pricey 1172½ Cormorant's Fable 1121¾ Outrun 12
LATEST WORKOUTS Jun 22 Aqu 3f fst :36⅕ h Jun 15 Aqu 5f gd 1:04⅘ b (d) Jun 8 Aqu 4f fst :51 b May 12 Aqu 5f fst 1:02⅘ hg

Love Lyric

Ch. f. 3, by Believe It—Hy's Stream, by Boldnesian
$30,000 Br.—Willcox Mr-Mrs A A (Fla) Tr.—Jerkens Steven T — 110
Own.—Willcox Mrs A A
Lifetime 7 0 1 1 $3,400 — 1984 7 M 1 1 $3,400 — 1983 0 M 0 0

21Jun84- 1Bel fst 1 :47⅕ 1:12⅘ 1:39⅕ Ⓕ Clm 20000 3 4 3 1½ 3 6½ 6 12 6 19 Bailey J D b 113 16.90 59-21 Bateau Road 1095 Tackful Queen 111hdWhisperingIrish1143 Tired 8
20May84- 2Bel fst 6f :23⅕ :47⅕ 1:13⅘ 3+ Ⓕ Md 30000 4 8 9 6 8 9½ 6 10 7 9 Gomez E R b 109 5.30 66-18 SilentMickey1131½OhMyLrk113hdMs.SemperFidlis1202¾ No factor 10
9May84- 1Bel fst 6f :23⅗ :47⅕ 1:11⅕ 3+ Ⓕ Md 45000 6 5 5 4½ 3 4½ 3 8½ 2 12½ Gomez E R b 109 6.40 73-21 Ruthie's Lassie 11312½ Love Lyric 1091½ZuppaInglesa1134¾ Rallied 6

24Apr84- 3Aqu my 6f :23 :47⅕ 1:13⅘ ⒻMd 45000 2 5 7¾ 6⁹ 6⁶½ 3⁵¾ Gomez E R b 117 13.60 66–21 StanfordGirl1212½MdelineSweetie1173½LoveLyric117hd Came out 7
23Mar84- 4Aqu fst 6f ⊡:22⅗ :47⅕ 1:14 ⒻMd Sp Wt 9 9 11¹¹ 9¹⁶ 9¹⁶ 9¹⁴¾ Gomez E R b 121 36.30 59–24 OnNightButy1165DrwingQulity1211½AdirondckMiss1212 Bore out 11
5Mar84- 9Aqu sly 6f ⊡:22⅘ :46⅗ 1:12⅘ ⒻMd Sp Wt 2 7 8⁷ 7⁹¾ 6¹² 5¹²¾ Gomez E R b 121 13.80 67–16 EvergreenMiss1213¾CinchToClinch121nkBrightCmlli1212¾ Outrun 9
13Feb84- 5Aqu fst 6f ⊡:22⅘ :46⅘ 1:13 ⒻMd Sp Wt 11 11 12¹⁴ 12¹⁷ 12²⁴ 11²⁰¾ Gomez E R 121 5.30e 59–18 Foolish River 1141¾ Sterner Stuff 1213¾Mt.Prospect1211½ Outrun 12
LATEST WORKOUTS Jun 18 Bel 4f fst :51 b Jun 13 Bel tr.t 5f fst 1:04 b Jun 4 Bel 7f gd 1:32 b May 29 Bel tr.t 3f my :38⅘ b (d)

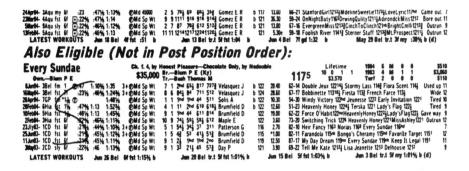

Also Eligible (Not in Post Position Order):

Every Sundae Ch. f. 4, by Honest Pleasure—Chocolate Only, by Nodouble
$35,000 Br.—Blum P E (Ky)
Own.—Blum P E Tr.—Bush Thomas M
117⁵ Lifetime 10 0 1 1 $3,570 | 1984 6 M 0 0 $510 | 1983 4 M 1 1 $3,060 | Turf 2 0 0 0 $110

8Jun84- 3Bel fm 1 Ⓣ:47 1:10⅘ 1:35 3↑ⒻMd Sp Wt 7 1 2hd 6⁵½ 8¹⁷ 7²⁷¾ Velasquez J b 122 20.40 62–14 Double Jeux 12214½ Stormy Lass 114¾ Flora Scent 114½ Used up 11
16May84- 3Bel fst 7f :23⅕ :46⅘ 1:24⅘ 3↑ⒻMd Sp Wt 8 6 8⁴½ 8⁴ 7¹¹ 5¹² Velasquez J b 124 28.60 67–17 Bobbinette 11310½ Fiesta 113¾ French Farce 113½ Wide 12
28Apr84- 7GP fm *1⅟₁₆ Ⓣ 1:48⅕ ⒻMd Sp Wt 1 1 1hd 1hd 4⁴ 5¹¹ Solis A b 122 10.30 54–30 Windy Victory 122hd Jeunesse 1222 Early Invitation 1221 Tired 10
28Feb84- 6Hia fst 1⅛ :47⅘ 1:13 1:52⅘ ⒻMd Sp Wt 4 1 1¹ 2hd 6¹⁰ 6¹⁸½ Brumfield D b 122 12.60 51–23 Heavenly Honey 1224½ Terska 1221 Lady's Flag 122½ Tired 9
10Feb84- 5Hia fst 1⅟₁₆ :48⅕ 1:13 1:45⅘ ⒻMd Sp Wt 9 1 1hd 4⁴ 6¹¹ 8¹⁴ Brumfield D 122 19.00 62–22 Force O'Habit122noHeavenlyHoney1222½Lady'sFlag122½ Gave way 9
2Feb84- 3Hia fst 6f :22⅘ :46⅗ 1:11⅗ ⒻMd Sp Wt 10 9 7⁴½ 5⁹½ 5⁸½ 6¹² Maple E 122 3.60 73–20 Switching Trick 1226 Heavenly Honey1221MissAshley1221 Outrun 12
23Jly83- 1CD fst 6f :21⅘ :44⅘ 1:10⅘ 3↑ⒻMd Sp Wt 5 1 5⁴½ 3⁴½ 3⁷ 3¹¹ Patterson G 116 2.70 82–10 Heir Fancy 1163 Norias 1168 Every Sundae 116hd 7
25Jun83- 1CD fst 6f :21⅘ :45⅕ 1:12⅘ 3↑ⒻMd Sp Wt 1 5 4¾ 5³ 4¹½ 5¹¾ Brumfield D 115 *1.00 82–11 Farandola 115nk Bongo's Cheramy 115hd Favorite Target 1151 12
11Jun83- 1CD fst 6f :21⅘ :45⅕ 1:11⅘ ⒻMd Sp Wt 9 1 2½ 1hd 1hd 2no Brumfield D 119 12.50 87–17 My Day Dream 119no Every Sundae 119nk Keep It Legal 1191 11
30May83- 2CD sly 6f :22⅘ :46 1:13⅘ ⒻMd Sp Wt 9 1 3² 2¹½ 4⁵ 5⁷¾ Day P 121 3.90 69–22 Tell Me Kate 1212½ Lisa Jeanette 1213 Delhousie 1212 9
LATEST WORKOUTS Jun 26 Bel 6f fst 1:15⅘ b Jun 20 Bel tr.t 5f fst 1:01⅘ b Jun 15 Bel 5f fst 1:03⅘ b Jun 3 Bel tr.t 5f my 1:01⅘ b (d)

Among Movie Queen's rivals, several had already competed under claiming tags, and none of these appeared to be worth more than $25,000. In addition, Movie Queen faced two first-starters, neither of which received any support at the betting windows, and two fillies dropping into the maiden-claiming ranks for the first time. Fabulous Ack had never finished close in maiden-special company, tiring in all four of her career starts, and was turning back from a mile on the grass into this six-furlong sprint. Paddy's Gift, on the other hand, had finished in the money three times in ten tries but had tired badly at route distances in her latest two races.

The fact that Fabulous Ack and Paddy's Gift ran first and third, split only by the first-starter She Speaks Well, speaks quite convincingly to our point. Dull form in maiden-special company often translates to "contender" (even "winner") in maiden-claiming competition.

At the beginning of this chapter we mentioned two exceptions to this rule. Early in two-year-old competition, the sharp maiden claimer with good speed figures often proves capable of moving successfully into maiden-special competition. Indeed, maiden-claiming winners with good figures often win again in allowance and even stakes company. And then the real runners begin to come to the races ...

Later as the three-year-old season progresses, the maiden-special ranks thin out. The more talented runners graduate, leaving their less-talented brethren to contest the issue in the better-grade maiden races. And once again, the maiden claimer with good figures assumes a more threatening posture. Let's take a look at the field for the second at Saratoga on August 15, 1984, a maiden sprint for older fillies.

One's first reaction might be to equate Saratoga racing with "class" and therefore toss out an animal like Naughty Sabrina, who

NINTH RACE
Belmont
JUNE 27, 1984

6 FURLONGS. ($1.08\frac{3}{5}$) MAIDEN CLAIMING. Purse $9,500. Fillies and Mares. 3-year-old and upward. Weight, 3-year-olds, 114 lbs. Older, 122 lbs. Claiming price $35,000; for each $2,500 to $30,000 allowed 2 lbs.

Value of race $9,500, value to winner $5,700, second $2,090, third $1,140, fourth $570. Mutuel pool $84,189. Triple Pool $187,481. OTB Triple Pool $313,991.

Last Raced	Horse	Eqt.	A.	Wt	PP	St	¼	½	Str	Fin	Jockey	Cl'g Pr	Odds $1
8Jun84 ^{3}Bel^{10}	Fabulous Ack		3	114	4	1	3^{2}	$4^{1\frac{1}{2}}$	$1^{\frac{1}{2}}$	1^{hd}	Davis R G	35000	11.90
	She Speaks Well		3	114	5	9	$7^{2\frac{1}{2}}$	$7^{1\frac{1}{2}}$	5^{2}	$2^{\frac{1}{2}}$	Migliore R	35000	25.60
11Jun84 ^{6}Bel^{10}	Paddy's Gift		3	114	8	7	4^{hd}	2^{hd}	$2^{1\frac{1}{2}}$	$3^{\frac{1}{2}}$	Cordero A Jr	35000	4.40
26Oct83 ^{9}Aqu^{4}	Sweet Missy G.		3	114	1	5	6^{2}	6^{2}	4^{1}	4^{nk}	Velasquez J	35000	8.40
19Apr84 ^{4}Aqu^{4}	Daddy's Slugger		3	110	3	6	5^{2}	5^{1}	$3^{\frac{1}{2}}$	5^{nk}	McCarron G	30000	4.70
21Jun84 ^{1}Bel^{6}	Love Lyric	b	3	110	11	11	$9^{1\frac{1}{2}}$	8^{4}	7^{7}	$6^{7\frac{1}{4}}$	Velez R I	30000	14.50
4Jun84 ^{3}Bel^{2}	Movie Queen	b	3	114	6	2	2^{2}	$1^{1\frac{1}{2}}$	$6^{\frac{1}{2}}$	7^{1}	Maple E	35000	1.50
18Jun84 ^{2}Bel^{12}	Come On Cotton		3	105	7	3	8^{hd}	9^{4}	8^{3}	8^{4}	Lopez V^{5}	30000	33.60
	Temple Goddess		3	109	9	8	11	11	10^{2}	9^{1}	Ward W A^{5}	35000	26.00
8Dec83 ^{3}Med^{3}	War Doll	b	3	114	2	4	$1^{\frac{1}{2}}$	3^{hd}	9^{2}	$10^{2\frac{1}{2}}$	Samyn J L	35000	10.40
20May84 ^{2}Bel^{9}	Ann's Gypsy Queen	b	3	110	10	10	10^{3}	$10^{\frac{1}{2}}$	11	11	Messina R	30000	49.00

OFF AT 5:18, Start good, Won driving Time, :$22\frac{4}{5}$, :$47\frac{3}{5}$, 1:$13\frac{4}{5}$ Track fast.

$2 Mutuel Prices:			
4-(D)-FABULOUS ACK	25.80	15.00	11.00
5-(E)-SHE SPEAKS WELL		24.00	10.60
8-(I)-PADDY'S GIFT			6.60

$2 TRIPLE 4-5-8 PAID $5,187.00.

B. f, by Ack Ack—Fabulous View, by Le Fabuleux. Trainer Suss-Kolyer R. Bred by Hancock III & Peters (Ky).

FABULOUS ACK, never far back, split horses leaving the turn to make her bid and lasted over SHE SPEAKS WELL in a long drive. The latter, wide into the stretch, was going well at the finish. PADDY'S GIFT made a run from the outside nearing the stretch and continued on with good energy. SWEET MISSY G. finished with good energy along the inside. DADDY'S SLUGGER rallied approaching the final furlong but wasn't good enough. LOVE LYRIC, off slowly, was going well at the finish while racing wide. MOVIE QUEEN opened a clear lead nearing the stretch but gave way under pressure. WAR DOLL was finished after going a half.

had failed to win in $25,000 claiming company. While the Saratoga meeting is possibly the "classiest" of the racing year, it does come in August, at a time when the older maiden ranks have lost their strongest runners. Three-year-olds debuting at this time of the year must be regarded suspiciously. Clearly, their careers have been delayed for some reason, most likely physical, or they would have been seen in action much sooner. It's usually a safe practice to eliminate first-starters this late in the year, demanding some evidence in actual competition before a bet is warranted.

Consequently, first-starters Printing Press, Falkara, and Floating can safely be ignored, even though the upstate audience chose the latter as their favorite. Based on established form, Faylizzie Times appeared, at least superficially, to be the logical favorite. Speed figures, however, painted a more condemning picture, revealing that the Olden Times filly had collapsed in the stretch during her career debut, earning a weak 94 speed figure.

Top O' The Li'l earned a slightly better figure (95) in her debut, but that was in May, and the filly had been inactive since.

Grape Tree's running line from her debut was quite promising, especially in light of her outside post. But it took her a month to get back to the races, then another month between that debacle and today's race. Obviously, this filly had problems.

2 **SARATOGA** 6 FURLONGS SARATOGA

6 FURLONGS. (1.08) MAIDEN SPECIAL WEIGHT. Purse $18,000. Fillies and Mares. 3-year-olds and upward. Weights, 3-year-olds, 117 lbs. Older, 122 lbs.

My Cliche — B. f. 3, by Spring Double—Kit's Charger, by Native Charger
Own.—Buckram Oak Farm — Br.—Binn M (NY) — Tr.—Paus A — 1107 — Lifetime 2 0 0 0 — 1984 2 M 0 0 — 1983 0 M 0 0
3Aug84- 5Sar fst 7f :22⅖ :46⅕ 1:25⅘ 3+ⒻMd Sp Wt 9 1 1hd 21 65½ 712½ Garrido O L7 110 43.20 63-19 Trios Lark 1171½ High Relief 117½ Slewbopper 122nk Tired 10
24Jun84- 5Bel fst 7f :23 :46⅕ 1:24⅘ 3+ⒻMd Sp Wt 4 6 83¾ 79 815 721½ Garrido O L7 107 49.70 56-22 Fiesta 1149 Agacerie 1144½ Current Miss 1143 No factor 14
LATEST WORKOUTS Aug 13 Sar 4f fst :48⅘ h ● Jly 29 Bel 6f fst 1:13⅘ h Jly 17 Bel 3f fst :35 h

Grape Tree — Gr. f. 3, by Tudor Grey—Pretty Poesy, by Hafiz
Own.—Kaufman W C III — Br.—Courtnery Evelyn T (Ky) — Tr.—Adams F Michael — 117 — Lifetime 2 0 0 0 $1,080 — 1984 2 M 0 0 $1,080 — 1983 0 M 0 0
14Jly84- 4Bel fst 7f :22⅘ :46⅘ 1:25⅕ 3+ⒻMd Sp Wt 12 6 74 64 912 1020¾ Lovato F Jr 116 4.90 55-19 Crumpets 111¾ Fetuccine 116nk Agacerie 1165 Wide 12
15Jun84- 5Bel fst 6f :22⅘ :46⅘ 1:12⅘ 3+ⒻMd Sp Wt 12 6 5¾ 1½ 21 44½ Lovato F Jr 114 18.40 76-18 Fleuve 114nk Slewbopper 1223 New Poems 1141 Weakened 13
LATEST WORKOUTS Aug 10 Sar 5f fst 1:00⅘ h Aug 2 Bel tr.t 3f fst :37⅕ b Jly 27 Bel tr.t 5f sly 1:03⅕ b Jly 24 Bel 3f fst :35⅘ h

Naughty Sabrina — B. f. 3, by Nasty And Bold—Bleep, by Assagai
Own.—Bus Boys Stable — Br.—Princess Farms (NY) — Tr.—Sedlacek Sue — 1125 — Lifetime 2 0 0 0 $840 — 1984 2 M 0 0 $840 — 1983 0 M 0 0
6Aug84- 9Sar fst 6f :22⅕ :45⅘ 1:11⅘ ⒻClm 25000 1 11 1½ 1hd 41½ 43 Lopez V5 111 24.90 79-20 Margogo 116¾ Shift Key 1161¾ Double Saucy 116½ Weakened 11
25Jly84- 6Bel fst 6f :22⅘ :46⅕ 1:12⅕ 3+ⒻMd Sp Wt 1 12 98½ 1115 1219 1219 Lopez V5 111 39.30 62-14 WhooPrincss1162FylizzTms116¾CornshImg116no Off slow,blocked 12
LATEST WORKOUTS Aug 3 Sar tr.t 3f fst :36⅘ h Jly 16 Aqu 5f fst 1:01 hg(d) Jly 9 Aqu 4f fst :48⅘ h Jun 26 Aqu 3f fst :36 h

Cinch To Clinch — Ch. f. 3, by Banquet Table—Banner, by To Market
Own.—Kimmel C P — Br.—Kimmel C P (Ky) — Tr.—Toner James J — 1107 — Lifetime 10 0 2 2 $11,980 — 1984 7 M 1 1 $5,860 — 1983 3 M 1 1 $6,120
28Jly84- 9Bel gd 6f :23 :46⅘ 1:12⅕ 3+ⒻMd 25000 4 3 12½ 1½ 63½ 64½ Bailey J D b 116 3.50 76-14 ⒹShift Key 116½ Iris Darlin 105nk Daddy'sSlugger116nk Weakened 11
19Apr84- 4Aqu fst 6f :22⅘ :47⅘ 1:13⅘ ⒻMd 25000 1 2 11 21½ 1110 1216 Bailey J D b 121 5.30 56-26 Holley Springs 1175 FrontLawn117nkHotliner1211½ Done after 1/2 12
14Apr84- 4Aqu sly 6f ⊡:23 :48 1:14 ⒻMd Sp Wt 3 4 64½ 98½ 1114 1114 Santagata N b 121 3.90 60-15 PreciousRoslie1161½Tmpstously1212Chiftin'sNtiv121no Fin. Early 11
24Mar84- 4Aqu fst 6f ⊡:22⅘ :46⅕ 1:12⅘ ⒻMd 70000 3 3 64½ 811 814 818½ Velasquez J 117 2.90 63-24 Silenciosa1171½LadyLitchfield1172MirrorOfHumnity1179½ Outrun 12
5Mar84- 9Aqu sly 6f ⊡:22⅘ :46⅗ 1:12⅘ ⒻMd Sp Wt 8 3 1½ 2hd 2½ 23¾ Santagata N 121 4.10 76-16 EvergrnMiss1213¾CinchToClinch121nkBrightCmlli1212¾ Game try 9
17Feb84- 6Aqu gd 6f ⊡:22⅘ :46⅗ 1:12 ⒻMd 70000 3 6 53 53 31½ 3½ Velasquez J 117 *2.80 83-14 Roy's Buck 110½ Precious Rosalie 119hdCinchToClinch1174 Hung 12
5Feb84- 6Aqu sly 6f ⊡:22⅘ :47⅘ 1:13 ⒻMd Sp Wt 1 1 31½ 56 912 913½ Velasquez J 121 7.70 66-25 Tax Dodge 1216RoyalBackground121noExplicitGal1212 Used early 12
21Dec83- 6Aqu fst 6f ⊡:22⅘ :47⅘ 1:14⅘ ⒻMd Sp Wt 2 5 42¾ 56 811 1211½ Velasquez J 117 *1.30 61-28 Jennifer'sChoice117½NorthernDamsel117¾CinderLass117¾ Bore in 12
11Aug83- 4Sar sly 5½f :22⅕ :46⅗ 1:05 ⒻMd Sp Wt 10 2 1½ 11½ 21½ 26½ Bailey J D 117 *2.60 85-20 MssOcn1176½CnchToClnch1174½StnnngPrncss117¾ Best of others 11
28Jly83- 3Sar fst 5½f :22⅕ :46⅕ 1:05⅘ ⒻMd Sp Wt 9 4 12½ 11½ 11½ 3½ Bailey J D 117 39.50 88-11 Stolen Title117½FullTimeWife117hdCinchToClinch1173 Weakened 12
LATEST WORKOUTS Aug 12 Sar 5f fst 1:01⅘ h Aug 6 Sar 5f fst 1:02⅘ b Jly 21 Aqu 5f fst 1:00⅘ hg Jly 15 Aqu 5f fst 1:03⅘ b

Jumping With Joy — B. f. 3, by Landscaper—High Rulerae, by Spring Double
Own.—Lucky Grace Stable — Br.—Murty Farm & Reinhart (Ky) — Tr.—Callejas Alfredo — 117 — Lifetime 2 0 0 0 — 1984 2 M 0 0 — 1983 0 M 0 0 — Turf 2 0 0 0
9Jly84- 4Bel gd 1¼ Ⓣ:48 1:39⅘ 2:06⅕ 3+ⒻMd Sp Wt 1 1 1hd 58½ 713 1121½ Graell A 116 44.80 42-35 Enhanced 1165¾ Flora Scent 116¾ Stormy Lass 1161½ Stopped 12
28Jun84- 4Bel fm 1$\frac{1}{16}$ Ⓣ:45⅘ 1:11 1:43⅘ 3+ⒻMd Sp Wt 8 6 98¾ 1214 1223 1224½ Santiago A 114 18.40 55-18 InstinctiveMove1144StormyLss1142¾QueenofZend114¾ Off slowly 12
LATEST WORKOUTS Aug 10 Bel tr.t 5f fst 1:02⅘ bg Aug 2 Bel tr.t 5f fst 1:02⅘ b Jly 7 Bel 4f sly :51⅘ b Jly 4 Bel 3f fst :35⅘ h

Printing Press — B. f. 3, by In Reality—Wealth of Nations, by Key To The Mint
Own.—Rokeby Stables — Br.—Mellon P (Va) — Tr.—Miller Mack — 1125 — Lifetime 0 0 0 0 — 1984 0 M 0 0 — 1983 0 M 0 0
LATEST WORKOUTS Aug 12 Sar 4f fst :48⅕ hg Aug 1 Sar 6f fst 1:13⅘ h Jly 26 Bel 6f fst 1:15 b Jly 21 Bel 5f gd 1:01⅘ hg

Falkara — Ch. f. 3, by Hail's Image—Sander Miss, by Gun Shot
Own.—Primavera J T — Br.—GAlvin M J (NY) — Tr.—Olsen Gary S — 1107 — Lifetime 0 0 0 0 — 1984 0 M 0 0 — 1983 0 M 0 0
LATEST WORKOUTS Jun 30 Aqu 3f fst :37⅘ b

Top O'The Li'l — Dk. b. or br. f. 3, by Top Command—Not So Lil, by Lil Fella
Own.—Cain Coralie — Br.—Cain Coralie (Ky) — Tr.—Turner William H Jr — 117 — Lifetime 1 0 0 0 — 1984 1 M 0 0 — 1983 0 M 0 0
11May84- 5Bel fst 6f :22⅘ :46⅘ 1:13⅕ ⒻMd Sp Wt 5 1 911 814 89 62½ Murphy D J 121 9.80 74-24 Statuesque 121½ Syrian City 121½ Estero 121½ No factor 9
LATEST WORKOUTS Aug 5 Sar 3f fst :36 hg Jly 26 Bel 5f fst 1:02 b Jly 19 Bel 3f gd :38⅘ b Jly 13 Bel 3f fst :35⅘ h

Faylizzie Times — Dk. b. or br. f. 3, by Olden Times—Frances V, by Carry Back
Own.—Michael R Jr — Br.—Michael R Jr (Ky) — Tr.—Michael Karen — 117 — Lifetime 1 0 1 0 $3,960 — 1984 1 M 1 0 $3,960 — 1983 0 M 0 0
25Jly84- 6Bel fst 6f :22⅘ :46⅕ 1:12⅕ 3+ⒻMd Sp Wt 5 3 11½ 12½ 12 22 Landicini C Jr 116 6.60 79-14 WhooPrincess1162FylizzieTimes116¾CornishImg116no Drifted out 12
LATEST WORKOUTS Aug 11 Sar 4f fst :47⅘ h Jly 9 Sar tr.t 5f fst 1:01⅘ b (d) Jun 30 Sar tr.t 4f fst :47⅘ b (d) Jun 27 Sar tr.t 3f gd :37⅘ b

Floating — B. f. 3, by Foolish Pleasure—Cloud Castle, by Graustark
Own.—Billings Michele — Br.—Greentree Stud (Ky) — Tr.—Johnstone Bruce — 117 — Lifetime 0 0 0 0 — 1984 0 M 0 0 — 1983 0 M 0 0
LATEST WORKOUTS Aug 12 Sar 4f fst :49⅕ bg Aug 1 Sar 5f fst 1:01 h Jly 4 Bel 3f fst :36⅘ b

Alaskan Oil — Dk. b. or br. f. 3, by Sauce Boat—Arctic Trader, by Nearctic
Own.—Evans E P — Br.—Evans E P (Va) — Tr.—Cantey Joseph B — 117 — Lifetime 1 0 0 0 — 1984 1 M 0 0 — 1983 0 M 0 0
25Jly84- 6Bel fst 6f :22⅘ :46⅕ 1:12⅕ 3+ⒻMd Sp Wt 12 4 21½ 22½ 42½ 85½ Maple E 116 21.40 75-14 WahooPrincess1162FylizzieTimes116¾CornishImge116no Used up 12
LATEST WORKOUTS Aug 11 Sar 6f fst 1:15⅘ b Aug 6 Sar 5f fst 1:00⅘ h Jly 22 Bel 5f sly 1:02 hg(d) Jly 17 Bel 6f fst 1:13⅘ h

Naughty Sabrina, on the other hand, had a far more interesting profile. She made her first appearance in the Faylizzie Times race, but inexperience (a slow start) and traffic problems eliminated her early. For her second start, trainer Sue Sedlacek chose a $25,000 open claiming contest for three-year-old fillies. The daughter of Nasty And Bold set the pace, despite another slow start, before succumbing to the more experienced and successful runners Margogo and Purse Keys by a small margin.

Naughty Sabrina's figure for that race was 98, four lengths superior to that of Faylizzie Times, and her pace figure was also faster, despite the slow start. The competition she faced on that occasion

Margogo
B. f. 3, by Salem—Priceless Princess, by Big Brave
$25,000 Br.—Clarke Helen D (Va)
Tr.—Barrera Oscar S
Own.—Barrera O S
116⁵ — Lifetime 20 3 5 3 $47,704 — 1984 16 3 5 1 $46,030 — 1983 4 M 0 2 $1,674 — Turf 2 0 0 0

1Aug84- 7Sar fm 1 3/16 Ⓣ:48 1:12 1:56 3↑ⒻAlw 22000 8 2 2hd 42 912 917½ Ward W A5 b 112 14.50 69-09 Marry Kay 112nk Secret Sharer 1172¾ Sultress 1171½ Tired 10
25Jly84- 1Bel fst 1 1/16 :47⅕ 1:12⅗ 1:45 3↑ⒻAlw 21000 3 1 2hd 11½ 13 15 Ward W A5 b 106 *1.40 77-14 Margogo 1065 Traipsin Lady 1111 Bartlett North 1136 Driving 6
20Jly84- 5Bel fst 6f :22⅗ :46⅖ 1:11⅗ 3↑ⒻAlw 20000 6 2 1hd 1½ 21 21½ Ward W A5 b 106 *.90 82-18 Foolish Clover 1171½ Margogo 1063½ Royal Offense 1115 Gamely 9
11Jly84- 5Bel fst 7f :22⅕ :45⅗ 1:24⅗ 3↑ⒻAlw 20000 7 4 1hd 1½ 11 2¾ Ward W A5 b 106 3.30 78-14 Hope So 117¾ Margogo 1062 Sarawilha 1111½ Weakeend 12
7Jly84- 2Bel sly 1 :46⅖ 1:11⅕ 1:36⅘ ⒻClm 25000 6 1 11 12½ 16 111 Ward W A5 b 111 *.90 81-16 Margogo 11111 Purse Keyes 1165½ Oh My Lark 1091½ Ridden out 7
25Jun84- 3Bel my 1 :45⅕ 1:10⅗ 1:37⅕ 3↑ⒻAlw 21000 7 2 1hd 2½ 22 22 Ward W A5 b 104 8.20 77-20 Winnebago Seven 1092 Margogo 1041 Native Beads1172¾ Gamely 10
8Jun84- 4Bel fm 1 1/16 Ⓣ:49 1:12⅖ 1:43⅘ 3↑ⒻAlw 21000 4 1 11 22 24 57½ Ward W A5 b 105 14.10 74-14 Salem Trials 1091¾ Lady President 1104 Scrutable 109¾ Tired 7
4Jun84- 1Bel fst 6f :22⅗ :46⅕ 1:12⅕ ⒻClm c-20000 7 2 32½ 42½ 41½ 4¾ Lopez V5 107 *1.80 80-19 Romeo'sMistress106nkFirRibbons109noNssu'sPrid116½ Weakened 7
24Apr84- 5Aqu my 6½f :22⅕ :45⅗ 1:18⅗ ⒻClm 30000 3 5 32½ 45½ 43 43½ Lopez V5 107 10.70 78-21 Cussle 1052 Purse Keyes 112nk Shimaleka 1161½ Hung 9
2Apr84- 8Key fst 7f :22⅗ :46⅕ 1:26 ⒻClm 22500 2 4 24 33½ 35½ 33½ Cole M A7 107 3.10 74-30 Breakage 1141¼ Cathy's Bluff 1162 Margogo 1071½ Weakened 7
LATEST WORKOUTS Jun 12 Bel tr.t 4f fst :49 b Jun 7 Bel tr.t 3f fst :36 h

Purse Keyes
Ch. f. 3, by Purse Finder—Laughing Keys, by Fast Hilarious
$25,000 Br.—Imbesi A (NJ)
Tr.—Moschera Gasper S
Own.—Davis A
116 — Lifetime 22 4 5 3 $62,675 — 1984 19 3 5 2 $56,940 — 1983 3 1 0 1 $5,735 — Turf 1 0 0 0 $1,050

7Jly84- 2Bel sly 1 :46⅖ 1:11⅕ 1:36⅘ ⒻClm 25000 7 2 21 22½ 26 211 MacBeth D b 116 4.70 70-16 Margogo 11111 Purse Keyes 1165½ Oh My Lark 1091½ 2nd Best 7
23Jun84- 3Bel fst 1 :46⅗ 1:12⅗ 1:38 ⒻClm 45000 1 4 44 45 47½ 412¼ MacBeth D b 112 10.60 63-22 Avanti Sassa 1128 Colorful Miss116nkOurAuntEdith1164 Even try 7
13Jun84- 2Bel fm 1 1/16 Ⓣ:48 1:12 1:45⅕ ⒻClm 35000 7 6 66 56 69½ 45½ Vega H7 b 105 9.00 70-16 Native Anna 107nk Undulant 116no Shady Cathy 1125 No factor 8
1Jun84- 5Bel fst 1 1/16 :46⅘ 1:11⅗ 1:44 ⒻClm 35000 4 5 55 88½ 918 720½ Cordero A Jr b 116 *2.20 61-20 Colorful Miss 1167 Avanti Sassa1164½Mickey'sLady114½ Fin. early 10
28May84- 3Bel fst 1 :46⅕ 1:12⅖ 1:39⅘ ⒻClm c-25000 3 6 54½ 2hd 14 16½ Velasquez J b 116 *1.20 66-17 Purse Keyes 1166½ Betrayed 1161½ Ms. Frenzy 107½ Driving 8
10May84- 3Bel fst 7f :23⅕ :47 1:25⅗ ⒻClm 30000 5 1 45 44 1½ 2½ Cordero A Jr b 114 *1.50 74-17 Season Saver 111½ Purse Keyes 1144¾ Colorful Miss1165¾ Gamely 6
2May84- 4Aqu fst 1⅛ :49⅕ 1:14 1:53⅗ ⒻClm 30000 7 7 63 52½ 32 33 Davis R G b 112 *2.30 64-29 Anselma 1092¼ Season Saver 116¾ Purse Keyes 112¾ Mild bid 7
24Apr84- 5Aqu my 6½f :22⅕ :45⅗ 1:18⅗ ⒻClm 30000 6 7 710 67¾ 54½ 22 Davis R G b 112 *1.40 80-21 Cussle 1052 Purse Keyes 112nk Shimaleka 1161½ Gained place 9
18Apr84- 3Aqu fst 170 ⊡:48⅘ 1:14⅕ 1:46 ⒻClm 25000 3 3 31 2hd 1hd 4½ Davis R G b 121 *1.20 69-16 Burned Toast 112nk Tackful Queen111hdAnselma118hd Weakened 5
13Apr84- 3Aqu fst 6f ⊡:22⅘ :46⅗ 1:12⅖ ⒻClm 45000 5 8 109¾ 99½ 89 53¾ Davis R G b 114 9.90 78-22 Thai Sox 114½ Majestic Flag 1092¾ Dusty Girl 112no Rallied 10
LATEST WORKOUTS Jly 27 Bel tr.t 4f sly :49⅗ h Jly 14 Bel tr.t 4f fst :49 b Jly 5 Bel tr.t 4f fst :48 h Jun 22 Bel tr.t 3f fst :37⅘ b

was probably tougher than these maidens could offer. Both Naughty Sabrina and Faylizzie Times were 9–2 on the board, as was Mack Miller's first-timer Printing Press. Floating, at 9–5, was favored. Was Naughty Sabrina the better bet? Was her class really suspect? Would another poor start compromise her chances?

Our point is that this late in the year, maiden-claiming animals with substantial figures do stand a reasonable chance against what remains in the maiden-special ranks. Indeed, Naughty Sabrina,

SECOND RACE
Saratoga
AUGUST 15, 1984

6 FURLONGS. (1.08) MAIDEN SPECIAL WEIGHT. Purse $18,000. Fillies and Mares. 3-year-olds and upward. Weights, 3-year-olds, 117 lbs. Older, 122 lbs.

Value of race $18,000, value to winner $10,800, second $3,960, third $2,160, fourth $1,080. Mutuel pool $183,277, OTB pool $137,640. Quinella Pool $232,492. OTB Quinella Pool $219,514.

Last Raced	Horse	Eqt.	A.Wt	PP	St	¼	½	Str	Fin	Jockey	Odds $1
6Aug84 9Sar4	Naughty Sabrina		3 112	2	5	6½	4hd	3hd	12¼	Lopez V5	4.70
25Jly84 6Bel2	Faylizzie Times		3 117	8	1	1½	13	12½	2nk	Landicini C Jr	4.70
14Jly84 4Bel10	Grape Tree		3 117	1	3	3½	2hd	2½	31¼	Lovato F Jr	11.70
9Jly84 4Bel11	Jumping With Joy		3 117	4	10	10	10	6½	4¾	Velasquez J	17.20
	Floating		3 117	9	2	21½	31½	44	5no	Cordero A Jr	1.90
	Printing Press		3 112	5	8	71	71	71½	62½	Ward W A5	4.90
25Jly84 6Bel8	Alaskan Oil		3 117	10	6	41½	53	51	72¾	Maple E	15.10
28Jly84 9Bel6	Cinch To Clinch	b	3 110	3	4	5½	61	81	81¾	Garrido O L7	16.70
	Falkara		3 110	6	9	95	920	10	9no	Delgado G7	42.10
11May84 5Bel6	Top O'The Li'l		3 117	7	7	84	82	92	10	Murphy D J	12.20

OFF AT 2:02. Start good, Won driving. Time, :22, :45⅖, 1:12 Track fast.

$2 Mutuel Prices:

3-(C)-NAUGHTY SABRINA	11.40	5.40	3.40
9-(I)-FAYLIZZIE TIMES		5.40	3.80
2-(B)-GRAPE TREE			6.40

$2 QUINELLA 3-9 PAID $28.80.

B. f, by Nasty And Bold—Bleep, by Assagai. Trainer Sedlacek Sue. Bred by Princess Farms (NY).

NAUGHTY SABRINA swung out while rallying leaving the turn and continued on gamely to wear down FAYLIZZIE TIMES and drew clear. The latter sprinted away to a clear lead while racing well out from the rail around the turn but wasn't able to withstand the winner. GRAPE TREE raced forwardly into the stretch while saving ground and continued on with good energy. JUMPING WITH JOY found best stride too late. FLOATING, a factor to the stretch, weakened. PRINTING PRESS failed to be a serious factor. ALASKAN OIL tired. CINCH TO CLINCH was finished early.

based on her performance against multiple winners, should have been favored in this field. Only the third of the three questions just raised really posed a serious threat to her chances.

As the race was run, Faylizzie Times ran the favored Floating into submission but was no match for the late charge of Naughty Sabrina. The reformed claimer returned $11.00 and needed only run to a figure of 98 to win.

Chapter 7

Beware the Impressive Maiden Winner

WHEREAS THE MAIDEN WINNER is said to have "graduated" from the maiden ranks, the victor in a restricted ("nonwinners other than") allowance race is said to have "lost a condition." All Thoroughbreds have three such "conditions"—eligibility to compete in "nonwinners of one," "nonwinners of two," and "nonwinners of three" allowance races.

The "nonwinners of one" (NW1) allowance race is meant to be a testing ground for developing young horses whose major claim to fame thus far in their career has been a maiden victory, and in some cases victories in claiming races. These "first-step" allowance contests often reveal horses on their way to stakes competition but are more likely to expose many of the contestants as nothing better than claiming animals.

The handicapper is usually confronted with several fairly standard "types" when analyzing an NW1 race. Which are to be preferred varies with the time of the year. These include:

(1) The horse that broke its maiden impressively in MSW company last time out.
(2) The horse that won an MSW race last time out with an average or subpar performance.
(3) The horse that graduated from the maiden-claiming ranks last time out.
(4) The horse that raced well in its only start in NW1 company.
(5) The horse that has raced well in a limited number (2–4) of starts in allowance company.
(6) The horse that has repeatedly failed to lose its NW1 condi-

tion, although possibly running in the money on several occasions.

(7) The horse that has failed to perform well in most of its allowance attempts.

(8) The three-year-old moving into NW1 company from the claiming ranks.

(9) The older claimer trying its luck in NW1 company.

Only on rare occasions are recent maiden graduates worth backing first time in allowance company. If they appear to have legitimate credentials, chances are they will be favored. And, of course, the horse with a proven record of futility in "nonwinners of one" company cannot be expected to change colors overnight.

My preference in these races has always been the lightly raced young horse with limited, though positive, experience against similar competition. The "lightly raced" aspect of this profile is important. A horse that made numerous attempts before breaking its maiden cannot realistically be expected to win a second try in NW1 company just because it may have placed or showed first time in that class. The horse that broke its maiden after two or three starts, then runs well, in good time, in allowance company next time out, has the "most preferred" profile for this kind of race if offered at a reasonable price. As the season wears on, however, the inherent ability that makes this kind of horse such a viable bet simply is not there—at least in most cases. Experience, even if it is gained in the claiming ranks, assumes more significance.

The following race includes several of the types listed above. It was run over seven furlongs at Aqueduct on May 16, 1984. We will discuss the 2–5 favorite, Eastern Viewpoint, first, then his opposition:

EASTERN VIEWPOINT

When this Damascus colt won his debut as the 8–5 favorite, posting "monster" pace and speed figures (110–106), many observers jumped on his bandwagon—concluding that this was the Belmont Stakes darkhorse, trainer Angel Penna's substitute for his ailing star Time For A Change. It would have been far safer to predict that the colt would be 2–5 for his second start.

While it might have been difficult to believe that Eastern Viewpoint could be beaten in NW1 company, there were a few warning signs the majority of the audience failed to notice. First, there is the

7 BELMONT

7 FURLONGS
BELMONT PARK

7 FURLONGS. (1.20⅘) ALLOWANCE. Purse $20,000. 3-year-olds and upward which have never won a race other than Maiden, Claiming or Starter. Weights, 3-year-olds, 113 lbs. Older, 124 lbs. Non-winners of a race other than claiming since April 15 allowed 3 lbs.

Highest Star

B. c. 3, by Hold Your Peace—Sunny Day III, by Solazo
Br.—Willcox Mr-Mrs A A (Fla)
Tr.—Schulhofer Flint S
Own.—Willcox A A
113 — Lifetime 2 1 0 0 $12,000 — 1984 2 1 0 0 $12,000 — 1983 0 M 0 0

28Apr84- 5Aqu fst 7f :22⅖ :45⅗ 1:23⅘ Alw 20000 2 3 31½ 33½ 32½ 43½ Graell A 122 2.20 78-21 TheSkeptic1172½BlindMan'sBluff1171½UpperStar117hd Weakened 8
17Apr84- 3Aqu fst 6f ⊡:22⅘ :46 1:11⅘ Md Sp Wt 2 2 1½ 11 12 11½ Graell A 122 3.50 80-15 Highest Star 1221½ Runaway Native122¾BoldNHonest1224 Driving 11
LATEST WORKOUTS ●May 11 Bel 7f fst 1:25⅘ h May 6 Bel 4f fst :47⅘ h Apr 25 Bel 4f fst :48 h Apr 8 Hia 4f fst :48⅘ b

Cathedral Aisle

B. c. 4, by Nostrum—Nice Bonnet, by Royal Levee
Br.—Freeman W C (NY)
Tr.—Freeman Willard C
Own.—Freeman W C
121 — Lifetime 10 1 4 0 $29,690 — 1984 4 0 2 0 $7,800 — 1983 4 0 1 0 $7,950 — Turf 1 0 0 0 $1,620

10May84- 5Bel fst 6f :23⅕ :46⅘ 1:11 3+Ⓢ Alw 24500 10 9 53 21½ 22½ 21½ Davis R G b 121 2.40 86-17 Mr. T. And Me 1121½ Cathedral Aisle 121¾ High Ice 1121¾ Gamely 12
21Apr84- 2Aqu fst 7f :24⅖ :48⅘ 1:26⅘ 3+Ⓢ Alw 24500 9 9 31½ 33½ 817 918 Cruguet J 121 *1.30 49-30 SincerWish1125½CommndrAlmy1212½GuyPbo121hd Stumbled gate 9
29Mar84- 9GP fst 7f :22⅘ :45⅗ 1:24 Alw 13000 7 7 68¾ 511 55 52 McCauley W H 117 5.60 82-26 Just A Miner 117¾ Rocky Knave 117no RightOnRed119nk Bumped 10
13Mar84- 7GP fst 6f :22 :44⅘ 1:10⅕ Alw 12000 6 7 55 35½ 34 21½ Cruguet J 117 3.30 87-17 Take It All 1171½ Cathedral Aisle 1171 Golden Break1173½ Rallied 8
21Jly83- 2Bel gd 1¼ Ⓣ:48⅘ 1:39 2:05⅘ 3+Ⓢ Alw 27000 2 5 52½ 74½ 68½ 54¾ Cruguet J 111 2.60 62-27 EsyChoice106½ⒹKnucklehdSmith1122½SpcificIntnt1111½ Bumped 9
21Jly83-Placed fourth through disqualification
7Jly83- 7Bel fst 7f :23⅘ :46⅘ 1:23⅘ 3+ Alw 20000 9 9 4¾ 2hd 86½ 88½ Murphy D J5 b 106 4.40 77-19 Galaxy Guide106hdWaitlist1171½BelieveTheQueen111¾ Forced out 10
22Jun83- 7Bel fst 1⅙ :46⅗ 1:10⅘ 1:43⅕ 3+Ⓢ Alw 28500 1 3 3½ 21½ 36½ 48½ Fell J 113 *.60 77-22 Sir Keys 1116½ Danderoo 1172 NewYorkCompany112no Weakened 8
11Jun83- 1Bel fst 1 :46⅘ 1:11⅗ 1:36⅘ 3+ Alw 21000 4 6 52½ 21½ 23½ 23½ Fell J 114 2.70 79-14 DaringGroom1043½CthedrlAisle1142½BrodwyHrry1123½ Held place 10
9Jly82- 4Bel fst 6f :22⅘ :46⅗ 1:11⅗ Md Sp Wt 2 3 42½ 3½ 12 15½ Fell J 118 *1.70 84-22 CthdrlAisl1185½DomintingDooly118nkNightTimBoogi118¾ Handily 11
18Jun82- 4Bel fst 5f :22⅘ :46⅘ :59⅕ Md Sp Wt 2 6 711 712 76½ 21 Fell J 118 10.90 97-15 Primitive Pleasure 1181 Cathedral Aisle1182½Lutyens118¾ Rallied 8
LATEST WORKOUTS May 6 Bel 5f fst :59 h May 1 Bel 6f fst 1:14⅘ h Mar 26 GP 6f fst 1:15 b Mar 21 GP 4f fst :49⅘ b

Delta Deity

B. c. 4, by Upper Nile—Deesse De Ridan, by Ridan
Br.—Carl W A (Ky)
Tr.—Goldberg Allen
Own.—Marcus Betty G
121 — Lifetime 3 1 0 1 $8,715 — 1983 3 1 0 1 $8,715 — 1982 0 M 0 0 — Turf 2 1 0 0 $7,560

16Aug83- 4Mth fm 1⅙ Ⓣ:49⅕ 1:13⅘ 1:45 3+ Md Sp Wt 12 9 96¾ 85½ 53½ 1hd Thornburg B 116 9.40 76-21 Delta Deity 116hd Wilhelm 1161 Competitiveness 116¾ Driving 12
5Aug83- 6Mth fm 1⅙ Ⓣ:47⅘ 1:11⅗ 1:44⅕ 3+ Md Sp Wt 3 9 1013 96½ 73½ 52 Vega A5 111 12.50 78-20 Quobow 116hd Wilhelm 116¾ Minstrel Time 116nk Rallied 12
9Jly83- 1Mth fst 6f :22⅘ :46 1:11⅗ 3+ Md Sp Wt 1 5 45 58½ 59 46½ Gonzalez M A 116 10.80 75-17 Late To Rise 1161½ NativeCourage1112ⒹBayMcCoy1113 Even try 7
9Jly83-Placed third through disqualification
LATEST WORKOUTS May 6 Mth 6f fst 1:15 b Apr 28 Mth 6f fst 1:17 b ●Apr 13 Aqu ⊡ 4f fst :46⅘ h

Bligh

B. c. 3, by Damascus—Maimiti, by Never Bend
Br.—Brant P M (Ky)
Tr.—Jolley Leroy
Own.—Brant B
110 — Lifetime 8 1 0 3 $20,730 — 1984 3 0 0 2 $7,350 — 1983 5 1 0 1 $13,380

14Apr84- 3SA fst 7f :22⅘ :45⅕ 1:22⅘ Alw 27000 2 7 711 711 58 37 Guerra W A b 120 14.10 79-16 Light Will 1203 Running Degree 1204 Bligh 1202 RAllied 8
4Mar84- 6SA fst 1⅙ :46⅘ 1:11 1:43⅕ Alw 23000 2 3 46 48 510 814¾ Castaneda M b 115 23.40 70-17 MightyAdversary1141¾HeavenlyPlain1176½Cazador118nk Fin. early 8
21Jan84- 6SA fst 6½f :21⅘ :44⅘ 1:16⅘ Alw 22000 3 6 65 65 44 37½ Pierce D b 120 7.10e 80-17 Rex Lake 1154 Montauk 1203½ Bligh 1201½ Rallied 8
26Dec83- 4SA fst 6f :22 :45⅗ 1:11⅘ Md Sp Wt 4 2 32½ 31 2hd 1no Pierce D b 118 12.50 81-16 Bligh 118no Carrizzo 118no Exclusive Arts 1186½ Driving 6
24Nov83- 6Aqu fst 1 :46⅘ 1:12⅘ 1:39 Md Sp Wt 3 6 44 54 55 511 Ycaza M b 118 5.60 60-24 Certain Treat 1185½RamblingRector1183ExclusiveRed118¾ Evenly 14
8Nov83- 4Aqu fst 6f :22⅘ :46⅕ 1:12⅕ Md Sp Wt 10 9 65 66 46 35 Ycaza M b 118 11.50f 75-26 Play On 118nk Circle Round 1184¾ Bligh 118¾ Mild response 14
12Sep83- 5Bel fst 7f :23⅕ :47 1:24 Md Sp Wt 12 9 72¾ 53 48 716½ Cruguet J b 118 14.00 65-22 Dr. Carter 1183 Country Manor 1188½ Exattic 119hd Tired 13
15Aug83- 6Sar fst 7f :22⅘ :45⅘ 1:24⅕ Md Sp Wt 12 8 73½ 32½ 44 45½ Cruguet J b 118 *1.80e 75-15 Hail Bold King 1182½ Gallant Hour 1182½ Exattic 118¾ Weakened 14
LATEST WORKOUTS May 10 Bel 6f fst 1:16⅘ b May 2 Bel 6f fst 1:14 b Apr 26 Bel 5f fst 1:00⅘ h

Troop Ship

B. g. 5, by Hoist the Flag—Fiddling, by Herbager
Br.—Clark Jane F (Ky)
Tr.—Barrera Oscar S
Own.—Barrera O S
116[5] — Lifetime 39 1 6 6 $48,150 — 1984 8 0 2 0 $7,810 — 1983 13 1 2 1 $17,240 — Turf 8 0 1 2 $10,440

12May84- 9Bel fst 7f :23⅕ :47 1:23⅘ Clm c-20000 6 10 94¾ 63½ 64½ 63½ Skinner K b 117 9.70 79-17 Gratification 117no Palimony 112hd J. Strap 1121½ In close early 12
24Apr84- 2Aqu my 7f :22⅘ :45⅘ 1:25 Clm 25000 6 9 86½ 85¾ 73½ 61½ Skinner K b 117 7.50 74-21 Creme De La Fete 113nk Storm Warrior 113hdSpyGame117¾ Wide 11
12Apr84- 5Aqu fst 170 ⊡:47⅘ 1:11⅘ 1:41⅗ Clm 35000 6 6 66½ 65¾ 612 716½ Skinner K b 117 8.20 75-19 Starbinia 1133½ Pearl Amber 113½ Great Hunter 1173¾ Outrun 8
9Apr84- 9Aqu fst 6f ⊡:23⅕ :47 1:12⅘ Clm 35000 4 10 86 55½ 24 2nk Skinner K b 117 21.40 81-19 Toss Across 117nk Troop Ship1172PartingCrack117nk Drifted out 12
12Mar84- 5Aqu fst 6f ⊡:23⅕ :47⅘ 1:12⅘ Clm 45000 5 8 95¾ 83½ 85½ 84½ Skinner K b 115 40.90 77-22 ⒹI'm So Merry 106¾ Quill Feather114½Fibak1101 Showed nothing 9
28Jan84- 7Aqu fst 1⅛ ⊡:47⅕ 1:12⅘ 1:45⅘ Alw 22000 11 6 107¾ 1114 1118 1125 Smith A Jr b 117 3.00e 58-20 Fast John 117no Righteous Anger 1103CanadianCalm1192 Outrun 11
21Jan84- 5Aqu fst 6f ⊡:23 :47 1:13 Alw 20000 9 10 77¾ 78½ 1016 1114¾ Lovato F Jr b 117 *3.20 64-30 Mc Michael112hdFlyingGeneral1124½PrideOfSatan1102½ Fell back 11
11Jan84- 5Aqu sl 6f ⊡:23⅕ :47⅘ 1:13⅘ Alw 20000 8 11 94¾ 75½ 42¾ 22 Lovato F Jr b 117 27.90 75-33 Sky Falcon 1122 Troop Ship 117nk Saint Stephan 117¾ Rallied 12
14Aug83- 2Sar gd 1⅛ Ⓣ:47⅘ 1:13 1:52 3+ Clm 40000 12 2 21½ 2½ 2½ 99½ Bailey J D b 117 41.10 70-25 ForceCommndr1172¾RichButtrfly1152½DivinMrquis113hd Stopped 12
3Aug83- 2Sar gd 1⅙ Ⓣ:47 1:12 1:45 3+ Clm 40000 7 8 811 98½ 85¾ 74½ Bailey J D b 117 18.50 68-20 Cancun 114¾ Millbank 1141¾ Skaran 1171½ Outrun 11
LATEST WORKOUTS May 15 Bel 3f fst :35⅘ h May 11 Bel 3f fst :39⅘ b May 5 Bel 4f my :48⅘ h Apr 21 Bel 4f fst :47⅘ h

Eastern Viewpoint

Ch. c. 3, by Damascus—Bonnie Blink, by Buckpasser
Br.—Phipps O (Ky)
Tr.—Penna Angel
Own.—Phipps O
113 — Lifetime 1 1 0 0 $10,800 — 1984 1 1 0 0 $10,800 — 1983 0 M 0 0

6May84- 2Aqu fst 7f :22⅘ :45⅘ 1:23⅘ Md Sp Wt 5 5 12½ 13½ 16 17¾ Cordero A Jr 122 *1.60 83-19 EsternViewpoint1227¾MjsticJbot1222Oscr'sGold1221½ Ridden out 8
LATEST WORKOUTS May 14 Bel 4f sly :47⅕ h May 2 Bel 4f fst :48 hg Apr 28 Bel 3f fst :36⅘ h Apr 26 Bel 7f fst 1:28 h

Greff

Ch. c. 3, by Angle Light—Abold Dame, by Bold Reasoning
Br.—Muckler Stables Inc (Ill)
Tr.—Shapoff Stanley R
Own.—Shapoff E L
110 — Lifetime 16 3 1 4 $51,440 — 1984 6 2 0 1 $27,120 — 1983 10 1 1 3 $24,320

25Apr84- 4Aqu gd 6f :22⅘ :46 1:11⅘ Clm 70000 4 6 64½ 33 34 3¾ Smith A Jr b 113 8.20 82-22 Fingers Inthe Till 113½ Award of Merit 113nk Greff113nk Fin. well 8
28Mar84- 7Aqu gd 170 ⊡:48⅘ 1:14⅕ 1:44 Alw 21000 3 7 64 79 711 715¾ Lovato F Jr b 117 2.90 64-22 Closed Corp117hdGoldenImmigrant1174CallMeRebel117nk Outrun 7
22Mar84- 1Aqu fst 6f ⊡:22⅘ :45⅘ 1:11⅕ Clm 70000 2 9 99¾ 99½ 67 44½ Lovato F Jr b 113 8.60 83-24 TrinbgoPride1083RstlssJohn119noBlindMn'sBluff1131½ No factor 9
7Mar84- 1Aqu fst 6f ⊡:22⅘ :46⅗ 1:11 Clm 70000 3 7 76 75½ 54 44 Velasquez J b 113 3.60 85-17 ⒹⒽStrikingRich103ⒹⒽRstlssJohn1131TrinbgoPrid1083 No factor 7
20Feb84- 3Aqu fst 6f ⊡:22⅘ :46⅘ 1:12⅘ Clm c-45000 8 12 117 96½ 52½ 1½ Velasquez J b 115 2.60 82-16 Greff 115½ Striking Rich 1172 Broadway Barry 117no Driving 12
2Feb84- 4Aqu fst 6f ⊡:22⅘ :46⅕ 1:11⅘ Clm 45000 2 6 77 67½ 33 1no Velasquez J b 113 10.90 86-22 Greff 113no Macho Devil 117½ Dixie's Island 1086 Driving 9
31Dec83- 3Aqu fst 6f ⊡:23⅕ :47⅕ 1:12 Clm 50000 5 5 41½ 43½ 56½ 510½ Lovato F Jr b 117 5.30 73-21 StrikingRich1175BlindMan'sBluff117nkSirCornwll1131½ Weakened 9
23Dec83- 3Aqu gd 6f ⊡:22⅘ :46⅗ 1:12 Clm 70000 4 7 54 53¾ 54½ 69½ Cordero A Jr b 113 2.90 75-21 MesuredResponse1084½Gemmology1173½TrinbgoPrid108½ No rally 10
7Dec83- 5Aqu fst 6f ⊡:22⅘ :46⅗ 1:12⅕ Clm 75000 5 2 3½ 3nk 32½ 44½ Bailey J D b 117 3.00 78-21 LandOfOz117hdBroadwayBarry1134½Cooper'sHwk117no Weakened 7
26Nov83- 3Aqu my 6f :22⅘ :46⅕ 1:11⅗ Clm 72500 1 6 65½ 34½ 22½ 22¾ McCarron G b 115 2.40 80-21 It's Frigid 1192¾ Greff 1151½ Cooper's Hawk 1131 Game try 6
LATEST WORKOUTS May 12 Bel 5f fst 1:00⅕ h May 7 Bel 4f fst :49⅘ b May 2 Bel tr.t 4f fst :51 b Apr 23 Bel 4f fst :49⅕ b

Solid Grip

B. g. 3, by Tom Swift—Tourniquette, by Dr Fager
Br.—Sommer Viola (Ky)
Tr.—Bush Thomas M
Own.—Sommer Viola
113 — Lifetime 2 1 0 0 $10,800 — 1984 2 1 0 0 $10,800 — 1983 0 M 0 0

24Apr84- 6Aqu my 7f :23 :46⅘ 1:25⅘ Md Sp Wt 6 2 41½ 43 1½ 1¾ Velasquez J 122 8.10 74-21 SolidGrip122¾AppointedHour1151½MjsticJbot1222¾ Wide; driving 6
11Apr84- 5Aqu fst 6f ⊡:22⅘ :46⅘ 1:11⅕ Md Sp Wt 7 4 1114 1120 919 614½ Velasquez J 122 35.50 73-18 Up Pops Awinner 1225½ Duomo 1223½ Atlantico 1221 Outrun 11
LATEST WORKOUTS May 15 Bel 3f fst :39 b May 11 Bel 5f fst 1:03 b May 3 Bel 4f fst :48⅘ b Apr 23 Bel 3f fst :36⅘ b

Irish Ore

Ch. c. 4, by Accipiter—Dianette, by Thorn
Br.—Equine Investments (Ky)
Tr.—O'Brien Charles
Own.—Delaney A
111[10] — Lifetime 13 1 2 3 $28,310 — 1984 11 1 1 3 $23,910 — 1983 2 M 1 0 $4,400

5May84- 3Aqu fst 6f :22⅘ :46 1:10⅘ 3+ Alw 20000 4 5 54 43 1½ 1¾ Espinosa R E10 111 30.10Ⓓ 88-16 ⒹIrish Ore 111¾ Le Voyeur 1244 Dancing Native1101 Bore in turn 7
5May84-Disqualified and placed fourth
28Apr84- 3Mth fst 6f :22⅘ :46⅕ 1:12⅕ 3+ Alw 11000 4 7 64½ 54½ 62½ 35 Deegan J C 119 3.70 74-22 Right AndRegal1062BalancingAct1173IrishOre1191 Fractious gate 8
14Apr84- 5Aqu sly 6f ⊡:22⅘ :47⅕ 1:12⅕ Alw 20000 1 6 44½ 2½ 2hd 21½ Deegan J C 117 13.00 82-15 Wandering Feet 1171½ Irish Ore 1171½ Flippydoo 112nk Game try 7
23Mar84- 8Aqu fst 170 ⊡:48 1:13⅘ 1:43⅘ Alw 21000 4 5 43½ 44 713 721 Deegan J C 117 11.70 62-24 Canadian Calm 11210 Mi TeSyd112noVaguelyBold117nk No factor 7
5Mar84- 6Aqu fst 6f ⊡:22⅘ :46⅗ 1:12 Md Sp Wt 4 6 64 33 21½ 1nk Deegan J C 122 10.70 84-22 Irish Ore 122nk Heads Will Roll 1221½ Oyster 1221½ Driving 8
25Feb84- 3Aqu gd 6f ⊡:22⅘ :46⅕ 1:10⅘ Md Sp Wt 9 8 36 41 35 37½ Santiago A 122 6.10 84-12 SummerTwilight122hdSilkPlesure1227½IrishOr1225 Lacked a rally 10
29Jan84- 1Aqu fst 170 ⊡:48 1:13⅘ 1:44⅕ Md Sp Wt 4 4 42 31½ 79 714 Deegan J C b 122 40.90 66-15 Young Naskra 122½ Vaguely Bold 1221 El Gourou 1171½ Tired 8
27Jan84- 6Aqu gd 6f ⊡:22⅘ :46⅘ 1:11⅘ Md Sp Wt 4 9 99¾ 86 43½ 43½ Murphy D J5 b 117 4.70 84-16 CourtProcdr1221¾WndrngFt1221½SmmrTwlght122nk Hesitated st. 9
21Jan84- 5Aqu fst 6f ⊡:23 :47 1:13 Alw 20000 5 11 109¾ 1012 912 78½ Murphy D J5 b 112 15.20 70-30 Mc Michael112hdFlyingGeneral1124½PrideOfSatan1102½ No factor 11
18Jan84- 4Aqu fst 6f ⊡:23⅘ :48⅘ 1:15⅘ Md Sp Wt 8 — — — 78½ 810½ Murphy D J5 117 *1.90 56-35 Verisimilar 117½ Wandering Feet 1223½ April FoolsBoy1221 Snow 12
LATEST WORKOUTS ●May 13 Aqu 4f fst :47 h Apr 27 Bel 3f fst :35⅕ h Apr 21 Bel 4f fst :49 b Apr 9 Bel tr.t 4f fst :48⅘ b

Steppin Battler — B. c. 3, by Crimson Battle—Steppin Stephanie, by Wa-Wa Cy
Own.—Mar-Rich Stable — Br.—Keller R C (Ky) — Tr.—Krenovich Joseph A — 110
Lifetime 10 1 1 1 $19,280 — 1984 4 1 0 0 $12,600 — 1983 6 M 1 1 $6,680

9May84- 8Bel	fst	1	:46⅘	1:12	1:36⅘	Withers	1	1	2hd	1018	1026	1040½	Cruguet J	b 126	110.30	42-21	Play On 126¹ Morning Bob 1262½ Back BayBarrister126¹	Stopped 10
26Jan84- 7Aqu	my	1 1/16 ⊡	:48	1:12⅘	1:44⅕	Alw 22000	8	3	3½	2hd	44½	513½	Rogers K L	b 122	23.40	78-10	Vanlandingham 117³ Charmed Rook 117nk LeroyS.117⁶	Gave way 9
19Jan84- 4Aqu	fst	1⅛ ⊡	:50	1:16⅘	1:56	Md Sp Wt	7	1	12½	11½	12½	111	Rogers K L	b 122	7.50	65-32	Steppin Battler122¹¹IceColdGold122⁶FlipN'Hold1222½	Ridden out 12
6Jan84- 6Aqu	fst	6f ⊡	:22⅘	:46⅘	1:12⅘	Md Sp Wt	12	1	21½	21½	2³	54½	Venezia M	b 122	10.30	76-24	Broadway Willy 122no I'mARounder1222½TheBondsman122¾	Tired 12
28Dec83- 6Aqu	sly	6f ⊡	:22⅘	:47⅘	1:14	Md Sp Wt	4	5	42½	41½	3½	3nk	Venezia M	b 118	19.00	74-29	Empravatar118nkMilitryOrder118hdSteppinBttler1182¾	Evenly late 12
8Dec83- 6Aqu	fst	6f ⊡	:22⅘	:46⅘	1:12	Md Sp Wt	10	1	2hd	2hd	9⁷	1111¾	Rogers K L	b 118	4.20	72-17	Expeditously 118nk CircleRound1182½LordMontague118¾	Stopped 12
19Nov83- 6Aqu	fst	6f	:22⅘	:45⅘	1:12⅕	Md Sp Wt	1	6	11½	11½	11½	21¾	Rogers K L	b 118	41.50	78-19	Spark Off 1181¾ Steppin Battler 118³ Romanoletti118nk	Game try 14
13Nov83- 4Aqu	fst	7f	:23⅕	:47	1:24⅘	Md Sp Wt	8	7	1¹	1½	2²	610¾	Rogers K L	b 118	18.20f	66-20	Counterfeit Money 1187¼ CertainTreat1181½Incite118nk	Gave way 13
21Oct83- 4Aqu	fst	1	:46⅘	1:12⅘	1:38	Md Sp Wt	4	4	65½	811	1118	1119½	Douglas R R5	b 113	76.50	56-20	Sly Boots 1185½ Upstart Broker 118³ Star Jet 1181½	Early foot 11
6Oct83- 4Bel	fst	7f	:23⅘	:46⅘	1:24⅘	Md Sp Wt	6	10	1013	1016	1028	1035	McCarron G	118	66.50	43-22	Chimes Keeper 118¹¹ Raise Alike 118½ Athena'sGlory118²	Trailed 10

LATEST WORKOUTS May 14 Bel 4f sly :48 h — May 5 Bel 7f my 1:31⅕ b — May 1 Bel 5f fst 1:01⅗ h — Apr 27 Bel 4f fst :48⅕ h

basic fact of racing life that the step from the maiden ranks into the "real world" is the steepest a horse must take. Then there is the simple matter that Eastern Viewpoint's courage went untested while racing on a clear (albeit exceptionally fast) lead in his debut. Add to these the even more significant factor of trainer methodology. Angel Penna is unquestionably at the top of his profession, yet his (better) animals seldom even compete in sprint races. Many debut at a mile and a sixteenth. If Penna regarded Eastern Viewpoint as a stakes prospect, his second start, if not his first, would have been at a route distance. But it was not, and knowing Penna's methodology, one could only conclude that Eastern Viewpoint was not as invincible as he may have appeared.

With any recent maiden winner, it helps to know the strength of the field it beat when graduating. Eastern Viewpoint had demolished, among others, two horses—Majestic Jabot and Appointed Hour—who had finished third and second, respectively, within two lengths of the winner, as favorite and second choice, in their first career starts.

Majestic Jabot — B. c. 3, by Majestic Light—Jabot, by Bold Ruler
Own.—Calumet Farm — Br.—Claiborne Farm (Ky) — Tr.—Whiteley David A — 122
Lifetime 1 0 0 1 $2,160 — 1984 1 M 0 1 $2,160 — 1983 0 M 0 0

24Apr84- 6Aqu	my	7f	:23	:46⅘	1:25⅘	Md Sp Wt	4	3	1hd	3³	2½	3²	MacBeth D	122	*1.40	72-21	Solid Grip122¾AppointedHour1151¼MajesticJabot1222¾	Weakened 6

LATEST WORKOUTS May 1 Bel 4f fst :48 h — Apr 23 Bel 3f fst :36⅘ h — Apr 20 Bel 4f fst :48⅘ b — Apr 16 Bel 4f sly :52 b (d)

Appointed Hour — B. g. 3, by Full Out—Gorgeous T, by Bold Hour
Own.—Spiegel R — Br.—MacLean A M (Ky) — Tr.—Schaeffer Stephen — 117⁵
Lifetime 1 0 1 0 $3,960 — 1984 1 M 1 0 $3,960 — 1983 0 M 0 0

24Apr84- 6Aqu	my	7f	:23	:46⅘	1:25⅘	Md Sp Wt	3	5	3½	22½	32½	2¾	Ward W7	115	3.30	73-21	Solid Grip 122¾ Appointed Hour1151¼MajesticJabot1222¾	Gamely 6

LATEST WORKOUTS May 3 Bel tr.t 4f fst :48⅘ h — ●Apr 20 Bel tr.t 6f fst 1:13⅘ h — Apr 13 Bel tr.t 5f fst 1:01⅗ hg — Apr 8 Bel tr.t 5f fst 1:00⅘ h

However, the winner of that maiden race, Solid Grip, who was one of Eastern Viewpoint's rivals today, earned a mediocre 97 for his performance on that occasion. It appeared, then, that Eastern Viewpoint had defeated sharp, though slow horses in his runaway debut performance. The primary consideration, though, was trainer Penna's apparent lack of confidence in his colt's ability and/or soundness.

And now, for the rest of this allowance field:

HIGHEST STAR

After getting away with a soft pace (96) in his winning debut (running a subpar 98 speed figure), Highest Star weakened when confronted with a stronger pace (106) in his second start. While his two-start profile is usually desirable in this type of race, Highest Star probably will not benefit from chasing the fleet Eastern Viewpoint through torrid early fractions.

CATHEDRAL AISLE

A New York-bred with an erratic history in NW1 company—both state-bred and open—Cathedral Aisle's presence in this race was suspicious, but in a positive sense. Once regarded a top prospect, the grandson of Dr. Fager was known to have sporadic back problems. After a sharp workout on May 6 and a sharp race (103 figure) on May 10 behind the then undefeated Mr. T And Me, trainer Freeman could have found an easier (and more lucrative) spot against state-breds. Instead, he rushed Cathedral Aisle back six days later in open company, despite being asked to spot a potential star eight pounds. In a ten-horse field one could dismiss the theory that he had been "drafted" by the racing secretary to help fill a race against a horse that had scared away much of its opposition. The only conclusion was that Freeman was trying to strike while the iron was hot. He had no guarantee of how Cathedral Aisle's back would feel in three days, or one week. The player therefore could feel fairly certain the horse was physically at his peak. Whether or not he was good enough was another question.

BLIGH

A closer shipping in from California for the powerful Leroy Jolley stable, Bligh's three allowance attempts had resulted in two good rallying efforts, the last "out of his conditions" in NW2 company. A logical contender, especially in light of the success California shippers enjoy in New York, with the preferred profile for this kind of race.

TROOP SHIP

This horse was claimed by Oscar Barrera from his last start, often the only recommendation a horse needs. However, Troop Ship was somewhat a typical Barrera claim in that he had no "back class."

His career to date had been a study in futility, with just one maiden-claiming win in thirty-nine starts, complemented by twelve in-the-money placings. A bridesmaid at best, he will probably be outclassed by the talented young horses usually found competing in the restricted allowance ranks during the spring and early summer. It would take at least a solid $50,000 claimer to win in NW1 company at this time of the year in New York—and an older one at that.

SOLID GRIP

We have already made the only comment necessary regarding this grass-bred gelding. He was a subpar maiden winner on April 24.

IRISH ORE

It took this horse nine tries before breaking his maiden, yet he has since competed successfully in allowance company, at the six-furlong distance anyway. He was a disqualified winner in this company last time, in slightly above-par time, and therefore a seemingly strong rival for Eastern Viewpoint. But there were two negative signs to consider: the potential physical problems hinted at by the "bore in" comment from his last start and the trip to Monmouth Park, suggesting the possible need for Lasix. Why else would a trainer ship a seemingly sharp horse to another track to run for an $11,000 purse when he could compete for $20,000 at home?

STEPPIN BATTLER

After breaking his maiden in his eighth start, then tiring badly in allowance company, this colt was laid off for more than three months, then returned to competition in the Withers Mile against horses prepping for the Belmont Stakes. Nonetheless, Steppin Battler was able to contest a strong pace (117 figure for six furlongs) before stopping badly. Now back in his proper element, he had a right to improve. If nothing else, he could prove the "fly in the ointment" for the favorite—the horse that would "look him in the eye" early, possibly engaging him in a suicidal speed duel for four or five furlongs.

We will have little to say about betting strategies or money management in this book. We do, however, have one word of advice here: The player is best advised to demand at least even money before placing a bet on any horse—indeed, to be very selective when wagering at odds lower than 2–1. And whenever a case can be made against an odds-on favorite like Eastern Viewpoint, to be aware that overlays can usually be found among its opponents.

If this particular race were to be played, it had to be on the opinion that Eastern Viewpoint could be had. And if he were beaten, chances are that his rivals for the early lead—Highest Star and Steppin Battler—would be beaten along with him. Of the five potential closers, only three made sense. Solid Grip's maiden figure left him too far behind, and the reluctant Troop Ship would require a major Oscar Barrera miracle to compete successfully at this level.

At 11–1, 12–1, and 8–1, respectively, Bligh, Cathedral Aisle, and Irish Ore were all overlays—with a reasonable upset possibility. Unless the player preferred one over the other two, and opted for a straight win bet, an exacta box was called for, possibly supplemented by straight-win bets on each of the three horses.

Steppin Battler did, in fact, challenge Eastern Viewpoint's supremacy early, battling with him to the head of the stretch, at which point Irish Ore took up the chase. Eastern Viewpoint succumbed from the constant pressure, but Irish Ore couldn't get the distance either. The New York-bred Cathedral Aisle, running possibly the race of his life, stormed by in the stretch. Bligh disappointed, never entering contention at any point of the race.

SEVENTH RACE
Belmont
MAY 16, 1984

7 FURLONGS. (1.20$\frac{2}{5}$) ALLOWANCE. Purse $20,000. 3-year-olds and upward which have never won a race other than Maiden, Claiming or Starter. Weights, 3-year-olds, 113 lbs. Older, 124 lbs. Non-winners of a race other than claiming since April 15 allowed 3 lbs.

Value of race $20,000, value to winner $12,000, second $4,400, third $2,400, fourth $1,200. Mutuel pool $101,438, OTB pool $111,964. Exacta Pool $244,408. OTB Exacta Pool $199,215.

Last Raced	Horse	Eqt.A.Wt	PP	St	¼	½	Str	Fin	Jockey	Odds $1
10May84 ^{5}Bel^{2}	Cathedral Aisle	b 4 121	2	6	$6^{\frac{1}{2}}$	5^{2}	$3^{1\frac{1}{2}}$	1^{4}	Davis R G	12.30
5May84 ^{3}Aqu^{4}	Irish Ore	4 111	7	8	$4^{1\frac{1}{2}}$	3^{hd}	1^{hd}	$2^{\frac{1}{2}}$	Espinosa R E^{10}	8.30
6May84 ^{2}Aqu^{1}	Eastern Viewpoint	3 113	5	3	2^{1}	$1^{\frac{1}{2}}$	$2^{1\frac{1}{2}}$	3^{2}	Cordero A Jr	.40
24Apr84 ^{6}Aqu^{1}	Solid Grip	3 113	6	7	8	8	5^{2}	$4^{\frac{3}{4}}$	Velasquez J	37.40
14Apr84 ^{3}SA^{3}	Bligh	b 3 110	3	2	7^{2}	7^{4}	6^{6}	5^{nk}	Velez R I	11.60
28Apr84 ^{5}Aqu^{4}	Highest Star	b 3 113	1	1	3^{2}	4^{3}	$4^{1\frac{1}{2}}$	$6^{6\frac{3}{4}}$	Graell A	16.40
12May84 ^{9}Bel^{6}	Troop Ship	b 5 116	4	4	$5^{1\frac{1}{2}}$	$6^{1\frac{1}{2}}$	$7^{\frac{1}{2}}$	7^{6}	Ward W A^{5}	7.50
9May84 ^{8}Bel^{10}	Steppin Battler	b 3 110	8	5	1^{hd}	$2^{1\frac{1}{2}}$	8	8	Cruguet J	49.20

OFF AT 4:06 Start good, Won ridden out. Time, :22$\frac{4}{5}$, :45$\frac{4}{5}$, 1:10$\frac{4}{5}$, 1:23$\frac{1}{5}$ Track fast.

$2 Mutuel Prices:			
2-(B)-CATHEDRAL AISLE	26.60	9.20	3.00
7-(I)-IRISH ORE		6.80	2.60
5-(F)-EASTERN VIEWPOINT			2.10

$2 EXACTA 2–7 PAID $186.40.

B. c, by Nostrum—Nice Bonnet, by Royal Levee. Trainer Freeman Willard C. Bred by Freeman W C (NY).

CATHEDRAL AISLE raced wide into the stretch while rallying, caught at the leaders leaving the furlong grounds and drew off. IRISH ORE loomed boldly from the outside leaving the turn but was no match for the winner. EASTERN VIEWPOINT showed speed to midstretch and weakened. HIGHEST STAR tired. TROOP SHIP had no apparent excuse. STEPPIN BATTLER tired badly from his early efforts.

Had the player invested $12.00 in an exacta box and covered himself with three $6.00 win bets, his total return on $30 invested would have been $266.20. In other words, he would have achieved odds of almost 8–1—that Eastern Viewpoint would fail to place.

Chapter 8

When a Young Horse Should Respect Its Elders

WHEN THREE-YEAR-OLDS LINE UP against older horses, the battlefield will probably be a restricted allowance contest. The major weapons: the physical maturity of the older horses versus the potential of the three-year-olds. Which predominates depends on several factors.

The four-or five-year-old Thoroughbred is a physically mature animal with a distinct advantage over its relatively immature sophomore rivals, all the more so toward the beginning of the year. This edge proves most significant over a distance of ground—anything over seven furlongs—and more than compensates for the weight the older horse is asked to concede to its younger rivals.

On the other hand, the fact that an older horse still remains eligible for restricted allowance races suggests that the animal is either lacking in ability or has seen its career delayed by physical or mental problems. It has had a full year longer than its younger rivals to advance to a higher plateau yet has failed to do so. This is most significant at the maiden and "nonwinners of one" allowance levels, and assumes decreasing importance as we move up the allowance ladder. The time of year when an older horse broke its maiden, or lost one of its allowance conditions, is also worth noting. A victory during a prime meet at age two or three over animals that later moved on to prove their merit as stakes horses might signify some latent class that has since failed to resurface due to physical problems.

The race we have chosen to analyze is the kind that is more likely to be won by an older horse. It was the eighth at Aqueduct on April 8, 1985, a "nonwinners of two" allowance contest at a flat mile, the first such race of the year open to both generations. Earlier,

8 AQUEDUCT

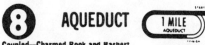

1 MILE. (1.33⅕) ALLOWANCE. Purse $25,000. 3-year-olds and upward which have never won two races other than Maiden, Claiming or Starter. Weights, 3-year-olds, 112 lbs. Older, 124 lbs. Non-winners of a race other than maiden or claiming at a mile or over since March 15 allowed 3 lbs.

Coupled—Charmed Rook and Bashert.

First Blast
Gr. c. 3, by Cannonade—Iron Hinge, by Iron Ruler
Br.—Morgan Nancy Penn (Ky)
Tr.—Toner James J
Own.—Kimmel C P
109
Lifetime 10 2 1 1 $32,960 | 1985 3 1 0 0 $13,800 | 1984 7 1 1 1 $19,160 | Turf 1 0 0 0

Entered 6Apr85- 8 GS
2Mar85-10GP fst 7f :22⅗ :45⅕ 1:22⅗ Swale 6 1 85¾ 810 811 812¼ Velasquez J 113 42.20 79-15 Chief'sCrown1223¼CremeFrich1173¼ChrokFst113ns Lacked a rally 9
18Feb85-10GP fst 1 1/16 :46⅗ 1:11⅕ 1:43⅗ Ftn Youth 1 5 88¼1424 1424 1228¼ MacBeth D 114 75.70f 55-22 Proud Truth112nk Stephan'sOdyssey1224DoItAgainDan1124¼ Tired 14
18Feb85-Grade II
6Jan85- 1Aqu fst 170 ⊡:48⅕ 1:12⅗ 1:42⅕ Alw 23000 5 3 3½ 2hd 2hd 1hd Migliore R 122 5.40 89-17 First Blast 122hd Passing Thunder1173¾Kilts'Nashua1121¾ Driving 6
29Dec84- 4Aqu fst 170 ⊡:46⅗ 1:11⅗ 1:42⅗ Md Sp Wt 1 3 26 24 1no 1no Migliore R 118 8.90 87-09 First Blast 118no MountGuard118hd ReviveTheEchoes1182¼ Driving 10
19Dec84- 6Aqu fst 6f ⊡:22⅗ :47 1:13⅕ Md Sp Wt 7 3 53¼ 53¼ 42¼ 32 Migliore R 118 9.70 76-25 Passing Thunder 118¾ DRewarded 1181¼ First Blast 118nk Rallied 12
19Dec84-Placed second through disqualification
12Dec84- 4Aqu fst 6f ⊡:23 :46⅗ 1:12⅗ Md Sp Wt 9 2 92¼ 79¼ 612 69¼ Migliore R 118 10.30 72-20 Another Doc 1184¾ Circle Flame 1181 Uene 118½ No factor 11
27Oct84- 4Aqu my 7f :22⅗ :45⅗ 1:22⅗ Md Sp Wt 7 7 109¾ 88 1120 818¼ Samyn J L 118 10.20f 69-16 Cream Fraiche 1183¼ Recognized 1185¼ScholarsTask1111¼ Outrun 13
13Oct84- 9Bel fm 1 1/16 Ⓣ:47 1:11⅕ 1:44⅗ Md Sp Wt 1 8 87¾ 78 87 55¼ MacBeth D 118 30.10 68-21 ForvrCommnd1151¾Numric1182RomnRivr1181¼ Pass'd tired ones 12
24Sep84- 4Bel fst 6f :23 :46⅗ 1:12 Md Sp Wt 10 6 3nk 2½ 43¼ 35¾ MacBeth D 118 42.40 76-21 Brookover 1185¼ Wollaston 118nk First Blast 1181¼ Weakened 14
13Sep84- 4Bel fst 6f :22⅗ :46⅕ 1:12 Md Sp Wt 13 10 1116 1112 812 78 Velasquez J 118 65.20 74-21 ScriptOhio118¾Cullendale1181¼MightyCourageous1181¼ No factor 14
LATEST WORKOUTS Apr 2 Aqu 3f fst :36⅗ b Mar 28 Aqu 6f fst 1:16⅕ h Mar 23 Aqu 4f fst :49⅖ h Feb 27 GP 5f fst 1:01⅗ h

Dead Piece Pack
B. c. 3, by Darby Creek Road—Etagere, by Rainy Lake
Br.—Stonewall Farm (Ky)
Tr.—Jerkens Steven T
Own.—Schwartz B K
109
Lifetime 12 2 1 0 $17,600 | 1985 2 0 0 0 | 1984 10 2 1 0 $17,600

1Mar85- 7Aqu fst 170 ⊡:46⅗ 1:11 1:41⅗ Alw 24000 4 6 612 614 512 511¼ Hernandez R b 117 19.90 81-25 Nordance 11710 Uene 119hd Feeling Gallant 1171¼ No factor 7
15Feb85- 5Aqu fst 6f ⊡:22⅗ :46 1:11⅗ Alw 23000 3 6 69 616 612 611¼ Moore D N5 b 112 22.90 74-26 Love That Mac 1123¼ Nordance 1173 Kilts' Nashua 119½ Outrun 6
31Dec84- 3Med fst 170 :48 1:13⅗ 1:44⅗ Alw 13000 1 4 44 33¼ 11¼ 13¼ Rocco J b 114 2.20 75-22 DeadPiecePack1143¼RedScreen1172¼FadedImage1092 Drew clear 6
19Dec84- 7Aqu fst 170 ⊡:49⅗ 1:15⅕ 1:45⅗ Alw 23000 8 7 67¼ 78¾ 76¼ 77 Alvarado R Jr b 117 4.50 66-25 Paths Of Glory 1174¾CrystalIceberg117nk UncleDaddy110½ Outrun 9
10Dec84- 5Aqu fst 6f ⊡:22 :45⅗ 1:12 Alw 22000 7 10 1014 1016 1010 52¾ Alvarado R Jr b 117 9.90 81-21 Shoot Pool 1171 Splendid Catch 117no FullofSpice117½ Slow start 11
27Nov84- 6Med fst 1 1/16 :48⅗ 1:13⅗ 1:47⅗ Alw 13000 1 7 74¾ 33 11 2no Castaneda K b 115 2.40 71-28 Promisino 114no Dead Piece Pack11512ManorParkway114nk Wide 7
16Nov84- 4Aqu fst 6f :23⅗ :47⅗ 1:13⅗ Md 45000 13 3 63 51¼ 31 11¼ Davis R G b 114 10.70f 74-35 DeadPiecePack1141¼Anconeus1141¼ConfirmedPtriot1072 Driving 14
28Sep84- 3Bel gd 7f :23 :46⅗ 1:25 Md 45000 5 3 96¼ 96 77¼ 47¼ Guerra W A b 114 16.30 69-26 Julies Bet 1165¼ Scholastic 118½ Fabulous Move 1181¾ Wide 9
16Sep84- 3Bel my 1 :46⅗ 1:11⅗ 1:38 Md 70000 2 8 76¼ 89 56 69¼ Migliore R 114 4.10 66-16 Radar Alarm 1141¾ Scholastic 114no Quintile 1142½ No factor 9
23Aug84- 6Sar sly 7f :22⅗ :46 1:24⅗ Md Sp Wt 11 2 86 610 47 57¾ Migliore R 118 8.00f 72-22 Coyote Dancer 1184¼ Haberdasher 1182¾ Foligno 118¾ Outrun 14
LATEST WORKOUTS Apr 6 Bel 5f fst 1:02 h Mar 27 Bel tr.t 6f fst 1:19⅗ b Mar 20 Bel tr.t 5f fst 1:04⅖ b Feb 25 Bel tr.t 6f fst 1:18⅕ b

Koch's Choice
B. g. 4, by Coastal—Charming Renee, by Cornish Prince
Br.—Blum P E (Ky)
Tr.—Jerkens H Allen
Own.—Blum P E
116[5]
Lifetime 3 2 0 0 $21,000 | 1985 3 2 0 0 $21,000 | 1984 0 M 0 0

30Mar85- 6Aqu fst 6f :23⅗ :46⅗ 1:10⅗ Alw 25000 1 5 41 34 57 57¾ Toro M 119 3.90 79-28 Water Skier 119½ Morning Thunder 119hd Vigumand 1122 Tired 6
8Mar85- 1Aqu fst 6f ⊡:22⅗ :45⅗ 1:10⅗ Alw 22000 8 1 2½ 21¼ 1hd 1nk Toro M 117 *1.60e 91-18 Koch's Choice 117nk BoldJulius1174¾HighlyRegarded112nk Driving 8
28Jan85- 1Aqu fst 6f ⊡:22⅗ :46⅗ 1:12⅕ Md 45000 2 3 1½ 1½ 14 13 Toro M 118 12.90 83-25 Koch's Choice 1183 Frosty Drone 122¾ Bold Bud1181¾ Ridden out 9
LATEST WORKOUTS Apr 6 Bel 5f fst 1:02 b Mar 24 Bel tr.t 1 fst 1:48 b Mar 20 Bel tr.t 6f fst 1:16⅗ b Mar 4 Bel tr.t 4f fst :49 b

Bold Bob's Dusty
B. c. 3, by Bob's Dusty—Victoire, by Crafty Admiral
Br.—Edwards H L (Fla)
Tr.—Galluscio Dominick
Own.—Winbound Farms
104[5]
Lifetime 18 3 10 1 $47,460 | 1985 4 2 1 0 $34,040 | 1984 14 1 9 1 $13,420

27Mar85- 8Aqu fst 7f :22⅕ :45 1:23⅗ Alw 25000 5 1 31¼ 3½ 45¼ 47¼ Cordero A Jr b 117 10.60 77-20 Trophy Hunter 1174¼ Koffkoff 117hd Centennial Lane 1222¾ Tired 5
18Feb85- 1Aqu fst 1 1/16 ⊡:48⅕ 1:13⅗ 1:48 Clm 75000 5 2 22 2½ 13 1¾ Moore D N5 b 114 *2.20 70-28 Bold Bob's Dusty 114¾ Olajuwon 115½ Helcin 112¾ Driving 8
6Feb85- 1Aqu gd 170 ⊡:48⅗ 1:14 1:44⅗ Alw 23000 1 1 11 12 15 15¼ Garrido O L5 b 112 8.80 76-27 Bold Bob's Dusty 1125¼ Natrac 112½ Olajuwon 1171¾ Ridden out 7
25Jan85- 3Aqu fst 1 1/16 ⊡:48⅗ 1:14 1:48⅕ Clm c-18000 6 1 11 11¼ 2½ 21¼ Moore D N5 b 108 *2.10 67-23 Gorsk 1081¼ Bold Bob's Dusty 1083CountryKitchen1171¼ 2nd best 9
26Dec84-10Crc fst 1 1/16 :48⅗ 1:15 1:49⅗ Clm c-12500 8 2 32 1hd 2hd 21¼ Soto S B b 114 4.00 69-22 SpruceTops1181¼BoldBob'sDusty114nk PopopsChoice114' Gamely 12
17Dec84-10Crc fst 1 :48⅗ 1:14⅗ 1:43⅗ Clm 12500 11 3 34¼ 31¼ 13 2hd DePass R b 114 *3.30 70-19 SprucTops114hd BoldBob'sDsty1143DomntngForc1141¼ Just failed 12
6Dec84-10Crc fst 1 1/16 :48⅗ 1:15⅗ 1:50 Clm 12500 5 2 21 1½ 1hd 2no DePass R b 114 10.50 69-23 RobbyRggs114no BoldBob'sDusty1142¾SprucTops114½ Drifted out 12
13Nov84- 2Crc fst 170 :50 1:15⅗ 1:47⅗ Clm 12500 6 1 11¼ 1hd 2hd 31¼ DePass R b 116 9.20 72-20 Rexson'sTrial1141Procasting116nk BoldBob'sDusty1162 Weakened 8
1Nov84- 8Crc fst 6f :22⅗ :46⅕ 1:13⅗ Clm 12500 2 1 2hd 22 67¼ 912¼ St Leon G b 116 4.00 70-20 Win Again 1141¾ Wiki Whim 116nk Sumpin Royal 116no Faltered 10
24Oct84- 3Crc fst 7f :22⅗ :46⅗ 1:27⅗ Clm 12500 6 2 31¼ 32 3½ 42 St Leon G b 116 *1.20 76-24 Sumpin Royal 1141¼ Leading Edge 106hd Crafty Beau116½ Evenly 9
LATEST WORKOUTS Apr 4 Bel tr.t 4f fst :48⅗ h Mar 23 Bel tr.t 4f fst :50⅖ b Mar 17 Bel tr.t 4f fst :49⅗ b Mar 11 Bel tr.t 3f fst :39 b

Doubter
Dk. b. or br. g. 4, by Roman Coffee—Saints Must C, by St Bonaventure
Br.—Wetherington E C (Fla)
Tr.—Barrera Oscar S
Own.—Barrera Oscar S
114[7]
Lifetime 36 5 4 9 $60,598 | 1985 12 1 2 2 $20,260 | 1984 14 2 1 5 $21,560 | Turf 2 0 0 1 $1,490

3Apr85- 1Aqu fst 7f :22⅗ :45⅖ 1:23 Clm 35000 5 5 64 75 66 63¾ Espinosa R E7 b 110 3.10e 82-18 On the Contrary1191¼LateToRise117nk RapidWing1151¼ No factor 10
28Mar85- 8Aqu fst 1⅛ :49⅗ 1:13⅗ 1:51⅕ Alw 25000 4 1 1½ 1hd 32 54¼ Espinosa R E7 b 110 13.40 74-25 Lord Ashdale117¾CharmedRook1173GoldenImmigrant122no Tired 6
23Mar85- 3Aqu fst 1⅝ :49 2:07⅗ 2:46⅗ Hcp 25000s 2 2 22 34 33 33¼ Day P b 115 6.20 66-23 Lively Teddy 116nk Arbitor's Image 1173Doubter1152¾ No excuse 8
20Mar85- 7Aqu fst 1⅛ :49⅕ 1:14⅖ 1:54 Alw 23000 2 3 3nk 3nk 52¼ 43 Garrido O L5 b 112 4.10 62-30 Attune 117nk Mr. Realtor 1172¼ Gallant Hour 117nk Weakened 8
15Mar85- 1Aqu fst 2 :49⅗ 3:05⅕ 3:31⅗ Hcp 16000s 2 3 21 22 26 28 Ward W A b 118 2.00e 29-40 Gene's Dream 1228 Doubter 1181¾ Milieu 11717 2nd best 7
10Mar85- 1Aqu fst 1⅛ ⊡:49⅗ 1:14 1:52 Clm 17500 1 2 41¼ 31¼ 1½ 13 Ward W A5 b 112 *1.10e 82-16 Doubter 1123 Raise The Bet 117nk Lord Howard 1086¼ Driving 7
8Mar85- 1Aqu fst 6f ⊡:22⅗ :45⅗ 1:10⅗ Alw 22000 6 6 88 89¾ 812 78¼ Garrido O L5 b 112 4.20e 83-18 Koch's Choice 117nk BoldJulius1174¾HighlyRegarded112no Outrun 8
3Mar85- 1Aqu fst 1⅝ ⊡:49⅗ 2:07⅗ 2:47⅗ Hcp 16000s 7 7 76¼ 44 55¾ 59¼ Ward W A 111 *1.80 66-17 Milieu 1123 Pitchpipe 120½ Arsalan 1174¾ No factor 8
23Feb85- 2Aqu fst 1 1/16 ⊡:48 1:12⅗ 1:46⅗ Clm c-14000 6 3 210 26 24 2¾ Migliore R 117 3.10 76-21 Mock Court 110¾ Doubter 1177 Big Ralph 1122¼ Sharp effort 12
11Feb85- 1Aqu fst 1¼ ⊡:48 1:39 2:05⅕ Clm 22500 1 8 53¼ 44 46¼ 34¾ Garrido O L5 110 9.30 84-14 Sum Total 117no Majestic Buck 1124¾ Doubter 1102¼ Rallied 10
LATEST WORKOUTS Feb 27 Bel tr.t 3f fst :37⅗ b

Feeling Gallant
Gr. c. 3, by Gallant Gambler—Dawnajay, by Grey Dawn II
Br.—Link Helen P (Tex)
Tr.—Picou James E
Own.—Link Helen Patricia
109
Lifetime 13 2 4 3 $51,856 | 1985 6 1 1 3 $32,096 | 1984 7 1 3 0 $19,760

22Mar85- 8Aqu fst 1⅛ :48⅕ 1:13⅗ 1:52⅗ Alw 25000 5 5 56¼ 53¼ 4¾ 32¼ Velasquez J 117 4.60 69-27 Helcin1172¼StrongSttmnt122hd FlingGllnt1173¼ In tight upper str 7
9Mar85- 6Aqu fst 170 ⊡:47 1:12 1:41⅗ Great Power 2 5 58 45 44¼ 45 Venezia M 115 32.80 88-16 Nordance 115½ Haberdasher 1152¼ Roo Art 1222 Evenly 6
1Mar85- 7Aqu fst 170 ⊡:46⅗ 1:11 1:41⅗ Alw 24000 6 4 46¼ 38 310 310 Venezia M 117 7.50 83-25 Nordance 11710 Uene 119hd Feeling Gallant 1171¼ Evenly 7
26Jan85- 6Aqu fst 170 ⊡:48 1:14⅕ 1:44⅗ Alw 23000 6 7 74¼ 73¼ 4¾ 1nk Venezia M 117 3.70 76-20 Feeling Gallant117nk CrystalIceberg117hd Haberdasher1122 Driving 10
16Jan85- 5Aqu fst 1⅛ ⊡:48⅗ 1:13⅗ 1:54 Alw 23000 5 4 31¼ 31 2hd 32 Cordero A Jr 117 5.00 70-27 UncleDaddy117no Haberdasher1122FeelingGallant11712 Weakened 6
4Jan85- 7Aqu fst 170 ⊡:48⅗ 1:13⅗ 1:44⅗ Clm 80000 8 8 73¾ 2½ 33 2nk Venezia M 114 6.40 76-21 FirstOneUp122nk FeelingGallant114nk Hberdsher107hd Just missed 8
28Dec84- 7Aqu sly 1 1/16 ⊡:47⅖ 1:12 1:44⅗ Alw 23000 8 9 86¾ 812 614 414 Venezia M 117 9.50 75-19 Romncer1177¼UncleDddy1104Lsit'sSilencer1122¼ P'ssd tired ones 10
19Dec84- 3Aqu fst 6f ⊡:23⅗ :47⅗ 1:12⅗ Clm 65000 6 4 63¼ 52¾ 24 23¼ Venezia M 117 6.70 77-25 Koffkoff 1133¼ Feeling Gallant 1171¾ ConfirmedPatriot1061 Wide 8
3Dec84- 5Aqu fst 7f :22⅗ :46 1:24⅗ Clm 60000 7 3 77¾ 75 47 26¾ Venezia M 113 19.70 71-29 Splendid Catch 1176¾FeelingGallant113½DistantOrbit108hd Rallied 8
12Nov84- 5Aqu gd 7f :23 :46 1:25 Clm 70000 3 6 84¼ 85¼ 815 817¼ Maple S 113 5.80e 58-25 First One Up 1132 Jet Wave 117hd Kilts' Nashua 1131¼ Outrun 8
LATEST WORKOUTS Apr 4 Bel tr.t 4f fst :51⅗ b Mar 29 Bel tr.t 4f fst :48⅖ h Mar 21 Bel tr.t 3f fst :38 b ●Mar 7 Bel tr.t 3f sl :37⅖ h

Charmed Rook
Dk. b. or br. c. 4, by Crow—Dear Irish, by Irish Castle
Br.—Pillar Stud Inc (Ky)
Tr.—Ferriola Peter
Own.—Nagle K
121
Lifetime 34 4 6 7 $106,260 | 1985 6 1 1 2 $21,460 | 1984 22 3 4 5 $81,830 | Turf 2 0 0 0

28Mar85- 8Aqu fst 1⅛ :49⅗ 1:13⅗ 1:51⅕ Alw 25000 5 5 52 3nk 2½ 2¾ Santagata N b 117 2.30 78-25 LordAshdale117¾CharmedRook1173GoldenImmigrnt122no Gamely 6
16Mar85- 5Aqu fst 1⅛ :49⅕ 1:14 1:54⅕ Clm c-35000 5 8 75¾ 54¼ 42¼ 3¾ Santagata N b 117 3.10 63-34 Lively Teddy 115nk Eecio 117½ Charmed Rook 117¾ Slow st. 8
27Feb85- 7Aqu fst 170 ⊡:47⅕ 1:12 1:42⅗ Alw 24000 3 6 610 58¼ 510 57¼ Santagata N b 117 13.00 80-24 Lord of theManor117no LordAshdale114¾TampaTown1175¼ Outrun 7
7Feb85- 5Aqu fst 1¼ ⊡:48⅖ 1:39⅗ 2:05⅗ Clm 70000 4 5 57 612 618 619 Migliore R b 113 3.30 68-24 Easy Choice 113½ Wild Chorus 1153¾ In the Ruff 113½ Outrun 7
31Jan85- 1Aqu fst 170 ⊡:47⅕ 1:12⅗ 1:43 Clm c-35000 5 7 78¼ 712 36 12¼ Santagata N b 117 5.70 85-25 CharmedRook1172¼Mr.Showbiz1172¾MarineBrss1132¼ Going away 10
12Jan85- 9Aqu fst 1 1/16 ⊡:47⅗ 1:13⅕ 1:46⅗ Clm 35000 8 7 87¼ 87¼ 76¼ 32 Santagata N b 117 13.20 74-24 Blue Quadrant 117nk Nice Pirate1171¾CharmedRook1171¼ Rallied 10
28Dec84- 3Aqu sly 170 ⊡:47 1:12⅗ 1:43⅕ Clm 50000 5 5 69 55¼ 49 410¼ Velasquez J b 117 *1.50 73-19 TrinbgoPride1132¾Cox'sKing1152¼FollowMyWord1175¼ No threat 6
19Dec84- 5Aqu fst 170 ⊡:48⅖ 1:14 1:44⅖ 3+ Clm 45000 9 7 79 75¾ 65¼ 44¾ Samyn J L b 111 13.10 73-25 Singh America 1133 Irish Waters117hd EspritDeRomeo1131¾ Wide 10
11Nov84- 1Aqu fst 1¼ :49⅕ 1:40⅕ 2:06⅗ Clm c-35000 1 5 55¼ 32 21 31¼ Samyn J L b 117 *1.70 61-25 Arbtr'sImg117no TwntytwBhm1171¼ChrmdRk1174½ Bid, weakened 7
17Oct84- 9Bel fst 1 :45⅗ 1:10⅗ 1:36⅗ Clm 35000 8 11 99 68¼ 37¼ 27¾ Samyn J L b 117 2.70 75-21 Vinny's Pride 1177¾ Charmed Rook 117no Sir Leader 1174 Wide 11
LATEST WORKOUTS Apr 5 Aqu 4f fst :49⅗ b Mar 14 Bel tr.t 4f fst :49 h Feb 21 Bel tr.t 4f fst :50 b

Bashert
Dk. b. or br. h. 5, by L'Heureux—Indian Hadassah, by Donut King
Br.—McMakin N (Ky)
Tr.—Ferriola Peter
Own.—Maggio C
121
Lifetime 22 3 4 2 $63,096 | 1985 1 1 0 0 $11,400 | 1984 10 0 2 0 $10,950 | Turf 2 0 0 0 $105

27Mar85- 3Aqu	fst	1	:46⅕	1:10⅘	1:36⅘	Clm 35000	4	4	52½	21	11	1½	Migliore R	b 117	3.70	83-20 Bashert 117½ Arabian Gift 1153½ Canadian Currency113hd	Driving	7
11Jly84- 3Bel	fst	1 1/16	:46⅗	1:10⅗	1:42⅗	Clm 70000	6	3	42½	43	43	44½	Migliore R	b 113	4.90	84-14 Meru 113½ Sharp Destiny 1131 Irish Waters 1133	Weakened	7
30Jun84- 1Bel	sly	1 1/16	:46⅖	1:11⅗	1:44⅕	Clm 35000	2	5	32	2½	1hd	2no	Migliore R	b 117	2.60	81-27 Irish Waters 117no Bashert 1178¾ Startop's Ace 1132	Brushed	6
20Jun84- 9Bel	fst	7f	:22⅗	:45⅘	1:24⅘	Clm c-25000	10	3	64½	86½	719	58½	Lopez V5	112	3.50	69-18 Gauguin Native 1102½ Act It Out 1173¾ Tarberry 1171	Outrun	11
13Jun84- 5Bel	fm	1 1/16	Ⓣ:46⅗	1:10⅖	1:42	Clm 35000	8	4	47	58	68½	78	Smith A Jr	113	14.40	78-16 Fearless Leader 117¾ Cannon Royal 1081 Full Concert1132¾	Tired	11
6Jun84- 3Bel	fst	7f	:22⅖	:45⅖	1:23⅘	Clm 30000	7	1	35	46	12½	2½	Lopez V5	108	36.90	82-20 To Erin 113½ Bashert 108½ Lord Hatchet 1172	Sharp	11
26May84- 1Bel	fst	6f	:22⅘	:46⅕	1:10⅖	Clm 35000	4	3	64½	56½	59½	811¾	Cordero A Jr	b 117	5.40	78-15 Harpers Bazaar 1154½ T. Dykes 117nk Meru 1086	Tired	8
12May84- 3Bel	fst	1⅛	:46⅘	1:11	1:49⅕	Clm 35000	1	1	11½	1½	43	45½	Lopez V5	b 112	13.20	75-17 Starbinia 117nk Terse 1171½ Bishen 1173¾	Tired	7
19Apr84- 7Aqu	fst	7f	:23	:46⅕	1:23⅘	Clm 45000	3	5	64½	66	68	58¾	Lopez V5	b 108	17.40	73-26 Starbinia 1133 Top Hat 117¾ Mighty Nasty 117hd	Outrun	8
25Mar84- 7Aqu	fst	1⅛	⊡:48⅗	1:13	1:51⅖	Alw 22000	7	5	64½	77	615	719½	Velasquez J	b 117	5.50	65-16 Share The Risk 117hd Morning Review 11910 Last Turn117¾	Tired	7

LATEST WORKOUTS Mar 22 Aqu 6f fst 1:15⅕ h

Golden Immigrant — B. g. 4, by Medaille D'Or—Ellis Island, by First Landing
Own.—Kluesener Mrs D K — Br.—Marydel Farm (Del) — Tr.—Nieminski Richard — **121**

Lifetime								
27 2 4 8	1985	6	1	2	3	$29,280
$64,440	1984	11	1	2	4	$29,280

28Mar85- 8Aqu	fst	1⅛	:49⅘	1:13⅘	1:51⅕	Alw 25000	1	4	31½	4nk	54½	33¾	Velasquez J	b 122	4.20	75-25 LordAshdale117¾ChrmedRook1173GoldenImmigrnt122no	Even try	6
17Mar85- 7Aqu	fst	1	:48	1:13⅗	1:39⅗	Alw 24000	6	1	1½	2½	33	32¾	Santagata N	b 122	3.20	66-33 Tampa Town 117nk Lord Ashdale 1122½ Golden Immigrant 1223		6
2Mar85- 9Aqu	fst	170	⊡:46⅗	1:11⅗	1:42⅗	Alw 23000	5	2	21	21	11½	14	Santagata N	b 117	*1.30	88-19 Golden Immigrant1174Cox'sKing117¾HaveABuck112nk	Drew clear	10
20Feb85- 7Aqu	fst	1 1/16	⊡:48⅖	1:13⅖	1:47	Alw 25000	8	2	2½	1½	2hd	2nk	Velasquez J	b 117	*2.30	75-23 Pitchpipe117nkGoldenImmigrant1173HaveABuck1103	Just missed	12
6Feb85- 7GP	fst	1 1/16	:47⅕	1:11⅘	1:44	Alw 15000	2	3	32	3nk	24	29	Bailey J D	117	*1.60	72-20 Silver Wraith 1179 GoldenImmigrant117nkAnecdote117½	Held 2nd	9
24Jan85- 7GP	fst	7f	:22⅕	:44⅘	1:21⅗	Alw 14000	4	6	44	64½	55¼	311	Maple E	117	12.40	85-18 Bright Ivor 11711 Tri For Size 122hdGoldenImmigrant117½	Rallied	12
26Dec84- 2Aqu	fst	1 1/16	⊡:47⅘	1:12⅖	1:45	Clm 70000	2	3	32½	42½	33	36	Skinner K	115	7.40	81-21 Vinny'sPride1131½Cooper'sHwk1134¾GoldnImmigrnt115¾	Mild bid	8
17Dec84- 6Aqu	fst	1 1/16	⊡:47⅖	1:12⅕	1:46⅕	Clm 50000	6	3	2½	32	2hd	2hd	Skinner K	117	10.00Ⓓ	81-19 Tomlin 113hd ⒹGolden Immigrant1172¾Vinny'sPride117nk	Bore in	12
17Dec84-Disqualified and placed third																		
24Nov84- 2Aqu	fst	6f	:22⅘	:46⅘	1:11⅘	Clm 50000	3	6	43	43	53	45½	Bailey J D	117	12.80	76-27 Darcy's Baby 1151¾ John TheRuler1172½DoubleJump1171½	Evenly	8
14Nov84- 4Aqu	fst	7f	:24⅕	:48	1:25⅕	Clm 50000	2	5	21	41¼	32	35¾	Skinner K	117	8.30	69-33 Drcy'sBby113½JohnTheRuler1155¼GoldnImmigrnt1171½	Weakened	7

Le Gosse — B. h. 5, by Nijinsky II—Quilly, by Bagdad
Own.—Borho R — Br.—Swettenham Stud & Partners (Ky) — Tr.—Van Wert Robert G — **121**

Lifetime						
13 2 1 4	1985	2	0	0	0	$1,380
$39,120	1984	8	2	1	4	$37,740
	Turf	4	0	0	1	$2,520

17Mar85- 7Aqu	fst	1	:48	1:13⅗	1:39⅗	Alw 24000	2	6	63	63	65½	610	McCarron G	b 117	4.10	59-33 TampaTown117nkLordAshdale1122½GoldenImmigrant1223	Trailed	6
9Mar85- 7Aqu	fst	6f	⊡:22	:45⅗	1:10⅗	Alw 23000	2	5	611	57	56½	46½	Bracciale V Jr	b 117	11.40	84-16 Water Skier 1172½MorningThunder1172¾ZephyrCove1171¼	Outrun	6
6Aug84- 7Sar	fst	1¼	:49	1:38⅕	2:03⅘	3+Alw 21000	8	7	75½	43½	31	1½	Davis R G	b 117	7.30	81-20 Le Gosse 117½ Traipsin Lady 1073 Errant Minstrel 1123	Driving	8
26Jly84- 5Bel	fst	1	:46⅗	1:11⅖	1:37⅕	3+Alw 21000	4	3	42	2hd	1hd	32½	Cordero A Jr	117	6.40	76-17 Dr. J. R. Howell 108¾ Gene's Dream 1131¾LeGosse1172	Weakened	9
29Jun84- 3Bel	fm	1 1/16	Ⓣ:45⅘	1:10⅖	1:41⅗	3+Alw 21000	9	7	77¾	76	37½	39	Cordero A Jr	117	5.70	79-20 No Man'sLand1175ContinentalDancer1114LeGosse1174¼	Wide str.	12
8Jun84- 8Bel	fst	1⅛	:47⅕	1:11⅗	1:48⅘	3+Nasau Cty H	6	2	21½	53½	715	717	Cruguet J	107	26.10	66-19 Moro 115¾ Canadian Factor 117nk Dance Caller 113hd	Tired	8
8Jun84-Grade II																		
25May84- 7Bel	fst	1	:46	1:11⅘	1:37⅗	3+Alw 21000	8	8	89½	64¼	36	24	Ward W A5	116	*3.10	73-23 Minstrel Star 1104 Le Gosse 1163½ Coast Range 1161½	LUgged in	8
13May84- 5Bel	fst	1 1/16	:46	1:10⅗	1:43	3+Alw 21000	2	8	76½	65¾	67½	39¾	Ward W A5	116	4.20	77-17 Nepal 1217½ Broadway Harry 1212½ Le Gosse 116no	Taken up	8
27Apr84- 6Aqu	fst	7f	:22⅘	:46⅗	1:24⅗	3+Md Sp Wt	7	1	21	21	1½	13½	Ward W7	117	*.80	78-21 Le Gosse 1173½ Adducer 1193½ Howie of Winloc117nk	Ridden out	8
9Apr84- 6Aqu	fst	6f	⊡:23⅗	:47⅕	1:11⅘	3+Md Sp Wt	7	3	55	25	311	38½	McCarron G	124	9.80	76-19 Rebeau's Ali 1122 Pauper Prince 1136½ Le Gosse 1241¾	Weakened	8

LATEST WORKOUTS ●Apr 3 Bel 6f fst 1:11⅗ h Mar 29 Bel tr.t 1 fst 1:48⅘ b Mar 26 Bel tr.t 4f fst :52⅖ b Mar 8 Bel tr.t 3f gd :36⅗ h

three-year-olds had been forced to compete against their own kind, as had older horses. The advanced condition of this race, the mile distance, and the time of year all favored the qualified older horse.

As with the "nonwinners of one" condition previously discussed, "nonwinners of two" races usually demand a nice win in the preceding classification (NW1) and no more than a few failures since advancing to NW2 competition. Some success in stakes competition would be encouraging but is not a prerequisite.

To analyze this race, we will look at the five older contestants first, starting with the favorite, Charmed Rook, and the eventual winner, Golden Immigrant:

CHARMED ROOK

If you like to bet 6-5 shots that have won only four times in 34 career starts, then this is your horse. Note that Charmed Rook has been claimed on three occasions since November—each time for $35,000, normally a positive sign, at least of physical well-being. However, since the first of those claims the horse has won only once in eight tries, hardly an improved rate, and hasn't been able to move up the claiming ladder. At least, that is, until its most recent claim by Peter Ferriola, regarded as one of the best at the claiming game on the New York circuit. Ferriola was able to coax a good race out of the horse in allowance company, with a significantly improved pace figure part of that performance. On the negative side, however, we note that Charmed Rook seems to run his good (and bad) races in pairs, and therefore would seem due for a down cycle. Another negative is the lack of evidence that the horse can carry the 121 pounds he's been assigned for this race.

GOLDEN IMMIGRANT

This gelding has been conceding weight in his latest two starts to fellow oldies like Charmed Rook and Lord Ashdale, the penalty for his top-figure victory in NW1 company on March 2. Although his two for twenty-seven career record is hard to take, the weight shift would seem to put him on equal terms with the favorite, at a far better price.

DOUBTER

This horse is obviously a cheaper animal than Charmed Rook, and he is still eligible for the NW1 condition. His March 8 and March 20 races were in that class, as anyone familiar with the NYRA purse structure would know. If set for a top effort, why not try for an easier spot in an NW1 race? The difference in total purse value is only $2,000.

KOCH'S CHOICE

This Allen Jerken's-trained gelding is making his first attempt at a route distance—long a Jerken's trump card—after failing to get to the races at age two or three. Pace and speed figures for his two victories were excellent, and stablemate Bold Julius, whom he edged on March 8, came right back eight days later with an impressive win in superb time. Although Koch's Choice's latest performance was disappointing, it did come in "nonwinners of three" company, one notch above the horse's conditions. The gelding appears to have some ability but probably has physical problems as well. Nonetheless, he's a threat to lead all the way.

LE GOSSE

Something definitely seems amiss here. Off the board only once (in a Grade II stakes) in eight starts in 1984, this five-year-old has failed to fire in both of his 1985 starts, with his second race being far less imposing than his first. The sharp six-furlong workout notwithstanding, this one will have to show something in the afternoon before a bet is warranted.

And now, for the three sophomores:

FIRST BLAST

Away from the races for five weeks since he appeared in two stakes events at Gulfstream Park, this colt appears to be well suited to the distance, having won a maiden race and an allowance contest in his first two dirt-track routes.

BOLD BOB'S DUSTY

Formerly a $12,500 claimer at Calder, this improved colt won consecutive routes in February—including an allowance contest—before resting for six weeks. He has the speed to contest the pace and is now "one-off-a-layoff."

FEELING GALLANT

All six of his starts in 1985 are decent, against better animals than either First Blast or Bold Bob's Dusty faced in New York during the winter. His latest effort was disappointing, however, coming against the weakest band he faced in 1985.

Speed figures were of little help in this race. They did, however, reveal that the three-year-olds were hard to separate and did indeed match up quite closely with Golden Immigrant and Koch's Choice. On average, the figures favored Charmed Rook by two or three lengths. But then, he was the bashful 6–5 favorite! The pace analysis of the race was complicated by the presence of two horses—Koch's Choice and Bold Bob's Dusty—possessing sprint speed. Neither figured to help the other's chances. How they would affect Golden Immigrant and First Blast, who preferred to race close to the pace, was hard to assess. The real crux of the matter, however, was whether the player was willing to support reformed claimers like Charmed Rook and Golden Immigrant against potentially good three-year-olds like First Blast and Feeling Gallant—animals that had been competing against such top-class runners as Chief's Crown, Proud Truth, Stephan's Odyssey, and Nordance. If either of these sophs had proven to be truly competitive against the best of his generation, he would have been hard to pass at the prevailing odds against such unimposing older horses. But then, the odds would have been much shorter if this had been the case.

The winner of the race, Golden Immigrant, did not have the ideal profile for an older horse in this kind of race. Although he was a quicker-than-average "nonwinners of one" winner three starts back and had raced well in "nonwinners of two" company since, he broke his maiden under a claiming tag as a three-year-old (no longer showing in his past performances), then won his "nonwinners of one" race as a four-year-old. Le Gosse had the more preferred look but (probably) lacked the physical condition to take advantage of it. However, Golden Immigrant could afford to be somewhat less than ideal because he didn't have a top-notch three-year-old to beat. He stalked the pace of Bold Bob's Dusty, took over entering the stretch, then won as his rider pleased.

EIGHTH RACE
Aqueduct
APRIL 8, 1985

1 MILE. (1.33⅕) ALLOWANCE. Purse $25,000. 3-year-olds and upward which have never won two races other than Maiden, Claiming or Starter. Weights, 3-year-olds, 112 lbs. Older, 124 lbs. Non-winners of a race other than maiden or claiming at a mile or over since March 15 allowed 3 lbs.

Value of race $25,000; value to winner $15,000; second $5,500; third $3,000; fourth $1,500. Mutuel pool $109,070, OTB pool $131,932. Exacta Pool $145,758. OTB Exacta Pool $145,110.

Last Raced	Horse	Eqt.	A.	Wt	PP	St	¼	½	¾	Str	Fin	Jockey	Odds $1
28Mar85 8Aqu3	Golden Immigrant	b	4	121	7	2	2¹	2hd	2¹½	1¹½	1²¾	Skinner K	5.80
27Mar85 8Aqu4	Bold Bob's Dusty	b	3	109	3	6	1½	1¹½	1hd	2⁴	2²¼	Ward W A†	13.40
22Mar85 8Aqu3	Feeling Gallant		3	109	5	4	8	7⁴	3¹½	3¹½	3hd	Venezia M	8.60
28Mar85 8Aqu2	Charmed Rook		4	121	6	5	6¹½	5½	7½	4hd	4½	Santagata N	1.20
2Mar85 10GP8	First Blast		3	112	1	8	7½	8	8	5hd	5²	Velasquez J	7.00
17Mar85 7Aqu6	Le Gosse	b	5	121	8	1	5½	4¹	5¹	6½	6¾	Davis R G	5.70
3Apr85 1Aqu6	Doubter	b	4	114	4	3	4½	6½	6½	7¹	7⁴	Espinosa R E7	24.10
30Mar85 6Aqu5	Koch's Choice		4	116	2	7	3½	3¹	4¹½	8	8	Garrido O L5	7.10

OFF AT 4:31. Start good, Won ridden out. Time, :23⅘, :46⅖, 1:11⅖, 1:36⅖ Track fast.

$2 Mutuel Prices:

8-(I)-GOLDEN IMMIGRANT	13.60	5.40	4.00
5-(D)-BOLD BOB'S DUSTY		11.60	6.20
7-(F)-FEELING GALLANT			5.20

$2 EXACTA 8-5 PAID $169.20.

B. g, by Medaille D'Or—Ellis Island, by First Landing. Trainer Nieminski Richard. Bred by Marydel Farm (Del).

GOLDEN IMMIGRANT caught BOLD BOB'S DUSTY nearing the stretch and proved clearly best under a hand ride. The latter saved ground while making the pace to the stretch and held on well to best the others. FEELING GALLANT made a run from the outside approaching the stretch but lacked the needed late response. CHARMED ROOK had no apparent excuse. FIRST BLAST, off slowly, raced wide. LE GOSSE raced forwardly until near the stretch and tired. DOUBTER tired. KOCH'S CHOICE was finished leaving the turn.

Our main point, remember, is not that Golden Immigrant was a clear-cut selection in this field—one could argue for Koch's Choice as well—but that even a moderate older horse like Golden Immigrant might be expected to defeat all but the best younger horses under the prevailing conditions.

Chapter 9

When Class Starts to Tell

IN THIS CHAPTER we will take a close look at the remaining type of restricted allowance race, those run under "advanced conditions" such as "nonwinners of three races other than maiden, claiming, or starter," and the occasional "nonwinners of four races other than maiden, claiming, or starter." These races differ quite significantly from their downstairs neighbors, the "nonwinners of one" and "nonwinners of two" races previously discussed. Class becomes the one factor most likely to provide the clue needed to unravel the mystery.

The weaker allowance conditions usually require that the handicapper look "backward" at how quickly each contestant advanced to its present level and look "sideways" at how well it has since competed at that level. The more advanced conditions also demand that the player look "forward" at how the horse has fared against classified allowance and stakes rivals.

These more advanced conditions place greater demands on the horses entered than do the weaker allowance conditions, demands that go beyond the obvious "one class difference" written into the conditions. Weaker allowance conditions often favor relatively inexperienced though possibly one-dimensional young horses who parlay good form into a quick rise up the allowance ladder. The advanced conditions demand a more well-rounded animal, one experienced at a variety of distances and against stakes and classified allowance runners. Fast-rising youngsters often prove to have neither the talent nor the experience to compete with such rivals, and the "nonwinners of three (four)" race is often the one to expose their weaknesses.

After a horse manages to win one or two allowance races its trainer (usually) begins looking around for stakes opportunities. Those who don't, and are not known for their cautious handling of young prospects, are tipping their hands, revealing a lack of confidence in their horse. They may as well have reached for the stars—many of the horses they will face in "nonwinners of three (four)" company have already been there.

Races carded under advanced allowance conditions often fail to fill, no doubt due in part to the fact that many of the horses eligible for such a race are looking elsewhere for better things—like stakes credentials. As a result, those looking for the allowance race must often change plans and run either at a less than desirable distance or against tougher competition at the classified level. It is either that or waiting until the next "nonwinners of three" race comes along in the condition book, and hoping that it fills this time. All of which adds up to the fact that most horses competing at the "nonwinners of three (four)" level have had their taste of higher forms of combat. And, in the process, have proven their merit to some extent, or had their limitations exposed.

Few allowance races run under advanced conditions offer as clear-cut a choice as did the fourth at Belmont on June 23, 1985, a "nonwinners of four" contest at a mile on the grass. Here's the field:

IS YOUR PLEASURE

Winner of the Grade I Jerome Mile at three over Track Barron, who is now regarded as a prominent "Horse Of The Year" candidate as a four-year-old. He also won the Saranac, a mile grass stake now one race removed from the bottom of his past performances. His first two starts at four were promising—Secret Prince, who beat him in "nonwinners of four" company on May 25 came out of that race to win the Nassau County Handicap. But that promise seemed to evaporate on June 9. In his defense, we must point out that Is Your Pleasure competed that day against classified rivals at a distance apparently short of his best trip. And while class cannot be used as an excuse for that performance, we will soon see that the majority of his rivals today have yet to earn (New York) classified status, not to mention graded stakes brackets. Is Your Pleasure is dropping sharply in class here, with the major open question relating to his condition. In that regard, we note that his trainer, E. I. Kelly, is not known for coming right back with a horse that is not physically at its best. What we have here, then, is a former Grade I horse seem-

4 BELMONT

1 MILE. (Turf). (1.33) ALLOWANCE. Purse $32,000. 3-year-olds and upward which have never won four races other than Maiden, Claiming or Starter. Weights, 3-year-olds 114 lbs. Older 122 lbs. Non-winners of two races other than Maiden or Claiming at a mile or over since May 15 allowed, 3 lbs. Of such a race since then 5 lbs.

Is Your Pleasure
Ch. c. 4, by Accipiter—I'm A Pleasure, by What A Pleasure
Br.—Isaacs H Z (Ky)
Tr.—Kelly Edward I
Own.—Brookfield Farms
117 Lifetime 18 4 6 2 $276,394 | 1985 3 0 0 1 $5,760 | 1984 9 2 4 0 $231,234 | Turf 4 1 1 0 $77,486
9Jun85- 7Bel gd 7f :22⅘ :46 1:23⅘ 3↑Alw 36000 6 7 74½ 73¾ 64½ 54½ Vasquez J b 117 *1.00 81-18 Mugatea 117hd Act It Out 119hd Momento II 1172 Sluggish st. 7
25May85- 5Bel fst 1 1/16 :45⅕ 1:09⅘ 1:41⅘ 3↑Alw 32000 6 4 43 42½ 34 32½ Vasquez J b 121 2.20 91-11 Secret Prince 121hd SteadyBeat1212½IsYourPleasure1213¼ Rallied 7
13May85- 8Bel fst 1 1/16 :46⅖ 1:10⅘ 1:42⅕ 3↑Alw 32000 6 2 21 32 46 47¼ Vasquez J b 121 *1.20 83-20 Special Care 121hd Silver Stark 1217¼ Exattic 121nk Tired 6
20Oct84- 3Bel fm 1 Ⓣ:46⅘ 1:10⅖ 1:35⅖ Envoy 2 3 31 42 52½ 53¾ MacBeth D b 122 *1.20e 84-12 Treasured One 115¾ A Gift 119nk So Vague 119no Weakened 7
8Oct84- 8Bel fst 1 :46⅘ 1:11⅕ 1:36⅘ Jamaica H 6 4 43½ 31½ 22½ 23 MacBeth D b 116 *1.80 79-28 Raja's Shark 1123 IsYourPleasure1162½LeroyS.117hd Second best 6
8Oct84-Grade III
3Sep84- 8Bel fst 1 :44⅕ 1:08⅘ 1:35⅕ Jerome H 5 8 75¾ 65½ 44 1¾ MacBeth D b 114 25.60 89-14 Is YourPleasure114¾TrackBarron1241ConcordeBound115¾ Driving 9
3Sep84-Grade I
14Jly84- 8Bel fm 1¼ Ⓣ:48⅕ 1:37 2:01⅕ Lexington 9 6 73½ 63½ 810 108¼ Cordero A Jr b 126 *1.90 79-11 Onyxly 1141 Dr. Schwartzman 1261½ Vision 1263 Outrun 13
14Jly84-Grade II
4Jly84- 7Bel fst 1⅛ :45⅘ 1:10 1:47⅘ Dwyer 5 5 43½ 33½ 39½ 414 MacBeth D b 123 10.30 74-11 TrackBarron11913½DrnThtAlrm123noSlewtheCoup114½ Weakened 7
4Jly84-Grade I
9Jun84- 7Bel fst 1⅛ :46⅖ 1:10⅘ 1:48⅕ ⓈColin 2 3 31½ 31 23 23 MacBeth D b 122 4.60 83-10 TrckBrron1173IsYourPlsur1224ImprilConcord1152 Best of others 7
3Jun84- 8Bel sf 1 1/16 Ⓣ:50⅖ 1:15 1:48⅘ Hill Prince 3 4 31½ 42 32 21½ Cordero A Jr b 126 *.80 53-46 A Gift 1141½ Is Your Pleasure 1264¾ Jesse's Hope 1172¾ Blocked 7
3Jun84-Grade III
LATEST WORKOUTS Jun 19 Bel tr.t 3f fst :37⅘ b Jun 8 Bel 3f fst :36⅕ b Jun 3 Bel 4f fst :49⅘ b May 24 Bel 4f fst :50⅕ b

Huckster
Dk. b. or br. h. 5, by Mr Prospector—Land Girl, by Sir Ivor
Br.—Tartan Farms (Fla)
Tr.—Galluscio Dominick
Own.—Winbound Farms
117 Lifetime 38 5 5 7 $126,325 | 1985 8 0 1 1 $19,600 | 1984 14 2 2 3 $54,625 | Turf 9 1 1 2 $17,945
8Jun85- 8Mth gd 6f :22⅘ :45⅘ 1:10 3↑Alw 20000 3 7 79½ 710 79 67¼ Hernandez R b 117 8.30 82-13 Rumptious 1191 Now's The Time 115½ Rocca Reale 1151 Outrun 7
20May85- 7Bel fst 7f :22⅘ :45⅘ 1:23⅕ 3↑Alw 30000 1 3 31½ 66½ 69 67¼ Migliore R b 121 13.30 78-22 Bienestar 1214¼ Big Box OfSweets1051½TalcPower1211 Brief foot 7
23Mar85- 6Aqu fst 7f :23⅘ :46⅘ 1:23⅘ Alw 28000 3 4 52¾ 53½ 44½ 44 Cordero A Jr b 117 2.40 80-23 KeyToTheFlg114noTlcPowr1122ElitSyncoption1172 Wide into str. 6
25Feb85- 8Aqu fst 6f ⊡:23 :46⅕ 1:11 Alw 36000 5 2 66½ 56 35 33 Hernandez R b 119 3.30 86-25 Mt.Livermore1151½AgileShobill1051½Huckstr1191½ Rallied outside 6
17Feb85- 7Aqu fst 170 ⊡:47⅗ 1:12⅘ 1:43 Alw 40000 5 7 76½ 63 43 44¼ Hernandez R b 119 3.60 80-25 I'm A Rounder 1151 Carjack 1103½ Barcelona 115hd Mild bid 7
31Jan85- 8Aqu fst 170 ⊡:49 1:13⅘ 1:43⅘ Alw 40000 9 9 84½ 75¾ 85 41¾ Lovato F Jr b 115 3.50 80-25 I'm So Merry 110nk I'm A Rounder 115nkBarcelona1151½ Late bid 9
26Jan85- 8Aqu fst 1⅛ ⊡:47⅘ 1:11⅘ 1:50⅖ 3↑Assault H 8 6 58½ 46½ 714 714 Ward W A b 108 13.70 76-20 Imp Society 1173¾ Verbarctic 115nk Regal Humor 1153 Tired 8
26Jan85-Grade III
12Jan85- 7Aqu fst 170 ⊡:48 1:13 1:42⅘ Alw 40000 1 8 96¾ 67½ 45 23 Lovato F Jr b 115 *2.10 84-24 Stoney Lonesome 1103 Huckster 1151½ Jacksboro1152½ Game try 9
28Dec84- 8Aqu sly 6f ⊡:22⅖ :45⅘ 1:11⅕ 3↑Alw 36000 2 6 86½ 86 43½ 1no Velasquez J b 115 2.60 88-19 Huckster 115no Shadowmar 117¾ Singh America 1151½ Driving 8
5Dec84- 5Aqu fst 6f ⊡:22⅕ :45⅘ 1:10⅕ 3↑Clm c-75000 3 5 67¾ 65½ 11 12 Cordero A Jr b 117 6.70 93-19 Huckster 1172 Tenifly 1132¾ Will Of Iron 1172¾ Driving 6
LATEST WORKOUTS Jun 20 Aqu Ⓣ 4f fm :50⅘ h ●Jun 3 Aqu ⊡ 4f fst :48⅘ b ●May 28 Aqu ⊡ 4f fst :47⅘ h May 16 Aqu Ⓣ 4f fm :49 b (d)

Welcome Suitor
Ch. c. 4, by Blushing Groom—Bold Pink, by Bold Bidder
Br.—Haefner W (Ky)
Tr.—Nickerson Victor J
Own.—Haefner W
119 Lifetime 9 3 0 1 $45,960 | 1985 7 2 0 1 $35,160 | 1984 2 1 0 0 $10,800 | Turf 3 2 0 0 $29,400
16Jun85- 8Bel sf 1⅜ Ⓣ:48⅕ 1:40 2:18⅕ 3↑Bowl Grn H 6 11 1428 1414 1313 1213 Venezia M 110 7.10 53-34 Sharannpour 1142¾ Flying Pidgeon 117nk Long Mick121hd Outrun 14
16Jun85-Grade I
20May85- 4Bel fm 1¼ Ⓣ:47⅘ 1:36⅕ 2:01⅕ 3↑Alw 26000 6 11 1114 67½ 32 12 MacBeth D 121 *1.70e 88-15 Welcome Suitor1212ColdFeetII1214½Pigwidgeon1211¾ Drew clear 11
28Apr85- 4Aqu fm 1⅛ Ⓣ:47⅕ 1:11⅘ 1:50⅘ 3↑Alw 23000 8 10 1010 63½ 1½ 11½ MacBeth D 121 6.80 90-09 Welcome Suitor 1211½ Numeric 1144 World Council 1213 Driving 11
27Mar85- 7Aqu fst 7f :22 :44⅘ 1:23⅘ Alw 24000 9 9 89¾ 87¾ 41½ 32½ Venezia M 117 *3.20 81-20 Silver Slate 117¾ Seagry 1171½ Welcome Suitor 117hd Rallied 12
20Feb85- 7Aqu fst 1 1/16 ⊡:48⅘ 1:13⅘ 1:47 Alw 25000 2 9 97½ 89½ 69 46¼ Venezia M 117 3.40 69-23 Pitchpipe 117nk GoldenImmigrant1173HaveABuck1103 Sluggishly 12
9Feb85- 7Aqu fst 1⅛ ⊡:47⅘ 1:13⅘ 1:54 Alw 23000 10 2 21 2½ 3nk 42 Venezia M 117 14.90 70-26 Coast Range 112nk Joey The K. 117¾ Great Amar 1101 Weakened 10
27Jan85- 7Aqu fst 6f ⊡:22⅘ :46⅕ 1:11⅘ Alw 22000 7 8 83½ 88¾ 98¾ 95½ McCarron G 117 12.20 79-20 Full Hard 112½ Hockey Fan 1171½ Crimson Medal 117hd Outrun 10
22Oct84- 9Bel fst 7f :23⅕ :46⅖ 1:24⅖ 3↑Alw 20000 8 9 94¾ 87½ 66½ 57 Venezia M 119 7.60 73-16 Royal Reunion 114no Sly Boots107½CrimsonMedal1171½ No factor 9
4Oct84- 6Bel fst 6f :22⅘ :47 1:12⅘ 3↑Md Sp Wt 11 12 66½ 11½ 12½ 11 Venezia M 119 13.10 80-26 Welcome Suitor 1191 CountrySinger119noIndication1191½ Driving 12
LATEST WORKOUTS ●Jun 13 Aqu Ⓣ 4f fm :48 h Jun 7 Aqu Ⓣ 5f yl 1:03⅘ b May 30 Aqu Ⓣ 4f sf :52 b (d) ●May 16 Aqu Ⓣ 4f fm :48⅘ h (d)

Condrillac
B. c. 4, by Sensitive Prince—Catty, by Never Bend
Br.—Alexander & Boone & Boone & Hoskins (Ky)
Tr.—Johnstone Bruce
Own.—Sugar Mill Farm
117 Lifetime 9 3 1 1 $51,899 | 1985 2 0 0 0 $170 | 1984 6 2 1 1 $37,701 | Turf 8 3 1 1 $51,729
11May85- 6Bel fm 6f Ⓣ:22 :45⅗ 1:09⅘ 3↑Alw 36000 7 2 1hd 11½ 53½ 913¾ Cordero A Jr 119 8.40 79-17 Sitzmark 1195½ Alev 121hd Alchise 1193¾ Gave way 11
24Apr85- 7Hia fst 7f :23 :45⅕ 1:22⅘ 3↑Alw 17000 7 2 2½ 21 34 76¾ St Leon G 119 18.10 83-14 Back Bay Barrister 117¾ Dr. George 119½ DervishHero1191½ Tired 7
8Oct84- 1Bel fm 6f Ⓣ:22 :45⅕ 1:10⅘ 3↑Alw 33000 5 4 21 22 46½ 610 Samyn J L 114 2.40 78-22 Whoop Up 116¾ Victorious 1151½ Scarlet Hobeau 1151½ Tired 7
5Aug84♦4Deauville(Fra) gd*6½f 1:16⅘ Ⓣ PrixMaurice deGheest(Gr2) 22 Piggott L 122 8.50 — — NeverSoBold1272 Condrillac122nk SpeedyGirl118hd Prom thruout 11
14Jly84♦2Lingfield(Eng) gd*7½f 1:31⅘ Ⓣ MarleyRoofTileStakes 11 Piggott L 120 *1.75 — — Condrillac 1201 FabulousHabit1173 FairDominion114hd Led fnl 2f 8
19Jun84♦3Ascot(Eng) gd 1 1:38⅘ Ⓣ StJamesPalaceStks(Gr.2) 725 Eddery P A 126 16.00 — — ChiefSinger 1268 Keen 126hd Kalim 1264 Pacemaker 6f 8
18May84♦5Newbury(Eng) gd 6f 1:13⅕ Ⓣ Hue-Williams Stakes 31½ Piggott L 126 *.60 — — Novello 1211½ Throne of Glory 121no Condrillac 1263 Bid,led 10
5May84♦3Haydock(Eng) fm*7f 1:28 Ⓣ Fairey Spring Trophy Stk 15 Eddery P A 112 *1.00 — — Condrillac 1125 WelshIdol 122¾ MrMeeka 1086 Prom,led fnl 2f 8
15Oct83♦4Newmarket(Eng) gd 7f 1:29 Ⓣ Houghton Stakes 11½ Piggott L 123 *1.60 — — Condrillac 1231½ Chaumiere 123¾ Luminate 123¾ Well pl,drvg 14
LATEST WORKOUTS Jun 18 Bel 7f fst 1:26⅘ h Jun 8 Bel 6f fst 1:13⅘ h Jun 2 Bel 6f fst 1:14 h May 21 Bel 7f fst 1:28⅕ b

Shining Out *
B. h. 5, by Full Out—All Agleam, by Gleaming
Br.—Greathouse D & E & J W Jr (Ky)
Tr.—Barrera Oscar S
Own.—Barrera O S
117 Lifetime 39 6 6 5 $92,848 | 1985 14 2 2 3 $38,960 | 1984 12 2 1 1 $42,260 | Turf 9 2 2 1 $7,088
20Jun85- 1Bel fst 7f :22⅘ :46⅕ 1:25⅕ Clm 35000 1 5 1½ 11 1hd 31 MacBeth D b 117 3.60 75-24 Lord Hatchet 112½ Sweet Devil 112½ Shining Out117nk Weakened 11
14Jun85- 5Bel fst 7f :23⅕ :46⅖ 1:23⅘ Clm 75000 8 1 74 68½ 816 817¼ Wynter N A5 107 7.00 65-24 Faces Up 1181½ Waitlist 122½ Mr. Tatt 111½ Unruly gate 9
10Jun85- 4Bel fst 6f :22⅗ :45⅘ 1:10⅖ Clm 35000 3 3 95¾ 65 33 31½ MacBeth D 117 *2.30 88-19 Strike A Coin 1171½ Big McCoy 117nk Shining Out 1172 Rallied 13
7Jun85- 2Bel fst 7f :22⅘ :45⅘ 1:24 Clm c-25000 13 6 41 31½ 1hd 2hd Migliore R b 117 4.80 82-19 Rapid Wing 119hd Shining Out 117¾ Ship Mint 117¾ Gamely 13
27May85- 2Bel fst 6f :22⅕ :45⅗ 1:10⅕ Clm 45000 12 10 54½ 66 76 95¾ Migliore R b 113 7.10 85-15 Ecstatic Pride 108nk Sir Leader 1171 See for Free 113¾ Tired 12
17May85- 8Bel fm 7f Ⓣ:22⅕ :44⅘ 1:20⅘ 3↑Alw 36000 6 4 43½ 66 514 613½ Migliore R b 119 18.80 86-11 RedWingDream1191½StayTheCourse1244DiscoCount124nk Outrun 8
28Apr85- 1Aqu fst 7f :22⅘ :45⅘ 1:23⅘ Clm 45000 7 3 31 31 32 33½ Migliore R b 115 *1.40 78-21 Fibak 1172½ Hueco 1171½ Shining Out 1151½ Evenly 8
19Apr85- 7Aqu sly 7f :22⅗ :45⅗ 1:23⅕ Clm 70000 5 2 33½ 22 22½ 22 Migliore R b 113 *1.90 83-22 Agile Shoebill 1172 Shining Out 113¾ Faces Up 1171¾ Gamely 6
8Apr85- 2Aqu fst 7f :22⅗ :45 1:23⅕ Clm 50000 2 7 54½ 42½ 2hd 1¾ Migliore R b 117 12.60 85-24 ShiningOut117¾FstAsThBrz113nkSpirtdBoy1101 Stumbd st., drvng 8
21Mar85- 7Aqu fst 6f :23⅕ :46⅘ 1:11⅘ Alw 24000 8 5 31 21 31½ 55 Migliore R b 117 3.00 77-34 MorningThunder1172Dixie'sIsland112¾BoldJulius1221½ Used early 8

Quick Dip
Ch. h. 5, by Vigors—Red Bikini, by One For All
Br.—Wimpfheimer J D (Ky)
Tr.—O'Connell Richard
Own.—Flying Zee Stables
117 Lifetime 47 7 7 8 $184,816 | 1985 5 0 1 0 $17,900 | 1984 18 4 3 5 $107,424 | Turf 28 5 6 7 $150,844
27May85-10LaD fm 1 1/16 Ⓣ:47 1:10⅘ 1:41⅘ 3↑Barkdale H 4 5 43 52½ 51¾ 21 Bourque K b 112 25.80 92-10 My Madness 1151 Quick Dip 1121 Shamtastic 114nk 10
1May85- 9LaD my 1 1/16 :50 1:15⅕ 1:46⅘ Alw 18000 1 3 49 526 531 429 Bourque K 114 9.10 49-33 Bright Baron 116½ Damen Hall 1185½ Shamtastic 11423 5
24Feb85-10FG sf *1⅛ Ⓣ:47⅕ 1:12⅘ 1:53⅘ F G Classic 8 7 69 76½ 69½ 56¼ Maple S b 113 68.00 60-34 Inevitable Leader 115hd Nassipour 1173 Bold Run 1173 No factor 11
24Feb85-Grade III
9Feb85-10FG fst 1 1/16 :46⅘ 1:11⅕ 1:44⅕ Alw 14500 6 5 512 512 69½ 610½ Romero R P b 114 10.50 81-15 RamblingNative114nkFreeForce1203ArtilleryAttack1141 No factor 7
27Jan85-10FG my 1 1/16 :47 1:11⅘ 1:43 Whirlaway H 1 2 31 44 512 413½ Maple S b 116 16.50 83-20 RapidGray1222HopefulWord1138SilverDiplomt1183½ Speed for 1/2 6
31Dec84-10FG fst 1 1/16 :46⅘ 1:11 1:43 3↑Handicap 1 7 712 715 724 732 Faul J H b 114 7.20 65-19 Aspro 1161 Silver Diplomat 117hd Free Force 113½ Trailed 7
15Nov84- 6Med yl 170 Ⓣ:48⅘ 1:14 1:45⅖ 3↑Alw 18000 4 6 42½ 21½ 35 35½ Samyn J L b 117 *.60e 57-37 Susie's Table 1171½ Jane's Dilemma1104QuickDip117nk Weakened 7
3Nov84- 4Aqu gd 1⅛ Ⓣ:49⅕ 1:13⅘ 1:51⅘ 3↑Alw 36000 1 3 31½ 41½ 22 32½ Samyn J L b 117 *2.00 84-18 Jump Shot 1191¾ Golden Champ II 110½ QuickDip117½ Weakened 8
18Oct84- 7Bel fm 1 1/16 Ⓣ:45⅗ 1:09⅕ 1:40⅖ 3↑Clm 175000 3 6 53 52½ 24 23 Samyn J L b 112 14.10 96-10 Disco Count 1073 Quick Dip 112no Lutyens 1133 Held place 8
10Oct84- 8Bel fm 1 Ⓣ:45⅕ 1:09⅖ 1:33 3↑Alw 36000 5 4 53 69 614 617½ Samyn J L b 117 18.10 82-12 Cozzene 1174 Sitzmark 1152¾ Alev 1152¾ Tired 6
LATEST WORKOUTS Jun 20 Bel Ⓣ 6f fm 1:15⅘ b Apr 26 LaD 5f fst 1:03 b

Dance Caller
Ch. h. 5, by Marshua's Dancer—All In, by Gallant Man
Br.—Morgan Nancy Penn (Ky)
Tr.—Jerkens H Allen
Own.—Hobeau Farm
117 Lifetime 29 4 1 5 $141,496 | 1985 6 0 0 1 $4,600 | 1984 9 0 1 1 $24,596 | Turf 5 1 0 2 $24,720
15Jun85- 7Bel fm 1 1/16 Ⓣ:45⅗ 1:09⅘ 1:41 3↑Alw 40000 10 6 64½ 66 54 44 Hernandez R 117 24.90 87-18 Fortnightly 1173 High Ice 117no Fearless Leader 1171 Late bid 10
17May85- 7GS my 170 :46⅕ 1:11 1:41⅕ Alw 20000 4 5 67 45½ 46½ 37½ Samyn J L 114 4.10 86-18 KingOfBridlewood1142½GallantPrelude1145DnceCller114½ Rallied 7
18Apr85- 8Aqu fst 1⅞ :50⅕ 2:33⅖ 3:12⅘ 3↑Handicap 2 4 67 622 637 633¾ Graell A 116 5.60 — — Erin Bright 118hd Eecio 10815½ Easy Choice 1181¾ Fell back 6
13Apr85- 8Aqu fst 1¼ :50⅘ 1:39⅖ 2:04⅕ 3↑Excelsior H 7 7 75½ 812 815 816¾ Graell A 109 23.50 58-21 Morning Bob 1122½ Lord of theManor1124¾LastTurn110nk Outrun 8
13Apr85-Grade II
4Apr85- 8Aqu fst 1 :46⅘ 1:10⅘ 1:36⅕ 3↑Alw 30000 4 7 714 714 713 711 Garcia G G b 121 10.40 74-19 Cooper's Hawk 117¾ Vinny's Pride 121nk Spender 1211 Outrun 7
23Mar85- 6Aqu fst 7f :23⅘ :46⅘ 1:23⅘ Alw 28000 4 6 62¾ 64 612 69¾ Skinner K b 117 12.20 74-23 Key To TheFlag114noTalcPower1122EliteSyncopation1172 Trailed 6
28Jly84- 8Bel sf 1½ Ⓣ:49⅕ 2:05⅘ 2:31 3↑Swd Dncer H 9 9 99½ 118 107¾ 109½ Velasquez J b 111 29.60 60-31 Majesty's Prince 1243½ Nassipour 1091½ Four Bases 112nk Outrun 11
28Jly84-Grade I

21Jly84- 8Bel sly 1½ :48⅗ 2:02 2:27⅘ 3+Brooklyn H 3 3 46½ 612 616 625 Miranda J b 111 10.80 58-21 Fit to Fight 12912½ Vision 1095 Dew Line 116hd Tired 8
21Jly84-Grade I
4Jly84- 8Bel fst 1¼ :47⅘ 1:35⅕ 2:00⅗ 3+Suburban H 2 6 65½ 68½ 69 57¾ Miranda J b 111 14.30 87-11 Fit to Fight 1263¾ Canadian Factor 116no Wild Again1164 Outrun 7
4Jly84-Grade I
8Jun84- 8Bel fst 1⅛ :47⅕ 1:11⅗ 1:48⅗ 3+Nasau Cty H 7 4 63¾ 42 42½ 31 Miranda J b 113 8.10 82-19 Moro 115¾ Canadian Factor 117nk Dance Caller 113hd Rallied 8
8Jun84-Grade II
LATEST WORKOUTS Jun 12 Bel 5f fst 1:06 b Jun 7 Bel tr.t 4f fst :48⅘ h Jun 2 Bel 4f fst :48⅕ h May 25 Bel 3f fst :36 b

Treasured One — Ch. c. 4, by Exclusive Native—Monteen, by Hail To Reason
Own.—Harbor View Farm
Br.—Harbor View Farm (Ky)
Tr.—Martin Frank
117 Lifetime 18 4 0 3 $85,227 | 1985 8 0 0 2 $12,867 | 1984 10 4 0 1 $72,360 | Turf 5 1 0 1 $38,803
20May85- 7Bel fst 7f :22⅘ :45⅘ 1:23⅕ 3+Alw 30000 6 4 53¾ 45 47 79½ Cruguet J 121 7.40 76-22 Bienestar 1214½ Big Box Of Sweets 1051½ Talc Power 1211 Tired 7
10May85- 8Bel fst 6f :22⅕ :45⅘ 1:11 3+Alw 36000 3 2 34 36 65½ 66½ Lovato F Jr b 121 5.80 80-20 Cozzene 1241½ Basket Weave124½MomentoII1192½ Finished early 7
27Apr85- 6Aqu fst 7f :24 :47⅕ 1:24⅕ 3+Alw 28000 7 1 4nk 53 41½ 4¾ Cruguet J b 121 3.50 79-26 ◻BigBoxOfSweets109nkMcMichel121nkIntntion124nk Raced wide 7
27Apr85-Placed third through disqualification
13Apr85-10OP fst 1⁄16 :46 1:10⅕ 1:42⅘ Alw 20000 10 4 32½ 42 34 510 Maple S b 118 5.00 79-17 Big Pistol 1213½ Shamtastic 1122 Dr. Spanky 1122½ Tired 10
20Feb85- 9GP fst 7f :22⅕ :44⅘ 1:22⅘ 3+Ft Laud'le H 1 4 44 33½ 31½ 55 Santos J A b 112 7.50 87-23 For Halo 122¾ Bright Ivor 113nk Jim Bracken 1134 Tired 6
12Feb85- 9GP fm 1⁄16 Ⓣ:46 1:10 1:40⅘ Alw 26000 3 4 44½ 53½ 33 33 Cruguet J b 119 *2.00e 93-05 Norclin 115hd Brother Liam 1153 Treasured One 1195 Evenly late 9
26Jan85- 9GP fm *1⁄16 Ⓣ 1:43 Alw 18000 8 7 88¼ 85¾ 711 711½ Santos J A b 117 2.10 79-08 Nagurski 117nk Dr. Carter 119no Glory O. So 117no Wide 1st turn 9
19Jan85- 7GP fm 1 Ⓣ:46 1:09⅘ 1:34⅘ 3+Appleton H 5 3 44 33 22 42 Santos J A b 112 4.90 95-07 Smart andSharp1171½Amerilad112½Dr.Schwartzman117no Bobbled 11
19Jan85-Grade III; Run in divisions
22Dec84- 6Aqu fst 6f ⊡:22⅕ :45 1:09⅗ 3+Alw 25000 5 4 42½ 32 3½ 1hd Cordero A Jr b 115 7.70 96-09 Treasured One 115hd Great Hunter 112no Whoop Up110nk Driving 8
1Dec84- 3Hol fst 7f :22⅘ :45⅕ 1:23⅕ 3+Alw 30000 6 3 — — — — Guerra W A 120 6.00 — — Somethingwonderful1173½SetFree117½ExplosivePssr1152½ Bolted 6
LATEST WORKOUTS Jun 20 Bel tr.t 5f fst 1:01⅘ h Jun 14 Bel tr.t 4f fst :48⅕ h Jun 8 Bel tr.t 4f fst :47⅗ h ●Jun 2 Bel tr.t 5f fst 1:00 h

Lt. Flag ✻ — B. c. 4, by Delta Flag—Stevens Stream, by Lt Stevens
Own.—Cedar Copse Stables
Br.—Shropshire Mrs J S (Ky)
Tr.—Lenzini John J Jr
117 Lifetime 21 9 3 2 $188,505 | 1985 3 0 1 0 $8,800 | 1984 7 3 2 0 $145,748
29Mar85- 8Aqu fst 1 :45⅘ 1:10⅖ 1:35⅘ Alw 40000 2 3 34 43½ 36½ 25¾ Santagata N 115 10.00 82-21 Mt. Livermore 1225¾ Lt. Flag 115¾ Eskimo 1172½ Rallies 7
23Mar85- 6Aqu fst 7f :23⅘ :46⅘ 1:23⅘ Alw 28000 5 2 1½ 2½ 56½ 58 Santagata N b 117 11.50 76-23 KeyToTheFlag114noTlcPower1122EliteSyncoption1172 Used early 6
18Jan85- 8Aqu fst 6f ⊡:22⅘ :45⅗ 1:10⅘ Handicap 5 5 43 712 78¾ 712 Ward W A 115 6.60 79-21 Sluggard 111hd Main Stem 112½ Leroy S. 117½ Fell back 7
28Dec84- 8Aqu sly 6f ⊡:22⅘ :45⅘ 1:11⅕ 3+Alw 36000 3 5 11 2hd 31½ 65½ Ward W A5 b 110 *2.10 83-19 Huckster 115no Shadowmar 117¾ Singh America 1151½ Tired 8
16Dec84- 8Aqu fst 1¼ ⊡:49⅘ 1:14⅘ 1:59⅘ Roamer H 7 1 1hd 11 614 617½ Samyn J L b 117 5.60 63-24 Fight Over 1151½ Tumbler 1131½ Regal Humor 1141¾ Gave way 7
7Apr84- 8Aqu fst 170 ⊡:47 1:11⅗ 1:40⅖ Gotham 2 2 22 21½ 24 24¾ Samyn J L 123 4.20 93-16 Bear Hunt 1144¾ Lt. Flag 1232 On The Sauce 11418 Gamely 5
7Apr84-Grade II
12Feb84- 8Aqu fst 1⁄16 ⊡:47⅘ 1:12⅘ 1:46⅗ Whirlaway 4 4 44 32 2½ 1nk Velasquez J 123 *1.00 79-24 Lt. Flag 123nk Wind Flyer 121½ Crude Ways 1218¾ Driving 6
28Jan84- 8Aqu fst 170 ⊡:48⅕ 1:12⅘ 1:42⅗ Count Fleet 6 2 21½ 2hd 11 12½ Velasquez J 117 6.10 88-20 Lt. Flag 1172½ Empravatar 117¾ Crude Ways 1192 Bore in, clear 9
14Jan84- 6Aqu fst 170 ⊡:49⅕ 1:14⅕ 1:42⅗ Handicap 3 1 1hd 2hd 21½ 22¾ Davis R G 112 3.10 85-17 ColdAndCloudy1122¾Lt.Flg11210NorthernFortress1141½ Game try 7
7Jan84- 5Aqu fst 1⁄16 ⊡:49 1:15 1:48 Alw 22000 1 1 11½ 1½ 12 16 McHargue D G 117 6.60 72-24 Lt. Flag 1176Vanlandingham1177½Cooper'sHawk1172½ Ridden out 7
LATEST WORKOUTS ●Jun 19 Aqu 5f fst 1:00⅖ h Jun 12 Aqu ⊡ 7f fst 1:27 h ●Jun 5 Aqu ⊡ 6f fst 1:15 h ●May 30 Aqu Ⓣ 5f sf 1:00 h (d)

Judge Costa — B. c. 4, by Determined Cosmic—Frampton Flight, by Misty Flight
Own.—Fink L R
Br.—Fink L R (NY)
Tr.—Schulhofer Flint S
119 Lifetime 22 4 2 5 $110,762 | 1985 8 1 2 3 $46,994 | 1984 11 3 0 1 $61,008 | Turf 10 3 2 2 $76,739
9Jun85- 4Bel sf 1 Ⓣ:46⅘ 1:12⅘ 1:39⅘ 3+Alw 29000 11 1 11 12½ 13 12¼ Vasquez J b 117 4.40 66-41 JudgeCosta1172¼QuickWork117¾TenderSovereign117½ Ridden out 11
27May85- 6Bel fm 1⁄16 Ⓣ:48 1:11⅘ 1:42⅕ 3+Alw 29000 3 2 2½ 2hd 2½ 24 Vasquez J b 121 *1.30 86-19 Go Go Regal 1214 Judge Costa 1212½ Harcolite 1141 Second best 8
15May85- 8Bel fm 1⁄16 Ⓣ:46 1:10 1:41⅘ 3+ⓈKingston 1 2 1½ 1½ 1hd 2nk Vasquez J b 1194 30.90 87-16 High Ice 119nk DHJudge Costa119DHFearlessLeader1191¾ Gamely 9
15May85-Dead heat
2May85- 7Aqu fm 1⁄16 Ⓣ:47⅘ 1:12⅗ 1:44⅘ 3+Alw 40000 1 3 31 2hd 2½ 32¾ Vasquez J b 119 2.90 80-17 Fray Star 1191½ StormyPuddles1191½JudgeCosta1191½ Weakened 10
12Apr85- 7Aqu fst 1⅛ :49⅕ 1:13 1:50⅘ 3+Alw 27000 7 1 11 1hd 3½ 32½ Vasquez J b 121 8.30 78-22 Lord Ashdale 121hd Bosun Mate 1212½JudgeCosta1213 Weakened 7
8Mar85- 8Hia fst 1⅛ :46⅘ 1:11 1:47⅗ Alw 13500 5 1 11½ 1½ 36 49 Guerra W A b 116 7.70 85-15 Rexson'sHope1165ContinentlDncer1164LordHtcht116hd Gave way 8
16Feb85- 7GP fm 1 Ⓣ:47 1:10⅘ 1:34⅗ Alw 18000 8 3 11 2½ 33 35 Cruguet J b 119 9.40 92-04 Cool 1192½ Audax 1192½ Judge Costa 1191 Weakened 11
25Jan85- 9GP fm *1 Ⓣ 1:38⅕ Alw 17000 4 3 46½ 58½ 56 55¼ Maple E b 1174 13.00 84-22 Cool 1171½ Rexson's Hope 1172 Nepal 1172 Weakened 10
25Jan85-Dead heat
23Nov84- 7Aqu gd 2 Ⓣ:48⅕ 3:05⅗ 3:30⅘ 3+Handicap 6 2 2½ 815 827 826¾ Guerra W A b 109 6.80 — — Putting Green1122CutTheMusic1102½EasyChoice106nk Used early 10
11Nov84- 8Aqu fst 1⅛ :47⅘ 1:12⅘ 1:52⅗ 3+ⓈMacarthur H 2 4 33 1hd 21 32 Davis R G b 110 7.70 71-25 Org 117¾ Talc Duster 1161½ Judge Costa 1101½ Bid, weakened 8
LATEST WORKOUTS Jun 17 Bel 4f gd :50⅘ b Jun 4 Bel 4f sly :53 b May 23 Bel 4f fst :50⅕ b May 10 Bel 4f fst :49 b

Nawannshar — B. c. 4, by The Minstrel—Neveen, by Sir Gaylord
Own.—Ceto R
Br.—HisHighness the AgaKhan (Ky)
Tr.—Olivares Luis
117 Lifetime 17 3 1 4 $34,289 | 1985 11 3 1 2 $31,280 | 1984 6 M 0 2 $3,009 | Turf 12 2 0 4 $23,709
9Jun85- 4Bel sf 1 Ⓣ:46⅘ 1:12⅘ 1:39⅘ 3+Alw 29000 7 10 87¾ 87¾ 54¾ 43½ Cruguet J b 119 23.90 62-41 Judge Costa 1172¼QuickWork117¾TenderSovereign117½ Wide str. 11
27May85-10LaD fm 1⁄16 Ⓣ:47 1:10⅘ 1:41⅘ 3+Barkdale H 7 8 911 86½ 97¾ 95¾ DelahoussyeDJ b 114 23.20 87-10 My Madness 1151 Quick Dip 1121 Shamtastic 114nk Outrun 10
14May85- 7Crc fm *1⁄16 Ⓣ 1:42⅘ 3+Alw 15700 4 4 21 22½ 34½ 58¾ Santos J A b 121 *1.80 86-05 Exclusive Member 1213 Crovero 1134½ Stepan 121¾ Tired 7
10May85- 7Crc fm *1⁄16 Ⓣ 1:44⅖ 3+Alw 13000 5 5 56½ 44 1hd 12 Santos J A b 123 3.20 85-21 Nawannshar 1232 Opal Fire 1232½ The Sunday Man 112nk Driving 8
4May85- 7Crc fm 1⁄16 Ⓣ:46 1:09⅗ 1:40⅗ Handicap 9 10 1017 1014 821 822 Santos J A b 112 17.30 80-01 Amerilad 115no Brother Liam 1187½ Bold Run 1184½ Checked 13
22Apr85- 8Hia fm *1⅛ Ⓣ 1:48⅘ 3+Alw 14000 2 8 94½ 54 23 1no Santos J A b 123 *2.70 87-19 Nawannshr123noCommnderRebeu1202½Mr.Celebrity117nk Driving 10
28Mar85- 8Hia fst 7f :23⅘ :46 1:23 Alw 14000 2 6 77 68½ 68½ 57 Santos J A b 122 6.60 81-20 Jovial 116no Soy Espada 1165 Frondeur 1161 No threat 8
20Mar85- 4Hia fst 1⅛ :48 1:12 1:51⅕ Md Sp Wt 2 5 4nk 31½ 2hd 2hd Santos J A b 122 *1.10 76-19 ◻Arctic Song 115hd Nawannshar 1223 Adorateur 1223 Bumped 12
20Mar85-Placed first through disqualification
13Mar85- 4Hia fst 7f :23 :45⅕ 1:24⅗ Md Sp Wt 2 11 97¾ 711 76¾ 21 Santos J A b 122 3.50 80-18 Riverboat 1221 Nawannshar 1221 Classic Bend 122½ Rallied 11
26Feb85- 8GP fm *1⁄16 Ⓣ 1:44⅕ Alw 17000 1 5 58½ 44 4nk 33 Soto S B b 117 4.90 82-15 Strawboy 1172½ Flying Flag 117¾ Nawannshar 117hd Rallied 10
LATEST WORKOUTS Jun 17 Bel tr.t 3f my :36⅘ b (d)

No Man's Land — B. g. 5, by Naskra—French Leave, by Damascus
Own.—Nagle K
Br.—Asbury & Forest Retreat Farm Inc (Ky)
Tr.—Ferriola Peter
117 Lifetime 18 3 3 5 $66,820 | 1985 1 0 0 0 | 1984 8 2 1 3 $40,220 | Turf 7 1 1 3 $27,900
Entered 22Jun85- 7 BEL
7Jun85- 1Bel fst 7f :23⅘ :46⅗ 1:23⅗ Clm c-50000 3 5 42 63¾ 616 620 Bailey J D b 117 3.00 64-19 Late To Rise 113¾ Fingers Inthe Till 1175 Fibak 1174¾ Tired 6
28Sep84- 8Bel yl 1⁄16 Ⓣ:47 1:12⅗ 1:44⅘ 3+Alw 25000 2 5 55½ 52½ 43 36½ Maple E 117 *2.00 65-36 Lutyens 1174¼ Go Go Regal 1132½ No Man's Land1171¼ Came out 8
27Aug84- 6Sar fm 1⁄16 Ⓣ:47 1:11⅕ 1:43⅘ 3+Alw 25000 3 5 53¾ 74½ 51¾ 31½ Maple E b 117 *1.70 77-17 Roman Bend 117½ Haste to Finish117¾NoMan'sLand117no Rallied 7
13Aug84- 6Sar fm 1⅜ Ⓣ:49⅘ 1:13⅖ 1:56⅘ 3+Alw 25000 1 1 1½ 11½ 21½ 43½ Maple E b 117 1.60 78-12 ChargingThrough1171MonkeyBread1191Nssipour1171½ Weakened 6
8Jly84- 7Bel fst 1⁄16 :46⅗ 1:10⅘ 1:42⅕ 3+Alw 22000 3 4 41½ 21½ 1hd 12½ Bailey J D b 122 4.10 91-15 NoMan'sLand1222½CanadianCalm1171¾Potentite1174½ Drew clear 9
29Jun84- 3Bel fm 1⁄16 Ⓣ:45⅘ 1:10⅗ 1:41⅗ 3+Alw 21000 3 4 41¾ 32 11½ 15 Bailey J D b 117 *3.20 88-20 NoMan'sLand1175ContinentalDncer1114LeGosse1174½ Ridden out 12
16Jun84- 3Bel fm 1⁄16 Ⓣ:46⅘ 1:11⅕ 1:43 3+Alw 21000 8 2 3nk 2hd 32½ 36 Bailey J D b 117 *3.60 75-20 Steepbank 1125 Penzance 1191 No Man's Land 117nc Weakened 12
6Jun84- 7Bel fst 7f :23 :46 1:23⅗ 3+Alw 20000 5 1 42 32 69¾ 712 Bailey J D b 117 *1.70 71-20 Pure Rascality 1092 Stomper 109¾ J. Strap 117¾ Tired 8
26May84- 5Bel fst 6f :22⅘ :45⅗ 1:11⅕ 3+Alw 20000 1 5 32 31½ 32 22 Bailey J D b 119 6.60 84-15 Nile River 1082 No Man's Land119hdWhoopUp1192¾ Gained place 8
30Sep83- 7Bel sly 1 :45⅗ 1:10⅗ 1:37 3+Alw 24000 7 6 31½ 2½ 31½ 35 Bailey J D b 113 *1.90 75-20 On The Turn 1134 Humbug I 1131 No Man's Land 1131 Tired 7
LATEST WORKOUTS Jun 3 Bel 4f fst :49 b ●May 25 Bel 6f fst 1:13 h May 19 Bel 5f fst 1:01 h May 9 Bel 4f fst :49⅘ b

ingly at the crossroads of its four-year-old season. At 7–2 odds, well worth a serious look.

WELCOME SUITOR

Just when I go on record saying that the American-based offspring of Blushing Groom show no preference for grass racing, along comes Welcome Suitor to win in "nonwinners of one" and "nonwinners of two" company his first two times on the sod. His first effort in stakes company, in the Grade I Bowling Green Handicap, was a painful experience, however. So we have here an animal that is still eligible for "nonwinners of three" races possessing no credentials above the "nonwinners of two" level. In addition, his late-running style seems unsuited to the mile distance, raising the possibility that this race might be for conditioning purposes only. Welcome Suitor is a false favorite.

CONDRILLAC

Placed in Group 2 company in France behind the ranking European sprinter, Never So Bold, in his final start before crossing the Atlantic, Condrillac has backed up badly in his three starts in this country. Certainly a factor in the early pace today, if not alone on the lead, and therefore a threat to be reckoned with. In American terms, Condrillac is still eligible for "nonwinners of three" company.

SHINING OUT

A claiming horse who has been unable to win in his first three starts since being claimed by Oscar Barrera. Shining Out is unlikely to do more than have a brief say in the early pace. He is still eligible for "nonwinners of two" company, as the purse for his March 21 race at Aqueduct reveals.

QUICK DIP

Seven lifetime wins point to this horse as a reformed claimer, one New Yorkers had seen perform on numerous occasions during 1983 and 1984. Although he woke up with a stakes placing at Louisiana Downs on May 27, Quick Dip is clearly a notch or two below Grade III company.

DANCE CALLER

Placed once in Grade II company ten starts back, Dance Caller hasn't been close since, indeed is winless in fifteen starts during 1984–1985. The horse's late running style seems ill suited to the mile distance of today's race.

TREASURED ONE

Since defeating Is Your Pleasure while winning the ungraded Envoy Stakes at Belmont on October 20, 1984 in his grass debut (as reported in another chapter in this book), Treasured One has been a perplexing disappointment. The colt bolted twice in two West Coast appearances late in 1984. His 1985 record to date classifies him a notch below Grade III quality.

LT. FLAG

Winless since earning his stakes brackets during the first few months of his three-year-old season, Lt. Flag woke up last time out in his third start as a four-year-old. But that was two and a half months ago. Why bring a horse to its peak, then lay it off and start all over again? Obviously something went wrong, and the fact that Lt. Flag is untested on the grass further complicates his task today.

JUDGE COSTA

A game, honest speed type coming off a "nonwinners of three' win, Judge Costa's best race to date was against state-bred stakes rivals of no particular merit. The presence of the speedy Condrillac will not help his cause.

NAWANNSHAR

Eligible for "nonwinners of three" company, with no credentials at or above that level, Nawannshar seems to lack sufficient class or early speed for this field. He was well beaten by Quick Dip last time.

NO MAN'S LAND

Another horse with reputed mental problems, No Man's Land ran poorly in $50,000 company in his first start of the year and was claimed by Peter Ferriola from Mack Miller. While running for Miller, the gelding failed to appear in any race above his eligibility conditions, suggesting that Miller harbored only limited hopes for the horse.

When a Grade I winner faces a group of ungraded horses, the selection is obvious, all the more so when the animal hails from one of the classier barns on the grounds. When such a horse starts at liberal odds, a prime wager is almost mandatory.

FOURTH RACE
Belmont
JUNE 23, 1985

1 MILE.(Turf). (1.33) ALLOWANCE. Purse $32,000. 3-year-olds and upward which have never won four races other than Maiden, Claiming or Starter. Weights, 3-year-olds 114 lbs. Older 122 lbs. Non-winners of two races other than Maiden or Claiming at a mile or over since May 15 allowed, 3 lbs. Of such a race since then 5 lbs.

Value of race $32,000; value to winner $19,200; second $7,040; third $3,840; fourth $1,920. Mutuel pool $163,891, OTB pool $132,363. Quin $139,918.Ex $173,919. OTB Quin $110,630.OTB Ex $152,227

Last Raced	Horse	Eqt.	A.	Wt	PP	St	¼	½	¾	Str	Fin	Jockey	Odds $1
9Jun85 ^{7}Bel^{5}	Is Your Pleasure	b	4	117	1	11	$9^{\frac{1}{2}}$	$7^{1\frac{1}{2}}$	5^{2}	$4^{1\frac{1}{2}}$	$1^{\frac{1}{2}}$	Cruguet J	3.50
15Jun85 ^{7}Bel^{4}	Dance Caller		5	117	6	5	$8^{1\frac{1}{2}}$	10^{2}	7^{1}	$5^{1\frac{1}{2}}$	2^{hd}	Hernandez R	8.40
9Jun85 ^{4}Bel^{1}	Judge Costa	b	4	119	9	1	4^{1}	5^{2}	4^{2}	$3^{\frac{1}{2}}$	3no	Vasquez J	4.60
16Jun85 ^{8}Bel^{12}	Welcome Suitor		4	119	2	10	11	11	10^{4}	7^{2}	$4^{5\frac{1}{2}}$	Venezia M	3.00
20May85 ^{7}Bel^{7}	Treasured One	b	4	117	7	7	7^{2}	4^{hd}	$3^{\frac{1}{2}}$	$2^{\frac{1}{2}}$	$5^{\frac{3}{4}}$	Samyn J L	9.70
9Jun85 ^{4}Bel^{4}	Nawannshar	b	4	117	10	9	10^{4}	$9^{\frac{1}{2}}$	8^{1}	8^{hd}	6^{nk}	Cordero A Jr	18.00
11May85 ^{6}Bel^{9}	Condrillac		4	117	3	8	$1^{1\frac{1}{2}}$	$1^{1\frac{1}{2}}$	$1^{1\frac{1}{2}}$	1^{hd}	7^{2}	Thibeau R J	29.60
27May85 ^{10}LaD^{2}	Quick Dip	b	5	117	5	2	2^{hd}	2^{2}	$2^{\frac{1}{2}}$	6^{hd}	8^{2}	Bailey J D	8.80
7Jun85 ^{1}Bel^{6}	No Man's Land	b	5	117	11	6	$6^{\frac{1}{2}}$	$6^{\frac{1}{2}}$	6^{1}	9^{4}	$9^{4\frac{3}{4}}$	Migliore R	18.00
29Mar85 ^{8}Aqu^{2}	Lt. Flag		4	117	8	3	5^{1}	$8^{\frac{1}{2}}$	11	10^{4}	10^{5}	Velasquez J	9.10
20Jun85 ^{1}Bel^{3}	Shining Out	b	5	117	4	4	$3^{1\frac{1}{2}}$	$3^{\frac{1}{2}}$	$9^{\frac{1}{2}}$	11	11	MacBeth D	40.60

OFF AT 2:40 Start good, Won driving. Time, :22$\frac{2}{5}$, :44$\frac{4}{5}$, 1:09$\frac{2}{5}$, 1:34$\frac{4}{5}$ Course firm.

$2 Mutuel Prices:			
1-(A)-IS YOUR PLEASURE	9.00	5.20	4.00
7-(G)-DANCE CALLER		9.00	4.20
10-(J)-JUDGE COSTA			2.80

$2 QUINELLA 1-7 PAID $51.40. $2 EXACTA 1-7 PAID $84.40.

Ch. c, by Accipiter—I'm A Pleasure, by What A Pleasure. Trainer Kelly Edward I. Bred by Isaacs H Z (Ky).

IS YOUR PLEASURE, off slowly, moved through along the inside at the turn, came out to continue his bid nearing the stretch and finished gamely to prevail. DANCE CALLER, taken up between horses entering the backstretch, was moving along the inside when steadied inside quick dip leaving the turn, came out to get around CONDRILLAC and TREASURED ONE just inside the final furlong and continued on with good courage. JUDGE COSTA, never far back, loomed a threat from the outside entering the stretch and finished with good energy. WELCOME SUITOR, outrun for six furlongs, finished well while racing wide. TREASURED ONE, bothered soon after entering the backstretch, made a run along the inside leaving the turn but gave way under pressure. CONDRILLAC was used up making the pace. QUICK DIP tired from his early efforts. NO MANS LAND tired. LT. FLAG showed brief speed. SHINING OUT gave way soon after a half.

We close with the warning that the "nonwinners of three (four)" race is not the ideal spot to try a horse—particularly a three-year-old—on the grass or at a distance for the first time. The competition will probably include older rivals with solid credentials on the turf, or at the distance, possibly earned in classified allowance or stakes competition. That experience, and possibly a slight age advantage as well, usually proves difficult to overcome.

Chapter 10

The Conditions Set the Stage

TO CATEGORIZE classified allowance races as either "weak" or "strong" based on the specific conditions of the race would be quite an oversimplification. A broad spectrum of race conditions fall somewhere between the extremes of "very weak" and "very strong." The weakest can easily fall to a claiming horse, while the strongest usually demand stakes class. The seasoned player realizes that he must read the conditions carefully to get an idea of the kind of animal it will take to win one of these races.

The strength of a classified allowance race is usually dictated by the time span written into the conditions and the number (and caliber) of wins allowed during that period to remain eligible for the race. As a general rule, conditions that go back a year or more, especially those that make ineligible any horse that won during that period, stamp a classified race as likely to fall into the "weak" category.

The seventh race at Aqueduct on January 5, 1985, read like a weak allowance sprint, yet it was of more than passing interest because of the presence of Chas Conerly and Don Rickles, each of whom was considered to be near the top of his generation at one point in his career. The race was for older horses that had not won a race worth $16,500 to the winner since the previous January 15.

One question that comes to mind immediately is why these two supposedly talented horses could be eligible for such a weakly conditioned race. Obviously, neither had a good year in 1984, and one had to wonder why. Were they damaged goods, possibly easy prey for seemingly lesser rivals? Let's take a closer look at the field:

7 AQUEDUCT

6 FURLONGS / INNER DIRT TRACK / AQUEDUCT (START / FINISH)

6 FURLONGS. (InnerDirt). (1.08⅘) ALLOWANCE. Purse $36,000. 4-year-olds and upward which have not won a race of $16,500 since January 15. Weight, 122 lbs. Non-winners of two races of $15,000 since December 1 allowed 3 lbs. Of such a race since then, 5 lbs. Of such a race since August 1, 7 lbs. (Maiden, claiming, starter and State-bred races not considered.)

Coupled—Stoney Lonesome and Singh America; Deemed Dividend and Space Mountain.

Hagley's Reward * — B. h. 5, by Hagley—Ortella, by Correlation
Br.—Dabru Stable (Pa)
Tr.—Lenzini John J Jr
Own.—Goldblatt B E
115 — Lifetime 23 7 4 5 $115,252 — 1984 7 0 0 2 $16,032 — 1983 15 7 4 3 $99,220

19Dec84- 8Key gd 6f :22 :45 1:10⅘ 3+Alw 16000 1 5 75 52¾ 21½ 42 Antley C W 112 6.20 86-22 Rocky Knave 113nk WillyWank111½MovingWind112nk Weakened 9
16Sep84- 8Key fst 7f :22⅘ :45⅗ 1:23⅕ 3+[S]Alw 20000 3 4 2½ 11 33½ 48 Lloyd J S 114 *1.80 83-21 Chocolate Dancer 1141½ Dr. Kroy 1176 Classic Steed 114½ Tired 6
3Sep84- 8Key fst 6f :21⅗ :44⅗ 1:10 3+Alw 16000 2 5 47½ 47 54½ 55½ Lloyd J S 116 3.30 86-26 Supreme Glow 1161½ Bill's Gulf 122no Bold Relic 1162½ Tired 5
23Jly84- 8Bel fst 6f :22⅘ :45⅗ 1:10⅕ 3+Alw 33000 2 6 59 611 611 78¾ Velasquez J 122 9.80 82-21 Muskoka Wyck 1192¾ Tarantara 117no I Enclose 1171 Outrun 7
20Feb84- 8Aqu fst 6f [•]:22 :45⅕ 1:09⅘ 3+Sport Plte H 11 9 95½ 62½ 53½ 33 Velasquez J 114 7.70 92-16 Entropy1121¾RockyMarriage1191½Hgley'sRewrd114no Fin. strong 11
21Jan84- 7Aqu fst 170 [•]:48⅗ 1:13⅗ 1:44⅘ Alw 38000 8 1 1hd 2hd 22 54½ Velasquez J 115 2.90 72-30 Snto'sJoe115hdFelingTooMuch115½AskMuhmmd1173½ Weakened 8
8Jan84- 7Aqu fst 170 [•]:48⅘ 1:14⅕ 1:44⅕ Alw 38000 10 1 1½ 1½ 2hd 3¾ Velasquez J 122 *1.20 79-21 To Erin 115¾ Pinstripe 115hd Hagley's Reward 1221½ Weakened 10
29Dec83- 8Aqu my 6f [•]:23 :46⅗ 1:11⅗ 3+Alw 35000 7 3 2½ 1hd 12½ 13 Velasquez J 117 *1.30 86-30 Hagley's Reward 1173AgileShoebill117hdElegantLife1131¾ Driving 10
17Dec83- 7Aqu fst 6f [•]:22⅘ :46 1:10⅘ 3+Alw 35000 3 3 11 12½ 15 14¾ Velasquez J 113 *1.30 92-19 Hagley's Reward 1134¾ Moro 1151¾ Special Care 1174 Ridden out 8
3Dec83- 6Med fst 6f :22⅘ :45 1:09⅘ 3+Alw 20000 2 5 1hd 13 13 13½ Wilson R 117 2.40 94-16 Hagley's Reward 1173½ NightMover1204I'mSoMerry1081½ Driving 6
LATEST WORKOUTS Dec 18 Med 3f fst :37 b Dec 10 Med 7f fst 1:33 b ●Dec 4 Med 6f gd 1:15⅖ h Nov 28 Med 5f fst 1:02 b

Good Ole Master * — Ch. g. 6, by Master Derby—Ole Honey, by Bold and Brave
Br.—Golden Chance Farm Inc (Ky)
Tr.—Henson Frank
Own.—Henson F
115 — Lifetime 50 10 6 8 $110,741 — 1984 20 6 2 3 $68,875 — 1983 12 2 1 2 $18,119 — Turf 1 0 0 1 $1,000

3Nov84- 8Key fst 7f :22⅘ :46⅕ 1:22⅘ 3+Quaker H 2 2 2½ 2hd 21½ 64½ Landicini C Jr 116 31.80 90-19 Eskimo 1142¾ North Glade 118nk Vittorioso 116no Tired 7
25Oct84- 8Med fst 6f :22⅘ :45⅗ 1:10⅘ 3+Alw 25000 5 2 43 54 57½ 510½ Lopez C C 119 9.20 79-23 Fortunate Prospect 1142 Ringside 1103 Rocky Knave 1192 Tired 6
4Oct84- 8Lri fst 6f :22⅘ :46⅕ 1:10⅘ 3+Alw 16000 8 2 3½ 2hd 2hd 11 Lopez C C 122 5.50 91-21 Good Ole Master 1221 Willard Scott 112no Near East122½ Driving 10
11Sep84- 8Key fst 6f :22 :44⅗ 1:08⅘ 3+Alw 16000 5 1 32½ 32½ 35 311 Lopez C C 120 10.10 86-19 Eillo 1209 Obgyn 1202 Good Ole Master 120¾ Evenly 6
25Aug84- 8Key fst 7f :22⅘ :45⅗ 1:23⅘ 3+Addy Boy H 4 2 1½ 1hd 32½ 53½ Lopez C C 116 12.90 84-22 Two Davids 119½ Rocca Reale 1161½ Lordly Love 1201 Tired 8
12Aug84- 8Key fst 6f :22⅕ :44⅘ 1:10⅘ 3+[R]Steelwood 5 2 21½ 22½ 24 32½ Lopez C C 118 3.00 86-20 Obgyn 118½ Rocca Reale 1162 Good Ole Master 1183½ Weakened 7
5Aug84- 10Suf fst 6f :21⅗ :44⅗ 1:10 3+Suf Sprnt H 1 5 116 1216 1225 1225½ Lopez C C 113 60.70 66-23 ConcordeBound1122½Commemorte1122¾LteToRise1051½ Bore out 12
5Aug84-Grade III
22Jly84- 8Key fst 6f :22⅕ :45 1:09⅘ 3+Alw 15000 3 3 1hd 1hd 11 13 Lopez C C 122 11.30 93-17 Good Ole Master 1223 Its Good 1121½ Near East1171½ Drew clear 8
14Jly84- 8Key fst 6f :22 :45⅕ 1:10⅕ 3+Squires H 10 5 61¾ 73¾ 910 911½ Lopez C C 117 10.30 78-20 Duke Mitchell 1192½ Main Stem 1151½ Dr. Kroy 112nk Outrun 10
16Jun84- 8Key fst 7f :22⅘ :44⅘ 1:21⅘ 3+Neshaminy H 2 2 11½ 1½ 2hd 21½ Lopez C C 116 4.80 96-19 Two Davids 1161½ Good Ole Master 1162½ Main Stem1172 Gamely 6
LATEST WORKOUTS ●Jan 2 Key 4f fst :48⅘ b ●Dec 26 Key 4f fst :47⅖ h

Stoney Lonesome — Dk. b. or br. g. 5, by Caro—Princess Red Wing, by Prince John
Br.—Morrisania Oaks Farm (Ky)
Tr.—Barrera Oscar S
Own.—Barrera O S
114⁵ — Lifetime 32 4 7 3 $103,520 — 1985 1 1 0 0 $15,000 — 1984 17 0 3 2 $28,800 — Turf 10 2 1 1 $37,100

1Jan85- 7Aqu fst 6f [•]:21⅘ :44⅗ 1:09⅗ Alw 25000 1 3 44 35 31½ 1nk Ward W A 117 2.30 96-13 Stoney Lonesome 117nkGreatHunter1122½WhoopUp1103½ Driving 5
22Dec84- 6Aqu fst 6f [•]:22⅕ :45 1:09⅗ 3+Alw 25000 8 6 73¾ 47 42½ 4nk Davis R G 117 *1.50 96-09 Treasured One 115hd Great Hunter 112noWhoopUp110nk Sluggish 8
14Dec84- 8Aqu fst 1⅟₁₆ [•]:48⅕ 1:12⅘ 1:44⅘ 3+Alw 40000 4 2 2½ 21 24 23¾ Davis R G 115 3.00 84-19 Verbarctic1153¾StoneyLonesome115½BowgonHrry119½ Held place 6
8Dec84- 3Aqu fst 6f [•]:22⅘ :46⅕ 1:11⅕ 3+Alw 25000 1 5 51¾ 61¾ 33 2nk Davis R G 117 4.00e 88-15 I'mARoundr115nkStonyLonsom1172½ElitSyncoption112nk Blocked 6
3Dec84- 8Aqu sly 1 :45⅗ 1:10⅘ 1:37 3+Alw 27000 2 3 44½ 33½ 25 36 Cruguet J 117 5.60 75-23 King'sSwn1173½Dr.J.R.Howell1152½StoneyLonsom1173¾ Weakened 8
28Nov84- 7Aqu fst 1 :46⅕ 1:11⅖ 1:38 3+Clm 70000 6 3 34 2½ 11 23 Cruguet J 113 2.30e 73-27 Last Turn 1133 StoneyLonesome1131IrishWaters113nk Weakened 8
22Nov84- 1Aqu gd 1⅟₁₆ (T):49⅕ 1:14⅘ 1:46⅕ 3+Clm 45000 3 1 1hd 1hd 2½ 31½ Ward W A5 108 4.10 73-26 CathedralBells117hdCrown1171½StoneyLonesome1081½ Weakened 8
18Nov84- 2Aqu fst 6f :22⅘ :45⅘ 1:11⅘ 3+Clm c-25000 7 6 32 56 98 910½ Skinner K 117 7.20 72-23 Satan's Charger 1152½ Snowgun 119½ Shekmatyar 113½ Tired 11
24Oct84- 9Aqu my 1 :45⅖ 1:09⅘ 1:35⅖ 3+Clm 25000 11 2 3½ 33½ 32 55½ Skinner K 117 27.40 83-14 Gauguin Native 117hd Marine Brass 1121¾ Mingo 1153½ Gave way 12
29Sep84- 10Med fst 1 :47⅖ 1:12⅗ 1:38⅖ 3+Clm 40000 7 7 78 89¾ 813 821½ Skinner K b 116 12.80 67-21 Dawn Encounter 1162 Youesaye 122hd Tarpaulin 1154½ Wide 8
LATEST WORKOUTS Dec 30 Bel tr.t 3f gd :36⅘ h (d) Nov 21 Bel tr.t 3f fst :36⅗ b Nov 11 Bel 4f fst :48 h

Chas Conerly — Dk. b. or br. h. 5, by Big Burn—Shall Return, by Fair Ruler
Br.—Lavezzo D H Jr (Ky)
Tr.—Jerkens H Allen
Own.—Hobeau Farm
108⁷ — Lifetime 21 5 3 4 $214,381 — 1984 4 0 1 1 $11,580 — 1983 9 4 0 2 $176,149

23Dec84- 8Aqu fst 6f [•]:21⅘ :44⅗ 1:09⅖ 3+Gravesend H 2 4 55½ 610 67¾ 89½ Miranda J b 119 8.10 88-17 Elegant Life 115no Tarantara 1203 Top Avenger 126½ Tired 8
6Dec84- 8Aqu sly 6f [•]:22⅘ :45⅘ 1:10⅕ 3+Alw 36000 1 3 2½ 33½ 33 32¾ Miranda J b 115 *1.40 90-12 Fight Over 113¾ Never Cye 1102 Chas Conerly 115no Weakened 6
25Nov84- 8Aqu fst 6f :22 :45⅗ 1:10⅘ 3+Sport Pg H 4 7 75 99 117¾ 116½ Miranda J b 123 *2.20 81-25 Tarantara117nkMuskokWyck114nkNewConnection1131½ No factor 13
25Nov84-Grade III
6Nov84- 7Aqu fst 6f :22⅘ :45⅗ 1:10⅖ 3+Alw 33000 5 3 31 42½ 23 2¾ Miranda J b 115 *2.00 88-20 Rollin on Over 117¾ Chas Conerly 115nk Tenifly 117¾ Gamely 7
22Oct83- 8Aqu fst 7f :22⅕ :45 1:21 3+Vosburgh 3 4 53½ 64 56½ 66 Miranda J b 123 3.40 90-19 A Phenomenon1231¾FittoFight126½DeputyMinister1261 No factor 8
8Oct83- 8Bel fst 6f :22⅕ :45⅗ 1:10⅖ 3+Fall Hwght H 4 2 52 3½ 1½ 1½ Miranda J b 136 3.20e 90-19 Chas Conerly 136½ Singh Tu 124½ Let Burn 1344 Drifted out 9
11Sep83- 8Bel fst 6f :22 :45⅕ 1:10⅗ 3+Boojum H 4 3 37½ 35½ 33 12 Miranda J b 118 14.40 89-22 Chas Conerly 1182 Gold Beauty1233¾Shimatoree1202½ Ridden out 4
29Aug83- 8Mth gd 1 :46⅘ 1:11 1:36⅘ 3+Alw 14000 1 1 1hd 1½ 1½ 1nk Miranda J b 113 *.60[D] 89-19 [D]Chas Conerly 113nk Valiant Lark 1151½ Tenifly 1185 Drifted out 5
29Aug83-Disqualified and placed third
21May83- 8Pim sly 1³⁄₁₆ :46⅘ 1:10⅗ 1:55⅗ Preakness 4 6 86 76 1115 1121¾ Skinner K b 126 68.20 71-11 DeputedTestmony1262¾DesrtWin1264HighHonors1261¾ Brief foot 12
23Apr83- 8Aqu fst 1⅛ :48⅕ 1:12⅕ 1:51 Wood Mem 5 5 42 53¾ 59 511¾ Fell J b 126 2.70 68-24 Slew O' Gold 126nk Parfaitement 126½ High Honors 1269¾ Tired 7
23Apr83-Run in two divisions 7th & 8th races
LATEST WORKOUTS Jan 3 Bel tr.t 4f gd :49 b Dec 21 Bel tr.t 4f fst :48 h ●Dec 18 Aqu [•] 4f fst :47⅖ h Dec 12 Bel 5f fst 1:02⅘ b

Singh America — Ch. h. 5, by Singh—Rikki Tikki Tavi, by Mongo
Br.—Warden Robin C (NY)
Tr.—Barrera Oscar S
Own.—Barrera O S
115 — Lifetime 40 5 8 7 $140,150 — 1984 24 4 1 5 $77,430 — 1983 16 1 7 2 $62,720 — Turf 10 0 5 1 $30,220

28Dec84- 8Aqu sly 6f :22⅘ :45⅗ 1:11⅕ 3+Alw 36000 7 4 64½ 65¾ 54 3¾ MacBeth D b 115 11.80 84-15 Huckster 115no Shadowmar 117¾ Singh America 1151½ Rallied 8
19Dec84- 5Aqu fst 170 [•]:48⅖ 1:14 1:44⅖ 3+Clm 45000 7 4 43 42½ 1½ 13 Velasquez J b 113 *2.60 78-25 SinghAmeric1133IrishWters117hdEspritDeRomo1131¾ Going away 10
13Dec84- 2Aqu fst 1⅟₁₆ [•]:47⅘ 1:12 1:44⅘ 3+Clm c-30000 11 5 55½ 66½ 612 613½ Velasquez J b 116 5.30e 75-19 Satan's Charger 117nk Terse 1101½ Cagle Springs 1176¾ Tired 11
30Nov84- 5Aqu fst 1⅜ :48 1:38⅘ 2:11⅘ 3+Clm 22500 4 1 2½ 2hd 13 16 Velasquez J b 115 2.50 80-23 Singh America 1156 Goumi 1135 Startop's Ace 110hd Driving 7
18Nov84- 2Aqu fst 6f :22⅘ :45⅘ 1:11⅘ 3+Clm 22500 10 9 42½ 46 43½ 55½ Velasquez J b 115 15.00 77-23 Satan's Charger 1152½ Snowgun 119½Shekmatyar113½ Raced wide 11
24Oct84- 9Aqu my 1 :45⅖ 1:09⅘ 1:35⅖ 3+Clm 25000 5 5 53½ 610 88 119½ Lopez V b 117 12.90 79-14 Gauguin Native 117hd Marine Brass 1121¾ Mingo 1153½ Gave way 12
14Oct84- 3Bel fst 1⅛ :46⅘ 1:12 1:51⅘ 3+Clm 25000 6 3 33 22½ 33 36 Lopez V b 117 4.50 62-28 Wimborn'sGtr1173GuguinNtiv1173SinghAmric1174½ Factor, wknd 7
3Oct84- 3Bel gd 1⅟₁₆ :47 1:12⅗ 1:46 3+Clm 25000 1 1 11½ 21½ 34½ 36¾ Lopez V b 117 5.40 65-26 Joy Hour 1156CremeDeLaFete113¾SinghAmerica1173¼ Weakened 7
26Sep84- 3Bel fst 1⅛ :46⅗ 1:12⅕ 1:52⅗ 3+Clm 32500 6 7 77½ 79½ 68½ 711½ Davis R G b 115 4.00e 53-25 Terse 1143½ Sailing Light 1124½ Ship Mint 110¾ Outrun 8
27Aug84- 3Sar fm 1⅛ [T]:47⅖ 1:11⅗ 1:50 3+Clm 50000 3 4 314 47½ 76 812½ Gomez E R b 117 22.00 78-17 Clarinet King 1191 Freon 1134½ The Ripleyite 117½ Tired 8
LATEST WORKOUTS Nov 25 Aqu 7f fst 1:30⅘ b Nov 11 Aqu 4f fst :49⅘ b

I'm A Rounder — Ch. c. 4, by Sauce Boat—I Encompass, by No Robbery
Br.—Brookfield Farms (Ky)
Tr.—Kelly Edward I
Own.—Brookfield Farms
114⁵ — Lifetime 14 4 3 3 $91,926 — 1984 13 4 3 3 $91,926 — 1983 1 M 0 0 — Turf 1 0 0 0

8Dec84- 3Aqu fst 6f [•]:22⅘ :46⅕ 1:11⅕ 3+Alw 25000 2 6 21 21 11½ 1nk Cordero A Jr b 115 *1.10 88-15 I'mARoundr115nkStonyLonsom1172½ElitSyncoption112nk Driving 6
24Nov84- 7Aqu fst 7f :23⅕ :46⅕ 1:23⅘ 3+Alw 25000 2 8 41½ 21½ 33 46¾ Cordero A Jr b 115 *3.40 77-27 On The Sauce 1151½ [D]King'sSwan1175SpecialCare117nk Impeded 9
24Nov84-Placed third through disqualification
24Oct84- 1Aqu my 6f :23 :46⅕ 1:09⅘ 3+Alw 33000 3 2 21 2hd 32 56 Davis R G b 112 *.80 86-14 Org 1154 Elite Syncopation 110½ On The Sauce 1121½ Gave way 6
6Oct84- 7Bel fst 6f :22⅘ :45⅗ 1:10⅗ 3+Alw 33000 4 4 1hd 3nk 1hd 2nk Davis R G b 112 6.80 89-17 UpPopsAwnnr112nkI'mARondr112noNorthrnTrdr116nk Just failed 8
18Jly84- 1Bel sly 6f :23 :46 1:11⅕ 3+Alw 23000 5 2 34½ 35 35 22½ Cordero A Jr b 113 *.70 83-19 Nile River 1122½ I'm A Rounder 113nk Agile Jet 106½ Wide 5
27Jun84- 7Bel fst 6f :22⅕ :45⅖ 1:10⅕ 3+Alw 23000 2 3 1hd 1hd 21½ 53½ Davis R G b 109 4.20 88-17 Lost Canyon 1132¾ On TheSauce109nkDaringGroom117nk Used up 9
10Jun84- 7Bel fst 6f :22⅕ :45⅖ 1:10⅘ 3+Alw 23000 2 6 66 65½ 65½ 3nk Davis R G b 111 5.70 88-20 TheWeddingGust112hdUnmistkn117nkI'mARoundr111no Came out 6
23May84- 8Bel fm 1 (T):45⅘ 1:10⅗ 1:35⅕ Saranac 4 2 64 56½ 913 1216¾ Davis R G b 114 2.60e 72-12 Is Your Pleasure 1142¾ Onyxly 1141¾ Loft 1233½ Stopped 12
23May84-Grade II
10May84- 6Bel fst 6f :23 :46⅖ 1:11⅖ 3+Alw 21000 4 4 4¾ 4¾ 12 11¾ Davis R G b 110 1.80 85-17 I'mARounder1101¾Dr.DavidNathan116nkFastEnough1102½ Driving 6
17Mar84- 8Aqu fst 6f [•]:22⅗ :46⅘ 1:11⅕ Bay Shore 8 1 2hd 2hd 3½ 34½ Cordero A Jr b 114 4.10 83-22 SecretPrinc1142½ThWddingGust1262½I'mARoundr114¾ Weakened 9
17Mar84-Grade III
LATEST WORKOUTS Dec 19 Bel tr.t 3f fst :38⅕ b Dec 2 Bel tr.t 4f fst :51 b Nov 23 Bel 3f fst :35⅘ h Nov 18 Bel tr.t 6f fst 1:16 b

Deemed Dividend * Dk. b. or br. g. 5, by Tentam—Buvette, by To Market
Br.—Kinghaven Farms Ltd (Ont-C)
Own.—Rory Green Stable Tr.—Sedlacek Michael C
1105 Lifetime 33 6 6 6 $85,135 | 1984 19 1 5 4 $31,850 | 1983 12 5 1 2 $52,625 | Turf 3 0 1 0 $2,640
23Dec84- 5Aqu fst 6f ⊡:22⅖ :45⅗ 1:11 3+Clm c-50000 8 6 74½ 42 1hd 3hd Cordero A Jr 117 4.30 89-17 TlcPower108noSpeedBrokr117noDmdDividnd117hd Bid, weakened 9
1Dec84- 7Grd fst 7f :24 :47⅗ 1:27 3+Alw 16000 1 2 55½ 55½ 34½ 42 Stahlbaum G b 117 7.60 78-29 Centenarian 114¾ Chic Boutique 117¾ Jacksboro 117½ Rallied 7
22Nov84- 9Grd fst 6½f :24 :47⅗ 1:20⅗ 3+ⓈAlw 16000 3 1 66½ 56 34 3¾ Swatuk B b 119 7.85 82-28 Centenarian 115¾ Feu D'enfer 121hdDeemedDividend1191¼ Rallied 7
31Oct84- 8Grd fst 6½f :23⅘ :47⅘ 1:19⅖ 3+Alw 16000 1 1 86½ 75½ 56 52½ Swatuk B b 119 4.00 86-21 Black Rule 119no Golden Robin 110hd Jacksboro 1241½ 9
20Oct84- 7WO fst 6f :22⅖ :45 1:10⅕ 3+Clm c-40000 1 6 53½ 43 22½ 2hd Wrayton E A5 b 112 *1.85 92-16 Centenarian 115hd Deemed Dividend 112⁵ Don't Bug Me 108½ 6
6Oct84- 6WO fst 7f :24⅕ :48 1:25⅕ 3+Clm 50000 1 5 41½ 52¼ 41 41¼ Lauzon J M b 117 3.05 81-23 Parnitha 117hd Feu D'enfer 117¹½ Life Master 116no No factor 5
22Sep84- 9WO fm 1¼ Ⓣ:46⅘ 1:37⅖ 2:03⅕ 3+ⓈSeagram CpH 5 9 109¼ 1212 1010 88¼ Lauzon J M b 112 27.40 82-09 Cool Northerner 116² Golden Birch 114²½ CoolTania116¹½ Outrun 14
9Sep84- 7WO fst 6½f :22⅖ :45 1:16⅘ 3+Alw 16000 6 4 52¾ 32½ 1½ 3hd Wrayton E A5 b 112 4.55 89-15 Shabu Shabu 117hd Feu D'enfer 119no Deemed Dividend 112¹½ 9
22Aug84- 6FE yl *7f Ⓣ:23⅕ :47⅗ 1:28 3+Clm 50000 8 7 69¼ 57 2½ 2no Lauzon J M b 117 6.55 76-33 Bad Rascal 117no Deemed Dividend 117² Aspirer 117¹¾ 8
6Aug84- 6WO fst 7f :23⅖ :46⅕ 1:24⅗ 3+Clm 47500 1 6 62½ 63¾ 34 24 Lauzon J M b 116 *1.70 82-24 Flag Ship 115⁴ Deemed Dividend 116nk Aspirer 117² 6
LATEST WORKOUTS Dec 22 Bel tr.t 3f sly :36⅗ h ●Nov 14 WO tr.t 4f fst :47 h

Barcelona Ch. c. 4, by Key To The Mint—Bold Honor, by Bold Ruler
Br.—Farish W S III & Jones W L (Ky)
Own.—French L R Jr Tr.—Lukas D Wayne
115 Lifetime 12 4 1 1 $80,020 | 1984 12 4 1 1 $80,020 | 1983 0 M 0 0 | Turf 1 0 0 0 $600
7Dec84- 7Med fr 1 :47 1:11⅗ 1:35 3+Alw 16000 1 1 1¹ 2hd 31½ 24½ Velasquez J b 114 *1.00 101-06 ⒹFlight of Time 116⁴½Barcelona114¾MorningReview116½ In tight 7
7Dec84-Placed first through disqualification
24Nov84- 7Aqu fst 7f :23⅕ :46⅕ 1:23⅖ 3+Alw 25000 9 3 3¹ 31½ 47 57¼ Velasquez J 117 3.80 77-27 On The Sauce115¹½ⒹKing'sSwan117⁵SpecialCare117nk Weakened 9
16Nov84- 7Aqu fst 6f :22⅗ :46⅕ 1:12⅕ 3+Alw 23000 2 3 42¼ 44½ 42 1nk Velasquez J 115 8.00 80-35 Barcelona 115nk Steppin Battler 115hdMinstrelGlory117¹½ Driving 10
4Oct84- 8Bel fst 6f :22⅘ :46⅔ 1:11 3+Alw 21000 1 2 2hd 2½ 65 711 Cordero A Jr b 114 2.70 76-26 EliteSyncoption114noStppinBttlr119nkNtivBiddr117³¾ Tired badly 7
26Apr84- 8Hol fm 1⅛ Ⓣ:48⅗ 1:12⅗ 1:42⅘ Alw 24000 5 2 3½ 2½ 3² 59½ Pincay L Jr b 117 1.80 75-17 Bedouin 114½ Armin 114² Known For Style 114³½ Tired 5
7Apr84- 4SA fst 1⅛ :45⅘ 1:10⅘ 1:43⅖ Alw 33000 5 3 2½ 2hd 1hd 31¾ Pincay L Jr b 117 2.70 82-18 Swivel 120¹ Bedouin 114¾ Barcelona 117¹½ Weakened 6
25Mar84-11FG fst 1⅛ :46⅗ 1:10⅘ 1:49⅗ La Derby 7 5 66¾ 66½ 68¼ 44½ Frazier R L b 118 27.30 91-18 Taylor's Special118¹SilentKing120¹FightOver123²½ No real threat 7
25Mar84-Grade II
14Mar84- 8SA gd 1⅛ :47⅕ 1:11⅕ 1:43⅗ ⓇS Catalina 1 1 3¹ 36 721 814¼ Valenzuela P A 115 13.60 69-26 Tights 120³ Prince True 117½ Gate Dancer 120¹¾ Fin. gamely 10
3Mar84- 7SA fst 6f :22 :45⅗ 1:09⅘ Alw 29000 5 1 2½ 2½ 2½ 1hd Valenzuela P A 120 *.90 89-14 Barcelona 120hd Lord Of The Wind 114⁷ TakkaTakka114¾ Driving 7
22Feb84- 8SA fst 6f :21⅘ :45⅕ 1:10 ⓇBolsa Chica 4 3 22½ 21½ 1½ 2hd Valenzuela P A 115 7.90 88-18 Artichoke 122hd Barcelona 115⁴½ Yukon's Star 114½ Just failed 6

Don Rickles Blk. c. 4, by Icecapade—I Got My Reasons, by Forli
Br.—Gamble Jane A (Ky)
Own.—Sabarese T M Tr.—Parisella John
117 Lifetime 14 4 4 0 $150,682 | 1984 10 2 3 0 $77,098 | 1983 4 2 1 0 $73,584 | Turf 2 0 0 0 $5,868
17Dec84- 8Aqu fst 1⁷⁰ ⊡:47⅗ 1:12⅕ 1:42⅕ 3+Alw 40000 5 1 1¹ 1½ 2½ 2² Davis R G b 113 3.20 87-19 King's Swan 115² Don Rickles 113³½ High Honors115hd Game try 7
25Nov84- 8Aqu fst 6f :22 :45⅗ 1:10⅘ 3+Sport Pg H 10 8 109 88 74½ 63 Davis R G 112 12.30 84-25 Tarantara117nkMuskokWyck114nkNewConnection113¹½ No threat 13
25Nov84-Grade III
10Nov84- 7Aqu fst 6f :22⅗ :45⅘ 1:11⅗ 3+Alw 25000 2 5 45 54 31½ 11¾ Davis R G 115 *1.80 84-23 Don Rickles 115¹¾ Agile Jet 115hd Huckster 112hd Riddenout 6
27Aug84- 6Sar fm 1⅛ Ⓣ:47 1:11⅕ 1:43⅘ 3+Alw 25000 5 1 1hd 1½ 1½ 41¼ Cordero A Jr 112 2.40 77-17 Roman Bend117½HastetoFinish117¾NoMan'sLand117no Weakened 7
5Aug84- 6Sar fst 6f :22 :44⅘ 1:09⅘ 3+Alw 23000 5 2 2½ 2½ 3² 23¾ Cordero A Jr b 112 *1.20 88-09 MajesticVenture112³¾DonRickles112¾GoGoRegl112¹ Gained place 6
3Jun84- 8Bel sf 1⅛ Ⓣ:50⅗ 1:15 1:48⅘ Hill Prince 2 2 2½ 2½ 4³ 48¾ Bailey J D 123 7.50 45-46 A Gift 114¹½ Is Your Pleasure 126⁴¾ Jesse's Hope 117²¾ Tired 7
3Jun84-Grade III
28May84- 9Key fst 1⅛ :47 1:11⅗ 1:49⅖ Pa Derby 1 1 1¹ 1hd 65½ 69 Vergara O b 122 9.70 79-17 Morning Bob 122hdAtTheThreshold122²½ⒹⒽBiloxiIndian122 Tired 7
28May84-Grade II
9May84- 8Bel fst 1 :46⅘ 1:12 1:36⅖ Withers 9 5 51¾ 3½ 85¾ 810½ Cordero A Jr b 126 *1.80 72-21 Play On 126¹ Morning Bob 126²½ Back Bay Barrister 126¹ Tired 10
9May84-Grade II
17Apr84- 8Aqu fst 6f ⊡:22⅖ :45 1:09⅘ 3+Alw 21000 1 4 3¹ 32½ 31½ 1¹ Cordero A Jr b 112 *.40 95-15 Don Rickles 112¹Sluggard119¹SuperCount112³¾ Off slowly, drvng 4
7Jan84- 9Crc fst 1⅛ :47⅖ 1:12⅘ 1:46 Trp Pk Dby 12 4 31½ 31½ 3¹ 33½ Cordero A Jr 121 2.50 85-14 Morning Bob 121¹½ ⒹRexson's Hope 121²DonRickles121½ Bore in 15
7Jan84-Grade II; Placed second through disqualification
LATEST WORKOUTS Dec 31 Bel tr.t 4f fst :49⅖ b Dec 14 Bel tr.t 4f fst :49⅖ b ●Dec 7 Bel tr.t 3f fst :35 h ●Nov 23 Bel tr.t 3f fst :35 h

Carjack * B. c. 4, by Cojak—Worlds Of Fun, by Dead Ahead
Br.—Ring Carolyn (Miss)
Own.—Leachman J Tr.—Ludwig Jack D
115 Lifetime 18 6 4 1 $68,952 | 1984 18 6 4 1 $68,952 | 1983 0 M 0 0 | Turf 1 0 1 0 $2,700
20Dec84- 8Med fst 6f :23⅕ :46⅘ 1:11⅗ 3+Alw 25000 2 4 2hd 52 52½ 65½ Graell A b 117 2.00 79-24 Faces Up 115¾ Habitonia 115² Now's The Time 110¹½ Tired 7
29Nov84- 9Grd fst 6½f :23⅕ :46⅘ 1:19⅘ 3+Handicap 4 1 2hd 1hd 13½ 13½ Attard L b 119 2.30 87-29 Carjack 119³½ Feu D'enfer 117¹½ Dance Corps 117¹½ Handily 5
10Nov84- 8Grd sly 6½f :23⅘ :47 1:19⅗ 3+Alw 16000 6 3 3³ 24½ 22 2½ Dos Ramos R A b 119 *1.10 87-29 The Accomodator 108½ Carjack 119⁵½ Parkpasser 117³½ 6
1Nov84- 9Grd fst 7f :23⅖ :46⅗ 1:25⅕ 3+Handicap 3 1 44 43 2½ 2nk Swatuk B b 114 5.30 89-26 New Connection 121nk Carjack 114³ Nancy's Champion 121²½ 7
21Oct84- 6WO fst 6f :21⅘ :44⅕ 1:09⅘ 3+Nearctic H 7 2 88½ 89 76½ 61½ Lauzon J M b 112 36.95 92-18 Diapason117nkNewConnection116½Commemorate121no No threat 8
21Oct84-Grade II-C
6Oct84-10WO fst 6f :23 :46⅕ 1:11⅗ 3+Alw 16000 1 5 1¹ 1² 12½ 12½ Swatuk B b 114 8.25 85-23 Carjack 114²½ Centenarian 111³ On Air 117hd Handily 9
20Sep84- 8WO fst 7f :22⅗ :45⅕ 1:23⅘ 3+Alw 14000 1 5 54½ 67½ 69 69½ Lauzon J M b 120 2.80 80-21 ReglPolicy117¹½DevotedAllince120²½TheAccomodtor117²½ Outrun 6
5Sep84- 7WO fst 1⁷⁰ :46⅔ 1:11 1:41⅘ 3+Alw 15400 7 5 5⁵ 44½ 43½ 42 Lauzon J M b 112 2.55 92-18 Center Ice 118¾ The Accomodator 115¹ Regal Policy 114nk 9
17Aug84- 8FE fst 6½f :23⅘ :46⅗ 1:16⅘ 3+Alw 13600 4 1 2¹ 2hd 1hd 11½ Lauzon J M b 120 *.80 95-16 Carjack 120¹½ Tri Tyson 115³ Charlemagne 117¹ Ridden out 6
4Aug84- 3WO fst 1⅛ :49 1:13⅗ 1:46⅕ Alw 17600 5 5 5⁵ 42 21½ 21½ Lauzon J M b 117 *1.45 77-21 Regal Policy 115¹½ Carjack 117⁴ Devoted Alliance 124¹½ 6
LATEST WORKOUTS Jan 4 Bel tr.t 3f fst :37⅕ h Dec 30 Bel tr.t 5f gd 1:05 b (d) Dec 15 Bel tr.t 4f fst :49 b Nov 22 WO tr.t 4f fst :50⅘ h

Space Mountain Ch. h. 6, by Night Invader—Action Lane, by In Reality
Br.—Happy Valley Farm (Fla)
Own.—Oak Manor Farm Tr.—Sedlacek Michael C
1105 Lifetime 42 7 12 3 $215,630 | 1984 11 1 4 0 $73,420 | 1983 14 3 4 2 $102,620 | Turf 3 0 0 0
28Dec84- 8Aqu sly 6f :22⅗ :45⅘ 1:11⅕ 3+Alw 36000 1 8 76½ 75¾ 64 42 Davis R G 115 16.30 83-15 Huckster 115no Shadowmar 117¾ SinghAmerica115¹½ Broke in air 8
7Jly84- 4Bel sly 7f :22⅗ :45⅕ 1:22⅘ Clm 75000 4 8 65 69 44½ 45 Lopez V5 107 5.50 83-16 Sky Falcon 112hd Irish Waters 112⁴ Huckster 122¹ Rallied 8
28Jun84- 9Bel fst 7f :22⅗ :45⅗ 1:22⅗ Clm 70000 7 11 99½ 66½ 34½ 26¾ Vega H7 106 10.70 82-19 Pinstripe117⁶¾SpaceMountain106²½HarpersBazar113nk Off slowly 11
26May84- 7Bel fst 1 :46 1:10⅗ 1:36⅕ 3+Alw 36000 1 9 914 916 713 614 Ward W A5 114 4.30e 70-15 Faces Up 119⁶ Nepal 119½ Starbinia 119⁵½ No factor 9
18May84- 8Bel fst 7f :23⅗ :47⅕ 1:23⅗ 3+Alw 33000 7 7 77¾ 77 66½ 56 Ward W A5 116 5.10 78-17 Vittorioso 119¹ Measured Response111¹½Mugatea119no No threat 7
21Apr84- 7Aqu fst 7f :23⅕ :46⅘ 1:25 3+Alw 33000 2 8 97¾ 96¾ 63½ 2hd Ward W7 112 4.20 76-30 Northern Ice 119hdSpaceMountain112½AgileShoebill116nk Gamely 9
8Apr84- 7Aqu fst 6f ⊡:22⅗ :46⅕ 1:10⅗ 3+Alw 33000 3 6 69 68½ 48 26¾ Ward W7 114 3.30 84-21 CannonShell121⁶¾SpceMountin114¾Stn'sChrger112½ Gained place 6
20Feb84- 8Aqu fst 6f ⊡:22 :45⅕ 1:09⅘ 3+Sport Plte H 3 10 64 83 65¾ 53½ Murphy D J 109 5.80 91-16 Entropy 112¹¾ Rocky Marriage119¹½Hagley'sReward114no Rallied 11
2Feb84- 7Aqu fst 1⁷⁰ ⊡:48 1:12⅘ 1:43⅖ Alw 38000 9 3 22½ 44 34 2¾ Murphy D J5 112 4.30 83-22 Medieval'sSon115¾SpaceMountain112nkHavagreatdte117³ Rallied 10
14Jan84- 8Aqu fst 1⅛ ⊡:47⅘ 1:12 1:50⅕ 3+Assault H 8 7 76½ 87 76½ 911¼ Graell A 110 7.40 83-17 Megaturn 115hd Moro 111¾ In the Ruff 117¹¾ Outrun 11
14Jan84-Grade III
LATEST WORKOUTS Dec 24 Aqu ⊡ 3f fst :36 h Dec 19 Aqu ⊡ 5f fst 1:01⅖ h Dec 13 Aqu ⊡ 5f fst 1:01⅖ h Dec 8 Aqu ⊡ 5f fst 1:04 b

HAGLEY'S REWARD

A top sprinter toward the end of his three-year-old season, the now five-year-old son of Hagley appeared to have suffered an injury either during or shortly after the 1984 Sporting Plate Handicap, in which he finished third to such solid runners as Entropy and Rocky Marriage, beating the likes of Cannon Shell. His return to the races at Keystone on December 19 was promising, hinting quite strongly that the horse was "sittin' on a win." One had to question, though, why the Meadowlands-based animal was shipped to Keystone for the prep. Were suitable races at the Meadowlands failing to fill? Or did trainer Lenzini feel that Hagley's Reward fit better with the Keystone set? Although now based in New York with several other Lenzini runners for the remainder of the winter, the Keystone option was still available, if needed, only a few hours away. But this time, Lenzini chose to remain at home and shoot for the big New York purse. That seemed to suggest that Hagley's Reward was set for his best effort, second try after a layoff, as so often happens.

GOOD OLE MASTER

A bona fide Keystone shipper, but coming off a two-month layoff and two poor races in similar company. If the trainer had a reputation for such a move . . . But he didn't.

STONEY LONESOME

It took Oscar Barrera's magic several races to get a win out of this horse, the animal's first in at least eighteen starts. He's not likely to step up from "nonwinners of three" company into the classified ranks and defeat solid classified runners.

CHAS CONERLY

Horses don't lay off from the races for a full year without good reason, especially when they're at the peak of their game. Obviously Chas Conerly suffered a serious injury. His best race since returning was his first, and the horse hasn't progressed since. It would be foolish to expect improvement.

BARCELONA

Although stakes-placed at Santa Anita early in the year, this three-year-old colt's recent win came in "nonwinners of two" company, and he has since failed against "nonwinners of three" rivals. He is not likely to prove competitive against older classified runners at this point.

DON RICKLES

Regarded a classics prospect at the start of the year, Don Rickles has been a bitter disappointment to his connections. His most recent win was against "nonwinners of three" rivals, and his subsequent loss was to a claiming runner who stalked his (fast) pace. He's the logical favorite and the horse to beat but is worth taking a shot against at 3–2 odds.

CARJACK

Carjack is a successful Canadian runner whose recent race in similar company at the Meadowlands made his form north of the border appear counterfeit.

SPACE MOUNTAIN

Winless since his first start of 1984, Space Mountain has recently been unable to handle claiming rivals at what would seem to be a more favorable seven furlongs.

Note how the various entrants satisfied the eligibility conditions. Wins for smaller purses out of town, or for weaker allowance conditions in New York, did not affect their eligibility for today's race.

With Don Rickles unreliable and Chas Conerly suspect, this kind of race could easily go to a claimer, a shipper, or a horse moving up from the restricted allowance ranks. Of these, Hagley's Reward seemed the logical upsetter. He was rounding to form and had es-

SEVENTH RACE
Aqueduct
JANUARY 5, 1985

6 FURLONGS.(InnerDirt). (1.08⅘) ALLOWANCE. Purse $36,000. 4-year-olds and upward which have not won a race of $16,500 since January 15. Weight, 122 lbs. Non-winners of two races of $15,000 since December 1 allowed 3 lbs. Of such a race since then, 5 lbs. Of such a race since August 1, 7 lbs. (Maiden, claiming, starter and State-bred races not considered.)

Value of race $36,000; value to winner $21,600; second $7,920; third $4,320; fourth $2,160. Mutuel pool $140,669, OTB pool $155,368. Exacta Pool $259,827. OTB Exacta Pool $257,856.

Last Raced	Horse	Eqt.	A.	Wt	PP	St	¼	½	Str	Fin	Jockey	Odds $1
19Dec84 ^{8}Key^{4}	Hagley's Reward		5	115	1	4	2½	2^{4}	1^{hd}	1½	Migliore R	6.10
17Dec84 ^{8}Aqu^{2}	Don Rickles	b	4	117	6	2	1^{1}	1^{hd}	2^{5}	2^{5}	Cordero A Jr	1.50
7Dec84 ^{7}Med^{1}	Barcelona	b	4	115	5	3	4½	3^{1}	3^{1}	3¾	Lovato F Jr	17.30
1Jan85 ^{7}Aqu^{1}	Stoney Lonesome		5	119	3	6	7^{hd}	4^{hd}	4½	4^{hd}	Davis R G†	3.60
28Dec84 ^{8}Aqu^{4}	Space Mountain		6	110	8	8	8	6^{1}	5^{hd}	5^{nk}	Ward W A^{5}	6.50
23Dec84 ^{8}Aqu^{8}	Chas Conerly	b	5	108	4	7	6^{hd}	8	6^{hd}	6¾	Privitera R^{7}	4.30
20Dec84 ^{8}Med^{6}	Carjack	b	4	115	7	1	5½	7^{2}	7^{5}	7^{8}	Graell A	18.80
3Nov84 ^{8}Key^{6}	Good Ole Master		6	115	2	5	3^{hd}	5^{hd}	8	8	Clayton M D	38.00

OFF AT 3:30 Start good, Won driving. Time, :22⅘, :46⅗, 1:09⅗ Track fast.

$2 Mutuel Prices:				
	2-(A)-HAGLEY'S REWARD	14.20	5.80	4.60
	7-(I)-DON RICKLES		3.40	2.80
	6-(H)-BARCELONA			5.40

$2 EXACTA 2-7 PAID $53.00.

B. h, by Hagley—Ortella, by Correlation. Trainer Lenzini John J Jr. Bred by Dabru Stable (Pa).

HAGLEY'S REWARD, attending DON RICKLES under hustling ractics drew abreast of him entering the stretch, and, going head-to-head until furlong out, proved superior, edging away in a swift run race. DON RICKLES, setting lively fractions, was unable to cope with winner during late stages, while remaining well in advance of others. BARCELONA had no excuse in decent effort. STONEY LONESOME failed to make presdence felt. SPACE MOUNTAIN raced wide. CHAS CONERLY never posed threat. CARJACK was unable to keep up. GOOD OLE MASTER stopped following flash of early foot.

tablished his class in New York stakes company. A win bet was called for, together with the insurance of a "place" bet in the form of an exacta with Don Rickles on top of Hagley's Reward. The insurance proved unnecessary, at least in the order prescribed. Hagley's Reward won the race, returning $14.60, with Don Rickles a solid second.

The seventh race at Belmont on July 18, 1985, appeared, at least on paper, to be capable of drawing a stronger field. The eligibility conditions were of the "nonwinners of two during the last half-year" variety. Indeed, the race did attract Solar Halo, regarded by many as the best three-year-old filly in the East at the end of the 1984 season. Her presence probably scared off a few fillies looking for an easy spot, but the race did attract several with recent stakes credentials and appeared to be a strong test for Solar Halo's first race of the year. But looks can be deceiving. Let's take a closer look at Solar Halo and her opposition:

SOLAR HALO

Solar Halo enjoyed a big reputation, but had she really earned it? A good-size filly, she was unraced at two, then won her first two starts at three in January. However, she did not race again until Saratoga, missing all the summer classics. Her only stakes victory came three days before Christmas against questionable opposition. However, she did precede that win with excellent placings behind the top-class fillies Heatherton and Sintra, earning the attention that was later elevated to stardom with her victory in the Firenze. As we mentioned, though, Solar Halo was a big filly and apparently prone to injury. A serious splint problem delayed her 1985 debut until July. And her size made it all the more difficult to train her up to a winning effort first race back. Indeed, with a talented filly having the Breeders' Cup as her ultimate goal, it would be surprising if young Bill Burch viewed this allowance race as anything more than a conditioner.

HARE BRAIN

At first glance, Hare Brain looks like a stakes filly, having won the O'Allison at Aqueduct in March and placed in a couple of other stakes since. A closer look, however, reveals that none of those races was the featured eighth race on their respective afternoons. Rather, they were all examples of a new trend—"black type" stakes

7 BELMONT

1 1/16 MILES. (1.40⅗) ALLOWANCE. Purse $40,000. Fillies and mares, 3-year-olds and upward which have not won two races of $16,500 at a mile or over since January 1. Weights, 3-year-olds, 116 lbs.; older, 122 lbs. Non-winners of a race of $15,000 at a mile or over since May 15 allowed 3 lbs.; of such a race since April 1, 5 lbs.; of such a race since February 1, 7 lbs. (Maiden claiming, starter and State-Bred races not considered.)

Dowery — B. f. 4, by Full Pocket—Vaguely Royal, by Vaguely Noble
Own.—Hillstead Farm | Br.—Hillstead Farm (Ky) | Tr.—Alexander Frank A
115 | Lifetime 17 11 1 2 $260,712 | 1985 4 1 0 2 $32,085 | 1984 9 6 1 0 $183,950 | Turf 1 0 0 0

6Jly85- 9Mth fst 1 1/16 :46⅕ 1:10 1:42⅘ 3+ⒻMly Ptchr H 8 4 31 2hd 2hd 33¼ Bracciale V Jr 115 38.10 89-17 Sefa's Beauty 119¾ Mitterand 1192¼ Dowery 1152¼ Weakened 11
6Jly85-Grade II
8Jun85- 9Crc fst 1 1/16 :49⅕ 1:13⅗ 1:47 3+ⒻMeadbk FmH 3 2 1½ 1½ 2½ 32¾ Velez J A Jr 122 *.70 81-15 Early Lunch 1132¾ Lament 115no Dowery 1222¾ Weakened 6
13May85- 7Crc fst 7f :23 :46⅕ 1:25⅕ ⒻAlw 15000 7 1 42½ 32 1½ 11½ Velez J A Jr 123 *.70 90-11 Dowery 1231½ Lauded Dancer 114½ Commended 1051½ Driving 7
13Feb85- 8GP fst 7f :22⅕ :45 1:23⅘ 3+ⒻShrly Jnes H 3 6 32½ 32½ 58 67¼ Perret C 121 5.80 78-24 Mickey's Echo 117½ Sugar's Image 117hd Nany 1224 Tired 10
1Dec84- 9Crc sly 1 1/16 :49⅘ 1:14⅖ 1:47⅖ 3+ⒻCoral Gbl H 5 3 3½ 12 13 2½ Velez J A Jr 121 *.80 81-24 Burst Of Colors 112½ Dowery 1215 Silvered Silk 121¾ Weakened 7
27Oct84- 8Key fst 1 1/16 :46⅖ 1:10⅘ 1:42⅘ ⒻCotillion 7 4 32½ 1½ 12½ 12 Bracciale V Jr 122 *1.00 91-15 Dowery 1222 Duo Disco 1225½ Hot Milk 1172¾ Ridden out 9
27Oct84-Grade III; Run In Divisions
13Oct84- 8Lrl fm 1 1/16 Ⓣ:46⅘ 1:12⅕ 1:43⅕ ⒻMarta WashH 9 2 2½ 2½ 44 1010¼ Bracciale V Jr 122 *1.40 77-14 Berkeley Court 1132 La Reine Elaine 1121½Tagalog110no Faltered 10
22Sep84- 8Lrl fst 1 :46⅗ 1:12 1:37 ⒻA Arundel H 2 1 1½ 1½ 13 13½ Black A S 118 *3.00 87-17 Dowery 1183½ Basie 1151½ Dumdedumdedum 114¾ Driving 13
1Sep84- 9Crc fst 1 1/16 :48⅖ 1:13⅗ 1:48⅖ 3+ⒻViscaya H 7 4 34½ 1½ 13 11 Lopez C 116 2.50 77-25 Dowery 1161 Silvered Silk 123½ Real Sunny 1102 Driving 8
15Aug84- 9Crc fst 1 1/16 :49⅖ 1:14⅗ 1:49⅖ ⒻBegonia 1 4 41¾ 21½ 1½ 11½ Velez J A Jr 115 *.80 72-22 Dowery1151½ClandestineAffir1151¾ErlyLunch1202 Boxed in,drvng 7
LATEST WORKOUTS Jun 1 Crc 6f fst 1:15 b | May 25 Crc 6f fst 1:19 b

Hare Brain — B. m. 5, by Naskra—Milina, by Nijinsky II
Own.—Terranova J P | Br.—Tartan Farms (Fla) | Tr.—Imperio Dominick A
117 | Lifetime 33 7 4 3 $185,434 | 1985 8 1 2 0 $69,334 | 1984 17 6 1 1 $105,700 | Turf 4 0 0 1 $2,280

6Jly85- 6Bel fst 6f :22 :45⅕ 1:11⅕ 3+ⒻThe Rose 1 5 614 612 610 69 McCarron G b 119 10.80 77-20 Ldy'sSecret1164¾FoolishIntntions115¾ProudClrionss115no Trailed 6
8Jun85- 2Bel sly 6f :22⅕ :45⅗ 1:10⅗ 3+ⒻGenuine Risk 5 10 911 74¾ 32½ 22¾ McCarron G b 119 29.50 86-12 Alabama Nana 1172¾ Hare Brain 1192½ Two Ours 119no 2nd best 10
20Apr85- 6Aqu gd 7f :22⅘ :45⅖ 1:22⅕ 3+ⒻSarsar 7 2 76¾ 65½ 58½ 48¼ Cordero A Jr b 121 3.80 82-10 Gracefully Yours 1197 Best Venture 119¾ Gene'sLady121½ Rallied 8
6Apr85- 6Aqu fst 6f :22⅘ :46 1:10⅗ 3+ⒻFair Mist H 5 5 64½ 42¾ 43 23 Cordero A Jr b 118 2.30 85-21 Gene's Lady1153HareBrain1183¾SharpLittleGirl1121¼ Second best 6
23Mar85- 7Aqu fst 1 :48⅕ 1:13⅕ 1:38 ⒻⓇO'alison 2 6 51½ 31 11½ 12¾ Cordero A Jr b 119 4.30 76-23 Hare Brain 1192¾ Best Venture 1173¼ Explicit Gal 115hd Driving 9
2Mar85- 7Aqu fst 1 1/16 ⊡:47⅗ 1:12⅘ 1:45⅘ ⒻAlw 40000 4 6 64½ 42 31½ 43¾ McCarron G b 117 11.60 77-19 Give Me A Hint 114nk Gene's Lady 1152¾ Owned By All115¾ Hung 7
2Feb85- 8Aqu my 1⅛ ⊡:47⅕ 1:12⅘ 1:53⅗ 3+ⒻRare Treat H 4 9 812 79¾ 815 815¾ McCarron G b 109 28.40 58-28 Bracalena 1135½ Duped 111½ Emphatic 1041½ Outrun 11
19Jan85- 8Aqu fst 1 1/16 ⊡:46⅘ 1:12 1:45⅗ 3+ⒻAffctntly H 2 6 69 55½ 54½ 59¼ McCarron G b 112 7.80 73-22 Sintrillium 1164 Emphatic 104½ Far Flying 1162¼ Outrun 7
19Jan85-Grade III; Run in Divisions
26Dec84- 7Aqu fst 170 ⊡:48⅖ 1:14 1:43⅘ 3+ⒻAlw 40000 5 5 53½ 52½ 1½ 15 McCarron G b 115 3.90 81-21 Hare Brain 1155 Yolanda 1133 Dusty Gloves 113no Easily 5
19Dec84- 8Aqu fst 6f ⊡:22⅘ :46⅗ 1:12⅕ 3+ⒻAlw 28000 7 1 96 66½ 51¾ 1¾ McCarron G b 117 *2.50 83-25 Hare Brain 117¾ Mepache 115¾ Gnash 1193 Driving 9
LATEST WORKOUTS Jly 15 Bel tr.t 4f fst :53⅖ b | Jly 2 Bel 4f fst :48⅕ b | Jun 26 Bel 5f fst 1:01⅕ h | Jun 23 Bel 4f fst :52⅕ b

Solar Halo — Dk. b. or br. f. 4, by Halo—Provenance, by Fleet Nasrullah
Own.—Edwards J F | Br.—Edwards J F (Md) | Tr.—Burch William E
115 | Lifetime 8 4 3 1 $155,875 | 1984 8 4 3 1 $155,875 | 1983 0 M 0 0 | Turf 2 0 1 1 $7,480

22Dec84- 8Aqu fst 1⅛ ⊡:47⅘ 1:11⅘ 1:49⅕ 3+ⒻFirenze H 8 7 72¾ 21½ 14 19 Davis R G 110 1.80 96-09 Solar Halo 1109 It's Fine 109¾ Quixotic Lady 115½ Handily 8
22Dec84-Grade II
24Nov84- 8Aqu fst 1¼ :49⅘ 1:38⅗ 2:04 3+ⒻLadies H 2 1 1hd 2½ 23 26¾ Velasquez J 112 3.50 69-27 Heatherten 1236¾ Solar Halo 1105 Key Dancer 113nk 2nd best 8
24Nov84-Grade I
11Oct84- 4Kee fst 1 1/16 :47⅕ 1:11⅕ 1:43⅖ ⒻQn Liz Cup 4 8 55 62½ 31½ 2no Day P 112 3.90 89-17 Sintra 112no Solar Halo 1122 Mr. T.'s Tune 1125 In close 12
21Sep84- 8Bel fst 1 1/16 :46⅘ 1:11⅖ 1:42⅘ 3+ⒻAlw 22000 3 3 31½ 12½ 110 113 Velasquez J 113 *.90 88-23 Solar Halo 11313 Oneezer 1132¾ Daddy's Dish 1131½ Ridden out 6
8Sep84- 6Bel fm 1 1/16 Ⓣ:45⅗ 1:09⅗ 1:42⅕ 3+ⒻAlw 22000 8 4 43 42½ 21 2hd Velasquez J 113 *2.20 85-16 Cosmic Sea Queen 117hd SolarHalo1135¼Disquieting113no Gamely 11
12Aug84- 5Sar fm 1 1/16 Ⓣ:47⅖ 1:11⅗ 1:42⅗ 3+ⒻAlw 22000 3 7 77¾ 76¾ 75¾ 34½ Davis R G 112 4.90 87-07 Secret Sharer 1173 Sultress 1141½ Solar Halo 112¾ Mild rally 9
21Jan84- 4Aqu fst 170 ⊡:50⅕ 1:17⅕ 1:48 ⒻAlw 22000 2 6 51½ 11½ 11½ 12½ Skinner K 116 2.60 61-30 Solar Halo 1162½ Optimus Girl 1211 Miss Cathy M. 1166 Driving 9
8Jan84- 6Aqu fst 6f ⊡:22⅗ :47⅕ 1:14⅕ ⒻMd Sp Wt 12 10 87¾ 55 23½ 1no Skinner K 121 7.40 73-21 Solar Halo 121no Second Glance 1212¾ Sunset Strait 1211 Driving 12
LATEST WORKOUTS Jly 10 Bel 6f fst 1:13⅘ h | Jly 4 Bel 5f fst :59⅘ h | Jun 27 Bel 5f fst 1:00 b | Jun 21 Bel 5f fst 1:02⅘ b

Sally The Shiek — Ch. m. 5, by Little Miracle—Dixie Deeny, by Prince Blessed
Own.—Fertile Acres Farm | Br.—Mistretta C (NY) | Tr.—Ortiz Paulino O
1107 | Lifetime 52 5 4 3 $150,562 | 1985 13 1 1 0 $45,980 | 1984 20 1 0 3 $41,322 | Turf 15 1 1 1 $33,862

26Jun85- 3Bel fm 1 1/16 Ⓣ:48⅗ 1:12⅘ 1:44⅘ ⒻClm 90000 5 4 53 64 64 73¼ Maple E 118 7.30 76-16 Marked Lady 112nkCosmicSeaQueen114¾TrickyTune112nk Outrun 8
19Jun85- 8Bel fst 1 :47⅖ 1:12⅕ 1:37⅗ 3+ⒻⓈHydeParkH 1 5 52½ 44 25 24 Maple E 111 12.20 73-28 Nany 1274 Sally The Shiek 1112 Flip's Pleasure1252½ Second best 9
12Jun85- 8Mth fm 1 1/16 Ⓣ:48⅕ 1:12⅖ 1:43⅖ 3+ⒻAlw 20000 7 6 64¾ 73½ 64½ 46 Ferrer J C 115 20.10 82-13 Miss Care 1222 Josalee 1151 Tagalog 1153 Outrun 7
3Jun85- 8Bel fst 1 :46⅖ 1:11⅕ 1:37⅖ 3+ⒻAlw 40000 6 6 69½ 612 617 65½ Samyn J L 119 10.80 72-13 Best Venture 1141 Robin's Rob 1172 Dis Hi Fi 117½ Outrun 6
24May85- 8Bel gd 1 Ⓣ:47 1:12⅖ 1:39⅗ 3+ⒻAlw 32000 5 5 55½ 45 44½ 45¼ Samyn J L 121 10.20 62-32 Tarifa 114nk Lotus Delight 1211¾ Maidenhead1213¼ No real threat 5
10May85- 6Bel fm 1 1/16 Ⓣ:47⅕ 1:11 1:43 ⒻClm 70000 8 7 1011 912 815 815¼ Samyn J L 113 13.10 66-22 Pull The Wool 117½ Dawna 113nk Reptile 1131¾ Outrun 11
23Mar85- 7Aqu fst 1 :48⅕ 1:13⅕ 1:38 ⒻⓇO'alison 9 5 62¾ 712 79 711¾ Samyn J L 119 12.70 64-23 HareBrin1192¾BestVenture1173¼ExplicitGl115hd Never prominent 9
8Mar85- 8Aqu fst 170 ⊡:48 1:13 1:43⅗ ⒻAlw 40000 4 3 32½ 21 12 1hd Samyn J L 115 12.70 82-18 Sally The Shiek 115hd For My Heart115nkToleration1153¼ Driving 9
1Mar85- 8Aqu fst 170 ⊡:48⅖ 1:13 1:44⅖ ⒻAlw 27000 4 4 54 56 59 410½ Guerra A A7 b 110 10.30 67-25 SuperlativeSue1123SourestRind1173¼ForMyHeart1174¼ No factor 6
23Feb85- 7Aqu fst 170 ⊡:48⅖ 1:13⅕ 1:44⅕ ⒻAlw 40000 2 2 31½ 76½ 610 68¼ Guerra A A7 b 108 14.20 71-21 Free Saint 1082¼ Irish Liberal 108hd Mepache 115½ Gave way 7
LATEST WORKOUTS Jly 15 Bel 4f fst :50 b | Jly 6 Bel tr.t 3f fst :38 b | Jun 10 Bel tr.t 4f fst :48⅖ h | May 18 Bel tr.t 4f gd :50 b

Gene's Lady — Ch. f. 4, by What a Pleasure—Lady T V, by T V Lark
Own.—Klein E V | Br.—Spreen R H (Fla) | Tr.—Lukas D Wayne
119 | Lifetime 38 6 8 11 $330,588 | 1985 10 2 2 3 $109,214 | 1984 19 2 2 6 $160,624 | Turf 6 0 1 0 $14,200

5Jly85- 8GS fst 6f :21⅕ :43⅘ 1:09⅖ 3+ⒻPrcss Shot H 3 5 59 57½ 44½ 34¾ Velasquez J b 119 4.30 90-15 Furash Folly 1161¾ Shanaleen 1173 Gene's Lady 1192 Rallied 5
8Jun85- 2Bel sly 6f :22⅕ :45⅗ 1:10⅗ 3+ⒻGenuine Risk 7 9 1012 96½ 54½ 45 Pincay L Jr b 122 *1.10e 84-12 Alabama Nana 1172¾ Hare Brain 1192¼ Two Ours 119no No threat 10
19May85- 7Bel fm 6f Ⓣ:22⅖ :45⅘ 1:09⅖ 3+ⒻYankee Girl 3 6 54 64½ 54½ 54¾ Velasquez J b 119 3.30 88-12 Mazatleca 1192 Foolish Intentions119¾Heartlight119hd No excuse 8
2May85- 8Aqu fst 1 :47⅕ 1:11⅘ 1:37⅕ 3+ⒻAlw 40000 5 1 1hd 1½ 14 14 Velasquez J b 121 *1.10 80-26 Gene's Lady 1214 ⒹQueen Alexandra 108¾LizMatizz1191¾ Handily 5
20Apr85- 6Aqu gd 7f :22⅘ :45⅖ 1:22⅕ 3+ⒻSarsar 3 8 53½ 54 37 37¾ Vasquez J b 121 *1.30 82-10 Gracefully Yours 1197 Best Venture 119¾ Gene'sLady121½ Rallied 8
6Apr85- 6Aqu fst 6f :22⅘ :46 1:10⅗ 3+ⒻFair Mist H 3 4 32 3nk 11½ 13 Vasquez J b 115 *1.80 88-21 Gene's Lady 1153 HareBrain1183¾SharpLittleGirl1121¼ Ridden out 6
25Mar85- 8Aqu fst 7f :23 :46⅖ 1:24⅗ ⒻAlw 36000 1 6 31½ 32½ 33 2½ Velasquez J b 117 2.50 77-35 Some For All 122½ Gene's Lady 1172¾ Slashing 1145 Gamely 6
10Mar85- 8Lrl fst 7f :23⅕ :46⅖ 1:24 3+ⒻFritchie H 6 4 11 3nk 41¼ 36 Murphy D J b 109 11.10 85-16 Flip's Pleasure 1154½ Applause 1201½ Gene'sLady1091¾ Weakened 8
10Mar85-Grade III; Run in divisions
2Mar85- 7Aqu fst 1 1/16 ⊡:47⅗ 1:12⅘ 1:45⅘ ⒻAlw 40000 2 1 1½ 11 11½ 2nk Lovato F Jr b 115 *1.50 81-19 Give Me A Hint 114nk Gene's Lady 1152¾OwnedByAll115¾ Gamely 7
19Jan85- 7Aqu fst 1 1/16 ⊡:47⅖ 1:12⅖ 1:45⅗ 3+ⒻAffctntly H 1 2 2hd 2hd 3½ 43¼ Murphy D J b 109 7.00 79-22 Descent 106½ Sweet Missus 1121¼ Bracalena 1141½ Weakened 7
19Jan85-Grade III; Run in Divisions
LATEST WORKOUTS Jun 30 Bel 4f fst :48⅖ h | Jun 23 Bel 4f fst :50⅖ b | Jun 3 Bel 4f fst :50⅘ b

Best Venture — B. f. 4, by Best Of It—Cassie, by Yatasto
Own.—Tresvant Stable | Br.—Graddy H III (Ky) | Tr.—Sedlacek Sue
1157 | Lifetime 39 7 11 6 $181,739 | 1985 14 3 3 2 $113,254 | 1984 13 3 3 3 $55,630 | Turf 2 0 0 0 $3,300

11Jly85- 8Bel fst 7f :22⅖ :45⅕ 1:23⅕ 3+ⒻHandicap 3 5 55 47 44½ 35½ Thibeau R J b 110 13.90 80-19 Alabama Nana1223½SharpLittleGirl1082½BestVenture1104¾ Rallied 5
21Jun85- 8Bel fm 1 Ⓣ:46⅗ 1:10⅖ 1:34⅕ 3+ⒻCaltha 4 3 42½ 411 421 437¾ Garrido O L b 117 11.60 56-14 Key Dancer 1172¼ Possible Mate 1225LuckyTouch10930½ Stopped 4
3Jun85- 8Bel fst 1 :46⅖ 1:11⅕ 1:37⅖ 3+ⒻAlw 40000 4 2 2hd 1hd 11½ 11 Garrido O L5 b 114 4.00 78-13 Best Venture 1141 Robin's Rob 1172 Dis Hi Fi 117½ Driving 6
16May85- 8Bel fst 7f :22⅘ :46 1:22⅘ 3+ⒻHandicap 2 6 64½ 66¾ 411 415 Garrido O L b 120 7.50 73-18 AlbmNn11411½Diplomette111nkDumdedumdedum1223¼ No threat 7
9May85- 7Bel fst 6f :22⅘ :46⅖ 1:12⅖ 3+ⒻAlw 30000 2 5 41¾ 53 2½ 12½ Garrido O L5 b 116 3.50 80-25 Best Venture 1162½ Two Ours 1211½ LotusDelight1212 Drew clear 7
28Apr85- 7Aqu fm 1 Ⓣ:47⅗ 1:12⅖ 1:36⅘ 3+ⒻHandicap 4 2 32½ 54½ 611 716¾ Velasquez J b 115 7.70 76-09 Possible Mate 1224 Lucky Touch 1102¼ Ida Lewis 1153¾ Tired 7
20Apr85- 6Aqu gd 7f :22⅘ :45⅖ 1:22⅕ 3+ⒻSarsar 2 5 3nk 32 27 27 Velasquez J b 119 27.20 83-10 Gracefully Yours 1197 Best Venture 119¾Gene'sLady121½ Gamely 8
6Apr85- 6Aqu fst 6f :22⅘ :46 1:10⅗ 3+ⒻFair Mist H 1 6 44 66¾ 68 58¾ Davis R G b 114 6.90 79-21 Gene's Lady 1153 Hare Brain 1183¾ Sharp Little Girl1121¼ Outrun 6
23Mar85- 7Aqu fst 1 :48⅕ 1:13⅕ 1:38 ⒻⓇO'alison 8 1 11 1hd 21½ 22¾ Davis R G b 117 3.20 73-23 Hare Brain 1192¾ Best Venture 1173¼ExplicitGal115hd Best others 9
3Mar85- 7Aqu fst 6f ⊡:22⅗ :46⅗ 1:12⅕ ⒻⓇC'flax Maid 5 8 53 52 41¼ 2¾ Garrido O L b 117 5.60 82-17 Satch 115¾ Best Venture 117¾ Gnash 115½ Rallied 9

Free Saint ✻ — B. m. 7, by Freepet—Mary Saint, by Lord Date
Own.—Spiegel R | Br.—North Star Ranch (Fla) | Tr.—Schaeffer Stephen
117 | Lifetime 92 14 13 17 $262,458 | 1985 9 2 1 2 $60,980 | 1984 24 3 4 6 $82,930 | Turf 13 0 2 2 $10,530

20Jun85- 8Bel fst 1⅛ :47⅘ 1:12⅖ 1:51⅗ 3+ⒻAlw 40000 1 3 31 36½ 311 314¼ Davis R G b 119 13.50 54-24 Basie 12213¼ Endear 1111¼ Free Saint 119¾ Even try 6
3Jun85- 8Bel fst 1 :46⅖ 1:11⅕ 1:37⅗ 3+ⒻAlw 40000 5 1 1hd 2hd 21½ 54 Davis R G b 117 2.50 74-13 Best Venture 1141 Robin's Rob 1172 Dis Hi Fi 117½ Tired 6
2May85- 8Aqu fst 1 :47⅕ 1:11⅘ 1:37⅕ 3+ⒻAlw 40000 4 2 4nk 41½ 45½ 46½ Privitera R5 b 116 6.70 73-26 Gene's Lady1214ⒹQueenAlexandra108¾LizMatizz1191¾ Weakened 5
2May85-Placed third through disqualification
6Apr85- 9GS fst 170 :46⅘ 1:11⅗ 1:42 ⒻAlw 25000 6 2 1hd 2½ 32½ 43½ Privitera R5 b 111 *1.70 — — Rose and Betty 114¾You'reTooSpecial1142¼Given114hd Weakened 7
22Mar85- 7Aqu fst 1 :47⅖ 1:12 1:38 ⒻClm 75000 2 3 1hd 11 11 11¾ Privitera R5 b 107 *1.50e 76-27 Free Saint 1071¾ Ida Lewis 1053½ Wench 1071¾ Driving 8
2Mar85- 7Aqu fst 1 1/16 ⊡:47⅗ 1:12⅘ 1:45⅘ ⒻAlw 40000 6 4 32 21 54 56½ Privitera R5 b 114 8.90 75-19 Give Me AHint114nkGene'sLady1152¾OwnedByAll115¾ Wide, tired 7
23Feb85- 7Aqu fst 170 ⊡:48⅖ 1:13⅕ 1:44⅕ ⒻAlw 40000 7 3 2hd 1½ 11 12½ Privitera R7 b 108 4.80 79-21 Free Saint 1082¼ Irish Liberal 108hd Mepache 115½ Drew off 7
25Jan85- 8Aqu fst 6f ⊡:22⅕ :45⅖ 1:10⅘ ⒻAlw 36000 1 6 67 69½ 68 47¾ Davis R G b 115 12.80 82-23 Jolly Mariner 1174¼ Yolanda 1172¼ Gnash 1151½ Never prominent 6
13Jan85- 3Aqu fst 6f ⊡:23 :46⅗ 1:12 ⒻClm 75000 5 5 53¼ 43½ 45½ 24 Privitera R7 b 105 14.70 80-27 Jolly Mariner 1174 Free Saint 1051½ Gnash 116¾ Rallied 7
12Nov84- 8Med gd 1 1/16 :47⅘ 1:13⅕ 1:46 3+ⒻAlw 25000 6 3 33 33½ 47 611 Privitera R7 b 108 2.50 68-28 Bright Choice 1155 Concord Hymn 110½ Al's Annie 115½ Tired 6
LATEST WORKOUTS ●Jly 11 Bel tr.t 6f fst 1:13⅘ h | Jly 5 Bel tr.t 4f fst :48⅖ h | Jun 29 Bel tr.t 4f fst :47⅘ h | Jun 18 Bel tr.t 4f gd :47⅘ h

races originally designed to give fillies more chances to gain the stakes placings that will adorn their catalog page when they or their offspring are offered at public auction. In actuality, most of these races are nothing more than classified allowances with names, perhaps sporting a purse $10,000 higher than the usual classified booty. Notice that Hare Brain's performance in the Grade III Affectionately was dismal. She would be no match for a real Grade I or II filly, like Solar Halo or any others she may encounter in this field.

SALLY THE SHIEK

Although recently placed against top-class state-bred rivals, while in receipt of gobs of weight, Sally The Shiek was only recently "outrun" by claiming rivals, and earlier had been no match for Hare Brain in the O'Allison. Her lifetime (and recent) win pecentage is alarmingly low for this kind of competition.

GENE'S LADY

A winner twice in 1985, once at six furlongs, Gene's Lady's form has fallen off of late. Her recent lack of early speed is a strong clue that the filly is in need of a freshening.

BEST VENTURE

A complicated study. Best Venture's grass races can be ignored, and her races behind the fleet Alabama Nana are not as bad as they first appear to be. However, she is no more than a good classified filly at best.

FREE SAINT

Winner of a classified race in February and a claiming race since, this seven-year-old mare is not of stakes quality.

DOWERY

A "feature-race" stakes winner at Calder, Keystone, and Laurel, Dowery has won eleven of her seventeen lifetime starts. More significant, however, is her recent performance in the Grade II Molly Pitcher Handicap at Monmouth, in which she raced competitively to the stretch call with the likes of Mitterand and Sefa's Beauty, two of the ranking handicap mares in the country, while in receipt of just four pounds from each. Anyone who wanted to take a shot against Solar Halo would have welcomed this filly's presence in the race. She had the kind of stakes quality needed to compete with Solar Halo and was clearly a notch or two above the other fillies in the race.

At first glance, 2–1 odds on Dowery might not seem enticing. But the fact that Solar Halo was being offered at an overly generous 6–5 suggested the obvious: The favorite was not seriously meant for this race. With that reassurance, Dowery was a great bet at 2–1 to outclass the remainder of this field. She did win, returning $6.60, with Solar Halo off the board.

SEVENTH RACE
Belmont
JULY 18, 1985

1 1/16 MILES. (1.40⅖) ALLOWANCE. Purse $40,000. Fillies and mares, 3-year-olds and upward which have not won two races of $16,500 at a mile or over since January 1. Weights, 3-year-olds, 116 lbs.; older, 122 lbs. Non-winners of a race of $15,000 at a mile or over since May 15 allowed 3 lbs.; of such a race since April 1, 5 lbs.; of such a race since February 1, 7 lbs. (Maiden, claiming, starter and State-Bred races not considered.)
Value of race $40,000; value to winner $24,000; second $8,800; third $4,800; fourth $2,400. Mutuel pool $116,620, OTB pool $83,794. Exacta Pool $200,601. OTB Exacta Pool $146,009.

Last Raced	Horse	Eqt.	A.	Wt	PP	St	¼	½	¾	Str	Fin	Jockey	Odds $1
6Jly85 9Mth3	Dowery		4	115	7	1	5²	3½	1¹	1¹½	1¾	Vasquez J	2.30
11Jly85 8Bel3	Best Venture	b	4	115	5	3	3¹	4²	3¹½	2¹	2²¼	Espinosa R E7	16.60
5Jly85 8GS3	Gene's Lady	b	4	119	4	2	1¹½	1¹	2hd	3²½	3⁴¼	Velasquez J	3.00
6Jly85 6Bel6	Hare Brain	b	5	117	1	7	6hd	5½	5⁶	4³	4¹½	McCarron G	11.40
22Dec84 8Aqu1	Solar Halo		4	115	2	6	2½	2¹½	4½	5¹	5nk	Migliore R	1.30
26Jun85 3Bel7	Sally The Shiek		5	110	3	4	7	7	6½	6¹½	6nk	Alvarez A7	13.00
20Jun85 8Bel3	Free Saint	b	7	117	6	5	4hd	6¹	7	7	7	Davis R G	31.90

OFF AT 4:09. Start good. Won driving. Time, :23⅕, :46, 1:10⅗, 1:36⅗, 1:43⅖ Track fast.

$2 Mutuel Prices:				
	7-(G)-DOWERY	6.60	3.80	2.80
	5-(E)-BEST VENTURE		8.40	4.60
	4-(D)-GENE'S LADY			3.20
	$2 EXACTA 7-5 PAID $75.40.			

B. f, by Full Pocket—Vaguely Royal, by Vaguely Noble. Trainer Alexander Frank A. Bred by Hillstead Farm (Ky).

DOWERY moved to the fore from the outside on the turn, settled into the stretch with a clear advantage and was roused to turn back BEST VENTURE. The latter rallied along the inside leaving the turn and continued on with good energy. GENE'S LADY showed speed to the stretch and tired. HARE BRAIN moved up along the inside leaving the turn but lacked a further response. SOLAR HALO tired. FREE SAINT was finished early.

Chapter 11

The Class Handicapper's Projection Method

In several racing locales the starter handicap/allowance has become the sport's American Buffalo—if not extinct, then at best a seriously endangered species. Racing secretaries complain that these races draw similar fields week after week, with a high percentage of winning favorites, both of which, they feel, add up to a lower than average handle. Needless to say, the starter handicap is replaced by something more likely to stimulate heavier betting action—a maiden-claiming race, for example!

I always welcomed the challenge offered by these races, and fondly recall the good old days in New York when Saturday's nightcap was usually the week's starter 'cap. And if a small group of horses seemed to dominate these races, they did so over a variety of route distances, on both dirt and turf, while carrying increasingly higher weights. The starter handicaps gave cheaper animals a chance to emulate their stakes-winning brethren, offering them, if successful, the chance to prove their weight-carrying ability, and to gain a special identity they could never have achieved in the claiming ranks.

The popular axiom about playing starter races is that the best bet is the horse that has recently won such a race. While our methodology in this chapter will be different, it will no doubt focus attention quite frequently on exactly these horses. However, we must point out that this will not be the case in our example race, the second at Belmont on June 20, 1984, due to the scarcity of starter races in New York that year.

Starter races are a class handicapper's delight. Although Thoroughbreds were not all created equal, the contestants in the typical

2 BELMONT

INNER TURF COURSE
1⅜ MILES
BELMONT PARK
START FINISH

1⅜ MILES. (InnerTurf). (2.11⅘) STARTER HANDICAP. Purse $14,000. 3-year-olds and upward, which have started for a claiming price of $16,000 or less since November 1, 1983. Weights Saturday, June 16. Declarations by 10:00 A.M., Monday, June 18.

Coupled—Superior Judge and Wimborne Castle; Mock Court and Heroic Spirit.

Superior Judge
Ro. g. 4, by Judger—Rain Dance, by Native Charger
Br.—Hancock III & Peters (Ky)
Tr.—DeBonis Robert
Own.—Misilipin Stable
108
Lifetime 30 4 2 4 $32,315 | 1984 12 0 1 2 $9,790 | 1983 18 4 1 2 $22,525 | Turf 2 0 0 0

14Jun84- 1Bel fst 1⅛ :47⅘ 1:13 1:51⅗ Clm 12000 8 8 89½ 46½ 47½ 49 Smith A Jr b 113 14.90 61-23 HughCpt119¾Rjb'sSon112nkRghtosAngs1177¾ Lacked a response 8
31May84- 1Bel sly 1¼ :48 1:38⅘ 2:05 Clm 16500 8 8 812 712 613 615¾ Vega H7 b 108 15.90 57-21 Milieu 1131 Protest 11511½ Jet Voyage 1123 No factor 8
19May84- 1Bel fst 1½ :50 2:07 2:32⅘ Clm 16000 4 7 79 78 611 618 Smith A Jr 117 11.60 40-26 Heroic Spirit 1157 Milieu 1132½ Sestrel 113hd No factor 7
7May84- 9Aqu fst 1⅛ :50⅘ 1:14⅘ 1:53⅗ Clm c-12500 9 4 42½ 32 21½ 51¾ Velasquez J b 117 *2.10 65-22 Sweet Believer 117nk Sestrel 119no Dissatisfaction 108nk Hung 9
26Apr84- 1Aqu fst 1⅛ :48⅘ 1:13⅘ 1:51⅘ Clm 16000 4 1 2hd 44 46½ 46½ Velasquez J b 117 2.90 69-26 John's Medicine 1131¾ HeroicSpirit1152LovingGesture1132½ Tired 7
2Apr84- 3Aqu fst 1⅛ ⊡:47⅘ 1:12 1:51⅘ Clm 30000 6 11 1112 1112 1014 913¼ Murphy D J b 113⁴ 18.60 70-17 Gauguin Native 1063¼ Bishen 1173¼ Full Concert 1131 Outrun 11
2Apr84-Dead heat
10Mar84- 9Aqu fst 1⅛ ⊡:48 1:13⅘ 1:53⅘ Clm 20000 11 12 1114 65 1½ 2¾ Velasquez J b 117 16.40 72-24 Jungle Marsh 114¾ Superior Judge 117hd Milieu 1176½ Game try 12
11Mar84- 3Aqu fst 1⅛ ⊡:51⅕ 1:15⅘ 1:54⅘ Clm 22500 3 10 109¾ 1010 66 45¼ Velasquez J b 115 20.90 66-23 Hall Of Honor 1171 Mr. Showbiz 1173 PurelyAPrince1081¼ Rallied 10
10Feb84- 1Aqu fst 1½ ⊡:49 2:08⅘ 2:35⅕ Hcp 10000s 3 8 813 32½ 35 37 Migliore R b 112 6.50 65-20 Lddy'sLuck1242PerlAmber1125SuperiorJudg112hd Bid; weakened 10
30Jan84- 3Aqu fst 1⅟₁₆ ⊡:48⅘ 1:14 1:47⅕ Clm 22500 8 12 129¼ 109¼ 77½ 65¼ Lovato F Jr b 115 10.30 71-25 Colonel Law 114¾SwapforPower119¾MorningReview1171¾ Outrun 12

LATEST WORKOUTS Jun 8 Bel tr.t 3f fst :37 b May 27 Bel tr.t 3f gd :38 b May 15 Bel tr.t 4f fst :50 b Apr 21 Aqu 5f fst 1:05 b

Commander Almy
B. g. 4, by Bold Commander—June Almy, by Whodunit
Br.—Snowden H Jr (NY)
Tr.—Nadler Herbert
Own.—Four Drake Stable
108
Lifetime 15 1 4 0 $22,650 | 1984 10 1 3 0 $19,850 | 1982 5 M 1 0 $2,800

10Jun84- 2Bel fst 7f :22⅘ :46 1:24⅗ Clm c-12000 2 9 87¼ 76½ 76½ 73¾ Davis R G b 113 4.20 75-20 Few Pence 114nk ComeUpPence108nkWimborneCastle119nk Wide 12
23May84- 1Bel fst 7f :22⅘ :46⅕ 1:24⅗ Clm 12000 5 5 74½ 43½ 31 2½ Davis R G b 113 6.20f 79-16 Rasselas 119½ CommanderAlmy1132BrightSearch117hd Outgamed 14
9May84- 9Bel fst 6f :23⅕ :46⅗ 1:11⅕ Clm 14000 11 6 99¼ 77½ 85¾ 85¼ Velasquez J 113 15.90 80-21 Creme De La Fete 119hd Rasselas 117½ No Heir 1032 Wide 11
29Apr84- 2Aqu fst 6f :22⅗ :46 1:11⅕ Clm 18000 1 7 54 54½ 63¼ 74¾ Bailey J D 113 7.30 80-18 Bouliabase 1131¾ I'm Peppy 117hd Jet Voyage 1151½ Weakened 10
21Apr84- 2Aqu fst 7f :24⅘ :48⅘ 1:26⅘ 3+ ⓈAlw 24500 2 4 73½ 55 29 25¼ Bailey J D 121 16.60 62-30 Sincere Wish 1125¼CommanderAlmy1212¼GuyPebo121hd Steadied 9
13Apr84- 7Aqu fst 1⁷⁰ ⊡:48⅘ 1:14 1:45⅕ 3+ ⓈAlw 26000 9 3 32½ 32 32½ 65 Davis R G 121 11.80 69-22 Triangulation 121hd Guy Pebo 121no Tenancy 1212½ Tired 10
1Apr84- 9Aqu fst 6f ⊡:22⅕ :45⅘ 1:11⅘ 3+ ⓈAlw 24500 11 2 78 76½ 64 43¾ Davis R G 121 7.90 82-19 Talc Duster 1121¾SincereWish113¾Tenancy1211½ Lacked final bid 12
18Mar84- 2Aqu fst 6f ⊡:23 :47⅘ 1:12⅘ ⓈAlw 24500 9 3 41½ 2hd 1hd 21½ Cordero A Jr 117 4.10 79-24 Fletcher 1171½ Commander Almy 117¾ Guy Pebo 117nk Gamely 10
3Mar84- 5Aqu fst 1⅟₁₆ ⊡:49⅘ 1:15⅕ 1:50 ⓈAlw 27000 1 1 1hd 1hd 2½ 54¾ Muino M M7 110 10.60 57-29 DamascusJet122hdWlkmileinmyshoes1123Loughre1171 Weakened 8
8Feb84- 2Aqu fst 6f ⊡:23⅕ :47⅘ 1:13 Md 12000 7 2 43½ 3½ 1½ 12 Muino M M7 111 4.50 79-19 CommnderAlmy1112RelStubborn1227½DesignrJns115¾ Drew clear 11

LATEST WORKOUTS Jun 14 Aqu ① 4f gd :51⅘ h (d) Jun 2 Bel tr.t 4f sly :51 b

Wimborne Castle
Dk. b. or br. h. 6, by Sir Wimborne—Amber Souffle, by Amberix
Br.—Whitney T P (NY)
Tr.—DeBonis Robert
Own.—Masilipin Stable
110
Lifetime 67 8 6 10 $213,980 | 1984 15 1 3 2 $19,800 | 1983 19 1 1 1 $22,650 | Turf 1 0 0 0

10Jun84- 2Bel fst 7f :22⅘ :46 1:24⅗ Clm 12000 7 7 76½ 64½ 42½ 3½ Smith A Jr b 119 14.00 78-20 FewPence114nkComeUpPence108nkWimborneCstle119nk In close 12
2Jun84- 3Bel sly 1⅟₁₆ :46⅘ 1:12 1:44⅗ Clm 12000 3 3 32½ 32 33 34½ Lopez V5 b 108 5.00 74-19 RighteousAngr1131¾SwpforPowr1172¾WimbornCstl108½ Even try 8
22May84- 5Mth fst 1⁷⁰ :47 1:11⅘ 1:44 3+ Clm 12500 3 2 1hd 2½ 2hd 2nk Santagata N b 116 2.80 76-25 Haligoluk 111nk Wimborne Castle 1161 Tamatar 1165 Gamely 6
18May84- 2Bel fst 6½f :23⅗ :46⅘ 1:18 Clm 15000 3 6 67½ 511 58½ 46½ Santiago A b 115 7.90 79-17 No Heir 1051½ Rasselas 1132½ Shy Hughes 1192¾ No factor 9
12May84- 9Bel fst 7f :23⅕ :47 1:23⅘ Clm 20000 9 8 74¾ 83½ 117½ 96 Bailey J D b 117 24.10 77-17 Gratification 117no Palimony 112hd J. Strap 1121½ Raced wide 12
24Apr84- 2Aqu my 7f :22⅘ :45⅘ 1:25 Clm 20000 5 11 1111 119¾ 94½ 92½ Squartino R A5 b 108 18.20 73-21 Creme De La Fete 113nkStormWarrior113hdSpyGame117¾ Outrun 11
17Apr84- 1Aqu fst 1⅜ ⊡:48⅕ 1:13⅕ 1:59 Clm c-16000 4 4 3nk 2½ 2½ 45¾ Samyn J L b 119 *1.40 77-15 Magic Michael 1171¾BeauJangles1122Roger'sPass1132 Weakened 8
31Mar84- 1Aqu gd 6f ⊡:22⅘ :45⅘ 1:11⅘ Clm 16000 7 11 109 1011 64 2no Santagata N b 119 10.30 87-15 NorthrnShrik113noWimbornCstl119½WhtAWbbt1121½ Just missed 12
21Mar84- 1Aqu fst 1⅛ ⊡:49⅘ 1:15⅕ 1:55 Clm 16000 11 3 31½ 61½ 2hd 1¾ Samyn J L b 117 *.90e 67-24 WmbrnCstl117¾FrAndSpnc1171¾ShtngDck117no Pocketed driving 12
17Mar84- 9Aqu fst 6f ⊡:23 :47⅘ 1:13 Clm 16000 5 10 108½ 96¾ 75½ 72½ Smith A Jr b 117 5.80 77-22 Royal Jove 117¾ Clinebell 115½ Bouliabase 112nk Showed little 11

*Jungle Marsh
Ch. g. 6, by Salt Marsh—Jungle Queen, by Claro
Br.—Haras La Quebrada (Arg)
Tr.—DeSanctis Ralph V
Own.—Vitale F J
115
Lifetime 37 8 3 6 $49,095 | 1984 16 5 2 2 $38,150 | 1983 8 0 0 2 $2,207 | Turf 8 2 0 0 $4,265

7Jun84- 3Bel fm 1⅜ Ⓣ:47⅕ 1:37⅘ 2:14⅗ Clm 35000 3 7 85½ 108½ 919 819½ Samyn J L 117 14.10 65-13 Oratavo 11210½ Palace 1172¾ Cannon Royal 112nk Outrun 12
28May84- 6Mth sly 1⅟₁₆ :47⅘ 1:13 1:45 3+ Clm 25000 6 — — — — — Thomas D B 116 14.20 76-19 Disco Dom 1164 Jungle Marsh 1164 Tahawas 1111½ Fog 9
21May84- 3Bel gd 1⅟₁₆ ①:47 1:12⅘ 1:44⅗ Clm 35000 2 11 1110 106½ 66 67½ Hernandez R 117 13.00 65-24 Amadandy 1122 Oliver List 1172 Kim's Chance 117¾ Wide 12
14May84- 9Bel fst 1 :45⅘ 1:11 1:35⅘ Clm 25000 5 12 1010 108½ 6 3 Hernandez R 117 16.10 75-17 Big Izzy 1139 Jet Voyage 1172 Jungle Marsh 117½ Mild rally 12
23Apr84- 1Aqu fst 1⅛ :47⅘ 1:13 1:51⅘ Clm 35000 2 5 67 65½ 59 58½ Garcia R L Jr10 109 10.70 66-20 Jet Steam 1132½ Laddy's Luck 1131¾ Terse 1172¾ Outrun 6
8Apr84- 4Aqu fst 1⅛ ⊡:47⅘ 1:12⅘ 1:51⅕ Clm 45000 5 11 118¾ 97¾ 710 915½ Hernandez R 114 31.50 71-21 Gauguin Native 1066¾ Minabchar 1171¾BlueQuadrant1171½ Outrun 12
31Mar84- 7Aqu gd 1⁷⁰ ⊡:47 1:12 1:41⅘ Clm 45000 5 9 88 96½ 811 811 Hernandez R 113 7.40 82-15 Gauley 113¾ On The Turn 1083 Jet Steam 1133½ Outrun 9
24Mar84- 9Aqu fst 1⁷⁰ ⊡:48⅕ 1:13⅘ 1:45⅗ Clm 30000 5 7 75½ 72 72½ 1no Messina R 113 9.10 73-24 JungleMarsh113noClerTheBses113hdEdgeOfWisdom113hd Driving 10
18Mar84- 9Aqu fst 1⅛ ⊡:48 1:13⅘ 1:53⅘ Clm 18000 6 9 914 77½ 41½ 1¾ Hernandez R 114 11.60 73-24 Jungle Marsh 114¾ Superior Judge 117hd Milieu 1176½ Driving 12
12Mar84- 3Aqu fst 1¼ ⊡:50⅘ 1:42⅘ 2:08 Clm c-14000 4 3 43½ 22 33 48¾ Murphy D J5 108 2.90 69-22 Creme De La Fete1157MagicMichael1131½Sestrel117nk No excuse 9

LATEST WORKOUTS Jun 15 Bel 1 fst 1:42 b May 6 Bel 6f fst 1:12⅕ h

Irish Bar
Ch. g. 4, by Barrera—Lady Regan, by King of the Tudors
Br.—Hinkle S D (Ky)
Tr.—Sallusto Justin
Own.—Sallusto J
107
Lifetime 20 3 3 1 $27,465 | 1984 10 1 1 0 $7,425 | 1983 10 2 2 1 $20,040 | Turf 4 1 0 0 $7,710

11Jun84- 5Atl fm *1⅟₁₆ ① 1:45⅕ 3+ Clm 13500 7 7 69½ 68 78½ 76½ Doran K7 105 14.10 84-11 Big Shot 1162½ Czar's Gold 1091 Gray Dude 1162 Outrun 9
2Jun84- 2Mth sly 1⅟₁₆ :47 1:12 1:45⅘ 3+ Clm 10500 6 4 410 57 56½ 6 Rocco J 112 4.20 69-21 Spellbounder 1191½ DistinguishedGent1172HastyFlight1141½ Tired 6
22May84- 5Mth fst 1⁷⁰ :47 1:11⅘ 1:44 3+ Clm 10500 5 5 55½ 57 69½ 510½ Smith A Jr b 115 2.20 66-25 Haligoluk 111nk Wimborne Castle 1161 Tamatar 1165 Outrun 6
16May84- 9Bel fst 1⅟₁₆ :46⅗ 1:11⅕ 1:44 Clm 13000 5 6 74½ 59 812 813¼ Garrido O L10 b 105 15.20 69-17 HeroicSpirit1172¾RighteousAnger117nkSweetBeliever1171 Outrun 11
5May84- 2Aqu gd 1 :47 1:12 1:37⅘ Clm 14000 5 4 53½ 42½ 47½ 48½ Smith A Jr b 113 5.30 68-16 Mock Court 1171 Heroic Spirit 1172¾Rasselas1174¾ Well up; tired 9
14Apr84- 2GP fst 1⅟₁₆ :47⅘ 1:12⅘ 1:44 Clm 10000 7 4 43½ 41¾ 32 11½ McCauley W H 117 *1.90 81-15 Irish Bar 1171½ Erd The Third 117no No Hunting1158½ Drew clear 11
17Mar84- 4GP fst 1⅟₁₆ :48⅘ 1:13 1:44⅘ Clm 16000 4 3 31½ 32 22 22 McCauley W H 117 5.10 75-17 Jungle Minister 1132 Irish Bar 1172 Humour 1171 Game try 8
5Mar84- 3Hia fst 7f :23 :45⅘ 1:23⅘ Clm 10000 7 4 74½ 57 56½ 44 McCauley W H 114 6.80 82-23 Dust Off The Mat 116½ CatchVilla1132CatchAndRun1161½ Rallied 10
15Feb84- 9Hia fst 7f :23⅘ :46 1:23⅕ Clm 18000 4 8 83¾ 87½ 65½ 64½ McCauley W H 112 15.60 82-19 Poppy Pepper 1161¾ Dragon Slayer 116nkTopCase1121½ No factor 12
20Jan84- 3Hia fst 7f :23 :46⅕ 1:23⅘ Clm 25000 8 9 85½ 104¾ 912 1010¾ Brumfield D 116 24.50 73-17 Apache Company 1161 Iron Hawk114noChocovicPark1172 Outrun 11

Nibroc
B. h. 5, by Roberto—Tremont Road, by Damascus
Br.—Phillips Mr-Mrs J W (Ky)
Tr.—Marcus Alan B
Own.—Marcus A B
106
Lifetime 20 1 5 0 $18,700 | 1984 9 0 1 0 $3,090 | 1983 10 1 4 0 $15,490 | Turf 1 0 0 0

11Jun84- 5Atl fm *1⅟₁₆ ① 1:45⅕ 3+ Clm 15500 1 9 914 910 66½ 65¾ Alvarado R Jr 116 3.90 85-11 Big Shot 1162½ Czar's Gold 1091 Gray Dude 1162 Outrun 9
23May84- 1Bel fst 7f :22⅘ :46⅕ 1:24⅗ Clm 12000 11 11 1413 1415 12 11 Velasquez J 113 31.00 69-16 Rasselas119½CommanderAlmy1132BrightSearch117hd Raced wide 14
12May84- 2Key fst 1⅟₁₆ :46⅗ 1:11⅕ 1:44⅗ 3+ Clm 11000 9 4 47½ 74¾ 67½ 44¾ D'Agusto J G 117 6.30 77-20 Swift And Proud 112no Plaza Prince 117hdBareTail1174¾ Mild bid 10
26Apr84- 5Aqu fst 7f :23⅗ :47⅘ 1:26⅗ Clm 10000 7 3 75 77 62½ 2¾ Velasquez J 117 7.50 68-26 Dancer's Moment 113¾ Nibroc 117¾ Jef Fix 117¾ Wide 8
21Apr84- 5Key fst 1⁷⁰ :46⅘ 1:12⅕ 1:42 Clm 12000 5 8 812 712 68½ 48½ Vega A 112 18.40 81-18 Hey Man 1163½ Goose Grease 1141½ Prontereno 1183¾ Rallied 8
12Mar84- 9Aqu fst 6f ⊡:23⅕ :47 1:13⅕ Clm 10000 9 12 1213 1215 128¾ 127½ Velasquez J 117 9.50 71-22 LeWshingtonin1072¾ExecutiveSwinger117noPrincePr108¾ Outrun 12
8Mar84- 3Aqu fst 6f ⊡:23⅕ :47⅘ 1:12⅘ Clm 12500 10 7 96¾ 107½ 66 64½ Ward W10 107 10.70 76-24 Clinebell 117¾ Son Number One 117nk No Additives 117¾ Wide 10
5Feb84- 9Aqu sly 6f ⊡:22⅘ :46⅘ 1:12⅘ Clm 16000 5 11 119¾ 1116 911 812 Graell A 117 17.70 70-25 FlyingGeneral1125RapidWing110¾DoubleDifference108hd Outrun 11
27Jan84- 9Aqu gd 6f ⊡:22⅕ :45⅘ 1:11 Clm 16000 6 7 55½ 1013 — — Graell A 117 11.40 — — Royal Duel 1174 Shaz 115hd Hawaiian Moonshine1141½ Lost irons 12
23Dec83- 2Aqu gd 6f ⊡:22⅘ :46⅘ 1:12⅘ 3+ Clm 25000 9 7 78½ 88½ 1011 109 Santagata N 117 42.00 72-21 Bright Search 117no Jeffery C. 1172TheBloodyBest117¾ No speed 10

LATEST WORKOUTS Jun 8 Bel tr.t 3f fst :39⅘ b ● Jun 7 Bel Ⓣ 5f gd 1:00⅘ b (d)

Lypharel
Ch. h. 5, by Lyphard—Arrelle, by Timmy My Boy
Br.—Guest R R (Va)
Tr.—Barbara R
Own.—Town Circle Stable
114
Lifetime 18 1 0 0 $11,160 | 1984 2 0 0 0 | 1983 10 0 0 0 $360 | Turf 7 1 0 0 $10,800

15Jun84- 2Bel fm 1¼ Ⓣ:50 1:40⅕ 2:05⅕ Clm 45000 7 2 1hd 77½ 817 819½ Santagata N 113 41.50 49-18 Monkey Bread 1133½ Val De La Meuse 117hd Broadly 1173½ Tired 10
27Jan84- 9Aqu gd 6f ⊡:22⅕ :45⅘ 1:11 Clm 16000 10 8 1012 1115 1015 1111¾ Santagata N 117 42.10 77-16 Royal Duel 1174 Shaz 115hd Hawaiian Moonshine 1141½ Outrun 12
14Nov83- 3Aqu fst 6f :23 :46 1:11⅘ 3+ Clm 14000 13 11 76½ 1114 1113 1110½ McNeil F A 117 44.40 73-24 Another Rodger 1131½ Ample Native 113nk Jef Fix 1171½ Outrun 14
10Nov83- 3Med sly 1⁷⁰ :47⅘ 1:13⅘ 1:45⅕ 3+ Clm 22500 5 3 56 515 417 531 McCauley W H 114 10.40 44-27 Hagline 1147 Floating Fury 11512½ Scarlet Invader 1197½ Outrun 6
7Nov83- 9Aqu fst 6f :22⅘ :45⅘ 1:11 3+ Clm 25000 2 9 710 713 714 714½ Thibeau R J b 117 27.80 72-22 CndinCurrency1173¾Meteorite1175½LitlHutch1152½ Broke slowly 9
17Oct83- 3Bel fst 6f :22⅘ :46 1:10⅕ 3+ Clm 25000 6 8 57 69 68 610½ Thibeau R J5 b 112 31.20 81-16 Ladies Fool 1152½ Come UpPence1152½Tarantara1152½ Slow start 8
29Sep83- 9Bel fst 6f :23 :46⅕ 1:11⅕ 3+ Clm 25000 9 10 75 96¾ 109½ 1013½ Douglas R R5 b 112 42.20 72-17 RighteousAngr1151¾JffryC.1171½ThundrBridg108¾ Stumbled early 10
4Sep83- 3Bel fst 6f :22⅘ :45⅘ 1:10⅘ 3+ Clm 30000 5 6 54¾ 64½ 75¾ 77¾ Bailey J D b 113 18.20 82-13 Fanny's Fox 117¾ Jeffery C. 117½ Prete Khale 1193 Tired 7
24Aug83- 2Bel fm 1¼ Ⓣ:48⅘ 1:38 2:02⅕ 3+ Clm 35000 2 4 31½ 66¾ 821 827¾ Rivera M A b 113 32.40 55-12 Rich Butterfly 1152 El Lute 1132 Explodent Bay 113no Tired 11
15Aug83- 3Sar fst 7f :22⅘ :45⅘ 1:22⅕ 3+ Clm 45000 3 8 53½ 54 611 916½ Rivera M A b 113 27.40 75-15 Bright Search 113¾ Crockford Lad 1174¾Moro1132 Steadied start 9

LATEST WORKOUTS Jun 14 Aqu ① 5f gd 1:05⅘ b (d) ● Jun 7 Aqu ① 7f fm 1:31 b (d) May 24 Aqu 6f gd 1:14⅘ h May 10 Aqu ① 3f fm :38⅘ b (d)

Amadandy
Gr. g. 4, by Greenough—Amadoll, by Amerullah
Br.—Hitching Post Farm (NC)
Tr.—Galimi Michael T
Own.—Berke M
116
Lifetime 25 3 1 1 $29,080 | 1984 15 2 0 1 $18,150 | 1983 10 1 1 0 $10,930 | Turf 2 1 0 0 $10,500

28May84- 2Bel fm 1⅛ ①:46⅘ 1:12⅘ 1:43⅘ Clm 45000 4 9 11⁵ 91⁴ 79 712¾ Skinner K 113 7.70 66-19 Crown 113¾ Fearless Leader 117hd Pumas Pride 115no Outrun 11
21May84- 3Bel gd 1⅛ ①:47 1:12⅘ 1:44⅘ Clm 35000 4 7 52½ 53 2½ 12 Giacomo A5 112 58.10 73-24 Amadandy 112² Oliver List 117² Kim's Chance 117¾ Drew clear 12
13May84- 9Bel fst 6f :22⅗ :46 1:11 Clm 12000 6 9 10⁹ 12⁹ 94½ 66 Skinner K 114 22.80 78-17 Rasselas 117½ Little Hutch 113⅘ Bright Search 117no Raced wide 12
4May84- 2Aqu gd 1⅛ :47⅗ 1:12 1:52 Clm 10000 2 2 2½ 2½ 33½ 45¾ Giacomo A5 112 11.30 69-24 DomAndJerry1171¼FourAndSixpence1172ShntyToCstl1172¼ Tired 8
26Apr84- 5Aqu fst 7f :23⅗ :47⅘ 1:26⅘ Clm 10000 5 6 1hd 41 84 87¼ Messina R b 119 6.40 62-26 Dancer's Moment 113¾ Nibroc 117¾ Jef Fix 117¾ Tired 8
13Apr84- 9Aqu fst 6f ⊡:23⅗ :47⅘ 1:11⅘ Clm 11500 9 6 52 52½ 45½ 57¾ Skinner K b 117 6.10 78-22 Boulibs1175¾NightlyBttl113noHwiinMoonshn1121 Wide, weakened 9
6Apr84- 9Aqu fst 6f ⊡:22⅘ :46⅘ 1:12⅘ Clm 10000 2 11 57½ 58 43 1hd Skinner K b 117 4.90 81-18 Amdndy117hdExprsswyHom106nkBbb'sPlsr112¾ Off slowly,drivng 11
31Mar84- 9Aqu gd 6f ⊡:22⅘ :45⅘ 1:10⅘ Clm 10000 2 5 21½ 33½ 36½ 36 Muino M M7 b 110 5.10 84-15 HandsomeDancer1082¾RainPrince1133¾Amadndy1103½ Weakened 7
21Mar84- 9Aqu fst 6f ⊡:22⅘ :46⅘ 1:12⅘ Clm 10000 1 10 64½ 56 54½ 53 Muino M M7 b 110 18.70 78-24 On the Helm 112² No Toast 117no Rain Prince 1081 Rallied 12
~~14Mar84- 9Aqu gd 1⅛ ⊡:48⅗ 1:13⅘ 1:54⅘ Clm 12500 2 2 21 76 99 914¾ Muino M M7 b 110 11.60 56-26 FourAndSixpence1173¾Runnymeade117noRdioNews1124¾ Stopped 9~~
LATEST WORKOUTS Jun 18 Aqu 6f fst 1:18⅗ b Jun 14 Aqu ① 4f gd :51 h (d) ●Jun 7 Aqu ① 6f fm 1:15⅘ h (d)

Ultimate Native
B. c. 4, by Native Host—Mahogany Lady, by Petrone
Br.—Wilson Constance S (Cal)
Tr.—Sciacca Gary J
Own.—Malkin P
109
Lifetime 43 2 5 3 $35,560 | 1984 8 1 1 0 $11,100 | 1983 23 1 2 3 $19,570 | Turf 8 0 0 2 $3,470

3Jun84- 10Mth fm 1 ①:47⅘ 1:11⅘ 1:38 3↑Clm 18000 1 5 74¾10⁸¾ 812 88¼ Skinner K b 114 43.50 77-09 ThrGrndson's113noGntry'sImg1141¼Rightorwrongfrnk117no Tired 11
2Jun84- 3Bel sly 1⅛ :46⅘ 1:12 1:44⅘ Clm 14000 1 5 64½ 57½ 55¼ 45 Messina R b 117 11.70 74-19 RighteousAngr1131¾SwpforPowr1172¾WimbornCstl108¾ Even try 8
21May84- 3Bel gd 1⅛ ①:47 1:12⅘ 1:44⅘ Clm 35000 5 3 31 74¾10⁹¾10¹2¼ Smith A Jr b 117 66.90 61-24 Amadandy 112² Oliver List 117² Kim's Chance 117¾ Tired 12
13May84- 1Bel fst 1 :46⅘ 1:11⅘ 1:36⅘ Clm 16000 5 1 53¾ 91³ 91⁶ 918¾ Smith A Jr b 117 24.90 63-17 Time Together 117nk Creme De La Fete 117³ Thaut 108no Tired 9
6Apr84- 3Aqu fst 1⁷⁰ ⊡:46⅘ 1:11 1:42⅘ Clm 19000 3 4 58¾ 91⁸ 92³ 925¾ Smith A Jr b 115 8.10 62-18 Palimony 1065¾ Rajab's Son 1174 J. Strap 1121 Tired 10
24Feb84- 9Aqu fst 1⅛ ⊡:47⅘ 1:12⅘ 1:52⅘ Clm 15000 8 2 2½ 1hd 1½ 1no Smith A Jr b 115 14.90 81-19 Ultimate Native 115noBeauJangles1171¼SpiritedSong113no Lasted 12
15Feb84- 2Aqu sly 1⁷⁰ ⊡:48⅘ 1:13⅘ 1:44⅘ Clm 12500 6 1 1½ 13 2½ 22¾ Smith A Jr b 117 11.20 77-23 Hall Of Honor 1172¾ UltimateNative117½Pitchpipe113¾ Weakened 10
13Jan84- 1Aqu fst 1⅝ ⊡:50⅘ 2:37⅘ 3:03⅘ Hcp 12500s 3 2 45 812 — — Messina R b 112 18.60 — — Lively Teddy 116¾ Laddy's Luck1221FactAndFable1119 Distanced 10
26Dec83- 9Aqu fst 1⅛ ⊡:49⅘ 1:16 2:00⅘ Clm 12500 2 1 11¼ 11½ 1½ 22 Messina R5 b 112 9.10 42-36 Fort Collins 117² Ultimate Native 1121¾HistoryBelle108nk Gamely 12
~~18Dec83- 9Aqu fst 1⅛ ⊡:48⅘ 1:14⅘ 1:49 Clm 16000 5 4 41¾ 65½ 65¾ 54¾ Davis R G b 117 11.10 62-25 Pitchpipe 1131½ John's Medicine 108¾ Fort Collins 117no No rally 12~~
LATEST WORKOUTS ●May 17 Aqu ① 3f gd :36⅘ h (d)

Masmak
B. g. 5, by Personality—Kitty Malone, by Better Bee
Br.—Varbest Stable (Ky)
Tr.—Marks Mervin
Own.—Shapiro T
112
Lifetime 26 2 4 4 $46,846 | 1984 1 0 0 0 $450 | 1983 6 1 0 0 $14,520 | Turf 11 0 3 1 $1,870

9Jun84- 3Pim fst 6f :23⅗ :46 1:10⅘ Clm 11500 4 5 56¾ 47¾ 48 49¾ Shaw N W 115 16.10 82-21 Chapel's Gold 1094¾ Powhattan 1132¾ Mafito 1192¾ Evenly 6
28Aug83- 8Pen fm 1 ① 1:35⅘ 3↑Alw 7500 4 7 89 711 711 714 Hutchinson C L5 108 19.40 73-18 Dr. Tipton 1131¼ SuenodeAmor114nkAdmiralWhiskers1103 Outrun 8
7Apr83- 8CT my 1⅛ :47⅘ 1:13⅘ 1:47⅘ Clm 16000 7 3 3¾ 4nk 66 710 Shaw N W 115 2.10 74-20 Mr. Frank T. 1161 Old South 1003 Eastern Counsel 1141 Tired 7
7Mar83- 7Aqu my 1⅛ ⊡:48 1:13 1:51⅘ Alw 23000 6 2 42 68¼ 724 726¼ Davis R G5 112 15.70 64-16 Groomed 117² Daring Bet 117¾ Gallant Gentleman 1172¾ Tired 7
2Feb83- 7Aqu fst 1⁷⁰ ⊡:47⅘ 1:13 1:43⅘ Alw 23000 1 3 35 67 617 720 Melendez J D5 114 16.00 65-24 Brae Axe 1101¾ Daring Bet 1174 No Heir 1221¾ Tired 7
15Jan83- 7Aqu sly 1⅛ ⊡:48⅘ 1:41 2:07⅘ Alw 22000 5 1 11¼ 11½ 14 13¾ Melendez J D5 112 9.70 80-22 Masmak 1123¾ The Mangler 1107¼ Starhitch 1173 Driving 8
7Jan83- 1Aqu gd 1⅛ ⊡:47⅘ 1:12⅘ 1:45⅘ Alw 22000 1 1 11 2hd 45¾ 411¾ Melendez J D5 112 8.40 73-16 Chapter One 1172¼ Starve Easy 117nk Ivan Lendl 1229¾ Gave way 7
18Dec82- 6Aqu fst 1⅛ ⊡:48⅘ 1:14⅘ 1:46⅘ 3↑Alw 22000 5 2 1hd 3¼ 32¼ 36¼ Miranda J 115 6.90 76-20 Cintula 115¾ Swallanga 1175¾ Masmak 115nk Weakened 8
10Dec82- 2Aqu fst 1⅛ ⊡:48⅘ 1:14⅘ 1:48⅘ 3↑Md 25000 8 2 11¼ 13 16 19¾ Miranda J 120 *.80 71-24 Masmak 1209¾ Spirited Song 116¾ Good Tune 1221¾ Ridden out 10
1Dec82- 3Aqu fst 1⁷⁰ ⊡:47⅘ 1:12⅘ 1:42⅘ 3↑Md 45000 5 2 22¾ 21¼ 21 2nk Miranda J 116 4.00 89-17 Pro 109nk Masmak 1165¼ Hugh Capet 11613 Game try 7
LATEST WORKOUTS May 5 CT 6f gd 1:20 b Apr 21 CT 4f sl :52⅘ b

***Coplis**
Ch. h. 6, by Flintham—Coplista, by Resuello
Br.—Haras San Javier (Arg)
Tr.—Aquilino Joseph
Own.—Gianca Stable
111
Lifetime 34 5 7 1 $37,239 | 1984 10 1 3 0 $17,310 | 1983 13 2 3 0 $12,404 | Turf 10 1 1 1 $5,129

14May84- 9Bel fst 1 :45⅘ 1:11 1:35⅘ Clm 25000 1 4 86¾ 87¾ 88¾ 512 Santagata N 117 16.50 74-17 Big Izzy 113¾ Jet Voyage 117² Jungle Marsh 117½ Early foot 12
2May84- 1Aqu fm 1⅛ ①:47 1:11⅘ 1:50⅘ Clm 30000 2 5 44¾ 64¾ 65¾ 75¾ Quartino R A5 108 17.20 85-09 Diwali 113¾ Oliver List 113¾ Gauguin Native 113² No factor 9
18Apr84- 5Aqu fst 6f ⊡:22⅘ :45⅘ 1:10⅘ Clm 32500 6 1 31¾ 44 55¾ 79¾ Santagata N 115 7.00 81-16 Amore Mio 1172¾ Spy Game 1132¾ Parting Crack 117hd Tired 8
5Apr84- 5Aqu sly 6f ⊡:23 :46⅘ 1:11⅘ Clm 22500 4 1 1½ 11½ 12 12¾ Santagata N 115 8.40 85-25 Coplis 1152¾ Spy Game 117² Starbinia 1172¾ Ridden out 9
11Mar84- 5Aqu fst 6f ⊡:22⅘ :46⅘ 1:12⅘ Clm 20000 7 2 42¾ 21¾ 21¾ 22¾ Skinner K 117 6.50 79-23 Rauschenberg 1142¾ Coplis 117no Ample Native 1171½ Gamely 12
3Mar84- 9Aqu fst 6f ⊡:22⅘ :47 1:13⅘ Clm 20000 7 8 53¾ 43¾ 43 23¾ Skinner K 117 7.60 74-29 Fleet Receiver 1103¾ Coplis 117no Ample Native 117hd Rallied 11
20Feb84- 1Aqu fst 6f ⊡:22⅘ :45⅘ 1:11⅘ Clm 16000 6 7 64¾ 52¾ 32¾ 2½ Skinner K 117 16.80 86-16 Our Man Valentine112½Coplis117nkDoubleDifference1101½ Rallied 10
15Feb84- 9Aqu sly 6f ⊡:22⅘ :46⅘ 1:11⅘ Clm 19000 2 6 46 45½ 55¾ 65 Skinner K 115 13.50 81-23 AppelAffirmed117¾KentuckyEdd1172Ruschenberg113¾ Weakened 12
26Jan84- 9Aqu my 6f ⊡:22⅘ :45⅘ 1:10⅘ Clm 20000 3 5 52¾10⁸¾10⁷¼10⁶¾ Skinner K 116 29.90 85-10 Bold Target 115¾ Spy Game 1131 J. Strap 110hd Outrun 10
14Jan84- 9Aqu fst 6f ⊡:22⅘ :46⅘ 1:11⅘ Clm 15000 7 6 42 55¾ 67 54¾ Graell A 115 11.30 80-17 Spy Game 1171½ Stage Gossip 1102 Bright Search 117½ Even try 12
LATEST WORKOUTS Jun 7 Aqu ① 4f fm :51 b (d) ●May 10 Aqu ① 5f fm 1:03 b (d)

Mock Court
Dk. b. or br. c. 4, by Naskra—Brown Paper Sack, by Stratmat
Br.—Johnson Karen & Kathy M & Rosenthal (Ky)
Tr.—Barrera Oscar S
Own.—Barrera O S
122
Lifetime 28 4 5 1 $60,525 | 1984 14 3 0 0 $29,220 | ~~1983 14 1 5 1~~ $31,305

17Jun84- 1Bel fst 1⅛ :45⅘ 1:10⅘ 1:50⅘ Clm 32500 2 1 13 21 710 713¾ Davis R G b 117 *2.20e 60-22 To Erin 1152¾ Promiser 11~~2nk Irish Waters 1160¾~~ Tired 8
14Jun84- 7Bel fst 6f :22⅘ :45⅘ 1:10⅘ Clm 35000 5 10 67¾ 69 64¾ 78¾ Cruguet J b 119 2.20e 82-23 Harpers Bazaar 119¾ AmpleNative115nkColdTrailin'106hd Outrun 10
9Jun84- 1Bel fst 7f :22⅘ :45⅘ 1:22⅘ 3↑Alw 21000 6 1 74¾ 54¾ 44¾ 48 Cruguet J b 122 8.50 82-10 Vigumand 1053 Slew the Coup 1145 It's Frigid 1121 Evenly 7
2Jun84- 1Bel sly 6f :22⅘ :45⅘ 1:10⅘ 3↑Alw 33000 3 7 78¾ 78¾ 713 716¾ Cruguet J b 117 4.40e 74-19 Will Of Iron 1173¾ Vincennes Road 117hd Rollin onOver117¾ Wide 7
28May84- 7Bel fst 1⅛ :46⅘ 1:10⅘ 1:42⅘ 3↑Alw 22000 5 1 16 16 17 110 Cruguet J b 119 8.40 91-17 Mock Court 11910 Cooper's Hawk 1094¾ InnerForce1095¾ Driving 6
25May84- 7Bel fst 1 :46 1:11⅘ 1:37⅘ 3↑Alw 21000 2 3 31 1hd 46¾ 510 Samyn J L b 121 5.60 67-23 Minstrel Star 1104 Le Gosse 1163¾ Coast Range 1161½ Tired 8
14May84- 9Bel fst 1 :45⅘ 1:11 1:35⅘ Clm c-25000 8 1 14 2hd 24 411¾ Samyn J L b 117 8.90 74-17 Big Izzy 113¾ Jet Voyage 117² Jungle Marsh 117½ Used up 12
5May84- 2Aqu gd 1 :47 1:12 1:37⅘ Clm 16000 9 2 2¾ 1½ 12¾ 11 Samyn J L b 117 5.40 77-16 Mock Court 1171 Heroic Spirit 1172¾ Rasselas 1174¾ Driving 9
~~28Apr84- 2Aqu fst 1 :45⅘ 1:10⅘ 1:37⅘ Clm 10500 12 1 13 14 13 1¾ Samyn J L b 113 6.60 77-21 MockCourt113¾VnshngPrnc1171½Chtnoogchch117½ Drifted, drvng 12~~
19Apr84- 9Aqu fst 7f :23 :46⅘ 1:24⅘ Clm 20000 4 10 76 76¾ 914 815 Samyn J L 117 3.30 65-26 What AWabbit1154I'mPeppy1174BankAccount117¾ Slow st, wide 10
LATEST WORKOUTS May 20 Bel tr.t 3f fst :35⅘ h

Walk The Beach
Dk. b. or br. h. 5, by Kennedy Road—Silver Sprite, by Herbager
Br.—Frances A Genter Stable (Fla)
Tr.—DiAngelo Joseph T
Own.—Cotilletta B
111
Lifetime 42 7 7 3 $73,138 | 1984 6 0 1 0 $2,970 | ~~1983 21 4 4 4~~ $56,808 | Turf 7 1 0 0 $7,350

7Jun84- 9Bel fst 1 :46 1:11⅘ 1:37⅘ Clm 17500 11 9 10¹1 98 78 68¾ Velasquez J 117 7.80 70-17 Rasselas 1132¾ Storm Warrior 117¾ Jet Voyage 1151½ No speed 12
25May84- 2Bel fst 7f :23⅘ :46⅘ 1:24 Clm 25000 7 13 13¹2¹2¹2 98¾ 76 Velasquez J 117 29.60 76-23 Palimony 1102¾ Midway Flyer 117¾ What A Wabbit 1121 Outrun 14
16Feb84- 9Aqu my 1⅛ ⊡:46⅘ 1:11⅘ 1:44⅘ Clm c-16000 2 10 10¹3 11¹3 98¾ 911¾ Hernandez R 117 *3.00 79-10 Proud Pauper 1151 Speier's Luck117²MassAppeal1171¾ No factor 11
~~28Jan84- 9Aqu fst 1⅛ ⊡:50⅘ 1:42 2:08 Clm 16000 2 8 811 76 52 22 Murphy D J5 112 7.10 76-20 PurelyAPrince1172WlkTheBch112½OnlyJustBgun1101½ Game try 9~~
18Jan84- 2Aqu fst 1⁷⁰ ⊡:49 1:15 1:45⅘ Clm 22500 1 9 — — 612 614¾ Santagata N 115 6.00 50-35 Haunted Lad1109¾MorningReview1172Eldag'sProspect1131 Snow 10
8Jan84- 2Aqu fst 1⅛ ⊡:49 1:14⅘ 1:54⅘ Clm 25000 3 10 911 88¾ 511 57¾ McHargue D G 122 5.50 63-21 Full Concert 117no Shy Hughes 1123¾MassAppeal1131¼ No factor 11
10Dec83- 9Med fst 1⁷⁰ :47⅘ 1:13 1:43⅘ 3↑Clm 20000 2 6 68 62¾ 21¾ 1½ Rocco J 119 *2.40 84-24 WalkTheBeach119½Swallanga1163BrzendBold1162 Wide str., drv. 9
3Dec83- 9Med fst 1⁷⁰ :46⅘ 1:11⅘ 1:42⅘ 3↑Clm 22500 6 5 411 46 22¾ 11¼ Rocco J 114 5.70 90-16 Walk The Beach 1141¼ Swallanga 1148 Bay Diplomat114¾ Driving 7
19Nov83- 5Med yl 1⅛ ①:48⅘ 1:14⅘ 1:48⅘ 3↑Clm 25000 1 6 98¾ 96¾ 912 77¾ Murphy D J5 111 8.60 52-40 Pink Buffalo 111hd Davrick 1162¾ Floating Fury 1141¾ No threat 11
7Nov83- 6Med fst 1 :48⅘ 1:13⅘ 1:38⅘ 3↑Alw 14000 7 5 43 45¾ 48 410¾ McCauley W H 116 2.40 78-22 Native Groogle 1111½ Flight of Time 1137¾ Bev's Boy 1081¼ Tired 7
LATEST WORKOUTS Jun 18 Bel tr.t 4f fst :51 b May 22 Bel 5f fst 1:01 h

Milieu
Dk. b. or br. h. 5, by Le Fabuleux—Minisquaw, by Chieftain
Br.—Live Oak Stud (Fla)
Tr.—Martin Jose
Own.—Old Glory Stable
114
Lifetime 42 7 5 2 $101,540 | 1984 15 2 2 2 $28,780 | 1983 11 1 1 0 $21,060 | Turf 9 1 0 0 $11,390

7Jun84- 3Bel fm 1⅜ ⊞:47⅘ 1:37⅘ 2:14⅘ Clm 35000 12 11 12¹1 55¾ 514 515¾ Miceli M b 117 22.60 70-13 Oratavo 11216¾ Palace 1172¾ Cannon Royal 112nk Lacked Fin. bid 12
31May84- 1Bel sly 1¼ :48 1:38⅘ 2:05 Clm 15500 5 7 710 35 24 11 Miceli M b 113 5.50 73-21 Milieu 1131 Protest 1151½ Jet Voyage 1123 Driving 8
25May84- 4Bel fst 1⅛ :47⅘ 1:12⅘ 1:51⅘ Clm 14000 3 8 86¾ 66 55¾ 42¾ Miceli M b 117 5.10 67-23 HughCpet112¾OnlyJustBegun1151¾John'sMedicine117nk Wide str 9
19May84- 1Bel fst 1½ :50 2:07 2:32⅘ Clm 14000 5 5 55¾ 54¾ 35 27 Santiago A b 113 8.10 51-26 Heroic Spirit 1157 Milieu 1132¾ Sestrel 113hd Best of others 7
16May84- 9Bel fst 1⅛ :46⅘ 1:11⅘ 1:44 Clm 12000 4 10 10¹3 10¹5 711 67¾ Miceli M b 113 11.50 74-17 Heroic Spirit 1172¾ RighteousAnger117nkSweetBeliever1171 Wide 11
~~7May84- 9Aqu fst 1⅛ :50⅘ 1:14⅘ 1:53⅘ Clm 12500 2 8 96¾ 98 87¾ 84 Miceli M b 117 3.10 63-22 Sweet Believer 117nk Sestrel 119no Dissatisfaction 108nk Outrun 9~~
26Apr84- 6Aqu fst 1¼ :49⅘ 1:40⅘ 2:05 Clm 20000 3 4 64¾ 69 614 613¾ Miceli M b 117 2.60 58-26 Magic Michael 1131¾ Rajab'sSon1195BeauJangles1084¾ Stumbled 6
18Mar84- 9Aqu fst 1⅛ ⊡:48 1:13⅘ 1:53⅘ Clm c-20000 1 10 10¹4 55 3¾ 3¾ Santiago A b 117 5.70 72-24 Jungle Marsh 114¾ Superior Judge 117hd Milieu 1176¾ Rallied 12
11Mar84- 3Aqu fst 1⅛ ⊡:51⅘ 1:15⅘ 1:54⅘ Clm 25000 9 7 62¾ 2½ 33¾ 64¾ Santiago A b 117 4.40 64-23 Hall Of Honor 1171Mr.Showbiz1173PurelyAPrince1081¼ Bid, tired 10
2Mar84- 5Aqu fst 1¼ ⊡:50⅘ 1:43⅘ 2:09⅘ Clm 22500 10 5 45 51¾ 22¾ 23 Santiago A b 117 5.80 68-28 Letter From Lucy1143Milieu1171¾Mr.Showbiz115¾ Best of others 10
LATEST WORKOUTS Jun 18 Bel tr.t 4f fst :49 b Jun 15 Bel tr.t 4f fst :49 b ●May 4 Bel tr.t 5f my 1:03⅘ b

Also Eligible (Not in Post Position Order):

Heroic Spirit — B. h. 5, by Naskra—Maia II, by Cipol — Br.—Whitney T P (Ky) — Tr.—Barrera Oscar S — Own.—Barrera O S — **120**

Lifetime 47 11 5 8 $162,330 — 1984 18 5 3 2 $61,470 — 1983 14 3 1 2 $52,680 — Turf 10 1 1 2 $26,620

15Jun84- 2Bel	fm	1¼	Ⓣ:50	1:40⅕	2:05⅕	Clm 45000	10	9	88½	87¾	79½	67	MacBeth D	b 113	10.80	61-18	Monkey Bread 1133½ ValDeLaMeuse117hdBroadly1173½	No factor	10
3Jun84- 5Bel	my	1¼		:48⅕ 1:38	2:03⅕	Clm 70000	7	8	87½	65½	66½	59¾	MacBeth D	b 113	3.20	72-23	Magic Michael 1131½HallOfHonor1136ClarinetKing117½	No factor	8
24May84- 5Bel	fst	1⅛		:47⅖ 1:11⅘	1:49⅕	Clm 25000	1	4	46	32½	15	16	MacBeth D	b 117	*.90e	81-15	Heroic Spirit 1176 Big Izzy 1171¾ Daring Bet 1121½	Ridden out	6
19May84- 1Bel	fst	1½		:50 2:07	2:32⅗	Clm 15000	2	3	33	12	15	17	MacBeth D	b 115	*.70	58-26	Heroic Spirit 1157 Milieu 1132¼ Sestrel 113hd	Drew off	7
16May84- 9Bel	fst	1 1/16		:46⅗ 1:11⅕	1:44	Clm 14000	1	7	53½	34½	21	12½	MacBeth D	b 117	*2.10	82-17	HeroicSpirit1172½RighteousAnger117nkSweetBlivr1171	Drew clear	11
12May84- 9Bel	fst	7f		:23⅕ :47	1:23⅘	Clm 19000	5	11	105	115½	85¾	53½	MacBeth D	b 115	6.50	80-17	Gratification 117no Palimony 112hd J. Strap 1121½	Late bid	12
5May84- 2Aqu	gd	1		:47 1:12	1:37⅘	Clm 16000	6	9	88	66½	35	21	Davis R G	b 117	2.70	76-16	Mock Court 1171 Heroic Spirit 1172¾ Rasselas 1174¾	Rallied	9
30Apr84- 4Aqu	fst	1⅛		:48⅗ 1:13⅖	1:51⅘	Clm 20000	5	4	48	33½	25	32	MacBeth D	113	2.20	74-23	SwpforPower1172MgicMichl115noHroicSpirit11312	Bid, weakened	5
26Apr84- 1Aqu	fst	1⅛		:48⅘ 1:13⅘	1:51⅘	Clm 15000	7	7	53½	55	36	21¾	MacBeth D	115	*1.00	74-26	John'sMedicine1131¾HeroicSpirit1152LovingGesture1132¾	Rallied	7
2Apr84- 3Aqu	fst	1⅛	⊡:47⅘	1:12	1:51⅘	Clm 32500	11	10	1011	97¾	810	48	MacBeth D	115	2.90e	75-17	Gauguin Native 1063½ Bishen 1173½ Full Concert 1131	Outrun	11

starter race were, at some point in their recent past, approximately equal. Each had to compete for a specific claiming price (or less) within a defined time frame in order to become eligible for the starter series. In our example, the conditions require a horse to have started for a claiming tag of $16,000 (or less) at some time since November 1, 1983. This, then, must be our starting point, and so we have drawn a line across the past performances of each entrant to indicate where it qualified for the starter series. The key to handicapping the race then becomes the simple matter of noting what each horse has done since or, in certain cases, what it was before dropping down to qualify. The prime contenders will be those horses that have moved farthest up the class ladder since qualifying, or those that were only recently racing well at a much higher level before dropping. The average starter race is won by a horse that is now valued two or three classes above the qualifying price for the race.

The race at Belmont provides a rather quick study, although it is potentially complicated by the fact that it was to be run on the grass. Only four of the starters had raced competitively above the $16,000 level since qualifying at that price, at least as far back as we can see in their past performances. These four include the 9–5 favored entry of Heroic Spirit and Mock Court, as well as Amadandy and Jungle Marsh. With the exception of Mock Court, as yet untried on turf, all qualify as competent grass runners. Note that, in this field, only Ultimate Native had recently appeared in a starter race.

The handicapping process now comes down to separating these four contenders, and this is made especially difficult because each raced poorly in its most recent start. Our task, in general, is to place a claiming tag on each horse, then choose the one with the highest current market value.

JUNGLE MARSH

A good second in the slop at Monmouth on May 28, and a closing third at a mile at Aqueduct on May 14, both for $25,000, and both at distances seemingly shorter than his best trip. It would seem fair to rate this horse somewhere between $20,000 and $25,000, and also important to note that he was soundly defeated by Amadandy on the grass between his recent good efforts.

AMADANDY

A grandson of Prince John, this gelding improved dramatically on the grass on May 21, then failed to enter contention one class higher in his next start. Clearly, he can be rated no higher than $35,000.

MOCK COURT

Top-weighted at 122 pounds, Mock Court was claimed by Oscar Barrera for $25,000 on May 14 and has won only one race since—a "nonwinners of two" allowance route that was taken off the grass. His pair of dismal performances for $35,000 since make his win suspect; he may have defeated a small band of "stuck" horses racing over a surface each detested. Mock Court's present value was clouded even more by his lack of experience on the grass. His sire, Naskra, has had only moderate success as a grass progenitor. At best, we can rate Mock Court between $20,000 and $25,000, possibly even as low as $16,000. But for grass, we can't be too certain.

HEROIC SPIRIT

This five-year-old moved as high as $25,000 for Barrera, winning very easily, but failed recently two and three classes higher. His recent race for $45,000 was certainly no worse than Amadandy's, and so his easy win for $25,000 suggests that he, too, be rated at $35,000. Four in-the-money finishes in ten races on the grass imply that class, not the surface, was the problem last time out.

Our conclusion is quite clear—Amadandy and Heroic Spirit are the class of this field. Provided they are fit, of course, and this is always a special problem with races like this. The horses we consider to be contenders in starter handicaps are usually once-cheaper animals, perhaps among the cheapest on the grounds, that have since moved up to possibly new heights but are always subject to drop back down to their previous depths. Physical problems are usually the reason they dropped low enough to qualify for these starter races, and these could surface again at any time. Unless, of course, the trainer was playing games with the claiming price, bluffing rival trainers with a possibly suspicious class drop, hoping to qualify the horse for the starter series.

In this case both horses proved fit enough to substantiate their class edge, Heroic Spirit holding off Amadandy's late charge by a nose. The winner returned $5.80, and the quinella paid a nice $14.80.

SECOND RACE
Belmont
JUNE 20, 1984

1 ⅜ MILES.(InnerTurf). (2.11⅘) STARTER HANDICAP. Purse $14,000. 3-year-olds and upward, which have started for a claiming price of $16,000 or less since November 1, 1983. Weights Saturday, June 16. Declarations by 10:00 A.M., Monday, June 18.

Value of race $14,000, value to winner $8,400, second $3,080, third $1,680, fourth $840. Mutuel pool $91,461, OTB pool $119,995. Quinella Pool $132,189. OTB Quinella Pool $151,157.

Last Raced	Horse	Eqt.	A.	Wt	PP	¼	½	¾	1	Str	Fin	Jockey	Odds $1
15Jun84 2Bel6	Heroic Spirit	b	5	120	12	7hd	7hd	6hd	2½	12½	1no	MacBeth D	b-1.90
26May84 2Bel7	Amadandy		4	116	7	62	61	71½	51	35	22	Skinner K	4.20
7Jun84 3Bel5	Milieu	b	5	114	11	52	52	3hd	11½	21	35½	Miceli M	9.40
10Jun84 2Bel7	Commander Almy		4	108	1	10½	91	91½	92	41	42¾	Fann B	18.60
11Jun84 5Atl6	Nibroc		5	106	5	81	82	82	61½	53	55	Alvarado R Jr	14.00
17Jun84 1Bel7	Mock Court	b	4	122	9	12	1hd	1½	31	6½	6¾	Velasquez J	b-1.90
15Jun84 2Bel8	Lypharel		5	114	6	2hd	41½	41	7½	7hd	7½	Davis R G	8.20
10Jun84 2Bel3	Wimborne Castle	b	6	110	2	41½	31	5½	81	84	82	Lopez V	6.50
7Jun84 9Bel6	Walk The Beach		5	111	10	9½	101	101	111	10½	9nk	Murphy D J	9.60
9Jun84 10Mth8	Ultimate Native	b	4	109	8	111½	111½	12	12	91½	106	Hernandez R	36.10
7Jun84 3Bel8	Jungle Marsh		6	115	3	3hd	2½	21½	4hd	11	11	Messina R	12.20
11Jun84 5Atl7	Irish Bar		4	107	4	12	12	111½	104	—	—	Thibeau R J	32.30

Irish Bar, Broke down.
b-Coupled: Heroic Spirit and Mock Court.

OFF AT 1:31 Start good, Won driving. Time, :24, :48⅖, 1:13, 1:38⅕, 2:03, 2:16, Course firm.

$2 Mutuel Prices:

1-(O)-HEROIC SPIRIT (b-entry)	5.80	3.20	2.80
8-(H)-AMADANDY		4.60	3.40
11-(N)-MILIEU			4.40

$2 QUINELLA 1-8 PAID $14.80.

B. h, by Naskra—Maia II, by Cipol. Trainer Barrera Oscar S. Bred by Whitney T P (Ky).

HEROIC SPIRIT moved fast to catch MILIEU nearing the stretch, quickly drew clear, was being confidently handled when challenged suddenly by AMADANDY in deep stretch and prevaield when roused. The latter rallied from the outside leaving the far turn, caught HEROIC SPIRIT a stride from the finish and just missed. MILIEU, never far back moved away to a clear lead on the far turn but weakened under pressure. COMMANDER ALMY wide into the stretch, failed to seriously menace. NIBROC moved up outside horses approaching the stretch but lacked a further response. MOCK COURT was used up making the pace. LYPHAREL tired badly. WIMBORNE CASTLE was finished at the far turn. WALK THE BEACH was always outrun. JUNGLE MARCH was finished before going a mile. IRISH BAR broke down after entering the stretch.

We conclude with one final point. In light of the outcome of this race, it would seem fair to rate it as the equivalent of a $35,000 claiming contest. Or perhaps at just $25,000, depending on whether we wish to rate Milieu, who finished third, beaten just two lengths, based on his recent races, or those better races at the bottom of his past performances.

You might call this the class handicapper's "projection method." But whatever you call it, all starter races should be classified in this way. Indeed, all claiming races, if not all races, should have their true class evaluated in this manner.

As noted above, our handicapping task in this race was simplified by the absence of starter races in the contestants' past performances. But on circuits where starter races are far more frequent than in New York, their appearance in the past performances tends to hide the current value of the contestants. The player who has accurately classified these races has a tremendous edge over his less-informed competitors at the track.

Chapter 12

A Horse of Another Color

OF THE MORE RECENT developments in Thoroughbred racing, one that has added still another piece to the handicapping puzzle is the proliferation of races restricted to state-breds. Offering higher than normal purses to inferior stock, these races have, among other things, contributed to the downfall of earnings calculations as credible indicators of class in the Thoroughbred.

Further confusing matters is the fact that comparisons observed in one state will probably prove useless in another. Where do state-breds fit with open company? How do state-bred claiming races measure up to open claiming events? What is the relationship between state-bred claiming and allowance company, and is it the same as for open competition? What is the top claiming price carded at the track? For state-breds? Answers found for New York, New Jersey, California, and Florida may in no way reflect the situation in Maryland, Pennsylvania, Illinois, or Louisiana. There is no uniform national answer to these questions.

I witnessed a good example of "class in the state-bred" during my 1983 visit to Arlington Park, where I was guest speaker at Scott McMannis's innovative handicapping center. The nightcap on August 13 was a "nonwinners of two" allowance sprint restricted to Illinois-breds. Odds-on favorite for the race was Bill's Buy Back, who had won both his career starts in impressive style. The ultimate winner of the race, Indian Terra, Jr., appeared—at least on paper, to this visitor from New York—to be the cheapest commodity in the field. Let's take a closer look.

Although he won his only two starts by large margins in actual times far superior to anything his rivals had recently clocked, Bill's Buy Back did so while racing clear on the early lead. Those races,

10th Arlington

6 FURLONGS. (1.08⅗) ALLOWANCE. Purse $11,640 (includes 20% ITBF). 3-year-olds and upward wihch have not won three races, Illinois registered, conceived and/or foaled. Weight, 3-year-olds, 117 lbs.; older, 122 lbs. Non-winners of $8,405 twice in 1983 allowed 3 lbs.; two races since July 2, 5 lbs.

Pick's Commando

B. c. 4, by Command Performer—P J's Pick, by Irish Lancer

Br.—Kenneke Edward H (Ill)		1983	11	0	2	0	$9,391
Own.—Kenneke E H	**117** **Tr.—Kenneke Edward H**	1982	18	2	1	1	$19,166
Lifetime 34 2 3 1 $28,820		Turf	2	0	0	0	

30Jly83-10AP	6f	:22^3 :46^3 1:13^{1}ft	23	117	10$^{9\frac14}$ 10^{12} 10$^{9\frac12}$ 8$^{6\frac12}$	Lasala J^9	[S]Aw12125	69-19	MystcSqur,GrtNPlck,CnnmonBob	10
21Jly83-6AP	6f	:22^1 :45^4 1:13^{2}gd	24	117	5^4 7$^{9\frac14}$ 5^7 5^5	Meier R^3	[S]Aw13260	70-28	SpecilRed,SmllButSlow,MysticSqur	7
22Jun83-3AP	1	:46^1 1:11^1 1:38^{1}ft	14	117	2$^{1\frac12}$ 3^5 4^8 5^{15}	Meier R^2	[S]Aw16120	55-24	MjesticZn,SmllButSlow,Crpntr'sMt	8
10Jun83-7AP	6f	:22^2 :45^4 1:11^{2}ft	35	117	3^2 4$^{1\frac12}$ 3$^{3\frac12}$ 4^4	Meier R^9	[S]Aw13750	81-27	Strate'nUp,MajesticZen,WiseNvjo	10
18May83-6Spt	1	:48 1:13 1:39^{1}ft	15	120	3^4 3$^{9\frac12}$ 3$^{8\frac12}$ 6^{11}	Jones R A^6	[S]Aw17490	73-19	HnovrConty,AllOfASddn,LytOnUm	8
3May83-8Spt	1	:49^4 1:14^4 1:40^{4}ft	3	120	1$^{\frac12}$ 1^{hd} 1^{hd} 2$^{1\frac14}$	Jones R A^4	[S]Aw17490	75-22	WcksPck,Pck'sCommndo,LytOnUm	7
25Apr83-9Spt	6½f	:23^3 :47^2 1:18^{4}ft	9¾	120	3$^{3\frac12}$ 3^4 3$^{3\frac12}$ 5$^{2\frac12}$	Jones R A^6	[S]Aw17710	80-19	SonofZen,LyitOnUm,FoolishDrive	10
12Apr83-7Spt	1	:48^4 1:14^3 1:40^{4}ft	33	120	1$^{\frac12}$ 1$^{\frac12}$ 2^{hd} 2no	Jones R A^6	[S]Aw18285	76-26	Verify,Pick'sCommando,LyitOnUm	8

Jun 20 AP 3f ft :37^1 b

Boy From Bliss

Ch. g. 4, by Pappa Steve—Flight Balcony, by First Balcony

Br.—Boyce Neil (Ill)		1983	11	0	1	3	$7,770
Own.—N & M Boyce Racing Sta Inc	**117** **Tr.—Boyce Neil**	1982	8	2	1	0	$15,543
Lifetime 22 2 2 4 $24,388		Turf	1	0	0	0	

30Jly83-10AP	6f	:22^3 :46^3 1:13^{1}ft	30	112^5	6$^{3\frac34}$ 5$^{4\frac12}$ 6$^{5\frac12}$ 7^6	Mills C^8	[S]Aw12125	70-19	MystcSqur,GrtNPlck,CnnmonBob	10
10Jly83-4AP	6f	:22^1 :45^3 1:11 ft	34	112^5	4^4 5^5 5^8 4^{16}	Mills C^4	[S]Aw14300	71-15	WiseNavajo,SpecialRed,GritNPluck	6
14Jun83-2AP	6f	:23^1 :46^2 1:11^{4}ft	*9-5	115	4$^{\frac34}$ 2$^{2\frac12}$ 2^2 3$^{7\frac12}$	Fires E^7	[S] 8000	75-23	Elmer'sLast,HndiJet,BoyFromBliss	8
14Jun83—Four wide early, faltered in the drive										
7Jun83-3AP	6f	:23 :47^1 1:13^{3}ft	3	115	4^1 4^1 2^2 3^4	Fires E^6	[S] 10000	70-27	DngrosDog,CortVctory,BoyFrmBlss	8
7Jun83—Rallied four deep late on turn										
27May83-4AP	6f	:23 :46^4 1:13 ft	*9-5	115	3^{nk} 2^{hd} 1^{hd} 3$^{\frac34}$	Fires E^7	[S] 10000	76-21	CortVctory,Msty'sLrk,BoyFrmBlss	7
14May83-9Spt	6f	:23^3 :47^2 1:13^{4}sy	4¾	112	2^{hd} 2^2 3$^{\frac12}$ 4^7	Evans R D^4	[S] 15000	74-19	EmerldLight,MeDunC,Don'tRuffIM	8
25Apr83-9Spt	6½f	:23^3 :47^2 1:18^{4}ft	12	120	4^5 4^6 7^9 8^9	Long B^2	[S]Aw17710	74-19	SonofZen,LyitOnUm,FoolishDrive	10
1Apr83-7Spt	6f	:23 :46^1 1:13 ft	22	120	2$^{\frac12}$ 3$^{1\frac12}$ 5$^{4\frac12}$ 5$^{4\frac12}$	GuajardoA^7	[S]Aw18480	80-18	RoringPet,IngrindBrss,FoolishDriv	10
1Apr83—Carried wide										
25Mar83-8Spt	6f	:24 :48^1 1:13^{4}ft	3½	120	2^1 2$^{1\frac12}$ 7$^{7\frac14}$ 7$^{9\frac12}$	Diaz J L^5	[S]Aw18480	71-20	‡CinnmonBob,GntlmnVc,InBtwnTm	7
11Mar83-8Spt	6f	:23^1 :47^1 1:13^{2}m	7	120	1^2 1^1 1^1 2$^{1\frac12}$	Diaz J L^1	[S]Aw17640	81-19	LunarFble,BoyFromBliss,LyitOnUm	8

Jly 27 AP 5f ft 1:02^2 b   Jly 6 AP 5f ft 1:01^2 h   Jun 19 AP 3f ft :38^2 b

Bill's Buy Back

B. c. 3, by Irish faberge—Cash Profit, by Handsome Boy

Br.—Wieland William A (Ill)		1983	2	2	0	0	$13,833
Own.—Wieland W A	**114** **Tr.—Rea Enoch**	1982	0	M	0	0	
Lifetime 2 2 0 0 $13,833							

29Jly83-9AP	6f	:22^4 :45^2 1:12^{2}ft	*1-2	112	1$^{1\frac12}$ 1$^{1\frac12}$ 1^3 1^7	PttersonA^9	[S]Aw11875	80-26	Bll'sByBck,CrmsonRmblr,PlsrDnc	12
10Jly83-3AP	6f	:22^2 :45^4 1:11^{3}ft	*9-5	115	1^1 1^2 1^5 1$^{6\frac14}$	Patterson A^{10}	[S]Mdn	84-15	Bill'sBuyBack,Mojimo,EmmyAwrd	12

Aug 11 AP 4f ft :49^3 b   Aug 5 AP 4f ft :52^2 b   Jly 27 AP 4f ft :48^3 h   Jly 23 AP 5f ft 1:02 b

Irish Flu

B. g. 4, by Irish Fabrege—Holme's Boo, by Noholme II

Br.—Wieland W A (Ill)		1983	9	1	0	1	$11,401
Own.—Fisher & Wiebe	**117** **Tr.—Adwell Paul T**	1982	12	1	2	1	$11,806
Lifetime 21 2 2 2 $23,207							

30Jly83-10AP	6f	:22^3 :46^3 1:13^{1}ft	16	117	1$^{1\frac12}$ 1^2 1$^{\frac12}$ 5^3	Meier R^7	[S]Aw12125	73-19	MystcSqur,GrtNPlck,CnnmonBob	10
10Jly83-4AP	6f	:22^1 :45^3 1:11 ft	5	119	2^1 2$^{1\frac12}$ 3$^{6\frac12}$ 6^{18}	Meier R^3	[S]Aw14300	69-15	WiseNavajo,SpecialRed,GritNPluck	6
25Jun83-9AP	6f	:23 :45^1 1:13^{1}ft	4¼	117	1$^{3\frac12}$ 1^4 1^5 1$^{5\frac12}$	Meier R^5	[S]Aw14420	76-24	Irish Flu, Call Me Friend, Kaiser	12
15Jun83-7AP	6f	:22^2 :45^4 1:13^{1}ft	21	117	1^1 1^3 1$^{3\frac12}$ 5$^{1\frac12}$	Meier R^1	[S]Aw13390	74-26	VikingChief,PlesureDnce,PrincRgis	9
4Jun83-6AP	6f	:22^2 :46^2 1:12^{3}ft	9½	117	1$^{1\frac12}$ 1^2 4$^{\frac34}$ 7^{10}	Meier R^4	[S]Aw12875	69-21	ViLusso,VikingChif,H'sPlumTough	9
26May83-9AP	6f	:23^1 :47^2 1:12^{3}ft	6¾	117	1$^{1\frac12}$ 1^3 3$^{\frac12}$ 5$^{9\frac12}$	Silva C H^6	[S]Aw12875	69-24	WiseNvjo,He'sPlumTough,ViLusso	12
16May83-9Spt	6f	:23^3 :47^2 1:13^{3}ft	*2¾	120	7$^{7\frac34}$ 8$^{6\frac34}$ 8^{11} 8^9	Silva C H^4	[S]Aw14520	73-20	Kharefor, No Jest, BigTomReeves	10
16May83—Stumbled at the break										
2May83-8Spt	6f	:23^3 :47^2 1:13^{3}ft	3¼	120	1$^{1\frac12}$ 1^2 1$^{1\frac12}$ 3$^{\frac34}$	Silva C H^8	[S]Aw14520	81-23	Ole Tooney,BigTomReeves,IrishFlu	9
2May83—Rushed up wide in drive										
22Apr83-9Spt	6f	:23^4 :47^4 1:14 ft	4½	120	1^2 1$^{1\frac12}$ 5$^{2\frac12}$ 9^{11}	Silva C H^1	[S]Aw15180	69-23	SltLkCity,NmblDncr,Lndy'sTomto	10
23Aug82-3AP	6f	:22^4 :46^1 1:11^{3}ft	15	112	1^2 1^{hd} 3$^{4\frac12}$ 7^{12}	Silva C H^1	[S]Aw12150	72-20	HulsSun,DemonWhisky,Crpntr'sMt	8

Jly 7 AP 4f ft :48^3 h   ●Jly 2 AP 4f sy :50^1 b   Jun 23 AP 5f ft 1:00^2 h

Cinnamon Bob

Dk. b. or br. g. 4, by Sir Cinnamon—Mousie, by Bolero
Br.—Bartholomew R Y (Ill) 1983 8 1 0 2 $11,716
Own.—Igoe, McNeill & Matthews 117 Tr.—Johnson Joseph M 1982 8 1 0 2 $6,991
Lifetime 16 2 0 4 $18,707

30Jly83-10AP	6f	:223	:463	1:131ft	14	117	95¾	75¼	53½	31¼	Fires E10	[S]Aw12125	75-19	MystcSqur,GrtNPlck,CnnmonBob	10
21Jly83-6AP	6f	:221	:454	1:132gd	18	117	64¼	58	712	713	SpencerSA6	[S]Aw13260	62-28	SpecilRed,SmllButSlow,MysticSqur	7
10Jly83-4AP	6f	:221	:453	1:11 ft	25	117	68½	69	611	517	SpencerSA6	[S]Aw14300	70-15	WiseNavajo,SpecialRed,GritNPluck	6
25Apr83-9Spt	6½f	:233	:472	1:184ft	6	120	1013	1012	911	99¼	SpencrSA10	[S]Aw17710	74-19	SonofZen,LyitOnUm,FoolishDrive	10
1Apr83-7Spt	6f	:23	:461	1:13 ft	4¼	120	98½	96	97¼	89½	SpencerSA3	[S]Aw18480	75-18	RoringPet,IngrindBrss,FoolishDriv	10
25Mar83-8Spt	6f	:24	:481	1:134ft	3½	120	44	31½	2hd	1nk†	SpencerSA4	[S]Aw18480	81-20	‡CinnmonBob,GntlmnVc,InBtwnTm	7

†25Mar83—Disqualified and placed third; Lugged in

11Mar83-8Spt	6f	:231	:471	1:132m	2¼	120	68½	54½	77½	712	SpencerSA5	[S]Aw17640	71-19	LunarFble,BoyFromBliss,LyitOnUm	8
25Feb83-9Spt	6f	:234	:472	1:124ft	5¾	120	57½	34½	34½	11½	SpencerSA7	[S]Aw13200	86-15	CinnmonBob,SonofZn,MtrcMoton	10
28Dec82-7Haw	6f	:214	:452	1:123sy	5¾	120	56¼	46½	35½	46¼	Lopez R D5	Aw9500	72-26	Slim'sBrothr,MrinEngin,PlyfulRook	7
15Dec82-9Haw	6½f	:224	:454	1:173ft	7¼	1145	2½	32½	22	312	Lasala J6	20000	73-20	BoldWork,FrSuspnson,CnnmonBob	8

Jly 6 AP 4f ft :49 b

Small But Slow

Dk. b. or br. g. 3, by Hula Chief—Tapping, by Our Michael
Br.—Perkins Dick (Ill) 1983 8 2 2 0 $24,945
Own.—Perkins & Stewart 112 Tr.—Weissman Michael F 1982 3 M 0 1 $1,216
Lifetime 11 2 2 1 $26,161

30Jly83-10AP	6f	:223	:463	1:131ft	4½	113	21½	43½	88½	1010	Clark K D1	[S]Aw12125	66-19	MystcSqur,GrtNPlck,CnnmonBob	10
21Jly83-6AP	6f	:221	:454	1:132gd	4½	115	21½	22½	22½	23	GallitanoG5	[S]Aw13260	72-28	SpecilRed,SmllButSlow,MysticSqur	7
8Jly83-7AP	6f	:22	:452	1:121ft	9	110	32½	32	22½	56¼	Evans R D9	[S]Aw16250	75-25	Carol Singhs,HandsomeU.,ViaLusso	9
22Jun83-3AP	1	:461	1:111	1:381ft	3	112	11½	12	11½	2¾	Fires E5	[S]Aw16120	69-24	MjesticZn,SmllButSlow,Crpntr'sMt	8
21May83-5Spt	6½f	:231	:462	1:174ft	4	110	11	1½	33	44½	Hirdes R JJr2	Aw19300	83-17	HighlndStrek,MinnsotRibot,ElAybl	6
1May83-8Spt	6f	:232	:472	1:141sy	5¾	114	33½	912	916	921	HltnM4	[S]Lnd Of Lin	58-26	RoylGrdnr,AllOfASuddn,InBtwnTim	9

1May83—Was carried out on the first turn

31Mar83-6Spt	6f	:224	:46	1:123ft	3¼	120	13	15	14	11½	HmiltonM4	[S]Aw15840	87-19	SmllButSlow,OurTerror,Gorg'sTurn	8
17Mar83-5Spt	6f	:233	:472	1:14 ft	*2-3e	119	14	13	14	16½	Richard D3	[S]Mdn	80-19	SmllBtSlow,Lndy'sTomto,OlToony	10
28Dec82-5Haw	6f	:214	:453	1:14 sy	3¾	120	1hd	22½	66½	69½	Lindsay R4	[S]Mdn	61-26	‡Extrneous,Khrefor,George'sTurn	12
17Dec82-2Haw	6f	:221	:46	1:121ft	5	120	12	2½	24	36¼	Richard D7	[S]Mdn	74-22	RrContinuity,Focoso,SmllButSlow	12

Aug 9 AP 4f ft :51 b Jly 7 AP 3f ft :36 h Jun 16 AP 5f ft 1:01 h

Indian Terra Jr.

B. c. 4, by Indian Terra—Rug Rat, by Mito
Br.—Cass Larry (Ill) 1983 5 0 0 2 $2,215
Own.—Ballis Ruth 117 Tr.—Salvino Noel P 1982 6 1 1 2 $14,790
Lifetime 27 2 1 11 $35,158

29Jly83-4AP	6f	:222	:462	1:13 ft	9¼	115	78½	68	62¾	32¼	Lopez R D3	[S] 8000	75-26	Pappouli, Son ofZen,IndianTerraJr.	9
13Jly83-2AP	7f	:223	:46	1:251ft	31	115	65	57	56½	36	Diaz J L12	[S] 10000	70-20	Bequested,Elmer'sLst,IndinTerrJr.	12
24Jun83-2AP	6f	:231	:471	1:121ft	20	115	83¾	75½	65	47½	Lopez R D7	[S] 10000	73-27	Hooli'sZinglong,DngrousDoug,HuB	8
7Jun83-3AP	6f	:23	:471	1:133ft	20	115	87¾	87¾	84½	45¼	Lopez R D4	[S] 10000	69-27	DngrosDog,CortVctory,BoyFrmBlss	8
22May83-2AP	6f	:222	:46	1:12 sy	8½	1105	46	57½	811	1017	Focareto S J4	12500	65-29	Missy'sLast,Tenshua'sBid,TwoBee	10
27Apr82-6Spt	1	:483	1:142	1:404ft	5½	112	64½	65¼	77¾	710	Evans R D5	[S]Aw18368	66-24	King Gone, TavernLadd,Mr.CleveT.	9
9Apr82-3Spt	1	:483	1:14	1:422ft	*8-5	112	33½	1hd	2½	12¼	Evans R D4	[S]Aw14750	68-19	IndinTrrJr.,WicksPick,ZnglongHom	8
26Mar82-9Spt	1	:483	1:142	1:412ft	*2	115	53	43	42	3¾	GuajardoA1	[S]Aw15930	72-19	Mr.United,BayofIntent,IndinTerrJr.	7
20Mar82-9Spt	6f	:232	:472	1:134sy	4¾	112	56	68	38	32½	SpencerSA1	[S]Aw12980	78-17	PollysPrfrmr,Shcky'sLd,IndnTrrJr.	9
6Mar82-1Spt	6f	:233	:473	1:132ft	3½	112	54	42	77	83½	SpencerSA8	[S]Aw14160	79-17	Deke, Metric Motion, Strumming	9

Aug 6 AP 3f ft :491 b Jly 9 AP 4f ft :491 b ●Jly 3 AP 5f gd 1:013 h Jun 21 AP 3f ft :374 b

Rare Continuity

B. c. 3, by Christopher R—Pride Chulm, by Asirio
Br.—Bartels W Jr (Ill) 1983 4 1 0 0 $10,573
Own.—Bartels Nadine & W 112 Tr.—Fedor James J 1982 3 1 0 0 $7,262
Lifetime 7 2 0 0 $17,835

30Jly83-10AP	6f	:223	:463	1:131ft	*7-5	112	43	32	42½	42½	GallitanoG5	[S]Aw12125	73-19	MystcSqur,GrtNPlck,CnnmonBob	10
16Jly83-4AP	6f	:222	:46	1:124ft	*8-5	112	1hd	1½	13	16½	GallitanoG8	[S]Aw13390	78-25	RreContinuity,Chiefo,Thundercloud	8
30Jun83-8AP	6f	:224	:462	1:124sy	18	112	1½	12	21	44	GallitanoG1	[S]Aw15900	74-32	ViLusso,LonesomeGeorge,WisNvjo	7
1Jan83-3Haw	6f	:221	:454	1:12 ft	*9-5	120	1½	1hd	3½	47¾	Long B4	[S]Aw14300	73-23	In Between Time, Kharefor, Calkay	7
17Dec82-2Haw	6f	:221	:46	1:121ft	3½	120	32	1½	14	15	Long B5	[S]Mdn	80-22	RrContinuity,Focoso,SmllButSlow	12
29Nov82-4Haw	6f	:221	:461	1:13 sy	4½	120	1hd	1hd	1hd	45½	Long B5	[S]Mdn	70-27	Billy'sFresho,InBtwnTim,Extrnous	12
11Nov82-2Haw	6f	:224	:464	1:14 sy	31	119	61¼	21	612	1020	Long B3	[S]Mdn	51-29	OurTerror,LwrencEr,GbtownHornt	12

Aug 9 AP 3f ft :36 h Jly 26 AP 4f ft :49 b Jly 14 AP 3f ft :37 b Jly 10 AP 5f ft 1:02 b

Grit N Pluck — B. g. 3, by Tartar Chief—Love Most, by Monastir

Br.—Price Virginia (Ill) — 1983 7 2 2 1 $22,350

Own.—Price Virginia **112** Tr.—Yarberry Jan — 1982 0 M 0 0

Lifetime 7 2 2 1 $22,350

30Jly83-10AP	6f	$:22^{3}$	$:46^{3}$	$1{:}13^{1}$ft	12	112	$3^{1\frac{1}{2}}$	2^{2}	$2^{\frac{1}{2}}$	2no	Gilligan L^{2}	[S]Aw12125	76-19	MystcSqur,GrtNPlck,CnnmonBob	10
10Jly83-4AP	6f	$:22^{1}$	$:45^{3}$	1:11 ft	3	112	$5^{5\frac{1}{2}}$	$4^{4\frac{1}{2}}$	$4^{6\frac{1}{2}}$	3^{12}	Strauss R^{5}	[S]Aw14300	75-15	WiseNavajo,SpecialRed,GritNPluck	6
30Jun83-8AP	6f	$:22^{4}$	$:46^{2}$	$1{:}12^{4}$sy	*9-5	113	6^{4}	$5^{4\frac{1}{2}}$	$5^{3\frac{1}{2}}$	$5^{7\frac{3}{4}}$	Strauss R^{2}	[S]Aw15900	70-32	ViLusso,LonesomeGeorge,WisNvjo	7
19Jun83-8AP	1	$:46^{3}$	1:12	$1{:}37^{2}$ft	9e	115	$1^{\frac{1}{2}}$	1^{hd}	$3^{2\frac{1}{2}}$	7^{14}	StrussR^{4}	[S]Isc Mrphy	60-26	LCouCou,AllOfASuddn,RoylGrdnr	11
12Jun83-9AP	1	$:46^{4}$	1:11	$1{:}37^{4}$ft	*7-5	112	$1^{1\frac{1}{2}}$	1^{3}	1^{4}	1^{2}	Strauss R^{7}	[S]Aw14750	72-27	GritNPluck,Lindy'sTomto,Violinist	12
4Jun83-7AP	6f	$:22^{2}$	$:45^{4}$	$1{:}11^{4}$ft	2	113	1^{hd}	$1^{1\frac{1}{2}}$	1^{2}	$2^{1\frac{3}{4}}$	Strauss R^{3}	[S]Aw12875	81-21	Mr.BoldTArr,GrtNPluck,GnrousRlr	10
25May83-1AP	6f	$:22^{4}$	$:46^{3}$	$1{:}13^{1}$ft	28	113	$1^{1\frac{1}{2}}$	$1^{2\frac{1}{2}}$	1^{5}	1^{11}	Strauss R^{2}	[S]Mdn	76-26	Grit N Pluck,Praeter,BiteEmRight	12

● Jly 26 AP 4f ft $:47^{2}$ hg Jly 8 AP 4f ft $:49^{3}$ b Jun 28 AP 4f sy $:50^{4}$ b

though impressive, offered no evidence as to how the colt would perform if challenged early. And in the field he would face, several of his rivals had front-running profiles. Each of Pick's Commando, Boy From Bliss, Irish Flu, Small But Slow, and Rare Continuity had run his best races after engaging the early lead. None of them had (at least recently) demonstrated any ability to come from off the pace. A superficial analysis of pace times revealed that Irish Flu (if none of the others) could run as fast as—if not faster than—Bill's Buy Back in the early stages.

If Bill's Buy Back were to be upset, his potential early rivals could not be considered the most likely to succeed. Their role would be to force the favorite to run hard early and soften him up for one of the stretch runners in the field. Another problem facing Bill's Buy Back was the negative-rail bias affecting the oucome of races at Arlington that week. Unless Pick's Commando recaptured his form and went for the lead, Bill's Buy Back could easily find himself the rail horse in a multihorse speed duel.

Of the contestants with proven stretch-running ability, Grit N Pluck was by far the most consistent, and also the one who would run closest to the early lead. Indeed, he was capable of contesting the early fractions himself, if his rider chose to do so. The other two, Cinnamon Bob and Indian Terra, Jr., came from farther behind, although neither with any great consistency. With his recent performances restricted to allowance company, Cinnamon Bob seemed the classier of the two. Yet Indian Terra Jr.'s last *Form* speed rating matched Cinnamon Bob's one day later, over a surface the *Form* considered seven lengths slower. If that figure was any measure, Indian Terra Jr. had to be accorded a chance. But the fact remained that he had been unable to win in state-bred $8,000 and $10,000 claiming company. Open "nonwinners of two" company in Chicago was worth at least $25,000. Was the same true in the state-bred ranks?

So much for our "uninformed" analysis of this race.

When an experienced handicapper finds himself attending the

races at an unfamiliar track, he is wise enough to proceed cautiously, aware that he must work without a full deck. Most likely, he will rely on the *Form* for "figs" and trip notes. He will constantly be nagged by the possibility that a horse that seemed to go off form last time out was in actuality the victim of a track bias or bad trip. Most of the local trainers will remain nothing more than names, their competence and pet ploys never to be discovered. In other words, the player will suffer from information gaps relating to three of the most crucial aspects of handicapping.

At Arlington I was fortunate to be in the good hands of Scott McMannis, a truly outstanding handicapper. Information Scott provided added significantly to our analysis of this particular race. To wit:

Scott's adjusted speed figures placed Bill's Buy Back clear of this field by a solid four lengths, and also rated Indian Terra Jr. at least the equal of the rest of this band. Scott also remarked that the jump from $8,000 claiming into allowance company within the Illinois-bred ranks was not nearly as steep as an outsider might suspect.

Scott's trip notes pointed out that Small But Slow had been badly shut off on the turn last time out, losing all chance in that race. His previous two starts produced contending speed figures—for second money, anyway. Scott's in-depth information also revealed that the owner of Indian Terra Jr. had changed trainers in mid-July and that the stable had been going well since. Two horses from the barn had shown improvement first time out for trainer Salvino, then improved again second time out. Indian Terra Jr. improved in his first start for Salvino and will do so again today if he follows the pattern. Actually, his last race was more impressive than it appears to be on paper. The horse raced on a dead rail that day, and today moves outside to the better part of the track, where he figures to get an easier trip.

In a similar vein, Grit N Pluck had also changed hands during the meet—sometime in mid-June. This time, however, the horses involved went off form. Although Grit N Pluck's last was close on figures, his performance that day was aided by a moderate early-speed bias.

With this additional information, and 1–2 odds on Bill's Buy Back complicating matters, the possible courses of action were limited—either concede the race to the favorite and make no bet or make a small action bet on Indian Terra Jr.

Apart from the state-bred issue, we are really trying to make two other points in this chapter. The first is that very few horses are worth bets as odds-on favorites, and no such horse is even worth considering if there is any question about its fitness or ability. Bill's Buy Back's character and courage had yet to be tested, and with these at issue, his odds-on proposition was unacceptable.

The second point to be made is that Indian Terra Jr. was worth serious consideration at the 55–1 odds at which he was being offered. The high odds compensated for the possibility that he might be outclassed in state-bred allowance company, and also for the animal's relatively low lifetime win percentage. He did appear to be rounding to form, though, and if a speed duel developed up front, he was one of only three horses in the field that were likely to be in position to capitalize.

The key to success at the races lies in the recognition and exploitation of overlay situations. Most successful players I know do well because they make serious wagers only when the horse they prefer goes off at odds that represent good value. I know of only one player who is able to stay ahead of this game while playing every race. His name is Phil Zipse, a friend of long standing who introduced me to this fascinating pastime and gave me my first handicapping lessons while we were studying for our doctorates at Rutgers back in the late 1960s. Phil's betting philosophy has always been quite simple: Look for the overlay with a reasonable chance of winning. On many occasions I've seen him bet against the horse he felt would win a race, playing instead an opponent whose chances were slimmer—

TENTH RACE
Arlington
AUGUST 13, 1983

6 FURLONGS. (1.08⅗) ALLOWANCE. Purse $11,640 (includes 20% ITBF). 3-year-olds and upward which have not won three races, Illinois registered, conceived and/or foaled. Weight, 3-year-olds, 117 lbs.; older, 122 lbs. Non-winners of $8,405 twice in 1983 allowed 3 lbs.; two races since July 2, 5 lbs.

Value of race $11,640, value to winner $6,984, second $2,328, third $1,281, fourth $698, fifth $349. Mutuel pool $103,143. Trifecta Pool $228,335.

Last Raced	Horse	Eqt.	A.	Wt	PP	St	¼	½	Str	Fin	Jockey	Odds $1
29Jly83 ^{4}AP^{3}	Indian Terra Jr.	b	4	117	7	9	9	8^{1}	5^{hd}	$1^{1\frac{1}{2}}$	Lopez R D	55.50
30Jly83^{10}AP^{3}	Cinnamon Bob	b	4	117	5	8	$6^{1\frac{1}{2}}$	$5^{1\frac{1}{2}}$	3^{1}	2^{3}	Fires E	5.60
30Jly83^{10}AP^{10}	Small But Slow	b	3	113	6	6	$3^{\frac{1}{2}}$	3^{1}	$2^{\frac{1}{2}}$	3^{1}	Louviere G P	16.00
30Jly83^{10}AP^{2}	Grit N Pluck	b	3	112	9	1	7^{4}	7^{6}	6^{3}	$4^{4\frac{1}{2}}$	Gilligan L	6.00
30Jly83^{10}AP^{4}	Rare Continuity	b	3	112	8	3	$5^{\frac{1}{2}}$	$4^{\frac{1}{2}}$	4^{hd}	5^{1}	Gallitano G	9.70
29Jly83 ^{9}AP^{1}	Bill's Buy Back		3	114	3	5	$1^{\frac{1}{2}}$	$1^{1\frac{1}{2}}$	1^{hd}	$6^{\frac{1}{2}}$	Patterson A	.50
30Jly83^{10}AP^{8}	Pick's Commando		4	117	1	7	8^{4}	9	9	$7^{1\frac{3}{4}}$	Lasala J	54.60
30Jly83^{10}AP^{7}	Boy From Bliss	b	4	117	2	4	$4^{\frac{1}{2}}$	$6^{\frac{1}{2}}$	$8^{1\frac{1}{2}}$	8^{5}	Clark K D	68.80
30Jly83^{10}AP^{5}	Irish Flu	b	4	117	4	2	2^{2}	2^{1}	7^{1}	9	Meier R	15.90

OFF AT 6:16 1/2. Start good. Won driving. Time, :22, :45⅘, :59, 1:12⅘ Track fast.

$2 Mutuel Prices:				
	7-INDIAN TERRA JR.	113.00	40.20	10.80
	5-CINNAMON BOB		6.40	4.20
	6-SMALL BUT SLOW			6.60

$2 TRIFECTA (7-5-6) PAID $4,077.40.

B. c, by Indian Terra—Rug Rat, by Mito. Trainer Salvino Noel P. Bred by Cass Larry (Ill).

INDIAN TERRA JR., outrun early, rallied wide after the half and outfinished CINNAMON BOB. The latter rallied inside horses in midstretch but unable to match strides with winner. SMALL BUT SLOW rallied between horses and loomed boldly furlong out, failed to sustain bid. GRIT N PLUCK rallied mildly while wide. RARE CONTINUITY tired between horses. BILL'S BUY BACK and IRISH FLU were used up dueling for lead. PICK'S COMMANDO was always outrun. BOY FROM BLISS was through late on turn.

though real—but whose odds offered far greater rewards. And I've seen his judgment vindicated regularly enough to make him a consistent winner.

Phil Zipse, originally from the Chicago area, learned the ABCs of handicapping at Arlington Park. Too bad he wasn't on hand for this race. He would probably have found the 55–1 odds on Indian Terra Jr. attractive. Wendy McMannis, Scott's wife and an excellent handicapper in her own right, was enticed, while Scott and I decided to pass the race rather than bet against the favorite. Wendy delayed our departure from the track that afternoon while she collected her $113.00 return!

As a footnote, we point out that Bill's Buy Back did not break from the gate too sharply, giving Boy From Bliss the opportunity to rush up for the early lead. When the latter stayed off the rail, jockey Patterson on the favorite altered course to the inside! Sharp handicappers, it seems, are usually far better attuned to biased racetracks than are the little men who ride the horses, and consequently figure to have the best opportunity to pick up on such things.

Chapter 13

The Bastard Distance

On several occasions I have heard the phrase "the bastard distance" used in reference to races at a mile and seventy yards. Indeed, speed handicappers believe that racing secretaries schedule races at this unusual distance solely to complicate their lives and confuse their calculations. They are forced to measure accurately the difference in time between this distance and the standard mile and a sixteenth, which is forty yards longer, so that their figures for the two distances are correctly aligned. Yet handicappers in general seem to make no conscious distinction between the two distances when handicapping a race or analyzing a performance at either distance. Both are considered typical middle-distance routes around two turns, and the shorter (by forty yards) run to the first turn at a mile and seventy yards is given little thought. Probably rightfully so.

If there is a "bastard" distance, however, then seven furlongs certainly deserves the accolade. To correctly align his figures with those at six panels, the speed handicapper must compare times at distances an eighth of a mile (220 yards) apart, a far more challenging assignment. In addition, handicapping criteria used to identify and separate contenders must be weighted differently at the two distances.

The makeup of the fields that gather for seven-furlong races often make the handicapper's task all the more difficult. Many of the contestants will have no demonstrated ability at the demanding distance. Identification of the probable pacesetters often proves to be a guessing game, with the player usually forced to choose from among horses (at best) able to prompt the pace at six furlongs, or set the pace at longer route distances.

One of the first questions a player must ask (and answer) for any race is, "Who will set the pace?" If this question cannot be answered with any degree of certainty, many serious players will pass the race, reasoning correctly that their chances of predicting the final outcome are seriously impeded if they cannot picture how the race will set up in its early stages. Races at seven furlongs, more than at any other distance, are likely to leave the answer to this question clouded. The following race, the second at Aqueduct on April 24, 1984, demonstrates the point. It is not atypical of seven-furlong races.

The first thing one might notice about this race is that of the eleven horses that started, only Cannon Royal had a recent history of taking the early lead. But his pacesetting efforts came around two turns, and the only sprint on his record found him midpack at the first call. It was certainly not obvious, then, who would set the pace in this race. It was however, obvious, that the pace would probably be slow.

Whenever he encounters a "paceless" race such as this one, whether it be at seven furlongs or some other distance, the experienced player is acutely aware that horses attempting to rally from well off the pace are at a decided disadvantage, more so than usual. Identifying the laggards, however, often proves as difficult as finding the early speed, with the jockey's awareness of the situation often the deciding factor dictating whether a horse prompts the pace or falls well back in the early stages.

In the race we are considering, Swap For Power (based on his last two races), Wimborne Castle (based on his races at six furlongs), Troop Ship, Storm Warrior (based on his sprints), and Stiff Upper Lip (based on the majority of his sprints) figure to be the rear guard, with J. Strap and Spy Game (the 6–5 favorite) not far ahead. This leaves Jeffrey C., Creme De La Fete, Cry For Help, and Cannon Royal as most likely to set the pace.

Another thing experienced players are well aware of is the unpredictable nature of paceless races. With the pace so much in question, no outcome should seem surprising. In such uncertain circumstances, the favorite is the last horse to play. A decent price is mandatory—a longshot highly desirable. At 6–5, Spy Game is very much an underlay, especially in light of his lack of early speed.

If a player insists on betting such races, he is best advised to look for a horse with the "winning attitude" (preferably at good odds) and a rider with a head on his shoulders. Whoever wins the race will do so because the rider took advantage of the unusual situation,

2 AQUEDUCT 7 FURLONGS (AQUEDUCT)

7 FURLONGS. (1.20⅕) CLAIMING. Purse $14,000. 4-year-olds and upward. Weights, 122 lbs. Non-winners of two races since April 1 allowed 3 lbs. Of a race since then 5 lbs. Claiming Price $25,000; for each $2,500 to $20,000, 2 lbs. (Races when entered to be claimed for $18,000 or less not considered.)

Coupled—Creme De La Fete and Rajab's Son; Spring Commander, Spy Game and Real Stubborn; Ample Native and J. Strap.

Charbonnel — B. h. 5, by Roberto—CHocolate Beau, by Beau Max
$20,000 Br.—Hanes Mrs J W (Ky) Tr.—Puentes Gilbert — 113
Own.—Garren M M
Lifetime 46 4 4 4 $41,855 | 1984 11 1 0 1 $8,280 | 1983 23 2 1 1 $27,600 | Turf 20 1 3 3 $9,505

19Apr84- 9Aqu fst 7f :23 :46⅘ 1:24⅕ Clm 20000 5 6 89 88¼ 813 713¼ Clayton M D b 117 17.00 67-26 What A Wabbit 1154 I'm Peppy 1174 Bank Account 117¾ Outrun 10
5Apr84- 5Aqu sly 6f ⊡:23 :46⅘ 1:11⅘ Clm 20000 7 3 96½ 913 713 610¼ Smith A Jr b 113 22.50 75-25 Coplis 1152¾ Spy Game 1172 Starbinia 1172¾ Outrun 9
17Mar84- 9Aqu fst 6f ⊡:23 :47⅘ 1:13 Clm 16000 6 8 97½ 76 53½ 51½ Clayton M D b 117 12.90 77-22 Royal Jove 117¾ Clinebell 115½ Bouliabase 112nk Clipped heels st 11
11Mar84- 5Aqu fst 6f ⊡:22⅘ :46⅘ 1:12⅘ Clm 20000 10 9 109¾ 66½ 87¾ 96½ Smith A Jr b 117 21.40 75-23 Rauschenberg 1142¾ Coplis 117no Ample Native 1171½ Outrun 12
3Mar84- 9Aqu fst 6f ⊡:22⅘ :47 1:13⅕ Clm 20000 1 11 1115 1112 1113 98½ Hernandez R b 117 11.40 69-29 Fleet Receiver 1103½ Coplis 117no Ample Native 117no No factor 11
23Feb84- 5Aqu fst 170 ⊡:48⅕ 1:14 1:44⅘ Clm 30000 9 8 87 77½ 77½ 76½ Smith A Jr b 113 18.80 72-22 Swap for Power 115¾ Hep Cat119nk GauguinNative1082 No factor 10
12Feb84- 9Aqu fst 6f ⊡:22⅘ :46⅘ 1:11⅘ Clm 16000 7 10 1011 77½ 3½ 14½ Smith A Jr b 117 8.90 85-24 Charbonnel 1174½ Royal Jove 117no WineAndWomen103½ Driving 12
3Feb84- 1Aqu fst 170 ⊡:48⅗ 1:14⅕ 1:46⅗ Clm 18000 3 9 914 812 98¼ 89¾ Hernandez R b 114 10.70 58-28 Letter FromLucy112noExuberance115¾WhatACharger1175 Outrun 10
27Jan84- 9Aqu gd 6f ⊡:22⅕ :45⅗ 1:11 Clm 16000 5 9 88¼ 66¾ 57½ 56 Smith A Jr b 117 *3.00 83-16 Royal Duel 1174 Shaz 115hdHawaiianMoonshine1141½ Lckd a rally 12
18Jan84- 9Aqu fst 6f ⊡:23⅘ :48⅘ 1:14 Clm 16000 10 2 73½ 75 66¼ 38½ Vega H7 110 14.30 65-35 Bold Target 1195 Rauschenberg 1223½ Charbonnel 1101¾ Rallied 12
LATEST WORKOUTS Apr 2 Bel tr.t 4f fst :47⅕ h Mar 25 Bel tr.t 5f fst 1:02⅘ b

Jeffery C. — Ch. g. 6, by Deer Isle—Sea Flare, by Neptune
$25,000 Br.—Thompson J W (NJ) Tr.—Fernandez Floreano — 117
Own.—Iron Lance Stables
Lifetime 74 13 12 15 $186,785 | 1984 5 0 0 1 $1,920 | 1983 27 1 7 9 $55,640 | Turf 3 0 0 0

20Apr84- 3Aqu fst 1 :46⅘ 1:12⅘ 1:38⅘ Clm 25000 2 5 31 22 22½ 33¾ Skinner K 117 7.60 69-28 WhatAChrger1172½CremeDeLFete1131½JefferyC 1171½ Weakened 8
17Mar84- 3Aqu fst 6f ⊡:23⅘ :47⅘ 1:13⅘ Clm 25000 8 3 41¾ 76 76½ 77 Cordero A Jr 117 8.30 70-22 Edge Of Wisdom 1171 I'm Peppy 1153½ Town Clown 112nk Tired 10
9Feb84- 9Aqu fst 6f ⊡:22⅘ :45⅕ 1:10⅕ Clm 30000 10 7 55 67 812 711½ MacBeth D 113 10.50 82-18 Bold Target 1136 Gauguin Native 1101½ Meru 1082½ Outrun 12
2Feb84- 2Aqu fst 170 ⊡:49 1:13⅕ 1:43⅕ Clm 35000 3 3 63½ 66 55 63½ Cole M A7 110 11.80 81-22 Surf Club 117¾ Big Izzy 117½ Full Concert 1131½ Early foot 10
12Jan84- 3Aqu fst 1⅙ ⊡:49⅕ 1:15 1:46 Clm 32500 2 8 73¾ 62¾ 73¾ 812½ Cole M A7 108 7.70 70-22 Share The Risk 1088¾ Feeling Too Much 115nkGauley1141 Outrun 12
30Dec83- 3Aqu fst 6f ⊡:23 :47 1:12⅘ 3+Clm 32500 9 1 65 66½ 66½ 55½ Davis R G 115 5.70 75-26 Creme De La Fete 117¾ Big Izzy 1171½ ⒹMeru 112no Evenly 9
23Dec83- 2Aqu gd 6f ⊡:22⅘ :46⅘ 1:12⅘ 3+Clm c-25000 7 1 32½ 22½ 21½ 2no Cordero A Jr 117 3.30 81-21 Bright Search 117noJefferyC.1172TheBloodyBest117¾ Just missed 10
28Nov83- 1Aqu my 7f :23⅕ :47 1:25 3+Clm 35000 3 3 34 32 32 35½ Samyn J L 117 4.30 70-30 Cold Trailin' 117hd Big Izzy 1135½ Jeffery C. 1172 No rally 8
10Nov83- 2Aqu fst 7f :23 :46⅘ 1:24⅘ 3+Clm 35000 3 6 63½ 43 24 22½ Zuniga M 117 4.50 75-24 Cold Trailin' 1172½ Jeffery C.1172½SurfClub1172½ Wide, stumbled 11
30Oct83- 3Aqu fst 6f :23 :46⅘ 1:11⅘ 3+Clm 35000 1 1 74 64¾ 53 3¾ Zuniga M 117 7.40 82-22 Tarantara 110hd Canadian Currency 113¾ Jeffery C. 117no Rallied 8
LATEST WORKOUTS Apr 11 Bel tr.t 4f fst :47⅘ hg Mar 15 Bel tr.t 4f fst :50 b

Swap for Power — Dk. b. or br. g. 6, by Seat of Power—Swipe, by Swaps
$25,000 Br.—Binn M (NY) Tr.—Martin Jose — 117
Own.—Mautner S
Lifetime 47 8 6 4 $200,724 | 1984 9 2 1 0 $25,830 | 1983 14 1 1 0 $16,350 | Turf 1 0 0 0

12Apr84- 5Aqu fst 170 ⊡:47⅘ 1:11⅘ 1:41⅘ Clm 32500 4 5 54½ 41¾ 56½ 512 Bailey J D b 115 5.00e 80-19 Starbinia 1133½ Pearl Amber 113½ Great Hunter 1173¾ Tired 8
2Apr84- 3Aqu fst 1⅛ ⊡:47⅘ 1:12 1:51⅘ Clm 32500 5 7 77½ 85¾ 912 913¼ Hernandez R b 1154 11.50 70-17 Gauguin Native 1063½ Bishen 1173½ Full Concert 1131 Outrun 11
2Apr84-Dead heat
24Mar84- 9Aqu fst 170 ⊡:48⅕ 1:13⅘ 1:45⅘ Clm 32500 6 2 32 41½ 61¾ 61½ Cordero A Jr b 115 *2.80 71-24 JungleMrsh113noClerTheBses113hdEdgeOfWisdom113hd Lckd rm. 10
10Mar84- 5Aqu fst 1⅛ ⊡:48⅘ 1:12⅘ 1:52⅕ Alw 38000 2 2 42 66½ 59½ 512¾ Lovato F Jr b 115 34.60 71-17 Startop's Ace 1151½ Letter From Lucy1105AlecGeorge1162½ Tired 7
23Feb84- 5Aqu fst 170 ⊡:49⅕ 1:14 1:44⅘ Clm 32500 4 3 21 21½ 2hd 1¾ Cordero A Jr b 115 4.00 78-22 Swap for Power 115¾ Hep Cat 119nk Gauguin Native 1082 Driving 10
12Feb84- 3Aqu fst 1⅛ ⊡:48⅘ 1:13⅘ 1:53⅘ Clm 32500 3 6 55½ 31½ 52½ 53½ Hernandez R 115 3.80e 73-24 Cagle Springs 115no Big Izzy 117nk Bishen 117no Lacked a rally 10
30Jan84- 3Aqu fst 1⅙ ⊡:48⅘ 1:14 1:47⅕ Clm 25000 6 6 52½ 11 2hd 2½ Hernandez R b 119 *3.10 75-25 ColonelLaw114½SwpforPower119¾MorningReview1171¾ Game try 12
12Jan84- 3Aqu fst 1⅙ ⊡:49⅕ 1:15 1:46 Clm 32500 6 3 42 51¾ 84 712 Hernandez R b 117 *2.00 70-22 ShreTheRisk1088¾FelingTooMuch115nkGuly1141 Steadied,lckd rm 12
2Jan84- 5Aqu fst 170 ⊡:47⅘ 1:12⅕ 1:42⅘ Clm 35000 3 4 57 46½ 32 11 Hernandez R b 117 7.40 87-21 Swap for Power 1171 To Erin 113½ Jet Steam 112¾ Driving 8
23Dec83- 5Aqu gd 1⅛ ⊡:48⅘ 1:13⅘ 1:52⅘ 3+Clm 70000 7 1 41½ 75¾ 910 912½ Vergara O b 113 5.90e 68-21 ⒹAccountReceivble117nkDd'sDl119noPurlyAPrinc1141¾ Fin. early 10
LATEST WORKOUTS Apr 20 Bel tr.t 3f fst :36⅘ h Apr 10 Bel tr.t 4f fst :50 b Mar 22 Bel tr.t 3f gd :35⅘ h Mar 17 Bel tr.t 4f fst :47⅘ h

Creme De La Fete * — Ch. g. 8, by Creme Dela Creme—Bridge Day, by Tudor Minstrel
$20,000 Br.—Collett & Polk Jr (Ky) Tr.—Barrera Oscar S — 113
Own.—Barrera O S
Lifetime 121 31 22 12 $374,725 | 1984 11 2 2 0 $28,040 | 1983 30 9 7 4 $127,240 | Turf 2 0 0 0 $174

20Apr84- 3Aqu fst 1 :46⅘ 1:12⅘ 1:38⅘ Clm 20000 8 3 52 44½ 34 22½ Lovato F Jr b 113 *.70e 70-28 What A Charger 1172½ Creme DeLaFete1131½JefferyC.1171½ Wide 8
9Apr84- 3Aqu fst 6f ⊡:23 :46⅘ 1:12 Clm 20000 9 2 42½ 56½ 46½ 52 Migliore R b 117 4.80e 82-19 Ample Native 117nk ⒹⒽStarbinia 119 ⒹⒽDebaj 119¾ No rally 11
28Mar84- 1Aqu fst 1¼ ⊡:46⅘ 1:39⅘ 2:05 Clm 20000 10 4 48 24 28 29 Cordero A Jr b 117 *1.70 84-22 PerlAmber1179CremeDeLFete1176MgicMichel1133 Best of others 10
26Mar84- 5Aqu fst 6f ⊡:23 :47⅕ 1:13⅕ Clm 22500 2 5 43½ 108 118¾ 95½ Cordero A Jr b 115 4.20 72-28 I'm Peppy 115hd Rauschenberg 1171½ J. Strap 108nk Stopped 12
12Mar84- 3Aqu fst 1¼ ⊡:50⅘ 1:42⅘ 2:08 Clm 15000 9 1 2hd 12 13 17 Cordero A Jr b 115 4.20 78-22 Creme De LaFete1157MagicMichael1131½Sestrel117nk Ridden out 9
7Mar84- 3Aqu fst 6f ⊡:22⅘ :46⅕ 1:11⅘ Clm 25000 9 2 73¾ 77½ 712 712½ Murphy D J5 b 112 3.50 75-17 Debaj 1173 Rauschenberg 1133 Just Any Time 1171½ Outrun 9
2Mar84- 7Aqu fst 6f ⊡:23⅕ :47 1:11⅘ Clm 45000 1 6 73½ 76 811 610 MacBeth D b 113 *2.20e 76-28 British Gunner 1082 Kaye's Prince 1132½ Fibak 1171 No factor 6
20Feb84- 5Aqu fst 6f ⊡:22⅕ :45⅘ 1:11⅘ Clm 70000 2 7 78 812 714 79 MacBeth D b 113 9.30 78-16 Measureable 113½ Tri Swaps 113hd I'm So Merry 108½ No speed 8
20Jan84- 9Aqu fst 1⅙ ⊡:49⅘ 1:14⅘ 1:48⅘ Clm 45000 9 2 31 98¼ 913 913¼ Smith A Jr b 115 5.90 56-29 Minabchar 117hd Taic Power 1135¾ Class Hero 115nk Stopped 11
12Jan84- 5Aqu fst 170 ⊡:48 1:13⅘ 1:42⅘ Clm 70000 10 2 33 64¾ 913 914¼ Smith A Jr b 114 3.90 75-22 Last Turn 1171½ Measureable 1131 Jordan's Gray 117nk Gave way 10

Cry For Help — B. g. 5, by Raise A Bid—Fifi Cat, by Crafty Admiral
$25,000 Br.—Dilibero C (Fla) Tr.—Schaeffer Stephen — 107[10]
Own.—Spiegel R
Lifetime 32 7 7 7 $57,066 | 1983 20 4 4 4 $35,126 | 1982 12 3 3 3 $21,940 | Turf 1 0 0 0 $255

15Dec83- 9Med fst 1⅙ :47⅘ 1:11⅘ 1:44⅘ 3+Clm 28000 2 3 31½ 31 32½ 39½ Messina R7 b 109 *1.70 78-18 Hagline 112nk Harpers Bazaar 1169 Cry For Help 1091 Tired 5
7Dec83- 7Med fst 6f :23 :46⅘ 1:12⅕ 3+Clm c-25000 3 3 54 43 1hd 14 Cordero A Jr b 119 3.30 82-26 Cry For Help 1194 RoyalJove109½Old'nWise1143 Forced out,clear 8
13Nov83- 8Suf gd 170 :47 1:12⅘ 1:44⅘ 3+Clm 21500 3 7 77½ 32 21½ 24 Elliott S b 117 *2.00 73-33 Self Pressured 1194CryForHelp1171OutAndAway1122½ Poor start 7
6Nov83- 8Suf sly 170 :48⅘ 1:14⅕ 1:45⅘ 3+Clm 21000 4 2 32½ 21 12 12 Elliott S b 122 5.40 72-38 Cry For Help 1222 Self Pressured 1192½ OutAndAway1146 Driving 7
28Oct83- 9Suf fst 170 :47 1:12⅕ 1:44⅘ 3+Alw 10500 5 4 41½ 31 2hd 31½ Elliott S b 122 13.40 75-27 Cozy Talk 115nk Mystery Jet 1061 Cry For Help 122½ Hung 6
15Oct83- 9Suf fst 1 :47 1:12⅕ 1:38⅘ 3+Alw 10000 7 4 42 1½ 11½ 1½ Elliott S b 114 2.70 84-23 Cry For Help 114½ Unnatural Joe 1172½ Cozy Talk 109nk Driving 7
8Oct83- 8Suf fst 6f :22⅘ :45⅘ 1:11 3+Clm 17500 3 6 3nk 32 33 2½ Elliott S b 117 12.70 85-22 Green Path 114½ Cry For Help 1172½ Andrew Scott 119½ Steadied 7
1Oct83- 7Suf fst 6f :22⅘ :45⅘ 1:11 3+Clm 16500 1 8 129½ 1111 910 48¾ Elliott S b 113 12.80 77-24 SkiResort1172½GreenPth1143¾AndrwScott1192½ Pass'd tired ones 12
17Sep83- 9Suf fst 170 :46⅘ 1:11⅕ 1:41⅘ 3+Clm 16500 6 2 21 35½ 36 312½ Elliott S b 113 10.50 80-19 Self Pressured 10912 BoldBlueStar114½CryForHelp1134½ Steadied 6
10Sep83- 8Suf fst 6f :22⅘ :45⅘ 1:10⅘ 3+Clm 17000 6 9 96½ 54½ 65 79½ Elliott S b 115 8.30 79-17 Runnymede Rambler 114nkⒹOratorical1142NuJacques1123½ Wide 9
LATEST WORKOUTS Apr 19 Bel tr.t 6f fst 1:13⅘ h Apr 13 Bel tr.t 5f fst 1:02⅘ b Apr 7 Bel tr.t 5f fst 1:01⅘ h Mar 23 Bel tr.t 3f fst :36⅘ h

Wimborne Castle — Dk. b. or br. h. 6, by Sir Wimborne—Amber Souffle, by Ambiorix
$20,000 Br.—Whitney T P (NY) Tr.—DeBonis Robert — 108[5]
Own.—Masilipin Stable
Lifetime 61 8 5 8 $209,140 | 1984 9 1 2 0 $14,960 | 1983 19 1 1 1 $22,650 | Turf 1 0 0 0

17Apr84- 1Aqu fst 1⅛ ⊡:48⅕ 1:13⅕ 1:59 Clm c-16000 4 4 3nk 2½ 2½ 45¾ Samyn J L b 119 *1.40 77-15 Magic Michael 1171¾BeauJangles1122Roger'sPass1132 Weakened 8
31Mar84- 1Aqu gd 6f ⊡:22⅘ :45⅘ 1:11⅘ Clm 16000 7 11 109 1011 64 2no Santagata N b 119 10.30 87-15 NorthrnShrik113noWimbornCstl119½WhtAWbbt1121½ Just missed 12
21Mar84- 1Aqu fst 1⅛ ⊡:49⅘ 1:15⅕ 1:55 Clm 16000 11 3 31½ 61½ 2hd 1¾ Samyn J L b 117 *.90e 67-24 WmbrnCstl117¾FrAndSpnc1171¾ShtngDck117no Pocketed driving 12
17Mar84- 9Aqu fst 6f ⊡:23 :47⅘ 1:13 Clm 16000 5 10 108½ 96¾ 75½ 72½ Smith A Jr b 117 5.80 77-22 Royal Jove 117¾ Clinebell 115½ Bouliabase 112nk Showed little 11
4Mar84- 9Aqu fst 1⅙ ⊡:48⅘ 1:14 1:46⅘ Clm 16000 9 3 32 2hd 22 23¾ Cordero A Jr b 117 4.50 75-21 HallOfHonor1173¾WimborneCstle1175Speier'sLuck117½ Hung str. 12
29Feb84- 9Aqu fst 6f ⊡:22⅘ :46⅘ 1:12⅘ Clm 16000 3 9 99½ 96¾ 86½ 73½ MacBeth D b 117 *3.70 77-24 Big Ralph 116noNorthernShrike113nkWineAndWomen107¾ Outrun 11
23Feb84- 3Aqu fst 6f ⊡:22⅘ :46⅕ 1:11⅘ Clm 20000 2 7 84¾ 78½ 75 55 MacBeth D b 117 *2.80 80-22 Stage Gossip 1101½ Rapid Wing 1171½ J. Strap 1171½ Mild bid 8
9Feb84- 9Aqu fst 6f ⊡:22⅘ :45⅕ 1:10⅕ Clm 32500 12 12 1210 1110 1012 811½ Smith A Jr b 115 9.30 81-18 Bold Target 1136 Gauguin Native 1101½ Meru 1082½ Outrun 12
29Jan84- 9Aqu fst 6f ⊡:22⅘ :46 1:11⅘ Clm 35000 9 11 117½ 1112 65½ 41 Smith A Jr b 117 25.30 84-15 WhatAWabbit113noEdgeOfWisdom117nkCrockfordLd117¾ Rallied 11
29Dec83- 8Aqu my 6f ⊡:23 :46⅘ 1:11⅘ 3+Alw 35000 2 10 98 911 914 711¾ Smith A Jr b 115 35.20 74-30 Hagley's Reward 1173AgileShoebill117hdElegantLife1131¾ Outrun 10
LATEST WORKOUTS Apr 12 Bel tr.t 3f fst :37 b

Spring Commander — Dk. b. or br. g. 5, by Spring Double—Little Debre, by Revoked
$20,000 Br.—Wetherington E C (Md) Tr.—Moschera Gasper S — 106[7]
Own.—Davis A
Lifetime 21 5 6 3 $66,740 | 1984 5 1 2 0 $17,710 | 1983 15 4 3 3 $45,290

19Mar84- 1Aqu fst 6f ⊡:23 :47⅘ 1:12⅘ Clm c-19000 9 6 21½ 32 43½ 57½ Squartino R A5 b 112 *.80 74-25 Starbinia 1192¾ Ample Native 1171½WhatAWabbit1082 Slow early 10
11Mar84- 9Aqu fst 6f ⊡:22⅘ :46⅘ 1:11⅘ Clm 32500 8 2 11½ 11½ 2½ 21¾ MacBeth D b 117 *1.40 85-23 FltRcivr1131¾SpringCommndr1175½PrtngCrck109¾ Best of others 11
1Mar84- 3Aqu fst 6f ⊡:22⅘ :46 1:12⅕ Clm 32500 4 8 1½ 12½ 15 13 Muino M M7 b 108 3.20 83-23 SpringCommnder1083SintStephn1101NotblPlsur117hd Ridden out 11
19Feb84- 9Aqu fst 6f ⊡:22⅘ :45⅘ 1:10⅘ Clm 35000 1 2 84¾ 85½ 42½ 41¾ Davis R G b 117 5.50 88-14 JetVoyage118½KentuckyEdd114¾Kim'sChance112½ Lacked a rally 11
1Jan84- 9Aqu fst 6f ⊡:23 :46⅘ 1:12⅕ Clm c-25000 10 1 12½ 1hd 2hd 2¾ Santiago A b 117 *3.40 82-22 FlyingGeneral112¾SpringCommander1172½ColonelLw106½ Gamely 12
18Dec83- 1Aqu fst 6f ⊡:22⅘ :46⅕ 1:11⅘ 3+Clm 35000 11 4 12½ 11½ 1½ 54¾ Santiago A b 117 12.70 82-25 CandinCurrency114hdBigIzzy1172TheBloodyBest1082½ Weakened 11
8Dec83- 5Aqu fst 6f ⊡:22⅕ :45⅕ 1:11 3+Clm 35000 3 6 33 44 45½ 45¾ Santiago A b 117 16.90 83-17 Kentucky Edd 117½ Cannon Shell 1101½ Big Izzy 1154 Weakened 10
6Nov83- 3Aqu fst 6f :22⅘ :46 1:11⅕ 3+Clm 75000 4 7 78½ 714 717 724½ Cruguet J b 119 6.50 60-29 Mighty Nasty 1172¾ Hereford Man 1081 Verbum 1063¾ Off slowly 7
16Oct83- 9Suf fst 6f :22⅘ :45⅘ 1:10⅘ 3+Alw 9500 3 2 2hd 2hd 2½ 21½ Bush W V b 122 *1.60 85-22 ⒹAurbar 1161½ Spring Commander 122no Minabchar 106hd Tired 5
16Oct83-Placed first through disqualification
3Oct83- 9Suf gd 6f :22⅕ :45⅘ 1:11 3+Alw 8500 5 2 21 1½ 12 14½ Bush W V b 119 *.70 86-23 SpringCommnder1194½TheGretFicco1161½DockStrik116nk Driving 6
LATEST WORKOUTS Apr 22 Bel tr.t 4f fst :49 b Apr 17 Bel tr.t 3f my :39 b (d) Apr 2 Bel tr.t 4f fst :48⅕ h Mar 23 Bel tr.t 4f fst :59⅘ b

Troop Ship — B. g. 5, by Hoist the Flag—Fiddling, by Herbager
Own.—Clark S C Jr — $25,000 — Br.—Clark Jane F (Ky) — Tr.—Watters Sidney Jr — 117
Lifetime 37 1 6 6 $48,150 — 1984 6 0 2 0 $7,810 — 1983 13 1 2 1 $17,240 — Turf 8 0 1 2 $10,440

pr84- 5Aqu fst 170 ⊡:47⅘ 1:11⅘ 1:41⅗ Clm 35000 6 6 66½ 65¾ 612 716¾ Skinner K b 117 8.20 75-19 Starbinia 1133½ Pearl Amber 113¾ Great Hunter 1173¾ Outrun 8
pr84- 9Aqu fst 6f ⊡:23⅕ :47 1:12⅗ Clm 35000 4 10 86 55½ 24 2nk Skinner K b 117 21.40 81-19 Toss Across 117nk Troop Ship1172PartingCrack117nk Drifted out 12
pr84- 5Aqu fst 6f ⊡:23⅕ :47⅖ 1:12⅖ Clm 45000 5 8 95¾ 83¾ 85¾ 84¾ Skinner K b 115 40.90 77-22 [D]I'm So Merry 106¾ Quill Feather114¾Fibak110¹ Showed nothing 9
n84- 7Aqu fst 1116 ⊡:47⅘ 1:12⅖ 1:45⅘ Alw 22000 11 6 107¾1114111811125 Smith A Jr b 117 3.00e 58-20 Fast John 117no Righteous Anger 1103CanadianCalm1192 Outrun 11
n84- 5Aqu fst 6f ⊡:23 :47 1:13 Alw 20000 9 10 77¾ 78½1016 1114¾ Lovato F Jr b 117 *3.20 64-30 Mc Michael112hdFlyingGeneral1124½PrideOfSatan1102½ Fell back 11
n84- 5Aqu sl 6f ⊡:23⅕ :47⅘ 1:13⅘ Alw 20000 8 11 94¾ 75½ 42¾ 22 Lovato F Jr b 117 27.90 75-33 Sky Falcon 1122 Troop Ship 117nk Saint Stephan 117¾ Rallied 12
83- 2Sar gd 1⅛ Ⓣ:47⅘ 1:13 1:52 3↑Clm 40000 12 2 21½ 2½ 2½ 99½ Bailey J D b 117 41.10 70-25 ForceCommndr1172¾RichButtrfly1152½DivinMrquis113hd Stopped 12
83- 2Sar gd 1116 Ⓣ:47 1:12 1:45 3↑Clm 40000 7 8 811 98½ 85¾ 74¾ Bailey J D b 117 18.50 68-20 Cancun 114¾ Millbank 1141¾ Skaran 1171½ Outrun 11
83- 3Sar fst 1⅛ :47⅕ 1:11⅕ 1:49⅗ 3↑Clm 50000 6 2 2½ 21½ 510 521½ Bailey J D b 117 10.30 65-13 Prete Khale 1156¾ Tumarshua 1158½ To Erin 115¾ Tired 7
83- 5Bel fst 6f :22⅖ :45⅗ 1:10⅕ Alw 20000 4 8 1011 97¾ 68 56¾ Murphy D J5 b 112 17.30 84-17 BelieveTheQuen1123½DigginDitchs1111¾Will'sFirst116no No threat 10
ATEST WORKOUTS Apr 21 Bel 4f fst :47⅘ h — Apr 8 Bel tr.t 3f fst :38⅗ b — Apr 3 Bel tr.t 4f fst :47 h — Mar 28 Bel tr.t 5f fst :59⅘ h

Also Eligible (Not in Post Position Order):

J. Strap — B. c. 4, by Sauce Boat—Sadie Mae, by Sadair
Own.—Sedlacek Sue — $20,000 — Br.—Jones W L Jr & Greathouse D (Ky) — Tr.—Sedlacek Sue — 108[5]
Lifetime 41 3 5 10 $68,970 — 1984 8 0 0 4 $8,910 — 1983 23 2 2 6 $40,050 — Turf 1 0 0 0

20Apr84- 3Aqu fst 1 :46⅘ 1:12⅗ 1:38⅘ Clm 20000 4 6 63½ 55 55 45 Lopez V5 108 5.80 68-28 What ACharger1172¾CremeDeLaFete1131½JefferyC 1171½ In close 8
6Apr84- 3Aqu fst 170 ⊡:46⅗ 1:11 1:42⅘ Clm 20000 8 10 814 716 412 39¾ Lopez V5 112 6.50 78-18 Palimony 1065¾ Rajab's Son 1174 J Strap 112¹ Rallied 10
26Mar84- 5Aqu fst 6f ⊡:23 :47⅕ 1:13⅕ Clm 20000 4 7 64½ 54½ 43 31½ Lopez V5 108 11.30 76-28 I m Peppy 115no Rauschenberg 1171½ J. Strap 108nk Willingly 12
17Mar84- 3Aqu fst 6f ⊡:23⅗ :47⅘ 1:13⅘ Clm 25000 1 5 52½ 54 54½ 66 Lopez V5 112 5.20 71-22 Edge Of Wisdom 117¹ I'm Peppy 1153¾TownClown112no Even try 10
23Feb84- 3Aqu fst 6f ⊡:22⅘ :46⅕ 1:11⅘ Clm c-20000 8 4 53½ 44 31 33 Vergara O 117 3.30 82-22 Stage Gossip 1101½ Rapid Wing 1171½ J. Strap 1171½ Evenly late 8
8Feb84- 5Aqu fst 6f ⊡:22⅖ :46⅖ 1:12⅕ Clm 25000 4 10 65 63¾ 44 42¾ Messina R5 112 5.20 80-19 I'm Peppy 1131¾ Shy Hughes 115nk Royal Due: 117¾ Evenly late 12
26Jan84- 9Aqu my 6f ⊡:22⅖ :45⅖ 1:10⅗ Clm 22500 2 8 63 54½ 52½ 31½ Messina R5 110 9.60 89-10 Bold Target 115½ Spy Game 113¹ J Strap 110no Rallied 10
16Jan84- 1Aqu fst 6f ⊡:23 :47⅗ 1:13⅘ Clm 25000 2 4 42 55 61½ 73½ Santagata N 117 6.60 71-41 Ample Native 113½ I'm Peppy 117½ Crockford Lad 117¹ Gave way 12
24Dec83- 1Aqu fst 6f ⊡:22⅗ :48⅘ 1:16⅘ Clm 25000 8 2 55½ 42½ 1hd 1½ Santagata N 117 8.00[D] 61-43 [D]J Strp117½Mirculously117½BrightestHope1121¾ Illegal whipping 12
24Dec83-Disqualified and placed second
30Nov83- 7Aqu fst 7f :23 :46⅕ 1:25⅗ Clm 25000 11 1 52¾ 51¾ 53¾ 44½ Davis R G 117 6.70 69-29 Miraculously 1171½ Prospero 117no Dr Frownfelter 1173 Evenly 12

Real Stubborn — Dk. b. or br. g. 4, by In Reality—Bellevarde, by Herbager
Own.—Davis A — $25,000 — Br.—Kimmell C P (Ky) — Tr.—Moschera Gasper S — 112[7]
Lifetime 17 1 7 1 $27,860 — 1984 6 1 3 1 $13,110 — 1983 11 M 4 0 $14,750

12Apr84- 9Aqu fst 6f ⊡:23 :46⅘ 1:12⅗ Md 25000 7 3 11 1hd 1hd 1no Cordero A Jr b 122 *1.60 81-19 Real Stubborn 122no Avid Dancer 1182½ Jason's Key118nk Driving 10
23Mar84- 9Aqu fst 6f ⊡:23 :48⅕ 1:14 Md c-20000 2 4 31½ 2hd 21½ 32½ Santagata N b 118 *1.20 72-24 MajestyCove118noAvidDancer1132½RealStubborn1185 No excuses 9
5Mar84- 6Aqu fst 6f ⊡:22⅘ :46⅗ 1:12 Md Sp Wt 6 5 53½ 63¾ 43½ 53¾ Murphy D J5 b 117 10.00 81-22 Irish Ore 122nk Heads Will Roll 1221½ Oyster 1221½ Evenly 8
8Feb84- 2Aqu fst 6f ⊡:23⅕ :47⅗ 1:13 Md 14000 5 1 2½ 2hd 2½ 22 Santagata N b 122 *1.00 77-19 CommnderAlmy1112RelStubborn1227½DesignerJns115¾ Game try 11
30Jan84- 9Aqu fst 6f ⊡:23 :46⅗ 1:13 Md 20000 11 3 4¾ 11 11 2nk Santagata N b 118 4.00 79-25 Makarios 115nk Real Stubborn 1182¾ Proudest Fellow 118nk Wide 12
5Jan84- 2Aqu fst 1116 ⊡:47⅘ 1:13⅗ 1:48⅘ Md 12000 5 1 14 16 13 2nk Messina R5 b 113 3.20 68-23 Vida De Oro 118nkRealStubborn1132¾RadioNews1111½ Just failed 12
29Dec83- 2Aqu my 6f ⊡:23⅕ :48⅕ 1:15⅕ 3↑Md 14000 7 7 5¾ 2hd 2½ 23 Messina R5 b 115 2.90 65-30 Delbarton 1163 Real Stubborn 115hd Solo 118¾ Led 'tween calls 7
21Dec83- 2Aqu fst 6f ⊡:23⅕ :47⅘ 1:13⅘ 3↑Md 20000 5 9 85½ 65¾ 68 78½ Davis R G b 116 6.80 68-28 Sky Falcon 1152½SummerTwilight120nkTheCableRock116¾ Outrun 11
30Nov83- 9Aqu fst 6f :23 :47⅕ 1:13⅕ 3↑Md 20000 10 3 2hd 2hd 32½ 43¾ Davis R G b 120 5.40 71-29 Morning Review 120hd Decatur 1202½ Ack Attack1201½ Weakened 12
21Nov83- 4Aqu fst 7f :23⅕ :46⅖ 1:25 3↑Md 35000 5 6 3nk 22 36 410½ Maple E b 116 4.00 65-23 MockCourt1204½SummerTwilight1166Jason'sKey116nk Weakened 10
LATEST WORKOUTS Apr 18 Bel tr.t 4f fst :48⅖ h — Apr 7 Bel tr.t 3f fst :35⅗ h — ●Mar 31 Bel tr.t 3f sly :35⅕ h

Rajab's Son — Ch. h. 5, by Rajab—Ever So Lovely, by Ever On
Own.—Barrera O S — $22,500 — Br.—Karutz W S (NY) — Tr.—Barrera Oscar S — 115
Lifetime 54 7 8 9 $158,234 — 1984 11 3 1 0 $33,670 — 1983 18 0 1 5 $24,468 — Turf 6 2 0 1 $39,588

20Apr84- 3Aqu fst 1 :46⅘ 1:12⅗ 1:38⅘ Clm 25000 6 2 21 32½ 44½ 55½ Squartino R A5 b 114 *.70e 67-28 What A Charger 1172¾ CremeDeLaFete1131½JefferyC.1171½ Tired 8
16Apr84- 5Aqu gd 1⅛ ⊡:48⅖ 1:12⅗ 1:51⅗ Clm 20000 1 2 2hd 11 12 13 MacBeth D b 117 *1.70 84-13 Rajab's Son 1173 Mr. Showbiz 1174½MachoDuck1172¾ Ridden out 6
6Apr84- 3Aqu fst 170 ⊡:46⅗ 1:11 1:42⅖ Clm 20000 10 3 36½ 25 25 25¾ MacBeth D b 117 5.20 82-18 Palimony 1065¾ Rajab's Son 1174 J. Strap 112¹ Best of others 10
19Mar84- 1Aqu fst 6f ⊡:23 :47⅖ 1:12⅖ Clm 19000 2 4 108½ 94¾ 65 48 MacBeth D b 117 5.00e 76-25 Starbinia 1192¾ Ample Native 1171½ What A Wabbit 1082 Rallied 10
11Mar84- 5Aqu fst 6f ⊡:22⅗ :46⅖ 1:12⅖ Clm 20000 1 7 85¾ 99 97¾ 75½ Murphy D J5 b 114 *2.30 76-23 Rauschenberg 1142¾ Coplis 117no Ample Native 1171½ No factor 12
7Mar84- 8Aqu fst 1116 ⊡:47⅗ 1:11⅘ 1:43⅗ 3↑[S]King Point H 9 5 74¾ 712 922 925½ Murphy D J b 106 5.40e 68-17 Jacque's Tip 118hd Startop's Ace 1078 Stiff UpperLip1113 Outrun 9
27Feb84- 5Aqu fst 170 ⊡:48⅗ 1:13⅘ 1:44⅗ Clm 20000 6 2 1hd 1hd 11½ 1¾ MacBeth D b 117 5.30 78-24 Rajab'sSon117¾LetterFromLucy114noOurMnVlentine1085 Driving 9
22Feb84- 9Aqu fst 6f ⊡:22⅗ :45⅗ 1:10⅘ Clm 45000 1 1 62¾ 85½1112 1111 Messina R5 b 108 8.70 79-25 Wild Moment 1173 Infinite Saga 113hd Cutter Sark 1122 Tired 12
19Feb84- 8Aqu fst 6f ⊡:22⅘ :45⅗ 1:10⅕ 3↑[S]H Hughes H 8 5 63 108½107½107½ Davis R G b 108 18.90 86-14 ColumbiHolme112nkMesuredResponse1071½EigntLif116no Outrun 10
12Feb84- 3Aqu fst 1⅛ ⊡:48⅗ 1:13⅘ 1:53⅘ Clm 32500 4 2 2hd 1hd 2hd 4nk MacBeth D b 115 4.30 76-24 Cagle Springs 115no Big Izzy 117nk Bishen 117no Weakened 10
LATEST WORKOUTS Mar 28 Bel tr.t 4f fst :47⅘ h — Mar 5 Bel tr.t 3f fst :36⅗ h

Spy Game — Dk. b. or br. c. 4, by Raja Baba—Konigsalpen, by Priamos
Own.—Davis A — $25,000 — Br.—Farish W S III (Ky) — Tr.—Moschera Gasper S — 117
Lifetime 37 6 9 6 $86,075 — 1984 9 2 3 1 $27,830 — 1983 27 4 6 5 $57,795 — Turf 1 0 0 0

18Apr84- 5Aqu fst 6f ⊡:22⅗ :45⅘ 1:10⅗ Clm 30000 1 4 43½ 33½ 22 22¾ Cordero A Jr b 113 3.00 88-16 Amore Mio 1172¾ Spy Game 1132¾ Parting Crack 117hd Game try 8
14Apr84- 1Aqu my 6f ⊡:22⅗ :45⅘ 1:11⅕ Clm 25000 8 11 1013 108¾ 66½ 32 Cordero A Jr b 117 *3.30 86-15 Meru 110no Jet Steam 1152 Spy Game 1171½ Rallied 12
5Apr84- 5Aqu sly 6f ⊡:23 :46⅖ 1:11⅘ Clm 25000 9 2 32 34½ 24 22¾ Cordero A Jr b 117 4.50 82-25 Coplis 1152¾ Spy Game 1172 Starbinia 1172¾ Game try 9
22Mar84- 5Aqu fst 6f ⊡:22⅖ :45⅖ 1:11⅖ Clm 35000 5 8 76½ 78 68 74 Samyn J L b 117 10.20 83-24 Debaj 117½ Shining Out 1171½ Parting Crack 115¹ Outrun 12
26Feb84- 9Aqu fst 6f ⊡:22⅘ :46⅗ 1:12⅕ Clm c-25000 9 6 77 75¾ 44½ 45¾ MacBeth D b 119 *3.70 77-29 WhtAChrger1171½[D]Ruschnbrg1083AmplNtiv1131½ lacked fin bid 12
18Feb84- 2Aqu fst 6f ⊡:23 :47⅕ 1:11⅗ Clm 25000 2 10 63½ 52½ 21½ 11½ MacBeth D b 117 2.80 86-12 SpyGm1171½WhtAWbbit1191½EdgOfWisdom117¾ Slow early, drvg 12
6Feb84- 5Aqu my 6f ⊡:23 :46⅗ 1:11 Clm c-20000 11 4 82½ 74½ 64¾ 54¾ MacBeth D b 117 2.50 84-19 Rajab's Son 1123 Ample Native 119¾ Miraculously 117no No rally 12
26Jan84- 9Aqu my 6f ⊡:22⅖ :45⅖ 1:10⅗ Clm 20000 6 9 84¾ 65 42 2½ Smith A Jr b 113 4.80 90-10 Bold Target 115½ Spy Game 113¹ J. Strap 110hd Rallied 10
14Jan84- 9Aqu fst 6f ⊡:22⅗ :46⅕ 1:11⅗ Clm 15000 4 1 73¾ 66 42½ 11½ MacBeth D b 117 3.70 87-17 SpyGame1171½StageGossip1102BrightSerch117½ Fractous st,clear 12
28Dec83- 9Aqu sly 170 ⊡:49 1:14⅘ 1:47⅖ Clm 20000 10 5 41¾ 32½ 22½ 42 Cordero A Jr b 113 *2.60 62-29 Only Just Begun 106½Speier'sLuck110hdProspero1121½ Weakened 10
LATEST WORKOUTS Mar 15 Bel tr.t 4f fst :47⅕ h — Mar 7 Bel tr.t 4f fst :47⅗ h

Cannon Royal — B. h. 5, by Cannonade—Royal Sense, by Sensitivo
Own.—Barge M — $25,000 — Br.—Drinkhouse M F (Fla) — Tr.—Sedlacek Roy — 117
Lifetime 42 7 4 5 $96,745 — 1984 7 0 1 0 $4,740 — 1983 19 4 0 2 $60,840 — Turf 8 1 1 1 $21,140

2Apr84- 3Aqu fst 1⅛ ⊡:47⅗ 1:12 1:51⅘ Clm 35000 9 2 1½ 43 1118 1123¾ Garcia R L Jr10 b 107 36.40 59-17 Gauguin Native 1063½ Bishen 1173½ Full Concert 113¹ Stopped 11
11Mar84- 9Aqu fst 6f ⊡:22⅗ :46⅖ 1:11⅖ Clm 32500 10 9 64 42½ 45 59¾ Miranda J b 115 21.70 77-23 FltRcivr1131¾SpringCommndr1175½PrtingCrck109¾ Lacked a rally 11
20Feb84- 2Aqu fst 1116 ⊡:47⅗ 1:12⅘ 1:46⅖ Clm 20000 10 1 11 1½ 1hd 2nk Davis R G b 117 3.70 80-16 Starbinia 117nk Cannon Royal 1172¾ Purple Emperor117½ Gamely 11
11Feb84- 2Aqu fst 170 ⊡:48 1:13⅗ 1:44⅕ Clm 45000 2 1 11½ 1hd 51¾ 78 Miranda J b 113 15.90 72-20 To Erin 1142½ Class Hero 115nk Rosalbin 117½ Tired 10
2Feb84- 7Aqu fst 170 ⊡:48 1:12⅖ 1:43⅗ Alw 38000 1 1 12½ 32 1014 1016 Graell A b 115 28.00 68-22 Medieval'sSon115¾SpaceMountain112nkHvgretdte1173 Used early 10
19Jan84- 3Aqu fst 6f ⊡:23⅗ :47⅗ 1:14⅕ Clm c-35000 4 3 — — — — Miranda J b 117 7.60 — — Wild Moment 115nk Cold Trailin' 113nk Am Dependable115no Fell 11
2Jan84- 5Aqu fst 170 ⊡:47⅖ 1:12⅕ 1:42⅘ Clm 35000 1 1 13 12½ 2½ 42½ Miranda J b 117 9.70 85-21 Swap for Power 117¹ To Erin 113½ Jet Steam 112¾ Weakened 8
24Dec83- 3Aqu fst 1116 ⊡:49⅗ 1:16⅕ 1:52⅖ 3↑Clm 35000 10 7 65¾ 45½ 66 711 Miranda J b 117 22.30 39-43 Gauley 112nk Badwagon Harry 117½ Rajab's Son 1151½ Tired 12
18Dec83- 2Aqu fst 1116 ⊡:48⅕ 1:13⅗ 1:47⅗ 3↑Clm 45000 10 5 52½ 77¾ 1015 1019½ Miranda J b 113 16.10 56-25 Laddy's Luck 115½ Righteous Anger 117½ShootingDuck1084 Tired 11
16Nov83- 6Med gd 1116 :47⅕ 1:12 1:45 3↑Clm 40000 4 1 12 12½ 12½ 1½ Miranda J b 116 20.50 84-18 Cannon Royal 116½ Poor Dad 1162 Red Light 115¾ Driving 8

Storm Warrior — B. c. 4, by Northern Jove—My Buck, by Buckpasser
Own.—Casetta Farm — $20,000 — Br.—Evans T M (Va) — Tr.—Campo John P — 113
Lifetime 19 1 3 0 $13,430 — 1984 6 0 0 0 $630 — 1983 9 0 1 0 $5,000

20Apr84- 3Aqu fst 1 :46⅘ 1:12⅗ 1:38⅘ Clm 20000 5 7 74 88½ 78 78¾ Miranda J 113 17.40 64-28 WhtAChrger1172¾CremeDeLFete1131½JeffryC.1171½ Lacked room 8
14Apr84- 3Pim sly 1116 :48⅖ 1:13⅕ 1:44⅕ Clm 25000 6 4 43 33 35½ 46½ Miranda J b 114 12.80 77-15 His Worship 114hd Hi Ho Racconto 1144½ Ixatapa 1152 Weakened 6
7Mar84- 3Aqu fst 6f ⊡:22⅘ :46⅕ 1:11⅗ Clm 25000 8 8 96¾ 88½ 611 59½ Miranda J b 117 38.00 78-17 Debaj 1173 Rauschenberg 1133 Just Any Time 1171½ No factor 9
18Feb84- 2Aqu fst 6f ⊡:23 :47⅕ 1:11⅗ Clm 25000 1 11 116½ 109¾ 98½ 99 Smith A Jr b 117 34.90 77-12 Spy Game 1171½ What A Wabbit1191½EdgeOfWisdom117¾ Outrun 12
19Jan84- 3Aqu fst 6f ⊡:23⅗ :47⅗ 1:14⅕ Clm 35000 6 6 910 910 811 88½ Hernandez R 117 27.80 65-32 Wild Moment 115nk ColdTrailin'113nkAmDependable115no Outrun 11
5Jan84- 5Aqu fst 6f ⊡:22⅖ :45⅗ 1:11⅗ Clm 50000 2 10 1016 1014 1012 98½ Hernandez R 117 43.40 78-23 Shining Out 113no Measureable 1172 The TimeIsNow113¾ Outrun 11
22Dec83- 5Aqu sly 170 ⊡:48 1:13 1:43⅕ Clm 75000 4 7 77¾ 63½ 616 618½ McHargue D G 112 15.40 66-25 Alchise 1142½ Last Turn 1144½ Macho Duck 1125½ Outrun 7
3Dec83- 3Aqu gd 1 :46⅕ 1:11 1:37⅕ Clm 75000 4 7 73½ 56½ 59 57½ Vergara O 117 35.90 73-20 In the Ruff 1131½ Joy Hour 1172½ Fibak 113no Outrun 8
24Nov83- 9Aqu fst 7f :22⅖ :45⅗ 1:24⅕ 3↑Alw 22000 5 7 97½ 913 1020 914¾ Skinner K b 115 34.20 65-24 SpecialCare117¾ScarletHobeau115¾CanadinCurrency1173½ Outrun 10
2Nov83- 5Aqu fst 1¼ :48⅖ 1:38⅘ 2:04⅘ 3↑Alw 24000 9 4 21½ 919 927 930½ Santagata N b 115 16.90 42-30 IndianLei1154½CandinCurrency1175½ChopperChrlie117nk Bore out 9
LATEST WORKOUTS Apr 11 Bel tr.t 4f fst :50 b — Apr 1 Bel tr.t 5f fst :59 hg — Mar 24 Bel tr.t 4f fst :49 b — Mar 20 Bel tr.t 4f fst :49 b

Ample Native — Ro. h. 5, by Shy Native—Ample Antics, by Funny Fellow
Own.—Sedlacek W — $22,500 — Br.—Sedlacek Sue (NY) — Tr.—Sedlacek Sue — 117
Lifetime 35 7 6 3 $108,530 — 1984 9 2 3 2 $30,040 — 1983 9 1 2 0 $12,230 — Turf 1 0 0 0

Date/Race	Cond	Dist	Fractions	Class	PP	St	1st	2nd	Str	Fin	Jockey	Wt	Odds	Speed	Top Finishers	Comment	Field
9Apr84- 3Aqu	fst	6f	⊡:23 :46⅘ 1:12	Clm 20000	5	1	3^{2}	2^{2}	$2^{1½}$	1^{nk}	Gomez E R	b 117	6.20	84-19	Ample Native 117^{nk} [DH]Starbinia 119 [DH]Debaj 119¾	Driving	11
19Mar84- 1Aqu	fst	6f	⊡:23 :47⅗ 1:12⅗	Clm 20000	7	2	$4^{3½}$	$2^{½}$	$1^{1½}$	$2^{2¾}$	Gomez E R	b 117	3.70e	79-25	Starbinia $119^{2¾}$ Ample Native $117^{1¼}$ What AWabbit 108^{2}	Bore out	10
11Mar84- 5Aqu	fst	6f	⊡:22⅗ :46⅖ 1:12⅖	Clm 20000	3	4	$5^{2½}$	$4^{1¾}$	$3^{1½}$	$3^{2¾}$	Gomez E R	b 117	9.60	79-23	Rauschenberg $114^{2¾}$Coplis117^{no}AmpleNative$117^{1¼}$	Lacked fin. bid	12
3Mar84- 9Aqu	fst	6f	⊡:22⅗ :47 1:13⅕	Clm 20000	11	1	2^{hd}	1^{hd}	$1^{1½}$	$3^{3½}$	Lopez V	b 117	7.10	74-29	Fleet Receiver $110^{3½}$ Coplis 117no Ample Native 117no	Tired	11
26Feb84- 9Aqu	fst	6f	⊡:22⅘ :46⅗ 1:12⅕	Clm 20000	11	1	$3^{½}$	2^{hd}	2^{hd}	$3^{4¼}$	Gomez E R	b 113	15.00	79-29	WhatAChrger$117^{1½}$[D]Ruschenberg108^{3}AmpleNtive$113^{1½}$	Steadied	12
26Feb84-Placed second through disqualification																	
15Feb84- 9Aqu	sly	6f	⊡:22⅕ :46⅕ 1:11⅗	Clm 20000	8	3	$3^{4½}$	3^{3}	$3^{2½}$	5^{5}	Gomez E R	b 119	3.90	81-23	AppelAffirmed117¾KentuckyEdd117^{2}Ruschenberg113¾	Weakened	12
6Feb84- 6Aqu	my	6f	⊡:23 :46⅖ 1:11	Clm 20000	10	3	2^{hd}	$3^{½}$	$2^{1½}$	2^{3}	Gomez E R	b 119	17.50	86-19	Rajab's Son 112^{3} Ample Native 119¾ Miraculously 117^{nc}	In tight	12
26Jan84- 9Aqu	my	6f	⊡:22⅖ :45⅖ 1:10⅗	Clm 20000	11	3	$7^{3¼}$	7^{5}	$6^{4¾}$	$9^{5¾}$	Gomez E R	b 115	8.00	85-10	Bold Target 115½ Spy Game 113^{1} J. Strap 110^{hd}	No factor	10
16Jan84- 1Aqu	fst	6f	⊡:23 :47⅗ 1:13⅘	Clm 20000	10	11	$9^{4¾}$	$8^{6¼}$	3^{hd}	$1^{½}$	Gomez E R	b 113	14.80	75-41	AmpleNtive113½I'mPeppy117¾CrockfordLd117^{1}	Ducked in drvng	12
27Dec83- 1Aqu	fst	6f	⊡:23⅕ :47⅖ 1:14⅘	3+Clm 12500	7	1	1^{1}	$1^{3½}$	1^{4}	$2^{1¼}$	Gomez E R	b 119	5.10e	69-31	The BloodyBest$117^{1¼}$AmpleNative119^{3}MajorMenuever$117^{1¼}$	Tired	9

LATEST WORKOUTS Apr 2 Aqu ⊡ 3f fst :35⅗ h

Stiff Upper Lip B. g. 4, by Upper Nile—Grinand Bearit, by Olympia
Own.—Lunetta J $22,500 Br.—Jones Brereton C & Humphrey G W Jr (NY) Tr.—Jerkens H Allen **115**

Lifetime									
17 3 0 2	$64,404	1984	4	1	0	1	$29,304
		1983	12	1	0	1	$20,700
		Turf	1	0	0	0	

Date/Race	Cond	Dist	Fractions	Class	PP	St	1st	2nd	Str	Fin	Jockey	Wt	Odds	Speed	Top Finishers	Comment	Field
9Apr84- 7Aqu	fst	6f	⊡:22⅘ :46⅖ 1:10⅘	Clm 45000	5	5	7^{5}	8^{13}	8^{17}	$8^{14¼}$	Velasquez J	b 113	4.90	76-19	Infinite Saga 117^{nk} Top Hat $117^{1¼}$ Fibak $106^{7½}$	Outrun	8
7Mar84- 8Aqu	fst	$1\frac{1}{16}$	⊡:47⅗ 1:11⅘ 1:43⅗	3+[S]King Point H	8	2	4^{2}	4^{5}	3^{5}	3^{8}	Velasquez J	b 111	4.90e	86-17	Jacque's Tip 118^{hd}Startop'sAce107^{8}StiffUpperLip111^{3}	Weakened	9
19Feb84- 8Aqu	fst	6f	⊡:22⅖ :45⅖ 1:10⅕	3+[S]H Hughes H	2	7	$7^{4½}$	$9^{5¾}$	$9^{3½}$	$4^{1½}$	Belmonte J E	b 109	2.70e	91-14	ColumbiHolme112^{nk}MesuredResponse$107^{1¼}$EightLif116^{hd}	Rallied	10
28Jan84- 5Aqu	fst	6f	⊡:23⅕ :47 1:12	[S]Alw 27000	5	2	$4^{2½}$	$1^{½}$	1^{hd}	1^{nk}	Belmonte J E5	b 112	9.20	84-20	Stiff Upper Lip112^{nk}ColumbiaHolme$117^{1¾}$McMichael117½	Driving	10
10Nov83- 7Aqu	fst	7f	:22⅖ :45⅘ 1:24⅗	3+[S]Alw 28000	5	7	$6^{4½}$	9^{7}	$7^{9½}$	$7^{8½}$	Clayton M D	b 115	26.10	70-24	GeorgeCinq120¾Jordan'sGray$115^{1¾}$NorthernExchnge115^{hd}	Outrun	10
31Oct83- 5Aqu	fst	1	:46⅕ 1:10⅘ 1:35⅖	3+[S]Alw 29500	7	6	$6^{3¾}$	6^{9}	6^{15}	$6^{20¼}$	Thibeau R J	b 114	23.20	69-24	MusicPrince$116^{3¾}$Jordan'sGry$114^{6¾}$NorthernExchnge114^{6}	Outrun	8
20Oct83- 3Bel	my	7f	:23 :46⅕ 1:23⅖	3+[S]Alw 28000	4	8	7^{7}	$7^{6½}$	7^{12}	$7^{11¼}$	Clayton M D	114	30.50	74-14	BoldTrumpetr$110^{1¼}$Jordn'sGry114^{hd}MusicPrinc119^{1}	Broke slowly	8
16Sep83- 9Bel	fst	6f	:22⅖ :46 1:11⅘	3+[S]Alw 28000	5	5	$7^{4½}$	$9^{6½}$	9^{7}	$8^{7¾}$	Clayton M D5	109	44.70	75-23	CrftyIrishmn112^{2}TimeTogethr$113^{2½}$WorldEmprior108^{no}	No factor	11
2Sep83- 8Bel	fst	6f	:23⅕ :46⅖ 1:10	3+Alw 24000	3	5	$6^{4½}$	$6^{7½}$	6^{14}	$6^{20¾}$	Thibeau R J5	108	31.80	71-16	Eskimo $115^{3½}$ Nearice 113^{3} Columbia Holme 113^{5}	Outrun	6
30Jun83- 6Bel	fm	1¼	[T]:51⅗ 1:41⅗ 2:06	3+[S]Alw 28500	3	8	$9^{9½}$	9^{14}	9^{20}	9^{22}	Velasquez J	112	7.90	42-27	Danderoo 117no KnuckleheadSmith112^{1}WimborneSky102^{4}	Outrun	9

LATEST WORKOUTS Apr 19 Bel 6f fst 1:15⅘ h   Apr 16 Bel 3f sly :38 b (d)   Apr 7 Bel tr.t 4f fst :51 b   Mar 28 Bel tr.t 7f fst 1:28⅗ h

or at least was not victimized by it, and because the horse "found a way" to win. A paceless race is just another in a long list of excuses that losing horses seldom overcome.

After eliminating the five horses that were most likely to comprise the rear echelon, and then the favored Spy Game, we may proceed to discard the disinterested Jeffrey C. (one win in thirty-two starts during 1983–84) and J. Strap (two wins in thirty-one starts), and the recently inactive Cry For Help. We are left with two possibilities: the aforementioned Cannon Royal, at 20–1, and the gallant old campaigner Creme De La Fete, long a favorite on the New York circuit, at 7–2. Based on his recent sharp performance at the similar one-turn mile distance, Creme De La Fete seemed the more logical selection. His career record of thirty-one wins in 121 starts made the 7–2 odds a small overlay, although perhaps not as much as one might hope for in such a race. Indeed, the horse would have been a more interesting betting proposition had he been coming off a pair of excusably poor performances—and still worth playing in a race as open as this one, based on his past history as a "winner."

Creme De La Fete needed all the grit and courage he could muster, overcoming traffic problems to charge from last to first in the last eighth mile, as nine horses finished within three lengths of the winner. The early pace was set by Stiff Upper Lip, whom our analysis had relegated to the rear guard.

Seven-furlong races become far more decipherable when the contention for the early lead can be readily identified—and especially so when only one such horse can be found. Actually, we have said nothing specific about seven-furlong races, but that will be the focus of the rest of this chapter.

There is a significant difference between the pace at six and seven furlongs. The horse able to lead early at the longer distance is

SECOND RACE **Aqueduct** **APRIL 24, 1984**

7 FURLONGS. (1.20⅘) CLAIMING. Purse $14,000. 4-year-olds and upward. Weights, 122 lbs. Non-winners of two races since April 1 allowed 3 lbs. Of a race since then 5 lbs. Claiming Price $25,000; for each $2,500 to $20,000, 2 lbs. (Races when entered to be claimed for $18,000 or less not considered.)

Value of race $14,000, value to winner $8,400, second $3,080, third $1,680, fourth $840. Mutuel pool $91,036, OTB pool $139,086. Quinella Pool $120,734. OTB Quinella Pool $179,955.

Last Raced	Horse	Eqt.A.Wt	PP	St	¼	½	Str	Fin	Jockey	Cl'g Pr	Odds $1
20Apr84 ^{3}Aqu^{2}	Creme De La Fete	b 8 113	3	3	3^{1½}	5^{hd}	1^{1}	1^{nk}	MacBeth D	20000	3.60
20Apr84 ^{3}Aqu^{7}	Storm Warrior	4 113	9	10	10^{hd}	10^{½}	8^{½}	2^{hd}	Cruguet J	20000	57.10
18Apr84 ^{5}Aqu^{2}	Spy Game	b 4 117	7	2	6^{hd}	7^{hd}	3^{1}	3^{¾}	Cordero A Jr	25000	1.30
20Apr84 ^{3}Aqu^{3}	Jeffery C	b 6 117	1	8	9^{3}	9^{1½}	6^{hd}	4^{nk}	Santagata N	25000	7.40
9Apr84 ^{7}Aqu^{8}	Stiff Upper Lip	b 4 116	10	5	1^{1}	1^{½}	1^{hd}	5^{nk}	Velasquez J	22500	14.90
12Apr84 ^{5}Aqu^{7}	Troop Ship	b 5 117	6	9	8^{1}	8^{2}	7^{½}	6^{nk}	Skinner K	25000	7.50
12Apr84 ^{5}Aqu^{5}	Swap for Power	b 6 117	2	6	7^{1}	6^{hd}	5^{½}	7^{nk}	Lovato F Jr	25000	24.80
20Apr84 ^{3}Aqu^{4}	J. Strap	4 108	11	1	2^{½}	2^{1½}	2^{1}	8^{½}	Lopez V^{5}	20000	15.20
17Apr84 ^{1}Aqu^{4}	Wimborne Castle	b 6 108	5	11	11	11	9^{2}	9^{¾}	Squartino R A^{5}	20000	18.20
2Apr84 ^{3}Aqu^{11}	Cannon Royal	b 5 117	8	4	4^{½}	3^{3}	4^{½}	10^{3}	Gomez E R	25000	20.70
15Dec83 ^{9}Med^{3}	Cry For Help	b 5 117	4	7	5^{2}	4^{½}	10^{½}	11	Migliore R†	25000	17.00

OFF AT 1:26 Start good Won driving Time, :22⅘, :45⅘, 1:11⅖, 1:25 Track muddy.

$2 Mutuel Prices:				
	4–(D)–CREME DE LA FETE	9.20	5.60	4.20
	9–(L)–STORM WARRIOR		33.00	11.80
	1–(J)–SPY GAME			2.60

$2 QUINELLA 4–9 PAID $419.80.

Ch. g, by Creme Dela Creme—Bridge Day, by Tudor Minstrel. Trainer Barrera Oscar S. Bred by Collett & Polk Jr (Ky).

CREME DE LA FETE close up early, dropped back between horses around the turn came out for the drive and finished boldly from the extreme outside to be up in the final strides. STORM WARRIOR, outrun to the stretch, finished with good energy while racing well out in the track. STIFF UPPER LIP showed speed to deep stretch while saving ground but weakened under pressure and came back cut on the right front leg. TROOP SHIP finished with good energy while racing wide. SWAP FOR POWER rallied along the inside nearing midstretch but wasn't good enough. J. STRAP was used up prompting the pace. CANNON ROYAL, a factor into the stretch, lacked a late response. CRY FOR HELP tired. WIMBORNE CASTLE raced with mud caulks.

seldom quick enough to head a pack of six-furlong types, Stiff Upper Lip being a case in point. An especially interesting situation arises when a single six-furlong speed type is entered in a seven-furlong "dash." The situation's profit potential increases significantly if that horse's record shows difficulty handling the sixth furlong—while (hopefully) revealing nothing about the animal's ability at seven furlongs. However, the lead his early speed will build, and the psychological advantage that comes with it, will often carry the horse to the winner's circle.

The race we have chosen to demonstrate this point is especially interesting in that, supeficially at least, three horses appeared to have six-furlong speed, a situation that, if true, would normally favor the closers in the field. Accurate pace figures, however, revealed that two of the three were bogus and that one horse figured to have the early lead all to himself.

The race we are referring to was the ninth at Belmont on June 1, 1985. A quick glance at first and second running positions identifies Bucket Ben, Pridemore, and Handful Of Steel as most likely to debate the issue in the early stages of the race.

What separated Bucket Ben, the 5–2 favorite, from the others

9 BELMONT

7 FURLONGS
BELMONT PARK

7 FURLONGS. (1.20⅘) CLAIMING. Purse $16,000. 3-year-olds, weight, 122 lbs. Non-winners of two races since May 1 allowed 3 lbs. Of a race since then, 5 lbs. Claiming Price $25,000; for each $2,500 to $20,000 2 lbs. (Races when entered to be claimed for $18,000 or less not considered).

Coupled—Soaring Romeo and Erne; Venture Beyond and Natrac.

Great Britain
Ch. c. 3, by Riva Ridge—Stay For Tea, by In Reality
$25,000 Br.—Huber G (Ky)
Tr.—Van Tuyl Barbara
Own.—Magid S E
1107
Lifetime 10 1 1 1 $12,640 — 1985 9 1 0 1 $10,440 — 1984 1 M 1 0 $2,200

13May85- 5Bel fst 7f :23 :46⅘ 1:25 Clm 35000 5 5 64½ 86 58 58½ Moore D N5 112 10.40 68-20 Charmed Destiny 1131½ Bolinger 1106½ Scholastic 115nk Outrun 8
29Apr85- 5Aqu fst 7f :23⅗ :47⅗ 1:26⅕ Clm 50000 1 7 1hd 53 77 611½ Moore D N5 112 37.90 58-33 Mr. Jimmy G. 115½ Big Stoop 1173½ Keep It Down 113nk Tired 8
17Apr85- 5Aqu fst 6f :23 :47 1:12⅘ Clm 50000 9 7 55½ 55½ 43½ 55½ Moore D N5 112 55.50 73-30 Mr. Jimmy G. 113½ FirstConquest1123½BeautifulTan115½ Even try 9
10Apr85- 4Aqu fst 1 :46⅘ 1:12 1:38⅘ Clm 50000 10 5 53½ 43½ 47 78½ Moore D N5 112 39.00 64-29 Dream Of Peace 1131½Mr.JimmyG.1131½TimelessTaste1133½ Tired 11
3Mar85- 6Aqu fst 6f ⊡:23 :46⅘ 1:12 Alw 22000 7 8 96½ 98½ 89½ 912½ Santagata N 117 41.20 71-17 Crossfield 119½ Splendid Catch 1172 Verbascum 1176 Outrun 9
23Feb85- 3Aqu fst 6f ⊡:23⅗ :47⅕ 1:13⅕ Md 70000 9 1 1hd 1hd 1½ 12½ Moore D N5 113 *2.70 78-21 Great Britain 1132½ Too MuchToDrink118½GrayLark1181½ Driving 10
6Feb85- 6Aqu gd 170 ⊡:49⅗ 1:15⅗ 1:46⅘ Md Sp Wt 9 4 75½ 713 712 714½ Moore D N5 117 10.30 54-27 DncinOnPins122nkPerfectPrde122½SometimSomwhr1221 Outrun 9
23Jan85- 4Aqu fst 6f ⊡:22⅘ :46⅘ 1:14 Md 50000 8 2 2hd 32 21 32 Moore D N5 117 3.60 72-24 Ron Rivers 1182 Quickest Of All118noGreatBritain117½ Weakened 12
19Jan85- 4Aqu fst 6f ⊡:22⅘ :46⅘ 1:12⅘ Md 70000 4 3 52½ 712 69 612½ Moore D N5 113 9.50 69-22 TylorRod1227½SpiceyBones118nkJogger'sDelight1182½ Rough trip 10
24Dec84- 4Aqu fst 6f ⊡:22⅘ :47 1:12⅘ Md 25000 4 5 22 23 24 23½ Moore D N 113 18.00 78-20 UltimatePower1183½GreatBritain1136½SimpleTruth113no 2nd best 10
LATEST WORKOUTS May 23 Aqu ⓣ 3f sf :38⅘ b (d) ●May 8 Aqu ⊡ 3f fst :35⅘ h ●Apr 25 Aqu 4f fst :48 h Apr 7 Aqu 6f fst 1:21⅘ b

Chez Revine
B. g. 3, by Darby Creek Road—Chez Ge, by Bold Commander
$25,000 Br.—McNaughton J R (Ill)
Tr.—Pagano George
Own.—Luckman S M
1125
Lifetime 6 1 0 0 $7,800 — 1985 5 1 0 0 $7,200 — 1984 1 M 0 0 $600

12May85- 5Bel fst 1⅛ :46 1:10⅘ 1:43⅕ Alw 25000 5 7 712 725 741 756 Moore D N5 b 112 38.70 31-19 Attribute 1173 Purple Mountain 1122½FreedomsEdge1178 Trailed 7
19Apr85- 9Aqu sly 1 :47 1:13⅕ 1:39 3↑Md 30000 2 8 42½ 22 2½ 1hd Davis R G b 110 10.50 71-22 Chez Revine 110hd Sirjac 1157 Sans Shame 1122½ Driving 12
3Apr85- 4Aqu fst 7f :22 :45⅘ 1:24⅘ 3↑Md 25000 12 7 75 44 41½ 43½ Santagata N b 112 16.60 75-18 NewAdventure1121½CommndBrek107noNicetoMtYou1052½ Evenly 13
24Mar85- 4Aqu fst 1⅛ :49 1:15 1:55⅘ Md 30000 5 4 4½ 3½ 89½ 815 Santagata N b 118 13.70 43-26 Fleet's Honor 1186½ New Monaker 1132 Gran Attache 118nk Tired 11
25Feb85- 6Aqu fst 1⅛ ⊡:49⅕ 1:15 1:56 Md 45000 8 10 84½ 96½ 95½ 97 Privitera R5 113 10.50 55-25 Upper Spy 1182½ New Monaker 113hd April Spark 1131½ Outrun 10
31Dec84- 5Aqu fst 6f ⊡:22⅘ :46⅘ 1:11⅘ Md 30000 7 9 108½ 917 415 415½ Migliore R 114 22.90 73-15 Love That Mac 1188½ Niceto Meet You1095½KeyBoat115½ Rallied 11
LATEST WORKOUTS May 28 Bel 5f fst 1:02⅘ b May 23 Bel Ⓣ 4f gd :50⅕ b (d) May 9 Bel Ⓣ 5f fm 1:02⅘ h (d) Apr 14 Bel 5f fst 1:01⅗ h

Bucket Ben
B. g. 3, by Elocutionist—Summertime, by Secretariat
$25,000 Br.—Strawbridge G Jr (Pa)
Tr.—Meschera Gasper S
Own.—Davis A
1107
Lifetime 8 1 1 1 $11,320 — 1985 6 0 1 1 $5,320 — 1984 2 1 0 0 $6,000

22May85- 1Bel fst 6f :22⅕ :45 1:10⅘ Clm 25000 6 5 2hd 2hd 2hd 22 Hernandez R b 117 7.10 88-14 Charmed Destiny 1192 BucketBen1176EddieBubbles112½ 2nd best 8
20Apr85- 2Aqu my 6f :22⅕ :45⅘ 1:11⅕ 3↑Clm 25000 9 3 1hd 1½ 3½ 84½ Migliore R b 117 9.20e 80-18 Mister G. 117½ Keep It Down 117nk Irv's Choice 1172½ Tired 11
6Apr85- 2Aqu fst 6f :22⅘ :46⅕ 1:11⅘ Clm 35000 7 3 11 22½ 44½ 68 Samyn J L b 117 7.30e 75-21 Fly Me Again 115½ Eddie Bubbles1102½DashingDennis1171½ Tired 9
27Mar85- 2Aqu fst 6f :22⅘ :45⅘ 1:11⅘ Clm 25000 10 1 12 2½ 32½ 33 Davis R G b 117 20.20 80-20 H. T. Willis 1121½ Stark Dancer 1121½ Bucket Ben117½ Weakened 10
9Feb85- 2Aqu fst 6f ⊡:23⅘ :47⅘ 1:13⅘ Clm 35000 12 1 31½ 56 920 920½ Davis R G b 117 15.10 55-26 Summitry 1124 Bolinger 1107 Fly Me Again 108nk Tired 12
1Jan85- 3Aqu fst 6f ⊡:21⅘ :45 1:11⅘ Clm c-35000 9 1 1hd 1hd 1hd 76 Lovato F Jr b 119 7.20 80-13 Top Talk 1192½ Student of Dance 108no ShiningTyson117nk Tired 9
20Dec84- 4Aqu fst 6f ⊡:22⅘ :47 1:14 Md 32500 4 5 1½ 12 13 14 Lovato F Jr b 116 *1.20 74-19 Bucket Ben 1164 Time Pays Off 1071½ Rich Gift1141½ Ridden out 12
9Dec84- 4Aqu fst 6f ⊡:23 :46⅘ 1:12⅘ Md 47500 3 4 1hd 3nk 53 56 Lovato F Jr 116 2.40 74-19 ConfirmedPtriot114hdNicetoMtYou114nkTylorRod114½ Weakened 11
LATEST WORKOUTS May 18 Bel 4f gd :48⅕ h May 8 Bel 4f fst :47⅘ h May 2 Bel 4f gd :50 b Apr 16 Bel 5f sly 1:01⅘ h

Gorsk
Dk. b. or br. c. 3, by Full Out—Hedging, by Hail To Reason
$22,500 Br.—Smith Anson B (Ky)
Tr.—Barrera Oscar S Jr
Own.—Sea Spray Farms
115
Lifetime 19 3 1 0 $27,030 — 1985 11 2 1 0 $22,560 — 1984 8 1 0 0 $4,470 — Turf 1 0 0 0

24May85- 1Bel fst 1 :46⅘ 1:12 1:39⅘ Clm 17500 4 5 68 65½ 74½ 21½ Cordero A Jr 117 6.60 66-18 Regal Trick 1081½Gorsk117hdThat'sTerrific117nk Blocked bumped 9
16May85- 1Bel fst 1⅟₁₆ :46⅕ 1:12 1:45⅕ Clm 20000 7 8 87½ 812 712 712 Bailey J D b 113 5.60 64-18 Hthrs'Myrrh1132½JptrAccord1171½MstrCmmnd1144½ Broke in air 8
4May85- 1Aqu fst 6f :23 :46⅘ 1:12⅕ Clm c-14000 8 1 73½ 77½ 68½ 46½ Wynter N A7 b 110 5.40 74-15 Pridemore 1124½ Norab 112hd Hy Shark 1131½ No threat 8
29Apr85- 1Aqu fst 1 :49 1:14⅘ 1:40⅘ Clm 22500 7 5 76½ 716 720 723½ Messina R 115 32.20 39-33 Scholastic 1176½ Creative Spirit 1153½ Gay Date 112½ Outrun 7
18Apr85- 5Aqu fst 1⅛ :48⅘ 1:13⅕ 1:55⅕ Clm 22500 6 9 914 811 58 65½ Espinosa R E7 108 18.10 53-30 ClassiValentine1171½Hethers'Myrrh115½JupiterAccord117no Wide 9
25Mar85- 1Aqu fst 1 :50⅕ 1:17⅘ 1:44⅘ Clm 14000 4 7 43½ 31 15 13½ Espinosa R E7 110 2.80 44-35 Gorsk 1103½ Military Victory 1132½ Mr. Recharge 117½ Driving 8
6Mar85- 4Aqu fst 1⅛ ⊡:48⅘ 1:14 1:53⅘ Clm 30000 1 11 1211 1217 1227 1229½ Garrido O L5 b 108 29.10 43-26 DebateACase113hdI'mABnker117noAccordingToLuke113nk Outrun 12
17Feb85- 4Aqu fst 170 ⊡:48⅘ 1:14⅘ 1:46⅘ Clm 35000 8 10 1013 86½ 711 710½ Garrido O L5 b 112 6.60 57-25 Fly Me Again 1081 Star de Cesica1153½JupiterAccord1132 Outrun 10
10Feb85- 3Aqu fst 1⅛ ⊡:48 1:13⅘ 1:53⅘ Clm 45000 1 11 119½ 119½ 810 55½ Garrido O L5 b 108 12.90 69-18 Glenn Brooke 1103½ Classi Valentine 117noNatrac113½ Slow early 11
25Jan85- 3Aqu fst 1⅟₁₆ ⊡:48⅘ 1:14 1:48⅕ Clm 18000 9 9 78½ 67½ 1½ 11½ Garrido O L5 b 108 13.40 69-23 Gorsk1081½BoldBob'sDusty1083CountryKitchen1171½ Going away 9
LATEST WORKOUTS ●May 9 Bel tr.t 3f fst :35⅘ h Apr 26 Aqu 3f fst :37⅘ b

Montriva
Ch. g. 3, by Monteverdi—Ridge Partner, by Riva Ridge
$22,500 Br.—Downing C G (Ky)
Tr.—Downer Harold
Own.—Colonnelle D
1087
Lifetime 13 1 1 4 $10,538 — 1985 4 0 0 1 $1,800 — 1984 9 1 1 3 $8,738

3Feb85- 1Aqu gd 6f ⊡:22⅘ :47⅕ 1:14⅘ Clm c-14000 10 3 65½ 611 712 810½ Giglio D Jr7 b 110 4.30 61-22 Stasera 117nk Czar's Fiddle 107hd Churning 112½ Outrun 10
25Jan85- 3Aqu fst 1⅟₁₆ ⊡:48⅘ 1:14 1:48⅕ Clm 20000 8 2 21 21½ 922 927½ Ward W A5 b 112 5.10 41-23 Gorsk 1081½ Bold Bob's Dusty 1083CountryKitchen1171½ Stopped 9
18Jan85- 5Aqu fst 6f ⊡:22⅘ :46⅘ 1:12⅘ Clm 25000 2 10 75 78 75½ 811 Ward W A5 b 112 5.30 70-21 ConfirmedPatriot1102½FirstNiteJitters117nkNaric1225 Slow start 11
4Jan85- 1Aqu fst 6f ⊡:23⅕ :47⅘ 1:12⅘ Clm 20000 8 4 5½ 23 23 34½ Ayarza I b 117 5.70 76-21 Gay Date 1082 Fly Me Again 1172½ Montriva 1171½ Wide, faltered 8
26Dec84-10Med fst 6f :23⅘ :47 1:13 Md 16000 2 7 11½ 11½ 13 12 Ayarza I b 118 *2.40 77-21 Montriva 1182 Power of Words 1183 He's AHeartake1182 Driving 10
17Nov84- 1Med fst 6f :23 :46⅘ 1:14 Md 28000 8 1 66½ 611 715 815 Ayarza I b 116 4.80 57-22 My Marisa 1084 Propeltor 118hd Leonard's Bunky 116½ No threat 9
26Oct84- 8Crc fst 6f :22⅘ :46⅘ 1:14 Md 25000 9 3 3½ 12 12½ 2½ Aviles O B b 118 7.60 80-17 Dacandina 118½ Montriva 1181½ Iron Fire 1182 Just failed 9
11Oct84-10Crc fst 6f :23 :46⅘ 1:14 Md 25000 7 4 42 42½ 65 67½ Aviles O B b 118 *3.20 74-19 Hail Taurus 1181½ Iron Fire 1182 Ells Do Much 118no Tired 12
1Oct84- 8Crc sly 6f :23 :47⅕ 1:14⅘ Md 25000 2 6 64 56½ 55 31½ Aviles O B 113 8.70 76-27 Parting Words 117½ Regal Force 1171 Montriva 1131 Rallied 12
13Sep84- 6Crc fst 7f :23⅘ :48⅕ 1:28⅕ Md 20000 4 1 1hd 1hd 1hd 42 Smith A Jr 117 *1.40 73-22 FlyingLord117noRobbyRaggs113nkExpectedMgic1171½ Weakened 12
LATEST WORKOUTS ●May 28 Aqu ⊡ 6f fst 1:16⅘ b ●May 24 Aqu ⊡ 5f fst 1:04 b May 5 Bel tr.t 5f fst 1:02⅘ b Apr 28 Bel tr.t 4f fst :51⅕ b

Pridemore
B. g. 3, by I'm For More—Ruthies Pride, by Jackal
$22,500 Br.—Poll D (Fla)
Tr.—Baeza Braulio
Own.—Mistretta Rose
115
Lifetime 11 2 4 1 $21,210 — 1985 8 1 2 1 $13,820 — 1984 3 1 2 0 $7,390

19May85- 3Bel fst 6f :23 :46⅘ 1:12⅕ Clm c-17500 2 1 23 24 22½ 21½ Moore D N5 b 112 *1.40 80-20 HndfulOfSteel1171½Pridemore1122½SprklingStte1171 Ducked out 10
4May85- 1Aqu fst 6f :23 :46⅘ 1:12⅕ Clm 14000 3 2 1hd 13 15 14½ Moore D N5 b 112 *1.40 80-15 Pridemore 1124½ Norab 112hd Hy Shark 1131½ Driving 8
19Apr85- 1Aqu fst 6f :23 :45⅘ 1:12 Clm 14000 5 2 45½ 38½ 210 27 Moore D N5 b 112 3.80 74-24 Bolinger 1127 Pridemore 1122½ SumpinRoyal1191½ Best of others 8
2Apr85- 2Aqu fst 7f :23⅕ :46⅘ 1:24⅘ Clm 14000 4 6 22 1½ 21½ 33½ Giglio D Jr7 b 110 2.30e 73-20 Sumpin Royal 1171½InstantRecall1172½Pridemore1102½ Weakened 10
4Feb85- 2GP fst 1⅟₁₆ :48⅕ 1:12⅘ 1:46⅘ Clm c-15000 5 5 64½ 78½ 1216 1214 Londono O J b 117 6.50 53-18 Bold Genius 122hd Flooey 117nk Secret Estate 1171½ Gave way 12
24Jan85- 4GP fst 6f :21⅘ :45 1:10⅘ Clm 20000 11 2 75½ 613 510 417 Londono O J b 117 6.90 70-18 Davey Do Good 1179 John One Six 1172 Mister Bid 1156 Outrun 12
17Jan85- 7GP fst 7f :22⅕ :45⅕ 1:24⅘ Clm 25000 12 1 53½ 42 42½ 54 Londono O J b 119 7.50 78-17 Crovero 117hd Wiles Road 113nk Stripe It Rich 122nk Weakened 12
2Jan85- 8Crc fst 6f :22⅘ :46 1:12⅘ Clm 30000 2 6 63½ 74½ 65½ 56½ Solis A b 120 20.60 80-16 UpperGrade116hdStrategyTalk1202½PrideofPortara1122 No factor 10
5Dec84- 4Crc fst 6f :22⅘ :46⅘ 1:14⅕ Md 25000 10 1 1½ 11½ 11 1½ Solis A b 120 *1.20 80-20 Pridemore 120½ Superb News 1201½ Princely Dream 1201 Driving 10
22Nov84- 1Crc fst 6f :22⅘ :46⅘ 1:13⅘ Md 20000 12 1 11 11 1hd 2½ Londono O J b 119 7.40 82-16 John One Six 119½ Pridemore1193VisibleJourney1192½ Weakened 12
LATEST WORKOUTS May 31 Bel tr.t 3f fst :36⅘ h May 27 Bel tr.t 5f fst 1:06 b

Soaring Romeo
B. g. 3, by Gallant Romeo—Soar Aloft, by Avatar
$20,000 Br.—November House Associates (Ky)
Tr.—Pascuma Warren J
Own.—Rogers Barbara D
113
Lifetime 11 3 0 0 $24,000 — 1985 11 3 0 0 $24,000 — 1984 0 M 0 0

22May85- 1Bel fst 6f :22⅕ :45 1:10⅘ Clm 22500 1 2 612 58½ 69½ 69½ MacBeth D b 115 20.20 81-14 Charmed Destiny1192BucketBen1176EddieBubbles112½ No factor 8
13May85- 5Bel fst 7f :23 :46⅘ 1:25 Clm 30000 8 1 54 42½ 814 817 MacBeth D b 113 12.70 60-20 Charmed Destiny 1131½ Bolinger 1106½ Scholastic 115nk Outrun 8
9Apr85- 4Aqu fst 7f :23 :47⅘ 1:25⅘ Clm c-25000 1 11 1218 1213 916 1115 Thibeau R J b 119 14.00 59-25 CharmedDestiny1103½TheRunningKind117hdMisterG.1175½ Outrun 12
27Mar85- 5Aqu fst 7f :22⅕ :45⅘ 1:22⅘ Clm 45000 5 8 1011 1013 821 819½ Thibeau R J b 113 21.40 68-20 Summitry 1174 Taylor Road 1175½ The RunningKind1132½ Outrun 10
17Mar85- 9Aqu fst 7f :23⅘ :48⅕ 1:28⅘ Clm 25000 12 1 116½ 118½ 22 1½ Thibeau R J b 119 5.50 59-33 Soaring Romeo 119½ Irv's Choice112½FrenchAnswer110no Driving 12
7Mar85- 2Aqu fst 6f ⊡:22⅘ :45⅘ 1:12⅘ Clm 25000 8 9 107½ 89½ 76½ 54 Thibeau R J b 119 9.90 78-21 Gay Date 114½ French Answer 1151½ Bolinger 112no Mild gain 11
1Mar85- 5Aqu fst 1⅟₁₆ ⊡:49 1:13⅘ 1:47⅘ Clm 45000 6 7 75½ 65½ 65½ 56½ Thibeau R J b 113 15.30 64-25 History Responds 113nk Natrac 109no Maggie'sMike115hd Outrun 7
18Feb85- 9Aqu fst 6f ⊡:22⅘ :46⅘ 1:13⅘ Clm 25000 7 8 97½ 810 43½ 1½ Thibeau R J b 117 46.10 75-28 SoaringRomeo117½StarkDancer117noStudentofDnce1143½ Driving 10
9Feb85- 2Aqu fst 6f ⊡:23⅘ :47⅘ 1:13⅘ Clm 35000 3 9 1215 1221 1224 1223½ McCarron G b 119 44.20 52-26 Summitry 1124 Bolinger 1107 Fly Me Again 108nk Far back 12
27Jan85- 9Aqu fst 6f ⊡:22⅘ :46⅘ 1:13 Clm 50000 4 11 117½ 1015 1011 1010½ McCarron G b 117 30.00 69-20 Anconeus 1082 Splendid Catch 117no Super Scope 117nk Outrun 12
LATEST WORKOUTS May 30 Bel tr.t 3f fst :36⅘ h ●May 9 Bel tr.t 6f fst 1:18 b May 5 Bel tr.t 3f fst :40 b

Handful Of Steel — Dk. b. or br. c. 3, by Cutlass—Handful of Joy, by All Hands
$25,000 Br.—Smith Paul P (Fla) Tr.—Shapoff Stanley R — 117
Own.—Cohen R B
Lifetime 6 2 0 0 $13,500 — 1985 4 1 0 0 $7,800 — 1984 2 1 0 0 $5,700

19May85- 3Bel fst 6f :23 :46⅘ 1:12⅕ Clm 17500 3 2 1³ 1⁴ 12½ 11½ McCarron G b 117 10.20e 81-20 Handful Of Steel1171½Pridemore1122¾SparklingState1171 Driving 10
6May85- 5Aqu fst 7f :22⅗ :46 1:24⅗ Clm 25000 1 5 2hd 4⁵ 69¾ 612 McCarron G b 117 28.20 65-23 Irv's Choice 1153½ Mister G. 119⁴ Creative Spirit 1172¼ Tired 7
20Apr85- 2Aqu my 6f :22⅕ :45⅘ 1:11⅘ 3+Clm 25000 1 5 98½111411131111¼ Ward W A 117 42.00 73-18 Mister G. 117¾ Keep It Down 117nk Irv's Choice 1172¼ Outrun 11
14Apr85- 4Aqu fst 7f :23⅗ :47⅕ 1:26 Clm 35000 7 5 98½ 88½ 913 810¾ McCarron G 117 23.40 60-22 Eddie Bubbles112nkTheRunningKind115noStardeCesica115¾ Wide 9
5Jly84- 4Bel fst 5½f :23⅘ :47⅘ 1:06⅘ Md 25000 6 2 5⁵ 4³ 3² 1nk McCarron G 118 *2.20 81-15 HndflOfStl118nkForCrtnDoc1182½AwsmIss1163½ Swerved, driving 7
27Jun84- 4Bel fst 5½f :23 :47⅕ 1:06⅗ Md 40000 8 5 6⁶ 712 612 5⁷ McCarron G 118 4.00 75-17 BernaCagney1111½EternlPrince1181½WesternChmp116⁴ No factor 9
LATEST WORKOUTS May 30 Bel tr.t 4f fst :49 b — May 26 Bel tr.t 4f fst :50⅕ b — May 18 Bel tr.t 3f gd :38⅘ b — May 12 Bel 4f fst :48 h

Niceto Meet You — Ch. c. 3, by Robin's Song—Great Encounter, by Impressive
$22,500 Br.—Peters L J (NY) Tr.—DeBonis Robert — 108⁷
Own.—Beltz Gail P
Lifetime 13 1 3 3 $28,940 — 1985 7 1 1 3 $22,720 — 1984 6 M 2 0 $6,220

18Apr85- 4Aqu fst 7f :22⅗ :45 1:25 3+[S]Md Sp Wt 12 2 73½ 51½ 1² 15½ Ward W A b 112 3.90 76-30 Niceto Meet You 1125½ Sea Coaster 107½ Exmoon 124⁴ Drew off 13
11Apr85- 4Aqu fst 6f :22⅗ :46⅗ 1:12⅘ 3+Md 25000 9 8 55½ 4⁴ 2½ 2¾ Maple E b 112 *1.30 76-24 Hey Hey Bay 112¾ Niceto Meet You 1122¾ Erne 112¾ Gamely 12
3Apr85- 4Aqu fst 7f :22 :45⅘ 1:24⅗ 3+Md 25000 9 1 3² 2¹ 1hd 31½ Espinosa R E⁷ b 105 5.20 73-18 NewAdventure1121½CommndBrek107noNictoMtYou1052½ Bore in 13
8Mar85- 4Aqu fst 1⅛ [•]:48⅘ 1:13⅗ 1:53⅘ [S]Md Sp Wt 4 2 54½117½ 8¹⁷ 817½ Davis R G b 122 5.00 57-18 Gallant Rake 122nk Romanizer 1225¾ Playfull John 1224½ Tired 12
11Feb85- 4Aqu fst 6f [•]:22⅘ :47 1:12⅘ [S]Md Sp Wt 8 1 4nk 42½ 3¹ 3¹ Davis R G b 122 2.60 79-14 CoolNwYorkr122hdTimlssTst1221NctoMtYou122nk Altered course 12
28Jan85- 4Aqu fst 6f [•]:23⅗ :48 1:14⅗ [S]Md Sp Wt 7 2 42½ 56½ 64½ 31¾ Davis R G b 122 5.20 70-25 HistoryResponds1221BigAlfie122¾NicetoMeetYou1221¾ Lugged in 12
9Jan85- 5Aqu fst 6f [•]:23⅕ :48⅕ 1:13⅘ Md 70000 5 2 4¾ 41½ 56½ 76¾ Privitera R⁷ b 111 13.10 68-26 ExclusivePartner1182½TaylorRoad118¾RadicalChnge1222½ Outrun 12
31Dec84- 5Aqu fst 6f [•]:22⅘ :46⅗ 1:11⅘ Md 32500 2 3 3³ 2⁶ 2⁸ 28¾ Privitera R⁷ b 109 *1.50 79-15 Love That Mac 1188¾ NicetoMeetYou1095¾KeyBoat115¾ 2nd best 11
15Dec84- 4Aqu fst 6f [•]:23⅕ :47⅘ 1:13⅕ Md 70000 3 4 2½ 4⁵ 57½ 59½ Davis R G b 114 *1.80 69-26 Jal's In Time 1181½Jogger'sDelight1142½FirstConquest1031½ Tired 9
9Dec84- 4Aqu fst 6f [•]:23 :46⅘ 1:12⅘ Md 45000 7 2 3½ 2hd 2¹ 2hd Davis R G b 114 6.50 80-19 ConfirmedPtriot114hdNicetoMetYou114nkTylorRod114¾ Sharp try 11

Creative Spirit — Gr. c. 3, by Fire Dancer—Indian Ghost, by Umbrella Fella
$25,000 Br.—Chak & Price Mmes (Fla) Tr.—Tufariello Frank — 117
Own.—Wood A
Lifetime 24 1 2 3 $20,130 — 1985 12 0 1 2 $9,080 — 1984 12 1 1 1 $11,050 — Turf 4 0 0 0

10May85- 2Bel fm 1 (T):45⅘ 1:11⅕ 1:37⅘ Clm 45000 6 2 1hd 3² 5³ 74½ Davis R G b 113 21.40 72-22 French Answer 113nk Roomie 117nkAnotherDoc117½ Used gamely 12
6May85- 5Aqu fst 7f :22⅗ :46 1:24⅗ Clm 25000 3 7 5⁴ 66½ 45½ 37½ Skinner K b 117 8.60 69-23 Irv's Choice 1153½ Mister G. 119⁴ Creative Spirit 1172¼ Rallied 7
29Apr85- 1Aqu fst 1 :49 1:14⅗ 1:40⅗ Clm 22500 2 4 64¾ 5⁸ 36½ 26½ Davis R G b 115 12.20 57-33 Scholastic 1176½ Creative Spirit 1153½ Gay Date 112½ Rallied 7
20Apr85- 2Aqu my 6f :22⅕ :45⅘ 1:11⅘ 3+Clm 22500 4 6 77½ 76½ 75½ 63¾ Davis R G b 115 32.40 81-18 Mister G. 117¾ Keep It Down 117nk Irv's Choice 1172¼ Outrun 11
9Apr85- 4Aqu fst 7f :23 :47⅗ 1:25⅗ Clm 25000 10 2 73½ 52¾ 5⁷ 4⁹ Skinner K b 117 15.50 65-25 ChrmedDestiny1103½ThRunningKind117hdMistrG.1175¾ No factor 12
14Mar85- 5Aqu fst 7f :23⅕ :46⅗ 1:26⅗ Clm 30000 11 1 103½ 73¾ 63¾ 6⁵ Lovato F Jr b 113 29.90 63-35 TheRunningKind1132½GayDate114hdMr.JimmyG.1172¼ Raced wide 11
7Mar85- 2Aqu fst 6f [•]:22⅗ :45⅘ 1:12⅗ Clm 25000 7 3 6⁵ 66½ 6⁶ 75¾ Lovato F Jr b 117 33.70 76-21 Gay Date 114¾ French Answer 1151¾ Bolinger 112no Outrun 11
28Feb85- 5Aqu fst 6f [•]:22⅗ :46 1:11⅗ Clm 35000 10 2 109½ 78½ 610 59½ Lovato F Jr b 117 50.80 77-22 Gay Date 1085¾ [D]Scholastic 117½ Mr. Jimmy G. 117nk Wide 12
17Feb85- 4Aqu fst 170 [•]:48⅗ 1:14⅘ 1:46⅗ Clm 35000 5 3 3⁴ 3³ 812 917¾ Murphy D J b 117 7.40 49-25 Fly Me Again 1081 Star de Cesica 1153½ JupiterAccord1132 Tired 10
26Jan85- 6Aqu fst 170 [•]:48 1:14⅕ 1:44⅘ Alw 23000 10 6 63¾ 52½ 78¾ 814 Murphy D J b 117 44.10 62-20 Feeling Gallant117nkCrystallceberg117hdHaberdasher1122 Outrun 10
LATEST WORKOUTS May 26 Bel tr.t 4f fst :48⅘ h — May 22 Bel tr.t 3f gd :35⅘ h — Apr 28 Bel 3f fst :38 b — ●Apr 7 Bel 3f fst :36 b

Eddie Bubbles — Dk. b. or br. g. 3, by Raise A Bid—Deeturman, by Turma-Now
$22,500 Br.—Yates F D (Fla) Tr.—Sedlacek Sue — 110⁵
Own.—Tresvant Stable
Lifetime 11 3 1 2 $28,167 — 1985 9 2 1 2 $24,860 — 1984 2 1 0 0 $3,307

22May85- 1Bel fst 6f :22⅕ :45 1:10⅘ Clm 25000 8 4 45½ 45½ 47½ 3⁸ Garrido O L⁵ 112 5.00 82-14 Charmed Destiny 119² Bucket Ben 117⁶EddieBubbles112½ Evenly 8
13May85- 5Bel fst 7f :23 :46⅗ 1:25 Clm 35000 7 3 7⁵ 75¾ 68½ 611½ Garrido O L⁵ 112 2.80 65-20 Charmed Destiny 1131½ Bolinger 1106½ Scholastic 115nk Outrun 8
25Apr85- 3Aqu fst 1 :47 1:12 1:38⅗ Clm 35000 2 4 4⁴ 42½ 42½ 32½ Garrido O L⁵ 112 7.70 71-25 KeepItDown117nkStardeCesica1172EddieBubbles1122¾ No mishap 8
14Apr85- 4Aqu fst 7f :23⅗ :47⅕ 1:26 Clm 35000 5 3 41½ 1½ 1¹ 1nk Garrido O L⁵ 112 2.60 71-22 EddieBubbles112nkTheRunningKind115noStardeCesic115¾ Driving 9
6Apr85- 2Aqu fst 6f :22⅘ :46⅕ 1:11⅗ Clm 32500 9 1 2¹ 12½ 12½ 2¾ Garrido O L⁵ 110 5.30 82-21 FlyMeAgin115¾EddieBubbles1102½DshingDnnis1171½ Couldn't last 9
7Mar85- 2Aqu fst 6f [•]:22⅗ :45⅘ 1:12⅗ Clm c-25000 4 5 42½ 44½ 4⁴ 42½ Brinkerhoff D 117 9.20 79-21 Gay Date 114¾ French Answer 1151¾ Bolinger 112no No excuse 11
28Feb85- 5Aqu fst 6f [•]:22⅗ :46 1:11⅗ Clm 35000 8 3 4² 3⁴ 2⁶ 46½ Murphy D J 117 15.30 79-22 Gay Date 1085¾ [D]Scholastic 117½ Mr. Jimmy G. 117nk Weakened 12
20Feb85- 4Aqu fst 6f [•]:22⅘ :45⅘ 1:11⅗ Clm 47500 1 11 3² 59½ 510 811¾ Brinkerhoff D 117 15.20 74-23 Splendid Catch1173½Summitry108⁴Maggie'sMike1131½ Slow early 12
30Jan85- 9Suf fst 6f :22⅘ :47⅗ 1:15 Alw 8000 7 1 1hd 11½ 12½ 11¾ Brinkerhoff D 119 *1.90 66-37 EddBbbls1191¾TrplBronz1223½HppyKngdm1192½ Unrly pre st, clr 8
29Dec84- 9Suf fst 6f :23⅗ :47⅘ 1:14⅕ Adult 8 3 1hd 1¹ 41½ 56¾ Brinkerhoff D 117 25.60e 63-36 African Prince 122½ Artie Baby 122² Flip For Ross 1172½ Tired 10

Erne — Ch. c. 3, by Son Excellence—Fly Bea Fly, by Cohoes
$25,000 Br.—Cohn S (NY) Tr.—Pascuma Warren J — 117
Own.—Cohn S
Lifetime 7 0 0 1 $1,800 — 1985 7 M 0 1 $1,800 — 1984 0 M 0 0

10May85- 9Bel fst 6f :22⅗ :46⅗ 1:12⅗ 3+Md 32500 7 9 6⁴ 10111117111¾ MacBeth D b 111 6.20 60-20 Naked Emperor 1132¾ Sweet River 1132½ Gran Fable113³ In tight 12
11Apr85- 4Aqu fst 6f :22⅗ :46⅗ 1:12⅘ 3+Md 25000 5 1 11½ 1¹ 1½ 33½ MacBeth D b 112 14.10 73-24 Hey Hey Bay 112¾ Niceto Meet You 1122¾ Erne 112¾ Lost whip 12
2Apr85- 6Aqu fst 6f :22⅗ :47⅕ 1:11⅘ 3+[S]Md Sp Wt 4 4 1½ 4¹ 914 918½ MacBeth D b 112 14.10 64-20 EverProud1122¾LegcyOfLove1073¾FvoriteHolm1121½ Brief speed 10
22Mar85- 3Aqu fst 6f :22⅗ :46⅗ 1:13 Md 20000 4 8 48½ 3⁶ 3⁵ 45½ Murphy D J b 118 12.50 70-27 BeautifulTan1223ColdAsACucumber1222GranFble122½ Weakened 14
15Mar85- 3Aqu fst 6f :23⅗ :48⅗ 1:14⅕ Md 20000 14 1 54½ 55½1117122¾ Samyn J L b 118 8.20e 47-40 H. T. Willis 1111¾ Sirjac 111½ Patato 1156½ Tired 14
22Feb85- 4Aqu fst 6f [•]:23 :47⅕ 1:14⅗ [S]Md Sp Wt 2 6 115½129¾1211113½ Davis R G b 122 13.50 57-22 FlyingSnowmobile122¾TimelessTaste1171½Romnizer122hd Outrun 12
7Feb85- 4Aqu fst 6f [•]:23⅕ :47⅘ 1:14 Md 25000 11 11 95½ 5⁶ 912 913¾ Davis R G b 122 6.00 60-24 DetermindRun1227SCostr118nkAmricnRomnc111hd Sluggish, wide 12
LATEST WORKOUTS May 26 Bel tr.t 4f fst :49⅗ b — May 19 Bel 6f fst 1:17 b — May 18 Bel tr.t 3f gd :39⅕ b — May 7 Bel 5f fst 1:01 h

Also Eligible (Not in Post Position Order):

Venture Beyond — Dk. b. or br. g. 3, by Great Above—New Blossom, by Brazen Brother
$20,000 Br.—Newchance Farm (Fla) Tr.—Barrera Oscar S — 108⁵
Own.—Barrera O S
Lifetime 22 2 1 2 $23,294 — 1985 14 1 0 1 $12,600 — 1984 8 1 1 1 $10,694

5May85- 1Aqu fst 1⅛ :48⅘ 1:14⅕ 1:53⅘ Clm 18000 6 3 4³ 54½ 713 816¾ Espinosa R E⁷ b 108 5.40 49-22 MsterCommnd1102½JupiterAccord1195OntheMoneyRd1082¾ Tired 8
29Apr85- 1Aqu fst 1 :49 1:14⅗ 1:40⅗ Clm 20000 1 2 53½ 4⁷ 4⁷ 4¹⁰ Espinosa R E⁷ b 106 5.60 53-33 Scholastic 1176½ Creative Spirit 1153½ Gay Date 112½ Weakened 7
26Apr85- 1Aqu fst 6f :23 :46⅗ 1:13⅕ Clm 17500 2 5 42½ 58½ 58½ 43¾ Espinosa R E⁷ b 112 3.20 71-23 Bolinger 1082½ Neat Sam112½OntheMoneyRed112¾ Lacked a rally 10
21Apr85- 1Aqu fst 1 :46⅗ 1:11⅗ 1:38 Clm 17500 3 3 3² 2⁴ 2¹ 1nk Espinosa R E⁷ b 110 4.30 76-21 VntrByond110nkWthrFront1156½InstntRcll1178½ Altrd course, drv 6
15Apr85- 3Aqu fst 6f :22⅗ :45⅘ 1:11⅗ Alw 22000 3 5 77¾ 814 88½ 85¾ Espinosa R E⁷ b 110 25.90 78-17 Broadway Tommy117hdTruthBeTold119½SuperScope117nk Outrun 8
12Apr85- 1Aqu fst 7f :23⅕ :46⅗ 1:25⅗ Clm 17500 2 3 1hd 1½ 2hd 31½ MacBeth D b 117 2.60e 70-22 Instant Recall 1171½ Stasera 106hdVentureBeyond1175 Weakened 7
9Apr85- 4Aqu fst 7f :23 :47⅗ 1:25⅗ Clm 25000 12 1 41½ 63¾ 7⁹ 811¾ Ward W A b 117 10.30 62-25 ChrmedDestiny1103½TheRunningKind117hdMistrG.1175¾ Fell back 12
2Apr85- 2Aqu fst 7f :23⅕ :46⅗ 1:24⅗ Clm c-14000 3 7 3² 4² 43½ 5⁷ Moore D N⁵ b 112 2.30e 70-20 Sumpin Royal 1171½ Instant Recall 1172½ Pridemore 1102½ Tired 10
17Mar85- 9Aqu fst 7f :23⅗ :48⅕ 1:28⅘ Clm 22500 11 3 62¾ 42½ 64¾ 5⁵ Moore D N⁵ b 110 17.70 54-33 Soaring Romeo 119¾ Irv's Choice 112¾ French Answer110no Wide 12
6Mar85- 4Aqu fst 1⅛ [•]:48⅘ 1:14 1:53⅘ Clm 30000 2 2 2¹ 52½ 913 918½ Moore D N⁵ b 108 20.10 54-26 Debate ACase113hdI'mABanker117noAccordingToLuke113nk Tired 12

Gallant Passer — B. c. 3, by Fast Passer—Prevail, by Chop Chop
$25,000 Br.—Howard F A (Va) Tr.—Campo Salvatore — 117
Own.—Asbell J
Lifetime 18 3 6 2 $32,985 — 1985 9 2 2 2 $22,600 — 1984 9 1 4 0 $10,385

15May85- 7GS fst 170 :46⅕ 1:11⅕ 1:41⅘ Clm 25000 6 6 4⁵ 44½ 1½ 2hd Rocco J b 115 3.20 90-12 Major Setback 115hd Gallant Passer 1151 Steal Steel118½ Gamely 10
27Apr85- 9GS fst 170 :47⅕ 1:12⅕ 1:42⅘ Clm 25000 2 3 52½ 32½ 3½ 3³ Antley C W b 118 *2.00 82-15 Le Wigg 115½ Count Upwards 1132½ Gallant Passer 1181½ Wide 6
19Apr85- 9GS fst 170 :45⅘ 1:11⅗ 1:43⅕ Clm 32000 6 3 2hd 1½ 1hd 3² Lloyd J S b 116 3.90 — — Rand Bill 1161¾ Makalite 114nk Gallant Passer 1163½ Drifted out 6
2Apr85- 1GS fst 1 1/16 :47⅗ 1:12⅕ 1:45 Clm 25000 3 1 1¹ 2hd 2¹ 2² Lloyd J S b 118 4.20 — — Ron Rivers 115² Gallant Passer 118² Makalite 115³ Gamely 7
23Mar85- 3Key sly 170 :47 1:12⅗ 1:45⅕ Clm 25000 7 2 2hd 1hd 1½ 1¾ Lloyd J S b 116 9.50 74-25 Gallant Passer 116¾ Say Gems 1181½ Son Of Pappa 1181½ Driving 7
22Feb85- 6Key fst 6f :22⅕ :45⅘ 1:11⅕ Clm 25000 5 8 62¾ 4⁴ 64½ 55½ Nied J Jr b 118 *1.90 80-21 Say Gems 116nk Satisfactory 1122½ Irv's Choice 1122½ No factor 9
18Feb85- 7Lrl fst 6f :22⅕ :45⅘ 1:12⅕ Alw 10000 7 4 45½ 68¾ 7⁸ 57¾ Lloyd J S b 115 13.70 74-20 RollDemBones1151¾AlongCameJones1143¾Ray'sBianchi115¾ Tired 8
24Jan85- 8Lrl fst 1 :46⅕ 1:11⅗ 1:37⅗ Alw 9500 6 1 1½ 3½ 2¹ 5⁷ Lloyd J S b 114 3.10 77-21 Little Bold John 1143½ Choix 117¾ Dubious Hands 1141 Tired 8
14Jan85- 5Key fst 7f :22⅘ :45⅗ 1:23⅗ Clm 25000 2 2 1hd 2hd 1hd 1½ Antley C W b 119 3.70 89-19 GallantPasser119½JumpingJackFlsh112¾MkingWves1141½ Driving 7
29Dec84- 1Med fst 6f :23 :46⅕ 1:11⅘ Md 25000 3 9 2½ 1½ 1½ 13½ Antley C W b 116 *1.70 83-16 Gallant Passer1163½HoutDeVert11610Leonard'sBunky1093 Driving 10
LATEST WORKOUTS May 30 GS 4f fst :48⅘ h — May 11 GS 4f fst :49 b — May 8 GS 4f fst :49 b — Apr 17 GS 4f fst :48 h

Natrac — B. g. 3, by Winged T—Twirl the World, by Frankie's Nod
$20,000 Br.—Greer Enterprises (Pa) Tr.—Barrera Oscar S — 113
Own.—Barrera O S
Lifetime 20 2 5 1 $31,730 — 1985 13 1 3 1 $26,020 — 1984 7 1 2 0 $5,710

16May85- 1Bel fst 1⅛ :46⅕ 1:12 1:45⅕ Clm 20000 8 6 74½ 6⁶ 67½ 48½ MacBeth D b 113 3.90 68-18 Hthrs'Myrrh1132½JptrAccrd1171½MstrCmmnd1144½ No real threat 8
25Apr85- 3Aqu fst 1 :47 1:12 1:38⅗ Clm 32500 7 5 5⁵ 58½ 611 711½ Velasquez J b 115 3.50 62-25 Keep It Down117nkStardeCesica1172EddieBubbles1122¾ Fell back 8
20Apr85- 2Aqu my 6f :22⅕ :45⅘ 1:11⅘ 3+Clm 25000 8 11 1114101³109½ 9⁶ Velasquez J b 117 3.60 79-18 Mister G. 117¾ Keep It Down 117nk Irv's Choice 1172¾ Outrun 11
6Mar85- 4Aqu fst 1⅛ [•]:48⅘ 1:14 1:53⅘ Clm 35000 10 8 74½ 62¾ 31½ 4nk Ward W A⁵ b 112 *1.70 73-26 DebateACase113hdI'mABnker117noAccordingToLuke113nk Rallied 12
1Mar85- 5Aqu fst 1 1/16 [•]:49 1:13⅗ 1:47⅘ Clm 45000 7 3 3¹ 2½ 2hd 2nk Ward W A⁵ b 108 *1.60 71-25 History Responds 113nkNatrac108noMaggie'sMike115hd Game try 7
25Feb85- 1Aqu fst 1 1/16 [•]:48⅕ 1:14⅕ 1:47 Alw 23000 1 3 3⁴ 31½ 3³ 53½ Ward W A⁵ b 112 7.10 71-25 GoldenChief1172Hberdsher112½ReviveTheEchos117nk Sluggish st. 7
22Feb85- 7Aqu fst 6f [•]:22⅗ :45⅘ 1:12 Alw 22000 9 11 11⁸ 10⁹ 75½ 5³ Moore D N⁵ b 112 25.80 81-22 Faded Image 112½ Aetolian 122nk Super Scope 1172½ Late bid 12
15Feb85- 1Aqu fst 1⅛ [•]:48⅘ 1:14⅗ 1:54⅘ Alw 23000 4 5 4⁷ 3³ 3⁵ 48½ Ward W A⁵ b 112 5.00 61-26 Uene 119⁴ Revive The Echoes 117½ Golden Chief 117² No rally 8
10Feb85- 3Aqu fst 1⅛ [•]:48 1:13⅗ 1:53⅘ Clm 45000 7 3 31½ 31½ 22½ 33½ Samyn J L b 113 *1.70 72-18 Glenn Brooke 1103½ Classi Valentine 117no Natrac113½ Weakened 11
6Feb85- 1Aqu gd 170 [•]:48⅗ 1:14 1:44⅘ Alw 23000 6 3 2¹ 3³ 3⁶ 25½ Moore D N⁵ b 112 *1.30 71-27 Bold Bob's Dusty 1125½ Natrac112½Olajuwon1171¾ Best of others 7
LATEST WORKOUTS Apr 17 Bel tr.t 3f fst :38 b — Apr 14 Bel tr.t 3f fst :39⅗ b

was the often-overlooked matter of pace figures. In both of his latest two starts, Bucket Ben faced an unusually fast pace for the class of animals involved—a 105 figure on both occasions. On April 20, he faltered late on a muddy track that was favoring closers. But on May 22, after a five-week freshening, he held on gamely, demonstrating significant improvement, while finishing six lengths clear of today's second choice, Eddie Bubbles. Bucket Ben's final figure for that race was superior to anything his rivals (with the exception of Eddie Bubbles) had ever recorded. All the more superior, in fact, in light of the quick pace that preceded it. Pridemore and Handful Of Steel figured to be gasping for air after chasing Bucket Ben for half a mile—and at least two lengths behind him.

As we have said, Bucket Ben was the 5–2 favorite in this field. Although a higher price would have been nice, the colt was so obviously superior to his opposition that the odds seemed a generous overlay. Three of his more formful rivals—Gorsk, Pridemore, and Handful Of Steel—had been competing against cheaper, and had given no indication that they had the ability to move up to the $25,000 level successfully. Two others—Great Britain and Chez Ravine—were dropping down, but there was no hint that $25,000 competition would be more to their liking. Three others—Montrivia, Soaring Romeo, and Venture Beyond—appeared to be off form.

NINTH RACE
Belmont
JUNE 1, 1985

7 FURLONGS. (1.20$\frac{2}{5}$) CLAIMING. Purse $16,000. 3–year–olds, weight, 122 lbs. Non–winners of two races since May 1 allowed 3 lbs. Of a race since then, 5 lbs. Claiming Price $25,000; for each $2,500 to $20,000 2 lbs. (Races when entered to be claimed for $18,000 or less not considered).

Value of race $16,000; value to winner $9,600; second $3,520; third $1,920; fourth $960. Mutuel pool $114,729, OTB pool $205,899. Triple Pool $285,404; OTB Triple Pool $422,006.

Last Raced	Horse	Eqt.	A.	Wt	PP	St	¼	½	Str	Fin	Jockey	Cl'g Pr	Odds $1
22May85 ^{1}Bel^{2}	Bucket Ben	b	3	110	3	1	$1^{1\frac{1}{2}}$	1^{4}	1^{3}	$1^{2\frac{3}{4}}$	Alvarez A^{7}	25000	2.50
13May85 ^{5}Bel^{5}	Great Britain		3	110	1	5	3^{2}	2^{2}	2^{4}	2^{3}	Wynter N A^{7}	25000	16.80
10May85 ^{2}Bel^{7}	Creative Spirit	b	3	117	9	6	7^{hd}	$5^{\frac{1}{2}}$	3^{4}	3no	Davis R G	25000	5.50
24May85 ^{1}Bel^{2}	Gorsk		3	115	4	9	11	11	$5^{\frac{1}{2}}$	4^{2}	Cordero A Jr	22500	4.70
19May85 ^{3}Bel^{2}	Pridemore	b	3	115	6	11	10^{2}	$10^{1\frac{1}{2}}$	4^{hd}	5^{nk}	Ward W A	22500	6.80
22May85 ^{1}Bel^{6}	Soaring Romeo	b	3	113	7	7	8^{1}	$9^{\frac{1}{2}}$	6^{2}	$6^{3\frac{3}{4}}$	MacBeth D	20000	14.30
5May85 ^{1}Aqu^{8}	Venture Beyond	b	3	108	11	4	4^{1}	$6^{1\frac{1}{2}}$	8^{5}	$7^{\frac{3}{4}}$	Privitera R^{5}	20000	25.40
22May85 ^{1}Bel^{3}	Eddie Bubbles		3	110	10	3	6^{hd}	8^{hd}	$7^{\frac{1}{2}}$	$8^{5\frac{3}{4}}$	Garrido O L^{5}	22500	4.50
3Feb85 ^{1}Aqu^{8}	Montriva	b	3	115	5	2	2^{2}	3^{3}	$9^{\frac{1}{2}}$	9no	Santagata N†	22500	63.10
19May85 ^{3}Bel^{1}	Handful Of Steel	b	3	117	8	10	$9^{\frac{1}{2}}$	$7^{\frac{1}{2}}$	11	$10^{1\frac{1}{2}}$	McCarron G	25000	10.90
12May85 ^{5}Bel^{7}	Chez Revine	b	3	117	2	8	$5^{1\frac{1}{2}}$	4^{hd}	$10^{\frac{1}{2}}$	11	Migliore R†	25000	34.60

OFF AT 5:41 Start good, Won driving. Time, :22$\frac{3}{5}$, :45$\frac{2}{5}$, 1:10$\frac{4}{5}$, 1:24$\frac{2}{5}$ Track fast.

$2 Mutuel Prices:			
4–(C)–BUCKET BEN	7.00	5.20	4.00
2–(A)–GREAT BRITAIN		13.60	10.80
10–(J)–CREATIVE SPIRIT			5.00

$2 TRIPLE 4–2–10 PAID $627.00.

B. g, by Elocutionist—Summertime, by Secretariat. Trainer Moschera Gasper S. Bred by Strawbridge G Jr (Pa).

BUCKET BEN quickly sprinted clear, drew off around the turn and held sway under good handling. GREAT BRITAIN raced forwardly to the stretch and continued on with good energy. CREATIVE SPIRIT raced well out in the track into the stretch and failed to seriously menace as his rider lost the whip with a sixteenth remaining. GORSK, very wide into the stretch, found best stride too late. PRIDEMORE raced wide into the stretch but lacked the needed rally. VENTURE BEYOND was finished early. EDDIE BUBBLES was always outrun. MONTRIVA tired badly. CHEZ REVINE tired badly. VENTURE beyond raced with mud caulks.

Creative Spirit simply didn't like to win. And Eddie Bubbles, after displaying some good form in April, had gone backward and was recently trounced by Bucket Ben.

The speed and pace figures clearly indicated that Bucket Ben would be an easy wire-to-wire winner in this field. Yet the bettors let him get away at a very liberal 5–2, probably because his record suggested that he wouldn't like seven furlongs. The evidence was quite convincing. The horse had tired in the stretch in all but one of his eight races, all at six furlongs. But our point is that despite what his record said, the horse figured to like seven furlongs under the prevailing conditions—an easy, uncontested pace, which would give him the chance to relax early—circumstances that would probably have a significant impact on the horse's stretch performance. And indeed they did!

Chapter 14

The Grass-Breeding Dream Race

GRASS-BREEDING aficionados, like the author, handicap certain kinds of turf races hoping they will find a clear-cut confrontation of a particular type, one that their knowledge of bloodlines will help them exploit. The protagonists will be grass-bred horses racing over that surface for the first (or second) time. The antagonists may come from either of two categories:

(1) Horses not bred for the grass that are moving to that surface for the first time, and whose recent good form on dirt hopefully will attract support at the betting windows.
(2) Horses with established form on the grass, the kind that finish in the money often but seldom win. These horses have become more or less "permanent residents" of the restricted allowance or claiming ranks and seem capable of winning only when they catch a field of horses with records of futility similar to their own.

Should both categories be represented in the same race, and one of them be favored, the profit potential of the situation is greatly enhanced. On the other hand, grass-bred neophytes become worthwhile betting propositions only when their odds are generous—at least 4–1 as a rule, although significantly higher odds would be necessary to compensate for poor dirt form.

The specific kinds of races we refer to are exactly those likely to favor three-year-olds—maiden races, restricted allowance races such as "nonwinners of one" and "nonwinners of two" contests, and claiming races exclusively for three-year-olds. Of course, other contenders may emerge in these races, such as lightly raced three-year-olds with established grass credentials, or European imports of stakes quality making their American debuts. These would obviously make the task of a first-time grass starter more difficult.

As an example, let's take a look at the seventh race at Belmont on June 10, 1985, a "nonwinners of one" allowance contest at a flat mile. Our task will be to identify the individual contestants as either "good guys" or "bad guys," "protagonists" or "antagonists." To help the reader identify grass bloodlines, we have prepared a table of statistics on numerous stallions, updating information found in *Thoroughbred Handicapping—State of the Art* through the 1985 season. This table can be found in the Appendix.

And now for the horses in the seventh at Belmont:

COUGAR EXPRESS

The 7–5 favorite coming off a pair of second-place finishes on the grass at Monmouth Park, Cougar Express has the earmarks of a nice grass prospect (in New Jersey)—or the potential to become a "permanent resident" of the allowance ranks. As a shipper, though, he has to be respected. But that respect was being carried too far. His favoritism was reportedly due, at least in part, to the trip handicappers in the audience, who had received word of the horrendous trip the colt nearly overcame on June 3 at Monmouth. But with so many grass first-timers in the field he had to be passed at the low odds and instead considered the prime antagonist in this field. The odds board often helps to make such choices crystal clear.

ANOTHER DOC

His recent starts, including two on the grass, indicate quite clearly that this horse belongs in the claiming ranks, and even there he seems to have difficulty winning. He's another antagonist but one not likely to attract much support at the betting windows.

WILLINGNESS

An impressive (maiden) winner of his grass debut as a two-year-old, this well-bred (for grass) colt has since disappointed on numerous occasions. His two allowance races in Florida, in particular, stamped him as likely to become a "permanent resident" of the

7 BELMONT

WIDENER TURF COURSE
1 MILE
BELMONT PARK
START
FINISH

1 MILE. (Turf). (1.33) ALLOWANCE. Purse $25,000. 3-year-olds which have never won a race other than maiden or claiming. Weight, 122 lbs. Non-winners of a race other than claiming at a mile or over since May 15, allowed 3 lbs.; of such a race since May 1, 5 lbs.

Coupled—Mr. Jimmy G. and Bolinger.

Cougar Express
B. c. 3, by Cougar II—Hasty Aysha, by Hasty Road
Own.—Firman Pamela H
Br.—Hancock & Jewell (Ky)
Tr.—Pierce Joseph H Jr
117
Lifetime 5 1 2 0 $17,200
1985 5 1 2 0 $17,200
1984 0 M 0 0
Turf 2 0 2 0 $5,200

3Jun85- 6Mth fm 1 1/16 ⓣ:49⅕ 1:12⅘ 1:43⅘ 3+Alw 13000 6 4 41½ 32 31½ 2no Perret C 114 *1.30 87-13 Arranan 118no Cougar Express 1142½ Lordship 118½ Game try 8
25May85- 7Mth gd 1 1/16 ⓣ:48⅗ 1:12⅘ 1:44⅗ 3+Alw 13000 4 4 44½ 21 1hd 22 Perret C 114 6.10 80-17 Out Lookin 1102 Cougar Express 1141½ SportingFree114¾ Gamely 12
27Apr85- 4Aqu fst 7f :23⅕ :47 1:25⅗ Alw 22000 4 6 51½ 74 88¾ 98¾ Lovato F Jr 122 22.10 65-26 Solgne 117¾ Area Rug 1121½ Haberdasher 117¾ Tired 11
19Apr85- 6Aqu sly 6f :22⅗ :46⅗ 1:12 3+Md Sp Wt 6 4 97¾ 811 76½ 1hd Lovato F Jr 113 17.70 81-22 Cougar Express 113hd Duomo 1242 Little's Brittle 112½ Driving 11
13Feb85- 6Aqu fst 6f ⊡:22⅕ :46 1:10⅘ Md Sp Wt 1 4 1hd 42 714 721½ Graell A 122 7.90 68-20 Crossfield 1227 Available Power 1178 Salvatore 1151½ Tired 9
LATEST WORKOUTS Jun 1 Mth 4f my :49⅗ b May 17 Mth 1 fst 1:41⅖ h Apr 26 Bel 3f fst :39 b Apr 13 Bel 4f fst :46⅘ h

Heaven's Gate
B. c. 3, by Great Above—Faithful Embassy, by Diplomat Way
Own.—Green R I
Br.—Clark B & Kay (Fla)
Tr.—Olivares Luis
117
Lifetime 26 5 7 2 $36,775
1985 10 2 2 0 $17,160
1984 16 3 5 2 $19,615
Turf 4 1 1 0 $8,390

1Jun85- 2Bel fst 1 1/16 :47 1:12 1:43⅘ Clm 75000 6 2 21½ 2½ 2hd 45¾ Velasquez J 113 17.00 78-11 According To Luke 112nk Helcin 1163¾ Olajuwon 1141½ Weakened 8
11May85- 6Crc sly 1 1/16 :47⅘ 1:13⅕ 1:47⅕ Clm 40000 7 3 23 35½ 921 925¾ Santos J A 116 2.50 57-17 DveyDoGood1144½Stn'sWy109½HndsomVrsion1167 Done after 3/4 9
16Apr85- 9Hia yl *1 1/16 ⓣ 1:45⅗ North Miami 1 2 3½ 2hd 58 616½ Santos J A 112 11.00 54-29 Foundation Plan 1196 Mr. Happy 117½ Crovero 117½ Faltered 8
2Apr85- 9Hia fst 1⅛ :46⅘ 1:11⅕ 1:50⅘ Alw 14000 10 3 2½ 17 2½ 22½ Solis A 114 3.00 77-17 Ells DoMuch1142½Heaven'sGate11410ForeverJune1141 Weakened 10
21Mar85- 8Hia fm *1⅛ ⓣ 1:50 Clm 35000 1 4 42½ 11½ 14 14 Santos J A 112 3.20 81-19 Heaven's Gate 1124 A Light Jet 1142½ PopopsChoice1101 Driving 12
8Mar85- 6Hia fst 6f :22 :44⅘ 1:10⅘ Clm 25000 10 10 84¾ 813 912 97¾ Soto S B 115 *2.80 80-15 Dwight D 115hd Regents Pride 1152 John One Six 115½ Outrun 11
28Feb85- 8GP fm *1 1/16 ⓣ 1:44 Alw 17000 7 3 33 52½ 62½ 56½ Santos J A 117 4.10 80-11 Dan N Den 1171½ Expected Magic 1173 My Shane 117¾ Tired 10
8Feb85-10GP fm *1 ⓣ 1:40⅘ Clm 45000 2 1 2hd 1½ 11½ 2hd Santos J A 117 11.00 76-24 Texolatic Tom 117hd Heaven's Gate 117¾ Stop Who117hd Gamely 10
11Jan85- 2GP fst 6f :23⅗ :45⅘ 1:11 Clm 10500 2 5 43 21½ 1½ 1nk Santos J A 113 3.00 84-16 Heaven's Gate 113nk Lukes Prospect 1153 Hasty Tex1143 Driving 12
3Jan85- 6Crc fst 7f :22⅘ :46 1:27⅕ Clm 16000 5 7 42½ 43 1015 1012½ Soto S B b 116 6.80 68-16 HurrBucphls114hdM'MnslICoocoo1181SnglBddr1182 Fin after 1/2 12
LATEST WORKOUTS Jun 8 Bel tr.t 4f fst :48 h Apr 13 Crc 4f sly :50 b (d)

Another Doc
B. g. 3, by Dr Valeri—Current Event, by Bald Eagle
Own.—Chuckolew Stable
Br.—Najemian G (Fla)
Tr.—DeBonis Thomas A
117
Lifetime 19 1 3 3 $35,906
1985 15 0 3 2 $20,606
1984 4 1 0 1 $15,300
Turf 2 0 0 1 $2,760

30May85- 9Bel fst 7f :22⅘ :46 1:25 Clm 50000 7 2 62½ 4¾ 1hd 2¾ Venezia M b 117 6.30 76-19 Gallant San 117¾AnotherDoc1175NakedEmperor110nk Stubbornly 10
22May85- 5Bel fst 1 :46⅘ 1:11⅘ 1:38⅘ Clm 50000 1 3 31½ 32 31 2nk Venezia M b 117 9.00 73-14 Bolinger 106nk Another Doc 1171 Equal Terms117hd Bumped late 11
10May85- 2Bel fm 1 ⓣ:45⅘ 1:11⅕ 1:37⅘ Clm 50000 5 5 64 42½ 32 3½ Venezia M b 117 23.60 75-22 French Answer 113nk Roomie 117nk Another Doc 117½ Rallied 12
26Apr85- 3Aqu fm 1⅛ ⓣ:47⅘ 1:12 1:49⅘ Clm 50000 6 6 53½ 63¾ 714 618½ Privitera R5 b 112 7.20 75-09 Exclusive Partner 113½ I'm ABanker1134Roomie11713¾ No factor 12
10Apr85- 4Aqu fst 1 :46⅗ 1:12 1:38⅗ Clm 50000 5 9 97¾ 86½ 88¾ 810½ Castaneda K b 117 5.20 62-29 Dream OfPeace1131½Mr.JimmyG.1131½TimelessTaste1133½ Outrun 11
4Apr85- 7Aqu fst 7f :23⅕ :46⅕ 1:23⅕ Alw 22000 4 5 52½ 64½ 76 66 Castaneda K b 117 26.10 79-19 Summitry 117½ Truth Be Told 1191½ See The Way 1173 No factor 7
25Mar85- 7Aqu fst 1 :47⅘ 1:13⅕ 1:40 Alw 23000 9 5 52½ 42 31½ 52½ Castaneda K b 117 31.70 63-35 Equalize 110hd Glenn Brooke 1121¾TruthBeTold122no Wide, hung 9
13Mar85- 7Aqu fst 7f :23⅕ :46⅘ 1:25⅕ Alw 25000 5 6 65½ 64 410 414¾ Castaneda K b 117 29.40 60-28 Eternal Prince 1226¾ SuperScope1172Verbascum1176 Raced wide 7
7Mar85- 1Aqu fst 170 ⊡:48⅘ 1:13⅘ 1:44⅘ Alw 23000 6 3 31½ 31½ 68½ 611¾ Rodriguez J C 117 11.60 66-21 Dungarvin King 1122¾ Olajuwon 1176¾StrongStatement1221 Tired 7
3Mar85- 2Aqu fst 6f ⊡:22⅘ :46⅘ 1:12 Clm 50000 1 7 84½ 86 67½ 511½ Venezia M 117 11.80 72-17 Determined Run 1131½ Gay Date108nkOverbought1172¾ No factor 8
LATEST WORKOUTS May 19 Bel 3f fst :39⅘ b May 5 Bel 3f fst :38⅖ b

Willingness
B. c. 3, by Affirmed—Mazurka, by Northern Dancer
Own.—Harbor View Farm
Br.—Harbor View Farm (Ky)
Tr.—Martin Frank
117
Lifetime 12 1 0 1 $23,667
1985 3 0 0 0 $300
1984 9 1 0 1 $23,367
Turf 9 1 0 1 $23,667

11Feb85- 9GP fm 1 ⓣ:47 1:11⅘ 1:35⅘ Gldn Grass 4 7 84¾ 65½ 45½ 67½ Cruguet J b 113 8.70 83-07 Verification 1133 Record Turnout 1141 TroutStream1132½ Outrun 13
11Feb85-Run in divisions
1Feb85- 8GP fm *1 ⓣ 1:37⅘ Alw 15800 9 8 86½ 87½ 815 815½ Guerra W A 117 *1.40 77-08 Our Diplomat 1171½ My Shane 1177 Booteka 117hd Needed rally 11
21Jan85- 8GP fm *1 1/16 ⓣ 1:45⅕ Alw 16000 1 4 42½ 74¾ 3nk 52½ Guerra W A 117 4.60 78-16 MillionDollarBoy1221ExpectedMgic117noNumeric1191 No mishap 10
15Dec84- 7Hol fm 1 ⓣ:47⅘ 1:12 1:37⅘ Alw 30000 9 6 52¾ 86 85¾ 86½ Hawley S 115 7.50 75-18 Savannah Dancer 110¾ Bolder Than Bold 1181½ Red Dusty 118hd 12
23Nov84- 8Hol fm 1 1/16 ⓣ:46⅘ 1:10⅕ 1:41⅘ Hoist Flag 2 4 66 1011 916 912½ Valenzuela P A b 115 29.20 78-13 Overtrump 1201 Right Con 1201½ Herat 120no Fell back 11
11Nov84- 4Hol fm 1 ⓣ:46⅕ 1:10 1:34⅘ Buckpasser 2 7 68½ 68½ 57½ 85½ Cruguet J b 115 19.40 89-08 Herat 122nk Sapient 1163½ Private Jungle 115nk Outrun 9
11Nov84-Run in Divisions
4Nov84- 8Aqu gd 1⅛ ⓣ:48⅕ 1:14⅕ 1:53⅕ Pilgrim 9 4 48½ 72½ 58½ 43½ Cruguet J b 113 4.20 75-26 Tent Up 1151¾ Space Rider 1131½ Nordance 113hd Evnely 10
4Nov84-Grade III
20Oct84- 4Bel fm 1 1/16 Ⓣ:47⅕ 1:11 1:41⅘ To Market 1 6 66½ 47 410 39¾ Cruguet J b 115 5.00 82-12 Herat 1178 Lightning Leap 1151¾ Willingness1153½ Mild response 8
20Oct84-Run in divisions
26Sep84- 6Bel yl 1 1/16 ⓣ:48 1:14 1:47⅕ Md Sp Wt 1 8 63½ 53½ 2½ 12¾ Cruguet J b 118 11.60 60-36 Willingness 1182¾ Roman River 1183SoundProof1181¾ Ridden out 12
LATEST WORKOUTS ●Jun 5 Bel tr.t 5f fst 1:00⅖ h May 30 Bel tr.t 3f fst :36⅕ h ●May 23 Bel tr.t 5f fst 1:00⅖ h ●May 17 Bel tr.t 4f fst :46⅘ h

Mr. Jimmy G.
B. g. 3, by Xoda—Banana Fudge, by Fred E
Own.—Barrera O S
Br.—Bates T A (Fla)
Tr.—Barrera Oscar S
112[5]
Lifetime 27 3 3 6 $59,330
1985 14 2 3 6 $53,460
1984 13 1 0 0 $5,870

25May85- 4Bel fst 7f :22⅘ :45⅘ 1:23⅕ 3+Alw 24000 3 2 52 52½ 62¾ 21½ Espinosa R E7 b 103 6.50 85-11 LordMontague1211½Mr.JimmyG.103nkAswnHigh112½ Wide, rallied 8
22May85- 4Bel fst 1 1/16 :46⅘ 1:11⅘ 1:43⅕ Alw 25000 2 4 31 41¾ 32½ 36 Espinosa R E7 b 110 3.30 80-14 Barbadian Reef 1174¾ Duluth 1171½ Mr. Jimmy G. 1105¾ Evenly 7
16May85- 9Bel fst 6f :23⅕ :45⅘ 1:11⅘ 3+Alw 24000 10 12 31 11½ 11 4¾ Espinosa R E7 b 103 8.00 84-18 Magicus 121nk Lord Montague 121nk TaylorRoad110nk Weakened 12
12May85- 1Bel fst 6f :22⅕ :45⅕ 1:11⅘ Clm c-45000 4 5 59½ 48 34 31 Migliore R b 118 2.90 84-19 MedievlMyhem1171DshingDennis113hdMr.JimmyG.1183 Wide str. 8
29Apr85- 5Aqu fst 7f :23⅗ :47⅘ 1:26⅕ Clm 45000 4 8 73¾ 42 2½ 1¾ Migliore R b 115 *2.10 70-33 Mr. Jimmy G. 115¾ Big Stoop 1173½ Keep It Down 113nk Driving 8
17Apr85- 5Aqu fst 6f :23 :47 1:12⅘ Clm 45000 4 8 77½ 33 2hd 1¾ Migliore R b 113 *1.60 79-30 Mr. Jimmy G. 113¾ First Conquest 1123¾BeautifulTan115½ Driving 9
10Apr85- 4Aqu fst 1 :46⅗ 1:12 1:38⅗ Clm 45000 7 4 31½ 2½ 2hd 21½ Migliore R b 113 *1.30 71-29 DreamOfPeace1131½Mr.JimmyG.1131½TimelessTaste1133½ Gamely 11
24Mar85- 1Aqu fst 6f :23 :47⅕ 1:12⅘ Clm c-35000 6 6 74½ 67½ 54¾ 45¾ Migliore R b 117 4.00 73-26 Silent Demon1121½GayDate1191½DScholastic1173 Struck by whip 9
24Mar85-Placed third through disqualification
14Mar85- 5Aqu fst 7f :23⅕ :46⅗ 1:26⅘ Clm 35000 10 7 62¾ 52½ 1hd 32½ Migliore R b 117 5.10 66-35 TheRunningKind1132½GayDate114hdMr.JimmyG.1172½ Wide, hung 11
28Feb85- 5Aqu fst 6f ⊡:22⅘ :46 1:11⅘ Clm 35000 7 12 1212 89½ 58 36½ Migliore R b 117 8.40 80-22 Gay Date 1085¾ DScholastic 117½ Mr. Jimmy G.117nk Bumped st. 12
28Feb85-Placed second through disqualification

The Home Secretary
Ch. c. 3, by Secretariat—Alaki Miss, by Olden Times
Own.—Whelan Elizabeth P
Br.—Fontainebleau Farm Inc (Ky)
Tr.—Kelly Edward I Jr
117
Lifetime 5 1 0 0 $6,900
1985 3 0 0 0 $300
1984 2 1 0 0 $6,600

22May85- 4Bel fst 1 1/16 :46⅘ 1:11⅘ 1:43⅕ Alw 25000 5 2 1½ 21½ 69 620½ Hernandez R b 117 30.10 65-14 Barbadian Reef 1174¾ Duluth 1171½ Mr. Jimmy G. 1105¾ Tired 7
2Mar85- 1GP fst 7f :22⅕ :44⅘ 1:22 Alw 16000 7 3 87¾ 713 715 624 Solis A b 117 33.70 70-15 Rhoman Rule 11710 J. O.'s Best 1224 Magloire 1192 Outrun 9
9Feb85- 8GP fst 6f :22⅕ :45⅘ 1:11 Alw 14800 10 3 85 107¾ 104½ 76 Solis A b 117 37.00 78-18 Honest Cut 117nk Warrior Country 1172LibertyRex1191 No factor 12
6Oct84- 3Crc fst 6f :22⅘ :45⅗ 1:12⅘ Alw 15400 6 5 67½ 46 44½ 42¾ Solis A b 112 9.10 84-20 HickoryHillFlyer1071½InstntRulr1121PltinumProspct119nk Outrun 6
6Aug84- 8Crc fst 6f :22⅘ :47 1:15 Md Sp Wt 8 1 1hd 12 1½ 1no Solis A b 116 4.60 76-28 The Home Secretary116noFlyerEscape1163½MadDoc1162½ Driving 9
LATEST WORKOUTS May 19 Bel 4f fst :48⅕ h May 8 Bel 5f fst 1:05⅗ b Apr 30 Bel 5f fst 1:03 b Apr 19 Hia 4f fst :49 b

Gran Fable
Ro. c. 3, by Gran Zar—Gallic Fable, by Le Fabuleux
Own.—Schott Marcia W
Br.—Schott Marcia W (Ky)
Tr.—Picou James E
117
Lifetime 7 1 0 3 $10,320
1985 7 1 0 3 $10,320
1984 0 M 0 0

29May85- 2Bel fst 6f :22⅘ :45⅘ 1:11⅘ 3+Md 35000 10 2 41½ 32 1hd 12 Velasquez J b 113 6.80 85-15 Gran Fable 1132 Circuitous 113¾ Midas Man 111nk Drew clear 14
10May85- 9Bel fst 6f :22⅘ :46⅘ 1:12⅘ 3+Md 35000 5 3 21½ 33 36 35 Velasquez J b 113 9.80 74-20 Naked Emperor 1132¾ Sweet River1132½GranFable1133 Weakened 12
17Apr85- 4Aqu fst 7f :23⅘ :47⅘ 1:27⅕ 3+Md 45000 2 7 76 88½ 68½ 77½ Ward W A b 108 21.10 58-30 Yes Sirree 1132 Everything 110¾ Naked Emperor 1121½ Outrun 11
1Apr85- 3Aqu fst 1⅛ :48⅘ 1:13⅘ 1:52⅘ 3+Md 50000 6 1 1½ 1hd 5½ 52 Velasquez J b 112 3.80 71-17 The Challenger 119nk Roque's Jewell1201½SansShame112hd Tired 6
22Mar85- 3Aqu fst 6f :22⅘ :46⅘ 1:13 Md 25000 9 7 57 410 49 35 Velasquez J b 122 4.10 71-27 BeautifulTn1223ColdAsACucumber1222GrnFble122½ Wide, rallied 14
20Feb85- 3Aqu fst 6f ⊡:23⅘ :47⅘ 1:14⅕ Md 35000 2 8 43½ 49½ 37 34½ Davis R G b 122 *2.90 69-23 Mister G. 1153¾ Catch The Redeye 118½ Gran Fable 122nk Rallied 12
23Jan85- 4Aqu fst 6f ⊡:22⅘ :46⅘ 1:14 Md 50000 10 11 1010 716 713 78 Davis R G b 122 30.10 66-24 RonRivers1182QuickestOfAll118noGreatBritain117¾ Bothered gate 12
LATEST WORKOUTS Jun 5 Bel 4f fst :47⅘ h May 28 Bel 3f fst :37⅕ b May 23 Bel 4f fst :48⅘ h May 17 Bel 4f fst :52 b

Wealthy Seamen
Ch. c. 3, by Key to the Mint—Sea Sister, by Sea-Bird
Own.—Buckland Farm
Br.—Evans T M (Ky)
Tr.—Campo John P
117
Lifetime 6 1 0 0 $11,400
1985 1 0 0 0
1984 5 1 0 0 $11,400
Turf 2 1 0 0 $11,400

22May85- 4Bel fst 1 1/16 :46⅘ 1:11⅘ 1:43⅕ Alw 25000 1 6 64½ 710 717 726½ Guerra W A 117 22.30 59-14 Barbadian Reef 1174¾ Duluth 1171½ Mr. Jimmy G. 1105¾ Outrun 7
18Oct84- 8Med fst 1 1/16 :46 1:11⅕ 1:45 Yng America 10 8 1125 1135 1141 1151¾ Bailey J D 119 111.10 32-22 Script Ohio 119¾ Spend A Buck 122nkTank'sProspect1192 Outrun 11
18Oct84-Grade I
30Sep84- 7Bel fm 1 ⓣ:45⅘ 1:10⅘ 1:36⅘ Donut King 7 5 56 510 712 711½ Lovato F Jr 115 6.80 71-27 Western Champ 117½ Don't Fool With Me 1173JonJan122nk Tired 10
29Aug84- 4Bel fm 1 1/16 ⓣ:47 1:11⅘ 1:43⅘ Md Sp Wt 9 3 32 32 3½ 11½ Lovato F Jr 118 5.70 78-14 Wealthy Seamen 1181½ Lathom 118nk No Latch 1183 Driving 11
18Aug84- 6Sar fst 6f :22⅘ :46⅕ 1:11⅘ Md Sp Wt 5 3 69 713 612 616½ Maple E 118 14.00 67-15 Lightning Leap 1185½ Anconeus 1183½ AlertResponse1181 Outrun 8
4Aug84- 4Sar fst 6f :22⅕ :45⅘ 1:11 Md Sp Wt 11 9 1114 813 514 513¾ Samyn J L 118 29.90 71-13 Vindaloo 1188 Anconeus 1184½ Radar Alarm 118¾ Rallied 13
LATEST WORKOUTS Jun 7 Bel tr.t 4f fst :48⅘ h May 30 Bel tr.t 3f fst :36 h May 15 Bel tr.t 4f fst :48⅘ h May 6 Bel 1 fst 1:43⅘ h

Equal Terms

```
Equal Terms                 B. c. 3, by Sauce Boat—Little Ferrous, by Iron Ruler                 Lifetime    1985 6 1 0 1   $8,760
                                Br.—Eaton Farms,Inc&Red Bull Stable (Ky)                 117   9 1 1 1    1984 3 M 1 0   $1,163
   Own.—Denmark Muriel          Tr.—Pascuma Warren J Jr                                          $9,923     Turf 3 0 1 0   $1,163
22May85- 5Bel fst 1   :46⅘ 1:11⅗ 1:38⅘      Clm 50000   5 1 1¹ 1¹ 2½ 3¹¼ MacBeth D  b 117 28.50  72-14 Bolinger 106nk Another Doc 117¹ Equal Terms117hd  Bumped late 11
3May85- 7Aqu sly 7f   :22⅘ :46⅕ 1:24⅕       Clm 70000   4 4 6² 6⁸½ 6³³ 6³¹½ MacBeth D  b 113 17.20  49-26 Taylor Road 117¾ Kilts' Nashua 117⁶½ Gallant San 117²½  Trailed 6
17Apr85- 5Aqu fst 6f  :23 :47 1:12⅘         Clm c-45000 5 5 8⁷½ 9¹⁰ 8¹² 8¹³½ McCarron G  b 113 3.70  66-30 Mr. Jimmy G. 113¾ First Conquest 112³¾BeautifulTan115½  Outrun 9
5Apr85- 4Aqu fst 6f   :22⅘ :45⅘ 1:11⅘ 3+Md 35000   10 5 3¹½ 2¹ 1½ 1²¾ McCarron G  b 114 20.10  84-23 EqualTerms114²¾TooMuchToDrink112³½FinlDuel108½  Going away 12
13Mar85- 3Aqu fst 7f  :23⅕ :47⅕ 1:26⅘        Md 75000    7 5 3nk 4¹¾ 9¹⁶ 10¹⁹½ McCarron G  b 122 16.00e  50-28 Spicey Bones 118hd Freedoms Edge 118nk Brucıefruit1137¾  Tired 13
4Feb85- 4Aqu fst 6f ⊡:23 :47⅘ 1:11⅘         Md Sp Wt    5 7 10¹³ 11²¹ 11²⁴ 11²⁷½ Murphy D J  122 10.60  58-21 Aetolian 122⁶ It's Affirmed 122⁴½ Alpine Raja 122½  Outrun 11
16Oct84♦2Redcar(Eng) gd 7f   1:23⅘ Ⓣ Captain Cook Stakes(Mdn)   4⁶¾ Eddery P A  126 6.00  — — Sojurn 123nk Paris Match 126²½ Changanoor 126⁴  Evenly 29
10Oct84♦1Goodwood(Eng) gd 6f 1:15 Ⓣ Hat Hill Stakes(Mdn)        4⁵½ Piggott L  126 *1.75  — — Great Northern 126no Chaise Lounge118¹½ IndianHal126⁴  Evenly 20
11Aug84♦1Newmarket(Eng) gd 6f 1:17 Ⓣ ColumbusTravelKiwiStk(Mdn   2³ Eddery P A  126 *3.00  — — BrveLouise118³ EqulTerms126² Rocky'sPrid126nk  Prom thruout 10
   LATEST WORKOUTS   Jun 6 Bel tr.t 5f my 1:02 h (d)   May 30 Bel tr.t 4f fst :48 h   May 18 Bel tr.t 5f gd 1:01⅘ h   ●May 10 Bel tr.t 1 fst 1:45 b
```

Haberdasher

```
Haberdasher                 Ch. c. 3, by Gummo—Lady Has A Bonnet, by Candy Spots                 Lifetime    1985 9 0 3 4   $38,452
                                Br.—Rose & Wagner (Ky)                                         19 1 4 6    1984 10 1 1 2  $17,690
  ˜Own.—Trevant Stable          Tr.—Sedlacek Sue                                         117     $56,142    Turf 1 0 0 0
    Entered 8Jun85- 7 BEL
18May85- 5Bel gd 1    :46⅘ 1:11⅘ 1:36⅘ 3+Alw 25000   7 7 7⁸½ 8⁹ 6⁷½ 6¹⁰ Velasquez J  b 111 2.10  73-15 Anecdote 121⁴¾ Geologist121¹NakedEmperor103hd  Lacked a rally 8
8May85- 3Bel fst 1⅟₁₆ :48⅕ 1:12⅘ 1:44⅘ 3+Alw 25000  7 3 2¹ 2² 3¹½ 3²½ Velasquez J  b 112 2.20  77-18 CleanMachine112¹½CoyoteDancer110¹½Haberdsher112¹  Weakened 7
27Apr85- 4Aqu fst 7f  :23⅕ :47 1:25⅘          Alw 22000   8 1 3½ 2hd 2½ 3²½ Velasquez J  b 117 3.70  72-26 Solgne 117¾ Area Rug 112¹½ Haberdasher 117¾  Weakened 11
9Mar85- 6Aqu fst 170 ⊡:47 1:12 1:41⅘          Great Power 1 3 3²½ 3² 2¹½ 2½ Velasquez J  b 115 11.50  92-16 Nordance 115½ Haberdasher 115²½ Roo Art 122²  Gamely 6
25Feb85- 1Aqu fst 1⅟₁₆ ⊡:48⅕ 1:14⅕ 1:47       Alw 23000   4 6 6⁶½ 7⁴½ 6⁴½ 2² Garrido O L⁵  b 112 *1.80  73-25 GoldenChief117²Haberdasher112¾ReviveTheEchoes117nk  In close 7
9Feb85- 8Aqu fst 1⅟₁₆ ⊡:48⅕ 1:13⅘ 1:46⅕       Whirlaway   5 11 7³½ 6²¾ 4⁴½ 4⁵½ Davis R G  b 117 6.20  74-26 First One Up 123nk King Babar117½TrophyHunter117⁴½  No threat 11
26Jan85- 6Aqu fst 170 ⊡:48 1:14⅕ 1:44⅘        Alw 23000   8 5 4¾ 1hd 1½ 3nk Garrido O L⁵  b 112 *1.40  76-20 FeelingGallant117nkCrystalIceberg117hdHberdsher112²  Weakened 10
16Jan85- 5Aqu fst 1⅛ ⊡:48⅗ 1:13⅘ 1:54          Alw 23000   4 2 2½ 1½ 3½ 2no Garrido O L⁵  b 112 3.60  72-27 UncleDaddy117noHaberdasher112²FeelingGallnt117¹²  Just missed 6
4Jan85- 7Aqu fst 170 ⊡:48⅗ 1:13⅘ 1:44⅘         Clm 75000   4 3 3²½ 6³ 4³½ 3½ Garrido O L⁵  b 107 7.50  75-21 FirstOneUp122nkFeelingGllnt114nkHbrdshr107hd  Wheeled, rallied 8
28Dec84- 7Aqu sly 1⅟₁₆ ⊡:47⅘ 1:12 1:44⅘       Alw 23000   3 6 5⁴½ 9¹³ 7¹⁷ 7¹⁸½ Garrido O L⁵  112 9.40  69-19 Romancer 117⁷½ Uncle Daddy 110⁴ Lasita's Silencer112²½  Outrun 10
   LATEST WORKOUTS   Jun 5 Aqu ⊡ 4f fst :48⅘ h   ●May 30 Aqu Ⓣ 3f sf :39⅘ b (d)   ●May 16 Aqu Ⓣ 3f fm :37⅘ b (d)   Apr 23 Aqu 5f gd 1:02⅘ h
```

*Carribean Song

```
*Carribean Song             Ch. c. 3, by Music Boy—Aruba, by Amber Rama                          Lifetime    1985 1 0 0 0
                                Br.—Warren Hill Stud-Mimika Financiera (Eng)             117   9 1 4 1    1984 8 1 4 1   $7,288
   Own.—Maxwell Adrian J        Tr.—Maxwell Adrian J                                             $7,288     Turf 8 1 4 1   $7,288
25May85- 9Bel fst 6f  :22⅕ :45⅘ 1:10⅘         Alw 24000   3 7 9⁷½ 10⁸½ 11¹⁵ 11¹⁶½ Vasquez J  117 25.80  73-11 Taylor Road 117² Lucky Belief 122²½ Bolinger 110½  Outrun 11
2Nov84♦3Newmarket(Eng) gd 5f  1:02⅘ Ⓣ PotterTrophyNurseryHcp    9⁵ Robinson P  126 *6.00  — — Perion 103¹ ExpressCar 105nk StellaGrande 126hd  Speed for 3f 15
18Oct84♦3Newmarket(Eng) gd 6f 1:13⅘ Ⓣ Fen Ditton Nursery Hcp    2² Robinson P  116 10.00  — — Sudden Impact 106² CarribeanSong116nk JeanneAvril115¾  Led 4f 14
4Oct84♦2Newmarket(Eng) gd 5f  1:01⅕ Ⓣ Bloodstock&GenInsNrsyHcp  3² Robinson P  120 25.00  — — Sunera 126² StormWarning 124hd CarribeanSong 120nk  Impeded 19
8Sep84♦1Thirsk(Eng) fm 5f      :58⅘ Ⓣ Highflyer Stakes          2⁴ Robinson P  123 1.75  — — MadamLoving120⁴ CarribeanSong123¹½ Rahash120⁵  Prom,no exc 6
30Aug84♦5Beverley(Eng) gd 5f  1:05 Ⓣ Figham Stakes               2no Robinson P  123 *2.00  — — HobornsRos113no CrrbnSong123²½ RcordGft123½  Set pace,nosed 11
14Jly84♦6Lingfield(Eng) gd 5f 1:00⅘ Ⓣ Croydon Nursery Hcp       8⁷½ Robinson P  133 *2.00  — — Axe Valley 121³ Halcyon Cove 112¹½ Abutaia 132²  Prom 3f 8
6Jly84♦1Sandown(Eng) gd 5f    1:01⅘ Ⓣ Inchcape Stakes           2² Robinson P  128 8.00  — — Bassenthwaite128² CarribenSong128nk BrownBerBoy123³  Led 4f 6
12Jun84♦1Yarmouth(Eng) fm*5f  1:05 Ⓣ JohnHoldrichStks(Mdn)      1⁴ Robinson P  126 6.00  — — CarribeanSong 126⁴ Saloum 126¹ Lord Jagged126²½  Led thruout 6
   LATEST WORKOUTS   Jun 7 Bel 3f fst :36⅘ h   ●Jun 3 Bel 4f fst :46⅘ h   May 31 Bel tr.t 4f fst :49 b   May 20 Bel 5f fst 1:00⅘ hg
```

Irv's Choice

```
Irv's Choice                Gr. g. 3, by El Rastro—Adversaria, by Tudor Way                      Lifetime    1985 12 1 3 4  $27,770
                                Br.—Katz Francine & J (Fla)                              117  21 3 4 5    1984 9 2 1 1   $13,300
   Own.—Town Circle Stable      Tr.—Barbara Robert                                               $41,070
2Jun85- 3Bel fst 1⅟₁₆ :46⅘ 1:11⅘ 1:44⅘        Clm 35000   9 2 2¹ 2½ 3½ 2nk Migliore R  b 117 5.60  80-19 DooleyDncer117nkIrv'sChoice117¾ChrmedDstiny117½  Just missed 9
6May85- 5Aqu fst 7f   :22⅘ :46 1:24⅘          Clm 22500   7 1 3¹ 2½ 1²½ 1³½ Migliore R  b 115 *1.80  77-23 Irv's Choice 115³½ Mister G. 119⁴ Creative Spirit 117²½  Driving 7
20Apr85- 2Aqu my 6f   :22⅕ :45⅘ 1:11⅕ 3+Clm 25000  7 2 5⁵ 5⁵ 4²½ 3¹ Cordero A Jr  b 117 4.20  84-18 Mister G. 117¾ Keep It Down 117nk Irv's Choice 117²¾  Rallied 11
14Apr85- 4Aqu fst 7f  :23⅘ :47⅕ 1:26           Clm 30000   8 2 1hd 3½ 2¹ 4¹ Cordero A Jr  b 113 4.50  70-22 EddieBubbles112nkTheRunningKind115noStrdCsic115¾  Weakened 9
6Apr85- 2Aqu fst 6f   :22⅘ :46⅕ 1:11⅘         Clm 30000   4 4 3³ 4⁵ 5⁴¾ 4⁴½ Cordero A Jr  b 113 *2.40  78-21 FlyMeAgain115¾EddieBubbles110²½DshingDennis117¹½  No excuse 9
17Mar85- 9Aqu fst 7f  :23⅘ :48⅕ 1:28⅘         Clm 25000   3 4 3½ 2hd 1² 2¾ Ward W A⁵  b 112 4.00  58-33 Soaring Romeo 119¾ Irv's Choice112¾FrenchAnswer110no  Gamely 12
8Mar85- 9Aqu fst 6f ⊡:22⅘ :46 1:12⅘          Clm c-17500 8 4 2¹ 2¹ 1hd 2¹½ Skinner K  b 117 4.10  79-18 Dash Mount108¹½Irv'sChoice117¹¾InstantRecall117nk  Just missed 12
22Feb85- 6Key fst 6f  :22⅕ :45⅘ 1:11⅕         Clm 20000   9 1 1½ 1½ 1² 3²¾ Rosales A G  b 112 17.20  82-21 Say Gems 116nk Satisfactory 112²½ Irv's Choice 112²½  Weakened 9
7Feb85- 7Lrl sly 6f   :22⅕ :46⅕ 1:11⅘         Clm 18500   3 2 6⁴½ 6⁸½ 4⁷ 3⁸½ Rosales A G  b 114 4.80  76-22 Departing Prints 114³¾Mr.AlLeeKat114⁴½Irv'sChoice114¹½  Rallied 9
27Jan85- 5Key fst 7f  :22⅘ :45⅘ 1:23⅘         Clm 18000   9 1 4² 2hd 2¹ 3⁴½ Rosales A G  b 115 2.60  83-20 Foxy Bud 115³ Daddy's A Caddy111¹½Irv'sChoice115²½  Weakened 9
   LATEST WORKOUTS   May 29 Aqu ⊡ 5f sly 1:03⅕ b (d)   May 23 Aqu Ⓣ 5f sf 1:04 b (d)
```

Also Eligible (Not in Post Position Order):

J. O.'s Best

```
J. O.'s Best                B. c. 3, by J O Tobin—Irish Course, by Irish Lancer                  Lifetime    1985 6 1 1 1   $14,780
                                Br.—Badgett B (Ky)                                       117   6 1 1 1    1984 0 M 0 0
   Own.—Morris J A Est of       Tr.—Stephens Woodford C                                          $14,780
16May85- 9Bel fst 6f  :23⅕ :45⅘ 1:11⅘ 3+Alw 24000  3 6 11¹¹ 10⁹ 9⁸½ 9⁶½ Maple E  110 4.20  78-18 Magicus 121nk Lord Montague 121nk Taylor Road 110nk  In close 12
8May85- 1Bel fst 6f   :22⅘ :45⅘ 1:11⅘         Alw 22000   7 6 1½ 2hd 2½ 3³½ Maple E  117 *.70  81-18 First Conquest 117¹½ Verbascum 117² J. O.'sBest117⁴½  Weakened 7
15Apr85- 3Aqu fst 6f  :22⅘ :45⅘ 1:11⅘         Alw 22000   6 6 3¹ 4²½ 4¹½ 4¾ Maple E  117 *1.00  83-17 BrodwyTommy117hdTruthBeTold119½SuperScop117nk  Weakened 8
2Mar85- 1GP fst 7f    :22⅕ :44⅘ 1:22          Alw 16000   4 5 1½ 1hd 2³ 2¹⁰ Maple E  122 2.60  84-15 Rhoman Rule 117¹⁰ J. O.'s Best 122⁴ Magloire 119²  No match 9
9Feb85- 8GP fst 6f    :22⅕ :45⅘ 1:11          Alw 14800   11 4 5²¾ 4¹½ 6¹¾ 5⁴¾ Brumfield D  122 *.90  79-18 Honest Cut 117nk Warrior Country 117² Liberty Rex119¹  Blocked 12
16Jan85- 4GP fst 6f   :22⅘ :45⅘ 1:10⅘         Md Sp Wt    6 4 1hd 1² 1hd 1no Maple E  122 4.00  87-20 J. O.'s Best 122no First Guess 122⁴ Nice Touch 122³  Driving 12
   LATEST WORKOUTS   Jun 8 Bel 5f fst 1:04 b   Jun 3 Bel 5f fst 1:00 h   ●May 30 Bel Ⓣ 4f sf :48⅘ h (d)   May 24 Bel 4f fst :49 b
```

Bahia Grande

```
Bahia Grande                Dk. b. or br. c. 3, by Coastal—Decorator, by Hoist The Flag          Lifetime    1985 3 1 1 1   $20,860
                                Br.—Live Oak Stud (Fla)                                  117⁵  3 1 1 1    1984 0 M 0 0
   Own.—Live Oak Plantation     Tr.—Kelly Patrick J                                              $20,860
1Jun85- 3Bel fst 1⅟₁₆ :48⅕ 1:12⅘ 1:43⅕        Alw 25000   7 6 5³ 4²½ 2⁴ 2⁴ Garrido O L⁵  117 1.70  82-11 Duluth 117⁴ Bahia Grande 117³½ General Grandi 117²  2nd best 8
20May85- 3Bel fst 1⅟₁₆ :47 1:12 1:43⅘ 3+Md Sp Wt  7 8 7⁴ 4¹½ 1½ 1⁴ Garrido O L⁵  108 4.40  84-22 BhGrnd108⁴Trn'nTogthr113hdBnnyThGrftr113⁵½  Steadied, driving 10
22Mar85- 6Aqu fst 6f  :23 :47⅕ 1:13⅕          Md 50000    10 12 9⁵½ 9⁸½ 6³½ 3¾ Garrido O L⁵  117 33.30  74-27 Intercostal113nkNakedEmperor122¾BhiGrnde117²½  Raced greenly 14
   LATEST WORKOUTS   Jun 8 Bel 3f fst :37⅕ b   May 28 Bel 4f fst :50⅘ b   May 16 Bel 4f fst :48⅘ h   May 12 Bel 4f fst :50 b
```

Lyphey

```
Lyphey                      Ch. c. 3, by Irish River—Lypatia, by Lyphard                         Lifetime    1985 4 1 0 2   $18,840
                                Br.—Mabee Mr-Mrs J C (KY)                                122   4 1 0 2    1984 0 M 0 0
   Own.—Brody J                 Tr.—Lukas D Wayne                                                $18,840
30May85- 6Bel fst 1   :46⅘ 1:10⅘ 1:36⅘ 3+Md Sp Wt  6 1 1¹ 1³ 1⁵ 1hd Velasquez J  113 2.70  82-19 Lyphey 113hd Lovely Bones 113⁴¾ Mamluk 113⁴¾  Lasted 7
17May85- 5Bel fst 7f  :23⅕ :46⅕ 1:24⅘ 3+Md Sp Wt  2 9 2hd 3½ 2½ 3⁴½ Velasquez J  113 4.70  75-19 Lucky Belief 113³¾ Mamluk 113¾ Lyphey 113½  Weakened 9
2May85- 6Aqu fst 6f   :23 :46⅘ 1:11⅘          Md Sp Wt    5 2 3½ 3²½ 3⁶ 3⁶ Velasquez J  122 4.10  78-26 Siberian Dancer 122¹ I Enrich 122⁵ Lyphey 122²  Even try 7
19Apr85- 6Aqu sly 6f  :22⅘ :46⅘ 1:12 3+Md Sp Wt    11 7 4¹ 4¹½ 3¹½ 5³ Velasquez J  112 15.60  78-22 Cougar Express 113hd Duomo 124² Little's Brittle112½  Weakened 11
   LATEST WORKOUTS   May 11 Bel 5f fst 1:00⅘ h
```

Naked Emperor

```
Naked Emperor               Ch. c. 3, by Fabled Monarch—No Bikini, by Miles Standish             Lifetime    1985 6 1 2 3   $19,720
                                Br.—Engles L R (Ky)                                      117   6 1 2 3    1984 0 M 0 0
   Own.—Elphand G               Tr.—O'Brien Leo                                                  $19,720
    Entered 9Jun85- 5 BEL
30May85- 9Bel fst 7f  :22⅘ :46 1:25           Clm 50000   5 4 7⁴ 6⁵½ 5⁶ 3⁵¾ Reed R L⁷  110 7.80  71-19 Gallant San 117¾ AnotherDoc117⁵NakedEmperor110nk  Went wide 10
18May85- 5Bel gd 1    :46⅘ 1:11⅕ 1:36⅘ 3+Alw 25000  5 4 6⁷½ 6⁶½ 4⁴ 3⁵¾ Espinosa R E⁷  103 20.20  77-15 Anecdote 121⁴¾ Geologist 121¹ Naked Emperor 103hd  Mild rally 8
10May85- 9Bel fst 6f  :22⅘ :46⅘ 1:12⅘ 3+Md c-35000 2 1 5²½ 2² 2² 1²¾ Migliore R  113 *1.40  79-20 Naked Emperor 113²¾ Sweet River 113²½ Gran Fable 113³  Driving 12
17Apr85- 4Aqu fst 7f  :23⅘ :47⅘ 1:27⅕ 3+Md 50000   11 1 3¹ 1½ 2½ 3²¾ Migliore R  b 112 *.90  62-30 Yes Sirree 113² Everything 110¾ Naked Emperor112¹½  Weakened 11
2Apr85- 3Aqu fst 6f   :22⅘ :46 1:10⅘ 3+Md 75000   2 4 2½ 2hd 2¹ 2²¾ Migliore R  b 112 2.80  84-20 HillsideView119²¾NakedEmperor112nkU.R.RiteNasty112²½  Gamely 11
22Mar85- 6Aqu fst 6f  :23 :47⅕ 1:13⅕          Md 50000    3 7 8⁵½ 4²¾ 1½ 2nk Gomez E R  b 122 *2.40  75-27 Intercostal113nkNakedEmperor122¾BahiaGrande117²½  Just failed 14
   LATEST WORKOUTS   May 25 Bel 3f fst :35⅘ h
```

Bolinger

```
Bolinger                    B. c. 3, by Bolger—Helofasnow, by Helioscope                         Lifetime    1985 16 3 4 2  $47,920
                                Br.—Plemmons J H (Wash)                                  112⁵ 23 4 4 3    1984 7 1 0 1   $8,097
   Own.—Barrera O S             Tr.—Barrera Oscar S                                              $57,017    Turf 2 0 0 0
30May85- 9Bel fst 7f  :22⅘ :46 1:25           Clm 45000   10 1 3¹ 3nk — — Espinosa R E⁷  b 108 5.40  — — Gallant San 117¾ Another Doc 117⁵ Naked Emperor 110nk  Fell 10
25May85- 9Bel fst 6f  :22⅕ :45⅘ 1:10⅘         Alw 24000   7 2 3nk 2½ 2¹½ 3⁴½ Espinosa R E⁷  b 110 13.80  84-11 Taylor Road 117² Lucky Belief 122²½ Bolinger 110½  Weakened 11
22May85- 5Bel fst 1   :46⅘ 1:11⅘ 1:38⅘        Clm 45000   7 2 2¹ 2¹ 1½ 1nk Espinosa R E⁷  b 106 *2.10  73-14 Bolinger 106nk Another Doc 117¹ Equal Terms 117hd  Driving 11
16May85- 7Bel fm 1  Ⓣ:45 1:09⅘ 1:35⅘          Alw 26000   2 1 1½ 1½ 3² 8¹⁰½ MacBeth D  b 117 6.20  78-13 DHWollaston 117³ DHKavazinga 117³ Olajuwon117¹  Used in pace 9
13May85- 5Bel fst 7f  :23 :46⅘ 1:25           Clm 35000   2 6 3³ 2¹½ 2²½ 2¹½ Espinosa R E⁷  b 110 *1.90  76-20 Charmed Destiny 113¹½ Bolinger 110⁶½ Scholastic 115nk  Gamely 8
10May85- 2Bel fm 1  Ⓣ:45⅘ 1:11⅕ 1:37⅘         Clm 45000   8 1 3½ 2hd 1hd 6¹½ Espinosa R E⁷  b 106 9.30  75-22 French Answer 113nk Roomie 117nk Another Doc 117½  Weakened 12
6May85- 5Aqu fst 7f   :22⅘ :46 1:24⅘          Clm c-22500 5 3 1hd 1½ 3²½ 4⁹¾ Decarlo C P¹⁰  b 105 3.10  67-23 Irv's Choice 115³½ Mister G. 119⁴ Creative Spirit117²½  Weakened 7
26Apr85- 1Aqu fst 6f  :23 :46⅘ 1:13⅕          Clm c-15500 9 1 1¹ 1⁵ 1⁵ 1²½ Privitera R⁵  b 108 *1.20  75-23 Bolinger 108²½ Neat Sam 112½ On the Money Red 112¾  Driving 10
19Apr85- 1Aqu fst 6f  :23 :45⅘ 1:12           Clm 14000   8 1 1³ 1⁷ 1¹⁰ 1⁷ Privitera R⁵  b 112 *1.70  81-24 Bolinger 112⁷ Pridemore 112²½ Sumpin Royal 119¹¾  Handily 8
27Mar85- 2Aqu fst 6f  :22⅘ :45⅘ 1:11⅘         Clm 25000   9 5 4³ 3¹ 8⁵½ 10⁹¾ Murphy D J  117 5.30  73-20 H. T. Willis 112¹¾ Stark Dancer 112¹½ Bucket Ben 117¾  Stopped 10
```

lower allowance ranks. A four-month layoff further complicates his task.

THE HOME SECRETARY

A son of Secretariat going on the grass for the first time—not a particularly interesting proposition. Early speed for six furlongs last time out in his first start after a layoff can be taken as a positive sign, although this is possibly negated by the lack of betting action then and now. This one can't be recommended as a serious grass-breeding play.

GRAN FABLE

Usually a maiden-claiming winner can be dismissed when moved into allowance company at this time of the year. But not so on the grass, if the breeding credentials are there. But who is Gran Zar?

WEALTHY SEAMEN

The Sea-Bird influence seemed to move this colt way up on the grass on August 29. But, in retrospect, the fields for that maiden contest and the subsequent Donut King Stakes were quite weak. The colt's three-year-old debut can be taken with a grain of salt, the race having been washed off the grass. However, it is hard to take this colt solely on the evidence of that one race as a two-year-old.

EQUAL TERMS

Unable to win (on grass) at relatively minor English tracks such as Redcar and Goodwood, this colt's bloodlines suggested a preference for slop rather than grass—but that was before his race at Aqueduct on May 3.

HABERDASHER

A fairly good example of an "antagonist of the first type"—good dirt form (except for his latest race)—but not bred very well for the grass. His one try on the grass (as a two-year-old) no longer shows among his running lines, but unfortunately is duly recorded in the turf line of his earnings box. If only he had tried the grass one race sooner, while his dirt form was good, he might have attracted some serious support at the betting windows.

CARRIBEAN SONG

The sharp workout on June 3 plus a trainer angle points to this horse as an upset possibility. Adrian Maxwell had great success on the grass during 1984 with European imports—horses brought to this country to be raced (briefly) and then sold. But this horse had two serious knocks. First of all, Maxwell did not have his favorite rider, Angel Cordero, in the irons. And second, the fact that seven of the horse's eight starts as a juvenile in England were at five furlongs suggested quite strongly that his former connections expected Carribean Song to amount to nothing more than a sprinter.

BAHIA GRANDE

This horse has the ideal profile for an NW1 race on the dirt—a maiden win in his second career start followed by a strong placing first time in allowance company. And the bloodlines on both sides of the pedigree said "most likely" to grass racing. Belmont winner Coastal, like Majestic Light, a son of Majestic Prince, was showing signs of becoming a good grass sire. Based on the results of his first two crops through the day of this race, the offspring of Coastal had won three of nine tries first and second times on grass. The dam, Decorator, was a fast, though apparently unsound, daughter of the great grass sire Hoist The Flag. Decorator herself raced just once on the turf, apparently suffering an injury that put an end to her three-year-old season. But the grass potential was in her genes.

LYPHEY

A front-running maiden victor in his latest start, Lyphey's immediate victim that day, Lovely Bones, came back within the week to break his maiden in impressive style, supporting Lyphey's case when entered back against winners. Once again, the breeding said "yes" to grass racing, reducing the risk usually associated with the move from maiden to allowance competition. Lyphey was from the first American crop of Irish River, champion two-year-old in France in 1978 and champion miler in that country the following season, while winning ten of twelve career starts at distances as long as a mile and an eighth. Irish River himself was a son of Riverman, an outstanding racehorse and one of Europe's most influential sires of the past ten years. Lyphey's dam was a stakes-placed (in Europe) daughter of Lyphard, another major European (and American) sire. A horse could hardly be better bred for a mile race on the grass.

Those of us who indulge in handicapping grass races by pedigree dream of races like this, where the choice is so clearcut and the results so perfect—two beautifully bred horses, in fine fettle, going greensward for the first time, both at enticing odds, and finishing heads apart, well clear of the rest of the field.

SEVENTH RACE
Belmont
JUNE 10, 1985

1 MILE.(Turf). (1.33) ALLOWANCE. Purse $25,000. 3-year-olds which have never won a race other than maiden or claiming. Weight, 122 lbs. Non-winners of a race other than claiming at a mile or over since May 15, allowed 3 lbs.; of such a race since May 1, 5 lbs.

Value of race $25,000; value to winner $15,000; second $5,500; third $3,000; fourth $1,500. Mutuel pool $129,907, OTB pool $127,462. Exacta Pool $241,655. OTB Exacta Pool $191,245.

Last Raced	Horse	Eqt.A.Wt	PP	St	¼	½	¾	Str	Fin	Jockey	Odds $1
30May85 6Bel1	Lyphey	3 122	10	9	7^{hd}	$5^{1\frac{1}{2}}$	$4^{\frac{1}{2}}$	$1^{\frac{1}{2}}$	1^{nk}	Velasquez J	7.40
1Jun85 3Bel2	Bahia Grande	3 117	11	11	10^{1}	$7^{\frac{1}{2}}$	$5^{\frac{1}{2}}$	$2^{1\frac{1}{2}}$	2^{2}	Garrido O L5	5.70
3Jun85 6Mth2	Cougar Express	3 117	1	8	11	10^{2}	$6^{\frac{1}{2}}$	$4^{1\frac{1}{2}}$	$3^{2\frac{1}{2}}$	Cordero A Jr	1.40
29May85 2Bel1	Gran Fable	b 3 117	5	3	1^{1}	$1^{\frac{1}{2}}$	2^{1}	$3^{\frac{1}{2}}$	$4^{4\frac{3}{4}}$	Davis R G	35.50
25May85 9Bel11	Carribean Song	3 117	9	7	6^{hd}	4^{hd}	$3^{\frac{1}{2}}$	5^{5}	$5^{2\frac{1}{4}}$	Ward W A	8.30
11Feb85 9GP6	Willingness	3 117	3	2	$3^{\frac{1}{2}}$	$3^{1\frac{1}{2}}$	7^{hd}	6^{6}	$6^{7\frac{1}{2}}$	Bailey J D	7.10
18May85 5Bel6	Haberdasher	b 3 117	8	10	$9^{\frac{1}{2}}$	8^{1}	8^{8}	$8^{2\frac{1}{2}}$	7^{2}	Venezia M	9.10
22May85 5Bel3	Equal Terms	b 3 117	7	1	4^{1}	2^{hd}	1^{hd}	7^{hd}	8^{2}	MacBeth D	28.60
30May85 9Bel2	Another Doc	b 3 117	2	5	8^{1}	11	9^{hd}	$9^{1\frac{1}{2}}$	9^{nk}	Santagata N	11.40
22May85 4Bel7	Wealthy Seamen	3 117	6	6	$5^{\frac{1}{2}}$	$9^{\frac{1}{2}}$	10^{1}	10^{5}	10^{6}	Guerra W A	26.60
22May85 4Bel6	The Home Secretary	b 3 117	4	4	2^{hd}	6^{hd}	11	11	11	Hernandez R	39.50

OFF AT 4:15 Start good, Won driving. Time, :23⅘, :48, 1:13, 1:39 Course yielding.

$2 Mutuel Prices:			
11-(O)-LYPHEY	16.80	9.40	3.60
12-(N)-BAHIA GRANDE		6.80	3.40
1-(A)-COUGAR EXPRESS			2.80

$2 EXACTA 11-12 PAID $60.80.

Ch. c, by Irish River—Lypatia, by Lyphard. Trainer Lukas D Wayne. Bred by Mabee Mr-Mrs J C (KY).

LYPHEY, between horses early, rallied inside BAHIA GRANDE approaching the stretch and outgamed that opponent under a strong hand ride. BAHIA GRANDE rallied wide into the stretch and finished with good determination. COUGAR EXPRESS, steadied back along the inside entering the backstretch, moved around HABERDASHER nearing the stretch, was taken back to the inside in upper stretch and finished willingly. GRAN FABLE weakened after making the pace racing off the rail. CARRIBBEAN SONG moved into contention between horses nering the turn but weakened after entering the stretch. WILLINGNESS, a forward factor while saving ground, fell back approaching the stretch and drifted out while tiring late. HABERDASHER tired. EQUAL TERMS prompted the pace from the outside, joined GRAN FABLE nearing the stretch but was finished soon after. ANOTHER DOC showed little. WEALTHY SEAMAN tired. THE HOME SECRETARY tired after prompting the pace from between horses.

However, we must warn the reader of the realities of the situation. The "grass-breeding dream race" occurs all too infrequently. Finding two solid plays in one race is quite rare. Even the best grass sires produce grass-debut winners only 20–25 percent of the time, with some who are recognized as grass influences as low as 15 percent. When two good-looking prospects like Lyphey and Bahia Grande appear in the same race, an exacta or quinella wager is called for, but not to the exclusion of straight-win bets on both horses. The risks are too high that one of the two will not take to the grass immediately (if at all).

Once again, we refer the interested reader to the Appendix, where statistical information on first and second grass performances for nearly 150 stallions can be found. The reader should be able to use this data to form his own conclusions about those sires he will use in his own betting portfolio.

We hope this chapter makes a more subtle point as well: Namely, that the grass-breeding angle goes beyond a list of prepotent stallions, and indeed involves young stallions, the broodmare and broodmare sire, and European influences.

With so much information being disseminated these days, many players are well aware of the established grass sires, so to maintain a significant edge over the competition, the serious player must dig a little deeper, expand his knowledge base at every opportunity, and keep abreast of current developments, such as emerging grass sires. This means reading through the past performances and result charts for all tracks covered in the local edition of the *Racing Form,* and subscribing to either of the two fine magazines, *The Thoroughbred Record* and *The Bloodhorse.* Both offer their subscribers an annual supplement called a "sire book," which contains detailed information about the bloodlines and racing and breeding performance of most of the country's stallions. These books are published to help breeders select appropriate stallions for their broodmares, but they can also provide interesting reading for handicappers intrigued by the pedigrees of the horses they bet. In short, they make for good reading on a cold winter's night.

As a concluding note, we wish to touch upon the fact that there is indeed a psychological side to the racing game. Some horses improve their first time on the grass because they have a real aptitude for racing on that surface; others because of the change of scenery. After you have read enough past performance profiles, you will realize that numerous horses run their best race on grass their first time on that surface. Possibly, the classification of that race realized the limits of their capabilities. More likely, though, the horse produced a superior effort because it was on edge due to the unusual circumstances. Whether it be grass for the first time, or a return to the grass following a winter of racing on dirt, or the first try around two turns, or at a different track, there are many horses that will "wake up" when their usual routine is altered.

Chapter 15

A Second Chance on the Grass

HORSES BRED FOR GRASS should be given at least two chances to demonstrate whether or not they have the aptitude for turf racing promised by their bloodlines. A horse may turn in an uninspiring performance its first time on the grass for reasons other than an inherent inability to handle that surface. The horse may have suffered a bad trip in its grass debut. Or it simply may not have been fit enough to give a peak effort, regardless of surface.

Or the horse may have been outclassed, entered well above its usual status to give the trainer a free look without the risk of losing the animal. Many horses jump up sharply under such conditions. Others do not but are able to handle their usual competition on grass, often at a decent price due to the misleading evidence from their grass debut. Their first try on the grass may be looked upon as a conditioning race, with the horse hopefully showing something during the running to suggest a liking for the surface.

Memorial Day has for years been the setting for the Metropolitan Mile, the premier handicap event at that distance on the East Coast. The 1985 edition featured all the top handicap stars east of the Rockies, and figured to be a competitive contest. Personally, I was somewhat skeptical of the talent of the contestants. My main interest for the day lay in the fourth race, a maiden contest on the grass, and specifically in a sorry-looking (on paper, at least) colt named Vatza Nice. While other fans debated the relative merits of the Metropolitan entrants, every other sentence from my mouth began "Vatza nice boy like you . . ."

Why Vatza Nice? Who was Vatza, his sire? Those who remembered recalled that Vatza was a son of European champion Nijinsky

II from the American champion mare Shuvee. If it were not for grass racing, however, this regally bred colt would have been regarded as a total failure on the racetrack. As it were, he won three times during his career, with at least two of these coming on the grass, including his debut over that surface. His lone stakes placing came in Belmont's grassy Hill Prince in May of his three-year-old season.

Considering his sire line and grass ability, Vatza was a stallion to watch as a potential sire of grass runners. Prior to Memorial Day, though, only one Vatza (to my knowledge) had run on the grass, that being a three-year-old colt named Vatza's Key. His turf debut at Hialeah on March 14 was stunning—a narrow loss by a nose at 120–1 odds, off dirt form even less imposing than Vatza Nice presented.

Vatza's Key — **B. c. 3, by Vatza—Key to the Heart, by Arts and Letters**
Own.—Stewart F — **Br.—Horne C J (Ky)** — **Tr.—Estevez Manuel A** — **119**

Lifetime							
6 0 1 0	1985	2	M	1	0	$1,980
$1,980	1984	4	M	0	0	
	Turf	1	0	1	0	$1,980

14Mar85- 7Hia	fm	*1 1/16 Ⓣ			1:43⅘	Md Sp Wt	4	6	6^{6}	$6^{4\frac{1}{2}}$	2^{1}	2no	Soto S B	b 119	120.40	79-25	Muffies Diver 119no Vatza's Key $119^{8\frac{1}{2}}$ DonEduardo119^{hd}	Bore in	9
18Jan85- 2Aqu	fst	1 1/16 ⊡	:48⅘	1:14⅖	1:48⅕	Md 30000	5	3	$3^{3\frac{1}{2}}$	7^{10}	8^{18}	7^{22}	Venezia M	118	41.20	47-21	Uncompromising$118^{11\frac{1}{2}}$Fleet'sHonor$122^{1\frac{3}{4}}$CommndBrk118^{hd}	Tired	9
26Dec84- 9Aqu	fst	1 1/16 ⊡	:49⅕	1:14⅘	1:47⅗	Md 25000	4	4	$4^{1\frac{1}{2}}$	6^{9}	8^{16}	$9^{21\frac{1}{2}}$	Ward W A5	b 113	25.50	52-21	PrivateLessons118^{no}ClassLeader$113^{2\frac{3}{4}}$MasterCommnd118^{10}	Tired	10
9Nov84- 9Aqu	fst	1⅛	:49⅕	1:15⅗	1:56	Md 35000	6	9	$8^{7\frac{3}{4}}$	$6^{6\frac{3}{4}}$	6^{19}	7^{20}	Kaenel J L	b 118	12.50	35-32	Flippnt118^{1}MstrCommnd114^{7}Uncompromisng$114^{2\frac{3}{4}}$	Showed little	10
26Oct84- 4Aqu	sly	1	:46⅖	1:11⅘	1:38⅖	Md 50000	5	7	9^{16}	9^{19}	9^{20}	$9^{26\frac{3}{4}}$	Cruguet J	b 118	13.30	47-22	FeelingGallant114^{nk}CreativeSpirit$118^{1\frac{3}{4}}$DancinOnPins114^{7}	Outrun	10
18Aug84- 4FE	fst	6½f	:22⅗	:45⅗	1:17⅕	Handicap	7	8	8^{13}	8^{16}	8^{17}	$8^{12\frac{1}{2}}$	Attard L	b 113	7.40e	80-12	PreEmptiveStrike$124^{1\frac{3}{4}}$TheRoyalFreeze123^{1}FightingChamp116^{nk}		8

After noting this colt's dramatically improved form on grass (he ran second again on April 3), I eagerly awaited the first Vatza to try the grass in New York. Vatza Nice was the one, on Memorial Day. An impressive work on the turf around the dogs the week before signaled a liking for the surface. My only question was whether trainer Freeman was using today's open-classification race for educational purposes with his New York-bred colt, but the heavy betting action seemed to suggest otherwise. Vatza Nice was part of an entry with a rather unimposing first-time starter, and it seemed that the Vatza colt was the one taking the play.

Metropolitan Day 1985 was not meant to be a happy memory. The best handicap horses in the East were routed by a grass horse from California. And Vatza Nice ran third, after moving too early over a course that had been favoring stretch-runners since the beginning of the meet. The important thing, however, was that the horse ran well for the first time in its career, indeed, even broke well. Obviously he liked the grass. There would always be another day.

For Vatza Nice, that day came one month later, on June 27. In the interim, Easton, who had finished second ahead of him on Memorial Day, came back to blast a similar field of maidens, adding a few points to our hero's stock.

4 BELMONT

1 1/16 MILES. (Turf). (1.39⅕) MAIDEN SPECIAL WEIGHTS. Purse $23,000. 3-three-olds and upward. Weights, 3-year-olds, 114 lbs. Older, 122 lbs.

Coupled—Mac At The Track and Paris Flight.

Endured
Ch. c. 3, by Exclusive Native—Quick-n-Crafty, by Crafty Admiral
Br.—Harbor View Farm (Ky)
Tr.—Martin Frank
Own.—Harbor View Farm
114
Lifetime 8 0 0 1 $4,610 | 1985 5 M 0 1 $4,610 | 1984 3 M 0 0 | Turf 7 0 0 1 $4,610

24May85- 6Bel gd 1⅜ Ⓣ:48⅘ 1:39⅗ 2:18 3+ Md Sp Wt 6 8 85¾ 85¾ 1213 1218½ Lovato F Jr b 113 7.50 49-32 MellowNative1136JuniorTerrce1041Singleminded113hd No excuse 14
8May85- 4Bel fm 1 1/16 Ⓣ:47⅘ 1:12⅘ 1:44⅕ Clm 70000 5 4 45 32 3½ 32½ Castaneda K b 113 33.40 77-23 Barbadian Reef 1172 I'm A Banker 113½ Endured 1134 Even try 8
26Apr85- 3Aqu fm 1⅛ Ⓣ:47⅖ 1:12 1:49⅘ Clm 50000 8 11 118 106½ 815 418½ Castaneda K b 117 36.90 77-09 Exclusive Partner 113½ I'mABanker1134Roomie11713½ No mishap 12
8Apr85- 6Aqu fst 1⅛ :48⅘ 1:13 1:52⅗ Md Sp Wt 8 6 54½ 812 925 929½ Lovato F Jr b 122 28.70 42-24 PurpleMountin1221½LovelyBones1222¾Turn'nTogthr1223½ Outrun 10
14Mar85- 7Hia fm *1 1/16 Ⓣ 1:43⅘ Md Sp Wt 1 8 78 78½ 714 615¼ Santos J A 119 4.90 63-25 Muffies Diver 119no Vatza'sKey119¾DonEduardo119hd No factor 9
19Nov84- 6Aqu sf 1 1/16 Ⓣ:50 1:16⅖ 1:51⅘ Md Sp Wt 6 5 62½ 42½ 59½ 69 Deegan J C 118 13.70 37-46 Olajuwon 1182 CleanMachine118¾ProAppeal11182½ Frcts into gate 8
8Oct84- 6Bel fm 1 1/16 Ⓣ:48 1:12⅖ 1:43⅗ Md Sp Wt 5 8 109 1010 814 714¼ Cruguet J 118 13.30 63-22 Danger's Hour 113¾ Space Rider 1186¾ WhiteFlannel1181¾ Outrun 12
25Sep84- 4Med gd 1 Ⓣ:48⅗ 1:13⅕ 1:39⅕ Md Sp Wt 10 7 74½ 87½1012 1016½ McCauley W H 118 3.30 61-19 Trout Stream 11810 JuniorTerrace1132Elloree'sChoice1181½ Tired 10
LATEST WORKOUTS Jun 21 Bel tr.t 4f fst :48 h Jun 15 Bel tr.t 4f fst :48⅖ h ●Jun 9 Bel tr.t 4f my :47 h Jun 2 Bel tr.t 5f fst 1:01⅘ h

Ok Fine
Dk. b. or br. c. 3, by J O Tobin—Fine Prospect, by Mr Prospector
Br.—Matthews Carla C (Ky)
Tr.—Jerkens Steven T
Own.—Stonewall Farm
114
Lifetime 1 0 0 0 | 1985 1 M 0 0 | 1984 0 M 0 0

29May85- 5Bel fst 7f :22⅖ :45⅕ 1:23⅕ Md Sp Wt 6 2 52½ 44 710 613½ Bailey J D 122 20.40 72-15 Dual Honor 1223¾ Air Wing 1223¾ Harley C. 122¾ Tired 7
LATEST WORKOUTS Jun 11 Bel 6f fst 1:16 b May 28 Bel 3f fst :35⅖ b Apr 27 Bel 7f fst 1:31⅗ b

Military Victory
B. g. 3, by Captain Cee Jay—Spicy Game, by King's Bishop
Br.—Volkert D G (Ky)
Tr.—Pascuma Warren J
Own.—Volkert D G
114
Lifetime 13 0 1 1 $6.170 | 1985 8 M 1 1 $5,510 | 1984 5 M 0 0 $660 | Turf 2 0 0 1 $2,760

9Jun85- 3Bel sf 1¼ Ⓣ:52 1:43⅘ 2:09 Clm 45000 5 5 55½ 21½ 34½ 34¾ MacBeth D 113 *2.60 44-41 RunwyBrokr1132¾ThRunnngKnd1132MltryVctory1133½ Weakened 7
3Jun85- 4Bel fm 1⅜ Ⓣ:48⅘ 1:38⅘ 2:17⅗ 3+ Md Sp Wt 13 11 119½ 109½ 76½ 53½ MacBeth D 114 37.90 65-28 Explosive Dancer 1141 Singleminded 114nk Deepdale1171½ Rallied 13
26Apr85- 2Aqu fst 1⅛ :48⅘ 1:14⅕ 1:54 3+ Md 25000 12 8 95½ 1212 1222 1225 MacBeth D 112 27.30 40-23 Hndsomely120noBuckyBdger103noTillitfreezesover1102½ Far back 12
11Apr85- 9Aqu fst 1⅛ :47⅘ 1:13⅖ 1:53⅖ 3+ Md 30000 11 2 44½ 88 919 826½ MacBeth D 112 24.80 41-24 New Monaker 1127¾ Dirty Thoughts 112no Rich Gift 112½ Tired 11
25Mar85- 1Aqu fst 1 :50⅕ 1:17⅖ 1:44⅖ Clm 12000 8 2 2hd 2hd 25 23½ Davis R G 113 13.10 41-35 Gorsk 1103½ Military Victory 1132½ Mr. Recharge 117¾ 2nd best 8
15Mar85- 3Aqu fst 6f :23⅗ :48⅗ 1:14⅕ Md 20000 9 9 119½ 1113 917 918½ Davis R G b 118 8.20e 51-40 H. T. Willis 1111½ Sirjac 111½ Patato 1156½ Outrun 14
24Feb85- 2Aqu fst 6f ⊡:22⅘ :46⅘ 1:14 Clm 14000 1 12 1212 1119 816 611½ Reed R L7 b 110 42.50 62-28 Even On Sunday 117nk Indulge 1062 Stasera 1192 Stumbled st. 12
1Jan85- 2Aqu fst 170 ⊡:49⅖ 1:14 1:45⅗ Md 25000 3 5 — — 817 818½ Thibeau R J b 122 5.20 54-13 Fulminator 120½ Best Target 1181 Gold Coup 1183½ Fog 10
16Dec84- 3Aqu fst 1 1/16 ⊡:50 1:16⅕ 1:50⅖ Md 45000 1 1 2hd 32 67½ 610½ MacBeth D b 114 15.10 49-24 I'm A Banker 114¾ Minus Two 1141 John Mosby 114½ Tired 7
7Dec84- 9Aqu fst 1 1/16 ⊡:48⅕ 1:13⅘ 1:47⅗ Md 25000 1 1 2hd 31½ 53½ 45¾ MacBeth D b 118 25.90 68-19 Cop A Plea 1163 Gallant Rake 1182 El Parador 114¾ Tired 10
LATEST WORKOUTS Jun 25 Bel tr.t 4f my :49⅖ b Jun 18 Bel tr.t 3f gd :37⅕ b May 31 Bel 3f fst :37⅖ b May 23 Bel tr.t 4f fst :50 b

Cuchulinn
Dk. b. or br. c. 4, by Irish Stronghold—Fly With Me, by Misty Flight
Br.—Entenmann Robert W (N.Y.)
Tr.—Alpers Sue
Own.—Woodside Stud
122
Lifetime 6 0 0 0 $2,010 | 1985 4 M 0 0 $1,610 | 1984 2 M 0 0 $400 | Turf 6 0 0 0 $2,010

9Jun85- 2Bel sf 1 1/16 Ⓣ:48⅖ 1:14 1:47⅖ 3+ Md Sp Wt 2 11 1113 119¾ 712 613¾ Skinner K b 122 18.00 45-41 Easton 1145½ Chestertown 1223¾ Divulge 1141½ Outrun 11
27May85- 4Bel fm 1 1/16 Ⓣ:47 1:12⅕ 1:43⅘ 3+ Md Sp Wt 8 7 76¾ 87 512 411½ Skinner K b 124 52.50 66-19 Lightsome 113nk Easton 1132¾ Vatza Nice 1138½ Rallied 10
10Apr85- 4Hia yl *1 1/16 Ⓣ 1:44 3+ Md Sp Wt 9 12 1211 1216 1218 1125 St Leon G b 124 38.00 53-22 Kavazinga 11212 Don Eduardo 1121½ Gypsy King 112hd Outrun 12
16Mar85-11Hia fm 1½ Ⓣ 2:30⅖ Clm 30000 8 5 57½ 1123 1122 1117¾ MacBeth D b 114 51.10 60-18 Stabalizer 114¾ Ⓓlam Charles Pet 112nk Elton's Song 112½ Tired 12
31Dec84- 2Crc fm *1⅛ Ⓣ 1:50⅖ 3+ Md Sp Wt 8 12 1115 109 87¼ 47¾ Cruguet J b 120 19.20 63-25 Tina's Double122¾BananaPeel1175½Scout'sDelight1201½ Mild gain 12
23Nov84- 4Aqu gd 1⅛ Ⓣ:49 1:14 1:53⅗ 3+ Md Sp Wt 4 7 76½ 711 713 719¾ Espinosa R E7 b 113 32.90 56-24 Husk 11311 Deepdale 1202½ Elegant Groom 1171 Outrun 9
LATEST WORKOUTS Jun 26 Bel 3f fst :37⅕ b Jun 19 Bel 4f fst :50⅗ b Jun 7 Bel 4f fst :50 b ●May 26 Bel tr.t 3f fst :37 b

Mac At The Track
B. c. 3, by Mac Diarmida—Native Prospect, by Restless Native
Br.—Goldberg Susan (Fla)
Tr.—Schulhofer Flint S
Own.—Goldberg Susan
114
Lifetime 13 0 0 1 $7,400 | 1985 7 M 0 0 $2,600 | 1984 6 M 0 1 $4,800 | Turf 12 0 0 1 $7,400

9Jun85- 3Bel sf 1¼ Ⓣ:52 1:43⅘ 2:09 Clm 45000 7 7 76½ 54 56½ 48½ Cruguet J 113 8.30 41-41 RunwyBrokr1132¾ThRunningKnd1132MltryVctory1133½ No factor 7
24May85- 6Bel gd 1⅜ Ⓣ:48⅘ 1:39⅗ 2:18 3+ Md Sp Wt 8 6 75½ 43½ 99½ 1117½ Samyn J L b 113 20.50 49-32 MellowNative1136JuniorTerrace1041Singleminded113hd Bid, tired 14
25Apr85- 6Hia fm *1⅛ Ⓣ 1:48⅘ 3+ Md Sp Wt 12 10 1014 99 88½ 67½ Vergara O 113 17.20 80-14 Pervader 1142½Vatza'sKey1131ChangeOfCommand118½ No factor 12
10Apr85- 4Hia yl *1 1/16 Ⓣ 1:44 3+ Md Sp Wt 8 10 96 54 56½ 514½ Hernandez C 112 10.70 63-22 Kavazinga 11212 Don Eduardo 1121½ Gypsy King 112hd Outrun 12
14Mar85-10Hia fm *1 1/16 Ⓣ 1:45⅗ Md Sp Wt 4 2 1hd 44 713 812½ Cruguet J 119 3.30 58-25 Profit Plus 119nk Beaux Ack 1193 Sangfroid 1191 Tired 10
19Feb85- 4GP fm *1 1/16 Ⓣ 1:47 Md Sp Wt 7 3 34½ 31 21½ 43½ Cruguet J 122 3.40 67-26 White Flannel 122½ Profit Plus 122no RoundRidge1223 Weakened 9
3Jan85- 3Crc fm *1 1/16 Ⓣ 1:46⅗ Md Sp Wt 7 6 56½ 77½ 77 75 Cruguet J 119 2.70 69-26 Don Le Moss109½Avey'sBrother119½OurDiplomat119½ Bore in str. 8
8Nov84- 6Aqu fst 1⅛ :49⅘ 1:15⅖ 1:54⅗ Md Sp Wt 4 8 89½ 78½ 621 629½ Cruguet J 118 5.20 32-26 Stack 1185¾ Dancin On Pins 1186½ Olajuwon 1188 Bothered st. 8
13Oct84- 9Bel fm 1 1/16 Ⓣ:47 1:11⅕ 1:44⅖ Md Sp Wt 2 9 98¾ 88½ 75½ 45 Davis R G 118 11.90 69-21 ForeverCommand1151¾Numeric1182RomanRiver1181½ No menace 12
8Oct84- 6Bel fm 1 1/16 Ⓣ:48 1:12⅖ 1:43⅗ Md Sp Wt 2 9 62½ 43 713 815¾ Samyn J L 118 *1.20 62-22 Danger's Hour 113¾ Space Rider 1186¾ White Flannel 1181¾ Tired 12
LATEST WORKOUTS Jun 22 Bel 4f fst :49⅕ b Jun 17 Bel 4f gd :49 h Jun 7 Bel 4f fst :49⅘ b May 16 Bel Ⓣ 4f fm :49⅘ b (d)

Backstreet
B. c. 3, by Darby Creek Road—Quimaule, by Quibu
Br.—Drogitis Mr-Mrs M (Ky)
Tr.—Drogitis Michael
Own.—Drogitis Heidee
114
Lifetime 7 0 0 0 $5,657 | 1985 1 M 0 0 $1,380 | 1984 6 M 0 0 $4,277 | Turf 5 0 0 0 $5,657

9Jun85- 2Bel sf 1 1/16 Ⓣ:48⅖ 1:14 1:47⅖ 3+ Md Sp Wt 9 10 96¾ 96½ 49½ 410½ Hernandez R 114 9.00 48-41 Easton 1145½ Chestertown 1223¾ Divulge 1141½ No factor 11
26Nov84- 4Aqu fst 1⅛ :49⅕ 1:14⅖ 1:54⅖ Md Sp Wt 10 8 97½ 76 88¾ 68½ Thornburg B b 118 9.70 54-25 Comedy Tonight 1181 ProAppeal118½SouthernSultan118¾ Outrun 10
4Nov84- 8Aqu gd 1⅛ Ⓣ:48⅕ 1:14⅕ 1:53⅕ Pilgrim 5 10 1017 107¾ 916 89½ Guerra W A 113 46.70 68-26 Tent Up 1151¾ Space Rider 1131½ Nordance 113hd Outrun 10
4Nov84-Grade III
20Oct84- 1Bel fm 1 1/16 Ⓣ:47⅖ 1:11⅘ 1:43⅖ To Market 1 6 68½ 64½ 57½ 46 Samyn J L 115 22.80 78-12 Danger's Hour 1151 Quintile 1153¾ ForCertainDoc1171½ No factor 7
20Oct84-Run in divisions
13Oct84- 9Bel fm 1 1/16 Ⓣ:47 1:11⅕ 1:44⅖ Md Sp Wt 7 10 1014 1014 910 66½ Cordero A Jr 118 22.70 68-21 Forever Command1151¾Numeric1182RomanRiver1181½ Went wide 12
5Oct84- 4Bel fm 1 1/16 Ⓣ:48⅘ 1:13 1:45⅕ Md Sp Wt 7 6 75½ 512 412 410½ Samyn J L 118 10.40 65-21 Quintile 1182½ Action Eddie 118no Abundant 1187¾ No factor 8
13Sep84- 4Bel fst 6f :22⅗ :46⅕ 1:12 Md Sp Wt 9 12 1419 1317 1216 1113½ Migliore R 118 40.30 68-21 Script Ohio 118¾ Cullendale1181½MightyCourageous1181½ Outrun 14
LATEST WORKOUTS Jun 5 Bel 4f fst :49 h May 30 Bel Ⓣ 6f sf 1:19 b (d) May 23 Bel Ⓣ 5f gd 1:03⅘ b (d) May 16 Bel Ⓣ 7f fm 1:31 b (d)

Feature This One
B. g. 3, by One For All—Magic To Do, by Exclusive Native
Br.—Thieriot C H (NY)
Tr.—Gullo Thomas J
Own.—Gampel H A
114
Lifetime 5 0 0 0 | 1985 3 M 0 0 | 1984 2 M 0 0

10Jun85- 2Bel fst 1 1/16 :47⅗ 1:13⅗ 1:46 3+ Md 30000 8 8 75½ 916 1025 1026½ Guerra W A b 110 46.30 46-19 Mating Dance 1145 Ocean Crossing 1181 April Spark1145½ Outrun 11
20May85- 3Bel fst 1 1/16 :47 1:12 1:43⅗ 3+ Md Sp Wt 2 2 85½ 1017 1027 1035½ Carter T10 b 103 23.60e 48-22 BhiGrnde1084Turn'nTogether113hdBnnyThGriftr1135½ Brief speed 10
10May85- 9Bel fst 6f :22⅘ :46⅗ 1:12⅗ 3+ Md 30000 10 6 42 77½ 713 914 Guerra W A b 109 22.00 65-20 NakedEmperor1132¾SweetRiver1132½GranFble1133 Finished early 12
29Nov84- 3Aqu gd 6f :23⅗ :48⅗ 1:15⅘ Md 25000 8 12 95 99½ 77½ 65¾ Bass S H7 b 111 5.20 56-35 Dash Mount 107no Intercostal 114¾ Park Lane 1141 Wide 14
2Nov84- 9Aqu fst 6f :23⅗ :48⅖ 1:14⅕ Md Sp Wt 10 4 84¾ 77½ 1012 1012¾ Espinosa R E7 111 52.10 57-35 Paths Of Glory 118¾ Yes Sirree 118¾ Verification118¾ Raced wide 12
LATEST WORKOUTS Jun 18 Bel tr.t 4f gd :50⅖ b May 27 Bel tr.t 3f fst :39⅗ b May 17 Bel tr.t 4f fst :49⅕ b May 8 Bel tr.t 3f fst :37 b

Vatza Nice
Ch. g. 3, by Vatza—Nice Bonnet, by Royal Levee
Br.—Freeman W C (NY)
Tr.—Freeman Willard C
Own.—Vatrano A J
114
Lifetime 5 0 0 1 $2,760 | 1985 2 M 0 1 $2,760 | 1984 3 M 0 0 | Turf 1 0 0 1 $2,760

27May85- 4Bel fm 1 1/16 Ⓣ:47 1:12⅕ 1:43⅘ 3+ Md Sp Wt 2 3 2hd 1½ 21 33 MacBeth D 113 3.90e 74-19 Lightsome 113nk Easton 1132¾ Vatza Nice 1138½ Weakened 10
6May85- 6Aqu fst 7f :22⅘ :46 1:25⅗ 3+ Ⓢ Md Sp Wt 5 11 1110 912 819 716 MacBeth D 113 21.40 57-23 Pekoe 1135 Hochmans Front 1132½ RomeoValentine113nk Outrun 13
30Nov84- 6Aqu fst 7f :22⅗ :45⅗ 1:25⅕ Ⓢ Md Sp Wt 14 14 109 910 811 811 Cruguet J 118 14.90 64-23 Club Fighter 118¾ Over the Wall 1182½ Casa Key 1157 Wide 14
12Nov84- 6Aqu gd 1 :47 1:13⅗ 1:40⅗ Ⓢ Md Sp Wt 11 12 61¾ 2½ 52 88¾ Maple E 118 16.20f 54-25 Classi Valentine118½ToCatchAKing1183½Mr.G.J.G.1182½ Squeezed 14
12Oct84- 5Bel fst 6f :23⅕ :47⅕ 1:13⅕ Ⓢ Md Sp Wt 7 11 1213 1212 1011 1010¾ MacBeth D 118 41.10 65-22 My Man John 1182½ WillSurprise118noFearlessTeddy1183½ Outrun 14
LATEST WORKOUTS Jun 20 Bel 6f fst 1:14⅘ h Jun 14 Bel 6f fst 1:17⅖ b Jun 3 Bel 4f fst :50 b ●May 16 Bel Ⓣ 6f fm 1:12⅘ h (d)

Paris Flight
Dk. b. or br. c. 3, by Super Concorde—Meg's Pride, by Sparkler
Br.—Willcox Mr-Mrs A A (Ky)
Tr.—Schulhofer Flint S
Own.—Willcox Mrs A A
114
Lifetime 4 0 0 0 $860 | 1985 3 M 0 0 $860 | 1984 1 M 0 0 | Turf 1 0 0 0

10Jun85- 2Bel fst 1 1/16 :47⅗ 1:13⅗ 1:46 3+ Md 35000 3 5 31 23 411 411½ Davis R G b 114 11.00 60-19 MtingDnce1145OcenCrossing1181AprilSprk1145½ Broke sluggishly 11
26May85- 6Bel fst 6f :22⅘ :46⅕ 1:11⅖ 3+ Md Sp Wt 3 8 106½ 89 98¾ 99½ Guerra W A b 113 58.00 76-13 Chimney Sweep 113¾ Wicked Wike 113¾GrittiPalace1132½ Outrun 10
11Feb85- 7GP fst 1 1/16 :47⅗ 1:13⅕ 1:47 Md Sp Wt 2 3 44 811 1026 932 Cruguet J b 122 30.60 34-26 FultlessOne122hdNorthernCool1225He'sSoPrtty1223 Speed for 1/2 10
22Oct84- 6Bel fm 1 1/16 Ⓣ:47⅕ 1:11 1:43⅗ Md Sp Wt 2 5 32½ 77 820 817¾ Samyn J L b 118 17.80 60-18 Space Rider 1181¾ Lord Ashley 1181½RoundRidge1181½ Off slowly 11
LATEST WORKOUTS Jun 24 Bel 4f fst :48 h Jun 18 Bel 4f fst :48 h Jun 7 Bel 4f fst :48 h Jun 2 Bel 4f fst :48 h

Air Wing
Ch. c. 3, by His Majesty—Beating Wings, by Bold Lad
Br.—Darby Dan Farm (Ky)
Tr.—Veitch John M
Own.—Darby Dan Farm
114
Lifetime 2 0 1 1 $7,480 | 1985 2 M 1 1 $7,480 | 1984 0 M 0 0

29May85- 5Bel fst 7f :22⅖ :45⅕ 1:23⅕ Md Sp Wt 4 5 65½ 67 25 23¾ Maple E 122 *1.10 82-15 Dual Honor 1223¾ Air Wing 1223¾ Harley C. 122¾ 2nd best 7
9May85- 6Bel fst 6f :22⅘ :46⅕ 1:11⅕ 3+ Md Sp Wt 3 5 68½ 48 37½ 34¾ Maple E 113 *1.80 81-25 Available Power 113hd Wicked Wike 1134¾ Air Wing1136¾ Rallied 6
LATEST WORKOUTS Jun 26 Bel 3f fst :36⅖ h ●Jun 22 Bel 5f fst 1:00⅖ h Jun 18 Bel 4f fst :49⅗ b Jun 12 Bel 4f fst :49 b

Roman River — B. c. 3, by Apalachee—Roman Grounder, by Proudest Roman
Own.—Schiff J M — Br.—Schiff J M (Ky) — Tr.—Kelly Thomas J — **114**
Lifetime 7 0 1 3 $10,900 — 1985 1 M 0 0 — 1984 6 M 1 3 $10,900 — Turf 3 0 1 2 $8,740

24May85- 5Mth fst 1 70	:47⅗ 1:13⅕ 1:45⅕	3↑ Md Sp Wt	1 2 4^{2} 5^{9} 8^{15} $9^{21\frac{1}{2}}$	Rocco J	b 114	5.00	48–25	Darrain $114^{\frac{3}{4}}$ Cyaneman 114^{2} In Control 114^{2}	Tired	9
5Nov84- 6Aqu my 1	:46⅗ 1:12⅘ 1:39⅕	Md Sp Wt	9 4 $4^{\frac{3}{4}}$ $5^{2\frac{1}{2}}$ $7^{8\frac{1}{4}}$ $7^{10\frac{3}{4}}$	Graell A	b 118	7.00	60–25	Numeric 118^{hd} Recognized $118^{2\frac{3}{4}}$ Cool Joe 118^{4}	Bore out	11
13Oct84- 9Bel fm 1 1/16 (T)	:47 1:11⅕ 1:44⅖	Md Sp Wt	6 4 4^{2} 5^{3} $4^{3\frac{1}{2}}$ $3^{3\frac{3}{4}}$	Graell A	b 118	7.50	70–21	ForeverCommand$115^{1\frac{3}{4}}$Numeric118^{2}RomnRiver$118^{1\frac{1}{2}}$	Lacked rally	12
28Sep84- 6Bel yl 1 1/16 (T)	:48 1:14 1:47⅕	Md Sp Wt	8 5 $3^{\frac{1}{2}}$ 3^{1} $1^{\frac{1}{2}}$ $2^{2\frac{3}{4}}$	Graell A	b 118	*1.50	57–36	Willingness $118^{2\frac{3}{4}}$ RomanRiver118^{3}SoundProof$118^{1\frac{3}{4}}$	Second best	12
14Sep84- 6Bel fm 1 1/16 [T]	:48 1:12⅖ 1:45⅕	Md Sp Wt	3 6 7^{5} 5^{5} 4^{3} $3^{3\frac{1}{4}}$	Graell A	118	3.90	72–23	Magnaminous $118^{\frac{3}{4}}$ Lathom $118^{2\frac{3}{4}}$ Roman River $118^{2\frac{3}{4}}$	Rallied	8
26Jly84- 6Bel fst 6f	:22⅗ :46⅕ 1:11⅗	Md Sp Wt	2 5 $9^{6\frac{3}{4}}$ $8^{7\frac{1}{4}}$ $7^{9\frac{1}{2}}$ 5^{11}	Graell A	118	9.20	73–17	Salem Drive $118^{\frac{3}{4}}$ Anconeus $118^{1\frac{1}{2}}$ Haberdasher 118^{4}	Outrun	10
9Jly84- 6Bel fst 5f	:22⅕ :45⅖ :57⅗	Md Sp Wt	2 5 6^{11} 6^{13} 5^{12} $3^{10\frac{1}{2}}$	Graell A	118	22.10	89–14	Ziggy's Boy $118^{6\frac{1}{2}}$ Varick $118^{3\frac{3}{4}}$ Roman River $118^{3\frac{3}{4}}$	Wide	8

LATEST WORKOUTS Jun 5 Bel 4f fst :48 h Apr 27 Hia 5f fst 1:01 h

Quick Secretariat — B. c. 4, by Secretariat—Princess Olympia, by Olympia
Own.—Laurin Mrs R — Br.—Laurin L (Ky) — Tr.—Laurin Roger — **122**
Lifetime 3 0 0 0 $140 — 1985 1 M 0 0 $140 — 1983 2 M 0 0 — Turf 3 0 0 0 $140

17Jan85- 5GP fm *1 1/16 (T)	1:45⅕	Md Sp Wt	2 6 4^{6} 3^{2} 4^{6} $6^{9\frac{3}{4}}$	MacBeth D	b 122	22.10	70–15	Nordico 122^{1} Lordship $122^{6\frac{1}{2}}$ Adorateur 122^{1}	No threat	10
8Sep83- 4Bel fm 1 1/16 (T)	:48 1:13 1:44⅘	Md Sp Wt	6 11 6^{4} 4^{3} 6^{8} $5^{12\frac{1}{2}}$	Hernandez R	b 118	12.20e	60–24	Cut The Music 118^{nk} Vision 118^{9} Anderson Spring $118^{\frac{3}{4}}$	Steadied	12
4Sep83- 4Bel fm 1 (T)	:47⅗ 1:12 1:38⅕	Md Sp Wt	4 10 $8^{4\frac{1}{2}}$ 6^{8} 6^{11} 6^{10}	Hernandez R	b 118	3.30	64–17	BoldJove$118^{1\frac{1}{2}}$ZephyrCove$118^{1\frac{1}{2}}$YukonBy118^{hd}	Lacked a response	11

LATEST WORKOUTS Jun 20 Bel [T] 6f fm 1:14⅘ h Jun 17 Bel 6f gd 1:18 b Jun 4 Bel 4f sly :49 b May 27 Bel 3f fst :36⅘ h

Vatza Nice was lucky enough to catch a relatively weak field on June 27. Eight of his eleven rivals had experience on the grass but had been found wanting. Air Wing, the 9–5 favorite, had run well in his two dirt starts but was not especially well bred for the grass. At 9–5, even a horse with the best grass bloodlines would have to be passed in its first try on the green.

More interesting at 45–1 was Feature This One, a son of the exceptional grass sire One For All from an Exclusive Native mare, who was making his first attempt on the grass after five dismal efforts on dirt, three for a claiming tag. If Vatza Nice could jump up on the grass (as he did), then so could this one. But, at 7–2, Vatza Nice was hard to pass, and definitely an overlay. Rating better than had been the case on Memorial Day, Vatza Nice moved smartly to the

FOURTH RACE **1 1/16 MILES.(Turf). (1.39⅕) MAIDEN SPECIAL WEIGHTS. Purse $23,000. 3-three-olds and upward. Weights, 3-year-olds, 114 lbs. Older, 122 lbs.**

Belmont

JUNE 27, 1985

Value of race $23,000; value to winner $13,800; second $5,060; third $2,760; fourth $1,380. Mutuel pool $97,164, OTB pool $109,554. Quin $82,405 OTB Quin $101,325. Ex $126,046 OTB Ex $125,155.

Last Raced	Horse	Eqt.	A.	Wt	PP	St	¼	½	¾	Str	Fin	Jockey	Odds $1
27May85 ^{4}Bel^{3}	Vatza Nice		3	114	8	5	5^{hd}	$5^{\frac{1}{2}}$	$4^{1\frac{1}{2}}$	1^{2}	1^{2}	MacBeth D	3.80
29May85 ^{5}Bel^{2}	Air Wing		3	114	10	9	9^{6}	9^{hd}	8^{1}	$4^{1\frac{1}{2}}$	$2^{1\frac{1}{2}}$	Maple E	1.80
10Jun85 ^{2}Bel^{10}	Feature This One	b	3	114	7	2	$3^{\frac{1}{2}}$	$4^{1\frac{1}{2}}$	$5^{\frac{1}{2}}$	$3^{\frac{1}{2}}$	3^{nk}	Santagata N	45.50
9Jun85 ^{2}Bel^{6}	Cuchulinn	b	4	122	4	10	11^{2}	11^{5}	11^{8}	$8^{1\frac{1}{2}}$	$4^{1\frac{1}{2}}$	Skinner K	26.70
9Jun85 ^{3}Bel^{3}	Military Victory		3	114	3	3	$7^{1\frac{1}{2}}$	7^{2}	7^{1}	$7^{\frac{1}{2}}$	5no	Bailey J D	11.80
29May85 ^{5}Bel^{6}	Ok Fine		3	114	2	1	$1^{\frac{1}{2}}$	2^{1}	$1^{\frac{1}{2}}$	2^{1}	$6^{2\frac{1}{2}}$	Velasquez J	18.80
24May85 ^{6}Bel^{12}	Endured	b	3	114	1	7	8^{1}	$8^{2\frac{1}{2}}$	9^{2}	9^{2}	7^{1}	Samyn J L	9.70
10Jun85 ^{2}Bel^{4}	Paris Flight	b	3	114	9	6	4^{4}	3^{hd}	3^{hd}	6^{hd}	$8^{1\frac{3}{4}}$	Davis R G	a-7.10
24May85 ^{5}Mth^{9}	Roman River	b	3	114	11	4	$2^{1\frac{1}{2}}$	$1^{\frac{1}{2}}$	2^{1}	5^{hd}	9^{nk}	Graell A	7.90
9Jun85 ^{2}Bel^{4}	Backstreet		3	114	6	11	12	12	12	12	$10^{\frac{3}{4}}$	Hernandez R	9.50
17Jan85 ^{5}GP^{6}	Quick Secretariat	b	4	122	12	8	6^{2}	$6^{1\frac{1}{2}}$	$6^{1\frac{1}{2}}$	10^{2}	11^{2}	Vasquez J	27.30
9Jun85 ^{3}Bel^{4}	Mac At The Track	b	3	114	5	12	$10^{\frac{1}{2}}$	10^{4}	$10^{\frac{1}{2}}$	$11^{1\frac{1}{2}}$	12	Cruguet J	a-7.10

a-Coupled: Paris Flight and Mac At The Track.

OFF AT 2:36. Start good. Won driving. Time, :23, :47, 1:11⅖, 1:37⅕, 1:43⅘ Course firm.

$2 Mutuel Prices:				
	8–(H)–VATZA NICE	9.60	3.80	3.60
	9–(J)–AIR WING		3.00	2.80
	7–(G)–FEATURE THIS ONE			11.80

$2 QUINELLA 8–9 PAID $11.60. $2 EXACTA 8–9 PAID $27.80.

Ch. g, by Vatza—Nice Bonnet, by Royal Levee. Trainer Freeman Willard C. Bred by Freeman W C (NY).

VATZA NICE, steadied along the inside at the turn, got through to make a bid nearing the stretch and, after drawing clear, held sway under a good handling. AIR WING split horses after entering the stretch and finished to gain the place. FEATURE THIS ONE raced within easy striking distance to the final furlong but lacked a rally. CUCHULINN rallied mildly between horses. MILITARY VICTORY had no apparent excuse. OK FINE was used up vying for the lead. ENDURED failed to be a serious factor. PARIS FLIGHT raced forwardly to the stretch and tired. ROMAN RIVER was used up vying for the lead. BACKSTREET was always outrun. QUICK SECRETARIAT tired while racing wide. MAC AT THE TRACK was always outrun.

lead in upper stretch and had no trouble holding off the late charge of Air Wing. Feature This One proved to be the best of the early contenders and held on for third money.

We found another interesting example of the "second try on grass" angle in the fifth race at Gulfstream on April 4, 1984. Three of the contestants—Gentle Pop, Flaming Color, and Green Ari—were trying the grass for the first time, but none had the bloodlines to warrant serious consideration. Angel From Above seemed to have gone off form. Both Peace Weapon and Julie's Bid seemed cheaper, based on the former's lack of success in allowance company following her victory for a claiming tag on January 18, in which the latter finished third. Neither Trinado (the 2–1 favorite) nor River Fete had raced since January. Lysine, who was herself absent for six weeks, was still a maiden. The logical selection seemed to be Little Mandy, second choice at 5–2.

Little Mandy seemed to have the most going for her. Two recent third-place finishes in the same company on the grass suggested fitness and a liking for the surface, as well as proper placement. However, the Little Current filly's record was beginning to take the shape of the standard "runner-up" profile, one of the prime "antagonist" types discussed in the preceding chapter. She had now failed on five occasions to win in "nonwinners of one" company, and her late-running style was not particularly suited to the short one-mile distance. Trinado, the favorite, also had the same running style, and clever players might have anticipated that she would eventually fall into the same "antagonist" category.

Obviously these two fillies could be beaten, and they were hardly worth backing as the public choices. But in a weak field, either could win without surprising too many people. Was there something in the field worth playing against them?

If either of these fillies were to be beaten, the logical selection had to be the maiden Lysine. Her sire, Majestic Light, was the hottest grass sire in the country at the time. Lysine's first try on the grass was excellent, even though she was checked sharply on the final turn. And that performance took on even more luster in light of the subsequent performance of the filly who beat her, Angel From Above, again a rival on April 4. That filly stamped her maiden win as "better than average" when she returned thirteen days later above her conditions in "nonwinners of two" company against previous allowance winners and raced quite creditably. Despite breaking from the outside post position, she fought tooth and nail for the lead for nearly a mile before cracking under the steady pressure. Apparently that effort drained her physically, if not mentally as

5 GULFSTREAM

TURF COURSE — ABOUT 1 MILE — GULFSTREAM — START — FINISH

ABOUT 1 MILE. (TURF). (1.36) ALLOWANCE. Purse $13,000. 3-year-old fillies which have never won a race other than Maiden or Claiming. Weights, 121 lbs. Non-winners of a race other than Claiming at a mile or over since February 15 allowed 3 lbs. Of such a race since January 15, 5 lbs.

Trinado
Dk. b. or br. f. 3, by Tri Jet—Valnado, by Tronado
Br.—Appleton Electric Co (Fla)
Tr.—Goldfine Lou M
Own.—Appleton A I
116
Lifetime 11 2 2 1 $13,435 | 1984 2 0 1 0 $3,080 | 1983 9 2 1 1 $10,355 | Turf 3 0 2 0 $5,360

30Jan84- 8Hia fm *1 1/16 Ⓣ 1:42⅘ ⒻAlw 14000 9 10 105½ 99 77¾ 44 DePass R 113 3.60 81-15 OakbrookLady1133½StillOurFront114nkSkimbleshnks113nk Rallied 12
12Jan84- 4Hia fm *1⅛ Ⓣ 1:49 ⒻAlw 14000 9 11 109¾109½ 32 22½ DePass R b 114 4.50 83-13 Powder Break 1132½ Trinado 1145½ Oakbrook Lady113½ Game try 12
28Dec83- 8Crc fm *1 1/16 Ⓣ 1:46⅗ ⒻAlw 12000 1 8 77½ 31½ 23 22½ DePass R b 114 14.20 71-23 Tres Noble 1112½ Trinado 1144½ Betchalife 1141½ Best of others 8
16Dec83- 3Crc sly 6½f :23 :47⅘ 1:21⅘ ⒻClm 12500 7 11 96¾ 66 32½ 12½ DePass R b 114 18.70 76-19 Trinado 1142½ Klubby Kaster 114½ PollyPrim112hd Steadied, clear 11
17Oct83- 1Haw fst 6f :22⅖ :47 1:15⅗ ⒻMd 15000 10 9 87½ 510 23½ 13½ Diaz J L b 119 2.10 63-30 Trinado 1193½ Matonka 114¾ Today Pleasure 116¾ Driving 12
3Oct83- 1Haw fst 5½f :22⅗ :47 1:06⅘ ⒻMd 15000 7 11 87 78 43½ 36 Diaz J L b 119 10.20 72-24 Arts 'N Crafts 1194 Miss Allthority 1192 Trinado 119no 12
2Sep83- 3AP fst 6f :22⅘ :46⅘ 1:13⅕ ⒻMd 20000 12 2 44½ 68½ 44½ 57¾ Diaz J L b 117 15.20 68-25 Sweet Hickory 1172½ Miss Beauty 1102½ La Donna's Star 1173 12
23Aug83- 3AP fst 5½f :23⅕ :47⅖ 1:07⅘ ⒻMd 20000 10 10 84 47½ 410 411½ Diaz J L b 117 5.60 64-29 Society Rose 1122½ La Donna's Star 1172 Awful 1177 10
13Jly83- 3AP fst 5f :22⅗ :47⅗ 1:01 ⒻMd 25000 8 9 87½ 68 56 45 Diaz J L b 117 11.50 76-20 Countess Inro 112¾ Shelly Menelly 117½ Society Rose 1173¾ 10
26Jun83- 5AP fst 5f :22 :45⅘ :59⅘ ⒻMd Sp Wt 6 9 97½ 913 812 811¾ Diaz J L 117 3.00e 77-22 Katrinka 1171½ Dancing Divy 1174 Landia 1171 10
LATEST WORKOUTS Mar 31 GP 3f fst :36⅗ h ● Mar 23 GP 5f fst 1:00 h Mar 16 GP 5f fst 1:02⅗ b Mar 9 GP 4f fst :50 b

River Fete
B. f. 3, by Mississipian—Festiva, by Espace Vital
Br.—Hunt N B (Ky)
Tr.—Winick Neal J
Own.—Summa Stable
116
Lifetime 5 1 1 0 $8,610 | 1984 1 0 0 0 $110 | 1983 4 1 1 0 $8,500 | Turf 2 1 0 0 $6,710

18Jan84- 10Hia yl *1⅛ Ⓣ 1:51⅕ ⒻClm 35000 9 4 46½ 67 99¼ 99¾ Bailey J D 117 *2.50 65-25 Peace Weapon 1081 Our Girl Chris 1101 Julie's Bid 111½ Tired 11
29Dec83- 5Crc fm *1 1/16 Ⓣ 1:48⅗ ⒻMd Sp Wt 3 3 42½ 3½ 11½ 11½ St Leon G 118 2.70 64-22 River Fete 1181½ Native Anna1182Sugarless1183½ Bore in. driving 8
5Oct83- 4LaD fst 170 :48⅕ 1:14 1:44⅘ ⒻMd Sp Wt 1 3 52½ 33 27 211 Maple S 119 16.30 62-23 Mary Fern 11911 River Fete 1195 Country Connection 119nk 12
16Sep83- 1LaD fst 6f :23 :46⅘ 1:13 ⒻMd Sp Wt 8 4 75¼1014 816 716 Maple S 119 41.10 62-21 Zinov's First 119hd Jill's Battle 1198 Sunny Weather 1195 12
29Jly83- 1LaD fst 6f :22⅖ :46⅕ 1:12⅕ ⒻMd Sp Wt 6 10 11131016 917 718¾ Maple S 119 45.10 63-21 Quick Justice 119nk Geevilla 11911 Mary Fern 119½ 12
LATEST WORKOUTS Apr 2 Hia 3f fst :38⅗ b Feb 22 Hia 7f gd 1:29⅖ b Feb 15 Hia 6f fst 1:16 b Feb 9 Hia 5f fst 1:02⅖ b

Candy Bowl
B. f. 3, by Majestic Light—Quick Cure, by Dr Fager
Br.—Firestone Mr-Mrs B R (Ky)
Tr.—Hough Stanley M
Own.—Firestone Mrs B R
116
Lifetime 5 1 1 1 $15,990 | 1984 3 1 0 1 $11,150 | 1983 2 M 1 0 $4,840 | Turf 3 1 1 1 $15,870

12Mar84- 6GP fm *1 1/16 Ⓣ 1:46⅕ ⒻAlw 13000 1 6 55½ 42 2½ 31½ Bailey J D 121 *1.10 73-21 Illaka 1161½ Battere 111no Candy Bowl 12114 Weakened 10
29Feb84- 7Hia fm 1 1/16 Ⓣ 1:43 Md Sp Wt 4 6 51½ 52½ 2hd 1nk Bailey J D 114 4.80 83-10 Candy Bowl 114nk Dissonance 1197 Errant Minstrel 119no Driving 12
10Feb84- 8Hia fst 7f :23⅕ :46⅗ 1:25 ⒻMd Sp Wt 6 8 66 66½ 512 614¼ Maple E 119 2.90 64-22 WinnebagoSeven1193½MerryChase119nkYearAfterYer1191 Outrun 12
17Oct83- 9Bel yl 1 1/16 Ⓣ :48⅗ 1:14⅕ 1:48 ⒻMd Sp Wt 10 5 32½ 31 23 22 Maple E 117 5.30 54-38 Qualique 1172 Candy Bowl 1172¾ Flora Scent 117¾ Lugged in 12
7Oct83- 6Bel fst 7f :23⅕ :47⅕ 1:26 ⒻMd Sp Wt 12 7 128¼ 76½ 69 79¾ Vasquez J 117 3.30 62-23 Second Sight 1171¾ Bett's Pleasure1173½FullSong1173¾ No threat 14
LATEST WORKOUTS Mar 31 Hia 6f fst 1:15⅗ b Mar 26 Hia 4f fst :50 b Mar 8 Hia 4f fst :50 b Feb 18 Hia 4f fst :47 h

Lysine
B. f. 3, by Majestic Light—Peace Movement, by Admiral's Voyage
Br.—Live Oak Stud (Fla)
Tr.—Kelly Patrick J
Own.—Live Oak Plantation
116
Lifetime 4 0 1 0 $2,400 | 1984 3 M 1 0 $2,400 | 1983 1 M 0 0 | Turf 1 0 1 0 $2,160

20Feb84- 9Hia fst 1⅛ :47⅗ 1:12⅗ 1:52⅕ ⒻMd Sp Wt 10 10 105½ 913 920 920 Gonzalez M A 118 3.10 51-16 Cancan Madame118nkSpring'sPromise118nkNativeAnna1181 Wide 12
31Jan84- 10Hia fm *1⅛ Ⓣ 1:49⅗ ⒻMd Sp Wt 6 5 57 64½ 42 2½ Gonzalez M A 118 33.40 82-14 Angel From Above 118½ Lysine118½CharmingPeggy1184 Checked 12
12Jan84- 10Hia fst 7f :23⅕ :46⅘ 1:25⅗ ⒻMd Sp Wt 11 3 53½ 55 97¾ 913 Gonzalez M A 119 10.20 63-18 Bygones 119½ Lucy Gayheart 1193 Bets Afire 1192 No factor 12
11Dec83- 6Aqu fst 6f ⊡:23⅗ :48⅗ 1:13⅗ ⒻMd Sp Wt 7 7 62½ 53½ 54¾ 58½ Murphy D J5 112 13.60 68-27 Suavite 1171 Tell Aunt Susan 1173¾ For My Heart 1172¾ Evenly 11
LATEST WORKOUTS Mar 28 Hia 4f fst :49⅘ b ● Mar 23 Hia 4f fst :40 b Mar 17 Hia 3f fst :37 b Mar 12 Hia 5f fst 1:01 b

*Skimbleshanks
Ch. f. 3, by Bold Lad—Thimblerigger, by Sharpen Up
Br.—Moyns Park Stud (Eng)
Tr.—DiMauro Stephen L
Own.—Dogwood Stable
116
Lifetime 12 1 2 2 $13,950 | 1984 5 0 1 1 $4,170 | 1983 7 1 1 1 $9,780 | Turf 2 0 1 1 $3,740

26Mar84- 8GP fst 1 1/16 :47⅗ 1:13 1:45⅗ ⒻAlw 13000 7 7 77 1116 1128 1135¼ Bailey J D 116 8.00 38-16 Montage 1161 ⒹBlonde Inflation 116nk Jillometti 1168 Outrun 12
7Mar84- 6GP fm 1 1/16 Ⓣ:48⅗ 1:13 1:44⅖ ⒻAlw 13000 12 3 2hd 1½ 11 2no Bailey J D 116 5.00 79-25 Megan Ann 116no Skimbleshanks 116nk Little Mandy 116nk Sharp 12
27Feb84- 7Hia fst 1 1/16 :46 1:10⅕ 1:44⅗ Alw 16000 1 3 34½ 38½ 712 721 Bailey J D 113 23.10 59-16 ⒹMontage 114no Madame Justice 1147 Peace Waters 1133 Tired 9
30Jan84- 8Hia fm *1 1/16 Ⓣ 1:42⅘ ⒻAlw 14000 10 5 3½ 1½ 2hd 33¾ Bailey J D 113 57.70 81-15 OkbrookLdy1133½StillOurFront114nkSkimblshnks113nk Weakened 12
25Jan84- 8Hia fst 6f :22 :45⅗ 1:11 ⒻAlw 14000 7 8 109¼ 1012 1011 1014½ Melendez J D 114 85.20 73-18 Twisted Relation 1141 StraightChick1143½Elaborately1093 Outrun 12
30Sep83- 7Med sly 1 :47⅘ 1:13 1:40 ⒻAlw 13000 4 5 45½ 89¾ 812 816¼ Melendez J D3 114 17.00 65-17 IngotWay109nkFullBonnet1122Lady'sReception117nk Roughed st. 8
17Sep83- 5Med fst 6f :23 :46⅘ 1:13 ⒻMd Sp Wt 6 1 42½ 1hd 1½ 1¾ Melendez J D3 115 6.20 78-17 Skimbleshanks 115¾ Hail To Star 1131 Canninvade 118½ Driving 7
24Aug83- 10Mth fst 6f :23 :46⅘ 1:13⅕ ⒻMd 35000 2 9 44 34½ 32½ 26 Melendez J D5 113 *3.30 68-26 AutumnBells1136Skimbleshnks1131½ApplBrownBtty114nk Rallied 12
12Aug83- 3Mth sly 5½f :23⅕ :47⅗ 1:07⅗ ⒻMd 35000 3 6 57 69½ 612 58¼ Melendez J D5 110 8.00 69-27 MinnieComputer1125ShotAbove117¾PintionQueen117½ No factor 8
3Aug83- 4Mth fst 5½f :23⅕ :47⅕ 1:07⅕ ⒻMd 35000 9 2 52¼ 43 54½ 33½ Melendez J D5 113⁴ 9.30 76-20 Knitted Top118¾PluckyDemand1142½ⒹⒽSkimbleshanks113 Rallied 12
3Aug83-Dead heat
LATEST WORKOUTS Mar 15 GP 3f fst :38 b Mar 5 GP 4f fst :49 b Feb 24 GP 4f fst :50 b Feb 16 GP 5f fst 1:06 b

Little Mandy
B. f. 3, by Little Current—Dear Editor, by Prince John
Br.—Knight L (Ohio)
Tr.—Owens Martin D
Own.—Knight L
116
Lifetime 7 1 0 2 $7,920 | 1984 5 0 0 2 $3,300 | 1983 2 1 0 0 $4,620 | Turf 5 0 0 2 $3,240

7Mar84- 6GP fm 1 1/16 Ⓣ:48⅗ 1:13 1:44⅖ ⒻAlw 13000 6 11 118¾ 97½ 53¼ 3nk Cruguet J 116 7.10 79-25 Megan Ann 116no Skimbleshanks 116nk LittleMandy116nk Rallied 12
28Feb84- 8Hia fst 1 1/16 :46⅗ 1:11⅕ 1:45⅕ ⒻAlw 18000 4 9 916 821 817 820½ Cruguet J 113 3.60 56-23 Christine's Pixie 113¾ Mamuska 1132 DanceAMoment1083 Outrun 9
6Feb84- 8Hia fm *1⅛ Ⓣ 1:49 ⒻAlw 14000 7 6 611 53½ 2½ 32½ Cruguet J 113 26.90 83-14 Disquieting 113no Vast Domain 1142½LittleMandy113no Weakened 10
21Jan84- 5Hia fm 1⅛ Ⓣ 1:50⅖ ⒻAlw 14000 9 12 1211 128¼ 77½ 64¼ Cruguet J 113 62.60 76-13 Scorched Panties113noⒹDisquieting114nkDesiredMiss1132 Outrun 12
12Jan84- 4Hia fm *1⅛ Ⓣ 1:49 ⒻAlw 14000 3 4 45½ 55¾ 98½ 915 Russ M L 113 20.10 71-13 Powder Break 1132½ Trinado 1145½ Oakbrook Lady 113½ Tired 12
28Dec83- 8Crc fm *1 1/16 Ⓣ 1:46⅗ ⒻAlw 12000 3 4 44 21½ 45½ 510 Russ M L 112 4.90 64-23 Tres Noble 1112½ Trinado 1144½ Betchalife 1141½ Tired 8
7Dec83- 6Tdn my 6f :23⅗ :49⅘ 1:17⅗ ⒻⓈMd Sp Wt 4 9 69¾ 34 13 13 Londono O A 117 *1.00 56-40 Little Mandy 1173 PleasantBreeze1171½PlunkATerry1172½ Driving 13
LATEST WORKOUTS ● Mar 27 GP Ⓣ 6f fm 1:19 b (d) Mar 17 GP 5f fst 1:05 b Feb 18 GP 7f fst 1:33 b

Gentle Pop
B. f. 3, by Gentle King—Strawberry Pop, by Vox Pop
Br.—Reich H R (Fla)
Tr.—Moos Joseph G
Own.—Mad Doc Stable
109⁷
Lifetime 11 5 2 1 $25,110 | 1984 10 4 2 1 $22,710 | 1983 1 1 0 0 $2,400

27Mar84- 3GP fst 7f :23 :45⅘ 1:24⅕ ⒻClm 16000 4 5 1hd 11 13 13 McCauley W H b 112 *1.20 83-18 Gentle Pop 1123 She's A Diplomat 116nk Retablo 1182½ Driving 9
17Mar84- 1GP fst 6f :23 :46⅗ 1:12⅕ ⒻClm 12500 8 3 2½ 21 1hd 13 McCauley W H b 118 *1.50 78-17 Gentle Pop 1183 Simple Answer1147FriskyJig116hd Bore in, clear 12
8Mar84- 5GP fst 7f :23⅕ :47⅕ 1:26 ⒻClm 12500 4 8 2hd 1½ 1hd 23½ Conner M J7 b 114 *1.00 70-22 Delta Cajun 1163½ Gentle Pop 1145½ Cold Test 1165 Game try 12
29Feb84- 2Hia fst 6f :23⅕ :47 1:12⅗ ⒻClm 10000 2 8 52½ 21½ 2½ 1nk Conner M J7 b 111 *1.40 81-20 Gentle Pop 111nk Liz Jr. 10910 I'm More Sugar 111no Driving 10
20Feb84- 7Hia fst 6f :22⅗ :45⅘ 1:11⅗ ⒻClm 10000 12 10 53½ 34½ 34½ 24 Conner M J7 b 113 3.80 81-16 TonktonPss1144GentlePop1133½I'mMorSugr111no Best of others 12
16Feb84- 6Hia fst 7f :23⅖ :46⅘ 1:25⅕ ⒻClm 15000 2 10 83¾ 83¾ 87½ 58½ Lee M A b 114 5.20 68-18 Retablo 1142 Just A Bid 1142 Edith Marie 1144 Wide str. 12
30Jan84- 7Hia fst 7f :23⅖ :46⅘ 1:25 ⒻClm 25000 5 10 74¾ 99½ 711 69½ Lee M A b 114 12.00 68-16 Casino Gal 107no Fancy N' Fair1144SpeedyOcalaFlyer1144 Outrun 11
24Jan84- 6Hia fst 7f :23⅕ :46⅗ 1:25⅘ ⒻClm 18000 12 5 64½ 63¾ 2½ 1½ Lee M A b 113 8.40 74-19 Gentle Pop 113½ Lena Ann 1091½ Custommade 1141 Driving 12
19Jan84- 8Hia fst 7f :23 :46⅖ 1:25 ⒻClm 19000 12 10 711 813 58 36½ Lee M A b 113 36.20 71-16 Chetski 1162½ Late Night Flight 1144 Gentle Pop 1134 Rallied 12
6Jan84- 8Crc fst 6f :22⅘ :46⅘ 1:13⅗ 3+ⒻClm c-12500 12 5 41½ 36½ 58½ 67¾ Fires E b 118 3.40 74-18 Beat The Tee 1143 Just A Bid 1122Mayihavethisdance1092½ Tired 12
LATEST WORKOUTS Mar 31 Crc 4f fst :53 b ● Feb 27 Crc 3f fst :37 b ● Feb 14 Crc 3f fst :36⅖ h

Flaming Color
B. f. 3, by Murtaugh—Southern Woman, by I'm For More
Br.—Panorama Farm (NY)
Tr.—Pace Jerry L
Own.—Cutrone J
109⁷
Lifetime 17 1 2 3 $8,039 | 1984 7 1 1 1 $4,277 | 1983 10 M 1 2 $3,762

20Mar84- 5GP fst 1 1/16 :48 1:13⅖ 1:46⅘ ⒻClm 16000 5 9 1011 1018 718 422 Fires E 118 2.90 45-22 Ruffians Revenge 11214 Tell TheFacts1117AspenMiss1121 Rallied 11
6Mar84- 10Tam fst 7f :23⅗ :47⅗ 1:27⅕ ⒻAlw 3900 1 5 43 43¾ 46½ 34½ Borden D A 122 *2.80 — — Native Regal 1224 Turkish Toast 116½ Flaming Color1222½ Evenly 7
18Feb84- 1Tam fst 1 1/16 :49 1:14⅗ 1:48⅕ Md Sp Wt 3 3 36 42 2½ 12 Borden D A 113 3.80 78-20 Flaming Color 1132 Finish The Fight1182G.B'sDream1131 Driving 9
3Feb84- 4Tam fst 1 1/16 :48⅕ 1:14 1:48⅖ ⒻMd Sp Wt 9 6 66¾ 65¾ 58 512¾ Crews W 118 11.30 64-24 Crowned Metal 1184 Love Serenade 1187JadeDust118¾ No factor 9
27Jan84- 3Tam fst 6f :23⅕ :47 1:13⅗ Md 15000 5 10 1212 1011 912 610 Luhr R D 115 4.70 67-27 Jewelry Thief 1174½Prenney'sPenny1202Bim'sBid1201½ No excuse 12
19Jan84- 6Tam gd 6f :23⅗ :48⅘ 1:15⅗ ⒻMd 15000 3 8 76½ 67 54½ 44½ Hilburn K D 118 7.30 63-32 SpeedyHands114¾Andrea'sPass1181½KristiK.1182½ Lacked fin. bid 11
3Jan84- 8Crc fst 7f :23⅖ :47⅘ 1:28⅗ ⒻClm 16000 9 1 87 88½ 51½ 21½ Lee M A 116 14.40 71-21 Disco Road 1071½ Flaming Color 1161½ Mary's Pet 116½ Rallied 10
22Dec83- 6Crc fst 6f :22⅗ :47⅕ 1:14⅘ ⒻMd 16000 7 12 1210 910 46 23 Lee M A 119 11.10 74-17 LadyEmily1193FlamingColor1192Mrshu'sTime110¾ Best of others 12
7Dec83- 2Aqu fst 170 ⊡:49⅗ 1:16⅘ 1:49⅗ ⒻMd 14000 8 9 87 54 410 310¼ Graell A 117 8.10 44-21 PokerRapture1137RegalStarlet1083½FlamingColor1171½ No threat 9
24Nov83- 4Aqu fst 6f :22⅘ :47 1:14 ⒻⓈMd Sp Wt 12 10 1011 1111 119½ 1011½ Miceli M 117 88.80 59-24 The Dell 117no Bold N Pink 1172¾ Miss Lee M. 117nk Outrun 14
LATEST WORKOUTS Feb 16 Tam 4f fst :49 b

Green Arri
Gr. f. 3, by Green Ticket—Flash Arri, by My Warrior
Br.—Tilson H G (Ky)
Tr.—Kassen David C
Own.—Adams A
116
Lifetime 4 1 0 0 $6,120 | 1984 2 1 0 0 $5,490 | 1983 2 M 0 0 $630

20Mar84-	1GP	fst	6f	:22⅘	:45⅘	1:13	ⒻMd 45000	10	2	41¼	31	2hd	11¼	Landicini C Jr	b 117	5.90	74-22	Green Arri117 1¼PrunersPleasure121hdLotsOfKlass121½ Drew clear	12
15Feb84-	4Hia	fst	6f	:22⅘	:46	1:11⅘	ⒻMd 40000	9	11	42	44	79	77¼	Brumfield D	b 119	2.50	76-19	Shot Above 114½ Usurper 119² Ell's Dusty Lark 119½ Sp'd for 1/2	12
7Nov83-	2CD	fst	7f	:23⅕	:47⅕	1:26⅕	ⒻMd Sp Wt	12	1	3½	2hd	56	715	McKnight J	b 118	5.40	61-23	Tomalu 118¾ Deck Chair 118⁸ Aracian 118nk	12
18Oct83-	2Kee	gd	6f	:22⅘	:46⅗	1:12	ⒻMd Sp Wt	5	5	11	2hd	31½	47	Brumfield D	b 119	3.50	75-16	Von Der Sonne 119¹ Sintra 119²½ Shamrock Boat 119³½	12

LATEST WORKOUTS Mar 28 Hia 4f fst :48⅖ b Mar 15 Hia 5f fst 1:01 b ●Mar 8 Hia 6f fst 1:14⅗ b Mar 2 Hia 5f fst 1:03 b

Angel From Above

Dk. b. or br. f. 3, by Great Above—Girl Kid, by Restore
Br.—McNichols W T (Fla)
Tr.—Seiden Stuart
Own.—Seiden C & S

118 Lifetime 7 1 1 2 $10,730 — 1984 4 1 0 1 $8,590; 1983 3 M 1 1 $2,140; Turf 4 1 0 1 $8,590

7Mar84-	6GP	fm	1⅟₁₆ Ⓣ	:48⅗	1:13	1:44⅖	ⒻAlw 13000	1	1	1hd	1013	1115	1115	Maple E	121	4.40	64-25	Megan Ann 116no Skimbleshanks116nkLittleMandy116nk Stopped	12
13Feb84-	6Hia	fm	*1⅟₁₆ Ⓣ			1:44⅖	ⒻAlw 16000	10	2	2½	2hd	2½	65	Velez J A Jr	114	13.70	71-22	Oakbrook Lady 120² Powder Break120nkRexson'sRose1141¼ Tired	10
31Jan84-	10Hia	fm	*1⅛ Ⓣ			1:49⅗	ⒻMd Sp Wt	2	3	33½	42½	1hd	1½	DePass R	118	10.60	83-14	Angel From Above 118½ Lysine 118½ CharmingPeggy118⁴ Drivng	12
6Jan84-	6Crc	fm	1⅟₁₆ Ⓣ	:48⅗	1:14⅕	1:46⅕	ⒻMd Sp Wt	6	3	2½	1hd	1½	32½	DePass R	119	12.90	71-18	BrooklynPrincss1142ByouBirdi119½AnglFromAbov119¾ Weakened	12
23Dec83-	6Crc	fst	7f	:23	:47⅖	1:27⅗	ⒻMd 30000	7	4	1hd	11½	11½	2½	DePass R	119	7.90	77-19	LadySkater119½AngelFromAbove119²OneForBeauty119no Gamely	12
6Dec83-	4Crc	fst	6f	:23	:47⅘	1:15⅗	ⒻMd 25000	7	3	1hd	1½	21	34½	Velez J A Jr	119	20.70	68-25	PoliticlRegent117½FriskyJig115⁴AngelFromAbove119¹ Weakened	12
23Nov83-	8Crc	fst	6f	:22⅕	:46⅗	1:14⅖	ⒻMd 40000	7	6	43	56½	1119	1115¾	DePass R	115	16.80	63-17	Irish Kay 117½ Lady Jet Setter 1191½Pm'sMoneyHoney119¹ Tired	12

LATEST WORKOUTS Mar 30 Crc 5f fst 1:02 b Mar 24 Crc 4f fst :49 h Mar 2 Crc 7f fst 1:30 b Feb 9 Crc 4f fst :49 h

Also Eligible (Not in Post Position Order):

Julie's Bid

Ch. f. 3, by Raise A Bid—Nanjo, by Su Ka Wa
Br.—Erinwood Farm (Fla)
Tr.—Olivares Luis
Own.—Pony Horse Stable

116 Lifetime 14 2 1 4 $10,810 — 1984 2 0 0 1 $1,220; 1983 12 2 1 3 $9,590; Turf 1 0 0 1 $1,100

22Mar84-	7GP	fst	1⅟₁₆	:48	1:12⅗	1:45⅕	ⒻClm 35000	8	8	76½	87½	1112	1013¾	Soto S B	b 116	15.40	61-17	Dahlonega 116½ Wonder Mar 116hd Quest For Justice114⁹ Outrun	12
18Jan84-	10Hia	yl	*1⅛ Ⓣ			1:51⅕	ⒻClm 30000	6	3	36½	31	31½	32	Soto S B	b 111	18.30	73-25	Peace Weapon 108¹ Our Girl Chris 110¹ Julie's Bid 111½ Evenly	11
22Nov83-	10Crc	fst	170	:49	1:15	1:48	ⒻClm 12500	3	8	66¾	55½	1hd	32½	St Leon G	b 118	*1.70	68-23	R. R.'s Reflection 1142½ FionaFlash112hdJulie'sBid118¾ Weakened	9
14Nov83-	3Crc	fst	1⅟₁₆	:50	1:16⅕	1:50⅗	ⒻClm 12500	5	5	44	1½	1hd	1½	St Leon G	b 116	6.70	66-20	Julie's Bid 116½ Disco Road 108³ Hot Water 107hd Driving	8
4Nov83-	2Crc	fst	6f	:23	:48	1:14⅘	ⒻMd 10000	10	1	54½	43	21	11½	Aviles O B	b 118	4.20	78-20	Julie's Bid 1181½ GorgeousGail1186½SweetestDancer111no Driving	11
28Oct83-	6Crc	fst	6f	:22⅘	:46⅗	1:15⅗	ⒻMd 12500	5	3	1116	1122	88¾	33½	Aviles O B	118	8.80	70-18	Proud Donna 1112½ Miss Barrister 1181½ Julie'sBid118nk Late bid	12
19Oct83-	2Crc	fst	1	:49⅘	1:16	1:44⅖	ⒻMd 12500	2	9	713	78½	53	96¾	Aviles O B	117	9.50	59-19	Disco Road 107¹ Proud Native 110½LaBelleSalange110½ No factor	10
5Oct83-	3Crc	fst	6f	:22⅘	:47	1:15⅕	ⒻMd 12500	5	2	43	57	813	79½	DePass R	118	5.00	66-15	Beat The Tee 118¹ Cool Lark 111³ Howie's Way 118¾ Tired	12
30Sep83-	4Crc	sly	6f	:23⅕	:47⅘	1:15⅗	ⒻMd 12500	5	4	73¾	74½	48	36½	DePass R	b 117	*1.80	68-21	Whatchagonadonow 110nk Mary's Pet 117⁶ Julie'sBid117½ Rallied	9
24Jun83-	4Crc	sly	5f	:23⅖	:47⅘	1:00⅗	ⒻMd 20000	1	2	53½	711	616	613	Lynch H D5	110	8.10	76-21	Gala Lingo 1154½ Mayihavethisdance1065½Jigevar106hd No factor	12

LATEST WORKOUTS Feb 18 Crc 5f fst 1:04 b Feb 11 Crc 4f fst :49⅘ h

Fair Ribbons

Gr. f. 3, by Native Royalty—Forest Kelly, by Warfare
Br.—Conrad Marian & M (Ky)
Tr.—Conway James P
Own.—Conrad J

116 Lifetime 4 1 0 0 $12,320 — 1984 2 0 0 0 $320; 1983 2 1 0 0 $12,000

3Mar84-	5Hia	fst	7f	:23⅗	:46⅗	1:24⅗	ⒻAlw 18000	6	10	108½	108½	911	77	Smith G P	117	22.70	72-13	High Exchange 114no Dahlonega 114½ Peace Waters 114⁴ Outrun	10
11Feb84-	4Hia	fst	6f	:22⅕	:45⅗	1:10⅗	ⒻAlw 14000	6	11	1022	1015	1014	1020½	Fires E	117	19.50	70-09	ScrtHrt1203½PrfctAffr120⁴ⒹBlondInfltn114nk Off slow, checked	11
11Dec83-	5Aqu	fst	6f ⊡	:23	:47⅖	1:13⅘	ⒻMd Sp Wt	8	6	67½	68	34	14½	Ycaza M	117	73.30	75-27	FairRibbons1174½Montage1171¾RoyalBackground117½ Ridden out	12
1Dec83-	6Aqu	fst	6f	:23⅗	:48	1:14⅗	ⒻMd Sp Wt	12	8	1219	1320	1316	1316¾	Ycaza M	117	26.40	52-29	Cantam 117¾ Accostage 117³ Lady's Bet 110½ Outrun	14

LATEST WORKOUTS ●Mar 29 GP 3f fst :36 h Mar 21 GP 4f fst :50 b Mar 16 GP 4f fst :49 b Feb 29 GP 3f fst :38 b

Dance A Moment

Dk. b. or br. f. 3, by For The Moment—Dance Guest, by Uppercut
Br.—Bowen R L (Ky)
Tr.—Hale Robert A
Own.—Hale R A

116 Lifetime 20 4 5 2 $29,260 — 1984 6 1 2 2 $14,090; 1983 14 3 3 0 $15,170

16Mar84-	8GP	fst	6f	:22⅘	:46	1:12⅕	ⒻClm 35000	4	9	66¾	55	2½	21	Duany A W10	b 109	3.20	77-21	ChimingJet1141DanceAMoment1092½SpeedyOclFlyer112no Rallied	9
13Mar84-	9GP	fst	7f	:22⅘	:44⅘	1:22⅘	ⒻAlw 14000	4	5	64½	69	45½	59½	Duany A W10	b 110	27.00	81-17	Enumerating 1161½ Madame Justice 121nk Proud Nova 118⁵	9
6Mar84-	9Hia	fst	7f	:23⅕	:45⅘	1:23⅗	ⒻClm 35000	5	5	41¼	42¾	37½	39	Duany A W5	b 108	10.00	76-17	Nastica 114⁷ Custommade 118² Dance A Moment108¹ L'ckd rally	11
28Feb84-	8Hia	fst	1⅛	:46⅗	1:11⅕	1:45⅕	ⒻAlw 18000	2	3	36	26	24	32¾	Squartino R A5	b 108	5.50	74-23	Christine'sPixie113¾Mamuska113²DanceAMoment108³ Weakened	9
24Jan84-	10Hia	fst	6f	:22⅘	:46	1:12	ⒻClm 30000	4	4	53½	34	3nk	1hd	Squartino R A5	b 107	17.60	83-19	DnceAMoment107hdOnToPerfection114hdChimingJt111nk Driving	12
6Jan84-	5Crc	fst	6½f	:22⅘	:46⅗	1:20⅗	ⒻClm c-20000	3	3	42½	41½	44½	24½	Bain G W	b 114	7.90	77-18	Speier'sImge1094½DnceAMomnt1141½NoBirds116¹ Best of others	7
27Dec83-	2Crc	fst	7f	:22⅘	:46⅕	1:27⅗	ⒻClm 13000	3	4	31½	31	21½	1½	Bain G W	b 114	4.10	78-17	Dance A Moment 114½ Naromo 112½ Miss Barrister 114nk Driving	10
5Dec83-	6Crc	fst	6f	:22⅘	:46⅘	1:15⅕	ⒻClm 12500	2	8	31	42	33	32½	Bain G W	b 116	*2.10	73-23	Beat The Tee 114²ⒹMamuska111nkDanceAMoment116½ Even try	12
5Dec83-Placed second through disqualification																			
28Nov83-	6Crc	fst	6f	:22⅘	:46⅕	1:13	ⒻClm 18000	1	10	31½	46½	410	812½	Bain G W	b 116	4.10	73-18	Simple Answer 1144½ Rainy Day Money 114³ Mary'sPet115½ Tired	10
17Nov83-	8Crc	fst	6f	:22⅕	:46⅕	1:13⅘	ⒻClm 20500	6	3	63½	64½	75½	43½	Bain G W	b 114	15.20	79-20	Mito'sTouch116¹NunbytheGlass114nkRainyDyMoney114² Late bid	9

Peace Weapon

Dk. b. or br. f. 3, by Hold Your Peace—Miss Gun Bow, by Gun Shot
Br.—Ocala Stud Farms Inc (Fla)
Tr.—Geiger Larry
Own.—Harris J R Jr

116 Lifetime 13 1 0 3 $10,875 — 1984 3 1 0 0 $7,430; 1983 10 M 0 3 $3,445; Turf 4 1 0 0 $7,540

7Mar84-	6GP	fm	1⅟₁₆ Ⓣ	:48⅗	1:13	1:44⅖	ⒻAlw 13000	3	9	94¾	1114	1012	810	Rydowski S R	b 116	6.90	69-25	Megan Ann 116no Skimbleshanks 116nk LittleMandy116nk Outrun	12
6Feb84-	8Hia	fm	*1⅛ Ⓣ			1:49	ⒻAlw 14000	6	7	814	85¾	54	42½	Squartino R A5	b 108	11.30	83-14	Disquieting 113no Vast Domain 1142½ Little Mandy 113no Rallied	10
18Jan84-	10Hia	yl	*1⅛ Ⓣ			1:51⅕	ⒻClm 35000	2	5	57	42½	41½	11	Squartino R A5	b 108	5.90	75-25	Peace Weapon 108¹ Our Girl Chris 110¹ Julie's Bid 111½ Driving	11
21Dec83-	2Crc	fst	170	:49⅗	1:15⅘	1:47⅗	ⒻMd 20000	2	5	63¾	65¾	52	3¾	Hernandez C	b 118	6.60	71-23	Oop La La 118¾ Native Anna 118no Peace Weapon 118¾ Rallied	8
14Dec83-	3Crc	fst	170	:49⅘	1:16⅕	1:48⅘	ⒻMd 22500	2	2	1hd	2½	21½	31½	Hernandez C	b 118	5.70	67-21	DreamsofLegend107nkOopLaLa118¹PeaceWepon1181½ Weakened	7
1Dec83-	6Crc	fst	1⅟₁₆	:50	1:15⅗	1:49⅗	ⒻMd Sp Wt	4	7	65½	79½	712	610½	Hernandez C	b 118	6.00	60-18	Auntie Betty 118² Bayou Birdie 1187½ Vague Idea 118¾ Outrun	9
11Nov83-	1Crc	fm	*1 Ⓣ			1:40⅕	Md Sp Wt	9	10	105½	77½	77½	63½	Squartino R A7	b 108	54.70	76-19	Mandarin Valley 118¹ Abri Fiscal 118¹ Solid Stuff 118¹ Late rally	10
1Nov83-	2Crc	sly	1	:49⅗	1:15⅗	1:43⅕	Md Sp Wt	1	6	66½	64¾	64¾	53	Squartino R A7	b 108	18.20	69-19	T. V. Aid 117½ Jose Hurray 117½ Our Zanzibar 117¹ No factor	9
10Oct83-	7Crc	sly	170	:48⅗	1:14⅘	1:47	ⒻMd Sp Wt	2	8	910	913	712	69	Rydowski S R	b 117	42.90	66-22	Silent Sword 1171½ Oop La La 117½ Guneva 117¹ No factor	9
30Sep83-	5Crc	sly	170	:49	1:15⅕	1:47⅕	ⒻMd Sp Wt	3	6	85	88	76½	55¾	Squartino R A7	b 109	31.90	68-21	MostPreciousLove116¾Gunev1161½CourgeousHert1163½ No factor	9

well. She folded up early in her latest start, against more appropriate "nonwinners of one" rivals. But her February 13 race suggested very strongly that she could compete in "nonwinners of one" company at her best. And if her victory over Lysine was questionable, as it appeared to be, the latter also figured to be competitive in that class, even though still a maiden. Had Lysine won that maiden race, she would have been a routine selection on April 4, as a grass-bred filly coming back again for the second time on the grass. At odds of 9–1, she was hard to pass! Ironically, that price might have been considerably higher if Angel From Above had not been among her rivals again on April 4. Those willing to dig for the information found in the latter's past performances—a natural point of inquiry—would have shared invaluable information the majority of the audience would have missed, had it not been right there in front of them.

Before accepting this maiden as a logical play against winners, however, one must question the trainer's motive for entering the horse in this spot. Was he merely looking for a prep race, while at the same time disguising the horse's form against tougher rivals than it would meet in a subsequent maiden race? Racing a horse above its proper conditions often entails losing a purse opportunity if the horse wins. If the horse were capable of winning a "nonwinners of one" allowance race, why not pick up the maiden purse before shooting for the allowance? A horse that breaks its maiden in allowance company is no longer eligible for maiden races, nor (most likely) for the NW1 allowance classification. The difference in purse value between MSW and NW1 races at most tracks is relatively small, especially when compared with the complete loss of the MSW purse. Since the former is far easier to win, why not try for it first?

Were it not for the fact that the Florida tracks (and several others around the country as well) card allowance races with conditions that read "nonwinners of two races" in addition to the standard "nonwinners of a race other than maiden, claiming, or starter," one would have to conclude that young Pat Kelly was using this allowance event as a prep race for Lysine. Or that she was an unsound filly who was doing especially well that week and Kelly wished to maximize his return by competing for the higher purse. But due to the wording of the race conditions in Florida, Lysine would remain eligible for one version of the NW1 race even if she were victorious on April 4 and consequently would have the opportunity to win two NW1 races and capture two NW1 purses.

Of the fillies in this field with grass experience, you might have noticed that only Angel From Above had early speed. This had to be in her favor, if she were fit. However, both Gentle Pop and Green Ari had speed on dirt, which, if translated to the grass, would hurt Angel From Above's chances of attaining an easy lead. It often happens, though, that indecision at the starting gate, caused by confusion or inexperience in new surroundings, can cost first-timers-on-the grass a few steps at the break, relegating them to the role of paceprompter rather than pacesetter. In this race, Green Ari broke sharply enough to contest the pace (Gentle Pop did not). Her early rival, however, was Lysine, and not Angel From Above. The latter showed no run at all during the race, completing a textbook example of the step-by-step deterioration of a horse's form cycle. Lysine drew off after the half and won laughing.

We do not mean to imply that the ability promised by grass bloodlines must surface immediately or not at all. There are times

FIFTH RACE
Gulfstream
APRIL 4, 1984

ABOUT 1 MILE.(turf). (1.36) ALLOWANCE. Purse $13,000. 3-year-old fillies which have never won a race other than Maiden or Claiming. Weights, 121 lbs. Non-winners of a race other than Claiming at a mile or over since February 15 allowed 3 lbs. Of such a race since January 15, 5 lbs.

Value of race $13,000, value to winner $7,800, second $2,340, third $1,430, fourth $650, balance of starters $130 each. Mutuel pool $53,843. Perfecta Pool $45,695. Trifecta Pool $54,433.

Last Raced	Horse	Eqt.A.Wt	PP	St	¼	½	¾	Str	Fin	Jockey	Odds $1
20Feb84 9Hia9	Lysine	3 116	3	1	1hd	1hd	14	16	18	Solomone M	9.00
30Jan84 8Hia4	Trinado	b 3 116	1	3	10	9hd	6hd	52½	2hd	Perret C	2.00
20Mar84 5GP4	Flaming Color	3 114	6	7	62½	5½	41	4hd	3no	Melendez A L7	99.60
18Jan84 10Hia9	River Fete	3 116	2	2	5½	62	72	31	41½	St Leon G	17.40
22Mar84 7GP10	Julie's Bid	b 3 116	9	6	43	42	2½	2hd	5nk	Vergara O	29.70
7Mar84 6GP3	Little Mandy	3 116	4	10	9½	8½	92	62	61	Fires E	2.60
7Mar84 6GP8	Peace Weapon	b 3 116	10	9	81½	10	10	71½	75	Hernandez C	9.60
7Mar84 6GP11	Angel From Above	3 118	8	8	7hd	71½	5hd	89	816	Rydowski S R	5.60
20Mar84 1GP1	Green Arri	b 3 116	7	4	24	21½	3hd	92	92½	Landicini C Jr	30.80
27Mar84 3GP1	Gentle Pop	b 3 109	5	5	31½	31½	8hd	10	10	Conner M J7	5.40

OFF AT 1:39 Start good, Won ridden out. Time, 1:39 Course firm.

$2 Mutuel Prices:				
	3-LYSINE	20.00	8.00	6.60
	1-TRINADO		4.20	3.40
	6-FLAMING COLOR			23.40

$2 PERFECTA 3-1 PAID $71.80. $2 TRIFECTA 3-1-6 PAID $2,419.20.

B. f, by Majestic Light—Peace Movement, by Admiral's Voyage. Trainer Kelly Patrick J. Bred by Live Oak Stud (Fla).

LYSINE broke to the inside into RIVER FETE, drew clear after a half, and was not threatened in the stretch run. TRINADO forced back at the start, was allowed to settle in stride, rallied between rivals coming to the head of the stretch moved along the backstretch, but lacked a closing response. RIVER FETE forced in at the start, was outrun. LITTLE MANDY showed little. PEACE WEAPON failed to reach contention. ANGEL FROM ABOVE raced wide on the second turn. GREEN ARRI had speed for a half. GENTLE POP was finished after a half.

when it pays to follow a grass-bred horse beyond its second race on turf, circumstances having prevented the animal from living up to its potential sooner.

Available Power seemed to be a case in point.

Available Power — Ch. c. 3, by Explodent—Always Available, by Executioner
Br.—Fuson Judith C (Ky)
Own.—Centennial Farms — Tr.—Jerkens H Allen — 108

Lifetime 11 1 3 1 $29,840 — 1985 11 1 3 1 $29,840 — 1984 0 M 0 0 — Turf 2 0 0 1 $3,000

23May85- 7Bel	gd	1 1/16	Ⓣ:48	1:12 3/5	1:45 1/5	3+ Alw 25000	4	1	12½	11	21½	33¼	Samyn J L		110	6.80	72-31	I'm A Banker 1101¾ Pervader1111½AvailablePower110¾	Weakened	8
17May85- 8Bel	fm	7f	Ⓣ:22 1/5	:44 3/5	1:20 4/5	3+ Alw 36000	2	6	65	55½	614	513½	Samyn J L		110	10.20e	86-11	RedWingDrem1191½StyTheCourse1244DiscoCount124nk	No threat	8
9May85- 6Bel	fst	6f	:22 4/5	:46 1/5	1:11 1/5	3+ Md Sp Wt	5	3	12	14	13	1hd	Samyn J L		113	3.00	86-25	Available Power 113hd Wicked Wike 1134¾ Air Wing1136¾	Driving	6
28Apr85- 6Aqu	fst	1 1/8	:49	1:13 4/5	1:53 3/5	3+ Md Sp Wt	8	1	1½	11½	11½	2½	Castaneda K		115	*2.60e	66-21	Pro Appeal113½AvailablePower1153½Darby'sTwist1124	Drifted out	8
19Apr85- 6Aqu	sly	6f	:22 3/5	:46 2/5	1:12	3+ Md Sp Wt	10	3	3½	31	43	75¾	Wynter N A10	b	103	2.60	75-22	Cougar Express 113hd Duomo 1242 Little'sBrittle112½	Wide; tired	11
10Apr85- 6Aqu	fst	7f	:23 3/5	:46 4/5	1:24 4/5	3+ Md Sp Wt	5	2	1hd	12	12½	2nk	Wynter N A10	b	102	9.20e	77-29	Swooping 112nk Available Power 1024¾ Oconto 1152½	Just failed	7
28Mar85- 6Aqu	fst	1	:45 3/5	1:10 2/5	1:38 3/5	Md Sp Wt	2	2	34	48	67	77	Cordero A Jr		122	4.40e	66-25	WhiteGovernor122½Turn nTogether122¾PurpleMountin1171	Tired	12
24Mar85- 6Aqu	fst	6f	:22 3/5	:46 2/5	1:11 4/5	Md Sp Wt	1	7	41½	78	79	511¾	Miranda J		122	9.10	70-26	Fly A Kite 122no Clever Wake 1223 Sarcophagus 1174	Tired	14
22Feb85- 6Aqu	fst	6f	⊡:23	:46 3/5	1:12 3/5	Md Sp Wt	6	2	2½	2hd	43½	66¼	Ward W A5		117	*1.50	75-22	First Conquest 1173¾ Truth Be Told 1221¾ Salvatore 122nk	Tired	11
13Feb85- 6Aqu	fst	6f	⊡:22 1/5	:46	1:10 4/5	Md Sp Wt	9	1	3½	1hd	23	27	Ward W A5		117	*2.80	83-20	Crossfield 1227 AvailablePower1178Salvatore1151¾	Best of others	9

LATEST WORKOUTS Jun 4 Bel 1 sly 1:42 b — May 30 Bel 4f fst :49 1/5 b — May 14 Bel 6f fst 1:16 b — May 6 Bel 7f fst 1:29 4/5 h

After an exceptionally fast maiden victory, Allen Jerkens wheeled the colt back in a classified allowance sprint on the grass—quite a difficult assignment for any recent graduate. That Available Power failed to enter contention in that race came as no surprise. In essence, his second start on the grass had to be looked upon as if it were his first, his prior start offering no real evidence regarding his ability to handle grass. But his performance the second time on turf was compromised by the soft conditions underfoot, which had made it almost impossible to win on the front end during the early stages of the Belmont meet. Available Power's race on May 23 certainly warranted another chance before giving up on the colt as a potentially first-rate grass runner or prime grass-breeding play.

Jerkens next entered the colt in the Ben Franklin Handicap, a grass stake at Garden State on June 8. It was not the spot I had been waiting for, and the colt's task was further complicated when assigned the twelve-post. Another misleading poor performance appeared to be on the horizon, one that could serve a purpose. It would add a few points to the colt's odds next time out, when he was entered back in "nonwinners of one" company, where he belonged at that point in his career. Instead, Available Power was scratched from the Franklin. However, the simple fact that Jerkens thought enough of the colt to enter him in a stake was significant, offering further reason to string along with the grass-bred colt and give him his third chance on that surface.

Unfortunately, Available Power suffered an injury before he could race again that meeting, one serious enough to have him sent to the farm for some rest and recuperation. When (if) he returned to the races, he would have to be looked upon in a different light.

Chapter 16

A Tribute to Exclusive Native

THIS CHAPTER IS IN PART a tribute to an old friend, one who is no longer with us. Popular recall identifies him as the sire of the great Affirmed, Triple-Crown winner and three-time Eclipse Award champion. I, for one, however, will always remember him for the numerous grass runners—horses like Qui Native, Native Courier, Sisterhood, Wild Injun, Give Me Strength, Geraldine's Store, and so on—whose immediate fondness for the turf added so much enjoyment to my afternoons at the races. Exclusive Native was one of the more prepotent grass sires in recent years, and a pleasant surprise at that. As a son of Raise A Native, one would never have expected him to attain that status.

Exclusive Native was "on a roll" during the autumn of 1984. On the September 7 card at Belmont alone, three of his offspring won at first or second asking on the grass: Greatest Legacy at $15.60, Agacerie at $12.20, and Exclusive One (in stakes company) at $20.40. Three days later at the Meadowlands, Compassion scored at $17.80 in her second grass start.

Of course, this rash of winners was only coincidental, the only thread connecting the four being the penchant of their common sire for getting runners that showed marked and immediate improvement when sent greensward for the first time. But when the group from Handicapping Expo '84 gathered at Belmont on October 20 for Jockey Club Gold Cup Day, the possibility that a fifth name would be added to the list was very real. Treasured One, a son of Exclusive Native from a Hail To Reason mare, was scheduled to make his grass debut in the day's third event, the Envoy stakes, at one mile on the Widener turf course.

Greatest Legacy — Ch. c. 4, by Exclusive Native—Hilitation, by Crafty Admiral
Br.—Harbor View Farm (Ky)
Own.—Harbor View Farm — Tr.—Martin Frank — **122**
Lifetime 13 0 2 3 $13,480 — 1984 6 M 1 2 $6,240 — 1983 2 M 1 0 $4,180 — Turf 1 0 0 1 $2,280

17Aug84- 5Sar	fm	$1\frac{1}{16}$	ⓣ:46⅗ 1:11⅗ 1:44⅗	3↑Md Sp Wt	5 3	4^{3} $3^{1\frac12}$ $3^{2\frac12}$ $3^{4\frac12}$	Guerra W A	122	4.50	69-17 ShyeMjesty117¾CrownThisOne$122^{3\frac34}$GretestLegcy$122^{6\frac12}$	Weakened	10
4Aug84- 9Sar	fst	7f	:23 :45⅘ 1:24⅖	3↑Md Sp Wt	8 3	$7^{3\frac12}$ 7^{8} $6^{5\frac12}$ $5^{4\frac12}$	Ward W A^5	117	15.00	75-13 Cool Welcome 117 1½ Incite 117½ Duomo 117¾	Wide	12
13Feb84- 4Hia	fst	7f	:23⅕ :46 1:23⅗	Md Sp Wt	5 4	3½ 2^{2} 2^{3} 3^{9}	Vasquez J	122	2.30	77-18 NskrDrummer122^{9}F.F.Dividend122^{1}GretestLegcy122^{hd}	Weakened	10
1Feb84- 3Hia	fst	6f	:22⅗ :45⅘ 1:10⅘	Md Sp Wt	7 3	3^{1} 2^{3} 2^{3} 2^{6}	Vasquez J	122	4.20	84-16 NativeBidder122^{6}GreatestLegcy122½Villmingo122^{5}	Best of others	10
23Jan84- 3Hia	fst	7f	:23 :45⅘ 1:22⅕	Md Sp Wt	7 5	$6^{5\frac12}$ $5^{4\frac12}$ 4^{11} $4^{18\frac12}$	Vasquez J	122	4.10	73-15 PurelyPleasure122^{12}NaskrDrummer122^{2}F.F.Dividend$122^{4\frac12}$	Outrun	12
8Jan84- 4Aqu	fst	6f	⊡:23 :46⅗ 1:11	Md Sp Wt	3 2	7^{6} 7^{11} 6^{18} 6^{22}	Miranda J	122	7.20	67-21 Minstrel Glory $122^{7\frac34}$ Wandering Feet 115^{3}IrishOre112½	No factor	9
28Dec83- 6Aqu	fst	6f	⊡:23⅕ :47⅗ 1:13⅘	3↑Md Sp Wt	8 3	4^{3} $4^{5\frac12}$ 4^{4} 2^{3}	Miranda J	120	6.80e	73-26 AppelAffirmed120^{3}GretestLegcy120^{hd}WnderingFeet113^{nk}	Rallied	10
19Dec83- 6Aqu	fst	6f	⊡:23⅗ :48⅕ 1:13⅘	3↑Md Sp Wt	8 7	3^{nk} $6^{4\frac12}$ $7^{9\frac34}$ $7^{12\frac12}$	Cordero A Jr	120	3.00e	64-26 I'mAHappyOne120^{1}HowieofWinloc$120^{4\frac34}$CanadianClm120^{nk}	Tired	9
10Oct82- 4Bel	fst	1	:47 1:13 1:39⅘	Md Sp Wt	2 6	$7^{7\frac12}$ $8^{5\frac34}$ $8^{9\frac34}$ $8^{13\frac12}$	MacBeth D	118	12.80	52-25 Chumming 118½ Moment of Joy 118^{2} Tanyosho 118^{1}	Tired	11
19Sep82- 6Bel	fst	6f	:22⅘ :46⅗ 1:12⅕	Md Sp Wt	6 8	$7^{6\frac12}$ $6^{2\frac12}$ 7^{6} 7^{7}	Fell J	b 118	3.80	74-20 Galaxy Guide 118¾ Balancing Act 118 1½ Law Talk 115 1¾	No factor	11

LATEST WORKOUTS Sep 6 Bel tr.t 3f fst :36⅘ b — Sep 4 Bel tr.t 4f sly :49 b — Aug 29 Bel tr.t 4f fst :47 h — Aug 15 Sar 4f fst :46⅗ h

Agacerie — B. f. 3, by Exclusive Native—Quiet Charm, by Nearctic
Br.—Tartan Farms (Fla)
Own.—Tartan Stable — Tr.—Nerud Jan H — **113**
Lifetime 7 1 1 3 $22,080 — 1984 6 1 1 3 $22,080 — 1983 1 M 0 0

13Aug84- 2Sar	fst	7f	:23⅕ :46⅗ 1:24⅘	3↑ⒻAlw 20000	3 5	2^{1} 2½ 1^{hd} 3½	Cruguet J	114	6.50	77-15 Scrutable 112½ Sweetest Gal 117no Agacerie 114 1½	Weakened	8
27Jly84- 6Bel	sly	1	:45⅘ 1:10⅘ 1:37⅕	3↑ⒻMd Sp Wt	8 3	2½ 1^{5} $1^{1\frac12}$ 1¾	Cruguet J	116	*1.60	79-21 Agacerie116¾Queen'sStatue116^{13}HlloweenQueen116^{no}	Ridden out	8
14Jly84- 4Bel	fst	7f	:22⅘ :46⅗ 1:25⅕	3↑ⒻMd Sp Wt	10 1	6^{3} $7^{4\frac12}$ $4^{2\frac12}$ 3^{1}	Velasquez J	116	*3.10	75-19 Crumpets 111¾ Fetuccine 116^{nk} Agacerie 116^{5}	Rallied	12
24Jun84- 5Bel	fst	7f	:23 :46⅕ 1:24⅘	3↑ⒻMd Sp Wt	2 3	1^{hd} $4^{2\frac12}$ 2^{5} 2^{9}	Velasquez J	114	5.80	69-22 Fiesta 114^{9} Agacerie $114^{4\frac12}$ Current Miss 114^{3}	Best of others	14
4Jun84- 6Bel	fst	7f	:23⅗ :46⅗ 1:25⅕	3↑ⒻMd Sp Wt	1 4	$4^{3\frac12}$ $4^{3\frac12}$ $3^{2\frac12}$ $3^{2\frac12}$	Velasquez J	114	5.90	73-19 Key Dancer 114no Elbarita $114^{2\frac12}$ Agacerie 114no	Rallied	7
24May84- 6Bel	fst	6f	:22⅘ :46⅗ 1:11⅘	ⒻMd Sp Wt	5 1	3^{nk} 3½ 3½ $8^{4\frac12}$	Velasquez J	121	9.20	80-15 Mine Only 121^{hd} Current Miss 121^{2} Reine Certaine 121 1½	Tired	13
1Dec83- 6Aqu	fst	6f	:23⅗ :48 1:14⅘	ⒻMd Sp Wt	10 2	$7^{2\frac12}$ $9^{8\frac12}$ 11^{11} $11^{11\frac12}$	Rogers K L	117	15.80	58-29 Cantam 117¾ Accostage 117^{3} Lady's Bet 110½	Outrun	14

LATEST WORKOUTS Sep 3 Bel 5f fst 1:02 b — Aug 12 Sar tr.t 5f fst 1:04 b — Aug 6 Sar tr.t 4f fst :50⅘ b — Jly 23 Bel tr.t 4f fst :49⅘ b

Exclusive Story — Ch. f. 2, by Exclusive Native—Dancer's Saga, by Northern Dancer
Br.—Evans T M (Ky)
Own.—Buckland Farm — Tr.—Campo John P — **116**
Lifetime 2 0 0 0 $1,080 — 1984 2 M 0 0 $1,080

21Jun84- 4Bel	fst	5½f	:22⅘ :46⅗ 1:06	ⒻMd Sp Wt	3 5	$4^{6\frac12}$ $4^{8\frac12}$ 5^{11} $7^{13\frac34}$	Bailey J D	117	4.70	71-21 Count Pennies 117^{2} Faster Than Fast $117^{2\frac12}$FrenchGold112^{6}	Tired	8
21May84- 4Bel	fst	5f	:22⅕ :45⅘ :58⅘	ⒻMd Sp Wt	6 8	6^{7} 5^{6} $5^{4\frac12}$ $4^{3\frac34}$	Cruguet J	117	2.30	89-09 [DH]Ldy'sSecret$117^{1\frac12}$[DH]Bonni'sAx$117^{1\frac12}$LunchingShot$117^{2\frac12}$	Evenly	8

LATEST WORKOUTS Aug 31 Bel tr.t 5f sly 1:04⅕ b — Aug 25 Sar 6f fst 1:13⅘ hg — Aug 22 Sar ⓣ 4f fm :47⅗ h — Aug 17 Sar ⓣ 7f fm 1:30⅘ h

Compassion — Ch. f. 3, by Exclusive Native—Movette, by Cyane
Br.—Exclusive Breeders (Ky)
Own.—Schwartz B K — Tr.—Jerkens Steven T — **117**
Lifetime 8 0 0 0 $2,280 — 1984 7 M 0 0 $2,280 — 1983 1 M 0 0 — Turf 1 0 0 0 $1,140

26Aug84- 4Sar	fm	1	ⓣ:47⅗ 1:13 1:39⅗	3↑ⒻMd Sp Wt	8 5	5^{5} $2^{2\frac12}$ $2^{1\frac12}$ 4^{7}	Davis R G	b 117	27.70	72-21 MaketheMagic$117^{1\frac34}$TrendyPhilly$122^{2\frac12}$DanceForDollrs$117^{2\frac34}$	Tired	10
3Aug84- 6Sar	fst	7f	:22⅘ :45⅘ 1:24⅕	3↑ⒻMd Sp Wt	2 6	2^{1} $2^{2\frac12}$ $5^{8\frac12}$ 7^{17}	Samyn J L	b 117	27.70	64-19 SweetestGal$117^{8\frac12}$MrkedLdy117^{nk}CornishImge$117^{1\frac12}$	Used in place	11
15Mar84- 4Aqu	fst	6f	⊡:23 :47⅕ 1:13⅕	ⒻMd Sp Wt	5 3	5^{5} $5^{5\frac12}$ 4^{6} 5^{8}	Samyn J L	121	9.60	70-25 SternerStuff$121^{2\frac12}$Satch114^{1}MirrorOfHumnity121^{3}	Lacked a rally	14
26Feb84- 6Aqu	fst	1⅛	⊡:50 1:16 1:56⅕	ⒻMd Sp Wt	7 1	1^{hd} 1½ 4^{11} $7^{18\frac34}$	Skinner K	121	8.70	45-29 Boat Hook 121^{5} Special Sue 116¾ Starlet Annie 121^{7}	Tired	8
13Feb84- 5Aqu	fst	6f	⊡:22⅘ :46⅗ 1:13	ⒻMd Sp Wt	10 8	$7^{4\frac34}$ $6^{6\frac12}$ 5^{7} $4^{6\frac34}$	Skinner K	121	5.30e	72-18 FoolishRiver$114^{1\frac34}$SternerStuff$121^{3\frac34}$Mt.Prospect$121^{1\frac12}$	No menace	12
27Jan84- 4Aqu	gd	6f	⊡:22⅗ :46 1:11⅕	ⒻMd Sp Wt	12 3	$3^{1\frac12}$ 3½ $4^{1\frac12}$ $5^{4\frac34}$	Skinner K	121	9.80	83-16 PossibleMte$121^{2\frac34}$EvrgrnMiss$121^{1\frac12}$RoylBckground121^{no}	Gave way	12
18Jan84- 6Aqu	fst	6f	⊡:24 :48⅘ 1:16	ⒻMd Sp Wt	3 9	– – 6^{5} $5^{2\frac12}$	Skinner K	121	27.90	61-35 Hope Chest 121¾ Land of the Brave121¾RoyalOffense116^{no}	Snow	11
1Dec83- 6Aqu	fst	6f	:23⅗ :48 1:14⅘	ⒻMd Sp Wt	5 4	2½ 4^{2} 12^{14} $12^{14\frac12}$	Skinner K	117	9.20	54-29 Cantam 117¾ Accostage 117^{3} Lady's Bet 110½	Tired	14

LATEST WORKOUTS Sep 7 Bel 7f fst 1:29 b — Sep 3 Bel 4f fst :48⅘ h — Aug 16 Sar ⓣ 4f fm :50⅘ b — Jly 31 Sar 5f fst 1:02 b

Had Treasured One been entered where his "conditions" warranted, in a "nonwinners of two" allowance contest on the grass, he would have been a mandatory selection, but no doubt at odds far shorter than the nearly 7–1 at which he started in the Envoy. He was a fresh and fit young horse, apparently on his way to better things.

For some reason the colt's career had been delayed, but now he seemed sound and appeared to be learning his lessons rapidly. After tiring at six furlongs on his return to the races on September 14, Treasured One was content to sit behind a slow pace ten days later, then come on to win at seven furlongs in excellent time, running the last eighth in :12 flat. Note two positive signs here—the early speed in his first race after a layoff and the quick return ten days later—both of which suggest sharpness and fitness. Based on that performance, Treasured One appeared to have some ability, and a future if he remained sound. At that time of the year, he certainly seemed capable of winning first try in allowance company. Which he did, again in faster than par time, again running his final eighth in :12 flat—all of which suggested that the colt would be able to compete successfully in "nonwinners of two" company and over a distance of ground. If he moved up at all on the grass, the sky was the limit on that surface.

3 BELMONT

1 MILE. (Turf). (1.33) 1st Running ENVOY STAKES. Purse $50,000 Added. 3-year-olds, weights, 122 lbs. Non-winners of two races of $25,000 allowed 3 lbs. Of such a race since then, 5 lbs. Of a race of $16,500 at a mile or over 7 lbs. ($50 to nominate; $100 to enter and $100 to start. (Closing Saturday, October 6). Closed with nominations.

Coupled—Is Your Pleasure and Inrhetoric.

Purple Comet

Dk. b. or br. c. 3, by Kohoutek—Lady Beddard, by Beddard
Br.—Reynolds D P (Md)
Own.—Reynolds D P **Tr.—Alexander Frank A**
122 Lifetime 12 8 1 1 $154,441 | 1984 12 8 1 1 $154,441 | 1983 0 M 0 0 | Turf 7 6 0 0 $122,407

28Sep84- 6Med yl 1⅜ Ⓣ:47⅘ 1:38 2:16⅗ Rutgers H 7 2 2⁴ 2½ 2²½ 4⁵¾ Bracciale V Jr 121 *2.90 76-20 Roving Minstrel 1151½ Raami 1172½ Dealaway 113² Weakened 8
28Sep84-Grade II; Run in divisions
15Sep84- 8Lrl fm 1⅟₁₆ Ⓣ:45⅘ 1:10⅔ 1:41⅗ Japn Assoc H 12 1 1¹½ 1¹ 1¹½ 1nk Bracciale V Jr 120 *1.60 95-10 PrplComt120nk RvngMnstrl116²Snwdn'sGld1123½ Drifted out, clea 12
3Sep84- 9Crc hd *1⅛ Ⓣ 1:45⅕ 3+ Calder H 8 3 3²½ 3¹½ 2¹ 1¹ Smith A Jr 116 *3.60 97-04 Purple Comet 116¹ Bold Frond 116½ Amerilad 116½ Driving 12
11Aug84- 8Crc hd *1⅛ Ⓣ 1:45⅘ Delray 7 3 3¹½ 1hd 1½ 1nk Smith A Jr 118⁴ 2.00 94-03 DH Amerild118nk DH PurplComt118nk FlyingPidgon112hd Rank early 9
11Aug84-Dead heat; Run in divisions
28Jly84- 7Mth fst 1⅟₁₆ :47 1:11⅕ 1:42⅘ Ⓢ Wav'gMonarh 4 5 4⁴ 3² 4⁵ 4⁶½ Bracciale V Jr 119 *1.60 85-14 Donna's Time 122¾ Evzone 1171½ Bald King 113⁴ Tired 5
11Jly84- 5Mth fm 1⅟₁₆ Ⓣ:48⅕ 1:11⅘ 1:42⅗+ 3+ Alw 16000 2 2 1¹ 1¹½ 1¹½ 1½ Bracciale V Jr 112 2.40 88-15 Purple Comet 112½ Mydrone 116⁴ Last of the Lot 116⁴ Driving 5
16Jun84- 7Crc sly 7f :22⅗ :46 1:24⅘ Alw 17300 1 5 3²½ 3½ 3nk 2¹ Solis A 118 2.20 91-18 No Room 112¹ Purple Comet 118nk Mo Exception 1122½ Gamely 6
LATEST WORKOUTS ●Oct 13 Lrl 6f fst 1:14⅘ b Aug 31 Crc 4f fst :50 b ●Aug 25 Crc 4f fst :48 h

Is Your Pleasure

Ch. c. 3, by Accipiter—I'm A Pleasure, by What A Pleasure
Br.—Isaacs H Z (Ky)
Own.—Brookfield Farms **Tr.—Kelly Edward I**
122 Lifetime 14 4 6 1 $270,634 | 1984 8 2 4 0 $231,234 | 1983 6 2 2 1 $39,400 | Turf 3 1 1 0 $77,486

8Oct84- 8Bel fst 1 :46⅗ 1:11⅕ 1:36⅗ Jamaica H 6 4 4³½ 3¹½ 2²½ 2³ MacBeth D b 116 *1.80 79-28 Raja's Shark 112³ IsYourPleasure1162½LeroyS 117hd Second best 6
8Oct84-Grade III
3Sep84- 8Bel fst 1 :44⅕ 1:08⅘ 1:35⅕ Jerome H 5 8 7⁵¾ 6⁵½ 4⁴ 1¾ MacBeth D b 114 25.60 89-14 Is YourPleasure114¾TrackBarron124¹ConcordeBound115¾ Driving 9
3Sep84-Grade I
14Jly84- 8Bel fm 1¼ Ⓣ:48⅕ 1:37 2:01⅕ Lexington 9 6 7³½ 6³½ 8¹⁰ 10⁸½ Cordero A Jr b 126 *1.90 79-11 Onyxly 114¹ Dr. Schwartzman 1261½ Vision 126³ Outrun 13
14Jly84-Grade II
4Jly84- 7Bel fst 1⅛ :45⅘ 1:10 1:47⅘ Dwyer 5 5 4³½ 3³½ 3⁹½ 4¹⁴ MacBeth D b 123 10.30 74-11 TrackBarron11913½DrnThtAlrm123noSlewtheCoup114½ Weakened 7
4Jly84-Grade I
9Jun84- 7Bel fst 1⅛ :46⅔ 1:10⅔ 1:48⅕ Ⓢ Colin 2 3 3¹½ 3¹ 2³ 2³ MacBeth D b 122 4.60 83-10 TrckBrron117³IsYourPlsur122⁴ImprilConcord115² Best of others 7
3Jun84- 8Bel sf 1⅟₁₆ Ⓣ:50⅔ 1:15 1:48⅘ Hill Prince 3 4 3¹½ 4² 3² 2¹½ Cordero A Jr b 126 *.80 53-46 A Gift 1141½ Is Your Pleasure 1264¾ Jesse's Hope 1172¾ Blocked 7
3Jun84-Grade III
23May84- 8Bel fm 1 Ⓣ:45⅘ 1:10⅔ 1:35⅕ Saranac 2 5 4²½ 2²½ 2hd 1²¾ Cordero A Jr b 114 2.60e 89-12 Is Your Pleasure 1142¾ Onyxly 1141½ Loft 1233½ Drew away 12
23May84-Grade II
13May84- 7Bel fst 6f :22⅕ :44⅘ 1:09⅕ Alw 21000 1 6 5⁵ 4⁷½ 2⁶ 2⁶½ Cordero A Jr b 117 12.00 89-17 Track Barron 1176½ Is Your Pleasure 117¾ Vigumand 112½ Wide 8
18Dec83- 7Aqu fst 1⅟₁₆ ⊡:48⅗ 1:14 1:47⅗ Alw 22000 6 3 3½ 2hd 2hd 1¾ Lovato F Jr b 117 *2.00 75-25 IsYourPlesure117¾Cooper'sHwk117³RovingMinstrel1171½ Driving 9
9Dec83- 7Aqu fst 1⅟₁₆ ⊡:49⅗ 1:14⅗ 1:46⅗ Alw 24000 2 5 5¹¾ 4³½ 2¹½ 2²¾ Lovato F Jr b 117 *.80 76-19 BerHunt1172¾IsYourPlesur1174½Cindy'sFrind1174½ Best of others 7
LATEST WORKOUTS Oct 18 Bel 3f fst :37⅕ b ●Oct 4 Bel 7f fst 1:26⅕ h Sep 27 Bel 3f fst :35⅗ b Sep 23 Bel 1 fst 1:41 h

Treasured One

Ch. c. 3, by Exclusive Native—Monteen, by Hail To Reason
Br.—Harbor View Farm (Ky)
Own.—Harbor View Farm **Tr.—Martin Frank**
115 Lifetime 4 2 0 0 $22,800 | 1984 4 2 0 0 $22,800 | 1983 0 M 0 0

3Oct84- 7Bel fst 7f :23 :47 1:24⅕ 3+ Alw 20000 4 9 8⁶¾ 5²½ 1hd 1¾ Cruguet J 119 7.60 81-26 TreasuredOne119¾CrimsonMedl112⁶¾BlindMn'sBluff1141½ Driving 9
24Sep84- 1Bel fst 7f :23⅗ :47⅗ 1:24 3+ Md Sp Wt 4 7 4²½ 7³½ 1hd 1²½ Cruguet J 118 *2.20e 82-21 Treasured One 1182½ Magnetize 118⁴ Duomo 118hd Ridden out 8
14Sep84- 3Bel fst 6f :22⅗ :46⅘ 1:11⅗ 3+ Md Sp Wt 12 2 2hd 1½ 2⁴ 5⁷½ Vergara O 118 3.10e 78-18 Another King117³RamblingRector1181½Magnetize1182¾ Gave way 12
4Apr84- 9Aqu fst 6f ⊡:23 :47 1:12⅗ Md Sp Wt 6 4 4¹¾ 4⁴ 6¹¹ 6¹¹½ Velasquez J 122 4.20 70-20 Mansei 1221½ Mega Luck 1223½ Oscar's Gold 1221½ Tired 12
LATEST WORKOUTS Oct 17 Bel tr.t 5f fst 1:01⅘ b Oct 10 Bel tr.t 4f fst :47⅘ h Oct 1 Bel tr.t 4f fst :48⅘ h Sep 21 Bel tr.t 4f fst :48⅘ h

*Cold Feet II

Ch. c. 3, by Arctic Tern—Ballarina, by King of the Castle
Br.—Tuttle W (Fra)
Own.—Tuttle Mrs W F L **Tr.—Nickerson Victor J**
115 Lifetime 10 1 2 0 $27,473 | 1984 6 0 0 0 $3,981 | 1983 4 1 2 0 $23,492 | Turf 10 1 2 0 $27,473

22Aug84♦5Deauville(Fra) gd*1 1:41⅘ Ⓣ Prix du Cercle 6⁴¾ Doleuze G b 119 20.00 — — TollTeller 119¾ AfricanJoy 1241½ PeakValue 119nk Well pl,wknd 8
7Aug84♦4Deauville(Fra) gd*1⅝ 2:39⅗ Ⓣ Prix de Menneval 9¹⁹ Doleuze G b 123 37.00 — — AgentDouble 123² Okeanos 128hd Bojador 123nk Led to stretch 9
5Jly84♦6Evry(Fra) gd*1⅜ 1:57⅕ Ⓣ Prix Athis Cars 4¹¾ Doleuze G 123 1.75 — — MidwayDancer132hd Rhapsodm132¹ OccuptionPrince119¾ Evenly 5
30Jun84♦4Evry(Fra) gd*1⅛ 1:50⅘ Ⓣ Prix Daphnis(Gr.3) 8⁷ Doleuze G 128 16.00 — — PlceMusic128no SettleSong1282½ EnchntdCstl128² Led to midstr 9
15Apr84♦6Longchamp(Fra) gd*1⅟₁₆ 2:12⅗ Ⓣ Prix de Guiche(Gr.3) 4⁹¾ Doleuze G 128 8.00 — — Yashgan 128nk Greinton 128⁸ Grand Orient 1281½ No threat 4
1Apr84♦2Longchamp(Fra) sf*1¼ 2:18⅕ Ⓣ Prix de Courcelles 4¹⁰ Doleuze G 123 *2.00 — — Duke ofSilver 128⁸ Micbol 128nk Tropular 123² Prom,wknd 7
21Nov83♦5StCloud(Fra) gd*1¼ 2:07⅗ Ⓣ Criterium deStCloud(Gr2) 8¹⁵ Doleuze G 121 3.00 — — Darshaan 121¾ Grand Orient 1211½ Real gold 118² Gave way 12
16Oct83♦3Longchamp(Fra) gd*1¼ 2:10⅗ Ⓣ Prix de Conde (Gr.3) 2³ Doleuze G 123 *.60 — — Long Mick 123³ Cold Feet 123⁸ Ina Sevile 120⁸ Well pl,no exc 5
1Oct83♦5Longchamp(Fra) fm*1⅛ 1:52⅕ Ⓣ Prix Saint Roman (Gr.3) 2hd Doleuze G 123 4.00 — — Truculent 123hd ColdFeetII1231½ DailyBusy120nk Bid,game finish 7
13Sep83♦7Evry(Fra) gd*1 1:46 Ⓣ Prix de Lamballe(Mdn) 1²½ Doleuze G 123 8.20 — — Cold Feet II 1232½ Polly's Ark 123³ Bojador 123½ Led thruout 14
LATEST WORKOUTS Oct 17 Aqu 4f fst :47⅘ h Oct 9 Aqu 4f fst :49⅕ b

So Vague *

B. c. 3, by Empery—Merry Says So, by Advocator
Br.—Cashman E C (Ky)
Own.—Gainey A **Tr.—Kegel Tim**
119 Lifetime 28 4 4 2 $114,735 | 1984 11 1 2 1 $19,336 | 1983 17 3 2 1 $95,399 | Turf 3 0 0 1 $1,980

28Sep84- 6Med yl 1⅜ Ⓣ:47⅘ 1:38 2:16⅗ Rutgers H 8 5 4⁸½ 4⁶ 5⁹ 6¹⁰¾ Ward W A 110 11.60 71-20 Roving Minstrel 1151½ Raami 1172½ Dealaway 113² Tired 8
28Sep84-Grade II; Run in divisions
7Sep84- 9Med fm 1⅟₁₆ Ⓣ:47⅗ 1:11⅗ 1:43⅕ 3+ Alw 18000 5 5 5⁶½ 5³½ 4² 3hd McCarthy M J 113 7.30 86-15 Charging Through 119hd Ayman 116no So Vague 1132½ Sharp 6
19Aug84- 9FL sly 1⅟₁₆ :46⅕ 1:12 1:48⅕ 3+ Rochester Cp 5 7 8¹⁵ 8¹¹ 7¹⁰ 5¹²½ Cooksey P J 110 5.70 62-30 NorthProspect112¹UnoRoberto118³BenMrino112½ Lacked a rally 9
23Jly84- 7RD fm 7½f Ⓣ:23⅗ :45⅗ 1:30 Alw 10000 4 7 6¹¹ 6⁷¾ 3² 1¾ Woods C R Jr 113 4.50 100-03 So Vague 113¾ Bim's Bid 1195½ Star's Robust 113² 8
23Jly84-Disqualified from purse money
13May84-10RD fst 1⅟₁₆ :47⅗ 1:11⅘ 1:46⅗ 3+ Alw 12000 6 10 9¹² 7¹⁰ 6⁴½ 5⁶¾ Cooksey P J 112 *1.60 69-23 Brooks N' Bruce 116no Sidi Bou Said 122nk Hard Four 122½ 10
5May84- 8CD fst 1¼ :47⅗ 1:36⅗ 2:02⅘ Ky Derby 4 15 15¹³ 16¹⁴ 12¹⁵ 11¹²½ Cooksey P J 126 9.90f 73-19 Swale 1263¼ Coax Me Chad 126² AtTheThreshold126nk No factor 20
5May84-Grade I
26Apr84- 7Kee fst 1⅛ :47⅗ 1:12⅗ 1:52⅕ Blue Grass 9 8 8¹⁷ 9¹⁹ 8¹⁹ 7²²¾ Cooksey P J 121 74.20 53-31 Taylor'sSpecial1213½SilentKing1212½CharmedRook121⁵ No threat 9
26Apr84-Grade I
19Apr84- 7Kee gd 7f :23⅕ :46 1:23⅗ Alw 29300 5 4 5⁹½ 5¹¹ 4⁸½ 2¹⁵ Cooksey P J 120 21.70 73-27 Devil's Bag 123¹⁵ So Vague 1201½ Triple Sec 123⁴ Best of others 5
1Apr84- 9Lat fst 1⅟₁₆ :46 1:10⅕ 1:42⅘ Jim Beam 9 12 12¹⁴ 9¹¹ 10¹⁶ 10¹⁷½ Cooksey P J 121 10.00 78-18 AtThThrshold121¹BoldSouthrnr121¹ThWddngGust121¾ No factor 12
1Apr84-Grade III
25Mar84- 8Lat sly 1 :46⅔ 1:10⅘ 1:38 Alw 10700 2 8 6⁹½ 4⁴½ 2½ 1¹ Cooksey P J 115 3.30 89-26 So Vague 115¹ A Gift 112no Raja's Shark 112⁸ Wide, clear 9
LATEST WORKOUTS ●Oct 13 FL 5f fst 1:01⅗ h Sep 19 FL 1 fst 1:45 b Sep 5 FL 3f fst :36⅘ h ●Aug 29 FL 5f fst 1:03⅘ b

A Gift

Ch. c. 3, by Shecky Greene—Mini Gift, by Minnesota Mac
Br.—Kellman J (Ky)
Own.—Asbury T **Tr.—Cantey Joseph B**
119 Lifetime 14 3 5 3 $95,970 | 1984 12 2 5 2 $82,770 | 1983 2 1 0 1 $13,200 | Turf 3 1 0 0 $43,680

21Sep84- 6Med fm 1⅟₁₆ Ⓣ:46⅕ 1:10 1:40⅘ 3+ Clf Hanger H 7 2 2¹½ 2¹ 5³ 6⁷½ MacBeth D 112 12.90 91-06 Late Act 113² Sitzmark 1111½ Quick Dip 112no Tired 10
21Sep84-Run in divisions
18Aug84- 5Sar fst 7f :22⅕ :44⅘ 1:22⅕ 3+ Alw 23000 4 4 3⁴½ 3⁷½ 3⁶ 3⁵½ MacBeth D 112 *1.50 85-15 Cut Away 117¾ Dancing Crown 1144¾ A Gift 1124¾ Wide str. 7
14Jly84- 8Bel fm 1¼ Ⓣ:48⅕ 1:37 2:01⅕ Lexington 8 5 6³ 5²½ 6⁸½ 5⁵½ MacBeth D 126 9.90e 82-11 Onyxly 114¹ Dr. Schwartzman 1261½ Vision 126³ Evenly 13
14Jly84-Grade II
30Jun84- 9Mth sly 1⅟₁₆ :46⅗ 1:12 1:44⅗ Lmplghtr H 1 6 3⁴½ 1hd 1hd 2² MacBeth D 118 2.40 81-19 Light Spirits 112² A Gift 118½ Dr. Schwartzman121⁵ Wide,gamely 9
30Jun84-Grade III
3Jun84- 8Bel sf 1⅟₁₆ Ⓣ:50⅔ 1:15 1:48⅘ Hill Prince 7 3 4² 3² 1½ 1¹½ MacBeth D 114 4.40 54-46 A Gift 1141½ Is Your Pleasure 1264¾ Jesse'sHope1172¾ Drew clear 7
3Jun84-Grade III
24May84- 1Bel fst 7f :22⅘ :45⅘ 1:22 Alw 21000 4 2 4¹¾ 3½ 2² 2⁴½ Maple E 117 4.10 87-15 Carr De Naskra 1174½ A Gift 1173½ Disastrous Night117¾ 2nd best 5
1Apr84- 6Lat fst 1 :49⅘ 1:13 1:39⅘ Alw 14400 7 5 3½ 2¹½ 2² 2hd Maple E 110 *.30 81-18 Dempsey's Brand 113hd A Gift 110⁵ Ada's Night 113¹ Failed 8
25Mar84- 8Lat sly 1 :46⅔ 1:10⅘ 1:38 Alw 10700 3 5 4² 3⁴½ 3³ 2¹ Snyder L 112 *1.90 88-26 So Vague 115¹ A Gift 112no Raja's Shark 112⁸ Rallied 9
14Mar84- 8OP fst 6f :21⅘ :45⅕ 1:09⅗ Alw 15000 2 4 3¹½ 4¹¾ 3²½ 2¾ Snyder L b 121 3.30 96-15 Locust Bayou 121¾ A Gift 121¹ Gold Policy 112⁵ Boxed in 8
20Feb84- 8OP fst 6f :21⅗ :44⅖ 1:09⅕ 3+ Alw 14000 3 5 4² 3³½ 2²½ 1¾ Snyder L b 112 *1.90 99-05 A Gift 112¾ Report For Duty 109² Lucky Larry 1121½ Driving 11
LATEST WORKOUTS Oct 16 Bel 7f fst 1:28⅕ h Oct 10 Bel 5f fst 1:02⅕ h Sep 18 Bel Ⓣ 7f fm 1:24⅕ h Sep 11 Bel 1 fst 1:39 h

Inrhetoric

Dk. b. or br. g. 3, by Elocutionist—Far Piece, by No Robbery
Br.—Isaacs H Z (Ky)
Own.—Brookfield Farms **Tr.—Kelly Edward I**
115 Lifetime 8 2 2 0 $27,040 | 1984 8 2 2 0 $27,040 | 1983 0 M 0 0 | Turf 3 1 2 0 $20,770

6Oct84- 5Bel fm 1 Ⓣ:46 1:10⅘ 1:36⅘ 3+ Alw 21000 3 6 3³½ 2hd 1hd 2¾ Davis R G b 114 3.60e 80-23 Solidified 119¾ Inrhetoric 1142½ Pigwidgeon 114no Gamely 11
23Sep84- 4Bel fm 1⅟₁₆ Ⓣ:47⅗ 1:11 1:42⅘ Clm 45000 1 2 2¹ 1hd 1¹½ 1³½ Davis R G b 113 *1.60 87-14 Inrhetoric 1133½ All Night Stand113¾MealTicket1171½ Ridden out 8

30Aug84- 5Bel fm 1 1/16 Ⓣ:45⅘ 1:10 1:42⅘ Clm 35000 6 3 22 1½ 2hd 2¾ Davis R G b 113 14.20 81-13 Titular Feast 113¾ Inrhetoric 1132¼ Andismo 1152 Gamely 9
29Jly84- 9Bel fst 6f :22⅗ :46⅗ 1:12⅘ 3+Md 25000 11 8 55 32 1½ 1½ Davis R G b 116 4.60 78-15 Inrhetoric 116½ Dr. Li Pera 107½ Effulgent 1162¾ Driving 12
19Jly84- 9Bel fst 6f :23 :46⅘ 1:12⅕ 3+Md 25000 8 12 44 22 45 48 Davis R G b 116 5.40 73-15 FightInfltion1221¾BoldBrmble1162¼FirstExperience1094 Checked 12
25Mar84- 4Aqu fst 6f ⊡:23 :47⅗ 1:13 Md Sp Wt 5 6 63½ 75½ 78 79½ MacBeth D b 122 33.60 69-16 Onyxly 1221½ Pauper Prince 1223½ Columbia Pride 1223 Tired 12
16Mar84- 7Aqu fst 6f ⊡:22⅗ :46⅗ 1:12⅘ Md Sp Wt 5 2 2½ 41½ 57½ 611 MacBeth D b 122 26.30 69-25 Perfect Double 122hd Mansei 1221¾ Milling Cove 1223¾ Stopped 8
22Feb84- 6Aqu fst 6f ⊡:22⅕ :46 1:12 Md Sp Wt 3 10 58½ 812 1026 1128 MacBeth D b 122 20.20 56-25 Chapparel 1222¾ Sir Ivor's Verdict 122¾ Moschini 1221 Outrun 11
LATEST WORKOUTS Oct 18 Bel tr.t 3f fst :36⅘ b Sep 30 Bel tr.t 4f fst :50⅘ b Sep 21 Bel tr.t 3f fst :37⅗ b

Winston's Gold
B. c. 3, by Sensitive Prince—Winston's Sapphire, by Icecapade
Br.—Sterlingbrook Farm (NJ)
Own.—Top The Marc Stable
Tr.—Jerkens H Allen
115
Lifetime 12 2 3 3 $46,522
1984 8 1 1 3 $27,229
1983 4 1 2 0 $19,293
Turf 3 0 1 2 $17,299

13Sep84- 8Med fm 1 1/16 Ⓣ:47⅗ 1:11 1:42⅕ 3+Ⓢ Jky Holow H 8 2 21½ 32½ 43 32¾ Perret C b 114 16.40 88-08 La Pawn 1142 Castle Guard 123¾ Winston's Gold1143 Came again 10
1Sep84- 8Mth fst 1 :46⅘ 1:11⅕ 1:36⅘ 3+Ⓢ J J Reilly H 6 5 53 54½ 45½ 67¾ McCarron G b 112 21.70 83-18 Special Mah1193AbstractThinker1143½CastleGuard1251 No factor 7
17Jly84- 9Mth fm 1 Ⓣ:46⅘ 1:11⅕ 1:36⅗ Ⓢ W LngbrnchH 5 4 42½ 21 1hd 23 Perret C b 116 2.90 89-14 LaPawn1183Winston'sGold1163RainbowCastle121½ Best of others 9
16Jun84- 8Atl fm 1 1/16 Ⓣ:47⅗ 1:12 1:42⅗ 3+Ⓢ A Imbesi H 3 1 2½ 1hd 3nk 34 Velez R I b 109 12.70 89-15 Always Up 1142 Rumptious 1202 Winston's Gold 1092½ Weakened 7
10May84- 8Mth fst 6f :23⅕ :46⅗ 1:12⅗ 3+Ⓢ Alw 13800 1 3 2½ 1hd 11 1¾ Perret C b 114 *.40 77-25 Winston's Gold 114¾ PrinceandProud1122TufTarbaby1072 Driving 6
3May84- 7Mth fst 6f :22⅘ :46 1:12⅕ 3+Ⓢ Alw 15000 1 3 2hd 1hd 2hd 3½ Perret C b 114 *1.30 78-24 RainbowCastle108nkRpidWing117nkWinston'sGold1147 Weakened 6
17Apr84- 7Aqu fst 6f ⊡:22 :45⅕ 1:10⅘ Alw 20000 7 2 52½ 43½ 45½ 56 Graell A b 117 25.40 86-15 AggressiveBid1174½DncingNtiv117¾BlindMn'sBluff110½ Weakened 8
7Apr84- 5Aqu fst 6f ⊡:22⅘ :46⅗ 1:11⅘ Alw 20000 5 1 54½ 610 612 513 Graell A 117 5.60 72-16 Coopr'sHwk1101RunningBold119hdRomnticTrditon1194¾ Far back 7
10Oct83- 10Suf fst 1 :48⅕ 1:13 1:38⅘ John Alden 6 4 42½ 59½ 57¾ 416½ Graell A 112 3.10 66-22 Don Bert B. 1141½ Adriatic Way 1142 HobbysSon12213 Weakened 6
14Sep83- 4Med fst 6f :22⅗ :46⅘ 1:13 Ⓢ Md Sp Wt 3 9 43 2hd 13 17 Graell A 118 *.60 78-17 Winston's Gold 1187 Twenty Count 1181½ Sea Glow 1111 Driving 12
LATEST WORKOUTS Oct 17 Bel 7f fst 1:33 b Oct 6 Bel 3f fst :37⅗ b Oct 1 Bel 7f fst 1:31⅘ b Sep 11 Bel 5f fst 1:02⅗ b

But could he win this soon in stakes company? Let's take a look at the opposition:

PURPLE COMET

This unfashionably bred colt came into the Envoy with winning credentials on the grass and Angel Cordero in the irons. The New York audience was duly impressed, making Purple Comet co-favorite at 6–5. Yet there was nothing in this colt's record to suggest New York stakes quality. For the most part, he had raced against—and narrowly beaten—horses whose names meant nothing in New York. Only Roving Minstrel's name was familiar, and he was regarded as nothing more than a nice allowance runner at the time he was beaten by Purple Comet in Maryland.

Purple Comet's most recent race was a cause for concern, though, raising the possibility that the colt had overextended himself at a difficult distance over a tiring surface. There was a very real possibility that the race could have a detrimental effect on Purple Comet's physical condition. With question marks concerning his class and fitness, plus the 122 pounds he was being asked to carry, Purple Comet looked beatable. But why had Cordero taken the mount on this shipper? And why did the New York crowd go overboard on his chances?

IS YOUR PLEASURE

One of the first lessons I learned at the racetrack was that "Kelly's horses are always ready," referring to E. I. Kelly (Sr.), trainer of Is Your Pleasure. I have seldom found reason to doubt that advice, but this was one instance. Is Your Pleasure was the established class of this field, and he liked the grass. The distance was perfect, and the weight no problem. I expected him to be heavily odds-on, yet he was being offered at an overly generous 6–5. Why?

The other four contestants were of questionable ability and/or fitness. In Rhetoric, the stablemate of Is Your Pleasure, would keep Purple Comet honest in the early running. So Vague was highly erratic. A Gift hadn't run really well since June, and his recent races were suspiciously spaced. And Winston's Gold had been competing against New Jersey-breds with only modest success. I would have backed Treasured One with great confidence against any of these four, and, at the prevailing odds, liked the bet against Purple Comet. It was Is Your Pleasure who worried me, yet many others in the audience seemed to feel otherwise. Their opinion made Is Your Pleasure seem less invincible than I had originally thought he would be.

The bet in the race was obvious: Treasured One to win, with an Is Your Pleasure-Treasured One exacta as a saver. The exacta bet proved unnecessary, because Is Your Pleasure turned in an uncharacteristically dull performance, confirming the crowd's suspicions. Treasured One, benefiting from a well-judged rail-hugging ride from Jean Cruguet, got up in the final yards and returned a nice $15.60.

THIRD RACE
Belmont
OCTOBER 20, 1984

1 MILE.(Turf). (1.33) 1st Running ENVOY STAKES. Purse $50,000 Added. 3-year-olds, weights, 122 lbs. Non-winners of two races of $25,000 allowed 3 lbs. Of such a race since then, 5 lbs. Of a race of $16,500 at a mile or over 7 lbs. ($50 to nominate; $100 to enter and $100 to start. (Closing Saturday, October 6). Closed with 30 nominations.

Value of race $53,000; value to winner $31,800; second $11,660; third $6,360; fourth $3,180. Mutuel pool $206,939, OTB pool $106,477. Track Exacta Pool $370,947. OTB Exacta Pool $239,094.

Last Raced	Horse	Eqt.	A.	Wt	PP	St	¼	½	¾	Str	Fin	Jockey	Odds $1
30ct84 ^{7}Bel^{1}	Treasured One		3	115	3	1	5^{1}	4^{hd}	5^{3}	$3^{1\frac{1}{2}}$	$1^{\frac{3}{4}}$	Cruguet J	6.80
21Sep84 ^{6}Med^{6}	A Gift		3	119	5	3	6^{5}	6^{6}	3^{1}	1^{hd}	2^{nk}	Maple E	6.70
28Sep84 ^{6}Med^{6}	So Vague		3	119	4	5	7	7	7	$4^{\frac{1}{2}}$	3no	Cooksey P J	28.00
28Sep84 ^{6}Med^{4}	Purple Comet		3	122	1	7	2^{hd}	2^{1}	$1^{\frac{1}{2}}$	$2^{\frac{1}{2}}$	$4^{2\frac{3}{4}}$	Cordero A Jr	1.30
80ct84 ^{8}Bel^{2}	Is Your Pleasure	b	3	122	2	6	$3^{\frac{1}{2}}$	3^{1}	$4^{\frac{1}{2}}$	5^{3}	5^{4}	MacBeth D	a-1.20
60ct84 ^{5}Bel^{2}	Inrhetoric	b	3	115	6	2	1^{1}	1^{hd}	$2^{\frac{1}{2}}$	6^{2}	$6^{\frac{3}{4}}$	Davis R G	a-1.20
13Sep84 ^{8}Med^{3}	Winston's Gold	b	3	115	7	4	$4^{\frac{1}{2}}$	$5^{\frac{1}{2}}$	$6^{\frac{1}{2}}$	7	7	Graell A	23.40

a-Coupled: Is Your Pleasure and Inrhetoric.

OFF AT 2:10 Start good, Won driving. Time, :23$\frac{1}{5}$, :46$\frac{3}{5}$, 1:10$\frac{2}{5}$, 1:35$\frac{2}{5}$ Course firm.

$2 Mutuel Prices:				
	3-(C)-TREASURED ONE	15.60	7.20	5.80
	6-(F)-A GIFT		7.40	5.40
	5-(E)-SO VAGUE			7.80
	$2 EXACTA 3-6 PAID $106.20.			

Ch. c, by Exclusive Native—Monteen, by Hail To Reason. Trainer Martin Frank. Bred by Harbor View Farm (Ky).

TREASURED ONE, reserved early, made a run along the inside entering the stretch and proved best under pressure. A GIFT raced wide while moving approaching the stretch, loomed boldly near the final furlong but wasn't good enough. SO VAGUE, very wide into the stretch, finished well while drifting out badly. PURPLE COMET quickly reached contention along the inside, took over approaching the stretch but weakened slightly in a stiff drive. IS YOUR PLEASURE, a factor to the stretch, lacked the needed late response. INRHETORIC was used up vying for the lead. WINSTON'S GOLD tired racing wide.

Chapter 17

Why Did They Wait So Long?

WHEN COZZENE FIRST CAME to the races in 1983, I had him ticketed for a career as a grass runner. As a son of Caro from a Prince John mare, he certainly had the bloodlines. When that first grass start never materialized (in 1983), I was puzzled. Jan Nerud, conditioner of his father's powerful Tartan Stable, certainly had no aversion to grass racing, having handled many top-class "daisy cutters" in recent years. Had Cozzene hinted in a workout somewhere down the line that grass was not to be his game?

Cozzene returned to the racing wars at four with a sharp effort behind Fit To Fight at seven panels. When Nerud entered him in the Metropolitan Mile on Memorial Day, I had other plans for the gray colt. On the back page of the previous Saturday's *Racing Form* was an entry blank for the supporting stakes events carded for Belmont Day two weeks hence. One was at a mile and a sixteenth on the turf, a perfect spot for Cozzene to make his long-awaited first appearance on the grass. I was hoping that he wouldn't run all that well in the Met, just well enough to suggest continued fitness. I got exactly what I had wished for when Cozzene chased a fast pace, then made a menacing move around the turn only to flatten out in the stretch and finish fourth.

Imagine my surprise when Cozzene was entered in a six-furlong stakes (The Jaipur) on Belmont Day! I had been anticipating that the colt would be my prime bet on the Belmont card, and I found it hard not liking him in that six-furlong event that was packed with early-speed types. Listed at 20–1 in the program, with Cordero scheduled to ride, Cozzene appeared to be quite the overlay. His prior record at six furlongs, before he began stretching out to longer distances, had been excellent. More than half of the punters with whom I spoke early on Belmont Day said that Cozzene would be their best value bet of the day. It still looked as if Cozzene could be the day's hero, and that his grass debut could be put off until another day.

You can imagine my disbelief when Cozzene opened a heavy favorite for the Jaipur. His odds never rose higher than 2–1. I had already invested too much in the horse, however, to bet against him, so I cut my bet in half and watched the race, knowing in my heart that he would run poorly. He did.

Horses often find it difficult to turn back to six furlongs later in their careers once they've become accustomed to racing at longer distances. The fact that Nerud chose a seven-furlong race for Cozzene's 1984 debut suggested that he felt the horse was no longer suited to the shorter six-furlong distance and had been trained with other things in mind.

Handicappers, on the other hand, often find it difficult to turn away from a horse they really like when its odds drop too low. Betting horses demands discipline. Backing away from a selection, even betting against it on another horse at more enticing odds, is the sternest test of that discipline. Committing oneself to a horse without acknowledging that value is an important part of the equation is a mistake. Unfortunately, it is one that most of us repeat time and time again.

On June 23, two weeks after Belmont Day, Cozzene (with stablemate Eskimo) showed up at Monmouth Park, set to make his grass debut. His task would not be an easy one, for among his rivals were Wild Again, winner of the Oaklawn and New Orleans Handicaps (and subsequent winner of the Breeders' Cup Classic), and Castle Guard, fresh from victory in the grassy Red Bank Handicap at Monmouth. Wild Again's most recent start had been his first on the grass, and he had been found wanting against horses I would have preferred Cozzene to on Belmont Day. Perhaps grass was not to be Wild Again's forte. Possibly something went wrong that day, as the subsequent brief layoff suggested. Or maybe the horse was simply in need of a short freshening.

With two serious rivals, odds of 2–1 would have represented minimum fair value on Cozzene. But one usually looks for more than fair value when a horse attempts something—like racing on the turf—for the first time. Was Cozzene worth a bet at 5–2 in this spot? Hindsight makes it easy to respond in the affirmative. He won nicely, returning $7.40, with his two major rivals checking in second and third behind him. The Cozzene-Wild Again exacta returned a juicy $21.00.

8 MONMOUTH

1 1-16 MILES
MONMOUTH PARK

1 1/16 MILES. (Turf). (1.42⅕) ALLOWANCE. Purse $19,000. 3-year-olds and upward which have not won $8,405 two times on the turf since July 10, 1983 other than maiden, claiming, starter or state bred. Weights, 3-year-olds, 113 lbs. Older, 122 lbs. Non-winners of $9,800 since May 18, allowed 3 lbs. $8,100 twice in 1984, 5 lbs. $8,100 in 1984, 7 lbs. (Maiden, claiming and starter races not considered)

Coupled—Eskimo and Cozzene.

*Colonel Sanders

Ch. h. 6, by On Your Mark—Purple Heron, by Great Heron
Br.—Tremaine W D (Ire)
Tr.—Crimean Joanne
Own.—Grace P
115
Lifetime 39 6 2 6 $33,075 | 1984 1 0 0 0 $285 | 1983 5 1 0 2 $19,300 | Turf 28 5 2 4 $31,000

15Jun84- 8Atl fm *1 ① 1:37⅘ 3+Alw 9500 10 8 78¾ 45 47 510½ Thomas D B 113 5.40 88-07 Dr. Tipton107¾GoldenStatue1085TomHagerty1132 Lacked fin. bid 10
19Jun83- 9Hol fm 1⅛ ①:47⅘ 1:12 1:42⅘ Clm 50000 7 11 107¾ 52½ 52 32¾ Sibille R 119 7.00 82-11 Tower Bridge 1112½ClearVerdict116nkColonelSanders119½ Rallied 12
5Jun83- 9Hol fm 1⅛ ①:48⅘ 1:12⅘ 1:42⅘ Alw 24000 6 5 31 1hd 54 66 Sibille R 120 5.80 79-11 Beldale Lustre 1142 Watchdog II115hdSargeantWilson1152½ Tired 7
5Jun83-Forced to steady off another horse's heels at 3/16
27May83- 9Hol fm 1⅛ ①:46⅗ 1:11⅕ 1:41⅘ Alw 22000 7 6 611 76½ 3½ 1no Sibille R 115 2.90 90-12 Colonel Sanders 115no Georgios 114½ Rich Watson 1141½ Driving 9
11May83- 9Hol fm 1⅛ ①:47 1:11⅗ 1:49 Alw 22000 4 9 913 97½ 4¾ 3¾ Sibille R 115 6.20 84-15 Fearsome Foursome 117nk Poor John 115½ ColonelSanders115nk 11
5May83- 9Hol fm 1 ①:47⅘ 1:11 1:35⅘ Clm 100000 5 6 58 56½ 64¾ 83½ Tejeira J 118 43.80 86-10 Lucullus 122no Maguei 118hd Tugoflove II 1161½ 8
17Nov82♦5Fairyhouse(Ire) sf 2 4:06⅖ Kilbride Plate (Hurdles) 87 Doran D 157 20.00 — — Brave George 1652 Ratheroghan 165¾ McSweeney 1512 Bid, tired 23
25Oct82♦5Limerick(Ire) sf 2½ 4:33⅕ Meadow Sweet Hcp (Hurdles) 722 Sleator M 139 5.00 — — Highway Girl1508 ELKekni1492 GortroeQueen1335 Well up, tired 11
14Oct82♦4Punchestown(Ire) yl 2 3:47⅕ Rathmore Plate (Hurdles) 69 Doran D 151 8.00 — — Tom Miller 1612 Buck House 1512½ Carriag Oir 1611 No threat 24
21Sep82♦3Listowel(Ire) gd 2 4:17⅘ Limited Hcp (Hurdles) 510 Doran D 135 10.00 — — Triggereo 1432½ Chinese Queen 140no Hi Harry 1512½ Fin. well 8
LATEST WORKOUTS Jun 14 Atl 3f sly :37⅕ b Jun 13 Del 3f fst :39 b

Eskimo

B. c. 4, by Northern Dancer—Dr Mary Lou, by Dr Fager
Br.—Tartan Farms (Fla)
Tr.—Nerud Jan H
Own.—Tartan Stable
108[7]
Lifetime 17 4 4 3 $101,810 | 1984 2 0 0 2 $23,250 | 1983 9 4 2 1 $66,320 | Turf 6 0 2 2 $15,840

2Jun84- 8Bel sly 1¼ :47⅘ 1:35⅘ 2:02⅕ 3+Red Smith H 4 4 48½ 37 39 311½ Cordero A Jr 112 *2.00 76-19 Hero's Honor 1177 Win 1144½ Eskimo 11216½ Weakened 5
11May84- 8Bel fm 7f ①:22⅘ :46 1:23⅕ 3+Alw 26000 4 1 52 31½ 31 31¾ Cordero A Jr 121 2.30 86-17 Wilhelm 121nk Charging Through 1211½ Eskimo 1213½ Hung 7
29Oct83- 9Aqu fst 1 :47⅕ 1:12⅗ 1:38⅘ 3+Alw 30000 5 2 21½ 1hd 1hd 11½ Rogers K L 114 9.50 72-28 Eskimo 1141½ Thalassocrat 1142 Unmistaken 114nk Driving 12
24Sep83- 8Med fst 6f :22 :45 1:10 3+Chief Pen H 1 5 66½ 78½ 67 85½ Rogers K L 108 2.90e 87-16 Monetary Gift 1141½ Star Gallant 1201½ Full Venture114nk Outrun 10
12Sep83- 6Med sly 6f :22⅘ :45⅗ 1:10⅗ 3+Alw 15000 3 1 57½ 45½ 34 21 Cordero A Jr 118 *.70 89-20 Valid Image 1121 Eskimo 1182½Hagley'sReward1165 Wide, rallied 6
2Sep83- 8Bel fst 6f :23⅕ :46⅖ 1:10 3+Alw 24000 1 1 43 3½ 11 13½ Cordero A Jr 115 1.90 92-16 Eskimo 1153½ Nearice 1133 Columbia Holme 1135 Ridden out 6
6Aug83- 4Sar fst 7f :22⅘ :45⅘ 1:23 3+Alw 20000 7 1 42½ 21 11 11¾ Cordero A Jr 112 *1.00 87-16 Eskimo 1121¾ No Man's Land 1073¾ Secretaire 1172½ Ridden out 7
7Jly83- 7Bel fst 7f :23⅘ :46⅘ 1:23⅘ 3+Alw 20000 1 3 3½ 3nk 1hd 42½ Cordero A Jr 111 *2.90 83-19 Galaxy Guide 106hdWaitlist1171½BelieveTheQueen111¾ Weakened 10
30May83- 9Bel my 7f :22⅘ :45⅗ 1:23⅕ 3+Alw 20000 9 1 41¾ 1hd 1hd 22 Cordero A Jr 112 6.10 84-11 Cold Remark 1082 Eskimo 1121¾ Private Sun 114no Gamely 9
19May83- 6Bel fm 1 ①:46⅘ 1:11⅗ 1:39 3+Alw 21000 1 3 41½ 32 22 31½ Fell J 113 *1.50 68-24 BundleofKisses119hdFeloniousFllow1141½Eskimo1131¾ Weakened 11
LATEST WORKOUTS Jun 15 Bel tr.t 4f fst :49⅕ b Jun 10 Bel tr.t 4f fst :48⅕ h May 25 Bel tr.t 4f fst :49 b May 19 Bel tr.t 4f fst :49⅕ b

Wild Again

Dk. b. or br. c. 4, by Icecapade—Bushel-N-Peck, by Khaled
Br.—Little W P (Ky)
Tr.—Timphony Vincent
Own.—Black Chip Stable
119
Lifetime 16 6 3 1 $363,725 | 1984 8 4 0 1 $330,025 | 1983 1 0 0 0 | Turf 1 0 0 0 $2,160

14May84- 8Bel gd 1⅛ Ⓣ:48⅘ 1:12⅗ 1:43⅗ 3+Alw 36000 5 1 1½ 2hd 2½ 43¾ Day P 124 2.90 80-22 Intensify1191½Erin'sTiger1212½DominatingDooley119hd Weakened 6
20Apr84- 9OP fst 1⅛ :45⅗ 1:09⅗ 1:46⅘ Oaklawn H 6 6 43 31½ 21½ 11 Day P 115 8.60 109-06 Wild Again 1151 Win Stat 1142 Dew Line 1181½ Driving 14
7Apr84- 9OP fst 1 1/16 :45⅗ 1:10 1:41⅗ Razorback H 1 1 2hd 2½ 31½ 87 Day P 116 *2.00 93-07 Dew Line 1161 Passing Base 1121¾ Win Stat 115¾ Tired 14
18Mar84-11FG fst 1¼ :47⅘ 1:36⅘ 2:02 N Orleans H 4 2 21½ 22½ 21½ 1nk Day P 112 10.50 99-17 Wild Again 112nk Explosive Bid 1122½ Crazy Moon 1103 Driving 10
2Mar84- 8SA fst 1 1/16 :46⅗ 1:10⅕ 1:42⅕ Alw 35000 3 1 22½ 24 21½ 12 Sibille R 119 3.00 90-18 Wild Again 1192 Paskanell 1142½ Debt 1145 Driving 7
20Feb84- 7SA fst 1 1/16 :46⅖ 1:10⅘ 1:42⅖ Alw 35000 5 1 2½ 1hd 1½ 32½ Sibille R 118 9.80 87-16 Ancestral 115nk Silent Fox 1132 Wild Again 1184 7
5Feb84- 5SA fst 1 :45⅗ 1:10⅗ 1:36⅘ Alw 28000 2 2 22 1½ 1½ 1nk Sibille R 115 10.40 84-17 Wild Again 115nk Stage Hand Johny1142½GoodFinish1171 Driving 9
21Jan84- 7SA fst 1 1/16 :46⅗ 1:11⅕ 1:44 Alw 27000 1 1 2hd 1hd 2hd 44½ Sibille R 115 12.10 76-17 NorthrxfrdDrv1152½StgHndJhny1141½Lghthwyhlm120¾ Weakened 12
22Dec83- 7Hol fst 7f :21⅗ :44 1:21⅗ 3+Alw 30000 1 7 68½ 710 68¾ 77½ Estrada J C 114 24.80 82-14 Paskanell 1161½ Estate 116hd Whelp 1202½ Outrun 8
30Oct82- 8SA fst 1 1/16 :45 1:09⅕ 1:41⅗ Norfolk 9 6 69 810 915 918½ Sibille R 118 40.80 74-10 Roving Boy 1184½ Desert Wine 1183½ Aguila 1181½ Outrun 9
LATEST WORKOUTS Jun 21 Bel 4f fst :48⅗ h Jun 16 Bel 5f fst 1:00⅘ h Jun 12 Bel 5f fst 1:00 h Jun 7 Bel 4f fst :49⅘ h

Cozzene

Gr. c. 4, by Caro—Ride The Trails, by Prince John
Br.—Nerud J A (Fla)
Tr.—Nerud Jan H
Own.—Nerud J A
115
Lifetime 9 3 3 0 $79,580 | 1984 3 0 1 0 $25,470 | 1983 6 3 2 0 $54,110

9Jun84- 6Bel fst 6f :22⅕ :44⅘ 1:09⅕ 3+Jaipur 3 10 64½ 55½ 68 67¾ Cordero A Jr 115 *2.00 88-10 Cannon Shell 1152 ChanBalum1152BelieveTheQueen1153 In close 12
28May84- 8Bel fst 1 :44⅘ 1:08⅘ 1:34 3+Metrop'ltn H 7 6 43 33 38 48½ Venezia M 114 13.10 87-17 Fit to Fight 124hd A Phenomenon 1267¼ Moro 1161 Tired 10
10May84- 8Bel fst 7f :23 :45⅘ 1:21⅕ 3+Alw 33000 5 4 42½ 32½ 24½ 27½ Venezia M 119 6.90 88-17 Fit to Fight 1247½ Cozzene 1192 Mugatea 1191 Wide stretch 7
20Oct83- 8Med fst 1 1/16 :46⅗ 1:10⅖ 1:43⅘ Palisades H 5 5 43½ 32 21 2hd Cordero A Jr 113 7.10 90-16 Bet Big 114hd Cozzene 113½ Jacque's Tip 1191 Just missed 7
9Oct83- 8Bel fst 1 :46 1:09⅗ 1:34 Jamaica H 8 4 53 33½ 57½ 510½ Bailey J D 113 8.10 84-10 Bounding Basque 1151½ A Phenomenon 1203 Bet Big 1155¾ Tired 8
5Sep83- 7Bel fst 7f :22⅗ :45⅘ 1:24⅕ 3+Alw 27000 1 6 21½ 2½ 11 11½ Cordero A Jr 115 *1.00 81-20 Cozzene 1151½ Dave The Dude 1172 Ecstatic Pride 1131½ Driving 9
17Aug83- 9Sar fst 6f :22⅕ :45 1:09⅗ 3+Alw 20000 11 9 21½ 2½ 1hd 12½ Cordero A Jr 112 *1.60 92-11 Cozzene 1122½ Stop Card 1145¾ CagleSprings112hd Brushed,drvng 12
27Jly83- 7Sar fst 6f :21⅘ :44⅘ 1:10⅗ 3+Alw 20000 6 9 65½ 37 34 23½ Migliore R 111 *1.90 85-13 Big McCoy 1063½ Cozzene 1112 Spring Fever 113nk Raced wide 11
25May83- 6Bel fst 6f :22⅗ :46 1:11⅕ 3+Md Sp Wt 3 11 53½ 21½ 2hd 13 Migliore R 113 *4.10 86-16 Cozzene 1133 Gallant Minded 113¾ Big McCoy113no Slow st-clear 12
LATEST WORKOUTS Jun 18 Bel 4f fst :48⅘ b ●Jun 4 Bel 4f gd :47 h ●May 25 Bel 5f fst :59⅗ h ●May 5 Bel 4f my :45⅘ h

Castle Guard *

B. h. 5, by Slady Castle—Chompelle, by Champion
Br.—Colonial Farms (NJ)
Tr.—Wells Harry
Own.—Colonial Farm
117[5]
Lifetime 43 13 10 4 $335,710 | 1984 5 3 1 1 $80,179 | 1983 13 3 3 1 $90,608 | Turf 5 2 1 1 $81,025

9Jun84- 9Mth fm 1 ①:47⅗ 1:10⅗ 1:35⅘ 3+Red Bank H 1 5 59 52½ 1½ 12½ Ferrer J C 118 4.70 96-09 Castle Guard 1182½ Super Sunrise 1232 Fray Star117½ Drew clear 10
9Jun84-Run in divisions
2Jun84- 9Mth sly 1 1/16 :47⅗ 1:12⅕ 1:44⅗ 3+ⓈLincroft H 3 4 44½ 31½ 2hd 1nk McCauley W H 122 *1.00 83-21 Castle Guard 122nk Rumptious 1203 Clone 117hd Driving 5
19May84- 7Mth fst 6f :22 :45 1:09⅕ 3+ⓈAlw 18000 3 5 65½ 63½ 33 11 Ferrer J C5 110 3.10 94-16 Castle Guard 1101 Duke Mitchell 122¾ Rumptious 1153 Driving 6
5May84- 8Mth fst 170 :45⅗ 1:10⅗ 1:41⅗ 3+Alw 17000 1 4 48½ 46 35 2½ Antley C W5 110 *1.10 88-20 A Native Yank 117½ Castle Guard 110½ Rollodka 1157 Rallied 6
28Apr84- 9Mth fst 6f :22⅗ :45⅗ 1:11⅗ 3+ⓈBrookdale H 2 11 106¾ 812 67½ 31½ Ferrer J C 119 4.80e 81-22 AbstractThinker112hdDukeMitchell1181½CastleGuard119hd Rallied 12
27Oct83- 8Med fst 1⅛ :47 1:11 1:49⅗ 3+Paterson H 4 7 96 86¾ 97½ 712¾ Perret C 114 63.10 72-20 Slewpy 115nk Bounding Basque 1176 Vittorioso 114nk No menace 11
10Oct83- 9Med fm 1 1/16 ①:47⅕ 1:11⅗ 1:44⅘ 3+ⓈJky Hollow H 4 7 84¾ 53¾ 21 12 Perret C 123 2.70e 80-19 Castle Guard 1232 Al Hadea 116hd Nickles Worth112½ Drew clear 10
20Sep83- 8Med fst 1 1/16 :46⅗ 1:10⅘ 1:45⅕ 3+ⓈHandicap 2 5 510 66¾ 32½ 1hd McCauley W H 122 *.50e 83-16 Castle Guard 122hd Conservatoire 1181½ Duke Me 1191½ Driving 6
3Sep83- 6Mth fst 170 :45⅘ 1:10⅗ 1:41⅕ 3+Alw 22000 5 7 88¾ 64½ 54 2½ McCauley W H 119 5.60 89-17 Otter Slide 119½ Castle Guard 119nk Hail Emperor 1171 Gamely 8
20Aug83- 9Mth fst 1⅛ :46⅗ 1:10⅕ 1:47⅕ 3+Monmouth H 4 8 914 911 917 919½ McCauley W H 112 50.40 79-16 Bates Motel 1242½ Island Whirl 124nk Linkage 1152½ Outrun 9
LATEST WORKOUTS Jun 21 Mth 4f fst :47⅘ b Jun 16 Mth 6f fst 1:14⅗ b Jun 8 Mth 3f fst :37⅘ b Jun 1 Mth 3f my :36 b

Doris's Rival

Ch. g. 5, by Double Edge Sword—Red's Landing, by Solo Landing
Br.—Steinberg O Y (Md)
Tr.—Vranas Barbara E
Own.—Steinberg O
110[5]
Lifetime 30 5 5 7 $49,857 | 1984 9 2 1 4 $23,562 | 1983 17 2 3 3 $18,999 | Turf 2 0 0 0

15Jun84- 7Pen fst 1 1/16 :47⅘ 1:11⅕ 1:44 3+ⓇRotunda 2 3 32 1½ 32 36½ Pino M G b 115 6.30 80-19 MoneyByOrlns1125St.Christophr1151½Doris'sRivl1157½ Weakened 6
2Jun84- 7Mth sly 1 :46⅕ 1:11⅗ 1:37⅕ 3+Alw 19000 3 1 18 12 11 31¾ Antley C W5 b 110 6.30 85-21 Rava Ruler 1151½ Northern Best 115½ Doris'sRival1102 Weakened 6
25May84- 5Mth fst 6f :22⅘ :45⅕ 1:11⅗ 3+Alw 13000 1 6 31 3½ 1½ 1no Antley C W5 b 112 4.40 83-21 Doris's Rival 112no Fortunate Way 117nk Red Medal 1101 Driving 6
12May84- 3Mth fst 1 :46⅖ 1:11 1:37⅘ 3+Alw 13500 5 2 2hd 31 31 31½ Antley C W5 b 114 7.40 84-18 Gaylord'sCarousel1191½Perfected119hdDoris'sRivl1145 Weakened 6
4May84- 8Mth gd 6f :22⅘ :46 1:11⅗ 3+Alw 13000 2 5 54½ 42 3½ 21½ Antley C W5 b 111 19.10 81-27 Donna's Time 1071½ Doris's Rival 111¾ Old 'n Wise 1181½ Rallied 5
15Mar84- 7Pim gd 1 1/16 :46⅕ 1:11 1:44⅕ Clm 30000 2 4 46 33 32 32¾ Kupfer T b 119 5.00 81-18 Pol Luka 1171½ On Watch 1151½Doris'sRival119nk Shuffled bk, st. 6
6Feb84- 6Bow gd 1 1/16 :48⅘ 1:13⅘ 1:45⅗ Clm 23500 4 1 13½ 12½ 12½ 16½ Kupfer T b 114 4.20 79-31 Doris's Rival 1146½ Mister Rouge 1133½ Jack Jouett 1098 Driving 6
20Jan84- 5Bow fst 7f :23 :45⅘ 1:23 Alw 11000 1 6 52 54½ 58½ 43¾ Kupfer T b 114 28.30 83-21 Humbug I 1221½ Divine Le Bon 1081½ Forty Love 1151 Evenly 6
2Jan84- 4Bow fst 7f :22⅘ :44⅘ 1:21⅗ Alw 11000 3 5 56 56 66½ 54 Kupfer T b 114 26.60 91-05 Pat's Addition 122hd KeyToCalamity1141JollyOop1091¾ No factor 7
21Dec83- 7Bow fst 7f :23 :45⅘ 1:22⅕ 3+Alw 11500 1 9 2hd 31½ 57 67¾ Kupfer T b 114 26.00 86-15 Gang Racer 1122 Key To Calamity 1123 Jolly Oop 112¾ Tired 10
LATEST WORKOUTS Jun 9 Mth 5f fst 1:04 b May 22 Mth 5f fst 1:02 b Apr 28 Mth 5f fst 1:02⅘ b

*Domynsky

Ch. c. 4, by Dominion—My Therape, by Jimmy Reppin
Br.—Webster C A (Eng)
Tr.—Curtis William Jr
Own.—Dogwood Stable
115
Lifetime 29 7 9 2 $146,201 | 1984 7 0 1 0 $15,556 | 1983 12 2 3 2 $101,809 | Turf 27 7 9 2 $146,061

9Jun84- 7Mth fm 1 ①:46 1:11⅗ 1:36⅘ 3+Red Bank H 7 6 57 62¾ 53 43½ Bracciale V Jr 114 12.40 90-09 Tough Mickey 1181½ Fortnightly 117no Roman Bend 1082 Wide 9
9Jun84-Run in divisions
9Apr84- 9GP sf *1 ① 1:39⅕ Alw 20000 10 3 42½ 63¾ 75¾ 65¾ Solomone M 115 3.40 78-21 Tarheel Lad 1191½ Davis Joy 119½ Groszewski 1151½ Tired 10
21Mar84- 9GP fm 1 ①:46⅗ 1:10⅗ 1:35 3+Appleton H 6 4 4¾ 31 43½ 44½ Solomone M 114 7.70e 91-08 GreatSubstence113½Dr.Schwartzmn1093½RisingRj113nk Weakened 10
21Mar84-Run in divisions
6Mar84- 8Hia fm 1 1/16 ① 1:41 Alw 24000 1 1 2hd 2hd 2hd 73½ Cruguet J 116 4.80 89-07 The Cerfer 119no Glory O. So 1141½ Persian Poet 113nk Tired 9
11Feb84- 6Hia fm 1 1/16 ① 1:41⅗ Alw 20000 10 5 53 42½ 41½ 58¾ Cruguet J 116 *1.50 82-08 Guston 1134½ Senior Citizen II 1192 Diverse Dude 1131½ Evenly 11
3Feb84- 9Hia fm *1 1/16 ① 1:40⅘ Alw 20000 8 9 86¾ 56 54½ 52½ Cruguet J 116 *1.10 92-07 GreatSubstence1191PrinceWestport113nkRisingRaj1141 Mild rally 12
21Jan84-10Hia fm 1 1/16 ① 1:42 3+Royal Palm H 3 2 2½ 12½ 2hd 21½ Cruguet J 115 4.90 87-13 Erin's Tiger 1161½ Domynsky 1154 Fort Guard 113¾ Gamely 11
21Jan84-Run in divisions
29Sep83- 8Med fm 1⅜ ①:48⅘ 1:38⅕ 2:14⅗ Rutgers H 8 4 46 1hd 31 65½ Brumfield D 116 6.40 86-11 Exile King 1132 Moon Spirit 1161 Fortnightly 118no Tired 9
29Sep83-Run in two divisions 6th & 8th races
LATEST WORKOUTS Jun 18 Mth 5f gd 1:03 b Jun 5 Mth 5f fst :59⅘ h ●May 29 Mth 7f my 1:28 b (d) May 23 Mth 4f fst :48⅘ b

Rava Ruler — Gr. g. 5, by Iron Ruler—Ravolia, by Noble Jay
Own.—Mamone R — Br.—Gilman Paper Co (Fla) — Tr.—Vincitore Michael — **122**
Lifetime 32 7 3 1 $61,047 — 1984 9 3 0 0 $29,490 — 1983 16 3 2 1 $27,622 — Turf 5 0 1 0 $3,820

9Jun84- 7Mth fm 1 ①:48 1:11⅗ 1:36⅗ 3↑Red Bank H 5 5 8¹⁰ 9⁸½ 7⁶ 8⁷ Thornburg B b 114 12.60 86-09 Tough Mickey 118¹½ Fortnightly 117no RomanBend108² Far back 9
9Jun84-Run in divisions
2Jun84- 7Mth sly 1 :46⅕ 1:11⅘ 1:37⅘ 3↑Alw 19000 4 2 2⁸ 2² 2¹ 1¹½ Thornburg B b 115 4.40 87-21 Rava Ruler 115¹½ Northern Best 115¾ Doris'sRival110² Drew clear 6
24May84- 7Mth fst 1 1/16 :47⅕ 1:12 1:44⅕ 3↑Alw 14500 1 2 2² 2^hd 1¹½ 1¹¾ Antley C W5 b 112 5.50 84-21 Rava Ruler 112¹¾ Late To Rise115¾RainbowCastle107⁸ Drew clear 6
14May84- 5Mth fst 6f :23 :46⅘ 1:12 3↑Alw 13000 1 6 6⁵½ 5⁴ 4⁴ 2^nk Ferrer J C5 b 112 11.00 80-26 ⓓLate To Rise 117^nk Rava Ruler112½Dependence119² Fin. strong 6
14May84-Placed first through disqualification
24Mar84- 6GP fst 7f :22⅘ :45⅕ 1:21⅘ Clm 50000 8 7 6²¾ 7⁴¾ 7¹² 8¹⁰½ Verge M E b 117 14.10 85-10 Northern Ocean 113¹½ Bag O'Bucks 117¾ Groszewski 117¹ Outrun 9
23Feb84- 7Hia fst 1 1/16 :46 1:10⅗ 1:41⅘ Alw 20000 8 6 6³ 6⁵ 5⁸½ 5⁹¾ Verge M E b 116 29.30 84-16 PurelyPlesure116¹½RedyToProve116¾SuperbMissile119⁷ No actor 9
14Feb84- 9Hia fst 1 1/16 :46⅕ 1:10⅗ 1:42⅗ Alw 18000 7 4 4³ 3⁵ 3⁵ 4⁶ Verge M E 116 14.50 85-16 Rising Raja 116¹ Cut Away 116⁴ Judge MyBudget111¹ Weakened 8
27Jan84- 8Hia fst 7f :23 :45⅗ 1:23 Alw 18000 10 5 9⁵½ 9⁷ 9¹¹ 9¹⁵½ Verge M E 116 19.20 72-22 Computer's Choice 116⁹ Garrigan116^nk EcstaticPride116⁴½ Outrun 10
18Jan84- 8Hia fm *1 1/16 ① 1:42⅘ Alw 18000 10 2 2¹ 2½ 6² 8⁴¾ Verge M E 116 19.60 81-14 The Cerfer 116¹ Cut Away 116¾ Sing One Song 116^hd Checked 11
19Dec83- 6Med fst 6f :22⅘ :46 1:10⅕ 3↑Alw 15000 5 7 7⁷¾ 5³½ 6⁵½ 5⁵½ Verge M E 116 4.70 87-11 B. J.'s Pleasure 109¹½Newsprobe116^noTahawas116^nk Lacked a bid 7
LATEST WORKOUTS May 5 Mth 4f my :50⅘ b

A few days after this race, I decided to ask Jan Nerud himself about Cozzene. What I learned was quite interesting.

I first asked Nerud why he hadn't tried Cozzene on the grass as a three-year-old. The answer proved quite logical. During the 1983 season, Tartan had an abundance of grass runners and grass prospects. Adding Cozzene to that list would have created scheduling conflicts. Cozzene would have been eligible for the same races as several of his stablemates. Since he was running well on the dirt anyway, Nerud decided to keep him there.

I next asked Nerud why he ran Cozzene in the six-furlong contest on Belmont Day. His answer was disturbing, simply because it involved information that was unavailable to the majority of players. Cozzene had suffered a mild setback shortly after the Metropolitan, missed a little training, and needed a tightener for future engagements. He might well have been 20–1 for that race had the public shared in this information.

Finally, I asked Nerud why he had chosen the Jersey race for Cozzene's grass debut. Did the horse need Lasix, which was per-

EIGHTH RACE
Monmouth
JUNE 23, 1984

1 1/16 MILES.(Turf). (1.42⅕) ALLOWANCE. Purse $19,000. 3-year-olds and upward which have not won $8,405 two times on the turf since July 10, 1983 other than maiden, claiming, starter or state bred. Weights, 3-year-olds, 113 lbs. Older, 122 lbs. Non-winners of $9,800 since May 18, allowed 3 lbs. $8,100 twice in 1984, 5 lbs. $8,100 in 1984, 7 lbs. (Maiden, claiming and starter races not considered)

Value of race $19,000, value to winner $11,400, second $3,800, third $2,090, fourth $1,140, fifth $570. Mutuel pool $111,297. Exacta Pool $109,652.

Last Raced	Horse	Eqt.A.Wt	PP	St	¼	½	¾	Str	Fin	Jockey	Odds $1
9Jun84 6Bel6	Cozzene	4 115	3	4	4½	4hd	4½	3¹½	1³	Swatuk B	a-2.70
14May84 8Bel4	Wild Again	4 119	2	2	2¹	2½	2²	1hd	2²	Perret C	2.40
9Jun84 9Mth1	Castle Guard	5 117	4	6	6	6	3hd	4⁶	3²	Ferrer J C5	.80
2Jun84 8Bel3	Eskimo	4 108	1	1	1hd	1hd	1½	2½	4⁶	Vega H7	a-2.70
15Jun84 7Pen3	Doris's Rival	b 5 110	5	5	5²	3½	5²½	5¹½	5¹	Antley C W5	24.70
9Jun84 7Mth8	Rava Ruler	b 5 122	6	3	3¹	5hd	6	6	6	Thornburg B	16.50

a-Coupled: Cozzene and Eskimo.

OFF AT 4:56. Start good, Won driving. Time, :23⅘, :47⅘, 1:11, 1:34⅘, 1:41 Course firm.

New Course Record

$2 Mutuel Prices:				
	1-COZZENE (a-entry)	7.40	3.60	2.20
	2-WILD AGAIN		3.60	2.20
	3-CASTLE GUARD			2.10

$2 EXACTA 1-2 PAID $21.00.

Gr. c, by Caro—Ride The Trails, by Prince John. Trainer Nerud Jan H. Bred by Nerud J A (Fla).

COZZENE, close up while saving ground, moved closer along the inside before a half, got through along the inside in midstretch to challenge and proved best under pressure. WILD AGAIN contested the pace outside ESKIMO and held on gamely. CASTLE GUARD, within striking distance early, raced three wide through the second turn then lacked a solid closing bid. ESKIMO vied for the lead while saving ground and tired. DORIS'S RIVAL, a forward factor while wide, tired. RAVA RULER tired from his early efforts.

missible medication at the shore oval? Again, Nerud's answer was reasonable but beyond the scope of the average player's information network. Nerud was pointing Cozzene for the United Nations Handicap at Atlantic City on July 4. He planned to prep Cozzene in a grass event at Belmont, but that race failed to fill. To make the Atlantic City race, Nerud was forced to look out of town and was fortunate to find the race at Monmouth on June 23.

Nerud concluded our conversation by telling me that he considered Cozzene to be the stable's major grass hope for 1984. He was half right, anyhow. Who's For Dinner, who ran coupled with Cozzene in the United Nations, was also to have a fine season in 1984. The Tartan entry finished second-third, separated by a nose, in the United Nations, behind Hero's Honor, the leading grass runner in the country at that stage of the 1984 season. The Hero's Honor-

EIGHTH RACE
Atlantic City
JULY 14, 1984

1 $\frac{3}{16}$ MILES.(Turf). (1.52⅘) 32nd Running THE UNITED NATIONS HANDICAP (Grade I). Purse $150,000 Guaranteed. (Plus $30,000 Breeders' Cup Prize Awards). 3-year-olds and upward. By subscription of $175 for each nomination on or before Monday, April 2, 1984 or $350 for each nomination made on or before Tuesday, June 12, 1984 or by supplementary nomination of $7,500 each by Wednesday, July 4, 1984. Fee to accompany the nomination, $750 to pass the entry box, $750 to start with $90,000 guaranteed the winner, $30,000 to second, $16,500 to third, $9,000 to fourth and $4,500 to fifth. Weights, Friday, July 6, 1984. The Atlantic City Racing Association reserves the right to assign or re-assign weight to any horse after the weights have been released. Starters to be named through the entry box by Thursday, July 12, 1984 (48 hour closing in effect.) $30,000 Breeders' Cup Prize Awards to be divided 54%, 27% and 9% to the owner of the first second and third horses provided they are nominated to the Breeders Cup. This event will not be divided, the field will be limited to 14 starters with three also eligibles. High weights on the scale preferred. Special "Early Bird" closing Monday, April 2, 1984 with 58 nominations. Late closing Tuesday, June 12, 1984 with 86 nominations. Supplementary nominations of $7,500 by Wednesday, July 4, 1984. Bredders' Cup Fund Awards to Hero's Honor, Cozzene and Who's For Dinner.
Total purse $180,000. Value of race $177,000, value to winner $106,200, second $38,100, third $19,200, fourth $9,000, fifth $4,500. Nominator Awards $3,000. Mutuel pool $125,550. Exacta Pool $92,115.

Last Raced	Horse	Eqt.A.Wt	PP	St	¼	½	¾	Str	Fin	Jockey	Odds $1
17Jun84 ^{8}Bel^{1}	Hero's Honor	b 4 123	5	3	2^{1}	1^{hd}	1^{hd}	$1^{3\frac{1}{2}}$	$1^{1\frac{1}{2}}$	Bailey J D	1.10
23Jun84 ^{8}Mth^{1}	Cozzene	4 114	8	5	4^{2}	4^{2}	3^{hd}	2^{1}	2no	Venezia M	a-9.70
7Jly84 ^{9}Mth^{8}	Who's For Dinner	b 5 110	10	2	1^{hd}	2^{2}	2^{1}	3^{hd}	3^{hd}	Swatuk B	a-9.70
11Dec83 ^{8}Hol^{8}	Majesty's Prince	5 125	4	4	6^{1}	5^{1}	5^{hd}	4^{1}	$4^{1\frac{1}{2}}$	Maple E	7.70
9Jun84 ^{9}Bel^{1}	Val Danseur	b 4 115	11	6	$3^{\frac{1}{2}}$	3^{hd}	4^{hd}	5^{2}	5^{nk}	Cordero A Jr	2.60
17Jun84 ^{8}Bel^{3}	Super Sunrise	b 5 121	7	9	11	11	10^{2}	7^{hd}	6^{2}	Perret C	7.10
1Jly84 ^{9}WO^{1}	Norwick	5 114	6	7	7^{hd}	9^{1}	8^{hd}	8^{hd}	7no	Davis R G	63.00
30Jun84 ^{9}Atl^{1}	Cost Control	5 114	1	1	9^{2}	7^{hd}	$7^{2\frac{1}{2}}$	6^{hd}	8^{1}	Velasquez J	10.50
9Jun84 ^{7}Mth^{3}	Roman Bend	b 4 107	3	10	5^{hd}	8^{1}	$6^{1\frac{1}{2}}$	9^{3}	$9^{2\frac{1}{2}}$	Antley C W	141.40
1Jly84 ^{8}Bel^{3}	Four Bases	b 5 112	9	8	10^{1}	10^{4}	$9^{\frac{1}{2}}$	10^{6}	10^{6}	Guerra W A	83.10
30Jun84 ^{9}Atl^{3}	Mucho Frio	4 111	2	11	8^{1}	6^{hd}	11	11	11	Landicini C Jr	222.20

a-Coupled: Cozzene and Who's For Dinner.

OFF AT 10:50 Start good, Won driving. Time, :24⅕, :48⅕, 1:11⅘, 1:35⅖, 1:54 Course firm.

$2 Mutuel Prices:				
	6-HERO'S HONOR	4.20	3.20	2.80
	1-COZZENE (a-entry)		6.20	9.20
	1-WHO'S FOR DINNER (a-entry)		6.20	9.20
	$2 EXACTA 6-1 PAID $34.80.			

B. c, by Northern Dancer—Glowing Tribute, by Graustark. Trainer Miller Mack. Bred by Mellon P (Va).

HERO'S HONOR, dueled for the early lead with WHO'S FOR DINNER while just off the inner rail, assumed command leaving the backstretch, made the pace off the rail into the stretch and was kept under lef-handed punishment while fully extended in the end. COZZENE, a forward factor off the rail, made a run along the inside on the final turn, continued on boldly and gamely held on for the pace. WHO'S FOR DINNER, failed to sustain his bid while prominent along the inner rail. MAJESTY'S PRINCE, reserved just off the leaders, made his run outside of rivals on the final turn, continued off the rail int he stretch lacking a strong finishing bid. VAL DANSEUR, showed good footing off the rail for six furlongs then steadily dropped back. SUPER SUNRISE, was outrun racing off the rail. COST CONTROL had no excuse.

Cozzene exacta, a logical saver for Cozzene backers, paid a generous $34.80. Exotics always seem to pay so well at the Jersey ovals!

We conclude by noting that Cozzene went on to win the Cliff Hanger Handicap on the grass in 1984, to place in several other major grass events, and finally to run third in the Breeders' Cup Mile (on the grass). The following season he won the Breeders' Cup Mile, his season-long objective.

Chapter 18

International Racing and the American Turf

IF NOTHING ELSE, the Breeders' Cup races have forced American handicappers to come to grips with the international racing scene. Although foreign runners have been competing in our grass stakes for years, the vast majority of American players—particularly those outside the New York and Los Angeles areas—have only a nodding acquaintance with European form.

The information that finds its way into the *Daily Racing Form* from the publication's continental counterparts is sketchy and well below American standards. Running lines are absent. The European pecking order, if such a thing exists, is hard to decipher solely from the company lines in the past performances. Quite simply, the player needs another source of information. And although the *Form*'s weekly reports from its foreign correspondents may be sufficient for some, many others prefer the coverage offered in either of the sport's weekly magazines, *The Thoroughbred Record* and *The Bloodhorse*.

To place the international scene in proper perspective, we must start at the ultimate source, the annual yearling sales held at Keeneland and Saratoga. If American racing—particularly turf racing—seems to have gone downhill during the past five years, there is good reason. A vast majority of the more fashionably bred yearlings—especially those bred to race on grass—are being sold to foreign interests. If the Englishman Robert Sangster doesn't make the final bid, then one of the Arab sheikhs will probably sign for the horse. The cream of each American yearling crop offered at public auction seems destined for the grass courses of Europe. For this reason, European grass form rates a notch or two above ours, and when these expatriates return to their native land, they often find the pickings easy. At least initially, anyway. After a few weeks in this country, many imports suffer through a period of "reverse acclimatization" during which they perform below their peak level, if they are able to race at all. But for that first race off the plane, horses considered to be only Group II or Group III in Europe are able to compete on a par with our best Grade I performers.

In this chapter we will look at the two Breeders' Cup II grass races, run at Aqueduct November 2, 1985. We will supplement our own comments with quotes from articles appearing in *The Thoroughbred Record* during the 1985 racing season, our point being, of course, that one's understanding of the European scene can be significantly enhanced by the information contained in these reports.

First let's look at the $2,000,000 Breeders' Cup Turf and start with Pebbles, the race favorite and the ultimate winner. Then we'll take the rest of the field in post-position order:

PEBBLES

Based on her two most recent races (between which she had been seriously ill), Pebbles must be regarded as the "Queen of the European Turf," certainly the leading European runner still in training. Indeed, Pebbles was now considered another in a long line of great European fillies. Her recent victory in the Dubai Champion Stakes at Newmarket was accomplished with consummate ease over a stellar field:

> Steve Cauthen took Slip Anchor into the lead from the start, pressed on his outside by Commanche Run, with Supreme Leader and Palace Music also prominent. Pebbles, meanwhile, was out back, last of the ten, and hanging left, as Pat Eddery gave her time to find her stride and settle into her rhythm.
>
> Eddery, who had never ridden the filly in a race before, never hustled her, while Cauthen up front had no option but to force the pace on Slip Anchor, harried all the while as he was by Commanche Run. With seven of the ten furlongs behind them, Cauthen had achieved his first and, it must have seemed, his major objective. Piggott was applying pressure, and Commanche Run was finding nothing. But by now Pebbles was collected and cantering, switching in towards the rail, picking off rivals nonchalantly.
>
> It was already apparent that Pebbles could take care of Slip Anchor and Commanche Run at any time Eddery chose, but the

6 AQUEDUCT

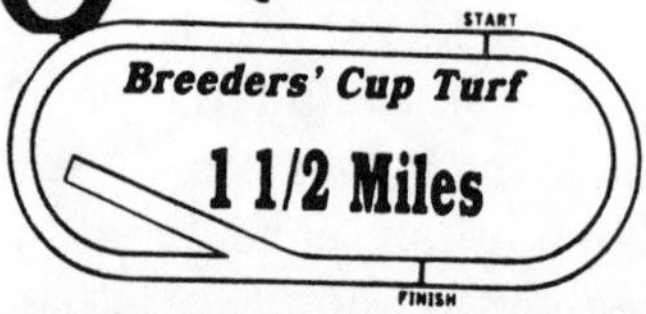

1 ½ MILES. (Turf). (2.28⅕) 2nd Running THE BREEDERS' CUP TURF (Grade I). Purse $2,000,000. 3-year-olds and upward. Weights, 3-year-olds, 122 lbs. 4-year-olds and older, 126 lbs. Fillies and Mares allowed 3 lbs. Value of race $2,000,000. Value to winner $900,000, second $450,000, third $216,000, fourth $140,000, fifth $100,000, sixth $20,000. Nominator Awards: Stallion, winner $50,000, second $25,000, third $12,000; Foal, winner $50,000 second, $25,000, third $12,000. Stallion awards will be paid only to the nominators of fully eligible stallions. Owners who supplement horses to Breeders' Cup Day races will be eligible for the Foal Nominator's Award in the case of a 12 per cent supplementary nomination or both the Foal Nominator's Award and the Stallion Nominator's Award in the case of a 20 per cent supplementary nomination. In accordance with the Breeders' Cup/European Breeders' Fund cross-registration agreement, nominator's awards will not be paid to horses eligible through E.B.F. All unpaid nominator's awards will remain the property of Breeders' Cup Limited. Supplementary nominee: GREINTON and PEBBLES

Coupled—Strawberry Road II, Bob Back and Theatrical; Shernazar and Lashkari.

***Strawberry Road II** — B. h. 6, by Whiskey Road—Giftisa, by Rich Gift
Br.—Pantos J (Aus)
Own.—Wildenstein D — Tr.—Biancone Patrick L — **126**
Lifetime 37 16 4 5 $1,051,327 — 1985 4 2 0 1 $217,380 — 1984 11 1 1 2 $244,500 — Turf 37 16 4 5 $1,051,327

21Sep85- 8Bel fm 1½ ⓣ:48⅘ 2:01⅕ 2:25⅘ 3+Trf Classic 8 5 57½ 54 42½ 35¼ Saint-Martin Y 126 3.20e 92-07 Noble Fighter 1193¼ Win 1261¾StrawberryRoadII126hd Came over 12
21Sep85-Grade I
27Jly85♦3Ascot(Eng) fm 1½ 2:27⅗ ⓣ KingGeoVI&QnElizStk(Gr1) 64 StMartin Y 133 12.00 — — Petoski 120nk Oh So Sharp 117½ Rainbow Quest1331½ Stride late 12
7Jly85♦5StCloud(Fra) gd*1⅝ 2:34⅖ ⓣ GrandPrix deStCloud(Gr1) 1nk StMartin Y 134 *.60 — — StrwberryRod134nk SeismicWve1311½ Treiziem1311½ Bid,led,held 7
8Apr85♦5Longchamp(Fra) sf*1¼ 2:18 ⓣ Prix d'Harcourt(Gr.2) 14 StMartin Y 130 *1.10 — — Strawberry Road 1304 Green Paradise1262½ Romildo1301½ Easily 7
25Nov84♦10Tokyo(Japan) fm*1½ 2:26⅕ ⓣ Japan Cup(Gr.1) 74½ Piggott L 126 9.50 — — KatsuragiAce1261½ Bedtime126hd SymboliRudolf121no No threat 14
10Nov84- 6Hol fm 1½ ⓣ:46⅘ 2:01⅘ 2:25⅘ 3+Br Cp Turf 3 1 11 2½ 21 41¾ Shoemaker W 126 5.20 93-01 Lashkari 122nk All Along 123½ Raami 122½ Weakened 11
10Nov84-Grade I
20Oct84- 8Lrl fm 1½ ⓣ:47⅘ 2:02⅘ 2:27⅘ 3+D C Intrnl 9 6 613 87¾ 75½ 33¼ Moore G 127 4.70 79-17 SettleSong1203PrsinTr124½StrwbrryRodII127nk Checked 3/8's pl 11
20Oct84-Grade I
7Oct84♦4Longchamp(Fra) sf*1½ 2:39 ⓣ Arc de Triomphe(Gr.1) 59 Starkey G 130 10.60 — — Sagace 1302 NorthernTrick 1206 AllAlong 127¾ Prom,led,wknd 22
2Sep84♦5BadenBaden(Ger) gd*1½ 2:29⅘ ⓣ GroserPreis vonBaden(Gr1) 1hd Thomson B 132 2.60 — — StrawberryRoad132hd EspritdeNord132½ Abry1324 Prom,led,held 8
24Aug84♦5BadenBaden(Ger) gd*1 1:39⅕ ⓣ Oettingen Rennen(Gr.3) 2no Heloury J 132 6.60 — — Hoyer 119no StrawberryRoad 1322½ Finian'sRainbow 1121 Cl,well 10
LATEST WORKOUTS Oct 31 Bel 5f fst 1:04 b Sep 19 Bel Ⓣ 6f fm 1:19 b (d)

Bob Back — Dk. b. or br. c. 4, by Roberto—Toter Back, by Carry Back
Br.—Allen J (Ky)
Own.—McNall B P — Tr.—Penna Angel — **126**
Lifetime 21 5 3 5 $343,905 — 1985 8 2 2 2 $268,385 — 1984 10 1 1 3 $46,459 — Turf 21 5 3 2 $343,905

12Oct85- 8Bel fm 1⅜ ⓣ:48⅕ 1:37⅘ 2:15⅘ 3+Man O War 1 6 83¾ 54½ 2½ 2nk Cordero A Jr 126 5.00 85-25 Win 126nk Bob Back 1262½ Baillamont 1211½ Brushed in dr 8
12Oct85-Grade I
8Sep85♦4PhoenixPk(Ire) sf*1¼ 2:09⅘ ⓣ PhoenixChampionStks(Gr1) 23 Raymond B 132 50.00 — — Commanche Run 1323 Bob Back 132¾ Damister 123no Fin,well 11
20Aug85♦3York(Eng) gd 1⅝ 2:18⅘ ⓣ Benson&HedgesGoldCup(Gr1) 612 Raymond B 132 18.00 — — Commanche Run 132¾ Oh So Sharp 1194 Triptych 1195 Prom 7f 6
6Jly85♦3Sandown(Eng) gd 1¼ 2:07⅕ ⓣ Coral-EclipseStakes(Gr.1) 33½ Raymond B 133 9.00 — — Pebbles 1302 RainbowQuest 1331½ BobBack 13320 Evenly 4
18Jun85♦2Ascot(Eng) gd 1¼ 2:05⅘ ⓣ Prince of WalesStake(Gr2) 11½ Raymond B 133 33.00 — — BobBck1331½ Pebbles130no CommncheRun13312 Trailed, up late 4
26May85♦6Rome(Italy) sf*1¼ 2:00⅘ ⓣ PrPresidente d'Rep(Gr1) 12½ Raymond B 132 *1.60 — — Bob Back 1322½ Reco 1182½ Dreyer 1182 Well pl,dr,clear 8
11May85♦5Evry(Fra) gd*1½ 2:30⅗ ⓣ GrandPrix d'Evry(Gr2) 713 Raymond B 121 5.75 — — Long Mick 121hd Palace Panther 1212½ Welnor 1302 Prom to str 9
27Apr85♦3Sandown(Eng) gd 1¼ 2:07⅘ ⓣ Westbury Stakes(Gr3) 3¾ Raymond B 120 11.00 — — Elegant Air 120½ Parliament 120hd Bob Back 120½ Closed well 12
11Nov84♦5Rome(Italy) sf*1⅜ 3:03 ⓣ Premio Roma(Gr.1) 55 Raymond B 121 5.00 — — ⒹOpale 1221 Yawa 1262 Alan Ford 126no Raced evenly 10
LATEST WORKOUTS Oct 31 Bel 4f fst :48⅘ b Oct 25 Bel Ⓣ 1 fm 1:46⅘ b (d) Oct 20 Bel Ⓣ 5f fm 1:00⅘ h Oct 10 Bel ⓣ 4f gd :52 b (d)

***Shernazar** — B. c. 4, by Busted—Sharmeen, by Val de Loir
Br.—H H Aga Khan (Ire)
Own.—H H Aga Khan — Tr.—Stoute Michael R — **126**
Lifetime 11 5 3 0 $92,356 — 1985 4 3 0 0 $73,052 — 1984 6 2 2 0 $18,406 — Turf 11 5 3 0 $92,356

6Oct85♦4Longchamp(Fra) gd*1½ 2:29⅘ ⓣ Arc de Triomphe(Gr1) 12 Swinburn W R 130 2.75e — — ⒹSagace130nk RainbowQuest1302 Kozana120nk Impeded entr str 15
6Sep85♦4Kempton(Eng) gd*1⅜ 2:16⅕ ⓣ September Stakes(Gr3) 1½ Swinburn W R 128 4.00 — — Shernazar128½ SlipAnchor12315 SupremeLeder1166 Well up,drvg 5
17Aug85♦4Newbury(Eng) gd*1⅜ 2:57 ⓣ Geoffrey Frer Stakes(Gr2) 12½ Swinburn W R 126 *.60 — — Shernazar 1262½ Spicy Story 1262 St Hilarion 11312 Led fnl 2f 5
2Aug85♦4Goodwood(Eng) gd 1½ 2:42⅘ ⓣ Alycidon Stakes 11½ Swinburn W R 127 10.00 — — Shernazar 1271½ Shardari 11410 Royal Coach 117½ Bid,handily 9
15Sep84♦4Doncaster(Eng) gd*1⅞ 3:09⅘ ⓣ St.Leger Stakes(Gr.1) 52 Swinburn W R 126 20.00 — — CommnchRun126nk Bynoun126½ Alphbtim126nk Bid then evenly 11
22Aug84♦4York(Eng) gd 1½ 2:28⅘ ⓣ GreatVoltigeurStakes(Gr2) 44½ Swinburn W R 119 8.50 — — RinbowQust1193 GoldAndIvory1191½ HdForHights123no Prom,led 7
31Jly84♦4Goodwood(Eng) gd 1½ 2:32⅘ ⓣ Gordon Stakes(Gr.3) 25 Swinburn W R 122 9.00 — — Commanche Run 1225 Shernazar 1228 GoldandIvory1226 Fin,well 8
4Jly84♦5Yarmouth(Eng) fm 1⅜ 3:04⅘ ⓣ Martham Stakes 14 Swinburn W R 135 *.80 — — Shernazar 1354 Geovale 1351 Vornorco 132½ Well pl,easily 6
14Jun84♦6Newbury(Eng) gd*1⅜ 2:53⅘ ⓣ Childrey Stakes(Mdn) 1½ Swinburn W R 126 *1.25 — — Shernazar 126½ Rhusted 1264 Ash Fair 1214 Bid,led fnl 3f 20
28May84♦6Doncaster(Eng) gd 1½ 2:40⅘ ⓣ Stand Stakes(Mdn) 27 Kimberley A 126 4.50 — — Commanche Run 1267 Shernazar1264 Bespoke126½ Prom thruout 17
LATEST WORKOUTS Oct 31 Aqu ⓣ 3f fm :38⅘ b

***Greinton** — B. c. 4, by Green Dancer—Crystal Queen, by High Top
Br.—Niarchos S (Eng)
Own.—Bradley Mary Jones — Tr.—Whittingham Charles — **126**
Lifetime 19 9 7 0 $1,210,730 — 1985 11 3 6 0 $1,061,900 — 1984 5 4 1 0 $127,873 — Turf 10 6 3 0 $388,830

5Oct85- 8Bel my 1½ :49⅘ 2:03 2:27 3+J C Gld Cup 3 4 31 54 615 724¼ Pincay L Jr 126 2.30 61-19 Vanlandingham 1262¼ Gate Dancer1267¼CremeFraiche1212¼ Tired 7
5Oct85-Grade I
14Sep85- 8Bel fst 1¼ :47 1:36⅕ 2:01⅕ 3+Marlboro H 1 2 31½ 52¾ 42 41 Pincay L Jr 122 *1.70 91-09 Chief'sCrown119nkGateDancer125¾Vanlandingham122hd Steadied 9
14Sep85-Grade I
25Aug85- 6AP yl 1¼ ⓣ:47⅗ 1:39⅘ 2:03⅘ 3+Bud Arl Mil 8 8 87¼ 66¼ 36 2¾ Pincay L Jr 126 *1.80e 76-27 Teleprompter 126¾ Greinton 1263¼ Flying Pidgeon 1261½ Gaining 13
25Aug85-Grade I
22Jly85- 8Hol fm 1½ ⓣ:50⅕ 2:02⅘ 2:25⅘ 3+Sunset H 3 3 31¼ 21 2½ 2hd Pincay L Jr 122 *.40 91-11 Kings Island 116hd Greinton 1221½ Val Danseur 114½ Just missed 5
22Jly85-Grade I
23Jun85- 8Hol fst 1¼ :46⅕ 1:34⅘ 1:58⅘ 3+Gold Cup H 4 4 22½ 22 2hd 11¾ Pincay L Jr 120 1.20 120 — Greinton 1201¾ Precisionist 1251½ Kings Island 1125 Driving 6
23Jun85-Grade I
9Jun85-10Hol fst 1 :45 1:08⅘ 1:32⅘ 3+Californian 1 4 35½ 33 11½ 12¾ Pincay L Jr 119 2.80 110-02 Greinton 1192¾ Precisionist 1263¼ Lord At War 1261½ Driving 4
9Jun85-Grade I
19May85- 8Hol fst 1 :44⅘ 1:08⅘ 1:32⅘ 3+Mrvn Lry H 1 5 53½ 33¼ 24 24 Pincay L Jr 121 2.70 105-08 Precisionist 1264 Greinton 1211 My Habitony 1151½ 2nd best 5
19May85-Grade II
13Apr85- 8SA fst 1⅛ :45 1:09 1:47 Sn Brndno H 4 4 45¼ 45¼ 2½ 1nk Pincay L Jr 120 *.80e 94-13 Greinton 120nk Precisionist 127hd Al Mamoon 11510 Driving 6
13Apr85-Grade II
3Mar85- 8SA fst 1¼ :45⅘ 1:34⅘ 2:00⅘ S. Anita H 1 3 35½ 32 22½ 21¾ McCarron C J 120 2.80 84-14 Lord At War 1251¾ Greinton 1201 Gate Dancer 1251½ Gamely 7
3Mar85-Grade I
3Feb85- 8SA fst 1¼ :45⅘ 1:34⅘ 2:00⅘ C H Strub 4 4 45¼ 2½ 2hd 2no Shoemaker W 117 4.30 88-12 Precisionist 125no Greinton 117½ Gate Dancer 12616 Just missed 5
3Feb85-Grade I
LATEST WORKOUTS Oct 29 Aqu ⓣ 5f fm 1:02 h (d) Oct 24 Aqu 1 fst 1:40⅕ b Oct 18 Bel 6f fst 1:13⅕ b Oct 12 Bel 3f fst :36⅕ b

Danger's Hour — Ch. c. 3, by Coastal—Lively Living, by Key to the Mint
Br.—Mellon P (Va)
Own.—Rokeby Stable — Tr.—Miller Mack — **122**
Lifetime 17 7 1 2 $447,020 — 1985 10 5 1 2 $389,087 — 1984 7 2 0 0 $57,933 — Turf 12 6 1 2 $364,937

18Oct85- 8Medfm 1⅜ ⓣ:47⅕ 1:36 2:13⅕ Rutgers H 9 8 96¾ 41½ 1hd 11¼ MacBeth D b 124 2.80 99-10 Dnger'sHour1241½SlewTheDrgon117½Divulg1163½ Lugged in, clear 12
18Oct85-Grade II
5Oct85- 6Bel my 1½ :48⅘ 2:02 2:30⅘ Law'c Realz 2 3 43 13 16 14¾ Bailey J D b 123 *1.00 68-19 Danger'sHour1234¾SilentSlander1143RegIDiplomt114¾ Easy score 5
5Oct85-Grade II; Run in Divisions
22Sep85- 7Pen fm 1⅛ ⓣ 1:39⅘ 3+Pa Gov Cp H 1 4 43 31¼ 14 16 Bailey J D b 116 *.70 92-13 Danger's Hour 1166 Arrowood Dream1122LittleLook1091½ Driving 7
22Sep85-Grade III
25Aug85- 5AP yl 1⅛ Ⓣ:48⅕ 1:12⅘ 1:44⅘ 3+Newmarket H 6 7 56¼ 23¼ 23 26¼ Bailey J D 114 3.70 72-27 Pass The Line 1156¼ Danger's Hour114¾BestOfBoth116¼ 2nd best 9
11Aug85- 8Sar fm 1⅛ ⓣ:47⅕ 1:10⅘ 1:47 3+B Baruch H 7 6 66 54¼ 44 45¼ Bailey J D 119 4.40 86-13 Win 124nk Cozzene 1204¼ Sitzmark 112¾ Mild rally 9
11Aug85-Grade II
13Jly85- 8Bel hd 1¼ Ⓣ:49⅕ 1:36⅘ 2:00⅘ Lexington 12 7 62¾ 2½ 1hd 11¼ Bailey J D 123 3.60 92-08 Dnger'sHour1231¼FoundtionPln123hdExclusivePrtner1142¾ Drivig 14
13Jly85-Grade II
22Jun85- 8Bel fm 1⅛ ⓣ:46⅘ 1:10⅘ 1:40⅘ Hill Prince 10 8 95¼ 64¼ 32 12 MacBeth D 119 6.40e 93-11 Dngr'sHor1192FondtnPln119¾ExclsvPrtnr1144 Lacked room,clear 13
22Jun85-Grade III
9Jun85- 4Bel sf 1 ⓣ:46⅘ 1:12⅘ 1:39⅘ 3+Alw 29000 10 5 41¾ 22¼ 33 54¾ Bailey J D 112 *2.00 62-41 Judge Costa1172¼QuickWork117¾TenderSovereign117½ Weakened 11
22May85- 8Bel sf 1 ⓣ:46⅘ 1:12⅘ 1:39 Saranac 6 7 74¾ 83¾ 54¼ 35¾ Guerra W A 114 16.60 64-30 Equalize 114¾ Verification 1143 Danger's Hour 114¾ Blocked 9
22May85-Grade II
8May85- 7Bel fm 7f ⓣ:23 :46 1:24 Alw 36000 2 5 33¼ 32 23 32¾ Bailey J D 122 7.10 81-23 Herat 1222¾ BroadwayTommy117hdDanger'sHour1221½ Weakened 7
LATEST WORKOUTS ●Oct 30 Bel 5f fst :59⅘ h Oct 25 Bel 4f fst :47⅕ b Oct 15 Bel 5f fst 1:00⅕ h Oct 12 Bel 3f fst :38⅘ b

***Mourjane** — Dk. b. or br. h. 5, by Pitskelly—Affaire d'Amour, by Tudor Music
Br.—McKinley W G (Ire)
Own.—Fernwood Stable — Tr.—Skiffington Thomas
126 — Lifetime 22 6 5 5 $226,177 — 1985 7 2 1 3 $108,183 — 1984 7 0 2 0 $19,092 — Turf 22 6 5 5 $226,177

20Oct85- 8Bel fm 1¼ [T]:50⅘ 1:38⅘ 2:02 3+Kelso H 7 7 7⁸ 65½ 42 1nk Migliore R 114 4.40e 84-18 Mourjane 114nk Cool 116½ Palace Panther 116½ Driving 9
20Oct85-Grade III
6Sep85- 8Bel fm 1⅛ [T]:49 1:12⅗ 1:42⅗ 3+Alw 36000 1 6 62½ 2½ 33 34½ Santos J A b 115 *.90 83-15 Garthorn 115nk Cornish Gem II 1154½ Mourjane 1154 Off slow 6
24Aug85- 9Mth fm 1⅜ ①:48⅕ 1:12⅗ 1:48⅗+ 3+Longfellw H 1 8 712 35 33 32¾ Santos J A b 117 4.20 95-09 Cozzene 122² Zoffany 114¾ Mourjane 117³ Mild bid 8
24Aug85-Grade II
27Jly85- 8Bel sf 1½ ①:51⅗ 2:07⅘ 2:33⅘ 3+Swrd Dancr 4 9 911 84½ 63½ 51¾ Cruguet J 118 10.80 56-42 Tri For Size 110¾ Talakeno 112hd Persian Tiara 113nk Raced wide 9
27Jly85-Grade I
16Jun85♦6Chantilly(Fra) gd*1 1:37⅘ ① PrChemindeFer duNord(Gr3) 2hd Piggott L b 123 *2.00 — — Pink 130hd Mourjane 123nk Majuscule 123² Bold bid, hung 8
2Jun85♦4Longchamp(Fra) gd*1⅛ 2:00⅘ ① Prix Dollar (Gr.2) 3¾ Piggott L 123 2.75 — — Yashgan 1271¼ Pink 127² Mourjane 123nk Finished well 8
27Apr85♦5Evry(Fra) gd*1 1:38⅘ ① Prix de Savigny 1½ Gibert A 119 *.80 — — Mourjane 119½ In Focus 119⁴ King Palace 113nk Bid, long drive 9
27Sep84♦3MLaffitte(Fra) sf*1¼ 2:08⅗ ① LaCoupe deMLaffitte(Gr3) 812 Gibert A 123 6.00 — — Estrapade 122⁴ Palace Music 121nk Bob Back 119nk No factor 11
26Aug84- 9AP fm 1¼ ①:48⅘ 1:37⅘ 2:01⅘ 3+Bud Arl Mil 2 11 108½1011 86½ 76½ Gibert A 126 10.60e 80-15 John Henry 1261¾ Royal Heroine 122³ Gato DelSol126no Far back 12
26Aug84-Grade I
11Aug84♦3Deauville(Fra) fm*1¼ 2:07⅗ ① Prix Gontaut Biron(Gr.3) 2no Head F 130 2.00 — — Bedtime 123no Mourjane 130⁶ Garthorn 123½ Bid,game try 6
LATEST WORKOUTS Oct 29 Bel [T] 5f fm 1:02⅘ b (d) Oct 10 Fai tr.t 6f fst 1:16⅕ b ●Oct 4 Fai tr.t 5f fst 1:00⅘ b Sep 30 Bel 3f fst :35 h

***Sharannpour** — Ch. h. 5, by Busted—Shamim, by Le Haar
Br.—Aga Khan H H (Ire)
Own.—Moss J S — Tr.—Frankel Robert
126 — Lifetime 14 7 1 4 $504,338 — 1985 6 4 0 0 $459,000 — 1984 8 3 1 4 $45,338 — Turf 14 7 1 4 $504,338

12Oct85- 8Med fm 1⅜ ①:49⅖ 1:38⅗ 2:15 3+Ballantine 8 5 44 1hd 2hd 1¾ Cordero A Jr 126 *1.80 90-13 Sharannpour 126¾ Late Act 1266½ Persian Tiara 123nk Driving 10
21Sep85- 8Bel fm 1½ ①:48⅘ 2:01⅕ 2:25⅘ 3+Trf Classic 5 9 812 65½ 64¾ 57¾ Pincay L Jr 126 6.20 89-07 Noble Fighter 1193½ Win 1261¾ StrawberryRoadII126no No threat 12
21Sep85-Grade I
22Jly85- 8Hol fm 1½ ①:50⅕ 2:02⅕ 2:25⅘ 3+Sunset H 4 5 55½ 52½ 44 42 Cordero A Jr 115 2.90 89-11 Kings Island 116hd Greinton 1221¼ Val Danseur 114½ No rally 5
22Jly85-Grade I
16Jun85- 8Bel sf 1⅜ [T]:48⅕ 1:40 2:18⅕ 3+Bowl Grn H 9 8 518 31½ 3nk 12¾ Cordero A Jr 114 *1.50 66-34 Sharannpour1142¾FlyingPidgeon117nkLongMick121hd Ridden out 14
16Jun85-Grade I
1Jun85- 8Bel sf 1¼ [T]:46⅗ 1:39 2:04⅕ 3+R Smith H 7 8 710 63½ 2hd 11¾ Cordero A Jr 112 *2.50 73-31 Sharannpour1121¾InevitbleLeder116¹ColdFeetII1102½ Ridden out 13
1Jun85-Grade II
19May85- 9Hol fm 1⅛ ①:46⅗ 1:10 1:40⅗ Clm 175000 2 4 47½ 35 3½ 12 Pincay L Jr 117 3.70 97-08 Sharannpour 117² Pol And Dic 1121¼ Go Dancer 116½ Driving 7
30Nov84♦6MLaffitte(Fra) sf*1½ 2:47⅕ ① Prix Zurbarab 22½ Guignard G 132 3.75 — — Darly 1282½ Sharannpour 132⁴ Octavio 123hd Rallied for 2nd 9
13Nov84♦5MLaffitte(Fra) sf*1½ 2:56⅗ ① PrixCharles&HenryRouher 11¼ StMartin Y 126 *.70 — — Shrnnpour1261¼ Mrtind'Ete126² OuiMonCptine126¾ Led thru str 7
4Nov84♦4Nantes(Fra) gd*1½ :00 ① Grand Prix de Nantes 37½ StMartin Y 128 — — — Pebble 1242½ Garthorn 132⁵ Sharannpour 128¹ Stride late 11
4Nov84-No time taken
14Oct84♦5Lyon(Fra) gd*1⅞ :00 ① Prix du Grand Camp 11¼ Mssard J 131 *.80 — — Sharannpour 1311¼ Centre Est 131¾ [D]Pot's Son 129² Bid,handily 9
14Oct84-No time taken
LATEST WORKOUTS Oct 27 Bel 7f fst 1:26⅘ b Oct 21 Bel 4f fst :50⅘ b Oct 6 Bel 7f gd 1:27⅕ b Sep 30 Bel 4f fst :51⅗ b

***Persian Tiara** — Ch. m. 5, by Persian Bold—Tarara Girl, by Major Portion
Br.—Finnegan M A (Ire)
Own.—Palm Beach Stable — Tr.—Maxwell Adrian J
123 — Lifetime 40 10 7 5 $722,990 — 1985 13 2 4 2 $335,798 — 1984 17 4 3 2 $373,093 — Turf 39 10 6 5 $719,630

19Oct85- 7Bel fm 1⅜ [T]:49 1:38⅘ 2:15⅘ 3+ⒻAthenia H 8 5 63½ 52 42 2¾ Velasquez J 119 *1.30 79-20 Videogenic 114¾ Persian Tiara 119¾ Key Witness 1082½ Gaining 13
19Oct85-Grade III
12Oct85- 8Medfm 1⅜ ①:49⅖ 1:38⅗ 2:15 3+Ballantine 2 7 910 74½ 47½ 37¼ Velasquez J 123 5.60 83-13 Sharannpour 126¾ Late Act 1266½ Persian Tiara123nk Closed well 10
21Sep85- 8Bel fm 1½ ①:48⅘ 2:01⅕ 2:25⅘ 3+Trf Classic 6 8 916111110111014 Velasquez J 123 16.60 83-07 Noble Fighter 1193½ Win 1261¾ Strawberry Road II 126hd Outrun 12
21Sep85-Grade I
22Aug85- 8Sar fm 1⅜ ①:50⅘ 2:03 2:40⅕ 3+Seneca H 2 5 66½ 2½ 31 73¾ Velasquez J 113 *1.50 80-15 Nassipour 112½ Morning Bob 108nk Act Away 112¹ Tired 12
22Aug85-Grade III
27Jly85- 8Bel sf 1½ ①:51⅗ 2:07⅘ 2:33⅘ 3+Swrd Dancr 3 7 78½ 62½ 52 3¾ Velasquez J 113 4.40 57-42 Tri For Size 110¾ Talakeno 112hd Persian Tiara 113nk Checked 9
27Jly85-Grade I
29Jun85- 8Bel gd 1⅜ [T]:49 1:38 2:16 3+ⒻSheepsh'd H 3 9 10131081 63½ 11¼ Velasquez J 116 5.60 77-21 Persian Tiara 1161¼ Key Dancer 118¾ Dictina 1121¼ Wide, clear 10
29Jun85-Grade II
14Jun85- 8GS fm 1½ ①:51⅗ 2:05⅕ 2:29⅗ 3+ⒻVineland H 5 4 43 1hd 2½ 21¼ Velasquez J 116 *1.10 — — Eastland 1101¼PersianTiara1165PowderBreak117¹ Led, weakened 10
14Jun85-Grade III; Run in divisions
11May85- 8Pim fm 1½ ①:49⅖ 2:02⅘ 2:27⅘ 3+Dixie H 7 5 67 21 31 2no Terry J 113 4.20 98-06 Nassipour115noPersianTiara1131¼[D]PssTheLine117no Just missed 8
11May85-Grade II
20Apr85-10Hia fm 1½ ① 2:27⅕ 3+Hia Cup H 1 9 112311112 89¾ 74 Terry J 114 13.70 90-11 Selous Scout 114¾ Flying Pidgeon116nkPassTheLine114nk Outrun 12
20Apr85-Grade I
30Mar85- 7Hia fm 1⅛ ① 1:49 ⒻKey Largo 10 7 79 62½ 1hd 22½ Maple E 122 *1.00 84-16 MarieD'Argonne1122½PersinTir1223½WimborneSky114hd 2nd best 10
30Mar85-Run in divisions
LATEST WORKOUTS Oct 31 Bel [T] 3f fm :36⅘ b (d) Oct 26 Bel [T] 6f fm 1:15 b Oct 10 Bel ① 3f gd :37⅘ b (d) Oct 3 Bel [T] 5f sf 1:05 b (d)

Baillamont — B. c. 3, by Blushing Groom—Lodeve, by Shoemaker
Br.—Romanoaks Farm (Ky)
Own.—Niarchos S S — Tr.—Boutin Francois
122 — Lifetime 9 3 1 2 $124,336 — 1985 7 2 0 2 $110,164 — 1984 2 1 1 0 $14,172 — Turf 9 3 1 2 $124,336

12Oct85- 8Bel fm 1⅜ ①:48⅗ 1:37⅘ 2:15⅘ 3+Man O War 7 8 63 2hd 3½ 32¾ Samyn J L 121 13.00 82-25 Win 126nk Bob Back 1262½ Baillamont 1218¼ Steadied 8
12Oct85-Grade I
8Sep85♦4PhoenixPk(Ire) sf*1¼ 2:09⅕ ① PhoenixChampionStks(Gr1) 54¾ Asmussen C 123 20.00 — — Commanche Run 132³ Bob Back 132¾ Damister 123no Evenly 11
29Jun85♦3Curragh(Ire) gd 1½ 2:29⅘ ① Irish Sweeps Derby(Gr1) 65 Asmussen C 126 16.00 — — Law Society 126½ Theatrical 1262½ Damister 126hd Stride late 13
9Jun85♦3Chantilly(Fra) sf*1⅝ 1:54⅗ ① PrixJean Prat(Gr 1) 1no Asmussen C 128 11.00 — — Baillamont 128no Metal Precieux 128⁶ Silvermine 124¾ Just up 8
8May85♦5Evry(Fra) gd*1⅛ 1:54⅗ ① Prix Matchem 12 Asmussen C 124 2.40 — — Baillamont 124² Envol 124nk Morespeed 124nk Going away 6
21Apr85♦6Longchamp(Fra) gd*1⅛ 2:13⅘ ① Prix de Guiche(Gr3) 31¼ Asmussen C 128 5.75 — — MetalPrecieux128½ LouisLeGrand128¹ Baillamont1281¼ Prom,led 8
8Apr85♦2Longchamp(Fra) sf*1¼ 2:23 ① Prix de Courcelles 53 Asmussen C 123 11.00 — — Publicity 123½ Bellwater 123² Envol 123nk Mild late rally 10
22Oct84♦2MLaffitte(Fra) sf*1 1:45⅗ ① Prix Sirtam(Mdn) 1hd Asmussen C 123 *1.10 — — Baillamont 123hd Keep Sun 1192½ Spartiate 123hd Prom,led,held 15
11Oct84♦2Evry(Fra) yl*1⅛ 2:06⅗ ① PrixSaintPierreAzif(Mdn) 2nk Asmussen C 123 *1.75 — — Premier Role 123nk Baillamont 1231¼ Narghile 123¾ Prom,led 9
LATEST WORKOUTS ●Oct 11 Bel 1 fst 1:43 b

Who's For Dinner — Dk. b. or br. h. 6, by Native Charger—Expectancy, by Intentionally
Br.—Tartan Farms (Fla)
Own.—Tartan Stable — Tr.—Nerud Jan H
126 — Lifetime 47 9 11 8 $633,126 — 1985 10 1 4 0 $191,590 — 1984 11 3 1 2 $278,993 — Turf 40 9 11 8 $632,106

12Oct85-10LaD fm 1⅜ ①:46⅗ 1:36⅕ 2:13⅕ 3+La Downs H 3 2 25 21½ 2hd 21¼ Guerra W A b 117 3.70 99-09 Semillero 1161¼ Who's ForDinner1171¼FlyingPidgeon118³ Gamely 7
30Sep85- 8Bel gd 1⅛ ①:47⅕ 1:11⅘ 1:43⅘ 3+Sea Bird 3 7 52½ 75½ 813 713¼ Cordero A Jr b 119 2.30 67-27 Zoffany 1172¾ Intensify 115hd Tri For Size 1192¾ Finished at 1/2 9
1Sep85- 8Bel gd 1¼ [T]:48⅘ 1:37⅘ 2:02 3+Manhttn H 3 6 53¾ 87 811 813¼ Cordero A Jr b 116 4.20 70-24 Cool 1122½ Win 1263¼ Sondrio 110½ Wide, tired 13
1Sep85-Grade I
10Aug85- 8Atl fm 1⅜ ①:45⅗ 1:11⅗ 1:54⅗ 3+U Nations H 11 3 33½ 2½ 42½ 22 Cordero A Jr b 116 *2.70 89-14 Ends Well 114² Who's For Dinner 116hd Cool 110¹ Gamely 11
10Aug85-Grade I
5Jly85- 8Bel fm 1⅜ ①:49 1:37⅗ 2:15⅘ 3+Tidal H 3 4 42½ 31½ 1½ 1¾ Cordero A Jr b 115 5.50 85-17 Who's For Dinner115¾Domynsky116nkFlyingPidgeon117nk Driving 11
5Jly85-Grade II
22Jun85- 7Bel fm 1¼ ①:46⅗ 1:35⅘ 2:00⅘ 3+Handicap 5 4 38 22 21½ 21¼ Cordero A Jr b 122 2.20 89-11 Act Away 1091¼ Who'sForDinner122½RovingMinstrel120¹ Bumped 8
30May85- 8Bel gd 1⅛ [T]:47⅗ 1:11⅘ 1:42⅘ 3+Handicap 5 4 42 51¾ 33¼ 24½ Cordero A Jr b 116 2.70 83-14 Cool 1094½ Who's For Dinner 116hdMrChromacopy117⁴ Game try 5
6May85- 8Aqu yl 1⅛ ①:47⅗ 1:12⅘ 1:46 3+Ft Marcy H 2 2 2½ 22½ 34¾ 55 Cordero A Jr b 116 3.00 70-25 Forzando II 120nk Native Raid 1154½ Solidified 113½ Tired 7
6May85-Grade III
24Apr85- 7Aqu fm 1 ①:48⅕ 1:12⅘ 1:37 3+Handicap 2 3 52½ 42½ 34½ 43¼ Cordero A Jr b 119 *.70e 87-12 NativeRaid1151½RegalHumor1102BadwagonHarry115nk Weakened 9
13Apr85- 1Aqu fst 7f :22⅗ :45⅕ 1:22⅘ 3+Handicap 4 7 716 719 723 724½ Cordero A Jr b 112 4.20e 64-21 Carr De Naskra 1221¾ LeroyS.116nkMr.Tatt1078½ Showed nothing 7
LATEST WORKOUTS Oct 28 Bel 5f fst :59⅘ h Oct 23 Bel 5f fst 1:01⅗ h Sep 24 Bel 5f sly 1:04 b Sep 19 Bel 5f fst 1:02 b

***Lashkari** — B. c. 4, by Mill Reef—Larannda, by Right Royal
Br.—Aga Khan S A (Eng)
Own.—H H Aga Khan — Tr.—De Royer Dupre Alain
126 — Lifetime 12 5 2 2 $982,285 — 1985 4 1 1 1 $25,691 — 1984 8 4 1 1 $956,594 — Turf 12 5 2 2 $982,285

25Aug85♦4Deauville(Fra) sf*1⅝ 3:14 ① GrandPrixdeDeauville(Gr2) 2½ St Martin Y 133 4.00 — — Air deCour 117½ Lashkari 133⁴ Noble Fighter 117¹ Bid, led 11
2Jly85♦7MLaffitte(Fra) gd*1⅞ 2:41 ① Prix Tertulien 11½ Poirier O 118 *.40 — — Lashkari 1181½ Nuoro 123³ Matin d'Ete 1232½ Bid, handily 10
27May85♦5StCloud(Fra) gd*1½ 2:35 ① PrixJean deChaudenay(Gr2) 42½ St Martin Y 134 1.75 — — Seurat 112¾ Romildo 134¹ Keep Sun 113½ No real threat 7
21Apr85♦2Longchamp(Fra) gd*1½ 2:38⅘ ① Prix d'Hedouville(Gr3) 32 St Martin Y 128 *.40 — — Darly 123¹ Temoignage 121¹ Lashkari 128nk Well pl, bore out 8
10Nov84- 6Hol fm 1½ ①:46⅗ 2:01⅘ 2:25⅘ 3+Br Cp Turf 2 6 62¾ 31½ 31½ 1nk Saint-Martin Y 122 53.40 94-01 Lashkari 122nk All Along 123½ Raami 122½ Driving 11
10Nov84-Grade I
21Oct84♦4Longchamp(Fra) st*1½ 2:46⅗ ① PrixConseil deParis(Gr2) 15 St Martin Y 121 3.90 — — Lashkari 121⁵ Darly 128³ Reine deGrace 1161½ Bid,drew away 8
11Sep84♦5Evry(Fra) gd*1½ 2:37⅗ ① Prix des Breviares 11 St Martin Y 126 *.80 — — Lashkari 126¹ Espoir deFerce 1271½ Kirigane 1221½ Bid,up late 12
7Aug84♦4Deauville(Fra) gd*1⅜ 2:39⅘ ① Prix de Menneval 42½ Samani H 123 4.00 — — AgentDouble 123² Okeanos 128hd Bojador 123nk Evenly 9
24Jun84♦4Longchamp(Fra) fm*1⅞ 3:14 ① GrandPrix deParis(Gr1) 73 Piggott L 123 4.00 — — At Talaq 123nk Woolskin 123hd SpicyStory123hd Bid, then evenly 11
10Jun84♦3Chantilly(Fra) yl*1½ 2:33⅕ ① Prix du Lys(Gr.3) 33 Carson W 121 *.90e — — IrisNoir 1242½ BlueSpleen 121½ Lashkari 1211½ Fin.well 9
LATEST WORKOUTS Oct 31 Aqu ① 5f fm 1:05⅘ b

***Teleprompter** — B. g. 5, by Welsh Pageant—Ouija, by Silly Season
Own.—Lord Derby — Br.—Stanley Estates & Stud Co (Eng) — Tr.—Watts J W
126 Lifetime 23 10 8 1 $789,882 — 1985 6 2 3 0 $653,420 — 1984 8 5 2 0 $105,104 — Turf 23 10 8 1 $789,882

Date / Race	Time	Race	Calls	Fin	Jockey	Wt	Odds	Result
28Sep85♦2Ascot(Eng) fm 1	1:38⅘	Ⓣ QueenElizabethIIStk(Gr2)		$2^{2\frac12}$	Ives T	b 133	3.50	— — Shadeed $126^{2\frac12}$ Teleprompter 133^{hd} Zaizafon116^{no} Checked twice 7
25Aug85- 6AP yl 1¼ Ⓣ:47⅗ 1:39⅖	2:03⅖	3↑Bud Arl Mil	1 1 $1^{1\frac12}$ $1^{\frac12}$ 1^{3}	$1^{\frac34}$	Ives T	b 126	14.20	77-27 Teleprompter $126^{\frac34}$ Greinton $126^{3\frac12}$ Flying Pidgeon $126^{1\frac12}$ Driving 13
25Aug85-Grade I								
20Jly85♦2Ayr(Scot) sf 1¼	2:13⅗	Ⓣ Land of Burns Stakes		2^{nk}	Ives T	b 134	*.70	— — Parliament 126^{nk} Teleprompter 134^{8} Mr. Meeka $134^{\frac12}$ Prom,led 8
6Jly85♦4PhoenixPk(Ire) fm 1⅛	1:47⅖	Ⓣ PacemakrInternt'lStk(Gr3)		1^{6}	Ives T	b 136	2.25	— — Teleprompter136^{6} NorthernPlin119^{3} FieryCelt131^{3} Led fnl 2 1/2f 6
17May85♦4Newbury(Eng) gd 1	1:38⅗	Ⓣ Lockinge Stakes(Gr2)		2no	Ives T	b 132	4.00	— — Prismatic 111no Teleprompter $132^{2\frac12}$ Sarab 127^{7} Prom,led 11
17Apr85♦4Newmarket(Eng) gd 1⅛	1:52⅗	Ⓣ Earl of Sefton Stks(Gr3)		8	Carson W	b 127	*1.75	— — King of Clubs 127^{hd} Parliament $127^{1\frac12}$ Kalim 122^{hd} Led 6f 8
29Sep84♦2Ascot(Eng) gd 1	1:42⅘	Ⓣ QueenElizbeth II Stk(Gr2)		1^{nk}	Carson W	b 126	5.50	— — Teleprompter126^{nk} Katies123^{6} Sackford130^{2} Headed,came again 6
29Aug84♦4Deauville(Fra) gd*1	1:33⅘	Ⓣ Prix Quincey(Gr.3)		1^{nk}	Rouse B	b 132	*1.60	— — Teleprompter132^{nk} Brocade$121^{1\frac12}$ Vacrme127^{6} With pace, gamely 10
18Aug84♦3Curragh(Ire) gd 1	1:36	Ⓣ Desmond Stakes(Gr.3)		$1^{2\frac12}$	Roche C	b 134	*1.75	— — Tlpromptr$134^{2\frac12}$ WstrnSymphony125^{3} Sign-of-Lif$120^{1\frac12}$ Led fnl 3f 8
21Jly84♦4Ayr(Scot) gd 1¼	2:05⅗	Ⓣ Land of Burns Stakes		$2^{2\frac12}$	Rouse B	b 134	3.00	— — Bedtime $126^{2\frac12}$ Teleprompter 134^{3} TrialByError 121^{3} Led 1 mile 7

LATEST WORKOUTS Oct 31 Aqu Ⓣ 3f fm :37⅖ b

***Pebbles** — Ch. f. 4, by Sharpen Up—La Dolce, by Connaught
Own.—Sheikh Mohammed AlMaktoum — Br.—Warren Hill Stud-Mimika Financiera (Eng) — Tr.—Brittain Clive E
123 Lifetime 14 7 4 0 $557,271 — 1985 4 3 1 0 $321,991 — 1984 4 2 2 0 $194,797 — Turf 14 7 4 0 $557,271

Date / Race	Time	Race	Fin	Jockey	Wt	Odds	Result
19Oct85♦2Newmarket(Eng) gd 1¼	2:04⅗	Ⓣ DubaiChampionStakes(Gr1)	1^{3}	Eddery P	126	4.50	— — Pebbles 126^{3} SlipAnchor 122^{hd} PalaceMusic 129 Bid, drew away 10
6Jly85♦3Sandown(Eng) gd 1¼	2:07⅕	Ⓣ Coral-EclipseStakes(Gr.1)	1^{2}	Cauthen S	130	3.50	— — Pebbles 130^{2} RainbowQuest $133^{1\frac12}$ BobBack133^{20} Prom,led fnl 2f 4
18Jun85♦2Ascot(Eng) gd 1¼	2:05⅘	Ⓣ Prince of WalesStake(Gr2)	$2^{1\frac12}$	Cauthen S	130	1.25	— — BobBck$133^{1\frac12}$ Pebbles130^{no} CommnchRun133^{12} Bid, then evenly 4
26Apr85♦3Sandown(Eng) gd 1	1:42	Ⓣ TrusthouseForte Mile(Gr2)	$1^{1\frac12}$	Cauthen S	130	*1.35	— — Pebbles $130^{1\frac12}$ Vacarme $126^{\frac12}$ Sarab $126^{2\frac12}$ Led fnl 2 1/2 f 7
20Oct84♦2Newmarket(Eng) gd 1¼	2:01	Ⓣ Dubai ChampionStakes(Gr1)	2^{nk}	Robinson P	119	7.50	— — Palace Music 122^{nk} Pebbles $119^{1\frac12}$ Raft 122^{nk} Strong late run 15
20Jun84♦4Ascot(Eng) gd 1	1:40⅗	Ⓣ Ⓕ Coronation Stakes(Gr.2)	$2^{1\frac12}$	Piggott L	130	*2.75	— — Katies $130^{1\frac12}$ Pebbles 130^{5} So Fine $126^{\frac34}$ Prom,led midstr 10
3May84♦4Newmarket(Eng) gd 1	1:38	Ⓣ Ⓕ 1,000GuineasStakes(Gr1)	1^{3}	Robinson P	126	8.00	— — Pebbles 126^{3} Meis El Reem 126^{nk} Desirable $126^{\frac34}$ Bid,dr.clear 15
19Apr84♦3Newmarket(Eng) gd 7f	1:24⅗	Ⓣ Ⓕ Nell Gwyn Stakes(Gr.3)	1^{1}	Robinson P	119	7.00	— — Pebbles 119^{1} Leipzig $119^{1\frac12}$ MeisElReem 119^{1} Bid,led fnl 2f 9
28Sep83♦3Newmarket(Eng) gd 6f	1:14⅘	Ⓣ Ⓕ CheveleyParkStakes(Gr1)	2^{nk}	Robinson P	123	33.00	— — Desirable 123^{nk} Pebbles 123no Prickle $123^{\frac34}$ Closed well 12
26Aug83♦3Goodwood(Eng) fm 7f	1:28⅗	Ⓣ Ⓕ Wat.CandelabraStks(Gr3)	$5^{5\frac34}$	Mercer J	121	3.30	— — Shoot Clear 121^{1} Satinette 121^{3} Tapaculo $118^{1\frac12}$ Evenly 8

LATEST WORKOUTS Oct 31 Aqu Ⓣ 3f fm :36⅘ h

***Theatrical** — B. c. 3, by Nureyev—Tree of Knowledge, by Sassafras
Own.—Firestone B R — Br.—Firestone B R & Mrs (Ire) — Tr.—Weld Dermot K
122 Lifetime 6 3 1 0 $80,389 — 1985 5 2 1 0 $78,681 — 1984 1 1 0 0 $1,708 — Turf 6 3 1 0 $80,389

Date / Race	Time	Race	Fin	Jockey	Wt	Odds	Result
8Sep85♦4PhoenixPk(Ire) sf*1¼	2:09⅕	Ⓣ PhoenixChampionStks(Gr1)	$7^{7\frac12}$	Kinane M J	123	8.00	— — Commanche Run 132^{3} Bob Back $132^{\frac34}$ Damister 123no Bid,wknd 11
29Jun85♦3Curragh(Ire) gd 1½	2:29⅘	Ⓣ Irish Sweeps Derby(Gr1)	$2^{\frac12}$	Kinane M J	126	6.00	— — Law Society $126^{\frac12}$ Theatrical $126^{2\frac12}$ Damister 126^{hd} Bid,led midstr 13
5Jun85♦3Epsom(Eng) gd 1½	2:36⅕	Ⓣ Derby Stakes(Gr.1)	7^{25}	Piggott L	126	10.00	— — Slip Anchor 126^{7} Law Society 126^{6} Damister 126no No threat 14
11May85♦3Leoaprdst'n(Ire) gd 1¼	2:13⅘	Ⓣ DerinstownStudDbyTrl(Gr2)	1^{4}	Kinane M J	123	*1.00	— — Theatrical 123^{4} NorthernPlain126^{2} LordDuke123^{3} Bid,drew away 8
27Apr85♦2Curragh(Ire) gd 1⅜	2:25⅖	Ⓣ Ballysax Plate	1^{2}	Piggott L	123	2.50	— — Theatrical123^{2} LedingCounsel131^{12} SnowPlnt123^{nk} Slow st,drvg 6
15Oct84♦4GowranPark(Ire) fm*1$\frac{1}{16}$	1:37⅖	Ⓣ Kilkenny Plate(Mdn)	1^{1}	Kinane M J	126	*1.10	— — Theatrical 126^{1} Pala Chief 126^{3} Jazz Ballet 126no Well up,easily 16

LATEST WORKOUTS Oct 31 Aqu Ⓣ 5f fm 1:01⅘ h

impudently confident jockey glanced over, saw a driving Willie Carson about to accomplish the same manoeuvre on Helen Street and cooly allowed that adversary first run.

Only after Helen Street had gained command did Eddery permit Pebbles to sail between Slip Anchor and the retreating Commanche Run, and only after she had cruised ahead of Helen Street did he let her down and ask her to stretch.

Memorably, Pebbles put three lengths between herself and her pursuers in a few strides. Then Eddery glanced both ways and stopped riding.

All went far from well for Pebbles after her historic victory in the Group I Coral Eclipse Stakes in July. Having become the first-ever distaff winner of that century-old Sandown feature, the four-year-old suddenly and inexplicably lost her appetite, even refusing the Guinness and eggs which form the most jealously relished part of her diet. Tests revealed nothing, but time cured all, and after the longest month of her conditioner's life, Pebbles began to eat and thrive again.

When he dismounted after the Champion, Eddery told Pebbles' lad that she was the best horse he had ever ridden. Coming from the man who won Derbies on Grundy and Golden Fleece and Arcs de Triomphe aboard Detroit and Rainbow Quest, that counts for something.

The Thoroughbred Record, October 26, 1985

Her earlier victory over eventual Arc winner (via disqualification) Rainbow Quest was nearly as impressive, though it was tainted somewhat by her victim's near nervous breakdown in the paddock and parade to the post:

> Predictably, August made the running, his task being to set an even, rather than a furious, gallop in order to help Rainbow Quest to settle. The ploy failed dismally, because in getting Rainbow Quest settled, Lequeux found himself behind Pebbles instead of tracking August and preparing to take command when his leader retreated.
>
> To be fair to Lequeux, he was entitled to take the view that his mount could be relied upon to produce sharp acceleration, but equally relevant was the fact that Rainbow Quest's natural distance was further than the mile and a quarter, whereas Pebbles was a classic winner at a mile.
>
> Effectively, Lequeux played into Cauthen's hands. The American knew he could afford to ignore August. He dictated the race's real pace, and he was presented with the opportunity to pick the optimum moment when he should kick for home and leave Rainbow Quest with too much to do in too short a time.
>
> The moment Cauthen chose came at the quarter pole, but then it seemed that even the timing to the challenge might not have mattered all that much. The gallop had been too slow, and the ground was too fast for Rainbow Quest to muster much in the way of acceleration so that he never posed a real threat to Pebbles. The filly galloped home triumphant by two easy lengths, with Rainbow Quest one and a half lengths in advance of Bob Back, whose Ascot acceleration was conspicuous by its absence this time.
>
> *The Thoroughbred Record,* July 13, 1985

STRAWBERRY ROAD

On paper Strawberry Road is a notch below Group I in Europe. This well-traveled six-year-old has had one decent race in this country, but only one workout since. As to why he came to this country early:

> There is no point in racing him against Sagace (heavy favorite for the Arc), as over a mile and a half, Strawberry Road is five lengths inferior.
>
> *The Thoroughbred Record,* July 13, 1985

BOB BACK

A marginal Group I performer in England, Bob Back's victory over Pebbles and Commanche Run at Ascot was regarded (at the time) as something of a joke:

> Perhaps because she had not been allowed to move when she obviously wanted to go, Pebbles chose to hang fire when the message was finally delivered. And by the time she found her best pace, the 33–1 shot Bob Back had flashed past both the surprised principals to bring off the shock of the season so far. Bob Back's astounding late burst took him one and a half lengths clear at the post, where Pebbles just nipped Commanche Run for second by a short head.
>
> There were numerous theories, explanations, and excuses connected with this extraordinary result, some of them possibly valid. But the fact remains that, as the race was run, Bob Back proved much the best horse on the day.
>
> *The Thoroughbred Record,* June 26, 1985

Bob Back's first race in this country was top-rate.

SHERNAZAR

A much improved runner at four, Shernazar, like Pebbles, holds a recent decision over the fleet Epson Derby winner Slip Anchor. He was reportedly flying in the Arc before losing all chance when he was severely impeded.

> One of the worst incidents came some four furlongs from home when Shernazar and Group I Italian Derby winner Don Orazio met on several occasions, and it was surprising that neither of the horses fell. Certainly, Shernazar had absolutely no chance once the field reached the straight.
>
> *The Thoroughbred Record,* October 12, 1985

GREINTON

Probably the most formidable of the American-based contingent, Greinton has had legitimate excuses in each of his last three races. He's possibly excuse-prone, though—always a negative in a large field—and has possibly been sent to the well once too often.

DANGER'S HOUR

A sharp three-year-old from the Mack Miller barn, Danger's Hour defeated the highly regarded Slew The Dragon in the Rutgers, but he has done little else of any merit lately. He has failed to impress in his efforts against older runners but has never been better.

MOURJANE

This horse is nothing more than a Grade III performer on either side of the Atlantic.

SHARANNPOUR

Though ungraded in Europe, this horse was an immediate Grade I performer in this country, which must be considered a strong indictment of the older American grass runners. Sharannpour shows a definite liking for soft conditions, which he will not find today.

PERSIAN TIARA

An American-based mare whose forte seems to be perseverance rather than brilliance, Persian Tiara is hardly in the same league as Pebbles.

BAILLAMONT

Though out of contention in major Group I races like the Irish Derby and Phoenix Champions, Baillamont was a strong challenger in the Man O'War until checked between horses in midstretch.

WHO'S FOR DINNER

This horse was a noncontender in this race last year at the tail end of a much better season.

LASHKARI

Last year's winner, and that's his only recommendation. Otherwise, has failed even to make an appearance in any of Europe's major races, this year or last.

TELEPROMPTER

A five-year-old gelding totally lacking in Group I credentials prior to stealing victory in the Arlington Million, Teleprompter would be a serious threat once again if he were allowed to race unchallenged on the early lead.

THEATRICAL

A serious challenger in the Irish Derby, but nowhere in the Epsom Derby and Phoenix Champions, this three-year-old has yet to prove his merit against his elders.

SIXTH RACE
Aqueduct
NOVEMBER 2, 1985

1 ½ MILES.(Turf). (2.28⅕) 2nd Running THE BREEDERS' CUP TURF (Grade I). Purse $2,000,000. 3-year-olds and upward. Weights, 3-year-olds, 122 lbs. 4-year-olds and older, 126 lbs. Fillies and Mares allowed 3 lbs. Value of race $2,000,000. Value to winner $900,000, second $450,000, third $216,000, fourth $140,000, fifth $100,000, sixth $20,000. Nominator Awards: Stallion, winner $50,000, second $25,000, third $12,000; Foal, winner $50,000 second, $25,000, third $12,000. Stallion awards will be paid only to the nominators of fully eligible stallions. Owners who supplement horses to Breeders' Cup Day races will be eligible for the Foal Nominator's Award in the case of a 12 per cent supplementary nomination or both the Foal Nominator's Award and the Stallion Nominator's Award in the case of a 20 per cent supplementary nomination. In accordance with the Breeders' Cup/European Breeders' Fund cross-registration agreement, nominator's awards will not be paid to horses eligible through E.B.F. All unpaid nominator's awards will remain the property of Breeders' Cup Limited. Supplementary nominee: GREINTON and PEBBLES

Total purse $2,000,000. Value of race $1,826,000; value to winner $900,000; second $450,000; third $216,000; fourth $140,000; fifth $100,000; sixth $20,000. $174,000 foal & stallion nom awards. Mutuel pool $557,304, OTB pool $255,702. Exacta Pool $538,062. OTB Exacta Pool $265,501.

Last Raced	Horse	Eqt.	A.	Wt	PP	¼	½	1	1¼	Str	Fin	Jockey	Odds $1
19Oct85 ^{2}Eng^{1}	(S)Pebbles		4	123	13	12^{2}	$13^{2\frac{1}{2}}$	7½	4½	1^{1}	1^{nk}	Eddery P	2.20
21Sep85 ^{8}Bel^{3}	Strawberry Road II		6	126	1	2^{hd}	$3^{1\frac{1}{2}}$	4½	$5^{1\frac{1}{2}}$	$2^{1\frac{1}{2}}$	$2^{1\frac{1}{4}}$	Cauthen S	a-3.80
20Oct85 ^{8}Bel^{1}	Mourjane		5	126	6	14	14	13^{1}	8^{hd}	3^{1}	3^{1}	Migliore R	51.20
25Aug85 ^{4}Fra^{2}	Lashkari		4	126	11	5^{1}	5^{2}	8½	$7^{1\frac{1}{2}}$	4^{1}	$4^{2\frac{1}{2}}$	St Martin E	b-7.70
18Oct85 ^{8}Med^{1}	Danger's Hour	b	3	122	5	7^{1}	7½	6^{hd}	6½	$7^{1\frac{1}{2}}$	5¾	MacBeth D	9.30
6Oct85 ^{4}Fra^{12}	Shernazar		4	126	3	10½	9^{hd}	12^{1}	12^{1}	8½	6no	Swinburn W R	b-7.70
5Oct85 ^{8}Bel^{7}	(S)Greinton		4	126	4	6½	6^{hd}	3½	1^{hd}	5½	7½	Pincay L Jr	2.60
28Sep85 ^{2}Eng^{2}	Teleprompter	b	5	126	12	1^{3}	1^{5}	1^{1}	2½	6^{hd}	8½	Ives T A	13.60
12Oct85 ^{10}LaD^{2}	Who's For Dinner	b	6	126	10	$3^{2\frac{1}{2}}$	2½	2½	3^{2}	9^{hd}	9^{nk}	Guerra W A	48.30
12Oct85 ^{8}Bel^{3}	Baillamont		3	122	9	11^{2}	12^{hd}	14	11^{1}	10^{hd}	10no	Asmussen C B	25.90
8Sep85 ^{4}Ire^{7}	Theatrical		3	122	14	$8^{1\frac{1}{2}}$	8^{1}	10½	10½	11½	11^{nk}	Piggott L	a-3.80
12Oct85 ^{8}Bel^{2}	Bob Back		4	126	2	9½	10½	11^{1}	9½	$12^{2\frac{1}{2}}$	$12^{2\frac{3}{4}}$	Cordero A Jr	a-3.80
19Oct85 ^{7}Bel^{2}	Persian Tiara		5	123	8	4½	4½	5^{1}	13^{4}	13^{4}	13^{4}	Velasquez J	47.90
12Oct85 ^{8}Med^{1}	Sharannpour		5	126	7	$13^{1\frac{1}{2}}$	$11^{1\frac{1}{2}}$	9^{hd}	14	14	14	McCarron C J	26.30

a–Coupled: Strawberry Road II, Theatrical and Bob Back; b–Lashkari and Shernazar.
(S) Supplementary nomination.

OFF AT 3:35. Start good, Won driving. Time, :24⅕, :48, 1:12⅖, 1:37, 2:02⅖, 2:27, Course firm.
New course record.

$2 Mutuel Prices:

11–(M)–PEBBLES	**6.40**	**4.20**	**3.20**
1–(A)–STRAWBERRY ROAD II (a–entry)		**4.80**	**3.40**
5–(F)–MOURJANE			**10.60**

$2 EXACTA 11–1 PAID $29.40.

Ch. f, by Sharpen Up—La Dolce, by Connaught. Trainer Brittain Clive E. Bred by Warren Hill Stud-Mimika Financiera (Eng).

PEBBLES, unhurried early, was blocked while moving well along the inside racing into the final turn, got through entering the stretch to reach the front nearing the final furlong and was all out to turn back STRAWBERRY ROAD II. the latter moved up along the inside approaching the end of the backstretch the final time, came out for room leaving the far turn and finished with good courage. MOURJANE, badly outrun early, finished well along the inside. LASHKARI dropped back through the run down the backstretch the final time, rallied from the outside after entering the stretch but wasn't good enough. DANCER'S HOUR moved up between horses on the backstretch, was steadied along while maintaining his position until near the stretch then lacked the needed rally. SHERNAZAR failed to be a serious factor. GREINTON, reserved behind the early leaders, rallied after entering the backstretch, caught the leader nearing the stretch but gave way under pressure. TELEPROMPTER sprinted away to a good lead before going a half, showed speed to the stretch while saving ground and tired. WHO'S FOR DINNER made a run entering the backstretch the final time, remained prominent to the stretch while racing between horses and gave way. BAILLAMONT was always outrun. THEATRICAL raced wide. BOB BACK moved up along the inside around the second turn but was finished before going a mile. PERSIAN TIARA tired badly. SHARANNPOUR was always outrun.

With the possible exception of Greinton, it was easy to dismiss the American contingent as outclassed on the world scale. As for the European runners that had raced recently at Belmont, one need only ask why they skipped the Arc de Triomphe, Europe's richest and most prestigious race. By coming to this country ahead of time, they ran the risk of suffering from problems associated with acclimatization by the time the Breeders' Cup was scheduled to be run. Eliminating these horses, we are left with just three: Pebbles, the favorite, Shernazar, better than his last suggests and running as an entry with the previous year's surprise winner, and Teleprompter, the lone speed in the race, although seemingly outclassed otherwise. Was Pebbles in a class by herself? Comparison through Slip Anchor suggested as much.

The $1,000,000 Breeders' Cup Mile painted a similar picture—the European contingent seemed to outclass their American rivals by a country mile. Only eight of the fourteen contestants deserve comment, so only those will be considered, starting with four American runners:

TSUNAMI SLEW

Campaigned mostly at the classic distances during 1985, Tsunami Slew's connections apparently did not consider him good enough to compete in the richer Breeders' Cup Turf and decided to take their shot in the Mile instead. He has the speed to take advantage of his rail position, but until his victory in the recent Carleton Burke at Santa Anita, had failed to win a Grade I race.

COZZENE

Pointed for this race since finishing third in the 1984 running, Cozzene's preparations were seriously hampered by wet conditions whenever an appropriate prep race came up. He was narrowly beaten by Win in the Grade II Baruch at Saratoga, which seems to be his proper classification. He has had problems breaking alertly in the past, and a slow beginning would seriously compromise his chances in this bulky field.

FORZANDO

An impressive, though surprising, winner of the Metropolitan Handicap in May, Forzando has been on the sidelines since late

4 AQUEDUCT

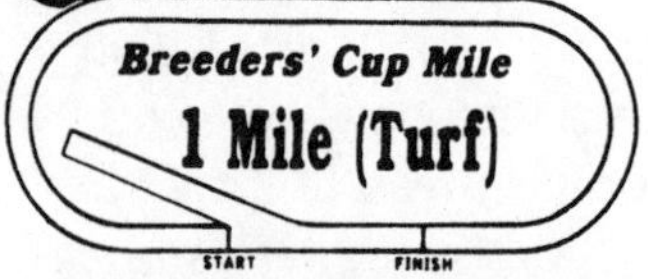

1 MILE. (Turf). (1.35⅓) 2nd Running THE BREEDERS' CUP MILE (Grade I). Purse $1,000,000. 3-year-olds and upward. Weights, 3-year-olds, 123 lbs. 4-year-olds and older, 126 lbs. Fillies and mares allowed 3 lbs. Value of race $1,000,000. Value to winner $450,000, second $225,000, third $108,000, fourth $70,000, fifth $50,000, sixth $10,000. Nominator Awards: Stallion, winner $25,000, second $12,500, third $6,000; Foal, winner $25,000, second, $12,500, third $6,000. Stallion awards will be paid only to the nominators of fully eligible stallions. Owners who supplement horses to Breeders' Cup Day races will be eligible for the Foal Nominator's Award in the case of a 12 per cent supplementary nomination or both the Foal Nominator's Award and the Stallion Nominator's Award in the case of a 20 percent supplementary nomination. In accordance with the Breeders' Cup/European Breeders' Fund cross-registration agreement, nominator's awards will not be paid to horses eligible through the E.B.F. All unpaid nominator's awards will remain the property of Breeders' Cup Limited. Supplementary Nominee: ROUSILLON

Coupled—Capture Him and The Noble Player.
Mutuel field— Chapel Cottage, Sitzmark.

Tsunami Slew — Dk. b. or br. c. 4, by Seattle Slew—Barbs Compact, by Barbizon
Br.—North Ridge Farm (Ky)
Tr.—Gregson Edwin
Own.—Whelan Elizabeth P — 126
Lifetime 27 10 4 1 $814,925 — 1985 11 4 2 0 $459,700 — 1984 14 5 2 1 $343,650 — Turf 16 7 3 0 $695,275

6Oct85- 8SA fm 1¼ ⓣ:46⅘ 1:35⅗ 1:59⅗ 3+C Burke H 3 2 21½ 21½ 21 12 Stevens G L 121 *1.20 89-13 Tsunami Slew 1212 Yashgan 1211¾ Best Of Both 1151 Drew out 7
6Oct85-Grade I
25Aug85- 6AP yl 1¼ ⓣ:47⅗ 1:39⅘ 2:03⅘ 3+Bud Arl Mil 7 3 31½ 2½ 23 79½ Meza R Q 126 8.60 67-27 Teleprompter 126¾ Greinton 1263½ Flying Pidgeon 1261¼ Tired 13
25Aug85-Grade I
11Aug85- 8Dmr fm 1⅛ ⓣ:48⅕ 1:11⅗ 1:46⅘ 3+E Read H 1 2 21½ 22½ 1hd 1½ Stevens G L 119 3.70 104-05 Tsunami Slew119½AlMamoon118¾BothEndsBurning1231¼ Driving 7
11Aug85-Grade II
4Jly85- 8Hol fm 1⅛ ⓣ:47⅗ 1:11 1:46⅕ 3+American H 5 1 12 11½ 12½ 11¾ Stevens G L 117 5.50 99-04 Tsunami Slew 1171¾ Al Mamoon 1173½ Dahar 1231¾ Driving 7
4Jly85-Grade II
1Jun85- 8Bel sf 1¼ Ⓣ:46⅗ 1:39 2:04⅕ 3+R Smith H 6 3 34 11 31½ 55¼ Delahoussaye E 119 3.70 68-31 Sharannpour1121¾InevitableLeder1161ColdFeetII1102¼ Weakened 13
1Jun85-Grade II
5May85- 8Hol fm 1⅛ ⓣ:46⅖ 1:10 1:46⅗ 3+Century H 6 2 21 2hd 21 54¼ Delahoussaye E 121 4.20 92-11 Dahar 1222¼ Both Ends Burning 122¾ Majestic Shore 120½ Wknd 7
5May85-Grade I
22Apr85- 8SA fm 1¼ ⓣ:46⅖ 1:34⅗ 1:59⅘ ⓈSn Jcnto H 7 1 12½ 12½ 12 11 Delahoussaye E 122 *1.20 88-19 Tsunami Slew 1221 Lofty 1191 Talakeno 1173½ Driving 7
10Mar85- 8SA fm 1¼ ⓣ:47⅕ 1:35 1:59⅗ Arcadia H 6 3 43½ 32½ 22½ 2hd Delahoussaye E 119 4.60 89-15 Fatih 116hd Tsunami Slew 119nk Swoon 113¾ Just missed 8
10Mar85-Grade II
18Feb85- 8SA fm 1¼ ⓣ:46⅕ 1:34⅗ 2:00⅗ S Nevada H 2 1 11 23 21½ 22 Delahoussaye E 119 3.00 82-15 Majestic Shore 1192 Tsunami Slew 119no Dahar 1251½ Ran early 6
18Feb85-Grade III
3Feb85- 8SA fst 1¼ :45⅗ 1:34⅗ 2:00⅕ C H Strub 3 3 33 513 514 523½ Delahoussaye E 119 12.70 64-12 Precisionist 125no Greinton 117½ Gate Dancer 12616 Fin early 5
3Feb85-Grade I
LATEST WORKOUTS ●Oct 30 Aqu ⓣ 5f fm 1:02 h (d) Oct 1 SA 5f fst 1:02⅕ h ●Sep 26 SA ⓣ 1 fm 1:38⅖ h (d) Sep 21 SA 7f fst 1:26⅘ h

***Chapel Cottage** — Dk. b. or br. f. 4, by Homing—Mayday Melody, by Highland Melody
Br.—Nurse Mrs R J (Eng)
Tr.—Ryan Michael
Own.—Ramsden T P — 123
Lifetime 12 4 2 2 $92,264 — 1985 7 2 2 0 $47,512 — 1983 5 2 0 2 $44,752 — Turf 12 4 2 2 $92,264

17Oct85♦4Newmarket(Eng) gd 7f 1:26 ⓣBisquitCognacStakes(Gr3) 2hd Robinson P 129 16.00 — — Efisio 128hd Chapel Cottage 129hd Powder Keg 128nd Bid led 8
4Aug85♦4Deauville(Fra) yl*6½f 1:16⅗ ⓣPrixMaurice deGheest(Gr2) 85¼ Robinson P 123 6.75 — — Spectacular Joke119nk Committed1231 RedMead1231½ No threat 13
11Jly85♦3Newmarket(Eng) gd 6f 1:11⅘ ⓣJuly Cup(Gr1) 54¾ Robinson P 129 11.00 — — NeverSoBold1322½ Committed129no Dayfyn120¼ Bid then evenly 9
21Jun85♦4Ascot(Eng) gd 5f 1:01⅗ ⓣKings Stand Stakes(Gr1) 53¾ Robinson P 126 9.00 — — NeverSoBold 1293 PrimoDominie121hd Committed126nk Fin well 15
16May85♦5York(Eng) gd 6f 1:13⅗ ⓣDuke of York Stakes(Gr3) 12 Robinson P 123 3.00 — — ChapelCottage1232 GreyDesire126¾ PollyDniels1104 Well pl drvg 10
4May85♦4Newmarket(Eng) gd 5f :59⅘ ⓣPalaceHouseStakes(Gr3) 21½ Robinson P 123 *2.50 — — Prince Sabo 1181½ Chapel Cottage 123½ PrinceReymo126½ Led 4f 11
20Apr85♦3Thirsk(Eng) gd 6f 1:13⅕ ⓣThirsk Hall Stakes 12 Robinson P 123 4.50 — — ChapelCottge1232 GreyDesire1405 FirwysGirl117nk Dwelt up late 10
10Sep83♦2Doncaster(Eng) sf 5f 1:02⅘ ⓣFlying Childers Stks(Gr2) 33½ Carson W 1234 4.50 — — Superlative 126½ Defecting Dancer 1263 DHReesh 1264 Stumbled 10
10Sep83-Dead heat
17Aug83♦5York(Eng) gd 6f 1:12⅕ ⓣⒻLowther Stakes(Gr.2) 32¾ Hide E 128 3.00 — — Prickle1232½ Desirable123nk ChapelCottage1281½ Bid then evenly 9
5Jly83♦4Newmarket(Eng) gd 6f 1:13⅖ ⓣⒻCherryHintonStakes(Gr3) 14 Hide E 122 *3.50 — — Chapel Cottage 1224 Nophe 125½ Sajeda 122no Bid easily 9
LATEST WORKOUTS Nov 1 Aqu ⓣ 3f fm :33⅘ h (d)

Capture Him — B. c. 4, by Mr Prospector—A Streaker, by Dr Fager
Br.—Reed W O (Ky)
Tr.—Gosden John H M
Own.—Sangster R E — 126
Lifetime 10 5 1 1 $89,967 — 1985 3 2 0 1 $42,230 — 1984 6 2 1 0 $45,695 — Turf 10 5 1 1 $89,967

14Sep85-11Bmf fm 1⅛ ⓣ:46⅖ 1:10⅖ 1:42⅘ 3+San Matean H 8 7 77¾ 76½ 53½ 3¾ Chapman T M 118 *1.60 93-04 Position's Best 117¾ Pair Of Aces 116no CaptureHim118no Rallied 10
24Apr85- 6Hol fm 1 ⓣ:45⅘ 1:09⅕ 1:33⅖ 3+Premiere H 3 6 64½ 53¾ 21½ 11¾ McCarron C J 1204 *1.30 96-06 DHRetsina Run 1161¾DHCaptureHim1201¾ValDanseur113¾ Driving 8
24Apr85-Dead heat. Run in divisions
4Apr85- 6GG fm 7½f ⓣ.24 :47⅘ 1:30⅘ Alw 18000 3 5 42½ 2½ 1½ 13 Baze R A 115 *.40 88-12 Capture Him 1153 Clear 116½ C. Howit Fitz 1144½ 6
11Nov84- 8Hol fm 1⅛ ⓣ:48⅖ 1:11⅘ 1:47⅖ Hol Derby 6 9 98¾ 85¾ 55½ 42¼ Eddery P b 122 8.50 91-08 Foscarini 122hd Roving Minstrel 122hd Bean Bag 1222 Rallied 10
11Nov84-Grade I; Run in Divisions
8Oct84♦3PhoenixPk(Ire) yl 1 1:50⅘ ⓣSwordlestown Stud Stakes 1no Eddery P b 127 *2.25 — — CaptureHim127no CongressPalace122nk RedRussell1302½ Just up 7
8Sep84♦3PhoenixPk(Ire) gd 7f 1:21⅗ ⓣBarronstown Stud Stakes 41½ Eddery P 125 *.65 — — Red Russell 1211 Neeyef 121½ Harlow 135hd Bid then evenly 8
19May84♦4Curragh(Ire) gd 1 1:38⅕ ⓣIrish2,000GuineasStk(Gr1) 41½ Eddery P 126 6.00 — — Sadler's Wells 126nk Procida 126½ Secreto 126½ Bid then evenly 9
12May84♦1PhoenixPk(Ire) gd 7f 1:20⅖ ⓣSwettenham Stud Stakes 1½ Eddery P 125 *.25 — — Capture Him 125½ Seafaring 1254 Mothers Word 1371 Led fnl 5f 4
21Apr84♦4PhoenixPk(Ire) gd 7f 1:24⅗ ⓣ2,000 Guineas Trial(Gr.3) 2no Eddery P 119 *.50 — — Hegemony 124no CaptureHim 1192½ Paymaster 1191 Bid,led 7
24Sep83♦1Curragh(Ire) gd 7f 1:30⅘ ⓣLee Plate(Mdn) 18 Eddery P 126 *.25 — — Capture Him 1268 Tomriland 1211½ Tridessus 126hd Easily 16
LATEST WORKOUTS ●Oct 31 Aqu ⓣ 3f fm :36⅕ h ●Oct 26 Hol 1 fst 1:39⅘ h ●Oct 21 Hol 7f fst 1:25⅕ h Oct 16 Hol 6f fst 1:15⅘ h

Dr. Schwartzman — B. c. 4, by Fluorescent Light—Stark Winter, by Graustark
Br.—Farish W S III & Hannibal Horse Co (Ky)
Tr.—Croll Warren A Jr
Own.—Levy Blanche P — 126
Lifetime 25 8 3 5 $260,347 — 1985 10 3 1 4 $124,979 — 1984 8 2 2 1 $87,671 — Turf 19 7 3 4 $244,035

25Oct85- 9Med fm 1⅛ ⓣ:47⅕ 1:10⅘ 1:41⅘ 3+Cl Virginian 3 8 77½ 64¾ 33½ 11¾ Perret C 119 4.20 93-09 Dr. Schwartzman 1191¾ Onyxly 1191½ RedBrigade1195 Going away 8
10Aug85- 8Atl fm 1⅜ ⓣ:45⅗ 1:11⅗ 1:54⅗ 3+U Nations H 10 5 58 53½ 68¼ 75¾ Antley C W 116 10.00e 85-14 Ends Well 1142 Who's For Dinner 116hd Cool 1101 Outrun 11
10Aug85-Grade I
15Jun85- 7Mth fm 1 ⓣ:49 1:12⅘ 1:37 3+Red Bank H 1 3 32 31 41½ 52½ Perret C 118 2.50 87-11 Castelets 115nk Evzone 117¾ Gothic Revival 1121½ Tired 8
15Jun85-Run in Divisions
4Jun85- 8Mth fm 1 ⓣ:48⅖ 1:12⅕ 1:36⅕ 3+Alw 20000 4 1 2hd 1hd 3nk 35 Perret C 122 *.70 89-11 Evzone 1225 Sun and Shine 115noDr.Schwartzman1223 Weakened 5
6Apr85-10Hia fm 1⅛ ⓣ 1:53⅘ 3+Bouginvla H 7 4 47½ 36 42 33½ Perret C 117 *1.40 86-13 Flying Pidgeon 1143 Nassipour114nkDr.Schwartzman117hd Evenly 9
6Apr85-Grade II Run in divisions
18Mar85- 9Hia fm 1⅛ ⓣ 1:41⅘ 3+Royl Palm H 3 6 614 55¾ 21 1hd Perret C 115 *1.50 89-11 Dr.Schwrtzmn115hdBoldRn1141½NorthrnFshn112hd Checked, drvg 11
18Mar85-Grade III
16Feb85- 9GP gd 1⅛ ⓣ:46⅕ 1:10 1:40 3+Can Turf H 5 5 57 43½ 32½ 21½ Perret C 116 8.30 99-04 Nepal 1121½ Dr. Schwartzman 116nk Roving Minstrel1201½ Rallied 12
16Feb85-Grade II. Run in divisions
5Feb85- 9GP fm *1⅛ ⓣ 1:45 Alw 25000 4 3 21½ 1hd 11½ 1¾ Perret C 115 *.90 81-23 Dr. Schwartzman 115¾ Bold Run 1222½ Ronbra 1221½ Driving 7
LATEST WORKOUTS ●Oct 19 Mth 6f fst 1:12⅘ h ●Oct 13 Mth 5f fst 1:00⅘ h Oct 7 Mth 1 fst 1:41 h ●Sep 30 Mth 6f fst 1:13 hg

Shadeed — B. c. 3, by Nijinsky II—Continual, by Damascus
Br.—CherryValleyFarmInc&TheGamelyCorp (Ky)
Tr.—Stoute Michael R
Own.—Maktoum Al Maktoum — 123
Lifetime 6 4 0 1 $180,029 — 1985 4 3 0 0 $166,707 — 1984 2 1 0 1 $13,322 — Turf 6 4 0 1 $180,029

28Sep85♦2Ascot(Eng) fm 1 1:38⅘ ⓣQueenElizabethIIStk(Gr2) 12½ Swinburn W R 126 *2.25 — — Shadeed 1262½ Teleprompter 133hd Zaizafon 116no Led fnl 4f 7
5Jun85♦3Epsom(Eng) gd 1½ 2:36⅕ ⓣDerby Stakes(Gr.1) 13 Swinburn W R 126 3.50 — — Slip Anchor 1267 Law Society 1266 Damister 126no Bid,gave way 14
4May85♦3Newmarket(Eng) gd 1 1:37⅖ ⓣ2,000 Guineas Stakes(Gr1) 1hd Piggott L 126 *.80 — — Shadeed 126hd Bairn 1261½ Supreme Leader 1265 Led fnl 3f 14
16Apr85♦3Newmarket(Eng) gd 1 1:38⅕ ⓣCraven Stakes(Gr3) 16 Swinburn W R 119 *2.25 — — Shadeed 1196 Damister 1193 Heraldiste 1192½ Led fnl 2f 6
20Oct84♦4Newmarket(Eng) gd 7f 1:25⅗ ⓣHoughton Stakes 12½ Swinburn W R 123 *1.10 — — Shadeed 1232½ Tiber Creek 120nk DHAl Riyadh 123nk Led fnl 2f 15
5Oct84♦6Newmarket(Eng) gd 7f 1:28⅕ ⓣWestley Stakes(Mdn) 31½ Swinburn W R 126 *1.25 — — Kala Dancer 1261½ Al Riyadh 126no Shadeed 1265 Fin.well 28
LATEST WORKOUTS Oct 31 Aqu ⓣ 5f fm 1:01⅗ h

Rousillon — B. c. 4, by Riverman—Belle Dorine, by Marshua's Dancer
Br.—Farish & Jones (Ky)
Tr.—Harwood Guy
Own.—Juddmonte Farms — 126
Lifetime 12 7 1 1 $380,722 — 1985 3 3 0 0 $284,792 — 1984 6 2 0 1 $66,840 — Turf 12 7 1 1 $380,722

8Sep85♦5Longchamp(Fra) gd*1 1:39 ⓣPrix du Moulin(Gr1) 11½ Starkey G 128 *1.50e — — Rousillon 1281½ Kozana 120½ Procida 128¾ Trailed,drvg 12
31Jly85♦4Goodwood(Eng) gd 1 1:41 ⓣSussex Stakes(Gr1) 12½ Starkey G 133 *2.00 — — Rousillon 1332½ Bairn 1221½ King ofClubs 133¾ Bid, drew away 10
18Jun85♦1Ascot(Eng) gd 1 1:40⅕ ⓣQueen Anne Stakes (Gr2) 12½ Starkey G 131 *2.75 — — Rousillon1312½ CelstilBounty114½ KingofClubs1342½ Going away 8
28Oct84♦3Longchamp(Fra) sf*7f 1:27 ⓣPrix de la Foret(Gr.1) 31½ Starkey G 137 6.50 — — Procida 1371½ Nikos 137hd Rousillon 137nk Well up,led 10
25Aug84♦3Goodwood(Eng) gd 1 1:43 ⓣWaterfordCrystalMile(Gr2) 1½ Starkey G 118 *.60 — — Rousillon 118½ Prego 126½ MeisElReem 119hd Bid,led,held 5

1Aug84♦4Goodwood(Eng) gd 1 1:38⅘ (T) Sussex Stakes(Gr.1) 2½ Starkey G 122 3.00 — — ChiefSinger 122½ Rousillon 122 7 Creag anSgor 122 2 Bore in 5
1Aug84-Disqualified and placed last
19May84♦4Curragh(Ire) gd 1 1:38⅘ (T) Irish2,000GuineasStk(Gr1) 5¾ Starkey G 126 2.10 — — Sadler's Wells 126nk Procida 126½ Secreto 126½ Bid then evenly 9
23Apr84♦4Longchamp(Fra) gd*1 1:35⅘ (T) PouleEssaiPoulains(Gr1) 6 3 Eddery P 128 2.75 — — Siberian Express 128¾ Green Paradise128nk Mendez128 1½ Slow st 14
7Apr84♦3Salisbury(Eng) gd 7f 1:27⅘ (T) 2000 GuineasTrailStk(Gr3) 1 1 Starkey G 122 *1.25 — — Rousillon 122 1 Chief Singer 127 7 Kalim 122 1 Bid,handily 17
24Sep83♦4Ascot(Eng) gd 1 1:41⅗ (T) Royal Lodge Stakes(Gr.2) 2 2 Starkey G 123 *1.20 — — Gold and Ivory 123 2 Rousillon 123 2½ TrojanFen 123 5 Bid,led 5
LATEST WORKOUTS Oct 31 Aqu (T) 4f fm :50 b

Al Mamoon

Ch. c. 4, by Believe It—Lady Winborne, by Secretariat
Br.—Haras de St George Ltd (Ky)
Own.—Firestone B R
Tr.—Frankel Robert
126
Lifetime 19 5 5 3 $400,139
1985 11 2 4 2 $377,200
1984 4 1 1 0 $12,670
Turf 13 5 3 0 $236,889

19Oct85- 8Med fst 1¼ :48 1:36 2:00⅘ 3+Med Cup H 6 4 4 3 1hd 3nk 3 7 Cordero A Jr 115 2.60 93-13 Bounding Basque113 4½WildAgain120 2½AlMamoon115 1½ Weakened 11
19Oct85-Grade I
14Sep85- 8Bel fst 1¼ :47 1:36⅕ 2:01⅕ 3+Marlboro H 2 4 5 3 6 2¾ 5 3 6 3½ Hawley S 116 18.90 88-09 Chief'sCrown119nkGateDncer125¾Vnlndinghm122hd Steadied turn 9
14Sep85-Grade I
25Aug85- 6AP yl 1¼ (T):47⅗ 1:39⅗ 2:03⅗ 3+Bud Arl Mil 10 6 5 6 4 4½ 6 6½ 6 7¾ Hawley S 126 25.80 69-27 Teleprompter 126¾ Greinton 126 3½ Flying Pidgeon126 1½ Bid,wknd 13
25Aug85-Grade I
11Aug85- 8Dmr fm 1⅛ (T):48⅕ 1:11⅗ 1:46⅘ 3+E Read H 2 4 4 2½ 4 4½ 3 2 2½ Hawley S 118 4.70 103-05 Tsunami Slew119½AlMamoon118 3½BothEndsBurning123 1½ Rallied 7
11Aug85-Grade II
4Jly85- 8Hol fm 1⅛ (T):47⅗ 1:11 1:46⅕ 3+American H 1 2 2 2 3 1½ 2 2½ 2 1¾ Delahoussaye E 117 3.60 97-04 Tsunami Slew 117 1¾ Al Mamoon 117¾ Dahar 123 1¾ Gamely 7
4Jly85-Grade II
16Jun85- 8Hol fm 1 1/16 (T):47 1:10⅗ 1:40⅕ 3+Inglwd H 4 4 4 1½ 4 2½ 2 1½ 1nk Delahoussaye E 116 3.10 98-08 Al Mamoon 116nk The Noble Player 118½ Swoon 114 1½ Driving 6
16Jun85-Grade III
19May85- 8Hol fst 1 :44⅘ 1:08⅗ 1:32⅘ 3+Mrvn Lry H 2 4 4 1¾ 5 6 4 6½ 4 6¾ Delahoussaye E 115 5.80 102-08 Precisionist 126 4 Greinton 121 1 My Habitony 115 1¾ Tired 5
19May85-Grade II
13Apr85- 8SA fst 1⅛ :45 1:09 1:47 Sn Brndno H 2 5 6 7 5 6 4 3 3nk Delahoussaye E 115 7.30 94-13 Greinton 120nk Precisionist 127hd Al Mamoon 115 10 Bumped St. 6
13Apr85-Grade II
24Mar85-10TuP fm 1 1/16 (T):47⅗ 1:12 1:42⅗ 3+Az Dwns H 8 3 3 2 2hd 1 4 1 4 McCarron C J 117 *.70 107 — Al Mamoon 117 4 Gemini Dreamer 116 4½ SecretHaven110hd Easily 9
3Mar85- 4SA fst 1 :45⅗ 1:09⅗ 1:35⅕ Alw 45000 1 3 1hd 1 2 1hd 2 2 McCarron C J 114 *.60 90-14 Forzando II 116 2 Al Mamoon 114 4PrairieBreaker118 1½ Weakened 7
LATEST WORKOUTS Oct 28 Bel 5f fst :57⅘ h ●Oct 12 Bel 6f fst 1:12 h ●Oct 6 Bel 6f gd 1:11⅕ h Sep 29 Bel 6f fst 1:13⅕ b

*Never So Bold

B. h. 5, by Bold Lad (Ire)—Never Never Land, by Habitat
Br.—Mount Rosa Stud (Ire)
Own.—Kessly E D
Tr.—Armstrong Robert W
126
Lifetime 22 10 4 3 $326,830
1985 5 4 0 0 $189,464
1984 8 3 4 1 $103,891
Turf 22 10 4 3 $326,830

6Oct85♦3Longchamp(Fra) gd*5f :55⅕ (T) Prix de l'Abbaye(Gr1) 4 1¾ Cauthen S 137 *.40 — — Committed 133hd Vilikaia 133¾ Parioli 133 1 Prom thruout 12
22Aug85♦3York(Eng) gd 5f :59 (T) WHillSprntChamp'ship(Gr1) 1 2 Cauthen S 126 *.65 — — NvrSoBold126 2 PrimoDomn122½ StormWrnng119 1½ Prom,handily 7
11Jly85♦3Newmarket(Eng) gd 6f 1:11⅘ (T) July Cup(Gr1) 1 2½ Cauthen S 132 *1.25 — — Never So Bold 132 2½ Committed 129no Dayfayna 120 1½ Bid,easily 9
21Jun85♦4Ascot(Eng) gd 5f 1:01⅗ (T) Kings Stand Stakes(Gr1) 1 3 Piggott L 129 4.00 — — NeverSoBold129 3 PrimoDomini121hd Committd126nk Bid,rdn out 15
28May85♦3Sandown(Eng) gd 5f 1:00⅗ (T) Temple Stakes(Gr3) 1½ Cauthen S 131 *2.25 — — Never So Bold131½ PrimoDominie122 3 Jonacris126nk Bid,led,held 6
27Sep84♦4Ascot(Eng) gd 6f 1:13⅗ (T) Diadem Stakes(Gr.3) 1 1½ Cauthen S 133 2.10 — — NeverSoBold133 1½ FortysecondStreet126 1 Habibti130 4 Led fnl 2f 9
8Sep84♦3Haydock(Eng) fm 6f 1:13 (T) Vernons Sprint Cup(Gr.2) 3½ Murray A 129 2.25 — — Petong 129no Habibti 126½ NeverSoBold 129 2 Bold bid,hung 9
17Aug84♦3Newbury(Eng) gd*7¼f 1:29⅗ (T) HungerfordStakes(Gr3) 2nk Cauthen S 131 *.70 — — Prego 126nk NeverSoBold 131 1 Sarab 118hd Bid,led 8
5Aug84♦4Deauville(Fra) gd*6½f 1:16⅗ (T) PrixMaurice deGheest(Gr2) 1 2 Cauthen S 127 *1.20 — — Never So Bold127 2 Condrillac122nk SpeedyGirl118hd Going away 11
12Jly84♦3Newmarket(Eng) gd 6f 1:11⅗ (T) JulyCup(Gr.1) 2 1½ Cauthen S 132 33.00 — — ChiefSinger123 1½ NeverSoBold132 3 Committed129 2½ Closed well 9
LATEST WORKOUTS Oct 31 Aqu (T) 4f fm :52⅕ b

Cozzene

Gr. h. 5, by Caro—Ride The Trails, by Prince John
Br.—Nerud J A (Fla)
Own.—Nerud J A
Tr.—Nerud Jan H
126
Lifetime 23 9 5 5 $528,152
1985 7 3 1 2 $168,480
1984 10 3 2 3 $305,562
Turf 11 5 2 4 $417,168

3Oct85- 8Med sly 1 1/16 :47 1:12⅕ 1:45 3+Clf Hngr H 6 4 5 2½ 5 5½ 5 13 6 16 Guerra W A 123 *1.00 62-25 Late Act 117nk Silver Surfer 116 2½PaxNobiscum116 7 Off sluggish 7
3Oct85-Grade III
24Aug85- 9Mth fm 1⅛ (T):48⅕ 1:12⅗ 1:48⅗+ 3+Longfellw H 6 4 3 8½ 4 5½ 1hd 1 2 Guerra W A 122 *.70 98-09 Cozzene 122 2 Zoffany 114¾ Mourjane 117 3 Driving 8
24Aug85-Grade II
11Aug85- 8Sar fm 1⅛ (T):47⅘ 1:10⅗ 1:47 3+B Baruch H 3 5 5 4 3 2 2hd 2nk Guerra W A 120 2.20 92-13 Win 124nk Cozzene 120 4½ Sitzmark 112¾ Bore out 9
11Aug85-Grade II
13Jly85- 9Mth fm 1 1/16 (T):48 1:11⅗ 1:42⅗ 3+Oceanport H 8 3 3 5 3 2½ 2hd 1 3 Guerra W A 121 *1.70 93-14 Cozzene 121 3 Stay The Course 119 3½ RovingMinstrel118 1 Driving 9
13Jly85-Grade III
8Jun85- 4Bel sly 6f :21⅘ :44⅗ 1:09⅕ 3+Jaipur 3 4 3 5 3 4 3 3½ 3 3½ Cordero A Jr 117 2.40 93-12 Mt. Livermore 119 2¾ Main Top 117½ Cozzene 117¾ Even try 7
27May85- 7Bel fm 7f (T):22⅗ :45 1:23 3+Wise Ship 2 7 4 4 2 4 2 2½ 3 1¾ Guerra W A 119 *.40e 87-19 Sitzmark 119 1 Red Wing Dream 119¾ Cozzene 119 1 Off slowly 7
10May85- 8Bel fst 6f :22⅕ :45⅗ 1:11 3+Alw 36000 7 7 5 6½ 4 6 2½ 1 1½ Guerra W A 124 5.10 87-20 Cozzene 124 1½ Basket Weave 124½ Momento II 119 2½ Driving 7
10Nov84- 4Hol fm 1 (T):45⅗ 1:08⅘ 1:32⅘ 3+Br Cp Mile 5 3 3 2½ 3½ 1hd 3 1¾ Guerra W A 126 3.80 103-01 Royal Heroine 123 1½ Star Choice 126nk Cozzene 126nk Weakened 10
10Nov84-Grade I
10Oct84- 8Bel fm 1 (T):45⅕ 1:09⅗ 1:33 3+Alw 36000 2 3 3 2 1 1½ 1 4 1 4 Guerra W A 117 *.90 100-12 Cozzene 117 4 Sitzmark 115 2¾ Alev 115 2¾ Ridden out 6
21Sep84- 8Med fm 1 1/16 (T):47 1:10⅗ 1:40⅗ 3+Cliff Hngr H 6 3 3 1 2hd 1hd 1½ Guerra W A 115 *1.00 100-06 Cozzene 115½ Ayman 112 1½ Pin Puller 114 4¾ Driving 6
• 21Sep84-Run in divisions
LATEST WORKOUTS Oct 30 Bel 4f fst :50⅗ b ●Oct 25 Bel 4f fst :46⅕ h Oct 20 Bel 4f fst :48⅗ b Oct 14 Bel 4f fst :48⅕ b

*Forzando II

Dk. b. or br. c. 4, by Formidable—Princely Maid, by King's Troop
Br.—Red House Stud (Eng)
Own.—Chillingworth S C
Tr.—Sullivan John
126
Lifetime 25 11 3 2 $441,009
1985 8 4 1 0 $369,405
1984 8 2 0 2 $43,807
Turf 22 9 3 2 $196,159

23Jun85- 8Hol fst 1¼ :46⅕ 1:34⅗ 1:58⅗ 3+Gold Cup H 5 2 4 4 4 5 4 7 5 10¾ Delahoussaye E 118 4.60 110 — Greinton 120 1¾ Precisionist 125 1½ Kings Island 112 5 Weakened 6
23Jun85-Grade I
27May85- 8Bel fst 1 :45⅘ 1:10⅕ 1:34⅗ 3+Metropltn H 4 7 7 3¾ 3 1½ 1 1½ 1 5¾ MacBeth D 118 23.60 93-15 Forzando II 118 5¾ Mo Exception 113 1½ TrackBarron125 1¾ Driving 8
27May85-Grade I
6May85- 8Aqu yl 1 1/16 (T):47⅗ 1:12⅗ 1:46 3+Ft Marcy H 3 4 4 4½ 5 5½ 2 1½ 1nk Velasquez J 120 *1.70 75-25 Forzando II 120nk Native Raid 115 4½ Solidified 113½ Driving 7
6May85-Grade III
20Apr85- 8SA fm *6½f (T):21⅗ :43⅕ 1:13⅗ Sn Smn H 8 2 7 11 8 7¾ 5 4½ 2hd Toro F 122 2.60 91-10 ChampagneBid121hdForzandoII122noSmartandSnrp118 1½ Gamely 8
20Apr85-Grade III
3Mar85- 4SA fst 1 :45⅗ 1:09⅗ 1:35⅕ Alw 45000 7 5 4 4½ 2 2 2hd 1 2 Toro F 116 7.60 92-14 Forzando II 116 2 Al Mamoon114 4PrairieBreaker118 1½ Ridden out 7
11Feb85- 8SA fm *6½f (T):20⅘ :43 1:14⅗ S Madre H 1 13 11 8½ 12 12 6 3¾ 1½ Toro F 117 11.80 87-13 Forzando II117½LuckyBuccaneer117 1½ChampagneBid121½ Driving 14
27Jan85- 5SA fm *6½f (T):21⅗ :43⅘ 1:13⅘ Alw 45000 7 9 9 6¾ 6 6½ 4 1½ 4 1¾ Valenzuela P A 115 7.50 88-14 Shananie 122½ Ayman 114 1½ Rocky Marriage 117hd Bumped st 12
27Jan85-Bumped, steadied start
13Jan85- 5SA fm *6½f (T):21⅕ :43⅗ 1:14⅗ Alw 42000 2 10 8 5¾ 7 7½ 5 3¾ 6 3¾ Valenzuela P A 119 11.70 82-16 Shananie 116nk Maxim Gorky 115 1 Bozina 119 1 Outrun 10
18Oct84♦4Newmarket(Eng) gd 7f 1:26 (T) BisquitCognacChalnge(Gr3) 3 3¾ Raymond B 128 5.50 — — Brocade 125 3 Prego 132¾ Forzando 128 4 Raced evenly 7
24Sep84♦6MLaffitte(Fra) sf*6f 1:12 (T) Prix deSeine etOise(Gr3) 3 5½ Raymond B 123 16.00 — — Proskona 120 5 Parioli 120nk Forzando 123hd Raced evenly 10
LATEST WORKOUTS ●Oct 31 Aqu (T) 5f fm 1:01 h Oct 25 SA (T) 5f fm 1:00 h (d) Oct 19 SA (T) 5f fm 1:00⅕ h (d) Oct 15 SA (T) 5f fm 1:04⅕ h (d)

Sitzmark

Dk. b. or br. h. 5, by J O Tobin—Aphonia, by Dunce
Br.—Lasater Farm (Ky)
Own.—Saldo Stable
Tr.—DeStasio Richard T
126
Lifetime 43 11 7 2 $300,280
1985 14 4 1 1 $135,231
1984 16 1 3 0 $84,796
Turf 21 5 4 1 $211,647

21Oct85- 6Bel fm 1 1/16 [T]:46⅗ 1:10⅗ 1:41⅗ 3+Alw 40000 2 4 4 2 4 1¾ 2hd 1hd Vasquez J b 117 2.70 93-19 Sitzmark 117hd Strong Dollar 115 3 Fearless Leader 115 3½ Driving 6
13Oct85- 6Bel gd 1 (T):46 1:10⅗ 1:36⅗ 3+Handicap 3 5 5 6¾ 5 13 5 16 4 17 Cordero A Jr b 116 9.00 66-25 Chief's Crown 125 2½ Intensify 114 2½ Smile 116 12 Outrun 5
14Sep85- 7Bel fm 1 (T):47 1:11⅕ 1:36 3+[R]Knightly Man 5 8 8 3¾ 7 3¾ 4 4 4 4½ Maple E b 117 7.60 81-19 Zoffany 119no Fearless Leader 115 3½ Aristocratical 119 1 In close 10
1Sep85- 8Bel gd 1¼ [T]:48⅘ 1:37⅘ 2:02 3+Manhttn H 13 1 1 2½ 7 6½ 12 16 12 17½ Maple E b 113 37.00e 66-24 Cool 112 2½ Win 126 3½ Sondrio 110½ Stopped 13
1Sep85-Grade I
11Aug85- 8Sar fm 1⅛ (T):47⅘ 1:10⅗ 1:47 3+B Baruch H 1 3 3 2 2½ 3 2 3 4¾ Vasquez J b 112 13.60e 87-13 Win 124nk Cozzene 120 4½ Sitzmark 112¾ Weakened 9
11Aug85-Grade II
3Aug85- 7Sar fm 1 1/16 (T):46⅗ 1:10⅗ 1:42 3+Alw 40000 7 4 3 2 2 1½ 3 2½ 2 2 Privitera R5 b 114 4.90 85-09 Aristocratical 115 2 Sitzmark 114no Onyxly 115½ Gained place 7
5Jly85- 8Bel fm 1⅜ (T):49 1:37⅗ 2:15⅗ 3+Tidal H 7 7 7 6 6 4 6 4 8 3½ Migliore R b 114 23.30 82-17 Wh'sFrDnnr115¾Dmynsky116nkFlyngPdgn117nk Needed response 11
5Jly85-Grade II
27Jun85- 6Bel fm 1 1/16 [T]:47⅗ 1:11⅕ 1:42⅗ 3+Alw 40000 4 3 3 2 3 1½ 3 1½ 1nk Vasquez J b 117 1.60 89-20 Sitzmark 117nk Vers La Caisse 112½ Spring Fever 117nk Driving 6
15Jun85- 9Mth fm 1 (T):46⅘ 1:10⅗ 1:35⅗ 3+Red Bank H 3 9 9 4¾ 4 2½ 4 2½ 4 1½ Antley C W b 119 *1.50 95-11 Ends Well 116½ Domynsky117hdBoldSoutherner115 1 Broke slowly 9
15Jun85-Run in Divisions
27May85- 7Bel fm 7f (T):22⅗ :45 1:23 3+Wise Ship 5 5 7 7 4 6 3 2½ 1 1 Vasquez J b 119 5.20 89-19 Sitzmark 119 1 Red Wing Dream 119¾ Cozzene 119 1 Driving 7
LATEST WORKOUTS Oct 7 Bel tr.t 5f fst 1:00⅘ b ●Sep 22 Bel tr.t 4f fst :48 h Sep 10 Bel tr.t 3f my :36⅘ b

Palace Music

Ch. c. 4, by The Minstrel—Come My Prince, by Prince John
Br.—Mereworth Farm (Ky)
Own.—Paulson A E
Tr.—Biancone Patrick L
126
Lifetime 10 4 3 1 $219,020
1985 3 1 0 1 $54,560
1984 7 3 3 0 $164,460
Turf 10 4 3 1 $219,020

19Oct85♦2Newmarket(Eng) gd 1¼ 2:04⅗ (T) DubaiChampionStakes(Gr1) 3 3 Lequeux A 129 14.00 — — Pebbles 126 3 SlipAnchor 122hd PalaceMusic 129 Fin well 10
26Sep85♦5MLaffitte(Fra) yl*1¼ 2:02⅕ (T) LaCoupe deMLaffitte(Gr3) 1¾ Legrix E 123 *.90 — — Palace Music 121¾ Iades 121nk Devalois 118 1½ Well pl. drvg 11
20Aug85♦3York(Eng) gd 1 5/16 2:18⅗ (T) Benson&HedgesGoldCup(Gr1) 4 9¾ St Martin Y 132 10.00 — — Commanche Run 132¾ Oh So Sharp 119 4 Triptych 119 5 Evenly 6
20Oct84♦2Newmarket(Eng) gd 1¼ 2:01 (T) Dubai ChampionStakes(Gr1) 1nk St Martin Y 122 18.00 — — Palace Music 122nk Pebbles 119 1½ Raft 122nk Bid,led,held 15

27Sep84 ♦ 3MLaffitte Fra sf*1¼ 2:06⅗ Ⓣ LaCoupe deMLaffitte(Gr3) 24 St Martin Y 121 2.40e — — Estrapade 1224 Palace Music 121nk Bob Back 119nk Fin well 11
19Aug84 ♦ 4Deauville Fra gd*1 1:34⅘ Ⓣ PrixJacquesLeMarois(Gr1) 24 Legrix E 121 32.00 — — Lear Fan 1214 Palace Music 121¾ SiberianExpress1211½ Fin well 10
15Jly84 ♦ 5MLaffitte Fra gd*1 1:37⅕ Ⓣ Prix Messidor(Gr.3) 21 Legrix E 117 12.00 — — Mille Balles 1261 Palace Music 117¾ Blue BellPearl113¾ Fin well 13
30Jun84 ♦ 4Evry Fra gd*1⅛ 1:50⅘ Ⓣ Prix Daphnis(Gr.3) 1no Legrix E 128 5.60 — — PalaceMusic128no SeattleSong1282½ EnchntedCstle1282 Just up 9
23Apr84 ♦ 4Longchamp Fra gd*1 1:35⅘ Ⓣ PouleEssaiPoulains(Gr1) 12 Piggott L 128 9.00 — — SiberianExpress128¾ GreenParadise128nk Mendez1281½ Gave way 14
29Mar84 ♦ 1StCloud(Fra sf*7½f 1:47⅘ Ⓣ Prix Phebe(Mdn) 11½ Head F 123 *1.50 — — Palace Music 1231½ River's Wave 1232 Percival 123¾ Bid, easily 11

The Noble Player — Ch. h. 5, by The Minstrel—Noble Mark II, by On Your Mark II
Own.—Sangster R E — Br.—Swettenham Stud (Ky) — Tr.—Gosden John H M — 126
Lifetime 28 7 8 5 $297,276 — 1985 6 1 3 0 $138,400 — 1984 7 2 3 1 $95,270 — Turf 28 7 8 5 $297,276

5Oct85- 8BM fm 1⅛ Ⓣ:47⅖ 1:11 1:48⅘ 3+Tanforan H 6 4 46 55 21 21½ Shoemaker W 119 2.30 94-04 BothEndsBurning1231½TheNoblePlayer1192½NakAck115nk Gamely 6
5Oct85-Grade III
25Aug85- 6AP yl 1¼ Ⓣ:47⅗ 1:39⅘ 2:03⅘ 3+Bud Arl Mil 2 5 66½ 77½ 56½ 55¾ Shoemaker W 126 27.80 71-27 Teleprompter 126¾ Greinton1263½FlyingPidgeon1261½ No menace 13
25Aug85-Grade I
10Aug85- 8Haw fm 1¼ Ⓣ:47⅗ 1:36 2:00⅖ 3+Arlington H 7 4 33 21 1½ 2no Toro F 118 *.90 114 — PssTheLine113noTheNoblePlyer118½ExecutivPrid1134½ Just failed 7
10Aug85-Grade I
4Jly85- 8Hol fm 1⅛ Ⓣ:47⅗ 1:11 1:46⅕ 3+American H 6 4 43 42 45 47 Lipham T 118 9.00 92-04 Tsunami Slew 1171¾ Al Mamoon 1173½ Dahar 1231¾ No rally 7
4Jly85-Grade II
16Jun85- 8Hol fm 1 1/16 Ⓣ:47 1:10⅖ 1:40⅕ 3+Inglwd H 1 3 2½ 2hd 11½ 2nk McCarron C J 118 2.30 98-08 Al Mamoon 116nk The Noble Player 118½ Swoon 1141¼ Gamely 6
16Jun85-Grade III
31May85- 8Hol fm 1 Ⓣ:45⅕ 1:09 1:33⅗ Alw 48000 4 5 510 42½ 3nk 11½ McCarron C J 115 3.10 95-10 The Noble Player 1151½ Val Danseur 115½ Gilgit 117hd Driving 8
5Nov84- 8SA fm 1¼ Ⓣ:47 1:36 2:01 3+ⓇH P Rsl H 4 4 45 31 11 11¼ McCarron C J 121 *.60 82-20 The Noble Player 1211¼ Trakady 117hd Dalby 1131¾ Ridden out 7
5Nov84-Disqualified from purse money
7Oct84- 8BM fm *1⅛ Ⓣ:47 1:11⅗ 1:50⅖ 3+Tanforan H 6 3 32 21½ 3½ 23½ Lipham T 118 17.00 92-04 BothEndsBurning1123½ThNoblPlyr1182EvningM'Lord116½ Gamely 9
7Oct84-Grade III
15Sep84-11Bmf fm 1 1/16 Ⓣ:47⅘ 1:11⅗ 1:43⅕ 3+Sn Matean H 5 5 53½ 31½ 1hd 1½ Lipham T 120 *1.70 92-06 TheNoblePlayer120½GreenwoodStar117nkPairOfAces1151½ Driving 9
25Aug84- 8Dmr fm 7½f Ⓣ:22⅗ :45⅘ 1:28⅘ 3+Escondido H 2 6 614 614 43½ 21¼ McCarron C J 121 *1.90 94-08 PairofDeuces1171¼TheNoblePlayer121nkFabulousDd1121¼ Gamely 8
25Aug84-Run in divisions
LATEST WORKOUTS Oct 31 Aqu Ⓣ 4f fm :51⅘ b ●Oct 26 Hol 7f fst 1:26⅖ h Oct 14 Hol 5f fst 1:01 h Oct 2 Hol 5f fst 1:02 h

Late Act * — B. h. 6, by Stage Door Johnny—Dunce Cap II, by Tom Fool
Own.—Greentree Stable — Br.—Greentree Stud Inc (Ky) — Tr.—Reinacher Robert Jr — 126
Lifetime 25 7 5 3 $533,344 — 1985 5 1 3 0 $117,370 — 1984 7 2 1 1 $216,716 — Turf 17 4 4 3 $457,724

12Oct85- 8Med fm 1⅜ Ⓣ:49⅖ 1:38⅖ 2:15 3+Ballantine 6 6 76 3½ 1hd 2¾ Maple E b 126 2.60 89-13 Sharannpour 126¾ Late Act 1266½ Persian Tiara 123nk Gave way 10
3Oct85- 8Med sly 1 1/16 :47 1:12⅕ 1:45 3+Clf Hngr H 2 7 63 31½ 2hd 1nk Bailey J D b 117 5.80 78-25 Late Act 117nk Silver Surfer 1162½ Pax Nobiscum 1167 Driving 7
3Oct85-Grade III
21Sep85- 8Med fm 1 1/16 Ⓣ:46 1:09⅗ 1:40⅗ 3+John Henry 8 8 63½ 42½ 23½ 21¼ Bailey J D b 113 2.90 — — Onyxly 1171¼ Late Act 1131½ Crazy Moon 117¾ Fin well 10
16Feb85-10GP fm 1 1/16 Ⓣ:46 1:09⅗ 1:40⅗ 3+Can Turf H 13 12 1214 128¾ 61¼ 53½ Maple E b 120 7.70 94-04 Solidified 113hd Selous Scout 1132 Jack Slade 1221 Late bid 13
16Feb85-Grade II Run in divisions
19Jan85- 9GP fm 1 Ⓣ:46⅕ 1:10⅖ 1:34⅖ 3+Appleton H 2 7 77 74¼ 34 27½ Maple E b 121 3.40 90-07 Star Choice 1187½ Late Act 121nk Solidified 114nk Railied 10
19Jan85-Grade III; Run in divisions
8Dec84- 9Crc fm *1⅛ Ⓣ 1:45⅘ 3+Hurricanes H 11 9 99 84¼ 109¼ 107½ Maple E b 123 *1.60 86-09 FlyingPidgeon112noDHPurpleComet117DHAmrild113½ Raced wide 11
8Dec84-Run in divisions
10Nov84- 9Hol fm 1⅛ Ⓣ:47⅕ 1:10⅗ 1:46⅗ 3+Stk 1000000 12 12 106¾ 105 84¼ 21¼ Maple E b 124 *1.90 96-01 Zoffany 1141¼ Late Act 1241 Johnotable 114hd Gaining 12
28Oct84- 8SA fm 1½ Ⓣ:45 2:00⅕ 2:25⅘ 3+Oak Tree 2 5 69 1½ 32 66 Maple E b 126 18.30 82-12 Both Ends Burning 1261 Gato DelSol1262¾Raami121nk Weakened 12
28Oct84-Grade I
14Oct84-10LaD sf 1⅜ Ⓣ:49⅕ 1:40⅕ 2:19⅕ 3+La Dwns H 11 12 104¾ 11½ 17 11½ Maple E b 118 *2.40 71-36 Late Act 1181½ Inevitable Leader1165FlyingPidgeon1111½ Driving 14
LATEST WORKOUTS Oct 30 Bel 4f fst :46⅗ h Oct 25 Bel 4f fst :47⅗ h Oct 20 Bel 4f fst :48⅖ b Oct 10 Bel 4f fst :50 b

June with a broken bone in his knee. Prior to the Met and the injury, he was only a Grade III performer on the grass.

AL MAMOON

Runner-up to Tsunami Slew on two occasions, Al Mamoon has been working bullets in the mornings. Post position 14 will not help his cause, however.

And now, for the foreign contingent, inner posts first:

NEVER SO BOLD

This horse was regarded as the premier sprinter in Europe prior to his stunning defeat at 2–5 in the Prix de l'Abbaye at Longchamp. Can he stay the mile?

> Rumor was confounded again, as Never So Bold produced all his familiar dash to race home two lengths clear of Primo Dominie, and, to universal satisfaction, he, this time, made it back to the winner's enclosure without the distressing symptoms which followed his Ascot and Newmarket victories. On both those occasions, he had become temporarily, but undeniably lame on pulling up, a circumstance veterinarians eventually ascribed to a

> leaky knee joint. This time there was no sign of unsoundness, and trainer Robert Armstrong felt confident about announcing plans to send Never So Bold to Aqueduct for the Grade I Breeders' Cup Mile in November.
>
> This is unquestionably the best sprinter in Europe, maybe the best sprinter seen in these parts for many years, but according to regular pilot, Steve Cauthen, the fact that his best form here is at five and six furlongs will not make him a forlorn hope over the longer distance in New York. "He's sure to get a mile there," says the Kentucky-born champion.
>
> *The Thoroughbred Record,* August 31, 1985

PALACE MUSIC

Campaigned in top company at the classic distances as a four-year-old, Palace Music was an accomplished miler in 1984 prior to defeating Pebbles in the Dubai Champion Stakes. The horse will be running late but is probably no longer quick enough to attain a good striking position early.

SHADEED

Rated an outstanding prospect in the spring, Shadeed is now coming off what is probably the best performance of his career.

> Back in the Spring, when he stormed home in the Group III Craven Stakes, Shadeed had looked every handsome inch a potential Horse Of The Year, but the seemingly inevitable Group I General Accident Two Thousand Guineas victory came in an undignified manner, with all the stops pulled out, and his lacklustre effort in the Group I Ever Ready Derby, in which he was virtually pulled up, made him seem a back number.
>
> We cynics were convinced that we would not hear from him again, and when we learned that he had been turned out at Rutland Stud, we scarcely needed further confirmation. But that was by no means the end.
>
> Without a race for nearly four months, Shadeed was tossed back in at the deep end against the likes of Grade I Budweiser-Arlington Million hero Teleprompter and Bairn, the three-year-old who had all but robbed him of the Guineas and had since gained Group II honors in the St. James Palace Stakes and taken second behind Rousillon in the Group I Swettenham Stud Sussex Stakes.

Teleprompter was provided with a pacemaker, but he could not go fast enough for the free-running Shadeed, who passed him at the end of the third furlong and was never headed in the five which followed. Poor Teleprompter could never get close enough to the pace to threaten a repeat of his Chicago victory, and though he battled on to secure second place inside the last furlong, Shadeed was then easing down, yet still traveling fast enough to set a new course record for the Ascot mile.

We are inclined to regard the rehabilitation of Shadeed as the supreme effort of Michael Stoute's career to date, and one of the most striking expositions of the trainer's art in our experience. Remember that Shadeed was not just physically jaded at the time of his Derby debacle. His blood count was wrong, his attitude to racing was suspect, and to many observers he was a nervous, fretful wreck incapable of coping with the stresses of training. To have brought him back as a relaxed, thoroughly competitive athlete to crack the Ascot course record in the best company at the first time of asking was nothing short of a masterpiece.

The Thoroughbred Record, October 12, 1985

ROUSILLON

This horse had been regarded by many as the best miler in Europe during 1985, at least, that is, before Shadeed returned to the races in late September.

There were 12 runners in the Moulin, including the classic winners No Pass No Sale and Silvermine. Rousillon was noted to be at a physical peak while parading in the paddock and was eventually backed down to 6-to-4 favoritism. As usual, the son of Riverman was slowly into his stride, but by the time the field had gone a furlong, the colt was handily placed in sixth position as his pacemaker Cataldi took the field along.

Cataldi was still in the lead at the entrance to the straight, with Heraldiste, River Mist, and Vin de France all close up in front of Comrade In Arms, Rousillon, and Kozana. Now moved out to make his challenge on the outside, Rousillon began to make rapid progress from two furlongs out, and he took the lead off Vin de France and the fading Cataldi with a little more than a furlong left to run. The colt then stretched out well and was never in danger of defeat throughout the final furlong.

Greville Starkey had a completely trouble-free ride on Rousillon, and his post-race comments were: "He's certainly the best miler I have ever sat on and throughout the final furlong we were only hacking along." Starkey continued, "If Rousillon had had a pacemaker in all his races, his career would have been even more distinguished."

Rousillon is now unbeaten in all his three races this season. He made his debut in the Group II Queen Anne Stakes, which he took from Celestial Bounty, King Of Clubs, and his pacemaker Cataldi, and then went on to land an impressive victory in the Group I Swettenham Stud Sussex Stakes at Goodwood from Bairn. Obviously, he is still a fresh horse, and it is going to take a good one to beat him in the Breeders' Cup Mile.

The Thoroughbred Record, September 14, 1985

From my vantage point, it seemed that a Rousillon-Shadeed quinella was inevitable, as close to a sure thing as any bet on the card that day. That is, until post positions were drawn, and the two foreign stars found themselves on the far outside—a problem that figured to hurt Shadeed, a speed type, more than the late-running Rousillon. But this was a problem that their class edge figured to help them overcome.

When Shadeed paddocked well, the first major obstacle was hurdled. The start of the race was another matter. Although he broke cleanly, Shadeed never overcame his position and was forced to race at least three-wide around both turns. Rousillon, known for being a problem starter, broke five lengths behind the field. In Europe, that wouldn't have been a serious problem. But at Aqueduct, where position going to the final turn is so important, it proved fatal. A horse must be within striking distance going to that turn, preferably on the inside, or face an uphill battle to the winner's circle. The outside move is not the prescription for success on the tightly turning grass course at Aqueduct. This was a problem the riders of both Rousillon and Pebbles would have to confront, and their reaction could very easily determine the outcome of their respective races.

Probably aware of this, jockey Greville Starkey aboard Rousillon panicked, rushing his horse into contention along the rail on the backstretch. This premature, though dramatic move left the horse with little to give during the final run to the wire. Shadeed, on the other hand, came up flat in the drive after his wide trip. Benefiting from a relatively easy and uneventful trip, Cozzene drew off in the last eighth to win rather easily.

FOURTH RACE
Aqueduct
NOVEMBER 2, 1985

1 MILE.(Turf). (1.34⅗) 2nd Running THE BREEDERS' CUP MILE (Grade I). Purse $1,000,000. 3–year–olds and upward. Weights, 3–year–olds, 123 lbs. 4–year–olds and older, 126 lbs. Fillies and mares allowed 3 lbs. Value of race $1,000,000. Value to winner $450,000, second $225,000, third $108,000, fourth $70,000, fifth $50,000, sixth $10,000. Nominator Awards: Stallion, winner $25,000, second $12,500, third $6,000; Foal, winner $25,000, second, $12,500, third $6,000. Stallion awards will be paid only to the nominators of fully eligible stallions. Owners who supplement horses to Breeders' Cup Day races will be eligible for the Foal Nominator's Award in the case of a 12 per cent supplementary nomination or both the Foal Nominator's Award and the Stallion Nominator's Award in the case of a 20 percent supplementary nomination. In accordance with the Breeders' Cup/European Breeders' Fund cross–registration agreement, nominator's awards will not be paid to horses eligible through the E.B.F. All unpaid nominator's awards will remain the property of Breeders' Cup Limited. Supplementary Nominee: ROUSILLON
Total purse $1,000,000. Value of race $913,000; value to winner $450,000; second $225,000; third $108,000; fourth $70,000; fifth $50,000; sixth $10,000. $87,000 foal & stallion nom awards. Mutuel pool $505,974, OTB pool $204,384. Ex Pl $366,058 OTB $162,666. Quin Pl $171,641. OTB $123,041.

Last Raced	Horse	Eqt.	A.	Wt	PP	St	¼	½	¾	Str	Fin	Jockey	Odds $1
30Oct85 ^{8}Med^{6}	Cozzene		5	126	6	4	$3^{1\frac{1}{2}}$	3^{1}	3^{2}	$2^{1\frac{1}{2}}$	$1^{2\frac{1}{4}}$	Guerra W A	3.60
19Oct85 ^{2}Eng^{3}	[D]Palace Music		4	126	9	13	$11^{\frac{1}{2}}$	9^{1}	9^{1}	$6^{\frac{1}{2}}$	2no	Cruguet J	16.10
19Oct85 ^{8}Med^{3}	Al Mamoon		4	126	14	6	$1^{2\frac{1}{2}}$	1^{1}	$1^{1\frac{1}{2}}$	$1^{\frac{1}{2}}$	3no	Cordero A Jr	18.10
28Sep85 ^{2}Eng^{1}	Shadeed		3	123	12	7	2^{1}	$2^{1\frac{1}{2}}$	2^{hd}	$3^{2\frac{1}{2}}$	$4^{\frac{3}{4}}$	Swinburn W R	5.30
25Oct85 ^{9}Med^{1}	Dr. Schwartzman		4	126	4	2	10^{1}	$11^{\frac{1}{2}}$	7^{1}	$4^{\frac{1}{2}}$	5^{1}	Perret C	65.40
6Oct85 ^{8}SA^{1}	Tsunami Slew		4	126	1	1	4^{1}	$7^{\frac{1}{2}}$	$8^{1\frac{1}{2}}$	7^{3}	$6^{\frac{3}{4}}$	Pincay L Jr	3.70
5Oct85 ^{8}BM^{2}	The Noble Player		5	126	10	8	7^{hd}	$13^{1\frac{1}{2}}$	$12^{\frac{1}{2}}$	8^{hd}	7^{hd}	Shoemaker W	a-16.80
12Oct85 ^{8}Med^{2}	Late Act	b	6	126	11	12	14	14	13^{4}	10^{1}	$8^{1\frac{1}{2}}$	Maple E	54.40
8Sep85 ^{5}Fra^{1}	(S)Rousillon		4	126	13	14	12^{2}	$6^{\frac{1}{2}}$	$4^{\frac{1}{2}}$	5^{1}	9^{nk}	Starkey G	3.00
6Oct85 ^{3}Fra^{4}	Never So Bold		5	126	5	11	$13^{1\frac{1}{2}}$	12^{1}	$10^{\frac{1}{2}}$	$9^{\frac{1}{2}}$	10^{1}	Cauthen S	9.10
21Oct85 ^{6}Bel^{1}	Sitzmark	b	5	126	8	10	$6^{\frac{1}{2}}$	8^{hd}	$11^{1\frac{1}{2}}$	11^{1}	$11^{2\frac{1}{4}}$	Vasquez J	f-36.30
23Jun85 ^{8}Hol^{5}	Forzando II		4	126	7	3	$5^{\frac{1}{2}}$	$5^{1\frac{1}{2}}$	$5^{\frac{1}{2}}$	12^{4}	$12^{4\frac{3}{4}}$	McCarron C J	18.50
17Oct85 ^{4}Eng^{2}	Chapel Cottage		4	123	2	9	$8^{1\frac{1}{2}}$	4^{hd}	$6^{1\frac{1}{2}}$	13^{7}	$13^{10\frac{1}{2}}$	Robinson P	f-36.30
14Sep85 ^{11}Bmf^{3}	Capture Him	b	4	126	3	5	9^{2}	10^{hd}	14	14	14	Delahoussaye E	a-16.80

[D]–Palace Music Disqualified and placed ninth.
a–Coupled: The Noble Player and Capture Him.
f—Mutuel field.
(S) Supplementary nomination.
OFF AT 2:22; Start good for all but ROUSILLON, Won driving. Time, :22⅘, :46⅖, 1:11⅕, 1:35 Course firm.

$2 Mutuel Prices:

5–(F)–COZZENE	9.20	5.60	4.00
11–(N)–AL MAMOON		13.60	8.60
9–(L)–SHADEED			5.60

$2 EXACTA 5–11 PAID $108.40. $2 QUINELLA 5–11 PAID $178.80.

Gr. h, by Caro—Ride The Trails, by Prince John. Trainer Nerud Jan H. Bred by Nerud J A (Fla).

COZZENE, never far back, made a run from the outside leaving the far turn, caught AL MAMOON just inside the final furlong and drew clear under pressure. PALACE MUSIC raced wide into the stretch while moving, lugged in leaving the furlong grounds intefering with TSUNAMI SLEW and ROUSILLON and continued on gamely to gain the place. PALACE MUSIC was disqualified and placed ninth following a stewards inquiry. AL MAMOON quickly sprinted clear, saved ground while making the pace into the stretch and weakened during the drive. SHADEED, prominent to the final furlong, lacked the needed rally. DR. SCHWARTZMAN, steadied along the inside on the far turn, finished well while being forced to steady again just prior to the finish. TSUNAMI SLEW dropped back along the inside on the backstretch, came out on the far turn and was moving between horses when impeded by PALACE MUSIC during the drive. THE NOBLE PLAYER failed to be a serious factor. LATE ACT was without speed. ROUSILLON off slowly, was blocked attempting to split horses nearing the end of the backstretch, raced within easy striking distance to the upper stretch and was weakening when bothered. NEVER SO BOLD lacked room racing to the first turn. SITZMARK tired. FORZANDO II was finished leaving the far turn. CHAPEL COTTAGE was taken up along the inside on the first turn, moved up when clear approaching the far turn, but was finished nearing the stretch. CAPTURE HIM raced wide.

The result of this race left me wondering about European milers. Were they merely second-rate citizens of the European turf competing at the eight-furlong distance because they lacked the class to contest the major prizes at the classic distances? Did the almost casual training style of Europe properly prepare them for the quick pace American milers would throw at them? I remembered the 1984 Breeders' Cup Mile and a horse named Lear Fan, whom I considered the best bet that day.

Lear Fan B. c. 3, by Roberto—Wac, by Lt Stevens
Own.—Salman A Br.—Karpidas C P (Ky) Tr.—Harwood Guy

123 Lifetime 7 5 1 1 $165,857

1984	4	2	1	1	$103,957
1983	3	3	0	0	$61,900
Turf	7	5	1	1	$165,857

9Sep84◆5Longchamp(Fra) yl*1	1:43⅗	Ⓣ Prix du Moulin(Gr 1)	2½	Starkey G	123	*.60	- --	Mendez 123½ Lear Fan 123^{hd} Meis El Reem 120^{2½}	Well up,led	7
19Aug84◆4Deauville(Fra) gd*1	1:34⅘	Ⓣ PrixJacquesLeMarois(Gr1)	1^{4}	Eddery P	121	3.10	-- -	LearFan121^{4} PlceMusic121¾ SiberinExpress121^{1½}	Bid,drew away	10
5May84◆3Newmarket(Eng) fm 1	1:37⅗	Ⓣ 2,000 Guineas Stakes(Gr1)	3^{6½}	Rouse B	126	3.50	- -	El Gran Senor 126^{2½} Chief Singer 126^{4} Lear Fan 126^{3}	Led for 6f	9
17Apr84◆3Newmarket(Eng) gd 1	1:38	Ⓣ Craven Stakes(Gr.3)	1no	Starkey G	124	*.80	- --	Lear Fan 124no Rainbow Quest 119^{7} Telios 119^{5}	Set pace,held	5
9Sep83◆3Doncaster(Eng) gd 7f	1:28	Ⓣ L.PerrierChampagneStk(Gr2	1^{3}	Clark A	126	*.25	-- --	Lear Fan 126^{3} Kalim 126^{6} Handstand 126^{2½}	Led final 5f	4
27Aug83◆2Newmarket(Eng) gd 1	1:40⅕	Ⓣ Fitzroy House Stakes	1^{8}	Clark A	130	*.35	-	Lear Fan 130^{8} Gold and Ivory 119½ Tropare119^{3}	Long lead,eased	5
5Aug83◆6Newmarket(Eng) gd 7f	1:27⅘	Ⓣ Isleham Stakes(Mdn)	1^{8}	Starkey G	126	*2.00	- -	LearFan 126^{8} Millside 126^{4} Plaits 123^{1½}	Prom,drew away	20

While the performances of Rousillon and Shadeed could be excused to some extent, I heard no explanation for Lear Fan's no-challenge off-the-board performance. Was I missing something? Since so few of the top European milers compete in this country—except on Breeders' Cup Day—it may take a few years to properly assess the situation.

Throughout this chapter our emphasis has been on turf racing. Grass, not dirt, is the horse's natural footing. It is asking too much to expect a horse to travel thousands of miles and take up residence in a foreign country, then handle a surface with which it is totally unfamiliar. Playing an American-based horse first time on turf is one thing. Backing a European runner in one of the Breeders' Cup dirt races is quite another. So far, no horse has managed to come even close.

Chapter 19

Beware Lightly Raced European Imports

WHEN TEN FILLIES WERE ENTERED in the fourth at Belmont on May 11, 1984, a maiden event on the grass, casual handicappers no doubt quickly concluded that the only real form in the race belonged to the two components of the Patrick Kelly-trained entry of Plasma and Damask Sky. Double Jeux, who had raced well on two occasions in France, had been an early scratch.

Both Plasma and Damask Sky "woke up" in their latest starts. Coincidentally, each moved from fourth in the early stages to contest the lead entering the stretch, then battled to midstretch. At that point, Damask Sky weakened, while Plasma spooked from the temporary railing across the chute, swerved, and unseated her rider. It could be said that each now had the powerful "bid, hung" angle in her favor. Their supporters could only wonder why Kelly was racing them as an entry, and not reserving one for the next scheduled maiden grass contest. Both appeared ready to win, and either seemed to be a logical selection in this race.

Serious players attuned to the international racing scene, however, looked at this race from a completely different perspective. For them, the race was between Refill and Double Jeux, and they no doubt welcomed the news that one of the two had been scratched.

European-trained horses race far less frequently than do their American counterparts. Consequently, many retain their "conditions," remaining eligible for moderate allowance competition when brought to this country. If such a horse had previously managed to win or place in top-class stakes events in Europe (Group 1, 2, or 3), it often far outclasses the competition it finds in restricted allowance or maiden contests in this country.

4 BELMONT

1 1/16 MILES. (TURF). (1.39⅘) MAIDEN SPECIAL WEIGHT. Purse $19,000. Fillies and Mares, 3-year-olds and upward. Weights, 3-year-olds, 113 lbs. Older 124 lbs.

Coupled—Purple Aura and Reactionist; Plasma and Damask Sky.

Double Jeux — B. f. 4, by Exclusive Native—Double Sham, by Sham
Br.—Spendthrift Farm (Ky)
Tr.—Penna Angel Jr
Own.—Combs L II
124 — Lifetime 2 0 1 1 $5,062 — 1983 2 M 1 1 $5,062 — 1982 0 M 0 0 — Turf 2 0 1 1 $5,062
25Oct83♦5Longchamp(Fra) gd*1¼ 2:11⅘ Ⓣ ⒻPrix de la Sorbonne(Mdn) 2½ Machado R 116 *2.00 — — Riviere Doree 118½ Double Jeux 116no Surentina 123½ Fin.well 8
8Oct83♦6Evry(Fra) gd*1⅛ 1:55⅘ Ⓣ ⒻPrix de Lisses 3² Machado R 116 7.75 — — Hard HeartedHanna124hd Surentina123² DoubleJeux116½ Fin.well 14
LATEST WORKOUTS May 9 Bel 4f sly :49 b — May 3 Bel 3f fst :35⅘ h — Mar 20 Hia 5f fst 1:00⅘ h

Golden Palette — Gr. f. 3, by Icecapade—Palette, by Post Card
Br.—Bach & Deters (Ky)
Tr.—Dunham Bob G
Own.—Four Fifths Stable
113 — Lifetime 5 0 0 0 — 1984 4 M 0 0 — 1983 1 M 0 0
24Apr84- 3Aqu my 6f :23 :47⅕ 1:13⅘ ⒻMd 45000 7 1 44½ 711 711 712½ Venezia M 117 8.80 60-21 StanfordGirl1212½MadelineSweetie1172½LoveLyric117hd Fin. early 7
4Apr84- 2Aqu fst 170 ⊡:49 1:15⅗ 1:46⅘ ⒻMd 45000 1 6 66 78½ 512 518½ Santagata N 117 *2.40e 47-20 Heavenly Splash 1174½ Dorset 1172½ Iris Darlin 1172 Raced wide 9
26Mar84- 6Aqu fst 6f ⊡:23⅕ :48⅕ 1:14⅕ ⒻMd Sp Wt 1 8 912 1113 1120 1123 Venezia M b 121 19.80 50-28 Outofthequestion1211½PreciousRosli1162½ForstWitch121½ Outrun 11
15Mar84- 4Aqu fst 6f ⊡:23 :47⅕ 1:13⅕ ⒻMd Sp Wt 13 12 1315 1316 1420 1418½ Venezia M 121 33.90e 60-25 Sterner Stuff 1212½ Satch 1141 Mirror OfHumanity1213 Far back 14
1Dec83- 6Aqu fst 6f :23⅘ :48 1:14⅘ ⒻMd Sp Wt 4 11 1320 1422 1420 1421½ Venezia M 117 10.10e 48-29 Cantam 117½ Accostage 1173 Lady's Bet 110½ Outrun 14
LATEST WORKOUTS May 7 Aqu 4f fst :49⅘ h — May 3 Aqu 4f fst :49⅘ h — Apr 22 Aqu 3f fst :37⅘ b — Apr 18 Aqu 5f fst 1:02⅘ b

***Refill II** — Dk. b. or br. f. 3, by Mill Reef—Regal Twin, by Majestic Prince
Br.—Waresley Park Stud (Eng)
Tr.—Skiffington Thomas
Own.—Kronfeld E N
113 — Lifetime 4 0 1 0 $5,173 — 1983 4 M 1 0 $5,173 — Turf 4 0 1 0 $5,173
8Sep83♦5Doncaster(Eng) gd 1 1:40⅘ Ⓣ ⒻMay Hill Stakes(Gr.3) 8 Hide E b 118 11.00 — — Satinette 1181½ Nepula 1181½ Shoot Clear 1253 No factor 9
26Jly83♦7Goodwood(Eng) gd 7f 1:28⅘ Ⓣ ⒻNewham Stakes(Mdn) 7 Cook P 123 *1.50 — — Stinette123½ ExctlyLikeYou1232½ CelticAssmbly1232½ Bid, wknd 14
5Jly83♦5Newmarket(Eng) gd 6 1:13⅘ Ⓣ ⒻCherryHintonStakes(Gr3) 44½ Cauthen S 119 4.50 — — ChapelCottage 1224 Nophe 125½ Sajeda 122no Fin. well 9
9Jun83♦4Newbury(Eng) gd 6f 1:16⅘ Ⓣ ⒻKingsolere Stakes 24 Eddery P 117 2.25 — — Pebbles 1174 Refill 1171 Valkyrie 1203 Bumped at start 7
LATEST WORKOUTS May 6 Bel 5f fst 1:00⅕ h — Apr 30 Bel 4f fst :48 h

Winning Birdie — B. f. 3, by Proud Birdie—Winning Run, by Towson
Br.—Marablue Farm (Fla)
Tr.—Morgan Jack B
Own.—Snipes B
113 — Lifetime 4 0 0 0 $1,140 — 1984 4 M 0 0 $1,140 — 1983 0 M 0 0
28Apr84- 6Aqu fst 6f :22⅘ :46⅘ 1:12 ⒻMd Sp Wt 7 13 128½ 99 913 1012½ Hernandez R b 121 33.00f 68-21 MrthMoonshin1213½JollyVictory121noLdyLitchfld1212½ Slow start 13
21Apr84- 4Aqu fst 7f :24⅕ :49⅕ 1:28⅕ ⒻMd Sp Wt 8 11 94½ 52½ 66 811½ Smith A Jr b 121 11.20 48-30 Sunset Strait 121nk GuideBoat1213½Spring'sPromise1212½ Outrun 13
10Mar84- 6Aqu fst 6f ⊡:22⅘ :47⅘ 1:13⅕ ⒻMd Sp Wt 10 7 97½ 54½ 57 59½ Hernandez R 121 3.40 69-24 DHRoylOffense121noDHBrightCmlli121noClock'Em1216 No factor 12
5Mar84- 9Aqu sly 6f ⊡:22⅘ :46⅘ 1:12⅘ ⒻMd Sp Wt 3 8 65 44 43½ 46½ Hernandez R 121 3.50 73-16 ErgrnMss1213½CnchTClnch121nkBrhtCmll1212½ Slow early, green 9
LATEST WORKOUTS ●Apr 19 Bel tr.t 3f fst :35⅘ h — Apr 14 Bel 5f fst 1:02⅘ h — Apr 7 Bel tr.t 6f fst 1:16⅘ b — Mar 17 Bel tr.t 3f fst :36⅘ h

***Thunderflash II** — B. f. 3, by Northfields—Catherine Wheel, by Roan Rocket
Br.—Roncon Ltd (Fra)
Tr.—Johnson Philip G
Own.—Brookway Stable
113 — Lifetime 3 0 0 0 — 1984 1 M 0 0 — 1983 2 M 0 0
28Apr84- 6Aqu fst 6f :22⅘ :46⅘ 1:12 ⒻMd Sp Wt 10 11 84½ 1010 1119 1119½ Migliore R 121 5.00e 61-21 MrthMoonshn1213½JllyVctry121noLdyLtchfld1212½ Bumped start 13
7Aug83- 4Sar fst 6f :22⅘ :45⅘ 1:11⅘ ⒻMd Sp Wt 13 12 107 1217 1324 1328½ Fell J 117 6.80e 54-15 PrincessPatelin1173½LdyLitchfield1122½LdyRipley117½ Very wide 14
15Jly83- 6Bel fst 5½f :23⅕ :46⅘ 1:05⅘ ⒻMd Sp Wt 1 3 21 63½ 1016 1025½ Maple E 117 *2.10 63-17 Some For All 1174½ Dash of Hope 1174½ Estero 1172½ Stopped 10
LATEST WORKOUTS Apr 26 Bel 3f fst :35 h — Apr 20 Bel tr.t 5f fst 1:01⅕ h

Ms. Semper Fidelis — B. f. 4, by Fifth Marine—Golden Sword, by Herbager
Br.—Swift G H Jr (Va)
Tr.—Destasio Richard A
Own.—Gargano P
117[7] — Lifetime 14 0 3 0 $7,810 — 1984 7 M 2 0 $6,710 — 1983 7 M 1 0 $1,100 — Turf 1 0 0 0
4May84- 1Aqu gd 6f :23 :47⅘ 1:13 3↑ⒻMd 35000 1 6 43 64 33 2¾ Muino M M7 b 117 3.80e 75-24 ErinTerry113¾Ms.SemperFidlis117hdWingdEmotions1102½ Rallied 9
26Apr84- 7Aqu fst 7f :23⅕ :47 1:25⅘ 3↑ⒻMd Sp Wt 8 7 64 43½ 57½ 78 Muino M M7 b 117 15.80e 66-26 Speriance 112nk Robin Of Winloc 112½ Indian House 1171½ Tired 12
8Mar84- 6Aqu fst 1⅛ ⊡:49⅕ 1:14⅘ 1:48⅘ ⒻMd Sp Wt 5 4 22 24 415 624½ MacBeth D b 122 13.80 44-24 Nutcracker Sweet 1124 Alusha 1229 Winged Buffet 1227½ Tired 7
26Feb84- 4Aqu fst 170 ⊡:49 1:15⅘ 1:47⅘ ⒻMd Sp Wt 1 1 2½ 22½ 59 716½ Davis R G b 122 4.00 48-29 Counselorette 1223½ Alusha 1224½ NutcrackerSweet1223 Stopped 8
16Feb84- 3Aqu my 1⅛ ⊡:47⅘ 1:13⅘ 1:45⅘ ⒻMd Sp Wt 7 1 15 11½ 12½ 21½ Davis R G b 122 17.30 82-10 Vndy'sJoy1221½Ms.SemperFidelis122nkCounselortt122½ Game try 7
25Jan84- 6Aqu sly 6f ⊡:22⅘ :46⅘ 1:12⅘ ⒻMd Sp Wt 7 2 52½ 43½ 58 613½ Davis R G b 122 25.50 68-18 Huga Baba 1224½ Fairway Fantasy 1225 Cidelsia 1172½ Tired 8
15Jan84- 3Aqu fst 6f ⊡:23⅘ :49⅕ 1:15⅘ ⒻMd Sp Wt 2 7 73½ 97½ 89½ 915½ Davis R G b 122 12.90 50-30 Baba Au Plum 1171½ Lisalane 122½ Dreamy Native 115hd Outrun 10
4Jly83- 5Bel hd 1⅛ Ⓣ:46⅘ 1:10⅘ 1:43⅘ 3↑ⒻMd Sp Wt 2 1 1½ 2½ 47½ 715½ McCarron G b 116 14.30 67-05 Good Economics 1227½ Born A Classic 116½ Pirate Den116½ Tired 8
28Mar83- 6Tam gd 6f :23⅘ :47⅘ 1:13⅘ Md Sp Wt 7 1 66½ 710 715 818½ Rivera H Jr b 113 3.90 58-27 Miss Edith 1135 Iam Charles Pet 1184½ Shanghai Red1184 Outrun 8
18Mar83- 7Tam fst 1⅛ :49⅘ 1:15⅘ 1:52⅘ ⒻMd Sp Wt 2 1 12 11½ 11 2¾ Johnson P A b 118 8.70 57-37 FloweryFuture118¾Ms.SemperFidlis1186FuturChiftss1187 Gamely 8
LATEST WORKOUTS Apr 20 Bel tr.t 4f fst :49⅕ h — Apr 14 Bel tr.t 3f fst :37 b — Apr 7 Bel tr.t 4f fst :49⅘ b — Mar 26 Bel tr.t 3f fst :36⅘ h

Fabulous Ack — B. f. 3, by Ack Ack—Fabulous View, by Le Fabuleux
Br.—Hancock III & Peters (Ky)
Tr.—Picou James E
Own.—DeMatteis F
106[7] — Lifetime 3 0 0 0 — 1984 3 M 0 0 — 1983 0 M 0 0
5May84- 1Aqu gd 7f :23 :46⅘ 1:26⅕ ⒻMd Sp Wt 2 3 43 77½ 79 612 Davis R G 121 16.60 58-16 Boldara 1213 Handsewn 116nk Elbarita 1211½ Fin. early 8
14Apr84- 4Aqu sly 6f ⊡:23 :48 1:14 ⒻMd Sp Wt 10 2 1hd 43½ 912 1012½ Davis R G b 121 7.50 61-15 PreciousRoslie1161½Tempestously1212Chieftin'sNtive121no Tired 11
2Apr84- 6Aqu fst 6f ⊡:22⅘ :46⅘ 1:12⅘ ⒻMd Sp Wt 4 2 42 710 714 816½ Davis R G 121 8.40 64-17 Lassie's Lady 121½ Hidden Point 1213½ Em An Aye 1214 Tired 10
LATEST WORKOUTS May 1 Bel 4f fst :49⅕ b — Apr 26 Bel 1 fst 1:43 b — Apr 21 Bel 6f fst 1:15⅕ b — Apr 13 Bel tr.t 3f fst :36⅘ b

I Merrily — Gr. f. 3, by King Pellinore—Invision, by Grey Dawn II
Br.—Isaacs H Z (Ky)
Tr.—Kelly Edward I
Own.—Brookfield Farm
113 — Lifetime 4 0 0 0 — 1984 1 M 0 0 — 1983 3 M 0 0 — Turf 1 0 0 0
4Jan84- 6Aqu fst 1⅛ ⊡:48⅕ 1:14⅕ 1:51 ⒻMd Sp Wt 1 3 511 612 811 710½ Davis R G b 121 6.90 47-25 Marry Kay 1212½ Accostage 1163 Sweet Miranda 121½ Tired 9
4Dec83- 6Aqu sly 7f :23⅘ :47⅘ 1:25⅘ ⒻMd Sp Wt 2 7 54 711 714 718½ Cordero A Jr b 117 7.10 54-25 Daddy'sDish1172½SunsetStrit1172½MissIceQueen1177½ No mishap 9
16Nov83- 4Aqu gd 7f :22⅘ :45⅘ 1:24⅘ ⒻMd Sp Wt 13 7 75½ 107½ 1215 1223½ Davis R G b 117 4.00 56-19 Full Song 1173½ Lady Litchfield 1173½ Paddy's Gift 117nk Outrun 13
17Oct83- 9Bel yl 1⅛ Ⓣ:48⅘ 1:14⅕ 1:48 ⒻMd Sp Wt 8 8 63½ 46 47½ 58 Davis R G b 117 *3.60 48-38 Qualique 1172 Candy Bowl1172½FloraScent117½ Off slowly, stdied 12
LATEST WORKOUTS May 6 Bel 6f fst 1:17 b — May 3 Bel tr.t 5f fst 1:05 b — Apr 28 Bel tr.t 5f fst 1:04 b — Apr 23 Bel tr.t 5f fst 1:03⅘ b

Purple Aura — Dk. b. or br. f. 3, by Mac Diamida—Madonna Red, by My Dad George
Br.—Tersney P J (Fla)
Tr.—Schulhofer Flint S
Own.—Tersney J M
113 — Lifetime 3 0 0 0 $200 — 1984 3 M 0 0 $200 — 1983 0 M 0 0 — Turf 2 0 0 0 $110
30Apr84- 1Aqu fm 1⅛ Ⓣ:48⅘ 1:14⅘ 1:47⅕ 3↑ⒻMd Sp Wt 8 2 2hd 43½ 511 720½ Graell A 112 2.80e 48-26 Pouska 1123 Jealous One 1154 La Reine Rose 1241½ Gaveway 10
6Apr84- 5GP fm *1⅛ Ⓣ 1:44⅘ ⒻMd Sp Wt 10 2 2½ 32½ 34 64½ McCauley W H 121 25.60 76-14 Battere 1213½ Restless Wendy 1211 Valdance 1211½ Gave way 10
15Feb84- 4Hia fst 6f :22⅘ :46 1:11⅘ ⒻMd 40000 6 12 1016 1130 1130 1135 Cruguet J 119 30.30 49-19 Shot Above 114½ Usurper 1192 Ell's Dusty Lark 119½ Outrun 12
LATEST WORKOUTS Apr 26 Bel 4f fst :49⅘ b — Apr 4 Hia 4f fst :49⅘ b — Mar 30 Hia 4f fst :49⅘ b — Mar 25 Hia 4f fst :49⅘ b

Plasma — Ch. f. 3, by Noholme II—Tokamak, by Tim Tam
Br.—Live Oak Stud (Fla)
Tr.—Kelly Patrick J
Own.—Live Oak Plantation
113 — Lifetime 6 0 0 0 $1,020 — 1984 5 M 0 0 $1,029 — 1983 1 M 0 0 — Turf 3 0 0 0 $760
30Apr84- 1Aqu fm 1⅛ Ⓣ:48⅘ 1:14⅘ 1:47⅕ 3↑ⒻMd Sp Wt 2 3 41½ 2hd — — Murphy D J b 112 11.10 — — Pouska 1123 Jealous One 1154 La Reine Rose 1241½ Lost rider 10
12Mar84- 6GP fm *1⅛ Ⓣ 1:46⅕ ⒻAlw 13000 9 9 910 86½ 79½ 415½ Rivera M A b 116 115.20 59-21 Illaka 1161½ Battere 111no Candy Bowl 12114 Outrun 10
25Feb84- 6Hia fst 6f :22⅘ :45⅘ 1:09⅘ ⒻMd Sp Wt 6 7 73½ 711 1020 1031½ Rivera M A b 119 50.10 65-11 ValleyProspector119noLadySusan119noPoliticalPrincess119½ Outrun 12
17Jan84- 6Hia fst 7f :22⅘ :46⅘ 1:25 ⒻMd Sp Wt 10 1 2hd 2hd 913 926 Vasquez J b 119 29.60 52-19 Aneka 119hd Year After Year 1191½ Gentle Ram 1197 Gave way 11
6Jan84- 6Crc fm 1⅛ Ⓣ:48⅘ 1:14⅕ 1:46⅕ ⒻMd Sp Wt 12 8 63½ 911 1221 1228½ Rivera M A b 119 18.60 46-18 BrooklynPrincess1142ByouBirdie119½AngelFromAbove119½ Wide 12
29Oct83- 4Aqu fst 6f :23⅕ :48⅕ 1:14⅕ ⒻMd Sp Wt 4 3 618 618 523 523 Murphy D J5 112 12.40 47-28 Disquieting 1171 Bett's Pleasure 1175 Shavie 11711 Outrun 7
LATEST WORKOUTS May 6 Bel 4f fst :48 b — Apr 24 Bel 3f sly :39⅕ b (d) — Apr 15 Bel tr.t 5f sly 1:04 b — Apr 10 Bel tr.t 4f fst :50⅘ b

Minstrely — Ch. f. 4, by The Minstrel—Politely, by Amerigo
Br.—DuPont Mrs R C (Md)
Tr.—Jerkens H Allen
Own.—Bohemia Stable
124 — Lifetime 1 0 0 1 $2,640 — 1983 1 M 0 1 $2,640 — 1982 0 M 0 0
6Nov83- 6Aqu fst 1⅛ :49⅘ 1:14⅘ 1:52⅘ 3↑ⒻMd Sp Wt 2 3 24 24 39 327 Bailey J D 120 2.20 44-29 Fois Gras 12019 Vandy's Joy 1208 Minstrely 1206 Unruly st. 7
LATEST WORKOUTS May 8 Bel tr.t 1 fst 1:47⅕ b — Apr 28 Bel tr.t 7f fst 1:30 b — Apr 21 Bel 6f fst 1:18⅘ bg — Apr 17 Bel 4f sly :49⅘ b

Syrian Splendor — B. f. 3, by Damascus—Magnificence, by Graustark
Br.—Tartan Farms Corp (Fla)
Tr.—Nerud Jan H
Own.—Tartan Stable
113 — Lifetime 2 0 0 0 — 1984 2 M 0 0 — 1983 0 M 0 0
14Apr84- 4Aqu sly 6f ⊡:23 :48 1:14 ⒻMd Sp Wt 11 1 74½ 66½ 710 79 Migliore R b 121 25.00 65-15 PreciousRosalie1161½Tempestously1212Chieftin'sNtive121no Wide 11
2Apr84- 6Aqu fst 6f ⊡:22⅘ :46⅘ 1:12⅘ ⒻMd Sp Wt 5 9 84½ 44 511 614½ Migliore R b 121 35.50 67-17 Lassie's Lady 121½ Hidden Point 1213½ Em AnAye1214 Slow start 10
LATEST WORKOUTS May 5 Bel tr.t 4f my :48⅕ h (d)

Also Eligible (Not in Post Position Order):

Damask Sky — B. f. 3, by Damascus—Peaceful Sky, by Tim Tam — Br.—Live Oak Stud (Fla) — Tr.—Kelly Patrick J — **113**
Own.—Live Oak Plantation
Lifetime 2 0 0 0 $650 — 1984 2 M 0 0 $650 — 1983 0 M 0 0 — Turf 1 0 0 0 $550

26Apr84-10GP	fm *1 1/16 ⓣ			1:47⅗	ⒻMd Sp Wt	5	9	4 2½	1hd	2hd	4 7½	Vergara O	121	3.70	61-27	Dictina121¾ⒹTriplePrincess121noFrnciscnOrder121¾	Weakened	10
11Apr84- 7GP	fst 6f	:22⅕	:45⅘	1:10⅘	ⒻMd Sp Wt	6	9	11 15	10 23	7 15	7 13½	Solomone M	121	2.90	73-21	Dupree 121⁶ Hold Your Whisper 121² Brenda's Bridges 121¾	Dull	11

LATEST WORKOUTS Apr 7 Hia 5f fst 1:01 bg Mar 31 Hia 4f fst :48 bg Mar 27 Hia 3f fst :36 bg ●Mar 24 Hia 3f my :36⅘ bg

Reactionist — B. f. 3, by Big Burn—Flighty Princess, by Misty Flight — Br.—Hyams J (Fla) — Tr.—Schulhofer Flint S — **113**
Own.—Haven M
Lifetime 6 0 0 1 $2,110 — 1984 6 M 0 1 $2,110 — 1983 0 M 0 0

9Apr84- 5GP	fst 1 1/16	:48⅕	1:13⅘	1:45⅘	ⒻMd Sp Wt	11	4	3 2½	3 1½	4 3½	5 5½	McCauley W H	121	8.00	69-20	Acute Beau 116½ Honey Bee Kind 121½ Usurper 114⁴	Weakened	11
31Mar84- 4GP	fst 1 1/16	:49⅘	1:14⅘	1:46	ⒻMd Sp Wt	4	8	7 4½	9 5½	5 7	4 6	Venezia M	121	19.50	65-14	Year After Year 121½ Be My Life121 1½Witwatersrand121⁴	Outrun	12
12Mar84- 5GP	fst 1 1/16	:48⅘	1:14⅕	1:46⅘	ⒻMd Sp Wt	6	5	2 1	2½	2 2½	3 12	Maple E	121	34.90	55-19	MerryChase121⁷AcuteBeu121⁵Rectionist121 1½	Well up, weakened	12
17Feb84- 8Hia	fst 6f	:22⅘	:46⅕	1:11⅘	ⒻMd Sp Wt	4	10	8 5½	7 10	6 9½	7 13¾	Cruguet J	119	48.40	71-18	Laurie'sAngel119¹LdyTecher119⁴½ⒹCherokeeQueen119nk	Outrun	12
10Feb84- 8Hia	fst 7f	:23⅕	:46⅘	1:25	ⒻMd Sp Wt	5	12	10 14	10 17	*8 15	7 18½	Cruguet J	119	34.90	60-22	WinnebagoSeven119¾MerryChse119nkYerAfterYer119¹	No factor	12
28Jan84- 2Hia	fst 6f	:22⅘	:46⅘	1:12⅘	ⒻMd Sp Wt	5	12	10 10	8 12	8 11	7 13	Cruguet J	119	8.50	68-15	Regent's Walk 119³ China Bee 119hd Affirmable 119¾	Off slowly	12

LATEST WORKOUTS May 10 Bel tr.t 3f fst :37⅘ b May 3 Bel tr.t 4f fst :50⅕ b Apr 25 Bel tr.t 4f fst :50 b Apr 20 Bel tr.t 4f fst :49⅘ h

Refill, for example, had raced well in the Group 3 Cherry Hinton Stakes at Newmarket, narrowly missing the place behind runaway winner Chapel Cottage. Although unraced since September, she was now trained by young Tom Skiffington, a former steeplechase rider who had quickly gained a reputation with grass runners and was also a trainer whose runners generally race well fresh. No doubt Refill had been working well in the spring at Skiffington's South Carolina headquarters, and her two on-track works since arriving in New York were good. Everything pointed to a near-peak performance, which is exactly what Refill delivered, winning as she pleased by more than ten lengths at a very liberal 5–2. It was the

FOURTH RACE
Belmont
MAY 11, 1984

1 1/16 MILES.(turf). (1.39⅗) MAIDEN SPECIAL WEIGHT. Purse $19,000. Fillies and Mares, 3-year-olds and upward. Weights, 3-year-olds, 113 lbs. Older 124 lbs.

Value of race $19,000, value to winner $11,400, second $4,180, third $2,280, fourth $1,140. Mutuel pool $117,743, OTB pool $100,123. Quinella Pool $166,221. OTB Quinella Pool $143,193.

Last Raced	Horse	Eqt.A.Wt	PP	St	¼	½	¾	Str	Fin	Jockey	Odds $1
8Sep83 5Eng8	Refill II	3 113	2	5	5 3½	4½	4 1½	1 3	1 10¾	Cordero A Jr	2.70
30Apr84 1Aqu	Plasma	b 3 113	8	8	8 4	7 1½	7 6	7 7	2 1¼	Maple E	a-1.60
26Apr84 10GP4	Damask Sky	3 113	10	7	6 1½	6 3	6 2	5 1½	3¾	Murphy D J	a-1.60
30Apr84 1Aqu7	Purple Aura	3 113	7	2	1½	2 1½	2 1	2 1	4nk	Graell A	19.30
4May84 1Aqu2	Ms. Semper Fidelis	b 4 117	5	4	4 3	5 5	5 3	3 1	5 4¾	Muino M M7	9.00
14Apr84 4Aqu7	Syrian Splendor	b 3 113	9	3	3 3	3 2½	3hd	6½	6 1¼	Migliore R	12.80
28Apr84 6Aqu11	Thunderflash II	3 113	4	1	2 1½	1hd	1½	4hd	7 2	Samyn J L	12.20
24Apr84 3Aqu7	Golden Palette	3 113	1	6	9 1½	9 3	8 3	8 2½	8 2¾	Venezia M	37.50
4Jan84 6Aqu7	I Merrily	b 3 113	6	9	10	10	10	9 5	9 12½	Davis R G	3.70
28Apr84 6Aqu10	Winning Birdie	b 3 113	3	10	7 1	8 2	9 1½	10	10	Hernandez R	29.40

a-Coupled: Plasma and Damask Sky .

OFF AT 2:33. Start good, Won ridden out. Time, :23, :46, 1:11⅖, 1:37⅗, 1:44 Course firm.

$2 Mutuel Prices:				
	3-(C)-REFILL II	7.40	3.60	3.20
	1-(J)-PLASMA (a-entry)		3.00	3.00
	1-(M)-DAMASK SKY (a-entry)		3.00	3.00
	$2 QUINELLA 1-3 PAID $9.40.			

Dk. b. or br. f, by Mill Reef—Regal Twin, by Majestic Prince. Trainer Skiffington Thomas. Bred by Waresley Park Stud (Eng).

REFILL II, steadied along looking for room behind the leaders approaching the stretch, came out leaving the turn and drew off rapidly after catching the leaders. PLASMA, wide into the stretch, finished well to best the others. DAMASK SKY moved through between horses near midstretch but failed to seriously menace. PURPLE AURA dueled for the lead to the upper stretch and gave way. MS. SEMPER FIVELIS made a run from the outside leaving the turn but lacked a further response. SYRIAN SPLENDOUR raced forwardly to the stretch and tired. THUNDERFLASH II was used up vying for the lead. I MERRILY showed nothing.

3 BELMONT

1 MILE. (Turf). (1.33) MAIDEN SPECIAL WEIGHTS. Purse $19,000. Fillies and mares, 3-year-old an dupward, weights, 3-year-olds, 114 lbs. Older, 122 lbs.

Stormy Lass
B. f. 3, by Take by Storm—My Lass, by Determine
Br.—Flynn & Nolan (Fla)
Tr.—Sciacca Gary J
Own.—Betancourt H
114
Lifetime 7 0 1 0 $4,480 | 1984 6 M 0 0 $1,950 | 1983 1 M 1 0 $2,530 | Turf 1 0 0 0 $1,140

10May84- 1Bel fst 1⅛ :47⅘ 1:13⅘ 1:46 ⒻMd Sp Wt 6 4 42 59 514 517 Smith A Jr 121 26.40 55-17 TraipsinLady1212½JealousOne121¾LdyLitchfield11610½ Wide, tired 6
30Apr84- 1Aqu fm 1⅛ Ⓣ:48⅘ 1:14⅘ 1:47⅕ 3+ⒻMd Sp Wt 4 1 1hd 31½ 35 48½ Smith A Jr 112 22.60 60-26 Pouska 1123 Jealous One 1154 La Reine Rose 1241½ Weakened 10
25Apr84- 2Aqu gd 7f :23⅕ :46⅘ 1:26⅘ ⒻMd 25000 6 2 43½ 56 77½ 69½ Smith A Jr 121 10.50 59-22 Mickey's Lady 1212 Winged Emotions 1211½ Amy T. 1121¾ Tired 7
24Feb84- 2Aqu sly 6f ⊡:23 :47⅘ 1:12⅘ ⒻMd 50000 12 9 87 1011 916 1017½ Muino M M7 114 22.30 65-16 PalaceTreasure1171½OneNightBeuty1172½LdyLitchfield1217 Wide 12
13Feb84- 5Aqu fst 6f ⊡:22⅘ :46⅘ 1:13 ⒻMd Sp Wt 12 10 108¾ 1011 1017 1016¾ Doran K7 114 21.60 62-18 Foolish River 1141¾ Sterner Stuff 1213¾Mt.Prospect1211¼ Outrun 12
12Jan84- 6Aqu fst 1⅛ ⊡:49 1:15⅘ 1:49 ⒻMd 50000 3 3 22 45 511 417¾ Santiago A 121 *1.00 49-22 J. C. Hon 1179¾ Erudite 1172¼ Koo 1216 Tired 6
31Dec83- 4Aqu fst 170 ⊡:48⅗ 1:14⅘ 1:46 ⒻMd 30000 2 1 1hd 12 12 2nk O'Hara S10 103 8.90e 71-21 Miss CathyM.117nkStormyLass1031TackfulQueen1175½ Just failed 9
LATEST WORKOUTS ●May 27 Aqu 5f fst 1:02 h Apr 20 Aqu 4f fst :48 h Apr 14 Aqu ⊡ 5f gd 1:04 b Apr 9 Aqu ⊡ 5f fst 1:03⅘ h

New Poems
B. f. 3, by Arts and Letters—Across The Bar, by Cyane
Br.—Christiana Stables (Ky)
Tr.—Maloney Deborah A
Own.—Christiana Stables
114
Lifetime 1 0 0 0 | 1983 1 M 0 0

16Nov83- 4Aqu gd 7f :22⅘ :45⅘ 1:24⅘ ⒻMd Sp Wt 3 11 1212 1314 1317 1324½ McCarron G 117 4.20e 54-19 Full Song 1173½ Lady Litchfield 1173½ Paddy's Gift 117nk Outrun 13
LATEST WORKOUTS ●Jun 2 Bel 4f sly :47⅘ h May 23 Bel 4f fst :48⅕ h May 17 Bel Ⓣ 5f fm 1:02⅖ b (d) May 14 Bel 3f sly :35 hg

Bit of Raja
Ch. f. 3, by Raja Baba—Mary Laurel, by Hasty Road
Br.—Maple Leaf Farm (Pa)
Tr.—Myer Patrick
Own.—Thorington Anne F
114
Lifetime 3 0 0 0 | 1984 3 M 0 0 | 1983 0 M 0 0 | Turf 1 0 0 0

19May84- 9Del yl 1 Ⓣ:47⅗ 1:14 1:40⅘ 3+ⒻMd Sp Wt 2 7 39 41¾ 77½ 715½ Clayton M D b 112 10.60 56-29 Silver Sequel 1127 With Surety 115nk Chili Petine 1122½ Ret. sore 12
15Mar84- 4Aqu fst 6f ⊡:23 :47⅕ 1:13⅕ ⒻMd Sp Wt 12 13 75½ 66 79½ 712½ Migliore R 121 28.90f 65-25 Sterner Stuff 1212½ Satch 1141 Mirror Of Humanity 1213 Outrun 14
23Feb84- 6Aqu fst 6f ⊡:23 :47⅗ 1:13⅘ ⒻMd Sp Wt 7 7 85½ 108½ 812 812½ Migliore R 121 51.30 63-22 Cinder Lass 1213½ Evergreen Miss 1211½ Explicit Gal 1212 Outrun 12
LATEST WORKOUTS Jun 4 Bel 5f gd 1:00⅘ h May 28 Bel 5f fst 1:01⅗ h May 17 Bel Ⓣ 4f fm :59⅖ b (d) May 11 Bel 7f fst 1:28⅘ b

Shift Key
B. f. 3, by Upper Case—The Old Blitz, by Native Charger
Br.—V & S Investments (ky)
Tr.—Puentes Gilbert
Own.—Lizza Karen
114
Lifetime 4 0 0 0 | 1984 4 M 0 0 | 1983 0 M 0 0

1Jun84- 6Bel fst 7f :23⅕ :46⅘ 1:25⅖ ⒻMd Sp Wt 5 13 74½ 62¾ 55¾ 810½ McCarron G b 121 17.60 64-20 Hence 1211 Carol Jane 1216 French Farce 116nk Off slowly 13
24May84- 6Bel fst 6f :22⅗ :46⅗ 1:11⅗ ⒻMd Sp Wt 9 9 116¾ 116¾ 75 94¾ Lopez V5 b 116 9.20 79-15 Mine Only 121hd Current Miss 1212 Reine Certaine 1211½ Outrun 13
11May84- 5Bel fst 6f :22⅘ :46⅘ 1:13⅕ ⒻMd Sp Wt 2 6 46 58 77 86¾ Lopez V5 b 116 65.00 69-24 Statuesque 121½ Syrian City 121½ Estero 121½ Tired 9
5May84- 1Aqu gd 7f :23 :46⅘ 1:26⅕ ⒻMd Sp Wt 7 4 32½ 53½ 811 814¾ Lopez V5 b 116 25.80 55-16 Boldara 1213 Handsewn 116nk Elbarita 1211½ Tired 8
LATEST WORKOUTS May 23 Bel tr.t 3f fst :36⅕ b ●May 18 Bel tr.t 5f fst 1:01⅖ h Apr 24 Bel 4f sly :49⅘ bg(d) Apr 19 Bel tr.t 4f fst :49 b

Flora Scent
Gr. f. 3, by FLuorescent Light—Native Nan, by Raise A Native
Br.—Hawkeye Farm (Ky)
Tr.—LaBoccetta Frank
Own.—Anchel Judith
114
Lifetime 10 0 1 1 $8,800 | 1983 10 M 1 1 $8,800 | Turf 3 0 1 1 $7,480

16Dec83- 4Aqu fst 170 ⊡:48⅖ 1:14 1:45⅘ ⒻMd Sp Wt 2 4 45 67 68 610 Messina R5 b 112 20.20 63-21 Sarawilha 117no Bett's Pleasure 1177½ Pricey 1171¾ In tight 10
7Dec83- 4Aqu fst 1⅛ ⊡:48⅕ 1:14⅕ 1:47⅘ ⒻMd Sp Wt 2 5 65½ 89 511 512½ Hernandez R b 117 10.10 61-21 Shavie 1173½ Boat Hook 1174¾ Surprise Special 1171½ No threat 12
4Nov83- 4Aqu fst 1⅛ :48⅘ 1:14 1:54⅖ ⒻMd Sp Wt 7 3 43½ 45½ 718 922 Hernandez R b 117 4.60 41-27 Coastal Breeze 1172 Maharadoon 1171 Scrutable 1178 Tired 11
17Oct83- 9Bel yl 1⅛ Ⓣ:48⅗ 1:14⅕ 1:48 ⒻMd Sp Wt 2 6 94¾ 811 58½ 34¾ Hernandez R b 117 4.40 51-38 Qualique 1172 Candy Bowl 1172¾ Flora Scent 117¾ Rallied 12
19Sep83- 6Bel fm 1 Ⓣ:47⅗ 1:12⅖ 1:37⅘ ⒻMd Sp Wt 4 9 64 2½ 21 2nk Hernandez R b 117 29.40 76-17 Class Play 117nk Flora Scent 1174 Qualique 1173 Forced out 9
10Sep83- 9Bel fm 1⅛ Ⓣ:47 1:11⅗ 1:44⅘ ⒻMd Sp Wt 11 10 97¾ 1014 818 714½ Hernandez R b 117 11.70 58-15 Salem Trials 117hd Heartlight 1173 Qualique 1172¾ No factor 12
29Aug83- 9Bel my 1 :47 1:11⅗ 1:37⅘ ⒻMd Sp Wt 4 6 76 66 43½ 43 Hernandez R b 117 13.70 73-15 Distaff Magic117noMiaNordica1173LandoftheBrave112hd Mild bid 8
14Aug83- 4Sar fst 6f :22⅘ :46⅗ 1:13 ⒻMd Sp Wt 2 11 107½ 118¾ 88½ 54½ Hernandez R b 117 51.70 71-12 My Lady Love 117½ Salem Trials 117noSunsetStrait1171½ Late bid 14
31Jly83- 4Sar fst 6f :22⅕ :45⅘ 1:11⅗ ⒻMd Sp Wt 6 11 1414 1316 1012 710¾ Hernandez R b 117 15.30f 72-12 Tina's Ten 1176¾ Heartlight 117¾ Silver Sequel 1171½ No threat 14
8Jly83- 4Bel fst 5f :23 :47 1:00 ⒻMd Sp Wt 8 8 812 815 814 810¾ Douglas R R7 b 110 34.80 78-18 Mrs. Flagler 1171 Mayslick Miss117noLoran117no Broke slow,wide 8
LATEST WORKOUTS ●Jun 7 Aqu 3f fst :35⅖ h Jun 2 Aqu 6f sly 1:15⅕ h May 24 Aqu 4f gd :51⅗ b (d) May 17 Aqu Ⓣ 5f gd 1:03⅘ h (d)

Nan's Gone
Ro. f. 3, by The Axe II—nan's Gone Native, by Native Charger
Br.—Forest Retreat Farms Inc (Ky)
Tr.—Hertler John O
Own.—Murphy V B Jr
114
Lifetime 0 0 0 0 | 1984 0 M 0 0 | 1983 0 M 0 0

LATEST WORKOUTS Jun 7 Aqu Ⓣ 4f fm :49⅘ b (d) May 28 Aqu 4f fst :52⅖ b May 10 Aqu Ⓣ 5f fm 1:05 b (d) May 3 Aqu 5f fst 1:04 b

Christmas Chime
B. f. 3, by Believe It—Christmas Wind, by Nearctic
Br.—Mellon P (Va)
Tr.—Miller Mack
Own.—Rokeby Stables
109⁵
Lifetime 5 0 1 0 $7,180 | 1984 2 M 0 0 $1,140 | 1983 3 M 1 0 $6,040

10May84- 1Bel fst 1⅛ :47⅘ 1:13⅗ 1:46 ⒻMd Sp Wt 1 2 2½ 32½ 48½ 414 Ward W A5 b 116 3.00 58-17 Traipsin Lady 1212¾ Jealous One 121¾ LadyLitchfield11610½ Tired 6
28Apr84- 6Aqu fst 6f :22⅘ :46⅗ 1:12 ⒻMd Sp Wt 13 7 95½ 88½ 811 79¾ Ward W5 b 116 5.00 71-21 MarthaMoonshine1213¾JollyVictory121noLdyLitchfield1212¾ Wide 13
24Oct83- 4Aqu sly 1 :47⅘ 1:13⅕ 1:39 ⒻMd Sp Wt 1 1 11 2hd 2hd 2nk Bailey J D b 117 3.00 71-25 Oneezer 112nk Christmas Chime 117½ Daddy'sDish1175 Just failed 7
13Oct83- 6Bel my 6f :22⅘ :46⅖ 1:12 ⒻMd Sp Wt 6 7 65 56½ 67½ 54 Bailey J D b 117 *.90 78-15 Wine Taster 1171½ True Pattern 117¾ Glorious Reason1171½ Wide 9
23Sep83- 4Bel fst 6f :22⅘ :46⅗ 1:12⅘ ⒻMd Sp Wt 5 7 76¾ 98½ 87 44½ Bailey J D 117 4.90 74-21 Avtr'sCourt1173Life'sLight117¾Forthetimbing117¾ Mild response 11
LATEST WORKOUTS Jun 5 Bel 4f fst :47⅗ h May 23 Bel 5f fst 1:01⅕ h May 17 Bel 4f fst :48⅖ b May 5 Bel 4f my :46⅘ h

Every Sundae
Ch. f. 4, by Honest Pleasure—Chocolate Only, by Nodouble
Br.—Blum P E (Ky)
Tr.—Bush Thomas M
Own.—Blum P E
122
Lifetime 9 0 1 1 $3,570 | 1984 5 M 0 0 $510 | 1983 4 M 1 1 $3,060 | Turf 1 0 0 0 $110

16May84- 3Bel fst 7f :23⅕ :46⅘ 1:24⅗ 3+ⒻMd Sp Wt 8 6 84½ 84 711 512 Velasquez J b 124 28.60 67-17 Bobbinette 11310½ Fiesta 113¾ French Farce 113½ Wide 12
20Apr84- 7GP fm *1⅛ Ⓣ 1:48⅕ ⒻMd Sp Wt 1 1 1hd 1hd 44 511 Solis A b 122 10.30 54-30 Windy Victory 122hd Jeunesse 1222 Early Invitation 1221 Tired 10
28Feb84- 6Hia fst 1⅛ :47⅘ 1:13 1:52⅖ ⒻMd Sp Wt 4 1 11 2hd 610 618½ Brumfield D b 122 12.60 51-23 Heavenly Honey 1224½ Terska 1221 Lady's Flag 122½ Tired 9
10Feb84- 5Hia fst 1⅛ :48⅕ 1:13 1:45⅗ ⒻMd Sp Wt 9 1 1hd 44 611 814 Brumfield D 122 19.00 62-22 Force O'Habit122noHeavenlyHoney1222½Lady'sFlag122½ Gave way 9
2Feb84- 3Hia fst 6f :22⅘ :46⅖ 1:11⅗ ⒻMd Sp Wt 10 9 74½ 59½ 59½ 612 Maple E 122 3.60 73-20 Switching Trick 1226 Heavenly Honey1221MissAshley1221 Outrun 12
23Jly83- 1CD fst 6f :21⅗ :44⅘ 1:10⅗ 3+ⒻMd Sp Wt 5 1 54½ 34½ 37 311 Patterson G 116 2.70 82-10 Heir Fancy 1163 Norias 1168 Every Sundae 116hd 7
25Jun83- 1CD fst 6f :21⅘ :45⅕ 1:12⅖ 3+ⒻMd Sp Wt 1 5 4¾ 53 41½ 51¾ Brumfield D 115 *1.00 82-11 Farandola 115nk Bongo's Cheramy 115hd Favorite Target 1151 12
11Jun83- 1CD fst 6f :21⅘ :45⅕ 1:11⅘ ⒻMd Sp Wt 9 1 2½ 1hd 1hd 2no Brumfield D 119 12.50 87-17 My Day Dream 119no Every Sundae 119nk Keep It Legal 1191 11
3May83- 2CD sly 6f :22⅖ :46 1:13⅘ ⒻMd Sp Wt 9 1 32 21½ 45 57¾ Day P 121 3.90 69-22 Tell Me Kate 1212½ Lisa Jeanette 1213 Delhousie 1212 9
LATEST WORKOUTS Jun 3 Bel tr.t 5f my 1:01⅘ b (d) May 24 Bel tr.t 4f gd :50⅗ b May 12 Bel 5f fst 1:01⅖ h Apr 8 Hia 4f fst :50 b

Cousin Jane
B. f. 4, by Tom Rolfe—Colonade, by Boldnesian
Br.—McBean P (Ky)
Tr.—Pierce Joseph H Jr
Own.—Greenberg M
122
Lifetime 6 0 1 2 $6,820 | 1984 1 M 1 0 $4,180 | 1983 5 M 0 2 $2,640 | Turf 3 0 1 2 $6,820

20May84- 4Bel fm 1⅛ Ⓣ:47 1:11⅗ 1:44⅕ 3+ⒻMd Sp Wt 5 6 65½ 42½ 33 23 Davis R G b 124 15.10 77-13 Tweedling 1133 Cousin Jane 1244 Purple Aura 113nk Wide str. 8
6Nov83- 6Aqu fst 1⅛ :49⅖ 1:14⅗ 1:52⅘ 3+ⒻMd Sp Wt 4 4 57½ 718 738 762¾ Migliore R b 120 11.40 — — Fois Gras 12019 Vandy's Joy 1208 Minstrely 1206 Fin. early 7
31Oct83- 5Med gd 1⅛ Ⓣ:47⅘ 1:13⅗ 1:46⅖ 3+ⒻMd Sp Wt 8 10 109½ 95½ 42½ 35½ Perret C b 117 5.50 65-24 PreciousPerfect1214NorcliffesSlkt1171½CousinJn1171½ Mild rally 10
18Oct83- 4Med yl 1⅛ Ⓣ:47⅘ 1:13⅗ 1:47⅘ 3+ⒻMd Sp Wt 8 6 65½ 44½ 44½ 37 Perret C b 117 20.70 56-32 Belle Glade 1174 Masters Wonder 1173 Cousin Jane 117½ Rallied 9
8Oct83- 5Med fst 6f :22⅕ :45⅘ 1:11⅗ 3+ⒻMd Sp Wt 8 10 1022 1022 1023 925½ Cordero A Jr b 118 12.50 60-14 Teriyaki Stake 1138 Pleasure On Hi 1181PirateDen1131 No factor 10
21Sep83- 4Bel fst 6f :22 :46 1:12⅘ 3+ⒻMd Sp Wt 13 11 1215 1322 1422 1421½ Fell J 118 18.10f 56-17 Hero'sCoin1181½SunshineO'MyLife1181StrictlyRaised118½ Outrun 14
LATEST WORKOUTS Jun 2 Mth 5f my 1:03 b May 16 Mth 7f fst 1:29 b ●May 6 Mth 7f fst 1:29 b Apr 28 Mth 7f fst 1:34 b

Plasma
Ch. f. 3, by Noholme II—Tokamak, by Tim Tam
Br.—Live Oak Stud (Fla)
Tr.—Kelly Patrick J
Own.—Live Oak Plantation
114
Lifetime 7 0 1 0 $5,200 | 1984 6 M 1 0 $5,200 | 1983 1 M 0 0 | Turf 4 0 1 0 $4,940

11May84- 4Bel fm 1⅛ Ⓣ:46 1:11⅗ 1:44 3+ⒻMd Sp Wt 8 8 713 78 77 210¾ Maple E b 113 *1.60e 65-17 Refill II 11310¾ Plasma 1131½ Damask Sky 113¾ Wide str. 10
30Apr84- 1Aqu fm 1⅛ Ⓣ:48⅘ 1:14⅘ 1:47⅕ 3+ⒻMd Sp Wt 2 3 41¾ 2hd — — Murphy D J b 112 11.10 — — Pouska 1123 Jealous One 1154 La Reine Rose 1241½ Lost rider 10
12Mar84- 6GP fm *1⅛ Ⓣ 1:46⅕ ⒻAlw 13000 9 9 910 86¾ 79½ 415½ Rivera M A b 116 115.20 59-21 Illaka 1161½ Battere 111no Candy Bowl 12114 Outrun 10
25Feb84- 6Hia fst 6f :22⅗ :45⅖ 1:09⅗ ⒻMd Sp Wt 6 7 73½ 711 1020 1031½ Rivera M A b 119 50.10 65-11 ValleyProspector1198LadySusan1196PoliticalPrincess119½ Outrun 12
17Jan84- 6Hia fst 7f :22⅘ :46⅖ 1:25 ⒻMd Sp Wt 10 1 2hd 2hd 913 926 Vasquez J b 119 29.60 52-19 Aneka 119hd Year After Year 1191½ Gentle Ram 1197 Gave way 11
6Jan84- 6Crc fm 1⅛ Ⓣ:48⅗ 1:14⅕ 1:46⅕ ⒻMd Sp Wt 12 8 63½ 911 1221 1228½ Rivera M A b 119 18.60 46-18 BrooklynPrincess1142ByouBirdie119½AngelFromAbove119¾ Wide 12
29Oct83- 4Aqu fst 6f :23⅕ :48⅕ 1:14⅕ ⒻMd Sp Wt 4 3 618 618 523 523 Murphy D J5 112 12.40 47-28 Disquieting 1171 Bett's Pleasure 1175 Shavie 11711 Outrun 7
LATEST WORKOUTS Jun 2 Bel tr.t 4f sly :51⅗ b May 29 Bel tr.t 5f my 1:05⅗ b (d) May 23 Bel 5f fst 1:05 b May 17 Bel tr.t 3f fst :37 b

Double Jeux
B. f. 4, by Exclusive Native—Double Sham, by Sham
Br.—Spendthrift Farm (Ky)
Tr.—Penna Angel Jr
Own.—Esuites Stable
122
Lifetime 2 0 1 1 $5,062 | 1983 2 M 1 1 $5,062 | 1982 0 M 0 0 | Turf 2 0 1 1 $5,062

25Oct83♦5Longchamp(Fra) gd*1¼ 2:11⅘ Ⓣ ⒻPrix de la Sorbonne(Mdn 22½ Machado R 116 *2.00 — — Riviere Doree 1182½ Double Jeux 116no Surentina 123½ Fin.well 8
8Oct83♦6Evry(Fra) gd*1⅛ 1:55⅗ Ⓣ ⒻPrix de Lisses 32 Machado R 116 7.75 — — Hard HeartedHanna124hd Surentina1232 DoubleJeux116½ Fin.well 14
LATEST WORKOUTS Jun 3 Bel 4f sly :48⅕ h May 26 Bel 5f fst 1:03⅗ b May 20 Bel 5f fst 1:02⅘ b May 9 Bel 4f sly :49 b

Fabulous Ack
B. f. 3, by Ack Ack—Fabulous View, by Le Fabuleux
Br.—Hancock III & Peters (Ky)
Tr.—Suss-Kolyer R
Own.—DeMatteis F
114
Lifetime 3 0 0 0 | 1984 3 M 0 0 | 1983 0 M 0 0

5May84- 1Aqu gd 7f :23 :46⅘ 1:26⅕ ⒻMd Sp Wt 2 3 43 77¾ 79 612 Davis R G 121 16.60 58-16 Boldara 1213 Handsewn 116nk Elbarita 1211½ Fin. early 8
14Apr84- 4Aqu sly 6f ⊡:23 :48 1:14 ⒻMd Sp Wt 10 2 1hd 43½ 912 1012¾ Davis R G b 121 7.50 61-15 PreciousRoslie1161½Tempestously1212Chieftin'sNtive121no Tired 11
2Apr84- 6Aqu fst 6f ⊡:22⅘ :46⅗ 1:12⅗ ⒻMd Sp Wt 4 2 42 710 714 816¾ Davis R G 121 8.40 64-17 Lassie's Lady 121¾ Hidden Point 1213½ Em An Aye 1214 Tired 10
LATEST WORKOUTS Jun 2 Bel 5f sly 1:02⅘ b May 28 Bel 4f fst :47⅕ h May 22 Bel 1 fst 1:42 b May 12 Bel 5f fst 1:00⅗ hg

first of four victories for Refill that summer, before illness put a premature end to her campaign. Note that the favored entry finished second and third.

Due possibly to a combination of physical problems and/or poor weather conditions, Double Jeux did not appear again in the entries until June 8, in the third race at Belmont. The field she faced was quite weak. Plasma was back for another try, and Cousin Jane, who had placed in each of her three grass starts, looked a threat. The latter, however, with her closing style and penchant for runner-up finishes, fit perfectly the model for one of the "antagonist" types discussed in an earlier chapter.

Based on her second-place finish at Longchamp, France's premier track, Double Jeux was a standout in this field. Her trainer, Angel Penna, Jr., worked especially well with grass horses and figured to have her ready for her first start of the year. Double Jeux breezed by almost fifteen lengths and returned a fair $5.40. Later that summer, she placed third behind Sabin in the Grade II $100,000-added Sheepshead Bay Handicap at Belmont.

THIRD RACE
Belmont
JUNE 8, 1984

1 MILE.(Turf). (1.33) MAIDEN SPECIAL WEIGHTS. Purse $19,000. Fillies and mares, 3-year-old an dupward, weights, 3-year-olds, 114 lbs. Older, 122 lbs.

Value of race $19,000, value to winner $11,400, second $4,180, third $2,280, fourth $1,140. Mutuel pool $96,845, OTB pool $101,417. Exacta Pool $214,054; OTB Exacta Pool $186,516.

Last Raced	Horse	Eqt.	A.	Wt	PP	St	¼	½	¾	Str	Fin	Jockey	Odds $1
25Oct83 ^{5}Fra^{2}	Double Jeux		4	122	10	8	5^{1}	$3^{1\frac{1}{2}}$	$1^{2\frac{1}{2}}$	1^{7}	$1^{14\frac{1}{2}}$	Cordero A Jr	1.70
10May84 ^{1}Bel^{5}	Stormy Lass		3	114	1	10	9^{2}	8^{4}	8^{3}	$4^{1\frac{1}{2}}$	$2^{\frac{3}{4}}$	Smith A Jr	51.10
16Dec83 ^{4}Aqu^{6}	Flora Scent		3	114	4	6	$8^{1\frac{1}{2}}$	$7^{1\frac{1}{2}}$	5^{1}	3^{1}	$3^{\frac{1}{2}}$	Migliore R	7.60
20May84 ^{4}Bel^{2}	Cousin Jane	b	4	122	8	7	$7^{\frac{1}{2}}$	6^{1}	$2^{1\frac{1}{2}}$	2^{1}	4^{7}	Davis R G	3.40
11May84 ^{4}Bel^{2}	Plasma	b	3	114	9	3	4^{1}	5^{1}	7^{1}	6^{2}	5^{1}	Maple E	6.10
10May84 ^{1}Bel^{4}	Christmas Chime	b	3	109	6	4	2^{1}	1^{hd}	$3^{\frac{1}{2}}$	5^{4}	6^{4}	Ward W A^{5}	6.40
16May84 ^{3}Bel^{5}	Every Sundae	b	4	122	7	2	$1^{\frac{1}{2}}$	$2^{\frac{1}{2}}$	$6^{\frac{1}{2}}$	8^{2}	$7^{2\frac{3}{4}}$	Velasquez J	20.40
	Nan's Gone		3	114	5	11	11	11	11	11	8^{hd}	Clayton M D	37.90
1Jun84 ^{6}Bel^{8}	Shift Key	b	3	114	3	9	10^{8}	9^{1}	9^{6}	9^{4}	$9^{1\frac{1}{4}}$	MacBeth D	26.50
5May84 ^{1}Aqu^{6}	Fabulous Ack		3	114	11	1	3^{1}	$4^{\frac{1}{2}}$	4^{hd}	7^{hd}	10^{3}	Samyn J L	14.30
19May84 ^{9}Del^{7}	Bit of Raja	b	3	114	2	5	$6^{\frac{1}{2}}$	10^{14}	10^{12}	10^{1}	11	Murphy D J	37.50

OFF AT 2:03 Start good, Won ridden out. Time, :23⅖, :47, 1:10⅗, 1:35 Course firm.

$2 Mutuel Prices:			
11-(K)-DOUBLE JEUX	5.40	4.00	2.80
1-(A)-STORMY LASS		23.00	11.80
5-(E)-FLORA SCENT			5.20

$2 EXACTA 11-1 PAID $222.60.

B. f, by Exclusive Native—Double Sham, by Sham. Trainer Penna Angel Jr. Bred by Spendthrift Farm (Ky).

DOUBLE JEUX moved to the fore with a rush from the outside approaching the stretch and drew off under a hand ride. STORMY LASS, very wide into the stretch, finished well to gain the place. FLORA SCENT rallied from the outside leaving the turn but lacked a late response. COUSIN JANE made a run approaching the stretch and weakened. PLASMA tired badly. CHRISTMAS CHIME and EVERY SUNDAE were used up vying for the lead. FABULOUS ACK tired badly. BIT OF RAJA was finished early.

Chapter 20

Like Mother, Like Son

PART OF THE FASCINATION OF Thoroughbred handicapping comes from the sport itself and the continuity of its bloodlines. Once a player has been around the races for a few years, he begins to see the offspring of horses he watched perform. At times, a memory of the peculiarities, the likes and dislikes of the sire and/or dam, proves very helpful. The Sword Dancer Handicap, a mile-and-a-half grass event run over a damp grass course at Belmont on July 28, 1984, was a case in point.

Glowing Tribute, the dam of morning-line favorite Hero's Honor, was an outstanding race mare in her time and something of a freak. She was one of the few Graustark's who moved up on the grass, a surface over which she was a multiple stakes winner. Glowing Tribute had her limitations, however. Despite her stout bloodlines—she was from a Hail to Reason mare—Glowing Tribute raced best at the middle distances, not really wanting to go as far as a mile and a quarter. And she definitely did not like soft footing. The author vividly recalls beating her under such conditions with an otherwise inferior runner called Welsh Pearl, to the tune of $17.00. Glowing Tribute was heavily favored on that occasion.

Hero's Honor's entire grass career can be seen in his past performances for the Sword Dancer. One third-place finish marred an otherwise perfect record on the grass. Hero's Honor seemed to have overcome his dam's distance limitations, even though his own sire's get have long been suspected of preferring the first mile and a quarter. But Hero's Honor had yet to run over a soft or yielding course, the kind he would be confronted with in the Sword Dancer. That, plus the fact that he was being asked to tote 126 pounds over the mile-and-a-half distance, made Hero's Honor an unattractive propo-

8 BELMONT

1½ MILES. (Turf). (2.24⅘) 10th Running THE SWORD DANCER HANDICAP (Grade I). Purse $200,000 added. (Plus $50,000 Breeders' Cup Premium Awards.) 3-year-olds and upward. By subscription of $500 each, which should accompany the nomination; $3,200 to pass the entry box, with $200,000 added. The added money and all fees to be divided 60% to the winner, 22% to second, 12% to third and 6% to fourth. Weights, Monday, July 23. Starters to be named at the closing time of entries. Trophies will be presented to the winning owner, trainer and jockey. The New York Racing Association reserves the right to transfer this race to the Main Course. Closed Wednesday, July 11, 1984 with 29 nominations.

Fortnightly

B. c. 4, by Dance Spell—Out Cold, by Etonian — Br.—Bwamazon Farm (Ky) — Tr.—Parisella John — Own.—Sabarese T M

114 — Lifetime 19 4 8 2 $325,634 — 1984 2 0 2 0 $36,310 — 1983 10 2 3 2 $182,256 — Turf 17 4 8 2 $325,634

4Jly84- 9AP fm 1⅛ ①:45⅗ 1:09⅘ 1:41⅘ 3+Strs Strps H 4 13 1412 1311 64 21½ Venezia M b 115 3.20 101-09 Tough Mickey 1191½ Fortnightly 1151½ Jack Slade 1131½ Wide 15

9Jun84- 7Mth fm 1 ①:48 1:11⅘ 1:36⅘ 3+Red Bank H 3 7 67½ 21 1½ 21½ Perret C b 117 7.30 92-09 Tough Mickey 1181½ Fortnightly 117no RomanBend1082 Game try 9

9Jun84-Run in divisions

15Oct83- 7Kee fst 1⅛ :47⅘ 1:11⅘ 1:48⅘ 3+Fayette H 3 5 58½ 58¾ 512 — Sellers M S b 115 13.70 — — DH Frost King 1232 DH Cad 1162 Bold Style 1202 Eased 5

29Sep83- 8Med fm 1⅜ ①:48⅘ 1:38⅕ 2:14⅗ Rutgers H 7 9 914 5¾ 21 33 Day P b 118 *1.90 89-11 Exile King 1132 MoonSpirit1161Fortnightly118no Drifted, brushed 9

29Sep83-Run in two divisions 6th & 8th races

18Sep83- 8Bel fm 1½ ①:49⅕ 2:03⅘ 2:28⅘ Lwrnce Rlztn 1 5 53½ 75½ 44½ 45½ Velasquez J b 123 2.20 77-17 Moon Spirit 114½ Win 1142¾ Tough Mickey 1142 Checked 10

5Sep83- 8AP fm 1½ ①:49⅘ 2:06⅕ 2:32⅘ Secretariat 5 9 711 21 11½ 11¾ Day P b 117 *1.40 77-19 Fortnightly 1171¾ Jack Slade 1146¾ Reap 1141½ Wide, driving 13

18Aug83- 8Sar sf 1⅛ ①:49⅘ 1:14⅘ 1:55⅕ 3+Alw 32000 4 3 21 2hd 41½ 31½ Velasquez J b 112 *.60 50-54 Sir Pele 117¾ Woozley 114½ Fortnightly 112½ Weakened 6

7Aug83- 8Sar fm 1⅛ ①:46⅕ 1:10⅘ 1:48⅖ 3+B Baruch H 3 8 813 77½ 32 2no Velasquez J b 113 2.80 85-16 Fray Star 114no Fortnightly 113¾ Who's For Dinner 1091¾ Gaining 9

7Aug83-Run in two divisions; 6th & 8th races

13Jly83- 8Bel fm 1¼ Ⓣ:47 1:35⅘ 2:00⅘ Lexington 2 4 38 33½ 23 2hd Velasquez J b 126 4.40 91-12 Kilaue114hdFortnightly1263½TopCompetitor114hd Steadied,lug in 10

LATEST WORKOUTS Jly 26 Bel Ⓣ 4f fm :49 b (d) Jly 20 Bel ① 1 yl 1:40⅘ h Jly 14 Bel tr.t 5f fst 1:02⅘ b ●Jun 28 Bel Ⓣ 5f fm :59⅘ h (d)

Win *

B. g. 4, by Barachois—Par Ci Par La, by Buckpasser — Br.—Wehle R G (NY) — Tr.—Bailie Sally A — Own.—Ephraim F

113 — Lifetime 21 7 5 1 $305,213 — 1984 5 2 1 0 $127,580 — 1983 15 5 4 1 $177,633 — Turf 9 4 1 0 $143,823

1Jly84- 8Bel sly 1⅜ :46⅕ 1:37⅘ 2:18⅘ 3+Tidal H 1 1 1hd 12½ 15 111 Graell A b 111 *1.10 87-20 Win 11111 Anne's Lover 1089 Four Bases 1125¾ Ridden out 6

17Jun84- 8Bel fm 1⅜ Ⓣ:48⅕ 1:35⅘ 2:14 3+Bwlng Grn H 5 5 32½ 21½ 23½ 55½ Graell A b 114 6.20 82-20 Hero's Honor 1201¾ Nassipour 110½ SuperSunrise1232½ Weakened 11

2Jun84- 8Bel sly 1¼ :47⅘ 1:35⅘ 2:02⅕ 3+Red Smith H 5 2 21½ 24 24 27 Graell A b 114 2.40 80-19 Hero's Honor 1177 Win 1144½ Eskimo 11216½ No match 5

24May84- 8Bel fst 1⅛ :45⅘ 1:10⅘ 1:43⅘ 3+Alw 36000 4 3 2½ 1hd 11 12¾ Graell A b 119 8.60 85-15 Win 1192¾ Mr. Badger 1214 Hero's Honor 12111½ Driving 5

28Apr84- 7Aqu fm 1 ①:47⅘ 1:13⅘ 1:39⅘ 3+Alw 36000 3 4 54½ 54 55 57½ Graell A b 121 5.00 70-21 ToughMickey1213Erin'sTigr1212½DomintingDooly119¾ Weakened 9

8Nov83- 6Aqu gd 1⅜ ①:49⅕ 1:41 2:17⅘ 3+Knickrbckr H 10 6 31½ 3nk 2½ 42½ Graell A b 113 5.30 79-21 Four Bases 105¾ Moon Spirit 114nk Ask Me 1171½ Wide 10

8Nov83-Run in Two Divisions: 6th & 8th Races

15Oct83- 7Bel sf 1½ ①:49⅘ 2:07 2:33⅘ 3+Handicap 1 3 34½ 21 32 43¾ Graell A b 114 *1.90 53-42 Dilmoun 113¾ Piling 115hd Four Bases 1053 Weakened 8

29Sep83- 6Med fm 1⅜ ①:47⅘ 1:36⅘ 2.14⅕ Rutgers 1 3 44½ 43 31½ 11¾ Graell A b 114 3.60 94-11 Win 1141½ Bounding Basque 115hd Hero's Honor 114¾ Drew clear 9

29Sep83-Run in two divisions 6th & 8th races

18Sep83- 8Bel fm 1½ ①:49⅕ 2:03⅘ 2:28⅘ Lwrnce Rlztn 6 4 43½ 1hd 1½ 2½ Graell A b 114 8.40 81-17 Moon Spirit 114½ Win 1142¾ Tough Mickey 1142 Gamely 10

31Aug83- 8Bel fm 1⅜ Ⓣ:49⅕ 1:39⅘ 2:16⅘ 3+Alw 30000 4 3 32½ 22½ 1hd 1nk Graell A b 114 8.90 73-27 Win 114nk Katyusha 1127 Juanca 1191 Driving 7

LATEST WORKOUTS Jly 24 Bel 5f fst 1:06⅖ b Jly 18 Bel 1 fst 1:38⅘ h Jly 12 Bel Ⓣ 5f gd 1:04⅘ b (d) Jly 8 Bel 4f gd :50⅘ b

Dr. Schwartzman

B. c. 3, by Fluorescent Light—Stark Winter, by Graustark — Br.—Farish W S III & Hannibal Horse Co (Ky) — Tr.—Croll Warren A Jr — Own.—Levy Blanche P

112 — Lifetime 13 5 2 1 $135,368 — 1984 6 2 2 1 $87,671 — 1983 7 3 0 0 $47,697 — Turf 7 4 2 0 $119,056

14Jly84- 8Bel fm 1¼ Ⓣ:48⅕ 1:37 2:01⅕ Lexington 2 7 85½ 95½ 57½ 21 Perret C 126 4.40e 87-11 Onyxly 1141 Dr. Schwartzman 1261½ Vision1263 Steadied, blocked 13

30Jun84- 9Mth sly 1⅛ :46⅘ 1:12 1:44⅘ Lmplghtr H 4 7 76½ 2hd 2hd 32½ Perret C 121 *2.20 80-19 Light Spirits 1122 A Gift 118½ Dr.Schwartzman1215 Unruly pre st. 9

16Jun84- 9Mth fm 1 ①:47⅕ 1:10⅘ 1:35 Long Branch 1 3 35½ 33½ 32½ 1nk Perret C 118 *.70 100-05 Dr. Schwartzman 118nk Stay The Course1123ForHalo1142 Driving 8

11Apr84- 9GP fm 1⅛ ①:46⅘ 1:11⅘ 1:42⅘ Spect'lr Bid 9 3 33½ 21 1hd 41 Perret C 119 *.50 87-12 Klaytone 1141 Amerilad 119hd Marine 117no Bore in 10

21Mar84- 9GP fm 1 ①:46⅘ 1:10⅘ 1:35 3+Appleton H 2 3 2½ 11 11½ 2½ Rocco J 109 2.40 94-08 GreatSubstence113½Dr.Schwartzmn1093½RisingRj113nk Weakened 10

21Mar84-Run in divisions

18Feb84- 8Hia fm 1⅛ ① 1:41⅘ Dade County 11 1 1hd 1½ 13 12 Perret C 119 *1.40 90-11 Dr. Schwartzman 1192 Klaytone 112nk Calejucam 113½ Drew clear 14

26Nov83- 7Crc fm *1⅛ ① 1:41⅘ City Miami 4 4 411 34 1hd 14½ Perret C 114 *2.70 98-05 Dr. Schwartzman1144½D.White1141Rexson'sHope1195½ Drew clear 10

26Nov83-Run in Two Divisions: 7th & 9th Races

5Nov83- 8Med fst 1⅛ :46⅕ 1:11⅘ 1:45⅕ Yng America 13 11 1013 913 817 717½ Perret C 119 17.20f 65-20 Swale 122no Disastrous Night 1193 Dr. Carter 1196 No menace 16

19Oct83- 8Aqu sly 1⅛ :48 1:13 1:50⅕ Pilgrim 7 4 47 53 411 411¾ Perret C 115 2.70 72-20 Vision1135½TheAccomodtor1134¾RovingMinstrl1131¾ Raced wide 7

19Oct83-Run in two divisions 7th & 8th races

LATEST WORKOUTS Jly 20 Mth 5f fst 1:02 b Jly 13 Mth 3f fst :35 h Jly 9 Mth 7f fst 1:26⅕ h Jun 29 Mth 3f gd :37 b (d)

Norwick

B. h. 5, by Far North—Shay Sheery, by A Dragon Killer — Br.—Jones Brereton C (Ky) — Tr.—Sedlacek Michael C — Own.—Stronach F

112 — Lifetime 33 8 4 3 $433,526 — 1984 9 1 0 3 $153,900 — 1983 7 2 0 0 $80,400 — Turf 30 7 4 1 $339,626

14Jly84- 8Atl fm 1⅜ ①:48⅕ 1:11⅘ 1:54 3+U Nations H 6 7 96½ 85½ 87¾ 75½ Davis R G 114 63.00 89-14 Hero's Honor 1231½ Cozzene 114no Who's ForDinner110hd Outrun 11

1Jly84- 9WO fst 1¼ :48⅘ 1:39⅘ 2:04⅘ 3+Dom'n Day H 8 6 66¾ 12 16 110 Stahlbaum G 123 *2.35 83-22 Norwick 12310 George Dinkle 115½ Juan De Fuca 116½ In hand 10

17Jun84- 8Bel fm 1⅜ Ⓣ:48⅕ 1:35⅘ 2:14 3+Bwlng Grn H 8 6 86½ 109½ 98¾ 66½ MacBeth D 114 27.80 81-20 Hero's Honor 1201¾ Nassipour 110½ SuperSunrise1232½ No factor 11

6May84- 8GG fm 1⅜ ①:47⅘ 1:35⅘ 2:13 3+Goldengate H 3 5 614 616 615 414 Chapman T M 114 26.10 89-09 John Henry 1252 Silveyville 1176 Lucence 1166 Evenly 6

22Apr84- 8SA fm *1¾ ①:47⅘ 2:26⅘ 2:48 San Juan H 7 7 75½ 54 47½ 36½ McCarron C J 115 16.60 80-15 Load The Cannons 1192½ Jenkins Ferry 1144 Norwick 1151½ Wide 9

1Apr84- 8SA fm 1½ ①:48⅖ 2:02⅘ 2:26⅘ 3+San Luis Rey 10 7 85 86½ 89 77½ Shoemaker W 126 18.40 74-17 Interco 126nk Gato Del Sol 126½ John Henry 1263½ Outrun 10

23Mar84- 7SA fst 1⅛ :46⅕ 1:10⅕ 1:41⅕ Alw 45000 6 6 613 611 57½ 34 McCarron C J 114 3.10 91-17 Fighting Fit 1222½ Hula Blaze 1221½ Norwick 114½ Rallied 6

4Mar84- 4SA fst 1⅛ :47⅘ 1:12 1:43⅘ Alw 45000 2 5 54½ 42 42½ 3½ McCarron C J 121 6.10 83-17 Count Gema 121½ Croeso 116hd Norwick 1211½ Shfl'd back early 6

23Feb84- 8SA fm 1⅛ ①:47⅘ 1:12⅘ 1:48⅘ Alw 45000 4 4 55 64½ 64½ 76 McCarron C J 116 5.80 77-17 Major Sport 122½ Handsome One 1141½ Ten Below1221 No factor 7

16Oct83- 9WO yl 1⅝ ①:51⅕ 1:42 2:45 3+Rothmans Int 11 8 78½ 54 68¾ 65¾ Stahlbaum G 126 74.70 69-25 All Along 1232 Thunder Puddles126¾Majesty'sPrince126nk Evenly 11

LATEST WORKOUTS Jun 13 Aqu 4f fst :49⅘ b Jun 7 Aqu 6f fst 1:12⅘ h

Four Bases

Ch. h. 5, by Diplomat Way—Bunting, by Hitting Away — Br.—Farnsworth Farm (Fla) — Tr.—Puentes Gilbert — Own.—Garren M M

110 — Lifetime 50 10 7 8 $327,143 — 1984 10 1 1 2 $112,788 — 1983 21 5 2 3 $136,337 — Turf 30 9 6 4 $291,333

14Jly84- 8Atl fm 1⅜ ①:48⅕ 1:11⅘ 1:54 3+U Nations H 9 10 107½ 95½ 1011 109 Guerra W A b 112 83.10 85-14 Hero's Honor 1231½Cozzene114noWho'sForDinner110hd No factor 11

1Jly84- 8Bel sly 1⅜ :46⅕ 1:37⅘ 2:18⅘ 3+Tidal H 4 4 414 46½ 38 320 Velasquez J b 112 8.00 67-20 Win 11111 Anne's Lover 1089 Four Bases 1125¾ Lacked a bid 6

17Jun84- 8Bel fm 1⅜ Ⓣ:48⅕ 1:35⅘ 2:14 3+Bwlng Grn H 6 2 53 56 77½ 97½ Thibeau R J b 114 17.30 80-20 Hero's Honor 1201¾ Nassipour 110½ Super Sunrise 1232½ Tired 11

2Jun84- 8Bel sly 1¼ :47⅘ 1:35⅘ 2:02⅕ 3+Red Smith H 1 3 35½ 520 527 539½ Samyn J L b 116 9.90 48-19 Hero's Honor 1177 Win 1144½ Eskimo 11216½ Tired 5

21Apr84- 9GP fm 1½ ①:48⅕ 2:01 2:26⅘ 3+Pan Amer'n H 8 2 22½ 716 719 622½ Solis A b 113 4.10 68-13 Tonzarun 1121½ Ayman 1141 Nassipour 110½ Tired 9

7Apr84- 9GP fm 1⅛ ①:45⅘ 1:09⅘ 1:40 3+Can Turf H 2 6 613 85¾ 77½ 94½ Solis A b 114 3.00 97-01 Ayman 112nk Smart andSharp1101¾Guston114nk Shuffled back st. 11

25Feb84- 11Hia fm 1½ ① 2:26⅘ 3+Hia Tf Cup H 3 1 1hd 1½ 1hd 2no Solis A b 113 16.20 96-04 Nijinsky's Secret 126no Four Bases1134Tonzarun1133½ Just failed 11

4Feb84- 10Hia fm 1⅜ ① 1:52⅘ 3+Bougainvla H 7 3 32½ 2½ 1½ 1½ Solis A b 111 68.00 95-11 Four Bases 111½ Tonzarun 111¾ Super Sunrise 1172½ Driving 14

21Jan84- 8Hia fm 1⅛ ① 1:41 3+Royal Palm H 7 7 77½ 75 89½ 98½ Velez R I b 113 5.10 84-13 Out Of Hock 113½ Gorytus 1132½ Mac The Sailor 1122½ Outrun 11

21Jan84-Run in divisions

5Jan84- 9Crc fm 1½ ①:51⅘ 2:07⅕ 2:31⅕ 3+W Mcknight H 4 2 12 1hd 2hd 32½ Velasquez J b 114 30.10 80-14 Nijinsky's Secret1241½DomMenotti112¾FourBases1142 Weakened 11

5Jan84-Run in Divisions

LATEST WORKOUTS Jly 26 Bel tr.t 4f fst :48⅘ b Jly 21 Bel 4f gd :48⅘ hg Jly 9 Bel tr.t 6f fst 1:18 b Jun 28 Bel tr.t 5f fst 1:05 b

Nassipour

Ch. c. 4, by Blushing Groom—Alama, by Aureole — Br.—Prince S A Aga Khan (Ky) — Tr.—DiMauro Stephen — Own.—Dogwood Stable

109 — Lifetime 18 3 2 4 $94,316 — 1984 9 0 2 3 $83,791 — 1983 8 3 0 1 $10,525 — Turf 17 3 2 4 $94,156

13Jly84- 8Bel fm 1⅜ Ⓣ:47⅘ 1:36⅕ 2:14 3+Handicap 5 8 69½ 45 33½ 33½ Samyn J L b 116 *2.00e 84-16 Domynsky 116nk Native Raid 1153 Nassipour 1164½ Rallied 11

17Jun84- 8Bel fm 1⅜ Ⓣ:48⅕ 1:35⅘ 2:14 3+Bwlng Grn H 3 9 911 87½ 33½ 21¾ Samyn J L b 110 26.40 85-20 Hero's Honor 1201¾ Nassipour 110½ Super Sunrise1232½ Wide str. 11

7Jun84- 7Bel fm 1⅜ ①:49⅘ 1:38 2:14⅕ 3+Alw 25000 1 7 66 42 23 22½ Samyn J L b 117 3.10 89-13 Talakeno 1172½Nassipour1174HeadoftheHouse119½ Best of others 7

20May84- 7Bel fm 2 ①:51 2:55⅘ 3:20⅘ 3+Handicap 3 6 32 34 33½ 34½ Samyn J L b 120 *2.10 93-13 Anne's Lover 1142¾ Erin Bright 1171¾ Nassipour 1202¾ Evenly 10

12May84- 9Pim sf 1½ ①:53⅘ 2:13⅕ 2:41 3+Dixie H 3 7 611 68¾ 512 412½ Saumell L b 113 *1.20e — — Persian Tiara 1092½CrazyMoon1128CanadianFactor1182 No factor 8

21Apr84- 9GP fm 1½ ①:48⅕ 2:01 2:26⅘ 3+Pan Amer'n H 2 8 913 611 46½ 32½ Velez J A Jr 110 24.90 88-13 Tonzarun 1121½ Ayman 1141 Nassipour 110½ Rallied 9

4Apr84- 8GP fm *1⅛ ① 1:44⅘ Alw 16000 6 9 814 811 84¾ 46 Solis A b 117 15.60 76-17 Baroque 117½ Norclin 1171 Northern Best 1174½ Rallied 9

24Mar84- 7GP fst 7f :22⅘ :44⅘ 1:21⅘ Alw 16000 8 3 911 913 89 67½ Solis A b 117 51.80 87-10 Magnetic Field II 1171½ Cut Away 117½ Derby Double1171 Outrun 9

12Mar84- 8GP fm *1⅛ ① 1:44⅘ Alw 16000 2 6 79½ 88 814 710½ Bailey J D b 119 10.20 71-21 Davis Joy 1171½ Baroque 1194½ Banker Baron 1191½ Outrun 9

19Oct83 ♦2Sandown(Eng) gd 1⅝ 2:59⅘ ① Meadowlands Hcp 12 McCarron C b 134 4.50 — — Nassipour 1342 Karablake 1358 RegalStreet140nk Far back, clear 8

LATEST WORKOUTS Jly 26 Bel Ⓣ 5f fm 1:05 b (d) Jly 24 Bel 3f fst :37⅘ b Jly 5 Bel Ⓣ 6f fm 1:14⅕ h (d) Jly 3 Bel 3f fst :37 b

Papal Bull

B. c. 4, by Alleged—Confess, by Cornish Prince — Br.—Valentine Mrs M (Pa) — Tr.—Imperio Dominick A — Own.—Terranova J P

110 — Lifetime 16 4 4 1 $75,100 — 1984 10 2 1 1 $41,850 — 1983 6 2 3 0 $33,250 — Turf 13 2 4 1 $54,100

15Jly84- 4Bel fm 1¼ Ⓣ:49 1:37 2:01⅕ 3+Alw 25000 4 5 31½ 21 31 1¾ Cordero A Jr 117 6.10 88-14 Papal Bull 117¾ Nepal 119nk Crazy Moon 1171½ Driving 6

```
6Jun84- 9Hol fst 1⅛  :45⅘ 1:10⅕ 1:41⅘  Alw 24000  6 6 513 57½ 44 1½  Hawley S  114 6.70  86-20 Papal Bull 114½ Poly Test 1144 Lord Protector 1175  Driving 7
28May84- 9Hol fm 1⅛ Ⓣ:47⅗ 1:11⅕ 1:48⅘  Alw 24000  6 6 78½ 85¾ 86¾ 73½  Toro F  115 4.10  85-08 Vigorous Vigors 120¾ Bertocelli 115½ CountySeat120hd  No factor 10
25Apr84- 9Hol fm 1⅛ Ⓣ:47⅘ 1:12 1:47⅘  Alw 24000  6 7 76½ 75½ 76 41  Toro F  115 4.10  90-04 Best Of Both 120no County Seat 120½ Chivalry 114½  Rallied 10
11Apr84- 4SA fm 1¼ Ⓣ:48⅕ 1:37⅘ 2:01⅘  Alw 33000  3 3 21½ 2½ 23 21½  Drexler H  116 5.40  78-17 Bosto 1141½ Papal Bull 116nk Allied Commander 1203  Wide 6
28Mar84- 5SA fm 1¼ Ⓣ:46⅕ 1:35⅗ 2:00⅘  Alw 35000  7 3 37½ 52½ 46½ 34  Drexler H  116 46.10  79-17 Top Competitor1201½AlliedCommander1202½PapalBull1161½  Wide 8
4Mar84- 5SA fm 1¼ Ⓣ:47 1:36 2:01⅗  Alw 32000  8 11 1112 1111 1011 119¾  Sibille R  116 40.70  69-19 Favoloso 1091½ Top Competitor 1201¾ Chivalry 115½  Never close 11
21Jan84- 7SA fst 1⅛  :46⅗ 1:11⅕ 1:44  Alw 27000  6 9 108¾ 1111 1117¾ 109¾  Fell J  120 18.40  71-17 NorthrxfordDrv1152½StgHndJohny1141½Lghthwyholm120¾  Outrun 12
15Jan84- 5SA fm 1⅛ Ⓣ:45⅘ 1:11⅕ 1:49⅗  Alw 26000  7 7 87½ 84½ 84½ 84  Sibille R  120 15.30  75-21 Ablantin 115½ Bruckner 115no Pair Of Aces 114hd  Outrun 10
1Jan84- 5SA fm 1¼ Ⓣ:48⅖ 1:38⅗ 2:02⅘  Alw 27000  2 2 21 2½ 53¾ 78½  Sibille R  118 3.60  66-26 Strong Dollar 1143½ Debonair Herc 115hd Ablantin 115¾  Tired 8
LATEST WORKOUTS  Jly 26 Bel Ⓣ 1 fm 1:42⅘ b (d)  ●Jly 12 Bel Ⓣ 7f gd 1:28⅘ h (d)  Jly 3 Bel tr.t 1 fst 1:44 b  Jun 28 Bel 5f fst 1:01⅘ h
```

Majesty's Prince

```
Majesty's Prince    Ch. h. 5, by His Majesty—Pied Princess, by Tom Fool
                    Br.—Marsh J D (Va)
Own.—Marsh J D      Tr.—Cantey Joseph B
124   Lifetime 36 9 10 9  $1,184,402   1984 1 0 0 0 $9,000   1983 13 2 1 7 $531,008   Turf 24 8 5 6 $1,096,872

14Jly84- 8Atl fm 1⅜ Ⓣ:48⅕ 1:11⅘ 1:54  3+U Nations H  4 6 54½ 51½ 44½ 41½  Maple E  125 7.70  92-14 Hero's Honor 1231½ Cozzene 114no Who's ForDinner110hd  Evenly 11
11Dec83- 8Hol gd 1⅜ Ⓣ:49⅘ 1:40 2:16⅗ 3+Turf Cup  6 12 1213 107½ 109½ 88½  Delahoussaye E  126 10.40  64-27 John Henry 126½ Zalataia 1231½ Palikaraki 1261½  Outrun 12
12Nov83- 8Lrl yl 1½ Ⓣ:51⅘ 2:08⅘ 2:35  3+D C Int'l  7 7 84½ 23½ 26 36  Cordero A Jr  127 5.50  38-56 All Along 1243½ WelshTerm1272½Majesty'sPrince127hd  Weakened 8
16Oct83- 9WO yl 1⅝ Ⓣ:51⅕ 1:42 2:45  3+Rothmans Int  2 7 911 75¾ 46½ 32¾  Maple E  126 3.45  72-25 AllAlong1232ThunderPuddles126¾Mjesty'sPrinc126nk  Closed well 11
1Oct83- 8Bel sf 1⅜ Ⓣ:52⅘ 1:43⅘ 2:23⅘ 3+Man O' War  5 3 44 32 32 1½  Maple E  126 7.60  44-56 Majesty's Prince 126½ Erins Isle 1261¾ L'Emigrant 1215½  Driving 11
28Aug83- 9AP gd 1¼ Ⓣ:50⅗ 1:41⅗ 2:04⅖ 3+Arl Million  12 14 1411 1412 1115 1211¾  Maple E  126 10.40  60-28 Tolomeo 118nk John Henry 126½ Nijinsky's Secret 1262  No speed 14
24Jly83- 8Bel sf 1½ Ⓣ:50⅖ 2:08 2:34⅘ 3+Swd Dancer H  7 6 715 77¾ 54 11  Maple E  120 3.90  52-48 Mjsty'sPrinc1201ⒹHushDr118hdThundrPuddls118¾  Steadied, drvg 9
2Jly83- 8Atl fm 1⅜ Ⓣ:47 1:10⅗ 1:53⅖ 3+U Nations H  1 10 75¾ 62¾ 63½ 33  Maple E  120 *2.80  94-08 Acaroid 113½ Trevita 1162½ Majesty's Prince 120no  Rallied 13
19Jun83- 8Bel fm 1⅜ Ⓣ:48⅗ 1:37⅘ 2:14⅘ 3+Bwlg Green H  2 7 712 74½ 65 31¾  Maple E  122 3.30  81-25 Tantalizing 113¾ Sprink 1131 Majesty's Prince 122¾  Steadied 7
7May83- 8GG fm 1⅜ Ⓣ:48⅗ 1:38⅘ 2:16⅘ 3+G Gate H  4 8 822 68½ 56 34  Nemeti W  122 2.90  82-19 Silveyville 1153 Ask Me 1151 Majesty'sPrince122¾  Altered course 9
LATEST WORKOUTS  Jly 24 Bel 7f fst 1:26⅘ h  Jly 10 Bel 6f fst 1:13⅕ h  ●Jly 5 Bel Ⓣ 1 fm 1:39⅘ h (d)  Jun 27 Bel 1 fst 1:40⅘ h
```

Dance Caller

```
Dance Caller        Ch. c. 4, by Marshua's Dancer—All In, by Gallant Man
                    Br.—Morgan Nancy Penn (Ky)
Own.—Hobeau Farm    Tr.—Jerkens H Allen
109   Lifetime 22 4 1 4  $136,896   1984 8 0 1 1 $24,596   1983 11 4 0 3 $111,100   Turf 3 1 0 2 $22,320

21Jly84- 8Bel sly 1½  :48⅗ 2:02 2:27⅘ 3+Brooklyn H  3 3 46½ 612 616 625  Miranda J  b 111 10.80  58-21 Fit to Fight 12912½ Vision 1095 Dew Line 116hd  Tired 8
4Jly84- 8Bel fst 1¼  :47⅗ 1:35⅕ 2:00⅗ 3+Suburban H  2 6 65½ 68½ 69 57¾  Miranda J  b 111 14.30  87-11 Fit to Fight 1263¾ Canadian Factor 116no Wild Again1164  Outrun 7
8Jun84- 8Bel fst 1⅛  :47⅕ 1:11⅘ 1:48⅘ 3+Nassau Cty H  7 4 63¾ 42 42½ 31  Miranda J  b 113 8.10  82-19 Moro 115¾ Canadian Factor 117nk Dance Caller 113hd  Rallied 8
25Mar84- 8Aqu fst 170 ⊡:47⅗ 1:12 1:41⅘ 3+Westchster H  4 6 89¾ 811 66¾ 66½  Velasquez J  b 114 4.40e  85-16 Jacque'sTip114nkMinstrelGlory107½Havagreatdate1111½  No factor 8
10Mar84- 8Aqu fst 1⅛ ⊡:47⅘ 1:12⅗ 1:51⅗ 3+Grey Lag H  4 4 49½ 44½ 44½ 45  Velasquez J  b 116 4.20  82-17 Moro 1224½ Morning Review 109nk ToErin107nk  Failed to menace 6
18Feb84- 8Aqu fst 1⅛ ⊡:47⅕ 1:11 1:48⅖ 3+Stymie H  8 5 74½ 108¾ 1011 813½  Miranda J  b 122 *1.00e  89-12 Gen'l Practitioner 119hd Jacque's Tip113nkPuntivo115¾  Far back 14
29Jan84- 8Aqu fst 1⅛ ⊡:47⅘ 1:12⅕ 1:43⅖ 3+Aqueduct H  7 8 74½ 75½ 64¾ 55½  Miranda J  122 4.30  89-15 Moro 120¾ Jacksboro 1202 Ask Muhammad 1172  No rally 9
18Jan84- 7Aqu fst 170 ⊡:49⅕ 1:14⅘ 1:45⅗  Alw 38000  5 5 67 57½ 33½ 2nk  Miranda J  119 4.80  73-35 Dave The Dude 117nk Dance Caller1193¾Thalassocrat1173½  Rallied 6
18Dec83- 8Aqu fst 1⅛ ⊡:50 1:14⅕ 1:59  Roamer H  1 7 63½ 66 55½ 56½  Miranda J  122 *2.10  77-25 Megaturn 113½ Galaxy Guide 1132 Majestic Solo 1141½  No rally 7
10Dec83- 8Aqu fst 1⅝ ⊡:49 2:05⅘ 2:45⅘ 3+Galant Fox H  4 5 54 35½ 32 1nk  Miranda J  118 *2.00  83-17 Dance Caller 118nk Fleet Pirate 1181½ Moro 1117½  Up in time 7
LATEST WORKOUTS  Jly 21 Bel tr.t 3f fst :37⅘ b  Jly 18 Bel 6f fst 1:13⅘ h  Jly 11 Bel tr.t 3f fst :36⅘ b  Jly 1 Bel 1 sly 1:42⅘ b
```

Hero's Honor

```
Hero's Honor        B. c. 4, by Northern Dancer—Glowing Tribute, by Graustark
                    Br.—Mellon P (Va)
Own.—Rokeby Stable  Tr.—Miller Mack
126   Lifetime 14 8 1 2  $486,785   1984 5 4 0 1 $411,810   1983 9 4 1 1 $74,975   Turf 7 6 0 1 $364,805

14Jly84- 8Atl fm 1⅜ Ⓣ:48⅕ 1:11⅘ 1:54  3+U Nations H  5 2 1hd 1hd 13½ 11½  Bailey J D  b 123 *1.10  94-14 Hero's Honor 1231½ Cozzene 114no Who's ForDinner110hd  Driving 11
17Jun84- 8Bel fm 1⅜ Ⓣ:48⅕ 1:35⅗ 2:14  3+Bwlng Grn H  7 1 11 11½ 13½ 11¾  Bailey J D  b 120 *2.80  87-20 Hero's Honor 1201¾ Nassipour 110½SuperSunrise1232½  Drew clear 11
2Jun84- 8Bel sly 1¼  :47⅖ 1:35⅘ 2:02⅕ 3+Red Smith H  3 1 11½ 14 14 17  Bailey J D  b 117 2.40  87-19 Hero's Honor 1177 Win 1144½ Eskimo 11216½  Ridden out 5
24May84- 8Bel fst 1⅛  :45⅗ 1:10⅗ 1:43⅖ 3+Alw 36000  1 1 1½ 2hd 31½ 36¾  Bailey J D  b 121 1.50  78-15 Win 1192¾ Mr. Badger 1214 Hero's Honor 12111½  Weakened 5
7May84- 8Aqu gd 1⅛ Ⓣ:48 1:12⅘ 1:43⅘ 3+Fort Marcy H  9 1 11 12½ 14 12  Bailey J D  b 115 3.40  87-22 Hero's Honor 1152 SuperSunrise1263¾Reinvested1131  Ridden out 9
29Sep83- 6Med fm 1⅜ Ⓣ:47⅖ 1:36⅘ 2:14⅕  Rutgers  7 4 34 31 1hd 31½  Bailey J D  b 114 3.40  92-11 Win 1141½ Bounding Basque 115hd Hero's Honor 114¾  Wide 9
29Sep83-Run in two divisions 6th & 8th races
19Sep83- 5Bel fm 1¼ Ⓣ:49⅗ 1:37⅘ 2:00⅘ 3+Alw 30000  2 1 14 1½ 1½ 1hd  Fell J  b 113 *.90  90-17 Hero's Honor 113hdBoltFromTheBlue113¾Hypertee1151½  Driving 7
10Sep83- 5Bel fm 1 Ⓣ:46⅕ 1:10⅖ 1:36  3+Alw 26000  5 4 42½ 21½ 1hd 11¾  Bailey J D  b 118 2.90  85-15 Hero'sHonor1181¾NtiveRid1131¾ChrgingThrough113nk  Drew clear 8
3Sep83- 9Bel fm 1⅛ Ⓣ:47⅕ 1:11⅘ 1:43  3+Alw 24000  4 4 32 21½ 11½ 13  Bailey J D  b 113 10.60  81-20 Hro'sHonor1133Cynsong115nkHilColumbus113hd  Lugged in,drvng 12
27Aug83- 9Bel fst 7f  :22⅖ :45⅗ 1:23⅘ 3+Alw 24000  2 9 64 89½ 1018 1022¾  Bailey J D  b 113 6.40  61-12 American Standard 1127 Brave Squire 1171Nivernay113nk  Outrun 11
LATEST WORKOUTS  Jly 26 Bel 4f fst :47⅘ h  Jly 21 Bel 4f gd :48⅘ h  Jly 12 Bel 4f gd :48⅖ h  ●Jly 7 Bel 1 sly 1:40⅘ h
```

*Persian Tiara

```
*Persian Tiara           Ch. f. 4, by Persian Bold—Tarara Girl, by Major Portion
                         Br.—Finnegan M A (Ire)
Owr.—Donoghue Mrs T P    Tr.—Maxwell Adrian J
109   Lifetime 20 5 2 2  $113,534   1984 10 1 2 1 $99,435   1983 9 4 0 1 $14,099   Turf 19 5 1 2 $110,174

15Jly84- 8Bel fm 1⅜ Ⓣ:47⅕ 1:35⅗ 2:12⅘ 3+ⒻShpshd BayH  5 7 721 714 711 66  Terry J  112 32.60  87-14 Sabin 1252 Thirty Flags 114¾ Double Jeux 111¾  No factor 9
12May84- 9Pim sf 1½ Ⓣ:53⅗ 2:13⅕ 2:41  3+Dixie H  2 6 712 11 12½ 12½  Shelton R L  109 19.50  32-65 PersianTiar1092½CrzyMoon1128CndinFctor1182  Lugged in,driving 8
29Apr84- 8Del fst 1⅛  :47⅗ 1:12 1:45⅖ 3+ⒻⓇKissMeKate  1 7 716 79¾ 34 2½  Terry J  112 32.10  80-19 Lying Lady 117½ Persian Tiara 112nk Virgin Bride 114¾  Rallied 7
20Apr84- 9GP fm *1⅛ Ⓣ  1:46⅘  ⒻAlw 20000  4 8 710 53½ 43½ 52½  Terry J  115 8.60  69-30 Melanie Frances 1151½ Bezique 115hd Miss First Lady 115¾  Hung 9
27Mar84- 9GP gd *1⅛ Ⓣ  1:45⅕  ⒻAlw 20000  6 8 87½ 712 511 410½  Terry J  115 17.70  70-22 Top Nice 1221½ Aspen Rose 1171 Forest Maiden 1178  No factor 8
9Mar84- 9GP fm *1⅛ Ⓣ  1:43⅘  ⒻAlw 20000  3 9 108½ 85½ 44½ 34½  Terry J  115 21.20  82-14 Thinghatab 1153 National Banner 1171½ Persian Tiara115½  Rallied 10
20Feb84- 8Hia fm 1⅛ Ⓣ  1:42⅕ 3+ⒻColumbianaH  1 14 1419 1417 1217 1213¾  Velez R I  107 48.70f  73-13 Sabin 1222 Aspen Rose 111hd Silver in Flight 1161  No threat 14
11Feb84- 8Hia fm 1⅛ Ⓣ  1:48  ⒻKey Largo  6 11 105 119¾ 75½ 74  Vasquez J  112 35.80  88-08 Silver in Flight 119no Erudite II 115½ Sulemeif 114¾  Outrun 12
27Jan84- 9Hia fm *1⅛ Ⓣ  1:49⅕  ⒻAlw 20000  5 7 614 66 43½ 23  Vasquez J  113 36.70  82-15 MissFrmpton1193PersinTir113hdCongressFlier113hd  Gained place 8
19Jan84- 9Hia fm *1⅛ Ⓣ  1:43⅖  ⒻAlw 20000  10 10 1018 1024 1014 1014½  St Leon G  114 28.60  67-16 ⒹMiss Frampton 1163½ Josalee 119¾ Queen's Era 1162½  Outrun 10
19Jan84-Placed ninth through disqualification
LATEST WORKOUTS  Jly 26 Fai tr.t 4f fst :49 b  Jly 10 Fai tr.t 4f fst :49 b  Jly 8 Fai tr.t 4f fst :49 b  ●Jly 4 Fai tr.t 4f fst :49 b
```

sition as morning-line favorite. The astute New York audience reached this same conclusion in surprising numbers, establishing Majesty's Prince instead as their favorite and sending Hero's Honor to the post as their 5-2 second choice.

Majesty's Prince was somewhat of a plodder (if that could be said of a member of racing's exclusive millionaire's club), with his best races coming over a distance of ground under soggy conditions. On the other hand, Majesty's Prince was a fresh horse, having made just one start thus far in 1984. That resulted in an "even" performance, just a length and a half behind a seasoned Hero's Honor, in the United Nations Handicap, while conceding that rival two pounds. With a four-pound weight shift in his favor, the soggy conditions, and normal improvement, Majesty's Prince appeared to be the logical selection in the Sword Dancer.

A few of the other contestants in the race deserve some comment:

FORTNIGHTLY

Sharp and fresh, this four-year-old colt had to be respected. However, the evidence suggests that Fortnightly did not appreciate soft footing. Sharp performances in the Baruch (against older horses) and Secretariat (at the Sword Dancer distance) were split by a lackluster performance in allowance company on soft grass.

WIN

This gelding couldn't handle Hero's Honor in either the Red Smith or Bowling Green, but the weight concessions are far more favorable this time. As the only other early speed in the race, Win could be extremely dangerous under more favorable dry conditions, for if he wanted the early lead Hero's Honor, under 126 pounds, was not likely to contest the point too vehemently, too soon. Under a clever ride, Win might be able to dictate comfortable early fractions and stay in front all the way.

DR. SCHWARTZMAN

A (sharp) three-year-old challenging quality older horses at a classic distance—always a tough assignment.

NASSIPOUR

After a good second to Hero's Honor, how can one excuse his modest performance in allowance company on July 13? This horse appears to have lost his will to win since he arrived in this country, as evidenced by nine consecutive defeats.

PAPAL BULL

Winner of two straight in allowance company, this improving four-year-old was taking his first shot at stakes competition, and doing so in a Grade I event. A difficult assignment.

PERSIAN TIARA

An impressive win over a soft course against males in the Dixie at Pimlico points this filly out. However, the competition on that occasion in no way compares with Grade I New York runners.

The race ran almost as expected. Hero's Honor did not relish the conditions and faded badly after chasing Win to the stretch. Majesty's Prince, on the other hand, was at home on the soft footing and won going away. He paid a paltry $5.40. Was he an underlay? Perhaps so. But there can be no denying the role course conditions played in the outcome of this race, and should have played in the selection of its fairly obvious winner. American handicappers as a group know how to react when the dirt surface turns up sloppy. But many of us remain unaware of the difference between firm and soft conditions on the grass, how they affect the outcome of races, and how some horses prefer one to the other. Awareness of a preference for or against soft footing—from proven performance or heredity—was the key to handicapping the 1984 Sword Dancer Handicap.

EIGHTH RACE
Belmont
JULY 28, 1984

1 ½ MILES.(Turf). (2.24⅘) 10th Running THE SWORD DANCER HANDICAP (Grade I). Purse $200,000 added. (Plus $50,000 Breeders' Cup Premium Awards.) 3-year-olds and upward. By subscription of $500 each, which should accompany the nomination; $3,200 to pass the entry box, with $200,000 added. The added money and all fees to be divided 60% to the winner, 22% to second, 12% to third and 6% to fourth. Weights, Monday, July 23. Starters to be named at the closing time of entries. Trophies will be presented to the winning owner, trainer and jockey. The New York Racing Association reserves the right to transfer this race to the Main Course. Closed Wednesday, July 11, 1984 with 29 nominations. Breeders' Cup Fund Award to Majesty's Prince.
Total purse $299,700. Value of race $276,700, value to winner $176,820, second $54,934, third $29,964, fourth $14,982. $3,000 Nominator Awards $20,000 Reverts to Breeders'Cup Fund Mutuel pool $236,155, OTB pool $282,113. Exacta Pool $249,486. OTB Exacta Pool $257,748.

Last Raced	Horse	Eqt.A.Wt	PP	¼	½	1	1¼	Str	Fin	Jockey	Odds $1
14Jly84 ^{8}Atl^{4}	Majesty's Prince	5 124	8	5^{hd}	6^{hd}	5^{hd}	4^{hd}	1^{2}	$1^{3\frac{1}{2}}$	Maple E	1.90
13Jly84 ^{8}Bel^{3}	Nassipour	b 4 109	6	$8^{2\frac{1}{2}}$	$7^{1\frac{1}{2}}$	7^{1}	6^{hd}	6^{1}	$2^{1\frac{1}{4}}$	Samyn J L	16.50
14Jly84 ^{8}Atl^{10}	Four Bases	b 5 112	5	2^{3}	2^{3}	2^{1}	$2^{1\frac{1}{2}}$	2^{hd}	3^{nk}	MacBeth D	30.20
15Jly84 ^{4}Bel^{1}	Papal Bull	4 110	7	$10^{1\frac{1}{2}}$	10^{hd}	$9^{\frac{1}{2}}$	8^{hd}	$4^{\frac{1}{2}}$	4^{1}	Cruguet J	38.90
14Jly84 ^{8}Atl^{7}	Norwick	5 112	4	$7^{\frac{1}{2}}$	$8^{2\frac{1}{2}}$	8^{3}	7^{hd}	7^{2}	5^{nk}	Davis R G	58.30
4Jly84 ^{9}AP^{2}	Fortnightly	b 4 114	1	6^{1}	$4^{\frac{1}{2}}$	3^{hd}	$5^{1\frac{1}{2}}$	3^{hd}	6no	Cordero A Jr	5.20
1Jly84 ^{8}Bel^{1}	Win	b 4 113	2	$3^{\frac{1}{2}}$	$3^{\frac{1}{2}}$	4^{1}	3^{hd}	5^{hd}	$7^{1\frac{1}{2}}$	Graell A	11.00
15Jly84 ^{8}Bel^{6}	Persian Tiara	4 110	11	11	11	11	10^{2}	$9^{1\frac{1}{2}}$	8^{nk}	Terry J	31.30
14Jly84 ^{8}Bel^{2}	Dr. Schwartzman	3 113	3	$4^{1\frac{1}{2}}$	5^{1}	6^{hd}	9^{2}	$8^{\frac{1}{2}}$	$9^{1\frac{1}{4}}$	Perret C	5.30
21Jly84 ^{8}Bel^{6}	Dance Caller	b 4 114	9	9^{3}	9^{4}	10^{1}	11	10^{5}	10^{12}	Velasquez J	29.60
14Jly84 ^{8}Atl^{1}	Hero's Honor	b 4 126	10	$1^{\frac{1}{2}}$	1^{hd}	11	$1^{\frac{1}{2}}$	11	11	Bailey J D	2.70

OFF AT 5:20 Start good, Won ridden out. Time, :26⅘, :49⅕, 1:14, 1:39⅘, 2:05⅗, 2:31, Course soft.

$2 Mutuel Prices:			
8-(H)-MAJESTY'S PRINCE	5.80	3.80	2.80
6-(F)-NASSIPOUR		9.80	5.80
5-(E)-FOUR BASES			11.40

$2 EXACTA 8–6 PAID $73.40.

Ch. h, by His Majesty—Pied Princess, by Tom Fool. Trainer Cantey Joseph B. Bred by Marsh J D (Va).

MAJESTY'S PRINCE reserved behind the leaders to the far turn, split horses to loom boldly leaving the far turn and drew away under intermittent urging. NASSIPOUR moved up along the inside racing into the far turn, came out between horses nearing the stretch and finished well to best the others after getting through FOUR BASES, prominent from the outset, raced forwardly to midstretch and weakened. PAPAL BULL made a run from the outside leaving the far turn but hung. NORWICK moved within easy striking distance nearing the end of the backstretch but failed to seriously menace while close quarters between horses during the drive FORTNIGHTLY, never far back while saving ground, made a bid between horses after entering the stretch but tired under pressure. WIN, close up early, rallied from the outside nearing the stretch, remained a factor until near the final furlong and gave way. PERSIAN TIARA was without speed. DR. SCHWARTZMAN, well placed until near the stretch, lacked a further response while racing wide. DANCE CALLER was always outrun. HERO'S HONOR moved to the inside at the first turn, saved ground while showing speed to the stretch and stopped suddenly.

Chapter 21

Track Bias on the Grass

THE TERM "TRACK BIAS" IS not reserved for dirt tracks. Grass courses also go through periods of bias, usually of the speed vs. closers nature. A period of intense heat and no rain can leave the course baked out, resulting in a steady stream of races won on the front end, with the victor leaving his victims behind in a cloud of dust. A considerable amount of rainfall can have the opposite effect—a soft course that (usually) favors closers.

When a handicapper visits an out-of-town track he is at a disadvantage with respect to track bias and trip information. He simply doesn't know when a poor performance is the direct result of a bad trip, possibly due to a biased racetrack on that occasion. Or when a seemingly good performance cannot be accepted at face value, having resulted from a perfect trip, possibly aided by a biased surface. It usually takes time to catch on when a bias does exist, especially one on the grass. With the limited number of races run on that surface, it can be days before a bias is noticed.

When I joined the participants of Handicapping Expo '84 at the Meadowlands on October 18, 1984, it was my first visit to the New Jersey oval since the first week of its existence back in 1977. I had no idea whether or not the main course was in the midst of one of its periods of "positive rail" bias. And although the weather had been dry and warm for that time of the year, my long-standing impression was that the Meadowlands' grass course tended to favor closers.

The seventh race that evening, coupled in the late daily double with the $500,000 Young America Stakes to follow, was an allowance contest on the grass restricted to "nonwinners of two other

7 MEADOWLANDS

TURF COURSE
1 1-16 MILES
MEADOWLANDS
START FINISH

1 1/16 MILES. (Turf). (1.40⅖) ALLOWANCE. Purse $14,000. 3-year-olds and upward which have not won two races other than Maiden, Claiming or Starter. Weights, 3-year-olds 118 lbs. Older 122 lbs. Non-winners of a race other than Maiden, Claiming or Starter at a mile or over since September 15 allowed 3 lbs. Such a race since August 15, 6 lbs.

Tarpaulin *

B. g. 4, by Dewan—Rain Lilly, by Jim J
Br.—Thomas Elizabeth F (Ky)
Tr.—Sava Vincent J
Own.—Sava Mr-Mrs V
119
Lifetime 26 4 3 7 $37,630 | 1984 14 3 3 4 $25,160 | 1983 8 0 0 2 $4,745 | Turf 5 1 1 0 $7,035

8Oct84- 5Med gd *1⅛ (T) 2:17⅘ 3+Clm 32000 3 3 32½ 31½ 44½ 57¾ Terry J b 119 12.20 — — Case Back 1072½ Oratavo 1122¾ Major Event 1191½ Weakened 9
29Sep84-10Med fst 1 :47⅘ 1:12⅘ 1:38⅘ 3+Clm 35000 2 3 33½ 1hd 3nk 32 Terry J b 115 6.40 87-21 Dawn Encounter 1162 Youesaye 122hd Tarpaulin 1154½ Wide 8
15Sep84- 7Med sly 1 1/16 :47⅗ 1:13⅗ 1:47⅗ 3+Alw 14000 6 3 4¾ 12½ 12 21½ Terry J b 122 3.30 70-24 Stabalizer 1191½ Tarpaulin 1222 OrYourMoneyBack113¾ 2nd best 7
4Sep84- 8Med sly 1 1/16 :47⅗ 1:12 1:44⅘ 3+Alw 13000 3 2 21½ 2hd 1hd 11 Terry J b 117 7.20 86-18 Tarpaulin 1171WorldAssembly1145½FrenchSovereign122nk Driving 7
25Aug84- 4Atl fm 1⅛ (T):49⅕ 1:13⅕ 1:51⅘ 3+(R)Hcp 15000 6 1 1½ 2hd 2½ 22 Terry J b 113 5.80 75-23 Big Shot 1172 Tarpaulin 1131 Memory Rock 1151½ Gamely 9
21Aug84-10Mth fm 1⅛ (T):48⅘ 1:12⅘ 1:50⅘+ 3+Clm 20000 8 1 1½ 1hd 32 55½ Terry J b 116 50.50 82-16 Delta Deity 116no Magnus Pater 1151½ Dissatisfaction 107¾ Tired 11
11Aug84- 3Mth fst 6f :22⅘ :45⅘ 1:09⅘ 3+Clm 20000 4 5 31½ 44½ 79½ 712 Santagata N b 112 24.80 79-12 Propaganda 1153 Creme Dela Corps 115½ Cap's Choice1162 Tired 7
28Jly84- 4Mth fst 170 :46⅗ 1:12 1:42⅕ 3+Clm c-16000 4 2 1hd 11 22 36 Bracciale V Jr b 116 6.50 79-14 Admiral's Gin 1146 Catfish Cohen 116no Tarpaulin1162 Weakened 7
21Jly84- 3Atl yl *5½f (T) 1:07 3+Clm 14500 1 2 2hd 22 21 1½ Landicini C Jr b 114 *1.60 78-28 Tarpaulin 114½ October Wind 1161 Enterprising 1181 Driving 6
9Jly84- 7Atl fst 5½f :22 :45⅘ 1:05 3+Clm 12000 6 2 32 2½ 1½ 14 Landicini C Jr b 116 *1.00 89-23 Tarpaulin 1164 Major Menuever 1091½ Easter 1122 Ridden out 9
LATEST WORKOUTS Sep 12 Med 4f fst :48⅘ h ●Sep 1 Atl 4f fst :47⅘ h

*Old Faithful

B. c. 3, by Red Regent—Ebullient, by Darius
Br.—Casey P (Ire)
Tr.—Mayberry Brian A
Own.—Siegal M
112
Lifetime 7 2 0 1 $8,015 | 1984 2 1 0 0 $6,430 | 1983 5 1 0 1 $1,585 | Turf 7 2 0 1 $8,015

26Jly84- 8Atl fm *1 (T) 1:39⅕ 3+Alw 7000 8 9 914 715 816 811¾ Madrid S O 113 11.70 79-09 Pink Buffalo 1163½ Reliable Jeff 1141 Mass Appeal 1162 Outrun 9
14Apr84♦5Curragh(Ire) gd 7f 1:31⅘ (T) Madrid Hcp 11 Lynch M 114 4.00 — — OldFaithful1141 RizlaBlue1203 DynmicLeder120¾ With pace drvg 15
7Sep83♦3Galway(Ire) gd*1 1/16 1:46⅘ (T) Long Walk Plate (Mdn) 11 Shanahan P 126 *.65 — — Old Faithful 1261 Royal Tender 1262 Dochas 1231 Bid,drvg 13
13Aug83♦2Curragh(Ire) fm 6f 1:16 (T) Dunmurry Plate(Mdn) 31½ Shanahan P 126 5.00 — — Inflation Beater126¾ PrinceofRondo126¾ OldFaithful1264 Rallied 8
29Jly83♦2Galway(Ire) fm 7f 1:28⅘ (T) Tuam Plate 47½ Shanahan P 124 10.00 — — Heavenly Plain 1242½ Action Girl 1211 Arcanum 1194 No threat 5
25Jun83♦2Curragh(Ire) gd 6f 1:13⅘ (T) Tyros Stakes 118¾ Shanahan P 123 20.00 — — Paymaster 126nk Productivity 123nk Deasys Delight129hd Outrun 17
11Jun83♦1Naas(Ire) gd 6f 1:16⅘ (T) Eadestown Plate 65 Shanahan P 119 16.00 — — Paymaster 122nk Late Sally 119½ Heavenly Plain 122nk Rallied 16
LATEST WORKOUTS Oct 12 Med 5f fst 1:02 b Oct 5 Med 5f fst 1:03⅘ b Sep 22 Med 4f fst :50 b Sep 5 Med 5f fst 1:03⅘ b

Case Back

Dk. b. or br. g. 4, by Upper Case—Y'All Come Back, by Carry Back
Br.—Triple Crown Breeders Group I Ltd (Fla)
Tr.—Pregman John Jr
Own.—Barrick J J
111[5]
Lifetime 41 9 4 4 $64,685 | 1984 9 3 1 1 $18,495 | 1983 22 3 3 3 $25,925 | Turf 27 6 4 4 $44,040

8Oct84- 5Med gd *1⅛ (T) 2:17⅘ 3+Clm 28000 8 1 12½ 11½ 12½ 12½ Conner M J5 b 107 31.40 — — Case Back 1072½ Oratavo 1122¾ Major Event 1191½ Driving 9
24Sep84- 8Med fm 170 (T):46⅘ 1:11⅕ 1:40⅘ 3+Alw 14000 3 1 1hd 63½ 711 922 Ward W A5 b 111 12.20 64-17 Gateshead 1223 Q. Naskra 1166 Strike the Set 1144 Faded 10
8Sep84- 8Del fm 1 (T):46⅘ 1:11 1:36⅘ 3+Clm 20000 9 2 21 15 15 14¾ Intelisano GPJr b 116 4.30 91-12 Case Back 1164¾ Memory Rock 1152 Spirited Song 112no Driving 12
25Aug84- 6Atl fm 1⅛ (T):48⅕ 1:13⅕ 1:52⅘ 3+(R)hcp 15000 5 1 1hd 1hd 11 22 Antley C W b 114 3.40 70-23 Mucho Frio 1242 Case Back 114nk Hasty Flight 1111½ Gamely 8
17Aug84- 6Atl fm 1⅛ (T):47⅗ 1:12 1:51⅗ 3+Clm 15500 1 1 11 12 1hd 3¾ Nied D b 120⁴ 5.90 78-18 Lypharel 112nk New Years Day 114½ DH Case Back 120 Weakened 11
17Aug84-Dead heat
1Aug84- 6Atl fm *1 1/16 (T) 1:48⅕ 3+Clm 13500 5 1 11 14 17 12 Nied D b 112 4.90 76-22 Case Back 1122 New Years Day 116½ Little Gold 112no Driving 10
21Jly84- 3Atl yl *5½f (T) 1:07 3+Clm 15500 4 6 43½ 45½ 45½ 42½ Pagano S R b 116 7.90 75-28 Tarpaulin 114½ October Wind 1161 Enterprising 1181 Evenly 6
19Feb84-11FG fm *1 1/16 (T):47⅘ 1:13⅕ 1:46⅘ Clm 27500 7 2 35 1220 — — Milligan E RJr5 b 111 47.70 — — Flakesaway 1153 Sargeant Wilson 114¾ NowAndThen1133½ Eased 12
1Feb84- 9FG fm *5½f (T):22⅘ :47 1:05⅘ Alw 10000 4 8 910 99½ 97¾ 86¾ Morgan M R b 113 42.70 84-09 Royal Roast 1141 Hawaiian Lady 111no Willow Drive1151½ Outurn 9
5Nov83- 9Med gd 1 1/16 (T):46⅘ 1:11⅘ 1:43⅘ Clm 25000 6 9 911 85 86½ 88½ Chavez S N b 115 45.40 75-22 Stay Secure 1135½ Pink Buffalo 113no Dr. Gaston 113½ No threat 12
LATEST WORKOUTS Sep 18 Med 4f fst :49⅕ b

Q. Naskra

Ch. c. 4, by Naskra—Princess Q, by Prince John
Br.—Beller S (Ky)
Tr.—Pierce Joseph H Jr
Own.—Beller S
116
Lifetime 15 2 3 0 $28,830 | 1984 9 0 2 0 $7,250 | 1983 3 1 0 0 $7,200 | Turf 10 2 2 0 $24,650

24Sep84- 8Med fm 170 (T):46⅘ 1:11⅕ 1:40⅘ 3+Alw 14000 4 8 84¾ 53 23 23 McCauley W H 116 4.10 83-17 Gateshead 1223 Q. Naskra 1166 Strike the Set1144 Best of others 10
25Aug84- 9Mth fm 1⅛ (T):48 1:11⅗ 1:49 + 3+Longfellw H 5 6 68½ 63¾ 64½ 64 Ferrer J C 108 29.00 91-08 Tough Mickey 1202 Intensify 115¾ Castle Guard 118hd Outrun 7
25Aug84-Grade II
14Aug84- 8Mth fm 1 1/16 (T):47⅘ 1:11⅘ 1:43⅘+ 3+Alw 13500 4 5 66½ 44 23 22 Antley C W5 113 3.40 82-22 Beagle 1182 Q. Naskra 1133 Escapade 118¾ Gamely 7
3Aug84- 9Mth fm 1 1/16 (T):47⅘ 1:11⅗ 1:43⅕ 3+Alw 13500 9 11 1111 106½ 65½ 43¾ Rujano M 118 15.90 91-17 Run the Ship 113¾ Northair 1182 Upmost 1131 Mild late bid 12
25Jly84- 8Mth fm 1 1/16 (T):49 1:13 1:44 + 3+Alw 13500 1 6 51½ 62¾ 52 51½ Rujano M 118 24.30 80-19 Snowcot 108hd Run the Ship 118nk Bev's Boy 120½ Evenly 9
14Jly84-10Mth fm 1 1/16 (T):47⅘ 1:11 1:43⅕+ 3+Clm 50000 10 8 811 107¾ 1214 1010½ Antley C W5 111 11.80 75-11 King's Swan 1162 Upmost 114½ King Neptune 116nk Outrun 12
11Jun84- 8Mth fm 1 (T):47⅘ 1:10⅗ 1:36⅘ 3+Alw 12500 5 5 57½ 43½ 53½ 53½ McCauley W H 118 2.90 89-09 Mucho Frio 115½ Northair 1183 Fuddy Dud 114hd Tired 7
4Jun84- 7Mth fst 1 1/16 :48⅕ 1:13 1:44⅘ 3+Alw 12500 1 5 52½ 57 619 629 Thornburg B 118 6.00 54-22 Sir Hasten 110½ Mucho Frio 1151½ Snowcot 1086 Outrun 6
12May84- 2GP fm 1 1/16 (T):48⅕ 1:12⅕ 1:43⅕ Alw 16000 7 4 41½ 31½ 62½ 55½ McCauley W H 117 4.60 80-14 Luigi Tobin 122nkPetanque117hdKhyberMountain1221½ Weakened 7
7Jly83- 8Mth fm 1 (T):47⅕ 1:11⅗ 1:37⅘ 3+Alw 12000 8 8 79 42½ 21½ 1nk McCauley W H 112 *2.20 86-20 Q. Naskra 112nk Prodata 1182 Perfected 1121½ Driving 11
LATEST WORKOUTS Oct 13 Med 3f fst :40 b Oct 5 Med 5f fst 1:02 b Sep 20 Med 5f fst 1:02 h Sep 14 Med 3f fst :37 b

Duet For One

Ch. g. 5, by Dance Spell—Reluctant Pearl, by Cohoes
Br.—Christiana Stables (Ky)
Tr.—Hine Hubert
Own.—Salvo F
116
Lifetime 19 2 4 1 $18,960 | 1984 10 1 1 1 $9,930 | 1983 9 1 3 0 $9,030 | Turf 3 0 0 1 $1,790

24Sep84- 8Med fm 170 (T):46⅘ 1:11⅕ 1:40⅘ 3+Alw 14000 9 9 1011 1010 812 513 Perret C b 119 19.70 73-17 Gateshead 1223 Q. Naskra 1166 Strike the Set 1144 No factor 10
8Sep84- 6Med fst 1 :46⅘ 1:11⅗ 1:38⅘ 3+Alw 14000 5 5 58 68½ 53½ 42 Davis R G b 119 8.20 85-18 FlightofTime116noEscapade116¾SmoothSunsation1061½ Mild gain 6
17Aug84- 8Atl fm 1 1/16 (T):48 1:12⅘ 1:44⅕ 3+Alw 7000 4 3 44½ 34 35 34 Hernandez R Z b 122 7.90 81-18 Reliable Jeff 1121½ Joy Hour 1162½ Duet For One 1223½ Evenly 6
28Jly84- 5Atl fst 1 1/16 :46⅗ 1:11⅗ 1:44⅘ 3+Alw 6500 1 6 45 44½ 21½ 1¾ Davis R G b 116 4.00 83-17 Duet For One 116¾ Peruber 10914 Tagliar 1122 Driving 6
25Jun84- 8Bow fst 1 1/16 :48 1:13 1:47 3+Alw 8500 6 4 46 45 42½ 54 Hernandez R Z b 119 3.60e 62-29 Tripledairya 107¾ Wise Mike 112¾ Fire Walker 1131½ No rally 8
7Jun84- 9Pim fst 1 1/16 :46 1:10⅘ 1:43⅘ 3+Alw 10000 7 7 79½ 78½ 48 49½ Hernandez R Z b 119 12.10 78-14 CllTheTun119nkContinntlDncr1142½TopRnking1107 Lacked a rally 8
30May84- 8Pim sly 1 1/16 :46⅘ 1:12 1:44⅘ 3+Alw 10000 1 4 34 33½ 35 46¾ Hernandez R Z b 119 6.20 74-19 Castelets 117no Top Ranking 1106½ Tripledairya 107½ Bore out 7
15May84- 5Pim fst 1 1/16 :46⅘ 1:10⅘ 1:42⅘ Clm 25000 4 3 46½ 48½ 512 518½ Adams J K b 114 5.30 75-15 Subarctic 1147½ Gallant A. 119¾ Willie Dee 114hd Tired 6
7May84- 5Pim sly 1 1/16 :46⅕ 1:10⅘ 1:43⅘ Alw 10000 3 3 33½ 24 25 29 Adams J K b 114 3.10e 79-20 Subarctic 1149 Duet For One 1147 Stabalizer 1224 2nd best 6
24Apr84- 8Pim gd 1 1/16 :47⅘ 1:12⅘ 1:44⅘ Alw 10000 5 2 23½ 31½ 36½ 411½ Adams J K b 114 14.10 72-23 HiHoRacconto1143½Tht'sAttrctive1148Luck[illegible]el117no Weakened 7
LATEST WORKOUTS Oct 15 Med 4f fst :48⅘ b Oct 8 Med 4f fst :49⅘ bg Sep 17 Med 4f fst :50⅗ b Aug 29 Pim 5f fst 1:02 b

Escapade

Gr. c. 4, by Icecapade—Kitty Malone, by Better Bee
Br.—Burke R J (Ky)
Tr.—Curtis William Jr
Own.—Burke R J
116
Lifetime 26 2 4 4 $37,255 | 1984 14 1 2 2 $18,035 | 1983 8 1 1 1 $11,520 | Turf 6 1 0 1 $9,525

29Sep84-10Med fst 1 :47⅘ 1:12⅘ 1:38⅘ 3+Clm 40000 8 4 67½ 79¾ 712 719½ Perret C b 116 7.80 69-21 Dawn Encounter 1162 Youesaye 122hd Tarpaulin 1154½ Tired 8
15Sep84- 7Med sly 1 1/16 :47⅗ 1:13⅗ 1:47⅗ 3+Alw 14000 4 1 2½ 710 717 722½ Perret C b 116 *1.40 49-24 Stabalizer 1191½ Tarpaulin1222OrYourMoneyBack113¾ Gave way 7
8Sep84- 6Med fst 1 :46⅘ 1:11⅗ 1:38⅘ 3+Alw 14000 3 4 43 33 32 2no Perret C b 116 9.50 87-18 FlightofTime116noEscapde116¾SmoothSunstion1061½ Just missed 6
23Aug84- 9Mth gd 1 (T):47⅘ 1:11⅗ 1:37⅘ 3+Alw 12000 2 6 78 69½ 716 718 Edwards J W 116 8.20 69-15 Bev's Boy 1201 Prince Quid 120½ Swaps Qui 1136 Outrun 7
14Aug84- 8Mth fm 1 1/16 (T):47⅘ 1:11⅘ 1:43⅘+ 3+Alw 13500 7 4 43½ 32½ 46½ 35 Edwards J W 118 52.00 79-22 Beagle 1182 Q. Naskra 1133 Escapade 118¾ Rallied 7
3Aug84- 9Mth fm 1 1/16 (T):47⅘ 1:11⅗ 1:43⅕ 3+Alw 13500 11 5 53½ 84¾ 129½ 1111¾ Edwards J W 118 46.20 83-17 Run the Ship 113¾ Northair 1182 Upmost 1131 Outrun 12
23May84- 7Mth fst 1 :46⅘ 1:11⅕ 1:37⅘ 3+Alw 12500 5 3 55 615 618 527½ Thornburg B 121 11.20 58-22 Evzone 114nk Sir Hasten 1094 Tumbler 11314 Tired 7
15May84- 8Mth fst 1 1/16 :47⅕ 1:11⅗ 1:43⅘ 3+Alw 12500 6 5 56 511 621 621¾ Rocco J 121 3.10 64-22 Right And Regal 1137 Sir Hasten 1109 Downthehatch119½ Outrun 6
7May84- 8Mth fst 170 :46⅘ 1:11⅗ 1:41⅘ 3+Alw 12500 6 1 11½ 11 31 35 Melendez J D 121 *1.90 82-23 Walnut Street Bank 121no Evzone 1095 Escapade 1211 Steadied 10
17Apr84- 8GP fst 1 1/16 :49 1:14 1:45⅘ Alw 14000 4 1 14 1½ 2hd 23 McCauley W H 122 2.60 69-28 Prospect Bay 1173 Escapade 1221BraveAndShining117½ Game try 7
LATEST WORKOUTS Oct 17 Med 3f fst :36⅘ b Oct 12 Med 5f fst 1:01⅖ b Oct 6 Med 4f fst :49 b Sep 27 Mth 3f fst :37 h

Strike the Set

B. c. 3, by Stage Door Johnny—White Reason, by Hail to Reason
Br.—Northridge Farm (Ky)
Tr.—Meyer Jerome C
Own.—White Fox Farm
112
Lifetime 14 2 2 3 $23,470 | 1984 14 2 2 3 $23,470 | 1983 0 M 0 0 | Turf 5 2 0 1 $16,420

8Oct84- 9Med gd *170 (T) 1:40⅘ 3+Alw 16000 4 8 88¾ 84¾ 65½ 57½ Rocco J b 112 7.70 — — Muscatite 1161 Jane's Dilemma 1136 Mucho Frio 116no Outrun 9
24Sep84- 8Med fm 170 (T):46⅘ 1:11⅕ 1:40⅘ 3+Alw 14000 2 5 72¾ 42½ 34 39 Deegan J C b 114 4.70 77-17 Gateshead 1223 Q. Naskra 1166 Strike the Set 1144 No threat 10
26Aug84- 9FE fm 1 1/16 (T):47 1:11⅕ 1:41⅘ Intrnatnl H 4 5 56½ 55½ 713 811½ Beckon D b 115 8.25 91 — Axe T. V. 1181¾ Hurontario 120¾ Ten Gold Pots 1173 Tired 8
26Aug84-Grade III-C
2Aug84- 9Mth fm 1 1/16 (T):48 1:11⅗ 1:43 + 3+Alw 12500 7 3 32½ 21 21½ 1hd Deegan J C b 113 4.30 86-22 Strike the Set 113hd Swaps Qui 1142 Noelito 118no Driving 11
24Jly84- 7Mth fst 1 1/16 :47⅘ 1:12⅘ 1:45⅕ 3+Alw 12500 6 5 43 41½ 22 21¾ Deegan J C b 113 12.80 77-20 Aram Jackes 1081¾ Strike the Set 1133HailToNauset1124 Gamely 7
10Jly84- 4Mth fm 1 (T):47⅕ 1:12⅕ 1:38⅕ 3+Md Sp Wt 10 5 65½ 42½ 2½ 11½ Deegan J C b 115 4.40 84-16 Strike the Set 1151½ Evoke 1153 Guy's Gold 1101 Bore out, clear 12
27Jun84- 4Mth fst 6f :22⅘ :45⅘ 1:11⅗ 3+Md Sp Wt 6 7 86 79 89½ 810 Deegan J C b 115 4.90 72-18 Dee's Bright Boy 115hdChatisun115nkJetronic1101 Roughed early 11
6Jun84- 1Mth fst 6f :23 :46⅕ 1:11⅕ 3+Md Sp Wt 2 6 2½ 2½ 21½ 23 Deegan J C b 115 10.10 81-18 Silver Surfer 1153 StriketheSet1151½KingofWales1153 Held place 7
28May84- 3Mth sly 6f :23 :46 1:10⅖ 3+Md Sp Wt 5 — — — 48 38½ Deegan J C b 115 13.90 80-19 No Conceit 110nk Silver Surfer 1158 Strike the Set 115hd Fog 11
19May84- 3Key fst 6f :22 :45⅕ 1:11⅕ Md Sp Wt 4 2 21½ 22 35 58½ Russo A Jr b 122 10.90 76-18 Major Dude 122hd Sakima 1226½ Distinctively Gold 122nk Wide 7
LATEST WORKOUTS ●Sep 21 Med 6f fst 1:13 h Sep 13 Med 5f fst 1:02 b ●Aug 22 FE Tr.(T) 6f fm 1:14 h Aug 18 FE Tr.(T) 1 sf 1:47⅘ h

than." On paper, the outcome seemed obvious: Q. Naskra was the obvious class of his field. He had soundly defeated four of his rivals when second on two recent occasions, and those placings sandwiched an impressive performance in the Longfellow Handicap at Monmouth, where he was beaten only a few lengths by the top-class New York runners Tough Mickey and Intensify.

The seventh was the second race run on the grass that evening. The fourth, a claiming event for three-year-olds, had been won in wire-to-wire fashion. That in itself was not unusual, although the manner in which the winner, Rising Jet, accomplished his victory proved quite significant.

Rising Jet — B. c. 3, by Tri Jet—Special Team, by Specialmante — $22,500 Br.—Hooper F W (Fla) Tr.—Plesa Edward Jr — 111[5]

Own.—Hooper F W

Lifetime 9 1 3 0 $13,450 — 1984 7 1 3 0 $13,450 — 1983 2 M 0 0

27Sep84- 1Bel	fst	1⅛	:47⅘	1:13	1:54⅕	3+ Md 25000	4	3	1^1	1^3	1^4	1^6	Miranda J	b 118	*1.20	56-31	RisingJet118^{6}ExcutivProducr118^{8}AppointdHour111^{no}	Ridden out	7
21Sep84- 3Bel	fst	1$\frac{1}{16}$	:46⅘	1:12	1:46⅕	3+ Md 35000	4	5	$4^{2½}$	3^4	3^2	$2^{1¼}$	Miranda J	b 118	*3.20	70-23	ShipMint109^{1¼}RisingJet118^{nk}AppointedHour107½	Between horses	9
31Aug84- 3Bel	gd	1	:46⅕	1:11⅘	1:37⅘	3+ Md 35000	6	1	1½	2½	2^5	2^{10}	Miranda J	b 117	30.80	67-13	Time ofEssence117^{10}RisingJet117^{4½}ShipMint113^{hd}	Best of others	11
25Jun84- 9Bel	fst	7f	:23	:47	1:26⅖	3+ Md 35000	8	9	$10^{5½}$	$8^{8¾}$	7^{11}	$7^{8½}$	Ward W A^5	109	8.70	61-16	Splitter 112^{hd} Country Road 118^{1¼}TaxableIncome107^{3½}	No threat	12
9Feb84- 2Aqu	fst	1⅛ [•]	:49⅖	1:15⅕	1:55	Md 45000	3	2	$4^{2¼}$	9^7	9^{13}	9^{17}	Santagata N	118	9.70	53-18	Razliv 118^{8½} Informal 117^1 Between Stops 120½	Gave way	11
22Jan84- 9Aqu	fst	1$\frac{1}{16}$ [•]	:49⅘	1:15⅖	1:50⅕	Md 50000	12	2	3^{nk}	5^5	8^{11}	$8^{8½}$	McHargue D G	122	4.70	52-25	Call Me Rebel 117½ Plenty of Fun 118½ BetweenStops118^{nk}	Tired	12
2Jan84- 2Aqu	fst	1$\frac{1}{16}$ [•]	:48⅖	1:14	1:48⅕	Md 32500	4	2	2^{hd}	1^{hd}	1½	2½	McHargue D G	120	6.20	70-21	Rivator 122½ Rising Jet 120^{4¾} Cojak's Boy 111½	Weakened	11
15Dec83- 2Aqu	my	1 70 [•]	:47⅘	1:14	1:45	Md 30000	2	3	3^5	$2^{1½}$	4^3	5^8	McHargue D G	114	30.40	68-17	ShooBertAli109^{2¾}OurMichaelSmith116^{2¼}HeavenlyCase107^{1¼}	Tired	10
25Nov83- 3Aqu	sly	7f	:23⅖	:47⅕	1:28⅖	Md 50000	6	11	11^{16}	11^{22}	11^{26}	11^{24}	Skinner K	118	17.60	35-38	BackwardPleasure114^{hd}FrenchFlame114¾FlyingGold114^{nk}	Trailed	11

LATEST WORKOUTS Oct 11 Bel 4f fst :51⅖ b — Oct 5 Bel 4f fst :50 b — Sep 14 Bel tr.t 4f fst :50 b — Sep 8 Bel 4f fst :48⅗ b

Breaking not so sharply from the outside (post 9), Rising Jet ran the first quarter in a blistering 22⅖, yet was able to dig in gamely through the lane in his first race out of the maiden ranks. His performance suggested quite emphatically that the grass course was

FOURTH RACE
Meadowlands
OCTOBER 18, 1984

1 MILE 70 YARDS.(Turf). (1.38) CLAIMING. Purse $11,000. 3-year-olds. Weights, 121 lbs. Non-winners of two races at a mile or over since September 2 allowed 3 lbs. Such a race since then 6 lbs. Claiming Price $25,000; if for $22,500, 2 lbs. (Races where entered for $20,000 or less not considered.)

Value of race $11,000; value to winner $6,600; second $2,200; third $1,210; fourth $660; fifth $330. Mutuel pool $121,446. Trifecta Pool $249,764.

Last Raced	Horse	Eqt.A.Wt	PP	St	¼	½	¾	Str	Fin	Jockey	Cl'g Pr	Odds $1
27Sep84 ^{1}Bel^1	Rising Jet	b 3 111	9	7	2^{hd}	2^{hd}	1½	1^1	$1^{1¼}$	Ward W A^5	22500	6.50
8Oct84 ^{3}Med^4	Paris Blade	3 115	1	1	4^{hd}	4^{hd}	$6^{½}$	$3^{1½}$	$2^{¾}$	Perret C	25000	3.00
12Oct84 ^{4}Bel^4	Lotsa Socks	b 3 118	7	8	6^1	$5^{2½}$	3^2	$2^{½}$	3^{nk}	Guerra W A	25000	1.80
10Oct84 ^{7}Key^3	Share A Lot	b 3 115	6	4	5^{hd}	$6^{½}$	5^{hd}	$4^{2½}$	4^4	McCauley WH†	25000	8.20
7Oct84 ^{8}Del^5	Regal Prince	3 115	5	6	8^5	$8^{2½}$	$8^{1½}$	$6^{1½}$	5^5	Nied J Jr	25000	6.00
8Oct84 ^{3}Med^6	Sovereign Secret	b 3 106	4	5	$3^{2½}$	$3^{2½}$	2^1	5^4	$6^{1¼}$	Birklin A^7	22500	46.60
13Oct84 ^{2}Med^2	Pepper Jr.	b 3 114	2	3	7^{hd}	7^3	7^1	7^4	7^7	Thornburg B	22500	13.80
5Oct84 ^{9}Bel^6	Bold Movement	b 3 118	8	9	9	9	9	9	8^1	Thomas D B	25000	10.80
8Oct84 ^{3}Med^5	Le Roi Roque	b 3 113	3	2	1½	1½	4^{hd}	8^3	9	Rocco J†	22500	21.70

OFF AT 9:17 Start good, Won driving. Time, :22⅖, :46, 1:10⅘, 1:36⅗, 1:40⅗ Course firm.

$2 Mutuel Prices:

10–RISING JET	15.00	6.40	3.80
1–PARIS BLADE		5.60	3.00
7–LOTSA SOCKS			2.60

$2 TRIFECTA 10–1–7 PAID $244.80.

B. c, by Tri Jet—Special Team, by Specialmante. Trainer Plesa Edward Jr. Bred by Hooper F W (Fla).

RISING JET forced the pace outside, gained a short lead entering the second turn and slowly drew clear. PARIS BLADE, well placed early, was angled out after a half, came widest of all for the drive and finished well for the place. LOTSA SOCKS, within striking distance early, moved to a challenging position on the outside after five furlongs but lacked a further bid. SHARE A LOT advanced inside on the second turn, moved between rivals approaching the stretch then lodged a mild bid inside. REGAL PRINCE was not a threat. SOVEREIGN SECRET, close up early, engaged the leaders from the inside before a half but tired in the drive. BOLD MOVEMENT was wide. LE ROI ROQUE vied for the lead for five furlongs and faded.

biased very strongly in favor of early speed. And in the seventh race, the early speed was quite obviously going to be Case Back.

If the grass course had not been biased, one would hardly have given Case Back a second look. He was clearly just a claiming horse over his head in allowance company. He had been soundly trounced by Q. Naskra when they met on September 24 while apparently in the peak of form. But, given the bias, Case Back became the clear alternative to the 7–10 favorite, and the sharp Meadowlands crowd was quick to pick up on this. Case Back, running on the front end all the way, won at odds of just 4–1. The exacta with the heavy favorite, who rallied strongly against the bias, paid a liberal $25.00. Those who made a habit of paying attention to little things—such as a quarter-mile time in a route race—were rewarded for their diligence.

SEVENTH RACE
Meadowlands
OCTOBER 18, 1984

$1\frac{1}{16}$ MILES.(Turf). (1.40⅗) ALLOWANCE. Purse $14,000. 3–year–olds and upward which have not won two races other than Maiden, Claiming or Starter. Weights, 3–year–olds 118 lbs. Older 122 lbs. Non–winners of a race other than Maiden, Claiming or Starter at a mile or over since September 15 allowed 3 lbs. Such a race since August 15, 6 lbs.
Value of race $14,000; value to winner $8,400; second $2,800; third $1,540; fourth $840; fifth $420. Mutuel pool $110,042. Exacta Pool $150,631.

Last Raced	Horse	Eqt.	A.Wt	PP	St	¼	½	¾	Str	Fin	Jockey	Odds $1
8Oct84 ^{5}Med^{1}	Case Back	b	4 111	3	2	$1^{1\frac{1}{2}}$	1^{2}	1^{hd}	$1^{2\frac{1}{2}}$	1^{1}	Ward W A^{5}	4.00
24Sep84 ^{8}Med^{2}	Q. Naskra		4 116	4	5	$6^{\frac{1}{2}}$	6^{1}	$5^{1\frac{1}{2}}$	$3^{2\frac{1}{2}}$	2^{5}	Velasquez J	.70
8Oct84 ^{5}Med^{5}	Tarpaulin	b	4 119	1	3	$2^{1\frac{1}{2}}$	2^{6}	2^{6}	$2^{1\frac{1}{2}}$	3^{4}	Terry J	10.50
29Sep84 ^{10}Med^{7}	Escapade	b	4 116	6	7	$5^{1\frac{1}{2}}$	5^{hd}	$4^{1\frac{1}{2}}$	$6^{1\frac{1}{2}}$	4no	Santagata N	22.00
8Oct84 ^{9}Med^{5}	Strike the Set	b	3 112	7	4	$3^{\frac{1}{2}}$	$3^{\frac{1}{2}}$	$3^{\frac{1}{2}}$	$4^{2\frac{1}{2}}$	5^{nk}	Deegan J C	3.30
24Sep84 ^{8}Med^{5}	Duet For One	b	5 116	5	1	4^{hd}	4^{1}	$6^{\frac{1}{2}}$	$5^{\frac{1}{2}}$	6^{3}	McCauley W H	18.40
26Jly84 ^{8}Atl^{8}	Old Faithful		3 114	2	6	7	7	7	7	7	Thornburg B	24.60

OFF AT 10:35 Start good, Won driving. Time, :23⅗, :46⅘, 1:10⅘, 1:36⅕, 1:42⅘ **Course firm.**

$2 Mutuel Prices:				
	3–CASE BACK	**10.00**	**3.80**	**2.60**
	4–Q. NASKRA		**2.80**	**2.40**
	1–TARPAULIN			**3.00**

$2 EXACTA 3–4 PAID $25.00.

Dk. b. or br. g, by Upper Case—Y'All Come Back, by Carry Back. Trainer Pregman John Jr. Bred by Triple Crown Breeders Group I Ltd (Fla).

CASE BACK set the pace, repulsed a bid by TARPAULIN on the second turn, opened a clear lead in upper stretch then had to be kept to pressure to hold Q. NASKRA safe. The latter; unhurried early, commenced a bid on the second turn and finished well to be second best. TARPAULIN, closest to the pace, engaged the winner from the outside after a half but tired in the drive. ESCAPADE was not a threat. STRIKE THE SET tired as did DUET FOR ONE.

One other contestant in this field deserves some comment—the Irish import Old Faithful. Capable of winning at the Curragh, Ireland's premier track, Old Faithful's American form and class remain a mystery. His miserable showing at Atlantic City could probably be ignored, based on the assumption that the horse had failed to acclimate to this country at that time. The subsequent layoff suggested as much. If he is now acclimated, Old Faithful could prove a factor in tonight's race, possibly even challenge for the early lead, as fresh horses often (inexplicably) do.

Old Faithful is not the type of horse the serious player makes one

SIXTH RACE
Belmont
JUNE 1, 1985

1 1/16 MILES.(Turf). (1.39⅘) ALLOWANCE. Purse $25,000. 3-year-olds and upward which have never won two races. Weights, 3-year-olds, 114 lbs. Older, 122 lbs. Non-winners of a race other than claiming at a mile or over since May 15 allowed 3 lbs. Of such a race since May 1, 5 lbs.

Value of race $25,000; value to winner $15,000; second $5,500; third $3,000; fourth $1,500. Mutuel pool $182,645, OTB pool $145,898. Exacta Pool $313,866. OTB Exacta Pool $207,967.

Last Raced	Horse	Eqt.	A.Wt	PP	St	¼	½	¾	Str	Fin	Jockey	Odds $1
29Jun84 ^{3}Bel^{4}	Stormgrey		4 117	5	8	9^{10}	$9^{1\frac{1}{2}}$	6^{3}	3^{2}	1^{hd}	Cordero A Jr	5.40
17May85 ^{2}Bel^{5}	Imperial Realm	b	5 117	4	7	7^{1}	7^{1}	3^{3}	$2^{2\frac{1}{2}}$	$2^{1\frac{1}{2}}$	Venezia M	8.80
15Oct84 ^{4}Eng^{11}	The Villain		4 117	9	6	6^{4}	4^{1}	$2^{\frac{1}{2}}$	1^{1}	3^{5}	Migliore R	9.80
23May85 ^{7}Bel^{4}	Anwar's Spirit		5 117	6	1	$2^{1\frac{1}{2}}$	2^{hd}	$4^{\frac{1}{2}}$	4^{2}	4^{1}	Ward W A	11.50
13May85 ^{7}Bel^{4}	Tongue Tied	b	3 112	2	9	10	10	9^{2}	$6^{\frac{1}{2}}$	5^{5}	Velasquez J	8.30
23May85 ^{3}Bel^{4}	World Assembly	b	4 117	3	5	3^{hd}	3^{1}	$5^{1\frac{1}{2}}$	$7^{1\frac{1}{2}}$	$6^{\frac{1}{2}}$	Cruguet J	3.30
13May85 ^{7}Bel^{5}	Mighty Courageous		3 109	10	3	$1^{\frac{1}{2}}$	$1^{1\frac{1}{2}}$	$1^{1\frac{1}{2}}$	$5^{\frac{1}{2}}$	7^{hd}	Samyn J L	5.80
25May85 ^{4}Bel^{7}	Run Lad		4 110	7	4	$5^{\frac{1}{2}}$	6^{1}	$7^{\frac{1}{2}}$	8^{6}	8^{7}	Guerra A A^{7}	40.00
11May85 ^{4}Bel^{2}	Crowning Chapter		4 117	8	2	$4^{\frac{1}{2}}$	5^{hd}	10	10	$9^{1\frac{1}{2}}$	Santagata N	5.10
22May85 ^{4}Bel^{5}	Siberian Dancer		3 109	1	10	$8^{\frac{1}{2}}$	$8^{2\frac{1}{2}}$	8^{hd}	9^{hd}	10	Shoemaker W	8.30

OFF AT 3:56 Start good, Won driving. Time, :23⅗, :48, 1:13⅗, 1:40, 1:46⅗ Course soft.

$2 Mutuel Prices:			
7-(H)-STORMGREY	12.80	5.40	5.00
6-(G)-IMPERIAL REALM		8.00	6.40
11-(R)-THE VILLAIN			8.80

$2 EXACTA 7-6 PAID $133.00.

Ro. c, by Vigors—Latest Model, by Nantallah. Trainer Penna Angel Jr. Bred by Clay A & R (Ky).

STORMGREY raced wide into the stretch while rallying and finished strongly to wear down IMPERIAL REALM. The latter made a run from the outside approaching the stretch, caught THE VILLAIN leaving the furlong grounds and fought it out gamely. THE VILLAIN made a bid leaving the turn but weakened in a long drive. ANWAR'S SPIRIT tired. TONGUE TIED passed tired horses while racing wide. WORLD ASSEMBLY qwas finished soon after going five furlongs. MIGHTY COURAGEOUS showed speed to the stretch and faltered. RUN LAD showed some early foot. CROWNING CHAPTER tired badly. SIBERIAN DANCER bobbled slightly after the start and was always outrun.

EIGHTH RACE
Belmont
JUNE 1, 1985

1¼ MILES.(InnerTurf). (1.58⅗) 25th Running THE RED SMITH HANDICAP (Grade II). $125,000 Added. (Plus $25,000 Breeders' Cup Premium Awards). 3-year-olds and upward. By subscription of $250 each, which should accompany the nomination; $2,000 to pass the entry box, with $125,000 added. The added money and all fees to be divided 60% to the winner, 22% to second 12% to third and 6% to fourth. Weights Monday, May 27. Starters to be named at the closing time of entries. Trophies will be presented to the winning owner, trainer and jockey. The New York Racing Association reserves the right to transfer this race to the main course. Closed Wednesday, May 15, 1985 with 46 nominations. Breeders' Cup Fund Awards to: Sharrannpour and Cold Feet II.

Total purse $193,500. Value of race $184,250; value to winner $114,600; second $37,070; third $22,470; fourth $10,110. $1,750 Nominator Awards;$7,500 Reverts to Breeders' Cup Fund Mutuel pool $199,255, OTB pool $228,504. Exacta Pool $240,394. OTB Exacta Pool $231,693.

Last Raced	Horse	Eqt.	A.Wt	PP	St	½	¾	1	Str	Fin	Jockey	Odds $1
19May85 ^{9}Hol^{1}	Sharannpour		5 112	7	$8^{2\frac{1}{2}}$	$7^{\frac{1}{2}}$	$5^{\frac{1}{2}}$	6^{2}	$2^{1\frac{1}{2}}$	$1^{1\frac{3}{4}}$	Cordero A Jr	2.50
11May85 ^{8}LaD^{3}	Inevitable Leader		6 116	9	9^{hd}	10^{2}	$10^{\frac{1}{2}}$	$4^{\frac{1}{2}}$	1^{hd}	2^{1}	Maple E	11.40
20May85 ^{4}Bel^{2}	Cold Feet II		4 110	13	12^{4}	11^{3}	$9^{\frac{1}{2}}$	$7^{1\frac{1}{2}}$	4^{1}	$3^{2\frac{1}{4}}$	Venezia M	f-8.70
23May85 ^{8}Bel^{2}	Lutyens		5 108	10	10^{4}	9^{1}	$12^{1\frac{1}{2}}$	$12^{1\frac{1}{2}}$	6^{2}	4^{nk}	Davis R G	f-8.70
5May85 ^{8}Hol^{5}	Tsunami Slew		4 119	6	$3^{\frac{1}{2}}$	3^{hd}	4^{1}	1^{1}	$3^{\frac{1}{2}}$	$5^{\frac{3}{4}}$	Delahoussaye E	3.70
11May85 ^{8}Pim^{4}	Pass The Line		4 113	2	4^{1}	4^{3}	$3^{\frac{1}{2}}$	$5^{\frac{1}{2}}$	$5^{\frac{1}{2}}$	6^{3}	Lovato F Jr	23.00
9May85 ^{8}Bel^{3}	Ends Well	b	4 113	3	$6^{1\frac{1}{2}}$	$6^{\frac{1}{2}}$	7^{hd}	$10^{\frac{1}{2}}$	8^{6}	$7^{\frac{1}{2}}$	Velasquez J	6.40
27Apr85 ^{8}GS^{2}	Hail Bold King		4 119	5	13	12^{hd}	11^{1}	$2^{\frac{1}{2}}$	$7^{\frac{1}{2}}$	8^{6}	Shoemaker W	4.70
18May85 ^{6}Bel^{4}	Masterful		4 110	12	$7^{\frac{1}{2}}$	8^{2}	$8^{\frac{1}{2}}$	8^{1}	9^{1}	9^{1}	Guerra W A	f-8.70
27May85 ^{8}GS^{1}	Broadway Harry	b	5 109	11	5^{4}	$5^{2\frac{1}{2}}$	6^{1}	11^{1}	11^{1}	10^{hd}	Graell A	25.50
19May85 ^{7}AP^{5}	Badwagon Harry	b	6 111	8	11^{hd}	13	13	13	10^{hd}	11^{1}	Migliore R	f-8.70
18May85 ^{6}Bel^{2}	Roving Minstrel		4 116	4	$11^{\frac{1}{2}}$	1^{hd}	$2^{1\frac{1}{2}}$	3^{1}	12^{7}	12^{12}	MacBeth D	11.60
6May85 ^{8}Aqu^{2}	Native Raid	b	5 115	1	2^{1}	2^{4}	1^{hd}	$9^{\frac{1}{2}}$	13	13	McCarron G	14.70

f—Mutuel field.

OFF AT 5:08, Start good, Won ridden out. Time, :22⅘, :46⅗, 1:11⅘, 1:39, 2:04⅕ Course soft.

$2 Mutuel Prices:			
8-(I)-SHARANNPOUR	7.00	4.20	3.40
9-(K)-INEVITABLE LEADER		8.80	5.00
16-(P)-COLD FEET II (f-field)			4.20

$2 EXACTA 8-9 PAID $61.80.

Ch. h, by Busted—Shamim, by Le Haar. Trainer Frankel Robert. Bred by H H Aga Khan (Ire).

SHARANNPOUR moved up between horses approaching the end of the backstretch was steadied along around the far turn came out for the drive and outfinished INEVITABLE LEADER under a hand ride. The latter

made a run from the outside approaching the stretch, caught TSUNAMI SLEW soon after straightening away and continued on with good energy. COLD FEET II, off slowly, was caught in close along the inside on the far turn, then finished well after getting out for the drive and pulled up lame. LUTYENS lacked room on the far turn angled out to make a run entering the stretch but failed to sustain his rally. TSUNAMI SLEW, never far back, moved to the fore approaching the stretch but weakened under pressure. PASS THE LINE a factor to the upper stretch, tired. ENDS WELL dropped back along the inside around the far turn and failed to seriously menace HAIL BOLD KING, badly outrun early, moved boldly around horses to loom a threat approaching the stretch but had nothing left. MASTERFUL checked midway of the far turn, lacked a further response. BROADWAY HARRY was finished soon after going six furlongs. BADWAGON HARRY was always outrun. ROVING MINSTREL tired badly from his early efforts. NATIVE RAID stopped suddenly after showing speed to the far turn.

of his prime wagers. Rather, he is the kind that may surface as an action bet, or one that cannot be excluded from an exotic wager if the situation warrants. He figures to be a longshot. But if he appears "live" on the oddsboard, he has to be regarded as a darkhorse contender. The oddsboard at the Meadowlands that evening was silent, however. Old Faithful entered the gate as the longest price in his field, and ran accordingly. There were no hints beforehand—stable betting, workouts, the jockey chosen—to suggest that he was about to run back to his European form. Until there is some such hint with an imported horse like this, it is wise to steer clear.

The exact opposite kind of grass bias—one caused by heavy rains—was prevalent during the first few weeks of the 1985 spring meeting at Belmont Park. I like to call it the "Last Shall Be First" bias. To say that it penalizes early speed hardly tells the whole story. The first, and often second, wave of horses to run at the early leaders usually find themselves leg weary by midstretch. During such periods of extreme bias, grass races are most likely to be won by the last horse to make its move (although not necessarily the horse running last early, which may not move at all). Obviously this places a heavy premium on the jockeys' patience and sense of timing, not to mention their awareness of the situation underfoot.

Heavy rains during the early morning hours on Saturday, June 1, compounded already less-than-firm conditions and set the stage for at least two days of extreme bias. The result charts from Saturday's sixth and eighth races give a feeling for what usually happens under such conditions. But the full impact of the bias was not seen until Sunday's feature, the New York Handicap for fillies and mares at a mile and a quarter on the turf.

As originally cast, the race shaped up featuring a potentially killing speed duel between the co-favorites Agacerie and Love Smitten, with one of the three late closers—Annie Edge, Dictina, and Powder Break—picking up the pieces in the stretch, whichever managed to time her move after the other two. The other three fillies entered looked hopelessly outclassed or out of shape.

However, Agacerie was an early scratch, leaving Love Smitten

8 BELMONT

INNER TURF COURSE
1¼ MILES
BELMONT PARK

1¼ MILES. (InnerTurf). (1.58⅘) 41st Running THE NEW YORK HANDICAP (Grade II). $75,000 Added. (Plus $25,000 Breeders' Cup Premium Awards) Fillies and mares, 3-years-old and upward. By subscription of $150 each, which should accompany the nomination; $1,200 to pass the entry box with $75,000 added. The added money and all fees to be divided 60% to the winner, 22% to second, 12% to third and 6% to fourth. Weights, Tuesday, May 28. Starters to be named at the closing time of entries. Trophies will be presented to the winning owner. The New York Racing Association reserves the right to transfer this race to the main course. Nominations Closed Wednesday, May 15, 1985.

Powder Break
Own.—Green R I
Dk. b. or br. f. 4, by Transworld—Bold Gee Gee, by Boldnesian
Br.—Farnsworth Farm & Williamson R (Fla)
Tr.—Olivares Luis
115 Lifetime 31 6 5 4 $164,890 | 1985 6 2 2 0 $63,415 | 1984 12 3 3 2 $92,515 | Turf 17 5 5 2 $153,680

27Apr85- 10Hia fm 1⅛ Ⓣ 1:47⅘ 3+ ⒻBlk Helen H 10 7 79 73½ 32½ 24½ Santos J A b 117 5.40e 91-14 Isayso 1184½ Powder Break 117hd Marie D'Argonne 113hd Wide 14
27Apr85-Grade II
30Mar85- 9Hia fm 1⅛ Ⓣ 1:49 ⒻKey Largo 4 7 712 78½ 46 1no Santos J A b 119 2.10 87-16 Powder Break 119no Id Am Fac 1171½MelanieFrances1171 Driving 8
30Mar85-Run in divisions
10Mar85- 10FG fm *1⅜ Ⓣ:49 1:40 2:19 ⒻBayou H 1 9 109½ 75½ 610 69¾ Faul J H b 117 4.20 81-13 Over YourShoulder1142¾CostaDelSol1162EruditeII1131 No threat 12
15Feb85- 9GP fm *1 1/16 Ⓣ 1:42⅗ ⒻAlw 27200 6 6 64 55½ 45½ 25 Soto S B b 117 *1.00 88-12 Isayso 1155 Powder Break 1171½ Illaka 117½ Rallied 9
9Feb85- 9GP fm *1 1/16 Ⓣ 1:43 ⒻAlw 26200 3 5 54½ 53½ 12½ 16 Soto S B b 117 2.40 91-06 Powder Break 1176 For Beauty115½PullTheWool117hd Ridden out 8
16Jan85- 7GP fm 1 Ⓣ:46 1:10⅘ 1:35⅘ 3+ ⒻSwnee RvrH 10 10 1010 77½ 86½ 89¾ Soto S B b 115 12.40 82-09 Early Lunch 112hd Eva G. 1147 Maidenhead 111nk Outrun 11
16Jan85-Grade III. Run in Divisions
28Jly84- 9Crc fm *1⅛ Ⓣ 1:45⅘ ⒻOffice Queen 4 8 86 52½ 1hd 13 Soto S B b 115 *2.50 94-05 Powder Break 1153 Delta Mary118½ScorchedPanties1152½ Driving 13
4Jly84- 8Crc fm 1 Ⓣ:47⅘ 1:11⅘ 1:36⅕ ⒻAlw 18600 4 5 55½ 32 21½ 1¾ Soto S B b 112 2.80 95-09 Powder Break 112¾ Early Lunch 1153 Gentle Screen1121¾ Driving 9
16Jun84- 10LaD fm *1 1/16 Ⓣ:46⅘ 1:10⅗ 1:40⅗ ⒻLyrique 11 10 74½ 75½ 513 38¾ Soto S B b 110 4.70 91-03 Nettie Cometti 1118 Carrysport 113¾ Powder Break 1103 Bore in 11
16Jun84-Run in Divisions
LATEST WORKOUTS May 31 Bel tr.t 5f fst 1:03⅗ b Apr 19 Crc 5f fst 1:02 b (d) Apr 6 Crc 4f fst :53 b (d)

Love Smitten
Own.—Chase D G
B. f. 4, by Key to the Mint—Square Angel, by Quadrangle
Br.—Taylor E P (Ont-C)
Tr.—Gregson Edwin
116 Lifetime 8 4 1 1 $94,300 | 1985 5 2 1 0 $67,850 | 1984 3 2 0 1 $26,450 | Turf 6 3 1 0 $79,950

12May85- 7Hol fm 1⅛ Ⓣ:47⅘ 1:11⅘ 1:48 3+ ⒻⓈSmthgryl H 1 1 11 11 1hd 65½ Pincay L Jr 119 *1.30 84-10 Capichi 117nk Red Ember 1182 Our Best Tell 1161½ Tired 8
14Apr85- 8SA fm 1¼ Ⓣ:46⅘ 1:35⅘ 2:01⅗ ⒻSta Brbra H 5 1 1½ 12 12 2no Pincay L Jr 117 4.50 79-25 Fact Finder 118no Love Smitten 1171 Salt Spring 1145 Just failed 6
14Apr85-Grade I
28Mar85- 7SA fm 1⅛ Ⓣ:47 1:11⅘ 1:47⅘ ⒻAlw 35000 6 1 1½ 11½ 12 11 Pincay L Jr 117 *1.20 88-12 Love Smitten 1171PromisingGirl1146FleetSecretariat1192 Driving 8
2Mar85- 5SA fm *6½f Ⓣ:21⅕ :44⅘ 1:15⅗ Alw 30000 3 8 54¾ 64½ 3½ 11½ Pincay L Jr 116 3.50 82-17 Love Smitten 1161½ Buena Fe II 114½ Lady Maureen 1143 Driving 12
30Jan85- 7SA fm *6½f Ⓣ:21 :45⅗ 1:14⅗ ⒻAlw 28000 8 4 31½ 1hd 3½ 47½ Delahoussaye E 116 *1.20 79-16 Danzadar 1151½ LadyMaureen1145WeddingFlower116¾ Weakened 11
4May84- 9Hol fm 1 1/16 Ⓣ:46⅘ 1:11⅗ 1:41⅗ ⒻAlw 22000 9 1 15 12½ 13 13 Pincay L Jr 117 2.60 92-06 Love Smitten 1173 Pronto Miss 1152 Shy Bride 1141½ Handily 10
12Apr84- 4SA fst 6f :21⅘ :45⅗ 1:11 ⒻAlw 26000 2 5 44½ 43½ 33½ 32¾ Delahoussaye E 119 *.40 80-18 Kyflaca 114¾ Luv's Force 1192 Love Smitten 1191¾ Lugged out 6
11Mar84- 3SA fst 6f :21⅘ :45⅗ 1:10⅗ ⒻMd Sp Wt 8 1 32 22 21 11¾ Delahoussaye E 117 5.10 86-18 Love Smitten 1171¾ Circular 1175 Queen Of Mirador1173½ Driving 9
LATEST WORKOUTS ● May 31 Bel 3f fst :34⅕ h May 7 Hol 5f fst 1:01⅗ h May 1 Hol 6f fst 1:13⅕ h Apr 25 Hol Ⓣ 5f fm 1:00⅗ h (d)

*Dictina
Own.—Seltzer E A
Ch. f. 4, by Dictus—Cesarina, by Milesian
Br.—Haras des Coludraies (Fra)
Tr.—Trotsek Harry E
114 Lifetime 14 3 2 1 $170,795 | 1985 4 0 1 1 $54,560 | 1984 10 3 1 0 $116,235 | Turf 12 3 2 1 $170,555

27Apr85- 10Hia fm 1⅛ Ⓣ 1:47⅘ 3+ ⒻBlk Helen H 4 13 1413 139½ 118 911½ Soto S B 117 *1.90e 85-14 Isayso 1184½ Powder Break 117hd Marie D'Argonne 113hd Outrun 14
27Apr85-Grade II
20Apr85- 10Hia fm 1½ Ⓣ 2:27⅘ 3+ Hia Cup H 5 8 719 67½ 33 41½ Soto S B 110 21.10 93-11 Selous Scout 114¾ Flying Pidgeon116nkPassTheLine114nk Rallied 12
20Apr85-Grade I
2Feb85- 10GP fm 1 1/16 Ⓣ:47⅕ 1:11⅕ 1:42 3+ ⒻOrchid H 10 7 61¾ 61¾ 32 31¾ Hernandez C 117 4.30e 88-10 Aspen Rose 116½ OverYourShoulder1141½Dictina117nk Evenly late 14
2Feb85-Grade II; Run in Divisions
1Jan85- 7Crc fm 1½ Ⓣ:49⅕ 2:03⅘ 2:28⅘ 3+ ⒻL'prvynte H 6 6 68 54¾ 42½ 2hd Hernandez C 117 3.50e 94-07 Persian Tiara 120hd Dictina 117½ Silver in Flight 1151½ Rallied 11
1Jan85-Grade III; Run in divisions
27Oct84- 7Crc fm *1⅛ Ⓣ 1:46⅘ 3+ ⒻGrassland H 6 7 77¾ 65 44½ 11½ Hernandez C 116 4.70 88-14 Dictina 1161½ You Snapped 1141 Winfield Honor 1111¾ Driving 9
27Oct84-Run in Divisions
7Oct84- 10LaD yl *1⅜ Ⓣ:48⅘ 1:40⅘ 2:17⅘ 3+ ⒻG Harvest H 6 7 78½ 94 67¾ 56¾ Delahoussaye D J 113 21.60e 87-13 Persian Tiara 1153½ Salt Spring 116¾ Aspen Rose 1182 Steadied 13
7Oct84-Grade II
1Sep84- 8AP gd 1⅜ Ⓣ:50⅘ 1:14⅘ 2:01⅕ 3+ ⒻModesty H 8 6 69½ 66 42½ 22½ Evans R D 109 5.90e 59-35 Jay's Sue 1232½ Dictina 1091½ Pretty Perfect 113½ Gamely 9
5Aug84- 8AP fm 1⅛ Ⓣ:48⅕ 1:13⅗ 1:51⅖ ⒻPucker Up 4 7 713 65½ 32 12½ Diaz J L 112 16.40e 80-20 Dictina 1122½ Nettie Cometti121¾PrincessMoran1161½ Drew clear 7
5Aug84-Grade III; Run in divisions

Distaff Magic
Own.—Corrado F L
Dk. b. or br. f. 4, by Fluorescent Light—Secondtimearound, by Double Jay
Br.—Corrado F L (Ky)
Tr.—Nickerson Victor J
106 Lifetime 30 3 5 4 $103,683 | 1985 3 0 0 0 $150 | 1984 16 2 5 2 $83,853 | Turf 17 2 5 2 $83,883

12May85- 8Bel fm 1 1/16 Ⓣ:46⅕ 1:09⅘ 1:40⅗ 3+ ⒻBeaugay H 4 4 65½ 710 48 56¾ Cruguet J 107 18.90 86-17 Possible Mate 1191½ Make the Magic 1091 Annie Edge1144 Tired 8
13Apr85- 8Hia st *1 1/16 Ⓣ 1:48⅗ 3+ ⒻColumbmaH 10 7 89½ 1012 1022 1025 Solis A 110 14.00 31-44 Isayso 1161 Rash But Royal 1137 Brindy Brindy 1131½ Outrun 10
13Apr85-Grade III: Run in Divisions
26Mar85- 8Hia fm *1⅛ Ⓣ 1:50⅘ ⒻAlw 15000 2 3 43 74¾ 85½ 99½ Cruguet J 116 4.80 68-27 Ark 1163 Dawna 116nk Eva G. 116hd Tired 10
10Nov84- 8Lrl yl 1⅛ Ⓣ:47⅘ 1:13 1:53 3+ ⒻChrysnthm H 5 8 99½ 1011 910 85¾ Grove P 111 26.80 66-19 GoodEconomcs1131½MddlnMgg1071½ThrtyFlgs115¾ In tight qrtrs. 12
10Nov84-Grade III
7Oct84- 8Bel fm 1⅜ Ⓣ:48⅘ 1:37⅕ 2:14⅘ 3+ ⒻAthenia H 4 6 83¾ 107½ 57½ 58 Davis R G 112 15.00 75-17 Key Dancer 1115 Surely Georgie's 107½ Rossard 123hd Outrun 11
7Oct84-Grade III
29Sep84- 3Bel gd 1 1/16 Ⓣ:49⅗ 1:13⅗ 1:45 ⒻLady Pitt 8 3 31 31 21 21 Maple E 114 2.40 75-22 Proud Nova 1141 Distaff Magic 114nk Lotus Delight116nk Gamely 8
8Sep84- 8Medfm 1 1/16 Ⓣ:46 1:10 1:41⅘ ⒻBolng Spg H 2 10 109½ 107¾ 63 2¾ Maple E 113 5.20 92-08 Possible Mate 116¾ Distaff Magic 113no MissAudimar1122 Rallied 13
8Sep84-Grade III
28Aug84- 9Mth fm 1 1/16 Ⓣ:48 1:12 1:44 ⒻL Silver H 3 9 85¾ 41¾ 22 21 Cruguet J 114 3.00 90-10 Wonder Mar 1161 Distaff Magic 114¾ Heartlight 121no Game try 10
5Aug84- 9Sar fm 1 1/16 Ⓣ:47⅗ 1:11⅕ 1:42⅖ 3+ ⒻAlw 25000 3 5 63 34 22 25¾ Cruguet J b 114 4.30 79-13 Hertlight1125¾DistffMgic1142¾RoylExplosion114no Best of others 11
14Jly84- 9Mth fm 1 1/16 Ⓣ:48⅗ 1:12⅗ 1:43⅗ 3+ ⒻEatontown H 2 5 63½ 85½ 84¾ 42½ Guerra W A b 106 16.40 91-11 Jubilous 1181¾ Maidenhead 113no High Schemes 118¾ Rallied 13
LATEST WORKOUTS May 25 Aqu ⊡ 5f fst 1:04⅘ b May 20 Aqu ⊡ 5f fst 1:04 b May 8 Aqu ⊡ 5f fst 1:02⅗ b ● May 4 Aqu 5f my 1:01⅕ h (d)

*Annie Edge
Own.—Augustin Stables
Ch. m. 5, by Nebbiolo—Friendly Court, by Be Friendly
Br.—Douglas Mrs H (Ire)
Tr.—Sheppard Jonathan E
112 Lifetime 19 5 3 5 $185,033 | 1985 2 0 0 1 $12,982 | 1984 5 3 0 1 $112,525 | Turf 19 5 3 5 $185,033

12May85- 8Bel fm 1 1/16 Ⓣ:46⅕ 1:09⅘ 1:40⅗ 3+ ⒻBeaugay H 8 6 54 45 33 32½ Velasquez J 114 3.20 91-17 Possible Mate 1191½ MaketheMagic1091AnnieEdge1144 Wide str. 8
20Apr85- 9Pim fm 1 1/16 Ⓣ:46⅗ 1:10⅗ 1:41⅗ 3+ ⒻGallorette H 12 10 77 77 58½ 43½ Dufton E 117 *2.20 100 — La Reine Elaine 113¾ Stufida1152½LadyEmerald107no Raced wide 12
20Oct84- 8Medfm 1⅜ Ⓣ:48⅘ 1:37⅗ 2:15 3+ ⒻQ Charlotte 3 9 811 52½ 43½ 54½ Castaneda K 118 *1.50 86-12 High Schemes 117nk Bezique 1102 If Winter Comes 1141 Hung 11
20Oct84-Grade II
14Oct84- 9Del fm 1¼ Ⓣ:50 1:14⅗ 1:50⅘ 3+ ⒻW'tz Song H 3 4 45½ 41¾ 2hd 12½ Castaneda K 123 *.80 90-21 Annie Edge 1232½ Good Economics 1111 Marsellesa113nk Handily 6
23Jun84- 8Bel fm 1¼ Ⓣ:48⅗ 1:37⅕ 2:02⅕ 3+ ⒻNew York H 9 3 54 86½ 44 1nk Velasquez J 112 15.70 83-18 Annie Edge 112nk Thirty Flags 114½Geraldine'sStore121no Driving 11
23Jun84-Grade II
6Jun84- 8Mth fm 1 1/16 Ⓣ:47⅗ 1:12⅕ 1:43 3+ ⒻAlw 19000 1 3 31½ 21 32 33 Ruane J 119 *.80 97-05 Mintage 1151 Doblique 1152 Annie Edge 119no Steadied,in tight 7
28Apr84- 9Pim yl 1 1/16 Ⓣ:49⅗ 1:14⅕ 1:45⅘ 3+ Riggs H 7 4 44½ 32 1½ 12½ Ruane J 107 17.60 83-21 Annie Edge 1072½ Crazy Moon 109no Tim Tamber 1144½ Driving 11
28Apr84-Grade III
13Oct83 ♦ 4Newmarket(Eng) gd 7f 1:24⅕ Ⓣ BisquitCognacChingeS(Gr3 812 Barclay A 125 11.00 — — Salieri 1282 Noalcoholic 1321 Sandhurst Prince 1322½ Bid, tired 10
8Sep83 ♦ 3Doncaster(Eng) gd 7f 1:26⅘ Ⓣ Kiveton Park Stakes 1no Barclay A 116 12.00 — — Annie Edge 116no Salieri 1292½ Drumalis 1291½ Bid, up late 8
6Jly83 ♦ 3Newmarket(Eng) gd 1 1:41⅕ Ⓣ ⒻChild Stakes(Gr.3) 512 Mercer J 117 7.50 — — RoyalHeroine1172 Flamenco1201½ LindasFantsy1173 Never close 8

Agacerie
Own.—Tartan Stable
B. f. 4, by Exclusive Native—Quiet Charm, by Nearctic
Br.—Tartan Farms (Fla)
Tr.—Nerud Jan H
118 Lifetime 13 6 1 3 $147,150 | 1985 2 1 0 0 $33,060 | 1984 10 5 1 3 $114,090 | Turf 5 5 0 0 $125,070

26May85- 7Bel fm 1 Ⓣ:46⅕ 1:11⅗ 1:36 3+ ⒻPucker Up 5 2 21 2½ 11½ 15 Cordero A Jr 119 *.70 85-16 Agacerie 1195 Proud Nova 1191½DanceForDollars1191 Ridden out 5
20Apr85- 6Aqu gd 7f :22⅘ :45⅗ 1:22⅕ 3+ ⒻSarsar 6 6 88¾ 88 712 712½ Cruguet J 124 9.40 78-10 Gracefully Yours 1197 Best Venture 119¾ Gene's Lady 121½ Wide 8
17Nov84- 4Aqu gd 1 1/16 Ⓣ:48 1:13⅕ 1:46⅘ ⒻKerala 3 2 22 1hd 11 11½ Cruguet J 121 *.70 71-25 Agacerie 1211½ Berkeley Court 121hd Proud Nova 121½ Handily 6
20Oct84- 2Bel fm 1 1/16 Ⓣ:47⅗ 1:11 1:42 3+ ⒻMoon Maiden 4 2 2½ 12 11 11½ Cruguet J 112 *1.20 86-12 Agacerie 1121½ Possible Mate 119¾ Descent 1201 Ridden out 9
27Sep84- 7Bel fm 1 1/16 Ⓣ:46 1:10⅗ 1:41⅘ 3+ ⒻAlw 22000 4 3 34½ 1½ 16 17½ Cruguet J 115 *1.90 87-22 Agacerie 1157½ Ark 113½ Safe Process 1171¾ Ridden out 12
7Sep84- 7Bel fm 1 1/16 Ⓣ:45⅗ 1:10⅘ 1:43⅕ 3+ ⒻAlw 21000 4 4 34½ 11½ 13½ 12½ Guerra W A 113 5.10 80-25 Agacerie 1132½ Enhanced 1135¾ Trios Lark 1133½ Ridden out 11
18Aug84- 2Sar fst 7f :23⅕ :46⅗ 1:24⅘ 3+ ⒻAlw 20000 3 5 21 2½ 1hd 3½ Cruguet J 114 6.50 77-15 Scrutable 112½ Sweetest Gal 117no Agacerie 1141½ Weakened 6
27Jly84- 6Bel sly 1 :45⅘ 1:10⅘ 1:37⅕ 3+ ⒻMd Sp Wt 8 3 2½ 15 11½ 1¾ Cruguet J 116 *1.60 79-21 Agacerie116¾Queen'sStatue11613HlloweenQueen116no Ridden out 8
14Jly84- 4Bel fst 7f :22⅘ :46⅗ 1:25⅕ 3+ ⒻMd Sp Wt 10 1 63 74½ 42½ 31 Velasquez J 116 *3.10 75-19 Crumpets 111¾ Fetuccine 116nk Agacerie 1165 Rallied 12
24Jun84- 5Bel fst 7f :23 :46⅕ 1:24⅘ 3+ ⒻMd Sp Wt 2 3 1hd 42½ 25 29 Velasquez J 114 5.80 69-22 Fiesta 1149 Agacerie 1144½ Current Miss 1143 Best of others 14
LATEST WORKOUTS May 21 Bel 4f fst :48⅕ b Apr 30 Bel 4f fst :49⅘ b Apr 14 Bel 4f fst :51⅗ b

Pull The Wool — Ro. m. 5, by All Oop—Fond Deceit, by Poker
Br.—Stiles M (Ky)
Tr.—Hough Stanley M
Own.—Hough S M
107 — Lifetime 46 7 6 11 $134,289 — 1985 8 1 1 3 $30,460 — 1984 12 1 0 3 $18,126 — Turf 19 3 1 7 $57,955

10May85- 6Bel fm 1 1/16 (T):47 1/5 1:11 1:43 (F)Clm 75000 11 6 6^6 4^3 3^3 1/2 1^1/2 Guerra W A 117 2.30 81-22 Pull The Wool 117 1/2 Dawna 113^nk Reptile 1131 1/2 Driving 11
4May85- 6Aqu fst 1 1/8 :48 3/5 1:12 4/5 1:51 (F)Clm 90000 3 5 53 1/2 3^2 3^3 2^3 Guerra W A 118 5.50 77-15 Ida Lewis 111^3 Pull The Wool 118^2 Whats Forever 114^1 Game try 5
6Apr85- 6Hia fm 1 1/16 (T) 1:42 3/5 (F)Alw 18000 10 5 72 1/2 77 1/2 7^11 3^3 Solis A 119 13.30 83-13 Mazatleca 116 1/2 Real Sunny 1192 1/2 Pull The Wool 119^hd Rallied 12
23Mar85- 9Hia yl 1 1/16 (T) 1:45 3/5 (F)Alw 17000 7 7 98 1/2 8^21 8^13 68 1/2 St Leon G 119 7.60 64-26 Princess Claire 119 1/2 Permissive 122 1/2 Warglo 1194 1/2 No threat 12
22Feb85- 9GP fst 1 1/16 :49 3/5 1:14 1:45 3/5 (F)Alw 26000 6 6 76 1/2 66 1/2 77 1/2 66 1/2 Santos J A 115 5.00 66-23 ScorchedPanties1191FacetheVerdict1152ForBeuty1152 No factor 8
9Feb85- 9GP fm *1 1/16 (T) 1:43 (F)Alw 26200 8 7 7^10 77 1/2 4^6 36 1/2 Guerra W A 117 6.20 84-06 Powder Break 117^6 For Beauty 115 1/2 Pull The Wool 117^hd Rallied 8
31Jan85- 9GP fm *1 1/16 (T) 1:44 3/5 (F)Alw 25000 2 8 77 1/2 76 1/2 62 1/2 3 1/2 Guerra W A 117 3.20 83-11 Nadias Charm 115^nk LantanaLady115^nk PullTheWool1171 1/2 Rallied 5
18Jan85- 9GP fm *1 (T) 1:38 1/5 (F)Alw 25000 8 10 10^16 10^10 87 1/2 7^4 Guerra W A 115 26.60 85-16 Princess Claire 115 1/2 Coup de Rouge 117 1/2 Permissive1191 1/2 Outrun 10
15Nov84- 8Aqu fst 7f :23 3/5 :46 4/5 1:25 1/5 3+(F)Alw 36000 1 4 52 1/2 65 1/2 68 1/2 58 1/2 Bailey J D 115 6.10 66-29 Duped 119 1/2 Liz Matizz 1142 1/2 Magaro 115^3 Outrun 6
21Oct84- 3WO gd 1 1/4 (T):47 3/5 1:38 2:04 1/5 3+(F)E P Taylor 9 10 10^11 109 1/2 7^12 79 1/2 Dos Ramos R A 123 102.35 77-15 ReinMthild1172 1/2 BoundingAwy117^nk Bldski'sHolidy117 1/2 No factor 11
21Oct84-Grade II
LATEST WORKOUTS May 23 Bel 3f fst :35 1/5 h May 18 Bel 5f gd 1:03 b May 2 Bel 5f gd 1:02 1/5 h Apr 26 Bel 5f fst 1:02 h

Ida Lewis — Dk. b. or br. m. 5, by Restive—Big Mad, by Hail To Reason
Br.—Martin T B (Fla)
Tr.—Sedlacek Michael C
Own.—Jcj Racing Stable
105 — Lifetime 43 6 9 8 $179,270 — 1985 9 3 2 2 $82,920 — 1984 20 1 6 3 $52,490 — Turf 8 0 1 2 $19,960

12May85- 8Bel fm 1 1/16 (T):46 1/5 1:09 4/5 1:40 4/5 3+(F)Beaugay H 3 8 75 1/2 69 1/2 58 1/2 46 1/2 Thibeau R J 107 18.90 87-17 PossibleMate1191 1/2 MaketheMagic1091AnnieEdge1144 No menace 8
4May85- 6Aqu fst 1 1/8 :48 3/5 1:12 4/5 1:51 (F)Clm 85000 4 4 42 1/2 42 1/2 1^1 1^3 Moore D N5 111 *.60 80-15 Ida Lewis 1113PullTheWool1182WhatsForever1141 Drifted easily 5
28Apr85- 7Aqu fm 1 (T):47 3/5 1:12 3/5 1:36 4/5 3+(F)Handicap 1 6 6^11 66 1/2 5^7 36 1/2 Davis R G 115 10.50 86-09 Possible Mate 122^4 Lucky Touch 1102 1/2 Ida Lewis 1153 1/2 Rallied 7
15Apr85- 5Aqu fst 1 :46 1/5 1:11 1/5 1:37 3/5 3+(F)Alw 30000 1 4 3^3 45 1/2 3^4 22 1/2 Moore D N5 116 *1.60 76-17 Jennifer's Choice 1212 1/2 Ida Lewis 116^hd SecondGlance121^nk Wide 6
22Mar85- 7Aqu fst 1 :47 3/5 1:12 1:38 (F)Clm 75000 3 5 2^hd 31 1/2 2^1 21 1/2 Giglio D Jr7 105 3.30 74-27 Free Saint 1071 1/2 Ida Lewis 1053 1/2 Wench 1071 1/2 Drifted 9
14Feb85- 8Aqu fst 1 3/4 [.] 3:04 (F)Handicap 8 4 5^3 1^4 1^8 112 1/2 Davis R G 110 *2.10 81-28 Ida Lewis11012 1/2RoseofAshes1121 1/2MagicCircle1143 Drifted, easily 8
28Jan85- 8Aqu fst 1 1/16 [.]:49 1:14 1/5 1:46 4/5 (F)Alw 25000 6 4 3 1/2 3^1 1^hd 1 1/2 Giglio D Jr7 110 7.70 76-25 Ida Lewis 110 1/2 Pistachio 1123 1/2 Halloween Queen 1171 Driving 7
23Jan85- 7Aqu fst 6f [.]:22 4/5 :46 4/5 1:12 1/5 (F)Alw 23000 2 11 9^4 10^5 55 1/2 4^5 Giglio D Jr7 110 8.40 78-24 Mt. Prospect 122^3 Pistachio 112^1 Hjerdish 117^1 Slow early 11
6Jan85- 6Aqu fst 1 1/16 [.]:49 1/5 1:14 1:47 3/5 (F)Alw 24000 2 2 2^2 2^1 3^3 31 1/2 Giglio D Jr5 112 5.20 70-17 GiveMeAHint112^hd SheerExtravgnce1171 1/2IdLewis1121 1/2 Drifted str 9
26Dec84- 1Aqu fst 1 1/16 [.]:48 4/5 1:14 1/5 1:47 3/5 3+(F)Clm c-50000 4 3 3^2 31 1/2 2 1/2 31 1/2 MacBeth D 117 4.90 73-21 Charsky 1171 1/2 Harlem Queen 113^nk Ida Lewis 117^3 No excuse 8
LATEST WORKOUTS May 28 Aqu [.] 4f fst :48 h ●Apr 12 Aqu 3f fst :35 4/5 h ●Apr 3 Aqu 6f fst 1:13 1/5 h

the lone speed, and placing trip handicappers in a quandary. Under ordinary circumstances, a top-class horse allowed to set an uncontested pace is hard to beat. But these were not ordinary circumstances that faced Love Smitten. However, as New Yorkers had learned several times already during 1985, California shippers were almost unbeatable in local stakes events. Just six days earlier, a California-based grass horse named Forzando ran away from the best handicap horses on the East Coast to win the Metropolitan Handicap, the premier mile event in that part of the country. And only the day before, Sharannpour invaded from Los Angeles to capture the Red Smith Handicap on the grass. His only start in California had been under a $175,000 claiming tag.

It was quite surprising, then, when a horse with so much going for it, including Angel "Mr. Bias" Cordero in the irons, was not favored. The New York audience appeared to be closely attuned to the condition of the grass course. Or were they? They made Annie Edge their 7–5 favorite over Love Smitten at 8–5. Of the three closers, she was the worst choice they could have made because of the bias. Her running style suggested that she, not Dictina or Powder Break, would make the first move at Love Smitten and Cordero. Indeed, as favorite, it was her rider's "obligation" to play "watchdog." With Love Smitten alone on the lead, it appeared that Annie Edge would be forced to make her move earlier than she would have liked, or was accustomed to—and consequently be swallowed up by the bias, along with Love Smitten.

Given this scenario, it was easy to conclude that the two favorites had very little chance of winning. Under the biased conditions, the winner had to be either Dictina (at 5–1) or Powder Break (at almost 7–1). Looking beyond their most recent performances in the

Black Helen at Hialeah, Dictina appeared to be the classier of the two. She had raced well in graded stakes, most notably the Hialeah Turf Cup, in which she had finished a most commendable fourth behind the likes of Selous Scout. Perhaps the strain of that effort knocked her out, which would explain her failure to lift her heels in the Black Helen.

If Dictina regained her form, she would be the likely winner. Otherwise, it would be Powder Break's race. Both had been away from the races for five weeks—a natural gap in their schedule at this time of the year. Had they been New York-based horses, their fitness might have been questioned. But they were shippers—normally a positive sign and especially so for Dictina, who came to town accompanied by Pat Day, one of the country's leading riders. Clearly both were well-meant.

It proved to be Powder Break's day, though, as she charged past Annie Edge in midstretch to win rather handily. The latter stalked the pace of Love Smitten and took over with a "winning move" entering the stretch only to be caught by the winner, who made a later move. Dictina, racing at the back of the field early, in ideal position to make the last move, failed to run at all. Love Smitten faded to last.

EIGHTH RACE
Belmont
JUNE 2, 1985

1 ¼ MILES.(InnerTurf). (1.58⅘) 41st Running THE NEW YORK HANDICAP (Grade II). $75,000 Added. (Plus $25,000 Breeders' Cup Premium Awards) Fillies and mares, 3-years-old and upward. By subscription of $150 each, which should accompany the nomination; $1,200 to pass the entry box with $75,000 added. The added money and all fees to be divided 60% to the winner, 22% to second, 12% to third and 6% to fourth. Weights, Tuesday, May 28. Starters to be named at the closing time of entries. Trophies will be presented to the winning owner. The New York Racing Association reserves the right to transfer this race to the main course. Closed Wednesday, May 15, 1985 with 28 nominations. Breeders' Cup Fund Award to Annie Edge.

Total purse $113,800. Value of race $95,550; value to winner $53,280; second $26,286; third $10,656; fourth $5,328. $750 Nominator Awards. $17,500 Reverts to Breeders'Cup Fund. Mutuel pool $156,649, OTB pool $116,701. Track Exacta Pool $220,172. OTB Exacta Pool $151,659.

Last Raced	Horse	Eqt.	A.	Wt	PP	¼	½	¾	1	Str	Fin	Jockey	Odds $1
27Apr85^{10}Hia^{2}	Powder Break	b	4	115	1	5^{4}	5^{6}	5^{6}	5^{4}	2^{3}	$1^{3\frac{1}{4}}$	Bailey J D	6.90
12May85 ^{8}Bel^{3}	Annie Edge		5	112	5	$2^{\frac{1}{2}}$	2^{1}	$2^{\frac{1}{2}}$	$1^{\frac{1}{2}}$	$1^{\frac{1}{2}}$	2^{2}	Velasquez J	1.40
10May85 ^{6}Bel^{1}	Pull The Wool		5	107	6	4^{1}	4^{1}	$4^{\frac{1}{2}}$	3^{1}	$3^{\frac{1}{2}}$	3^{nk}	Guerra W A	19.20
12May85 ^{8}Bel^{5}	Distaff Magic		4	106	4	$3^{2\frac{1}{2}}$	3^{3}	3^{2}	$4^{\frac{1}{2}}$	4^{1}	$4^{2\frac{1}{4}}$	Cruguet J	25.80
27Apr85^{10}Hia^{9}	Dictina		4	114	3	$6^{1\frac{1}{2}}$	7	$6^{\frac{1}{2}}$	$6^{1\frac{1}{2}}$	6^{3}	$5^{2\frac{3}{4}}$	Day P	5.60
12May85 ^{8}Bel^{4}	Ida Lewis		5	105	7	7	$6^{\frac{1}{2}}$	7	7	7	$6^{1\frac{3}{4}}$	Thibeau R J	16.40
12May85 ^{7}Hol^{6}	Love Smitten		4	116	2	1^{2}	1^{1}	$1^{1\frac{1}{2}}$	$2^{2\frac{1}{2}}$	$5^{1\frac{1}{2}}$	7	Cordero A Jr	1.60

OFF AT 5:04 Start good, Won driving. Time, :25⅖, :49⅘, 1:13⅖, 1:38⅕, 2:03⅗ Course good.

$2 Mutuel Prices:

1–(A)–POWDER BREAK	15.80	5.00	3.20
5–(E)–ANNIE EDGE		3.00	2.40
6–(G)–PULL THE WOOL			3.60

$2 EXACTA 1–5 PAID $44.20.

Dk. b. or br. f, by Transworld—Bold Gee Gee, by Boldnesian. Trainer Olivares Luis. Bred by Farnsworth Farm & Williamson R (Fla).

POWDER BREAK, reserved to the far turn, came out to launch a bid nearing the stretch, caught ANNIE EDGE just inside the final furlong and drew away under brisk urging. ANNIE EDGE prompted the pace, took over approaching the stretch but was no match for the winner. PULL THE WOOL rallied from the outside nearing the stretch but weakened during the drive. DISTAFF MAGIC, naver far back saved ground into the stretch but lacked the needed late response. DICTINA was always outrun. IDA LEWIS was never close. LOVE SMITTEN, showed speed for a mile but had nothing left.

Chapter 22

The Swiftest of the Swift

SHORT DASHES ON the grass have enjoyed renewed popularity during the past few years, particularly in the Northeast. Since the majority of these races are run at either five or five-and-a-half furlongs, one might suspect that their solution is rather straightforward: Simply select the swiftest contender with sufficient class, then sit back and watch the animal lead its rivals a merry chase from flagfall to finish.

It's not that easy. Because of the unusually short distance, grass sprints tend to attract precisely the fleetest horses on the grounds eligible for the classification. The majority of grass-sprint races are overloaded with early speed types. And, perhaps surprisingly, many of these fields tend to bunch up during the last eighth of a mile. It is not uncommon to see a horse come from dead last to nail the early speed right on the wire, even at five furlongs.

The typical grass sprint, packed as it usually is with speedballs, provides as good a setting as any in which to discuss the following questions:

(1) How does one approach sprint races in which all of the logical contenders tend to race on the early lead?
(2) Does too much early speed kill? And whom?

To begin answering these questions, one must look at each speed horse in the race and ask, "How can this horse win? Must it be on the early lead? Alone? Can it drop a length or two off the pace, then come on in the stretch? If need be, can the horse run from several lengths off the lead?" After getting answers to these questions, the player will usually find that his choice resolves to one of the following:

(1) He may play the horse he perceives to be the quickest in the race, hoping that it will discourage its rival speedballs and leave them staggering in the path of the closers. Identifying the swiftest of the swift, however, may prove no simple task. If comparative handicapping fails to provide the clue, the player must resort to pace figures. Yet no speed number (for pace or final time) could be more unreliable than one for a grass sprint, there being so little evidence on which to base an accurate daily variant.

(2) Alternately, the player may choose to back a speed type that has proven its gameness under fire as well as its ability to rate just off the pace and move to the lead when asked. With that kind of versatility, the horse doesn't need everything breaking its way in order to win.

(3) As a final option, the player may conclude that the speed horses will kill themselves off and instead play a horse that is likely to benefit from the speed duel that figures to develop up front. Of course, late closers are the least likely to win under most circumstances, so the player should consider only those with solid winning records. And be aware that the horse will probably either have to swing out around the dueling leaders or attempt to weave its way through them. In neither case does the horse figure to get an easy trip, and the odds should reflect this before a bet is warranted.

By way of example, we will analyze the split divisions of the Sports Palace Handicap, a five-and-a-half furlong grass sprint run September 22, 1985, at Laurel Racecourse. The stakes was named in honor of the innovative new facility opened the following weekend at the Maryland oval.

The first division of the Sports Palace was the more speed-oriented of the two, yet it was captured by a speed horse. Of course, a high incidence of speed types in a race reduces the number of potential closers in the field even before form is considered. Let's take a closer look:

PRINCE VALID

The proven closer in the field, Prince Valid is a stakes winner in Maryland and a grass-sprint winner as well. Both wins were at five furlongs, and the six-year-old came from fourth at the first call on

6 LAUREL

Start · 5½ FURLONGS LAUREL · TURF COURSE · Finish

5½ FURLONGS. (Turf). (1.03⅘) 1st Running THE SPORTS PALACE HANDICAP (1st Div.) Purse $35,000 added. A handicap for 3-year-olds and upward. By subscription of $50 each, which should accompany the nomination, $175 to pass the entry box, $175 additional to start with $35,000 added to which 65% of all monies to the winner, 20% to second, 10% to third and 5% to fourth. Weights five days before the race. Starters to be named through the entry box by the usual time of closing. Closed Tuesday, September 3 with 29 nominations.

Prince Valid

B. h. 6, by Valid Appeal—Princess Clem, by Clem
Br.—Greyhound Stable (Fla)
Tr.—Gaudet Dean
Own.—Cohen I

116 — Lifetime 44 15 10 4 $258,651 — 1985 8 3 2 1 $55,052 — 1984 4 0 1 2 $11,810 — Turf 5 2 1 0 $20,310

7Sep85- 8Pim fst 6f :23 :45⅘ 1:10⅘ 3+Terrapin H 4 6 56 46 55¾ 68¾ Nicol P A Jr 116 3.70 84-18 ⒹChiefStewrd1141½VincnnsRod1161½FltrOnThQuy1161½ Steadied 8

7Sep85-Placed fifth through disqualification

6Jly85- 7Mth fst 5f :22⅗ :45⅗ :57⅘ 3+Handicap 6 3 53½ 51½ 52½ 55 Nicol P A Jr 119 *1.60 92-17 Mayanesian 1151½ Sharp Little Girl 1123 Reliable Jeff 121½ Wide 7

22Jun85- 7Bow fst 7f :22⅘ :45⅘ 1:23 3+Alw 21000 1 2 21½ 1hd 13½ 1½ Nicol P A Jr 119 *1.70e 87-18 PrinceVlid119½CountDisco117hdVincennsRod122½ Lost whip,drvg. 8

1Jun85- 8Pim fst 5f :22⅕ :45⅖ :57⅖ 3+Mister Diz H 4 3 42 31½ 1½ 12½ Nicol P A Jr 117 2.10 98-17 Prince Valid 1172½ Whoop Up 116no Ryburn 1161½ Drew clear 7

25May85- 6Pim fst 5f :22⅕ :45⅖ :57⅘ 3+Alw 22000 4 5 51½ 42 2hd 3nk Nicol P A Jr 117 2.10 97-12 Ryburn 117nk ⒹWhoop Up 117no Prince Valid1172½ Squeezed bk. 7

25May85-Placed second through disqualification

17May85- 8Pim sly 6f :22⅘ :45⅕ 1:10⅘ 3+Alw 22000 1 1 35 34½ 34 37 Nicol P A Jr 117 3.40 87-14 Vincennes Road 1172½ ASipOfJulep1224½PrinceValid1172¾ Evenly 6

4May85- 5Pim fm 5f Ⓣ:22⅗ :46⅘ :59⅘ Alw 15000 7 3 42 33 2hd 11½ Nicol P A Jr 114 *1.20 89-16 Prince Valid 1141½ Ryburn 115½ Warlock's Revenge 1153 Driving 8

20Apr85- 7Pim fst 6f :23 :45⅘ 1:10 Alw 17000 6 1 32 32 31½ 21½ Nicol P A Jr 114 2.60e 94-12 Vincennes Road 1191½ Prince Valid1141½LordDuck119no Game try 8

17Mar84- 7Pim fst 6f :23 :45⅘ 1:10⅘ Alw 22000 6 4 36½ 34½ 23 21 Byrnes D 114 3.10 93-17 Jordana's Count 1141 Prince Valid1142BachelorBoo122no Gamely 7

11Mar84- 8Aqu fst 6f ⊡:21⅘ :45⅖ 1:10⅖ 3+Toboggan H 7 8 74½ 71½ 42 52 Byrnes D 118 37.10 90-23 Top Avenger 1201½ Main Stem 109½ Elegant Life 116hd No threat 9

11Mar84-Grade III

LATEST WORKOUTS Sep 17 Pim 4f fst :48 h — Aug 27 Pim 6f gd 1:13 b — Aug 21 Pim 5f my 1:02⅖ b — Aug 15 Pim 5f fst 1:01⅖ h

Hope Me Die

B. g. 6, by Dancing Count—Maria Queen, by Jim J
Br.—Leatherbury K T Assoc Inc (Md)
Tr.—Leatherbury King T
Own.—The Jim Stable

110 — Lifetime 56 17 13 8 $213,464 — 1985 10 5 3 2 $44,560 — 1984 13 3 4 0 $47,260 — Turf 1 0 0 0 $1,140

10Sep85- 8Pim fst 6f :23 :46 1:11 3+Alw 15000 1 4 1hd 1½ 1½ 32 Delgado A b 117 *1.50 89-23 Semaj 1171½ Double Door Prize 112½ HopeMeDie117nk Weakened 7

2Sep85- 7Pha fst 7f :22⅕ :44⅘ 1:23 3+Clm 45000 8 4 3½ 2hd 1hd 2½ Miller D A Jr b 115 3.70 91-15 Proud Dhabi 119½ Hope Me Die 115hd Duke Me 116no Stubbornly 10

13Aug85- 7Pim fst 6f :23 :45⅘ 1:10⅘ 3+Clm 40000 7 5 3½ 21 1hd 1no Delgado A b 119 *1.40 92-15 HopeMeDie119noGary'sFriend1151½DoubleDoorPrize1173½ Driving 7

27Jly85- 4Pim my 6f :23⅕ :46 1:11⅕ 3+Clm 50000 5 2 11 12 14 12 Delgado A b 115 *1.10 90-18 Hope Me Die1152WoodbineRoad117¾Hardi117no Bobbled st.,clear 5

24Jun85- 1GS fst 6f :22 :44⅘ 1:09⅖ 3+Clm 40000 1 4 11½ 2hd 2½ 3¾ Antley C W b 116 *1.10 94-16 King's Bluff 114½ Sir Damascus 116nk HopeMeDie1166 Weakened 7

14May85- 7Pim fst 6f :23⅘ :46⅕ 1:10⅘ Clm 40000 6 3 13½ 16 16 17 Bracciale V Jr b 115 *1.00 93-15 Hope Me Die 1157 Hardi 114no Antiash 117no Driving 6

19Apr85- 7Pim fst 6f :23 :45⅘ 1:10⅖ Clm 30000 2 1 11 14 14 12½ Bracciale V Jr b 115 *1.30 94-19 Hope Me Die 1152½ Near East 115½ Stag a Lee 1091½ Driving 8

30Mar85- 7Pim sly 6f :23⅕ :46⅕ 1:11⅘ Clm 30000 7 5 1hd 1hd 2hd 23½ Delgado A b 114 *1.80 84-16 Gary's Friend 1153½ Hope Me Die 114½ Mr. Baggins 1142 Failed 7

21Feb85- 7Lrl fst 6f :22⅖ :46⅖ 1:12⅖ Clm 25000 6 2 42 11 1hd 1¾ Delgado A b 114 *.90 81-23 Hope Me Die 114¾ Canter Hill 1191½ Hi Ho Racconto114¾ Driving 7

23Jan85- 5Lrl fst 7f :22⅖ :45 1:22⅖ Clm 30000 1 2 1hd 1½ 2½ 21½ Kaenel J L b 115 3.50 96-14 King'sBluff1171½HopeMeDi1151½DoublExplosion115hd Weakened 8

LATEST WORKOUTS Aug 10 Pim 3f fst :37 h

Felter On The Quay

B. c. 3, by Full Out—Tampature, by Weather Bureau
Br.—Greathouse J W & Sons (Ky)
Tr.—Connors Robert F
Own.—Limestone Farm

115 — Lifetime 18 8 5 2 $157,134 — 1985 12 6 4 1 $124,910 — 1984 6 2 1 1 $32,224

7Sep85- 8Pim fst 6f :23 :45⅘ 1:10⅘ 3+Terrapin H 2 2 11 1hd 2hd 32¾ Vigliotti M J 116 *1.20 90-18 ⒹChiefStwrd1141½VincnnsRod1161½FltrOnThQuy1161½ Lost whip 8

7Sep85-Placed second through disqualification

10Aug85- 6Mth fst 6f :22⅗ :44⅘ 1:09⅘ S. Greene 2 1 12½ 1hd 1hd 1½ Vigliotti M J 122 2.00 92-13 Felter OnTheQuay122½YankeeBird1145BoltingHolme1151½ Driving 5

23Jly85- 8GS fst 6f :21⅘ :44⅘ 1:09⅘ 3+Alw 20000 6 1 13 1½ 11 11¾ Vigliotti M J 111 *1.20 94-16 Felter On TheQuay1111¾SirDamascus1124AhSoTony112no Handily 6

29Jun85- 8GS my 6f :21⅗ :44⅖ 1:09⅘ Del Vally H 5 2 11 12½ 12 12 Vigliotti M J 114 2.80 93-15 FelterOnTheQuay1142DoublyCler1207Urigo115no Drifted out,clear 10

6Jun85- 8GS fst 6f :22 :45 1:09⅘ 3+Alw 15000 4 1 11½ 11 12 1¾ Vigliotti M J 111 *1.10 94-19 FelterOnTheQuay111¾RockN'Roller1182½MedievlLove1133 Driving 6

25May85- 7Bel fst 6f :21⅘ :44⅘ 1:09⅕ Dance Spell 1 1 11½ 1hd 21 35½ MacBeth D 115 7.00 90-11 Tiffany Ice 1221¾Ziggy'sBoy1153¾FelterOnTheQuay1151½ Brushed 5

23Apr85- 8GS fst 6f :22 :45 1:09 3+Alw 15000 2 1 12½ 1½ 11½ 11½ Vigliotti M J 110 *.60 97-13 Felter On The Quay 1101½ Rock N' Roller1126HaiStar1237 Driving 5

6Apr85- 7Kee gd 6f :21⅘ :45 1:10⅘ Lafayette 4 2 1hd 1hd 1hd 2no Allen K K 112 4.60 88-21 ProudestHour121noFltrOnThQuy1123½Don'tHsitt1213 Just missed 7

4Mar85- 7GP fst 7f :22 :44⅘ 1:23 Alw 17000 7 1 11 12½ 12 21½ MacBeth D 117 3.60 87-19 Script Ohio 1191½ Felter On TheQuay1171½Violado1179 Weakened 7

21Feb85- 5GP fst 6f :21⅘ :45 1:10⅖ Alw 16000 3 3 11 11 13 2½ MacBeth D 117 3.30 86-24 HonestCut122½FelterOnTheQuay1176ColderThan1192½ Weakened 8

LATEST WORKOUTS ●Aug 30 Del 4f fst :48 b — ●Aug 8 Del 4f sly :48 h

Starbet

B. g. 3, by Ribet—Cornish Hussy, by Pontoise
Br.—Calantoni Mr-Mrs S (Ky)
Tr.—Rowan Stephen C
Own.—Calantoni Victoria

113 — Lifetime 11 6 2 0 $50,009 — 1985 11 6 2 0 $50,009 — 1984 0 M 0 0 — Turf 2 2 0 0 $17,100

7Sep85- 7Pha fst 5f :21⅘ :44⅗ :57⅖ Handicap 1 1 1hd 11 12 14½ Colton R E 112 3.00 101-14 Starbet 1124½ Flunky Home 1111 Fast Caz 1151 Driving 6

2Sep85- 7Pen fm 5f Ⓣ :57⅘ 3+Handicap 1 5 52½ 41½ 41½ 11½ Colton R E 117 *1.10 93-17 Starbet 1171½ Cold Dawn 1151 Hear Hear 115½ Altrd crse-clear 5

10Aug85- 6Mth fst 6f :22⅗ :44⅘ 1:09⅘ S. Greene 5 2 32½ 31 33½ 58¾ Lloyd J S 113 15.70 83-13 Felter On The Quay122½YankeeBird1145BoltingHolme1151½ Tired 5

27Jly85- 6Atl my 6f :22⅕ :45⅖ 1:10⅘ ⓇMckee City 1 3 1½ 13½ 11 21½ Lloyd J S 117 2.50 86-22 Embi's Drone 1121½ Starbet 1175½ Flunky Home1134 Second best 6

29Jun85- 8GS my 6f :21⅗ :44⅖ 1:09⅘ Del Vally H 9 4 76½ 67¾ 58½ 613 Colton R E 114 33.60 80-15 Felter On TheQuay1142DoublyClear1207Urigo115no Lacked a rally 10

23Jun85- 8Del fm 5f Ⓣ:21⅘ :45⅗ :57⅘ Double Jay H 2 8 84¾ 64 31 11 Colton R E 118 4.10 93-13 Starbet 1181 Strike Up 1221½ Running Memories 118½ Driving 10

7Jun85- 8Mth fst 6f :22⅘ :45⅕ 1:09⅘ 3+Alw 14000 5 1 21 2½ 22 24 Colton R E 113 2.90 87-17 Ultra Mod 1164 Starbet 1131 Sacred Motion 1165 Game try 7

28May85- 8Pim fst 6f :22⅗ :45⅕ 1:10⅕ 3+Alw 12500 4 4 33½ 31½ 21 1¾ Colton R E 114 17.80 95-10 Starbet 114¾ Dandy Danny 1093½ T. Farnon 113½ Driving 5

17May85- 6Pen sly 6f :23 :46 1:12⅘ Alw 6500 6 4 2hd 11½ 12 13½ Colton R E 116 3.20 81-30 Starbet 1163½ Royal Shadow 1092 Fast Gordy 1221½ Driving 7

4May85- 7Pen fst 6f :23⅕ :46⅖ 1:13⅕ Md 7500 7 8 22 12 15 15¾ Colton R E 118 *2.50 78-22 Starbet 1185¾ Prince Moravin 1151½ Twin Tom 1182 Ridden out 11

LATEST WORKOUTS ●Sep 19 Pen 5f fst 1:00 h — ●Aug 30 Pen 4f fst :47⅘ h — ●Aug 20 Pen 3f fst :35 h — ●Jly 25 Pen 4f fst :49⅕ h

Proud Clarioness *

B. f. 4, by Tri Jet—Forest Murmurs, by Proud Clarion
Br.—Burke W J (Fla)
Tr.—Jerkens H Allen
Own.—Lou-Roe Stable

110 — Lifetime 17 6 1 5 $181,539 — 1985 5 0 0 3 $22,116 — 1984 7 3 0 2 $121,833 — Turf 1 0 0 1 $6,624

17Aug85- 1Sar fst 6f :21⅖ :44⅖ 1:09⅕ 3+ⒻRevidere H 2 1 13½ 11½ 22 35 Cordero A Jr 113 4.90 89-08 WeddingPicture1122½LeSlew1122½ProudClrionss113no Weakened 5

9Aug85- 8Sar fst 7f :21⅘ :44⅕ 1:22⅘ 3+ⒻBallerina 7 2 11½ 1hd 911 923½ Cordero A Jr 116 7.80 66-19 Lady's Secret 117no Mrs. Revere 1162¾ Solar Halo 116¾ Stopped 9

9Aug85-Grade II

29Jly85- 8Bel gd 7f Ⓣ:23⅗ :46⅘ 1:24 3+ⒻLily White 4 2 11½ 12 1½ 31¾ Samyn J L 115 3.90 82-22 Vers La Caisse 122½ Tarifa 1151½ProudClarioness1155½ Weakened 6

17Jly85- 8Bel fst 1$\frac{1}{16}$:45⅘ 1:10⅕ 1:44 3+ⒻAlw 40000 6 1 11½ 1hd 2hd 44½ Cordero A Jr 115 2.80e 78-18 Tearupthetickets 1151 Le Slew 1151½BrindyBrindy1152 Weakened 7

6Jly85- 6Bel fst 6f :22 :45⅕ 1:11⅕ 3+ⒻThe Rose 3 2 1½ 1hd 22 35½ Skinner K 115 4.20 80-20 Ldy'sSecret1164¾FoolishIntentions115¾ProudClrionss115nk Tired 6

16Jun84- 8Bel fst 1⅛ :45⅗ 1:09⅗ 1:48⅘ ⒻMther Goose 3 1 11 2½ 519 527½ Davis R G 121 17.20 56-22 Life's Magic 1213½ Miss Oceana 121¾WildApplause1214½ Stopped 5

16Jun84-Grade I

26May84- 8Bel fst 1 :45⅗ 1:10⅖ 1:35⅘ ⒻAcorn 1 1 11½ 1½ 33½ 35¾ Samyn J L 121 31.20 80-15 MissOceana121nkLife'sMgic1215½ProudClrioness121no Weakened 9

26May84-Grade I

12May84- 8Bel fst 7f :22 :44⅖ 1:23⅕ ⒻComely 7 1 2hd 21½ 25 36½ Samyn J L 116 2.90 80-17 Wild Applause1133½Suavite1132¾ProudClarioness1162½ Weakened 7

12May84-Grade III

25Apr84- 8Aqu fst 6f :23 :46⅕ 1:10⅘ ⒻPrioress 6 1 12 11½ 11½ 1¾ Samyn J L 115 *.70 89-22 Proud Clarioness115¾Dumdedumdedum1121¾Suavite112hd Driving 6

5Apr84- 1Aqu sly 6f ⊡:21⅘ :44⅘ 1:10⅘ 3+ⒻAlw 33000 6 1 14 16 15 12½ Samyn J L 109 *.70 90-25 ProudClarioness1092½LizMtizz114nkGiftOfTheMgi1171 Ridden out 6

LATEST WORKOUTS Sep 18 Bel tr.t 4f fst :49 b — ●Aug 6 Bel 5f fst 1:00 b — ●Jly 24 Bel 4f fst :45⅘ h

*Dr. Manet

Dk. b. or br. h. 6, by Minera II—Julie Manet, by Martins Rullah
Br.—Haras La Doma (Arg)
Tr.—Fisher John R S
Own.—Watriss J B

112 — Lifetime 22 5 4 2 $27,946 — 1985 4 0 2 0 $4,510 — 1984 5 2 0 0 $15,732 — Turf 20 5 4 2 $27,778

6Sep85- 4Bel fm 1$\frac{1}{16}$ Ⓣ:45⅘ 1:09⅕ 1:41⅗ 3+Clm 50000 8 2 25 35½ 917 1023½ Velasquez J 117 9.40 65-15 World Assembly 117¾ Vulnerability 117no Persian Poet117¾ Tired 12

17Aug85- 4Pim hd 1$\frac{1}{16}$ Ⓣ:49⅗ 1:13⅗ 1:43⅘ 3+Clm 50000 3 1 11 11 14 2no Terry J 115 3.50 84-12 AmericanArtist117noDr.Mnet1152½BenjminII117no Drifted,bumped 6

3Aug85- 6Pim fm 5f Ⓣ:22⅕ :45⅘ :58⅕ 3+Clm 40000 7 4 3½ 32 21 2¾ Davidson J 117 *1.90 94-06 Sir Prize Birthday 115¾ Dr. Manet 117nk Canter Hill1152 Willingly 7

23Jly85- 8Mth fm 5f Ⓣ:22⅕ :44⅘ :57 3+Alw 20000 8 5 5¾ 53 86¾ 87 Perret C 115 8.80 91-06 Perfect Remedy 115no Chas Conerly 115nkSunandShine1151 Wide 8

7Dec84- 9Hol fst 1 :44⅕ 1:08⅘ 1:34⅘ 3+Clm 80000 4 2 32 511 717 723½ Shoemaker W 116 7.50 74-08 Right On Red 1191½ Unbeknownst to Me 1165½ Espontaneo1161½ 7

18Nov84- 8Hol fm 5f Ⓣ:21⅘ :43⅘ :56 3+Meteor H 7 3 43½ 54½ 84½ 96½ Lipham T 115 11.90 92-07 Famous Star 1171½ Debonaire Junior 121hd Shananie 115nk Tired 11

27Oct84- 7Lrl fm 5½f Ⓣ:22⅗ :45⅖ 1:03⅘ 3+Alw 14000 5 4 11½ 11½ 12½ 11½ Miller D A Jr 115 2.10 103-08 Dr. Manet 1151½ Pink Buffalo 115nk Fed Funds 119hd Driving 8

6Oct84- 9Del fm 5f Ⓣ:22⅕ :45⅗ :57⅘ 3+J O Tobin H 7 4 2½ 2hd 33½ 45½ Terry J 115 4.30 90-16 Shananie 1153¾ Jeff 1241½ Hear Hear 115no Weakened 9

21Sep84- 8Lrl fm 5½f Ⓣ:22⅘ :45⅖ 1:03⅖ 3+Alw 10500 2 4 11 12 14 14½ Bracciale V Jr 116 6.00 103-03 Dr. Manet 1164½ Key To Calamity 1162½ Hawklike 1143½ Driving 7

4Sep83 ♦ 1Hipodromo(Arg) fst*5f :55⅘ Premio Mountdrago(Alw) 46 Orcellet D 126 14.95 — — Ubicado 1193 Raigras 1191½ Juzgado 1121½ 5

LATEST WORKOUTS Sep 19 Fai tr.t 3f fst :35⅖ b — ●Sep 14 Fai tr.t 4f fst :48⅘ b — Aug 31 Fai 5f fst 1:03 b — ●Aug 14 Fai tr.t 4f fst :49⅕ b

Whoop Up — Own.—Edwards R L

Ch. h. 5, by Divine Royalty—Balanced Melody, by Balance Of Power
Br.—Edwards R L (Wash)
Tr.—Nesky Kenneth A

112 — Lifetime 26 4 4 6 $99,510 — 1985 10 1 3 3 $40,950 — 1984 16 3 1 3 $58,560 — Turf 4 1 1 0 $23,800

13Sep85- 8Med	fm	5f	Ⓣ:22⅕ :45⅘ :58⅕	3↑Alw 20000	8	3	1hd	2hd	2hd	2nk	Guerra A A7	112	5.50	92-15 Feed The Fire 112nk Whoop Up 112¾ Awesome Rebel1152	Gamely 12
15Aug85- 7Sar	fst	6f	:21⅘ :44⅖ 1:09	3↑Alw 36000	1	1	1½	21½	34	59¼	Wynter N A7	108	3.60	85-08 MjesticVenture1157¼TheWeddingGust115noNrThStorm110½	Tired 7
7Aug85- 6Sar	fm	1	Ⓣ:46⅗ 1:11 1:36⅖	3↑Alw 40000	3	1	12	11½	24	57¼	Wynter N A7	108	15.80	86-14 Judge Costa 1153¾ Fearless Leader 115nk Sondrio1152	Weakened 10
14Jly85- 6Bel	fst	7f	:22⅗ :45⅘ 1:23⅖	3↑Alw 27000	3	2	12½	12	15	13¾	Guerra A A7	110	2.60	85-21 Whoop Up 1103¾GoldenImmigrant1173½SirLeader117½	Drew clear 6
1Jun85- 8Pim	fst	5f	:22⅕ :45⅖ :57⅖	3↑Mister Diz H	5	1	1½	1hd	3½	22¼	Kupfer T J	116	4.80	96-17 Prince Valid 1172¼ Whoop Up 116no Ryburn 1161½	Game try 7
25May85- 6Pim	fst	5f	:22⅕ :45⅖ :57⅗	3↑Alw 22000	5	1	1½	2hd	3nk	2nk	Pino M G	117	4.50Ⓓ	97-12 Ryburn 117nk ⒹWhoop Up 117no Prince Valid 1172¼	Bore in 7
25May85-Disqualified and placed third															
15Feb85- 7Aqu	fst	6f	⊡:22⅗ :46 1:11⅕	Alw 25000	6	1	1½	11	2hd	21¼	Guerra A A7	110	3.40	87-26 Mt. Livermore 1191¼ Whoop Up 1101½ Cooper'sHawk1191	Gamely 7
27Jan85- 8Aqu	fst	6f	⊡:22⅕ :45⅖ 1:10⅕	Coaltown	5	2	21	45	510	510¾	Samyn J L	114	18.30	82-20 DHEntropy 1234 DHMuskoka Wyck1144MainStem1173¾	Gave way 6
11Jan85- 8Aqu	fst	6f	⊡:23⅕ :47⅕ 1:11⅗	Alw 25000	2	3	11	2hd	31	34¾	Guerra A A7	110	2.50	81-30 EcstaticPride112½BlindMn'sBluff1194¼WhoopUp1106½	Weakened 6
1Jan85- 7Aqu	fst	6f	⊡:21⅘ :44⅗ 1:09⅗	Alw 25000	6	1	12	11	2½	32¼	Guerra A A7	110	6.30	93-13 StoneyLonesome117nkGretHunter1122¼WhoopUp1103¾	Weakened 6

LATEST WORKOUTS ●Sep 9 Aqu 4f fst :47 h ●Sep 3 Aqu 5f fst :58⅗ h Aug 29 Aqu 3f fst :36⅖ h ●Aug 24 Sar tr.t 4f fst :48 h

A Sip Of Julep — Own.—Davison Rosalee

Dk. b. or br. h. 5, by Accipiter—Fast Exchange, by Swaps
Br.—Davison Mrs R (Md)
Tr.—Ferris Richard D

115 — Lifetime 36 9 15 2 $142,306 — 1985 11 4 4 0 $76,616 — 1984 8 0 6 0 $19,860

17Aug85- 8Mth	fst	6f	:22⅖ :44⅘ 1:09	3↑Aloma's Rlr	1	2	1hd	2hd	23	69¼	Kupfer T J	b 119	9.20	86-10 Aeronotic 1195 Silent Hour 115¾ For Halo 1192¼	Tired 8
25May85- 8Mth	fst	6f	:22⅖ :45⅖ 1:10⅕	3↑Handicap	2	4	12½	12½	2hd	25	Miller D A Jr	b 115	3.30	84-22 Ringside 1115 A Sip Of Julep 1153½ For Halo 1243	Best of others 7
17May85- 8Pim	sly	6f	:22⅘ :45⅕ 1:10⅖	3↑Alw 22000	6	2	11	12½	1hd	22½	Miller D A Jr	b 122	2.30	91-14 VincennesRod1172½ASipOfJulep1224½PrincVlid1172¾	Second best 6
25Apr85- 8GS	fst	5f	:21⅘ :44⅖ :56⅗	3↑Bld Rsng H	3	4	1hd	2hd	32½	45	Baltazar C	b 117	2.70	95-13 FortunteProspect1152MjsticVntur1173ChifStwrd113no	Weakened 8
25Apr85-Run in divisions															
6Apr85- 9Pim	fst	6f	:22⅖ :45⅕ 1:09⅘	3↑J E Hoover H	1	3	13	12	1½	11¾	Baltazar C	b 115	2.40	98-15 A Sip Of Julep 1151¾ Roast 1113¾ Vincennes Road 1111½	Driving 5
10Mar85- 7Lrl	fst	6f	:22⅖ :45⅗ 1:11	3↑Handicap	7	1	14	16	13½	13½	Baltazar C	b 116	3.20	88-16 A Sip Of Julep1163½AMagicSpray113noKaye'sPrince121nk	Driving 8
22Feb85- 8Lrl	fst	6½f	:22 :45⅕ 1:18	Alw 16000	6	4	1hd	2hd	11½	11	Baltazar C	b 119	4.20	— — ASipOfJulp1191MortggMn1161NorthrnRtrt118½	Drifted out,drvng 6
2Feb85- 8Lrl	sly	6f	:22⅘ :46⅘ 1:12⅖	3↑Chesapeake H	7	5	41½	77½	721	723½	Miller D A Jr	b 115	7.90	57-36 Never Cye 114no Jyp 1233¾ Ultramate 1145½	Faltered 7
26Jan85- 7Lrl	fst	6f	:22⅕ :45⅘ 1:11⅕	Alw 15000	7	2	11	13	11	22	Baltazar C	b 119	4.10	85-24 Kye'sPrinc1152ASipOfJulp1192½Computr'sChoic1091½	Drifted out 8
12Jan85- 7Bow	fst	6½f	:22⅘ :45⅘ 1:16⅗	Alw 15000	7	4	2hd	12	1½	11	Baltazar C	b 115	2.90	105-14 ASipOfJulep1151DukeOfHerts115nkComputer'sChoic1092	Driving 8

LATEST WORKOUTS Sep 18 Lrl 5f fst 1:01⅕ h ●Sep 7 Bow 4f fst :46⅗ h ●Jly 31 Bow 4f fst :47⅗ h

Bryantown — Own.—Clark Mrs H S

Ch. g. 4, by Dundee Marmalade—Restless Turk, by Restless Native
Br.—Clark Mrs H S-DuPont-Glengar Farm (Md)
Tr.—Clark Henry S

110 — Lifetime 13 6 1 4 $50,270 — 1985 6 3 0 3 $31,380 — 1984 4 1 1 0 $7,790 — Turf 1 1 0 0 $5,700

23Aug85- 7Pim	fst	6f	:23⅕ :46⅕ 1:11	3↑Alw 16000	5	2	1hd	1hd	1½	11¼	Davidson J	119	3.40	91-16 Bryantown 1191¼ Count The Dots 117¾ Hatchet Boy 1171	Driving 7
1Aug85- 8Pim	fst	6f	:24 :48 1:12⅕	3↑Alw 12500	5	2	11	1½	1½	12¾	Davidson J	117	*1.50	85-24 Bryantown 1172¾ Urigo 1123½ Jan R.'s Boy 117¾	Driving 5
23Jly85- 8Pim	fst	6f	:23⅖ :47 1:11⅘	3↑Alw 12500	1	2	1hd	1hd	11½	33½	Miller D A Jr	117	*.70	83-20 Stop Card 1171½ Urigo 1142¼ Bryantown 11713	Weakened 5
10Jly85- 8Bow	fst	6f	:22⅕ :45⅕ 1:10⅖	3↑Alw 16000	7	4	3nk	1hd	1hd	3¾	Davidson J	119	*1.90	87-20 Rambler Red 122nk Semaj 117½ Bryantown 119¾	Weakened 7
19Jun85- 8Bow	fst	6f	:22 :44⅖ 1:09⅘	3↑Alw 16000	2	4	22½	22½	21½	1¾	Davidson J	117	*.80	91-23 Bryantown 117¾ Onion Juice 1174 Rapid Robber 112¾	Driving 8
12Jun85- 8Bow	fst	6½f	:22⅗ :45⅕ 1:16⅗	3↑Alw 10500	2	2	2½	21	2hd	3nk	Davidson J	117	12.60	104-07 Woodbine Road117nkColdCreation117hdBryantown1171½	Willingly 6
13Dec84- 8Bow	fst	6½f	:22⅗ :46 1:18⅘	3↑Alw 10000	6	5	2½	44	719	735¼	Kaenel J L	115	10.30	62-29 Corsican Lt. 1151½ See for Free 115no Woodbine Road115hd	Tired 7
9Nov84- 8Lrl	fst	6f	:22⅗ :46⅖ 1:10⅘	3↑Alw 10000	1	2	2½	44	79½	713¼	Miller D A Jr	116	3.70	75-20 Never Cye 1182¾ Woodbine Road 1141 He's Bad 1096	Faltered 8
2Nov84- 8Lrl	fm	5½f	Ⓣ:22⅗ :45⅗ 1:04⅖	3↑Alw 9500	3	1	1½	11	11½	1¾	Edwards J W	115	*1.60	98-12 Bryantown 115¾ Sober Parson 116½ Fresh Hope 111hd	Hard dr. 7
23Oct84- 8Lrl	fst	6f	:22⅗ :46⅘ 1:12⅕	3↑Alw 9500	3	1	3½	1½	2½	21	Edwards J W	115	3.90	81-21 So West 1171 Bryantown 1151 Northern Retreat 115¾	Drifted out 6

LATEST WORKOUTS Sep 17 Pim 5f fst 1:01⅗ h ●Sep 11 Pim 5f fst 1:02⅗ b Sep 4 Pim 5f fst 1:03 b Aug 30 Pim 5f fst 1:04⅖ b

both occasions. A 35 percent winner lifetime, Prince Valid is now set for his second start after a two-month layoff. His liberal 9–2 odds are due at least in part to an apparently lackluster performance first time back, although the horse didn't have the clearest of sailing on that occasion. An interesting possibility considering the number of speed horses in front of him. If he could slip through along the rail . . .

HOPE ME DIE

Basically a speed horse, Hope Me Die has only recently demonstrated both the gameness and tractability we look for in a field of this type. However, he is basically a claiming animal, with no proven record on the grass. It's a tough spot.

FELTER ON THE QUAY

A three-year-old making his first start on the grass, Felter On The Quay has not been headed at either of the first two calls in any of the races showing on his record. Whether he can reproduce that speed on the grass is at least open to question, and whether he can outgame older horses in such a contentious contest is debatable. As 2–1 favorite, he's hardly worth the risk.

STARBET

A three-year-old that has captured both his turf starts at five furlongs, albeit at Delaware Park and Penn National, Starbet has been able to win on the lead and from eighth at the first call at short-dash distances. Whether the former $7,500 maiden will be competitive in this field is doubtful, however. He was no match for the favorite on two occasions during the summer.

PROUD CLARIONESS

This four-year-old filly hasn't won in seventeen months, although she's been clear on the early lead on most occasions. There is no evidence as to how she will perform against males, but there is sufficent evidence of her lack of gameness, making her hard to take as 4–1 co-second choice in this field.

DR. MANET

One usually doesn't prepare a horse for a sprint stakes with middle-distance routes, but then Dr. Fisher isn't your ordinary horseman. In this case, however, we must pass, reasoning that the August 17 race knocked Dr. Manet out—a conclusion that seems confirmed by the "drifted" comment in the *Form* for that race, and by the horse's dismal performance on September 6, when he failed to produce any semblance of his accustomed early lick.

WHOOP UP

Although seldom out of the picture at the half-mile call, Whoop Up has managed just one win in ten starts during 1985—and that after getting clear early at seven furlongs on July 14. The five-year-old demonstrated his gameness and present fitness in his latest race, and his record shows a game effort behind Mt. Livermore, one of the year's top sprinters. However, he was solidly trounced by Prince Valid at five furlongs on June 1.

A SIP OF JULEP

This horse is another bullet from the gate, but he's making his grass debut. A Sip of Julep's soundness must be questioned. He is making his first start in five weeks, that coming on the heels of a thirteen-week layoff. Not likely to have the foundation to compete with this caliber horse.

BRIANTOWN

A game front-runner that can rate just off the pace, Briantown has won his only start on grass, at today's distance. However, the gelding is making his stakes debut with only limited experience against classified rivals. His rise in class appears too sharp, and he's likely to find himself parked on the outside the entire trip.

In the absence of accurate pace figures—difficult to come by, considering the number of tracks involved, especially the grass courses—one can only guess which of perhaps seven horses has the most early speed. It does seem, however, that the New York invader Whoop Up holds a class and/or gameness advantage over each of his rivals for the early lead, making him the speed type most likely to succeed in this race. And even if he were not clearly the fastest or gamest of the early contenders, he certainly is the most enticing at nearly 13–1 odds. If one wishes to bet a horse that's likely to get caught up in a speed duel, then decent odds are certainly a prerequisite for the bet.

Even though the course was on the hard side of firm, the compet-

SIXTH RACE
Laurel
SEPTEMBER 22, 1985

5 ½ FURLONGS.(Turf). (1.03⅖) 1st Running THE SPORTS PALACE HANDICAP (1st Div.) Purse $35,000 added. A handicap for 3-year-olds and upward. By subscription of $50 each, which should accompany the nomination, $175 to pass the entry box, $175 additional to start with $35,000 added to which 65% of all monies to the winner, 20% to second, 10% to third and 5% to fourth. Weights five days before the race. Starters to be named through the entry box by the usual time of closing. Closed Tuesday, September 3 with 29 nominations.
Value of race $38,875; value to winner $25,269; second $7,775; third $3,887; fourth $1,944. Mutuel pool $52,895. Exacta Pool $80,477.

Last Raced	Horse	Eqt.A.Wt	PP	St	¼	⅜	Str	Fin	Jockey	Odds $1
13Sep85 8Med2	Whoop Up	5 112	7	2	1hd	1½	1hd	1no	Guerra A A	13.90
23Aug85 7Pim1	Bryantown	4 114	9	3	3½	21	21½	21½	Davidson J	21.40
7Sep85 8Pim5	Prince Valid	6 116	1	4	4½	4½	32	31¾	Nicol P A Jr	4.60
7Sep85 7Pha1	Starbet	3 115	4	6	61½	62	4hd	41¼	Miller D A Jr	4.30
6Sep85 4Bel10	Dr. Manet	6 115	6	7	9	81	71½	51	Bracciale V Jr	8.10
10Sep85 8Pim3	Hope Me Die	b 6 111	2	8	82	7hd	86	6nk	Delgado A	15.20
7Sep85 8Pim2	Felter On The Quay	3 115	3	1	21	3½	51	71	Vigliotti M J	2.40
17Aug85 1Sar3	Proud Clarioness	4 114	5	5	51	51	6½	811	Morgan M R	4.30
17Aug85 8Mth6	A Sip Of Julep	b 5 115	8	9	71	9	9	9	Kupfer T J	11.30

OFF AT 3:31 Start good, Won driving. Time, :22⅗, :45⅘, :57⅗, 1:03⅗ Course firm.

$2 Mutuel Prices:				
	7-WHOOP UP	29.80	12.00	7.40
	9-BRYANTOWN		18.60	7.80
	1-PRINCE VALID			5.60
	$2 EXACTA 7-9 PAID $566.80.			

Ch. h, by Divine Royalty—Balanced Melody, by Balance Of Power. Trainer Nesky Kenneth A. Bred by Edwards R L (Wash).

WHOOP UP came in slightly near the five eighths pole, disputed the pace inside BRYANTOWN and gamely edged that one in a hard drive. BRYANTOWN challenged outside the winner through the stretch and just missed. PRINCE VALID hung. STARBET had a mild rally. DR. MANET passed tired ones. FELTER ON THE QUAY weakened along the rail. PROUD CLARIONESS, steadied when shuffled back near the five eighths pole, drifted wide entering the stretch and weakened. An objection by the rider of PROUD CLARIONESS against the winner for alleged interference soon after the start was not allowed.

itive situation up front seemed to favor Prince Valid, who figured to tuck in behind the early leaders from his rail post, save ground around the turn, then attempt to get through in the stretch. A very plausible theory, except that the horse was pushed early—often a necessity from the rail post—then swung out around a few horses entering the stretch, and hung in the late stages. Whoop Up, however, parlayed speed and gameness into a narrow decision over Briantown to earn his first stakes victory.

The second division of the Sports Palace featured a smaller field, but one that included three New York shippers, each looking at least as imposing on paper as Whoop Up had prior to his victory. Here's the field:

RELIABLE JEFF

A (disqualified) stakes winner at Delaware Park under similar conditions, Reliable Jeff's last three races have been at middle distances, and his best efforts of late have been against state-bred competition in New Jersey. He was unable to handle rival Mayanesian on July 6 and isn't likely to turn the tables today.

CHAS CONERLY

A once-classier performer that has found his "Fountain of Youth" on the grass, Chas Conerly has been "right there" in his two grass sprints, with off-the-pace performances on both occasions. If Hall of Fame trainer Allen Jerkins thinks enough of the horse to ship him to Maryland, then his last race can be regarded as a conditioner and the horse considered a serious stretch threat.

ALEV

A hard-hitting performer in New York, on both dirt and turf, Alev appears to be a more reasonable favorite than Felter On The Quay in the first division. But is he quick enough to win at five-and-a-half furlongs? With such an important matter subject to question, it's hard to recommend a bet on the favorite.

MILADY'S EAGLE

A fleet filly with an abundance of early speed, Milady's Eagle is clearly the one to catch. How she will stand up to pressure from

8 **LAUREL**

5½ FURLONGS. (Turf). (1.03⅘) 1st Running THE SPORTS PALACE HANDICAP (2nd Div.). Purse $35,000 added. A handicap for 3-year-olds and upward. By subscription of $50 each, which should accompany the nomination, $175 to pass the entry box, $175 additional to start with $35,000 added to which 65% of all monies to the winner, 20% to second, 10% to third and 5% to fourth. Weights five days before the race. Starters to be named through the entry box by the usual time of closing. Closed Tuesday, September 3 with 29 nominations.

Reliable Jeff — Ch. g. 4, by Czar Alexander—Foiled, by Crafty Admiral
Own.—Seahorse Stable — Br.—Baer S M (NJ) — Tr.—Graci Joseph J III — **120**
Lifetime 38 14 8 5 $217,949 — 1985 15 5 4 2 $150,345 — 1984 15 6 3 2 $49,084 — Turf 9 4 2 1 $29,191
Entered 21Sep85- 8 MED
12Sep85- 8Medfst 170 :46⅖ 1:11⅕ 1:41⅕ 3+ⓈHandicap 6 1 11½ 11 11½ 11 Black A S b 121 3.10 93-22 Reliable Jeff 1211 Jewelry Sale 116nk Derby Hat 1143½ Driving 7
13Aug85- 8Mth fm 1⅟₁₆ Ⓣ:48 1:11⅗ 1:42 + 3+Alw 25000 5 1 11 21 42½ 46 Black A S b 122 3.70 85-13 Crazy Moon 1152½ Chas Conerly 1152 Arranan 1151½ Tired 8
25Jly85- 8GS sly 1⅟₁₆ :46⅘ 1:11 1:45 3+ⓈBlackwood H 5 2 22 2½ 1½ 2¾ Black A S b 123 3.40 82-23 Bill Wheeler 115¾ Reliable Jeff 123hd Duke Me 1133 Bore out in 7
6Jly85- 7Mth fst 5f :22⅖ :45⅗ :57⅘ 3+Handicap 3 2 2hd 3nk 41½ 34½ Black A S b 121 2.20 93-17 Mayanesian 1151½ Sharp Little Girl1123ReliableJeff121½ Steadied 7
21Jun85- 8GS fst 6f :22 :44⅘ 1:10 3+ⓈCinamnsn H 4 2 2½ 3nk 1½ 11 Black A S b 122 2.80 92-13 Reliable Jeff 1221 R. Philip 112½ Chip's Knight 1161 Driving 5
8Jun85- 9Mth gd 6f :22⅖ :44⅘ 1:09⅖ 3+ⓈBrookdale H 6 1 31 33½ 44½ 47 Nied J Jr b 124 *1.80 86-13 Chip's Knight 115no Duke Me 1166 Jewelry Sale 1141 Tired 7
27May85- 5GS fst 1 :46⅕ 1:10 1:35⅗ 3+ⓈVly Forge H 7 2 2½ 2hd 11½ 1¾ Nied J Jr b 122 7.10 97-08 Reliable Jeff 122¾ Duke Me 116no La Pawn 1196½ Driving 7
12May85- 8Del fm *5f Ⓣ:22⅖ :46 :58⅕ 3+Post Card H 2 4 2hd 2½ 1hd 1¾ Nied J Jr b 126 *1.20Ⓓ 99-04 ⒹRelibleJeff126¾HereComesRed1131LowellPremir113nk Broe out 10
12May85-Disqualified and placed third
25Apr85- 8GS fst 5f :21⅘ :44⅖ :56⅗ 3+Bld Rsng H 2 2 42½ 54½ 57 57½ Vigliotti M J b 115 6.90 92-13 FortunteProspect1152MjesticVntur1173ChifStwrd113nk No threat 8
25Apr85-Run in divisions
8Apr85- 8GS fst 6f :21⅘ :44⅗ 1:09⅖ 3+ⓈHandicap 8 1 2½ 2½ 12 11½ Black A S b 122 *1.80 — — Reliable Jeff 1221½ Duke Me 1123 Bold Julius 115½ Driving 8
LATEST WORKOUTS Sep 4 Pha 5f fst 1:01⅘ b

Chas Conerly — Dk. b. or br. h. 5, by Big Burn—Shall Return, by Fair Ruler
Own.—Hobeau Farm — Br.—Lavezzo D H Jr (Ky) — Tr.—Jerkens H Allen — **113**
Lifetime 30 6 5 5 $247,181 — 1985 9 1 2 1 $32,800 — 1984 4 0 1 1 $11,580 — Turf 4 1 2 0 $30,600
14Sep85- 7Bel fm 1 Ⓣ:47 1:11⅕ 1:36 3+ⓇKnightly Man 3 1 1hd 31½ 76½ 710½ Velasquez J b 115 4.70e 74-19 Zoffany 119no Fearless Leader 1153½ Aristocratical 1191 Tired 10
1Sep85- 7Bel gd 6f Ⓣ:23 :46⅖ 1:11⅘ 3+Alw 36000 6 1 31 2½ 1hd 1¾ Velasquez J b 115 2.60 81-24 ChsConerly115¾BigBoxOfSweets1122DomintingDooly1171 Driving 9
13Aug85- 8Mth fm 1⅟₁₆ Ⓣ:48 1:11⅗ 1:42 + 3+Alw 25000 2 4 32½ 11 11½ 22½ Toro M b 115 3.30 89-13 Crazy Moon 1152½ Chas Conerly 1152 Arranan 1151½ Weakened 8
23Jly85- 8Mth fm 5f Ⓣ:22⅕ :44⅘ :57 3+Alw 20000 5 8 72 63½ 33 2no Rocco J b 115 11.90 98-06 PerfectRemedy115noChasConerly115nkSunndShine1151 Lost whip 8
4Jly85- 7GS fst 6f :21⅗ :44 1:09⅕ 3+Alw 20000 2 4 512 413 49 34 Toro M b 115 3.40 92-12 Best By Test 1143 American Diabolo1151ChasConerly1152 Rallied 5
9Jun85- 7Bel gd 7f :22⅘ :46 1:23⅗ 3+Alw 36000 5 2 32 42 53¾ 65½ Toro M b 117 9.60 80-18 Mugatea 117hd Act It Out 119hd Momento II 1172 Weakened 7
26May85- 3Bel fst 6f :22⅖ :45⅗ 1:10 3+Alw 36000 6 1 2hd 1½ 3½ 54¾ Migliore R b 119 2.70 87-13 Main Top 119hd Momento II 119¾ Daring Groom 119hd Gave way 6
15Apr85- 8Aqu fst 7f :23⅕ :46 1:23 3+Alw 36000 1 4 2½ 43½ 46 58½ Wynter N A10 b 109 7.30 78-17 Waitlist 1213½ Steady Beat 1191½ Northern Ice 1193 Tired 7
5Jan85- 7Aqu fst 6f ⊡:22⅖ :46⅗ 1:09⅗ Alw 36000 4 7 63½ 88½ 66¾ 68½ Privitera R7 b 108 4.30 87-17 Hagley's Reward 1151½ Don Rickles1175Barcelona1151½ No threat 8
23Dec84- 8Aqu fst 6f ⊡:21⅘ :44⅗ 1:09⅖ 3+Gravesend H 2 4 55½ 610 67¾ 89½ Miranda J b 119 8.10 88-17 Elegant Life 115nk Tarantara 1203 Top Avenger 126½ Tired 8
LATEST WORKOUTS Sep 12 Bel 4f fst :50⅖ b — Aug 11 Bel 4f fst :49⅕ b — Aug 7 Bel 4f fst :48⅗ b — Aug 3 Bel 4f fst :48⅘ b

***Alev** — Ch. g. 6, by Hot Spark—St Citrus, by Relic
Own.—Spiegel R — Br.—Whitsbury Manor Stud (Eng) — Tr.—Schaeffer Stephen — **118**
Lifetime 54 14 4 6 $237,771 — 1985 12 4 2 2 $126,840 — 1984 18 5 1 3 $83,480 — Turf 44 12 3 4 $164,367
7Sep85- 3Bel fst 1⅟₁₆ :45⅘ 1:10⅕ 1:42⅕ 3+Clm 450000 4 1 21 32½ 46½ 412½ Santagata N b 112 4.00 78-14 Waitlist 114½ Act It Out 1127¾ Tampa Town 1124½ Tired 4
25Aug85- 7Sar sly 7f :22⅗ :45⅗ 1:23⅘ 3+Handicap 3 1 1½ 2hd 14 13½ Santagata N b 117 1.70 83-19 Alev 1173½ Roving Minstrel 122nk Main Top 10911 Ridden out 4
18Aug85- 7Sar fm 1⅟₁₆ Ⓣ:47⅖ 1:11⅗ 1:42⅘ 3+ⓇNtve Courier 4 1 1½ 2½ 2½ 62½ Santagata N b 115 2.90 89-15 A Gift 117¾ Mighty Louis 115¾ Aristocratical 115no Weakened 7
31Jly85- 7Sar sf 1⅟₁₆ Ⓣ:49 1:14 1:45⅖ 3+Daryl's Joy 5 2 25 22½ 25 36½ Santagata N b 117 4.70 63-30 Roving Minstrel 1196½ Four Bases 115hd Alev 117½ Weakened 6
8Jly85- 7Bel fm 1 Ⓣ:45⅖ 1:09⅘ 1:35 3+Handicap 3 2 21½ 3nk 1hd 1nk Santagata N b 117 9.10 90-14 Alev 117nk Mr Chromacopy 112¾ Aristocratical 1121½ Stiff drive 9
30Jun85- 7Bel fm 6f Ⓣ:21⅘ :44⅗ 1:09⅖ 3+Alw 36000 4 3 43 23 21½ 11 Velasquez J b 119 *1.80 93-18 Alev 1191 Equalize 114½ River Demon 1173¾ Driving 6
16Jun85- 7Bel my 7f :22⅖ :44⅘ 1:23 3+Alw 36000 3 2 21½ 31½ 2½ 15 Velasquez J b 117 1.80 87-17 Alev 1175 Alcnise 117nk River Demon 1171 Ridden out 4
6Jun85- 8Bel gd 6f :22⅕ :44⅘ 1:10⅖ 3+Handicap 6 1 45 67 34½ 31½ Velasquez J b 115 3.30 88-15 Basket Weave 114hd River Demon 1101½ Alev 115½ Rallied outside 7
27May85- 7Bel fm 7f Ⓣ:22⅗ :45 1:23 3+Wise Ship 4 3 54½ 56 43 42¾ Velasquez J b 119 10.20 86-19 Sitzmark 1191 Red Wing Dream 119¾ Cozzene 1191 Even try 7
11May85- 6Bel fm 6f Ⓣ:22 :45⅖ 1:09⅖ 3+Alw 36000 5 5 42¾ 32 22½ 25½ Velasquez J b 121 *.90 88-17 Sitzmark 1195½ Alev 121hd Alcnise 1193¾ Saved place 11
LATEST WORKOUTS ●Sep 20 Bel tr.t 3f fst :36 h — Sep 15 Bel tr.t 4f fst :48⅗ b — Sep 2 Bel tr.t 4f fst :50 b — Aug 14 Sar tr.t 4f fst :51 b

Milady's Eagle — B. m. 5, by Spring Double—Save The Eagle, by Bald Eagle
Own.—Casey Eleanor — Br.—Casey J W (Md) — Tr.—Casey James M — **116**
Lifetime 24 7 5 6 $95,060 — 1985 7 4 1 2 $59,340 — 1984 7 1 3 2 $20,490 — Turf 5 3 2 0 $50,600
24Aug85- 7Mth fm 5f Ⓣ:22 :44⅘ :57 3+ⒻRed Cross 7 3 1hd 11 12 11 Antley C W b 119 *.40Ⓓ 98-09 ⒹMilady's Eagle 1191 Often 1171½ Nick's Nag 117¾ Bore out late 9
24Aug85-Disqualified and placed second
3Aug85- 7Mth fm 5f Ⓣ:21⅘ :44⅖ :57⅕ 3+ⒻPhnm Belle 3 3 11 12½ 13 12½ Antley C W b 120 *.40 97-09 Milady's Eagle 1202½ Cedar Town 1141 Doris J. 109½ Driving 8
16Jly85- 5Mth fst 5f :22⅕ :45 :56⅘ 3+Alw 20000 2 1 11½ 1½ 21½ 34½ Melendez J D b 117 4.70 97-17 DigginDitches1224½MjesticVntur120noMildy'sEgl1171½ Weakened 4
4Jly85- 7Mth fm 5f Ⓣ:21⅗ :44 :56⅖ 3+ⒻⓇVeryLucky 11 1 13 13 14 15½ Antley C W b 113 2.10 101-07 Milady's Eagle 1135½ Cedar Town 113¾ Applause 117no Driving 11
20Jun85- 8Mth fm 5f Ⓣ:22⅕ :44⅘ :57⅕ 3+ⒻAlw 15000 4 2 12 15 15 14½ Miller D A Jr b 116 *1.50 97-11 Milady's Eagle 1164½ Classy Cut1101½GingerRock1162½ Riden out 6
10Jun85- 7Mth fst 6f :22⅗ :45⅘ 1:10⅘ 3+ⒻAlw 14000 4 5 11½ 11½ 11½ 36½ Miller D A Jr b 116 3.90 80-17 Tabayour 114nk Just Smashing 1146Milady'sEagle1162 Weakened 7
31May85- 5Mth fst 6f :22⅖ :45⅗ 1:13 3+ⒻClm 40000 4 4 1½ 13 16 19 Miller D A Jr b 116 2.80 75-21 Milady's Eagle 1169 Lady Counselor 116¾ SoDoI1162½ Ridden out 6
21Jly84- 7Mth sly 5f :21⅘ :45⅕ :57⅘ 3+ⒻⓇVery Lucky 5 3 52½ 44 44 21½ Melendez J D b 114 12.00 96-16 Second Glance 1091½ Milady's Eagle 114nkBigDreams1233 Rallied 9
9Jly84- 8Mth fst 5f :21⅘ :45⅖ :57⅘ 3+ⒻAlw 17000 1 4 11 11½ 2½ 34½ Melendez J D b 115 7.10 92-17 Chic Belle 122½ Second Glance 1124Milady'sEagle115¾ Weakened 6
27Jun84- 8Mth fm 5f Ⓣ:22⅖ :45⅕ :57⅗ 3+ⒻAlw 14000 6 8 62¾ 31 2½ 2nk Melendez J D b 116 6.90 95-01 LaReineElaine115nkMilady'sEagle116nkMissSharpe1162 Stumbled 8
LATEST WORKOUTS ●Jly 30 Mth Ⓣ 3f sf :34⅘ b (d)

Mayanesian — Ch. h. 6, by Bold Hour—Cozumel, by T V Lark
Own.—Gordonsdale Farm — Br.—Madden Preston (Ky) — Tr.—Zito Nicholas P — **116**
Lifetime 66 9 12 5 $273,209 — 1985 12 1 3 0 $47,592 — 1984 12 2 3 0 $68,195 — Turf 11 2 4 1 $93,060
26Aug85- 5Sar sly 6f :22⅕ :45⅘ 1:11 3+Alw 36000 2 1 12 11 2hd 22 Santos J A b 115 2.80 83-21 Cannon Shell 1192 Mayanesian 115½ Archregent 1165¾ No match 6
17Aug85- 5Sar fst 6f :21⅘ :44⅗ 1:09⅗ 3+A Phenomenon 4 1 11½ 12½ 1½ 22 Santos J A b 117 10.10 90-08 Cognizant 1172 Mayanesian 117½ Spender 117½ No match 7
19Jly85- 7Bel fm 6f Ⓣ:21⅗ :44⅖ 1:09⅘ 3+Alw 36000 6 2 31½ 33½ 32½ 21¼ Cordero A Jr b 122 2.70 90-14 Zany Tactics 1221¼ Mayanesian 122½ River Demon 1152¾ Rallied 6
6Jly85- 7Mth fst 5f :22⅖ :45⅗ :57⅘ 3+Handicap 5 1 3nk 4¾ 31 11½ Cordero A Jr b 115 6.40 97-17 Mayanesian 1151½ SharpLittleGirl1123ReliableJeff121½ Drew clear 7
30Jun85- 7Bel fm 6f Ⓣ:21⅘ :44⅗ 1:09⅖ 3+Alw 36000 5 2 21½ 43½ 55 45½ Ward W A b 117 9.20 88-18 Alev 1191 Equalize 114½ River Demon 1173¾ Tired 6
15Jun85- 7Bel fm 1⅟₁₆ Ⓣ:45⅖ 1:09⅖ 1:41 3+Alw 40000 1 8 74½ 77 68 67¾ Ward W A 117 10.70 83-18 Fortnightly 1173 High Ice 117no Fearless Leader 1171 No factor 10
6Jun85- 8Bel gd 6f :22⅕ :44⅘ 1:10⅖ 3+Handicap 1 4 33 35 65½ 63½ Ward W A b 113 10.20 87-15 Basket Weave 114hd River Demon 1101½ Alev 115½ No excuse 7
10May85- 8Bel fst 6f :22⅕ :45⅖ 1:11 3+Alw 36000 5 6 711 716 716 716½ Falcone J10 b 114 8.10 71-20 Cozzene1241½BasketWeve124½MomentoII1192½ Rider lost control 7
25Apr85- 6GS fst 5f :22 :44⅕ :56⅕ 3+Bld Resong H 3 4 31 54¾ 48½ 59½ Ward W A b 115 8.40 92-13 Rollin on Over 1122½ Roast 1104 Burts Star 1161½ Tired 6
25Apr85-Run in divisions
27Mar85- 9Hia fst 6f :21⅗ :44⅗ 1:09 Kendall 7 1 1½ 11½ 45½ 610¾ Bailey J D b 119 20.90 85-17 FortunteProspect117nkMjsticVntur1176RoxburyPrk1171 Faltered 7
LATEST WORKOUTS Sep 18 Bel 4f fst :47⅘ h — Sep 13 Bel Ⓣ 5f gd 1:03 b — Aug 10 Sar 4f fst :47 h — Aug 3 Sar 3f fst :34⅕ h

Ringside — B. h. 5, by Sir Ivor—Middle Cornish, by Speak John
Own.—Charlton — Br.—Kilroy W S (KY) — Tr.—Forbes John H — **115**
Lifetime 45 11 10 1 $201,777 — 1985 11 2 2 0 $83,772 — 1984 14 4 4 1 $69,055 — Turf 5 0 1 0 $6,389
13Sep85- 8Medfm 5f Ⓣ:22⅕ :45⅘ :58⅕ 3+Alw 20000 1 4 2hd 32 42½ 53¾ Perret C b 119 3.00 88-15 Feed The Fire 112nk Whoop Up 112¾ Awesome Rebel 1152 Tired 12
6Aug85- 9Mth fst 1 :46⅖ 1:10⅖ 1:36 3+Sal Mile H 8 7 43 1½ 4nk 910¾ Verge M E b 115 16.80 82-12 Valiant Lark 116no Pat's Addition 1152 Rumptious 1162 Tired 10
6Aug85-Grade III
27Jly85- 8Mth fst 6f :23 :45⅘ 1:10⅕ 3+Ahoy 2 6 63¾ 63¾ 64¾ 64¾ Verge M E b 119 1.90 84-13 Fuddy Dud 1151½ For Halo 119no Aeronotic 1222 Shuffled st 6
6Jly85- 8GS fst 6f :21⅘ :44 1:08⅖ 3+J Kilmer H 4 7 86¾ 89 62¾ 22½ Verge M E b 117 4.20 98-14 Sagittarian 1112½ Ringside 1171½ Mortgage Man 112½ Rallied 8
15Jun85- 7Mth fm 1 Ⓣ:49 1:12⅗ 1:37 3+Red Bank H 6 2 1hd 2hd 2hd 42½ Verge M E b 116 4.80 87-11 Castelets 115nk Evzone 117¾ Gothic Revival 1121½ Weakened 8
15Jun85-Run in Divisions
1Jun85- 8GS fst 6f :22 :44⅘ 1:08⅘ 3+Equus H 4 3 32 3½ 12½ 15½ Verge M E b 115 5.40 98-12 Ringside1155½Hgley'sRwrd1142½AmricnLgion1141 Drifted in, clear 5
1Jun85-Run in divisions
25May85- 8Mth fst 6f :22⅖ :45⅖ 1:10⅕ 3+Handicap 5 3 22½ 22½ 1hd 15 Verge M E b 111 8.30 89-22 Ringside 1115 A Sip Of Julep 1153½ For Halo 1243 Driving 7
9Apr85- 8GS fst 6f :22⅖ :45⅕ 1:09⅖ Alw 30000 6 1 1½ 1½ 11½ 2hd Krone J A b 122 18.20 — — Tarnish 117hd Ringside 1221½ Now's The Time 115¾ Just failed 6
23Mar85- 8Key sly 6f :22 :45⅖ 1:10⅕ 3+Newtown H 4 2 32 45½ 55½ 56 Krone J A b 113 10.20 84-25 Rocky Knave 115½ Burts Star 1201½ Tarnish 1141½ Tired 6
26Jan85- 8Key fst 7f :22⅖ :45⅕ 1:23 3+Gallnt Bob H 11 3 3½ 41½ 911 912½ Krone J A b 117 9.60 80-22 Rocky Knave 115nk Reliable Jeff 116no Obgyn 1152 Tired 12
LATEST WORKOUTS Sep 9 Med 5f fst 1:02 b — ●Aug 26 Mth 5f my 1:00⅘ hg — Aug 22 Mth 5f my 1:05⅕ b — Aug 2 Mth 4f fst :48⅘ b

No No Romeo — Ch. g. 3, by Romeo—Tup Take, by Tarleton Oak
Own.—Double H Stable
Br.—Honeycut Paul (Ky)
Tr.—Hollis Barbara
113

Lifetime							
12 5 2 1	1985	12	5	2	1	$51,717
$51,717	1984	0	M	0	0	
	Turf	1	0	0	0	$577

2Sep85-10Tdn	fst	6f		:22	:44⅗	1:10⅕	N Randall	8	1	2 1½	3 5	4 8	5 8	Arnold M W	119	3.10	85-19	Near The Storm 122 3 Avator's Best 117 1½ Dusty'sDynamite119 2½	8
17Aug85-10RD	gd	6f		:21⅗	:45	1:10⅗	Eagle	1	3	1 ½	1 3	1 1	2 1	Arnold M W	124	*1.70	89-26	Smart Bask 119 1 No No Romeo 124 5 Vannelli 119 hd	8
3Aug85-10Det	fst	6f		:22⅗	:45⅕	1:10⅘	Dearborn	5	1	1 1½	1 1½	1 3	1 1½	Arnold M W	123	4.80	86-22	No No Romeo 123 1½ Dusty's Dynamite 113 1 Grand Reward 123 2	6
13Jly85- 8Bml	fst	6f		:24⅗	:47⅗	1:13⅖	3+ Crete H	3	1	1 1	1 ½	1 hd	3 2½	Arnold M W	114	*1.40	89-22	Chimes Keeper 117 no Roman Sabotage 120 2½ No NoRomeo114 2½	5
29Jun85- 9EIP	fst	6f		:22	:45⅖	1:10⅘	Brentwood	8	1	1 hd	1 1½	1 4	1 3½	Arnold M W	117	5.70	91-21	No No Romeo 117 3½ Rented Condo 120 2 Rhubick 113 nk	9
16Jun85- 9RD	fst	5½f		:21⅘	:44⅗	1:05	Alw 10000	3	3	1 ½	1 ½	1 2	1 5	Arnold M W	119	3.40	90-24	No No Romeo 119 5 King's Piper 116 1½ Check Our Song 114 4	6
26May85-10RD	fm	1	Ⓣ	:47	1:12⅖	1:37⅕	Spartacus	11	2	1 hd	1 hd	2 ½	6 8¾	Walt B A	118	53.30	85-03	Sparkling Jay 118¾ Crazy Life 124 3 Rough Choice 121 4	12
15May85- 9RD	sly	6f		:22⅕	:45⅗	1:12	Alw 14000	4	2	1 1½	1 hd	1 2	1 no	Walt B A	119	25.90	83-32	No No Romeo 119 no Sparkling Jay 121 1½ Avator's Best 118 1½	7
26Apr85- 4RD	fst	6f		:22⅕	:45⅗	1:10⅘	3+ Alw 6000	4	4	5 7½	5 9¼	5 6	2 10	Neff S	113	3.40	79-25	Avator's Best 114 10 No No Romeo 113 1 Bennett's Coin 112 3	6
13Apr85- 4Kee	fst	7f		:23⅘	:46⅘	1:25⅕	Alw 16000	1	8	1 hd	6 3	11 11	11 14¼	Brumfield D	115	12.00	66-19	Nashua Night 108 1 Cormorant's Party 118 2 Quibble 112 nk	12

LATEST WORKOUTS ●Aug 31 Tdn 3f my :37 b Aug 1 Det 3f fst :36⅕ b

male rivals is hard to gauge, however. Her July 16 effort against the boys in allowance company at Monmouth was her worst in a year's time. As co-favorite, she's not worth the risk.

MAYANESIAN

A horse that no rival could outrun for the early lead in previous seasons. Mayanesian has been slow to come around in 1985, but his latest two races seem to signal a return to his 1984 form and style. If so, he and Milady's Eagle figure to run each other dizzy before they reach the stretch.

RINGSIDE

This sprinting son of Sir Ivor seems to have lost the good form he enjoyed in late spring and has only one in-the-money finish to show from five tries on the grass. Not likely here.

NO NO ROMEO

A three-year-old invader from the smaller midwestern circuits, this gelding's class can best be measured from the bottom line of his past performances—an awful finish at Keeneland, which was quickly followed by improved performances at River Downs. Apparently his form at the smaller tracks must be taken with a grain of salt. Class notwithstanding, his early speed puts him at a disadvantage against (and outside) the likes of Milady's Eagle and Mayanesian.

Unlike the first division, only two horses figured to dominate the pace in this race. Both were impetuous types, though, and neither would be denied the early lead or be likely to tolerate the other's presence. It was a no-win situation for both of them and, with the small field spread out behind them on the backstretch, a relatively uncomplicated spot for a closer.

The conclusion here is simple: If one wishes to pass on the co-favorites Alev and Milady's Eagle as underlays and rule out the two early speed horses as likely to self-destruct, the value play must obviously be Chas Conerly. Value plays don't always win, however. But, if correctly gauged, they win often enough to produce long-term profits. In this case, Chas Conerly managed to come from last and close a five-length gap in the last eighth mile to catch and pass a tired Milady's Eagle, who had assumed command a few strides out of the gate. Mayanesian showed little interest once he'd been outrun for the early lead.

EIGHTH RACE
Laurel
SEPTEMBER 22, 1985

5 ½ FURLONGS.(Turf). (1.03⅖) 1st Running THE SPORTS PALACE HANDICAP (2nd Div.). Purse $35,000 added. A handicap for 3–year–olds and upward. By subscription of $50 each, which should accompany the nomination, $175 to pass the entry box, $175 additional to start with $35,000 added to which 65% of all monies to the winner, 20% to second, 10% to third and 5% to fourth. Weights five days before the race. Starters to be named through the entry box by the usual time of closing. Closed Tuesday, September 3 with 29 nominations. Value of race $38,525; value to winner $25,041; second $7,705; third $3,853; fourth $1,926. Mutuel pool $43,136. Exacta Pool $72,342.

Last Raced	Horse	Eqt.	A.	Wt	PP	St	¼	⅜	Str	Fin	Jockey	Odds $1
14Sep85 ^{7}Bel^{7}	Chas Conerly	b	5	114	2	7	7	7	3^{1}	1^{2}	Morgan M R	5.30
24Aug85 ^{7}Mth^{2}	Milady's Eagle	b	5	116	4	1	$1^{1\frac{1}{2}}$	$1^{2\frac{1}{2}}$	1^{5}	$2^{\frac{3}{4}}$	Edwards J W	2.20
12Sep85 ^{8}Med^{1}	[D]Reliable Jeff	b	4	120	1	5	2^{1}	2^{2}	$2^{\frac{1}{2}}$	3^{nk}	Lopez C	8.50
7Sep85 ^{3}Bel^{4}	Alev	b	6	118	3	6	5^{2}	5^{1}	$4^{1\frac{1}{2}}$	$4^{4\frac{1}{4}}$	Miller D A Jr	2.10
26Aug85 ^{5}Sar^{2}	Mayanesian	b	6	116	5	2	4^{1}	$3^{\frac{1}{2}}$	5^{4}	$5^{4\frac{1}{2}}$	Bracciale V Jr	3.30
13Sep85 ^{8}Med^{5}	Ringside	b	5	115	6	4	6^{2}	6^{hd}	7	6^{1}	Delgado A	15.30
2Sep85 ^{10}Tdn^{5}	No No Romeo		3	115	7	3	$3^{\frac{1}{2}}$	$4^{\frac{1}{2}}$	6^{1}	7	Arnold M W	28.60

[D]–Reliable Jeff Disqualified and placed fourth.

OFF AT 4:32 Start good, Won driving. Time, :22⅖, :45⅗, :57⅘, 1:03⅗ Course firm.

Equals Course Record

$2 Mutuel Prices:				
	2–CHAS CONERLY	**12.60**	**6.80**	**4.40**
	5–MILADY'S EAGLE		**4.40**	**2.80**
	4–ALEV			**2.40**

$2 EXACTA 2–5 PAID $71.40.

Dk. b. or br. h, by Big Burn—Shall Return, by Fair Ruler. Trainer Jerkens H Allen. Bred by Lavezzo D H Jr (Ky).

CHAS CONERLY swung wide entering the stretch and closed with a flourish to sweep passed MILADY'S EAGLE in deep stretch. MILADY'S EAGLE sped to the front, set the pace racing slightly off the rail and could not hold off the winner. RELIABLE JEFF drifted out approaching the eighth pole and again near the sixteenth pole, both times carrying out ALEV. Following a stewards' inquiry and an objection by the rider of ALEV, RELIABLE JEFF was disqualified and placed fourth. ALEV, steadied inside MAYANESIAN around the turn, was bothered through the stretch. MAYANESIAN weakened. RINGSIDE raced wide. NO NO ROMEO faltered.

You will note that grass breeding played no role in our analysis of these races. The typical grass stallion has a distance pedigree, and his offspring are usually not noted for the precocity needed to win at the shortest of sprint distances. Conversely, one should refrain from jumping to conclusions about a stallion's propensity for siring grass runners based on the evidence of the results of a few grass sprints. One is best advised to demand proven ability to sprint as well as some evidence of grass form—even if only a pacesetting effort in a grass route—before backing a horse in a turf sprint.

Chapter 23

When the Rains Come and Wash Away the Grass

ONE OF THE MAJOR DIFFERENCES between the sport in this country and in Europe is the racing surface itself. In America, the grass course is an option racing secretaries love. In Europe, it's the only game in town.

The show must go on in Europe, whether it rains or the sun shines. And European horses may be forced to compete over courses that more closely resemble bogs than the near-concrete highways to which Americans have grown accustomed during the hot summer months. In this country, on the other hand, heavy rains usually force scheduled grass races to be transferred to the damp main track, with numerous scratches often reducing the fields to small bands of misfits and stuck horses—those requesting to scratch but forced to stay in the race to help maintain reasonable field size.

How does the player sort out the wheat from the chaff, the horses with serious intentions from those likely to be severely inconvenienced by the prevailing track conditions? Many players don't even try, routinely passing races that have been taken off the grass. In many cases they are right to do so. But this isn't always so.

In restricted allowance and maiden races, many of the contestants have rather limited experience on the grass anyway, and these races can be analyzed based on the horses' established (or lack of) dirt form. A knowledge of which bloodlines tend to move up in the slop often proves helpful.

But when a field of older grass specialists gathers, and is then forced to the main track, the situation is far more difficult. We will take a close look at two such races and hopefully make a few points that will convince some skeptics that it is not always wise to sit back and passively watch these races and that good "action" bets can be found if one knows what to look for.

First, let's analyze the second (and last) race at Belmont on Saturday, June 30, 1984, a high-priced claiming event originally carded at a mile-and-a-quarter on the inner grass course. The heaviest rains in many years forced this race to be moved to the swamped main track, and subsequently washed out the remainder of the day's program (not to mention the rug in my family room). Four of the original cast of eleven were scratched, leaving a field of seven to face the starter. Co-favorites on the board at 5–2 were Clarinet King and Crown.

Let's take a look at the contestants:

EL FANTASMA

An invader from the Argentine, this horse's five career wins all came on the grass. Although his first race in this country appeared promising—enough to make the horse a serious longshot possibility had the race remained on the grass—El Fantasma had to be considered an unknown quantity over the sloppy course. Add to this the fact that his conditioner, L. C. Alvarez, was a relatively unknown member of the New York trainer colony, and we have a true mystery horse to deal with.

FREON

A career grass specialist whose seventeen wins all came on turf, Freon was winless in eighteen dirt starts and was being asked to race over a distance that was probably beyond his best trip.

CLARINET KING

Under such dismal track conditions, why take a "chance" with the favorite? Clarinet King raced under "similar" conditions two starts back and was able only to "clunk up" for third money. Otherwise, his dirt form of late was rather unimpressive.

CROWN

An Irish-bred colt, Crown's first two starts in this country revealed a definite dislike for the main track—even under dry conditions. Even

2 BELMONT

INNER TURF COURSE
1¼ MILES
BELMONT PARK
START FINISH

1⅛ MILES. (InnerTurf). (1.58⅘) CLAIMING. Purse $23,000. 4-year-olds and upward weights, 122 lbs. Non-winners of two races over a mile since June 1, allowed 3 lbs. Of such a race since then, 5 lbs. Claiming price $75,000 to $70,000. Races when entered to be claimed for $65,000 or less not considered).

*El Fantasma
B. h. 6, by Kasteel—Espiritosa, by Immortality
$70,000 Br.—Haras Los Cerrillos (Arg) Tr.—Alvarez L C
Own.—Singing Frog Stable
113
Lifetime 24 5 5 4 $19,911 | 1984 4 0 0 1 $1,650 | 1983 8 3 1 1 $5,969 | Turf 16 5 2 1 $16,393

13Jun84- 5Bel fm 1⅛ Ⓣ:46⅗ 1:10⅗ 1:42 Clm 40000 4 5 57½ 47 47 44¼ Cordero A Jr 117 6.40 81-16 Fearless Leader 117¾ CannonRoyal108¹FullConcert1132¾ Mild bid 11
9Mar84 ♦10Hipodromo(Arg) fst*1¼ 2:04 Premio Figurita(Alw) 41⁹ Fajardo J 123 1.30 — — Manguero 119¹¹ Picarel 126nk Chapulin 120⁹ 6
24Feb84 ♦10Hipodromo(Arg) hy*1¼ 2:04⅗ Clasico Labrador Hcp 61⁹ Pezoa C 117 6.00 — — Categorico 110³ El Cantabro 118⁶ Brady 131³ 8
1Jan84 ♦6SanIsidro(Arg) fm*1¼ 1:58⅗ Ⓣ Clasico Botafogo(Gr.3) 32½ Pezoa C 133 3.05 — — Maspicante 132¾ Sol Dorado 1321½ El Fantasma 133⁵ 12
22Dec83 ♦5Hipodromo(Arg) fst*1¼ 2:04 Premio Mitla Hcp 21½ Pezoa C 117 *1.00 — — Jumbler 1241½ El Fantasma 117⁶ Wizzo 1262½ 7
25Nov83 ♦6Hipodromo(Arg) fst*1⅛ 1:49⅕ PremioArturoLavallolHcp 71⁵ Centeno V 116 *1.55 — — Jumbler 119² Wizzo 126nk Prophet 1131½ 8
20Oct83 ♦11SanIsidro(Arg) fm*1¼ 2:00⅗ Ⓣ Pr.A.deCastroPerez(Alw) 1⁵ Pezoa C 126 *.95 — — ElFantasma 126⁵ Veremos 119¾ Kadlero 119¾ 12
27Aug83 ♦9SanIsidro(Arg) sf*1¼ 2:03 Ⓣ Premio Alan Breck Hcp 51¹ Pezoa C 120 *1.40 — — Picarel 122no Milimil 126⁴ Bacardi 117³ 6
9Jly83 ♦6SanIsidro(Arg) gd*1½ 2:28⅗ Ⓣ Gran Premio 9 deJulio(Gr1 92¹ Pezoa C 134 19.10 — — New Dandy 134⁵ Mezcalero 1342½ El Temido 1341½ 11
25May83 ♦9SanIsidro(Arg) fm*1⅛ 1:48⅕ Ⓣ Premio Campero(Alw) 1hd Pezoa C 126 1.95 — — El Fantasma 126hd Lester 119⁴ Fray Gaston 1101½ 7
LATEST WORKOUTS Jun 26 Aqu 4f fst :51 b ●Jun 19 Aqu 3f my :36⅗ h (d) Jun 5 Aqu 7f fst 1:28⅕ b May 14 Aqu 4f gd :51⅗ b

Current Charge
B. h. 7, by Little Current—Midway Island, by Turn-To
$75,000 Br.—Nydrie Stud (Va) Tr.—DiMauro Stephen
Own.—McKibbin D A
110⁷
Lifetime 33 4 4 5 $90,415 | 1984 3 0 0 0 $1,200 | 1983 5 0 2 1 $17,500 | Turf 33 4 4 5 $90,415

20Jun84- 5Bel fm 1⅛ Ⓣ:46 1:10⅗ 1:41⅗ Clm 75000 8 11 94¾ 64½ 1011 1014½ Vega H⁷ 110 26.80 75-17 Lutyens 108² Meru 1171½ Freon 113¹ Outrun 12
28Jan84- 9Hia fm 1⅛ Ⓣ 1:48⅕ Alw 20000 9 8 96½ 88 1011 1109 Melendez J D 113 5.00 82-13 Secret Ward 119hd Reap 114nk Senior Citizen II 114½ Outrun 11
13Jan84- 9Hia fm *1⅛ Ⓣ 1:40⅘ Alw 20000 7 7 56½ 56 55½ 49 Melendez J D 113 29.50 85-08 Super Sunrise 116¹ Out Of Hock 119²WorldAppeal119⁶ No factor 11
4Aug83- 7Sar fm 1 Ⓣ:46⅗ 1:11⅗ 1:37 3+Alw 37000 4 7 78½ 85¾ 23 2nk Samyn J L 115 8.80 91-20 AskClrence115nkCurrentChrge115nkAmricSluts115hd Just missed 8
23Jly83- 7Bel gd 1 Ⓣ:47 1:10⅗ 1:36 3+Alw 37000 3 7 75 34 33½ 31½ Samyn J L 117 4.50 83-23 HexgreaveStar119nkAskClrence1171½CurrentChrge1176¾ Wide str. 7
14Jly83- 8Bel fm 1¼ Ⓣ:49⅕ 1:37⅗ 2:01⅗ 3+Handicap 3 5 67½ 54 55 42¾ Samyn J L 114 20.20 82-18 Erin's Tiger 122nk Four Bases 113² Kentucky River 114½ Evenly 7
3Jly83- 8Bel fm 1⅜ Ⓣ:48⅗ 1:36⅗ 2:12⅗ 3+Tidal H 3 7 79 86½ 816 820 Bailey J D 117 43.80 73-15 Hush Dear 117hd John's Gold 1171½ Late Act 1112½ Outrun 8
7Apr83- 9Hia fm *1⅛ Ⓣ 1:41 Alw 15000 6 9 108½ 86½ 52¾ 24 McCauley W H 116 17.90 90-11 A Sure Hit 113⁴ Current Charge 116nk No HomeRun116nk Rallied 10
19Oct82- 8Lrl fm 1½ Ⓣ:48 2:02⅗ 2:27⅗ 3+Lrl Tf Cup H 11 10 98½ 1010 99 88¾ Hernandez C 114 6.60 71-19 Royal Roberto 1143½ Uncle Jeff 111¹ Forkali 1151½ No factor 13
3Oct82- 9WO yl 1¼ Ⓣ:47⅗ 1:40⅗ 2:08⅕ 3+Jky Club H 2 5 57½ 65½ 42¾ 31½ Hernandez C 116 10.55 65-34 Frost King 1311½ Nijinsky's Secret 119hd Current Charge 1163½ 9
LATEST WORKOUTS Jun 26 Bel 3f fst :37 b

Freon
Dk. b. or br. g. 7, by Icecapade—Miss Summons, by Helioscope
$70,000 Br.—Walden B P (Ky) Tr.—Moschera Gasper S
Own.—Davis A
113
Lifetime 73 17 14 9 $278,590 | 1984 5 0 1 1 $13,380 | 1983 13 4 3 2 $102,840 | Turf 55 17 12 6 $258,870

20Jun84- 5Bel fm 1⅛ Ⓣ:46 1:10⅗ 1:41⅗ Clm 70000 6 6 74 53½ 35 33½ Bailey J D 113 5.30 85-17 Lutyens 108² Meru 1171½ Freon 113¹ Mild bid 12
11Jun84- 7Bel hd 1⅛ Ⓣ:45⅕ 1:09⅗ 1:39⅗ Clm 75000 11 6 63 31½ 46 47¾ Cordero A Jr 113 3.70 89-14 Persian Poet 122no Crown 1123¾ Clarinet King 112⁴ Weakened 11
27May84- 7Bel fm 1 Ⓣ:46⅗ 1:12 1:37⅗ Clm 75000 4 7 83½ 21 2½ 21½ MacBeth D 112 *2.70 76-34 Persian Poet 1121½ Freon 112¾ Alchise 107⁷ Gamely 9
23May84- 2Bel fm 1⅛ Ⓣ:45⅗ 1:09⅗ 1:41⅕ Clm 70000 7 7 78 44 32½ 42½ Bailey J D 113 *2.30 84-12 Quick Dip 1131¾ Clarinet King 117nk Roulette Wheel 108½ Rallied 11
17May84- 7Bel fm 1⅛ Ⓣ:46⅗ 1:10⅗ 1:41⅗ Clm 175000 4 6 64 55¾ 62½ 44½ Santagata N 112 3.80e 85-16 DHRed Brigade 116² DHRemanded II 112²FrayStar1142½ Even try 9
30Oct83- 2Aqu gd 1⅛ Ⓣ:47⅗ 1:13 1:52⅕ 3+Clm 75000 7 9 98½ 74 75½ 45½ Davis R G 117 *3.40 77-24 Red Brigade 119¾ Clarinet King 1171¾ No Neck 113³ Wide str. 12
23Oct83- 5Aqu sf 1 Ⓣ:49⅕ 1:15⅗ 1:43⅗ 3+Clm 250000 5 7 75¾ 54½ 45½ 33½ Davis R G 112 7.80 53-61 Ten Below 114¾ Prosper 116³ Freon 112⁶ Wide str 7
15Oct83- 7Bel sf 1½ Ⓣ:49⅗ 2:07 2:33⅗ 3+Handicap 2 4 57½ 67 69 88¾ Davis R G 111 4.50 48-42 Dilmoun 113¾ Piling 115hd Four Bases 105³ Fin after 1m 8
9Oct83- 7Bel gd 1 Ⓣ:48 1:13⅗ 1:39⅕ 3+Alw 40000 4 5 68½ 59 45 2½ Murphy D J⁵ 114 3.50 68-30 Forkali 115½ Freon 114hd Kilauea 1141½ Rallied 8
3Oct83- 7Bel gd 1⅛ :47⅗ 1:12 1:43⅗ 3+Handicap 5 2 42 46 39 38¾ Davis R G 115 3.10 75-19 Disco Count 1182¾ Clarinet King 113⁶ Freon 115⁶ Wide 5
LATEST WORKOUTS Jun 28 Bel tr.t 4f fst :49⅗ b ●Jun 7 Bel tr.t 4f fst :48⅕ h May 26 Bel tr.t 3f fst :36 b May 15 Bel tr.t 5f fst 1:02⅗ b

Quick Dip
Ch. c. 4, by Vigors—Red Bikini, by One For All
$70,000 Br.—Wimpfheimer J D (Ky) Tr.—Puentes Gilbert
Own.—Flying Zee Stables
115
Lifetime 30 5 4 3 $92,322 | 1984 6 2 1 0 $32,830 | 1983 15 0 2 3 $27,892 | Turf 15 3 3 2 $61,030

20Jun84- 5Bel fm 1⅛ Ⓣ:46 1:10⅗ 1:41⅗ Clm 75000 1 8 116¾ 109 76½ 65¾ Maple E b 119 6.50 83-17 Lutyens 108² Meru 1171½ Freon 113¹ Lacked room 12
8Jun84- 6Bel fm 1⅛ Ⓣ:45⅗ 1:09⅗ 1:42⅗ 3+Alw 22000 5 7 75½ 51¾ 1hd 11¾ Maple E b 117 15.20 83-14 Quick Dip 1171¾ Sir Roland 109hd Go Go Regal 109½ Driving 8
28May84- 7Bel fst 1⅛ :46⅗ 1:10⅗ 1:42⅕ 3+Alw 22000 1 4 26 49 413 420 Hernandez R b 119 5.30 71-17 Mock Court 119¹⁰ Cooper's Hawk 1094½ Inner Force 1095¾ Tired 6
23May84- 2Bel fm 1⅛ Ⓣ:45⅗ 1:09⅗ 1:41⅕ Clm 70000 1 6 42½ 21½ 2½ 11¾ Samyn J L b 113 4.60 87-12 Quick Dip 1131¾ ClarinetKing117nkRouletteWheel108½ Drew clear 11
11May84- 2Bel fm 1¼ Ⓣ:48⅗ 1:37⅗ 2:02⅗ Clm 50000 5 3 31½ 12½ 12½ 21 Samyn J L b 117 6.40e 81-17 Lutyens 108¹ Quick Dip 117¾ Class Hero 115½ Game try 10
28Apr84- 1Aqu fm 1⅛ Ⓣ:48 1:13⅗ 1:53 Clm 50000 3 2 21½ 21 57¾ 510¾ Squartino R A⁵ b 112 7.20 68-21 Full Deck 1133½ Ski Jump 1123½ Limit Position 1132½ Gave way 9
3Nov83- 5Aqu gd 1⅛ Ⓣ:48⅗ 1:14⅗ 1:53⅗ Clm 50000 6 2 2hd 31 68 716 Murphy D J⁵ b 112 7.30 60-23 Val DeLaMeuse113½CagleSprings1196¾AncientBarrister113³ Tired 12
6Oct83- 6Bel fst 1⅛ :48 1:12⅗ 1:44⅗ Clm 75000 2 5 21½ 32 44½ 58 Rivera M A b 117 4.60 72-22 Gallant Minded 117nk Joy Hour 113⁴ Super Rolfe 108³ Tired 7
29Sep83- 8Bel fm 1 Ⓣ:44⅗ 1:09⅕ 1:34⅗ 3+Alw 40000 7 3 37 34½ 56 78½ Rivera M A b 114 5.50e 81-17 HuntedLd1151¾BrightSecretry1124½CommndAttention117nk Tired 8
10Sep83- 3Bel fm 1 Ⓣ:46 1:09⅗ 1:35⅕ Clm 80000 2 5 31 2½ 1½ 21¾ Rivera M A b 114 5.20 87-15 Pulsate 1121¾ Quick Dip 114² The Ghost 122¾ Game try 8
LATEST WORKOUTS Jun 16 Bel tr.t 5f fst 1:02⅗ b Jun 5 Bel tr.t 5f fst 1:02 b May 19 Bel tr.t 5f fst 1:02 b May 5 Bel tr.t 6f my 1:14⅗ h (d)

Top Mechanic
Dk. b. or br. g. 6, by Lord Rebeau—Top Dare, by Top Gallant
$75,000 Br.—Evans & Saybe (Ohio) Tr.—Shapoff Stanley R
Own.—Corrado A G
117
Lifetime 27 4 7 8 $50,600 | 1983 13 0 2 5 $16,225 | 1982 14 4 5 3 $34,375 | Turf 2 0 0 1 $3,360

27Nov83- 9Tdn fst 170 :47⅗ 1:12⅗ 1:42⅗ 3+Alw 9000 9 11 87½ 75 66 67 Rivera H Jr 114 *1.70 84-20 Double Hits 122½ Sizeable Profit 1172½ Nashua's Armor 117¹ 11
19Nov83- 9Dar gd 1⅛ :47⅕ 1:12⅗ 1:51⅕ 3+American H 7 5 77½ 52 56¾ 513¾ Perrotta M 115 19.20 75-21 Bill Monroe 125nk Mitey J. 125¹²¾ Exterminate 115nk No factor 7
5Nov83- 9Tdn my 170 :48⅗ 1:14⅗ 1:47 3+Alw 9000 4 6 48 47 37½ 35½ Rivera H Jr 114 2.60 64-33 Brent's Clarion 115⁵ Nashua's Armor 116½ Top Mechanic 114¹ 9
9Oct83- 9Tdn my 170 :47⅗ 1:12⅗ 1:44⅗ 3+Alw 9000 8 7 69½ 34 2½ 3hd Rivera H Jr 114 *3.10 83-23 Fast Benny 122hd Brent's Clarion 115no Top Mechanic 1142½ 9
25Sep83- 9Dar fst 1⅛ :47⅗ 1:12⅕ 1:45 3+SAlw 12000 3 5 52½ 32 32½ 2nk Perrotta M 114 7.40 82-21 Exterminate 113nk Top Mechanic 1143½ Advance 113½ 8
17Sep83- 9Tdn my 170 :47⅗ 1:13⅕ 1:44⅗ 3+Alw 9000 2 5 47 34½ 36 43½ Borden D A 113 3.60 79-28 My Z. Bomb 1191½ Nashua's Armor 119¹ Dr. Canning 115¹ 7
31Jly83- 2Sar fm 1⅛ Ⓣ:46⅗ 1:10⅕ 1:49⅕ 3+Clm 75000 3 10 1018 1014 911 98½ McCarron G 117 11.40 85-08 Clarinet King 113½ King Neptune 117¾ Lava 117½ No speed 11
21Jly83- 5Bel gd 1⅛ Ⓣ:45⅗ 1:11 1:44⅕ Clm 80000 8 8 819 815 813 35½ McCarron G 114 30.40 70-27 Act It Out 1163¾ Fan Letter 1091½ Top Mechanic 114nk Rallied 8
19Jun83- 7Tdn fst 1⅛ :47⅗ 1:12⅗ 1:44⅗ 3+Fathers H 10 10 913 817 614 517 Borden D A 114 2.90 69-21 Joker Joseph1181½SecondQuarter1209½CurrentData114³ No speed 10
11Jun83- 8Tdn fst 170 :48⅕ 1:13 1:43⅗ 3+Alw 9500 1 4 48 36 32 22½ Borden D A 113 *1.00 85-19 Reggie's Winner1142½TopMechanic1131½Stiver'sTiger122² Rallied 6
LATEST WORKOUTS Jun 26 Bel 4f fst :48⅗ h Jun 20 Bel 1 fst 1:43⅗ b Jun 14 Bel Ⓣ 1 fm 1:42⅗ b (d) Jun 7 Bel 5f fst :59⅗ h

*Come To London
Ch. g. 5, by Comeram—Kalizma, by Tour du Monde
$70,000 Br.—Glen Appin Stud V (Aus) Tr.—Brennan Pat
Own.—Brennan B F
108⁵
Lifetime 26 4 7 4 $63,005 | 1984 3 0 0 0 $1,380 | 1983 15 2 6 2 $45,945 | Turf 26 4 7 4 $63,005

20Jun84- 5Bel fm 1⅛ Ⓣ:46 1:10⅗ 1:41⅗ Clm 70000 5 10 84½ 76 46 44½ Samyn J L b 113 19.10 84-17 Lutyens 108² Meru 1171½ Freon 113¹ Evenly late 12
9Jun84- 9Bel hd 1⅛ Ⓣ:45⅗ 1:09⅗ 1:40 3+SBlue Larkspr 1 6 42½ 76½ 714 718½ Graell A b 122 30.20 77-07 Val Danseur 1152½ Intensify 117⁷ Charging Through 1153¾ Tired 8
9Jun84-Run in divisions
27May84- 7Bel fm 1 Ⓣ:46⅗ 1:12 1:37⅗ Clm 100000 5 4 41½ 98¾ 710 610¾ Graell A b 122 24.60 67-34 Persian Poet 1121½ Freon 112¾ Alchise 107⁷ Lacked room 9
5Nov83 ♦8Flemington(Aus) fm*1¼ 2:01⅗ Ⓣ The Grey-Smith Stakes 4 Clarke M 120 5.00 — — Penny Edition 123¹ Dynamo 120nk Holsam 117 15
22Oct83 ♦5MooneeVly(Aus) sf*1½ 2:09 Ⓣ W.S.Cox Plate(Gr.1) 13 Didham E 126 100.00 — — Strawberry Road 1303½ Kiwi Slave 1301½ Mr. McGinty 126 13
12Oct83 ♦7Caulfield(Aus) sf*1¼ 2:06⅗ Ⓣ Coongy Hcp(Gr.3) 2nk Thomson B 118 5.00 — — La Cocotte 113nk Come to London 1181½ No Peer 123 9
5Oct83 ♦5Cranbourne(Aus) fm*1¼ 2:05⅗ Ⓣ Cranbourne Cup Hcp 3³ Thomson B 118 3.00 — — Noble Comment 116½ Warri Symbol 1122½ Come To London 118 14
22Sep83 ♦7Caulfield(Aus) sf*1⅛ 1:53⅗ Ⓣ Royal Show Hcp 2no Clarke M 122 4.50 — — Mevron Boy 116no Come To London 122½ Prime Walk 102 15
14Sep83 ♦6Geelong(Aus) sf*1⅛ 1:49 Ⓣ Kilmore Hcp 1¾ Clarke M 113 6.00 — — Come To London 113¾ Rare Decision 1151½ Glen Moriston 119 14
6Sep83 ♦7Sandown(Aus) sf*1 1:48⅗ Ⓣ Mulgrave Hcp 8 Thomson B 124 4.50 — — Power Cord 115nk Rossie Boy 111⁴ Expert 116 12
LATEST WORKOUTS Jun 26 Bel 4f fst :48 h Jun 7 Bel Ⓣ 3f gd :38 b (d) May 24 Bel 4f gd :49 hg May 20 Bel 6f fst 1:17 b

Clarinet King
Dk. b. or br. g. 8, by His Majesty—Chateau Quille, by Chateaugay
$70,000 Br.—Franklin Mrs J M (Md) Tr.—Ribaduo Robert
Own.—East Country Stable
113
Lifetime 94 16 17 17 $302,173 | 1984 7 0 1 3 $13,820 | 1983 17 5 5 1 $109,170 | Turf 37 8 9 7 $158,416

11Jun84- 7Bel hd 1⅛ Ⓣ:45⅕ 1:09⅗ 1:39⅗ Clm 75000 6 10 108½ 75 35½ 33¾ Smith A Jr 112 3.40e 93-14 Persian Poet 122no Crown 1123¾ Clarinet King 112⁴ Rallied 11
3Jun84- 5Bel my 1¼ :48⅕ 1:38 2:03⅕ Clm 75000 5 7 76 55 56 37½ Smith A Jr 117 4.10 74-23 Magic Michael 1131½ Hall OfHonor113⁶ClarinetKing117½ Wide st. 8
23May84- 2Bel fm 1⅛ Ⓣ:45⅗ 1:09⅗ 1:41⅕ Clm 75000 10 9 812 79½ 67 21¾ Smith A Jr 117 3.20e 85-12 Quick Dip 1131¾ Clarinet King 117nk Roulette Wheel 108½ Wide 11
6May84- 7Aqu gd 1⅛ Ⓣ:48⅗ 1:13⅗ 1:45⅗ Clm 75000 5 6 53 32½ 36½ 35 Smith A Jr 117 3.30 73-20 Ski Jump 1081½ Full Deck 1133¾ Clarinet King 117² Rallied 9
28Apr84- 7Aqu fm 1 Ⓣ:47⅗ 1:13⅗ 1:39⅗ 3+Alw 36000 5 9 914 89¾ 78½ 67¾ Smith A Jr 119 15.00 70-21 Tough Mickey121³Erin'sTiger1212½DominatingDooley119¾ Outrun 9
13Feb84- 1Aqu fst 1⅛ ⊡:48⅗ 1:13 1:51⅗ Clm 75000 10 10 107¾ 87 712 69 Smith A Jr 117 8.20 78-18 Mr. Badger 113⁵ Blue Quadrant 113½ Last Turn 117½ Outrun 10
2Feb84- 6Aqu fst 1⅛ ⊡:47⅗ 1:12 1:45⅗ Clm 175000 5 6 510 611 66½ 66½ Smith A Jr 113 16.40 78-22 Mortgage Man 1171¾Pinstripe1222½LarkOscillation114½ No threat 6
20Nov83- 7Aqu fst 1⅜ :50 1:41⅗ 2:21 3+Handicap 8 7 79 68 611 610½ Smith A Jr 111 3.00 65-23 Fleet Pirate 1121½ Field Cat 122³ Ten Below 1131¾ No factor 8
30Oct83- 2Aqu gd 1⅛ Ⓣ:47⅗ 1:13 1:52⅕ 3+Clm 75000 6 8 87½ 63½ 42½ 2¾ Smith A Jr 117 4.90 82-24 Red Brigade 119¾ Clarinet King 1171¾ No Neck 113³ Rallied 12
15Oct83- 7Bel sf 1½ Ⓣ:49⅗ 2:07 2:33⅗ 3+Handicap 4 6 69 78 79½ 78½ Smith A Jr 113 8.20 48-42 Dilmoun 113¾ Piling 115hd Four Bases 105³ Outrun 8
LATEST WORKOUTS Jun 28 Bel tr.t 3f fst :35⅗ h Jun 1 Bel tr.t 4f gd :48⅗ h

*Crown
B. h. 5, by Realm—Moneycashen, by Hook Money
$70,000 Br.—Exors of the late LtCol D S Cripps (Ire) Tr.—Gullo Thomas J
Own.—Corrado F L
113
Lifetime 29 5 4 4 $56,992 | 1984 5 1 1 0 $18,240 | 1983 7 0 0 2 $2,855 | Turf 27 5 4 4 $56,992

23Jun84- 7Bel fm 6f Ⓣ:22 :45⅘ 1:09⅘ 3+Alw 33000	10 8 106½ 88½ 84½ 53	Davis R G	117	4.10	89-18 Sitzmark 1171½ Meru 1171½ Rollin on Over 117½	Rallied 12
11Jun84- 7Bel hd 1 1/16 Ⓣ:45⅕ 1:09⅖ 1:39⅘ Clm 75000	8 4 21 2½ 2½ 2no	Davis R G	112	*2.70	97-14 Persian Poet 122no Crown 1123¾ Clarinet King 1124	Gamely 11
26May84- 2Bel fm 1 1/16 Ⓣ:46⅘ 1:12⅗ 1:43⅖ Clm 45000	6 4 31 2hd 13½ 18½	Davis R G	113	7.40	79-19 Crown 1138½ Fearless Leader 117hd Pumas Pride115no	Drew clear 11
18May84- 9Bel fst 7f :23⅕ :46⅘ 1:24⅖ Clm c-35000	6 6 31 64½ 88½ 77½	Terry J	117	5.60	72-17 The Time Is Now 1171½ Jet Steam 117hd Meru 1082½	Tired 12
9May84- 8Pim fst 1 1/16 :46⅗ 1:10⅘ 1:42⅕ Alw 18000	1 4 44½ 44½ 56½ 513½	Terry J	114	27.10	80-16 DeputdTstmony1146½HushHushFlsh1144¾BlckiDw1141½	Stumbled 8
5Nov83◆7Doncaster(Eng) gd 1 1:43⅗ Ⓣ Last Post Hcp	31	Oldroyd G	124	33.00	-- Star of a Gunner 112½ RomanBeach118½ Crown124hd	Closed well 27
17Aug83◆7York(Eng) gd 1⅛ 1:53⅕ Ⓣ Falmouth Hcp	14	Oldroyd G	115	14.00	-- Whisky Talk 1203 Music Lover 119nk Sagamore 1151½	Prom 6f 17
19Jly83◆3Ayr(Scot) gd 1 1:41⅘ Ⓣ Souter Johnie Hcp	73	Oldroyd G	136	11.00	-- DnishExpress118¾ WibisRnge130no RingBidder132hd	Led entr str 8
10Jun83◆3York(Eng) gd 1⅛ 1:50⅖ Ⓣ ElCapistranoVillasHcp	67½	Oldroyd G	119	5.50	-- Banoco 105no Wibis Range 1152 Silver Snow 1021	Speed 7f 11
2May83◆4Kempton(Eng) sf 1 1:55⅗ Ⓣ Jubilee Hcp	8	Oldroyd G	123	5.50	-- Elmar 1222 Minamax 1163 Lion City 117½	Bid,tired 12

LATEST WORKOUTS Jun 7 Bel tr.t 4f fst :49 b ●Jun 1 Bel tr.t 3f gd :35⅗ h May 24 Bel tr.t 3f gd :38 b May 17 Bel 3f fst :37 b

Majesty's World *
B. g. 9, by His Majesty—Spirit World, by Prince John
$70,000 Br.—Marsh J D (Va)
Tr.—Tammaro John III
Own.—Marsh J D
113
Lifetime 84 15 14 8 $425,023
1984 2 0 0 1 $2,125
1982 9 2 1 0 $117,305
Turf 15 2 1 0 $50,860

16Jun84- 5Mth fst 1 1/16 :48⅕ 1:12 1:43⅘ 3+Clm 50000	4 5 514 512 512 49	Bracciale V Jr	b 116	2.80	78-18 Acolyte 1076 Private Showing 1163 Disco Dom 112no	Evenly 6
26May84- 6Mth fst 1 :46 1:11 1:38⅖ 3+Clm 50000	5 6 622 516 510 39	Rocco J	b 116	7.60	72-19 VgbondSergent1164Admirl'sGin1075Mjsty'sWorld1161½	No threat 6
24Jun82- 8Bel fst 1 3/16 :46⅕ 1:11⅕ 1:56 3+Handicap	4 6 617 614 611 69¾	MacBeth D	b 118	5.50	91-12 Lueders 111nk Indian Toast 1124½ Switch Point 1101	Far back 6
13Jun82- 8Bel sf 1⅜ [T]:52⅖ 1:44⅘ 2:24⅘ 3+Bowlg Grn H	3 10 1011 75½ 86¾ 77¾	Nemeti W	b 112	63.30	25-67 Open Call 1244JohnnyDance1142½BaltimoreCanyon1161	No factor 10
8May82- 8Pim fm 1½ Ⓣ:48⅘ 2:04⅖ 2:30⅕ 3+Dixie H	9 13 1323 1314 1216 1012½	Bracciale V Jr	b 116	8.80	74-16 Robsphere 1201 Present TheColors113½RichandReady1154	Outrun 13
1May82- 7Pim fst 1 1/16 :45⅗ 1:09⅗ 1:41 Alw 23800	2 8 816 820 617 59½	Black A S	b 116	5.10	90-08 LuxuriantMan119½[D]TimTamber1198PrivateShowing114½	Bumped 8
28Mar82- 7Aqu fst 1 3/16 :48⅕ 1:12⅘ 1:56⅘ Handicap	2 7 714 710 713 616½	MacBeth D	b 123	2.30	61-27 Bar Dexter 11710 ReturnForGlory1071¾Bucksplasher109no	Outrun 7
13Mar82- 7Aqu fst 1⅝ ⊡:49⅗ 2:07⅖ 2:45⅘ Handicap	6 8 87½ 61½ 11 11½	MacBeth D	b 122	4.50	83-17 Mjesty'sWorld1221½NicePirte1183RturnForGlory1114¾	Ridden out 8
6Mar82- 8Bow gd 1¼ :48⅖ 1:38⅗ 2:03⅖ 3+J Campbell H	10 10 1013 85½ 43½ 1no	Black A S	b 112	29.60	103-20 Mjesty'sWorld112noSunnyWintrs114noThirtyEightPcs123½	Driving 10
20Feb82- 7Aqu fst 2 ⊡:25 2:39⅕ 3:29⅖ Handicap	1 5 43 1hd 32 22	MacBeth D	b 120	3.00	75-17 Nice Pirate 1152 Majesty's World 120no Wimpfybell1121¾	Gamely 6

LATEST WORKOUTS Jun 13 Mth 5f fst 1:04⅖ b May 23 Mth 5f fst 1:01⅘ b May 15 Mth 6f fst 1:13⅕ h May 8 Mth 5f fst 1:02 b

Dr. David Nathan
Dk. b. or br. c. 4, by Full Out—Misty Bride, by Hethersett
$75,000 Br.—Meadowhill (Ky)
Tr.—Johnson Philip G
Own.—Meadowhill
117
Lifetime 14 3 1 3 $56,100
1984 3 0 1 1 $7,260
1983 11 3 0 2 $48,840
Turf 7 2 0 3 $31,200

27May84- 7Bel fm 1 Ⓣ:46⅗ 1:12 1:37⅖ Clm 100000	1 6 63½ 87½ 811 712¾	Samyn J L	122	3.30	65-34 Persian Poet 1121½ Freon 112¾ Alchise 1077	No menace 9
19May84- 7Bel fm 1 1/16 Ⓣ:47 1:11 1:42⅕ 3+Alw 22000	1 5 44 44½ 46½ 35½	Davis R G	121	2.90	80-14 Onyxly 1132½ Fatih 1243 Dr. David Nathan 1212½	Lacked fin.bid 7
10May84- 6Bel fst 6f :23 :46⅖ 1:11⅗ 3+Alw 21000	5 5 67¾ 67¾ 67½ 21¾	Ward W A5	116	16.20	83-17 I'mARounder1101¾Dr.DavidNathan116nkFastEnough1102½	Gaining 6
8Nov83- 2Aqu fst 1 :45⅘ 1:10⅗ 1:37⅘ Clm 100000	5 7 66 56½ 55½ 1no	Samyn J L	122	4.50	77-26 Dr.DavidNathn122noWill'sFirst114nkTmpTown122nk	Wide, driving 7
27Oct83- 9Med fst 1 1/16 :47⅗ 1:12⅖ 1:44⅘ 3+Alw 14000	1 6 66½ 53½ 33 42¾	Samyn J L	112	2.30	82-20 LdiesFool1161½WlkTheBech116nkNtiveGroogle1111½	Stumbled st. 7
10Oct83- 3Bel fst 6f :21⅘ :44⅘ 1:10⅕ 3+Alw 24000	5 6 713 711 56 43½	Samyn J L	114	22.70	88-15 CauseForAppluse117noNerice1141½PmsMcAllister1171¾	No factor 7
2Oct83- 4Bel my 1 1/16 :46⅘ 1:11 1:42⅘ 3+Alw 26000	1 6 67 89½ 78½ 67¾	Samyn J L	114	3.50e	80-14 Lutyens 1142 North Glade 1191¾ Joycapade 1174	Fin.early 8
14Aug83- 5Sar gd 1⅛ [T]:48⅕ 1:13 1:52⅖ 3+Alw 21000	8 3 54½ 52½ 2½ 1hd	Samyn J L	117	9.60	78-25 Dr.DvidNthn117hdRogus'Wlk117nkHilColumbus1171	Wide, driving 9
1Aug83- 1Sar fm 1⅜ Ⓣ:39 2:28⅘ 2:42⅘ 3+Alw 21000	3 6 67 58 59½ 510¾	Samyn J L	b 112	6.00	60-29 RoyalContractor1176¾TrecleTom1121½ImperilRelm112½	No factor 7
16Jly83- 9Bel fm 1 1/16 Ⓣ:47⅗ 1:12⅖ 1:44⅕ 3+Md Sp Wt	11 7 41¾ 31½ 11 1nk	Samyn J L	b 116	3.80	75-16 Dr.DavidNathan116nkRogues'Walk1221½HilColumbus1165¾	Driving 12

LATEST WORKOUTS Jun 27 Bel tr.t 5f fst 1:04 b Jun 23 Bel 6f fst 1:15⅕ h Jun 18 Bel 4f fst :47⅘ h Jun 13 Bel 4f fst :53 b

Nicene
Ch. c. 4, by Believe It—Polyandry, by Marino
$75,000 Br.—Ohrstrom G (Ky)
Tr.—Jensen Kay E
Own.—Ohrstrom G
117
Lifetime 22 3 0 0 $20,112
1984 3 0 0 0
1983 12 2 0 0 $10,921
Turf 20 3 0 0 $20,112

20Jun84- 5Bel fm 1 1/16 Ⓣ:46 1:10⅖ 1:41⅖ Clm 75000	7 12 127½ 98 66½ 55	Davis R G	b 117	19.80	84-17 Lutyens 1082 Meru 1171½ Freon 1131	Late bid 12
26May84- 7Bel fst 1 :46 1:10⅗ 1:36⅕ 3+Alw 36000	7 5 68½ 815 920 925½	Maple E	b 119	24.90	59-15 Faces Up 1196 Nepal 119½ Starbinia 1195½	Tired 9
10May84- 8Bel fst 7f :23 :45⅘ 1:21⅕ 3+Alw 33000	7 6 74 712 726 729½	Skinner K	b 119	78.90	66-17 Fit to Fight 1247½ Cozzene 1192 Mugatea 1191	Wide 7
18Nov83◆6MLaffitte(Fra) gd*1 1:39 Ⓣ Prix Ocarina	711	Desaint J C	123	25.00	-- Val Danseur 128¾ Tameen 120hd Pale Crystal 1192	No threat 10
31Oct83◆4StCloud(Fra) gd*1 5/16 2:17⅕ Ⓣ Prix de Corbon Hcp	51¾	Desaint J C	120	*3.00e	-- Super Great 112hd Hijar 108hd Really Fabulous 1241½	Fin.well 17
27Sep83◆3Evry(Fra) gd*1¼ 2:03⅖ Ⓣ Prix duGrandMorinHcp	55½	Desaint J C	121	2.90e	-- Fiona 108½ Campera 110½ Angel Face 1132½	Raced evenly 11
5Sep83◆3CrLaroche(Fra) gd*1⅛ :00 Ⓣ Prix Ville deMarcqHcp	56½	Desaint J C	131	--	-- Vallee des Sauges 1174 Moonsilk 123nk Axylos 111¾	No threat 11
5Sep83-No time taken						
18Aug83◆4Deauville(Fra) gd*1¼ 2:06⅗ Ⓣ Prix d'Alencon Hcp	83½	Depalmas M	116	6.00	-- Bylly theKid132no Abdonski1081½ SingingBoy128½	No real threat 20
8Aug83◆4Clairfont'e(Fra) gd*1⅛ 1:50⅘ Ⓣ PrixGerard deChavagnac	43	Desaint J C	123	--	-- Val Danseur 128nk SquadronLeader123¾ TakeAStep1202	Fin.well 10

LATEST WORKOUTS Jun 27 Bel 4f fst :48⅕ h ●Jun 17 Bel 5f fst 1:00⅘ h Jun 9 Bel tr.t 4f fst :48⅗ h Jun 6 Bel tr.t 3f fst :36⅘ b

though he appeared to be the only speed in the race, he was hardly worth the risk at 5–2 odds, which were no doubt the direct result of good recent form on the grass.

MAJESTY'S WORLD

A nine-year-old gelding, this former graded stakes winner was making only his third start after a two-year layoff. As a shipper moving up in class, he seemed well-meant, at least for the scheduled grass race. Although assigned a mud-mark by the *Daily Racing Form,* the old, physically-suspect gelding did not figure to be helped by the laboring track he would face.

DR. DAVID NATHAN

A lightly raced four-year-old also extending beyond his pedigree, the "doc's" only offtrack effort showing was dull. His most recent performance was unexpectedly bad, and the subsequent five-week layoff further clouded the horse's current fitness. Was this "grass contest" meant to be a conditioning race?

NICENE

A French import with two awful dirt efforts, Nicene's latest race showed signs of life ("late bid"). The difference between this horse and Crown is that Nicene was bred in this country—indeed, was a son of Believe It, an outstanding racehorse capable of defeating Alydar in the Remsen as a two-year-old over a wet track the son of In Reality figured to relish. Nicene therefore had to be considered the horse with the bloodlines best suited for the flooded conditions. That, plus the hint of improvement last time, made him an interesting proposition at 12–1, the longest price on the board.

Under the conditions these horses would face, a decent price was mandatory. In this respect, Nicene had the most to offer. And, indeed, he ran right to his In Reality-line pedigree.

SECOND RACE
Belmont
JUNE 30, 1984

1 ¼ MILES. (1.59⅗) CLAIMING. Purse $23,000. 4–year–olds and upward weights, 122 lbs. Non–winners of two races over a mile since June 1, allowed 3 lbs. Of such a race since then, 5 lbs. Claiming price $75,000 to $70,000. Races when entered to be claimed for $65,000 or less not considered). (Originally carded to be run at 1 1/4 miles turf course.)

Value of race $23,000, value to winner $13,800, second $5,060, third $2,760, fourth $1,380. Mutuel pool $59,344, OTB pool $110,553. Quinella Pool $77,766. OTB Quinella Pool $166,456.

Last Raced	Horse	Eqt.A.Wt	PP	¼	½	¾	1	Str	Fin	Jockey	Cl'g Pr	Odds $1
20Jun84 ^{5}Bel^5	Nicene	b 4 117	7	7	5^2	$1^{1/2}$	1^1	1^1	$1^{4\frac{1}{2}}$	Maple E	75000	12.20
20Jun84 ^{5}Bel^3	Freon	7 113	2	1^{hd}	1^2	$2^{1\frac{1}{2}}$	$2^{1/2}$	2^2	$2^{1/2}$	Venezia M	70000	7.40
11Jun84 ^{7}Bel^3	Clarinet King	8 113	3	4^{hd}	3^2	3^4	3^6	3^8	3^{11}	Davis R G	70000	2.60
27May84 ^{7}Bel^7	Dr. David Nathan	4 117	6	5^3	6^2	5^2	$4^{1\frac{1}{2}}$	4^2	4^2	Migliore R	75000	4.40
16Jun84 ^{5}Mth^4	Majesty's World	b 9 113	5	$6^{1/2}$	7	6^3	$5^{1/2}$	$5^{1/2}$	$5^{1\frac{1}{2}}$	Hernandez R	70000	4.20
13Jun84 ^{5}Bel^4	El Fantasma	6 113	1	3^2	$4^{1/2}$	4^{hd}	6^8	6	6	Cordero A Jr	70000	7.70
23Jun84 ^{7}Bel^5	Crown	5 113	4	2^5	2^{hd}	7	7	—	—	Cruguet J	70000	2.90

Crown, Eased.

OFF AT 1:31 Start good, Won driving. Time, :24⅘, :49⅕, 1:14⅗, 1:40⅗, 2:06⅘ Track sloppy.

$2 Mutuel Prices:				
	11-(K)-NICENE	**26.40**	**11.60**	**5.40**
	3-(C)-FREON		**7.00**	**5.00**
	7-(G)-CLARINET KING			**3.40**
	$2 QUINELLA 3-11 PAID $95.20.			

Ch. c, by Believe It—Polyandry, by Marino. Trainer Jensen Kay E. Bred by Ohrstrom G (Ky).

NICENE moved through inside horses to make a bid at the far turn, made the pace into the stretch and drew away under brisk urging while remaining well out from the rail. FREON, prominent to the final furlong, was no match for the winner. CLARINET KING moved up while racing well out in the track on the backstretch, remained a factor to the stretch and weakened. DR. DAVID NATHAN failed to be a serious factor. MAJESTY'S WORLD was always outrun. EL FANTASMA tired badly. CROWN gave way soon after going a half and was eased when unable to keep up.

Many trainers prepare for the possibility of rain by entering off-track specialists in grass contests. If the rains materialize as forecast, the horse will race; otherwise it will be scratched. While this practice is especially prevalent in stakes races, one should be alert to the possibility whenever heavy rains cancel a scheduled grass contest.

For handicappers, the trick lies in the proper identification of such horses beforehand. In some states, such as New York, they can be quite easy to spot. The rules allow horses to be entered with the stipulation "dirt only" and to be placed on the also-eligible list pending a change in track conditions. This rule aside, many of these horses stick out as "not belonging"—until the rains come.

Let's take a look at the first race at Belmont on September 15, 1984, another mile-and-a-quarter contest switched to the main track by heavy rains. Originally eight horses—less than a full field—were entered in the body of the race, with two more names appearing on the also-eligible list, presumably set to compete only if the race were switched to the main track. When the rains came, four of the original eight were scratched, leaving a field of six to contest the issue:

WESTERN

Winless in thirteen starts in 1984, this horse has performed poorly in New York on the heels of four consecutive third-place finishes at Hollywood Park. His record shows no evidence of ability to handle an off track, or an eastern track, for that matter.

LUTYENS

Part of the favored entry, Lutyens has become a turf specialist over the years but has apparently performed well in the past over wet surfaces—better than his recent performance in the aptly named Tidal Handicap might suggest.

HARCOLITE

An Irish-bred three-year-old facing his elders, Harcolite has returned to his best form since moving back to the grass, a surface over which he won in Europe as a two-year-old. However, the sloppy conditions and age difference make him an unlikely winner.

BAG O' BUCKS

A Canadian invader winless in twelve starts on the grass, Bag O' Bucks has been on the board in twenty-one of thirty-four lifetime starts on dirt. But his ability to handle the slop remains an unknown, as does his proper placement in New York, although the high-priced claiming ranks hardly seem overly ambitious. Even though this horse's latest start came in a marathon grass stake in Canada, one gets the feeling that this "grass maiden" would not object if the race were switched to the main track.

1 BELMONT

INNER TURF COURSE
1¼ MILES
BELMONT PARK
START · FINISH

1¼ MILES. (InnerTurf). (1.58⅘) CLAIMING. Purse $28,000. 3-year-olds and upward. Weights, 3-year-olds, 118 lbs.; older, 122 lbs. Claiming price $200,000; for each $5,000 to $175,000, 2 lbs.

Coupled—Palace, Lutyens and In the Ruff.

Palace
Ch. h. 7, by Golden Palace—Miss Newberry, by Killam II
$175,000 Br.—Marsh Thoroughbred Farm (Va)
Tr.—Moschera Gasper S
Own.—Davis A
107⁵
Lifetime 62 11 15 7 $199,328 | 1984 9 1 4 1 $29,710 | 1983 13 1 4 1 $33,280 | Turf 28 7 12 3 $134,710

10Sep84- 1Bel fm 1⅜ Ⓣ:49⅕ 1:38⅗ 2:17⅕ 3↑Clm c-40000 7 9 96½ 64 53 22¼ Cordero A Jr 119 *1.80 74-20 El Fantasma 1172¼ Palace 119nk Turn To Johnny 117no Gamely 11
25Aug84- 4Sar gd 1⅜ [T]:50⅗ 1:41⅘ 2:20 3↑Clm 40000 8 8 86¾ 52 1½ 1nk Cordero A Jr 117 *1.20 68-32 Palace 117nk Pumas Pride 1132¼ Turn To Johnny 1171½ Drivng 10
11Aug84- 2Sar fm 1⅛ Ⓣ:48 1:12 1:49⅘ 3↑Clm 40000 3 4 42 54 42½ 2hd Velasquez J 117 *2.10 78-22 Freon 117hd Palace 1172¼ Esprit De Romeo 112hd Game try 11
1Aug84- 2Sar fm 1⅜ Ⓣ:48⅕ 1:12⅕ 1:55⅕ 3↑Clm 45000 4 7 75 64½ 33¼ 21½ Velasquez J 113 6.10 89-09 Lord Calvert 1171½ Palace 1131¼ King Neptune 117½ Wide 11
8Jly84- 2Bel fst 1¼ :48⅘ 1:37⅕ 2:01⅘ 3↑Clm 35000 5 7 44 48 312 416½ Samyn J L 117 6.40 73-15 Startop's Ace 1179 Share The Risk 1176½ HeroicSpirit119¾ Evenly 8
7Jun84- 3Bel fm 1⅜ [T]:47⅕ 1:37⅖ 2:14⅖ Clm 35000 7 5 63½ 2hd 27 210½ Cordero A Jr 117 *3.20 75-13 Oratavo 11210½ Palace 1172¾ Cannon Royal 112no 2nd best 12
21May84- 5Bel gd 1⅛ Ⓣ:46⅕ 1:11 1:43⅕ Clm 35000 2 8 84 98¼ 68 34¼ Santagata N 117 5.10 75-24 Gottagetup 1171½ Ski Jump 1193 Palace 1172 No menace 12
14May84- 9Bel fst 1 :45⅘ 1:11 1:35⅘ Clm c-25000 7 3 34 66¾ 78½ 712¾ Murphy D J 117 11.60 73-17 Big Izzy 1139 Jet Voyage 1172 Jungle Marsh 117½ Tired 12
5May84- 4Aqu fst 6½f :22⅘ :45⅘ 1:17 Clm 25000 7 7 84¾109 94½ 84¾ Murphy D J 117 24.70f 85-16 Jet Voyage 1152¾ Stiff Upper Lip 115no I'm Peppy 113nk Outrun 13
16Oct83- 1Bel fst 1 :45 1:10⅗ 1:36⅘ 3↑Clm 30000 8 6 1014 1011 911 813¾ Ayarza I 113 9.70 67-14 Alec George 115no Exuberance 1172¼ WimborneCastle117½ Wide 10
LATEST WORKOUTS Jly 26 Aqu Ⓣ 4f fm :49⅘ h

Western
B. h. 6, by Ack Ack—Restless Wave, by Restless Native
$175,000 Br.—Jones Aaron U (Ky)
Tr.—Barrera Lazaro S
Own.—Jones Aaron U
112
Lifetime 50 7 9 12 $334,660 | 1984 13 0 1 4 $36,125 | 1983 12 3 2 3 $182,700 | Turf 23 2 3 9 $138,400

1Sep84- 1Bel fm 6f Ⓣ:22⅕ :44⅘ 1:08⅘ 3↑Clm 180000 4 5 614 618 612 57 Skinner K b 115 8.80 91-14 Alev 113hd Unmistaken 1121½ Aristocratical 1145¾ Outrun 6
9Aug84- 5Sar fm 1⅛ Ⓣ:46⅘ 1:10⅘ 1:41⅘ 3↑Clm 200000 3 3 56 611 614 618½ Guerra W A b 122 4.60 69-19 Disco Count 1128¼ Fray Star 114hd Quick Dip 1126½ Tired 8
22Jly84- 7Hol fm 1⅛ Ⓣ:46⅘ 1:10⅘ 1:41 Alw 45000 1 3 32 42 2½ 3nk McCarron C J b 115 *1.00 94-08 Iron Leader 115nk Twin's Tornado 117hd Western1152½ Weakened 6
21Jun84- 8Hol fm 1⅛ Ⓣ:48 1:11⅕ 1:46⅘ Alw 40000 3 2 2½ 2½ 31½ 33¼ Black K b 116 11.10 95-05 TheNoblePlayer1152GreenwoodStr1151½Western1161½ WEakened 6
3Jun84- 9Hol fm 1⅛ Ⓣ:46⅗ 1:09⅘ 1:40⅕ Alw 40000 6 5 54½ 66 52¾ 34¼ Black K b 116 11.30 94-05 Vin St Benet 1172 Pin Puller 1222¼ Western 1161½ Rallied 6
25May84- 8Hol fm 1 Ⓣ:47⅘ 1:10⅘ 1:34⅕ Alw 40000 5 7 63¾ 54½ 56½ 36 Fell J b 115 22.10 91-04 Go Dancer 1152 Scrupules 1174 Western 1153 Mild gain 8
17May84- 8Hol fst 1 :46⅕ 1:10⅗ 1:36 Alw 35000 7 6 64¾ 55½ 610 610 Fell J b 114 7.00 76-18 Cyril's Choice 1144 EbonyBronze114¾Espontaneo1142½ No factor 7
4May84- 7Hol fst 6½f :22 :44⅘ 1:15⅘ Alw 40000 8 2 76½ 810 611 610 Fell J b 115 10.60 81-18 Motivity 1151 Haughty but nice 117noGeminiDreamer1195 Outrun 8
23Mar84- 7SA fst 1⅛ :46⅕ 1:10⅕ 1:41⅕ Alw 45000 4 3 38 59½ 611 612 Sibille R b 115 9.50 83-17 Fighting Fit 1222¼ Hula Blaze 1221½ Norwick 114½ Tired 6
4Mar84- 4SA fst 1⅛ :47⅘ 1:12 1:43⅘ Alw 45000 6 3 31½ 21½ 21½ 42 Garcia J A⁵ b 109 *1.30 82-17 Count Gema 121½ Croeso 116hd Norwick 1211½ Well up, no rally 6
LATEST WORKOUTS Sep 9 Bel 5f fst 1:00 h Aug 29 Bel tr.t 5f fst 1:02 b Aug 18 Sar 5f fst 1:01⅕ h Jly 18 Hol 4f fst :49⅘ h

Lutyens *
Ch. c. 4, by Avatar—Flying Buttress, by Exclusive Native
$175,000 Br.—Brant P M (Ky)
Tr.—Moschera Gasper S
Own.—Davis A
112
Lifetime 47 8 1 6 $148,656 | 1984 16 3 1 2 $63,576 | 1983 22 5 0 3 $79,920 | Turf 18 4 1 3 $82,416

6Sep84- 1Bel gd 1 Ⓣ:47 1:11⅕ 1:36⅘ 3↑Clm c-75000 1 6 54½ 55 43 23½ Cordero A Jr 114 4.80 77-27 Red Brigade 1183½ Lutyens 1141½ Freon 116no Best of others 8
29Aug84- 5Bel fm 1⅛ [T]:48 1:11⅘ 1:42⅘ 3↑Clm 75000 1 3 43 53½ 52 43 Ward W A⁵ 112 *2.20 86-14 Red Brigade 119¾ Come To London 119¾ Beagle 1151½ Weakened 7
8Aug84- 9Mth fm 1⅛ Ⓣ:49⅘ 1:12⅕ 1:42⅘+ 3↑Alw 17000 6 3 33 51¾ 44 45 Antley C W⁵ 110 3.20 84-13 Data Swap 115no Always Up 1153 St. Brendan 1152 Tired 6
30Jly84- 8Bel gd 1⅛ [T]:48⅕ 1:12 1:43 3↑[R]Viceregal 6 6 66½ 65½ 711 49 Guerra W A 115 18.50 77-29 Intensify 1227 Quick Dip 1151¾ Nepal 115nk Rallied 8
23Jly84- 6Bel yl 1⅛ [T]:48 1:12⅘ 1:45⅘ Clm 175000 6 7 614 58½ 44½ 33¾ Maple E 113 5.70 70-29 Quick Dip 1123½ Fray Star 114nk Lutyens 113½ Rallied 8
12Jly84- 5Bel gd 1 Ⓣ:47 1:11⅗ 1:36⅘ Clm 175000 10 5 63½ 51¾ 2½ 1no Lopez V⁵ 107 15.60 83-24 Lutyens 107no Fray Star 114nk Quick Dip 1124½ Driving 10
1Jly84- 8Bel sly 1⅜ :46⅕ 1:37⅘ 2:18⅗ 3↑Tidal H 3 2 2hd 34½ 515 529½ Lopez V 105 6.40 57-20 Win 11111 Anne's Lover 1089 Four Bases 1125¾ Tired 6
20Jun84- 5Bel fm 1⅛ Ⓣ:46 1:10⅗ 1:41⅗ Clm 70000 10 5 42¾ 22 11 12 Lopez V⁵ 108 17.10 89-17 Lutyens 1082 Meru 1171½ Freon 1131 Ridden out 12
7Jun84- 7Bel fm 1⅜ Ⓣ:49⅘ 1:38 2:14⅕ 3↑Alw 25000 7 2 42 3½ 43½ 46¾ Cruguet J 117 8.60 84-13 Talakeno 1172¼ Nassipour 1174 Head of the House 119½ Tired 7
20May84- 7Bel fm 2 Ⓣ:51 2:55⅗ 3:20⅘ 3↑Handicap 4 5 53½ 44½ 44½ 47½ Venezia M 112 11.70 91-13 Anne's Lover1142¾ErinBright1171¾Nassipour1202¾ Lacked fin. bid 10
LATEST WORKOUTS Aug 22 Bel 3f fst :36⅘ b Jly 20 Bel tr.t 3f fst :36 h

*Come To London
Ch. g. 5, by Comeram—Kalizma, by Tour du Monde
$175,000 Br.—Glen Appin Stud V (Aus)
Tr.—Brennan Pat
Own.—Brennan B F
112
Lifetime 33 5 9 6 $93,889 | 1984 10 1 2 2 $32,264 | 1983 15 2 6 2 $45,945 | Turf 31 5 9 6 $93,889

9Sep84- 9Del fm 1⅛ Ⓣ:47⅘ 1:11⅘ 1:48⅘ 3↑Royal Vale H 5 4 45 43½ 31½ 3nk Solomone M b 116 3.20 100-11 Castelets 114nk GeneralStrike114noComeToLondon116nk Fin. well 6
29Aug84- 5Bel fm 1⅛ [T]:48 1:11⅘ 1:42⅘ 3↑Clm 75000 5 7 75½ 63½ 63 2¾ Maple E b 119 2.80 88-14 Red Brigade 119¾ Come To London 119¾ Beagle 1151½ Gamely 7
24Aug84- 5Sar yl 1⅜ Ⓣ:49⅘ 1:15 1:59⅘ 3↑Clm 75000 5 1 1½ 3nk 12½ 18 Maple E b 113 2.70 69-40 Come To London 1138 Lord Calvert 112¾ Upmost1166 Ridden out 7
17Aug84- 3Sar fm 1⅜ Ⓣ:46⅘ 1:10⅕ 1:55 3↑Clm 70000 9 2 2½ 2hd 1hd 31½ Maple E b 113 4.30 89-17 GoldnChmpII1131½CrstldLun108nkComToLondon1131¾ Weakened 9
1Aug84- 5Sar fm 1⅜ Ⓣ:47⅘ 1:11 1:54⅕ 3↑Clm 50000 9 1 11½ 1½ 2½ 21½ Day P b 117 12.10 94-09 Red Brigade 1171½ Come To London 117¾ Broadly 115½ Gamely 10
21Jly84- 9Bel sly 1⅛ :46 1:11 1:43⅘ Clm 70000 6 7 819 717 728 739¼ Cruguet J b 113 17.40 44-21 King's Swan 1173 Beagle 1135 Jumbler 1105½ Outrun 8
6Jly84- 5Bel fst 1⅛ :46⅘ 1:11⅘ 1:43⅕ Clm 50000 7 4 31 43½ 813 719 Velasquez J b 117 5.80 67-18 Super Rolfe 1134½ Act It Out 1131 Lord Calvert 1171½ Tired 8
20Jun84- 5Bel fm 1⅛ Ⓣ:46 1:10⅗ 1:41⅗ Clm 70000 5 10 84½ 76 46 44½ Samyn J L b 113 19.10 84-17 Lutyens 1082 Meru 1171½ Freon 1131 Evenly late 12
9Jun84- 9Bel hd 1⅛ Ⓣ:45⅘ 1:09⅘ 1:40 3↑[R]Blue Larkspr 1 6 42½ 76½ 714 719½ Graell A b 122 30.20 77-07 Val Danseur 1152½ Intensify 1177 Charging Through 1153¾ Tired 8
9Jun84-Run in divisions
27May84- 7Bel fm 1 Ⓣ:46⅘ 1:12 1:37⅘ Clm 100000 5 4 41½ 98¾ 710 610¾ Graell A b 122 24.60 67-34 Persian Poet 1121½ Freon 112¾ Alchise 1077 Lacked room 9
LATEST WORKOUTS Jly 29 Bel tr.t 5f fst 1:01⅗ h Jly 15 Bel 4f fst :53 b

*Harcolite
Ch. c. 3, by Wolverlife—Born Friendly, by Takawalk II
$185,000 Br.—Osthus Mrs K (Ire)
Tr.—O'Brien Leo
Own.—Dileo P
112
Lifetime 18 4 1 2 $44,948 | 1984 11 3 0 2 $43,020 | 1983 7 1 1 0 $1,928 | Turf 13 4 1 1 $42,488

27Aug84- 6Sar fm 1⅛ Ⓣ:47 1:11⅕ 1:43⅘ 3↑Alw 25000 4 2 2hd 2½ 2½ 54 Migliore R 117 4.60 74-17 Roman Bend 117½ Haste to Finish 117¾ NoMan'sLand117no Tired 7
19Aug84- 7Sar fm 1⅜ Ⓣ:49⅕ 1:14⅕ 1:58⅕ 3↑Alw 22000 4 1 11 11 14 14 Migliore R 117 9.80 75-20 Harcolite 1174 Sir Star 119no Penzance 1171¾ Ridden out 10
9Aug84- 7Sar fm 1⅛ Ⓣ:48 1:12⅘ 1:43⅘ 3↑Alw 21000 9 1 13 1½ 12½ 13 Migliore R 112 11.60 78-19 Harcolite 1123 Ends Well 1124¾ Altered Style 1122½ Driving 12
2Aug84- 2Sar fm 1⅛ Ⓣ:48 1:12⅘ 1:49⅘ Clm 50000 8 3 31½ 3½ 1hd 32 Migliore R 117 3.80 76-19 All Night Stand 113¾ Star Coral 1101½ Harcolite 1172 Off slowly 10
22Jly84- 5Bel gd 1⅛ :45⅘ 1:10 1:42⅘ Clm 50000 1 2 21½ 31 34 37 Migliore R 117 7.60 83-13 Banquet I 1133½ Engadine 1193½ Harcolite 1172½ Tired 7
16Jly84- 2Bel fm 7f Ⓣ:23⅕ :46 1:23⅘ Clm 75000 10 1 52½ 41½ 43½ 73½ Migliore R 112 23.20 81-15 ColonialDays1121MrChromacopy118hdUpPopsAwinner116no Tired 12
18Jun84- 5Bel fm 1⅛ Ⓣ:47 1:12 1:44 Clm 45000 1 2 11 1hd 1½ 11 Migliore R 113 5.10 76-25 Harcolite 1131 My Friend Shep 108nk Sonspree 1136 Driving 10
1Apr84- 7Key fst 6f :22⅘ :45⅘ 1:10⅘ Alw 10500 6 8 75½ 77½ 615 614¾ Ruane J 115 17.90 73-25 Finest Light 1202¾ Robinsboy 1106¾ Chris Stork 1152½ No factor 8
28Mar84- 8Aqu gd 170 [•]:48 1:13⅘ 1:43⅘ Alw 21000 1 2 23½ 44½ 611 619 Deegan J C 117 45.30 63-22 Inner Force 1193¾ Kick Stand 1222 Upper Star 1172½ Tired 7
10Feb84- 7Aqu fst 6f [•]:22⅘ :46⅕ 1:11⅘ Alw 20000 2 9 95½ 810 816 819½ Deegan J C 117 24.80 65-20 I'm A Rounder 1222½ Greyfield 1225½ Gemmology 1101½ Outrun 9
LATEST WORKOUTS Sep 13 Aqu 4f fst :50⅘ b Sep 8 Aqu 4f fst :47⅘ h

Red Brigade
B. g. 5, by Daryl's Joy—Red Gossip, by Hard Work
$175,000 Br.—Mufson Rhoda (Fla)
Tr.—Barrera Luis
Own.—Happy Valley Farm
112
Lifetime 42 14 10 4 $260,240 | 1984 11 5 2 0 $80,980 | 1983 13 4 3 2 $102,620 | Turf 37 13 10 4 $254,240

6Sep84- 1Bel gd 1 Ⓣ:47 1:11⅕ 1:36⅘ 3↑Clm 90000 2 5 43 22½ 11½ 13½ Guerra W A b 118 2.90 81-27 Red Brigade 1183½ Lutyens 1141½ Freon 116no Ridden out 8
29Aug84- 5Bel fm 1⅛ [T]:48 1:11⅘ 1:42⅘ 3↑Clm 75000 2 2 31 31 3½ 1¾ Guerra W A b 119 3.20 89-14 Red Brigade 119¾ Come To London 119¾ Beagle 1151½ Driving 7
19Aug84- 5Sar fm 1 [T]:47 1:11⅕ 1:36⅘ 3↑Clm 85000 7 3 32½ 36½ 25 25½ Cordero A Jr b 116 2.40 87-20 Disco Count 1225½ Red Brigade 1162½ Forkali 118no Wide 7
12Aug84- 2Sar fm 1 [T]:46⅘ 1:10⅘ 1:36⅕ 3↑Clm 80000 9 5 3½ 2hd 11 1hd Cordero A Jr b 114 *2.00 95-07 Red Brigade 114hd Upmost 1123½ Forkali 1171½ Driving 10
5Aug84- 5Sar fm 1⅛ [T]:48⅘ 1:12⅘ 1:50 3↑Clm 75000 2 2 21½ 1hd 1½ 2hd Cordero A Jr b 117 *1.00 90-13 El Fantasma 117hd RedBrigade1172¾BlueEmmanuelle113½ Gamely 8
1Aug84- 5Sar fm 1⅜ Ⓣ:47⅘ 1:11 1:54⅕ 3↑Clm 50000 1 4 32½ 33 1½ 11½ Cordero A Jr b 117 4.50 95-09 Red Brigade 1171½ Come To London 117¾ Broadly 115½ Driving 10
21Jly84- 9Bel sly 1⅛ :46 1:11 1:43⅘ Clm 70000 2 2 24 818 840 852½ Bailey J D b 113 5.90 31-21 King's Swan 1173 Beagle 1135 Jumbler 1105½ Stopped 8
12Jly84- 5Bel gd 1 Ⓣ:47 1:11⅗ 1:36⅘ Clm 180000 8 2 1hd 1hd 52½ 77 Bailey J D b 114 20.00 76-24 Lutyens 107no Fray Star 114nk Quick Dip 1124½ Gave way 10
20Jun84- 5Bel fm 1⅛ Ⓣ:46 1:10⅗ 1:41⅗ Clm 75000 9 2 2½ 32 97½ 99¼ Cordero A Jr b 117 *1.40 80-17 Lutyens 1082 Meru 1171½ Freon 1131 Gave way 12
9Jun84- 3Bel hd 1⅛ Ⓣ:45⅘ 1:09⅘ 1:40⅘ 3↑[R]Blue Larkspr 5 4 64½ 76 78½ 79¾ Day P b 117 6.80 84-07 NativeRaid1175½RemndedII1221¾Who'sForDinner117nk Early foot 9
9Jun84-Run in divisions
LATEST WORKOUTS Jly 19 Bel tr.t 4f gd :53 b (d)

Quick Dip
Ch. c. 4, by Vigors—Red Bikini, by One For All
$175,000 Br.—Wimpfheimer J D (Ky)
Tr.—O'Connell Richard
Own.—Flying Zee Stables
112
Lifetime 35 7 5 5 $146,814 | 1984 11 4 2 2 $87,322 | 1983 15 0 2 3 $27,892 | Turf 20 5 4 4 $115,522

17Aug84- 7Sar fm 1⅛ Ⓣ:47⅘ 1:12 1:42⅘ 3↑Alw 36000 8 9 85½ 93¾ 42½ 11½ Samyn J L b 117 4.60 83-17 Quick Dip 1171½ Lost Canyon 114nk Roman Bend 115½ Driving 9
9Aug84- 5Sar fm 1⅛ Ⓣ:46⅘ 1:10⅘ 1:41⅘ 3↑Clm 175000 5 6 66 56 38 38½ Samyn J L b 112 *2.40 80-19 Disco Count 1128¼ FrayStar114hdQuickDip1126½ Broke from gate 8
30Jly84- 8Bel gd 1⅛ [T]:48⅕ 1:12 1:43 3↑[R]Viceregal 1 8 88 76½ 69½ 27 Maple E b 115 7.40 79-29 Intensify 1227 Quick Dip 1151¾ Nepal 115nk 2nd best 8
23Jly84- 6Bel yl 1⅛ [T]:48 1:12⅘ 1:45⅘ Clm 175000 8 4 39 25 2½ 13½ Samyn J L b 112 3.50 74-29 Quick Dip 1123½ Fray Star 114nk Lutyens 113½ Drew clear 8
12Jly84- 5Bel gd 1 Ⓣ:47 1:11⅗ 1:36⅘ Clm 175000 1 10 75 62½ 31½ 3nk Samyn J L b 112 15.50 83-24 Lutyens 107no Fray Star 114nk Quick Dip 1124½ Rallied 10
20Jun84- 5Bel fm 1⅛ Ⓣ:46 1:10⅗ 1:41⅗ Clm 75000 1 8 116¾109 76½ 65¾ Maple E b 119 6.50 83-17 Lutyens 1082 Meru 1171½ Freon 1131 Lacked room 12
8Jun84- 6Bel fm 1⅛ Ⓣ:45⅗ 1:09⅘ 1:42⅘ 3↑Alw 22000 5 7 75½ 51¾ 1hd 11¾ Maple E b 117 15.20 83-14 Quick Dip 1171¾ Sir Roland 109hd Go Go Regal 109½ Driving 8
28May84- 7Bel fst 1⅛ :46⅕ 1:10⅘ 1:42⅕ 3↑Alw 22000 1 4 26 49 413 420 Hernandez R b 119 5.30 71-17 Mock Court 11910 Cooper's Hawk 1094½ Inner Force 1095¾ Tired 6
23May84- 2Bel fm 1⅛ Ⓣ:45⅘ 1:09⅘ 1:41⅘ Clm 70000 1 6 42½ 21½ 2½ 11¾ Samyn J L b 113 4.60 87-12 Quick Dip 1131¾ ClarinetKing117nkRouletteWheel108½ Drew clear 11
11May84- 2Bel fm 1⅜ [T]:48⅘ 1:37⅘ 2:02⅘ Clm 50000 5 3 31½ 12½ 12½ 21 Samyn J L b 117 6.40e 81-17 Lutyens 1081 Quick Dip 117¾ Class Hero 115½ Game try 10
LATEST WORKOUTS Sep 11 Bel 6f fst 1:13⅘ h Jly 19 Bel tr.t 5f gd 1:01 h (d)

Bag O'Bucks Ch. g. 4, by Beau Buck—Bag Of Stars, by Bagdad
$175,000 Br.—Salinas M (Cal) Tr.—Donato Robert A
Own.—Rich M
112 Lifetime 46 5 9 9 $129,097 1984 15 1 2 3 $41,488 1983 19 2 4 5 $63,214 Turf 12 0 0 2 $20,816
19Aug84- 9FE yl 1½ Ⓣ:49⅘ 2:33⅕ 3+Niagara H 5 5 69½ 67½ 47 44½ Driedger I 111 31.55 — — Cost Control 1152 Bold Run 1171½ DRocamadour II121½ Checked 9
19Aug84-Placed third through disqualification
29Jly84-10WO fm 1 [T]:46 1:10⅗ 1:35⅘ 3+Alw 21000 2 8 912 88 511 42½ Dos Ramos R A 119 29.45 96-09 GunCrrige117¾PxNobiscum124noNncy'sChmpion1211½ Belated bid 10
21Jly84-10WO fst 7f :23 :45⅘ 1:24⅗ 3+Alw 16000 4 3 85½ 88½ 66½ 32¾ Fell J 124 10.15 84-15 Son OfTheNorth114¾GoneToRoyalty1212BagO'Bucks124nk Rallied 11
7Jly84- 9WO gd 6f :22⅗ :45⅘ 1:12⅕ 3+Alw 16000 6 2 11 2hd 31½ 46½ Fell J • b 124 3.30 75-25 French Regency1172½Aspirer1192½ReddyRoadster1191½ Weakened 7
2Jly84- 7WO fm 7f Ⓣ:22⅘ :45 1:22⅗ 3+Alw 16000 2 2 76 811 79½ 610 Dittfach H b 121 40.40 88-16 Gun Carriage 1174½AmericaSalutes1171½VictoriousEmperor1191½ 9
1Jun84- 7WO fst 6½f :23 :46 1:17⅗ Alw 16000 3 4 1hd 21 22½ 45¾ Attard L b 121 *1.35 79-26 Determinant 1242 Juan De Fuca 1243½ Squire Cornwall 115nk 6
21May84- 9WO fst 1 1/16 :47⅗ 1:11⅘ 1:44⅗ Eclipse H 8 2 1hd 1hd 1hd 44½ Attard L b 115 34.60 83-22 AskMuhammad1191½Diapason1191½GoneToRoylty1201½ Gave way 9
13May84- 8WO fst 170 :46⅘ 1:12 1:43⅗ Alw 21000 6 3 3nk 12 11 23 Attard L b 115 3.45 83-18 Pax Nobiscum 1243 Bag O'Bucks 1152 Wayover 1153¾ 6
17Apr84- 9GP fst 7f :23 :45⅗ 1:22⅘ Alw 18000 1 3 1½ 12½ 14 13½ Cohen G b 115 4.80 90-28 Bag O'Bucks1153½ElPerico1191DNorthernOcean1151½ Ridden out 8
3Apr84- 9GP fst 7f :22⅗ :45 1:22⅗ Alw 18000 3 1 2½ 2½ 22 3¾ Swatuk B b 117 13.80 90-20 A Native Yank 122½BantheBlues122nkBagO'Bucks1171 Weakened 9
LATEST WORKOUTS Sep 12 WO tr.t 4f sly :48⅘ h ●Sep 8 WO 6f fst 1:13⅘ h Aug 26 WO tr.t 5f fst 1:01⅗ h Aug 17 WO tr.t 4f fst :51⅕ h

Also Eligible (Not in Post Position Order):

In the Ruff Ch. c. 4, by Prove Out—Fairway Flight, by Tom Fool
$175,000 Br.—Floyd William (Fla) Tr.—Meschera Gasper S
Own.—Davis A
112 Lifetime 25 7 3 2 $160,198 1984 13 1 1 1 $38,458 1983 12 6 2 1 $121,740 Turf 1 0 0 0
3Sep84- 9Med fst 1¼ :46⅗ 1:34⅘ 2:00⅘ 3+Med Cup H 9 7 711 811 815 719½ Antley C W 109 15.70e 80-09 WildAgain1156CanadianFactor114noInevitableLeader116nk Outrun 9
18Aug84- 1Sar fst 1⅛ :49 1:13⅕ 1:50⅕ 3+Bld Reason H 4 2 41¾ 54½ 53½ 53½ Day P 110 *1.80e 80-15 Moro 123nk Fast Gold 116nk Exattic 109hd Tired 6
1Aug84- 3Sar fst 7f :22⅗ :45 1:22⅕ 3+Clm 100000 8 1 97½ 99¾ 99½ 914½ Espinosa R E7 115 26.60 76-13 Pinstripe 122¾ Meru 1121¾ Fleet Receiver 1122¾ Outrun 11
20May84- 7Bel fm 2 Ⓣ:51 2:55⅗ 3:20⅘ 3+Handicap 1 8 1027 1035 1049 1060¾ Bailey J D 122 10.30 37-13 Anne's Lover 1142¾ Erin Bright 1171¾ Nassipour 1202¾ Outrun 10
5May84- 6Aqu fst 1⅛ :47⅘ 1:12⅕ 1:50 Clm 175000 6 5 66 — — — Cordero A Jr 112 2.10 — — High Ascent 112hd Sharp Destiny 1125¾ By The River 107½ Fell 6
14Apr84- 8Aqu sly 1¼ [•]:47⅕ 1:37⅘ 2:03 3+Excelsior H 2 2 21½ 69½ 615 819 MacBeth D 116 2.10e 84-15 CanadianFactor1171½LuvALibra1171½CanadinClm108½ Done early 8
4Apr84- 7Aqu fst 1⅛ [•]:47⅘ 1:12 1:50⅗ 3+Alw 36000 7 3 44 56½ 612 618 Muino M M7 117 4.80 72-20 Luv A Libra 121hd Reinvested 119hd Startop's Ace 1218½ Tired 8
26Mar84- 8Aqu fst 1½ [•]:50⅘ 2:08⅘ 2:34⅗ Handicap 5 3 2hd 12 13½ 13 Cordero A Jr 120 *1.50e 76-28 In the Ruff 1203 Fleet Pirate 118nk Erin Bright 119nk Driving 8
17Mar84- 6Aqu fst 170 [•]:48⅕ 1:13⅗ 1:43⅗ Alw 25000 8 4 42 21 1hd 2½ Cordero A Jr 117 *1.50 81-22 Luv A Libra 117½ In the Ruff 1176½ Special Care 1172 Game try 8
10Mar84- 8Bow fst 1¼ :48⅗ 1:38⅗ 2:04⅖ 3+J B Camp'l H 7 3 43½ 53¾ 86¾ 86½ Edwards J W 116 6.70 88-20 Island Champ 115no Forceful Intent 1161LuxuriantMan1113 Tired 10
LATEST WORKOUTS Sep 1 Bel tr.t 4f fst :49⅕ b Aug 27 Sar tr.t 5f fst 1:04⅗ b Aug 16 Sar tr.t 4f fst :50 b Aug 9 Sar tr.t 3f fst :38⅕ b

Waitlist Ch. h. 5, by Avatar—Renounce, by Buckpasser
$175,000 Br.—Phipps O M (Ky) Tr.—Penna Angel
Own.—Phipps O M
112 Lifetime 15 4 1 1 $69,140 1984 7 0 0 1 $9,540 1983 5 3 1 0 $48,800 Turf 1 0 0 0
1Aug84- 3Sar fst 7f :22⅗ :45 1:22⅕ 3+Clm 100000 7 8 87½ 109¾ 76¾ 45½ Davis R G 122 8.50 86-13 Pinstripe 122¾ Meru 1121¾ Fleet Receiver 1122¾ Wide 11
2Jly84- 1Bel gd 1 :44⅘ 1:09⅗ 1:34⅗ 3+Alw 36000 4 3 411 414 414 514½ Bailey J D 115 8.60 79-15 Slew O' Gold 1157½ Cannon Shell 1151½ NorthernIce1083½ Outrun 5
2Jly84-Awarded fourth purse money
25Jun84- 8Bel fst 7f :23⅕ :46⅕ 1:22⅕ 3+Alw 33000 3 5 54 32 47 48¾ Bailey J D 119 *1.30 82-16 Verbarctic1178¾McMichel117hdTlcDuster111no Lcked furthr resp. 5
1Jun84- 8Bel fst 7f :22⅗ :45⅘ 1:22⅘ 3+Alw 33000 5 5 77 75¾ 46 34¾ Davis R G 117 13.30 83-20 DMagnetic Field II 109nk Reinvested 1174½ Waitlist 1171½ Rallied 8
10Feb84- 8Aqu fst 170 [•]:48⅗ 1:13⅗ 1:42⅕ Alw 33000 1 6 43 57½ 514 520 Cordero A Jr 117 8.60 70-20 Puntivo 1222½ Jacque's Tip 11710 North Glade 1175½ No threat 6
29Jan84- 8Aqu fst 1 1/16 [•]:47⅘ 1:12⅕ 1:43⅗ 3+Aqueduct H 5 9 95 96½ 78¾ 710½ Lovato F Jr 112 7.30 84-15 Moro 120¾ Jacksboro 1202 Ask Muhammad 1172 No factor 9
13Jan84- 8Aqu fst 1⅛ [•]:49⅘ 1:14⅘ 1:52⅘ Alw 38000 2 6 31 41¾ 54½ 56½ Lovato F Jr 117 3.50 75-20 Lark Oscillation 1151½ Deedee's Deal1153½ToErin119hd Weakened 7
12Sep83- 8Bel fst 1⅛ :47⅗ 1:11⅗ 1:49 3+Alw 30000 5 3 3nk 1hd 14 15½ Bailey J D 119 *.70 82-22 Waitlist 1195½ Count Normandy 117hd Bashert 1135½ Ridden out 5
20Aug83- 1Sar fst 1⅛ :47⅕ 1:11 1:50 3+Alw 23000 3 3 32 33 33 11¾ Bailey J D 119 *1.10e 85-16 Waitlist 1191¾ Kleiglight 117no Luv A Libra 1121¾ Wide str., clear 7
30Jly83- 1Sar fst 1⅛ :47⅕ 1:11 1:49⅗ 3+Alw 21000 6 3 42½ 31½ 2hd 1no Bailey J D 117 2.30 87-14 Waitlist 117no Inner Circuit 1125½ Norclin 1113¾ Bumped, driving 7
LATEST WORKOUTS Sep 10 Bel 5f fst 1:00⅗ h Sep 3 Bel 4f fst :47⅗ h ●Aug 17 Sar tr.t 5f fst 1:02 h Aug 16 Sar tr.t 3f fst :39⅕ b

WAITLIST

One of the two also-eligibles entered in the hope for rain, Waitlist is the rare claiming animal from the Angel Penna barn—not a positive sign. Winless in 1984, the horse has clearly failed to live up to the expectations he raised the previous year. The wet track may help the grandson of Graustark, but there are no other positive signs to recommend him.

IN THE RUFF

The other horse entered for "dirt only," In The Ruff was bred for the slop, being a son of the mud-loving Prove Out. Like Lutyens, though, the only offtrack race in his past performances was poor, albeit in stakes company. A claiming animal as a three-year-old, In The Ruff gained prominence the preceding winter in New York, performing well in several distance stakes—indeed winning the marathon Display Handicap at two and a quarter miles. He has now made three starts following a two-month freshening, and while the second of those races gave hope that a winning performance was forthcoming, it was followed by a dull performance in the Meadowlands Cup on September 3. However, with the hot-riding Robbie Davis accepting the mount, it appeared that race could be overlooked, leaving the horse "sittin' on ready," and this looked like the right spot.

Although it was not difficult to identify In The Ruff as the logical selection in this race, whether he, along with stablemate Lutyens, was worth a wager at 6–5 odds was another matter. If only this had been an exacta race—Bag O' Bucks rallied nicely to secure second place in upper stretch.

FIRST RACE
Belmont
SEPTEMBER 15, 1984

1 ¼ MILES. (1.59⅗) CLAIMING. Purse $28,000. 3-year-olds and upward. Weights, 3-year-olds, 118 lbs.; older, 122 lbs. Claiming price $200,000; for each $5,000 to $175,000, 2 lbs. (Originally carded to be run at 1 1/4 miles inner turf course.) (16th Day. WEATHER RAINING. TEMPERATURE 57 DEGREES).

Value of race $28,000; value to winner $16,800; second $6,160; third $3,360; fourth $1,680. Mutuel pool $124,729, OTB pool $131,892.

Last Raced	Horse	Eqt.	A.	Wt	PP	¼	½	¾	1	Str	Fin	Jockey	Cl'g Pr	Odds $1
3Sep84 ^{9}Med^{7}	In the Ruff		4	112	6	1^{1}	1^{1}	$1^{1\frac{1}{2}}$	1^{5}	1^{6}	1^{9}	Davis R G	175000	a-1.20
19Aug84 ^{9}FE^{3}	Bag O'Bucks		4	112	4	4^{hd}	4^{hd}	$5^{\frac{1}{2}}$	3^{2}	$2^{1\frac{1}{2}}$	$2^{1\frac{1}{4}}$	Driedger I	175000	5.10
27Aug84 ^{6}Sar^{5}	Harcolite		3	112	3	2^{3}	$2^{2\frac{1}{2}}$	$2^{1\frac{1}{2}}$	2^{hd}	$3^{1\frac{1}{2}}$	$3^{\frac{1}{2}}$	Migliore R	185000	5.10
1Aug84 ^{3}Sar^{4}	Waitlist		5	112	5	5	5^{1}	6	6	6	$4^{\frac{1}{2}}$	Hernandez R	175000	2.40
6Sep84 ^{1}Bel^{2}	Lutyens		4	114	2	6	6	4^{1}	$5^{2\frac{1}{2}}$	$4^{1\frac{1}{2}}$	$5^{2\frac{3}{4}}$	Cordero A Jr	175000	a-1.20
1Sep84 ^{1}Bel^{5}	Western	b	6	114	1	3^{1}	3^{1}	3^{2}	4^{1}	5^{1}	6	Vergara O	175000	6.30

a-Coupled: In the Ruff and Lutyens.

OFF AT 1:30 Start good, Won ridden out. Time, :24⅕, :48, 1:12⅖, 1:37⅗, 2:03⅘ Track sloppy.

Official Program Numbers↘

$2 Mutuel Prices:				
	1-(J)-IN THE RUFF (a-entry)	4.00	2.80	2.20
	7-(H)-BAG O'BUCKS		3.80	2.60
	4-(E)-HARCOLITE			2.60

Ch. c, by Prove Out—Fairway Flight, by Tom Fool. Trainer Moschera Gasper S. Bred by Floyd William (Fla).

IN THE RUFF raced well out from the rail while making the pace, shook off HARCOLITE nearing the end of the backstretch and drew away while being ridden out. BAG O'BUCKS finished with good energy to gain the place. HARCOLITE saved ground while showing speed to the turn and tired. WAITLIST was always outrun. LUTYENS saved ground to no avail. WESTERN rallied racing into the turn but was finished soon after going six furlongs.

Chapter 24

When the Going Gets Tough

EVERYONE HAS HEARD THE old saw "When the going gets tough, the tough get going." In racing parlance, this might translate to "When the going gets wet, some horses endure it better than most." In many cases, identifying the horse that seems to revel in the off going proves the key to handicapping on rainy days.

Off-track racing presents its own special obstacles, to horses and players alike. Both the slippery surface underfoot and the flying mud affect the outcome of races, further complicating the issue. Determining which horse or horses will handle the conditions, however, can be a tricky proposition.

There can be a vast difference between a track termed "sloppy" and one designated "muddy." The horse that likes one might despise the other. Whether it be the size or shape of their feet, or the length of their stride, some horses get better traction over a sloppy surface than a muddy one, while others are more comfortable in the mud. The player must be careful when he declares that a given horse likes the off going and should be sure the horse likes the particular type of wet track he will be facing.

As a rule, wet tracks tend to favor front-runners, and this is no doubt due to the splashing mud that can easily discourage horses attempting to come from behind. The fact that a horse might rally strongly in the slop on one occasion, then fail to fire on a similar day, however, can probably be explained by position, if not form. The horse may have been racing on the outside when it ran well and was then buried along the rail when it raced poorly. Apart from the higher density of flying mud, the rail at many tracks offers the deepest, heaviest going and is without question the worst place to be on that racetrack.

The distance of races can also confound off-track form. A horse that goes wire-to-wire at a mile and a sixteenth in the slop has proven nothing about its ability to race from behind at sprint distances on wet racetracks. Conversely, the horse that has failed to rally in wet track sprints may not dislike the track conditions but simply resent the mud in its face. Given the chance to go on the lead in a route, such a horse might easily astound those who had incorrectly interpreted its (lack of) off track form.

The true mud lover, then, is the horse that can rally from behind while racing on the inside. The horse has proven that it can handle the surface and endure the conditions. To refine previous statements, then, the key to handicapping in the rain often proves to be the player's ability to identify the horse that has proven itself at the distance under similar conditions—and his awareness of the fact that many horses perform well in the slop or mud only when presented with specific circumstances that favor their running style and/or post position.

As an example, let's take a look at the field for the ninth race at Aqueduct on October 24, 1984, scheduled for the one-turn mile distance over a track labeled muddy. Earlier races on the card had been won by a mixed bag of horses, suggesting an unbiased racing surface. Four early scratches allowed Tarberry, George Cinq, Stoney Lonesome, and Gauguin Native into the race, in posts 9 through 12, respectively.

JOY HOUR

This horse raced well, earning a good figure in this class at Belmont two races back over a drying-out surface. But with just two wins in twenty-nine starts over the last two years, it would seem that a second win in three starts might be asking too much.

MARINE BRASS

Idle since July, is a very negative consideration over a track that might be "laboring" and place a premium on fitness. And since that July race was the five-year-old's only start of the year, his soundness has to be suspect as well. But then, why did Mike Sedlacek, one of New York's leading claiming trainers, add the horse to his string? And why did the usually astute New York audience establish him as their 3–1 favorite? Finally, just where did this allowance horse from Maryland fit into the New York claiming ranks? Probably in a higher classification, if he was still the runner he had been in 1983.

9 AQUEDUCT 1 MILE AQUEDUCT

1 MILE. (1.33⅕) CLAIMING. Purse $16,000. 3-year-olds and upward. Weight, 3-year-olds, 119 lbs. Older, 122 lbs. Non-winners of two races at a mile or over since October 1 allowed 3 lbs. Of such a race since then, 5 lbs. Claiming price $25,000; for each $2,500 to $20,000 allowed 2 lbs. (Races when entered to be claimed for $18,000 or less not considered.)

Coupled—Mingo and Creme De La Fete.

Tachycardia
B. m. 5, by Spanish Riddle—Gladys II, by All Serene
$25,000 Br.—Wilson J J (Va)
Tr.—Dutrow Richard E
Own.—Majorca D G
109 5
Lifetime 44 8 10 5 $59,250
1984 14 4 4 1 $29,665
1983 13 2 4 2 $17,175
Turf 2 0 0 0

12Oct84- 9Bel fst 7f :23 :46⅕ 1:24⅕ 3↑ⒻClm 30000 4 2 1hd 2hd 44½ 48 MacBeth D 113 15.50 73-22 Extemp 117hd Wench 1177 Tarpis 1171 Gave way 8
27Sep84- 3Lrl fst 6f :23 :47 1:12⅗ 3↑ⒻClm 25000 1 1 53 57 57½ 45 Jenkins J P5 110 *1.90 75-22 Nalees Blues 1144 Miss Self 111½ Net 115½ Evenly 7
23Aug84- 2Mth fst 1 :46⅘ 1:11⅗ 1:38⅘ 3↑ⒻClm 25000 4 2 21½ 21 31½ 24 Miller D A Jr 116 1.80 77-21 Fenian'sRainbow1194Tachycrdi116nkReglCopper1092½ Gained 2nd 6
6Aug84- 7Mth fst 170 :45⅘ 1:10⅘ 1:41⅗ 3↑ⒻClm 20000 8 1 15 12½ 1hd 34½ Melendez J D 116 4.80 83-20 Axe Me Nicely 116½ Ring On Doc 1114Tachycardia1162 Weakened 8
18Jly84- 5Mth sly 6f :22⅖ :45⅘ 1:12 3↑ⒻClm 25000 2 6 77½ 814 614 58½ Miller D A Jr 116 5.00 71-17 CommnderNThif1174½PickinPg119½Fnin'sRinbow116nk No factor 8
20Jun84- 5Mth fst 6f :22⅗ :45⅘ 1:11⅕ 3↑ⒻClm 32000 2 5 22½ 55½ 610 610½ Antley C W5 111 3.20 74-15 Extemp 114hd Sunshine Sandal 1115 Dareport 111nk Tired 6
23May84- 5Mth fst 1 1/16 :47⅕ 1:12⅘ 1:44 3↑ⒻClm 32500 5 2 1hd 11 2½ 21 Miller D A Jr 114 2.90 75-22 Czarland 1091 Tachycardia 1143 Something Fine 1142½ Came in 6
3May84- 6Mth fst 170 :47⅘ 1:12⅗ 1:43⅘ 3↑ⒻClm 30000 5 2 11 12½ 12 21½ Antley C W5 109 3.60 78-24 Great Land 1181½ Tachycardia 109nk Jennifer's Lady 1096 Gamely 6
10Apr84- 7Pim fst 1 1/16 :47 1:12⅕ 1:44⅘ ⒻAlw 17000 7 3 46½ 88¾ 814 918½ Jenkins J P5 112 5.50 63-19 Center Field 115hd Longwinner 1191 Ting A Ling 114½ Wide 9
8Mar84- 8Bow fst 1 1/16 :48⅗ 1:13⅗ 1:47 ⒻAlw 8000 4 1 11 12 12 1hd Hunter M T5 114 *1.60 71-35 Tachycardia 114hd R. K.'s Issue 1193½ Bishop's Fling 1141 Driving 6
LATEST WORKOUTS Oct 8 Aqu 4f fst :50⅘ b ●Sep 14 Lrl 6f fst 1:13 h

Joy Hour
Dk. b. or br. c. 4, by Bold Hour—J. A's Joy, by Johns Joy
$25,000 Br.—Mitchell & Johnson (Ky)
Tr.—Kelly Edward I Jr
Own.—Jayeff Stables
119
Lifetime 36 4 4 2 $57,560
1984 10 1 1 0 $11,840
1983 19 1 3 1 $36,366
Turf 12 2 1 1 $12,134

11Oct84- 3Bel fst 7f :23⅕ :46⅘ 1:24⅘ 3↑Clm 45000 6 2 51¾ 54½ 69½ 69¾ Cruguet J b 113 12.20 69-26 Hollywood Hendrson 1083 LordHatchet1081½BigMcCoy115½ Tired 7
3Oct84- 3Bel gd 1 1/16 :47 1:12⅘ 1:46 3↑Clm 22500 4 3 21½ 11½ 14 16 Cruguet J b 115 4.10 72-26 Joy Hour 1156 Creme De La Fete113¾SinghAmerica1173½ Handily 7
14Sep84- 5Bel fst 6f :22⅘ :46⅕ 1:10⅕ 3↑Clm 25000 3 7 64½ 66¾ 66¾ 45¾ Cruguet J b 117 12.60 85-18 BigMcCoy1075CanadianCurrency117½Jordan'sGry117nk Mild Rally 10
6Sep84- 7Bel gd 1 1/16 Ⓣ:50 1:14 1:44⅘ 3↑Alw 22000 5 1 1hd 89 821 817½ Cordero A Jr 117 19.40 59-27 Ends Well 1181¾ Fatih 117½ Steepbank 1131¾ Stopped 8
17Aug84- 8Atl fm 1 1/16 ①:48 1:12⅘ 1:44⅕ 3↑Alw 7000 5 4 34 2hd 23½ 21½ Terry J 116 4.00 83-18 Reliable Jeff 1121½ Joy Hour 1162½DuetForOne1223½ Second best 6
25May84- 2Bel fst 7f :23⅕ :46⅗ 1:24 Clm 25000 2 11 115½105¾ 77½ 86½ Cruguet J b 117 20.60 76-23 Palimony 1102½ Midway Flyer 107½ What A Wabbit 1121 Outrun 14
14May84- 9Bel fst 1 :45⅘ 1:11 1:35⅘ Clm 25000 9 5 24 33 58 914¾ Cruguet J b 117 4.00 71-17 Big Izzy 1139 Jet Voyage 1172 Jungle Marsh 117½ Tired 12
19Apr84- 7Aqu fst 7f :23 :46⅕ 1:23⅘ Clm 45000 7 2 53½ 76½ 711 712½ MacBeth D b 113 20.00 69-26 Starbinia 1133 Top Hat 117¾ Mighty Nasty 117hd Outrun 8
25Feb84- 1Aqu gd 1 1/16 ⊡:47⅘ 1:12 1:43⅘ Clm 75000 1 2 1hd 54½ 78¾1115½ MacBeth D b 117 18.30 79-12 Bidamex 1082¾ Last Turn 117hd Deedee's Deal 1175 Gave way 11
4Jan84- 5Aqu fst 1 1/16 ⊡:47⅘ 1:12⅘ 1:46⅕ Clm 75000 5 6 610 710 821 820½ Samyn J L b 117 5.70 60-25 Hollywood Hendrson 113nk LastTurn1173½HardKnot117nk Outrun 8
LATEST WORKOUTS Sep 30 Bel tr.t 4f fst :49⅘ b Sep 3 Bel 4f fst :48⅘ h

Stoney Lonesome
Dk. b. or br. g. 4, by Caro—Princess Red Wing, by Prince John
$25,000 Br.—Morrisania Oaks Farm (Ky)
Tr.—Watters Sidney Jr
Own.—Clark S C Jr
117
Lifetime 23 3 4 1 $61,340
1984 9 0 0 0 $1,620
1983 9 2 1 0 $34,340
Turf 9 2 1 0 $34,460

29Sep84-10Med fst 1 :47⅘ 1:12⅘ 1:38⅘ 3↑Clm 40000 7 7 78 89¾ 813 821½ Skinner K b 116 12.80 67-21 Dawn Encounter 1162 Youesaye 122hd Tarpaulin 1154½ Wide 8
22Sep84- 2Bel fst 1 :46⅘ 1:11⅘ 1:37⅘ 3↑Clm 50000 8 7 42½ 42½ 89½119½ Skinner K 117 31.40 69-19 Talc Power 108¾ Harpers Bazaar 1171½ Big McCoy 1131½ Tired 11
6Sep84- 5Bel fst 7f :22⅘ :46 1:23 3↑Clm 50000 8 6 94½ 54 86½ 76¾ Cruguet J 117 25.50 80-17 HrpersBzr1131¾Mr.Bdger113nkHollywoodHndrson1131½ No factor 9
19Aug84- 5Sar fm 1 Ⓣ:47 1:11⅘ 1:36⅘ 3↑Clm 100000 4 4 42½ 48 68¾ 718¾ Cruguet J 122 *.90e 73-20 Disco Count 1225½ Red Brigade 1162½ Forkali 118no Tired 7
12Aug84- 2Sar fm 1 Ⓣ:46⅘ 1:10⅘ 1:36⅕ 3↑Clm 100000 10 8 812 88¾ 63¾ 44¾ Cruguet J 122 18.10 90-07 Red Brigade 114hd Upmost 1123½ Forkali 1171½ Lacked fin.bid 10
1Aug84- 3Sar fst 7f :22⅘ :45 1:22⅕ 3↑Clm 100000 3 9 51¾ 65½1011 1021½ Cruguet J 122 39.90 70-13 Pinstripe 122¾ Meru 1121¾ Fleet Receiver 1122¾ Outrun 11
16Jly84- 8Bel fm 7f ①:23⅘ :46⅕ 1:22 3↑Alw 33000 2 6 63¾ 55½ 611 712 Lovato F Jr 115 10.90 82-15 Stay The Course 1098 Azarin 115hd Eskimo 1173 No threat. wide 7
25Jun84- 7Bel fst 1 1/16 :46⅘ 1:11⅕ 1:42⅘ 3↑Alw 25000 1 1 1½ 1hd 814 832½ Cruguet J 117 19.60 56-16 Vision 112½ Raja's Shark 111½ Super Rolfe 1176 Stopped 8
10Jun84- 7Bel fst 6f :22⅕ :45⅖ 1:10⅘ 3↑Alw 23000 8 8 87 89 812 812½ Cruguet J 117 37.40 75-20 TheWeddingGuest112hdUnmistken117nkI'mARoundr111no Trailed 8
5Sep83- 7Bel fst 7f :22⅘ :45⅖ 1:24⅕ 3↑Alw 27000 3 9 76½ 77 78 811½ Cruguet J 113 36.10 69-20 Cozzene 1151½ Dave The Dude 1172 Ecstatic Pride 1131½ Outrun 9
LATEST WORKOUTS Oct 18 Bel 4f fst :48 h Sep 17 Bel 5f fst 1:00⅘ h Sep 1 Bel 4f fst :46⅘ h

Tarberry
Ch. h. 6, by Avatar—Dawn Sky, by Imbros
$25,000 Br.—Asbury C A & T H (Ky)
Tr.—O'Connell Richard
Own.—Flying Zee Stable
117
Lifetime 52 8 6 6 $128,550
1984 15 0 2 1 $10,320
1983 13 3 0 2 $46,770
Turf 2 0 0 0

17Oct84- 2Bel fst 7f :22⅘ :45⅘ 1:24⅕ 3↑Clm 25000 6 9 55 35 42 42¾ Maple E b 117 18.00 78-21 J. Strap 1101½ Speier's Luck 117¾ Faded Poster 117¾ Weakened 13
15Sep84- 2Med sly 1 1/16 :47⅘ 1:12⅘ 1:45⅖ 3↑Clm 25000 5 4 43½ 58½ 511 517½ Rivera M A b 116 *2.60 64-24 Asticou 1164½ Bloomin Bliss 1164½ Here's to Paul 1195 Tired 7
5Sep84- 3Bel gd 7f :23⅕ :45⅗ 1:22⅘ 3↑Clm 25000 2 6 54 49 59 58 Cordero A Jr b 117 3.70 80-12 Sailing Light 113no Rauschenberg 1081 Palimony 1135¾ Evenly 7
26Aug84- 3Sar fst 6½f :22⅘ :45⅘ 1:17⅕ 3↑Clm 25000 5 11 108¾ 65½ 66½ 25¾ Cordero A Jr b 117 5.30 80-15 The Time Is Now 1195¾ Tarberry 117no Sailing Light113hd Rallied 12
9Aug84- 9Sar fst 6f :22⅘ :45⅖ 1:10 3↑Clm 30000 11 12 118¾1212 1215 1012½ Samyn J L b 113 9.00 78-14 CutterSrk1173¾JustAnyTime1171WildMomnt117no Always outrun 12
2Jly84- 3Bel fst 1 :45⅘ 1:11 1:36⅘ Clm 25000 6 8 88½ 55 24 21½ Maple E b 117 4.60 81-15 Gauguin Native 1121½ Tarberry 1173 Daring Bet 1083½ Rallied 9
20Jun84- 9Bel fst 7f :22⅘ :45⅘ 1:24⅘ Clm 25000 5 10 97½ 65½ 37 36½ Maple E b 117 6.20 72-18 Gauguin Native 1102½ Act It Out 1173¾ Tarberry 1171 Wide 11
3Jun84- 2Bel my 7f :22⅘ :46 1:23⅘ Clm 25000 10 10 106¾ 96½ 76½ 42 MacBeth D b 117 18.10 81-23 ColdTrailin'1101¾CraftyIrishman107hdCremeDeLFete117nk Rallied 12
28Apr84- 9Aqu fst 7f :22⅘ :45⅗ 1:23⅘ Clm 35000 4 10 54½ 812 914 1111½ Squartino R A5 b 112 14.60 70-21 What A Charger 117no Jet Steam 117no FearlessLeader117¾ Tired 12
24Mar84- 9Aqu fst 170 ⊡:48⅕ 1:13⅗ 1:45⅖ Clm 35000 2 1 11 2hd 31 83½ Muino M M7 b 110 5.00 70-24 JungleMrsh113noClerTheBses113hdEdgOfWisdom113hd Gave way 10
LATEST WORKOUTS Oct 14 Bel tr.t 4f fst :50 b ●Oct 7 Bel tr.t 5f fst 1:02⅖ b Aug 24 Sar tr.t 4f my :49⅘ h

Creme De La Fete *
Ch. g. 8, by Creme Dela Creme—Bridge Day, by Tudor Minstrel
$20,000 Br.—Collett & Polk Jr (Ky)
Tr.—Moschera Gasper S
Own.—Davis A
108 5
Lifetime 136 36 25 15 $422,345
1984 26 7 5 3 $75,660
1983 30 9 7 4 $127,240
Turf 3 0 0 0 $174

21Oct84- 3Bel fst 1 :46⅘ 1:12⅕ 1:37⅘ 3↑Clm c-15500 5 3 66 53½ 32 3nk Ward W A5 b 108 *1.40 76-21 Inner Circuit 108no Pitchpipe 115nk CremeDeLaFete1083¾ Rallied 10
12Oct84- 2Bel fst 7f :23⅘ :46⅘ 1:24⅘ 3↑Clm 15500 6 3 42 53 64 3½ Maple E b 113 5.30 79-22 Ample Native 115hd Mingo 117½ Creme De LaFete1131¾ Wide str 8
8Oct84- 2Bel fst 7f :23 :47⅕ 1:26 3↑Clm c-12000 7 8 83¾ 94¾ 31½ 1¾ MacBeth D b 115 *3.00 72-28 Creme De La Fete115¾GeorgeCinq1173½DComedion117nk Driving 14
3Oct84- 3Bel gd 1 1/16 :47 1:12⅘ 1:46 3↑Clm 20000 6 2 33 33½ 24 26 MacBeth D b 113 *.70e 66-26 JoyHour1156CremeDeLFete113¾SinghAmeric1173½ Best of others 7
28Sep84- 9Bel gd 7f :23 :46⅘ 1:24⅘ 3↑Clm 12000 8 1 41½ 85½ 63¾ 1nk MacBeth D b 113 *2.40 78-26 CremDLFt113nkGorgCinq117nkMidwyFlyr1171½ Came out, driving 8
27Jun84- 3Bel fst 1 :45⅘ 1:11⅕ 1:37⅘ Clm 16500 4 6 87 66½ 67 65½ Cordero A Jr b 115 *1.20e 71-17 Verbum 117no Dr. Butcher 1082½ Hugh Capet 1192¾ Raced wide 10
20Jun84- 9Bel fst 7f :22⅘ :45⅘ 1:24⅘ Clm 22500 7 2 31½ 43½ 820 911¾ MacBeth D b 115 3.30 66-18 Gauguin Native 1102½ Act It Out 1173¾ Tarberry 1171 Tired 11
3Jun84- 2Bel my 7f :22⅘ :46 1:23⅘ Clm 25000 12 1 42 53½ 45½ 31¾ Velasquez J b 117 *1.80 81-23 ColdTrailin'1101¾CrftyIrishmn107hdCremeDeLFete117nk Wide str 12
27May84- 2Bel fst 7f :23 :46⅖ 1:23⅖ Clm 17500 9 1 31 1hd 11 11 MacBeth D b 119 *1.50e 85-20 Creme De La Fete 1191 Rasselas 118¾ Jet Voyage 1192½ Driving 9
24May84- 5Bel fst 1⅛ :47⅖ 1:11⅘ 1:49⅕ Clm 22500 3 2 2½ 21½ 512 515½ Cordero A Jr b 115 *.90e 65-15 Heroic Spirit 1176 Big Izzy 1171¾ Daring Bet 1121½ Tired 6
LATEST WORKOUTS Sep 25 Bel tr.t 3f fst :37 b

Bold Amateur
B. c. 4, by Sea Songster—Never Speak, by Speak John
$22,500 Br.—Evans T M (Va)
Tr.—Galimi Michael T
Own.—Russo T
108 7
Lifetime 16 2 4 2 $25,550
1984 4 1 0 0 $6,040
1983 6 1 1 1 $13,660
Turf 1 0 1 0 $4,840

11Apr84- 1Kee fst 1 1/16 :48⅕ 1:13⅕ 1:41⅘ Clm 15000 1 3 33½ 34½ 33 1nk Melancon L b 112 6.30 99-20 Bold Amateur 112nk Appeal Judge 112nk Herreno 1124½ Driving 6
15Mar84- 8OP fst 1 1/16 :47⅖ 1:11⅘ 1:43⅕ 3↑Alw 14000 4 4 54 79 815 817½ Haire D b 161 34.30 75-10 Leavesumdouble 1123 Big Oar 1194 Kanchi 1061½ Tired 9
6Mar84- 8OP fst 1 1/16 :46⅘ 1:11⅗ 1:43⅖ 3↑Alw 14000 1 6 54 31 37 49 Haire D b 116 21.70 82-20 Chieftin'sHwk1065DemolitionDerby1212WitnessTr1122 Weakened 8
20Feb84- 8OP fst 6f :21⅗ :44⅖ 1:09⅕ 3↑Alw 14000 11 1 1112 1120 1121 1018 Agnello A b 124 43.80 81-05 A Gift 112¾ Report For Duty 1092 Lucky Larry 1121½ Outrun 11
31Dec83- 5Med fr 6f :22⅕ :45⅗ 1:10⅘ 3↑Md Sp Wt 7 2 65½ 42½ 31 1no Bracciale V Jr b 118 3.50 89-07 Bold Amateur 118no Relation 1131 Towson Native 1183 Driving 7
25Nov83- 6Aqu sly 1 :47 1:13⅗ 1:40⅘ 3↑Md Sp Wt 4 4 53 56 58½ 512½ McCarron G b 120 4.90 51-38 Sea Lord 1203¾ Peruber 120hd On A Streak 1203½ No factor 8
15Nov83- 5Lrl sly 1 :46⅘ 1:13⅕ 1:39⅘ 3↑Md Sp Wt 2 4 48 32½ 31½ 3nk Edwards J W 119 *3.00 75-19 Rushwin 119hd Duke Of Hearts 119nk Bold Amateur1198 Even try 9
3Nov83- 5Med fst 1 1/16 :47⅗ 1:13⅕ 1:46⅖ 3↑Md Sp Wt 6 1 11½ 1hd 42½ 47 McCarron G 118 3.90 70-24 Flintrock 118½ Crazy Moon 1182 Manhandle 1184½ Weakened 7
10Oct83- 2Bel fm 1¼ Ⓣ:50⅘ 1:41⅗ 2:06⅖ 3↑Md Sp Wt 11 2 21 2hd 1½ 22 McCarron G 119 21.90 60-28 Prodigals Path 1192 Bold Amateur 119½ Radiation119½ Weakened 12
20Sep83- 3Med fst 6f :22⅕ :45⅘ 1:11⅘ 3↑Md 25000 1 6 47 57½ 46 47½ Rocco J 118 3.40 77-16 Moe Baum 1092 Native Courage 1181½ Sable Princess1154 Evenly 7
LATEST WORKOUTS Oct 20 Aqu 4f fst :52⅘ b

Marine Brass
Gr. h. 5, by Fifth Marine—Moon Glitter, by In Reality
$25,000 Br.—Turner F D (Ky)
Tr.—Sedlacek Michael C
Own.—Lane Glenn
112 5
Lifetime 21 9 4 2 $89,400
1984 1 0 0 0
1983 8 4 3 0 $50,820
Turf 1 0 0 0

17Jly84- 8Bow fst 6f :22⅘ :45⅘ 1:10⅘ 3↑Alw 12000 7 1 52½ 54 56 58½ Adams J K 122 2.40 78-28 Semaj 1171¾ A Sip Of Julep 112¾ Willard Scott1101¾ Rallied wide 8
12Nov83- 2Lrl gd 1 :45⅕ 1:10⅕ 1:35⅘ 3↑Alw 16000 4 1 1½ 11½ 13 14½ Adams J K 122 *1.20 93-11 Marine Brass 1224½ Issue Joined 1154 Bronze Hill 117¾ Driving 9
5Nov83- 8Lrl fst 7f :22⅘ :45⅖ 1:23⅘ 3↑Alw 16000 5 1 33 32 12½ 1¾ Adams J K 119 *.80 92-12 Marine Brass119¾Disarco'sRib115nkMoneyByOrleans1133¾ Driving 6
24Sep83- 7Lrl fst 1 :46⅕ 1:10⅘ 1:36⅕ 3↑Alw 18000 6 1 1hd 11 12½ 12 Adams J K 117 4.30 91-17 Marine Brass 1172 Valiant Lark 1151½ Hail Emperor 1152 Driving 10
14Sep83- 7Lrl fst 1 :47 1:12⅕ 1:37⅘ 3↑Alw 19000 8 1 2hd 2hd 21 26 Adams J K 117 3.10 78-25 Shadowfax 1156 Marine Brass 1175 Her Pal 1194 Best of others 8
13Aug83- 7Mth fst 170 :46⅘ 1:10⅘ 1:40⅘ 3↑Alw 22000 4 2 2½ 51¾ 57½ 712 Adams J K 117 4.40 80-16 Courteous Majesty 115½ Hail Emperor 119½ Nemrac 1155 Tired 9
6Jly83- 8Bow fst 7f :23 :45⅗ 1:23 3↑Alw 16000 4 1 33 32½ 11½ 12½ Adams J K 114 *1.40 90-25 Marine Brass 1142½ Hatchet Boy 1221¾ Janet's Flash 1191 Driving 5
27Jun83- 8Bow fst 6f :22⅘ :45⅗ 1:10⅘ 3↑Alw 16000 4 2 2½ 21½ 21½ 22 Adams J K 114 2.90 85-19 Jay Mar's Buck 1192 MarineBrass1142GantletDancer1191 Gamely 6

18Jun83- 7Bow fst 7f :22⅘ :46⅕ 1:25⅕ 3↑Alw 16000 3 1 3^{1} 2^{1} 1^{1} 2^{1½} Adams J K 114 2.40 77-25 Hatchet Boy 119^{1½} Marine Brass 114^{¾} Nemrac 119^{¾} Steadied 7
4Dec82- 7Lrl sly 1 :45⅗ 1:11 1:37⅕ 3↑Alw 16000 7 1 1^{1} 1^{1½} 2^{½} 2^{3¼} Adams J K 116 *1.20 83-19 HushHushFlash113^{3¾}MrineBrss116^{1¾}PeceForPece119^{5} Weakened 9
LATEST WORKOUTS ●Oct 17 Aqu 5f fst :59⅗ h Sep 22 Lrl 4f fst :50⅘ b ●Sep 15 Lrl 6f fst 1:12⅘ h ●Sep 9 Pim 6f fst 1:15 h

J. Strap

B. c. 4, by Sauce Boat—Sadie Mae, by Sadair
$25,000 **Br.—Jones W L Jr & Greathouse D (Ky)**
Tr.—Martin Jose
Own.—Belle-C Stable
112^{5} Lifetime 51 5 5 12 $90,780 | 1984 18 2 0 6 $30,720 | 1983 23 2 2 6 $40,050 | Turf 1 0 0 0

17Oct84- 2Bel fst 7f :22⅘ :45⅗ 1:24⅕ 3↑Clm 22500 10 6 12^{11} 8^{9¾} 5^{3½} 1^{1½} Vega H^{5} 110 44.20 81-21 J. Strap 110^{1½} Speier's Luck 117^{¾} Faded Poster 117^{¾} Driving 13
14Sep84- 5Bel fst 6f :22⅘ :46⅕ 1:10⅘ 3↑Clm 22500 6 6 8^{6} 9^{9¾} 9^{14} 9^{13½} Vergara O 115 26.00 77-18 Big McCoy 107^{5}CanadianCurrency117^{½}Jordan'sGray117^{nk} Outrun 10
5Sep84- 3Bel gd 7f :23⅕ :45⅗ 1:22⅘ 3↑Clm 25000 1 4 4^{3½} 5^{9¼} 6^{9½} 6^{10} Maple E 117 10.10 78-12 Sailing Light 113no Rauschenberg 108^{1} Palimony 113^{5¾} Tired 7
9Aug84- 9Sar fst 6f :22⅗ :45⅗ 1:10 3↑Clm 32500 2 9 10^{7¾} 9^{7¾} 6^{8½} 6^{8} Maple E 115 12.60 82-14 CutterSrk117^{3¾}JustAnyTime117^{1}WildMoment117^{no} Broke slowly 12
30Jly84- 7Bel fst 7f :22⅘ :46⅕ 1:24 Clm 32500 3 9 9^{5½} 8^{3¾} 5^{4} 4^{4½} Cordero A Jr 115 *2.30e 77-19 Talc Power 117^{1½} Fibak 115^{3½} Love To Laugh 110^{hd} Rallied 11
12Jly84- 2Bel fst 7f :23 :46 1:23 Clm 35000 3 8 9^{6½} 9^{8} 9^{8¾} 9^{10½} Lovato F Jr 117 4.60e 77-17 Bright Rex 117^{2¾} Shifty Sheik 117^{¾} Act It Out 117^{½} Outrun 10
6Jun84- 7Bel fst 7f :23 :46 1:23⅗ 3↑Alw 20000 3 4 6^{4} 7^{4¾} 4^{5} 3^{2¾} Lovato F Jr 117 12.30 80-20 Pure Rascality 109^{2} Stomper 109^{¾} J. Strap 117^{¾} Rallied 8
20May84- 3Bel fst 6f :22⅗ :45⅘ 1:11⅗ Clm c-20000 4 5 6^{7} 5^{8½} 3^{5} 1^{3½} Lopez V^{5} 112 2.60e 85-18 J. Strap 112^{3½} Ample Native 117^{2½} Jet Voyage 117no Going away 8
12May84- 9Bel fst 7f :23⅕ :47 1:23⅗ Clm 20000 11 3 5^{3½} 9^{4½} 4^{3} 3^{hd} Lopez V^{5} 112 16.20 83-17 Gratification 117no Palimony 112^{hd} J. Strap 112^{1½} Rallied 12
24Apr84- 2Aqu my 7f :22⅘ :45⅘ 1:25 Clm 20000 11 1 2^{1} 2^{½} 2^{hd} 8^{2} Lopez V^{5} 108 15.20 74-21 Creme De LaFete113^{nk}StormWarrior113^{hd}SpyGame117^{¾} Stopped 11
LATEST WORKOUTS ●Oct 13 Bel tr.t 4f fst :48 h Oct 6 Bel tr.t 4f fst :47⅘ h ●Sep 12 Bel tr.t 3f fst :35 h Sep 2 Bel tr.t 4f fst :48⅘ h

Canadian Currency

Gr. g. 5, by Sinister Purpose—Miss Turnpenny, by Iron Ruler
$25,000 **Br.—Beechwood Farm Ltd (Ont-C)**
Tr.—O'Brien Colum
Own.—Jim Tim Stables
117 Lifetime 62 6 13 11 $128,106 | 1984 22 1 3 1 $26,970 | 1983 29 4 6 5 $77,290 | Turf 2 0 0 0

17Oct84- 2Bel fst 7f :22⅘ :45⅗ 1:24⅕ 3↑Clm 25000 5 3 4^{2} 2^{4} 3^{1½} 7^{4½} Lopez V b 117 9.00 77-21 J. Strap 110^{1½} Speier's Luck 117^{¾} Faded Poster 117^{¾} Tired 13
24Sep84- 5Bel fst 7f :22⅘ :46⅕ 1:24⅕ 3↑Clm 25000 5 2 3^{3} 3^{2} 1^{hd} 2^{1} Cordero A Jr b 117 7.80 80-21 Mingo 110^{1} Canadian Currency 117^{2½}FadedPoster117^{nk} Game try 7
14Sep84- 5Bel fst 6f :22⅘ :46⅕ 1:10⅘ 3↑Clm 25000 8 5 5^{4} 5^{3¾} 2^{5} 2^{5} Cordero A Jr b 117 6.40 86-18 Big McCoy 107^{5} CanadianCurrency117^{½}Jordan'sGray117^{nk} Rallied 10
1Sep84- 2Bel fst 1$\frac{1}{16}$:47⅗ 1:12⅗ 1:44 3↑Clm 25000 8 7 5^{4} 4^{3½} 4^{9} 4^{12¾} Migliore R b 117 8.10 69-13 FeelingTooMuch117^{3½}Speier'sLuck117^{1½}SuperRolf117^{8} No factor 8
26Aug84- 3Sar fst 6½f :22⅘ :45⅘ 1:17⅕ 3↑Clm 25000 4 6 5^{7} 5^{5½} 5^{6} 5^{7} Skinner K b 117 21.00 79-15 The Time Is Now 119^{5¾} Tarberry 117 :: Sailing Light 113^{hd} Hung 12
8Aug84- 9Sar fst 7f :22⅘ :45⅗ 1:24⅕ 3↑Clm 25000 9 1 4^{2½} 6^{5½} 6^{7} 10^{9¾} Skinner K b 117 8.50 71-16 TheTimeIsNow117^{hd}Rauschenberg106^{2}HndsomeDncer110^{nk} Wide 11
15Jly84- 3Bel fst 6f :22⅘ :45⅘ 1:10⅘ Clm 25000 1 1 4^{3½} 4^{2½} 2^{1½} 1^{2} Cordero A Jr b 117 7.70 88-17 Canadian Currency 117^{2} Fibak 117^{hd} Zeb's Hel Cat 117^{½} Driving 8
7Jly84- 3Bel sly 7f :22⅘ :45⅘ 1:24 Clm 25000 3 7 7^{5½} 7^{9½} 7^{14} 7^{13½} Lovato F Jr b 117 5.60 69-16 Handsome Dancer 115^{4¾} Spirit Of Alma113^{¾}Palimony110^{1} Outrun 8
28Jun84- 5Bel fst 6f :22⅘ :46⅕ 1:11⅘ Clm 25000 3 5 7^{3¾} 6^{4½} 5^{2} 4^{1½} Lovato F Jr b 117 10.70 82-19 Just Any Time 117^{½} Palimony 110^{¾} Zeb's Hel Cat 112no Rallied 11
20Jun84- 9Bel fst 7f :22⅗ :45⅗ 1:24⅘ Clm 25000 11 1 4^{2} 2^{1½} 2^{5} 4^{7¼} Lovato F Jr b 117 15.20 71-18 Gauguin Native 110^{2½} Act It Out 117^{3¾} Tarberry 117^{1} Weakened 11
LATEST WORKOUTS Sep 11 Aqu 4f fst :50⅘ b

Faded Poster

B. g. 5, by Poster Prince—Faded Lady, by Sadair
$25,000 **Br.—Murrell J R (NY)**
Tr.—Kelley Walter A
Own.—Kelley Mrs W A
117 Lifetime 19 6 3 5 $133,974 | 1984 5 0 0 2 $3,360 | 1982 10 5 1 3 $107,788

17Oct84- 2Bel fst 7f :22⅘ :45⅗ 1:24⅕ 3↑Clm 25000 9 11 10^{8½} 6^{7} 7^{4½} 3^{2} Guerra W A 117 5.30 79-21 J. Strap 110^{1½} Speier's Luck 117^{¾} Faded Poster 117^{¾} Rallied 13
24Sep84- 5Bel fst 7f :22⅘ :46⅕ 1:24⅕ 3↑Clm 25000 1 7 1^{hd} 1^{hd} 3^{1} 3^{3½} Guerra W A 117 6.60 78-21 Mingo 110^{1} Canadian Currency117^{2½}FadedPoster117^{nk} Slow start 7
9Sep84- 3Bel fst 7f :22⅘ :45⅘ 1:23⅗ 3↑Clm 35000 8 5 4^{2} 4^{1} 4^{3½} 5^{8} Guerra W A 117 3.80 75-18 NotTwoTms112^{1½}ThTmIsNow117^{1½}FlngTooMuch117^{½} Raced wide 9
13Aug84- 2Sar fst 7f :22⅗ :45⅕ 1:22⅗ 3↑Clm 45000 2 12 5^{3½} 5^{4} 8^{6} 9^{9½} Espinosa R E^{7} 106 11.80f 81-13 Mr. Tatt 106^{3} HarpersBazaar119^{1½}HollywoodHendrson113^{hd} Tired 13
4Aug84- 9Sar fst 6f :21⅘ :44⅘ 1:09⅘ 3↑Clm 50000 5 10 7^{6½} 10^{11} 8^{7} 7^{8¾} Espinosa R E^{7} 110 14.90 83-13 Sir Quasar 117^{1½} Hominy Hill 110^{2½}JusticeSanders112^{¾} No factor 12
28Jly82- 8Bel my 1 :47⅗ 1:11⅘ 1:37⅕ 3↑[S]EvanShipman 3 5 5^{2} 5^{5} 5^{8½} 6^{13¾} Cordero A Jr 112 *1.60 66-21 Prosper 117^{3½} Jan's Kinsman 110^{nk} Accipiter's Hope 126^{4} Tired 7
13Jly82- 8Bel fst 6f :23⅗ :47⅕ 1:11⅕ 3↑[S]Alw 35000 1 4 4^{2} 4^{¾} 1^{½} 1^{¾} Beitia E 113 *1.30 86-22 Faded Poster 113^{¾} Jan's Kinsman 113^{½} Furrow 115^{1½} Driving 5
27Jun82- 6Bel fst 7f :23⅗ :46⅗ 1:23⅘ [S]Handicap 4 9 4^{¾} 3^{1} 3^{1} 3^{hd} Beitia E 113 *1.70e 83-21 Majestic Kat 113no FearlessLeader116^{no}FadedPoster113^{nk} Evenly 10
2Jun82- 5Bel fst 6f :23⅗ :46⅗ 1:10⅕ 3↑[S]Alw 32500 6 4 3^{½} 1^{1} 1^{2} 1^{4½} Beitia E 109 *1.20 91-11 Faded Poster 109^{4½} Prosper 117^{¾} Jan's Kinsman111^{1½} Ridden out 6
17May82- 8Aqu fst 7f :22 :44⅗ 1:23⅕ [S]Albany H 7 5 5^{6} 5^{3½} 3^{2} 3^{1} Cordero A Jr 118 3.10 84-22 Majestic Kat 112^{½} Cupecoy's Joy 121^{½} Faded Poster 118^{2¾} Wide 9
LATEST WORKOUTS Oct 13 Bel tr.t 4f fst :49⅕ b Oct 6 Bel tr.t 4f fst :49⅘ b Oct 1 Bel tr.t 3f fst :37⅕ h Sep 17 Bel tr.t 4f fst :48⅘ b

Singh America

Ch. c. 4, by Singh—Rikki Tikki Tavi, by Mongo
$25,000 **Br.—Warden Robin C (NY)**
Tr.—Sedlacek Woodrow
Own.—Mack W L
117 Lifetime 34 3 8 6 $112,430 | 1984 18 2 1 4 $49,710 | 1983 16 1 7 2 $62,720 | Turf 10 0 5 1 $30,220

14Oct84- 3Bel fst 1⅛ :46⅘ 1:12 1:51⅘ 3↑Clm 25000 6 3 3^{3} 2^{2½} 3^{3} 3^{6} Lopez V b 117 4.50 62-28 Wimborn'sGtr117^{3}GuguinNtiv117^{3}SinghAmric117^{4½} Factor, wknd 7
3Oct84- 3Bel gd 1$\frac{1}{16}$:47 1:12⅗ 1:46 3↑Clm 25000 1 1 1^{1½} 2^{1½} 3^{4½} 3^{6¾} Lopez V b 117 5.40 65-26 Joy Hour 115^{6}CremeDeLaFete113^{¾}SinghAmerica117^{3½} Weakened 7
26Sep84- 3Bel fst 1⅛ :46⅗ 1:12⅕ 1:52⅗ 3↑Clm 32500 6 7 7^{7½} 7^{9½} 6^{8½} 7^{11½} Davis R G b 115 4.00e 53-25 Terse 114^{3½} Sailing Light 112^{4½} Ship Mint 110^{¾} Outrun 8
27Aug84- 3Sar fm 1⅛ [T]:47⅗ 1:11⅗ 1:50 3↑Clm 50000 3 4 3^{14} 4^{7½} 7^{6} 8^{12½} Gomez E R b 117 22.00 78-17 Clarinet King 119^{1} Freon 113^{4½} The Ripleyite 117^{½} Tired 8
5Aug84- 5Sar fm 1⅛ [T]:48⅘ 1:12⅘ 1:50 3↑Clm 75000 5 3 5^{4} 5^{3} 5^{9} 5^{10½} Lopez V^{5} b 114 10.90 80-13 El Fantasma 117^{hd} RedBrigade117^{2¾}BlueEmmanuelle113^{½} Outrun 8
23Jly84- 6Bel yl 1$\frac{1}{16}$ [T]:48 1:12⅗ 1:45⅗ Clm 175000 4 3 4^{11} 6^{8½} 6^{11} 6^{10¾} Lopez V^{5} b 107 13.40 63-29 Quick Dip 112^{3½} Fray Star 114^{nk} Lutyens 113^{½} Tired 8
12Jly84- 7Bel fst 1$\frac{1}{16}$:46⅗ 1:10⅘ 1:42⅗ 3↑[S]Alw 27500 1 2 2^{1½} 2^{1½} 1^{2} 1^{4½} Lopez V^{5} b 112 4.00 89-17 SinghAmeric112^{4½}Crey'sBoy111^{2½}TlentedJcques111^{1½} Drew clear 10
25Jun84- 5Bel fst 1¼ :47⅗ 1:37⅘ 2:04⅗ 3↑[S]Alw 27500 1 2 2^{½} 1^{2} 1^{1½} 3^{¾} Lopez V^{5} b 112 3.20 74-16 WhtsForevr104^{¾}ColumbiPrid112^{no}SinghAmric112^{½} Drifted out str 7
1Jun84- 7Bel fst 1 :47⅗ 1:11⅘ 1:36⅘ 3↑[S]Alw 27500 8 2 1^{hd} 3^{nk} 3^{1½} 3^{1½} Lopez V^{5} b 112 10.00 80-20 Bright Rex117^{½}TalentedJacques114^{¾}SinghAmerica112^{2¾} Willingly 8
24May84- 2Bel fst 7f :22⅘ :46⅗ 1:23⅕ 3↑[S]Alw 26000 12 12 11^{6¾} 10^{5½} 8^{7½} 8^{7¾} Lopez V^{5} b 116 22.70 78-15 Mr.T.AndMe113^{3½}RestlessFeet110^{½}Loughre121^{1} Sweved, lost iron 12
LATEST WORKOUTS Sep 13 Aqu 3f fst :36⅘ b Aug 24 Sar 3f gd :38 b

Fletcher

Dk. b. or br. c. 4, by Arbees Boy—Forwardly, by Native Charger
$20,000 **Br.—Woodside Stud Inc (NY)**
Tr.—Ferraiola Frank
Own.—Double G Farms
106^{7} Lifetime 28 3 6 2 $81,290 | 1984 17 2 3 1 $51,700 | 1983 11 1 3 1 $29,590

13Oct84- 5Bel fst 6f :22⅘ :46⅗ 1:12⅗ 3↑[S]Alw 26000 3 6 5^{5} 4^{4½} 3^{1½} 1^{1½} Espinosa R E^{7} 110 7.50 80-25 Fletcher110^{1½}TexasGentlemn114^{3}SweetDevil116^{½} Bore out,drvng 7
3Oct84- 2Bel gd 6f :22⅘ :47 1:12⅗ 3↑Clm 17500 7 5 4^{3} 4^{4½} 2^{1½} 2^{1} Ward W A^{5} b 112 6.70 79-26 Spy Game 117^{1} Fletcher 112^{2½} Great Hunter 117^{nk} Bore out 8
27Sep84- 2Med fst 6f :23⅕ :46⅗ 1:12 3↑Clm 20000 7 2 2^{1} 2^{hd} 5^{1½} 4^{3¾} Guerra W A b 116 5.70 78-23 Mister Rouge 109^{nk} Reven Too 109^{½} Old 'n Wise 114^{3} Weakened 8
12Sep84- 9Bel fst 6f :23 :46⅕ 1:10⅘ 3↑Clm 17500 8 9 3^{1½} 3^{1} 3^{2} 2^{4½} Guerra W A b 117 4.90 84-14 Miraculously 115^{4½} Fletcher 117^{1½} Town Clown 117^{2½} Game try 9
31Aug84- 5Bel fst 6f :22⅘ :45⅗ 1:09⅗ 3↑[S]Alw 26000 4 7 9^{9½} 9^{12} 8^{11} 6^{9} Guerra W A b 117 35.90 85-13 Venelli 112^{2½} High Ice 107^{1¾} Black Ore 112^{1¾} No factor 10
13Jun84- 8Bel fst 6f :23 :46⅖ 1:11⅗ 3↑[S]Alw 26000 7 6 3^{1½} 3^{3} 3^{4½} 5^{3¾} Migliore R b 117 22.90 81-18 Restless Feet 109^{1½} ComicFlare110^{2}[D]Carey'sBoy114^{nk} Weakened 8
13Jun84-Placed fourth through disqualification
30May84- 2Bel fst 7f :23 :46⅗ 1:23⅗ Clm 17500 7 8 6^{4} 6^{4½} 7^{7½} 7^{7½} Migliore R b 117 9.90 78-20 Creme De La Fete 119^{1} Rasselas 118^{¾} Jet Voyage119^{2½} No factor 9
20May84- 3Bel fst 6f :22⅗ :45⅘ 1:11⅗ Clm 20000 1 3 3^{3½} 3^{4} 4^{7} 4^{5½} Migliore R b 122 9.60 79-18 J. Strap 112^{3½} Ample Native 117^{2½} Jet Voyage 117no Weakened 8
5May84- 5Aqu fst 6f :22⅘ :46⅗ 1:11 3↑[S]Alw 26000 2 5 2^{2} 2^{hd} 2^{½} 5^{1½} Squartino R A^{5} b 116 9.60 84-16 French Tab 110^{¾} Sincere Wish 113^{¾} Bright Rex 121^{hd} Weakened 8
14Apr84- 3Aqu sly 6f [•]:22⅘ :46⅗ 1:11⅗ 3↑[S]Alw 26000 1 6 3^{½} 3^{3½} 4^{3½} 3^{4½} Squartino R A^{5} b 119 7.60 82-15 Joyer's Angle 113^{4½} French Tab 109^{hd} Fletcher 119^{nk} Even 9
LATEST WORKOUTS Sep 20 Aqu 3f fst :35 hg Sep 8 Aqu 3f fst :36 h Aug 25 Aqu 3f fst :36⅕ b

Mingo

Dk. b. or br. g. 5, by Knightly Sport—Creme Rhoda, by Creme Dela Creme
$22,500 **Br.—Carter Mrs M (Ky)**
Tr.—Moschera Gasper S
Own.—Davis A
110^{5} Lifetime 54 8 7 9 $100,175 | 1984 17 4 2 1 $36,100 | 1983 21 2 4 4 $37,975 | Turf 1 0 0 0

17Oct84- 2Bel fst 7f :22⅘ :45⅗ 1:24⅕ 3↑Clm 22500 7 10 7^{6¾} 5^{5½} 2^{1½} 5^{2¾} Samyn J L b 117 *2.90e 78-21 J. Strap 110^{1½} Speier's Luck 117^{¾} Faded Poster 117^{¾} Tired 13
12Oct84- 2Bel fst 7f :23⅗ :46⅗ 1:24⅗ 3↑Clm c-17500 5 4 3^{1½} 3^{2} 2^{½} 2^{hd} Ward W A^{5} b 117 *1.10e 80-22 Ample Native 115^{hd} Mingo117^{½}CremeDeLaFete113^{1¾} Just missed 8
6Oct84- 5Bel fm 1 (T):46 1:10⅘ 1:36⅘ 3↑Alw 21000 6 8 7^{8½} 6^{5½} 6^{6½} 6^{5¾} Vega H^{5} b 112 14.60e 75-23 Solidified 119^{¾} Inrhetoric 114^{2½} Pigwidgeon 114no No factor 11
3Oct84- 7Bel fst 7f :23 :47 1:24⅕ 3↑Alw 20000 5 5 5^{2¾} 7^{4½} 5^{3½} 5^{9} Ward W A^{5} b 112 4.10 72-26 TreasuredOne119^{¾}CrimsonMedl112^{6¾}BlindMn'sBluff114^{1½} Outrun 9
24Sep84- 5Bel fst 7f :22⅘ :46⅕ 1:24⅕ 3↑Clm 22500 6 4 5^{6½} 4^{6} 2^{hd} 1^{1} Ward W A^{5} b 110 *.80 81-21 Mingo110^{1}CandinCurrency117^{2½}FdedPoster117^{nk} Bore in, driving 7
19Sep84- 9Bel fst 6f :23⅗ :47⅕ 1:11⅘ 3↑Clm c-14000 1 1 5^{1½} 2^{2} 1^{½} 1^{2} Ward W A^{5} b 112 *2.90 83-19 Mingo 112^{2} No Heir 110^{2} Royal Jove 117^{¾} Drew clear 11
26Aug84- 3Sar fst 6½f :22⅘ :45⅘ 1:17⅕ 3↑Clm 20000 12 9 9^{8½} 4^{5} 4^{6} 4^{5¾} Ward W A^{5} b 108 7.30 80-15 The Time IsNow119^{5¾}Tarberry117^{no}SailingLight113^{hd} Raced wide 12
8Aug84- 9Sar fst 7f :22⅘ :45⅗ 1:24⅕ 3↑Clm 20000 7 11 6^{4} 5^{4¾} 4^{2} 4^{2½} Lopez V b 108 6.20 79-16 ThTmIsNw117^{hd}Rschnbrg106^{2}HndsmDncr110^{nk} Off slowly, brush 11
30Jly84- 3Bel fst 6f :22⅘ :46 1:11 Clm 18000 4 4 6^{3½} 5^{3} 2^{2} 3^{2¾} Lopez V^{5} b 110 3.40 84-19 Toss Across 113^{2} Clear The Bases 117^{¾} Mingo 110^{3} Weakened 7
23Jly84- 1Bel fst 7f :22⅘ :46⅗ 1:23⅗ Clm 17500 5 4 2^{½} 1^{hd} 2^{1½} 2^{4} Lopez V^{5} b 114 5.20 79-21 Speier's Luck 117^{4} Mingo 114^{hd} Mock Court 115^{1¾} Held 2nd 10
LATEST WORKOUTS Oct 1 Bel tr.t 3f fst :37 h Sep 9 Aqu 4f fst :49 b

He's Something

B. h. 8, by Figonero—She's Something, by Four-and-Twenty
$25,000 **Br.—Kuns V (Cal)**
Tr.—Glass O J Jr
Own.—Glass O J
117 Lifetime 28 5 0 7 $61,116 | 1984 4 1 0 0 $6,600 | 1982 4 1 0 2 $25,100 | Turf 1 0 0 1 $1,760

11Aug84- 6Aks fst 1$\frac{1}{16}$:48⅕ 1:21 1:44⅘ Clm 30000 1 3 2^{1½} 1^{½} 1^{1½} 1^{1} Kutz D 116 13.80 79-16 He's Something 116^{1} Claim the Throne 116^{2} Intermediary 112^{hd} 7
1Aug84- 8Aks fst 6f :22⅘ :45⅕ 1:11⅗ Alw 17500 1 7 7^{7½} 7^{9½} 8^{12} 8^{10¾} Smith M E 112 12.70 69-28 Big Bad Fred 112^{½} Skate 112^{1½} Maui Star 112^{3} 8
18Jly84- 8Aks fst 6f :22⅗ :44⅘ 1:09⅘ Alw 17200 4 4 3^{1} 4^{9} 7^{13} 7^{15½} Hall D C 114 14.90 75-19 Double Ready 118^{nk} Energetic King 112^{4½} Maui Star 112^{½} 7
7Jly84- 7Aks fst 6f :22⅗ :44⅘ 1:09⅗ Alw 16100 1 5 2^{hd} 4^{3½} 8^{14} 8^{16} Valovich C J 112 8.40 73-19 Smokite 118^{hd} Paradin' Cowboy 112^{5} Hold the Beans 112^{nk} 8
30Apr82- 8Hol fst 7f :21⅗ :44⅕ 1:21⅗ Alw 32000 1 7 6^{4¾} 7^{6} 7^{9½} 5^{6½} Steiner J J^{5} 110 14.70 83-15 Navarino II 122^{1½} Mister Wilder 117^{¾} Guarantee 113^{¾} 7
18Apr82- 5SA fst 1$\frac{1}{16}$:45⅗ 1:09⅗ 1:41⅕ Alw 30000 1 2 2^{½} 3^{1} 1^{hd} 1^{nk} Asmussen C B 114 8.50 95-07 He's Something 114^{nk} Veschaco 114^{½} Guarantee 114^{5} Driving 9
11Apr82- 5SA sly 6½f :22 :45⅕ 1:17 Alw 26000 7 3 4^{3½} 5^{5} 7^{5½} 3^{1½} Valenzuela P A 114 4.00 83-18 Tellaround 116^{1} Redoutable 114^{½} He's Something 114no 7
14Mar82- 7SA sly 6½f :21⅗ :44⅗ 1:18⅗ Alw 26000 1 6 5^{11} 5^{14} 5^{12} 3^{3½} Asmussen C B 114 5.70 75 — Terresto's Singer 115^{1½} Master Warrior117^{1¾}He'sSomething114^{½} 6
23Oct81- 7Haw 5 3 2^{1½} 2^{hd} 2^{½} 3^{3½} Silva C H 120 4.00 76 — 0
LATEST WORKOUTS Oct 20 Med 5f fst 1:02⅘ b Oct 4 Med 3f fst :38⅕ b

Double Atom — Dk. b. or br. h. 5, by Spring Double—Atom Princess, by Prince John
$20,000 Br.—Natoli D & Diane & Pascuma (NY) — Tr.—Pascuma James J Jr — 113
Own.—Santangelo F
Lifetime 36 3 4 6 $82,284 — 1984 10 0 0 0 $1,290 — 1983 10 1 1 2 $32,154 — Turf 4 0 0 0 $3,444

Date / Race	Cond	Dist	Fractions	Class	Running line	Jockey	Wt	Odds	Finishers	Comment	Field
12Oct84- 2Bel	fst	7f	:23⅗ :46⅗ 1:24⅘	3+Clm 17500	7 6 53 86½ 88 76	Skinner K	b 117	24.90	74-22 Ample Native 115hd Mingo 117½ Creme DeLaFete1131¾	No factor	8
30Jun84- 10Mth	sly	1 1/16	:46⅘ 1:11⅗ 1:44⅗	3+Clm 20000	3 5 68¾ 712 814 815	McCauley W H	b 115	10.60	66-19 Anne's Rainbow 113¾ Don Big Shot 1159 Top Case 1151	Tired	10
20Jun84- 9Bel	fst	7f	:22⅗ :45⅘ 1:24⅘	Clm 22500	1 8 118¾ 98½ 619 68¾	Skinner K	b 115	41.30	69-18 Gauguin Native 1102½ Act It Out 1173¾ Tarberry 1171	Wide	11
7Jun84- 3Bel	fm	1⅜ [T]	:47⅕ 1:37⅘ 2:14⅘	Clm 35000	11 2 2½ 76½ 1121 1125	Skinner K	b 117	*3.20e	60-13 Oratavo 11210½ Palace 1172¾ Cannon Royal 112nk	Tired	12
21May84- 3Bel	gd	1 1/16 Ⓣ	:47 1:12⅗ 1:44⅗	Clm 35000	11 2 1½ 2hd 53 57½	Skinner K	b 117	27.10	66-24 Amadandy 1122 Oliver List 1172 Kim's Chance 117¾	Weakened	12
3May84- 5Aqu	fst	1	:45⅗ 1:10⅘ 1:37	Clm 30000	7 8 710 712 715 816	McCarron G	b 113	22.90	65-24 Great Hunter 1171½ Startop's Ace 1175 Kim's Chance117½	Outrun	10
23Apr84- 1Aqu	fst	1⅛	:47⅘ 1:13 1:51⅘	Clm 35000	1 2 21½ 53¾ 611 616½	McCarron G	b 117	8.90	59-20 Jet Steam 1132½ Laddy's Luck 1131¾ Terse 1172¾	Tired	6
10Mar84- 3Aqu	fst	170 [•]	:47⅘ 1:13⅕ 1:43⅗	Clm 45000	1 8 86 87½ 58 411½	McCarron G	113	23.10	71-17 British Gunner 1138½ Full Deck 1171¾ CanadianCalm1171½	Outrun	8
1Mar84- 5Aqu	fst	1 1/16 [•]	:48⅗ 1:13⅘ 1:47⅕	Clm 47500	9 11 1012 96½ 910 1111½	Smith A Jr	115	13.40	65-23 Bishen 1151½ Talc Power 117¾ Alamacani 117¾	Outrun	12
3Feb84- 3Aqu	fst	6f [•]	:23 :46⅗ 1:12	Clm 47500	7 5 117½ 96¾ 77½ 77	Smith A Jr	115	26.00	77-28 Top Hat 1172½ Cutter Sark 117nk Gratification 1122	No factor	11

LATEST WORKOUTS ●Oct 9 Aqu 4f fst :48⅘ h — Oct 4 Aqu 6f fst 1:14⅘ b — Sep 29 Aqu 4f my :48⅕ h (d) — Sep 23 Aqu 4f fst :50⅘ b

Also Eligible (Not in Post Position Order):

George Cinq — Dk. b. or br. g. 4, by Determined King—Miss Georgene, by Stella Aurata
$20,000 Br.—Ocala Stud Fm Inc-Ofarrell Jr-Wiest (NY) — Tr.—Alvarez Louis C — 115
Own.—Martinez G
Lifetime 27 4 3 4 $78,330 — 1984 8 1 2 0 $11,560 — 1983 12 3 1 3 $62,720 — Turf 1 0 0 0 $120

Date / Race	Cond	Dist	Fractions	Class	Running line	Jockey	Wt	Odds	Finishers	Comment	Field
15Oct84- 9Bel	fst	1 1/16	:47⅕ 1:12⅗ 1:45⅗	3+Clm c-14000	11 8 83¾ 22 11 11½	Guerra W A	117	*2.10	74-27 George Cinq 1171½ Comedion 1171 Cry For Help 1063	Driving	12
8Oct84- 2Bel	fst	7f	:23 :47⅕ 1:26	3+Clm 14000	10 12 104¾ 72¾ 1hd 2¾	Guerra W A	117	5.60	71-28 Creme De La Fete115¾GeorgeCinq1173½[D]Comedion117nk	Gamely	14
28Sep84- 9Bel	gd	7f	:23 :46⅗ 1:24⅘	3+Clm 14000	6 2 63½ 52½ 1hd 2nk	Guerra W A	117	17.60	78-26 Creme DeLaFete113nkGeorgeCinq117nkMidwayFlyer1171½	Gamely	8
30Jly84- 1Bel	fst	1	:45⅗ 1:11 1:37⅕	Clm 17500	4 4 44 58½ 610 612	Cruguet J	117	10.20	67-19 Hugh Capet 1172¾ Time Together 115½ Dr. Butcher 1083	Tired	7
23Jly84- 1Bel	fst	7f	:22⅗ :46⅗ 1:23⅘	Clm 17500	2 7 75½ 87 79½ 610½	Hernandez R	117	14.30	72-21 Speier's Luck 1174 Mingo 114hd Mock Court 1151¾	No factor	10
6Jly84- 5Bel	fst	1 1/16	:46⅗ 1:11⅗ 1:43⅕	Clm 45000	5 7 74¾ 63¾ 612 820	Cruguet J	113	12.80	66-18 Super Rolfe 1134½ Act It Out 1131 Lord Calvert 1171½	Outrun	8
31Jan84- 5Hia	fm	*1 1/16 Ⓣ	1:54⅘	Clm 50000	8 5 68½ 75½ 1112 1113½	Thornburg B	116	52.80	76-14 Palace Tower 116½ Magna Mark 116½ Cancun 1142	Fell back	12
23Jan84- 5Hia	fst	1 1/16	:47⅘ 1:11⅘ 1:43	Clm 50000	5 5 52½ 53¾ 612 623	Encinas R I	116	4.70	65-15 Right On Red 1165 Kan Reason 11411 Manila Bay 1121	Outrun	6
28Dec83- 8Aqu	sly	1 1/16 [•]	:48⅗ 1:14 1:47⅗	3+[S]Alex M Robb	4 4 52 97½ 911 918¾	McCarron G	114	15.60	55-29 Ask Muhammad 1223½ Mugatea 116½ Shy Groom 119½	Early foot	9
4Dec83- 9Aqu	sly	7f	:23⅗ :46⅘ 1:23⅗	3+Alw 27000	4 4 31½ 35 715 617½	Ycaza M	117	13.60	66-25 Tarantara 1126¾ North Glade 1171½ Native Raid 1174½	Tired	9

LATEST WORKOUTS Sep 21 Bel tr.t 4f fst :49⅘ b — Sep 16 Bel tr.t 3f my :39 b

Gauguin Native — B. g. 6, by Raise A Native—Royal Portrait, by Ribot
$25,000 Br.—Hobeau Farm Inc (Fla) — Tr.—Hernandez Sandino — 117
Own.—Rand R
Lifetime 73 15 11 12 $234,385 — 1984 23 5 4 4 $75,410 — 1983 9 0 1 0 $9,265 — Turf 15 1 5 3 $48,845

Date / Race	Cond	Dist	Fractions	Class	Running line	Jockey	Wt	Odds	Finishers	Comment	Field
14Oct84- 3Bel	fst	1⅛	:46⅘ 1:12 1:51⅘	3+Clm 25000	7 1 12½ 12½ 2hd 23	Velasquez J	b 117	*1.80	65-28 Wimborne'sGter1173GuguinNtive1173SinghAmric1174½	No match	7
4Oct84- 5Bel	gd	1 1/16 Ⓣ	:46 1:11⅗ 1:44⅗	3+Clm 35000	10 6 89½ 711 78 67¾	Velasquez J	b 113	19.50	65-27 [DH]EspritDeRomeo1121[DH]SkiJump1131EasyChoice113½	No factor	12
26Sep84- 3Bel	fst	1⅛	:46⅗ 1:11⅕ 1:52⅗	3+Clm 35000	3 2 32 45 44½ 48½	Cordero A Jr	b 117	1.90	55-25 Terse 1143½ Sailing Light 1124½ Ship Mint 110¾	Tired	8
19Sep84- 3Bel	fst	6f	:22⅗ :46⅘ 1:10⅘	3+Clm 35000	4 4 2½ 41 32 31¾	Cordero A Jr	b 117	8.90	86-19 Sailing Light 108no BigMcCoy1081¾GauguinNative1172	Weakened	7
31Aug84- 2Bel	gd	1¼ [T]	:47⅘ 1:38⅘ 2:04⅘	3+Clm 35000	3 1 12½ 11½ 2hd 24	Velasquez J	b 117	*1.50	66-31 Uncle Sal 1174 Gauguin Native 1172 Goumi 117¾	No match	6
23Aug84- 9Sar	sly	1⅛	:47 1:11⅗ 1:51⅕	3+Clm 25000	5 1 12½ 16 15 17½	Velasquez J	b 117	*4.30	79-22 GuguinNtive1177½Speier'sLuck115½MdvlMovmnt117¾	Ridden out	12
10Aug84- 1Sar	fst	1¼	:47 1:37⅘ 2:03⅕	3+Clm 25000	5 4 43 11½ 21 36½	Velasquez J	b 117	7.20	77-13 Bold 'n Cold1171½ABigFortune1135GauguinNative1172	Weakened	8
29Jly84- 5Bel	fst	1 1/16	:46⅕ 1:10⅘ 1:42⅕	Clm 45000	4 4 65 710 710 613½	Espinosa R E7	b 106	19.10	77-15 CanadianCalm1131½ShareTheRisk1133Startop'sAce115nk	Fin.early	8
19Jly84- 6Bel	fst	1⅜	:49 1:39⅘ 2:18⅘	Clm 45000	4 7 76 54 48 412½	Espinosa R E7	b 106	7.80	74-15 ClrintKing1174HroicSpirit1133½EspritDRomo1085	Lacked fin. bid	7
12Jly84- 2Bel	fst	7f	:23 :46 1:23	Clm 32500	6 6 74½ 77 54½ 55¾	Hernandez R	b 115	3.90	81-17 Bright Rex 1172¾ Shifty Sheik 117¾ Act It Out 117½	Wide str.	10

Reggae Man — Ro. g. 5, by Near Man—Down Beat, by Native Dancer
$20,000 Br.—Triple Crown Breeders Group III Ltd (Fla) — Tr.—DiAngelo Joseph T — 113
Own.—Two Anns Stable
Lifetime 30 10 3 2 $62,740 — 1984 9 1 0 1 $10,685 — 1983 16 9 3 0 $51,165 — Turf 2 0 0 0 $95

Date / Race	Cond	Dist	Fractions	Class	Running line	Jockey	Wt	Odds	Finishers	Comment	Field
4Jly84- 10Crc	fm	*1⅛ Ⓣ	1:47⅕	3+Clm 20000	2 1 1hd 1224 1243 1235½	Lee M A	b 113	33.60	51-09 El PequenoGato1171Avago1174Joycapade117no	Done after 1/2 ml.	12
25Jun84- 8Crc	gd	6f	:23 :47 1:13	Clm 20000	7 4 72¾ 77¾ 713 616	Rojas E E	b 116	3.20	70-21 King Of Bridlewood 109½ Lesion 1202½ Anne'sDarling112½	Outrun	8
8Jun84- 10Crc	fst	6½f	:22⅗ :46⅘ 1:20	3+Clm 32500	3 3 1hd 3nk 712 817¾	Gonzalez B	b 115	11.10	67-20 Salariado 117¾ Big Win 1102 Karel Van Kaat 115hd	Gave way	9
15May84- 9GP	fst	6f	:22 :45 1:11⅘	Alw 20000	5 2 42¾ 67¾ 613 610½	Gonzalez B	b 115	13.60	72-23 Hamlet 115¾ Those Eyes 1151 Just A Miner 1154	Tired	6
13Apr84- 6GP	sly	7f	:22⅗ :45⅗ 1:23	Clm c-25000	6 2 1hd 2hd 2hd 3¾	Hernandez C	b 119	*2.10	88-19 My Sail 122½ Gust of Reason 122nk Reggae Man 1191½	Weakened	8
3Apr84- 7GP	fst	1 1/16	:46⅘ 1:11⅕ 1:43	Clm 40000	8 1 16 11½ 21½ 45¾	Hernandez C	b 113	6.90	80-20 Superb Missile 1171½ Nancy's Shadow1173Solano1131½	Weakened	8
17Mar84- 7GP	fst	6f	:22⅗ :45⅕ 1:09⅘	Alw 18000	3 5 1½ 1hd 42¾ 89	Hernandez C	b 115	8.40	82-17 Compo'sTempo1193½NumberOnSpcil122noThosEys1151½	Faltered	10
22Feb84- 6Hia	fst	6f	:21⅘ :44⅘ 1:09⅕	Clm 32000	2 4 1½ 12½ 11½ 11½	Hernandez C	b 116	10.30	97-14 Reggae Man 1161½ Ancient Briar 116no Big Win 1163	Driving	9
14Jan84- 9Hia	fst	7f	:22⅘ :45⅘ 1:22⅘	Alw 20000	6 5 14 14 44½ 813	Bailey J D	b 115	--	78-11 Fast Reason 1221 Gallant Prelude 117nkRaiseALine1195	Gave way	10
14Jan84- No wagering, tote malfunction											
12Nov83- 7Tdn	my	1 1/16	:47 1:12⅘ 1:48⅕	3+Handicap	9 1 11½ 11 1½ 21	Martin E Jr	b 122	2.40	68-34 Camp Robber 1211 Reggae Man 1222½ Sizeable Profit 1152		

LATEST WORKOUTS Oct 6 Bel 5f fst 1:05 h — Oct 1 Bel 5f fst 1:03⅘ b — Sep 24 Bel tr.t 4f fst :49⅘ b — Sep 17 Bel tr.t 4f fst :49 b

Apparently, though, physical problems have compromised his ability. Or, at least, Sedlacek wants rival trainers to think so.

J. STRAP

Another infrequent winner (less than 10 percent of his starts over the past two years), this son of Sauce Boat figures to like the wet conditions. However, he failed to hang on at seven furlongs in the mud at Aqueduct on April 24, and so has to be suspect at the added distance today. In addition, he will probably be trying to rally from an inside post.

FADED POSTER

With two recent good races in this class after a two-year hiatus, this former state-bred stakes competitor has to be respected. Note his close finish behind Majestic Kat and Cupecoy's Joy in May of 1982.

However, his only effort in the mud was poor and, preceding his long layoff, suggested the possibility that the horse injured himself in that race, with the track conditions being a contributing factor. The animal might prove cautious over a similar racing surface today and has to be considered a risky betting proposition.

SINGH AMERICA

A third infrequent winner, with no visible off-track form, Singh America nevertheless has early speed in his favor.

FLETCHER

A state-bred worth at most $17,000 on the open market. Outclassed here.

MINGO

An interesting study. Mingo is a horse with a well-known preference for racing from behind on the inside—exactly the kind of racing style that would get him into trouble under the prevailing conditions. If taken to the inside, the splashing mud might stop him. If steered to the outside, he won't do his best under any condition. With no record in the mud to suggest that he might be able to overcome an inside trip, he's a poor risk.

DOUBLE ATOM

Never close this year, including a recent poor performance in the slop at Monmouth against cheaper.

TARBERRY

Winless in fifteen starts this year, is sufficient reason to dismiss him out of hand.

GEORGE CINQ

Woke up when dropped down to the $14,000 level, but has no apparent back class to suggest that he can handle the significant rise in class forced by his recent claim.

STONEY LONESOME

Although dropping sharply in class, this grass-bred gelding has shown nothing in 1984. Previous drops in class haven't helped, so why should this one?

GAUGUIN NATIVE

A lifetime winner of fifteen races, this well-bred six-year-old's best recent effort came in the slop at Saratoga. His figure for that race far exceeded his norm, suggesting that the horse was indeed a mudlark. Note also that his previous winning race was preceded by an improved effort forecasting the win. In similar fashion, Gauguin Native's race on October 14 suggests that a peak performance is forthcoming, and the track conditions are apparently working out to his advantage. Or are they? The race at Saratoga was over a surface termed sloppy. Today's was labeled muddy. In addition, Gauguin Native enjoyed a clear early lead at Saratoga, a luxury that did not appear likely in today's field. But the generous 4–1 odds seemed to compensate for the possibility that the horse might prefer slop to

NINTH RACE
Aqueduct
OCTOBER 24, 1984

1 MILE. (1.33⅕) CLAIMING. Purse $16,000. 3-year-olds and upward. Weight, 3-year-olds, 119 lbs. Older, 122 lbs. Non-winners of two races at a mile or over since October 1 allowed 3 lbs. Of such a race since then, 5 lbs. Claiming price $25,000; for each $2,500 to $20,000 allowed 2 lbs. (Races when entered to be claimed for $18,000 or less not considered.)

Value of race $16,000; value to winner $9,600; second $3,520; third $1,920; fourth $960. Mutuel pool $101,048, OTB pool $190,789. Triple Pool $191,013. OTB Triple Pool $310,413.

Last Raced	Horse	Eqt.	A.	Wt	PP	St	¼	½	¾	Str	Fin	Jockey	Cl'g Pr	Odds $1
14Oct84 3Bel2	Gauguin Native	b	6	117	12	1	14	42	22	21½	1hd	Velasquez J	25000	4.10
17Jly84 8Bow5	Marine Brass		5	112	2	6	3hd	1½	11½	1½	2¾	Ward W A5	25000	3.30
17Oct84 2Bel5	Mingo		5	115	7	7	9½	8½	53	43	33½	Samyn J L†	22500	12.30
17Oct84 2Bel4	Tarberry	b	6	117	9	9	102	102½	81½	6½	4hd	Maple E	25000	7.80
29Sep84 10Med8	Stoney Lonesome		4	117	11	2	21	31	33	31	5½	Skinner K	25000	27.40
15Oct84 9Bel1	George Cinq		4	115	10	3	61	91	71	71½	6¾	Cordero A Jr	20000	11.60
13Oct84 5Bel1	Fletcher		4	106	6	5	41½	2hd	4½	5hd	71¼	Espinosa R E7	20000	12.40
17Oct84 2Bel3	Faded Poster		5	117	4	12	111	11½	10½	9hd	8¾	Guerra W A	25000	8.00
12Oct84 2Bel7	Double Atom		5	113	8	4	71	6hd	9½	10½	9¾	Deegan J C	20000	38.00
11Oct84 3Bel6	Joy Hour	b	4	119	1	10	8hd	7hd	11½	112½	10hd	Cruguet J	25000	7.90
14Oct84 3Bel3	Singh America	b	4	117	5	8	52	55	6½	81½	11¾	Lopez V	25000	12.90
17Oct84 2Bel1	J. Strap		4	112	3	11	12	12	12	12	12	Vega H5	25000	10.60

OFF AT 4:49 Start good, Won driving. Time, :22⅗, :45⅖, 1:09⅘, 1:35⅖ Track muddy.

$2 Mutuel Prices:			
12-(N)-GAUGUIN NATIVE	10.20	4.80	3.20
2-(D)-MARINE BRASS		4.60	3.60
7-(J)-MINGO			7.40

$2 TRIPLE 12-2-7 PAID $452.00.

B. g, by Raise A Native—Royal Portrait, by Ribot. Trainer Hernandez Sandino. Bred by Hobeau Farm Inc (Fla).

GAUGUIN NATIVE showed good early foot while racing wide on the backstretch, dropped over at the turn to go after MARINE BRASS and continued on gamely to prevail in a long drive. The latter took over while saving ground nearing the end of the backstretch, opened a clear lead before going six furlongs and held on well. MINGO rallied from the outside after entering the stretch and continued on with good energy while lugging in. TARBERRY failed to seriously menace with a mile late response. STONEY LONESOME raced forwardly to midstretch and gave way. FLETCHER was finished soon after going a half. FADED POSTER broke slowly. JOY HOUR was always outrun. SINGH AMERICA gave way after going a half.

mud. Also, regular New York players, who had watched this horse race for several seasons, knew that he did not need a clear lead early to win.

This field includes several horses that simply do not like to win. Such a horse will find an excuse not to win, and the muddy track gives him a good one. Unless the horse shows a special fondness for wet conditions—its record includes a strong effort over a damp track—it can safely be ignored as a serious contender and dismissed as a potential bet.

Everything else considered, Gauguin Native seems the logical selection. He's apparently fit, can win at this level, and likes (?) the track conditions. The outside post will not hurt him, not nearly as much as it would have if the race had been around two turns. Indeed, he might be able to use the famous "Ussery's Alley" to his advantage, racing well out from the rail down the backstretch, then taking the "downhill" route into the turn. Many horses have gained several lengths at this stage of a race at Aqueduct by employing this strategy.

The race did not run exactly to expectations. Gauguin Native opened a four-length lead by the first quarter, then dropped back to fourth before coming again to wear down Marine Brass in the final yards. Mingo managed to rally mildly for third from the outside while lugging in, looking for the apparent security of the rail.

Chapter 25

Who Is Glenn Brooke?

In *Thoroughbred Handicapping—State of the Art,* I made a point of mentioning the hazards of using the company lines in the past performances to compare the relative merits of horses that, though not racing against one another recently, may have competed against common opponents. Unless the player knows the exact circumstances surrounding each performance upon which such comparisons are based, he is treading on thin ice. We do not mean to imply that comparative handicapping cannot be done effectively, however, only that the typical once-a-week player usually has insufficient information to do so.

Often however, proper identification of just one name in a horse's past performances proves the key to correctly gauging that horse's ability. The Manassa Mauler, a seven-furlong overnight stakes for three-year-olds run on Wood Memorial Day, April 20, 1985, at Aqueduct provided a typical example.

Of the five horses entered, only Meghan's Deal—unsuccessful recently in maiden-claiming company in New York prior to winning twice at Garden State in ordinary times—could be eliminated, and this partly because he had the rail on a track exhibiting an outside closers' bias.

Favored at 8–5 was Summitry, a reformed claimer that had won its last two races while earning speed figures that were clearly the best in today's small field. However, his recent victory in allowance company had come at the direct expense of Truth Be Told, who had only recently won the "Jacques Who Award" as the "bridesmaid of the meet" for the just concluded winter meeting at Aqueduct. Based on this comparison, I concluded that Summitry was a favorite worth betting against.

5 AQUEDUCT 7 FURLONGS AQUEDUCT

7 FURLONGS. (1.20⅕) 1st Running THE MANASSA MAULER STAKES. Purse $50,000 Added (Closing Wednesday, April 10). 3-year-olds which have never won a race of $25,000, 122 lbs. Non-winners of a race of $20,000 allowed, 3 lbs. Of two races other than maiden or claiming, 5 lbs. Of a race other than maiden or claiming, 7 lbs. $100 to nominate; $200 to enter and $200 to start. (Maiden, Claiming, Starter and State-Bred Races not considered.) A trophy will be presented to the owner of the winner. Closed with nominations.

Meghan's Deal Ch. c. 3, by Regal And Royal—Sir For Her, by Traffic Whirl
Own.—Murphy J P Br.—Murphy J P (Fla) Tr.—Scanlon Robert N
117 Lifetime 7 2 0 0 $15,930 1985 4 2 0 0 $15,600 1984 3 M 0 0 $330
9Apr85- 5GS fst 6f :22 :45⅕ 1:10⅘ Alw 14000 5 3 54½ 53½ 3½ 1¹ Antley C W b 120 3.00 — — Meghn'sDel120¹PlumWin114²DncingInThAir115⁶ Drifted, driving 8
2Apr85- 5GS fst 6f :22⅕ :46 1:11⅕ Md Sp Wt 5 6 52½ 41½ 2¹ 1½ Antley C W b 120 5.80 — — Meghan's Deal 120½ Break Dancing120½BatterPile120ⁿᵈ Driving 8
22Mar85- 6Aqu fst 6f :23 :47⅕ 1:13⅕ Md 50000 9 2 73½ 54½ 5³ 5⁴ Murphy D J 122 19.70 71-27 Intercostal 113ⁿᵒ Naked Emperor 122½ Bahia Grande 1172½ Wide 14
15Mar85- 4Key fst 6f :22⅗ :46⅘ 1:12⅘ Md Sp Wt 11 5 78½ 88½ 85½ 65½ Antley C W 122 21.00 71-26 Hurdy Gurdy Man 122½ Just Like Jo122½BatterPile122³ No factor 11
7Aug84- 6Mth fst 5½f :22⅘ :47 1:06⅕ Md 40000 10 1 84½ 10¹¹ 10¹³ 10¹²½ Deegan J C 118 28.60 72-16 Green Hills 113½ Cool Scruff 1171½ Western Champ 116³ Wide 11
26Jly84- 6Mth fst 5½f :23 :47 1:06⅘ Md 50000 2 4 66 76½ 79 75½ Deegan J C 118 27.00 77-20 ClearMyStage118²RacetrackRomeo118ⁿᵒOurDiplomat113¹ Outrun 12
10Jly84- 6Mth fst 5f :22⅕ :46 :59⅕ Md Sp Wt 1 3 33½ 47½ 49 58½ Vega A 116 36.70 81-20 Tree Hawk 118⁴ Jusavik 118² Noholme's Best 118¹ Tired 8
LATEST WORKOUTS Apr 18 GS 4f fst :49 b Mar 30 GS 4f fst :48 h Mar 9 GS 6f fst 1:13⅘ h Mar 2 GS 5f fst 1:01 hg

Summitry Dk. b. or br. c. 3, by National Zenith—Eureka Time, by Jig Time
Own.—Nagle K Br.—Twin Pines Farm Inc (Fla) Tr.—Ferriola Peter
117 Lifetime 15 5 3 1 $56,730 1985 6 3 1 0 $39,800 1984 9 2 2 1 $16,930
4Apr85- 7Aqu fst 7f :23⅕ :46⅕ 1:23⅕ Alw 22000 3 7 41½ 42 2½ 1½ Santagata N 117 *1.20 85-19 Summitry117½TruthBeTold1191½SeeTheWay117³ Slow st., driving 7
27Mar85- 5Aqu fst 7f :22⅕ :45⅘ 1:22⅘ Clm 50000 9 5 31½ 3ⁿᵏ 1³ 1⁴ Santagata N b 117 *1.00 88-20 Summitry 117⁴ Taylor Road 1175½ TheRunningKind1132½ Handily 10
20Feb85- 4Aqu fst 6f ⊡:22⅘ :45⅘ 1:11⅘ Clm 45000 8 5 43 25 24 23½ Garrido O L⁵ b 108 *2.40 83-23 Splendid Catch 1173½ Summitry 108⁴Maggie'sMike1131½ 2nd best 12
9Feb85- 2Aqu fst 6f ⊡:23⅘ :47⅘ 1:13⅘ Clm 35000 4 6 21 2½ 1³ 1⁴ Garrido O L⁵ b 112 3.70 76-26 Summitry 112⁴ Bolinger 110⁷ Fly Me Again 108ⁿᵏ Ridden out 12
30Jan85- 3Aqu fst 6f ⊡:23 :46⅘ 1:13⅘ Clm c-25000 6 7 44½ 57 79½ 610 Murphy D J 117 *1.60 66-25 FlyMeAgin110ⁿᵈⒹAccordingToLuke1192½Bolingr117⁴ Bumped st 7
30Jan85-Placed fifth through disqualification
16Jan85- 7Aqu fst 6f ⊡:22⅘ :46 1:11⅘ Alw 22000 5 10 78 65 88½ 79½ Ayarza I 117 37.10 78-22 Love That Mac 1124½ Full of Spice 117½SchoarsTask117½ Outrun 10
29Dec84- 4Med fst 6f :23 :46⅕ 1:11⅘ Clm 32000 8 9 96½ 52½ 1¹ 12½ Morgan M R 117 8.90 84-16 Summitry 1172½ Now We've Got Him 117½Satyrically117½ Driving 10
9Dec84- 6Aqu fst 1⅟₁₆ ⊡:48⅘ 1:13 1:46 Alw 23000 8 7 73½ 65½ 512 513½ Morgan M R 117 39.50 68-19 TrophyHunter1172½UncleDddy110³ComedyTonight122³ No factor 8
3Dec84- 5Aqu fst 7f :22⅘ :46 1:24⅘ Clm 60000 3 7 67½ 42½ 58 47½ Privitera R⁷ 106 17.70 71-29 SplendidCatch1176½FeelingGallnt113½DistntOrbit108ⁿᵒ No factor 8
20Nov84- 3Med fst 6f :23⅘ :48⅘ 1:15 Clm 28000 2 4 44 43½ 43 2² Ayarza I 112 8.80 65-30 Spoiled Preppie 118² Summitry 112ⁿᵒ StardustLight118ⁿᵈ Rallied 6
LATEST WORKOUTS Apr 15 Aqu 6f fst 1:14⅘ h ●Mar 24 Aqu 5f fst 1:01 h ●Mar 20 Aqu 6f fst 1:13⅘ h

Equalize Gr. c. 3, by Northern Jove—Zenta, by Dr Fager
Own.—Tartan Stable Br.—Tartan Farms (Fla) Tr.—Nerud Jan H
117 Lifetime 3 2 0 0 $25,800 1985 3 2 0 0 $25,800 1984 0 M 0 0
25Mar85- 7Aqu fst 1 :47⅘ 1:13⅕ 1:40 Alw 23000 3 4 2¹ 2¹ 2½ 1ⁿᵈ Guerra A A⁷ 110 6.90 66-35 Equalize 110ⁿᵈGlennBrooke1121½TruthBeTold122ⁿᵒ Off sluggishly 9
15Mar85- 6Aqu fst 7f :23⅕ :47⅘ 1:27 Md Sp Wt 13 3 5³ 4½ 2ⁿᵈ 1½ Guerra A A⁷ 115 58.60 66-40 Equalize 115½ Clever Wake 122² Cost Conscious 1225½ Driving 13
4Mar85- 6Aqu fst 6f ⊡:23 :46⅘ 1:11⅘ Md Sp Wt 10 8 75½ 915 915 814 Guerra A A⁷ 115 17.60e 73-22 EternlPrince122⁸ChngeThLock122ⁿᵏAlx'sGm122ⁿᵒ Raced greenly 10
LATEST WORKOUTS Apr 13 Bel tr.t 4f fst :51⅗ b Apr 5 Bel tr.t 4f fst :53 b Mar 23 Bel tr.t 4f fst :52⅘ b Mar 13 Bel tr.t 4f gd :51⅕ b
17Nov84- 9Lrl fst 6f :23 :47⅕ 1:12⅘ Md Sp Wt 7 11 58½ 3³ 6¹² 10¹⁹½ Delgado A 118 7.30 59-19 Celtic Lad 118⁵ Dashing Dennis 1182½ KingOfLove118ⁿᵈ Fell back 11
LATEST WORKOUTS Apr 18 Aqu 3f fst :35⅕ h ●Apr 5 Bow 3f fst :35⅘ h ●Mar 16 Bow 3f fst :35⅘ h Mar 9 Bow 5f fst 1:01 h

Sport Jet Ro. c. 3, by Amasport—Solojet, by Solo Landing
Own.—Reiber E W Br.—Keyes F (Fla) Tr.—Perlsweig Daniel
119 Lifetime 14 4 2 3 $67,582 1985 7 1 2 2 $42,077 1984 7 3 0 1 $25,505
6Apr85- 8GS fst 1 :45⅘ 1:10 1:35⅘ Cherryhill H 13 2 22½ 22 26 412½ Allen R D Jr b 114 42.60f — — Spend A Buck122¹⁰½IAmTheGame115½KingBabar1161½ Weakened 14
16Mar85- 10Tam fst 1⅟₁₆ :47⅘ 1:12⅘ 1:46⅘ Bud Tam Dby 10 6 62½ 41½ 3² 32½ Allen R D Jr b 118 20.60 83-17 Regal Remark 122² Verification 122ⁿᵏ Sport Jet 1181½ Brushed 14
16Mar85-Grade III
6Mar85- 9Tam fst 7f :23 :47⅘ 1:27 Sam F Davis 2 10 89½ 87 31½ 43 Rivera J R b 118 10.50 86-26 Tamao's Gray118ⁿᵏSparklingJay1201½JetCadet1151½ Stumbled st. 13
16Feb85- 9Tam fst 7f :23⅘ :47⅕ 1:26⅕ Ocala Brdrs 6 2 2ⁿᵈ 2½ 2¹ 33½ Rivera H Jr b 118 1.70 89-20 Tajawa 115ⁿᵈ Sparkling Jay 1183½ Sport Jet 118¹¹ Weakened 7
6Feb85- 9Tam sly 6f :22⅘ :46⅘ 1:12⅘ Gr'tno Rice 2 5 57 33½ 3¹ 11½ Rivera H Jr b 122 2.30 81-23 Sport Jet 1221½ Devil's Millhopper 1193½ Scatbird 1225½ Driving 5
23Jan85- 9Tam fst 6f :22⅘ :46⅕ 1:11⅘ Spect'ar Bid 8 3 2¹ 2ⁿᵈ 2½ 21½ Rivera H Jr b 116 3.10 85-20 Scatbird 1131½ Sport Jet 1161½ Sparkling Jay 116ⁿᵈ 2nd best 9
9Jan85- 9Tam fst 6f :22⅘ :46⅘ 1:12⅘ ⓇAffirmed 5 3 54½ 43½ 42½ 2½ Rydowski S R 113 *1.10 81-24 Sparkling Jay 119½ Sport Jet 113² Scatbird 112½ Rallied 7
15Dec84- 8Tam fst 6f :23⅕ :47⅘ 1:15⅕ Fla Brd Cham 3 5 4½ 41½ 31½ 3ⁿᵏ Breen R b 117 *1.10 69-29 Tamao'sGray122ⁿᵏCherokeeFst119ⁿᵈSportJet117½ Steadied, bmpb 11
6Dec84- 8Tam fst 6f :23⅘ :47⅘ 1:14 Bay Harbor 3 2 2ⁿᵈ 1ⁿᵈ 1½ 12½ Luhr R D b 115 2.60 75-38 Sport Jet 1152½ Sparkling Jay 1201½ BeauMonde1122½ Ridden out 9
15Nov84- 9Crc fst 6f :22⅖ :46 1:12⅘ Clm 40000 1 3 1½ 1½ 1½ 1ⁿᵒ Breen R b 116 37.10 89-22 Sport Jet 116ⁿᵒ Valatory 1161½ Hickory Hill Flyer 1071½ Driving 9
LATEST WORKOUTS ●Apr 19 GS 3f fst :34⅘ h ●Apr 5 GS 3f fst :35⅕ h Mar 30 GS 5f fst 1:00 h ●Feb 27 Tam 5f fst 1:03 h

Bolting Holme B. c. 3, by Noholme II—Bolt, by Tom Rolfe
Own.—Braude H M Br.—Silver & Smith & Williamson (Fla) Tr.—Wheeler Robert E
119 Lifetime 13 4 3 1 $95,865 1985 4 1 2 0 $21,730 1984 9 3 1 1 $74,135 Turf 1 0 0 0
16Mar85- 6Pim fst 6f :23⅕ :46⅕ 1:11⅘ Alw 22000 7 5 66½ 56 3³ 2ⁿᵈ Bracciale V Jr 119 3.50 89-15 BeaQulity114ⁿᵈBoltingHolme1191½RollDemBones115⁷ Just missed 7
2Mar85- 8Lrl fst 1 :46⅘ 1:12⅕ 1:38 ⓇDncing Count 7 5 4² 3¹ 3⁴ 23½ Miller D A Jr 119 4.70 79-26 AlongCmeJones1123½BoltingHolm1191½JyBryn1191½ Wide, rallied 7
18Feb85- 8Lrl fst 1 :46⅕ 1:11⅘ 1:37⅘ Gen George 3 5 42½ 64½ 64½ 68½ Lloyd J S 119 14.60 75-20 Roo Art 122² Joyfull John 112⁴ I Am The Game 1191½ Tired 8
26Jan85- 7Key fst 7f :22⅘ :45⅘ 1:25⅘ ⓇHolly 4 2 4² 3ⁿᵏ 1ⁿᵈ 1² Lloyd J S 120 *1.50 80-22 BoltingHolm120²Jck'sGoldrunnr113ⁿᵏExubrntWy115½ Drew clear 7
17Nov84- 8Aqu fst 1⅛ :49 1:12⅘ 1:53⅕ Remsen 2 7 77 6⁵ 4⁷ 47½ Passmore W J 115 37.70 61-31 Stone White 113³ Mighty Appealing 1222½ Hot Debate 117¹ Wide 11
17Nov84-Grade I; Awarded third purse money
4Nov84- 8Key fst 7f :22⅘ :45 1:23⅘ ⓇAnniversary 3 6 53½ 55½ 43½ 11½ Passmore W J 118 6.80 90-17 Bolting Holme 1181½ DandyDanny118²BanjoDancing121ⁿᵈ Driving 6
6Oct84- 8Lrl fst 1⅟₁₆ :46⅘ 1:12⅘ 1:43 Laurel Fty 1 7 94½ 109½ 79½ 513 Pino M G 122 91.70 80-15 MightyAppeling1222½CutlssRelity122ⁿᵈRhomnRul122¹⁰ No factor 12
6Oct84-Grade I
22Sep84- 7Lrl sly 1 :47⅘ 1:14 1:40⅘ Alw 10000 5 5 54½ 41½ 34½ 1² Miller D A Jr 115 2.50 70-26 Bolting Holme 115² Alikazammie115ⁿᵈCleverNow115³ Drew clear 12
15Sep84- 5Bel sly 7f :22⅘ :46 1:23⅕ Futurity 1 5 32½ 5⁴ 819 821 Maple E 122 55.60 65-18 SpectacularLove122¹Chief'sCrown1223½Mugzy'sRullah1222½ Tired 8
15Sep84-Grade I
22Aug84- 5Sar fm 1 ⓣ:47⅘ 1:12⅘ 1:38⅕ Alw 21000 9 7 65½ 67½ 86½ 68½ MacBeth D 117 3.60 76-20 WstrnChmp117½NicklBck117ⁿᵏDon'tFoolWithM1173½ Forced out 10
LATEST WORKOUTS Apr 14 Lrl 6f fst 1:15 h ●Apr 3 Lrl 6f fst 1:13 h Mar 14 Lrl 4f gd :50⅘ b Mar 1 Lrl 3f fst :36⅘ b

Second choice at 2–1 was the Maryland invader Bolting Holme. Although away from the races for five weeks, he seemed to be the class of the field. He was already a two-time stakes winner at the seven-furlong distance, once after a nine-week layoff. Although he had failed on three previous excursions to New York (twice in Grade I events), this was a softer spot, and he figured to have the bias working in his favor. Front bandages on this shipper posed a problem, though. Were they standard equipment? Or were they protecting an injury related to the colt's recent layoff?

Third choice at 5–2 was Sport Jet, probably second best to Spend A Buck in the Cherry Hill Mile at Garden State two weeks earlier. In that race, he finished within two lengths of stakes winners I Am The Game and King Babar, after chasing the eventual Derby winner for seven furlongs. King Babar had been the victor in the Swift Stakes at Aqueduct early in March. Sport Jet's sharp blowout for this race suggested that he might be the pacesetter in a field seemingly devoid of front-running speed.

Also interesting (at 4–1) was Equalize, the winner of two straight in New York. In his recent allowance victory, he defeated Truth Be Told by two lengths, a margin larger than Summitry had managed, despite being far less seasoned than Summitry at that time. Based on this comparison alone, Equalize seemed a far better bet than Summitry at the prevailing odds, especially since Summitry figured to be rail speed and Equalize appeared likely to rally from the two- or three-path. But to take Equalize seriously against two colts with stakes credentials, one had to answer the question "Who Is Glenn Brooke?" Glenn Brooke, of course, was the horse that charged at Equalize on March 25.

In situations like this, the professional (every day) player holds a decided edge over his once-a-week rival and would probably be able to identify Glenn Brooke as a New York-bred that had won only two races in sixteen starts, including his narrow loss to Equalize—information that would convince most players to make their choice between Bolting Holme and Sport Jet in this race. Indeed, information that, in this case at least, would have led most players astray, because Equalize rallied gamely in the final yards to wear down the front-running Sport Jet, with Summitry right there in third.

FIFTH RACE
Aqueduct
APRIL 20, 1985

7 FURLONGS. (1.20⅕) 1st Running THE MANASSA MAULER STAKES. Purse $50,000 Added (Closing Wednesday, April 10). 3–year–olds which have never won a race of $25,000, 122 lbs. Non–winners of a race of $20,000 allowed, 3 lbs. Of two races other than maiden or claiming, 5 lbs. Of a race other than maiden or claiming, 7 lbs. $100 to nominate; $200 to enter and $200 to start. (Maiden, Claiming, Starter and State–Bred Races not considered.) A trophy will be presented to the owner of the winner. Closed with nominations.
Value of race $53,900; value to winner $32,340; second $11,858; third $6,468; fourth $3,234. Mutuel pool $233,796, OTB pool $114,243.

Last Raced	Horse	Eqt.	A.	Wt	PP	St	¼	½	Str	Fin	Jockey	Odds $1
25Mar85 7Aqu1	Equalize		3	117	3	4	4 1½	3 1½	3 1	1 nk	Cordero A Jr	4.30
6Apr85 8GS4	Sport Jet	b	3	119	4	2	1 hd	1 hd	2 2½	2 ¾	Allen R D Jr	2.60
4Apr85 7Aqu1	Summitry	b	3	117	2	3	2 1½	2 3	1 hd	3 1¼	Santagata N	1.70
16Mar85 6Pim2	Bolting Holme		3	119	5	1	3 1	4 2½	4 2½	4 2¼	Velasquez J	2.30
3Apr85 5GS1	Meghan's Deal	b	3	117	1	5	5	5	5	5	Vasquez J	12.20

OFF AT 3:19 Start good, Won driving. Time, :23⅕, :45⅗, 1:09⅘, 1:22⅗ Track muddy.

$2 Mutuel Prices:			
3–(D)–EQUALIZE	10.60	5.20	2.80
4–(E)–SPORT JET		3.60	2.40
2–(B)–SUMMITRY			2.40

Gr. c, by Northern Jove—Zonta, by Dr Fager. Trainer Nerud Jan H. Bred by Tartan Farms (Fla).

EQUALIZE, never far back while racing well out in the track, finished strongly to wear down SPORT JET. The latter raced outside SUMMITRY while vying for the lead to deep stretch and continued on with good courage. SUMMITRY saved ground while vying for the lead to deep stretch and weakened slightly. BOLTING HOLME dropped back around the turn, then failed to seriously menace with a mild late response. MEGHAN'S DEAL was always outrun.

Those who were unable to identify Glenn Brooke on April 20 found their answer the following day. Glenn Brooke was entered in

9 AQUEDUCT

7 FURLONGS (AQUEDUCT)

7 FURLONGS. (1.20⅕) ALLOWANCE. Purse $25,500. 3-year-olds and upward foaled in New York State and approved by the New York State-bred Registry which have never won a race other than maidern, claiming or starter. Weights, 3-year-olds, 112 lbs. lbs. Older, 124 lbs. Non-winners of a race other than claiming since April 1, allowed 3 lbs.

How About Now

Ch. c. 3, by For The Moment—Naskranaut, by Naskra
Br.—Johnson & Whitney (NY)
Tr.—Johnson Philip G
Own.—Cobble View St

109 Lifetime 9 1 0 2 $22,050 | 1985 5 1 0 2 $22,050 | 1984 4 M 0 0

5Apr85- 5Aqu	fst	1	:46 1:10⅘ 1:37⅕	3+[S]Alw 27000	4 6 86½ 911 911 89¼	Samyn J L		112	8.70	71-23 CaptainMarvel1141½HistoryResponds1091¼IrishCuvee1212 Outrun	9
17Mar85- 5Aqu	fst	1	:48 1:14⅘ 1:42⅕	[S]Md Sp Wt	12 11 89¾ 89¾ 43 13	Samyn J L		122	6.10	55-33 How About Now 1223 Playfull John 122¾ Root Canal1222 Driving	14
8Mar85- 4Aqu	fst	1⅛ ⊡	:48⅖ 1:13⅗ 1:53⅖	[S]Md Sp Wt	2 8 86 74½ 512 410½	Samyn J L		122	4.90	65-18 Gallant Rake122nkRomanizer1225¾PlayfullJohn1224½ Lost stirrups	12
21Feb85- 6Aqu	fst	1 1/16 ⊡	:49⅗ 1:15⅖ 1:49⅖	[S]Md Sp Wt	5 4 41¾ 1hd 32 38½	Samyn J L	b	122	5.50	55-29 Poniard 1224 Noisy WhenHot1174½HowAboutNow1228 Weakened	12
4Feb85- 9Aqu	fst	1⅛ ⊡	:47⅗ 1:13⅘ 1:54⅖	[S]Md Sp Wt	2 5 52½ 3½ 21 36½	Samyn J L	b	122	5.00	63-21 GlennBrook1171¾Ponird1224¾HowAboutNow1221¾ Altered course	11
29Dec84- 4Aqu	fst	170 ⊡	:46⅖ 1:11⅖ 1:42⅘	Md Sp Wt	4 9 1014 916 710 710½	Skinner K		118	3.30e	77-09 First Blast 118noMountGuard118hdReviveTheEchoes1182½ Outrun	10
2Dec84- 4Aqu	fst	6f	:23⅕ :47⅖ 1:14⅕	[S]Md Sp Wt	8 4 55¾ 59 59½ 55½	Samyn J L		118	13.30	65-24 Pico De Gallo118¾GlennBrooke1113¾LuckySkipper111½ No threat	12
22Nov84- 6Aqu	fst	6f	:22⅘ :46⅗ 1:12⅘	Md Sp Wt	4 14 119½ 1119 910 812	Cordero A Jr		118	27.80e	65-29 MedievlMrket1132½WightInGold118¾TruthBTold1181¼ Slow early	14
11Nov84- 2Aqu	fst	6f	:22⅗ :46⅘ 1:13⅘	Md Sp Wt	6 9 1011 1013 1012 1013½	Samyn J L		118	15.10	61-25 Romancer 1182 [D]Easton 1181¼ Uene 113nk Bore out st.	11

11Nov84-Placed ninth through disqualification

LATEST WORKOUTS Apr 18 Bel tr.t 3f fst :38 b · Apr 3 Bel 4f fst :50⅘ b · Mar 30 Bel tr.t 4f fst :51⅕ b · Mar 25 Bel tr.t 4f fst :51⅕ b

Neat Sam

Ro. c. 3, by My Old Friend—Nora The Decorator, by Rip 'n Skip
Br.—Star L D (NY)
Tr.—Barrera Oscar S Jr
Own.—Star L D

104⁵ Lifetime 10 1 1 0 $15,027 | 1984 10 1 1 0 $15,027

19Dec84- 2Aqu	fst	6f ⊡	:23 :47 1:13⅘	Clm 30000	3 6 41½ 55 74 75½	Davis R G	b	113	16.20	70-25 Top Talk 113hd Super Scope 1081¾ [D]Student ofDance108hd Tired	11
16Dec84- 6Aqu	fst	6f ⊡	:23⅕ :46⅘ 1:13⅕	[S]Alw 25500	2 8 31½ 34 712 812¾	Davis R G	b	117	10.40	65-24 Pico De Gallo 122¾ Club Fighter 1193½ Silent Slander 1172½ Tired	9
7Oct84- 1Bel	fst	7f	:23⅕ :46⅘ 1:26⅕	[S]Alw 24500	4 3 11½ 2hd 42 610½	Cruguet J	b	117	19.00	60-25 Artie Baby 1192½ Hot Debate 1222½ Scottish Cross 1171½ Tired	7
23Sep84- 9FL	fst	6f	:22⅘ :46⅖ 1:13	[S]Ny Brdrs Fty	8 9 87¾ 89½ 910 1014½	Cook R W	b	122	23.60	69-20 Rollick 'NRoll1221ScottishCross1223LoveYouSis1192 Stumbled st	12
9Sep84- 8FL	fst	6f	:22⅘ :47 1:13⅘	[S]Aspirant	6 9 76 54½ 33 45½	Hernandez R	b	122	2.50e[D]	74-26 Rollick 'N Roll 122½ SincereRullah1223ScottishCross1222 Bore in	9

9Sep84-Disqualified and placed fifth

17Aug84- 8Sar	fst	6f	:22⅖ :45⅘ 1:11⅘	[S]Empire	7 11 67½ 66 54½ 45	Hernandez R	b	115	22.50	76-21 BazookaBabe116noLittleVenture1174¾QueenBreeze116nk Wide str	12
2Aug84- 6Mth	fst	6f	:22⅗ :45⅗ 1:11⅗	Clm 35000	6 4 1hd 2½ 22½ 22½	McCauley W H	b	113	11.60	80-20 I'mARutabaga1082½NeatSam1136FootbllCoch113½ Best of others	9
13Jun84- 3Bel	fst	5½f	:23⅕ :47⅘ 1:07⅕	Md 25000	3 5 32 32 2½ 1½	Garrido O L7		111	3.60	79-18 Neat Sam 111½ Poppops Josh 1147 Hidden Surprise 1185 Driving	8
7Jun84- 4Bel	fst	5f	:22⅕ :46 :59⅕	[S]Md Sp Wt	5 4 58½ 58½ 58½ 610	Gomez I		118	6.40	81-17 LittleVenture1183½CleverChamp1182½CaptinMrvel1181¼ No factor	8
23May84- 4Bel	fst	5f	:22⅘ :47⅕ 1:00⅖	[S]Md Sp Wt	4 3 32½ 44½ 42¾ 41½	Gomez I		118	32.90	84-16 Who's The Judge 118nk Loyal Lynn 115nk SteelCity118¾ Willingly	7

LATEST WORKOUTS Apr 19 Bel tr.t 3f fst :35⅘ h · ●Apr 15 Bel tr.t 3f fst :36⅕ h · Apr 12 Bel tr.t 5f fst 1:02⅗ b · ●Apr 8 Bel tr.t 3f gd :35 h

According To Luke

B. c. 3, by Robin's Song—Joy For Daddy, by Daryl's Joy
Br.—Pineau A L & Patricia (NY)
Tr.—Daggett Michael H
Own.—Kern Margarite

109 Lifetime 16 2 2 3 $22,302 | 1985 10 1 1 3 $17,820 | 1984 6 1 1 0 $4,482 | Turf 1 0 0 0

13Apr85- 9Aqu	fst	1	:47 1:12 1:37⅘	3+[S]Alw 27000	6 8 75½ 54 33½ 25¾	Samyn J L	b	109	8.00	72-21 AnothrSmmr1125¾AccordngToLk109nkTkATlc121½ Best of others	11
29Mar85- 6Aqu	fst	1	:47⅘ 1:12 1:38	Clm c-25000	4 3 31 42 4¾ 3¾	Cordero A Jr	b	117	*1.20	75-21 Scholastic 117½ Southern Joe 117nkAccordingToLuke1173 Evenly	8
14Mar85- 7Aqu	fst	1⅛	:48⅘ 1:13⅘ 1:52⅘	Alw 23000	7 7 77 86½ 816 816½	Ward W A5	b	112	7.70	55-35 StrongStatement1193CrystlIceberg117noTruthBeTold1227 Outrun	8
6Mar85- 4Aqu	fst	1⅛ ⊡	:48⅖ 1:14 1:53⅘	Clm 30000	4 12 96½ 84½ 52 3hd	Samyn J L	b	113	4.80	73-26 DebateACase113hdI'mABnker117noAccordingToLuke113nk Rallied	12
3Mar85- 9Aqu	fst	1 1/16 ⊡	:47⅗ 1:13⅖ 1:46⅘	[S]Alw 27000	5 7 84¾ 73½ 41½ 5¾	Samyn J L	b	117	10.00	75-17 Revive The Echoes 117no Glenn Brooke 114nk Poniard122nk Hung	10
15Feb85- 1Aqu	fst	1⅛ ⊡	:48⅖ 1:14⅗ 1:54⅘	Alw 23000	1 8 814 86¾ 614 613½	Graell A	b	117	5.90	54-26 Uene 1194 Revive The Echoes 117½ Golden Chief 1172 Outrun	8
7Feb85- 7Aqu	fst	6f ⊡	:22⅕ :46⅕ 1:11⅘	[S]Alw 25500	9 12 1212 1120 79¾ 36¾	Davis R G	b	117	7.60	78-24 RdiclChnge1126½HistoryRsponds122½AccordingToLuk117½ Rallied	12
30Jan85- 3Aqu	fst	6f ⊡	:23 :46⅘ 1:13⅗	Clm 25000	5 1 76½ 78½ 34½ 2hd	Davis R G	b	119	5.90[D]	76-25 FlyMAgin110hd[D]AccordingToLuk1192½Bolingr1174 Broke out st.	7

30Jan85-Disqualified and placed seventh

25Jan85- 3Aqu	fst	1 1/16 ⊡	:48⅗ 1:14 1:48⅕	Clm c-20000	3 3 44½ 79½ 613 514¾	Miceli M	b	117	3.30	54-23 Gorsk1081½BoldBob'sDusty1083CountryKitchn1171½ Showed little	9
5Jan85- 3Bow	sly	6½f	:22⅘ :45⅘ 1:20⅕	Clm 18500	6 4 58½ 46 33 11½	Kaenel J L	b	115	*1.80	86-22 AccordingToLuke1151½GllntSolo114nkBurntFthrs1154½ Drew clear	6

LATEST WORKOUTS Apr 11 Bel tr.t 4f fst :48⅘ b · Apr 6 Bel tr.t 5f fst 1:05⅕ b · Mar 26 Bel tr.t 3f fst :38 b · Feb 25 Bel tr.t 4f fst :49⅗ hg

Effective Action

Dk. b. or br. c. 3, by Kirby Lane—Dem's Pleasure, by Noholme II or Selari
Br.—DeLuke D J (NY)
Tr.—Drogitis Michael
Own.—Assunta Louis Farm

112 Lifetime 7 1 0 2 $22,020 | 1985 2 1 0 0 $15,420 | 1984 5 M 0 2 $6,600

13Apr85- 9Aqu	fst	1	:47 1:12 1:37⅘	3+[S]Alw 27000	3 4 43½ 31½ 23 46½	Vasquez J	b	112	26.80	71-21 AnotherSummr1125¾AccordingToLuk109nkTkATlc121½ Weakened	11
2Apr85- 4Aqu	fst	6f	:23 :46⅘ 1:12⅖	3+[S]Md Sp Wt	13 1 41½ 2hd 1½ 11½	Vasquez J	b	112	16.30	79-20 Effective Action 1121½ Exmoon 124nk Pekoe 1121 Drew clear	13
30Nov84- 6Aqu	fst	7f	:22⅗ :45⅗ 1:25⅕	[S]Md Sp Wt	12 12 53 31 57½ 510¾	Davis R G	b	118	12.80	64-23 Club Fighter 118¾ Over the Wall 1182½ Casa Key 1157 Tired	14
1Oct84- 9Bel	sly	7f	:22⅖ :46⅗ 1:25⅘	[S]Md Sp Wt	5 4 46 31½ 22 36½	Davis R G		118	6.00	67-24 AuctionEvder1186½GlnnBrook111noEffctivAction1185½ Weakened	11
23Sep84- 9FL	fst	6f	:22⅖ :46⅖ 1:13	[S]Ny BrdrsFty	11 4 65½ 54½ 78 912½	McCauley W H		122	15.30	71-20 Rollick 'N Roll 1221 Scottish Cross 1223LoveYouSis1192 No rally	12
16Sep84- 4Bel	my	6f	:22⅘ :46⅘ 1:11⅘	[S]Md Sp Wt	7 4 77 63¾ 56½ 46½	Davis R G		118	6.50	76-16 HotDebate1183¾FearlessTeddy1181½AuctionEvder1131½ No factor	11
5Sep84- 6Bel	fst	6f	:22⅘ :46⅖ 1:12⅖	[S]Md Sp Wt	7 9 98½ 89¾ 55¾ 31½	Davis R G		118	43.80	79-12 Artie Baby 1181½TheTinkerman118hdEffectiveAction1182½ Rallied	13

LATEST WORKOUTS Apr 11 Bel tr.t 4f fst :52 b · Mar 29 Bel tr.t 5f fst 1:02⅘ b · Mar 10 Bel tr.t 4f fst :49 h · ●Mar 4 Bel tr.t 6f fst 1:18 b

Glenn Brooke

Gr. c. 3, by Flip Sal—Gay Bonny, by Lord Gaylord
Br.—Old Westbury Assoc I (NY)
Tr.—Sedlacek Sue
Own.—Tresvant Stable

105⁵ Lifetime 18 2 6 3 $64,530 | 1985 10 2 3 1 $48,040 | 1984 8 M 3 2 $16,490

13Apr85- 9Aqu	fst	1	:47 1:12 1:37⅘	3+[S]Alw 27000	2 11 108½ 97½ 76½ 69½	Garrido O L5		106	*2.00	68-21 AnotherSummer1125¾AccordingToLuke109nkTkeATlc121½ Outrun	11
4Apr85- 7Aqu	fst	7f	:23⅕ :46⅕ 1:23⅕	Alw 22000	2 6 74¾ 74½ 64 45½	Garrido O L5		112	8.80	80-19 Summitry 117½ Truth Be Told 1191¾ See The Way 1173 Mild gain	7
25Mar85- 7Aqu	fst	1	:47⅖ 1:13⅕ 1:40	Alw 23000	5 8 74 54 41½ 2hd	Garrido O L5		112	13.50	66-35 Equalize 110hd Glenn Brooke1121¾TruthBeTold122no Sharp effort	9
14Mar85- 7Aqu	fst	1⅛	:48⅘ 1:13⅘ 1:52⅘	Alw 23000	8 8 88 76 611 613	Garrido O L5		112	4.50	58-35 StrongSttement1193CrystlIcebrg117noTruthBTold1227 No factor	8
3Mar85- 9Aqu	fst	1 1/16 ⊡	:47⅗ 1:13⅖ 1:46⅘	[S]Alw 27000	4 10 106½ 51½ 1hd 2no	Garrido O L5		114	4.40	76-17 ReviveTheEchoes117noGlennBrook114nkPonird122nk Sharp effort	10
18Feb85- 1Aqu	fst	1 1/16 ⊡	:48⅕ 1:13⅘ 1:48	Clm 70000	4 6 68½ 65½ 54½ 54½	Garrido O L5		110	4.10	66-28 Bold Bob's Dusty 114¾ Olajuwon 115½ Helcin 112¾ Evenly	8
10Feb85- 3Aqu	fst	1⅛ ⊡	:48 1:13⅗ 1:53⅖	Clm 45000	11 5 54 41½ 12½ 13½	Moore D N5		110	6.50	75-18 Glenn Brooke 1103½ Classi Valentine 117no Natrac 113½ Driving	11
4Feb85- 9Aqu	fst	1⅛ ⊡	:47⅗ 1:13⅘ 1:54⅖	[S]Md Sp Wt	3 4 42½ 41 11 11¾	Garrido O L5		117	3.20	70-21 GlnnBrook1171¾Ponird1224¾HowAboutNow1221¾ Lugged in, clear	11
28Jan85- 6Aqu	fst	6f ⊡	:23 :47⅘ 1:14⅕	[S]Md Sp Wt	5 2 75½ 66½ 42 3¾	Garrido O L5		117	*1.40	72-25 HsRoylHghnss122½BlldogDrmmnd122nkGlnnBrk1171¾ Cont'd well	12
10Jan85- 9Aqu	fst	6f ⊡	:22⅘ :46⅗ 1:12⅘	[S]Md Sp Wt	2 5 54½ 44 31½ 2½	Garrido O L5		117	*3.10	79-22 Dewan Light 122½ Glenn Brooke 1172½RareDiligence1171¾ Gamey	12

LATEST WORKOUTS Apr 19 Aqu 3f fst :37⅖ b · Feb 28 Aqu ⊡ 3f fst :37 b

Joaleo

Dk. b. or br. g. 4, by Red Anchor—Hidden Agenda, by Handsome Boy
Br.—Taub A & J (NY)
Tr.—Sciacca Gary J
Own.—Taub Stables

111¹⁰ Lifetime 16 1 0 2 $9,870 | 1985 6 0 0 1 $2,850 | 1984 9 1 0 1 $7,020

10Apr85- 1Aqu	fst	6f	:23⅕ :46⅘ 1:12⅖	Clm 13000	6 1 2½ 21½ 24 3½	Lalman D10	b	107	6.40	78-29 Dancing Native 113no Another Tina 112½ Joaleo 107½ Weakened	9
1Apr85- 7Aqu	fst	6f	:22⅕ :45⅗ 1:10	3+[S]Alw 25500	13 1 2½ 3½ 36 69½	Lalman D10	b	111	14.20	82-17 GllopRhythm1126½AnotherSummer109hdStrOfBordux1122½ Faded	13
17Mar85- 4Aqu	fst	7f	:23 :47⅕ 1:27	[S]Alw 25500	6 2 21½ 2hd 2½ 4¾	Lalman D10	b	107	26.20	65-33 WrightSkipper117noBudOut117¾Herecomesthchif117hd Weakened	11
2Mar85- 4Aqu	fst	6f ⊡	:22⅗ :46⅗ 1:12	[S]Alw 25500	6 3 3nk 31 44 88½	Lalman D10	b	107	35.80	76-19 Iron Face 1176 Timperature 110¾ I'm Up Top 117nk Tired	12
23Feb85- 9Aqu	fst	1 1/16 ⊡	:48⅗ 1:14⅕ 1:48	Clm 13000	4 1 12 41½ 1012 1015¾	Lalman D10		105	38.80	54-21 Abacus Boy 117nk Josiah W. 1122½ Palimony 1173 Stopped	11
28Jan85- 9Aqu	fst	6f ⊡	:23 :47⅗ 1:13	Clm 15500	6 5 31½ 86½ 1014 1015½	Lalman D10	b	105	18.90	63-25 Big Ralph 1131 Startop 117¾ What A Charger 1172 Tired	10
29Dec84- 9Aqu	fst	6f ⊡	:22⅖ :45⅗ 1:11⅗	Clm 12000	4 8 11½ 1½ 1hd 31½	Lalman D10	b	105	53.20	86-09 Proud Stock 117½ Randall H. 117¾ Joaleo 105¾ Grudgingly	10
19Dec84- 1Aqu	fst	6f ⊡	:23 :47⅕ 1:13	Clm 12000	11 1 2hd 88 1024 1027½	Gomez E R	b	113	24.50	52-25 Dumb Pomme 1083½ Oscar's Gold 112nk Another Tina 1171 Tired	11
9Dec84- 9Aqu	fst	6f ⊡	:22⅖ :46⅕ 1:12⅘	Clm 14000	9 2 22 37 1011 1113½	Gomez E R		117	36.20	66-19 Adirondack Pride 1171½ Gretzky 1171½ Sea Glow 115nk Stopped	11
9May84- 2Bel	fst	7f	:23 :47⅕ 1:25⅗	Clm 16000	1 1 1hd 77 1124 1132½	Gomez E R		117	21.20	42-21 One Winner 1191¼ El Professor 1173½ Camino Joe 1133¾ Stopped	11

LATEST WORKOUTS Mar 27 Aqu 3f fst :36⅖ h · ●Mar 10 Aqu 3f fst :35⅘ h

My Sondance

Dk. b. or br. c. 4, by Flying Error—Dancing Dana, by Bold Monarch
Br.—Cardile S (NY)
Tr.—Cardile Saverio
Own.—Cardile S

114⁷ Lifetime 28 1 0 0 $19,560 | 1985 8 0 0 0 $2,250 | 1984 20 1 0 0 $17,310

14Apr85- 1Aqu	fst	6f	:23⅕ :46⅖ 1:11⅕	Clm 25000	8 2 63¾ 108 97½ 910¾	Guerra A A7		110	14.20e	74-22 Ecstatic Pride 114¾ Act It Out 1171¾ Fletcher 1131½ Fin. early	12
5Apr85- 5Aqu	fst	1	:46 1:10⅘ 1:37⅕	3+[S]Alw 27000	1 1 1hd 3nk 64½ 78½	Guerra A A7		114	20.60	71-23 Captain Marvel 1141½ HistoryResponds1091¼IrishCuvee1212 Tired	9
1Apr85- 7Aqu	fst	6f	:22⅕ :45⅗ 1:10	3+[S]Alw 25500	7 3 105½ 65½ 67½ 48½	Guerra A A7		114	5.70f	82-17 GllpRhythm1126½AnthrSmmr109hdStrOfBrdx1122½ Overland route	13
25Mar85- 9Aqu	fst	7f	:23⅖ :47⅘ 1:26⅖	Clm 17500	9 1 41½ 31½ 42 46½	Guerra A A7		110	39.30	63-35 AccountReceivable1193½Nostranaut117½Mr.Rdius1172½ Weakened	9
17Mar85- 4Aqu	fst	7f	:23 :47⅕ 1:27	[S]Alw 25500	4 3 43½ 42 31½ 53½	Guerra A A7		110	62.20	63-33 WrightSkipper117noBudOut117¾Herecomesthchif117hd No excuse	11
6Mar85- 2Aqu	fst	6f ⊡	:23⅕ :47 1:12⅗	Clm 17500	2 3 67 817 819 818	Guerra A A5	b	112	41.10	63-26 Dancing Native 1121 Fancy Talker117nkAnotherTina1173½ Outrun	10
2Mar85- 4Aqu	fst	6f ⊡	:22⅗ :46⅗ 1:12	[S]Alw 25500	5 9 108½ 1211 1214 1114½	Garrido O L5	b	112	65.80	69-19 Iron Face 1176 Timperature 110¾ I'm Up Top 117nk Outrun	12
14Jan85- 1Aqu	fst	6f ⊡	:22⅖ :45⅘ 1:12⅗	[S]Alw 25500	8 5 98¾ 822 815 711½	Privitera R5		112	34.10	70-20 Adirondack Pride 1173 Caramba 117nk Gretzky 112hd Outrun	10
26Dec84- 5Aqu	fst	6f ⊡	:22⅖ :46⅖ 1:12⅗	3+[S]Alw 25500	1 1 22 43½ 46½ 75¾	Moore D N5		110	47.70	75-21 Joyful Promise 1153 Columbia Pride 115¾ Bud Out 115nk Tired	8
14Dec84- 6Aqu	fst	6f ⊡	:23⅕ :47 1:12	3+[S]Alw 25500	3 5 74½ 712 711 812	Moore D N5		110	45.30	72-19 Vital Chum 1121¼ What APhilip115¾NorthernCondor1152¾ Outrun	8

LATEST WORKOUTS Mar 30 Bel tr.t 3f fst :41 b

Razalu — Ch. c. 4, by Jungle Savage—Hospiday, by Hawaii
Own.—Surazal Stable — Br.—Lazarus M (NY) — Tr.—Aquilino Joseph — 121
Lifetime 8 1 2 0 $27,580 — 1985 4 1 0 0 $13,800 — 1984 4 M 2 0 $13,780

17Mar85- 4Aqu fst 7f :23 :47⅕ 1:27 (S)Alw 25500 9 6 54½ 63 87 87½ Migliore R b 117 4.00 59-33 Wright Skipper 117no Bud Out117¾Herecomesthechief117hd Tired 11
10Feb85- 6Aqu fst 1 1/16 ⊡:47⅘ 1:12⅘ 1:45⅘ (S)Alw 27000 3 9 1111 106½ 89½ 78¾ Migliore R b 117 9.10 72-18 Ivor'sRobbed115nkHerecomesthchif1171½ArmsRc1121¾ No threat 12
2Feb85- 4Aqu my 6f ⊡:23⅖ :47⅗ 1:12⅗ (S)Alw 25500 10 8 104½ 68 812 914¾ Migliore R b 119 3.70 66-28 Omas Josh 1175 Ivor's Robbed 115¾ Gretzky 112no Wide 11
7Jan85- 6Aqu fst 6f ⊡:22⅖ :46⅗ 1:12⅘ (S)Md Sp Wt 3 7 43½ 32½ 2hd 1no Migliore R b 122 *1.00 80-27 Razalu 122no Change Nights 117¾ Irish Cuvee 1173½ Just up 12
24Dec84- 9Aqu fst 1 1/16 ⊡:49⅕ 1:14⅘ 1:47⅖ 3+(S)Md Sp Wt 9 7 62½ 21½ 23 2¾ Cordero A Jr b 120 *1.30 74-20 Timperature 120¾ Razalu 1208 Roque's Jewell 1202 2nd best 10
14Dec84- 6Aqu fst 6f ⊡:23⅕ :47 1:12 3+(S)Alw 25500 5 8 31 32½ 44½ 44¾ Cordero A Jr 115 5.20 79-19 VitalChum1121½WhtAPhilip115¾NorthernCondor1152¾ Weakened 8
5Dec84- 6Aqu fst 170 ⊡:49⅕ 1:14⅖ 1:44⅗ 3+(S)Md Sp Wt 4 8 43 42½ 47½ 410 Messina R 120 *.40 67-19 PoppaChrlieK.1208¼Honey'sSeven120noJoey'sMoney1201¾ Evenly 10
16Nov84- 9Aqu fst 1 :47⅕ 1:12⅘ 1:40⅖ 3+(S)Md Sp Wt 6 10 86¾ 47½ 34 2¾ Messina R 120 15.70 63-35 Columbia Gold 120¾ Razalu 1201¼ Timperature 1205 Blckd turn 12
LATEST WORKOUTS Apr 18 Aqu 4f fst :48 h ●Apr 13 Aqu 3f fst :34⅘ h Mar 11 Bel tr.t 5f fst 1:03⅘ b Mar 4 Bel tr.t 3f fst :39⅖ b

Ever Proud — Ch. c. 3, by Effervescing—Proud Tribute, by Proudest Roman
Own.—Entenmann R — Br.—Linder B N (NY) — Tr.—Imperio Dominick A — 112
Lifetime 1 1 0 0 $13,800 — 1985 1 1 0 0 $13,800 — 1984 0 M 0 0

2Apr85- 6Aqu fst 6f :22⅗ :47⅕ 1:11⅘ 3+(S)Md Sp Wt 5 8 31 1½ 11 12¾ Vasquez J 112 *1.00 82-20 EverProud1122¾LegcyOfLove1073¾FvoriteHolme1121½ Ridden out 11
LATEST WORKOUTS ●Apr 18 Bel tr.t 4f fst :47⅕ h ●Apr 12 Bel 5f fst 1:00 h ●Mar 29 Bel tr.t 6f fst 1:12⅘ hg Mar 22 Bel tr.t 4f fst :50 b

Con Lune — Gr. g. 3, by Iron Constitution—Pleine Lune, by Barachois
Own.—Mangurian H T — Br.—Mangurian H T Jr (NY) — Tr.—Root Richard R — 109
Lifetime 5 1 0 0 $13,200 — 1985 1 0 0 0 — 1984 4 1 0 0 $13,200

24Mar85- 8Aqu fst 6f :22⅗ :46⅕ 1:10⅗ (S)Catskill 7 5 54 810 1019 1025 Velasquez J b 114 6.90e 63-26 Radical Change 1148 Artie Baby 120¾ Silent Slander 114hd Tired 10
7Oct84- 1Bel fst 7f :23⅕ :46⅘ 1:26⅕ (S)Alw 24500 6 6 53 711 721 734½ Davis R G b 122 3.60 36-25 Artie Baby 1192½ Hot Debate 1222½ ScottishCross1171½ Fin. early 7
23Sep84- 9FL fst 6f :22⅖ :46⅖ 1:13 (S)Ny Brdrs Fty 6 7 99¼ — — — Rodriguez W b 122 2.20e — — Rollick 'N Roll 1221 Scottish Cross 1223 Love YouSis1192 Bolted 12
16Sep84- 6Bel gd 6f :22⅖ :45⅘ 1:10⅘ (S)Md Sp Wt 5 1 11½ 12½ 16 18 Velasquez J b 118 16.50f 88-10 Con Lune 1188 Over the Wall 1181½ GlennBrooke1112 Ridden out 13
22Aug84- 4Sar fst 6f :22⅘ :46⅘ 1:12⅗ (S)Md Sp Wt 7 6 64¾ 88 813 817¼ Velasquez J b 118 15.00 60-21 Scottish Cross 1182½HotDebate1182½SilentSlander118nk Steadied 13
LATEST WORKOUTS Apr 17 Bel tr.t 4f fst :50⅕ b Apr 11 Bel tr.t 4f fst :49⅘ b Apr 5 Bel tr.t 3f fst :36⅘ h Mar 21 Bel tr.t 3f fst :38⅘ b

Honey's Seven — B. c. 4, by Jackknife—Honey Pep, by Peppy Jay
Own.—Lostritto J A — Br.—Karutz W S (NY) — Tr.—Lostritto Joseph A — 111 10
Lifetime 15 1 2 1 $27,494 — 1985 7 1 0 0 $15,270 — 1984 8 M 2 1 $12,224 — Turf 1 0 0 0

13Apr85- 9Aqu fst 1 :47 1:12 1:37⅗ 3+(S)Alw 27000 1 9 1111 1111 1113 1116¼ Davis R G b 121 61.20 61-21 AnotherSummr1125¾AccordingToLuk109nkTkATlc121½ No factor 11
28Mar85- 7Aqu fst 1⅛ :49⅗ 1:14⅗ 1:54⅘ (S)Alw 27000 9 8 53 31 915 1017 Migliore R b 117 40.90 44-25 LittlOlCtpn1121IntrpidFront114nkHrcomsthchf1172¾ Bid, stopped 10
13Mar85- 2Aqu fst 7f :23⅘ :48⅖ 1:28 (S)Md Sp Wt 8 9 65½ 41½ 12 12 Santagata N b 122 15.30 61-28 Honey's Seven 1222 Change Nights 1176½ Exmoon 122hd Driving 11
27Feb85- 6Aqu fst 1 1/16 ⊡:49⅗ 1:16 1:49⅕ (S)Md Sp Wt 5 5 31 51½ 56½ 412½ Rolon E M10 b 112 30.60 51-24 Intrepid Front 1156 Change Nights 1176½Joey'sMoney117nk Tired 11
13Feb85- 3Aqu fst 6f ⊡:22⅖ :46⅗ 1:13 (S)Md Sp Wt 2 11 1111 1219 913 710½ Samyn J L b 122 12.90 68-20 IrishCuvee117nkPowerhousePet1221½ChngNights1172½ Slow early 12
28Jan85- 1Aqu fst 6f ⊡:22⅘ :46⅗ 1:12⅕ Md 45000 3 5 79½ 716 715 611½ Davis R G b 118 12.80 71-25 Koch's Choice 1183 Frosty Drone 122¾ Bold Bud 1181¾ Outrun 9
7Jan85- 6Aqu fst 6f ⊡:22⅖ :46⅗ 1:12⅘ (S)Md Sp Wt 2 6 66 98½ 87¾ 88 Santagata N 122 13.70 72-27 Razalu 122no Change Nights 117¾ Irish Cuvee 1173½ Outrun 12
24Dec84- 9Aqu fst 1 1/16 ⊡:49⅕ 1:14⅘ 1:47⅖ 3+(S)Md Sp Wt 10 8 84 54 410 410¾ Santagata N 120 8.60 64-20 Timperature 120¾ Razalu 1208 Roque's Jewell 1202 No rally 10
5Dec84- 6Aqu fst 170 ⊡:49⅕ 1:14⅖ 1:44⅗ 3+(S)Md Sp Wt 9 2 2½ 2½ 24 28¼ Santagata N 120 7.30 69-19 PoppChrlieK.1208¼Honey'sSvn120noJoy'sMony1201¾ Held second 10
16Nov84- 9Aqu fst 1 :47⅕ 1:12⅘ 1:40⅖ 3+(S)Md Sp Wt 4 6 41¾ 35½ 58¼ 57½ Santagata N 120 9.10 56-35 Columbia Gold 120¾ Razalu 1201¼ Timperature 1205 Weakened 12
LATEST WORKOUTS Apr 11 Bel tr.t 3f fst :39 b Mar 24 Bel tr.t 4f fst :51 bg

Root Canal — Dk. b. or br. c. 3, by Robin's Song—Tooth For Tooth, by Boldnesian
Own.—Peters L J — Br.—Peters M Elena (NY) — Tr.—Johnstone Bruce — 109
Lifetime 6 1 1 3 $28,280 — 1985 5 1 1 2 $25,640 — 1984 1 M 0 1 $2,640

29Mar85- 9Aqu fst 1 :46⅗ 1:11⅘ 1:38⅖ (S)Md Sp Wt 1 3 11 11 11 1¾ Vasquez J 122 3.40 74-21 Root Canal 122¾ Ethics Aside 1227½ Romanizer 122¾ Driving 12
17Mar85- 5Aqu fst 1 :48 1:14⅘ 1:42⅕ (S)Md Sp Wt 8 3 13 15 12 33¾ Migliore R b 122 5.70 51-33 How About Now 1223 PlayfullJohn122¾RootCanal1222 Weakened 14
28Feb85- 4Aqu fst 6f ⊡:23⅕ :47⅖ 1:14 (S)Md Sp Wt 8 5 1hd 14 13 2¾ Migliore R b 122 4.40 73-22 AnotherSummer122¾RootCnl1222SiempreFidlius122nk Weakened 12
24Jan85- 7Aqu fst 1 1/16 ⊡:47⅕ 1:11⅘ 1:46⅕ (S)Alw 27000 1 8 87½ 1115 1019 1017½ Murphy D J 117 16.80 61-21 Silent Slander117nkRadicalChange1175¾OvertheWall122no Outrun 12
13Jan85- 6Aqu fst 1 1/16 ⊡:48⅖ 1:14⅗ 1:49⅖ (S)Md Sp Wt 1 4 36 23 26 36 Migliore R 122 6.00 57-27 Over the Wall 1225½ Gallant Rake122¾RootCanal12213½ Lugged in 12
19Jly84- 5Bel fst 5½f :22⅘ :47 1:06 (S)Md Sp Wt 3 9 59½ 44 33½ 34 Murphy D J b 118 *2.30 81-15 Lady Whooo 1101 Romanizer 1183 Root Canal 1183½ Off slowly 10
LATEST WORKOUTS Apr 15 Bel 4f fst :48⅕ h Apr 9 Bel 4f fst :48⅖ h ●Mar 26 Bel tr.t 4f fst :48⅗ h Mar 11 Bel tr.t 5f fst 1:04⅕ b

the ninth race, a "nonwinners of one" allowance contest for state-breds at seven furlongs. And this time, the company line provided the right answer.

What made Glenn Brooke appear a standout on April 21 was the fact that he was the only horse in the field that had successfully competed in open allowance company—against such known quantities as Equalize and Summitry. None of his state-bred rivals could come close to matching such credentials. Indeed, the figures Glenn Brooke earned in open competition placed him lengths ahead of his rivals.

To accept Glenn Brooke as a good bet in this field, however, one had to resolve two problems: Would there be sufficient pace in the race for his stretch run to prove effective? And did he have an excuse for his dull performance last time out, when he showed nothing as the 2–1 favorite in the same classification?

As we will see when analyzing the opposition, the prospects were good for a lively pace. As for Glenn Brooke's latest race, trip handicapping provided the excuse, as it so often does. The track on April 13 favored early speed types racing on or near the rail. Only two horses—Morning Bob and Sois Sage—were able to rally from behind the first three to win that day, and Morning Bob had a big class edge over his rivals. To further complicate his task, Glenn Brooke was asked to rally from last against a relatively slow pace. Trip handicappers knew that race could be thrown out, but many of the weekend players in attendance took his performance at face value, allowing Glenn Brooke to start at generous odds of 9–2 on April 21.

And now, for a closer look at his opposition:

HOW ABOUT NOW

Very slow maiden win, then trailed in first (and only) allowance try. Nothing to recommend him.

NEAT SAM

First start since December. Could have early speed, but the anticipated competition for the early lead would make the seven-furlong trip difficult at this point in his campaign.

ACCORDING TO LUKE

This colt finished second, ahead of Glenn Brooke, last time out at 8–1. His best efforts against open company, though, came in claiming races for tags as high as $30,000. Notice, however, the colt's dismal failures against open allowance company on February 15 and on March 14. It would have been nice if the crowd had favored this one over Glenn Brooke, but unfortunately it didn't.

EFFECTIVE ACTION

Bid and hung last time in his second start after a layoff and first try at the mile distance, finishing three lengths ahead of Glenn Brooke that day. Certainly eligible to improve, and an interesting alternative at 11–1.

JOALEO

Early speed, but with only one win in sixteen career starts. This four-year-old has been unable to win at rock-bottom claiming levels and certainly figures to be no match for a younger colt able to compete with allowance runners.

MY SONDANCE

Nothing lately, for as low as $17,500 claiming.

EVER PROUD

The favorite at 7–5 off his debut win in average time for state-bred maidens. This colt's ability will be tested today in allowance competition. Will be with the pace, but will have company. A false favorite—as many debut winners are in their second career starts.

CON LUNE

This horse was far back in his only start of the year—in state-bred stakes competition. His maiden win at two came after a similar dull effort in his debut, and his winning figure that day was excellent—the only horse in the field with a figure even threatening Glenn Brooke's best. He could have early speed, as he did in his maiden win, and he's worth considering at 21–1.

HONEY'S SEVEN

Made a move in his first allowance test March 28 but stopped badly. Apparently ran out of gas on that occasion and probably needs a freshening.

ROOT CANAL

Likely early speed, but last three (maiden) efforts resulted in very subpar speed figures.

With several six-furlong speed types in the field, a contested, potentially fast pace was assured. Consequently, the stretch-running Glenn Brooke could be bet with some confidence, especially in light of the exploits of Equalize and Summitry the day before. At 9–2, he was a generous overlay. At his best, he deserved to be favored.

Players who wanted an exotic supplement to their win bet had some interesting possibilities. The favored Ever Proud and co-third choices According To Luke and Root Canal (both at 6–1) hardly looked more enticing than the longer-priced Effective Action, a definite threat to improve, and Con Lune, a good possibility to surprise. Unfortunately, it was According to Luke and Ever Proud who completed the triple behind Glenn Brooke, proving once again that when the win odds are right, the bulk of one's wager should go into that pool.

NINTH RACE
Aqueduct
APRIL 21, 1985

7 FURLONGS. (1.20⅘) ALLOWANCE. Purse $25,500. 3-year-olds and upward foaled in New York State and approved by the New York State-bred Registry which have never won a race other than maiden, claiming or starter. Weights, 3-year-olds, 112 lbs. lbs. Older, 124 lbs. Non-winners of a race other than claiming since April 1, allowed 3 lbs.
Value of race $25,500; value to winner $15,300; second $5,610; third $3,060; fourth $1,530. Mutuel pool $132,616, OTB pool $172,991. Triple Pool $317,345. OTB Triple Pool $399,565.

Last Raced	Horse	Eqt.A.Wt	PP	St	¼	½	Str	Fin	Jockey	Odds $1
13Apr85 ^{9}Aqu^{6}	Glenn Brooke	3 107	5	3	7½	6½	4^{2}	1^{nk}	Garrido O L^{5}	4.50
13Apr85 ^{9}Aqu^{2}	According To Luke	b 3 112	3	10	10^{3}	8^{1}	1^{1}	$2^{2½}$	Migliore R	5.90
2Apr85 ^{6}Aqu^{1}	Ever Proud	3 112	8	8	3^{hd}	1^{hd}	2^{1}	$3^{1¼}$	Vasquez J	1.40
13Apr85 ^{9}Aqu^{4}	Effective Action	b 3 112	4	9	5^{hd}	5^{hd}	3^{1}	4^{nk}	Ward W A	11.60
13Apr85 ^{9}Aqu^{11}	Honey's Seven	b 4 111	10	5	9^{3}	9^{1}	5^{4}	5^{1}	Rolon E M^{10}	80.30
29Mar85 ^{9}Aqu^{1}	Root Canal	3 109	11	6	6^{hd}	4^{hd}	6½	6^{3}	Velasquez J	6.00
10Apr85 ^{1}Aqu^{3}	Joaleo	b 4 111	6	2	2^{hd}	2½	7^{4}	7no	Lalman D^{10}	13.90
14Apr85 ^{1}Aqu^{9}	My Sondance	4 114	7	1	8^{2}	10^{5}	8^{2}	$8^{1¼}$	Guerra A A^{7}	25.10
5Apr85 ^{5}Aqu^{8}	How About Now	3 109	1	11	11	11	11	$9^{1¼}$	Samyn J L	30.00
24Mar85 ^{8}Aqu^{10}	Con Lune	b 3 109	9	4	$4^{1½}$	7½	9^{1}	$10^{2½}$	Thibeau R J	21.50
19Dec84 ^{2}Aqu^{7}	Neat Sam	b 3 104	2	7	1^{hd}	3½	10^{3}	11	Privitera R^{5}	18.80

OFF AT 5:04, Start good, Won driving. Time, :23⅕, :45⅕, 1:11⅗, 1:24⅘ Track fast.

$2 Mutuel Prices:				
	5-(E)-GLENN BROOKE	11.00	5.60	3.40
	3-(C)-ACCORDING TO LUKE		7.20	4.00
	8-(I)-EVER PROUD			2.60
	$2 TRIPLE 5-3-8 PAID $157.00.			

Gr. c, by Flip Sal—Gay Bonny, by Lord Gaylord. Trainer Sedlacek Sue. Bred by Old Westbury Assoc I (NY).

GLENN BROOKE never far removed from leaders, altered course after entering stretch and charging down middle of the track collared ACCORDING TO LUKE seventy yards out. The latter rallying extremely wide into stretch continued run gaining clear lead with furlong remaining and lugged in striving to stay was not equal to task. EVER PROUD, rushed into contention following sluggish getaway turned for home showing way, then showing signs of efforts gave way while drifting. EFFECTIVE ACTION between horses during drive wanted for room briefly. Jockey W. Ward's claim of foul against ACCORDING TO LUKE and ever proud for alleged stretch interference was dismissed. HONEY'S SEVEN passed tired horses. ROOT CANAL raced wide.JOALEO flattened out. MY SONDANCE was outrun. HOW ABOUT NOW raced poorly. CON LUNE retired early.

Chapter 26

The Improving Three-Year-Old

IN ALMOST ALL claiming races, the player is confronted with the problem of deciding how to deal with horses that are either moving up or dropping down in class. These matters will be discussed in some depth in this and the following two chapters.

Does the horse on the rise really have a chance against better company? Or is it in over its head, possibly just prepping for a future engagement? What do its speed figures reveal about its chances in faster company?

Is the drop down returning to its proper level? Or is it trying to establish its current value? There is a significant difference. Are there signs of physical problems or overracing that might prevent the animal from performing well regardless of the competition? Should the reduction in value be regarded with suspicion?

The answers to most of these questions are often directly related to the trainer and his/her usual methodology with claiming animals—a subject that will not be discussed in specific detail in this book but one that is nevertheless of paramount importance to all players. Trainer handicapping is one of the game's last frontiers. The player is encouraged to learn as much as possible about the trainers on his circuit. The time invested will prove to be time well spent.

When dealing with class rises, there are two standard profiles with which every player should become familiar. One deals basically with three-year-olds and is the subject of this chapter. The other relates primarily to older horses and will be discussed in the next chapter.

The three-year-old Thoroughbred is in the developing stage of its career. Physically, it has yet to reach full maturity, which comes at age five. The trainer may still be experimenting with such things as distance, surface, and running style, hoping to properly assess the animal's true aptitude as a racehorse.

As a rule, the three-year-old claiming animal is overpriced relative to the claiming tags carried by older animals of comparable ability, because owners refuse to drop a young horse before giving it every chance to display its ability. Many horses do not establish their true value until well into their three-year-old season. In the meantime, they are likely to fluctuate up and down in claiming value. More to the point of this chapter, however, is the fact that a three-year-old can suddenly find its legs and parlay good form into a steady rise up the claiming ladder. Although many players would be reluctant to back an older horse attempting to move up into a class where it has no previous record of success, this should not be the case with a three-year-old.

The focal point of this chapter will be a three-year-old colt by the name of Charmed Destiny. We meet him first as the 8–5 favorite in the second race at Aqueduct on April 20, 1985, a $25,000 claiming sprint for three-year-olds run over a muddy track.

At this stage in his career Charmed Destiny fit the mold of the improving three-year-old almost to a tee. After two unsuccessful attempts at the rock-bottom $14,000 claiming level, the colt suddenly woke up, winning three in succession, the last two on the rise, with steadily improving speed figures each time. Yet there were three good reasons for expecting Charmed Destiny's streak would come to an end on April 20.

With the track termed muddy after rain overnight and during the preceding day, one had to be alert to the possibility of a biased racing surface. As a rule, the day's first race cannot provide sufficient evidence, one way or the other, about the existence of a bias. However, the first race on April 20 just happened to present pretty convincing proof of a negative-rail closers' bias. The odds-on favorite in that race, Sweet Ridge, faltered late to finish out of the money, after setting the pace into the stretch while racing along the rail.

My selection in the race was Irish Point, a daughter of a Herbager mare, which is strong mud breeding. She never got into gear while racing along the inside throughout (and then came back to win impressively in her next start). The victorious Highland Singh came with a late rush on the far outside. As likely speed on the rail, Charmed Destiny could easily fall victim to the same bias even if he was still on the up side of his form cycle.

Sweet Ridge B. f. 3, by Riva Ridge—Run Royal Run, by Might
$70,000 Br.—Kubat & Smith & Viking Farms Ltd (Ky) **112** Lifetime 14 5 1 2 $60,250 1985 6 3 0 0 $40,920 1984 8 2 1 2 $19,330
Own.—Chasrigg Stable Tr.—DeBonis Robert

11Mar85- 5Aqu fst 6f ⊡:22⅘ :46⅕ 1:11⅘ ⒻAlw 22000 6 1 2hd 1½ 14 11 Migliore R 116 2.60 85-18 Sweet Ridge 1161FlyingHeat116¾SaraThompson1065 Bled, driving 6
2Mar85- 6Aqu fst 6f ⊡:22⅘ :47 1:13 ⒻAlw 22000 8 2 3½ 2½ 31 46½ Davis R G 116 4.60 72-19 Halo Country 1182¾ Dream Puss 1163 K.'s Solution 116¾ Faltered 11
13Feb85- 7Aqu fst 1⅟₁₆ ⊡:48 1:13⅗ 1:48⅗ ⒻAlw 24000 8 1 11 2½ 46½ 517¾ Davis R G 116 *.80e 49-20 Lady on the Run 1166½ Waltha 1096 Adda Girl 1161½ Tired 8
2Feb85- 1Aqu my 1⅟₁₆ ⊡:48⅕ 1:14⅕ 1:48⅘ ⒻClm 60000 3 1 12 1hd 13 12½ Davis R G 112 *2.10 68-28 Sweet Ridge 1122½ Adda Girl1128½StrategicAsset1122 Ridden out 7
24Jan85- 9Aqu fst 6f ⊡:22⅗ :45⅘ 1:11⅘ ⒻClm 45000 4 4 1½ 11 11 13 Davis R G 112 22.10 85-21 Sweet Ridge 1123 Regal Lynco 1072½ Right Girl 112hd Driving 12
10Jan85- 3Aqu fst 6f ⊡:22⅘ :46⅗ 1:12⅗ ⒻClm 45000 4 3 41½ 41½ 62½ 62¾ Garrido O L5 107 17.80 78-22 Flying Hope 1161 Dawn's Answer 105hd Regal Lynco 109no Tired 9
19Dec84- 6Med fst 6f :22⅘ :46⅗ 1:13 ⒻAlw 12000 7 1 2hd 1½ 2½ 36 Antley C W 114 *2.40 71-23 Lu Lu's Girl 1206 My Marisa 108hd Sweet Ridge 1142 Tired 7
6Dec84- 5Aqu sly 6f ⊡:22 :45⅘ 1:11⅘ ⒻClm 62500 1 5 3nk 3½ 88 815¾ MacBeth D b 114 3.30 69-12 Nell Diamond 116½ Carnegie Hill 1052½ Singing Praise112nk Tired 8
23Oct84- 8Med gd 6f :22⅗ :45⅘ 1:11⅕ ⒻAlw 12000 2 4 31½ 31½ 23 26 Blackstun KM7 b 107 4.50 80-20 Grand Glory 1126 Sweet Ridge 107nk UmbrellaRig1202 Held place 7
13Oct84- 6Med fst 1 :46⅗ 1:12⅗ 1:40⅗ ⒻⓇElmwd Pk 1 2 32½ 48½ 714 822½ Guerra W A b 114 10.70 56-19 Eloquack 1189 Ordinary Housewife 1181 Trade Name 114½ Tired 9
LATEST WORKOUTS Apr 12 Bel tr.t 3f fst :36⅕ h Apr 6 Bel tr.t 5f fst 1:02⅖ h Mar 30 Bel tr.t 5f fst 1:04 b Feb 23 Bel tr.t 4f fst :50⅘ b

Irish Point B. f. 3, by Irish Castle—Grey Doreen, by Grey Dawn II
$75,000 Br.—Mereworth Farm (Ky) **116** Lifetime 9 1 2 1 $13,270 1985 7 1 1 1 $11,400 1984 2 M 1 0 $1,870
Own.—Walsh Mrs T M Tr.—Walsh Thomas M

8Apr85- 7Aqu fst 1 :46⅘ 1:12⅕ 1:39⅖ ⒻAlw 24000 3 2 41½ 1hd 65½ 65½ Maple E 116 18.40 63-24 Vaguely Foolish 116no Why Did I 1163 Daraly 116no Tired 7
24Mar85- 3Aqu fst 1 :47⅖ 1:13⅕ 1:39⅖ ⒻClm 100000 6 5 52½ 64¾ 715 718 Samyn J L 121 11.30 53-26 Lady on the Run 1216½ AddaGirl104nkHighlandSingh1133½ Trailed 7
16Mar85- 7Aqu fst 1 :47 1:12⅗ 1:39⅘ ⒻAlw 23000 2 3 31 64½ 44 37¾ Samyn J L 116 7.90 59-34 DmGris1165¾ToonInTomorrow1112IrshPont1162½ Pss'd tired ones 6
6Mar85- 3Aqu fst 6f ⊡:24⅕ :49 1:14⅗ ⒻMd 35000 10 1 41½ 11 14 14¾ Samyn J L 121 3.70 72-26 Irish Point 1214¾ Lady Jessica 1171½ Bet The Rent 1143 Driving 12
22Feb85- 2Aqu fst 6f ⊡:23⅕ :48 1:15 ⒻClm 17500 6 4 51½ 21 21 21½ Samyn J L 116 7.40 68-22 Cousin Bette 1091½ Irish Point 116½R.J.'sWoman1167¾ Weakened 8
10Jan85- 4Aqu fst 170 ⊡:49⅘ 1:16⅕ 1:47⅗ ⒻMd 35000 3 5 32 32 711 816½ Deegan J C b 121 10.20 46-22 Strategic Asset 1213½ Nazizi 1214 Final Destiny 1211½ Bid. wknd 10
4Jan85- 2Aqu fst 1⅟₁₆ ⊡:49⅕ 1:14⅘ 1:47⅖ ⒻMd Sp Wt 6 3 75 99½ 819 823½ Clayton M D b 121 16.10 50-21 Grand Creation 1218Mlle.Kerouac1165½WhyDidI1212½ Brief speed 12
3Dec84- 2Aqu fst 1 :47⅕ 1:13⅘ 1:42 ⒻMd 25000 5 4 31 31½ 32½ 22¾ Clayton M D b 1174 8.50 53-29 SpringLndng1132[DH]IrshPont117[DH]RglChoc1077¾ Altered course 8
3Dec84-Dead heat
19Nov84- 4Aqu fst 7f :24 :48⅘ 1:29⅕ ⒻMd 50000 8 9 74½ 1010 1114 1014 Miranda J 117 31.90 41-33 Flight N Fantasy 113noSuddenShower117hdBabyChris1131 Outrun 11
LATEST WORKOUTS Apr 16 Bel 4f sly :48⅗ h Apr 2 Bel 4f fst :51⅕ b Mar 13 Bel tr.t 4f gd :51⅖ b

FIRST RACE
Aqueduct
APRIL 20, 1985

7 FURLONGS. (1.20⅕) CLAIMING. Purse $22,000. Fillies, 3-year-olds. Weight, 121 lbs. Non-winners of two races since April 1 allowed 3 lbs. Of a race since then, 5 lbs. Claiming price $75,000 for each $2,500 to $70,000, 2 lbs. (Races when entered to be claimed for $65,000 to less not considered.) (34th Day. WEATHER CLOUDY. TEMPERATURE 56 DEGREES).

Value of race $22,000; value to winner $13,200; second $4,840; third $2,640; fourth $1,320. Mutuel pool $136,623, OTB pool $137,642.

Last Raced	Horse	Eqt.A.Wt	PP	St	¼	½	Str	Fin	Jockey	Cl'g Pr	Odds $1
29Mar85 7Aqu5	Highland Singh	b 3 116	6	4	7	65	44	12½	Maple E	75000	3.80
11Apr85 3Aqu1	Too Sunny	3 107	7	2	52	3½	1hd	2½	Ramirez M R5	70000	10.70
2Mar85 6Aqu6	Brutish Beast	3 116	3	6	3hd	52	3hd	3nk	Vasquez J	75000	11.10
11Mar85 5Aqu1	Sweet Ridge	3 112	1	3	1½	1hd	22	43½	Migliore R	70000	.90
13Apr85 7Aqu7	Easy Way	b 3 107	2	5	22	2½	5½	5nk	Garrido O L5	70000	8.50
8Apr85 7Aqu6	Irish Point	3 116	4	7	6½	7	7	62	Velasquez J	75000	7.20
14Apr85 9Aqu10	Love You Sis	3 116	5	1	4½	41½	61½	7	Ward W A	75000	10.20

OFF AT 1:00 Start good, Won driving. Time, :22⅘, :46, 1:11, 1:24⅕ Track muddy.

Official Program Numbers

$2 Mutuel Prices:			
6-(G)-HIGHLAND SINGH	9.60	5.00	3.60
7-(H)-TOO SUNNY		7.80	4.60
3-(D)-BRUTISH BEAST			5.60

Ch. f, by Singh—Ex Landlady, by Executioner. Trainer Brennan Pat. Bred by Bell Bloodstock Co (Ky).

HIGHLAND SINGH angled out whilemoving after entering the stretch and drew off after catching the leaders near the final sixteenth. TOO SUNNY moved to the leaders from the outside on the turn, dueled for command to the final sixteenth but was no match for the winner. BRUTISH BEAST, a factor to the stretch while saving ground, continued on with good energy SWEET RIDGE saved ground while showing speed to the final sixteenth but was no match for the winner. BRUTISH BEAST, a factor to the stretch while saving ground, continued on with good energy. SWEET RIDGE saved ground while showing speed to the final sixteenth and weakened. EASY WAY was used up vying for the lead. IRISH POINT saved ground to no avail. LOVE YOU SIS tired. SWEET RIDGE raced with mud calks.

Owners— 1, Lynch J W; 2, Wilson C T Jr; 3, Rosenthal Mrs M; 4, Chasrigg Stable; 5, Tresvant Stable; 6, Walsh Mrs T M; 7, Alibrandi Elsya.

Trainers— 1, Brennan Pat; 2, Hernandez Ramon M; 3, Johnson Philip G; 4, DeBonis Robert; 5, Sedlacek Sue; 6, Walsh Thomas M; 7, DiAngelo Joseph T.

Scratched—Etoile Joyeux (5Apr85 3Aqu1).

A second problem for Charmed Destiny was the speedy Bucket Ben, who was dropping back down to the $25,000 level, where he had run third on March 27. His pace figures were slightly faster than the favorite's—not so his final speed figures, though—and he figured to keep Charmed Destiny pinned in along the rail.

2 AQUEDUCT 6 FURLONGS

6 FURLONGS. (1.08⅕) CLAIMING. Purse $15,000. 3-years-olds, 122 lbs. Non-winners of two races since April 1 allowed 3 lbs. Of a race since then, 5 lbs. Claiming price $25,000; for each $2,500 to $20,000, 2 lbs. (Races when entered to be claimed for $18,000 or less not considered.)

Coupled—Natrac and Venture Beyond; Bucket Ben and Keep It Down.

Handful Of Steel — Dk. b. or br. c. 3, by Cutlass—Handful of Joy, by All Hands
$25,000 Br.—Smith Paul P (Fla) Tr.—Shapoff Stanley R — 117
Own.—Cohen R B
Lifetime 3 1 0 0 $5,700 — 1985 1 0 0 0 — 1984 2 1 0 0 $5,700

14Apr85- 4Aqu fst 7f :23⅘ :47⅕ 1:26 Clm 35000 7 5 9¾ 8¾ 913 810¼ McCarron G 117 23.40 60-22 Eddie Bubbles112nk TheRunningKind115no StardeCesica115¾ Wide 9
5Jly84- 4Bel fst 5½f :23⅘ :47⅘ 1:06⅘ Md 25000 6 2 55 43 32 1nk McCarron G 118 *2.20 81-15 HndflOfStl118nk ForCrtnDoc118²½ AwsmIss1163½ Swerved, driving 7
27Jun84- 4Bel fst 5½f :23 :47⅕ 1:06⅗ Md 40000 8 5 66 712 612 57 McCarron G 118 4.00 75-17 BernaCagney1111½ EternlPrince1181½ WesternChmp1164 No factor 9
LATEST WORKOUTS Apr 10 Bel 4f fst :49⅘ b — Apr 4 Bel 6f fst 1:16⅘ hg — Mar 31 Bel tr.t 6f fst 1:19⅗ b — Mar 27 Bel tr.t 5f fst 1:05⅕ b

Full of Fortune — B. c. 3, by Key to the Kingdom—Matriculation, by Arts and Letters
$25,000 Br.—Mjaka I Stable (Ky) Tr.—Field Kenneth — 117
Own.—Trillora
Lifetime 11 2 0 1 $12,250 — 1985 5 0 0 0 $310 — 1984 6 2 0 1 $11,940 — Turf 1 0 0 0

10Apr85- 4Aqu fst 1 :46⅗ 1:12 1:38⅗ Clm 45000 1 1 2hd 32 68 912¼ Maple E b 113 26.10 61-29 Dream Of Peace 1131½ Mr.JimmyG.1131½ TimelessTaste1133¼ Tired 11
28Mar85- 7Pim fst 6f :22⅘ :46⅕ 1:12⅕ Clm 40000 4 4 44 53½ 54 72¼ Kupfer T J b 114 6.40 82-20 Do RightMan114¾ MechanicalKid114nk WildcatFortySix112nk Tired 7
16Mar85- 6Pim fst 6f :23⅕ :46⅕ 1:11⅘ Alw 22000 5 6 54¾ 68¼ 68¼ 59¼ Saumell L b 115 31.00 79-15 Bea Quality 114hd Bolting Holme 1191½ RollDemBones1157 Outrun 7
4Feb85- 8GP fst 1$\frac{1}{16}$:46⅗ 1:11⅗ 1:44⅘ Alw 16000 3 1 1½ 66¾ 1033 1033 Velez J A Jr b 117 266.00 46-18 ProudTruth1176 CrowningHonors1171½ SecretryGnrl117½ Bore out 10
23Jan85- 7GP fst 7f :22 :45 1:24⅘ Alw 16200 5 7 79 1015 1012 1013¼ Maple E b 117 137.10 69-22 Sir Leon 1173¾ Colder Thana 122nk Bowladrome 122½ Outrun 12
15Oct84- 7Lrl fst 7f :22⅘ :46⅕ 1:25⅗ Alw 10000 5 3 3nk 33½ 58¼ 615¼ Miller D A Jr b 119 5.10 68-20 BnjoDncing1156 EsternTrdition119hd VictoryAtNewport1192¼ Tired 7
29Sep84- 4Lrl sly 6f :22⅘ :46⅗ 1:12 Alw 9500 2 1 1hd 21 1hd 11 Miller D A Jr b 115 2.80 83-16 Full of Fortune 1151 Satan's Flame 1152 Galleynipper1152 Driving 7
20Sep84- 7Lrl fst 6f :22⅕ :46⅕ 1:12⅖ Alw 9500 6 7 76½ 78 55½ 36¼ Miller D A Jr b 115 20.30 75-25 Rain Shelter 1156 Clever Now 117nk Full of Fortune115hd Rallied 7
22Aug84- 5Sar fm 1 ⓣ:47⅘ 1:12⅘ 1:38⅕ Alw 21000 5 10 1012 1014 1018 920¾ Murphy D J 117 35.00 64-20 WstrnChmp117¾ NclBc117nk Dn'tFlWthM1173¼ Checked, bore out 10
LATEST WORKOUTS Apr 8 Pim 4f fst :51 b — Mar 27 Pim 3f fst :37⅕ h — Mar 13 Pim 4f fst :50⅘ b — Mar 3 GP 4f fst :50 b

Charmed Destiny — Dk. b. or br. c. 3, by Winged T—Miss Charming, by Final Ruling
$22,500 Br.—Bowman T (Md) Tr.—Wilson R — 112⁵
Own.—Twin Bee Stable
Lifetime 14 4 1 0 $31,310 — 1985 7 3 1 0 $26,210 — 1984 7 1 0 0 $5,100

9Apr85- 4Aqu fst 7f :23 :47⅘ 1:25⅘ Clm 22500 9 4 2½ 1hd 14 13½ Moore D N5 b 110 2.80e 74-25 ChrmedDstiny1103½ ThRunningKind117hd MistrG.1175¾ Ridden out 12
24Mar85- 2Aqu fst 6f :23⅗ :47⅕ 1:12⅘ Clm 17500 6 3 1hd 15 110 19 Moore D N5 b 112 *.80 77-26 CharmedDestiny1129 SparklingState114¾ UltimtePower1173 Easily 9
15Mar85- 9Aqu fst 7f :23⅗ :47⅘ 1:27⅘ Clm 14000 2 6 4nk 11 16 110 Moore D N5 b 112 6.00 62-40 Charmed Destiny 11210 Sharpe Writer 1171¾ Stasera 112nk Easily 12
24Feb85- 2Aqu fst 6f ⊡:22⅘ :46⅗ 1:14 Clm 14000 7 11 33 33 23 44¾ Hernandez R b 117 *1.70e 70-28 Even On Sunday 117nk Indulge 1062 Stasera 1192 Broke in tangle 12
2Feb85- 3Aqu my 170 ⊡:50 1:15⅘ 1:46⅘ Clm 14000 2 1 2hd 2hd 25 29 Hernandez R b 117 2.90 57-28 Natrac 1129 Charmed Destiny 117hd Mr. Recharge1172 Held place 8
18Jan85- 5Aqu fst 6f ⊡:22⅘ :46⅗ 1:12⅗ Clm 20000 5 6 12 11 52¼ 610¾ Hernandez R b 113 7.70 70-21 Confirmed Patriot 1102¼ First Nite Jitters 117nk Narica1225 Tired 11
1Jan85- 3Aqu fst 6f ⊡:21⅘ :45 1:11⅗ Clm 30000 5 7 53¾ 33 75¼ 86¼ Hernandez R b 113 4.20 80-13 Top Talk 1192¼ Student of Dance 108no ShiningTyson117nk Tired 9
15Nov84- 3Aqu fst 6f :23 :47 1:13⅖ Clm c-30000 4 5 3nk 3nk 31½ 55¼ McCarron G 113 6.10 69-29 WrriorInOrbit110hd UnclDddy1083 ⒹShiningTyson112hd Weakened 9
4Nov84- 7Lrl fst 6f :22⅘ :46 1:12 Alw 9000 8 7 67¼ 58¼ 77¾ 65¼ Wright D R 115 22.90 77-22 Ramten 1151 The Great Escaper 115no LittleBoldJohn1194 Outrun 8
25Oct84- 8Lrl gd 1 :46⅘ 1:13⅕ 1:38⅗ Alw 9500 1 2 21½ 1hd 43½ 715 Wright D R 115 6.70 64-22 DoubleLeaFast1191½ TournamentPlay1198 Athabasc1091½ Faltered 8
LATEST WORKOUTS Feb 20 Aqu ⊡ 4f fst :49⅕ b

Creative Spirit — Gr. c. 3, by Fire Dancer—Indian Ghost, by Umbrella Fella
$22,500 Br.—Chak Phyllis & Price Judith L (Fla) Tr.—Tufariello Frank — 115
Own.—Wood A
Lifetime 20 1 1 2 $14,590 — 1985 8 0 0 1 $3,540 — 1984 12 1 1 1 $11,050 — Turf 3 0 0 0

9Apr85- 4Aqu fst 7f :23 :47⅘ 1:25⅘ Clm 25000 10 2 73½ 52¾ 57 49 Skinner K b 117 15.50 65-25 ChrmedDestiny1103¼ ThRunningKind117hd MistrG.1175¾ No factor 12
14Mar85- 5Aqu fst 7f :23⅕ :46⅗ 1:26⅗ Clm 30000 11 1 103½ 73¾ 63¾ 65 Lovato F Jr b 113 29.90 63-35 TheRunningKind1132¼ GayDate114hd Mr.JimmyG.1172¼ Raced wide 11
7Mar85- 2Aqu fst 6f ⊡:22⅘ :45⅘ 1:12⅖ Clm 25000 7 3 65 66½ 66 75¾ Lovato F Jr b 117 33.70 76-21 Gay Date 114¾ French Answer 1151¾ Bolinger 112no Outrun 11
28Feb85- 5Aqu fst 6f ⊡:22⅗ :46 1:11⅗ Clm 35000 10 2 109½ 78½ 610 59¼ Lovato F Jr b 117 50.80 77-22 Gay Date 1085¾ ⒹScholastic 117½ Mr. Jimmy G. 117nk Wide 12
17Feb85- 4Aqu fst 170 ⊡:48⅗ 1:14⅘ 1:46⅗ Clm 35000 5 3 34 33 812 917¾ Murphy D J b 117 7.40 49-25 Fly Me Again 1081 Star de Cesica 1153¼ JupiterAccord1132 Tired 10
26Jan85- 6Aqu fst 170 ⊡:48 1:14⅕ 1:44⅘ Alw 23000 10 6 63¾ 52¼ 78¾ 814 Murphy D J b 117 44.10 62-20 Feeling Gallant117nk CrystalIceberg117hd Haberdasher1122 Outrun 10
19Jan85- 2Aqu fst 1$\frac{1}{16}$ ⊡:48⅗ 1:14 1:48⅗ Clm 45000 2 1 11 11 41½ 32¼ Murphy D J b 113 35.40 65-22 Helcin 112nk Another Doc 1172 Creative Spirit 113½ Weakened 12
11Jan85- 9Aqu fst 6f ⊡:23⅕ :47⅗ 1:13⅖ Clm 40000 4 4 2hd 3nk 62¼ 77¼ Murphy D J b 117 15.50 69-30 Gay Date 113hd Student of Dance 1171½ Mr. Jimmy G.1133¾ Tired 9
19Dec84- 3Aqu fst 6f ⊡:23⅖ :47⅘ 1:12⅘ Clm 60000 8 1 41½ 42½ 711 78¾ Velasquez J b 113 7.90 71-25 Koffkoff 1133¼ Feeling Gallant 1171¾ ConfirmedPatriot1061 Tired 8
3Dec84- 5Aqu fst 7f :22⅘ :46 1:24⅗ Clm 65000 4 5 33 32 36 58¼ Davis R G b 117 4.00 69-29 Splendid Catch 1176¾ Feeling Gallant113½ DistantOrbit108hd Tired 8
LATEST WORKOUTS ●Apr 7 Bel 3f fst :36 b — Apr 3 Bel tr.t 5f fst 1:02⅖ h — Mar 29 Bel tr.t 5f fst 1:02⅘ h

Mister G. — Dk. b. or br. c. 3, by Cinteelo—Missy G, by Knightly Manner
$25,000 Br.—Gargano P (Ky) Tr.—DeStasio Richard T — 117
Own.—Gargano P
Lifetime 7 1 0 1 $9,480 — 1985 5 1 0 1 $7,800 — 1984 2 M 0 0 $1,680

9Apr85- 4Aqu fst 7f :23 :47⅘ 1:25⅘ Clm 25000 4 7 52½ 42½ 24 33½ Vasquez J b 117 9.50 71-25 ChrmedDstiny1103¼ ThRunningKind117hd MistrG.1175¾ Bid, evenly 12
27Mar85- 2Aqu fst 6f :22⅖ :45⅘ 1:11⅗ Clm 25000 6 6 33 43 53 53¾ Reed R L7 b 110 12.10 79-20 H. T. Willis 1121¾ Stark Dancer 1121½ Bucket Ben 117¾ Tired 10
14Mar85- 5Aqu fst 7f :23⅕ :46⅗ 1:26⅗ Clm 35000 7 3 2hd 41½ 74¾ 76½ Reed R L7 b 112 42.40 62-35 The Running Kind 1132¼ Gay Date 114hd Mr. JimmyG.1172¼ Tired 11
3Mar85- 2Aqu fst 6f ⊡:22⅗ :46⅘ 1:12 Clm 50000 7 1 61¾ 75 79½ 713¾ Reed R L7 b 110 24.40 70-17 Determined Run 1131½ Gay Date 108nk Overbought 1172¾ Outrun 8
20Feb85- 3Aqu fst 6f ⊡:23⅖ :47⅘ 1:14⅕ Md 35000 11 1 2½ 1½ 12 13¾ Reed R L7 b 115 4.20 73-23 Mister G. 1153¾ Catch The Redeye 118½ Gran Fable 122nk Driving 12
27Jun84- 4Bel fst 5½f :23 :47⅕ 1:06⅗ Md 40000 2 1 2hd 2½ 33½ 46¾ MacBeth D b 118 *1.90 75-17 BernaCgney1111½ EternlPrince1181½ WesternChmp1164 Weakened 9
27Apr84- 4Aqu fst 4½f :23⅕ :47 :53⅘ Md Sp Wt 2 5 43½ 34 35¾ Smith A Jr 118 2.50Ⓓ 87-07 CrystlIcebrg118½ StrongAppl1185½ ⒹMistrG.118¾ Steadied, lugged 6
27Apr84-Disqualified and placed fourth
LATEST WORKOUTS Apr 18 Bel tr.t 3f fst :37⅕ b — Apr 5 Bel tr.t 5f fst 1:04 b — Mar 22 Bel tr.t 6f fst 1:20 b — Mar 11 Bel tr.t 4f fst :52⅕ b

Cop A Plea — B. g. 3, by Good Counsel—Coming Spring, by Graustark
$22,500 Br.—Galbreath J W (Ky) Tr.—Gulio Thomas J — 115
Own.—Gulio T J
Lifetime 7 1 1 0 $9,460 — 1985 1 0 0 0 — 1984 6 1 1 0 $9,460

1Jan85- 3Aqu fst 6f ⊡:21⅘ :45 1:11⅗ Clm 30000 2 9 98¾ 88¼ 85¼ 55 Garrido O L5 b 108 17.80 81-13 Top Talk 1192¼ Student of Dance108no ShiningTyson117nk Outrun 9
7Dec84- 9Aqu fst 1$\frac{1}{16}$ ⊡:48⅕ 1:13⅗ 1:47⅗ Md 22500 2 6 31½ 2hd 12 13 Cordero A Jr b 116 2.40 74-19 Cop A Plea 1163 Gallant Rake 1182 El Parador 114¾ Driving 10
30Nov84- 2Aqu fst 1⅛ :48⅗ 1:14⅖ 1:54⅖ Md 22500 10 6 42½ 21½ 44½ 47½ Cordero A Jr b 116 4.10 55-23 Jupiter Accord 1184 Minus Two1183 SharpeWriter114½ Weakened 12
15Nov84- 2Aqu fst 1 :47⅖ 1:14 1:42 Md 30000 9 6 51½ 4½ 55 57¼ Graell A b 114 5.20 48-29 Angelic Bliss 114hd Jupiter Accord 1183 GoldCoup114½ Weakened 12
4Nov84- 4Aqu fst 6f :23⅗ :47⅘ 1:13⅗ Md 25000 4 12 104 86½ 710 713½ Deegan J C b 118 *3.00 61-25 Warrior In Orbit 111¾ Mr. G.J.G. 118½ Cedar Lane 1186¾ Wide 12
26Oct84- 4Aqu sly 1 :46⅖ 1:11⅘ 1:38⅘ Md 45000 4 3 45 610 815 818½ Deegan J C b 114 3.60 55-22 FelingGllnt114nk CrtivSpirit1181¾ DncinOnPins1147 Brk slwly, tired 10
19Oct84- 4Bel fst 6f :23 :47⅕ 1:12⅖ Md 45000 10 10 55 45 48 29¼ Deegan J C b 114 14.40 70-21 Kilts' Nashua 1189¼ Cop A Plea 114nk Creative Spirit 118hd Wide 13
LATEST WORKOUTS Apr 17 Bel tr.t 3f fst :37 b — Apr 14 Bel tr.t 4f fst :51 b — Mar 27 Bel tr.t 4f fst :52⅘ b — Mar 20 Bel tr.t 5f fst 1:03 b

Irv's Choice — Gr. g. 3, by El Rastro—Adversaria, by Tudor Way
$25,000 Br.—Katz Francine & J (Fla) Tr.—Barbara Robert — 117
Own.—Town Circle Stable
Lifetime 18 2 3 4 $25,870 — 1985 9 0 2 3 $12,570 — 1984 9 2 1 1 $13,300

14Apr85- 4Aqu fst 7f :23⅘ :47⅕ 1:26 Clm 30000 8 2 1hd 3½ 21 41 Cordero A Jr b 113 4.50 70-22 EddieBubbles112nk TheRunningKind115no StrdCsic115¾ Weakened 9
6Apr85- 2Aqu fst 6f :22⅘ :46⅕ 1:11⅗ Clm 30000 4 4 33 45 54¾ 44¼ Cordero A Jr b 113 *2.40 78-21 FlyMeAgain115¾ EddieBubbles1102¼ DshingDennis1171½ No excuse 9
17Mar85- 9Aqu fst 7f :23⅗ :48⅕ 1:28⅖ Clm 25000 3 4 3½ 2hd 12 2¾ Ward W A5 b 112 4.00 58-33 Soaring Romeo 119¾ Irv's Choice112¾ FrenchAnswer110no Gamely 12
8Mar85- 9Aqu fst 6f ⊡:22⅗ :46 1:12⅘ Clm c-17500 8 4 21 21 1hd 21½ Skinner K b 117 4.10 79-18 Dash Mount1081½ Irv'sChoice1171¾ InstantRecall117nk Just missed 12
22Feb85- 6Key fst 6f :22⅕ :45⅘ 1:11⅕ Clm 20000 9 1 1½ 1½ 12 32¾ Rosales A G b 112 17.20 82-21 Say Gems 116nk Satisfactory 1122¼ Irv's Choice 1122¼ Weakened 9
7Feb85- 7Lrl sly 6f :22⅕ :46⅕ 1:11⅘ Clm 18500 3 2 64¼ 68½ 47 38¼ Rosales A G b 114 4.80 76-22 Departing Prints 1143¾ Mr.AlLeeKat1144¼ Irv'sChoice1141½ Rallied 9
27Jan85- 5Key fst 7f :22⅘ :45⅖ 1:23⅘ Clm 18000 9 1 42 2hd 21 34¼ Rosales A G b 115 2.60 83-20 Foxy Bud 1153 Daddy's A Caddy1111½ Irv'sChoice1152¼ Weakened 9
14Jan85- 5Key fst 7f :22⅘ :45⅖ 1:23⅗ Clm 20000 3 1 52¾ 31½ 42½ 42¼ Appleby D L Jr b 114 16.00 86-19 GallantPsser119½ JumpingJckFlsh112¾ MkingWves1141½ Weakened 7
4Jan85- 7Key fst 6f ●:22⅗ :46⅗ 1:12⅕ Clm 25000 9 1 84¼ 53½ 32 46¼ Appleby D L Jr b 116 65.90 74-31 Narica 1201½ Lone Roan 1205 Jumping JackFlash116no Weakened 10
19Dec84- 5Key gd 6½f :22⅘ :46 1:19⅖ Clm 25000 9 1 73¾ 78 58½ 65¼ Knight L C b 117 25.10 71-22 NowWe'vGotHim1091 JumpingJckFlsh1131½ RlxingPt114no Outrun 10
LATEST WORKOUTS Apr 4 Bel 3f fst :34⅘ h — Mar 25 Bel tr.t 3f fst :38⅕ b — Mar 15 Bel tr.t 4f fst :51 b

Natrac — B. g. 3, by Winged T—Twirl the World, by Frankie's Nod
$25,000 Br.—Greer Enterprises (Pa) Tr.—Barrera Oscar S — 117
Own.—Barrera O S
Lifetime 17 2 5 1 $30,650 — 1985 10 1 3 1 $24,940 — 1984 7 1 2 0 $5,710

6Mar85- 4Aqu fst 1⅛ ⊡:48⅖ 1:14 1:53⅘ Clm 35000 10 8 74½ 62¾ 31½ 4nk Ward W A5 b 112 *1.70 73-26 DebateACase113hd I'mABnker117no AccordingToLuke113nk Rallied 12
1Mar85- 5Aqu fst 1$\frac{1}{16}$ ⊡:49 1:13⅖ 1:47⅘ Clm 45000 7 3 31 2½ 2hd 2nk Ward W A5 b 108 *1.60 71-25 History Responds 113nk Natrac108no Maggie'sMike115hd Game try 7
25Feb85- 1Aqu fst 1$\frac{1}{16}$ ⊡:48⅕ 1:14⅕ 1:47 Alw 23000 1 3 34 31½ 33 53¼ Ward W A5 b 112 7.10 71-25 GoldenChief1172 Hberdsher112½ ReviveTheEchos117nk Sluggish st. 7
22Feb85- 7Aqu fst 6f ⊡:22⅗ :45⅘ 1:12 Alw 22000 9 11 118 109 75½ 53 Moore D N5 b 112 25.80 81-22 Faded Image 112½ Aetolian 122nk Super Scope 1172¼ Late bid 12
15Feb85- 1Aqu fst 1⅛ ⊡:48⅖ 1:14⅗ 1:54⅘ Alw 23000 4 5 47 33 35 46½ Ward W A5 b 112 5.00 61-26 Uene 1194 Revive The Echoes 117½ Golden Chief 1172 No rally 8
10Feb85- 3Aqu fst 1⅛ ⊡:48 1:13⅗ 1:53⅖ Clm 45000 7 3 31½ 31½ 22½ 33¼ Samyn J L b 113 *1.70 72-18 Glenn Brooke 1103¼ Classi Valentine 117no Natrac113½ Weakened 11
6Feb85- 1Aqu gd 170 ⊡:48⅗ 1:14 1:44⅘ Alw 23000 6 3 21 33 36 25¼ Moore D N5 b 112 *1.30 71-27 Bold Bob's Dusty 1125¼ Natrac112½ Olajuwon1171¾ Best of others 7
2Feb85- 3Aqu my 170 ⊡:50 1:15⅘ 1:46⅘ Clm c-14000 8 2 3½ 1hd 15 19 Ward W A5 b 112 *.80 66-28 Natrac 1129 Charmed Destiny 117hd Mr.Recharge1172 Ridden out 8
26Jan85- 9Lrl fst 6½f :22⅘ :46⅖ 1:19⅗ Clm 18500 8 8 912 78½ 63½ 41¾ Delgado A b 114 7.50 — — Taurus The Bull114nk BostonBlackie114nk OnlyCourse1151½ Rallied 10
7Jan85- 7Key my 7f :22⅗ :46 1:26⅘ Clm 18000 3 3 1hd 1½ 22 21½ Lloyd J S b 116 6.90 71-26 Empire Lock 1221½ Natrac 116½ Heathers' Myrrh 1184 Gamely 11
LATEST WORKOUTS Apr 17 Bel tr.t 3f fst :38 b — Apr 14 Bel tr.t 3f fst :39⅗ b

Bucket Ben — B. g. 3, by Elocutionist—Summertime, by Secretariat
$25,000 Br.—Strawbridge G Jr (Pa) Tr.—Moschera Gasper S — 117
Own.—Davis A
Lifetime 6 1 0 1 $7,800 — 1985 4 0 0 1 $1,800 — 1984 2 1 0 0 $6,000

6Apr85- 2Aqu fst 6f :22⅘ :46⅕ 1:11⅗ Clm 35000 7 3 11 22½ 44½ 68 Samyn J L b 117 7.30e 75-21 Fly Me Again 115¾ Eddie Bubbles1102¼ DashingDennis1171½ Tired 9

27Mar85- 2Aqu fst 6f :22⅘ :45⅘ 1:11⅗ Clm 25000 10 1 1^{2} $2^{1/2}$ $3^{2\frac12}$ 3^{3} Davis R G b 117 20.20 80-20 H. T. Willis $112^{1\frac34}$ Stark Dancer $112^{1\frac14}$ Bucket Ben$117^{3/4}$ Weakened 10
9Feb85- 2Aqu fst 6f ⊡:23⅗ :47⅘ 1:13⅗ Clm 35000 12 1 $3^{1\frac12}$ 5^{6} 9^{20} $9^{20\frac34}$ Davis R G b 117 15.10 55-26 Summitry 112^{4} Bolinger 110^{7} Fly Me Again 108^{nk} Tired 12
1Jan85- 3Aqu fst 6f ⊡:21⅘ :45 1:11⅗ Clm c-35000 9 1 1^{hd} 1^{hd} 1^{hd} 7^{6} Lovato F Jr b 119 7.20 80-13 Top Talk $119^{2\frac34}$ Student of Dance 108no ShiningTyson117^{nk} Tired 9
20Dec84- 4Aqu fst 6f ⊡:22⅗ :47 1:14 Md 32500 4 5 $1^{1/2}$ 1^{2} 1^{3} 1^{4} Lovato F Jr b 116 *1.20 74-19 Bucket Ben 116^{4} Time Pays Off $107^{1\frac34}$ Rich Gift$114^{1\frac12}$ Ridden out 12
9Dec84- 4Aqu fst 6f ⊡:23 :46⅘ 1:12⅘ Md 47500 3 4 1^{hd} 3^{nk} 5^{3} 5^{6} Lovato F Jr 116 2.40 74-19 ConfirmedPtriot114^{hd}NicetoMtYou114^{nk}TylorRod$114^{3/4}$ Weakened 11
LATEST WORKOUTS Apr 16 Bel 5f sly 1:01⅘ h Apr 3 Bel tr.t 4f fst :49⅖ h Mar 26 Bel tr.t 3f fst :38 b Mar 20 Bel tr.t 4f fst :50⅕ b

Scholastic **Ch. c. 3, by Buckaroo—United Scholar, by Scholar Gypsy**
$25,000 Br.—Dearborn Ltd (Ky)
Own.—Garren M M Tr.—Puentes Gilbert
117 Lifetime 30 2 6 2 $40,780 **1985 14 1 0 1 $18,480** **1984 16 1 6 1 $22,300**

14Apr85- 4Aqu fst 7f :23⅖ :47⅕ 1:26 Clm 30000 1 4 $5^{2\frac14}$ 5^{6} 6^{9} $6^{5\frac34}$ Santagata N b 113 13.30 65-22 EddieBubbles112^{nk}TheRunningKind115^{no}StrdeCsic$115^{3/4}$ No factor 9
6Apr85- 2Aqu fst 6f :22⅘ :46⅕ 1:11⅗ Clm 32500 1 2 4^{3} $7^{8\frac12}$ 8^{10} $8^{10\frac34}$ Santagata N b 115 4.00 72-21 FlyMeAgain$115^{3/4}$EddieBubbles$110^{2\frac12}$DashingDennis$117^{1\frac12}$ Fin. early 9
29Mar85- 6Aqu fst 1 :47⅗ 1:12 1:38 Clm 25000 5 1 1^{hd} 2^{1} 2^{hd} $1^{1/2}$ Santagata N b 117 3.00 76-21 Scholastic $117^{1/2}$ Southern Joe117^{nk}AccordingToLuke117^{3} Driving 8
24Mar85- 1Aqu fst 6f :23 :47⅕ 1:12⅖ Clm 35000 5 4 $6^{3\frac14}$ $4^{6\frac12}$ $4^{4\frac12}$ $3^{2\frac34}$ Santagata N b 117 6.40e[D] 76-26 SilentDemon$112^{1\frac12}$GayDate$119^{1\frac12}$[D]Scholastic117^{3} Illegal whipping 9
24Mar85-Disqualified and placed fourth
14Mar85- 5Aqu fst 7f :23⅕ :46⅗ 1:26⅗ Clm 35000 1 11 $7^{2\frac34}$ $6^{2\frac34}$ $8^{5\frac34}$ $8^{6\frac12}$ Venezia M b 117 11.20 61-35 The RunningKind$113^{2\frac14}$GayDate114^{hd}Mr.JimmyG.$117^{2\frac14}$ Slow early 11
6Mar85- 4Aqu fst 1⅛ ⊡:48⅖ 1:14 1:53⅘ Clm 35000 7 4 $4^{1\frac12}$ 3^{1} 6^{6} 6^{8} Venezia M b 117 9.20 65-26 Debate ACase113^{hd}I'mABanker117^{no}AccordingToLuke113^{nk} Wide 12
28Feb85- 5Aqu fst 6f ⊡:22⅗ :46 1:11⅗ Clm 35000 6 9 $7^{5\frac12}$ 6^{8} $3^{6\frac12}$ $2^{5\frac34}$ Samyn J L b 117 11.00[D] 80-22 Gay Date $108^{5\frac34}$ [D]Scholastic $117^{1/2}$ Mr. Jimmy G. 117^{nk} Bore out 12
28Feb85-Disqualified and placed third
20Feb85- 4Aqu fst 6f ⊡:22⅘ :45⅘ 1:11⅗ Clm 47500 4 7 6^{4} $6^{9\frac12}$ 6^{10} $6^{8\frac34}$ Santagata N b 115 6.50 77-23 Splendid Catch$117^{3\frac14}$Summitry108^{4}Maggie'sMike$113^{1\frac12}$ No mishap 12
11Feb85- 7Aqu fst 6f ⊡:22 :45⅗ 1:11⅗ Alw 22000 4 6 $6^{7\frac12}$ $6^{8\frac14}$ 6^{7} $4^{4\frac12}$ Santagata N b 117 14.40 82-14 Koffkoff $112^{1\frac12}$ Dashing Dennis $117^{1\frac34}$ Anconeus $112^{1\frac12}$ Late bid 6
6Feb85- 1Aqu gd 1^{70} ⊡:48⅗ 1:14 1:44⅘ Alw 23000 5 6 $5^{4\frac12}$ 6^{9} 7^{20} $7^{16\frac34}$ Samyn J L b 117 5.30 59-27 Bold Bob's Dusty $112^{5\frac14}$ Natrac $112^{1/2}$ Olajuwon $117^{1\frac34}$ Never close 7
LATEST WORKOUTS Mar 22 Bel tr.t 4f fst :50 b

Also Eligible (Not in Post Position Order):

Keep It Down **Ch. c. 3, by Native Uproar—Tehama, by Cohoes**
$25,000 Br.—Bettersworth J R (Ky)
Own.—Davis A Tr.—Moschera Gasper S
117 Lifetime 18 2 1 1 $23,568 **1985 9 0 0 1 $2,640** **1984 9 2 1 0 $20,928**

6Apr85- 2Aqu fst 6f :22⅘ :46⅕ 1:11⅗ Clm 35000 3 6 8^{11} 9^{11} $7^{9\frac34}$ 7^{8} Lovato F Jr 117 7.30e 75-21 Fly Me Again $115^{3/4}$EddieBubbles$110^{2\frac12}$DashingDennis$117^{1\frac12}$ Outrun 9
24Mar85- 1Aqu fst 6f :23 :47⅕ 1:12⅖ Clm 35000 7 5 5^{3} $7^{7\frac34}$ $6^{8\frac34}$ 6^{10} Thibeau R J b 117 *1.20e 69-26 Silent Demon $112^{1\frac12}$ Gay Date $119^{1\frac12}$ [D]Scholastic 117^{3} No factor 9
14Mar85- 5Aqu fst 7f :23⅕ :46⅗ 1:26⅗ Clm 35000 4 5 1^{hd} $3^{1/2}$ $9^{6\frac12}$ 9^{13} Garrido O L5 112 *1.50e 55-35 The Running Kind $113^{2\frac14}$ GayDate114^{hd}Mr.JimmyG.$117^{2\frac14}$ Faltered 11
28Feb85- 5Aqu fst 6f ⊡:22⅗ :46 1:11⅗ Clm 35000 9 8 $11^{9\frac34}$ 12^{14} 7^{12} $6^{9\frac12}$ Henderson J C10 107 45.20 77-22 Gay Date $108^{5\frac34}$ [D]Scholastic $117^{1/2}$ Mr. Jimmy G. 117^{nk} No factor 12
20Feb85- 4Aqu fst 6f ⊡:22⅘ :45⅘ 1:11⅗ Clm 45000 11 1 $11^{8\frac12}$ 12^{30} 12^{32} $12^{31\frac14}$ Venezia M b 113 33.20 55-23 Splendid Catch $117^{3\frac14}$ Summitry 108^{4} Maggie's Mike $113^{1\frac14}$ Dull 12
6Feb85- 1Aqu gd 1^{70} ⊡:48⅗ 1:14 1:44⅘ Alw 23000 3 2 $3^{1\frac12}$ 4^{8} 6^{15} 6^{16} Ward W A5 112 7.80 60-27 Bold Bob's Dusty $112^{5\frac14}$ Natrac $112^{1/2}$ Olajuwon $117^{1\frac34}$ Tired 7
27Jan85- 9Aqu fst 6f ⊡:22⅗ :46⅖ 1:13 Clm 45000 5 3 3^{1} 7^{7} 7^{5} $7^{3\frac12}$ Ward W A5 108 3.90 75-20 Anconeus 108^{2} Splendid Catch 117^{no}SuperScope117^{nk} No mishap 12
14Jan85- 2Aqu fst 6f ⊡:22⅗ :46⅗ 1:12⅘ Clm 60000 9 1 $3^{1/2}$ 3^{1} 2^{1} 3^{hd} Miranda J 113 3.40e 80-20 Golden Chief 115no Super Scope 113no Keep It Down $113^{1\frac34}$ Wide 9
3Jan85- 5Aqu fst 6f ⊡:23⅕ :47⅗ 1:12⅗ Clm 50000 9 2 1^{1} 1^{hd} $2^{1/2}$ $6^{2\frac12}$ Migliore R 117 5.30 78-19 SilentDemon117^{nk}SuperScope108^{nk}UltimatePower108^{1} Gave way 9
28Dec84- 7Aqu sly $1\frac{1}{16}$ ⊡:47⅖ 1:12 1:44⅗ Alw 23000 2 4 6^{5} 10^{19} 10^{25} 9^{29} Santagata N b 117 23.50 60-19 Romancer$117^{7\frac12}$UncleDaddy110^{4}Lsit'sSilencer$112^{2\frac12}$ Showed little 10
LATEST WORKOUTS Apr 4 Bel tr.t 4f fst :50 b Mar 8 Bel tr.t 4f gd :52⅘ b Feb 27 Bel tr.t 3f fst :38⅘ b

More condemning, however, was the simple fact that Charmed Destiny was not being moved up another notch in claiming price, as he had for his prior two victories. His performance on April 9 certainly warranted another boost in value, yet trainer Wilson obviously thought otherwise. Why? What had he observed in the interim to suggest taking a more cautious posture? Why this sudden lack of confidence in his horse?

Among the other contestants, second-choice Natrac was dropping in class off a six-week layoff and turning back to six furlongs after three routes. The distance appeared to be too short, making the dropdown seem especially suspicious. Third in the betting, Irv's Choice looked good on paper but had neither the pace nor the final-time figures to match strides with Charmed Destiny.

Of the others, Handful Of Steel could conceivably repeat his one-off-a-layoff form reversal of the previous summer. But his long layoff following that win was suspicious, as was the lack of betting action on April 14 and for today's race. Full Of Fortune showed good speed for six furlongs in his local debut and was now dropping sharply in price to a seemingly more suitable distance. He seemed a more serious threat but nevertheless remained somewhat of a mystery. Both Creative Spirit and Keep It Down had shown little in recent starts. Cop A Plea had been away since January 1 and showed nothing in his only start out of the maiden ranks. And Scholastic, with only two wins from thirty lifetime starts (already!), was dull in his last two starts, although at a higher level.

Finally, there was Mister G., a lightly raced colt who bid and hung in his latest start, finishing only three-and-a-half lengths behind the favorite. His sire, Cinteelo, was one of the great off-track runners in recent years, a genetic consideration that, by itself, could make a difference of several lengths. If the favorite failed to run his best race, or was victimized by a possible bias, Mister G. appeared as likely as anyone to beat him—which is exactly what happened.

SECOND RACE
Aqueduct
APRIL 20, 1985

6 FURLONGS. (1.08⅘) CLAIMING. Purse $15,000. 3-years-olds, 122 lbs. Non-winners of two races since April 1 allowed 3 lbs. Of a race since then, 5 lbs. Claiming price $25,000; for each $2,500 to $20,000, 2 lbs. (Races when entered to be claimed for $18,000 or less not considered.)

Value of race $15,000; value to winner $9,000; second $3,300; third $1,800; fourth $900. Mutuel pool $161,925, OTB pool $141,140. Quinella Pool $254,031. OTB Quinella Pool $237,637.

Last Raced	Horse	Eqt.	A.	Wt	PP	St	¼	½	Str	Fin	Jockey	Cl'g Pr	Odds $1
9Apr85 ^{4}Aqu^{3}	Mister G.	b	3	117	5	7	3^{2}	3^{3}	$1^{\frac{1}{2}}$	$1^{\frac{3}{4}}$	Vasquez J	25000	6.50
6Apr85 ^{2}Aqu^{7}	Keep It Down		3	117	11	1	6^{2}	6^{1}	5^{2}	2^{nk}	Bailey J D	25000	a-9.20
14Apr85 ^{4}Aqu^{4}	Irv's Choice	b	3	117	7	2	$5^{\frac{1}{2}}$	$5^{\frac{1}{2}}$	4^{hd}	$3^{2\frac{3}{4}}$	Cordero A Jr	25000	4.20
9Apr85 ^{4}Aqu^{1}	Charmed Destiny	b	3	112	3	4	$2^{1\frac{1}{2}}$	$2^{\frac{1}{2}}$	2^{hd}	4no	Moore D N^{5}	22500	1.70
14Apr85 ^{4}Aqu^{6}	Scholastic	b	3	117	10	8	10^{5}	9^{2}	8^{2}	5^{hd}	Santagata N	25000	22.40
9Apr85 ^{4}Aqu^{4}	Creative Spirit	b	3	115	4	6	$7^{\frac{1}{2}}$	7^{4}	7^{2}	6^{hd}	Davis R G	22500	32.40
10Apr85 ^{4}Aqu^{9}	Full of Fortune	b	3	117	2	9	$4^{1\frac{1}{2}}$	4^{1}	$6^{\frac{1}{2}}$	$7^{\frac{3}{4}}$	Maple E	25000	11.40
6Apr85 ^{2}Aqu^{6}	Bucket Ben	b	3	117	9	3	1^{hd}	$1^{\frac{1}{2}}$	3^{2}	$8^{1\frac{1}{4}}$	Migliore R	25000	a-9.20
6Mar85 ^{4}Aqu^{4}	Natrac	b	3	117	8	11	11	$10^{\frac{1}{2}}$	10^{4}	$9^{1\frac{1}{4}}$	Velasquez J	25000	3.60
1Jan85 ^{3}Aqu^{5}	Cop A Plea	b	3	115	6	10	$8^{\frac{1}{2}}$	$8^{\frac{1}{2}}$	9^{hd}	$10^{4\frac{1}{4}}$	Messina R	22500	28.20
14Apr85 ^{4}Aqu^{8}	Handful Of Steel		3	117	1	5	9^{hd}	11	11	11	Ward W A	25000	42.00

a-Coupled: Keep It Down and Bucket Ben.

OFF AT 1:31 Start good, Won driving. Time, :22⅕, :45⅗, 1:11⅕ Track muddy.

$2 Mutuel Prices:				
	6-(G)-MISTER G.	15.00	7.80	6.00
	1-(P)-KEEP IT DOWN (a-entry)		9.00	5.40
	8-(I)-IRV'S CHOICE			4.40
	$2 QUINELLA 1-6 PAID $56.40.			

Dk. b. or br. c, by Cinteelo—Missy G, by Knightly Manner. Trainer DeStasio Richard T. Bred by Gargano P (Ky).

MISTER G., close up early reached the front from the outside after entering the stretch and was under pressure to turn back KEEP IT DOWN. The latter, wide into the stretch, was going well at the finish. IRV'S CHOICE, never far back, finished with good energy between horses. CHARMED DESTINY saved ground while showing speed to midstretch and weakened. SCHOLASTIC rallied mildly while racing wide. CREATIVE SPIRIT saved ground to no avail. FULL OF FORTUNE weakened. BUCKET BEN gave way after showing speed to midstretch. NATRAC was always outrun. CREATIVE SPIRIT raced with mud caulks.

We believe Charmed Destiny was a better win selection on April 9, however. He embodied all of the textbook requirements for the "rising three-year-old" angle on that occasion: a win, then another win on the rise, then another rise in class. Although facing seemingly classier animals that appeared capable of producing faster figures—pace as well as final time—the power of this angle is such that the improving horse will, often enough, improve even further and run to whatever figures are needed to do the job. The fact that Charmed Destiny overcame a four-horse speed duel to draw away at seven furlongs on February 24 was reassuring, speaking well of the horse's courage under fire.

Let's take a closer look at his opposition on April 9:

4 AQUEDUCT — 7 FURLONGS

7 FURLONGS. (1.20⅕) CLAIMING. Purse $15,000. 3-year-olds. Weights, 122 lbs. Non-winners of two races since March 15 allowed 3 lbs. Of a race since then 5 lbs. Claiming price $25,000; for each $2,500 to $20,000 2 lbs. (Races where entered to be claimed for $18,000 or less not considered.)

Coupled—Dash Mount and Charmed Destiny; Creative Spirit and Uncompromising; Venture Beyond and Blue Flack.

Soaring Romeo

B. g. 3, by Gallant Romeo—Soar Aloft, by Avatar
$25,000 Br.—November House Associates (Ky)
Tr.—Sedlacek Roy
Own.—Barge Marc
119 — Lifetime 8 3 0 0 $24,000 — 1985 8 3 0 0 $24,000 — 1984 0 M 0 0

Race	Fractions	Class	Running line	Jockey	Wt	Odds	Speed / Finish / Comment
27Mar85- 5Aqu fst 7f	:22⅕ :45⅗ 1:22⅗	Clm 45000	5 8 1011 1013 821 819½	Thibeau R J	b 113	21.40	68-20 Summitry 1174 Taylor Road 1175½ The RunningKind1132¾ Outrun 10
17Mar85- 9Aqu fst 7f	:23⅗ :48⅕ 1:28⅘	Clm 25000	12 1 116¾ 118¾ 22 1¾	Thibeau R J	b 119	5.50	59-33 Soaring Romeo 119¾ Irv's Choice112¾FrenchAnswer110no Driving 12
7Mar85- 2Aqu fst 6f	⊡:22⅗ :45⅘ 1:12⅘	Clm 25000	8 9 107¾ 89½ 76½ 54	Thibeau R J	b 119	9.90	78-21 Gay Date 114¾ French Answer 1151¾ Bolinger 112no Mild gain 11
1Mar85- 5Aqu fst 1⅛	⊡:49 1:13⅗ 1:47⅘	Clm 45000	6 7 75½ 65½ 65½ 56¾	Thibeau R J	b 113	15.30	64-25 History Responds 113nk Natrac 108no Maggie'sMike115hd Outrun 7
18Feb85- 9Aqu fst 6f	⊡:22⅖ :46⅗ 1:13⅘	Clm 25000	7 8 97¾ 810 43½ 1½	Thibeau R J	b 117	46.10	75-28 SoaringRomeo117½StarkDancer117noStudentofDnce1143½ Driving 10
9Feb85- 2Aqu fst 6f	⊡:23⅗ :47⅘ 1:13⅗	Clm 35000	3 9 1215 1221 1224 1223¾	McCarron G	b 119	44.20	52-26 Summitry 1124 Bolinger 1107 Fly Me Again 108nk Far back 12
27Jan85- 9Aqu fst 6f	⊡:22⅗ :46⅖ 1:13	Clm 50000	4 11 117¾ 1015 1011 1010½	McCarron G	b 117	30.00	69-20 Anconeus 1082 Splendid Catch 117no Super Scope 117nk Outrun 12
7Jan85- 4Aqu fst 6f	⊡:23 :47⅖ 1:14⅕	Md 30000	6 4 3nk 2hd 1hd 1¾	McCarron G	b 118	6.60	73-27 Soaring Romeo 118¾ Black Elk 118hd Rich Gift 1222½ Driving 12

Allotment

B. g. 3, by Sauce Boat—Hard To Get, by Sir Gaylord
$25,000 Br.—Bettersworth J R (Ky)
Tr.—Hertler John O
Own.—Cobble View Stable
110⁷ — Lifetime 8 2 0 0 $11,398 — 1985 5 0 0 0 $1,140 — 1984 3 2 0 0 $10,258

Race	Fractions	Class	Running line	Jockey	Wt	Odds	Speed / Finish / Comment
27Mar85- 2Aqu fst 6f	:22⅖ :45⅘ 1:11⅗	Clm 25000	4 4 75½ 66 64½ 64½	Guerra A A7	110	20.80	79-20 H. T. Willis 1121¾ Stark Dancer 1121½ Bucket Ben117¾ No mishap 10
17Mar85- 9Aqu fst 7f	:23⅗ :48⅕ 1:28⅘	Clm 25000	7 5 41 31 43½ 75¾	Guerra A A7	110	17.80	53-33 Soaring Romeo 119¾ Irv's Choice 112¾ French Answer110no Tired 12
28Feb85- 5Aqu fst 6f	⊡:22⅗ :46 1:11⅗	Clm 30000	12 11 64 57 47½ 79¾	Guerra A A7	106	27.00	76-22 Gay Date 1085¾ [D]Scholastic 117½ Mr. Jimmy G. 117nk No factor 12
9Feb85- 2Aqu fst 6f	⊡:23⅗ :47⅘ 1:13⅗	Clm 35000	5 3 52 67 311 512½	Lovato F Jr	b 117	10.00	63-26 Summitry 1124 Bolinger 1107 Fly Me Again 108nk No excuse 12
3Jan85- 5Aqu fst 6f	⊡:23⅕ :47⅗ 1:12⅗	Clm 45000	5 3 76½ 74 63 41½	Giglio D Jr7	107	16.90	79-19 Silent Demon 117nk Super Scope108nkUltimatePower1081 Rallied 9
19Dec84- 2Aqu fst 6f	⊡:23 :47 1:13⅗	Clm c-35000	4 5 2hd 2½ 2½ 85½	Cordero A Jr	117	*.90e	70-25 Top Talk 113hd Super Scope 1081½ [D]Student ofDance108hd Tired 11
28Nov84- 9Med fst 6f	:22⅖ :46 1:13⅗	Clm 25000	7 3 33 3nk 1½ 11	Krone J A	117	3.20	73-25 Allotment 1171 Misery Bay 117hd Viable Proposition 1103 Driving 8
6Nov84- 1CD gd 6f	:22⅖ :46⅕ 1:13⅗	Md 25000	8 2 3½ 12 11 1½	Day P	121	*.90	76-22 Allotment 121½ Botcha's Bid 121¾ Debate A Case 1212 Driving 11

LATEST WORKOUTS Mar 14 Bel tr.t 5f fst 1:06 b Mar 8 Bel tr.t 5f gd 1:05⅘ b

Fast Travler

Ch. g. 3, by Mount Hagen—So Saucy, by Chateaugay
$20,000 Br.—Dogwood Farm Inc (Ky)
Tr.—Casse Mark
Own.—Casse N E
103¹⁰ — Lifetime 11 1 3 0 $12,405 — 1985 3 0 0 0 — 1984 8 1 3 0 $12,405

Race	Fractions	Class	Running line	Jockey	Wt	Odds	Speed / Finish / Comment
17Feb85- 4Aqu fst 170	⊡:48⅗ 1:14⅘ 1:46⅗	Clm 30000	2 1 21 1012 1022 1030½	Wynter N A10	b 103	14.40	37-25 Fly Me Again 1081 Star de Cesica 1153½ JupiterAccord1132 Tired 10
10Feb85- 3Aqu fst 1⅛	⊡:48 1:13⅗ 1:53⅖	Clm 50000	10 4 43½ 53½ 1116 1115½	Migliore R	117	6.30	60-18 Glenn Brooke 1103½ Classi Valentine 117no Natrac 113½ Tired 11
4Jan85- 7Aqu fst 170	⊡:48⅗ 1:13⅗ 1:44⅘	Clm 80000	6 1 11 41½ 76½ 714¾	Migliore R	114	14.40	61-21 First One Up122nkFeelingGallant114nkHaberdasher107hd Stopped 8
8Nov84- 3CD fst 1 1/16	:49⅗ 1:14⅕ 1:46⅖	Alw 11425	4 1 11 11½ 1hd 2hd	Woods C R Jr	112	26.90	76-19 Nordic Scandal 115hd Fast Travler 1121 Fuzzy 1183 Gamely 7
27Oct84- 3Kee fst *7f	1:30⅖	Alw 13340	1 6 2½ 3½ 614 615½	McKnight J	112	15.90	55-25 Diamond Rich 115½ Magloire 1171 Stop Who 1172½ Stopped 6
11Oct84- 6Kee fst 1 1/16	:48⅗ 1:13⅕ 1:46⅖	Alw 15800	4 3 44½ 31½ 22 25	Woods C R Jr	112	2.90	69-17 Grand Native 1155 Fast Travler1124OutLookin1156 Best of others 5
22Sep84- 5Lat fst 1	:49⅕ 1:14 1:41⅗	Md Sp Wt	5 2 1½ 15 17 19	Woods C R Jr	120	3.40	71-18 Fast Travler 1209 Palekh 1202½ Lunada Bay 117hd 9
9Sep84- 1Lat fst 1	:49⅗ 1:15⅗ 1:44⅖	Md Sp Wt	7 3 2hd 21½ 39 417½	Foster D E	120	4.00	39-32 Gunman's Gauntlet 1202½SeldomStill12013SpreadTotheRight1172 9
29Aug84- 2CD fst 6f	:22⅕ :45⅘ 1:12⅕	Md Sp Wt	4 6 67 710 714 613¾	McKnight J	118	5.30e	71-20 Come Summer 1185 Red Liquor 1182½ Color Me Gone 1182 10
15Aug84- 4CD fst 6f	:22⅕ :45⅘ 1:11⅘	Md Sp Wt	1 5 55½ 55½ 56½ 59¾	Woods C R Jr	118	*1.70	77-14 Night Above 118nk Pickwick Landing 1183 Step Proud 1186½ 7

LATEST WORKOUTS Apr 5 Bel 5f fst 1:02 h Mar 17 Bel tr.t 5f fst 1:03⅘ b Mar 9 Bel tr.t 4f gd :50 b Feb 16 Bel tr.t 3f fst :38⅘ b

Flippant

Gr. c. 3, by Flip Sal—Ebony Rock, by Rock Talk
$25,000 Br.—Pepitone B (NY)
Tr.—Puentes Gilbert
Own.—Garren M M
117 — Lifetime 16 1 1 2 $10,900 — 1985 3 0 0 0 — 1984 13 1 1 2 $10,900

Race	Fractions	Class	Running line	Jockey	Wt	Odds	Speed / Finish / Comment
1Apr85- 7Aqu fst 6f	:22⅕ :45⅗ 1:10	3↑[S]Alw 25500	6 10 85 107 1011 1112	Cordero A Jr	b 109	5.70f	79-17 GllopRhythm1126½AnotherSummr109hdStrOfBordux1122½ Outrun 13
24Mar85- 1Aqu fst 6f	:23 :47⅕ 1:12⅘	Clm 32500	4 1 21 21 34½ 56¾	Davis R G	b 115	6.40e	72-26 Silent Demon 1121½ Gay Date 1191½ [D]Scholastic 1173 Tired 9
18Feb85- 1Aqu fst 1 1/16	⊡:48⅕ 1:13⅗ 1:48	Clm 70000	8 1 12 1½ 66½ 710½	Santagata N	b 113	25.10	60-28 Bold Bob's Dusty 114¾ Olajuwon 115½ Helcin 112¾ Tired 8
28Dec84- 7Aqu sly 1 1/16	⊡:47⅗ 1:12 1:44⅗	Alw 23000	9 3 3½ 56 921 1029¾	Miranda J	b 117	49.50	59-19 Romancer 1177½ Uncle Daddy 1104 Lasita'sSilencer1122½ Stopped 10
16Dec84- 6Aqu fst 6f	⊡:23⅕ :46⅗ 1:13⅕	[S]Alw 25500	4 4 2hd 21 24 67¾	Samyn J L	b 117	10.90	70-24 Pico De Gallo 122¾ Club Fighter 1193½ Silent Slander 1172½ Tired 9
9Dec84- 8Aqu fst 1⅛	⊡:49⅕ 1:14⅕ 1:53	[S]B F Bongard	6 2 21½ 32 510 613½	Davis R G	b 115	33.10	63-19 Hot Debate 122no Romancer 1177 Royal Bocha 117nk Used early 9
23Nov84- 9Aqu fst 1	:47⅗ 1:13 1:39⅘	[S]Alw 27000	1 7 71¾ 77½ 44 66	Davis R G	b 117	15.10	61-29 MyManJohn117¾Romancer1121¾WinWonSoon117hd Flattened out 10
9Nov84- 9Aqu fst 1⅛	:49⅕ 1:15⅗ 1:56	Md 35000	8 2 2½ 2hd 13 11	Davis R G	b 118	*2.00	55-32 Flippant 1181 MasterCommand1147Uncompromising1142¾ All out 10
29Oct84- 4Aqu my 6f	:23 :47 1:11⅘	Md 32500	11 11 53 32½ 35½ 34¾	Cruguet J	b 116	3.70	77-18 Stark Dancer 1141¾ Casting For 1133Flippant1163¾ Sluggish start 14
25Oct84- 2Aqu gd 1	:47 1:12⅖ 1:39⅘	Md c-25000	4 8 1hd 12 11 31	Cruguet J	b 118	*2.30e	67-21 Sudden Stroke 118nk Park Lane 114¾ Flippant 118nk Off Slowly 14

LATEST WORKOUTS ●Apr 8 Bel 3f gd :34⅘ h Mar 30 Bel tr.t 3f fst :36⅖ h Mar 22 Bel tr.t 5f fst 1:01⅘ h Mar 17 Bel tr.t 4f fst :49 b

Mister G.

Dk. b. or br. c. 3, by Cinteelo—Missy G, by Knightly Manner
$25,000 Br.—Gargano P (Ky)
Tr.—DeStasio Richard T
Own.—Gargano P
117 — Lifetime 6 1 0 0 $7,680 — 1985 4 1 0 0 $6,000 — 1984 2 M 0 0 $1,680

Race	Fractions	Class	Running line	Jockey	Wt	Odds	Speed / Finish / Comment
27Mar85- 2Aqu fst 6f	:22⅖ :45⅘ 1:11⅗	Clm 25000	6 6 33 43 53 53¾	Reed R L7	b 110	12.10	79-20 H. T. Willis 1121¾ Stark Dancer 1121½ Bucket Ben 117¾ Tired 10
14Mar85- 5Aqu fst 7f	:23⅕ :46⅗ 1:26⅗	Clm 35000	7 3 2hd 41½ 74¾ 76½	Reed R L7	b 112	42.40	62-35 The Running Kind 1132½ Gay Date 114hd Mr. JimmyG.1172½ Tired 11
3Mar85- 2Aqu fst 6f	⊡:22⅗ :46⅗ 1:12	Clm 50000	7 1 61¾ 75 79½ 713¾	Reed R L7	b 110	24.40	70-17 Determined Run 1131½ Gay Date 108nk Overbought 1172¾ Outrun 8
20Feb85- 3Aqu fst 6f	⊡:23⅗ :47⅗ 1:14⅕	Md 35000	11 1 2½ 1½ 12 13¾	Reed R L7	b 115	4.20	73-23 Mister G. 1153¾ Catch The Redeye 118½ Gran Fable 122nk Driving 12
27Jun84- 4Bel fst 5½f	:23 :47⅕ 1:06⅗	Md 40000	2 1 2hd 2½ 33½ 46¾	MacBeth D	b 118	*1.90	75-17 BernaCqney1111½EternlPrince1181½WesternChmp1164 Weakened 9
27Apr84- 4Aqu fst 4½f	:23⅕ :47 :53⅗	Md Sp Wt	2 5 43½ 34 35¾	Smith A Jr	118	2.50[D]	87-07 CrystlIcebrg118½StrongAppl1185½[D]MistrG.118¾ Steadied, lugged 6

27Apr84-Disqualified and placed fourth

LATEST WORKOUTS Apr 5 Bel tr.t 5f fst 1:04 b Mar 22 Bel tr.t 6f fst 1:20 b Mar 11 Bel tr.t 4f fst :52⅕ b Feb 28 Bel tr.t 3f fst :38⅘ b

Dash Mount

B. c. 3, by Mount Hagen—Maidsmorton, by Bold Ruler
$25,000 Br.—Proskauer Mrs Susan & Todd R (Ky)
Tr.—Wilson R
Own.—Anchel E
110⁷ — Lifetime 9 2 0 0 $13,200 — 1985 5 1 0 0 $7,200 — 1984 4 1 0 0 $6,000 — Turf 1 0 0 0

Race	Fractions	Class	Running line	Jockey	Wt	Odds	Speed / Finish / Comment
24Mar85- 1Aqu fst 6f	:23 :47⅕ 1:12⅘	Clm 35000	2 3 42 98½ 914 915½	Espinosa R E7	b 110	20.50	64-26 Silent Demon 1121½ Gay Date 1191½ [D]Scholastic 1173 Early foot 9
8Mar85- 9Aqu fst 6f	⊡:22⅗ :46 1:12⅘	Clm 15500	1 8 64½ 56 32 11½	Espinosa R E5	b 108	33.70	80-18 Dash Mount 1081½ Irv's Choice 1171¾ Instant Recall117nk Driving 12
24Feb85- 2Aqu fst 6f	⊡:22⅗ :46⅖ 1:14	Clm 12000	6 2 43½ 610 713 712½	Messina R	b 113	*1.70e	62-28 Even On Sunday 117nk Indulge 1062 Stasera 1192 Tired 12
3Feb85- 1Aqu gd 6f	⊡:22⅗ :47⅕ 1:14⅗	Clm 12000	7 7 55½ 510 67½ 53½	Messina R	b 113	14.30	68-22 Stasera 117nk Czar's Fiddle 107hd Churning 112¾ No factor 10
4Jan85- 1Aqu fst 6f	⊡:23⅕ :47⅗ 1:12⅘	Clm 18000	7 1 4¾ 78 716 717½	Privitera R7	b 106	8.20	62-21 Gay Date 1082 Fly Me Again 1172½ Montriva 1171¾ Brief foot 8
29Nov84- 3Aqu gd 6f	:23⅗ :48⅗ 1:15⅘	Md 20000	4 5 2hd 1½ 2½ 1no	Privitera R7	b 107	15.30	62-35 Dash Mount 107no Intercostal 114¾ Park Lane 1141 Driving 14
19Nov84- 6Aqu sf 1 1/16	ⓣ:50 1:16⅖ 1:51⅘	Md Sp Wt	4 2 2hd 76¾ 816 817½	Espinosa R E7	b 111	35.70	29-46 Olajuwon 1182 Clean Machine 118¾ Pro Appeal 1182½ Bore out 8
29Oct84- 4Aqu my 6f	:23 :47 1:11⅘	Md 30000	14 1 21 45½ 716 918¾	Migliore R	114	6.40e	63-18 Stark Dancer 1141¾ Casting For 1133 Flippant 1163¾ Tired 14
1Oct84- 4Bel gd 6f	:22⅗ :46⅗ 1:12⅗	Md 35000	12 8 911 912 911 1011¾	Venezia M	118	47.30	67-21 Trophy Hunter 1161 Confirmed Patriot118½CastingFor1111¾ Wide 12

LATEST WORKOUTS Apr 3 Aqu 5f fst 1:02⅗ b Mar 17 Aqu 4f fst :49⅘ h Mar 4 Aqu ⊡ 4f fst :50⅕ b Feb 14 Aqu ⊡ 4f fst :51⅗ b

Stark Dancer

B. c. 3, by Graustark—Dancing Gull, by Northern Dancer
$25,000 Br.—Newstead Farm (Va)
Tr.—Lake Robert P
Own.—Cohen M
112⁵ — Lifetime 14 1 3 1 $19,150 — 1985 4 0 2 0 $6,600 — 1984 10 1 1 1 $12,550

Race	Fractions	Class	Running line	Jockey	Wt	Odds	Speed / Finish / Comment
27Mar85- 2Aqu fst 6f	:22⅖ :45⅘ 1:11⅗	Clm 25000	5 3 22 1½ 11½ 21¾	Moore D N5	b 112	*3.40	81-20 H. T. Willis 1121¾ Stark Dancer 1121½ Bucket Ben117¾ Weakened 10
18Feb85- 9Aqu fst 6f	⊡:22⅖ :46⅗ 1:13⅘	Clm c-25000	6 1 1hd 1hd 1hd 2½	Migliore R	b 117	3.80	74-28 SoaringRomeo117½StarkDancer117noStudentofDnce1143½ Gamely 10
27Jan85- 9Aqu fst 6f	⊡:22⅗ :46⅖ 1:13	Clm 45000	6 4 2hd 1hd 31 52½	Hernandez R	b 114	34.20	77-20 Anconeus 1082 Splendid Catch 117no SuperScope117nk Gave way 12
19Jan85- 2Aqu fst 1 1/16	⊡:48⅗ 1:14 1:48⅗	Clm 50000	11 3 31 21 55½ 87½	Hernandez R	b 117	13.30	60-22 Helcin 112nk Another Doc 1172 Creative Spirit 113½ Tired 12
28Dec84- 7Aqu sly 1 1/16	⊡:47⅗ 1:12 1:44⅗	Alw 23000	4 7 97½ 45½ 511 514¾	Hernandez R	b 117	23.40	74-19 Romancer 1177½UncleDaddy1104Lasita'sSilencer1122½ No mishap 10
12Dec84- 1Aqu fst 170	⊡:50⅗ 1:15⅗ 1:46	Clm 40000	2 2 2hd 1hd 1½ 2hd	Hernandez R	b 113	3.30	70-20 Helcin 104hd Stark Dancer 1135½ Angelic Bliss 113hd Just failed 7
24Nov84- 3Aqu fst 6f	:23 :47⅖ 1:13⅗	Clm 45000	6 7 62½ 43 44½ 46½	Hernandez R	b 113	5.40	68-27 Splendid Catch 117¾ My Marisa 1075 The RunningKind117½ Wide 8
15Nov84- 3Med fst 6f	:22⅖ :46 1:12⅘	Clm 45000	4 5 67½ 56½ 58 54¾	Hernandez R	b 114	7.30	73-22 Distant Orbit 109nk Dwight D. 1171 Put It In Park 1201 No factor 6
29Oct84- 4Aqu my 6f	:23 :47 1:11⅘	Md 30000	9 5 41½ 21½ 11½ 11¾	Hernandez R	b 114	6.40e	82-18 Stark Dancer 1141¾ Casting For 1133 Flippant 1163¾ Driving 14
28Sep84- 3Bel gd 7f	:23 :46⅗ 1:25	Md 45000	2 7 53 51½ 54¾ 510	Hernandez R	b 114	20.30	67-26 Julies Bet 1165½ Scholastic 118½ Fabulous Move 1181¾ No factor 9

LATEST WORKOUTS Mar 14 Aqu 4f fst :49⅘ b

Shining Tyson

B. g. 3, by Cutlass—Mrs Mansfield, by Dewan
$25,000 Br.—Carrion J S (Fla)
Tr.—Agati James
Own.—Vignone F
117 — Lifetime 20 1 3 3 $21,546 — 1985 8 0 0 1 $4,080 — 1984 12 1 3 2 $17,466

Race	Fractions	Class	Running line	Jockey	Wt	Odds	Speed / Finish / Comment
27Mar85- 2Aqu fst 6f	:22⅖ :45⅘ 1:11⅗	Clm 25000	7 7 109½ 89 106½ 87¾	Lovato F Jr	117	36.80	75-20 H. T. Willis 1121¾ Stark Dancer 1121½ Bucket Ben 117¾ Wide 10
17Mar85- 9Aqu fst 7f	:23⅗ :48⅕ 1:28⅘	Clm 25000	2 7 1hd 1hd 75½ 910¾	Murphy D J	b 117	23.30	48-33 Soaring Romeo 119¾ Irv's Choice 112¾ French Answer110no Tired 12
3Mar85- 2Aqu fst 6f	⊡:22⅗ :46⅗ 1:12	Clm 45000	6 6 2hd 53½ 810 817½	Williams A C7	b 106	41.20	66-17 Determined Run 1131½ Gay Date 108nk Overbought1172¾ Stopped 8
28Feb85- 5Aqu fst 6f	⊡:22⅗ :46 1:11⅗	Clm 35000	2 5 31 45 913 1015½	Santagata N	b 117	31.80	71-22 Gay Date 1085¾ [D]Scholastic 117½ Mr. Jimmy G. 117nk Fin. early 12
9Feb85- 2Aqu fst 6f	⊡:23⅗ :47⅘ 1:13⅗	Clm 35000	8 4 41½ 35½ 412 614½	Guerra A A7	110	12.30	62-26 Summitry 1124 Bolinger 1107 Fly Me Again 108nk Tired 12
23Jan85- 1Aqu fst 6f	⊡:23⅕ :47⅖ 1:12⅘	Clm 35000	3 2 21½ 2½ 31½ 43½	Santagata N	117	4.70	77-24 Gay Date 1152 Bolinger 1171½ Mr. Jimmy G. 117no Tired 5
11Jan85- 9Aqu fst 6f	⊡:23⅕ :47⅗ 1:13⅗	Clm 37500	7 1 61½ 2hd 2½ 45	Santagata N	b 115	6.60	72-30 Gay Date 113hd Student of Dance 1171½ Mr. Jimmy G.1133¾ Tired 9
1Jan85- 3Aqu fst 6f	⊡:21⅘ :45 1:11⅗	Clm 35000	6 2 4¾ 54 53 32½	Graell A	117	8.70	84-13 Top Talk 1192½ Student of Dance 108no Shining Tyson117nk Wide 9
19Dec84- 2Aqu fst 6f	⊡:23 :47 1:13⅗	Clm 35000	9 1 31 32½ 52 52½	Zuniga M	b 117	7.60	74-25 TopTalk113hdSuperScope1081¾[D]StudentofDance108hd Weakened 11
19Dec84-Placed fourth through disqualification							
16Dec84- 1Aqu fst 170	⊡:48⅕ 1:13⅗ 1:45⅘	Clm 70000	3 2 32 34 710 612¾	Privitera R7	b 106	26.80	58-24 Lasita'sSilencer1082½KeepItDown117noKilts'Nshu117no Fin. early 7

LATEST WORKOUTS Apr 3 Bel tr.t 4f fst :49 h Mar 15 Bel tr.t 3f fst :37⅗ b Mar 10 Bel tr.t 5f fst 1:05 b Feb 18 Bel tr.t 3f fst :35⅘ h

The Running Kind — Dk. b. or br. g. 3, by Batonnier—Nu Regards, by No Robbery
$25,000 Br.—Rafsky & Seltzer (NY) | 117 | Lifetime 10 2 1 2 $25,060 | 1985 6 1 1 1 $16,780 | 1984 4 1 0 1 $8,280
Own.—Gampel H A Tr.—Gullo Thomas J

27Mar85- 5Aqu fst 7f :22⅕ :45⅗ 1:22⅘ Clm 45000 7 1 66 55½ 49 39¼ Davis R G b 113 5.50 78-20 Summitry 1174 Taylor Road 1175½ The RunningKind1132¾ Rallied 10
14Mar85- 5Aqu fst 7f :23⅕ :46⅘ 1:26⅗ Clm 30000 8 9 116½ 94½ 42½ 12½ Davis R G b 113 7.60 68-35 The Running Kind 1132½ Gay Date 114hd Mr.JimmyG.1172½ Driving 11
20Feb85- 4Aqu fst 6f ⊡:22⅘ :45⅘ 1:11⅗ Clm 45000 5 9 128¾ 814 812 58¼ Giglio D Jr7 b 106 55.00 77-23 SplendidCatch1173½Summitry1084Maggie'sMike1131½ Raced wide 12
10Feb85- 3Aqu fst 1⅛ ⊡:48 1:13⅘ 1:53⅘ Clm 45000 6 2 2hd 21 79¾ 910¼ Giglio D Jr7 b 106 25.60 64-18 Glenn Brooke 1103½ Classi Valentine 117no Natrac 113½ Stopped 11
26Jan85- 6Aqu fst 170 ⊡:48 1:14⅕ 1:44⅘ Alw 23000 5 10 1011 109¼ 811 712¼ Giglio D Jr7 b 110 51.40 64-20 Feeling Gallant117nk CrystalIceberg117hd Haberdasher1122 Outrun 10
12Jan85- 3Aqu fst 170 ⊡:48⅘ 1:15⅕ 1:47 Clm c-35000 10 2 21 21½ 23 23¾ Graell A b 117 *1.60e 61-24 Fulmintor1173¾TheRunningKind1171½ReglTrick1171¼ Second best 10
27Dec84- 6Aqu gd 1$\frac{1}{16}$ ⊡:49⅘ 1:15⅘ 1:48⅖ Clm 50000 8 3 21 31½ 714 712¼ Graell A b 116 10.50 57-28 Silent Slander 1152 Helcin 1112¾ Captain Marvel 109hd Tired 9
3Dec84- 5Aqu fst 7f :22⅘ :46 1:24⅗ Clm 65000 5 4 47 89 818 716¾ Cordero A Jr 117 *1.80 61-29 SplendidCatch1176¾FeelingGallnt113½DistntOrbit108hd Dull effort 8
24Nov84- 3Aqu fst 6f :23 :47⅖ 1:13⅖ Clm 50000 3 6 73¾ 76½ 78½ 35¾ Cordero A Jr 117 2.30 68-27 SplendidCatch117¾MyMaris1075TheRunningKind117½ Sluggish st 8
22Jly84- 4Bel my 5½f :23 :46⅘ 1:05⅘ Md 40000 8 2 12½ 11½ 15 17½ Graell A 118 *3.10 88-21 The Running Kind 1187½ Flippant1143½BroStache1141 Ridden out 8
LATEST WORKOUTS Apr 4 Bel tr.t 4f fst :49⅕ h Mar 10 Bel tr.t 3f fst :37⅘ b

Gorsk — Dk. b. or br. c. 3, by Full Out—Hedging, by Hail To Reason
$22,500 Br.—Smith A B (Ky) | 108[7] | Lifetime 14 3 0 0 $23,070 | 1985 6 2 0 0 $18,600 | 1984 8 1 0 0 $4,470 | Turf 1 0 0 0
Own.—Don-Nick Stable Tr.—Puccio Donald

25Mar85- 1Aqu fst 1 :50⅕ 1:17⅘ 1:44⅘ Clm 14000 4 7 43½ 31 15 13½ Espinosa R E7 110 2.80 44-35 Gorsk 1103½ Military Victory 1132½ Mr. Recharge 117¾ Driving 8
6Mar85- 4Aqu fst 1⅛ ⊡:48⅘ 1:14 1:53⅘ Clm 30000 1 11 1211 1217 1227 1229¾ Garrido O L5 b 108 29.10 43-26 DebateACase113hd I'mABnker117no AccordingToLuke113nk Outrun 12
17Feb85- 4Aqu fst 170 ⊡:48⅗ 1:14⅘ 1:46⅗ Clm 35000 8 10 1013 86½ 711 710¼ Garrido O L5 b 112 6.60 57-25 Fly Me Again 1081 Star de Cesica1153½JupiterAccord1132 Outrun 10
10Feb85- 3Aqu fst 1⅛ ⊡:48 1:13⅘ 1:53⅖ Clm 45000 1 11 119¾ 119½ 810 55½ Garrido O L5 b 108 12.90 69-18 Glenn Brooke 1103½ Classi Valentine 117no Natrac113½ Slow early 11
25Jan85- 3Aqu fst 1$\frac{1}{16}$ ⊡:48⅗ 1:14 1:48⅕ Clm 18000 9 9 78½ 67½ 1½ 11½ Garrido O L5 b 108 13.40 69-23 Gorsk1081½BoldBob'sDusty1083CountryKitchen1171½ Going away 9
4Jan85- 1Aqu fst 6f ⊡:23⅕ :47⅖ 1:12⅘ Clm 18000 1 8 74½ 55 48 46 Moore D N5 108 28.30 74-21 Gay Date 1082 Fly Me Again 1172¾Montriva1171¾ Pssd tired ones 8
18Dec84- 2Med fst 6f :23⅘ :48⅖ 1:13⅘ Clm 16000 1 8 63½ 76¾ 78½ 610½ Moore D N5 b 112 53.50 63-21 Gay Date 113hd Natrac 1172 Wexelar 1173 No threat 9
9Nov84- 1Med fst 6f :23 :46⅘ 1:12⅘ Clm 16000 5 8 99¾ 914 918 818 Santagata N b 117 17.80 62-20 GayDte1133½RoylChristopher1174NowWe'veGotHim1172½ Outrun 9
30Oct84- 2Med fst 170 :47⅕ 1:13 1:45⅕ Clm 25000 1 5 56½ 712 714 716½ Santagata N 117 5.80 57-24 ⊡Influenced 117nk Uncle Daddy 1107 Dr. Orsini 1121 Tired 9
25Oct84- 5Aqu gd 7f :23 :46⅖ 1:24⅕ Clm 45000 8 1 75½ 78 612 610½ Privitera R7 106 38.80 69-21 Keep It Down 1174¾ First OneUp1171½SavageRunner113nk Outrun 8
LATEST WORKOUTS Mar 2 Aqu ⊡ 3f fst :37⅕ b

Charmed Destiny — Dk. b. or br. c. 3, by Winged T—Miss Charming, by Final Ruling
$22,500 Br.—Bowman T (Md) | 110[5] | Lifetime 13 3 1 0 $22,310 | 1985 6 2 1 0 $17,210 | 1984 7 1 0 0 $5,100
Own.—Twin Bee Stable Tr.—Wilson R

24Mar85- 2Aqu fst 6f :23⅘ :47⅕ 1:12⅘ Clm 17500 6 3 1hd 15 110 19 Moore D N5 b 112 *.80 77-26 CharmedDestiny1129SparklingState114½UltimtePower1173 Easily 9
15Mar85- 9Aqu fst 7f :23⅗ :47⅘ 1:27⅘ Clm 14000 2 6 4nk 11 16 110 Moore D N5 b 112 6.00 62-40 Charmed Destiny 11210 Sharpe Writer 1171¾ Stasera 112nk Easily 12
24Feb85- 2Aqu fst 6f ⊡:22⅘ :46⅖ 1:14 Clm 14000 7 11 33 33 23 44½ Hernandez R b 117 *1.70e 70-28 Even On Sunday 117nk Indulge 1062 Stasera 1192 Broke in tangle 12
2Feb85- 3Aqu my 170 ⊡:50 1:15⅘ 1:46⅘ Clm 14000 2 1 2hd 2hd 25 29 Hernandez R b 117 2.90 57-28 Natrac 1129 Charmed Destiny 117hd Mr. Recharge1172 Held place 8
18Jan85- 5Aqu fst 6f ⊡:22⅖ :46⅗ 1:12⅗ Clm 20000 5 6 12 11 52½ 610¾ Hernandez R b 113 7.70 70-21 Confirmed Patriot 1102½ First Nite Jitters 117nk Narica1225 Tired 11
1Jan85- 3Aqu fst 6f ⊡:21⅘ :45 1:11⅗ Clm 30000 5 7 53¾ 33 75½ 86¼ Hernandez R b 113 4.20 80-13 Top Talk 1192½ Student of Dance 108no ShiningTyson117nk Tired 9
15Nov84- 3Aqu fst 6f :23 :47 1:13⅗ Clm c-30000 4 5 3nk 3nk 31½ 55½ McCarron G 113 6.10 69-29 WrriorInOrbit110hd UnclDddy1083⊡ShiningTyson112hd Weakened 9
4Nov84- 7Lrl fst 6f :22⅘ :46 1:12 Alw 9000 8 7 67½ 58½ 77¾ 65½ Wright D R 115 22.90 77-22 Ramten 1151 The Great Escaper 115no LittleBoldJohn1194 Outrun 8
25Oct84- 8Lrl gd 1 :46⅘ 1:13⅕ 1:38⅘ Alw 9500 1 2 21½ 1hd 43½ 715 Wright D R 115 6.70 64-22 DoubleLeaFast1191½TournamentPlay1198Athabasc1091¼ Faltered 8
8Oct84- 6Lrl fst 6f :22⅖ :46⅖ 1:12⅕ Alw 9500 7 4 68 53½ 63¼ 64¼ Wright D R 115 7.60 78-19 Warm Season 115hd One Up His Sleeve 1152 Unless 1192 Outrun 8
LATEST WORKOUTS Feb 20 Aqu ⊡ 4f fst :49⅕ b

Creative Spirit — Gr. c. 3, by Fire Dancer—Indian Ghost, by Umbrella Fella
$25,000 Br.—Chak Phyllis & Price Judith L (Fla) | 117 | Lifetime 19 1 1 2 $13,690 | 1985 7 0 0 1 $2,640 | 1984 12 1 1 1 $11,050 | Turf 3 0 0 0
Own.—Wood A Tr.—Tufariello Frank

14Mar85- 5Aqu fst 7f :23⅕ :46⅗ 1:26⅗ Clm 30000 11 1 103½ 73¾ 63¾ 65 Lovato F Jr b 113 29.90 63-35 TheRunningKind1132½GayDate114hd Mr.JimmyG.1172½ Raced wide 11
7Mar85- 2Aqu fst 6f ⊡:22⅗ :45⅘ 1:12⅘ Clm 25000 7 3 65 66½ 66 75¾ Lovato F Jr b 117 33.70 76-21 Gay Date 114¾ French Answer 1151½ Bolinger 112no Outrun 11
28Feb85- 5Aqu fst 6f ⊡:22⅗ :46 1:11⅗ Clm 35000 10 2 109½ 78½ 610 59½ Lovato F Jr b 117 50.80 77-22 Gay Date 1085¾ ⊡Scholastic 117½ Mr. Jimmy G 117nk Wide 12
17Feb85- 4Aqu fst 170 ⊡:48⅗ 1:14⅘ 1:46⅗ Clm 35000 5 3 34 33 812 917¾ Murphy D J b 117 7.40 49-25 Fly Me Again 1081 Star de Cesica 1153½ JupiterAccord1132 Tired 10
26Jan85- 6Aqu fst 170 ⊡:48 1:14⅕ 1:44⅘ Alw 23000 10 6 63¾ 52½ 78¾ 814 Murphy D J b 117 44.10 62-20 Feeling Gallant117nk CrystalIceberg117hd Haberdasher1122 Outrun 10
19Jan85- 2Aqu fst 1$\frac{1}{16}$ ⊡:48⅗ 1:14 1:48⅗ Clm 45000 2 1 11 11 41½ 32½ Murphy D J b 113 35.40 65-22 Helcin 112nk Another Doc 1172 Creative Spirit 113½ Weakened 12
11Jan85- 9Aqu fst 6f ⊡:23⅕ :47⅗ 1:13⅖ Clm 40000 4 4 2hd 3nk 62½ 77¼ Murphy D J b 117 15.50 69-30 Gay Date 113hd Student of Dance 1171½ Mr. Jimmy G 1133¾ Tired 9
19Dec84- 3Aqu fst 6f ⊡:23⅖ :47⅖ 1:12⅘ Clm 60000 8 1 41½ 42½ 711 78¾ Velasquez J b 113 7.90 71-25 Koffkoff 1133½ Feeling Gallant 1171¾ConfirmedPatriot1061 Tired 8
3Dec84- 5Aqu fst 7f :22⅘ :46 1:24⅗ Clm 65000 4 5 33 32 36 58½ Davis R G b 117 4.00 69-29 Splendid Catch 1176¾ Feeling Gallant113½DistantOrbit108hd Tired 8
12Nov84- 5Aqu gd 7f :23 :46 1:25 Clm 75000 4 8 74½ 43 44 43½ Davis R G b 117 16.20 72-25 First One Up 1132 Jet Wave 117hd Kilts' Nashua 1131½ Wide 8
LATEST WORKOUTS ●Apr 7 Bel 3f fst :36 b Apr 3 Bel tr.t 5f fst 1:02⅖ h Mar 29 Bel tr.t 5f fst 1:02⅘ h

Student of Dance — Dk. b. or br. g. 3, by I'm For More—Odd Student, by Odd Dancer
$25,000 Br.—Guerrera & Lyons (Fla) | 117 | Lifetime 14 2 2 2 $24,175 | 1985 7 1 2 1 $19,180 | 1984 7 1 0 1 $4,995
Own.—Casper B Tr.—Dutrow Richard E

27Mar85- 2Aqu fst 6f :22⅖ :45⅘ 1:11⅗ Clm 25000 8 2 54½ 54 42½ 43¾ Migliore R 117 7.80 79-20 H. T. Willis 1121¾ Stark Dancer 1121¼ BucketBen117¾ Raced wide 10
14Mar85- 5Aqu fst 7f :23⅕ :46⅗ 1:26⅗ Clm 32500 6 2 93½ 105½ 1010 1015 Hernandez R 115 6.60 53-35 The Running Kind 1132½ Gay Date 114hd Mr.JimmyG.1172½ Outrun 11
18Feb85- 9Aqu fst 6f ⊡:22⅘ :46⅗ 1:13⅘ Clm c-25000 4 2 2hd 2hd 2hd 3½ Ward W A5 114 *1.40 74-28 SoringRomeo117½StrkDncer117no StudentofDnce1143½ Weakened 10
8Feb85- 1Aqu gd 6f ⊡:24 :50 1:16⅗ Clm c-20000 7 2 43 31 11½ 17 Hernandez R 117 *1.00 61-34 Student of Dance 1177 Churning 113¾ Giant Colony 113½ Easily 7
26Jan85- 6Aqu fst 170 ⊡:48 1:14⅕ 1:44⅘ Alw 23000 1 2 1hd 84½ 912 917¼ McCarron G 117 11.10 59-20 Feeling Gallant 117nk CrystalIceberg117hd Haberdasher1122 Tired 10
11Jan85- 9Aqu fst 6f ⊡:23⅕ :47⅗ 1:13⅖ Clm 40000 1 9 51¼ 4¾ 3½ 2hd McCarron G 117 7.60 77-30 GayDate113hd StudentofDance1171½Mr.JimmyG.1133¾ Sluggish st. 9
1Jan85- 3Aqu fst 6f ⊡:21⅘ :45 1:11⅗ Clm c-30000 1 5 63¾ 43½ 42½ 22½ Ward W A5 108 *2.50 84-13 Top Talk 1192½StudentofDance108no ShiningTyson117nk Game try 9
19Dec84- 2Aqu fst 6f ⊡:23 :47 1:13⅗ Clm 30000 2 8 63 67 41½ 31¾ Moore D N5 108 7.40⊡ 74-25 TopTlk113hd SuperScope1081¾⊡StudentofDnce108hd Swerved out 11
19Dec84-Disqualified and placed sixth
9Nov84- 8Crc fst 6f :22⅖ :46⅖ 1:13⅗ Clm c-16000 7 3 64¾ 53½ 22½ 45¾ Wilson B G 116 *1.60 77-21 Stripe It Rich 114¾ Win Again 1163 Hot Actor 1142 Bid,evenly 9
29Oct84- 3Crc fst 6½f :23 :46⅗ 1:19⅖ Clm 20000 6 1 45 32½ 32 33½ Wilson B G 114 4.40 84-26 ChchiMn1142WhtTrouble1141½StudntofDnc1143½ Brushed, evenly 7
LATEST WORKOUTS Mar 25 Aqu 3f fst :37⅖ b Mar 8 Bel tr.t 4f gd :50⅘ b Mar 1 Bel tr.t 4f fst :52⅕ b

Venture Beyond — Dk. b. or br. g. 3, by Great Above—New Blossom, by Brazen Brother
$25,000 Br.—Newchance Farm (Fla) | 117 | Lifetime 15 1 1 1 $11,714 | 1985 7 0 0 0 $1,020 | 1984 8 1 1 1 $10,694
Own.—Barrera O S Tr.—Barrera Oscar S

2Apr85- 2Aqu fst 7f :23⅕ :46⅗ 1:24⅘ Clm c-14000 3 7 32 42 43½ 57 Moore D N5 b 112 2.30e 70-20 Sumpin Royal 1171½ Instant Recall 1172½ Pridemore 1102½ Tired 10
17Mar85- 9Aqu fst 7f :23⅗ :48⅕ 1:28⅘ Clm 22500 11 3 62¾ 42½ 64¾ 55 Moore D N5 b 110 17.70 54-33 Soaring Romeo 119¾ Irv's Choice 112¾ French Answer110no Wide 12
6Mar85- 4Aqu fst 1⅛ ⊡:48⅘ 1:14 1:53⅘ Clm 30000 2 2 21 52½ 913 918¼ Moore D N5 b 108 20.10 54-26 Debate ACase113hd I'mABanker117no AccordingToLuke113nk Tired 12
17Feb85- 4Aqu fst 170 ⊡:48⅗ 1:14⅘ 1:46⅗ Clm 32500 7 2 11 12 41½ 56¾ Moore D N5 b 110 12.70 60-25 Fly Me Again 1081 Star de Cesica 1153½ JupiterAccord1132 Tired 10
19Jan85- 2Aqu fst 1$\frac{1}{16}$ ⊡:48⅗ 1:14 1:48⅗ Clm 50000 10 2 21 64 109½ 1110¾ Moore D N5 b 112 31.60 56-22 Helcin 112nk Another Doc 1172 Creative Spirit 113½ Tired 12
11Jan85- 9Aqu fst 6f ⊡:23⅕ :47⅗ 1:13⅖ Clm c-40000 3 3 4nk 1hd 1½ 55½ Miranda J b 117 6.30 72-30 Gay Date 113hd StudentofDance1171½Mr.JimmyG.1133¾ Gave way 9
1Jan85- 3Aqu fst 6f ⊡:21⅘ :45 1:11⅗ Clm 35000 7 4 3nk 64½ 65 42½ Davis R G b 119 6.40 83-13 Top Talk 1192½ Student of Dance 108no Shining Tyson117nk Wide 9
28Nov84- 7Grd fst 1 :48⅘ 1:14⅕ 1:42⅕ Md 32000 3 2 21½ 1½ 13 13 King R Jr b 122 7.85 69-29 Venture Beyond 1223 Bobino 117hd Wild Style 1141½ Handily 9
31Oct84- 4Grd fst 1 :46 1:13 1:41⅗ Md 40000 6 1 12½ 12 1hd 75½ Fell J b 122 *1.40 67-21 Classy Fiero 1162½ Bobino 112nk Gothic Prince 117hd 10
27Oct84- 7WO gd 6f :22⅗ :46⅕ 1:11⅗ Md Sp Wt 10 9 119 1011 813 714¾ Fell J b 122 5.60 70-27 Nodoublerinker 1178½ Old Gun Powder 1172¾ Dustman 117hd 11
LATEST WORKOUTS Mar 28 Aqu 4f fst :49 b Mar 1 Aqu ⊡ 4f fst :49 b ●Feb 12 Aqu ⊡ 4f gd :48⅗ h

Also Eligible (Not in Post Position Order):

Uncompromising — Dk. b. or br. c. 3, by Proud Clarion—Cabin Queen, by Cabildo
$25,000 Br.—Southwind Farm (Miss) | 117 | Lifetime 9 1 1 2 $12,320 | 1985 3 1 0 1 $8,640 | 1984 6 M 1 1 $3,680
Own.—Wood A Tr.—Tufariello Frank

6Mar85- 4Aqu fst 1⅛ ⊡:48⅘ 1:14 1:53⅘ Clm 30000 6 3 31 73¾ 812 814 Murphy D J 113 54.90 59-26 Debate ACase113hd I'mABanker117no AccordingToLuke113nk Tired 12
7Feb85- 1Aqu fst 1$\frac{1}{16}$ ⊡:48⅘ 1:15⅕ 1:47⅗ Clm 25000 5 1 12 11½ 24 38½ Murphy D J b 119 3.60 64-24 StrdCsic1137½MstrCommnd115¾Uncompromising1194½ Weakened 7
18Jan85- 2Aqu fst 1$\frac{1}{16}$ ⊡:48⅘ 1:14⅖ 1:48⅕ Md 30000 3 1 11½ 12 16 111¼ Murphy D J b 118 5.10 69-21 Uncmprmsng11811½FltsHnr1221½CmmndBr118hd Speed in reserve 9
7Dec84- 9Aqu fst 1$\frac{1}{16}$ ⊡:48⅕ 1:13⅗ 1:47⅗ Md 25000 6 3 41¾ 42 813 815½ Lovato F Jr b 118 4.00 58-19 Cop A Plea 1163 Gallant Rake 1182 El Parador 114¾ Fell far back 10
25Nov84- 4Aqu fst 1⅛ :49⅖ 1:15⅗ 1:56⅘ Md 30000 4 4 21½ 21½ 25 26½ Lovato F Jr b 114 8.60 45-25 Lsit'sSilncr1186½Uncompromisng1146½GllntRk1143 Best of others 11
15Nov84- 2Aqu fst 1 :47⅖ 1:14 1:42 Md 30000 5 3 2hd 52¾ 67 67¾ Lovato F Jr b 114 4.40 48-29 Angelic Bliss 114hd Jupiter Accord 1183 Gold Coup 114½ Faltered 12
9Nov84- 9Aqu fst 1⅛ :49⅕ 1:15⅗ 1:56 Md 30000 4 1 1½ 1hd 38 38 Lovato F Jr b 114 5.70 47-32 Flippant1181MsterCommnd1147Uncompromising1142¾ Weakened 10
29Oct84- 4Aqu my 6f :23 :47 1:11⅘ Md 30000 7 14 86 811 816 714¾ Privitera R7 107 16.00 67-18 Stark Dancer 1141¾ Casting For 1133 Flippant 1163¾ Poor start 14
8Oct84- 4Bel fst 7f :23⅕ :47⅘ 1:28⅖ Md 25000 11 11 84½ 65½ 77 73¾ Cruguet J 118 8.40 56-28 SavageRunner118⊡DH WrriorInOrbit118⊡DH Infltionism113¾ Outrun 14
LATEST WORKOUTS Apr 8 Bel 5f gd 1:04 bg Apr 2 Bel 4f fst :49⅘ b Feb 26 Bel tr.t 6f fst 1:19⅘ b Feb 18 Bel tr.t 4f fst :51⅗ b

Blue Flack — Dk. b. or br. c. 3, by Cyane—Hecate, by Ack Ack
$20,000 Br.—Christiana Nursery Trust (Pa) | 113 | Lifetime 6 1 1 0 $8,200 | 1985 5 1 1 0 $8,200 | 1984 1 M 0 0
Own.—Barrera O S Tr.—Barrera Oscar S

27Mar85- 2Aqu fst 6f :22⅖ :45⅘ 1:11⅗ Clm 22500 1 10 86½ 109½ 95¾ 99 Cordero A Jr b 115 4.20 74-20 H. T. Willis 1121¾ Stark Dancer 1121¼ Bucket Ben 117¾ Slow st. 10
8Mar85- 9Aqu fst 6f ⊡:22⅗ :46 1:12⅘ Clm c-17500 4 7 34 1115 1213 1116½ Lovato F Jr b 119 *3.10 64-18 Dash Mount 1081½ Irv's Choice 1171¾ Instant Recall117nk Outrun 12
1Mar85- 2Aqu fst 6f ⊡:22⅗ :46⅖ 1:13⅗ Md 20000 9 1 31 12 12 13 Santagata N b 118 *2.80 77-25 Blue Flack 1183 Sparkling State 1172½ Patato 115¾ Driving 11
22Feb85- 3Aqu fst 6f ⊡:23 :47 1:14 Md 20000 1 2 12 14 14 21½ Garrido O L5 b 113 18.90 73-22 Norab 1221½ Blue Flack 1132½ Black Elk 1222¾ Weakened 11
27Jan85- 3Aqu fst 6f ⊡:22⅗ :47 1:13⅗ Md 20000 10 3 11 45 915 921½ Migliore R b 118 10.90 56-20 Upper Swell 1224 Sacred Sun 1223 Sum Alimoney 1224½ Stopped 12
31Dec84- 5Aqu fst 6f ⊡:22⅗ :46⅗ 1:11⅘ Md 30000 4 4 23 38 616 720½ Garrido O L5 b 109 11.90 68-15 Love That Mac 1188¾ Niceto Meet You 1095¾ Key Boat115¾ Tired 11
LATEST WORKOUTS Feb 16 Aqu ⊡ 4f fst :53⅘ b Feb 11 Aqu ⊡ 4f fst :53⅘ b

SOARING ROMEO

Although a winner twice in three tries for $25,000, and seemingly ideally suited to seven furlongs, this gelding's winning speed figures were not likely to prove competitive in this field.

ALLOTMENT

This horse's last four races were dull, including the latest two in this class.

FAST TRAVLER

This horse is a confirmed router prepping at seven furlongs for future engagements. The drop in class off a seven-week layoff is suspicious, especially since the distance is not ideal for a winning effort.

MISTER G.

This horse had yet to show the signs of life that made him an interesting proposition on April 20.

DASH MOUNT

Charmed Destiny's stablemate, Dash Mount attempted to move up too far last time. His two winning speed figures do not compare favorably with the others in this field.

STARK DANCER

On paper this well-bred colt looks competitive with Charmed Destiny, their pace and speed figures being about equal. There is one disturbing note, though: Why did trainer Lake rest the horse for six weeks rather than move him up in class after claiming him on February 18? One must suspect unsoundness, especially in light of the horse's regal bloodlines.

SHINING TYSON

This horse finished far back in his last five starts and didn't even flash his customary early speed last time.

THE RUNNING KIND

With the best speed figures in the field based on his latest two starts, The Running Kind is the favorite. Why, then, is he dropping this low? Summitry, who beat him last time, had since repeated in allowance company. The gelding had previously established himself as a solid contender at the $35,000 level. A suspicious class drop, worth betting against.

CREATIVE SPIRIT

There's nothing to recommend this one, judging by his last five starts.

STUDENT OF DANCE

His two good races in February produced a good speed figure off a slow pace (February 8), then a much slower speed figure off a faster pace (February 18). His latest effort appears promising, coming two off a four-week freshening. Although both pace and speed figures

FOURTH RACE Aqueduct APRIL 9, 1985 — **7 FURLONGS. (1.20⅕) CLAIMING. Purse $15,000. 3-year-olds. Weights, 122 lbs. Non-winners of two races since March 15 allowed 3 lbs. Of a race since then 5 lbs. Claiming price $25,000; for each $2,500 to $20,000 2 lbs. (Races where entered to be claimed for $18,000 or less not considered.)**

Value of race $15,000; value to winner $9,000; second $3,300; third $1,800; fourth $900. Mutuel pool $86,473, OTB pool $117,181. Qu Pl $86,202 OTB Qu $117,573 Ex Pl $122,682 OTB Ex $126,910

Last Raced	Horse	Eqt.	A.	Wt	PP	St	¼	½	Str	Fin	Jockey	Cl'g Pr	Odds $1
24Mar85 2Aqu1	Charmed Destiny	b	3	110	9	4	2½	1hd	14	13¼	Moore D N5	22500	a-2.80
27Mar85 5Aqu3	The Running Kind	b	3	117	8	9	96	73	4hd	2hd	Davis R G	25000	2.10
27Mar85 2Aqu5	Mister G.	b	3	117	4	7	5hd	4½	22	35¾	Vasquez J	25000	9.50
14Mar85 5Aqu6	Creative Spirit	b	3	117	10	2	72	51	5½	4nk	Skinner K	25000	15.50
27Mar85 2Aqu6	Allotment		3	110	2	10	10½	81½	85	5nk	Guerra A A7	25000	34.90
27Mar85 2Aqu2	Stark Dancer	b	3	117	6	5	1½	22	31	62	Deegan J C†	25000	7.40
27Mar85 2Aqu4	Student of Dance		3	117	11	3	3½	3hd	61½	7hd	Cordero A Jr	25000	7.50
2Apr85 2Aqu5	Venture Beyond	b	3	117	12	1	41	6½	72	83¼	Ward W A	25000	10.30
27Mar85 2Aqu8	Shining Tyson		3	117	7	6	8hd	101½	10½	9no	Graell A	25000	22.20
24Mar85 1Aqu9	Dash Mount	b	3	110	5	12	116	112	11½	10no	Espinosa R E7	25000	a-2.80
27Mar85 5Aqu8	Soaring Romeo	b	3	119	1	11	12	12	9½	114½	Thibeau R J	25000	14.00
17Feb85 4Aqu10	Fast Travler	b	3	103	3	8	61	9½	12	12	Wynter N A10	20000	63.50

a-Coupled: Charmed Destiny and Dash Mount.

OFF AT 2:27 Start good for all but DASH MOUNT, Won ridden out. Time, :23, :47⅖, 1:12⅖, 1:25⅖ Track fast.

$2 Mutuel Prices:				
	1-(K)-CHARMED DESTINY (a-entry)	7.60	4.20	2.80
	9-(I)-THE RUNNING KIND		3.80	3.00
	6-(E)-MISTER G.			5.40

$2 QUINELLA 1-9 PAID $12.20; $2 EXACTA 1-9 PAID $26.00.

Dk. b. or br. c, by Winged T—Miss Charming, by Final Ruling. Trainer Wilson R. Bred by Bowman T (Md).

CHARMED DESTINY showed good early foot, drew away entering the stretch and held sway under good handling. THE RUNNING KIND, wide into the stretch, was going well at the finish. MISTER G. came out while moving leaving the turn and continued on with good energy. CREATIVE SPIRIT tired. STARK DANCER was used up vying for the lead. STUDENT OF DANCE gave way leaving the turn. VENTURE BEYOND tired DASH MOUNT dwelt at the start. FAST TRAVELER was finished early.

were on the slow side, the horse raced wide throughout. He had yet to prove, however, that he could put a fast-pace figure together with a respectable final-time figure.

VENTURE BEYOND

Oscar Barrera off a claim—often all that need be said in New York circles. However, this is a three-year-old, not an older horse with back class, as are most of Barrera's successful claims.

After running his fastest half-mile pace figure of late while dueling with Stark Dancer and Student of Dance, Charmed Destiny continued to improve, pulling away through upper stretch, and winning rather handily, earning what appeared to be the best speed figure of his young career.

Chapter 27

What Goes Down Might Come Back Up

THERE IS A SIGNIFICANT DIFFERENCE between a young horse (two-or three-year-old) attempting to move up the claiming ladder and an older animal making a similar move. That difference is quite simple: The older horse, at least to some extent, has established its true class—a claiming range in which it can compete successfully. When the horse moves outside that range—either above it or below—it must be regarded suspiciously, and its chances of winning are usually worse than they appear to be at first glance. The younger horse, on the other hand, is still in the process of maturing and learning, looking to establish its proper class niche. It is a better bet to handle the class rise successfully, if qualified to do so. Of course, we make these statements under the assumption that the horse has not been introduced to medication recently, either legal or illegal. Horses "under the influence" often take inexplicable steps up in company, making a joke of what traditionalists term "class."

There is one notable situation, however, in which older horses can be played confidently while on the rise—the exception that proves the rule, so to speak. It involves the animal that had fallen upon hard times—most likely caused by injury and/or overracing—and suffered through the embarrassment of a series of unsuccessful drops down through the claiming ranks. At some point, however, the cycle is reversed—probably in conjunction with a change in management and/or a layoff—and the horse begins to climb back up the class ladder, asserting its "back class." It also provides those who "remembered when" with a few good bets along the way, as the horse avenges defeats absorbed on its way down.

This pattern is usually easy to spot. The precipitous class drop often shows in the past performances, as might the back class—wins or good efforts in better company prior to the drop down. And then, suddenly, a good race, followed by a rise in class. As long as the horse continues to improve and move up in class, it remains a good bet. Even, sometimes, when it attempts to rise above its former peak level.

The race we have chosen to demonstrate this point was the third at Aqueduct on January 6, 1985, a claiming race for older males. We chose this race not only because it was won by Alamacani, a horse with back class winning for the third consecutive time on the rise, but also because the race provides a good example of the benefits of the "collegial" classification system as applied to Thoroughbreds.

The Thoroughbred population at any given track can be thought of as split into four distinct groups, just like the students at a university. The two-year-olds are freshmen, the three-year-olds the sophomores, four-year-olds are the juniors, and anything older, the seniors. The distinction between the juniors and the seniors is a fine one and is usually not even worth noting. Its major point of application is to the kind of race we are about to discuss—claiming events that include newly turned four-year-olds, none of which had previously competed against older horses while racing for a claiming tag. Classifying such horses based on claiming races restricted to three-year-olds late in their three-year-old season can prove misleading, since the price tags on the three-year-olds may still be inflated, even that late in the year.

Let's take a close look at the twelve horses entered, starting with the eventual winner, Alamacani:

ALAMACANI

The past performances still show the deterioration in Alamacani's form cycle, starting with two fair efforts for $35,000 in early summer, right through the final decline—two off-the-board finishes for $17,500. The subsequent nine-week layoff obviously cured the horse's ailments. Had the rest come three races sooner, back-class advocates would have missed out on $21.60, $7.40, and $26.40 mutuels as the horse reestablished its value. Was Alamacani worth backing on January 6 against $50,000 horses? Indeed, was he a good bet at 12–1 on December 23, breaking from post 11 against $35,000 animals? How far the five-year-old could move back up depended to

3 **AQUEDUCT**

1 1/16 MILES
INNER DIRT TRACK
AQUEDUCT

1 1/16 MILES. (InnerDirt). (1.42) CLAIMING. Purse $22,000. 4-year-olds and upward. Weight, 122 lbs. Non-winners of two races at a mile or over since December 1 allowed 3 lbs. Of such a race since then, 5 lbs. Claiming price $50,000; for each $2,500 to $45,000 allowed 2 lbs. (Races when entered to be claimed for $40,000 or less not considered.)

Coupled—Canadian Currency and Cagle Springs.

Canadian Currency
Gr. g. 6, by Sinister Purpose—Miss Turnpenny, by Iron Ruler
Own.—Davis A $45,000 Br.—Beechwood Farm Ltd (Ont-C)
Tr.—Moschera Gasper S
113 Lifetime 70 7 13 15 $146,226
1985 1 0 0 0
1984 29 2 3 5 $45,090
Turf 2 0 0 0

3Jan85- 3Aqu fst 6f ⊡:22⅗ :46⅗ 1:10⅘ Clm 35000 8 6 74½ 53¾ 811 99¾ Graell A 117 *2.50e 80-19 Royal Rollick1174½I'mSoMerry108½BalancingAct117no No mishap 11
26Dec84- 3Aqu fst 170 ⊡:48⅘ 1:14⅕ 1:44⅘ 3+Clm c-25000 8 3 1hd 2hd 21 32½ Lovato F Jr b 117 *1.90 74-21 Clear TheBases1081½GeorgeCinq112½CanadianCurrency1173 Tired 8
14Dec84- 3Aqu fst 6f ⊡:22⅗ :46⅕ 1:11⅗ 3+Clm 30000 6 2 64½ 64¾ 35 34½ Lovato F Jr b 113 9.40 81-19 Balancing Act 1121½ Skirl 1173½ CanadianCurrency113¾ Mild rally 6
6Dec84- 1Aqu sly 6f ⊡:21⅘ :45⅕ 1:10⅕ 3+Clm 30000 5 6 77¾ 66¾ 54½ 56½ Lovato F Jr b 113 5.90 87-12 Great Hunter 1081 Tarpaulin 108¾ Balancing Act 112½ No factor 8
26Nov84- 3Aqu fst 6f :23 :46⅗ 1:11⅘ 3+Clm 30000 1 5 63½ 63½ 42 41½ Lovato F Jr b 115 10.10 83-25 Satan's Charger 117½ Mingo 115nk Skirl 117½ Late bid 9
18Nov84- 3Aqu fst 7f :23⅕ :46⅗ 1:24⅗ 3+Clm 30000 4 2 52¾ 62½ 53 32 Lovato F Jr b 115 9.30 76-23 DHJordan'sGray117 DHMingo1132CanadianCurrency115no Rallied 7
9Nov84- 5Aqu fst 6f :22⅘ :46⅖ 1:12 3+Clm 30000 1 2 41¾ 41½ 2hd 1½ Lovato F Jr b 114 5.90 81-32 CndinCurrency114½NotTwoTimes1082¼ColumbiHolm117nk Driving 5
29Oct84- 2Aqu my 6f :22⅗ :45⅖ 1:10 3+Clm 25000 3 4 32 32½ 33½ 35¾ Migliore R b 117 8.80 85-18 JustAnyTime1195½CremeDeLFete113½CndinCurrency117hd Evenly 10
17Oct84- 2Bel fst 7f :22⅗ :45⅗ 1:24⅕ 3+Clm 25000 5 3 42 24 31½ 74½ Lopez V b 117 9.00 77-21 J. Strap 1101½ Speier's Luck 117¾ Faded Poster 117¾ Tired 13
24Sep84- 5Bel fst 7f :22⅘ :46⅕ 1:24⅕ 3+Clm 25000 5 2 33 32 1hd 21 Cordero A Jr b 117 7.80 80-21 Mingo 1101 Canadian Currency 1172½FadedPoster117nk Game try 7
LATEST WORKOUTS Jan 2 Bel tr.t 3f gd :36⅕ b (d)

Alamacani
Dk. b. or br. h. 5, by Irish Ruler—Classic Dance, by Board Marker
Own.—Denmark Muriel $47,500 Br.—Regal Oak Farm (Fla)
Tr.—Pascuma Warren J
115 Lifetime 44 8 2 10 $110,231
1984 20 3 1 2 $41,010
1983 19 3 1 6 $55,578
Turf 2 0 0 0

23Dec84- 9Aqu fst 1⅛ ⊡:48⅘ 1:13⅕ 1:51⅘ 3+Clm 32500 11 1 31½ 41½ 32 1hd MacBeth D b 115 12.20 83-17 Alamcni115hdGuguinNtive115hdCgleSprings1176½ Alt.course, drvg 11
7Dec84- 1Aqu fst 1⅛ ⊡:48⅖ 1:14 1:52⅖ 3+Clm 25000 3 1 1hd 1hd 11 1½ MacBeth D b 117 2.70 80-19 Alamacani 117½ Dancing Zulu 1154 Super Rolfe 1153 Driving 8
28Nov84- 5Aqu fst 7f :23 :45⅗ 1:24⅕ 3+Clm 22500 7 1 31 32 31 2nk Maple E b 115 9.40 80-27 Great Hunter 108nk Alamacani 1153½ Tarpaulin 1121½ Wide 9
17Nov84- 9Aqu fst 7f :23⅘ :47⅗ 1:26 3+Clm 17500 4 3 3½ 2hd 1hd 1½ MacBeth D b 117 9.80 71-31 Alamacani 117½ Stiff Upper Lip 1101¾ Tarberry 1171½ Driving 10
12Sep84- 9Bel fst 6f :23 :46⅕ 1:10⅘ 3+Clm 17500 6 3 65 67½ 710 47¾ MacBeth D b 117 4.30 80-14 Miraculously 1154½ Fletcher 1171½ Town Clown 1172½ Rallied 9
1Sep84- 3Bel fst 7f :23 :46 1:23⅗ 3+Clm 17500 3 3 2½ 55½ 611 68¾ MacBeth D 117 4.30 75-13 SailingLight1171½HndsomeDncer117nkDr.Butcher1082 Brief speed 10
10Aug84- 1Sar fst 1¼ :47 1:37⅘ 2:03⅕ 3+Clm 25000 3 1 31 34½ 56 511 MacBeth D b 117 7.80 73-13 Bold 'n Cold 1171½ A Big Fortune 1135 Gauguin Native1172 Tired 8
30Jly84- 7Bel fst 7f :22⅘ :46⅕ 1:24 Clm 32500 8 3 62½ 94½ 1111 1012¾ MacBeth D b 115 3.50e 69-19 Talc Power 1171½ Fibak 1153½ Love To Laugh 110hd Wide 11
12Jly84- 2Bel fst 7f :23 :46 1:23 Clm 32500 4 2 31½ 43 64¾ 44 MacBeth D b 115 10.40 83-17 Bright Rex 1172¾ Shifty Sheik 117¾ Act It Out117½ Lacked a rally 10
14Jun84- 7Bel fst 6f :22⅘ :45⅗ 1:10⅕ Clm 35000 4 1 45 47½ 44 46½ MacBeth D b 117 13.80 84-23 Harpers Bazaar 1196½ Ample Native115nkColdTrailin'106hd Evenly 10
LATEST WORKOUTS Jan 3 Bel tr.t 5f gd 1:03 b Dec 29 Bel tr.t 3f sly :37⅘ b Dec 20 Bel tr.t 5f fst 1:03 b Dec 14 Bel tr.t 4f fst :49 b

Terse
Ch. h. 5, by Good Behaving—Cutty, by Smart
Own.—Treavant Stable $45,000 Br.—Schmidt C E (Ky)
Tr.—Sedlacek Sue
1067 Lifetime 34 3 9 3 $91,810
1984 19 1 5 1 $38,390
1983 12 2 3 1 $47,580
Turf 1 0 0 0

28Dec84- 6Aqu sly 1⅛ ⊡:48 1:12⅕ 1:51 3+Clm 45000 5 5 54½ 54½ 69½ 611½ Garrido O L5 b 108 6.70 75-19 Cagle Springs 1131 Class Hero 1131½ Bold Trumpeter1101 Outrun 7
13Dec84- 2Aqu fst 1 1/16 ⊡:47⅘ 1:12 1:44⅘ 3+Clm 35000 2 3 31 22 2½ 2nk Espinosa R E7 b 110 5.30e 88-19 Satan's Charger 117nk Terse 1101½CagleSprings1178¾ Just missed 11
30Nov84- 7Aqu fst 1⅛ :47⅗ 1:12 1:50⅕ 3+Clm 45000 7 6 84½ 86 610 611½ Espinosa R E7 b 106 7.60 73-23 Wild Chorus 1171½ Waitlist 1133½ Ask Mikey 113hd Outrun 9
14Nov84- 6Aqu fst 1⅛ :49⅘ 1:15⅖ 1:54⅘ 3+Clm 45000 7 3 33 4¾ 2hd 21½ Espinosa R E7 b 106 15.30 60-33 Tuned Out 1131½ Terse1064¾FeelingTooMuch110hd Best of others 7
18Oct84- 1Bel fst 1⅛ :45⅘ 1:10⅗ 1:49⅗ 3+Alw 22000 4 6 79 713 614 514½ Lopez V3 b 114 6.90 64-24 High Honors 1173½ Mi Te Syd 1176½LordoftheManor1161½ Outrun 7
26Sep84- 3Bel fst 1⅛ :46⅗ 1:12⅕ 1:52⅗ 3+Clm 35000 7 6 55 34 3½ 13½ Lopez V3 b 114 4.00e 64-25 Terse 1143½ Sailing Light 1124½ Ship Mint 110¾ Blocked, drvng 8
22Sep84- 2Bel fst 1 :46⅘ 1:11⅘ 1:37⅖ 3+Clm 45000 2 9 94¾ 96½ 910 87 Garrido O L7 b 106 12.70 71-19 Talc Power 108¾ Harpers Bazaar 1171½ Big McCoy 1131½ Outrun 11
13Sep84- 6Bel fst 1⅛ :45⅘ 1:09⅘ 1:48⅘ 3+Alw 22000 5 5 47 510 58½ 511¾ Garrido O L7 b 110 10.20 71-21 Bosun Mate 1133½ Last Turn 117½ Spitalfields 1137 Outrun 6
2Sep84- 1Bel fst 1 1/16 :46⅕ 1:10⅗ 1:43 3+Clm 45000 1 5 65½ 54½ 42 2¾ Garrido O L7 b 106 5.70 86-17 Irish Waters 113¾ Terse 1061 Hollywood Hendrson 113½ Game try 7
5Aug84- 1Sar fst 1⅛ :46⅕ 1:12 1:49⅖ 3+Alw 36000 5 2 31 34 48 58½ Ward W A5 b 110 8.80 79-09 Turkey Shoot 115no Sitzmark 1154¾ Weekend Surprise 1132 Tired 5
LATEST WORKOUTS Dec 8 Aqu ⊡ 4f fst :51⅗ b

Husk
Ch. c. 4, by Judger—Hira, by Hawaiino
Own.—Live Oak Plantation $45,000 Br.—Live Oak Stud (Fla)
Tr.—Kelly Patrick J
1105 Lifetime 11 2 0 1 $32,520
1984 11 2 0 1 $32,520
1983 0 M 0 0
Turf 4 1 0 0 $13,740

26Dec84- 2Aqu fst 1 1/16 ⊡:47⅘ 1:12⅗ 1:45 Clm 70000 8 7 711 811 818 717 Garrido O L5 b 110 18.30 70-21 Vinny'sPride1131½Cooper'sHwk1134¾GoldenImmigrnt115¾ Outrun 8
14Dec84- 7Aqu fst 170 ⊡:48⅘ 1:13⅗ 1:42⅖ 3+Alw 24000 1 4 52 56½ 514 413¾ Garrido O L5 b 115 7.30 73-19 Harry L. 1154½ Last Turn 1175½ Dr. J. R. Howell 1154 No factor 5
3Dec84- 7Aqu sly 1⅛ :48⅗ 1:13 1:52⅖ 3+Alw 23000 2 3 33½ 33½ 11½ 14 Garrido O L5 b 115 7.90 73-23 Husk 1154 Beal Boru 115¾ Twentytwo Bahama 115½ Drew clear 6
23Nov84- 4Aqu gd 1⅛ Ⓣ:49 1:14 1:53⅗ 3+Md Sp Wt 3 3 32½ 2½ 15 111 Garrido O L7 b 113 8.00 76-24 Husk 11311 Deepdale 1202½ Elegant Groom 1171 Easily 9
19Nov84- 3Aqu fst 1 :49 1:15 1:40 3+Md Sp Wt 1 8 84½ 66½ 67¾ 59½ Garrido O L7 b 113 14.70 56-33 Magnetize 120hd Cox's King 120¾ Sacred Motion 120¾ No factor 8
8Nov84- 1Aqu fst 1⅜ :49⅖ 1:43⅕ 2:23⅗ 3+Md Sp Wt 6 3 31½ 3nk 33 32½ Garrido O L7 b 113 4.20 61-26 Crescent Club 120no Deepdale 1202½ Husk 1136¾ Evenly 7
18Oct84- 3Bel fm 1 1/16 Ⓣ:47⅕ 1:11 1:42 3+Md Sp Wt 3 4 47 611 411 411½ Garrido O L7 112 15.50 80-10 Longest Straw 1192 RomanDiplomat1191¾DoubleAlias1197½ Tired 8
12Oct84- 4Bel fm 1 1/16 Ⓣ:46⅖ 1:11 1:43⅕ Clm 40000 3 8 109½ 1010 911 68½ Garrido O L7 110 45.30 72-20 Arbitor's Image 116¾ Fire Tab 113¾ Pemetic 1133 No factor 11
23Sep84- 9Bel fm 1 1/16 Ⓣ:45⅖ 1:09⅘ 1:41⅘ 3+Md Sp Wt 4 7 816 819 717 615¾ Garrido O L7 111 31.10 71-14 Solidified 1186½ Special Agent1182¾LongestStraw1181½ No factor 12
28Jan84- 4Aqu fst 1 1/16 ⊡:48⅕ 1:14⅖ 1:48⅕ Md Sp Wt 7 8 85¾ 75½ 64¾ 44¾ Santiago A 122 16.20 66-20 Tobin's Dream 1221½ Ice Cold Gold 122nk First Tent 1223 Rallied 9
LATEST WORKOUTS Jan 2 Bel tr.t 4f gd :48 h (d) Dec 21 Bel tr.t 3f fst :37⅕ b Dec 10 Bel tr.t 4f fst :52⅖ b Nov 30 Bel tr.t 4f fst :51⅖ b

Epilogue *
B. g. 4, by Jolly Johu—All for Scarlet, by One For All
Own.—Cohen N L $45,000 Br.—Small Mr-Mrs D R (Md)
Tr.—Small Richard W
115 Lifetime 30 9 2 5 $127,270
1984 20 7 1 2 $109,940
1983 10 2 1 3 $17,330
Turf 5 1 0 1 $20,495

Entered 5Jan85- 8 KEY
26Dec84- 2Aqu fst 1 1/16 ⊡:47⅘ 1:12⅗ 1:45 Clm 70000 6 8 811 711 611 46¾ Hernandez R 115 5.00 80-21 Vinny'sPride1131½Cooper'sHwk1134¾GoldnImmigrnt115¾ Late bid 8
14Dec84- 8Bow fst 1 1/16 :48⅗ 1:13⅗ 1:45⅘ 3+Alw 18000 4 5 613 610 43 1nk Bracciale V Jr 115 5.00 72-29 Epilogue 115nk Issue Joined 117¾NearEast1174½ Brushed, just up 7
23Nov84- 2Aqu fst 1⅛ :49 1:14⅗ 1:53 Clm 47500 1 1 1½ 41½ 21 11¾ Hernandez R 115 8.40 70-29 Epilogue 1151¾ Fifth Facade 117¾ Errant Minstrel 1172¾ Driving 10
27Oct84- 6Aqu my 1 :45⅖ 1:09⅗ 1:35⅗ Clm 50000 5 12 1111 917 812 710 Kaenel J L 117 6.60 79-16 HighestStar1081½MostlyMichael1083½Drcy'sBby113hd Raced wide 13
20Oct84- 9Lrl fst 1 :46⅖ 1:11⅗ 1:36⅗ 3+Alw 15000 6 8 1011 1011 812 67 Byrnes D 111 23.80 82-12 Semaj 117no Shadowfax 1175 Hatchet Boy 115½ Outrun 11
12Sep84- 7Lrl fst 1 :46⅘ 1:12⅗ 1:38⅖ 3+Alw 16000 3 8 813 711 512 510½ Nicol P A Jr 110 6.70 69-31 Rollodka 1151½ St. Brendan 1157½ Shadowfax 119½ No factor 8
9Aug84- 1Sar fm 1 1/16 Ⓣ:47 1:11⅘ 1:44 Clm 90000 1 9 916 911 77 65 McCarron G 118 6.10 72-19 Pied A' Tierre 122nk Ice Bucket 117¾ColonialDays1161½ No factor 9
4Jly84- 8Bow fst 1⅛ :47⅖ 1:12 1:49⅕ Gov's Cup H 1 9 96¾ 98½ 711 513 Jenkins J P 110 12.00 85-20 Big Pistol 120nk Carr De Naskra 11411 Raja's Shark 1181 Outrun 9
4Jly84-Grade III
23Jun84- 7Bow fst 1 1/16 :47⅘ 1:12⅘ 1:44⅘ Alw 18000 5 6 611 67 54½ 41½ Passmore W J 119 1.90e 75-26 Donna's Time 117¾ All Is Peaceful 114hd Sir Brilliant 109¾ Evenly 7
9Jun84- 8Pim fst 1 1/16 :45⅗ 1:09⅘ 1:42⅖ Annapolis H 3 7 79½ 67½ 32½ 3¾ Passmore W J 116 2.80 92-21 Donna's Time 122¾ Spring Itch 109nk Epilogue 116no Wide str. 7
LATEST WORKOUTS ●Dec 24 Pim 4f fst :47 h

Equity Kicker
B. g. 4, by Cormorant—Silkys Angle, by Angle Light
Own.—Heilsen Stable $50,000 Br.—Sonnenblick J E (NY)
Tr.—Hertler John O
1125 Lifetime 18 5 2 1 $90,040
1984 16 4 2 1 $73,300
1983 2 1 0 0 $16,740
Turf 2 0 1 1 $9,290

26Dec84- 2Aqu fst 1 1/16 ⊡:47⅘ 1:12⅗ 1:45 Clm 70000 5 5 58½ 56½ 47 68½ Guerra A A5 108 8.10 78-21 Vinny'sPride1131½Coopr'sHwk1134¾GoldnImmigrnt115¾ No threat 8
6Dec84- 6Aqu sly 170 ⊡:47⅗ 1:12⅖ 1:41⅗ Clm 50000 6 5 43½ 2hd 1hd 11½ Ward W A5 112 2.60 92-12 Equity Kicker 1121½ Double Jump 1173½ Closed Corp113½ Driving 6
11Nov84- 8Aqu fst 1⅛ :47⅘ 1:12⅖ 1:52⅖ 3+ⓈMacarthur H 3 8 78¾ 77½ 66½ 67½ Ward W A 109 13.50 66-25 Org 117¾ Talc Duster 1161½ Judge Costa 1101½ No factor 8
27Oct84- 7Aqu my 1⅛ :47⅖ 1:10⅘ 1:48⅘ 3+Alw 25000 7 7 78½ 67 57 46½ Ward W A5 111 7.00 84-16 Regal Humor1142DesertChief1161½BroadwayHarry1173 No factor 8
11Oct84- 5Bel fm 1 Ⓣ:45⅗ 1:09⅘ 1:35⅗ Clm 80000 3 7 67½ 63¾ 54½ 32½ Privitera R7 107 4.60 85-12 Ice Bucket 118½ Steepbank 1132 Equity Kicker 1073 Rallied 8
1Oct84- 6Bel sly 1 1/16 :47⅕ 1:12⅕ 1:44⅕ 3+ⓈAlw 27500 6 6 52 3½ 14 12¾ Ward W A5 109 *1.70 81-24 Equity Kicker 1092¾ Tuned Out 114½ Carasco 1194 Driving 7
15Sep84- 9Bel sly 1 :45⅖ 1:11 1:36⅘ 3+ⓈAlw 27500 5 6 75½ 32 33½ 22¾ Ward W A5 108 7.90 78-18 High Ice 1132¾ Equity Kicker 1081TalentedJacques1135 Wide str. 11
20Aug84- 9Sar fm 1⅛ Ⓣ:47⅖ 1:12 1:50⅘ 3+ⓈAlw 27500 11 9 915 76½ 21½ 2nk Cruguet J 112 15.80 86-19 StormyPuddls117nkEquityKickr112½TundOut1122¾ Best of others 12
9Aug84- 2Sar fst 7f :21⅘ :44⅗ 1:23 3+ⓈAlw 26000 8 3 812 68½ 44 41½ Ward W A5 107 24.70 86-14 Comic Flare 117¾ Flying Skipper 114no High Ice 114½ Wide 10
23Jly84- 2Bel fst 1 1/16 :47⅕ 1:12⅗ 1:45⅘ Clm 25000 7 8 63½ 54½ 1½ 12 Ward W A5 112 *2.20 73-21 Equity Kicker 1122 Great Amar 113nk DQMr. Radius 117¾ Driving 10
LATEST WORKOUTS Nov 27 Bel tr.t 3f fst :37 b Nov 9 Bel tr.t 3f fst :37 b

Class Hero
Ch. h. 6, by Determined King—Fabulous Rose, by Night Invader
Own.—Santangelo Barbara $45,000 Br.—Braman & Pierce (Fla)
Tr.—Pascuma James J Jr
113 Lifetime 72 9 20 10 $231,900
1984 20 1 5 4 $58,100
1983 15 3 3 0 $56,810
Turf 14 1 3 2 $32,090

28Dec84- 6Aqu sly 1⅛ ⊡:48 1:12⅕ 1:51 3+Clm 45000 1 1 12 11½ 2hd 21 MacBeth D b 113 3.50 86-19 Cagle Springs 1131 Class Hero 1131¾ BoldTrumpeter1101 Gamely 7
19Dec84- 5Aqu fst 170 ⊡:48⅖ 1:14 1:44⅖ 3+Clm 45000 5 3 32½ 32 55½ 57½ Santagata N b 113 2.80 70-25 SinghAmeric1133IrishWters117hdEspritDeRomeo1131¾ Weakened 10
9Dec84- 2Aqu fst 1 1/16 ⊡:47⅕ 1:12⅕ 1:45⅕ 3+Clm 45000 5 4 33 21 21 21 Santagata N b 113 13.00 85-19 Waitlist 1171 Class Hero 1132 Tenifly 1154 Sharp effort 10
30Nov84- 7Aqu fst 1⅛ :47⅗ 1:12 1:50⅕ 3+Clm 50000 8 7 73½ 54 910 913 Santagata N b 117 5.40 71-23 Wild Chorus 1171¾ Waitlist 1133½ Ask Mikey 113hd Showed little 9
13Nov84- 8Med fst 170 :46⅖ 1:13⅕ 1:44⅕ 3+Alw 25000 5 5 76½ 74½ 56½ 38¾ Santagata N b 115 11.70 69-28 Castle Guard 1192½ Bill Wheeler 1176½ Class Hero 1153 No threat 7
2Nov84- 6Aqu fst 7f :23⅗ :47⅗ 1:25⅘ 3+Clm 45000 5 2 63¾ 32 2hd 2hd Santagata N b 113 16.20 72-35 Tenifly115hdClassHero1132½NorthernExchange1171½ Sharp effort 7
22Oct84- 2Bel fst 6f :22⅕ :45⅗ 1:11 3+Clm 45000 4 8 913 1017 109¾ 84½ Santagata N b 113 30.30 82-16 Snowgun 113no Big McCoy 1132¾ Sixth of May 113nk Outrun 10
2Jun84- 6Bel sly 7f :22⅗ :45⅗ 1:22⅘ Clm 47500 3 6 77¾ 711 612 611 Skinner K b 115 11.30 77-19 Meru 1154 Cutter Sark 1175 I'm So Merry 112½ Outrun 7
26May84- 2Bel fm 1 1/16 Ⓣ:46⅘ 1:12⅖ 1:43⅖ Clm 47500 11 6 41½ 712 56 48½ Santagata N b 115 7.60e 70-19 Crown 1138½ Fearless Leader 117hd Pumas Pride 115no Steadied 11
21May84- 1Bel gd 1⅜ Ⓣ:50⅘ 1:40 2:17⅖ Clm 50000 2 1 1½ 43 56½ 57¾ Santagata N b 117 3.60 62-24 Broadly 113¾ Full Deck 1174 Goumi 1132¾ Tired 6
LATEST WORKOUTS Dec 17 Aqu ⊡ 4f fst :49⅘ b Dec 7 Aqu ⊡ 4f fst :49⅕ b Nov 28 Aqu 4f fst :49 b Nov 20 Aqu 4f fst :49⅘ b

Deedee's Deal — Dk. b. or br. g. 8, by Hickory—Me Carla, by Gallant Romeo — $45,000 — Br.—Amiung R (Fla) — Tr.—Ribaudo Robert — 108⁵
Own.—Martini Mrs N A
Lifetime 90 19 17 17 $386,602 — 1984 8 0 3 1 $26,100 — 1983 19 6 1 5 $123,510 — Turf 27 4 4 4 $83,560

19Dec84- 5Aqu fst 170 ⊡:48⅘ 1:14 1:44⅖ 3+Clm 47500 4 6 65 64½ 87¾ 711¼ Moore D N5 b 110 12.40 67-25 Singh America 1133IrishWaters117hdEspritDeRomeo1131¾ Outrun 10
22Jun84- 1Bel fm 1⅛ [T]:47 1:10⅘ 1:42⅘ Clm 50000 4 3 31½ 54 43 65½ Cordero A Jr b 117 2.10 82-19 Fearless Leader 113nk Beagle 1132½ Full Deck 117¾ Tired 7
11Jun84- 7Bel hd 1⅛ Ⓣ:45⅕ 1:09⅖ 1:39⅘ Clm 75000 4 11 1118 1016 914 614 Cruguet J b 112 3.40e 83-14 Persian Poet 122no Crown 1123¾ Clarinet King 1124 Outrun 11
23May84- 2Bel fm 1⅛ Ⓣ:45⅗ 1:09⅘ 1:41⅘ Clm 75000 2 5 66½ 66½ 54 64 Cordero A Jr b 117 3.20e 83-12 Quick Dip 1131¾ Clarinet King 117nk Roulette Wheel 108½ Evenly 11
25Feb84- 1Aqu gd 1⅛ ⊡:47⅗ 1:12 1:43⅗ Clm 75000 2 4 63½ 32½ 23 32¾ Cordero A Jr b 117 *1.30 92-12 Bidamex 1082¾ Last Turn 117hd Deedee's Deal 1175 Saved ground 11
16Feb84- 5Aqu my 170 ⊡:48⅘ 1:13 1:40⅘ Clm 85000 3 3 33 3nk 22½ 23 Smith A Jr b 116 1.90 95-10 ShreTheRisk1073Deed'sDl1161½HollywoodHndrson1203¾ 2nd best 5
26Jan84- 8Aqu my 170 ⊡:47⅕ 1:11 1:40 Alw 38000 1 2 23½ 22½ 21½ 24 Cordero A Jr b 115 2.60 97-10 Mortgage Man 1144Deedee'sDeal115¾FabulousFind1152 Game try 7
13Jan84- 8Aqu fst 1⅛ ⊡:49⅘ 1:14⅘ 1:52⅘ Alw 38000 3 2 1½ 2hd 21 21½ Cordero A Jr b 115 *2.10 80-20 Lark Oscillation 1151½ Deedee's Deal 1153½ To Erin119hd Brushed 7
31Dec83- 5Aqu fst 170 ⊡:47⅕ 1:12⅕ 1:41⅘ 3+Clm 85000 1 3 35½ 21½ 3½ 3nk Cordero A Jr b 116 2.80 92-21 Moro 117no Mortgage Man 117nk Deedee's Deal 1166¾ Weakened 8
23Dec83- 5Aqu gd 1⅛ ⊡:48⅗ 1:13⅗ 1:52⅘ 3+Clm 75000 1 6 74½ 52¾ 32 2nk Cordero A Jr b 119 2.40 81-21 [D]AccountRecivbl117nkDd'sDl119noPurlyAPrinc1141¾ Just missed 10
23Dec83-Placed first through disqualification
LATEST WORKOUTS Dec 15 Bel tr.t 5f fst 1:04⅘ b — Dec 8 Bel tr.t 5f fst 1:02⅘ b — Nov 25 Bel tr.t 4f fst :51 b

Lively Teddy — Ch. g. 6, by Teddy's Courage—Lively Debate, by Wolfram — $47,500 — Br.—Edwards R L (NY) — Tr.—Barrera Oscar S — 115
Own.—Barrera O S
Lifetime 31 5 3 4 $83,240 — 1985 1 0 0 0 — 1984 12 3 1 3 $58,470 — Turf 2 0 0 0

1Jan85- 5Aqu fst 1½ ⊡:50⅕ 2:07⅕ 2:33⅘ Clm c-25000 7 5 54 710 712 711¾ Skinner K b 117 7.10 69-13 Errant Minstrel 1173 Bold 'nCold117¾Wimborne'sGater117¾ Tired 8
23Dec84- 9Aqu fst 1⅛ ⊡:48⅗ 1:13⅕ 1:51⅘ 3+Clm 35000 4 8 86 95¾ 1018 916¾ Skinner K b 117 7.70 66-17 Alamacani 115hd Gauguin Native 115hd Cagle Springs 1176¼ Wide 11
9Dec84- 2Aqu fst 1⅟16 ⊡:47⅕ 1:12⅕ 1:45⅕ 3+Clm 50000 4 10 915 911 611 59½ Skinner K b 117 7.90e 77-19 Waitlist 1171 Class Hero 1132 Tenifly 1154 Sluggish st 10
7Jun84- 7Bel fm 1⅜ Ⓣ:49⅘ 1:38 2:14⅕ 3+Alw 25000 4 4 32 79 625 628¾ Skinner K b 117 10.40 62-13 Talakeno 1172½ Nassipour 1174 Head of the House 119½ Tired 7
16May84- 8Bel fm 1⅛ Ⓣ:47⅘ 1:11⅗ 1:41⅘ 3+[S]Kingston 9 13 104¼ 76½ 67¾ 77¼ Skinner K b 117 7.20e 80-16 Slewpy 1212 Limit Position 117hd Prosper 1171¼ Outrun 13
5May84- 6Aqu fst 1⅛ :47⅘ 1:12⅕ 1:50 Clm 175000 1 6 56 34 37 46½ Skinner K b 112 3.70 79-16 High Ascent 112hd Sharp Destiny1125¾ByTheRiver107½ Weakened 6
6Apr84- 8Aqu fst 1⅛ ⊡:46⅘ 1:11⅗ 1:52 3+[S]Alw 27500 1 5 46 31 1½ 12¾ Skinner K b 121 8.20 82-18 Lively Teddy 1212¾ Groom's Image 111¾ Tuned Out 1118¾ Driving 6
12Mar84- 7Aqu fst 170 ⊡:48⅖ 1:13⅗ 1:44⅖ [S]Alw 28500 3 3 22½ 32½ 36 37¼ Skinner K b 119 *2.30 72-22 SpiritOfAlm1177StormyPuddls117nkLvlyTddy1191¼ Lacked lt. rally 7
25Feb84- 2Aqu gd 1⅟16 ⊡:47⅗ 1:12 1:45⅗ [S]Alw 28500 5 6 64 64¾ 21½ 3¾ Skinner K b 122 7.80 83-12 NorthrnExchng117½StormyPuddls117nkLvlyTddy1222½ Weakened 9
16Feb84- 1Aqu my 1⅛ ⊡:48⅕ 1:13⅗ 1:51⅗ [S]Alw 27000 6 3 2hd 1hd 1hd 1¾ Skinner K b 117 *1.50 88-10 Lively Teddy 117¾ Tenancy 1175½ Hogan's Hideaway1171¼ Driving 6
LATEST WORKOUTS Jan 4 Bel tr.t 3f fst :37⅗ h — Dec 31 Aqu ⊡ 4f fst :54 b — Dec 17 Aqu ⊡ 4f fst :50⅗ b — Dec 5 Aqu ⊡ 1 fst 1:43 b

Torontonian — B. h. 6, by Timeless Moment—Northern Lisa, by Northern Dancer — $47,500 — Br.—Beechwood Farm Ltd (Ont-C) — Tr.—Sedlacek Michael C — 110⁵
Own.—Stronach F
Lifetime 15 3 3 1 $55,693 — 1984 2 0 0 0 — 1983 11 1 3 1 $40,453 — Turf 3 0 1 0 $11,355

22Dec84- 6Aqu fst 6f ⊡:22⅕ :45 1:09⅘ 3+Alw 25000 7 2 52¾ 57½ 68½ 69½ Ward W A5 112 22.40 86-09 Treasured One 115hd Great Hunter 112no Whoop Up110nk Outrun 8
22Nov84- 9Grd fst 6½f :24 :47⅘ 1:20⅘ 3+[S]Alw 16000 7 2 54½ 66 610 67 Leblanc J B 117 6.95 76-28 Centenarian115¾FeuD'enfer121hdDeemedDividend1191½ No factor 7
16Jly83- 9WO fm 1¼ Ⓣ:46⅘ 1:37⅕ 2:03 [S]Can Mat'y 9 3 53¾ 3½ 43½ 73¾ Attard L 126 4.80 88-08 Twice An Angel 121nk Regency Gold 121½ Briar Wind 1261½ Tired 11
8Jly83- 8WO fm *1⅛ [T]:46⅘ 1:01⅕ 1:48⅘ 3+[S]Alw 21000 7 3 45 79½ 78¾ 64¾ Attard L 115 3.05 97-06 Cool Tania 1151½ Captain Sunburst 108½ Bridle Path 119½ Outrun 8
5Jun83- 9WO fm 1⅟16 Ⓣ:48⅕ 1:12⅗ 1:46 [S]ConaughtCup 5 4 54½ 54 42½ 21½ Attard L 1154 17.50 72-18 FiddleDncerBoy1151½[DH]Torontonin115[DH]BridlePth1211½ Gamely 10
5Jun83-Dead heat
18May83- 8WO fst 1⅟16 :48 1:12⅘ 1:45⅘ 3+Alw 15100 4 3 2hd 3nk 2hd 1hd Attard L 1184 *.70 80-19 [DH]Torontonian 118hd [DH]Diapason 113hd Sir Khaled 114no Driving 6
18May83-Dead heat
7May83- 9WO fst 7f :23 :45⅗ 1:22⅘ Vigil H 5 3 3½ 2½ 32 22 Attard L 114 7.50 94-20 Jacksboro 1182 Torontonian 114nk Ask Muhammad 118½ Rallied 9
23Apr83- 9Grd fst 7f :23 :46⅘ 1:25⅕ [S]J Cartier 7 7 53½ 43½ 42¾ 33 Attard L 114 8.35 86-20 Regent Cat 1151½ Frost King 1311¾ Torontonian 1141½ Rallied 7
9Apr83- 9Grd fst 6½f :23⅗ :47⅗ 1:19⅘ Bld Ventre H 2 1 53½ 41½ 42 4nk Attard L 113 24.35 87-22 Play The Hornpipe 115hdJacksboro117hdFraudSquad118no Rallied 8
26Mar83- 7Aqu fst 1⅛ :47⅘ 1:12⅗ 1:50⅖ Alw 23000 8 4 55¾ 95¾ 1011 914¾ Venezia M 117 5.50 68-19 Gauley 1127 Daring Bet 117hd Sad Trombone 117¾ Tired 11
LATEST WORKOUTS Dec 31 Aqu ⊡ 6f fst 1:16⅕ b — Dec 7 Aqu ⊡ 4f fst :49⅘ b — Nov 20 WO tr.t 3f fst :36 b — ●Nov 14 WO tr.t 5f fst :59⅘ b

Satan's Charger — Dk. b. or br. h. 5, by Native Royalty—Evil, by Rash Prince — $45,000 — Br.—Mike S (NY) — Tr.—O'Brien Colum — 108⁵
Own.—Jimtim Stable
Lifetime 38 9 7 3 $216,147 — 1984 18 6 3 2 $79,275 — 1983 10 2 1 0 $44,964

31Dec84- 1Aqu fst 170 ⊡:48⅘ 1:12⅘ 1:42 3+Clm c-35000 2 1 11½ 12 14 13 Ward W A5 b 117 *.70 90-15 Satan'sCharger1173GauguinNative1151½Bienestr1151¼ Ridden out 8
17Dec84- 1Aqu fst 170 ⊡:47⅗ 1:12⅗ 1:42⅕ 3+Clm 70000 1 5 54½ 53½ 21½ 2¾ Ward W A5 b 108 2.50 88-19 MagneticFieldII113¾Satn'sChrger1083¾EsyChoice1131 Poor start 5
13Dec84- 2Aqu fst 1⅟16 ⊡:47⅗ 1:12 1:44⅘ 3+Clm 32500 3 1 1hd 12 1½ 1nk Samyn J L b 117 *1.40 88-19 Satan's Charger 117nk Terse 1101½ Cagle Springs 1178¾ Driving 11
3Dec84- 3Aqu fst 1 :46 1:10⅘ 1:36⅘ 3+Clm 32500 1 1 12 13 13 13½ Samyn J L b 115 *.70 84-29 Stn'sChrger1153½EspritDeRomeo1176ClrinetKing1144 Ridden out 6
26Nov84- 3Aqu fst 6f :23 :46⅘ 1:11⅖ 3+Clm 35000 5 7 21 1hd 1½ 1½ Samyn J L b 117 *.70e 84-25 Satan's Charger 117½ Mingo 115nk Skirl 117½ Driving 9
22Nov84- 2Aqu fst 1 :46⅘ 1:12⅗ 1:38⅖ 3+Clm c-25000 13 3 23 2½ 14 18 Davis R G b 117 *3.30 74-29 Satan's Charger 1178 Speier'sLuck117½MightyNasty110hd Handily 14
18Nov84- 2Aqu fst 6f :22⅗ :45⅘ 1:11⅘ 3+Clm 22500 5 7 52½ 35 31½ 12½ Davis R G b 115 2.00e 82-23 Satan's Charger 1152½ Snowgun 119½ Shekmatyar 113½ Driving 11
10Nov84- 3Aqu fst 6f :22⅘ :46⅗ 1:11⅗ 3+Clm c-17500 2 8 75½ 65½ 64¾ 52¾ Privitera R7 110 4.30 80-23 Sailing Light 112hd Faded Poster115½GeorgeCinq119nk No threat 9
1Nov84- 5Aqu fst 7f :24 :47⅖ 1:24 3+Clm 17500 10 1 51¾ 3½ 2hd 2hd Privitera R7 110 4.50 81-21 Sailing Light 110hdSatan'sCharger1104¾FunnyCap1171½ Game try 10
29Oct84- 2Aqu my 6f :22⅘ :45⅖ 1:10 3+Clm 20000 5 5 107¾ 99¼ 713 811¼ Privitera R7 106 7.00 80-18 JustAnyTime1195½CremeDeLFete113½CndinCurrency117hd Outrun 10

Tivo — Ch. g. 4, by Restivo—Dancer Of Peace, by Peace Corps — $45,000 — Br.—Heubeck E Jr & Harriet (Fla) — Tr.—Kelly Michael J — 108⁵
Own.—Heubeck Mrs E Jr
Lifetime 12 3 0 1 $39,084 — 1985 1 0 0 0 — 1984 4 0 0 0 $1,050 — Turf 2 1 0 1 $23,750

1Jan85- 7Aqu fst 6f ⊡:21⅘ :44⅘ 1:09⅘ Alw 25000 4 5 54½ 58 57½ 58 Velasquez J b 117 16.90 88-13 Stoney Lonesome 117nk GreatHunter1122½WhoopUp1103¾ Outrun 6
12Mar84- 9OP sly 6f :21⅗ :45⅕ 1:10⅘ Alw 17500 1 7 714 79½ 55 44¾ McKnight J b 115 12.50 86-16 Big Pistol 1152 Secret Mountain 121nk Matsaco 1122½ Rallied 7
2Mar84- 8OP fst 1 :45 1:09⅗ 1:35⅕ Alw 17500 3 6 66½ 67½ 713 721 Haire D b 121 8.20 — — Vanlandingham 12110 Dirty Birdie 1212½ SharperThan112½ Outrun 7
25Feb84- 9OP fst 6f :21⅕ :44 1:09⅘ Handicap 2 7 56½ 45 55 64¾ Sorrows A G Jr 115 30.80 93-03 AtThThrshld120¾WndrdPrspct1201½St.JEprss1171 Lacked fin. bid 7
10Feb84- 8OP fst 5½f :21⅘ :45 1:03⅕ Alw 25000 7 11 119½ 915 1019 1015¾ Romero R P b 120 11.20 86-15 Wondered Prospect 112nk St. Joe Express1123¾Whitebrush1122½ 12
10Sep83-11LaD fm 1 Ⓣ:48 1:11⅘ 1:37⅗ Minstrel 1 5 41¾ 42¾ 32 1nk Romero R P 114 *2.70 86-10 Tivo 114nk Sovereign Exchange 1142½ A Hard Ten 1141 Driving 10
10Sep83-To be run in two division, 6th & 11th races
27Aug83- 8AP sly 7f :22⅘ :46 1:27 Arl Wash Fty 1 12 65 1116 1420 1322¾ Romero R P 122 5.40f 44-36 All Fired Up 1221½ Holme On Top 122no SmartNSlick1221 Outrun 17
30Jly83- 9LaD fm *7½f Ⓣ:22⅘ :46 1:30 Grady Madden 3 9 710 76 42½ 31½ Whited D E 114 16.00 88-09 Mississippi Man 112nk Sandy Cat 1141½ Tivo 114nk Rallied 10
10Jly83- 9LaD fst 6f :22⅕ :45⅗ 1:12⅘ Envoy 8 6 53½ 65½ 64½ 52¾ Hiett J K 112 5.10 76-22 Mickey'sRod112hdMtsco112hdStrkDcision1121½ Bobbled; steadied 8
17Jun83- 5LaD fst 5½f :22⅘ :46⅘ 1:07 Alw 12000 4 5 41½ 2hd 13½ 18 Hiett K5 117 *1.20 85-21 Tivo 1178 Intrepid Spy 1181 Plenty A Dreams 1144 6
LATEST WORKOUTS Dec 10 Bel tr.t 4f fst :50⅘ b

a great extent on his back class—his best efforts as a four-year-old, or perhaps even late in his three-year-old season. But these races no longer show in his running lines. However, the resourceful player who took the time to reference old *Racing Forms*—the editions of June 14 and then January 14, for example—would have remembered that, early in the year, Alamacani had been competitive for $50,000; indeed for $70,000 during the latter part of his three-year-old season. Therefore, he had a right to beat $35,000 horses on December 23 and was eligible to repeat against $50,000 rivals on January 6. All the more so, in fact, in light of his game performance on December 23—a troublesome outside trip from post 11 adding luster to an otherwise ordinary-looking winning effort.

Alamacani — Dk. b. or br. c. 4, by Irish Ruler—Classic Dance, by Board Marker
Own.—Denmark Muriel — $35,000 — Br.—Regal Oak Farm (Fla) — Tr.—Pascuma Warren J — 117
Lifetime 34 5 1 10 $75,611 — 1984 10 0 0 2 $6,390 — 1983 19 3 1 6 $55,578 — Turf 2 0 0 0

18May84- 9Bel	fst	7f	:23⅕ :46⅘ 1:24⅖	Clm 35000	10	3	41¼	53¾	46	55½	MacBeth D	b 117	11.10	74-17	The Time Is Now 1171½ Jet Steam 117hd Meru 1082½	Tired	12
11May84- 2Bel	fm	1¼	Ⓣ:48⅖ 1:37⅖ 2:02⅖	Clm 50000	3	6	69½	1016	1023	1027¼	MacBeth D	b 117	25.80	55-17	Lutyens 1081 Quick Dip 117¾ Class Hero 115½	Tired	10
27Apr84- 9Aqu	fst	1	:46 1:10⅕ 1:36⅖	Clm 50000	2	8	83½	108¾	67	53¾	MacBeth D	b 117	20.20	80-21	Seagry 117hd Talc Power 1172 Cagle Springs 1131¼	Raced wide	11
18Apr84- 7Aqu	fst	1 3/16	⊡:48⅖ 1:12⅗ 1:56⅗	Clm 50000	2	4	33½	32	47	49½	MacBeth D	b 117	27.00	86-16	Pearl Amber 1133½ On The Turn 1123½ Last Turn1172¼	Weakened	8
25Mar84- 7Aqu	fst	1⅛	⊡:48⅗ 1:13 1:51⅗	Alw 22000	4	2	22	53½	715	618¾	MacBeth D	b 117	11.40	66-16	Share The Risk117hdMorningReview11910LastTurn117¾	Gave way	7
1Mar84- 5Aqu	fst	1 1/16	⊡:48⅖ 1:13⅗ 1:47⅕	Clm 50000	4	3	42	52¼	64¼	32¼	MacBeth D	b 117	9.30	74-23	Bishen 1151½ Talc Power 117¾ Alamacani 117¾	Evenly	12
20Feb84- 9Aqu	fst	1⅛	⊡:48⅕ 1:13⅗ 1:52⅕	Clm 50000	1	2	23½	22	3½	3¾	Clayton M D	b 117	22.30	83-16	Bishen117noCndinCurrency117¾Almcni1173¾	Lckd needed respon	10
12Feb84- 2Aqu	fst	6f	⊡:22 :45⅗ 1:11⅕	Clm 50000	10	6	53½	63½	74¼	73½	MacBeth D	b 117	16.00	84-24	Tri Swaps 119nk I'm SoMerry107¾TheTimeIsNow117nk	Weakened	12
21Jan84- 3Aqu	fst	6f	⊡:23⅕ :47⅖ 1:12⅗	Clm 70000	7	2	96	118½	118	119½	MacBeth D	b 113	17.10	71-30	Northern Ice 1132 Full Deck 1133 Pams McAllister 113½	Outrun	11
14Jan84- 7Aqu	fst	6f	⊡:22⅕ :45⅘ 1:11	Alw 22000	5	2	44	44	810	713¾	MacBeth D	b 117	8.90	75-17	Cannon Shell 1172¼ Special Care 1174¾ Forgot theRing117¾	Tired	8

LATEST WORKOUTS Jun 10 Bel tr.t 6f fst 1:16⅗ b — Jun 4 Bel tr.t 4f fst :48 h — May 9 Bel tr.t 4f gd :49⅘ b — May 4 Bel tr.t 4f my :47⅗ h

Alamacani — Dk. b. or br. c. 4, by Irish Ruler—Classic Dance, by Board Marker
Own.—Denmark Muriel — Br.—Regal Oak Farm (Fla) — Tr.—Pascuma Warren J — 117
Lifetime 24 5 1 8 $69,221 — 1983 19 3 1 6 $55,578 — 1982 5 2 0 2 $13,643 — Turf 1 0 0 0

29Dec83- 5Aqu	my	6f	⊡:23⅖ :47⅖ 1:12⅖	3↑ Clm 75000	3	5	3nk	2½	31½	31	Samyn J L	b 115	7.70	81 30	Tarberry 1101 Jet Voyage 108hd Alamacani 1153	Well up,no rally	7
19Nov83- 5Aqu	fst	7f	:22⅗ :45⅖ 1:23⅖	Clm 75000	8	4	94¾	96¾	88½	46	Murphy D J5	b 107	11.40	78 19	Verbarctic 1141¼ Northern Ice 1221 Will's First 1183¾	Rallied	9
31Oct83- 7Aqu	fst	7f	:23⅕ :45⅗ 1:23⅘	3↑ Alw 24000	6	1	41½	33	44½	45¾	MacBeth D	b 114	32.40	76 24	Nearice 1144¾ Moment of Joy 114no Intention 1091	Even try	7
21Sep83- 9Bel	fst	6f	:22 :45⅕ 1:10⅘	Clm c-50000	2	1	33	44½	56	55¾	Bailey J D	b 117	*1.80	82 17	Will's First 117nk Diggin Ditches1174Importunity1171½	Early foot	9
2Sep83- 3Bel	fst	6f	:22⅘ :45⅗ 1:10⅕	Clm 70000	1	2	21½	32	34½	34¾	Bailey J D	b 113	4.20	86 16	NumberOneSpecial112hdHailtoLeder1174¾Almcni1131¼	Weakened	6
7Aug83- 1Sar	fst	6½f	:22⅕ :45⅖ 1:17	Clm 50000	7	1	11½	1hd	1hd	11¼	Bailey J D	b 119	2.80	87-15	Alamacani 1191¼ Diggin Ditches 1171¼ King Billy 1122¾	Driving	7
4Aug83- 5Sar	fst	6f	:22⅕ :45⅕ 1:10⅕	Clm 70000	9	1	32½	32	42¾	53	Bailey J D	b 113	5.30e	86 16	WriteOff117noNumberOneSpecl1122¾TorpdoLos117[illegible]	Weakened	9
23Jly83- 5Bel	fst	7f	:23⅕ :47 1:25⅗	Clm 70000	4	1	3nk	3½	12	35¼	Bailey J D	b 113	3.60e	69 30	Last Turn 1133¼ Cold Remark 1172 Alamacani 1133	Weakened	8
9Jly83- 3Bel	fst	7f	:23⅕ :46⅕ 1:24⅕	Clm 50000	4	3	1½	2½	1½	11	Bailey J D	b 117	*2.30e	81 23	Alamacani 1171 Transonic 110½ Brightest Hope 1132	Drifted, dr	9
4Jly83- 2Bel	fst	7f	:22⅕ :45⅖ 1:25	Clm 70000	3	1	34	43½	42	64½	Bailey J D	b 113	3.70e	72 17	Proud Capital 117nk Brouder's Tip 1081 Gallant George113¾	Tired	11

LATEST WORKOUTS Jan 12 Bel tr.t 4f fst :50⅖ h — Jan 7 Bel tr.t 4f fst :50 h — Jan 5 Bel tr.t 4f fst :51 b — Dec 28 Bel tr.t 3f fst :37⅕ b

CANADIAN CURRENCY

A horse with just two wins in thirty starts over the last twelve months doesn't figure to be much of a threat when moving up in class off a dull effort, especially if it's still in "jail" following a recent claim. However, Canadian Currency's new trainer was an Oscar Barrera-protégé by the name of Gaspar Moschera. In addition, the horse figured to be "speed on the rail," usually dangerous over Aqueduct's inner course. The fact remained, however, that his route effort against $25,000 claimers on December 26 was relatively slow, and the six-year-old didn't appear to have the back class to handle the class rise, as did Alamacani.

TERSE

With just one win—and five seconds—in nineteen starts during 1984, Terse is an unlikely winner, even though competitive twice recently for $45,000. A good horse to bet against.

HUSK

One of a quartet of four-year-olds in the field, Husk quickly deteriorated after impressive maiden and allowance victories at Thanksgiving time. The horse showed nothing against $70,000 three-year-olds recently and is consequently unlikely to fare well against slightly cheaper older horses.

EPILOGUE

An erratic four-year-old yet to face his elders in the claiming ranks, Epilogue's "out of the clouds" running style is not favored by Aqueduct's inner course. His winning performance on November 23 was so out of character—note the early speed—as to suggest the possibility that a "betting coup" was engineered on that occasion. Does the stable have similar intentions today?

EQUITY KICKER

A third four-year-old coming out of the Vinny's Pride race on December 26, this state-bred can apparently handle any kind of surface. His recent win for $50,000 says that he fits well here. But can he handle five-and six-year-olds?

CLASS HERO

This is another horse cursed with the "Jacques Who Syndrome"—ten in-the-money finishes during 1984 but just one win. Class Hero competes almost exclusively at the $50,000 level, with an occasional good race—but never two in a row.

DEEDEE'S DEAL

This hard-hitting eight-year-old appears to have lost interest—or suffered a compromising injury. Since laying off for three months early in 1984, the gelding raced poorly three times, then rested again for six months, apparently to no avail.

LIVELY TEDDY

An atypical Oscar Barrera claim, with suspect (allowance) back class against state-breds, Lively Teddy has no back speed figures of any merit. It would take a minor miracle, but . . .

TORONTONIAN

This once classy Canadian invader—note the two good races behind Jacksboro, who became a successful classified allowance runner in New York—shows a sixteen-month gap in his record and two dull efforts since returning. He's apparently not the same horse he was in 1983.

SATAN'S CHARGER

The 5–2 favorite breaking from the 11-post rather than his customary inside position. A successful Oscar Barrera claim, Satan's Charger improved from $25,000 to $70,000 and was then suspiciously cut back to $35,000 for his latest start and was claimed away from Barrera—never a positive sign. In light of this and the outside post position, Satan's Charger is a false favorite to exploit.

TIVO

As if the 12-post weren't bad enough, this former stakes winner hasn't won since September of 1983 at Louisiana Downs, and has only recently returned from a ten-month layoff.

One final note here: A speed figure analysis of the race clearly favors Satan's Charger—ignoring the fact that his figures were earned from inside posts and the horse will be breaking from the outside today. On the other hand, the figures rated Alamacani no

THIRD RACE
Aqueduct
JANUARY 6, 1985

1 $\frac{1}{16}$ MILES.(InnerDirt). (1.42) CLAIMING. Purse $22,000. 4-year-olds and upward. Weight, 122 lbs. Non-winners of two races at a mile or over since December 1 allowed 3 lbs. Of such a race since then, 5 lbs. Claiming price $50,000; for each $2,500 to $45,000 allowed 2 lbs. (Races when entered to be claimed for $40,000 or less not considered.)

Value of race $22,000; value to winner $13,200; second $4,840; third $2,640; fourth $1,320. Mutuel pool $101,758, OTB pool $129,751. Exacta Pool $213,715. OTB Exacta Pool $254,755.

Last Raced	Horse	Eqt.	A.Wt	PP	St	¼	½	¾	Str	Fin	Jockey	Cl'g Pr	Odds $1
23Dec84 ^{9}Aqu^{1}	Alamacani		5 115	2	2	2^{1}	2^{hd}	$2^{1\frac{1}{2}}$	1^{hd}	$1^{\frac{3}{4}}$	MacBeth D	47500	4.80
3Jan85 ^{3}Aqu^{9}	Canadian Currency	b	6 113	1	1	$1^{1\frac{1}{2}}$	$1^{\frac{1}{2}}$	1^{hd}	$2^{1\frac{1}{2}}$	2no	Graell A	45000	15.20
26Dec84 ^{2}Aqu^{4}	Epilogue		4 115	5	5	11^{3}	10^{hd}	$6^{1\frac{1}{2}}$	4^{hd}	$3^{2\frac{1}{4}}$	McCarron G	45000	5.30
19Dec84 ^{5}Aqu^{7}	Deedee's Deal	b	8 108	8	7	$3^{\frac{1}{2}}$	5^{1}	3^{hd}	3^{1}	4^{3}	Moore D N^{5}	45000	16.90
26Dec84 ^{2}Aqu^{6}	Equity Kicker		4 114	6	4	12	12	8^{hd}	$8^{\frac{1}{2}}$	5^{hd}	Ward W A	50000	14.00
31Dec84 ^{1}Aqu^{1}	Satan's Charger	b	5 113	11	8	6^{hd}	4^{hd}	4^{1}	5^{2}	6^{1}	Lovato F Jr†	45000	2.80
26Dec84 ^{2}Aqu^{7}	Husk	b	4 110	4	10	$8^{\frac{1}{2}}$	11^{3}	9^{hd}	$9^{\frac{1}{2}}$	7^{hd}	Garrido O L^{5}	45000	38.30
1Jan85 ^{5}Aqu^{7}	Lively Teddy	b	6 115	9	11	10^{2}	8^{1}	7^{2}	$7^{\frac{1}{2}}$	8no	Migliore R	47500	9.50
28Dec84 ^{6}Aqu^{2}	Class Hero	b	6 113	7	3	4^{1}	3^{hd}	5^{1}	6^{hd}	$9^{1\frac{3}{4}}$	Davis R G	45000	5.40
28Dec84 ^{6}Aqu^{6}	Terse	b	5 106	3	9	5^{hd}	9^{hd}	10^{1}	10^{4}	$10^{6\frac{1}{4}}$	Espinosa R E^{7}	45000	11.20
1Jan85 ^{7}Aqu^{5}	Tivo	b	4 113	12	12	$9^{\frac{1}{2}}$	6^{1}	12	12	11^{hd}	Santagata N	45000	19.70
22Dec84 ^{6}Aqu^{6}	Torontonian		6 115	10	6	$7^{\frac{1}{2}}$	$7^{\frac{1}{2}}$	11^{11}	11^{hd}	12	Gomez E R	47500	35.10

OFF AT 1:27. Start good, Won driving. Time, :23$\frac{4}{5}$, :47$\frac{4}{5}$, 1:12$\frac{1}{5}$, 1:38, 1:44$\frac{3}{5}$ Track fast.

$2 Mutuel Prices:				
	2-(B)-ALAMACANI	11.60	6.80	4.80
	1-(A)-CANADIAN CURRENCY		14.60	12.60
	5-(E)-EPILOGUE			4.60
	$2 EXACTA 2-1 PAID $146.20.			

Dk. b. or br. h, by Irish Ruler—Classic Dance, by Board Marker. Trainer Pascuma Warren J. Bred by Regal Oak Farm (Fla).

ALAMACANI, ideally positioned immediately, went after CANADIAN CURRENCY approaching stretch, and, heading him, with little over furlong remaining, slowly edged away. CANADIAN CURRENCY, displaying decent speed setting fractions, went well to the end in game effort. EPILOGUE, allowed to drop out of it, lodged bid racing widest, and closing powerfully final quarter-mile, was rapidly getting to top two. DEEDEE'S DEAL, never far back most of way, weakened final eighth. EQUITY KICKER found stride late. SATAN'S CHARGER, forced to race, wide flattened out. HUSK was never formidable. LIVELY TEDDY lacked response. CLASS HERO faltered. TERSE was outrun. TIVO and TORONTONIAN were far back.

better than such older rivals as Terse, Class Hero, and Deedee's Deal, and the four-year-olds Husk, Epilogue, and Equity Kicker. Of course, Alamacani's most recent figure was earned from the 11-post.

Our point, however, goes beyond speed figures. It is simply that Alamacani's back class pointed him out as likely to move up in class again and prove successful against the other older horses in this field, and the subtle age difference made him appear preferable to the newly turned four-year-olds he would face, colts who had yet to establish their real value in the older claiming ranks. Of course, neither the back class nor the slight age advantage hurt him during a tough stretch drive.

Chapter 28

The Downward Spiral

ON A RECENT TRIP to New Haven, I found myself having lunch at Connecticut's futuristic Teletrack facility, "attending" the races at "nearby" Belmont Park. I had not anticipated an afternoon at the races, so I did not purchase the *Form* or look over the day's entries. I decided to stay away from the betting windows and just watch the races closely in the hope of spotting a future bet. I didn't have long to wait.

While viewing the first race, I noticed a horse making a sharp move on the turn, way out in the four-path. I watched the replays closely, learned that the filly's name was Anselma, and that although her move was sharp, it also was rather short-lived, spanning three sixteenths of a mile at most. I asked a gentleman sitting at the same table what her form looked like going into the race and learned what I hoped to hear. Anselma was a fresh filly, making only her second start after a five-month layoff. In many cases, a "bid-hung" performance is a sign of an overraced horse tapping its energy reserve as a prelude to going completely off form. Anselma did not fall into that category, and I confidently predicted to those present that she would need at most two starts before finding the winner's circle.

Anselma had been dropped into the claiming ranks for her first start after her recent layoff and was dropping again for the October 11 race. At the time of my trip to Connecticut, I was planning to write a chapter for this book on the subject of dropdowns and was looking for an appropriate race as an example. Anselma appealed to me as a potential future bet based on her wide "bid-hung" trip. I had no idea that she would emerge as the heroine of this chapter. As a matter of fact, her dropdown pattern gave me sufficient second thoughts about her physical well-being to cut back somewhat on the size of my bets in her next two starts, on November 4 and November 9.

It is useless to make broad statements about horses dropping in class. Dropdowns come in many different shapes. The context—as revealed in the horse's past performance profile—tells whether the drop in class should be viewed in a positive or negative sense. I find it useful to distinguish seven different, although at times overlapping, categories of dropdowns:

(1) The horse dropping back to its proper level after failing to stand a rise in class. If still fit and not discouraged from chasing classier animals, it is a likely contender no matter what its recent form may resemble.

(2) The horse dropping back to its proper level after racing itself into shape against better animals following a recent layoff. Many trainers use this maneuver to avoid a claim and drop the horse precisely when they believe it is ready to win.

(3) The off-form horse dropping down seeking its proper level, possibly descending below its most recently established competitive level. Where the downward spiral will end is anybody's guess. If the animal drops without showing any improvement whatsoever, don't expect another drop to make much difference. This pattern is often seen in horses that parlay an extended period of fitness and good form into a sharp rise up the claiming ladder only to tumble back down when overexertion or a minor injury robs them of their fitness or enthusiasm for racing.

(4) The horse dropping from allowance company down into the claiming ranks for the first time of late. The age of the horse, its recent form in allowance company, its status in the allowance ranks, and the claiming tag for which it is entered, all have some bearing on the proper interpretation of this maneuver.

(5) The horse dropping in its first start after a layoff, seldom a good sign. Unless the layoff was the result of a compromising injury, the trainer would probably race the animal back into winning condition in a higher classification. That way, he would receive good value for the horse if he lost it on a claim.

(6) The horse dropping after a good race, again usually a negative sign. Why drop a sharp horse, one that others may see as capable of winning at a higher level, unless the animal has serious physical ailments that may soon surface and compromise its form? The horse may have one good race left, but the odds are usually too low to warrant a bet. The question is

often whether or not a player should bet against such a horse, and an understanding of trainer methodology often provides the answer.

(7) The lightly raced older animal now being dropped for the first time, suggesting that whatever ailments have kept the animal on the sidelines over the years have grown more acute.

Of course, no analysis of dropdowns can be complete without reference to trainer methodology. Some trainers thrive with dropdowns. Others drop only ouchy animals, hoping to rid themselves of a problem. Some use the drop as a bluff—at least on occasion—hoping rival trainers will suspect problems that don't exist. The occasional successful (healthy) dropdown is used to bait rival trainers into a false sense of security, hopefully encouraging one of them to halter an unsound animal at some later date.

Now let's continue with the Anselma story by taking a look at the second race at Aqueduct on November 9, 1985. Here's the field for this $14,000 claiming sprint at six furlongs:

LOYAL DIPLOMAT

A confirmed front-runner that has raced in this class all year long, Loyal Diplomat won for the first time in 1985 last time out—but that was on September 12. An eight-week layoff following a win must be regarded as suspiciously as a drop in class on the heels of victory. With a competitive pace likely today, and her recent winning figure subpar, she's not a likely repeater.

LAST GIRL

A winner the last four times she competed at this level, Last Girl has been consistently unsuccessful against better and now drops down once again where she fits best. She's a reasonable favorite here, but her inability to win one class higher suggests that any reasonable dropdown might pose a serious threat. Also, in light of an exceptionally poor performance last time out at the Meadowlands, one had to wonder about her current conditioner, Joseph Aquilano. What were his credentials? Had he lost control of the horse? A relative unknown on the New York circuit, Aquilano didn't claim Last Girl from an Oscar Barrera or a Peter Ferriola. Rather, his immedi-

2 AQUEDUCT 6 FURLONGS

6 FURLONGS. (1.08⅕) CLAIMING. Purse $12,000. Fillies and Mares, 3-year-olds and upward. Weights, 3-year-olds 120 lbs. Older 122 lbs. Non-winners of two races since October 15 allowed 3 lbs. Of a race since then 5 lbs. Claiming price $14,000; for each $1,000 to $12,000 2 lbs. (Races when entered to be claimed for $10,000 or less not considered.)

Coupled—Last Girl and Our Mutual Friend; Pair Of Queens and Rialto Ripple.

Loyal Diplomat

Ch. m. 6, by Diplomat Way—Loyal Subject, by Roman Patrol
Own.—Krohn Deborah
$14,000 Br.—Giglia S (Fla)
Tr.—Krohn Nat
117 Lifetime 46 7 6 4 $91,885 1985 12 1 1 1 $13,640 1984 15 4 2 0 $35,960

12Sep85- 4Bel fst 7f :23 :46⅗ 1:25⅘ 3+ⒻClm 13000 8 2 2hd 1hd 12 1¾ Santagata N 115 24.60 73-23 Loyal Diplomat 115¾ Croatia 110hd Rebel Love 1062½ Driving 10
4Sep85- 1Bel fst 6f :23⅕ :47⅕ 1:12⅕ 3+ⒻClm 13000 8 1 11 2hd 65½ 810¾ Santagata N 115 7.80 70-21 Last Girl 1101½ Our Trisha 1171 Croatia 1101¾ Tired 9
9Aug85- 6Mth fst 6f :22⅗ :45⅘ 1:11⅗ 3+ⒻClm 14000 4 5 3½ 32 41½ 44 Thomas D B 113 19.00 78-19 RunforOscar116hdInkiePinkie1163LanguorousBeu1121 Weakened 7
27Jly85- 9Bel fst 6f :22⅖ :46 1:11⅖ 3+ⒻClm 13000 5 5 11½ 1hd 1½ 54½ Santagata N 115 13.70 80-10 Last Girl 1103 Pleasant Bid 113½ For Naught 1151 Stopped 8
12Apr85- 3Aqu fst 6f :23⅕ :47⅖ 1:12⅗ ⒻClm 16500 7 1 32½ 21½ 43½ 58 Moore D N5 110 3.80 70-22 Goodwill Mission 1131¾ Croatia 112¾ Speier's Image 1174¾ Tired 8
2Apr85- 1Aqu fst 6f :23⅕ :47⅕ 1:11⅘ ⒻClm 17500 6 7 72½ 63¾ 65½ 67½ MacBeth D 117 7.70 75-20 Speier'sImage117¾KyraMaria1191¾PairOfQueens1133 Broke in air 7
20Mar85- 1Aqu fst 1 :48⅖ 1:14⅕ 1:40⅖ ⒻClm 15500 1 1 12 1½ 2½ 24 Santagata N 113 6.10 60-30 WgonDggon1194LoylDplmt1134½KyTKnsngtn117no Best of others 6
14Mar85- 3Aqu fst 6f :22⅘ :47⅖ 1:13⅖ ⒻClm 17500 8 1 12 2½ 53½ 77½ Garrido O L5 b 112 19.90 67-35 Maggie Carta 1122¾ Lucas Lou1141½GoldenGreens117hd Gave way 12
25Feb85- 4Aqu fst 6f ⊡:22⅘ :47 1:13⅘ ⒻClm c-12000 5 2 2hd 21 21 32 Espinosa R E7 b 106 3.10 73-25 So Fun 1171½ Pair Of Queens 117¾LoyalDiplomat1063½ Weakened 8
21Feb85- 1Aqu fst 6f ⊡:22⅘ :46⅘ 1:13⅖ ⒻClm 15500 4 6 23 32½ 34 44¾ Espinosa R E7 106 3.70 72-29 Charismata 1121½ Iwasonlyakid 1172¾ Artic Moss 117½ No excuse 10
LATEST WORKOUTS Oct 18 Bel tr.t 3f fst :37⅘ b

*Last Girl

Dk. b. or br. m. 5, by Last Rore—Snow Brusch, by Snow Cat
Own.—Surazal Stable
$14,000 Br.—Haras Noroma (Arg)
Tr.—Aquilino Joseph
110[7] Lifetime 30 8 4 3 $51,112 1985 15 5 2 1 $43,480 1984 9 0 2 0 $3,921 Turf 1 0 0 0 $161

2Nov85- 3Med fst 6f :23 :46⅖ 1:11⅘ 3+ⒻClm 18000 1 6 52¾ 65 77½ 711½ Vasquez M M7 107 2.70 73-18 Beanalee 1093½ Squirrel Run 1192 Donut Flash 1133 No factor 10
7Oct85- 1Bel fst 1 :47⅖ 1:12⅗ 1:39⅕ 3+ⒻClm c-14000 5 8 42 1½ 11½ 1½ Rolon E M7 110 *1.30 69-23 Last Girl 110½ Mucchinette 1174 Jungle Secret 1142 Driving 8
28Sep85- 2Bel fst 7f :23⅕ :46⅘ 1:24⅗ 3+ⒻClm 17500 1 4 32 52¾ 31 43¾ Rolon E M7 112 4.20 76-18 Video Queen 110hd Our Trisha 1173 Majennique 108hd Weakened 10
4Sep85- 1Bel fst 6f :23⅕ :47⅕ 1:12⅕ 3+ⒻClm c-14000 2 7 32 31½ 1½ 11½ Rolon E M7 110 2.30 81-21 Last Girl 1101½ Our Trisha 1171 Croatia 1101¾ Driving 9
27Jly85- 9Bel fst 6f :22⅖ :46 1:11⅖ 3+ⒻClm 14000 3 2 43½ 42 2½ 13 Guerra A A7 110 *2.50 85-10 Last Girl 1103 Pleasant Bid 113½ ForNaught1151 Lost whip, clear 8
21Jly85- 1Bel fst 7f :23 :46⅗ 1:25⅗ 3+ⒻClm 17500 5 2 31½ 2hd 1½ 32½ Guerra A A7 110 9.70 71-16 Lady Nizon 1101½ Goodwill Mission1101½LastGirl110no Weakened 7
1Jly85- 2Bel fst 6f :22⅗ :45⅘ 1:11 ⒻClm 17500 9 3 42 33 37½ 612 Rolon E M7 110 11.10 75-17 SunSounds1176Speier'sImge1102½GoodwillMission1081 Gave way 13
19Jun85- 3Bel fst 6f :22⅘ :47 1:13 ⒻClm 35000 1 2 42 52½ 65 87 Guerra A A7 110 50.70 70-28 Elbarita 1171¾ Lady Kinsman 117hd So Fun 113no Tired 10
14Jun85- 1Bel fst 6f :23⅕ :47⅕ 1:12⅕ ⒻClm 25000 5 3 53½ 55 56 510½ Rolon E M7 110 14.10 70-24 So Fun 1151¾ Conveyance 117¾ Sun Sounds 1173 Evenly 7
28Apr85- 9Aqu fst 7f :23⅕ :46⅗ 1:26⅘ ⒻClm 14000 3 6 52½ 42½ 21½ 12 Rolon E M10 107 5.00 67-21 LstGirl1072RiltoRippie1122Story'sVeryRich113hd Bore in, driving 10
LATEST WORKOUTS Oct 31 Aqu 3f fst :37 b Oct 26 Aqu 5f fst 1:03⅕ b ●Oct 20 Aqu 4f fst :47⅗ h

Anselma

Ch. f. 4, by Auberge—Lady Warfare, by Warfare
Own.—Tresvant Stable
$12,000 Br.—Gray E & H (Va)
Tr.—Reid Mark J
106[7] Lifetime 31 6 3 4 $92,700 1985 11 2 1 0 $34,360 1984 20 4 2 4 $58,340 Turf 5 0 1 0 $5,770

4Nov85- 9Aqu fst 7f :22⅖ :46 1:25⅕ 3+ⒻClm 14000 6 9 96¼ 64½ 44 510½ Decarlo C P7 110 5.90 65-19 Poco Lolo 1152¾ Croatia 1121¾ Macha Of Ulster 1122½ Outrun 12
11Oct85- 1Bel fst 7f :23 :46⅘ 1:24⅘ 3+ⒻClm 22500 11 7 73½ 41 86½ 910½ Rini W5 110 12.20 67-22 Solo Energy 1103 Miss Puckett 1171 Video Queen 106½ Tired 13
29Sep85- 1Bel fst 6f :23⅕ :47 1:11⅗ 3+ⒻClm 35000 3 4 64¼ 62¾ 56½ 59¾ Decarlo C P7 110 9.00 74-19 Speier's Image 117¾MachaOfUlster1174Kouklamou1192 No factor 7
24Apr85- 8GS fst 1 :46⅗ 1:11⅕ 1:36⅗ ⒻAlw 35000 4 6 67½ 69 512 616 Marquez C H Jr7 112 9.20 76-13 Miss Arrowood 1175½ Bharal 1154 Tyrolean Miss 1155 No factor 7
15Apr85- 6GS fst 6f :22⅖ :45⅕ 1:10⅕ 3+ⒻAlw 16000 5 5 63 69¾ 67¾ 58½ Marquez C H7 114 *1.00 — — Sour Dancer 1192½ Majestic Flag 1192 Bride To Be 1194 Outrun 7
23Mar85- 1Aqu fst 7f :23⅖ :47 1:25⅗ ⒻAlw 23000 4 1 52¾ 42½ 1hd 1½ Garrido O L5 117 2.80 73-23 Anselma117½VideoQueen122nkFirstEmerald117no Hard drive, bled 6
13Mar85- 8Aqu fst 6f :23⅖ :47⅖ 1:12⅖ ⒻAlw 25000 8 8 75½ 51¾ 21 2½ Garrido O L5 117 9.00 78-28 Tiny Butterfly 117½ Anselma 117no FirstEmerald1171½ Went wide 8
4Mar85- 7Aqu fst 6f ⊡:23⅕ :46⅖ 1:12⅖ ⒻAlw 22000 2 6 54½ 56½ 21 1hd Garrido O L5 112 13.50 82-22 Anselma 112hd No Mur Murs 1122¼ Apple Too 1121½ Stiff drive 7
10Feb85- 7Aqu fst 1$\frac{1}{16}$ ⊡:48 1:13⅕ 1:45⅗ ⒻAlw 23000 7 5 63½ 42½ 42½ 46½ Garrido O L5 112 12.30 75-18 Current Miss 117½ Tenatell 1173 Miss Puckett 1173 No mishap 8
31Jan85- 6Aqu fst 1¼ ⊡:50 1:42⅘ 2:10⅕ ⒻAlw 23000 7 4 32 43½ 55½ 74¾ Garrido O L5 112 15.20 59-25 Magic Circle 117½ Miss Puckett 117hdImprovising119¾ No mishap 9
LATEST WORKOUTS Sep 17 Aqu 5f fst 1:02⅖ b Sep 11 Aqu 4f gd :49⅖ b (d)

So Little Time

Ro. f. 4, by Little Current—Time For Art, by Nearctic
Own.—Boyan T
$14,000 Br.—Furgatch H (Ky)
Tr.—Galluscio Dominick
110[7] Lifetime 41 4 4 9 $47,380 1985 12 1 0 1 $10,755 1984 18 3 3 4 $30,025

3Oct85- 3Med sly 6f :23 :46⅘ 1:12⅘ 3+ⒻClm 16000 2 6 45½ 67½ 58½ 513½ Santagata N b 116 12.60 65-25 Sail Or Cerf 1191½ Tiki Taylor 1145½ Croatia 1095½ Outrun 7
11Aug85- 9Suf fst 6f :21⅘ :45⅕ 1:11 3+ⒻAlw 11000 6 3 21½ 36½ 511 618 Baez R b 114 34.60 68-23 Crozier'sTea1223½FrillsandRibbons1222½BrvelyStted1194 Stopped 6
5Aug85- 9Suf fst 6f :22⅕ :45⅘ 1:12⅕ 3+ⒻAlw 10500 3 4 32½ 56½ 58½ 59½ Bush W V b 122 38.10 70-25 Sea Trip 122¾ Fast Lane Gal 1223½ Now It's Gone 114½ Fin. early 5
24Jly85- 8Suf fst 6f :22⅖ :46⅕ 1:13⅕ 3+ⒻAlw 10500 5 4 31½ 33 44 68 Bush W V b 119 41.20 67-31 RunnngCousn122½GrkWy1193½Blh'sFolly1172½ Squeezed back st. 6
3Jly85- 6Suf fst 6f :22 :46 1:10⅘ 3+ⒻAlw 10500 6 3 1hd 21½ 67 615½ Bush W V b 122 10.90 72-16 Charmful 1151 Greek Way 1222½ Stormy Welcome 1141 Stopped 6
28Jun85- 9Suf sly 1 :46⅘ 1:13⅘ 1:40⅘ 3+ⒻAlw 10000 1 2 21 47 518 538¾ Bush W V b 117 3.80 35-24 FrillsandRibbons11211CourtUnion1142¾LadyCrlton1145½ Stopped 5
12May85- 9Suf fst 6f :22⅗ :46⅖ 1:12 3+ⒻAlw 10000 3 3 11½ 11½ 13 11½ Bush W V b 122 10.10 81-23 SoLittleTime1221½BonniBluSky1223FrillsndRibbons1222¼ Driving 6
4May85- 9Suf fst 6f :22⅖ :46 1.12 3+ⒻAlw 10000 3 5 11½ 11½ 1½ 43½ Vargas J L b 122 12.40 77-20 Homera 122hd Bonnie Blue Sky 1221½ MyOwnSunshine1222 Tired 6
19Apr85- 7Rkm fst 6f :22⅕ :45⅗ 1:11⅖ 3+ⒻPrimonetta H 2 7 65 67½ 69½ 712½ Bush W V b 115 6.90e 74-20 FurshFolly1201½RunningCousin1214¾ImptuousPunch1204½ Outrun 10
11Apr85- 5Aqu fst 6f :23⅕ :47 1:12⅖ ⒻClm 25000 9 2 3nk 1hd 2hd 32½ Espinosa R E7 b 110 3.10e 77-24 Our Trisha 1101½ GoldenGreens1071SoLittleTime110hd Weakened 10
LATEST WORKOUTS ●Oct 28 Aqu 4f fst :47⅗ h Oct 14 Aqu 4f fst :49 b Sep 29 Aqu 4f fst :48⅘ h Sep 25 Aqu 4f my :49⅘ b

Shimaleka

B. f. 4, by Salem—Sally M B, by At Forty
Own.—Hop Stables
$14,000 Br.—Ballenger W H (Va)
Tr.—Olsen Gary S
117 Lifetime 31 3 3 5 $58,465 1985 12 0 1 3 $16,900 1984 19 3 2 2 $41,565 Turf 1 0 0 0

6Jun85- 7Bel gd 6f :22⅖ :45⅗ 1:10 3+ⒻAlw 25000 3 1 21 44½ 69½ 730¾ Cordero A Jr b 117 10.90 61-15 KamikazeRick1094¾FavorbleReview1143GrndCretion1094 Stopped 7
15May85- 5Bel fst 6f :22⅗ :46⅗ 1:11⅘ 3+ⒻAlw 25000 3 8 1½ 1½ 32½ 56¾ Davis R G b 121 13.40 76-17 Carrie's Dream110nkFindHappiness1101¾ScreenLanding1212 Tired 8
26Apr85- 7Aqu fst 6f :23⅖ :47⅕ 1:11⅘ 3+ⒻAlw 24000 2 2 21½ 22 37 38¾ Davis R G b 121 7.30 73-23 Promethia 1126¾ Ashley'sRainbow1212Shimaleka1211½ Weakened 6
5Apr85- 6Aqu fst 6f :23 :46⅗ 1:11⅗ 3+ⒻAlw 23000 2 3 11 1½ 1hd 33¾ Davis R G b 121 4.90 79-23 Top Issue 1091¾ Screen Landing 1212 Shimaleka 121½ Weakened 8
23Mar85- 1Aqu fst 7f :23⅖ :47 1:25⅗ ⒻAlw 23000 5 2 11½ 11 3½ 4¾ Davis R G b 117 10.20 72-23 Anselma 117½VideoQueen122nkFirstEmerald117no Set pace, wknd 6
13Mar85- 8Aqu fst 6f :23⅖ :47⅖ 1:12⅖ ⒻAlw 25000 7 1 2½ 2hd 42 63 Santagata N b 117 6.20 76-28 Tiny Butterfly117½Anselma117noFirstEmerald1171½ Flattened out 8
3Mar85- 3Aqu fst 6f ⊡:23 :47 1:12⅗ ⒻAlw 23000 7 1 21 2hd 21 44¼ Ward W A5 b 112 3.00 77-17 SueeSuprem117¾TinyButtrfly1172¼FirstEmrld1191¼ Wide,faltered 7
21Feb85- 8Aqu fst 6f ⊡:22⅗ :46⅗ 1:12⅗ ⒻAlw 25000 7 1 21 1½ 21 33½ Davis R G b 117 *1.40 77-29 Explicit Gal 1172 Shavie 1171½ Shimaleka 1172½ Weakened 7
4Feb85- 8Aqu fst 6f ⊡:22⅗ :46 1:11⅘ ⒻAlw 25000 2 5 11 11 12 2no Guerra A A7 b 110 14.90 85-21 Tearupthetickets112noShimaleka1102½OurTrish112hd Just missed 7
23Jan85- 7Aqu fst 6f ⊡:22⅘ :46⅘ 1:12⅕ ⒻAlw 23000 6 9 21 21½ 44½ 79½ Guerra A A5 112 20.70 73-24 Mt. Prospect 1223 Pistachio 1121 Hjerdish 1171 Lost whip 11
LATEST WORKOUTS Oct 31 Aqu Ⓣ 5f fm 1:02⅘ h Oct 24 Aqu Ⓣ 5f fm 1:04⅕ b (d) Oct 16 Aqu 4f fst :49 hg Oct 2 Aqu 3f fst :37⅘ b

Pair Of Queens

Ch. f. 4, by What Luck—Minstrel Queen, by King Of the Tudors
Own.—Iron Lance Stable
$12,000 Br.—Arky & Warner (Ohio)
Tr.—Fernandez Floreano
113 Lifetime 27 3 3 3 $36,180 1985 11 0 2 2 $9,100 1984 16 3 1 1 $27,080

23Oct85- 2Aqu fst 7f :22⅘ :46⅖ 1:24⅗ 3+ⒻClm 12000 12 2 62½ 63¾ 912 1012½ Santos J A b 113 32.00 66-17 Mucchinette 1171 Buckfinder's Joy 109½ Our Trisha 1173¾ Wide 12
22Jun85- 2Bel fst 6f :22⅘ :47 1:13⅘ ⒻClm 14000 10 9 54 63½ 75¾ 84½ Cruguet J b 117 14.20 68-23 Fighting Spirit 110nk Blue Bride 113nk Sun Sounds 117nk Wide 13
10Jun85- 1Bel fst 7f :23⅗ :47⅕ 1:25⅕ ⒻClm 14000 3 5 31 32 36 410 Velasquez J b 117 2.80 66-19 Copepod 1193 Ducky Duchesse 1176½ Lovely Mesa108½ Weakened 6
19May85- 9Bel fst 7f :23⅕ :47⅕ 1:24⅗ ⒻClm 14000 2 10 44 53 714 922 Ramirez M R5 b 112 4.80 57-20 Copepod 11312 Promise Kept 115no Tiki Taylor115no Broke in air 10
2Apr85- 1Aqu fst 6f :23⅕ :47⅕ 1:11⅘ ⒻClm 15500 3 6 4nk 3½ 31 32½ Santagata N b 113 2.40 79-20 Speier's Image 117¾ Kyra Maria 1191¾ Pair OfQueens1133 Evenly 7
27Mar85- 1Aqu fst 6f :22⅘ :46⅖ 1:11⅘ ⒻClm 14000 7 2 31 2½ 12 2no Santagata N b 117 7.30 82-20 KyraMaria114noPairOfQueens1178½FabulousAck117nk Just missed 12
18Mar85- 2Aqu fst 7f :23⅗ :48⅖ 1:27⅘ ⒻClm 14000 11 3 31 2hd 1½ 45½ Santagata N b 117 14.80 56-38 SweetAmbition117¾KyraMari1144½BitterChocolte113nk Weakened 14
4Mar85- 2Aqu fst 6f ⊡:23 :47 1:12⅕ ⒻClm 15550 1 5 33½ 35 58½ 711¾ Thibeau R J b 113 5.40 71-22 So Fun 1177½ Ebullient 108½ Ducky Duchesse 112hd Faltered 10
25Feb85- 4Aqu fst 6f ⊡:22⅘ :47 1:13⅘ ⒻClm 14000 8 4 43 34 32 21½ Thibeau R J b 117 4.80 74-25 So Fun 1171½ Pair Of Queens 117¾ Loyal Diplomat 1063½ Rallied 8
9Feb85- 9Aqu fst 6f ⊡:23⅕ :47⅘ 1:14⅕ ⒻClm 15500 10 2 42½ 45½ 46½ 33½ Thibeau R J b 113 19.10 69-26 Last Girl 1073½ Croatia 117hd Pair Of Queens 1131 Wild, rallied 11
LATEST WORKOUTS Oct 8 Bel tr.t 4f fst :50⅘ b

Our Mutual Friend

Dk. b. or br. m. 5, by Ivorson—L'Jackae, by Presented
Own.—Nevins G
$12,000 Br.—Denning J (Md)
Tr.—Aquilino Joseph
108[5] Lifetime 56 12 9 2 $80,045 1985 8 1 0 0 $6,120 1984 23 4 5 1 $41,525 Turf 2 0 0 0

23Oct85- 2Aqu fst 7f :22⅘ :46⅖ 1:24⅗ 3+ⒻClm 13000 8 7 83½ 98¼ 1012 710¼ Jones B S7 b 112 39.30 68-17 Mucchinette 1171 Buckfinder's Joy 109½ Our Trisha 1173¾ Outrun 12
11Oct85- 3Med fst 6f :23 :47 1:12⅗ 3+ⒻClm 11500 8 7 79¾ 77½ 62¼ 11¼ Decarlo C P7 b 107 14.40e 79-18 Our Mutual Friend 1071¼ May Bay 116nk LadyFunfair1162 Driving 9
7Oct85- 1Bel fst 1 :47⅖ 1:12⅗ 1:39⅕ 3+ⒻClm 13000 7 3 64½ 79 717 616½ Decarlo C P7 b 108 16.40 52-23 Last Girl 110½ Mucchinette 1174 JungleSecret1142 Finished early 8
28Sep85- 2Bel fst 7f :23⅕ :46⅘ 1:24⅗ 3+ⒻClm 15500 5 6 74 107½ 914 812 Davis R G b 113 11.40 67-18 Video Queen 110hd Our Trisha 1173 Majennique 108hd Outrun 10
12Sep85- 4Bel fst 7f :23 :46⅗ 1:25⅘ 3+ⒻClm 13000 9 9 86¾ 97½ 87½ 43¼ Alvarado R Jr b 115 51.40 70-23 Loyal Diplomat 115¾ Croatia 110hd Rebel Love 1062½ Wide str. 10
4Sep85- 1Bel fst 6f :23⅕ :47⅕ 1:12⅕ 3+ⒻClm 13000 3 2 912 810 99 79 Alvarado R Jr b 115 10.80e 72-21 Last Girl 1101½ Our Trisha 1171 Croatia 1101¾ Outrun 9
13Jan85- 1Aqu fst 6f ⊡:23⅕ :47⅘ 1:13⅗ ⒻClm 13000 2 6 42½ 56½ 44½ 55½ Guerra A A5 b 110 11.70 70-27 Perfect Gift 114½ Radiant Gem 1132 Future Friend 1142½ No rally 12
7Jan85- 1Aqu fst 170 ⊡:49 1:15⅗ 1:48 ⒻClm 13000 8 1 11½ 11½ 24 710½ Blackstun KM5 b 110 15.20 49-27 Saturna 1084½ M. V. On Five 117¾ Vicky's Holly 112nk Stopped 9
5Dec84- 1Med fst 6f :23 :46⅘ 1:13⅕ 3+ⒻClm 10000 3 5 43½ 55½ 68 69¾ Blackstun KM7 b 109 4.30 66-24 Snow Maid 1161½ Lady Sheffield 114no Shelly'sTomboy1196 Tired 10
27Nov84- 2Med fst 1$\frac{1}{16}$:48 1:14 1:49 3+ⒻClm 10000 4 1 1hd 67¾ 1015 1021½ Messina R b 116 2.40e 42-28 Lure the Lady 1163 Bravest Girl 1163 Subtlety 1162½ Stopped 10
LATEST WORKOUTS Sep 22 Aqu 4f fst :50 b

Rialto Ripple

B. f. 4, by Empery—Roundelay, by Mr Prospector
Own.—Golden Field Farm
$13,000 Br.—Tartan Farms (Fla)
Tr.—Fernandez Floreano
110[5] Lifetime 46 2 6 4 $35,500 1985 16 1 4 2 $19,740 1984 22 1 2 2 $15,130 Turf 3 0 0 0

```
13Oct85- 2Bel fst 6f  :23⅗ :47⅗ 1:12⅗ 3+ⒻClm 14000   8 1 1hd 1½ 43½ 68     Alvarez A7     110 11.20  71-19 Rebel Love 1142 Goodwill Mission 1122¼ Croatia 110no   Used up 8
12Sep85- 4Bel fst 7f  :23  :46⅗ 1:25⅘ 3+ⒻClm 14000   2 4 43 42 98½ 98¾       Cruguet J      117 14.10  64-23 Loyal Diplomat 115¾ Croatia 110hd Rebel Love 1062½   Tired 10
4Sep85- 1Bel fst 6f   :23⅕ :47⅕ 1:12⅕ 3+ⒻClm 14000   5 4 54 42½ 55 58        Cruguet J      117 12.70  73-21 Last Girl 1101¼ Our Trisha 1171 Croatia 1101¾   Tired 9
5Jly85- 3Bel fst 6f   :22⅘ :45⅘ 1:10⅕   ⒻClm 20000   5 7 59 612 726 727¾     Cruguet J      113 27.40  63-17 Outofthequestion 1174¾DevotedAna1191¼ExplicitGal1171¼   Outrun 7
1Jly85- 2Bel fst 6f   :22⅘ :45⅘ 1:11    ⒻClm 15500   7 10 89 912 1117 1320¼  Cruguet J      113 7.90   66-17 SunSounds1176Speier'sImge1102¼GoodwillMission1081   Fell back 13
29May85- 1Bel fst 6f  :23  :45⅗ 1:11⅗   ⒻClm 14000   2 1 52½ 2½ 11½ 1hd      Cruguet J      117 *1.30  85-15 Rialto Ripple 117hd April Miracle 117hd Tiki Taylor 1152   Driving 8
9May85- 3Bel fst 6f   :23⅕ :47⅗ 1:13⅕   ⒻClm 14000   7 4 62½ 21 22 22¾      Ramirez M R5   112 7.00   73-25 Croatia1102¾RialtoRipple112¾GoodwillMission115¾   Altered course 11
28Apr85- 9Aqu fst 7f  :23⅕ :46⅗ 1:26⅘   ⒻClm 14000   1 10 1½ 11 11½ 22      Ramirez M R5   112 4.30   65-21 Last Girl 1072 Rialto Ripple 1122Story'sVeryRich113hd   Weakened 10
18Apr85- 3Aqu fst 6f  :22⅘ :46⅕ 1:13⅖   ⒻClm 14000   4 6 75 78 55 33½       Ramirez M R5   112 5.60   71-30 Millionaire Jen 117no Last Girl 1073¼ Rialto Ripple1122¼   CHecked 11
22Mar85- 4Aqu fst 7f  :23⅗ :47⅕ 1:26⅗   ⒻClm 14000   6 4 2½ 2hd 11½ 31      Guerra A A7    110 10.40  67-27 Gentle Ram1131GoodwillMission106noRialtoRipple1102   Weakened 9
LATEST WORKOUTS   Oct 27 Bel tr.t 4f fst :48 h   Oct 11 Bel tr.t 4f fst :49⅘ b
```

Croatia

```
Croatia                      B. f. 4, by Irish Ruler—Fast and Fancy, by Baffle            Lifetime     1985 19 1 5 3   $26,900
                     $14,000 Br.—Wolftrap Farms Inc (Va)                            1125  49 8 11 8    1984 24 5 6 3   $38,537
Own.—Wooton Mary L           Tr.—Lake Diane E                                             $74,737      Turf 1 0 0 0
4Nov85- 9Aqu fst 7f   :22⅘ :46  1:25⅕ 3+ⒻClm 14000   7 3 31 1½ 12 22¾       Rini W5        112 7.50   72-19 Poco Lolo 1152¾ Croatia 1121¾ Macha Of Ulster 1122¼   Game try 12
13Oct85- 2Bel fst 6f  :23⅗ :47⅗ 1:12⅗ 3+ⒻClm 14000   1 3 2hd 74½ 33 34¾     Decarlo C P7   110 *2.60  74-19 Rebel Love1142GoodwillMission1122¼Croatia110no   Lacked fin.bid 8
3Oct85- 3Med sly 6f   :23  :46⅘ 1:12⅘ 3+ⒻClm 16000   4 2 55½ 35 33½ 36¾     Decarlo C P7   109 5.90   71-25 Sail Or Cerf 1191¼ Tiki Taylor 1145½ Croatia 1095½   Tired 7
12Sep85- 4Bel fst 7f  :23  :46⅗ 1:25⅘ 3+ⒻClm 14000   10 1 53½ 54 32½ 2¾     Decarlo C P7   110 3.20   72-23 Loyal Diplomat 115¾ Croatia 110hd Rebel Love 1062½   Rallied 10
4Sep85- 1Bel fst 6f   :23⅕ :47⅕ 1:12⅕ 3+ⒻClm 14000   7 3 64½ 64½ 42 32½     Decarlo C P7   110 *1.30e 79-21 Last Girl 1101¼ Our Trisha 1171 Croatia 1101¾   Rallied 9
9Aug85- 6Mth fst 6f   :22⅘ :45⅘ 1:11⅗ 3+ⒻClm 16000   6 1 63½ 66¾ 64½ 54¾    Verge M E      116 11.90  77-19 Run forOscar116hdInkiePinkie1163LanguorousBeau1121   Steadied 7
27Jly85- 9Bel fst 6f  :22⅘ :46  1:11⅘ 3+ⒻClm 14000   8 7 64½ 3½ 32 44½      Jones B S7     110 3.50   80-10 Last Girl 1103 Pleasant Bid 113½ For Naught 1151   Weakened 8
11Jly85- 2Bel fst 7f  :22⅘ :46⅗ 1:25⅗   ⒻClm 14000   10 1 22 1½ 1½ 22½     Jones B S7     110 11.10e 72-19 Explicit Gal 1102¼ Croatia 1101¼ Pleasant Bid 113½   Gamely 11
1Jly85- 2Bel fst 6f   :22⅘ :45⅘ 1:11    ⒻClm 15500   13 6 32 43½ 58 512     Espinosa R E7  106 *1.60e 75-17 SunSounds1176Speier'sImg1102¼GoodwillMission1081   Weakened 13
22Jun85- 2Bel fst 6f  :22⅘ :47  1:13⅘   ⒻClm 14000   9 4 64 75½ 97½ 94½     Alvarez A7     110 7.00   68-23 Fighting Spirit 110nk Blue Bride 113nk Sun Sounds 117nk   Wide 13
LATEST WORKOUTS   Oct 30 Aqu 4f fst :48⅘ h   Sep 23 Aqu 4f fst :49 b
```

Bonnie's Poker

```
Bonnie's Poker               Dk. b. or br. f. 3, by Poker—What a Surprise, by Wise Margin   Lifetime     1985 8 0 0 0
                     $14,000 Br.—Garland Mr-Mrs S E (Ky)                            115   12 1 1 1     1984 4 1 1 1    $11,440
Own.—Gampel H A              Tr.—Gullo Thomas J                                           $11,440      Turf 2 0 0 0
24Jly85- 3Bel fst 7f  :22⅘ :45⅗ 1:24⅗    ⒻClm 20000  4 8 88½ 811 510 67¼    Santagata N   b 112 21.10  72-17 CoolRoyalty1094½FancyMissNncy1161½JungleSecret114nk   Outrun 8
14Jly85- 4Bel fst 6f  :22⅘ :46⅗ 1:13⅕    ⒻClm 22500  1 9 913 89½ 69 68      Santos J A    b 114 22.30  68-21 Berna Cagney 1163SweetRenee1111SingingPraise1161¼   No factor 10
3Jly85- 7Bel fm 1  Ⓣ:46⅘ 1:11  1:35⅘    ⒻAlw 25000  3 2 2½ 65¼ 1113 1115¼   Santagata N   b 116 69.60  71-12 Bailrullah 116¾ KeenResponse1161¾CrooningWater1161¾   Stopped 11
20Jun85- 4Bel fst 6½f :23  :47⅘ 1:19⅘    ⒻClm 22500  7 8 64¾ 43½ 43½ 68¼    Santagata N   b 114 43.20  69-24 Femininity 1184 Singing Praise116nkHawaiiDrone1163¼   Weakened 13
12Jun85- 1Bel fst 1⅛  :47⅖ 1:12⅖ 1:45    ⒻClm 25000  5 3 63 612 621 628¼    Guerra W A    b 116 8.70   48-17 Cousin Belle 11614½ Seconds Ago 1162 Bet The Rent 1161¼   Tired 8
23May85- 5Bel fm 1 Ⓣ:47 1:13  1:41⅕     ⒻClm 35000  12 6 54½ 53 55 510¼    Guerra W A    b 116 8.30   48-31 Jilladella 116nk Visible Marie 1163¼ Rebel Love 1162   No factor 12
13Apr85- 4Aqu fst 6f  :22⅘ :46  1:12     ⒻClm 45000  7 6 74½ 68½ 611 710¾   Vasquez J     b 112 17.60  70-21 Regal Lynco 111hd Proximal 1162 Baby Chris 1121¾   No factor 8
8Apr85- 3Aqu fst 6f   :22⅘ :46  1:11⅗    ⒻClm c-35000 1 5 54 77½ 713 515    Vasquez J     b 116 3.70   68-24 Proximal 1166¼ Sweet Renee 112½ Jetting Lass 1165   Outrun 7
6Dec84- 5Aqu sly 6f ⊡:22  :45⅘ 1:11⅘     ⒻClm 60000  7 4 41½ 62¾ 64½ 55¾    Ward W A5     b 107 *1.20e 79-12 Nell Diamond 116½ Carnegie Hill 1052¼ Singing Praise112nk   Wide 8
21Nov84- 6Med fst 1   :48⅕ 1:14⅗ 1:43⅗   ⒻAlw 13000  6 1 1½ 45 45½ 37¼     Ward W A5     b 109 *1.50  55-28 Mama Caba 1146¼ Doubiruby 1141 Bonnie's Poker 1092   Steadied 6
LATEST WORKOUTS   Oct 26 Bel tr.t 4f fst :51⅘ b   Oct 7 Bel tr.t 4f fst :50⅗ b
```

Tams Deb

```
Tams Deb                     Dk. b. or br. f. 3, by Mullineaux—Optimistic Deb, by Up Spirits Lifetime    1985 7 0 1 1    $4,440
                     $14,000 Br.—Shaw & Tamily (NY)                                 115   14 1 1 1     1984 7 1 0 0    $14,670
Own.—Tamily Margaret         Tr.—Cruguet Denise                                           $19,110
3May85- 9Aqu fst 1    :47⅗ 1:13⅗ 1:40  3+ⒻⓈAlw 28500  5 1 2hd 64½ 820 923¾   Gomez E R     b 110 14.50  42-26 Wild Tune 1212½ Madeline Sweetie 1212 Right Girl 1113¼   Tired 10
25Apr85- 1Aqu fst 7f  :22⅘ :46⅗ 1:27⅖ 3+ⒻClm 15500  9 3 1½ 11 2hd 21¼     Cruguet J     b 112 7.20   63-25 Rebel Love 1161¼ Tams Deb 112hd Angela's Song 1061¾   Gamely 11
12Apr85- 4Aqu fst 6f  :22⅗ :46⅗ 1:11⅘ 3+ⒻⓈAlw 25500  1 10 129¼ 1414 1319 1216¾ Santagata N  b 111 12.80f 65-22 DHCrmllSwts1135¾DHPilinor'sPrd1135¾BocBrd1211¼   Lacked room 14
28Mar85- 2Aqu fst 1   :46⅘ 1:11⅘ 1:39⅘   ⒻClm 14000  3 6 53½ 42½ 58½ 510¾   Espinosa R E7   109 6.70   58-25 FncyMissNncy1074¾SpringLnding1134PrinciplAsst1141¾   No factor 9
18Mar85- 7Aqu fst 7f  :23⅗ :48  1:27⅘   ⒻⓈAlw 25500  13 2 64¾ 55 1120 1225¼ Thibeau R J     116 30.60f 39-38 Asleep In Church 1168 Red Hot Penny1091½AddaGirl116nk   Outrun 13
4Mar85- 1Aqu fst 6f ⊡:23⅗ :47⅘ 1:14⅖    ⒻClm 20000  10 3 — 21 32 34¾      Privitera R5    111 12.80  67-22 Flight N Fantasy 116nk Away You Go 1164½ Tams Deb 1113   Snow 11
24Feb85- 5Aqu fst 1⅟₁₆ ⊡:49⅗ 1:15⅕ 1:48⅘ ⒻⓈAlw 27000  8 1 21 98½ 919 924¾  Vergara O       116 35.30  41-28 Casa Key 116¾ Asleep In Church 1215 Adda Girl 1165   Stopped 9
21Dec84- 5Aqu fst 170 ⊡:48⅖ 1:14⅘ 1:45⅖ ⒻⓈAlw 27000  8 10 1013 1015 1031 1032¼ Moore D N5  b 111 44.30  41-22 Tryjen 1165½ Lady Abingdon 1161¾ Luke's Girl 1164¾   Outrun 10
19Nov84- 9Aqu fst 7f  :23⅖ :47⅘ 1:26⅗   ⒻⓈAlw 25500  11 1 52½ 85½ 1122 1128¼ Cruguet J    b 116 21.40  39-33 Easy Step 1162¾TallGlassO'Water1213¾CarbonRun1163¼   Fell back 11
31Oct84- 8Aqu fst 1   :46⅘ 1:12⅕ 1:39⅕   ⒻⓈEast View 6 1 2½ 620 618 827¾   Cruguet J     b 117 16.70  42-19 Queen Alexandra 1196 Jeremiah Bullfrog 1191 Tryjen 117nk   Tired 8
LATEST WORKOUTS   Nov 7 Bel 3f gd :37⅕ bg   ●Oct 17 Sar Ⓣ 5f yl 1:05 b (d)   Oct 13 Sar tr.t 4f gd :49⅖ b   Oct 9 Sar tr.t 3f fst :39⅖ b
```

Fleeting Love

```
Fleeting Love                B. f. 3, by Son Ange—Love You Angel, by Gallant Romeo          Lifetime     1985 7 1 0 1    $9,300
                     $12,000 Br.—Gaver & Snowden (Ky)                               1065  7 1 0 1      1984 0 M 0 0
Own.—Gold Mill Farm          Tr.—Jerkens Steven T                                         $9,300
23Oct85- 2Aqu fst 7f  :22⅘ :46⅖ 1:24⅗ 3+ⒻClm 12000  2 10 118½ 108½ 67 57¼   Vasquez M M5    105 26.50  71-17 Mucchinette 1171 Buckfinder's Joy 109½ Our Trisha 1173¾   Outrun 12
13Oct85- 2Bel fst 6f  :23⅗ :47⅗ 1:12⅗ 3+ⒻClm 13000  7 2 52½ 64 74½ 44½     Marquez C H Jr5 107 6.50   74-19 Rebel Love 1142 Goodwill Mission 1122¼ Croatia 110no   Wide 8
23Sep85- 6Med fst 6f  :22⅘ :46⅖ 1:12⅕    ⒻClm 20000  5 6 911 99½ 88½ 89½    Marquez C H Jr5 109 17.30  71-26 Bubbly Water 1181 Nunny Jo 1153½ Moody Monday 1153½   Outrun 9
1Sep85- 2Bel fst 6f   :22⅗ :46⅕ 1:12⅕ 3+ⒻMd 30000   8 2 32 23 2hd 12½     Marquez C H Jr5 109 46.30  81-16 Fleeting Love 1092½ Clever Kitty 1131 LadyJessica118   Drew clear 13
28Jly85- 1Mth fst 1   :47⅘ 1:13⅘ 1:40⅖ 3+ⒻMd 20000   7 5 64½ 74½ 64½ 68½   Perret C        115 2.10   62-16 C'est Si Chic 115¾ Wild Anticipation 1151½Virturella1152½   Outrun 7
9Jly85- 9Bel fst 6f   :23⅕ :47⅕ 1:12⅕ 3+ⒻMd 30000   4 9 55 43 47½ 411½    Wynter N A7     105 *2.30  69-16 Rocco's Girl 1117 Excuse My Dust1121½It'sMaria1123   In close st 10
19Jun85- 2Bel fst 6f  :22⅘ :47⅕ 1:14⅖ 3+ⒻMd 30000   7 3 35 37 35 31½      Wynter N A7     103 38.80  68-28 What Knott 110¾ Plugged In 110¾ Fleeting Love 1033¾   Even try 13
LATEST WORKOUTS   Nov 7 Bel 3f gd :37⅕ b   Oct 11 Bel 3f fst :39 b   Sep 19 Bel tr.t 5f fst 1:03⅘ b   Sep 14 Bel tr.t 4f fst :54 b
```

Blue Bride

```
Blue Bride                   Dk. b. or br. f. 4, by Fairway Pleasure—Bridget, by Devil Diver Lifetime    1985 16 1 3 1   $30,635
                     $12,000 Br.—Johnson J E III (NY)                               113   22 1 5 2     1984 6 M 2 1    $13,180
Own.—Kenworthy Janet W       Tr.—Kenworthy J J                                            $43,815      Turf 1 0 0 0
28Sep85- 2Bel fst 7f  :23⅕ :46⅘ 1:24⅗ 3+ⒻClm 15500  2 5 42½ 65½ 1015 1018   MacBeth D     b 113 15.60  61-18 Video Queen 110hd Our Trisha 1173 Mojennique 108no   Fin. early 10
4Sep85- 1Bel fst 6f   :23⅕ :47⅕ 1:12⅕ 3+ⒻClm 14000  9 8 21 1hd 2½ 44      MacBeth D     b 117 9.70   77-21 Last Girl 1101¼ Our Trisha 1171 Croatia 1101¾   Tired 9
16Aug85- 2Mth fst 6f  :23⅕ :47  1:12⅕ 3+ⒻClm 12500  4 6 63¾ 73½ 75¼ 35     Morgan M R    b 116 21.20  74-17 Donut Flash 1164 Languorous Beau 1161 Blue Bride 116nd   Rallied 8
27Jly85- 9Bel fst 6f  :22⅘ :46  1:11⅘ 3+ⒻClm 12000  1 1 32 52½ 52½ 76¾     Skinner K       115 5.90   78-10 Last Girl 1103 Pleasant Bid 113½ For Naught 1151   Tired 8
21Jly85- 1Bel fst 7f  :23  :46⅗ 1:25⅗ 3+ⒻClm 15500  1 6 21 1hd 2½ 42¾     MacBeth D     b 113 9.00   71-16 Lady Nizon 1101¼ Goodwill Mission1101¼LastGirl110nk   Weakened 7
8Jly85- 2Bel fst 6f   :22⅘ :46  1:12  3+ⒻⓈAlw 27500  1 3 78½ 813 89½ 86½   Decarlo C P10 b 107 23.50  75-16 Adda Girl 1111 Femininity 113hd Our Lady Tingle 116½   Outrun 11
22Jun85- 2Bel fst 6f  :22⅘ :47  1:13⅘    ⒻClm 12000  4 1 1½ 1hd 1hd 2nk     MacBeth D     b 113 18.00f 73-23 Fighting Spirit 110nk Blue Bride 113nk SunSounds117nk   Sharp try 13
6Jun85- 4Bel sly 7f   :22⅕ :45⅘ 1:24⅘ 3+ⒻⓈAlw 27500  7 8 1215 1111 911 1018¾ Graell A       117 14.00f 59-17 Video Talc 1116½ Stoke The Fire112hdHatInTheRing1131¼   Outrun 14
25May85- 2Bel fm 1 Ⓣ:46⅗ 1:12⅕ 1:39⅘ 3+ⒻⓈAlw 29000 8 7 1014 1019 1126 1125½ Skinner K     121 28.40  43-24 Skip And Run 1052¾ Got The Edge 1105½Cath'sTurn121nc   Outrun 11
12Apr85- 4Aqu fst 6f  :22⅗ :46⅗ 1:11⅘ 3+ⒻⓈAlw 25500  8 8 1412 1313 1114 1013¼ Skinner K     121 56.50  69-22 DHCrmllSwts1135¾DHPilinor'sPrd1135¾BocBrd1211¼   Raced wide 14
LATEST WORKOUTS   ●Nov 7 Bel 3f gd :36 h   Oct 24 Bel 4f fst :52 b   Sep 26 Bel 4f fst :52 b   Sep 21 Bel 3f fst :35⅘ h
```

ate predecessors with the filly, Juan Cultino and Paulino Ortiz, were cut from the same mold as Aquilano, and most players would not know whether the move to Aquilano's barn was for better or worse.

ANSELMA

After that sharp move on October 11, Anselma was dropped to rock-bottom (by New York standards) $14,000 claiming on November 4 and staged a repeat performance. Once again, she made a bold wide move on the turn, this time carrying her speed to the eighth pole before hanging—a promising performance by a relatively fresh horse, suggesting that improvement in form was imminent. However, since her October 11 race had raised the same possibilities, the subsequent drop down to $14,000 is hard to explain. The original drop to $35,000 off the layoff, and the subsequent one to $22,500, both seem reasonable when put in perspective. Anselma's past performances show that she has been racing in "nonwinners of one/two" allowance events restricted to older (four and up) fillies and mares during the winter months of early 1985, races usually filled with the preceding season's claimers moving up to fill a vacuum created by the logistics of winter racing in New York. Indeed, as a three-year-old, Anselma won four of twenty races, competing at the $35,000-$50,000 level during the latter half of the year.

Although her overall performance since returning warrants today's drop, the promise hinted at by those performances does not. Today's race looks like a serious try, though. The trainer has entered her for $12,000 in a race with a top claiming price of $14,000 and has acquired the services of a seven-pound apprentice rider. Both moves are designed to reduce weight, which is often a sign of trainer intent, if nothing else. That, plus the fact that Anselma is coming back within five days of her most recent race, suggests quite emphatically that she is well-meant and deserves serious consideration in this field.

SO LITTLE TIME

This former New England allowance runner was recently purchased by a New York outfit, for whom she raced at the Meadowlands. That she raced poorly in New Jersey came as no surprise. Her last good race at Suffolk Downs was on May 12, and the class drop from Suffolk allowances to $16,000 claiming at the Meadowlands was more apparent than real.

SHIMALEKA

Like Anselma, a winter allowance filly now dropping down to bargain-basement claiming, the difference being that Shimaleka is making the drop in one precipitous leap following a layoff, while Anselma took three races to hit bottom. Note that Anselma finished ahead of Shimaleka on two occasions in March. Based on her history, Shimaleka is a reliable early-speed type, assuring an honest pace. But even that must be questioned, considering the layoff and sharp class drop.

PAIR OF QUEENS

This horse is winless in eleven starts—all at this level—during 1985. Although she is making her second start after a layoff, there was nothing encouraging about her return.

OUR MUTUAL QUEEN

The weaker half of the favored entry, this horse's only decent effort of late came at the Meadowlands. If that performance revealed anything about relative class at the two tracks, then her stablemate's failure in New Jersey is all the more suspicious.

RIALTO RIPPLE

A winner only twice in forty-six career starts, Rialto Ripple was out of the money at this level in her last three starts.

CROATIA

Second or third in her last five starts, all coming at today's level, and a winner only once in nineteen starts during 1985, this filly clearly has bridesmaid tendencies. Of the four fillies to finish ahead of Anselma in that November 4 race, the only one back in this field, and a prime candidate to become the victim of a form reversal.

BONNIE'S POKER

Away since July 24, this filly has been dropping down slowly, seeking her proper niche, over a considerable period of time. So far, she has met with little success and drops again today upon her return.

TAM'S DEB

This horse alternates between state-bred allowance company and \$15,000-\$20,000 claiming, with moderate success in the latter. The horse fits well at this level but hasn't raced since May—and wasn't prepped for this race in allowance company.

FLEETING LOVE

This horse hasn't shown much since breaking her maiden for \$30,000, including two dull races in October at today's level.

BLUE BRIDE

Back at her proper level after a brief freshening, Blue Bride's early speed will be compromised by the outside (13) post position. Only one for twenty-two lifetime, hard to take.

As often happens in the lower claiming ranks, most of the entrants in this race either have no recent form to speak of or are dropping suspiciously. Even the "stable" members of this field, Last Girl and Croatia, have their faults. The first-named is the favorite—always hard to take at this level—and seems beatable if any of the dropdowns prove to be worth more than $14,000. The latter, although consistent of late, simply doesn't want to win.

The first prerequisite for a bet in a field of this type is a good price. The second, a reason for wanting to bet on a particular horse, some positive signs hinting of fitness and stable intent. Anselma fit the bill here, if one wished to believe the signs in her recent record and conclude that her downward spiral was about to come to an end, and possibly even reverse itself. As we mentioned at the beginning of this chapter, that is exactly what did happen.

SECOND RACE
Aqueduct
NOVEMBER 9, 1985

6 FURLONGS. (1.08⅕) CLAIMING. Purse $12,000. Fillies and Mares, 3-year-olds and upward. Weights, 3-year-olds 120 lbs. Older 122 lbs. Non-winners of two races since October 15 allowed 3 lbs. Of a race since then 5 lbs. Claiming price $14,000; for each $1,000 to $12,000 2 lbs. (Races when entered to be claimed for $10,000 or less not considered.)
Value of race $12,000; value to winner $7,200; second $2,640; third $1,440; fourth $720. Mutuel pool $104,834, OTB pool $82,562. Quinella Pool $161,550. OTB Quinella Pool $132,648.

Last Raced	Horse	Eqt.	A.	Wt	PP	St	¼	½	Str	Fin	Jockey	Cl'g Pr	Odds $1
4Nov85 ^{9}Aqu^{5}	Anselma		4	107	3	9	9^{hd}	8^{hd}	$3^{\frac{1}{2}}$	$1^{1\frac{3}{4}}$	Decarlo C P^{7}	12000	8.80
23Oct85 ^{2}Aqu^{10}	Pair Of Queens	b	4	113	6	3	$8^{1\frac{1}{2}}$	$7^{\frac{1}{2}}$	$4^{1\frac{1}{2}}$	2no	Thibeau R J	12000	b-14.30
24Jly85 ^{3}Bel^{6}	Bonnie's Poker	b	3	115	10	12	6^{1}	4^{1}	$2^{1\frac{1}{2}}$	3^{hd}	Santagata N	14000	22.20
4Nov85 ^{9}Aqu^{2}	Croatia		4	112	9	2	$3^{\frac{1}{2}}$	2^{1}	1^{hd}	$4^{\frac{3}{4}}$	Rini W^{5}	14000	3.80
23Oct85 ^{2}Aqu^{7}	Our Mutual Friend	b	5	108	7	8	10^{2}	9^{3}	6^{2}	$5^{1\frac{1}{2}}$	Vasquez M M^{5}	12000	a-2.00
2Nov85 ^{3}Med^{7}	Last Girl		5	110	2	7	7^{hd}	6^{2}	$5^{\frac{1}{2}}$	$6^{4\frac{3}{4}}$	Rolon E M^{7}	14000	a-2.00
3Oct85 ^{3}Med^{5}	So Little Time	b	4	117	4	6	1^{1}	$1^{\frac{1}{2}}$	7^{2}	7^{2}	Migliore R†	14000	12.30
28Sep85 ^{2}Bel^{10}	Blue Bride	b	4	113	13	1	$5^{\frac{1}{2}}$	10^{2}	9^{2}	$8^{\frac{3}{4}}$	Deegan J C	12000	34.80
12Sep85 ^{4}Bel^{1}	Loyal Diplomat		6	117	1	4	$4^{\frac{1}{2}}$	3^{hd}	$8^{1\frac{1}{2}}$	$9^{\frac{3}{4}}$	MacBeth D	14000	8.30
23Oct85 ^{2}Aqu^{5}	Fleeting Love		3	107	12	11	13	11^{4}	$10^{1\frac{1}{2}}$	$10^{1\frac{3}{4}}$	Marquez C H Jr^{5}	12000	20.20
6Jun85 ^{7}Bel^{7}	Shimaleka	b	4	117	5	10	$11^{\frac{1}{2}}$	12^{2}	12^{6}	11^{nk}	Murphy D J	14000	5.00
13Oct85 ^{2}Bel^{6}	Rialto Ripple	b	4	110	8	5	$2^{\frac{1}{2}}$	$5^{\frac{1}{2}}$	$11^{1\frac{1}{2}}$	12^{9}	Jones B S^{5}	13000	b-14.30
2May85 ^{9}Aqu^{9}	Tams Deb		3	115	11	13	12^{hd}	13	13	13	Cruguet J	14000	24.10

a-Coupled: Our Mutual Friend and Last Girl; b-Pair Of Queens and Rialto Ripple.
OFF AT 12:57. Start good, Won driving. Time, :22⅖, :46⅕, 1:11⅗ Track fast.

$2 Mutuel Prices:				
	4-(C)-ANSELMA	19.60	10.00	6.80
	2-(F)-PAIR OF QUEENS (b-entry)		14.60	7.40
	8-(J)-BONNIE'S POKER			14.20
	$2 QUINELLA 2-4 PAID $140.80.			

Ch. f, by Auberge—Lady Warfare, by Warfare. Trainer Sedlacek Sue. Bred by Gray E & H (Va).

ANSELMA, blocked midway of the turn, came out after getting through between horses entering the stretch and finished strongly to prove clearly best. PAIR OF QUEENS finished with good courage between horses to gain the place. BONNIE'S POKER loomed boldly from the outside leaving the turn but weakened slightly in a long drive. CROATIA made a bid between horses leaving the turn but wasn't good enough in a stiff drive. OUR MUTUAL FRIEND, wide into the stretch, rallied mildly. LAST GIRL made a run along the inside entering the stretch but hung. SO LITTLE TIME was used up making the pace. BLUE RIDGE showed brief speed. LOYAL DIPLOMAT a factor to the stretch, gave way. SHIMALEKA was always outrun. RIALTO RIPPLE tired badly.

Chapter 29

The Muscle-Sore Rebound

FEW OF MY HANDICAPPING acquaintances own crystal balls. Those who do use them infrequently. Thoroughbred racing is so complex that even trainers find it difficult to look beyond their horse's next race. There is simply too much that can happen to cloud the view.

Handicappers, however, often fall into the trap of tabbing a horse they've just seen race as a probable winner next time out. They do so without knowing how well the horse came out of that race, where or when the trainer will next race the animal, the nature of its opposition, and the track conditions or biases it may face for that race. In spite of all this, experienced players can do quite well gazing into their crystal balls, provided they are wise in their selection of "future plays" and are able to back off when the situation demands.

When Proud Truth edged Stephan's Odyssey in the 1985 Fountain of Youth Stakes at Gulfstream Park, my crystal ball lit up and revealed a chain of events encompassing the Florida Derby and the Flamingo Stakes. It told me in no uncertain terms that Proud Truth would beat Stephan's Odyssey a more substantial margin in the upcoming Florida Derby, then lose to his rival in the Flamingo at Hialeah four weeks later. In both instances, the crystal ball was picking the underdog and reasoning counter to the tenets of conventional handicapping wisdom. Both selections were based on the same premise, one that will repeatedly give the player at least two chances to zig while others zag, to borrow a phrase made popular by Gordon Jones. This is exactly what the winning player needs—a chance to bet logically against popular opinion, at good odds. It also provides at least one sound basis for predicting a horse's behavior over its next two or three races with some reasonable chance of being correct, at least often enough to make the effort worthwhile.

Proud Truth and Stephan's Odyssey met for the first time in the Fountain of Youth on February 18, 1985. I preferred Proud Truth for two reasons: his solid victory in a prep race two weeks earlier and a ten-pound pull in the weights. Stephan's Odyssey, on the other hand, was making his first start in two months. If Proud Truth was the horse I thought he was (or would soon become), I had little doubt he would find the winner's circle that day, especially with the cards seemingly stacked in his favor.

In the Fountain of Youth, the two colts rallied extremely wide around the turn, then battled as a team to the wire, with Proud Truth, inside his rival all the way, gaining the decision. After the race, I changed my opinion, concluding quite logically that Stephan's Odyssey was at least the equal of Proud Truth and would be favored over his rival when competing at level weights in the Florida Derby. I was also aware that Stephan's Odyssey might not perform at peak level in the Florida Derby because of something called "muscle soreness." Like human athletes, the Thoroughbred race horse can "tighten up" after its first hard exercise of the year (or after a layoff) and suffer from sore muscles for two or three weeks thereafter. If asked to race during that period, the horse's performance may leave something to be desired. The probability that Stephan's Odyssey might be prone to such a malady was higher than normal, in fact, there being a possible precedent in his record. Muscle soreness might have been the explanation for his only loss as a two-year-old. This, of course, would increase the likelihood of a repeat performance in the Florida Derby. His workout activity preceding that race was suspiciously light for a promising young colt preparing for the classics, lending further credence to our muscle soreness theory.

Stephan's Odyssey   **Dk. b. or br. c. 3, by Danzig—Kennelot, by Gallant Man**   Lifetime 5 3 1 0 $677,360   1985 1 0 1 0 $26,260
Own.—DeKwiatkowski H   **Br.—Kennelot Stables Ltd (Ky)**   **122**   1984 4 3 0 0 $651,100
Tr.—Stephens Woodford C

18Feb85-10GP	fst	1 1/16	:46 3/5	1:11 1/5	1:43 3/5	Ftn Youth	11	11	11^{12}	$9^{6\frac{1}{4}}$	$5^{\frac{1}{2}}$	2^{nk}	Maple E	122	2.70	83-22	ProudTruth112^{nk}Stphn'sOdyssy122^{4}DoItAginDn$112^{4\frac{1}{2}}$	Just missed 14
18Feb85-Grade II																		
16Dec84- 8Hol	gd	1 1/16	:45 3/5	1:10 3/5	1:43 2/5	Hol Futy	8	12	10^{9}	$4^{2\frac{1}{4}}$	$1^{1\frac{1}{2}}$	1^{1}	Maple E	121	11.20	— —	Stephan's Odyssey 121^{1} FirstNorman$121^{1\frac{1}{4}}$RightCon121^{hd}	Driving 13
16Dec84-Grade I																		
2Dec84- 3Hol	fst	6f	:22	:45 2/5	1:09 3/5	Alw 22000	1	6	$6^{5\frac{1}{2}}$	$3^{1\frac{1}{2}}$	2^{hd}	1no	Pincay L Jr	118	3.90	101-05	Stephn'sOdyssey118^{no}ImgeofGretness118^{5}ProBowlr$118^{3\frac{1}{2}}$	Driving 6
28Oct84- 6Aqu	gd	7f	:22 1/5	:45	1:22 3/5	Alw 20000	3	6	$5^{3\frac{3}{4}}$	$3^{1\frac{1}{2}}$	3^{2}	$4^{3\frac{1}{2}}$	McCarron G	122	*1.90	84-14	Another Reef $117^{\frac{1}{2}}$ Secretary General $117^{2\frac{3}{4}}$SkipTrial117^{nk}	Drifted 7
21Oct84- 6Bel	fst	6f	:22 4/5	:46 2/5	1:12	Md Sp Wt	4	7	4^{3}	$3^{2\frac{1}{2}}$	$2^{\frac{1}{2}}$	$1^{1\frac{1}{4}}$	Day P	118	*.70	82-21	Stphn'sOdyssy$118^{1\frac{1}{4}}$RllngMnstrl$118^{5\frac{3}{4}}$DmscsSm118^{2}	Bumped,clear 11

LATEST WORKOUTS   **Feb 27 Hia 5f fst 1:00 4/5 h**   **Feb 16 Hia 4f fst :49 b**   **●Feb 12 Hia 1 fst 1:40 2/5 b**   **●Feb 7 Hia 6f fst 1:11 h**

The Florida Derby ran pretty much to my expectations, with Proud Truth the winner at 2-1 and Stephan's Odyssey a dull sixth at even money. After the race, and prior to the Flamingo on March 30, one heard several excuses offered to explain Stephan's Odyssey's subpar performance in the Florida Derby. To quote from Joe Hirsch's column in the March 5 *Racing Form*:

> Stephan's Odyssey, the 11–10 favorite for the Florida Derby, finished sixth and was obviously not at his best. Breaking from post 1, he was closer to the pace than usual, but on the other hand it was a leisurely pace—the first six furlongs in 1:11.2—and it couldn't have taken much out of him.
>
> "He had a touch of ringworm after the Fountain of Youth," trainer Woody Stephens said Monday. "That could have taken a little of the edge off. In addition, we've had some coughing at the barn and while his temperature was normal, he was souring slightly when he shipped to Gulfstream Saturday. He seemed composed in the paddock, though he did break out just a bit. It was a warm day, and that could have accounted for it, but when you put everything together, he simply didn't run his race and we've got to give him another chance."

Another reporter mentioned a skin rash that was bothering the horse at that time. Still another reported that the horse came out of the Florida Derby "leg weary," which if true, would support our theory.

With the average maiden, allowance, or claiming horse, we seldom find anything in the press to help us fill the gaps between its past performance lines and can only guess at possible explanations for poor performances. Muscle soreness offers one scenario upon which such guesses may be based. With stakes horses, however, we are often forced to sort out conflicting reports, many of which are no doubt fabricated by stable connections to help protect the horse's reputation. This is especially true with highly promising colts, which may have a potentially lucrative stud career ahead of them, and a reputation that must be protected by any means.

One thing was certain after the Florida Derby, however. Proud Truth had not improved very much, if at all. He defeated Irish Sur, a "Calder horse," by a very small margin. The third-place horse, Do It Again Dan, an overraced, unspectacular sort with bridesmaid tendencies, was only a length behind. Had Stephan's Odyssey run his best race, he would probably have won the Florida Derby.

As we mentioned at the beginning of this chapter, it is difficult to project too many races into a horse's future. By Flamingo time four weeks later, juvenile champion Chief's Crown had entered the pic-

11 HIALEAH

1⅛ MILES
HIALEAH
START · FINISH

1 ⅛ MILES. (1.46⅖) 56th Running FLAMINGO STAKES (Grade I). Purse $265,000 Guaranteed. 3-year-olds by subscription of $500 each if made on or before Saturday, February 2, 1985, or by supplementary nomination of starters to pay $2,000 additional with $265,000 guaranteed. The added money and all fees to be divided 60% to the winner, 20% to second, 11% to third, 6% to fourth and 3% to fifth. Weights, colts and geldings, 122 lbs. Fillies 117 lbs. Non-winners of a Sweepstakes allowed 4 lbs. Starters to be named through the entry box by the usual time of closing. Flamingo Cup to winning owner. Replica to the trainer. Nominations closed Saturday, February 2, 1985 with 94 nominations Supplementary nominations of $12,500 each may be make at closing time of entries. Closed with 94 nominations, 1 supplementary nomination: Important Business.

Mr. Happy
Ch. c. 3, by Little Current—Maiden Bell, by Nashua
Br.—Red Oak Farm (Fla)
Own.—Red Tree Farm
Tr.—Anderson Pete
118
Lifetime 8 3 0 1 $33,758 | 1985 3 2 0 1 $28,058 | 1984 5 1 0 0 $5,700 | Turf 3 2 0 1 $28,058

5Mar85- 8GP fm *1⅛ ⓣ 1:44⅘ Alw 19000 7 5 510 34½ 12 14 Bailey J D 122 3.60 84-17 Mr Happy 1224 ⓑCrovero 1191 Hector J 119¾ Driving 10
11Feb85- 8GP fm 1 ⓣ:48⅕ 1:11⅗ 1:35⅕ Gldn Grass 2 6 84¾ 45 33 33¾ Bailey J D 113 15.10 98-07 ⓑFoundtionPln119nk CovertOpertion1193¼Mr.Hppy1133 Mild gain 13
11Feb85-Run in divisions
11Jan85- 8GP fm *1 ⓣ 1:39⅘ Alw 17200 7 7 73¾ 61½ 41 1hd Guerra W A 117 23.80 81-16 Mr. Happy 117hd Hector J. 122nk Verification119¾ In tight, driving 10
22Dec84- 9Crc fst 170 :49⅕ 1:14 1:44⅘ Wht A Plesre 2 7 99¾ 913 911 610¾ Gonzalez M A 112 110.00 75-18 Covert Operation 112½EmergencyCall1171IrishSur1153½ No threat 9
22Dec84-Run in Divisions
1Dec84- 5Crc fst 1 1/16 :50⅘ 1:16 1:48⅘ Alw 13700 3 5 64 64½ 65½ 48½ Hernandez C 112 14.50 69-23 CovertOpertion1161½DremABit112hdMillionDollrBo··1144¾ Outrun 6
8Nov84- 4Lrl fst 1 :46⅘ 1:13 1:39⅘ Md Sp Wt 7 6 77½ 76¾ 63½ 1no Baltazar C 118 27.20 74-23 Mr. Happy 118no Platinum Fox 118¾ Sir Concorde 116 Driving 8
13Oct84- 9Lrl fst 6f :22⅘ :46⅘ 1:11⅘ Md Sp Wt 7 10 1118 1013 1014 1014 Passmore W J 118 9.20 70-14 Dandy Danny 1183 Medieval Love 1181½ T. Farnon 1182½ Outrun 12
20Jun84- 6Mth fst 5f :22⅘ :46⅕ :58⅘ Md Sp Wt 9 8 1111 1212 813 68½ Gonzalez M A 118 23.90 83-15 SilverDrling1183SovereignSong1181WhoTughtWho1184 No factor 12
LATEST WORKOUTS Mar 17 Hia 4f fst :50⅘ b Mar 2 Hia 4f fst :48⅘ b Feb 24 Hia 3f fst :37⅕ b Feb 7 Hia 4f fst :48⅘ h

Important Business
B. c. 3, by Codex—Suite Of Dreams, by Tentam
Br.—Tartan Farms (Fla)
Own.—Custom Taylored Stable
Tr.—Jolley Leroy Jr
118
Lifetime 6 2 0 2 $18,835 | 1985 2 1 0 0 $7,950 | 1984 4 1 0 2 $10,885

22Mar85- 8Hia sly 1⅛ :47⅕ 1:11⅗ 1:49 Alw 13000 6 2 22½ 21½ 12 16 Vasquez J 114 19.60 87-16 ImportntBusiness1146ClipprClss120noClockTowr1142½ Ridden out 9
20Feb85- 7GP fst 6f :22⅘ :45⅘ 1:10⅘ Alw 15000 4 9 87½ 56½ 79¾ 68¾ Guerra W A 117 22.70 77-23 First Guess 1227½ Leakey 119nk Night Detective 117½ No factor 9
24Dec84-10Crc fst 170 :48⅘ 1:14⅕ 1:46⅘ Clm 35000 8 9 88¾ 98½ 913 813½ St Leon G 114 *3.30 65-20 Iron Fire 1171¾ For Real's First 1181½ Raging Fever 1142 Outrun 11
29Nov84- 7Crc fst 170 :50⅕ 1:15⅘ 1:46 Clm 40000 1 5 63 64 58 38½ St Leon G 114 *1.30 71-21 RcordTrnot1204TomTomWrror1134½ImprtntBsnss1141½ Steadied 7
5Nov84- 5Crc fst 7f :23⅘ :47⅘ 1:26⅕ Clm 40000 1 6 65 67½ 55½ 33½ St Leon G 116 4.40 81-18 HonestCut1161½TomTomWrrior1132ImportntBusinss1161½ Rallied 6
18Oct84- 6Crc fst 6½f :22⅘ :46⅘ 1:20⅘ Md 35000 7 9 97½ 76½ 52½ 1½ St Leon G 118 2.40 82-19 ImportntBusiness118½PureRdnce1141½SpecilCompny114½ Driving 9
LATEST WORKOUTS Mar 29 Hia 3f fst :38⅘ b Mar 20 Hia 4f fst :48⅘ b Mar 11 Hia 7f fst 1:28⅘ b Mar 4 Hia 1 fst 1:41⅘ h

Alfred
B. c. 3, by Our Liberty—Locanto Bolina, by Southern Brook
Br.—Abel R L (Fla)
Own.—Bosso Jr & Hinson
Tr.—Hinson Al W
118
Lifetime 8 3 1 0 $39,653 | 1985 2 0 0 0 | 1984 6 3 1 0 $39,653 | Turf 1 0 1 0 $9,190

16Mar85-10Hia fst 1⅛ :48⅘ 1:12 1:47⅘ Everglades 7 2 32 42¾ 610 617 Molina V H b 112 33.30 76-13 Rhoman Rule 1128 Creme Fraiche 1176 Irish Sur 119hd Tired 8
16Mar85-Grade II
2Mar85-10GP fst 7f :22⅘ :45⅕ 1:22⅘ Swale 1 8 61½ 75 912 912¾ Molina V H b 115 21.40 79-15 Chief'sCrown1223½CremeFriche1173½CherokeeFst113nk Fell back 9
10Nov84- 8Crc fm 1 1/16 ⓣ:48 1:12⅕ 1:43⅕ City Miami 1 10 107¾ 43½ 23 24½ Molina V H b 114 3.00 84-09 FoundtionPln1144½Alfred114¾CovertOpertion1121¾ Couldn't gain 10
27Oct84- 8Aqu my 1⅛ :48⅕ 1:12⅕ 1:49⅕ Champagne 3 6 64 65½ 611 612½ Molina V H b 122 8.90 77-16 ForCertinDoc122noMightyAppeling1224Tnk'sProspct122nk Outrun 6
27Oct84-Grade I
10Oct84- 9Crc fst 170 :48⅕ 1:13⅘ 1:45⅘ Alw 20800 4 5 53½ 1hd 13 113½ Molina V H b 112 *1.50 81-23 Alfred 11213½ Mr. Introienne 1121 Hopalong Justice11211 Handily 5
12Sep84- 9Crc fst 7f :22⅘ :46⅘ 1:25⅘ Foolish Plsr 3 5 31½ 31½ 44 48½ Smith A Jr 116 4.40 83-20 EmergencyCll1184½Bobbin'sKey116nkMr.Introinn1161½ Weakened 7
15Aug84- 2Crc fst 6f :22⅘ :46⅕ 1:13⅘ Alw 13400 9 3 85½ 71½ 3½ 11½ Smith A Jr 116 7.10 82-22 Alfred 1161½PlatinumProspect114nkHickoryHillFlyer1181½ Driving 9
8Aug84- 4Crc fst 6f :22⅘ :47⅘ 1:15⅕ Md 25000 6 11 610 66 2½ 12½ Wagers P 116 16.70 75-23 Alfred 1162½ Cherokee D'Or 1164 Prince Case 1161½ Drew clear 11
LATEST WORKOUTS ●Mar 27 Crc 3f fst :36⅘ h (d) Mar 9 Hia 1⅛m fst 1:52⅘ h ●Feb 28 Crc 4f fst :49⅘ b (d) Feb 16 Crc 6f fst 1:16⅘ b

Stephan's Odyssey
Dk. b. or br. c. 3, by Danzig—Kennelot, by Gallant Man
Br.—Kennelot Stables Ltd (Ky)
Own.—DeKwiatkowski H
Tr.—Stephens Woodford C
122
Lifetime 6 3 1 0 $677,360 | 1985 2 0 1 0 $26,260 | 1984 4 3 0 0 $651,100

2Mar85-11GP fst 1⅛ :47⅘ 1:11⅘ 1:50 Fla Derby 1 3 53½ 42 55 64½ Maple E 122 *1.10 78-15 Proud Truth 122nk Irish Sur 1221 Do ItAgainDan1221½ Weakened 11
2Mar85-Grade I
18Feb85-10GP fst 1 1/16 :46⅘ 1:11⅕ 1:43⅘ Ftn Youth 11 11 1112 98½ 5½ 2nk Maple E 122 2.70 83-22 ProudTruth112nkStphn'sOdyssy1224DoItAginDn1124½ Just missed 14
18Feb85-Grade II
16Dec84- 8Hol gd 1 1/16 :45⅘ 1:10⅘ 1:43⅘ Hol Futy 8 12 109 42½ 11½ 11 Maple E 121 11.20 — — Stephan's Odyssey 1211 FirstNorman1211½RightCon121hd Driving 13
16Dec84-Grade I
2Dec84- 3Hol fst 6f :22 :45⅘ 1:09⅘ Alw 22000 1 6 65½ 31½ 2hd 1no Pincay L Jr 118 3.90 101-05 Stephn'sOdyssey118noImgeofGretness1185ProBowlr1183½ Driving 6
28Oct84- 6Aqu gd 7f :22⅕ :45 1:22⅘ Alw 20000 3 6 53¾ 31½ 32 43½ McCarron G 122 *1.90 84-14 Another Reef 117½ Secretary General 1172¾SkipTrial117nk Drifted 7
21Oct84- 6Bel fst 6f :22⅘ :46⅘ 1:12 Md Sp Wt 4 7 43 32½ 2½ 11½ Day P 118 *.70 82-21 Stphn'sOdyssy1181½RllngMnstrl1185¾DmscsSm1182 Bumped,clear 11
LATEST WORKOUTS Mar 29 Hia 3f fst :36⅘ b Mar 25 Hia 6f fst 1:12⅘ h ●Mar 20 Hia 7f fst 1:26 h Mar 16 Hia 6f fst 1:13⅘ h

Chief's Crown
B. c. 3, by Danzig—Six Crowns, by Secretariat
Br.—Rosen C (Ky)
Own.—Star Crown Stable
Tr.—Laurin Roger
122
Lifetime 10 7 2 0 $951,682 | 1985 1 1 0 0 $30,792 | 1984 9 6 2 0 $920,890

2Mar85-10GP fst 7f :22⅘ :45⅕ 1:22⅘ Swale 9 2 2hd 2hd 11 13½ MacBeth D 122 *.30 92-15 Chief'sCrown1223½CremeFriche1173½CherokeFst113nk Ridden out 9
10Nov84- 1Hol fst 1 :45 1:10 1:36⅕ Br Cp Juv 5 6 64¾ 32½ 21 1¾ MacBeth D 122 *.70 — — Chief's Crown 122¾Tank'sProspect122¾SpendABuck1226½ Driving 10
10Nov84-Grade I
27Oct84- 8SA fst 1 1/16 :46⅘ 1:10⅘ 1:42⅘ Norfolk 6 2 2½ 1hd 1hd 11½ MacBeth D 118 *.30 89-13 Chief's Crown 1181½ MatthewT.Parker1189VivaMaxi118hd Driving 6
27Oct84-Grade I
6Oct84- 8Bel fst 1 :45⅘ 1:10⅘ 1:36⅘ Cowdin 4 4 21 12 13 16 MacBeth D 122 *.50 82-17 Chief's Crown 1226BionicLight12212½ScriptOhio1221½ Ridden out 8
6Oct84-Grade I
15Sep84- 5Bel sly 7f :22⅘ :46 1:23⅕ Futurity 5 2 68 64 34 21 MacBeth D 122 *.70 85-18 SpectculrLove1221Chif'sCrown1223½Mugzy'sRullh1222¾ Wide str. 8
15Sep84-Grade I
26Aug84- 8Sar fst 6½f :21⅘ :44⅘ 1:16 Hopeful 3 4 33½ 3½ 1½ 13¾ MacBeth D 122 *1.10 92-15 Chief'sCrown1223¾TiffanyIce1223¾Mugzy'sRullah122½ Ridden out 9
26Aug84-Grade I
3Aug84- 8Sar fst 6f :22⅘ :46 1:10⅕ Sar Spec'l 4 3 33 2hd 1hd 12¾ MacBeth D 117 *2.10 89-19 Chief'sCrown1172¾DoItAginDn117hdSkyCommnd122¾ Ridden out 6
3Aug84-Grade II
5Jly84- 6Bel fst 5½f :22⅘ :45⅘ 1:04⅘ Md Sp Wt 5 1 1hd 2hd 11 15 MacBeth D 118 *1.10 93-15 Chief's Crown 1185 Desert War 1182½TigerBidder1184 Ridden out 9
22Jun84- 4Bel fst 5½f :22⅕ :46⅕ 1:05⅘ Md Sp Wt 1 1 43½ 46½ 34½ 21 MacBeth D 118 5.20 86-21 Secretary General 1181 Chief's Crown1181½TiffanyIce1189 Rallied 10
13Jun84- 4Bel fst 5f :22⅘ :46⅘ :58⅘ Md Sp Wt 8 8 46½ 613 513 411½ Cordero A Jr 118 3.10 81-18 Don'tFoolWithMe1189Attribute118nkMountRlity1183½ Carried out 8
LATEST WORKOUTS ●Mar 25 Hia 6f fst 1:11⅘ h Mar 15 GP 6f fst 1:15 b ●Mar 9 GP 5f fst 1:00 h ●Feb 26 GP 6f fst 1:12 h

Now I Can
B. c. 3, by Fire Dancer—Dama Antiqua, by Cundro
Br.—Kelly Barbara & N H (Fla)
Own.—Kelly Barbara & N H
Tr.—Kelly Nathan H
118
Lifetime 13 2 1 1 $27,890 | 1985 6 1 1 1 $17,340 | 1984 7 1 0 0 $10,550 | Turf 1 0 0 0 $180

16Mar85-10Hia fst 1⅛ :48⅘ 1:12 1:47⅘ Everglades 5 7 68¾ 68½ 58½ 515 Solomone M b 112 98.10 78-13 Rhoman Rule 1128 Creme Fraiche 1176 Irish Sur 119hd No factor 8
16Mar85-Grade II
5Mar85- 8GP fm *1⅛ ⓣ 1:44⅘ Alw 19000 3 9 819 813 912 811 Smith A Jr b 122 23.20 73-17 Mr. Happy 1224 ⓑCrovero 1191 Hector J. 119½ No factor 10
14Feb85- 9GP fst 1 1/16 :47⅕ 1:11⅘ 1:45⅘ Alw 17000 5 5 55¾ 56½ 32½ 32¾ Smith A Jr b 122 6.50 71-23 Lautaro 117nk L'Enrogue 1222½ Now I Can 122nk Rallied 7
30Jan85- 5GP fst 1 1/16 :47 1:11⅘ 1:45⅕ Alw 16000 6 7 610 64¾ 11½ 2hd Londono O J b 117 19.10 75-24 ⓑClock Tower 117hd Now I Can 1173 Block Party 1222 Snarp 11
30Jan85-Placed first through disqualification
15Jan85- 8GP fst 1 1/16 :48⅕ 1:13 1:45⅕ Alw 15000 7 9 97 76¾ 65½ 56 Valdivieso H A b 117 13.20 69-21 L'Enrogue 117¾ Numeric 119nk Travaux 117½ No threat 10
5Jan85- 3Crc fst 6f :22⅘ :46⅘ 1:12⅕ Alw 10000 5 9 76½ 54½ 31½ 21¾ Valdivieso H A b 112 20.80 88-14 Verification 1151¾ Now ICan1122¾LibertyRex1172¾ Best of others 9
26Dec84- 8Crc fst 7f :22⅘ :45⅘ 1:25⅕ Alw 10000 5 10 1111 811 65½ 77½ Valdivieso H A b 114 43.30 83-22 Proud Truth 1193 Bowladrome 1142 Regal Brek 113hd No factor 12
18Dec84- 9Crc fst 6f :22⅘ :45⅘ 1:13⅘ Alw 11800 7 11 1110 106½ 74¾ 42½ Valdivieso H A b 114 94.30 82-22 Platinum Prospect 119hdWaterGate112hdLibertyRex1142 Late bid 12
6Nov84- 8Crc fst 6f :22⅕ :46⅕ 1:12⅘ Alw 15400 10 9 106½ 107½ 610 511½ Valdivieso H A b 116 20.80 77-21 PeaceOfMyHeart116nkTropicalClimate1162DremABit1123¾ Outrun 10
8Oct84- 5Crc fst 170 :50 1:15⅘ 1:47⅘ Alw 13000 2 4 42½ 66¾ 711 716 Solis A 118 8.30 57-23 Lautaro 113hd Covert Operation 116no Satan's Way 1147½ Tired 7
LATEST WORKOUTS ●Mar 24 Crc 3f fst :36⅘ h (d) Mar 21 Crc 4f fst :51 b (d) Mar 3 Crc 3f fst :38⅘ b (d) Feb 21 Crc 3f fst :36⅘ h

Proud Truth — Ch. c. 3, by Graustark—Wake Robin, by Summer Tan — Br.—Galbreath Mrs J W (Ky) — Tr.—Veitch John M — 122 — Lifetime 6 5 0 0 $325,197 — 1985 4 3 0 0 $307,197 — 1984 2 2 0 0 $18,000

Own.—Darby Dan Farm

2Mar85-11GP fst 1⅛ :47⅘ 1:11⅗ 1:50 Fla Derby 7 6 64½ 65½ 33½ 1nk Velasquez J 122 2.00 82-15 ProudTruth122nkIrishSur1221DoItAgainDn1221½ Steadied, driving 11

2Mar85-Grade I

18Feb85-10GP fst 1$\frac{1}{16}$:46⅘ 1:11⅕ 1:43⅘ Ftn Youth 9 10 910 86½ 3nk 1nk Velasquez J 112 *1.90 83-22 ProudTruth112nkStephan'sOdyssey1224DoItAgainDn1124½ Driving 14

18Feb85-Grade II

4Feb85- 8GP fst 1$\frac{1}{16}$:46⅗ 1:11⅗ 1:44⅗ Alw 16000 2 5 63½ 41½ 11 16 Velasquez J 117 *.80 79-18 ProudTruth1176CrowningHonors1171½ScrtryGnrl117½ Ridden out 10

5Jan85- 9Crc fst 1$\frac{1}{16}$:48⅕ 1:13 1:46⅘ Trop Pk Dby 15 11 1316 915 68 42¾ Velasquez J 121 *1.60 83-14 Irish Sur 1211½ Artillerist 121½ Banner Bob 121¾ Rallied 16

5Jan85-Grade II

26Dec84- 8Crc fst 7f :22⅘ :45⅘ 1:25⅕ Alw 10000 1 12 77½ 58 52½ 13 Velasquez J 119 *1.10 90-22 ProudTruth1193Bowladrome1142RegIBrek113hd BrkeInTangle,Clr 12

2Dec84- 6Aqu fst 6f :22⅘ :47 1:12⅘ Md Sp Wt 2 7 84½ 76½ 31 12¾ Velasquez J 118 2.10e 79-24 Proud Truth 1182¾ Take Control 1181½ Buckner 1183 Handily 10

LATEST WORKOUTS ●Mar 29 Hia 3f fst :35⅗ b ●Mar 24 Hia 7f fst 1:26⅕ b Mar 19 Hia 6f fst 1:14⅘ b Mar 14 Hia 4f fst :49⅘ b

Sir Leon — Dk. b. or br. c. 3, by Private Account—Oh So Sweet II, by Ballymoss — Br.—Fox Carolyn & Holland (Fla) — Tr.—Rose Harold J — 122 — Lifetime 8 3 1 1 $35,760 — 1985 5 3 0 1 $33,510 — 1984 3 M 1 0 $2,250

Own.—Geranis Lucille

20Mar85- 9Hia fst 7f :22⅘ :44⅘ 1:23 ⒺJ M Ofarrell 7 8 815 712 33½ 1¾ Cruguet J 119 5.00 88-13 Sir Leon 119¾ Cherokee Fast 119nk Cameo King 119½ Driving 8

6Feb85- 9GP fst 7f :21⅘ :44⅘ 1:21⅗ Hutcheson 10 5 64½ 83 76½ 710¼ Velez J A Jr 112 15.90 86-20 Banner Bob 1142½DoItAgainDan1143CremeFraiche1141½ Outrun 12

6Feb85-Grade III

23Jan85- 7GP fst 7f :22 :45 1:24⅗ Alw 16200 1 5 58 66½ 3½ 13¼ Santos J A 117 6.10 82-22 Sir Leon 1173¼ Colder Thana 122nk Bowladrome 122½ Driving 12

14Jan85- 7GP fst 7f :22⅘ :45⅘ 1:24⅕ 3↑Md Sp Wt 4 4 2½ 51½ 13 18¼ Santos J A 122 2.90 83-22 Sir Leon 1228¼ Upper Bend 1224 Pragmatist 1224 Ridden out 12

1Jan85- 4Crc fst 6f :22⅕ :45⅘ 1:13⅕ Md Sp Wt 4 5 32 42½ 33 32 Bain G W 120 10.50 83-17 Handsome Version 120½ Flyer Escape 1201½ SirLeon1202½ Evenly 12

22Dec84- 5Crc fst 7f :22⅘ :46 1:26 Md Sp Wt 4 3 31 52½ 33 44 Bain G W 120 9.60 82-18 Quckerbow1201MedievlKin120½DremOfPec1202½ Lacked response 12

15Dec84- 4Crc fst 6f :22 :45⅗ 1:13⅕ Md Sp Wt 6 10 96 77½ 58½ 56½ Bain G W 120 4.90 79-20 Cruise the Sea 1202½ Key Charger 1202½ Shedac 120½ Outrun 11

28Nov84- 6Crc fst 6f :22⅘ :46⅗ 1:13⅘ Md Sp Wt 3 7 1½ 31 22 34¾ Bain G W 119 5.50 79-18 Trap Shoot 1193¾ ⒹShedac 1191 Sir Leon 1193 Weakened 9

28Nov84-Placed second through disqualification

LATEST WORKOUTS Mar 27 Crc 4f fst :50⅘ b Mar 19 Crc 4f fst :50 b

ture and, in a race devoid of early speed, held a tactical advantage over Proud Truth and Stephan's Odyssey, both stretch-runners.

John Veitch, the trainer of Proud Truth, was well aware of the situation and had his colt stalk Chief's Crown from the start. Stephan's Odyssey lay back, as usual. Nevertheless, the two colts finished on almost equal terms, one length behind the victorious Chief's Crown. The winner was disqualified at the track for allegedly drifting out in front of Proud Truth repeatedly during the stretch run—a decision that was reversed several days later, setting a dangerous precedent for the industry. Many observers felt, however, that it was Proud Truth who had trouble keeping a straight course and that he had bothered Stephan's Odyssey to some extent.

At equal weights, with Chief's Crown and Proud Truth both offered at 6–5 and Stephan's Odyssey at 7–2, who was the logical bet? Was Stephan's Odyssey even worth considering? If his poor performance in the Florida Derby was the direct result of muscle soreness, then the horse certainly was eligible to return (as he did) to the performance level he established in the Fountain Of Youth or Hollywood Juvenile, on what is called the "muscle sore rebound." Four weeks is usually sufficient time to recover from muscle soreness and any subsequent damage caused by racing while in that condition.

Anyone who incorporates the "muscle sore" and "muscle sore rebound" angles into his handicapping methodology would have recognized Stephan's Odyssey as a legitimate threat in the Flamingo and consequently would have passed on Chief's Crown and Proud Truth as underlays at 6–5, each with two rivals to beat. Of the three logical contenders in the race, only Stephan's Odyssey offered a value bet. And although he didn't win, he did run a big race, despite the controversial stretch run and the slow pace that did him no good. In the process, he confirmed the form he had established head to head with Proud Truth in the Fountain Of Youth.

We should point out, however, that stakes horses are not the

ELEVENTH RACE
Hialeah Park
MARCH 30, 1985

1 ⅛ MILES. (1.46⅖) 56th Running FLAMINGO STAKES (Grade I). Purse $265,000 Guaranteed. 3–year–olds by subscription of $500 each if made on or before Saturday, February 2, 1985, or by supplementary nomination of starters to pay $2,000 additional with $265,000 guaranteed. The added money and all fees to be divided 60% to the winner, 20% to second, 11% to third, 6% to fourth and 3% to fifth. Weights, colts and geldings, 122 lbs. Fillies 117 lbs. Non–winners of a Sweepstakes allowed 4 lbs. Starters to be named through the entry box by the usual time of closing. Flamingo Cup to winning owner. Replica to the trainer. Nominations closed Saturday, February 2, 1985 with 94 nominations Supplementary nominations of $12,500 each may be make at closing time of entries. Closed with 94 nominations, 1 supplemental nomineeImportant Business.

Value of race $265,000; value to winner $150,000; second $50,000; third $27,500; fourth $15,000; fifth $7,500; balance of starters $5,000 each. Mutuel pool $280,680. Perfecta Pool $109,508. Trifecta Pool $78,433.

Last Raced	Horse	Eqt.	A.	Wt	PP	St	¼	½	¾	Str	Fin	Jockey	Odds $1
2Mar85 ^{10}GP^{1}	[D]Chief's Crown		3	122	5	1	$1^{\frac{1}{2}}$	1^{hd}	1^{1}	$1^{2\frac{1}{2}}$	1^{1}	MacBeth D	1.30
2Mar85 ^{11}GP^{1}	Proud Truth		3	122	7	4	$2^{\frac{1}{2}}$	$2^{1\frac{1}{2}}$	$3^{1\frac{1}{2}}$	2^{hd}	2^{nk}	Velasquez J	1.20
2Mar85 ^{11}GP^{6}	Stephan's Odyssey		3	122	4	6	$4^{1\frac{1}{2}}$	$4^{1\frac{1}{2}}$	$4^{1\frac{1}{2}}$	$3^{\frac{1}{2}}$	$3^{3\frac{1}{2}}$	Maple E	3.50
22Mar85 ^{8}Hia^{1}	(S)Important Business		3	118	2	3	3^{1}	$3^{\frac{1}{2}}$	2^{hd}	4^{5}	4^{8}	Santos J A	22.00
20Mar85 ^{9}Hia^{1}	Sir Leon		3	122	8	7	6^{2}	5^{1}	5^{4}	5^{5}	$5^{1\frac{1}{2}}$	Cruguet J	34.70
16Mar85 ^{10}Hia^{6}	Alfred	b	3	118	3	5	$7^{1\frac{1}{2}}$	$7^{1\frac{1}{2}}$	7^{4}	6^{1}	6^{5}	Molina V H	70.90
16Mar85 ^{10}Hia^{5}	Now I Can	b	3	118	6	8	8	8	$6^{\frac{1}{2}}$	7^{6}	$7^{5\frac{1}{2}}$	Solomone M	67.50
5Mar85 ^{8}GP^{1}	Mr. Happy		3	118	1	2	5^{hd}	$6^{1\frac{1}{2}}$	8	8	8	Baltazar C	38.00

[D]–Chief's Crown Disqualified and placed second.
(S) Supplementary nomination.

OFF AT 5:54, Start good, Won driving. Time, :24⅗, :48⅘, 1:12⅖, 1:36⅕, 1:48⅖ Track fast.

$2 Mutuel Prices:			
7–PROUD TRUTH	4.40	2.40	2.40
5–CHIEF'S CROWN		2.40	2.40
4–STEPHAN'S ODYSSEY			2.80

$2 PERFECTA 7–5 PAID $11.60. $2 TRIFECTA 7–5–4 PAID $19.80.

Proud Truth—Ch. c, by Graustark—Wake Robin, by Summer Tan. Trainer Veitch John M. Bred by Galbreath Mrs J W (Ky).

CHIEF'S CROWN quickly moved to the fore, shook off a challenge from IMPORTANT BUSINESS on the second turn, drew clear in midstretch, drifted out slightly through the final sixteenth while under left-handed pressure and held off PROUD TRUTH. Following a stewards inquiry CHIEF'S CROWN was disqualified and placed second for causing interference to PROUD TRUTH in the final sixteenth. PROUD TRUTH had speed from the outset, was outside CHIEF'S CROWN along the backstretch, dropped back slightly on the turn, came to CHIEF'S CROWN at the head of the stretch, could not keep pace in midstretch, went out into STEPHAN'S ODYSSEY inside final sixteenth while behind CHIEF'S CROWN and then was taken out into STEPHAN'S ODYSSEY again in the late stages to avoid CHIEF'S CROWN'S heels. STEPHAN'S ODYSSEY, well-placed along the outside and in contention throughout, responded to pressure coming to the head of the stretch to gain a narrow advantage over PROUD TRUTH inside the final eighth, was forced out by that one inside the final sixteenth, then close to the finish and was outfinished by PROUD TRUTH. IMPORTANT BUSINESS racing inside, gained a narrow lead for a couple strides between calls leaving the backstretch, was unable to keep pace in early stretch, but continued on well to the finish. SIR LEON was prominent to the head of the stretch, weakened and came back sore. ALFRED failed to be a serious threat in the drive. NOW I CAN was outrun. MR. HAPPY had some speed for a half.

ones that are most likely to suffer from muscle soreness. The better candidates are cheaper horses that overexert themselves in their first start after a layoff, running harder than their training regimen has prepared them to do. Stakes horses are generally prepared more meticulously for their return to the races. Cheaper horses are often brought to a certain level of fitness in their training, then allowed to race to a peak of fitness. If they find themselves in a competitive situation before reaching that peak, muscle soreness is often the result. And a subsequent losing effort as favorite often goes hand in hand, as the crowd goes overboard on the sharp returnee that "can only improve." After the disappointing race, these same horses often score at a big price, on the "muscle sore rebound."

To get a (possibly) different perspective on "muscle soreness," I spoke with Skippy Shapoff, a successful trainer on the New York circuit for many years, and one of the finest gentlemen I have met in this game. His comments were quite interesting, and are well worth repeating.

Shapoff first remarked that even if it is brought up to the race in good condition, a horse's first race after a layoff is usually a severe physical shock to the animal's entire system. The horse comes out of the race physically tired—and Shapoff emphasized that "tired" was a better choice of words than "sore." He did note, however, that if the layoff was caused by physical problems, these can show up again after the first race back, seriously affecting the horse's performance in subsequent races.

Shapoff went on to say that most horses need at least ten days to recover from the jolt to their system, and that racing back too soon can only compound the problem. He also pointed out that horses that win their return to the races usually move up in class for their next race, and the tougher competition alone can make them look bad on that occasion, although many observers will mistakenly blame "muscle soreness" for the poor performance.

To get back to our friends Proud Truth and Stephan's Odyssey, the two colts managed to stay out of each other's way until they met in the Kentucky Derby. Benefiting from a rail-hugging ride, the latter got up in deep stretch to capture second money. Proud Truth, on the other hand, saw his chances (for second) sabotaged when he was taken out into the seven-path on the final turn. Despite this tremendous loss of ground, he finished within three lengths of Stephan's Odyssey.

Both colts chose to skip the Preakness and use Belmont's Peter Pan as their fine tune-up for the Belmont Stakes. Having defeated his arch rival three times in Florida, Proud Truth seemed the logical selection. But the race would offer a prime betting opportunity only if the casual Sunday audience was led astray by the misleading evidence from the Derby—which most had seen—and made Stephan's Odyssey a heavy favorite over Proud Truth.

Handicappers should get into the habit of analyzing not only past performances but also anticipated crowd reaction to them. They should go to the track armed not only with their selections for the day and their own morning line for each race but also with a feeling for how the crowd will bet each race. They should ask the vital question, "How might others in the crowd be fooled so that my horse will become a value bet?" If they can't foresee this happening, then either the odds on their selection will be unappetizing or seemingly attractive odds could easily signal lack of stable confidence.

In the Peter Pan, Proud Truth started at 3–2, with Stephan's Odyssey at even money. While these odds might not seem enticing in a race relatively devoid of early speed—unfavorable circumstances for either horse—or tilted sufficiently in favor of Stephan's Odyssey to call for a bet on Proud Truth, they at least proved that trip handicappers do not govern the odds board at the NYRA tracks—at least not this day.

Proud Truth, rallying on the rail, edged away from the pacesetting longshot Cutlass Reality through the stretch, despite suffering an injury that forced him to miss the Belmont two weeks later. Stephan's Odyssey did little running, finishing fourth, then fooled form handicappers with a strong second-place finish in the Belmont itself—demonstrating once again that horses prepping for major stakes events are often not asked for their best in the prep race.

EIGHTH RACE
Belmont
MAY 26, 1985

1⅛ MILES. (1.45⅘) 32nd Running THE PETER PAN (Grade I). Purse $75,000 Added. (Plus $25,000 Breeders' Cup Premium Awards). 3–year–olds. By subscription of $150 each, which should accompany the nomination; $1,200 to pass the entry box, with $75,000 added. The added money and all fees to be divided 60% to the winner, 22% to second, 12% to third and 6% to fourth. 126 lbs. Non–winners of a race of $75,000 at a mile or over allowed 3 lbs.; of a race of $35,000 at any distance, 6 lbs. of three races other than maiden or claiming, 9 lbs. Of two races other than maiden or claiming, 12 lbs. Starters to be named at the closing time of entries. A trophy will be presented to the winning owner. Closed Wednesday, May 8, 1985 with 39 nominations. Breeders' Cup Fund Awards to Proud Truth & Salem Drive.

Total purse $114,250. Value of race $105,000; value to winner $67,050; second $19,635; third $12,960; fourth $5,355. Nominator Awards $1,750, $7,500 Reverts Breeders' Cup Fund Mutuel pool $160,535, OTB pool $128,605. Exacta Pool $178,564. OTB Exacta Pool $129,360.

Last Raced	Horse	Eqt.	A.	Wt	PP	St	¼	½	¾	Str	Fin	Jockey	Odds $1
4May85 ^{8}CD^{5}	Proud Truth	b	3	126	3	5	$5^{1/2}$	4^{hd}	$4^{1/2}$	1^{hd}	$1^{1\frac{1}{4}}$	Velasquez J	1.50
18May85 ^{8}Pim^{5}	Cutlass Reality	b	3	114	1	3	1^{hd}	2^{1}	1^{hd}	2^{2}	$2^{1\frac{1}{2}}$	Cordero A Jr	11.00
28Apr85 ^{5}Aqu^{3}	Salem Drive		3	114	4	2	3^{1}	$3^{1\frac{1}{2}}$	3^{1}	$3^{2\frac{1}{2}}$	$3^{2\frac{1}{4}}$	Maple E	14.00
4May85 ^{8}CD^{2}	Stephan's Odyssey		3	126	6	4	6^{1}	$5^{1/2}$	5^{1}	4^{2}	4^{4}	Pincay L Jr	1.00
8May85 ^{8}Bel^{3}	Concert		3	120	7	1	7	7	6^{5}	5^{5}	$5^{10\frac{3}{4}}$	McCarron G	11.20
20May85 ^{4}Bel^{11}	Clean Machine		3	114	5	7	$2^{1/2}$	$1^{1/2}$	$2^{1/2}$	6^{8}	$6^{7\frac{1}{2}}$	Migliore R	32.50
8May85 ^{8}Bel^{6}	Stone White	b	3	123	2	6	$4^{1/2}$	6^{1}	7	7	7	Lovato F Jr	18.80

OFF AT 5:03 Start good, Won driving. Time, :23⅗, :46⅗, 1:10⅘, 1:35⅕, 1:47⅗ Track fast.

$2 Mutuel Prices:

3–(C)–PROUD TRUTH	5.00	3.20	3.00
1–(A)–CUTLASS REALITY		7.60	4.80
4–(D)–SALEM DRIVE			7.40

$2 EXACTA 3–1 PAID $64.20.

Ch. c, by Graustark—Wake Robin, by Summer Tan. Trainer Veitch John M. Bred by Galbreath Mrs J W (Ky).

PROUD TRUTH never far back, made a run along the inside nearing the stretch, bumped with CUTLASS REALITY leaving the turn, dueled with that rival to the final furlong and proved clearly best while drifting out slightly. CUTLASS REALITY alternated for the lead while racing slightly out from the rail. Bumped with PROUD TRUTH while vying for the lead leaving the turn and continued on with good courage to best the others. SALEM DRIVE, close up early, made a bid from the outside midway of the turn, remained prominent to the upper stretch but wasn't good enough. STEPHAN'S ODYSSEY raced outside horses while remaining within easy striking distance until near the stretch and weakened under pressure. CONCERT moved through along the inside approaching the stretch but lacked a further response. CLEAN MACHINE, sent up between horses leaving the chute, showed speed until near the stretch and tired badly. STONE WHITE was finished early.

Chapter 30

Out Well After the Finish

HANDICAPPERS OF THE MID-1980s are far better informed and educated than were their counterparts of twenty, even ten, years ago. In 1965, there was very little literature on the subject of Thoroughbred handicapping. By 1975, we had the works of Tom Ainslie, but little else, from which to learn both the basics and the finer points of the game. In the past ten years, however, we have witnessed a literary explosion, with the excellent works of Beyer, Davis, Davidowitz, Jones, Quinn, Scott, Sartin, and others guiding us through the techniques of speed and trip handicapping, the riddles of form and fitness, and the mysteries of class. Educators like Henry Kuck in New York, Scott McMannis in Chicago, Ron Cox in San Francisco, Lee Rousso, Jim Selvidge, and John Meyer in the Los Angeles area, Greg Lawlor in San Diego, George Kaywood in Omaha, Paul Braseth in Seattle, and Rick Beau in Vancouver have helped spread the word to the masses through their seminars, newsletters, and services. Trainer studies are now being made available to those who are willing to purchase this critical information.

As a group we have taken handicapping know-how to the very edges of its frontiers. And we have often asked each other, "What is coming next?" "Where do we go from here?" If enough people share the same knowledge base, all will have to work a little harder to find that slight edge, that one weapon that few others are aware of, or are simply unable or unwilling to master.

The consensus, as I hear it, seems to be that those weapons will be visual by nature—the ability to watch races intelligently, to accurately appraise horses in the paddock or during the post parade and warm-ups, to observe and understand a jockey's communications with his horse and its response thereto as the race is being run, to watch a horse's behavior after the race as it is pulled up and led back to the unsaddling area.

In this chapter we will focus on one particular aspect of a horse's performance after the race is over: how the horse is handled during the eighth of a mile after the finish line. A horse that continues to run after the wire, and covers that additional furlong in good time, is said to have finished "out well." In actuality, this "training move" may have covered two furlongs, actually starting when the horse was asked for its run at the eighth pole.

The "out well" angle has not yet caught on with very many players. The proper identification of horses' "out well" takes considerable effort, demanding that the player:

(1) Clock the race through the extra eighth mile beyond the finish line, then compare that time with the final time to get a number for the additional furlong.
(2) Chart the horses at the imaginary "finish line," noting lengths behind the first horse to "finish."

Obviously the player must have a stopwatch, a good eye, a vantage point near the clubhouse turn, and ideally, an assistant. Few will have the persistence to bother.

The "out well" got its start as a by-product of trip handicapping. John Pricci of *Newsday* and Paul Mellos, a storied professional player from New York, made a habit of observing horses visually after the finish, hoping to pick up on training maneuvers staged by certain trainers. A few years later, Mark Berner joined Pricci at *Newsday* and suggested timing the additional furlong and charting the field at the secondary finish line. Indeed, the three of them—Pricci, Mellos, and Berner—must be considered the founding fathers of the "out well" as it is now defined. Mark Berner, in fact, makes a point of disseminating "out well" information to *Newsday* readers in his weekly "Horses to Watch" column.

A horse that finishes "out well" is telling observers in no uncertain terms that it is fit, or at least gaining in conditioning. The animal is also suggesting that it would prefer to go longer—"out wells" seldom turn back in distance successfully. In many cases the "out well" is tipping trainer intentions. Many trainers use the "out well" move as the finishing touch on a horse's training regimen and go for the money next time out. If the trainer moves the horse up in class, this is probably just a measure of his confidence, and is typically ac-

Mark Berner's Horses to Watch

The horses that finish out-well are the ones that gallop out strongly after the finish of the race.

Aroundback was out-well in 13 4/5 seconds in her debut, which she won by 9¼ lengths, versus $35,000 maiden-claimers at 6 furlongs on Wednesday. This 3-year-old filly by Disc-Wayin the Back is trained by Harry Wendell and should be watched in a non-winners-of-1 allowance race in her next start.

Momento was out in 14 1/5 versus $75,000 claimers at 6 furlongs Thursday. The 6-year-old horse by Proposal-Mundana, trained by Oscar Barrera, was steadied on the turn, swung wide entering the stretch and finished well on the outside. Watch for him versus similar at the distance or greater.

Likely Gain finished out in 15 seconds while racing in a non-winners-of-2 allowance event at 6 furlongs, also on Thursday. This 4-year-old daughter of Co-jak and Piccadilly Daisy is trained by John Parisella. Watch for her to race back in the same class at the distance or greater.

Cherry Jubilee was out in 13 3/5 on Thursday against classified allowance rivals at 6 furlongs. The 4-year-old filly by Costal-Cherry Willow is trained by H. Allen Jerkens and should be watched at the same level while racing around two turns.

Of the 179 horses that have appeared here and raced back, 37 have won in their next start. A $2 win bet on each would have produced a $119.20 profit.

companied by a good price. If the horse drops down, it is nonetheless a solid proposition, still often at good odds. With the "out well" signaling fitness and trainer intentions, proper placement is the major open question. As long as the trainer isn't doing something outlandish in that respect, the horse is worth following.

Just what constitutes an "out well" finish? How fast does a horse have to cover that extra furlong in order to qualify? Unfortunately, there is no simple answer. Any aspect of time is relative to the individual racing surface and its present condition. As a general rule of thumb, however, any finish between twelve and fifteen seconds, depending on the track, the class of the animal, and the distance of the race, can be considered "out well." The reader is advised, however, to establish his own standards for his local circuit.

Anyone who pursues this methodology will find several "out wells" each day, with a far higher ratio of occurrence among classier animals. He also will notice that a follow-up bet on each and every "out well" is unwarranted. To be successful, play on "out wells" must be selective, either focusing on trainers with a known history with the move or on horses whose "out well" was either the best of the day or the best of the day at a route distance or unusually good for the class of the horse involved. Many horses just happen to continue on after the wire and qualify as "out wells," with their trainer unaware of the situation. Unless theirs was the best of the day, they are usually not worth following.

The following race will help to demonstrate the potential power of this angle. It is very unlikely that you, the reader, will be able to pick either the winner or third-place finisher using standard handi-

9 AQUEDUCT

1⅛ MILES INNER DIRT TRACK AQUEDUCT

1⅛ MILES. (InnerDirt). (1.48⅘) CLAIMING. Purse $12,500. Fillies and mares, 4-year-olds and upward. Weight, 122 lbs. Non-winners of two races at a mile or over since Janaury 1 allowed 3 lbs. Of such a race since then, 5 lbs. Claiming price $14,000; for each $1,000 to $12,000, 2 lbs. (Races when entered for $10,000 or less not considered.)

Coupled—Jumping With Joy and Silent Hush.

Photojournalist

Ch. m. 6, by Journalist—Viewfinder, by Rambunctious
Own.—Fernandez F — $12,000 — Br.—Herman H (Md) — Tr.—Fernandez Floreano — 106 7
Lifetime 46 3 5 5 $42,818 | 1985 2 0 0 0 $750 | 1984 14 0 1 2 $5,220 | Turf 2 0 0 0

13Jan85-	1Aqu	fst	6f	⊡:23⅕ :47⅘ 1:13⅗	ⒻClm 13000	12	2	86	916	812	810½	Privitera R7		108	25.00	66-27	Perfect Gift 114½ Radiant Gem 1132 Future Friend 1142½	Outrun	12
7Jan85-	1Aqu	fst	170	⊡:49 1:15⅖ 1:48	ⒻClm 12000	6	7	67½	69¾	67¾	45½	Privitera R5		108	26.10	54-27	Saturna 1084¼ M. V. On Five 117¾ Vicky's Holly 112nk	Slow st	9
19Dec84-	9Aqu	fst	1⅛	⊡:48⅘ 1:15 1:55⅘	3↑ⒻClm 13000	3	10	88½	1011	1021	1031	Garrido O L5	b	110	37.80	32-25	Torsions Pet 1172¾ Lucas Lou 1127 Sweet Missy G 1011	Outrun	11
14Dec84-	1Aqu	fst	6f	⊡:23 :47⅘ 1:14	3↑ⒻClm 13000	4	8	813	815	89½	78¾	Garrido O L5	b	110	26.70	65-19	Charismata 1031 Future Friend 108½ Jay's Gem 1111½	No factor	9
21Nov84-	1Aqu	fst	6f	:24⅕ :48⅖ 1:14⅕	3↑ⒻClm 15500	5	4	56½	58	58	512½	Blackstun KM7	b	106	17.60	58-33	Our Trisha 1102 Tara K. 1172 Golden Greens 1171¾	Outrun	6
19Oct84-	9Bel	fst	7f	:22⅗ :47⅖ 1:26⅗	3↑ⒻClm 15500	2	8	86½	85½	69½	511½	Maple S	b	113	26.30	57-21	Tara K. 1123¾ Lovely Mesa 1071½ Golden Greens 1176	Raced wide	9
12Oct84-	1Bel	fst	1 1/16	:46⅗ 1:12⅖ 1:45⅗	3↑ⒻClm 15500	7	4	47	611	614	520½	Delgado G7	b	106	14.30	53-22	Lady Nizon 117¾ Oceanic View 1179 Torsions Pet 11510	Fin. early	7
21Aug84-	3Mth	fst	6f	:23⅕ :46⅘ 1:12	3↑ⒻClm 10000	1	7	712	78½	45½	33	Gonzalez M A	b	116	17.60	77-17	MissJupiterJt1162PuffAwy1091Photojournlist1163	Sluggish early	7
27Jly84-	1Bel	sly	7f	:22⅘ :46⅖ 1:24⅕	ⒻClm 14000	4	3	32½	44½	616	619¼	Delgado G7	b	110	6.10	62-21	Loyal Diplomat 1155 Be A Reality1101¾SingingPartner1151¾	Tired	7
18Jly84-	3Bel	sly	1 1/16	:47⅕ 1:13 1:46⅖	ⒻClm 19000	4	3	3nk	34	35½	313¼	Delgado G7	b	106	11.00	56-19	TorsionsPet11710OurMutulFriend1133¼Photojournlist1063½	Tired	6

LATEST WORKOUTS Jan 1 Bel tr.t 4f gd :51⅖ b

Halcyon Hour

B. m. 5, by Hold Your Peace—Mon Cherie, by Promise
Own.—Chernay S R — $12,000 — Br.—Tayloe W Randolph (Fla) — Tr.—Olsen Gary S — 113
Lifetime 38 3 5 3 $39,775 | 1985 3 0 0 0 | 1984 20 2 1 2 $18,010 | Turf 2 0 0 0

28Jan85-	2Aqu	fst	1 1/16	⊡:48⅕ 1:14⅘ 1:50	ⒻClm 12000	11	3	31	52¾	47½	56½	Santagata N	b	113	22.30	54-25	M.SnsitivK116½JumpingWithJoy1082¾StyOnCours1171	No mishap	12
23Jan85-	2Aqu	fst	6f	⊡:23 :47⅕ 1:13⅗	ⒻClm 12000	7	6	73½	85½	74¾	76½	Santagata N	b	113	26.20	71-24	MaggieCart1122Lyphrd'sChoice106hdFutureFriend113½	No factor	12
7Jan85-	1Aqu	fst	170	⊡:49 1:15⅖ 1:48	ⒻClm 12000	2	6	77½	810	57½	58¼	Santagata N	b	113	12.70	51-27	Saturna 1084¼ M. V. On Five 117¾ Vicky's Holly 112nk	No factor	9
19Dec84-	9Aqu	fst	1⅛	⊡:48⅘ 1:15 1:55⅘	3↑ⒻClm 12000	1	11	1112	87	816	823¼	Vergara O	b	113	25.80	40-25	Torsions Pet 1172¾ Lucas Lou 1127 Sweet Missy G. 1011	Outrun	11
23Nov84-	3Aqu	fst	1	:47⅘ 1:14 1:40⅕	3↑ⒻClm 12000	7	3	3½	43½	412	517½	Cordero A Jr	b	113	10.30	47-29	Torsions Pet 1171½ Bell Carmel 1177½ Shofoose 1134	Weakened	7
14Nov84-	1Aqu	fst	7f	:23⅗ :49⅕ 1:29⅗	3↑ⒻClm 13000	6	3	63¾	72¾	56½	58¼	MacBeth D	b	115	9.70	46-33	Bell Carmel 117nk Charismata 107¾ Looking Gap 1134	No factor	8
26Oct84-	1Aqu	sly	7f	:23⅕ :46⅖ 1:25⅗	3↑ⒻClm 14000	1	4	41½	21	22	31½	Cruguet J	b	117	5.00	72-22	Lucas Lou 1121½ Bell Carmel113noHalcyonHour1176¾	Good effort	6
28Sep84-	5Bel	yl	1 1/16	[T]:47⅗ 1:13⅕ 1:47	3↑ⒻClm 35000	6	5	410	77½	712	717½	Cruguet J	b	113	19.90	48-36	Ma Gonzesse 1135¾ Fairly II 113½ Baker's Bet 113¾	Outrun	8
13Sep84-	2Bel	fst	7f	:23 :46⅖ 1:24⅖	3↑ⒻClm 14000	5	10	88½	109¾	913	914¼	Garrido O L7	b	110	10.70	65-21	Lady Nizon 1173½ Lucas Lou 112¾ Whitewalls 1173	Outrun	11
5Sep84-	9Bel	fst	1 1/16	:46⅗ 1:12 1:44⅖	3↑ⒻClm 14000	3	9	63½	43½	21	33½	Garrido O L7	b	110	17.00	77-12	Quiet Glory 1172½ Lucas Lou 117¾ Halcyon Hour 1104	Weakened	10

LATEST WORKOUTS Dec 10 Aqu ⊡ 3f fst :38 b

Demean's Gold

B. f. 4, by Gold And Myrrh—Demean, by Dewan
Own.—Diangelo J T — $12,000 — Br.—Wilmot W F (NY) — Tr.—DiAngelo Joseph T — 113
Lifetime 20 3 1 3 $25,853 | 1985 2 0 0 0 | 1984 14 2 0 1 $11,924

25Jan85-	1Aqu	fst	170	⊡:47⅘ 1:13⅗ 1:45⅖	ⒻClm 15500	1	9	1011	109½	814	811¾	Lovato F Jr	b	114	25.00	61-23	Bell Carmel 1134¾ Christamela 108hd Golden Greens117nk	Outrun	10
13Jan85-	1Aqu	fst	6f	⊡:23⅕ :47⅘ 1:13⅗	ⒻClm 12000	1	7	53½	714	77½	67½	Davis R G	b	113	23.90	69-27	Perfect Gift 114½ Radiant Gem 1132FutureFriend1142½	No threat	12
29Dec84-	1Aqu	my	1 1/16	⊡:47⅘ 1:12⅖ 1:45⅘	ⒻClm 15500	5	8	56½	55½	68	67	Davis R G	b	112	14.50	76-17	Conshohockn112nkJumpingWithJoy107nkMistAStright109nk	Wide	8
6Dec84-	2Aqu	sly	1 1/16	⊡:47⅘ 1:13⅕ 1:45⅖	ⒻClm 15500	2	7	79½	77½	49	410½	Davis R G	b	112	6.80	75-16	PrettyNiche1164¾MistAStraight1051¾Vicky'sHolly1123¾	No factor	10
28Nov84-	1Aqu	fst	1	:47⅖ 1:13⅕ 1:40⅘	ⒻClm c-12000	5	8	97½	911	99½	78½	Santagata N	b	112	8.60	54-27	Purse Keyes 1142 Thai Sox 1141½ Mist A Straight 105¾	Outrun	10
10Nov84-	5FL	sly	170	:48⅖ 1:13⅗ 1:45⅘	3↑Ⓕ[S]Clm 10000	4	5	54	46½	21½	13	Hulet L	b	112	*1.70e	72-21	Demean's Gold 1123 Fast 'N Square 1154 Neo 112nk	Driving	9
4Nov84-	6FL	fst	1 1/16	:48⅘ 1:14⅘ 1:49⅕	3↑[S]Clm 10000	7	4	45	44	46½	48	Cook R W	b	109	12.30	62-17	Aggi's Boy 1122 Spring Alibi 1172 Elby Bee 1104	Evenly	7
5Oct84-	7FL	fst	6f	:22⅘ :47 1:13⅕	3↑ⒻAlw 5500	5	6	68	78½	710	59	Laiz G	b	113	12.30	74-25	ShdbushShimmr1132PrincssO'Hr113¾DuckyDuchss1136	No factor	7
2Sep84-	8FL	gd	1 1/16	:49⅕ 1:15⅗ 1:50⅕	3↑Ⓕ[S]Alw 9900	6	2	1½	11	1hd	31	Laiz G	b	114	14.70	64-25	Fast'NSquare116¾LovelyMesa111nkDemean'sGold1141½	Weakened	7
10Aug84-	8FL	fst	170	:47⅕ 1:12 1:43⅖	3↑[S]Alw 9900	9	7	813	1120	1125	1130¼	Laiz G	b	112	8.40e	53-18	Syn Capade 1224½ Saxon Prince 1222½ Chenango 1156	Outrun	11

LATEST WORKOUTS Jan 11 Bel tr.t 3f fst :37⅕ b

Sweet Missy G.

B. f. 4, by Winged T—Missy G, by Knightly Manner
Own.—Gargano P — $12,000 — Br.—Gargano P (Ky) — Tr.—DeStasio Richard T — 103 10
Lifetime 14 1 1 2 $14,860 | 1984 10 1 1 1 $12,460 | 1983 4 M 0 1 $2,400 | Turf 1 0 1 0 $3,850

29Dec84-	1Aqu	my	1 1/16	⊡:47⅘ 1:12⅖ 1:45⅘	ⒻClm 15500	1	4	66¾	68¼	43½	4½	Reed R E10		102	11.40	82-17	Conshohockn112nkJumpingWthJoy107nkMstAStrght109nk	Rallied	8
19Dec84-	9Aqu	fst	1⅛	⊡:48⅘ 1:15 1:55⅘	3↑ⒻClm 12000	5	6	78½	64	55¾	39¾	Reed R E10		101	26.00	53-25	Torsions Pet 1172¾ Lucas Lou 1127 Sweet Missy G 1011	Rallied	11
28Nov84-	1Aqu	fst	1	:47⅖ 1:13⅕ 1:40⅘	ⒻClm 13000	3	9	86½	86½	77	56½	Reed R E10		104	10.40	55-27	Purse Keyes 1142 Thai Sox 1141½ Mist A Straight 105¾	Outrun	10
2Nov84-	3Aqu	fst	1⅛	:50⅕ 1:16 1:56	3↑ⒻClm 12000	2	4	54	67	612	611¼	Velasquez J		115	3.70	43-35	Bell Carmel 113½ Lucas Lou 1121¾ Shofoose 113hd	Tired	6
17Oct84-	5Bel	fst	7f	:23 :47⅕ 1:25⅗	ⒻClm 25000	5	5	115¾	116½	109¾	89½	Davis R G		116	*3.10	65-21	WhispringIrish1122½JosElSgundo1131½MissLilZ.109hd	Raced wide	11
24Sep84-	9Bel	fm	1 1/16	Ⓣ:47 1:10⅘ 1:43⅗	ⒻClm 40000	9	7	76	78	35	22½	Davis R G		116	17.20	76-20	DoubleSucy1122½SwtMissyG.116nkForMyHrt116nk	Best of others	12
8Sep84-	9Bel	fst	1⅛	:47 1:11⅘ 1:51⅕	ⒻClm 35000	10	6	914	915	816	613½	Velasquez J		116	*3.70	57-17	Anselma 1091¾ Tackful Queen 1113½ Video Queen 1162	Outrun	10
4Aug84-	1Sar	fst	7f	:22 :45 1:24⅖	ⒻClm 50000	7	9	916	920	811	68½	Miranda J		116	9.30	71-13	Fast Lane Gal1112½LadyLitchfield1091½SilentMickey1163½	Outrun	9
12Jly84-	1Bel	fst	7f	:22⅘ :46 1:24⅖	3↑ⒻMd 35000	5	1	86¾	68¾	14	15¾	Velasquez J		116	*1.40	80-17	Sweet Missy G. 1165¾ Daddy's Slugger 1123ShiftKey112no	Driving	8
27Jun84-	9Bel	fst	6f	:22⅘ :47⅗ 1:13⅗	3↑ⒻMd 35000	1	5	66½	64½	42½	41	Velasquez J		114	8.40	72-17	Fabulous Ack 114hd She Speaks Well114½Paddy'sGift114½	Rallied	11

LATEST WORKOUTS Jan 29 Bel tr.t 6f fst 1:17⅖ b — Jan 5 Bel tr.t 3f gd :37 b

Vicky's Holly

B. f. 4, by Full Out—Northern Orbit, by Royal Orbit
Own.—O'Neill J C — $12,000 — Br.—Quammen L D (Ky) — Tr.—Howe Peter M — 113
Lifetime 20 1 0 2 $11,130 | 1985 2 0 0 1 $1,500 | 1984 15 1 0 1 $9,630 | Turf 2 0 0 0 $1,230

28Jan85-	2Aqu	fst	1 1/16	⊡:48⅕ 1:14⅘ 1:50	ⒻClm 14000	10	2	2hd	22	914	912	Samyn J L	b	117	3.30	48-25	M.SensitiveKae116½JumpingWithJoy1082¾StyOnCourse1171	Tired	12
7Jan85-	1Aqu	fst	170	⊡:49 1:15⅖ 1:48	ⒻClm 14000	7	4	21½	21½	34	35¼	Moore D N5	b	112	3.10	55-27	Saturna 1084¼ M. V. On Five 117¾ Vicky's Holly 112nk	Bumped	9
17Dec84-	2Aqu	fst	6f	⊡:23 :47 1:13⅗	ⒻClm 17500	1	8	42	43	64¼	78½	Samyn J L	b	116	6.90	68-19	Miss Lil Z. 1091½ Resonner 1112½ Wildeyed Beauty 1092¾	Tired	10
6Dec84-	2Aqu	sly	1 1/16	⊡:47⅘ 1:13⅕ 1:45⅖	ⒻClm 15500	10	3	3nk	11	23	36½	Samyn J L	b	112	28.50	78-16	PrettyNiche1164¾MistAStright1051¾Vicky'sHolly1123¾	Weakened	10
30Nov84-	3Aqu	fst	7f	:22⅘ :46⅖ 1:25⅖	ⒻClm 20000	11	3	76¾	73¾	1111	1113	Samyn J L	b	112	25.50	61-23	JoseElSegundo105nkWkUpLilSuzy116¾Ddddy'sSluggr1161½	Outrun	11
14Nov84-	2Aqu	fst	7f	:23⅗ :48⅖ 1:28⅗	ⒻClm 17500	5	10	85¼	98¼	68½	45¾	Samyn J L	b	116	11.40	52-33	Resonner 105½ Bateau Road 1123½ Purse Keyes 1162	No factor	12
9Nov84-	9Med	yl	170	Ⓣ:49⅘ 1:15⅕ 1:46⅗	3↑ⒻClm 32000	7	5	54½	65	69	711¾	Samyn J L	b	113	7.40	45-44	Palace Mischief 1161 Artic Moss 109½ Blazon Sara 1059	Outrun	7
15Oct84-	4Bel	fm	1 1/16	[T]:47⅘ 1:12⅘ 1:44⅘	ⒻClm 45000	2	5	57¾	42	31	43	Samyn J L	b	112	28.30	74-23	For My Heart 1121 Anselma 106½ Lady President1161½	Weakened	8
2Jly84-	2Bel	gd	1	:46⅖ 1:12 1:38⅗	ⒻClm 35000	8	4	55	1014	1020	1027	Fann B	b	116	29.60	45-15	Gettis 1162¾ Romeo's Mistress1162½[DH]HolleySprings109	Fin.early	10
21Jun84-	1Bel	fst	1	:47⅕ 1:12⅘ 1:39⅕	ⒻClm 25000	4	2	21	48	715	724	Brumfield D	b	116	13.70	45-21	Bateau Road 1095 Tackful Queen 111hdWhisperingIrish1143	Tired	8

Lady Nizon

B. m. 5, by Nizon—Neil's Mor Mor, by Etonian
Own.—Spataro J M — $14,000 — Br.—Dogwood Farm Inc (Fla) — Tr.—Nadler Herbert — 122
Lifetime 36 12 3 4 $73,227 | 1985 4 2 0 0 $18,600 | 1984 21 7 3 1 $45,166 | Turf 1 0 0 0

2Feb85-	2Aqu	my	170	⊡:49⅗ 1:15⅖ 1:46⅕	ⒻClm 32500	9	2	2hd	21	85½	911	Graell A	b	115	*2.90	58-28	Torsions Pet108nkCourageousKaren1152½GuideBoat107¾	Stopped	10
26Jan85-	2Aqu	fst	170	⊡:49 1:15 1:44⅗	ⒻClm 25000	3	4	43½	2½	11	12½	Graell A	b	117	*1.30	77-20	Lady Nizon 1172½ Poco Lolo 1126 Mia Reale 1171½	Driving	10
12Jan85-	2Aqu	fst	1 1/16	⊡:47⅗ 1:14⅕ 1:48⅖	ⒻClm 17500	3	6	28	25	14	15½	Graell A	b	117	3.60	68-24	Lady Nizon 1175½ Bell Carmel 117no Pistachio 1174¾	Handily	12
3Jan85-	9Aqu	fst	1⅛	⊡:47⅘ 1:13⅖ 1:54	ⒻClm 25000	9	9	813	57½	45	56	Ward W A5	b	114	*2.60	66-19	Romalane 1171½ TorsionsPet1141LucasLou1081¾	Raced sluggishly	9
22Dec84-	1Aqu	gd	1 1/16	⊡:47⅘ 1:13⅖ 1:44⅕	3↑ⒻClm 25000	1	9	911	75	33½	32½	Ward W A5	b	114	4.40	76-09	Maggie Carta 113¾ Oceanic View1171¾LadyNizon114¾	Sluggish st.	9
12Dec84-	6Med	fst	170	:47⅗ 1:12⅖ 1:43⅘	3↑ⒻAlw 13000	3	6	512	59½	43	1¾	Ward W A5	b	111	3.50	80-22	Lady Nizon 111¾ Miss Precisely116¾CancanMadame1133½	Driving	8
28Nov84-	7Med	fst	1	:48 1:13⅘ 1:41⅖	3↑ⒻClm 18000	2	6	66½	21½	21	21	Vergara O	b	115	2.90	73-25	Daisy's Debut 1161 Lady Nizon 1155 Pistachio 111¾	Gamely	8
19Nov84-	3Med	fst	170	:49⅕ 1:14⅗ 1:46	3↑ⒻClm 16000	1	3	1hd	11½	2hd	2½	Ward W A	b	119	*.80	68-30	AutumnChngs116½LdyNizon1194Christml1074	Angled out, gamely	6
31Oct84-	9Aqu	fst	1	:46⅘ 1:12 1:37⅗	3↑ⒻClm 22500	4	12	105¾	96½	66¾	49	Cruguet J	b	115	5.60	69-19	Oceanic View 115hd Tachycardia 1175 Party CutUp1174	No threat	12
12Oct84-	1Bel	fst	1 1/16	:46⅗ 1:12⅖ 1:45⅗	3↑ⒻClm 17500	4	5	35	1½	14	1¾	Cruguet J	b	117	*2.00	74-22	Lady Nizon 117¾ Oceanic View 1179 Torsions Pet 11510	Driving	7

LATEST WORKOUTS Jan 23 Aqu ⊡ 4f fst :49⅕ b — ●Jan 9 Aqu ⊡ 4f fst :48⅘ h — Dec 7 Aqu ⊡ 4f fst :52 b

Mist A Straight

B. f. 4, by Poker—Foggy Crossing, by Misty Flight
Own.—Ferrara V — $14,000 — Br.—Ellis J (NY) — Tr.—Imperio Joseph — 117
Lifetime 27 3 3 3 $46,245 | 1985 2 0 0 0 | 1984 22 2 2 3 $25,665 | Turf 1 0 0 0 $1,560

19Jan85-	3Aqu	fst	1 1/16	⊡:49 1:14⅗ 1:48⅘	Ⓕ[S]Alw 27000	7	7	912	714	715	68½	Blackstun K M5		112	12.00	57-22	Count On Karen 117½ Kyra Maria 112no Deerish 1125¾	Outrun	9
7Jan85-	7Aqu	fst	1⅛	⊡:49⅖ 1:14⅘ 1:55⅕	Ⓕ[S]Alw 27000	2	7	64	53½	55½	69	MacBeth D		117	4.50	57-27	Lovely Mesa 117¾ Promise Kept 1173 Deerish 114hd	Broke in air	9
29Dec84-	1Aqu	my	1 1/16	⊡:47⅘ 1:12⅖ 1:45⅘	ⒻClm 16500	7	6	78¾	89¾	54	3½	Blackstun K M5		109	4.40	82-17	Conshohockn112nkJumpingWthJoy107nkMstAStrght109no	Rallied	8
20Dec84-	5Aqu	fst	1 1/16	⊡:48⅗ 1:13⅘ 1:47	3↑Ⓕ[S]Alw 27000	9	11	117¾	1012	79¾	715	Blackstun K M5		110	16.20	62-19	Skipper's Angel1156½Marianivor1152½AprilMiracle1124¾	No factor	12
6Dec84-	2Aqu	sly	1 1/16	⊡:47⅘ 1:13⅕ 1:45⅖	ⒻClm 15500	7	4	46½	54	34	24¾	Blackstun K M7		105	11.90	80-16	PrttyNich1164¾MistAStrght1051¾Vcky'sHolly1123¾	Best of others	10
28Nov84-	1Aqu	fst	1	:47⅖ 1:13⅕ 1:40⅘	ⒻClm 12000	4	7	75½	74½	43	33½	Blackstun KM7		105	44.10	58-27	Purse Keyes 1142 Thai Sox 1141½ Mist A Straight 105¾	Rallied	10
23Nov84-	3Aqu	fst	1	:47⅘ 1:14 1:40⅕	3↑ⒻClm 13000	2	7	77½	712	720	622	Privitera R7	b	106	27.10	43-29	Torsions Pet1171½BellCarmel1177½Shofoose1134	Showed nothing	7
14Nov84-	2Aqu	fst	7f	:23⅗ :48⅖ 1:28⅗	ⒻClm 16500	11	2	64½	55½	810	79	Privitera R7	b	107	29.50	49-33	Resonner 105½ Bateau Road 1123½ Purse Keyes 1162	No factor	12
3Nov84-	9Aqu	fst	1	:47⅗ 1:13⅖ 1:40	3↑Ⓕ[S]Alw 26000	4	12	1211	1119	917	919¾	Velasquez J		115	31.80	46-24	Wild Tune 1151¾ Adirondack Miss 1103½ Marianivor 115½	OUtrun	12
22Oct84-	4Bel	fm	1¼	[T]:48 1:37⅗ 2:03⅕	3↑Ⓕ[S]Alw 26000	1	6	79	813	513	410¾	Guerra W A		114	39.20	67-18	Silver BluffRoad1174¾KyraMaria1141Deerish1145	P'ssd tired ones	11

LATEST WORKOUTS Jan 30 Bel tr.t 3f fst :38⅗ b

Annie Blueeyes — B. f. 4, by Teddy's Courage—Maid Of Sorrow, by Wolfram
Own.—Tresvant Stable — $12,000 — Br.—Gulick B (Fla) — Tr.—Sedlacek Sue
108⁵ — Lifetime 19 1 2 1 $13,300 — 1985 3 0 0 0 — 1984 16 1 2 1 $13,300 — Turf 4 0 1 0 $3,030

28Jan85- 2Aqu fst 1 1/16 ⊡ :48⅕ 1:14⅗ 1:50 ⒻClm 12000 2 10 1112 1014 1015 710½ Garrido O L5 b 108 11.90 50-25 M.SensitivK116½JumpingWithJoy108¾StyOnCours1171 No factor 12
12Jan85- 2Aqu fst 1 1/16 ⊡ :47⅗ 1:14⅕ 1:48⅖ ⒻClm 16500 4 8 1019 1221 1219 920½ Garrido O L5 b 110 19.30 48-24 Lady Nizon 1175½ Bell Carmel 117no Pistachio 1174¾ Far back 12
3Jan85- 9Aqu fst 1⅛ ⊡ :47⅘ 1:13⅗ 1:54 ⒻClm 20000 3 6 611 814 816 713½ Wynter N5 b 108 15.20 58-19 Romalane 1171½ Torsions Pet 1141 Lucas Lou 1081¾ No factor 9
21Dec84- 2Med sly 1 1/16 :48⅕ 1:14 1:49⅗ 3↑ⒻClm c-12500 6 8 88¼ 78¼ 44½ 32¾ Blackstun KM5 b 111 6.00 58-23 ⒹDareport 111nk Ring On Doc 1192½AnnieBlueeyes111½ Mild rally 8
21Dec84-Placed second through disqualification
13Dec84- 3Med fst 170 :47⅗ 1:13 1:44 ⒻClm 16000 5 5 65½ 65½ 66 43¾ Blackstun KM5 b 113 8.90 75-20 Feeling Free 113¾ Ellen's Ad 108hd Streaking Sue 1143 Late bid 7
6Dec84- 3Med gd 1 :47⅗ 1:14⅘ 1:42 3↑ⒻMd 16000 6 6 46½ 2hd 15 110 Blackstun KM7 b 112 1.60 71-26 AnnieBlueeyes11210T.J.'sSong119nkHttrsPrincess1145 Ridden out 7
16Nov84- 7Med yl 1 1/16 Ⓣ:49⅕ 1:15⅗ 1:49⅕ ⒻClm 20000 2 7 34½ 42½ 62 73 Blackstun KM7 b 108 10.70 53-44 MissBattagli1151½WyetteCoghlin115½MidnightDelight107nk Tired 10
7Nov84- 4Med fst 170 :46⅗ 1:12⅘ 1:43⅗ ⒻClm 25000 9 6 712 88¾ 811 913½ Garrido O L7 b 108 19.50 67-19 Streaking Sue 108½ Slady's Princess 1083 Silverlust 1134 Tired 9
22Oct84- 3Med fm 1 1/16 Ⓣ:46⅘ 1:11⅕ 1:43 3↑ⒻMd Sp Wt 2 6 66½ 44 25 24 Santagata N b 117 7.80 83-13 IllustriousJonne1174AnnieBlueys117noStgDoorMmm1126 Gamely 7
4Oct84- 3Bel fst 1 :48 1:14⅕ 1:41⅗ 3↑ⒻMd 22500 13 9 76½ 47½ 44 43½ Santagata N b 117 10.70 53-26 JumpingWithJoy1191Drvton117¾WkUpLISuzy1191¾ Lacked a rally 13

Jumping With Joy — B. f. 4, by Landscaper—High Rulerae, by Spring Double
Own.—Rory Green Stable — $12,000 — Br.—Murty Farm & Reinhart (Ky) — Tr.—Sedlacek Michael C
108⁵ — Lifetime 15 1 3 0 $18,320 — 1985 2 0 1 0 $2,750 — 1984 13 1 2 0 $15,570 — Turf 2 0 0 0

28Jan85- 2Aqu fst 1 1/16 ⊡ :48⅕ 1:14⅗ 1:50 ⒻClm 12000 7 5 52¾ 42½ 22 2½ Moore D N5 b 108 7.00 59-25 M.SensitiveKe116½JumpingWithJoy108¾StyOnCours1171 Rallied 12
12Jan85- 2Aqu fst 1 1/16 ⊡ :47⅗ 1:14⅕ 1:48⅖ ⒻClm 15500 1 3 613 918 1117 1120½ Moore D N b 108 11.90 48-24 Lady Nizon 1175½ Bell Carmel 117no Pistachio 1174¾ Tired 12
29Dec84- 1Aqu my 1 1/16 ⊡ :47⅘ 1:12⅖ 1:45⅘ ⒻClm 15500 8 1 2hd 2hd 1hd 2nk Moore D N5 b 107 14.20 83-17 Conshohockn112nkJumpngWthJoy107nkMstAStrght109no Gamely 8
19Dec84- 9Aqu fst 1⅛ ⊡ :48⅘ 1:15 1:55⅘ 3↑ⒻClm 12000 2 4 45½ 33 35 410¾ Davis R G b 111 10.40 52-25 Torsions Pet 1172¾ Lucas Lou 1127 SweetMissyG.1011 Weakened 11
6Dec84- 2Aqu sly 1 1/16 ⊡ :47⅘ 1:13⅕ 1:45⅖ ⒻClm 15500 5 5 67½ 67 714 816½ Cordero A Jr b 112 5.40 69-16 Pretty Niche 1164¾ Mist A Straight 1051¾Vicky'sHolly1123¾ Tired 10
15Nov84- 5Aqu fst 1 :46 1:12 1:40 ⒻClm 30000 6 6 617 913 916 817 Moore D N5 107 13.50 49-29 Gentle Ram 1091½ Best Venture 1065 Heavenly Splash 1123 Tired 9
4Nov84- 9Aqu fst 6f :23⅕ :47⅖ 1:13⅘ ⒻClm c-17500 1 8 95 96¾ 65 53¾ Velasquez J 116 3.90 68-25 Pair Of Queens 1121 Resonner 109½ Purse Keyes 1161¾ No factor 10
27Oct84- 9Aqu my 1 :46⅗ 1:11⅕ 1:38 ⒻClm 18000 5 8 84¾ 611 68½ 65½ Velasquez J 114 3.60 70-16 Oh My Lark 116½ Tiki Taylor 1124 Harvard Whip 111¾ No factor 10
17Oct84- 5Bel fst 7f :23 :47⅕ 1:25⅗ ⒻClm 20000 11 1 62¾ 31 53¼ 44 Velasquez J 114 8.30 70-21 WhisperingIrish1122½JosElSgundo1131½MissLilZ.109hd Weakened 11
10Oct84- 5Bel fst 1 :47⅖ 1:13 1:39⅘ ⒻClm 20000 5 7 85¾ 74½ 45 22¾ Velasquez J 118 7.40 63-25 WildeyedBeuty1112¾JumpingWithJoy118hdPurseKeyes116no Wide 11

Stay On Course — Dk. b. or br. f. 4, by J O Tobin—T V Aglo, by T V Lark
Own.—Winchell V H — $14,000 — Br.—Winchell V H Jr (Ky) — Tr.—Brown Warren E
117 — Lifetime 17 1 1 1 $8,766 — 1985 3 0 0 1 $1,500 — 1984 14 1 1 0 $7,266

28Jan85- 2Aqu fst 1 1/16 ⊡ :48⅕ 1:14⅗ 1:50 ⒻClm 14000 12 1 1hd 12 12 33½ Davis R G b 117 45.40 57-25 M.SnsitivK116½JumpingWithJoy108¾StyOnCours1171 Weakened 12
25Jan85- 1Aqu fst 170 ⊡ :47⅘ 1:13⅗ 1:45⅖ ⒻClm 17500 7 5 44½ 65¾ 916 1016¾ Santagata N b 117 49.70 56-23 BellCarmel1134¾Christamela108hdGoldenGreens117no Fell far bck 10
11Jan85- 5Aqu fst 6f ⊡ :23⅗ :47⅗ 1:13⅖ ⒻClm 25000 8 7 73½ 813 816 915½ Santagata N b 117 61.20 61-30 Belgard 1192 Video Queen 117½ DHChiming Jet 110 Outrun 10
27Dec84- 1Med fst 6f :23⅕ :47⅕ 1:13⅕ 3↑ⒻMd 16000 3 7 3½ 32½ 32 1nk Santagata N b 118 11.40 76-16 StayOnCourse118nkHattarsPrincess1131½CrimsonRun1182 Driving 10
17Dec84- 1Med fst 1 :48⅕ 1:14⅕ 1:41⅗ 3↑ⒻMd 20000 3 3 34 67½ 58 511½ Garrido O L5 b 113 11.50 62-21 Bonnie Princess 1131½ T. J.'s Song116¾KomputerKathy1116 Tired 7
6Dec84- 3Med gd 1 :47⅗ 1:14⅘ 1:42 3↑ⒻMd 16000 3 5 56½ 45½ 49 415½ Santagata N b 119 3.40 56-26 AnnieBlueeyes11210T.J.'sSong119nkHattrsPrincess1145 No threat 7
21Nov84- 3Med fst 1 1/16 :48⅘ 1:14⅗ 1:50⅖ 3↑ⒻMd 22500 2 4 35½ 45½ 64½ 75¼ Davis R G b 115 8.50 52-28 Conshohocken 117¾ Derivation 1151½ Midnight Delight107¾ Tired 7
30Oct84- 3Med fst 6f :23⅕ :48 1:13⅗ 3↑ⒻMd Sp Wt 3 6 713 712 712 714¼ Antley C W b 118 12.60 59-24 Lady Joanne 1185 Jet On Back 119¾ Damask Sky 113¾ Outrun 7
23Oct84- 2Med gd 1 :47⅘ 1:14⅕ 1:41⅘ 3↑ⒻMd 22500 1 3 1hd 3½ 32 48¼ Ward W A5 b 110 2.50 64-20 Pick oftheHarem1173½MidnightDelight107¾Moira'sDeal1174 Tired 8
9Oct84- 4Med fst 6f :22⅘ :46⅖ 1:13⅘ 3↑ⒻMd 20000 9 1 42¾ 33½ 32½ 21 Conner M J5 b 113 25.60 72-22 Sizzling Skirt 1181 Stay On Course 1135 Sweepaway116hd Rallied 9
LATEST WORKOUTS Jan 23 Bel tr.t 5f fst 1:05 b Dec 24 Med 3f gd :36⅖ b Dec 14 Med 5f fst 1:02 b

Silent Hush — Dk. b. or br. f. 4, by Resound—Midnight Hush, by Sunrise Flight
Own.—Lane Glenn — $12,000 — Br.—Beau Val Farm (Va) — Tr.—Sedlacek Michael C
108⁵ — Lifetime 24 3 4 7 $33,540 — 1985 1 0 0 0 — 1984 20 3 3 7 $31,630 — Turf 1 0 0 1 $1,045

25Jan85- 1Aqu fst 170 ⊡ :47⅘ 1:13⅗ 1:45⅖ ⒻClm 15500 9 7 65¾ 55½ 68 67½ Moore D N5 b 108 6.40 66-23 Bell Carmel 1134¾Christamela108hdGoldenGreens117no Off slowly 10
26Dec84- 7Key fst 1 1/16 :47⅕ 1:13 1:46⅗ ⒻClm 12000 1 3 12 12½ 1hd 22¾ Nied J Jr b 112 3.70 68-25 Sarah Ashway 1162¾ Silent Hush1122½MakeHappen1202½ 2nd best 10
16Dec84- 6Key fst 170 :47⅖ 1:13⅗ 1:45⅗ ⒻClm 12000 3 5 57 3½ 2hd 3½ Simpson B H5 b 109 4.10 71-25 Make Happen 116hd Sarah Ashway 116½ Silent Hush 1095 Hung 11
21Nov84- 6Key fst 1 1/16 :47⅗ 1:12⅘ 1:46⅖ ⒻClm 11000 6 3 32½ 31 21 32½ Simpson B H5 b 113 *2.00 70-22 Miss Kiskadee 108½SarahAshway1161½SilentHush113nk Weakened 7
12Nov84- 7Key fst 170 :48⅖ 1:14⅗ 1:44⅘ ⒻClm 14000 6 4 45 53½ 58½ 59½ Cole M A5 b 108 9.40 66-28 Bovey Tracy1124MightyEchelon1183YenDancer1141 Bobbled gate 8
19Oct84- 5Key fst 170 :46⅖ 1:11⅘ 1:44⅕ ⒻClm 11000 3 4 2hd 2½ 2½ 2no Cole M A5 b 114 3.90 79-18 Cold Test 116no Silent Hush 114nk RamblingRobber117½ Steadied 9
10Oct84- 1Key fst 170 :47⅕ 1:12⅗ 1:43⅕ ⒻClm 14000 6 3 32½ 31 33½ 37½ Conner M J5 b 107 4.60 77-18 Yen Dancer 114nk Mighty Echelon 1167 Silent Hush 1072½ Evenly 8
26Sep84- 2Key fst 170 :47⅖ 1:14⅖ 1:46⅖ ⒻClm 11000 3 4 34 21½ 11½ 1½ Conner M J5 b 111 3.50 68-25 Silent Hush 111½ Cold Test 1191 Erin Terry 114hd Driving 9
15Sep84- 1Key sly 170 :47⅘ 1:13⅖ 1:44⅖ ⒻClm 10000 4 3 2hd 3nk 2hd 2no Conner M J5 b 109 3.10Ⓓ 78-21 Tall Tell 111noⒹSilentHush1091Elaine'sGift1082 Drifted; bumped 8
15Sep84-Disqualified and placed third
LATEST WORKOUTS Jan 19 Aqu ⊡ 4f fst :50⅘ b

Fantasia Agapi Mou — B. m. 5, by Mullineaux—Sweet Fantasy, by LE Fabuleux
Own.—Lostritto J A — $12,000 — Br.—Avraamides Andreas (NY) — Tr.—Lostritto Joseph A
113 — Lifetime 22 1 3 0 $34,370 — 1985 3 0 0 0 $750 — 1984 9 0 1 0 $9,350 — Turf 5 0 1 0 $4,180

28Jan85- 2Aqu fst 1 1/16 ⊡ :48⅕ 1:14⅗ 1:50 ⒻClm 12000 9 12 99¾ 86¾ 58 44½ Lovato F Jr 113 16.30 56-25 M.SensitiveKe116½JumpingWithJoy108¾StyOnCours1171 Rallied 12
13Jan85- 1Aqu fst 6f ⊡ :23⅕ :47⅘ 1:13⅗ ⒻClm 12000 3 9 96½ 816 1014 1014½ Deegan J C 113 18.80 61-27 Perfect Gift 114½ Radiant Gem 1132 FutureFriend1142½ No speed 12
3Jan85- 1Aqu fst 6f ⊡ :23⅕ :47⅕ 1:13⅕ ⒻClm 14000 3 8 85½ 76½ 62¾ 63¾ Ward W A5 112 15.80 74-19 GoldenGrns117hdDuckyDuchss113hdRdintGm1131¾ Overland route 11
22Jun84- 5Bel fm 1 1/16 Ⓣ:46⅘ 1:12 1:44⅖ 3↑ⒻⓈAlw 26000 9 11 107¾ 87½ 77 710½ Maple E 117 9.80 63-19 Danger Zone 1132 Wild Tune 1145¾ Shipboard Fling 112no Outrun 12
25May84- 9Bel fst 1 1/16 :47⅕ 1:13 1:46⅕ 3↑ⒻⓈAlw 26000 12 6 43½ 31½ 22½ 22 Maple E 121 17.90 69-23 Oedipus Rex1212FantasiaAgapiMou1213½MissCosmic113no Rallied 12
20May84- 1Bel fst 7f :23⅗ :47⅖ 1:25⅕ ⒻClm 18000 2 6 612 611 69½ 47½ Velasquez J 113 8.30 69-18 Listed 117½ Gala Ball 1172¾ Silver Judy 1174 Steadied 6
19Apr84- 8Aqu fst 1⅛ :49⅖ 1:14⅘ 1:54⅘ 3↑ⒻⓈAlw 26000 6 1 11 2½ 33 67¾ MacBeth D 121 24.30 53-26 Lotus Delight 1131½ PromiseKept1093EverHigher121no Weakened 10
13Apr84- 1Aqu fst 170 ⊡ :48⅖ 1:13⅗ 1:45 ⒻClm 30000 1 5 43 58 513 411½ Muino M M7 109 8.40 64-22 Bravest Girl 1174¾ Jay Netta Joe 106nk BongShik1146½ No factor 7
4Apr84- 3Aqu fst 170 ⊡ :48⅘ 1:14⅘ 1:45⅖ ⒻClm 20000 4 8 61¾ 76½ 46½ 46½ Lovato F Jr 113 31.50 66-20 BiggrEnough1155½TorsionsPt108½SomthingFin117¾ Lacked room 10
16Mar84- 3Aqu fst 1⅛ ⊡ :49 1:14⅗ 1:56⅕ ⒻClm 16000 12 8 89¾ 86½ 43½ 44 Lovato F Jr 117 59.70 57-25 History Belle 1131¾ Whitewalls 1121½LuretheLady117¾ Bid evenly 12
LATEST WORKOUTS Jan 11 Bel tr.t 3f fst :37⅖ b Dec 31 Bel tr.t 4f fst :50⅘ b Dec 23 Bel tr.t 3f fst :38⅕ b Dec 12 Bel tr.t 3f fst :38 b

Also Eligible (Not in Post Position Order):

Shofoose — Dk. b. or br. m. 6, by Silent Doon—Little Galla, by Completelea
Own.—Miller Josephine — $12,000 — Br.—Leonhard Jr & Miller (Pa) — Tr.—Rigione John H
106⁷ — Lifetime 65 12 3 11 $108,148 — 1985 1 0 0 0 — 1984 20 0 1 2 $7,280 — Turf 6 1 0 2 $6,285

23Jan85- 2Aqu fst 6f ⊡ :23 :47⅕ 1:13⅖ ⒻClm 12000 8 9 93¾ 75 63¾ 64¾ Privitera R7 106 11.20 72-24 MaggieCart1122Lyphrd'sChoice106hdFutureFriend113½ No factor 12
19Dec84- 9Aqu fst 1⅛ ⊡ :48⅘ 1:15 1:55⅘ 3↑ⒻClm 12000 4 1 11½ 11 45½ 514½ Cordero A Jr 113 6.80 49-25 Torsions Pet 1172¾ Lucas Lou 1127 SweetMissyG.1011 Weakened 11
23Nov84- 3Aqu fst 1 :47⅘ 1:14 1:40⅕ 3↑ⒻClm 12000 3 2 2½ 1hd 36 38¾ Gomez E R 113 9.10 56-29 Torsions Pet 1171½ Bell Carmel 1177½ Shofoose 1134 Weakened 7
2Nov84- 3Aqu fst 1⅛ :50⅕ 1:16 1:56 3↑ⒻClm 12000 4 2 2½ 2½ 31 32½ Gomez E R 113 16.60 53-35 Bell Carmel 113½ Lucas Lou 1121¾ Shofoose 113hd Weakened 6
20Sep84- 1Bel fst 1 :47⅖ 1:13⅖ 1:39⅗ 3↑ⒻClm 12000 6 4 69½ 614 621 623¾ Samyn J L 113 12.20 43-26 Quiet Glory 1191 Lucas Lou 1123½ Torsions Pet 1172 Tired 6
5Sep84- 9Bel fst 1 1/16 :46⅗ 1:12 1:44⅖ 3↑ⒻClm 12000 6 5 74¾ 1012 1021 1024½ MacBeth D 113 14.10 56-12 Quiet Glory 1172½ Lucas Lou 117¾ Halcyon Hour 1104 Outrun 10
29Aug84- 3Mth fst 1 :47⅖ 1:12⅖ 1:39⅕ 3↑ⒻClm 10000 1 1 1½ 2hd 44 47½ Conner M J5 110 2.00 69-23 MissDustyB.1111AutumnChnges1194Louie'sNtiv1152½ Drifted out 5
13Aug84- 7Mth fst 1 1/16 :48 1:12⅕ 1:44 3↑ⒻClm 14000 5 4 43 47 412 513 Thornburg B 114 10.00 72-16 Singing Oak 1092 Royal Courtesy 1165 Quiet Glory 1135 Evenly 9
13Aug84-Awarded fourth purse money
2Aug84- 4Mth fst 1 1/16 :49⅖ 1:14⅕ 1:46⅘ 3↑ⒻClm 12500 3 2 2hd 11 1½ 2¾ Conner M J5 111 10.80 70-20 Autumn Changes 114¾ Shofoose 111no Bossy Rose 1146 Gamely 7
LATEST WORKOUTS Feb 4 Bel tr.t 5f fst 1:03⅕ b Jan 14 Bel tr.t 5f fst 1:02 b

capping tenets. Most players would have taken a quick look at this field and caught an early train home! The race in question was the ninth at Aqueduct on February 7, 1985, a route contest for the cheapest fillies on the grounds.

At this lowly level one doesn't expect to find "winning" horses, and this race is no exception. Only Shofoose, breaking from the extreme outside post, had a decent career win percentage. Yet she hadn't won in at least twenty-one starts. To bet any of these animals, one needed something positive that was hidden from the average player—and a decent price. The "out well" provided the hidden information, and, in this case at least, the prices were right.

With Mark Berner's permission, we have reprinted his selections for this race exactly as they appeared in *Newsday*. I know for a fact that Mark loved Annie Blueeyes in this race based on her strong "out well" move. It is to his credit that he shared his information and enthusiasm with his readers rather than keep it to himself. For that matter, most public handicappers would have done the same. Picking winners in print is that important to them.

9 1 1/8 Miles. 4-Year-Olds & Up. F&M. Claiming $14,000-12,000. Purse $12,500.

			Jockey	Trainer	Wt.	ML
A	1	xxPhotojournalist	Guerra	Fernandez	106	20-1
B	2	Halcyon Hour	Santagata	Olsen	113	15-1
C	3	Demean's Gold	Davis	DiAngelo	113	20-1
D	4	xxxSweet Missy G.	Reed	DeStasio	103	5-1
E	5	Vicky's Holly	Samyn	Howe	113	12-1
F	6	Lady Nizon	Graell	Nadler	122	2-1
G	7	Mist A Straight	Santagata	J Imperio	117	8-1
H	8	xAnnie Blueeyes	Garrido	S Sedlacek	108	15-1
I	9a	xJumping With Joy	Moore	M Sedlacek	108	7-2
J	10	Stay On Course	Davis	Brown	117	12-1
K	11a	xSilent Hush	Moore	M Sedlacek	117	7-2
L	12	FantasAgapiMou	Lovato	Lostritto	113	12-1
M	13	xxShofoose	Privitera	Rigione	106	12-1

1. Annie Blueeyes. 2. Jumping With Joy. 3. Photojournalist. 4. Sweet Missy G.

Annie Blueeyes was bothered in the first turn and found her best stride too late in last; finished out-well. **Jumping With Joy** placed at this level in last besting many of these. **Photojournalist** finished out-well in last and tries two-turns again. **Sweet Missy G.** was freshened following a good effort; chance for part of triple.

Speaking with Berner a few weeks after this race, I learned the following details:

(1) Annie Blueeyes had finished "out well" in 14.4 seconds on January 28, the best of the day at a route distance.
(2) Photojournalist had finished "out well" in 14.2 seconds on January 13, the best "out well" of that day at any distance.
(3) Sweet Missy G had finished "out well" in 14.4 seconds on December 29, the best of that day at a route distance. It was now almost six weeks since that move, however,
(4) Mist A Straight was a marginal "out well" on January 19, finishing her extra furlong in 16 seconds.

Without this additional information, it would have been difficult to make a case for either Annie Blueeyes or Photojournalist. But when one of the cheaper horses on the grounds proves "best of the day" (or close to it) at something, that is worth noting and following up on. To suggest that either was worth a small wager at the prevailing odds is hardly stretching the point. If the two had been used to key a triple wager—an outlay of $108 with each of the nine others used in each position—the resulting ticket would have been worth $4970.00!!

NINTH RACE
Aqueduct
FEBRUARY 7, 1985

1 ⅛ MILES.(InnerDirt). (1.48$\frac{2}{5}$) CLAIMING. Purse $12,500. Fillies and mares, 4–year–olds and upward. Weight, 122 lbs. Non–winners of two races at a mile or over since Janaury 1 allowed 3 lbs. Of such a race since then, 5 lbs. Claiming price $14,000; for each $1,000 to $12,000, 2 lbs. (Races when entered for $10,000 or less not considered.)

Value of race $12,500; value to winner $7,500; second $2,750; third $1,500; fourth $750. Mutuel pool $81,050, OTB pool $205,333. Triple Pool $156,173. OTB Triple Pool $310,439.

Last Raced	Horse	Eqt.A.Wt	PP	St	¼	½	¾	Str	Fin	Jockey	Cl'g Pr	Odds $1
28Jan85 ^{2}Aqu^{7}	Annie Blueeyes	b 4 108	7	7	$4^{\frac{1}{2}}$	3^{1}	1^{2}	1^{8}	$1^{6\frac{3}{4}}$	Garrido O L^{5}	12000	15.40
19Jan85 ^{3}Aqu^{6}	Mist A Straight	4 117	6	3	8^{1}	9^{1}	9^{2}	5^{1}	$2^{1\frac{1}{4}}$	Santagata N	14000	5.00
13Jan85 ^{1}Aqu^{8}	Photojournalist	6 106	1	2	7^{hd}	7^{hd}	5^{hd}	3^{hd}	3^{nk}	Guerra A A^{7}	12000	32.70
29Dec84 ^{1}Aqu^{4}	Sweet Missy G.	4 103	4	11	11	11	11	7^{1}	$4^{\frac{1}{2}}$	Reed R L^{10}	12000	4.40
25Jan85 ^{1}Aqu^{6}	Silent Hush	b 4 108	9	8	3^{hd}	$4^{1\frac{1}{2}}$	$4^{\frac{1}{2}}$	4^{1}	5^{2}	Moore D N^{5}	12000	2.40
28Jan85 ^{2}Aqu^{4}	Fantasia Agapi Mou	5 113	10	10	$9^{1\frac{1}{2}}$	8^{1}	7^{1}	$6^{\frac{1}{2}}$	6^{2}	Lovato F Jr	12000	10.70
28Jan85 ^{2}Aqu^{5}	Halcyon Hour	b 5 113	2	1	$10^{\frac{1}{2}}$	10^{2}	8^{1}	8^{6}	$7^{1\frac{3}{4}}$	Migliore R	12000	17.60
28Jan85 ^{2}Aqu^{9}	Vicky's Holly	b 4 113	5	5	1^{1}	1^{1}	3^{1}	2^{hd}	$8^{6\frac{1}{2}}$	Samyn J L	12000	10.90
25Jan85 ^{1}Aqu^{8}	Demean's Gold	b 4 113	3	4	6^{4}	6^{2}	6^{hd}	10^{2}	$9^{\frac{3}{4}}$	Ward W A	12000	25.50
28Jan85 ^{2}Aqu^{3}	Stay On Course	b 4 117	8	6	$2^{1\frac{1}{2}}$	$2^{\frac{1}{2}}$	$2^{\frac{1}{2}}$	9^{1}	$10^{3\frac{1}{2}}$	Davis R G	14000	5.50
23Jan85 ^{2}Aqu^{6}	Shofoose	6 106	11	9	5^{1}	5^{hd}	10^{1}	11	11	Privitera R^{7}	12000	14.50

OFF AT 4:01 Start good, Won easily. Time, :23$\frac{2}{5}$, :48$\frac{3}{5}$, 1:14$\frac{4}{5}$, 1:42$\frac{4}{5}$, 1:56$\frac{3}{5}$ Track fast.

$2 Mutuel Prices:			
8–(H)–ANNIE BLUEEYES	32.80	12.60	10.20
7–(G)–MIST A STRAIGHT		6.60	4.80
2–(A)–PHOTOJOURNALIST			14.00

$2 TRIPLE 8–7–2 PAID $4,970.00.

B. f, by Teddy's Courage—Maid Of Sorrow, by Wolfram. Trainer Sedlacek Sue. Bred by Gulick B (Fla).

ANNIE BLUEEYES, stealing away from opposition leaving backstretch, reached finish with substantial margin proving much the best. MIST A STRAIGHT's late run earned her place share. PHOTOJOURNALIST wide during late stags, lasted over SWEET MISSY G. The latter, trailing initial six furlongs, finished with good energy SILENT HUSH lacked response. FANTASIA AGAPI MOU took overland route. HALCYON HOUR was never prominent. VICKY'S HOLLY stopped. DEMEAN'S GOLD was outrun. STAY ON COURSE faded midway of fina bend.

Serious players should never accept any handicapping concept—new or old—without proof. Does the "out well" angle really work? To help answer this question, and obtain some statistics, we asked Mark Berner if we could publish results based on his weekly "Horses to Watch" column in *Newsday*. He agreed, thereby putting his reputation, and that of his favorite angle, on the line. The following statistics cover all "out wells" mentioned in Berner's column, from its first appearance in February 1985 through the end of the 1985 season. The results are excellent, especially when one considers that there were no strings attached, no handicapping judgments required.

Horses	*Winners*	*Win Percent*	*Dollar Net*
179	37	20.7%	$2.67

These statistics, of course, reflect the "out well" at its best. The horses Berner mentions in his column are the cream of the "out well" crop—those with the best moves of the week or trained by the "right" trainers or most likely to benefit from the training move and show marked improvement next time out. Maidens and freshened horses are as likely as any candidates to benefit from such a move.

As we have already mentioned, this is precisely the way the "out well" angle should be played.

Berner's most interesting selection during the 1985 season was

Equalize Gr. c. 3, by Northern Jove—Zonta, by Dr Fager Lifetime 1985 1 M 0 0
Br.—Tartan Farms Corp (Fla) 1 0 0 0 1984 0 M 0 0
Own.—Tartan Stable Tr.—Nerud Jan H 1157
4Mar85- 6Aqu fst 6f :23 :46⅘ 1:11⅗ Md Sp Wt 10 8 75¼ 915 915 814 Guerra A A7 115 17.60e 73-22 EternlPrince1228ChngeThLock122nkAlx'sGm122no Raced greenly 10
LATEST WORKOUTS Mar 13 Bel tr.t 4f gd :51⅕ b Mar 2 Bel tr.t 4f fst :51⅕ b Feb 24 Bel tr.t 4f fst :50⅘ b Feb 4 Bel tr.t 4f fst :49 b

Equalize was "out well" in :14.3 seconds on March 4, the best move of that day, after breaking slowly and racing greenly. Nonetheless, he still finished only six lengths out of second place, behind runaway winner Eternal Prince. All signs pointed to an improved effort in his second start, which was at seven furlongs. That improvement paid off to the tune of $119.20!!! The victory was the first of three consecutive for the colt at that meet, the third coming in a minor stakes event on Wood Memorial Day. Many "out wells" do well in their second start after the training move, too, although the statistics we have presented focus only on the first start after the move.

Trainer Jan Nerud's runners seem to flourish on the heels of an "out well" performance, suggesting that Nerud schedules the additional furlong move as a routine part of his conditioning process. Another example during 1985 was the filly Ecorche, who broke her maiden on October 28 in her second career start.

Ecorche Dk. b. or br. f. 3, by Big Spruce—Idmon, by Dr Fager Lifetime 1985 2 1 0 0 $13,200
Br.—Tartan Farms (Fla) 2 1 0 0 1984 0 M 0 0
Own.—Tartan Stable Tr.—Nerud Jan H 115 $13,200
28Oct85- 9Aqu fst 7f :23⅕ :47⅘ 1:25⅘ 3+ⒻMd Sp Wt 2 8 1½ 1hd 1hd 11 Venezia M 119 4.10 74-26 Ecorche 1191 Roberto's Social 119¾ Dunsaname 1194¾ Driving 10
19Sep85- 2Bel fst 7f :22⅘ :45⅘ 1:25⅘ 3+ⒻMd Sp Wt 8 10 88½ 58½ 79 65½ Venezia M 118 3.80 69-20 I'mWllBrd1181EmbrcblSlw1181¾UnlimitdAccount118½ Raced wide 11
LATEST WORKOUTS Oct 23 Bel 4f fst :47⅗ h Oct 19 Bel tr.t 4f fst :48⅘ b Oct 12 Bel tr.t 4f fst :51⅖ b Sep 29 Bel 4f fst :48 b

On September 19, Ecorche finished out an extra eighth mile in :13.3 after racing wide the entire trip in a race whose shape was "fast-slow." Notice that the filly's odds increased only marginally from a well-backed 7–2 for her debut to 9–2 on October 28, following an apparently dull effort first time out. Obviously many in the New York audience that day were attuned to Nerud's use of a horse's first career start for educational and conditioning purposes.

While discussing Ecorche, we must question whether she merited support in her third start, a "nonwinners of one" allowance contest at a flat mile, for which she was installed the 7–5 favorite? Ordinarily one should refrain from supporting recent maiden graduates their first time in allowance company, unless the animal proved its competitiveness while accomplishing that initial victory in fast time. This is all the more so, in fact, as the season wears on and the quality of the maiden winner (and the animals it defeated) becomes suspect—especially if that maiden winner failed to get to the races until late in its three-year-old season. On the other hand, one might reason that while maiden fields get weaker as the racing season rolls along, so also do "nonwinners of one" fields, and a talented, though possibly unsound or injury-prone, animal may easily parlay temporary good condition into a quick pair of wins. Working in Ecorche's favor here is the fact that Nerud is noted for his ability to get a repeat win following a maiden victory. Only a couple of weeks before, a Nerud filly named Seminoli followed a weak-figure maiden win with a nine-length romp in allowance company. Like Ecorche, Seminoli had come to the races late in her career and had broken her maiden second time out. Ecorche followed suit on November 9, winning her first allowance test by nearly eleven lengths. Her time for that race surpassed par time for filly and mare stakes events at the same distance and was hardly forecast by the rather average time she posted breaking her maiden.

A horse has seldom, if ever, worked "out well" in as sensational a style as did Turkoman on October 16, 1985.

Turkoman — Dk. b. or br. c. 3, by Alydar—Taba, by Table Play
Own.—Saron Stable — Br.—Robertson Corbin J (Ky) — Tr.—Jones Gary — 122

Lifetime	1985	10 2 5 2	$228,610	
11 3 5 2	1984	1 1 0 0	$12,100	
$240,710				

16Oct85- 8Bel	fst	7f	:23⅕	:46⅘	1:22⅖	3+ Alw 27000	2	6	65½	43½	13½	110	Vasquez J	114	*.50	90–22	Turkomn11410PurplMountn1141½AccordngToLuk1145	Ridden out	6
17Aug85- 8Sar	fst	1¼	:48⅕	1:36⅕	2:01⅕	Travers	2	1	2½	2½	2½	22½	McHargue D G	126	7.60	92–08	Chief's Crown 1262½ Turkoman 1263 Skip Trial 126½	Weakened	7
17Aug85-Grade I																			
21Jly85- 8Hol	fst	1¼	:47	1:36	2:01⅘	Swaps	3	8	76½	63¾	31	2no	McHargue D G	115	*1.90	105–04	Padua 115no Turkoman 1153½ Don't Say Halo 1202½	Fast finish	8
21Jly85-Grade I																			
29Jun85- 7Hol	fst	1	:44⅘	1:08⅘	1:33⅘	Slvr Scrn H	2	9	910	89¾	56½	43½	McHargue D G	118	*1.50	100 —	Pancho Villa 118½ProudestDoon1182Nostalgia'sStar1181	Crowded	9
29Jun85-Grade II																			
16Jun85- 5Hol	fst	1	:45⅗	1:10	1:34⅕	Alw 32000	3	6	66½	33	12½	13½	McHargue D G	115	*.80	102–02	Turkoman 1153½ Ascension 1164 Sapient 1142½	Ridden out	7
20Apr85- 8GG	fst	1⅛	:47⅘	1:11⅗	1:48⅘	Cal Derby	9	8	75½	32	33½	22½	McHargue D G	115	*1.70	87–13	Hajji's Treasure1152½Turkoman115noNostalgia'sStar1163½	Gamely	10
20Apr85-Grade II																			
30Mar85- 8GG	fst	1 1/16	:45⅖	1:09⅘	1:41⅕	Gold Rush	10	8	911	85½	45	2hd	McHargue D G b	115	*1.60	97–13	Protect Yourself117hdTurkoman115nkFullHonor1151½	Just missed	10
3Mar85- 6SA	fst	1 1/16	:46⅕	1:10⅖	1:43⅖	Alw 28000	9	5	42½	42½	64	33	Hawley S b	114	*1.40	81–14	Bolder Than Bold 118noAscension1093Turkoman1141½	Drifted out	9
30Jan85- 9SA	fst	1 1/16	:47⅗	1:11⅘	1:43⅘	Alw 25000	5	6	74½	64½	33	31½	Hawley S b	114	*.50	81–17	RoyalOlympia1151½RelaunchATune114hdTurkomn1141½	Lugged in	7
13Jan85- 4SA	fst	1 1/16	:46⅖	1:11⅗	1:42	Alw 24000	5	6	63	3½	2½	22½	Hawley S b	114	3.60	88–13	Skywalker 1182½ Turkoman 1146 Royal Olympia 115½	Wide turn	7

LATEST WORKOUTS Oct 30 Aqu 4f fst :46⅗ h Oct 25 Bel 4f fst :47 b Oct 13 Bel 4f fst :46⅗ h

Prepping at seven furlongs for the Breeders' Cup Classic, the Alydar colt demolished his field on the turn with an eye-catching last-to-first move that encompassed no more than a sixteenth of a mile, while en route to a 1:22.2 clocking for the seven panels. Turkoman then worked an additional three furlongs, getting the mile in 1:34.3, nine furlongs in 1:47.4, and the full mile and a quarter in 2:01—all "racehorse" times, to say the least. Split into eighths, Turkoman went out three panels in :12.1, :13.1, and :13.1, respectively—all of which suggested that he had returned to the races a dramatically improved colt. Since he had been a reasonably close second to Classic favorite Chief's Crown in the Travers, it was relatively easy to project him as a probable winner of the $3,000,000 race. At 7–1 odds, he was hard to pass. However, a relatively slow start compounded by a total lack of racing room on the final turn and into the stretch, when the horse was full of run, prevented Turkoman from showing his true ability.

Chapter 31

A Change in Workout Pattern

A HORSE'S WORKOUT LINE can prove to be a significant supplement to its past performances. An especially sharp workout can signal improving form. The absence of workouts hints of physical problems.

More often than not, however, the workouts provide relatively insignificant information and can at times be misleading. The clockers miss some workouts and record others incorrectly. Indeed, the public remains ignorant of so much information on each workout—what the trainer hopes the horse will gain from the workout, for example—that the true significance of a workout is often beyond its comprehension.

When the 1984 Matron Stakes drew a small field of four juvenile fillies, with only three betting interests, Belmont officials carded it as the fifth race of the day, canceled the usual exacta, and combined it with the sixth race in an "instant" daily double. The key to that double lay in the recognition of not-so-subtle changes in the workout patterns of the favorites in the two races.

The Matron came down to a choice between Contredance, the leader protem of her division, and the Wayne Lukas-trained entry of Tiltalating and Fiesta Lady. Something seemed to have little chance. On breeding, Tiltalating did not figure to appreciate the final furlong, as her recent performance in Chicago seemed to prove. With everything breaking in her favor that day—a clear lead into the stretch over a sloppy track—she nevertheless succumbed to Contredance's late rush. Fiesta Lady, on the other hand, was the unknown factor in this field. She was a California shipper, just off the plane, making her first start in New York. And her West Coast form was good. After breaking her maiden going five-and-a-half furlongs at

5 BELMONT

7 FURLONGS

7 FURLONGS. (1.20⅘) 78th Running THE MATRON (Grade I). Purse $75,000 Added. Foals of Mares Served in 1981. (Filly Foals of 1982). Weights, 119 lbs. By subscription of $100 each if made on or before Tuesday, May 1, 1984 or $500 each on or before, Wednesday, August 15, 1984, fee to accompany the nomination. $300 to pass the entry box and $600 to start. The added money together with all nomination fees, entry and starting fees for The Matron of 1984 to be divided 60% to first, 22% to second, 12% to third and 6% to fourth, after original nominator awards of $5,000 to the winner, $2,500 to second, $1,250 to third. Starters to be named at the closing time of entries. Trophies will be presented to the winning owner, trainer and jockey. Supplementary nominations may be made at the time of entry by a payment of $3,750 each to pass the entry box and $7,500 to start with the provision that supplementary nominees are excluded from original nominator awards. The nominator awards will be presented to the first three original nominees to finish. Closed May 1, with 155 nominations at $100, closed August 15 with 12 additional at $500. Closed with one Supplementary nominee: Sociable Duck.

```
Coupled—Fiesta Lady and Tiltalating.

Sociable Duck     Dk. b. or br. f. 2, by Quack—Unsociable, by Never Bend      Lifetime   1984 3 1 1 0  $37,156
                  Br.—Bwamazon Farm (Ky)                               119   3 1 1 0
  Own.—Bwamazon Farm   Tr.—Casse Mark                                        $37,156
27Aug84- 8Sar fst 6f :22⅕ :45⅗ 1:11   ⒻSpinaway  7 1 2^1 2^1½ 2^1½ 2^1¼ Migliore R b 119 12.50 84-16 Tiltalating 1191¼ SociableDuck119¾Contredance1191¼ Held place 7
12Aug84- 4Sar fst 6f :22⅕ :45⅘ 1:11⅘  ⒻMd Sp Wt 10 2 2^1 1½ 1^5 1^9 Migliore R b 117 *1.90 82-15 SocibleDuck1179DncingPuddles1171½JuniperVlley117¾ Ridden out 12
11Jun84- 4Bel fst 5f :22⅗ :45⅘ :58⅗   ⒻMd Sp Wt 8 6 7^6 8^15 8^19 8^19 Migliore R 117 *1.30e 76-19 Gentle Kelly 1172¾ Golden Silence 1175½Sham'sBeauty1172¼ Wide 8
  LATEST WORKOUTS  ●Sep 24 Bel 4f fst :47 h   Sep 12 Bel 4f fst :47⅘ h   Aug 22 Sar 4f fst :47⅕ b   Aug 8 Sar 3f fst :36 h

Something         Ch. f. 2, by Superbity—Sweet Nothings, by Promsed Land      Lifetime   1984 6 2 3 0  $43,906
                  Br.—Massie Sandra M (Md)                             119   6 2 3 0
  Own.—Poulsen R J M   Tr.—Bond Bernard P                                    $43,906
15Sep84- 9Del sly 6f :22⅕ :45⅕ 1:11    Ⓕ(R)Unity Hall 6 2 2½ 1^3 1^6 1^3½ Kupfer T J b 112 2.90 86-31 Something 1123½ Bold Whim 1151 Heavenly Bound 11512 Driving 6
 4Aug84- 9Mth fst 6f :22⅗ :45⅕ 1:10⅘   ⒻSorority 12 1 4^1½ 5^3½ 6^8 7^12¾ Kupfer T b 119 37.10 73-13 Tiltalating 1195 Raise A Q. 119hd Schematic 1191 Fin. after 1/2 12
24Jly84- 8Mth fst 5½f :22⅗ :46⅗ 1:06⅕  ⒻColleen 3 2 2hd 2hd 1^1½ 2½ Kupfer T b 115 8.40 83-20 Count Pennies 115½ Something 1151½ Find 115nk Gamely 10
     24Jly84-Run in Divisions
13Jly84- 8Bow fst 5½f :22⅗ :46⅗ 1:05⅘  ⒻAlw 8000 4 1 1^1½ 1^2 1^2 2hd Kupfer T 119 *.50 91-20 Fleeting Glory111hdSomething119¾LadyLisaRuch1191 Just failed 6
 2Jly84- 8Bel fst 5½f :21⅘ :45⅘ 1:05⅕  ⒻAstoria 7 4 3^1½ 2hd 1^1 2^3 Kupfer T 113 4.80 86-15 Faster Than Fast 1103 Something113½QueenBreeze1121½ 2nd best 9
 8May84- 3Pim sly 5f :22 :46⅗ :59⅘      ⒻMd Sp Wt 2 2 1^1½ 1^3 1^2½ 1^1½ Kupfer T 119 2.20 86-20 Something 1191½ Dansez Seull 1197½ Chic AndSassy1191¾ Driving 8
  LATEST WORKOUTS  ●Sep 28 Lrl 3f sly :35 h   Sep 23 Lrl 4f fst :50 b   Sep 12 Lrl 4f fst :48⅘ b   ●Sep 5 Pim 6f my 1:14 h

Contredance *     B. f. 2, by Danzig—Nimble Folly, by Cyane                   Lifetime   1984 5 3 0 1  $292,086
                  Br.—Derry Meeting Farm (Pa)                          119   5 3 0 1
  Own.—Dokwiatkowski H   Tr.—Stephens Woodford C                             $292,086
 8Sep84- 8AP sly 7f :22 :45⅘ 1:26      ⒻArl Was Lass 2 2 3^2½ 3^2 2^1½ 1^1½ Day P 119 2.20 72-33 Contredance 1191½ Tiltalating 119¾ Miss Delice 1191¾ Driving 5
27Aug84- 8Sar fst 6f :22⅕ :45⅗ 1:11    ⒻSpinaway 5 7 7^14 5^9 3^4½ 3^4¾ Maple E 119 2.10 80-16 Tiltalting1191½SocibleDuck119¾Contrednce1191½ Stumbled start 7
16Aug84- 8Sar fst 6f :22⅕ :45 1:10⅗    ⒻAdirondack 4 1 1hd 1^2 1^2½ 1¾ Maple E 114 3.40e 88-21 Contredance 114¾ Outstandingly 1142½ Oriental 1144¾ Driving 7
 1Aug84- 8Sar fst 6f :22⅕ :46 1:11⅗    ⒻSchuylrville 4 3 2½ 2^2½ 6^8 8^12½ Maple E 114 *1.60 70-13 WeekendDelight1193Resembling114noWinters'Love1144½ Stopped 8
28Jun84- 6Bel fst 5f :22⅗ :46⅗ :59⅕    ⒻMd Sp Wt 2 2 1^1 1½ 1^3½ 1^4 Maple E 117 *.50 91-19 Contrednce1174FlyThruTheSkis1125ElinHmmings1174 Ridden out 6
  LATEST WORKOUTS  Sep 27 Bel 4f fst :48⅘ h   Sep 23 Bel 6f fst 1:13⅘ b   Sep 18 Bel 5f fst 1:00⅘ h   Sep 5 Bel 4f sly :46⅘ h

Fiesta Lady       Ch. f. 2, by Secretariat—Faneuil Girl, by Bolinas Boy       Lifetime   1984 6 2 2 0  $122,500
                  Br.—Brook & Stevens (Ky)                             119   6 2 2 0
  Own.—Klein Mr-Mrs E V   Tr.—Lukas D Wayne                                  $122,500
 2Sep84- 5Dmr fst 1 :45⅘ 1:12 1:38⅘    ⒻDebutante 6 6 6^4½ 2^1 1½ 1^2¾ Pincay L Jr 117 3.10 74-18 Fiesta Lady 1172¾ Doon's Baby 1192¾ Trunk 115no Drew clear 7
     2Sep84-Run in Divisions
20Aug84- 8Dmr fst 1 :46⅘ 1:11⅘ 1:37⅕   ⒻSorrento 5 5 3^3 4^2½ 4^4½ 4^3¾ Pincay L Jr 117 2.60 78-17 Wayward Pirate 114½ Doon's Baby 1203 Trunk 116nk Weakened 6
 8Aug84- 8Dmr fst 6f :22 :45⅕ 1:11⅕    ⒻJunior Miss 2 5 5^8 5^7 3^2½ 2^2½ Lamance C 117 3.00e 79-21 Doon's Baby 1172½ Fiesta Lady 1173 Trunk 117½ Game try 6
22Jly84- 6Hol fst 5½f :22⅗ :46⅗ 1:05   ⒻMd Sp Wt 7 1 1½ 1^2 1^5 1^9½ Valenzuela P A 116 *1.70 86-15 Fiesta Lady 1169½ Here Comes Love 1163½ Hydro Jet 116½ Easily 8
 4Jly84- 4Hol fst 5½f :22⅗ :46 1:05⅗  ⒻMd Sp Wt 10 1 2^1½ 4^3½ 4^4½ 2^4½ Black K 117 21.90 79-18 Neshia 1164½ Fiesta Lady 1171¾ Renew 1161½ Driving 10
17Jun84- 6Hol fst 5f :22⅗ :46⅕ :58⅘    ⒻMd Sp Wt 3 6 — — — — McCarron C J 116 6.20 — — Winters' Love 116½ Princess Cabrini1161½FolkArt1171¼ Pulled up 9
  LATEST WORKOUTS  Sep 14 Dmr 5f fst 1:02⅘ h   Aug 27 Dmr 5f fst 1:04 h   Aug 16 Dmr 3f fst :38⅘ h

Tiltalating       Dk. b. or br. f. 2, by Tilt Up—Linda Cubanita, by Proudest Roman   Lifetime   1984 6 4 2 0  $360,440
                  Br.—Winwoods Farm (Ky)                               119   6 4 2 0
  Own.—Klein E V   Tr.—Lukas D Wayne                                         $360,440
 8Sep84- 8AP sly 7f :22 :45⅘ 1:26      ⒻArl Was Lass 4 1 1½ 1^2 1^1½ 2^1½ Cordero A Jr 119 *.50 71-33 Contredance 1191½ Tiltalating 119¾ Miss Delice 1191¾ Gamely 5
27Aug84- 8Sar fst 6f :22⅕ :45⅗ 1:11    ⒻSpinaway 6 2 1^1 1^1½ 1^1½ 1^1½ Cordero A Jr 119 *1.10 85-16 Tiltalating 1191½ Sociable Duck 119¾ Contredance 1191½ Driving 7
11Aug84- 9Mth fst 6f :22⅕ :45⅕ 1:10⅘   Sapling 8 3 2^2 1hd 1^2 2^1 Valenzuela P A 119 2.00 87-12 Doubly Clear1221Tiltalating119¾DoItAgainDan1221½ Second best 10
 4Aug84- 9Mth fst 6f :22⅗ :45⅕ 1:10⅘   ⒻSorority 6 2 1^1 1½ 1^2½ 1^5 Valenzuela P A 119 *2.00 86-13 Tiltalating 1195 Raise A Q. 119hd Schematic 1191 Drew off 12
24Jly84- 9Mth fst 5½f :22⅗ :46⅖ 1:05⅗  ⒻColleen 10 2 1^1½ 1^1½ 1^2½ 1^3 Cordero A Jr 115 *.80 87-20 Tiltalating 1153 Sophisticated Lynn 1152½Don'tJoke1122½ Driving 10
     24Jly84-Run in Divisions
11Jly84- 6Bel fst 5f :22⅕ :45⅘ :58      ⒻMd Sp Wt 4 1 1^1½ 1^1½ 1^4 1^8 Rice H J 117 18.50 97-14 Tiltalating 1178 Smart Darlin 1175½ SuperbAssembly1173½ Driving 7
  LATEST WORKOUTS  Sep 24 Bel 6f fst 1:13⅘ h   Sep 19 Bel 5f fst 1:01⅘ h
```

Hollywood Park, she campaigned exclusively in stakes company at Del Mar, winning that track's premier event for juvenile fillies, the Debutante, in her most recent outing.

The key to the Matron could be found by comparing Contredance's final workout in preparation for the race with her final work (still showing) for the Arlington-Washington Lassie. Both were handy four-furlong moves, with the latter a sharp :46.4 in the slop and the former a relatively dull :48.4 over a fast track. That dull work had to raise some suspicion that Contredance would not be at her best for the Matron. The oddsboard reflected these suspicions, with Contredance and the entry going to the post at almost identical odds. One would have expected the Matron to be a coronation for Contredance, with the provincial New York crowd favoring her at odds possibly below 1–2.

With Contredance "ice" on the board, the entry, as the only alternative, had to be the pick. Tiltalating was strictly the one to catch and Fiesta Lady the only other possibility to catch her. Fiesta Lady did catch Tiltalating in deep stretch, with Contredance a distant third, and later found to be suffering from a bone chip in her ankle.

FIFTH RACE
Belmont
SEPTEMBER 29, 1984

7 FURLONGS. (1.20⅗) 78th Running THE MATRON (Grade I). Purse $75,000 Added. Foals of Mares Served in 1981. (Filly Foals of 1982). Weights, 119 lbs. By subscription of $100 each if made on or before Tuesday, May 1, 1984 or $500 each on or before, Wednesday, August 15, 1984, fee to accompany the nomination. $300 to pass the entry box and $600 to start. The added money together with all nomination fees, entry and starting fees for The Matron of 1984 to be divided 60% to first, 22% to second, 12% to third and 6% to fourth, after original nominator awards of $5,000 to the winner, $2,500 to second, $1,250 to third. Starters to be named at the closing time of entries. Trophies will be presented to the winning owner, trainer and jockey. Supplementary nominations may be made at the time of entry by a payment of $3,750 each to pass the entry box and $7,500 to start with the provision that supplementary nominees are excluded from original nominator awards. The nominator awards will be presented to the first three original nominees to finish. Closed May 1, with 155 nominations at $100, closed August 15 with 12 additional at $500. Closed with one Supplementary nominee: Sociable Duck.

Total purse $103,850. Value of race $95,100; value to winner $57,060; second $20,922; third $11,412; fourth $5,706. $8,750 Nominator Awards. Mutuel pool $129,607, OTB pool $57,668.

Last Raced	Horse	Eqt.A.Wt	PP	St	¼	½	Str	Fin	Jockey	Odds $1
2Sep84 ^{5}Dmr^{1}	Fiesta Lady	2 119	3	3	4	4	2^{6}	$1^{1\frac{3}{4}}$	Pincay L Jr	a-.80
8Sep84 ^{8}AP^{2}	Tiltalating	2 119	4	1	1^{hd}	1^{1}	$1^{2\frac{1}{2}}$	2^{14}	Cordero A Jr	a-.80
8Sep84 ^{8}AP^{1}	Contredance	2 119	2	4	3^{6}	$3^{2\frac{1}{2}}$	$3^{\frac{1}{2}}$	3^{6}	Maple E	.70
15Sep84 ^{9}Del^{1}	Something	b 2 119	1	2	$2^{2\frac{1}{2}}$	2^{5}	4	4	Kupfer T J	8.90

a–Coupled: Fiesta Lady and Tiltalating.

OFF AT 3:56. Start good, Won driving. Time, :22⅖, :45⅗, 1:11⅗, 1:24⅘ Track fast.

$2 Mutuel Prices: **1–(D)–FIESTA LADY (a–entry) .... 3.60 — —**
(Win Wagering Only)

Ch. f, by Secretariat—Faneuil Girl, by Bolinas Boy. Trainer Lukas D Wayne. Bred by Brook & Stevens (Ky).

FIESTA LADY, outrun early, came out while moving leaving the turn and finished strongly to wear down TILTALATING and draw clear. The latter raced well out from the rail while vying for the lead with SOMETHING put that one away approaching the stretch but wasn't able to withstand the winner while besting the others. CONTREDANCE was finished before going a half. SOMETHING saved ground while showing speed for a half and tired badly.

The second half of the double was the Wanda, a seven-furlong grass stake for fillies and mares. Co-favorites were the Woody Stephens entry of Quixotic Lady and Jubilous, and the Laz Barrera-trained Brorita.

Since seven furlongs looked at least one furlong too short for the late-running Jubilous, it appeared that those supporting the entry were backing the chances of Quixotic Lady, based on her recent placing behind the 1983 Eclipse Award winner Ambassador Of Luck. Her supporters, however, should have looked one race deeper into her past performances. They would have found the only grass race of her career, indeed the only poor performance appearing in her recent past performances. Since Quixotic Lady was not bred for the grass, one had to conclude that there was a very strong chance the filly simply did not like that surface.

Co-favorite Brorita, on the other hand, had won four of thirteen lifetime starts on the grass, and her latest two had been first-rate. A look at her workout line, however, revealed a pair of five-furlong

6 BELMONT

WIDENER TURF COURSE — START — 7 FURLONGS — BELMONT PARK — FINISH

7 FURLONGS. (Turf). (1.20⅘) 1st Running WANDA STAKES. Purse $40,000 Added. Fillies and Mares. 3-year-olds and upward. Weights, 3-year-olds, 118 lbs. Older, 122 lbs. Non-winners of a race of $30,000 since January 1, allowed 3 lbs. Of a race of $20,000 since then, 5 lbs. Of two races of $16,500 since then, 7 lbs. (Maiden, claiming, starter and state-bred races not considered.) $50 to nominate; $100 to enter and $100 to start. Closed Saturday, September 15 with 30 nominations.

Coupled—Quixotic Lady and Jubilous.

Rash But Royal — B. f. 4, by Royal Ski—Rash, by T V Lark
Own.—Berry M — Br.—Galbreath Enterprises Inc (Pa) — Tr.—Destasio Richard A — 122
Lifetime 22 5 4 1 $125,030 — 1984 15 3 4 0 $95,630 — 1983 6 1 0 1 $18,000 — Turf 5 3 2 0 $84,000

1Sep84- 6Med fm 1 1/16 Ⓣ:46⅗ 1:10⅗ 1:42⅕ 3↑ⒻViolet H 5 1 12 11½ 13½ 11 Kaenel J L 114 17.30 91-11 RashButRoyal1141HighSchemes1151CndlelightAffir110hd Driving 8
1Sep84-Run in divisions
12Aug84- 7Pen fm 1 1/16 Ⓣ 1:42 3↑ⒻBlue Bonnet 4 1 1½ 11½ 11½ 1hd Kaenel J L 114 2.10 80-22 Rash But Royal 114hd Virgin Bride121hdTyroleanMiss1123 Driving 9
26Jly84- 7Bel fm 1 1/16 Ⓣ:46⅗ 1:10⅗ 1:42⅘ 3↑ⒻAlw 22000 8 1 11½ 1½ 11½ 2hd Lovato F Jr 117 7.60 83-17 RoylExploson113hdRshBtRoy1173¾PlygrlPrncss1123¾ Drifted out 8
14Jly84- 2Bel fm 7f Ⓣ:23 :45⅗ 1:23 ⒻClm 75000 3 3 11 1½ 1½ 1½ Lovato F Jr 117 *2.90 89-11 RshButRoyl117½CosmicSeQueen1131½PoliticsNTricks113¾ Driving 10
13Jun84- 7Bel fm 7f Ⓣ:23 :46 1:22⅘ ⒻClm 70000 10 2 1hd 2hd 1½ 2¾ Lovato F Jr 113 27.90 91-16 DesertRainsong113¾RashButRoyl113nkLovingHomeII117¾ Gamely 12
4Jun84- 2Bel fst 1 :46⅘ 1:11⅗ 1:37 ⒻClm 50000 10 2 31½ 53¾ 88½ 914½ Davis R G 117 5.20 66-19 Harlem Queen 1171½ Tarpis 108nk Free Saint 1122½ Bore in start 10
25May84- 3Bel fst 6f :22⅘ :46⅘ 1:12⅘ ⒻClm 50000 4 2 52½ 33 22 2¾ Davis R G 117 6.70 79-23 No Limitations 117¾ Rash But Royal 117¾ Pentecost 1171 Rallied 7
5May84- 7Aqu fst 6f :22⅘ :46 1:10⅘ 3↑ⒻAlw 21000 6 2 53 45½ 511 513½ Muino M M7 114 25.00 74-16 Wild Applause 1104½ Future Fun1212SauceOfLife1212½ No factor 6
24Apr84- 8Aqu my 7f :23⅗ :46 1:23⅗ 3↑ⒻAlw 21000 6 2 63¾ 67 69½ 614½ Muino M M5 121 21.60 69-21 Queen for the Day 1125¾ Be Smart 113no Pistachio 1144½ Outrun 6
21Mar84- 7Aqu fst 6f ⊡:22⅘ :47⅕ 1:12⅘ ⒻAlw 21000 6 4 1hd 2hd 43 77¾ Velasquez J 117 3.40 74-24 Shawnee Creek 1172 T. V. Snow 117hd Our Trisha 112¾ Tired 8

Cosmic Sea Queen — B. f. 4, by Determined Cosmic—Sea Queen, by Prince John
Own.—Davis A — Br.—Fink L R (Fla) — Tr.—Moschera Gasper S — 115
Lifetime 24 7 5 2 $123,262 — 1984 11 5 4 1 $83,382 — 1983 9 2 1 0 $26,640 — Turf 18 6 5 1 $11[illegible].122

12Sep84- 5Bel fm 1 1/16 Ⓣ:48 1:11⅘ 1:42⅕ 3↑ⒻAlw 25000 1 2 21½ 1½ 1½ 2½ Davis R G 119 4.20 84-17 RoylExplosion113½CosmicSeQuen119nkSurlyGorgi's1151½ Gamely 11
8Sep84- 6Bel fm 1 1/16 Ⓣ:45⅘ 1:09⅗ 1:42⅕ 3↑ⒻAlw 22000 4 2 21 2hd 11 1hd Samyn J L 117 2.30 85-16 Cosmic Sea Queen 117hd SolarHalo1135½Disquieting113hd Driving 11
1Sep84- 6Med fm 1 1/16 Ⓣ:46⅗ 1:10⅗ 1:42⅕ 3↑ⒻViolet H 4 2 22 43 34½ 42 Cordero A Jr 111 5.50 89-11 RshButRoyl1141HighSchemes1151CndlelightAffir110hd Weakened 8
1Sep84-Run in divisions
27Aug84- 5Sar fm 1 Ⓣ:47⅘ 1:12⅘ 1:37⅘ 3↑ⒻAlw 22000 3 4 31½ 1½ 2hd 23½ Samyn J L 117 *1.00 85-17 Key Dancer 1123½ CosmicSeaQueen1174½Fiesta112hd Second best 10
22Aug84- 7Sar fm 1 Ⓣ:47 1:11⅘ 1:36 3↑ⒻHandicap 1 2 21 1hd 2hd 32 Samyn J L 111 *2.00 94-20 If WinterComes1161½Brorita111½CosmicSeaQueen111¾ Weakened 8
13Aug84- 1Sar fm 1 1/16 Ⓣ:47⅘ 1:12 1:42⅘ 3↑ⒻClm 175000 4 1 11½ 11½ 12½ 16 Samyn J L 112 *2.60 92-12 Cosmic SeaQueen1126AloneInParisII112hdTarifa1184½ Ridden out 7
6Aug84- 6Sar fm 1 Ⓣ:47⅘ 1:12 1:37⅕ 3↑ⒻClm 70000 1 1 1½ 11 12 13¾ Samyn J L 113 *1.00 90-17 CosmicSQun1133¾BlzonSr113hdAutumnBlossom119hd Ridden out 10
25Jly84- 5Bel fm 1 1/16 Ⓣ:46⅘ 1:11⅕ 1:42⅕ ⒻClm c-50000 2 3 33 2½ 15 18¾ Samyn J L 117 *1.20 85-15 Cosmic Sea Queen 1178¾ Latka 113noBlazonSara108no Ridden out 11
14Jly84- 2Bel fm 7f Ⓣ:23 :45⅗ 1:23 ⒻClm 70000 4 2 21 2½ 2½ 2½ Samyn J L 113 6.50 88-11 RshButRoyl117½CosmicSeQueen1131½PoliticsNTricks113¾ Gamely 10
3Mar84- 10Hia fm 1 1/16 Ⓣ 1:42⅘ ⒻAlw 18000 9 6 64½ 42½ 22½ 11¾ Perret C 116 2.50 85-13 Cosmic Sea Queen 1161¾Dwynwen116nk[illegible]MyCountry116 Driving 12
LATEST WORKOUTS ●Sep 28 Bel tr.t 3f gd :35⅘ h Sep 22 Bel tr.t 4f fst :49 h

Quixotic Lady — Gr. f. 4, by Quadratic—Lady Dulcinea, by Nantallah
Own.—Ross Valley Farms — Br.—Ryehill Farm (Md) — Tr.—Stephens Woodford C — 119
Lifetime 29 12 9 2 $475,729 — 1984 8 1 5 0 $107,424 — 1983 18 10 2 2 $341,335 — Turf 1 0 0 0

14Sep84- 8Bel fst 7f :23⅕ :46⅘ 1:23 3↑ⒻAlw 33000 1 2 31 32½ 32½ 2¾ Maple E 119 4.80 86-18 AmbssdorofLuck115¾QuixoticLdy1192¾MdmForbes122¾ Came out 6
22Aug84- 7Sar fm 1 Ⓣ:47 1:11⅘ 1:36 3↑ⒻHandicap 2 6 53 43 43½ 53 Maple E 120 3.40 93-20 If Winter Comes1161½Brorita111½CosmicSeaQueen111¾ No threat 8
9Aug84- 8Sar fst 7f :23 :46⅕ 1:22⅘ 3↑ⒻAlw 33000 5 4 31½ 21 22 21½ Maple E 119 *1.70 87-14 Appluse1191½QuixoticLdy1191½Mickey'sEcho1172½ Best of others 10
11Jly84- 1Bel fst 1 :46⅘ 1:11⅗ 1:36 3↑ⒻAlw 36000 1 4 32 21 2½ 1hd Maple E 117 *.50 85-14 QuixoticLady117hdMademoiselleForli1176¾DownStge117¾ Driving 5
4Jly84- 9Mth fst 1 1/16 :46 1:09⅘ 1:41⅘ 3↑ⒻM. Pitcher H 4 5 47 35½ 33½ 25 Maple E 118 2.40 92-14 Sultry Sun 1165 Quixotic Lady 1181 Nany 114¾ Gamely 10
10Jun84- 8Bel fst 1⅛ :47 1:11⅘ 1:49⅕ 3↑ⒻHempstead H 3 8 84 63 33½ 24 Maple E 118 6.10 77-20 Heatherten 1184 Quixotic Lady 118nk ThirtyFlags1143¾ Came out 10
31May84- 8Bel sly 6f :22⅘ :45⅘ 1:09⅕ 3↑ⒻAlw 33000 2 3 32½ 32½ 24 26½ Maple E 119 2.30 90-21 SultrySun1216½QuixoticLdy1191½MdemoislIForli1194 Second best 6
19May84- 8Bel fst 1 1/16 :46 1:10⅘ 1:43 3↑ⒻShuvee H 5 7 87½ 53½ 1½ 42½ Maple E 120 7.70 85-26 QueenofSong117hdTrySomethingNew1211½Narrate1161 Weakened 10
20Dec83- 8Med fst 1 1/16 :47⅕ 1:11⅘ 1:43⅘ ⒻHoney Bee H 5 5 52¾ 3½ 13 15 McCarron G 123 *1.10 91-19 Quixotic Lady 1235 It's Fine 1122 Concord Hymn 1081½ Driving 8
19Nov83- 8Aqu fst 1¼ :48⅘ 1:38 2:03⅘ 3↑ⒻLadies H 8 6 63¾ 62½ 23 25¾ Maple E 119 2.80e 73-19 Mademoiselle Forli 1135¾QuixoticLady119¾Mochila1132¾ Bumped 9
LATEST WORKOUTS Sep 27 Bel 4f fst :48 b Sep 23 Bel 5f fst 1:04 b Sep 10 Bel 4f fst :51 b Sep 6 Bel 5f fst 1:00 b

Hot Milk — Gr. f. 3, by Restless Native—Nuit Blanche, by Gray Phantom
Own.—Evans E P — Br.—Evans E P (Va) — Tr.—Johnson Philip G — 111
Lifetime 9 5 1 0 $108,765 — 1984 6 2 1 0 $40,860 — 1983 3 3 0 0 $67,905 — Turf 1 1 0 0 $19,800

6Sep84- 8Bel gd 7f Ⓣ:23⅗ :47 1:24⅘ 3↑ⒻAlw 33000 7 3 12 11 1½ 1no MacBeth D b 111 7.10 80-27 Hot Milk 111no Miss Frampton 1151½AloneInParisII119hd Driving 8
23Aug84- 5Sar sly 7f :22⅕ :44⅘ 1:23⅗ 3↑ⒻAlw 26000 1 5 32½ 32½ 68 59½ MacBeth D b 112 2.00 75-22 Pride's Crossing 1173 Strictly Raised 117½ Liz Matizz 1175¾ Tired 6
2Aug84- 8Sar fst 7f :21⅘ :44⅗ 1:22⅗ ⒻTest 9 1 76 810 69 610 MacBeth D 121 9.40 79-19 Sintra 1161½ Wild Applause 1211¾ Lucky LuckyLucky1244 Outrun 9
9Jly84- 8Bel fst 6f :22⅘ :45⅗ 1:09⅘ 3↑ⒻAlw 33000 1 4 21½ 22 22 22 MacBeth D 111 2.50 93-14 Medieval Moon 1152 Hot Milk 1114GratefulFriend1171½ Game try 7
26May84- 8Bel fst 1 :45⅗ 1:10⅘ 1:35⅘ ⒻAcorn 2 5 58 815 815 717¾ MacBeth D 121 5.10 68-15 MissOceana121nkLife'sMagic1215½ProudClrioness121no No factor 9
10May84- 7Bel fst 6f :22⅘ :45⅗ 1:09⅘ 3↑ⒻAlw 23000 4 4 21½ 2½ 2½ 1hd MacBeth D 111 *1.60 94-17 Hot Milk 111hd Ripley 1213¾ Buzz My Bell 1124 Lost whip, drvng 7
26Jly83- 9Mth fst 5½f :22⅘ :45⅗ 1:04⅘ ⒻColleen 7 2 43 43½ 21½ 11½ MacBeth D 121 *1.20 91-20 Hot Milk 1211½ Terrible TerriT.1152½SweetAlane115no Ridden out 8
6Jly83- 8Bel fst 5½f :22⅕ :45⅕ 1:04⅘ ⒻAstoria 7 6 75½ 44½ 32½ 1nk MacBeth D 112 2.90 92-10 HotMilk112nkTerribleTerriT.1122½BottlTop1141½ Lugged in, drvng 9
19Jun83- 4Bel fst 5f :22⅘ :47 :59⅘ ⒻMd Sp Wt 7 7 21½ 1hd 11½ 14¾ MacBeth D 117 2.00 92-15 Hot Milk 1174¾ MileHighLady117½Amyark1174¾ Rcd greenly,clear 8
LATEST WORKOUTS Sep 27 Bel 4f fst :51⅗ b ●Sep 22 Bel 4f fst :46⅘ h ●Aug 20 Sar tr.t 3f fst :34⅘ h ●Aug 15 Sar tr.t 6f fst 1:17⅘ b

Descent — Ch. f. 4, by Avatar—Alyne Que, by Raise a Native
Own.—Schuemann T P — Br.—Claiborne Farm (Ky) — Tr.—Jackson Evan S — 115
Lifetime 17 5 4 4 $115,021 — 1984 6 1 1 2 $35,451 — 1983 10 3 3 2 $73,070 — Turf 5 1 1 2 $35,451

13Sep84- 8Bel fm 1 1/16 Ⓣ:45⅗ 1:10⅘ 1:43⅕ 3↑ⒻAlw 36000 3 6 611 55 32½ 33½ Velasquez J 119 6.30 76-19 Brorita 1171¾ It's Fine 1171¾ Descent 1191¾ Rallied 6
1Sep84- 8Med fm 1 1/16 Ⓣ:47⅘ 1:10⅘ 1:42 3↑ⒻViolet H 6 3 32 31 54 56½ Davis R G 111 10.60 85-11 Aspen Rose 1141 It's Fine 112no If WinterComes1135½ Weakened 8
1Sep84-Run in divisions
1Aug84- 4Sar fm 1 Ⓣ:48 1:12 1:36⅘ 3↑ⒻAlw 28000 1 5 32 42 11½ 1nk Velasquez J 117 *1.30 94-09 Descent117nkAloneInParisII117hdMissAudimr114¾ Drifted out,dr. 8
14Jly84- 7Bel fm 1 1/16 Ⓣ:46⅗ 1:10⅕ 1:41 3↑ⒻHandicap 2 6 63½ 41½ 2½ 2hd Samyn J L 110 3.00 91-11 Top Nice 115hd Descent 1101 Rose Crescent 1154 Sharp 8
15Jun84- 6Bel fm 7f Ⓣ:24⅕ :47 1:22⅘ 3↑ⒻAlw 33000 7 6 64 53½ 33½ 31 Samyn J L 117 7.70e 91-18 If Winter Comes 117hd Smuggled 1171 Descent 1172½ Rallied 10
23May84- 7Bel fst 7f :22⅘ :45⅘ 1:22 3↑ⒻHandicap 3 5 43½ 43 614 624 Bailey J D b 114 6.60 68-16 Nany 1157½ High Schemes 1222½ Amanti 1181½ Fin. early 6
11Dec83- 8Aqu fst 170 ⊡:47⅘ 1:13 1:44⅘ ⒻBusher H 8 5 36½ 811 914 911½ McHargue D G b 116 8.90 66-27 Far Flying 1201½ DownStage116hdCaptivatingGrace1121¾ Stopped 10
19Nov83- 8Aqu fst 1¼ :48⅘ 1:38 2:03⅘ 3↑ⒻLadies H 1 4 74½ 51¾ 53¾ 511½ Venezia M b 112 6.80 67-19 Mademoiselle Forli 1135¾QuixoticLady119¾Mochila1132¾ Hung dr. 9
22Oct83- 7Aqu fst 1 :46⅕ 1:10⅘ 1:36 ⒻGrecian Coin 3 8 1011 66½ 22½ 11 Samyn J L b 114 7.30 86-19 Descent 1141RarelyLayte114½Propositioning1141¾ Wide str., drvg 10
2Oct83- 5Bel my 6f :22⅕ :45⅘ 1:10⅘ 3↑ⒻAlw 27000 3 6 55 33 21½ 21 Fell J b 116 2.50 88-14 RpidProspector1171Descent1164½SomSpkr1165½ Lacked room st. 6
LATEST WORKOUTS · Sep 25 Bel 6f fst 1:14⅕ h Sep 20 Bel 5f fst 1:02⅘ b Sep 8 Bel 4f fst :48 b Aug 31 Bel 3f sly :36⅘ b

Miss Frampton — Ch. m. 5, by Dike—Frampton Flight, by Misty Flight
Own.—Fink L R — Br.—Fink L R (Fla) — Tr.—Schulhofer Flint S — 115
Lifetime 37 6 7 5 $119,166 — 1984 15 3 4 0 $86,226 — 1983 5 1 2 2 $21,080 — Turf 29 5 7 5 $110,466

6Sep84- 8Bel gd 7f Ⓣ:23⅗ :47 1:24⅘ 3↑ⒻAlw 33000 3 2 22 21 2½ 2no Guerra W A 115 14.30 80-27 Hot Milk 111no Miss Frampton 1151½AloneInParisII119hd Gamely 8
27Aug84- 7Sar fm 1 Ⓣ:47⅘ 1:12⅘ 1:37 3↑ⒻAlw 36000 2 7 85¾ 97½ 97¾ 912 Davis R G 115 21.00 79-17 Sailing Hour 115¾ Barkerville Belle 1151½ Nany 119½ Outrun 9
13Aug84- 1Sar fm 1 1/16 Ⓣ:47⅘ 1:12 1:42⅘ 3↑ⒻClm 175000 3 3 35½ 45½ 49 611¾ Cruguet J 112 3.30 80-12 Cosmic Sea Queen 1126 Alone In Paris II 112hd Tarifa1184½ Tired 7
9Jly84- 1Bel gd 1 1/16 Ⓣ:48 1:13⅕ 1:46⅗ ⒻClm 175500 7 4 32 22 21½ 1nk Cruguet J 112 3.90 63-35 Miss Frampton 112nk Maidenhead 1131 Petit Ball 1121½ Driving 7
21Jun84- 5Bel fm 1 Ⓣ:47 1:11⅘ 1:36⅘ ⒻClm 185000 7 4 52½ 66½ 711 712 Velasquez J 116 *1.50 70-16 Tarifa 1021 Maidenhead 1121½ Huga Baba 1121 Tired 7
9Jun84- 5Bel hd 1 1/16 Ⓣ:45⅘ 1:10⅘ 1:41⅕ 3↑ⒻⓇTanya 6 6 74½ 41½ 2½ 53¾ Velasquez J 115 4.70e 86-07 Class Play 114¾ Proud Nova 107½ Top Nice 1222 Weakened 13
26May84- 6Bel fm 6f Ⓣ:22⅘ :46 1:11 3↑ⒻAlw 33000 3 1 2hd 2hd 12 21½ Cruguet J 119 9.50 83-19 HopflContrct1121½MssFrmpton1193BonEglg119nk Best of others 9
13May84- 8Bel fm 1 1/16 Ⓣ:46 1:10⅘ 1:42 3↑ⒻBeaugay H 7 6 64½ 74½ 85¾ 88½ Cruguet J 113 11.10 77-15 Thirty Flags 113¾ Jubilous 1143 Nany 111nk No factor 12
28Mar84- 9GP fm 1 Ⓣ:47⅕ 1:11⅘ 1:36⅘ 3↑ⒻSuwane Riv H 1 8 87 64½ 54½ 55¾ Perret C 115 4.50 80-17 Sulemeif 1133½ Jubilous 115½ Melanie Frances 1131 No factor 13
19Mar84- 9GP fm *1 Ⓣ 1:39⅘ ⒻAlw 20000 5 5 57½ 33½ 2hd 2nk Cruguet J 122 2.90 83-18 Rejoiceful115nkMissFrmpton1225Queen'sAngel115nk Just missed 8
LATEST WORKOUTS Sep 21 Bel 4f fst :50 b Sep 14 Bel 4f fst :52 b ●Aug 23 Sar Ⓣ 4f gd :48⅘ b Aug 6 Sar Ⓣ 4f fm :50⅕ b

Brorita — Ch. f. 4, by Caro—Mellow Marsh, by Seaneen
Own.—Green Dolly — Br.—Spendthrift Farm (Ky) — Tr.—Barrera Lazaro S — 119
Lifetime 24 5 4 2 $111,710 — 1984 6 2 2 0 $55,170 — 1983 16 3 2 2 $56,165 — Turf 13 4 2 1 $80,060

13Sep84- 8Bel fm 1 1/16 Ⓣ:45⅗ 1:10⅘ 1:43⅕ 3↑ⒻAlw 36000 6 3 21½ 12 12 11¾ Cordero A Jr 117 *2.30 80-19 Brorita 1171¾ It's Fine 1171¾ Descent 1191¾ Driving 6
22Aug84- 7Sar fm 1 Ⓣ:47 1:11⅘ 1:36 3↑ⒻHandicap 7 5 64 31½ 31½ 21½ Cordero A Jr 111 5.80 94-20 If Winter Comes1161½Brorita111½CosmicSeaQueen111¾ Game try 8
2Aug84- 7Sar fm 1 1/16 Ⓣ:46⅘ 1:11 1:42⅕ 3↑ⒻAlw 36000 5 4 42 22 43½ 610 Cordero A Jr 115 8.40 76-19 AspenRose115½Gerldine'sStore1172½RoseCrescent1154½ Gave way 7
5Jly84- 8Hol fm 1 1/16 Ⓣ:46⅘ 1:10⅘ 1:41⅘ ⒻAlw 40000 5 3 32½ 2½ 33 58½ Pincay L Jr 121 *1.20 83-11 Flag De Lune 1161 Colaxe 1143½ Skillful Joy 114no Tired 7
24Feb84- 8SA fm 1⅛ Ⓣ:46⅘ 1:12 1:49⅘ ⒻAlw 35000 6 3 31½ 31½ 12½ 13½ Meza R Q 118 5.00 78-22 Brorita 1183½ Caferana 114¾ Love Me True 115no Handily 9
5Jan84- 5SA fm *6½f Ⓣ:21⅕ :43⅘ 1:16 ⒻAlw 27000 5 8 55½ 511 35½ 21½ Meza R Q 118 4.20 77-21 Love Me True 1151½ Brorita 118½ Upatree 1131½ Rallied 11
27Nov83- 6Hol fm 1 1/16 Ⓣ:48⅕ 1:12⅗ 1:43⅘ 3↑ⒻⓇLa Zanzara 7 3 32½ 32 2hd 11½ Cordero A Jr 114 15.00 80-17 Brorita 1141½ Dontstop Themusic 1161½ Foggy Moon1142 Driving 7
8Oct83- 5SA fst 1 1/16 :46⅘ 1:11 1:43⅘ 3↑ⒻAlw 26000 11 7 57 56 613 816½ Pincay L Jr 117 8.60 68-16 Past Pleasures 1172½ Chain Of Gold 1173VoodooQueen1192 Wide 11
28Aug83- 5Dmr fm 1 1/16 Ⓣ:47 1:11⅗ 1:43⅕ 3↑ⒻAlw 21000 6 4 33 22 55½ 812¾ Pedroza M A 116 *1.40 80-07 Henley's Honey 1164½ Waynearina 1183½ Greenstone 121¾ Tired 10
11Aug83- 7Dmr fm 1 1/16 Ⓣ:47⅕ 1:11⅘ 1:43⅘ ⒻAlw 17000 1 3 33 2hd 11½ 14 Pincay L Jr 117 *1.70 90-10 Brorita 1174 Super Valentine 1161½ Classie Bishop 114hd Driving 9
LATEST WORKOUTS Sep 8 Bel 5f fst :59⅗ h ●Aug 30 Bel tr.t 5f fst 1:00 h Aug 18 Sar 5f fst :59⅘ h ●Aug 10 Sar tr.t 5f fst 1:02⅘ h

Jubilous — Dk. b. or br. f. 4, by Sir Ivor—Bring Out The Band, by One for All
Br.—Hickory Tree Farm (Va)
Own.—Hickory Tree Stable — Tr.—Stephens Woodford C — 122
Lifetime 21 7 6 3 $208,576 — 1984 12 4 3 1 $142,345 — 1983 8 2 3 2 $55,431 — Turf 20 7 5 3 $185,016

1Sep84- 8Medfm 1 1/16 Ⓣ:47⅖ 1:10⅘ 1:42 3+ⒻViolet H 8 5 43½ 75 79 710½ Maple E 117 3.60 81-11 Aspen Rose 1141 It's Fine 112no If Winter Comes 1135½ Tired 8
1Sep84-Run in divisions
13Aug84- 8Sar fm 1⅛ Ⓣ:47⅖ 1:11⅗ 1:48⅕ 3+ⒻDiana H 5 8 86½ 95¼ 922 930½ Maple E 118 4.40 55-12 WildAppluse1094PrettyPerfect109nkSpitCurl1124 Stumbled badly 9
14Jly84- 9Mth fm 1 1/16 Ⓣ:48⅗ 1:12⅖ 1:43⅗ 3+ⒻEatontownH 13 11 106¾ 95¾ 64½ 11¾ McCarron G 118 *2.20 94-11 Jubilous 1181¾ Maidenhead 113no High Schemes 118¾ Driving 13
28Jun84- 8Bel fm 1¼ Ⓣ:48⅕ 1:37⅗ 2:03 3+ⒻAlw 36000 1 6 78½ 32 31 11¾ Maple E 117 *1.10 79-18 Jubilous 1171¾ Bon Eglogue 117¾ Virgin Bride 1172 Driving 7
9Jun84- 5Bel hd 1 1/16 Ⓣ:45⅘ 1:10⅖ 1:41⅕ 3+ⒻⓇTanya 10 9 53½ 31½ 3½ 43 Maple E 115 *1.10 87-07 Class Play 114½ Proud Nova 107½ Top Nice 1222 Weakened 13
13May84- 8Bel fm 1 1/16 Ⓣ:46 1:10⅖ 1:42 3+ⒻBeaugay H 9 5 53½ 41 2hd 2¾ Maple E 114 *1.50 85-15 Thirty Flags 113¾ Jubilous 1143 Nany 111nk Rallied 12
14Apr84- 9GP sly 1 1/16 :46⅘ 1:10⅖ 1:41⅗ 3+ⒻOrchid H 5 6 57 59 22½ 24½ McCauley W H 114 7.00 89-12 Sabin 1254½ Jubilous 1141 Sulemeif 11514 Best of others 7
28Mar84- 9GP fm 1 Ⓣ:47⅗ 1:11⅘ 1:36⅘ 3+ⒻSuwane Riv H 2 11 108 97½ 32½ 23½ Maple E 115 *2.00 82-17 Sulemeif 1133½ Jubilous 115½ Melanie Frances 1131 Wide 13
5Mar84- 7Hia fm 1 1/16 Ⓣ 1:42⅗ ⒻAlw 25000 3 3 42½ 31½ 3½ 11½ Maple E 116 *.30 85-11 Jubilous 1161½ Bimini Flyer 1164 Court Union 1161 Driving 8
11Feb84- 8Hia fm 1⅛ Ⓣ 1:48 ⒻKey Largo 10 4 2hd 2hd 2½ 61½ Maple E 119 5.40 90-06 Silver in Flight 119no Erudite II 115½ Sulemeif 114¾ Bid,wknd 12
LATEST WORKOUTS Sep 23 Bel 6f fst 1:15 h — Sep 18 Bel 5f fst 1:02⅘ b — Sep 14 Bel 4f fst :48⅘ h — Aug 27 Sar 6f fst 1:14⅘ h

***Tarifa** — Gr. f. 4, by Pitskelly—Slap Up, by Gala Performance
Br.—Vigors T C (Eng)
Own.—Dileo P — Tr.—O'Brien Leo — 115
Lifetime 20 5 1 3 $51,522 — 1984 6 1 0 1 $24,340 — 1983 10 3 1 2 $25,543 — Turf 18 5 1 3 $51,522

20Sep84- 8Medfm 170 Ⓣ:45⅗ 1:10⅕ 1:39⅘ 3+ⒻAlw 20000 2 3 3½ 31½ 53½ 69¾ Espinosa R E7 108 9.80 81-14 Bon Eglogue 1154½ Down Stage 1151½ Alone In ParisII1172 Tired 8
22Aug84- 7Sar fm 1 Ⓣ:47 1:11⅗ 1:36 3+ⒻHandicap 8 1 11 65½ 611 821 Migliore R 111 23.70 75-20 If Winter Comes 1161½ Brorita 111½ Cosmic Sea Queen111¾ Tired 8
13Aug84- 1Sar fm 1 1/16 Ⓣ:47⅘ 1:12 1:42⅗ 3+ⒻClm 190000 6 2 21½ 21½ 22½ 36 Migliore R 118 6.60 86-12 Cosmic Sea Queen1126AloneInParisII112hdTarifa1184½ Weakened 7
28Jly84- 8Atl fm 1⅜ Ⓣ:47⅘ 1:11⅗ 1:53⅗ 3+ⒻMtchmker 5 4 45 42 37½ 411½ Migliore R 115 21.80 84-09 Sabin 1231½ Doblique 1136 Virgin Bride 1134 Evenly 8
9Jly84- 1Bel gd 1 1/16 Ⓣ:48 1:13⅕ 1:46⅗ ⒻClm 190000 6 1 12 12 11½ 42¾ Migliore R 118 3.70 60-35 Miss Frampton 112nk Maidenhead 1131 Petit Ball1121½ Gave way 7
21Jun84- 5Bel fm 1 Ⓣ:47 1:11⅗ 1:36⅗ ⒻClm 175000 2 3 1½ 14 14 11 Espinosa R E10 102 6.30 82-16 Tarifa 1021 Maidenhead 1121½ Huga Baba 1121 Bore out; drvng 7
14Nov83- 1Aqu fst 7f :23⅗ :47⅗ 1:25⅖ 3+ⒻClm 85000 7 1 64 75½ 711 716½ MacBeth D 114 22.70 57-24 Harlem Queen 112no Lady D. 1142¾ Sweet Laughter 107no Outrun 7
22Oct83- 7Aqu fst 1 :46⅕ 1:10⅗ 1:36 ⒻGrecian Coin 5 5 88½ 1019 1019 1020 Murphy D J 116 26.30 66-19 Descent 1141 Rarely Layte 114½ Propositioning 1141¾ Fell back 10
29Sep83- 7Bel fm 1 1/16 Ⓣ:47⅘ 1:11⅗ 1:43⅖ 3+ⒻAlw 30000 4 4 43½ 32 32 1hd Vasquez J 115 20.50 84-17 Tarifa 115hd Idle Gossip 113no Cryptic 113½ Driving 7
10Aug83♦2Salisbury(Eng) gd 6f 1:13⅗ Ⓣ Hare Warren Hcp 4¾ Hills M 107 *3.00 — — GuntripsCentenary 111hd Stereos114¾ Ismore110no Prom thruout 10
LATEST WORKOUTS Sep 19 Aqu 3f fst :37⅘ b — Sep 14 Aqu 4f fst :48⅘ h — Sep 8 Aqu 4f fst :49⅘ b — Aug 8 Sar Ⓣ 5f fm 1:01⅗ h

It's Fine — B. f. 4, by Sham—Finely, by Northern Dancer
Br.—Dupont Mrs R C (Md)
Own.—Golden R L — Tr.—Jerkens H Allen — 119
Lifetime 20 4 6 2 $116,509 — 1984 6 1 3 0 $57,260 — 1983 13 3 3 2 $59,249 — Turf 8 1 3 1 $45,524

13Sep84- 8Bel fm 1 1/16 Ⓣ:45⅗ 1:10⅖ 1:43⅕ 3+ⒻAlw 36000 4 2 32½ 22 22 21¾ Guerra W A 117 2.80 78-19 Brorita 1171¾ It's Fine 1171¾ Descent 1191¾ Gamely 6
1Sep84- 8Medfm 1 1/16 Ⓣ:47⅖ 1:10⅘ 1:42 3+ⒻViolet H 4 2 21½ 2½ 1½ 21 Guerra W A 112 18.60 91-11 Aspen Rose 1141 It's Fine 112no If Winter Comes 1135½ Gamely 8
1Sep84-Run in divisions
18Jly84- 8Bel sly 1 :46⅕ 1:10⅘ 1:36⅘ 3+ⒻAlw 36000 5 3 32 32½ 23 21¾ Samyn J L 119 3.80 79-19 Queen for the Day 1041¾It'sFine1193½NationalBanner1153 Rallied 7
2Jly84- 7Bel fst 1 :45⅗ 1:10 1:35⅗ 3+ⒻAlw 36000 6 2 21 12½ 12½ 11 Samyn J L 115 3.40 87-15 It's Fine 1151 National Banner 1153 Idle Gossip 1176 Driving 7
6Jun84- 8Bel fst 6f :22⅘ :46⅕ 1:10⅘ 3+ⒻAlw 33000 2 4 64 33 43½ 42¾ Samyn J L 117 4.00 85-20 Annie's Dream 117¾ T. V. Snow 117¾LotusDelight1091½ Weakened 6
21May84- 7Bel gd 1 1/16 Ⓣ:47⅗ 1:12⅕ 1:43⅘ 3+ⒻAlw 25000 6 4 31½ 21 3½ 43½ Cordero A Jr 121 7.00 79-24 Proud Nova 1102 Berkeley Court 110¾Maidenhead121½ Weakened 7
11Dec83- 8Aqu fst 170 ⊡:47⅗ 1:13 1:44⅗ ⒻBusher H 5 3 914 911 811 88½ Cordero A Jr 114 4.30 69-27 FarFlying1201½DownStage116hdCaptivatingGrace1121¾ Early foot 10
2Dec83- 8Medfst 1 1/16 :47⅕ 1:11⅗ 1:43⅗ ⒻHoney Bee H 4 8 711 75¾ 33 25 Antongeorgi W A 112 24.10 86-19 Quixotic Lady 1235 It's Fine 1122 Concord Hymn 1081½ Rallied 8
24Nov83- 9Medfst 170 :46⅘ 1:12⅕ 1:43 ⒻCedar Ridge 5 7 811 66½ 38½ 27½ Antongeorgi W A 116 12.90 78-21 Far Flying 1147½ It's Fine1161½SpringtimeSharon11610½ Game try 8
10Nov83- 6Medsly 1 1/16 :48⅗ 1:14 1:49 3+ⒻAlw 14000 2 5 55½ 36½ 32 12 Antongeorgi W A 108 *2.20 64-27 It's Fine 1082 Chafing Dish 119¾ Jackie U. 1135 Driving 7
LATEST WORKOUTS Sep 26 Bel 5f fst 1:06 b — Sep 22 Bel 5f fst 1:04⅘ b — Aug 27 Bel 1 fst 1:43⅘ b — ●Aug 22 Bel 7f fst 1:26⅘ h

Corn Acupa — Ch. f. 3, by Raise A Cup—Cornisara, by Cornish Prince
Br.—Brennan B F (NY)
Own.—Brennan & Bernard — Tr.—Brennan Pat — 111
Lifetime 19 4 3 2 $71,148 — 1984 15 3 3 1 $56,868 — 1983 4 1 0 1 $14,280 — Turf 2 0 0 0 $688

26Sep84- 5Medfst 5f :23 :46⅗ :58⅗ 3+ⒻAlw 30000 9 3 75½ 56 55 56½ Castaneda M 118 5.80e 87-25 Grecian Comedy 1191 Gnash 1172 Mavelous 1151½ No factor 10
12Sep84- 8Medfst 6f :23 :46⅕ 1:11⅘ 3+ⒻAlw 20000 3 4 21 1hd 31½ 35 Doran K7 111 10.60 81-21 ⒹMavelous 1152 Birdie Belle 1153 Corn Acupa 1112½ Weakened 6
23Aug84- 5Mth fst 6f :22⅕ :45⅗ 1:10⅕ 3+ⒻAlw 13000 5 3 32 1hd 1½ 1no Doran K7 106 8.10 89-21 Corn Acupa 106no Second Glance 1004 Be Smart 1157 Driving 6
4Aug84- 7Mth fm 5f Ⓣ:22 :45 :57⅘ ⒻⓇPlat'm Bel 3 5 43 64½ 61¾ 52½ McCauley W H 117 33.80 94-05 Big Monday 117½ Cantam 1131 Cedar Town 115¾ Evenly 10
25Jly84- 8Bel fst 6f :22⅘ :45⅗ 1:10 3+ⒻAlw 33000 6 1 34 34½ 58½ 59½ Graell A 109 32.70 82-14 Mallorca 1094¾ Secret Heart 1091½ I'm A Southpaw 117hd Tired 7
27Jun84- 8Bel fst 1 :45⅗ 1:10⅗ 1:35⅘ 3+ⒻⓈHydeParkH 1 2 32½ 58½ 920 937½ Graell A 108 36.40 49-17 Nany 11613½ Lotus Delight 1123½ Donna's World 1113¾ Stopped 9
17Jun84- 3Bel fm 1 Ⓣ:45⅘ 1:12 1:38 ⒻClm 75000 2 1 1hd 85¾ 923 925½ Graell A 116 8.10 50-20 Mickey's Lady 112hd Betrayed 1122½ Snakey 112no Stopped 9
28May84- 9FL sly 6f :22⅘ :47⅗ 1:14⅘ ⒻⓈNiagara 4 4 2½ 11½ 14 13½ Hulet L 117 *1.10 75-30 Corn Acupa 1173½ Caution Zone 117¾ Doctor's Pill 117¾ Handily 9
28May84-Run in divisions
14May84- 6Bel fst 6f :22⅘ :45⅗ 1:11 3+ⒻⓈAlw 26000 2 3 21½ 21 22½ 22¾ Graell A 110 6.30 84-17 Clock 'Em 1132¾ Corn Acupa 110¾ Leecoo 1059 No match 7
27Apr84- 5Aqu fst 6f :22⅘ :45⅘ 1:12 3+ⒻⓈAlw 26000 2 2 1hd 1½ 1hd 2no Graell A 109 6.10 81-21 Heartless 114no Corn Acupa 1092 Give Me AHint1212 Just missed 7
LATEST WORKOUTS Sep 21 Bel tr.t 4f fst :54 b — Sep 6 Bel 5f fst :58⅘ h — Aug 13 Bel 6f fst 1:14 h

Springset — Dk. b. or br. f. 4, by Maribeau—Jersey Baby J, by Convex
Br.—Imbesi A (NJ)
Own.—Imbesi J M — Tr.—Imbesi Joseph — 115
Lifetime 20 4 4 3 $33,912 — 1984 10 4 0 1 $21,388 — 1983 10 M 4 2 $12,524 — Turf 3 2 0 0 $11,700

18Sep84- 9Medfm 1 1/16 Ⓣ:48 1:11⅘ 1:42⅘ 3+ⒻAlw 14000 6 9 77½ 31 78 813 Terry J b 122 4.70 75-14 Hardly Regal 1132½ Chafing Dish 1161 Q. Native 1061 Tired 9
7Sep84- 6Medfm 1 1/16 Ⓣ:47 1:11⅗ 1:44⅕ 3+ⒻAlw 13000 2 6 66 1hd 1½ 14 Terry J b 116 8.40 81-15 Springset 1164 Tricky Sea 1121 Capay 112½ Driving 10
24Aug84- 7Mth fst 5f :22⅗ :45⅗ :58⅕ 3+ⒻAlw 11000 5 7 66¾ 68½ 812 88½ Edwards J W b 116 5.40 86-24 Silver Dora 1133½ Nahadeh 1112½ Puff Away 109¾ No Threat 8
9Aug84- 6Atl fm *5½f Ⓣ 1:05⅘ 3+ⒻClm 18000 5 4 78½ 2½ 11 16 Edwards J W b 114 8.10 84-21 Springset 1146 Beauty's Sonnata 112nk MissSharpe1184 Drew off 8
31Jly84- 2Mth fst 6f :22 :45⅕ 1:12 3+ⒻClm 10000 4 5 55 21½ 12½ 12 Edwards J W b 116 9.20 80-15 Springset 1162 Cyn Cl's Saint 1145 Twin Penny 116no Drew clear 9
16Jly84- 7Mth fst 6f :22⅕ :45⅘ 1:12⅕ 3+ⒻClm 14000 7 5 23 21 1hd 45½ Thomas D B b 113 18.80 73-20 Cher Cheval 1164 Miss Self 116½ Flobonaire 1161 Weakened 10
3Jly84- 5Mth fst 6f :22⅗ :46⅖ 1:11⅘ 3+ⒻClm 12500 2 4 54½ 75½ 58½ 37 Imparato J b 116 8.90 74-17 My Tara 1142 Tipsy's Second 1115 Springset 1161 Mild bid 7
21Jun84- 4Mth fst 6f :23 :46⅗ 1:12⅗ 3+ⓈMd 7500 2 6 11 12 13 16 Imparato J b 117 2.90 78-23 Springset 1176 Never Yield 115nk Kaz Giacomo 1151 Driving 10
14Jun84- 3Mth fst 6f :23 :47⅕ 1:14 3+ⓈMd 10000 5 8 79 511 510 410¾ Antley C W5 b 112 *2.50 59-20 Scheckelby 1103 Kaz Giacomo 115¾ Ms. Admirable1137 No threat 8
8May84- 9Mth fst 6f :22⅘ :46⅕ 1:12 3+ⒻⓈMd Sp Wt 7 3 52 68 719 723 Verge M E b 123 14.30 57-22 Brenda's Bridges 1104 Poetic Miss 115nk Parlay Bar 1107 Outrun 9

works prior to each of those races. But now, sixteen days from her most recent start, Brorita had failed to make even one appearance on the morning workout tabs. Why the change in training routine? Could Brorita be expected to reproduce her best form without her normal rigorous morning exercise? Could she have suffered a minor setback in the interim?

With these suspicions, the cautious player might have passed the race altogether. Others would have tried to capitalize on the situation by looking for overlays among the remaining fillies. Several had shown good form sprinting on the grass. Whether Descent, the eventual three-length winner at a $20.80 mutuel, made any more sense than Miss Frampton, Rash But Royal, or Hot Milk, who finished second, third, and fourth, respectively, is debatable. Our point is that awareness of a change in a seemingly sharp horse's workout pattern, and of another's probable dislike for the grass, helped eliminate the two favorites in this otherwise wide-open race. The Fiesta Lady-Descent daily double returned $41.20, and the sixth race quinella $132.00.

SIXTH RACE
Belmont
SEPTEMBER 29, 1984

7 FURLONGS.(Turf). (1.20⅘) 1st Running WANDA STAKES. Purse $40,000 Added. Fillies and Mares. 3-year-olds and upward. Weights, 3-year-olds, 118 lbs. Older, 122 lbs. Non-winners of a race of $30,000 since January 1, allowed 3 lbs. Of a race of $20,000 since then, 5 lbs. Of two races of $16,500 since then, 7 lbs. (Maiden, claiming, starter and state-bred races not considered.) $50 to nominate; $100 to enter and $100 to start. Closed Saturday, September 15 with 30 nominations.

Value of race $43,800; value to winner $26,280; second $9,636; third $5,256; fourth $2,628. Mutuel pool $183,496, OTB pool $119,973. Quinella Pool $260,659. OTB Quinella Pool $182,753.

Last Raced	Horse	Eqt.A.Wt	PP	St	¼	½	Str	Fin	Jockey	Odds $1
13Sep84 ^{8}Bel^{3}	Descent	4 115	5	7	9^{3}	8^{1}	3^{hd}	$1^{3\frac{1}{4}}$	Velasquez J	9.00
6Sep84 ^{8}Bel^{2}	Miss Frampton	5 115	6	2	6^{hd}	$7^{1\frac{1}{2}}$	$4^{1\frac{1}{2}}$	$2^{\frac{3}{4}}$	Davis R G	18.10
1Sep84 ^{6}Med^{1}	Rash But Royal	4 122	1	10	$1^{1\frac{1}{2}}$	1^{1}	1^{2}	3no	Pincay L Jr	5.10
6Sep84 ^{8}Bel^{1}	Hot Milk	b 3 111	4	5	2^{1}	2^{1}	2^{hd}	4no	MacBeth D	9.20
1Sep84 ^{8}Med^{7}	Jubilous	4 122	8	8	10^{2}	11	8^{hd}	5^{hd}	McCarron G	a-2.90
13Sep84 ^{8}Bel^{1}	Brorita	4 119	7	9	8^{1}	6^{1}	5^{hd}	$6^{\frac{1}{2}}$	Cordero A Jr	2.20
20Sep84 ^{8}Med^{6}	Tarifa	4 115	9	4	11	$10^{1\frac{1}{2}}$	$6^{\frac{1}{2}}$	$7^{\frac{1}{2}}$	Migliore R	55.80
12Sep84 ^{5}Bel^{2}	Cosmic Sea Queen	4 115	2	3	$3^{\frac{1}{2}}$	$3^{\frac{1}{2}}$	7^{1}	$8^{\frac{3}{4}}$	Samyn J L	9.00
13Sep84 ^{8}Bel^{2}	It's Fine	4 119	10	1	5^{2}	5^{hd}	$9^{\frac{1}{2}}$	$9^{1\frac{1}{2}}$	Guerra W A	9.40
14Sep84 ^{8}Bel^{2}	Quixotic Lady	4 119	3	11	$7^{\frac{1}{2}}$	$9^{\frac{1}{2}}$	10^{6}	$10^{5\frac{1}{4}}$	Maple E	a-2.90
18Sep84 ^{9}Med^{8}	Springset	b 4 115	11	6	4^{hd}	4^{1}	11	11	Terry J	68.40

a-Coupled: Jubilous and Quixotic Lady.

OFF AT 4:29. Start good, Won ridden out. Time, :23⅕, :46⅗, 1:10⅗, 1:23⅗ Course good.

$2 Mutuel Prices:				
	5-(E)-DESCENT	20.00	11.00	6.60
	6-(F)-MISS FRAMPTON		17.80	8.40
	2-(A)-RASH BUT ROYAL			4.60
	$2 QUINELLA 5-6 PAID $132.00.			

Ch. f, by Avatar—Alyne Que, by Raise a Native. Trainer Jackson Evan S. Bred by Claiborne Farm (Ky).

DESCENT rallied while racing wide after entering the stretch and drew off under intermittent urging. MISS FRAMPTON split horses leaving the turn and finished with good energy. RASH BUT ROYAL hustled to the front along the inside early, saved ground while making the pace into the stretch but weakened under pressure. HOT MILK prompted the pace into the stretch and weakened. JUBILOUS rallied mildly between horses. BRORITA moved up while racing well out in the course leaving the turn but lacked the needed late response. TARIFA raced very wide while moving leaving the turn but failed to sustain her rally. COSMIC SEA QUEEN raced forwardly to the stretch and gave way. ITS FINE tired. QUIXOTIC LADY, off slowly, saved ground to no avail.

Chapter 32

Big Pace as a Sign of Improvement

As the field paraded to the post for the first race at Aqueduct on Saturday, April 7, 1984, a couple of very interesting aspects of the form cycle were on display as well. To set the scene, the Inner dirt track at Aqueduct had for a number of days been heavily biased in favor of inside speed types. A mild breeze blew from left to right into the faces of the horses on the backstretch. While the direction of the wind could not help front-runners, its real effect on the day's races would not be known until a few races had been run.

Let's analyze the contestants:

ROYAL DUEL

One of three or four horses in the field capable of contesting the early lead and, unless displaced early, he'll probably be on the golden rail all the way. Royal Duel's latest race showed definite signs of improvement. For not only did the colt flash surprise early speed, and carry it to the eighth pole, but the pace he contested was extremely fast for the class—a sharp 106. As documented in my second book, *Thoroughbred Handicapping—State of the Art,* the big pace number, especially when posted by a freshened horse or one that had been off form, is a powerful angle. In combination with the form reversal and the ultimate tenth-place finish, it pointed quite clearly to an improving horse coming off a good tightener that would probably go to the post at good odds. Note the similarities to the colt's victory at almost 8–1 on January 27. Add to all of this a touch of back class (As recently as late January, the colt won for

1 AQUEDUCT

6 FURLONGS
INNER DIRT TRACK
AQUEDUCT

6 FURLONGS. (INNER-DIRT). (1.08⅘) CLAIMING. Purse $9,500. 4-year-olds and upward. Weights, 122 lbs. Non-winners of two races since March 1 allowed 3 lbs. Of a race since then, 5 lbs. Claiming price $12,500–$10,500, 2 lbs. Races when entered to be claimed for $8,500 or less not considered.

Royal Duel

Dk. b. or br. c. 4, by Soubej—Louise's Riddle, by Siama's Turn
$12,500 Br.—Liddell C M (Pa)
Tr.—O'Connell Richard
Own.—Roan Hero Stable
117
Lifetime 31 6 0 3 $58,698
1984 7 1 0 1 $8,640
1983 17 1 0 1 $17,092
Turf 1 0 0 0

31Mar84- 1Aqu	gd	6f	⊡:22⅘ :45⅘ 1:11⅘	Clm 15000	2	7	1hd	2 1½	3 2	10 6	Davis R G	b 115	20.80	81-15	NorthernShrk113noWimbornCstl119½WhtAWbbt112½	Gave way 12
19Mar84- 1Aqu	fst	6f	⊡:23 :47⅗ 1:12⅗	Clm 18000	8	8	5 3½	6 4	9 11	9 14½	Clayton M D	b 113	32.80	68-25	Starbinia 1192¾ Ample Native 1171½ What A Wabbit 1082	Outrun 10
26Feb84- 9Aqu	fst	6f	⊡:22⅘ :46⅗ 1:12⅕	Clm 25000	6	3	5 3½	4 3½	8 8¾	10 15½	Davis R G	b 117	12.60	68-29	What ACharger1171½[D]Rauschenberg1083AmpleNative1131½	Tired 12
15Feb84- 9Aqu	sly	6f	⊡:22⅕ :46⅕ 1:11⅗	Clm c-20000	7	5	8 11	9 14	9 13	8 8¾	Miranda J	b 117	4.50	77-23	Appeal Affirmed 117¾KentuckyEdd1172Rauschenberg113¾	Outrun 12
8Feb84- 5Aqu	fst	6f	⊡:22⅘ :46⅘ 1:12⅕	Clm 25000	5	1	2 1½	3 1½	2 1½	3 2	Miranda J	b 117	6.00	81-19	I'm Peppy 1131¾ Shy Hughes 115nk Royal Duel 117¾	Bore in 12
27Jan84- 9Aqu	gd	6f	⊡:22⅕ :45⅗ 1:11	Clm 16000	7	1	2 3	2hd	1 4	1 4	Miranda J	b 117	7.70	89-16	Royal Duel 1174 Shaz 115hd Hawaiian Moonshine 1141½	Drew out 12
18Jan84- 9Aqu	fst	6f	⊡:23⅗ :48⅘ 1:14	Clm 16000	2	6	5 2	5 2½	3 4½	5 10¾	Miranda J	b 117	16.20	63-35	Bold Target 1195 Rauschenberg 1223½ Charbonnel 1101¾	Tired 12
24Dec83- 1Aqu	fst	6f	⊡:22⅘ :48⅘ 1:16⅗	Clm 25000	1	8	2 4	8 7¾	10 14	10 15¾	Miranda J	b 117	20.40	45-43	[D]J Strap 117½ Miraculously 117½ Brightest Hope 1121¾	Tired 12
16Dec83- 5Aqu	fst	6f	⊡:22⅕ :45⅗ 1:11⅗	Clm 35000	9	6	4 3	4 1¾	7 4¾	10 6½	Miranda J	b 117	45.70	80-21	Just Any Time 117¾ Carpet Ride 117hd Saint Stephan 117nk	Tired 12
8Dec83- 5Aqu	fst	6f	⊡:22⅕ :45⅕ 1:11	3↑ Clm 35000	4	7	6 7½	6 8	7 11	9 10½	Miranda J	b 115	41.50	79-17	Kentucky Edd 117½ Cannon Shell 1101½ Big Izzy 1154	Outrun 10

LATEST WORKOUTS Mar 16 Bel tr.t 4f fst :49 b Mar 7 Bel tr.t 4f fst :48⅘ h Feb 24 Bel tr.t 3f sly :36 h

Raised Trouble

Dk. b. or br. g. 4, by Raise A Bid—Cassy Lou, by Reflected Glory
$10,500 Br.—Newchance Farm (Fla)
Tr.—Necella Vincent
Own.—Ferette M A
113
Lifetime 20 2 0 2 $18,415
1984 4 0 0 0
1983 10 1 0 1 $10,015

Entered 6Apr84- 9 AQU

31Mar84- 9Aqu	gd	6f	⊡:22⅘ :45⅘ 1:10⅘	Clm 10000	4	2	5 5	7 9½	7 15	6 11½	Davis R G	b 117	11.40	78-15	Handsome Dancer 1082¾ Rain Prince1133½Amadandy1103½	Outrun 7
8Mar84- 1Aqu	fst	6f	⊡:23⅗ :47⅕ 1:12⅗	Clm 10000	5	2	5 4½	6 8½	7 7½	6 9½	Muino M M7	110	16.10	71-24	Flippydoo 108no Bouliabase 1066½ Charlie's Star 107¾	No factor 12
19Feb84- 2Aqu	fst	6f	⊡:22⅕ :45⅗ 1:11⅗	Clm 11500	4	1	5 4½	6 7¾	8 8	8 3½	Muino M M7	109	10.90	82-14	Quiche 110½ Northern Shrike 117no No Additives 1121½	Tired 10
4Jan84- 1Aqu	fst	6f	⊡:22⅘ :46⅘ 1:12⅗	Clm 9000	7	1	7 4½	6 5½	7 5½	7 8½	Graell A	113	9.50	73-25	Major Menuever 1172¾ TimeTogether1171½Bouliabase108½	Outrun 8
30Dec83- 4Med	fr	6f	:22⅘ :45 1:10⅘	Clm 8000	3	4	7 5¾	6 6	4 7	3 5½	Graell A	115	7.50	85-10	Jonathan'sToy1154½OpinionLeader1151RisedTrouble1151	Mild bid 8
18Dec83- 9Aqu	fst	1 1/16	⊡:48⅘ 1:14⅘ 1:49	Clm 14000	10	5	10 6½	10 12	10 13	10 16¾	McHargue D G	113	17.10	50-25	Pitchpipe 1131½ John's Medicine 108¾FortCollins117no	Brief foot 12
16Dec83- 1Aqu	fst	6f	⊡:23 :46⅗ 1:12⅗	Clm 10500	5	3	4 1½	6 4	4 4½	4 1½	Santagata N	113	10.20	81-21	RapidStreak108¾ExecutiveSwinger117nkDearRichrd115nk	Late bid 8
14Nov83- 9Aqu	fst	7f	:23⅕ :47⅕ 1:25	Clm 14000	8	1	5 1½	8 5½	8 15	8 18½	Santagata N	b 117	40.90	57-24	J. Strap 1172½ Executive Swinger 1154½ Spy Game 1133½	Outrun 11
4Nov83- 9Aqu	fst	7f	:23⅗ :47⅗ 1:25⅘	Clm 14000	12	1	4 2½	11 7¾	10 15	10 20	Santagata N	b 117	19.70	52-27	VlidDecision1152ExecutiveSwinger1173DrRichrd1154	Raced wide 12
21Oct83- 1Aqu	fst	6½f	:23 :46⅘ 1:17⅘	Clm 14000	6	3	5 4½	5 3½	5 6	6 7½	Santagata N	b 117	20.60	78-20	VlidDecision1082½BitterWrth1082½ExecutivSwingr119hd	No factor 14

21Oct83-Placed fifth through disqualification
LATEST WORKOUTS Mar 21 Bel tr.t 4f fst :49⅗ b

Handsome Dancer

B. c. 4, by Fire Dancer—Alchemilla, by Quadrangle
$12,500 Br.—Newchance Farm & Raff (Fla)
Tr.—Galluscio Dominick
Own.—Ran-Sco Stable
114[5]
Lifetime 25 3 1 2 $28,020
1984 9 2 0 0 $10,800
1983 7 1 0 0 $9,780

31Mar84- 9Aqu	gd	6f	⊡:22⅘ :45⅘ 1:10⅘	Clm 9000	1	3	1 1½	1 3½	1 4	1 2¾	Belmonte J E5	b 108	7.60	90-15	Handsome Dancer 1082¾ RainPrince1133½Amadandy1103½	Driving 7
23Mar84- 1Aqu	fst	170	⊡:48⅗ 1:13⅗ 1:43⅗	Clm 10500	8	1	2½	2 1½	6 9¾	5 17¾	Belmonte J E5	b 109	25.00	64-24	Exuberance 11712 Hasty Flight1141HomeSecretary1171	Gave way 10
8Mar84- 1Aqu	fst	6f	⊡:23⅗ :47⅕ 1:12⅗	Clm 10000	2	8	4 3	4 5	4 2¾	5 8	Miranda J	b 117	24.00	73-24	Flippydoo 108no Bouliabase 1066½ Charlie's Star 107¾	No factor 12
27Feb84- 9Aqu	fst	6f	⊡:23 :47 1:12⅗	Clm 11500	2	10	7 4	8 6½	9 9½	9 6¾	Muino M M7	b 109	17.40	74-24	Nightly Battle 1131¾ Clinebell113hdPrinceofSport113hd	No factor 12
11Feb84- 9Aqu	fst	6f	⊡:22⅘ :46⅘ 1:12	Clm 12500	7	2	5 1½	6 4½	7 5¾	6 6¾	Belmonte J E5	b 114	18.40	77-20	NeedAPenny113noOurMnVlentine1174½BrightCurrnt1091½	Outrun 11
5Feb84- 9Aqu	sly	6f	⊡:22⅗ :46⅘ 1:12⅗	Clm 15000	6	8	6 5½	7 7½	7 10	7 11¾	Muino M M7	b 108	8.90	70-25	FlyingGenerl1125RpidWing1102½DoubleDifference108hd	Wide str 11
1Feb84- 9Aqu	fst	6f	⊡:23 :47⅗ 1:12⅘	Clm 18000	6	9	7 3¾	3 1½	1 1½	1 3	Muino M M7	b 110	13.80	80-18	Handsome Dancer 1103 Implosion 110hdDelbarton1171	Drew clear 12
27Jan84- 9Aqu	gd	6f	⊡:22⅕ :45⅗ 1:11	Clm 16000	2	4	7 7¾	7 7½	7 9	7 8½	Vega H7	b 110	22.10	81-16	Royal Duel 1174 Shaz 115hd HawaiianMoonshine1141½	No menace 12
18Jan84- 2Aqu	fst	170	⊡:49 1:15 1:45⅗	Clm 22500	10	3	—	—	—	—	Hernandez R	b 115	17.30	— —	HuntedLd1109¾MorningRview1172Eldg'sProspct1131	Snow, Eased 10
31Dec83- 6Bow	fst	7f	:22 :44⅕ 1:20⅘	3↑ Alw 10000	8	9	9 15	9 14	8 18	8 11½	Baltazar C	b 115	19.80	90-82	Humbug I 1171 Quill Feather 1142 King's Bluff 110hd	Outrun 9

LATEST WORKOUTS Mar 17 Bel tr.t 4f fst :49⅕ h

Swiss Connection

B. g. 5, by Poker—Swiss Policy, by New Policy
$12,500 Br.—Sabiston J T (Ont-C)
Tr.—Bolton Amos E
Own.—Rosencrans Barbara
117
Lifetime 57 7 2 8 $65,000
1984 4 0 0 0 $1,500
1983 25 2 2 4 $27,440
Turf 3 0 0 0

28Feb84- 1Aqu	fst	6f	⊡:22⅕ :45⅗ 1:11⅗	Clm 16000	8	10	10 17	10 13	10 15	8 9½	MacBeth D	b 117	6.80	77-16	OurManVlentine112½Coplis117nkDoubleDifference1101½	Dwelt st 10
12Feb84- 9Aqu	fst	6f	⊡:22⅘ :46⅘ 1:11⅘	Clm 16000	1	12	12 14	10 13	7 5¾	4 4¾	MacBeth D	b 117	18.10	80-24	Charbonnel 1174½ Royal Jove 117no Wine AndWomen103½	Rallied 12
19Jan84- 9Aqu	fst	1 1/16	⊡:48⅘ 1:14⅘ 1:49	Clm 16000	4	10	7 8	12 16	11 15	12 15½	Smith A Jr	b 117	10.50	51-32	No Heir 1173 Boomer Sooner 1171 Magic Michael 1171	Outrun 12
6Jan84- 3Aqu	fst	170	⊡:48⅘ 1:14 1:45⅗	Clm 16000	9	8	8 6	6 5½	3 4	4 4½	Smith A Jr	b 117	8.60	69-24	Fort Collins 117hd Spirited Song 1131½ Soudan 1172¾	Hung late 10
11Dec83- 4Aqu	fst	1 1/16	⊡:48⅘ 1:14⅘ 1:47⅕	3↑ Clm 19000	7	8	6 8½	5 6	4 6	5 5½	MacBeth D	b 115	10.40	70-27	Vanishing Prince 1151½Exuberance1173½Danderoo117nk	No factor 8
24Nov83- 2Aqu	fst	6½f	:23⅗ :47⅕ 1:19⅕	3↑ Clm 19000	1	11	8 5½	10 4	6 4	5 3½	MacBeth D	b 115	10.30	76-24	WhtAChrger113hdFlippydoo106¾TheBloodyBest1102½	No menace 11
13Nov83- 1Aqu	fst	1	:48 1:13⅕ 1:39⅕	3↑ Clm 19000	4	6	4 3½	4 6	4 5½	3 5¾	MacBeth D	b 115	5.70	64-20	Jet Voyage 1141½ Big Izzy 1124½ Swiss Connection115nk	Mild bid 8
7Nov83- 9Aqu	fst	6f	:22⅘ :45⅘ 1:11	3↑ Clm 22500	4	8	9 23	9 22	9 19	8 14¾	MacBeth D	b 115	14.50	71-22	CndnCurrency1173¾Meteorite1175½LittlHutch1152½	Jamed bk. st. 9
13Oct83- 5Bel	my	1 1/16	:46 1:10⅕ 1:42⅘	3↑ Clm 25000	1	8	8 15	8 21	8 16	7 16¾	Murphy D J5	b 112	11.30	73-15	Pride Of Satan 1171 Verbum 1172½ Laddy's Luck 1153½	Outrun 9
5Oct83- 1Bel	fst	6½f	:22⅘ :45⅘ 1:17⅘	3↑ Clm 30000	8	7	11 11	11 10	9 8½	7 3¾	MacBeth D	b 113	25.10	85-21	Cold Trailin' 117¾ Pride Of Satan 1131¾ Big Izzy 108½	No factor 11

LATEST WORKOUTS Mar 18 Bel tr.t 5f fst 1:00⅘ hg

Buck's Spirit

B. c. 4, by Crown Gift—Spirit of Ireland, by Up Spirits
$12,500 Br.—Waltsak Carol A (NY)
Tr.—Cincotta Vincent J
Own.—La Polla R
117
Lifetime 13 1 3 4 $37,860
1984 6 1 1 3 $27,500
1983 4 M 2 0 $7,480

10Mar84- 2Aqu	fst	6f	⊡:23 :47⅘ 1:12⅘	[S]Alw 24500	1	5	1hd	1hd	2hd	7 6¾	Murphy D J	b 114	13.30	73-24	Fletcher 1171½ Commander Almy 117¾ Guy Pebo 117nk	Gave way 10
1Mar84- 4Aqu	fst	6f	⊡:22⅘ :47⅗ 1:14⅕	[S]Md Sp Wt	5	1	2 2½	2 1½	1 2½	1 2	Murphy D J5	b 117	*1.60	73-23	Buck's Spirit 1172 Triangulation 117hd Spit Ball 1225	Drew clear 11
20Feb84- 4Aqu	fst	170	⊡:49⅗ 1:15 1:46	[S]Md Sp Wt	10	3	2 2	1hd	2 1½	3 2	Murphy D J5	b 117	2.50	69-16	Damascus Jet1222Triangulation117hdBuck'sSpirit1174½	Weakened 10
3Feb84- 4Aqu	fst	1 1/16	⊡:50⅕ 1:16 1:48⅘	[S]Md Sp Wt	12	1	1 1½	1 1½	2 6	3 16	Murphy D J5	b 117	5.10	52-28	BlushingBunny12214Triangultion1172Buck'sSpirit117½	Weakened 12
25Jan84- 4Aqu	sly	6f	⊡:22⅗ :46⅕ 1:12⅘	[S]Md Sp Wt	2	4	2hd	2 1½	1hd	2hd	Murphy D J5	b 117	*2.50	82-18	AprilFoolsBoy122hdBuck'sSpirt1171½ToyBulldog1172¾	Drifted out 12
5Jan84- 9Aqu	fst	6f	⊡:23⅕ :47 1:11⅘	[S]Md Sp Wt	8	2	3 2	4 1¾	2 3	3 6¾	Migliore R	b 122	7.10	78-23	Midway Flyer 1226¾ Blushing Bunny122noBuck'sSpirit122hd	Wide 11
9Dec83- 9Aqu	fst	6f	⊡:23⅕ :47⅕ 1:12⅕	3↑ Md 14000	4	5	1hd	1hd	1 1½	2 1½	Migliore R	b 120	3.00	82-19	Medieval Manor 1151½ Buck'sSpirit1204½LatinSailor1226¾	Gamely 11
30Nov83- 9Aqu	fst	6f	:23 :47⅕ 1:13⅕	3↑ Md 28000	7	6	4 8¾	1hd	4 2¾	5 7½	Rivera J S	b 120	8.90	67-29	Morning Review 120hd Decatur 1202½ Ack Attack 1201½	Weakened 12
30Jan83- 4Aqu	fst	1⅛	⊡:49⅕ 1:14⅘ 1:55⅗	[S]Md Sp Wt	1	1	1 1½	1hd	4 5½	5 15½	Migliore R	b 122	*2.40	53-20	Spirit Of Alma 1225½YoungNaskra1174Sirnonyma1225½	Weakened 9
3Jan83- 7Aqu	fst	6f	⊡:23⅗ :48⅘ 1:14⅘	[S]Md Sp Wt	6	2	1hd	2hd	2hd	2 2½	Migliore R	b 122	*1.30	78-25	NwYorkCompny1222½Buck'sSpirit1226ClrlyOutFront115¾	Gamely 9

Hawaiian Moonshine

Dk. b. or br. c. 4, by Hula Chief—Cathy's Moonsplash, by Moonsplash
$12,500 Br.—Avery D E (Tex)
Tr.—Krohn Nat
Own.—Krohn Deborah
112[5]
Lifetime 40 2 10 3 $30,090
1984 8 0 0 1 $1,920
1983 22 1 9 1 $23,515

Entered 6Apr84- 9 AQU

26Mar84- 9Aqu	fst	6f	⊡:23⅗ :48 1:13	Clm 12500	2	3	6 4½	4 3½	4 2½	5 4½	Samyn J L	117	6.80	74-28	No Additives 117½ Rasselas 1132 Clinebell 119¾	Lacked rally 10
12Mar84- 9Aqu	fst	6f	⊡:23⅕ :47 1:13⅕	Clm c-18000	6	1	7 5¾	5 4½	5 3½	4 3	Belmonte J E5	112	10.70	75-22	LWshingtonn1072½ExcutvSwngr117noPrncPr108¾	Finished willing 12
20Feb84- 1Aqu	fst	6f	⊡:22⅕ :45⅗ 1:11⅗	Clm 16000	10	9	9 6½	8 6¾	9 13	10 12½	Velasquez J	b 117	7.80	74-16	Our Man Valentine112½Coplis117nkDoubleDifference1101½	Outrun 10
6Feb84- 3Aqu	my	170	⊡:47⅘ 1:13⅗ 1:43⅗	Clm 16000	4	8	8 11	8 10	6 5¾	7 6½	Ayoub L5	114	7.20	75-19	ComputerCrlos115¾FourAndSixpenc1132RinPrinc1172½	No factor 10
27Jan84- 9Aqu	gd	6f	⊡:22⅕ :45⅗ 1:11	Clm 16000	1	10	11 13	9 10	6 7½	3 4	Ayoub L5	114	4.90	85-16	Royal Duel 1174 Shaz 115hd Hawaiian Moonshine 1141½	Rallied 12
21Jan84- 5Aqu	fst	6f	⊡:23 :47 1:13	Alw 20000	3	9	11 12	9 9¾	8 9¾	8 9½	Ayoub L5	114	25.00	70-30	Mc Michael112hdFlyingGeneral1124½PrideOfSatan1102½	No factor 11
19Jan84- 5Aqu	fst	1⅛	⊡:48⅗ 1:14⅘ 1:55⅗	Alw 22000	10	10	10 20	10 13	8 10	8 13½	Ayoub L5	115	20.30	55-32	[D]PuttingGreen1172½ColonelLaw1122½CanadinClm122¾	No factor 10
11Jan84- 5Aqu	sl	6f	⊡:23⅕ :47⅗ 1:13⅗	Alw 20000	3	12	12 12	12 13	7 6½	6 4½	Ayoub L5	113	27.30	72-33	Sky Falcon 1122 Troop Ship 117nk Saint Stephan 117¾	Rallied 12
27Dec83- 9Aqu	fst	6f	⊡:23 :47⅗ 1:14	Clm 12500	10	2	6 7	5 4	1hd	1 2½	Ayoub L	117	13.60	74-31	HwiinMoonshine1172½OurMnVlentin1175½ProudPupr117¾	Driving 11
23Dec83- 9Aqu	gd	6f	⊡:22⅕ :46 1:12⅗	Clm 15000	8	2	2 1½	4 3	6 11	6 8¾	Vega H7	108	18.60	73-21	Bold Target 1171¾ Spy Game 1191½ Flying General 117¾	Gave way 9

Rasselas

B. h. 6, by Key To The Kingdom—Lilac Hill, by Prince John
$12,500 Br.—Tinton Falls Stable (Md)
Tr.—Shapoff Stanley R
Own.—Cohen R B
117
Lifetime 43 7 5 6 $84,023
1984 1 0 1 0 $2,090
1983 9 1 0 1 $13,620
Turf 1 0 0 0

26Mar84- 9Aqu	fst	6f	⊡:23⅗ :48 1:13	Clm 10500	1	2	2 2½	2 1½	2 1	2 ½	Santagata N	b 113	6.10	78-28	No Additives 117½ Rasselas 1132 Clinebell 119¾	Gaining 10
12May83- 9Aqu	fst	6½f	:23⅕ :47 1:18⅗	Clm 16000	6	1	3 1½	2 1½	2 3	3 2½	Bailey J D	b 117	15.10	80-20	Kenny J 112½ Southern Shade 1172 Rasselas 1171½	Weakened 12
8Apr83- 2Aqu	my	7f	:22⅗ :45⅗ 1:22⅗	Clm 25000	4	8	10 6½	8 11	7 14	8 9½	Smith A Jr	b 117	8.10	78-17	Kenny J. 108nk Need A Penny 1121 DealingDiplomat115hd	Outrun 13
25Mar83- 3Aqu	fst	7f	:23⅗ :48⅕ 1:25⅗	Clm 30000	9	3	11 8½	9 7½	5 5	9 8½	Smith A Jr	b 113	6.20e	66-36	Prete Khale 1084 Term Paper 1121 Rigid 115¾	Wide str. 11
16Mar83- 3Aqu	fst	1	:46⅕ 1:11⅕ 1:37⅗	Clm 35000	9	11	12 7½	14 12	14 17	14 17½	Lovato F Jr	b 117	8.10	61-27	Hugh Capet 115¾ Startop'sAce1122½LetterFromLucy115no	Outrun 14
5Mar83- 1Aqu	fst	6f	⊡:23⅗ :46⅘ 1:11⅗	Clm 35000	5	2	6 4½	6 5½	6 4½	5 3½	Lovato F Jr	b 117	6.90	83-16	Bright Search1152¾CanadianCurrency117noFirstee110no	No threat 7
5Feb83- 3Aqu	fst	1 1/16	⊡:47⅗ 1:13⅗ 1:46⅗	Clm 37500	4	4	3 3	4 5	4 5½	4 6½	Gonzalez M A	b 115	5.50e	74-20	Boldeelee1143½AlecGeorg1132½Strtop'sAc112½	Lacked a response 10
22Jan83- 3Aqu	fst	6f	⊡:23 :45⅗ 1:10	Clm 40000	10	2	4 1½	4 1¾	4 3½	4 2¾	Kaenel J L	b 119	5.40	91-07	NorwegianPocket117noKentuckyEdd1122½RellySmrt117nk	Evenly 10
14Jan83- 5Aqu	fst	6f	⊡:23⅕ :46⅗ 1:11⅗	Clm 45000	1	1	4 1½	4 2½	5 2½	5 6¾	Kaenel J L	b 113	4.20	80-19	Happy Hooligan 1192½ Fanny's Fox 117½ Jeffery C. 1174	Tired 10
3Jan83- 4Aqu	fst	6f	⊡:23⅗ :47⅕ 1:12⅗	Clm 35000	8	1	3 1	3 1	1hd	1 2½	Kaenel J L	b 117	12.30	82-25	Rasselas 1172½ Pleasure Bid 117hd Rigid 1121	Drew clear 8

LATEST WORKOUTS Apr 3 Bel tr.t 4f fst :52 b Mar 23 Bel tr.t 5f fst 1:01⅘ h Mar 12 Bel tr.t 5f fst 1:01⅕ h Mar 7 Bel tr.t 4f fst :48⅘ h

Nightly Battle						Ch. g. 5, by Nightly's Pleasure—Battlesomma, by Battle Joined									Lifetime	1984 5 1 1 0	$8,090
Own.—Spiegel R						$12,500 Br.—Lindley J (Neb) Tr.—Schaeffer Stephen							117		45 9 8 6 $84,089	1983 14 2 2 1	$16,494
19Mar84- 3Aqu fst 6f	⊡:23⅘	:48	1:13	Clm 12500	9 1	1 1½	1 1	2 hd	2½	Cordero A Jr	119	8.40	78-25	Flippydoo 110½ Nightly Battle 119 2 LeWashingtonian 109 no		Gamely	10
27Feb84- 9Aqu fst 6f	⊡:23	:47	1:12⅘	Clm 10500	11 2	2½	2½	1½	1 1½	Santagata N	113	27.70	81-24	Nightly Battle 113 1½ Clinebell 113 hd Prince of Sport 113 hd		Driving	12
11Feb84- 9Aqu fst 6f	⊡:22⅘	:46⅘	1:12	Clm 10500	9 7	1 hd	1½	3 1½	8 9	Santagata N	113	28.00	75-20	NeedAPenny 113 no OurManVlentine 117 4½ BrightCurrent 109 1½		Tired	11
1Feb84- 9Aqu fst 6f	⊡:23	:47⅘	1:12⅘	Clm 10000	4 3	1 hd	1½	4 3	9 9½	Santagata N	117	4.20	78-18	Handsome Dancer 110 3 Implosion 110 hd Delbarton 117 1		Tired	12
18Jan84- 9Aqu fst 6f	⊡:23⅘	:48⅘	1:14	Clm 14000	4 3	2 hd	6 3	8 11	8 17½	Santagata N	b 113	9.70	57-35	Bold Target 119 5 Rauschenberg 122 3½ Charbonnel 110 1½		Gave way	12
26Dec83-11Med fr 6f	:22	:44⅘	1:09⅘	3+ Clm 14000	2 5	4 1½	2 3	2 2	2 3	Santagata N	b 114	11.90	93-10	Raise An Emperor 116 3 NightlyBattle 114 2½ Mafito 112 1½		Held place	11
6Dec83- 7Med sly 6f	:23	:47⅘	1:13⅘	3+ Clm 16000	6 4	1 hd	2 2½	6 5½	6 15	Migliore R	b 116	7.50	60-24	Newsprobe 119½ T. V. Table 116 1½ Clinebell 114 1		Tired	7
18Nov83- 7Med fst 6f	:22⅘	:46	1:11⅘	3+ Clm 14000	10 1	2½	2 hd	2½	4 5½	Migliore R	114	15.40	78-21	Newsprobe 119 hd Professor Vis 116 4½ Rich Saul 116 1		Weakened	12
8Nov83- 2Med fst 6f	:22⅕	:45⅘	1:11⅘	3+ Clm 12500	3 2	2 1	1 1	1 1½	1 1	Migliore R	116	11.50	84-22	Nightly Battle 116 1 Judge Grey 119 1½ Prune Pie 111 nk		Driving	7
22Oct83- 2Med fst 6f	:22⅘	:45⅘	1:12⅕	3+ Clm 12500	1 3	1½	2 1	2½	5 1½	Graell A	116	10.90	80-19	Fog A Balla 116 no Freedom Lad 116½ Judge Grey 119 1		Weakened	8
LATEST WORKOUTS	Apr 1 Bel tr.t 4f fst :48⅘ h				Mar 13 Bel tr.t 4f fst :49⅘ b							Mar 8 Bel tr.t 4f fst :49⅘ b			Feb 21 Bel tr.t 4f fst :50 b		

$16,000 and raced competitively for $25,000 before going off form.) and Royal Duel offered a little something for everyone—trip, speed, form, and class handicappers alike. As enticing an 8–1 shot as one is likely to find.

RAISED TROUBLE

This horse hasn't been close in his latest five races, four of which were in lower classifications.

HANDSOME DANCER

Like Royal Duel, this colt was coming off a race in which he set an exceptionally fast pace. Unlike Royal Duel, though, Handsome Dancer had enough left that day to maintain his pace to the wire. His figures (107–105) were outstanding and would demolish most $12,500 fields at Aqueduct. However, Handsome Dancer earned those figures against lesser competition ($10,000 claimers), while racing uncontested on the front end—both negative signs that many players will overlook. A third strike against Handsome Dancer was his lack of back class. All of his recent efforts against competition above the $10,000 level had proven unsuccessful. In summary, he'll probably be among the favorites, yet is outclassed and outpositioned by Royal Duel.

SWISS CONNECTION

A sluggish sort dropping to a new low, Swiss Connection is unlikely to contend at six furlongs over a speed-favoring track.

BUCK'S SPIRIT

A recent maiden graduate in the state-bred ranks, Buck's Spirit's winning figure on March 1 was several lengths inferior to average time for $12,500 claimers.

HAWAIIAN MOONSHINE

Another slow starter, this colt has won only once in the last two years (thirty starts), while finishing second on nine occasions—none of these in eight starts so far in 1984.

RASSELAS

The 9–5 favorite, Rasselas recently returned from a ten-month layoff with a strong effort in $12,500 company. With normal improvement, he's a likely "one off a layoff" winner, many would reason. But not every horse improves in its second try after a layoff. Most noteworthy are those forced into an all-out effort first race back. The common terminology used nowadays is "muscle soreness." Rasselas was doubly suspect in this respect. Note that the six-year-old dropped significantly just prior to his layoff, then dropped again upon returning from the layoff. The latter, especially, is a bad sign, suggesting unsoundness. Most trainers would race a claiming animal back into shape in a higher class, then drop it when ready for a winning effort. The fact that trainer Shapoff dropped Rasselas on March 26 suggested that the horse had not returned as well as might be expected, and the fact that Shapoff entered him for $10,500 against $12,500 rivals suggested that the horse was well-meant on that occasion, and that his connections probably didn't like his chances for an extended campaign. Rasselas was an excellent candidate for muscle soreness, and a great favorite to bet against.

NIGHTLY BATTLE

This gelding's last two races, in today's company, were excellent—or at least appeared so on paper. Pace and speed figures, however, revealed them to be almost identical and rather weak for the class. Both were run in subpar time, after significantly slow early fractions. As the outside speed facing swifter rivals inside over an inside-speed course, he's not likely to be a winner.

Royal Duel had too many things going for him to pass up at 8–1, even though the wind factor did not figure to help him. His performance that day, however, was completely out of character. Hustled to a long lead in the early stages, Royal Duel remained in front to the wire, despite tiring noticeably in deep stretch. He paid a liberal $19.20.

FIRST RACE
Aqueduct
APRIL 7, 1984

6 FURLONGS.(INNER DIRT). (1.08⅘) CLAIMING. Purse $9,500. 4-year-olds and upward. Weights, 122 lbs. Non-winners of two races since March 1 allowed 3 lbs. Of a race since then, 5 lbs. Claiming price $12,500–$10,500, 2 lbs. Races when entered to be claimed for $8,500 or less not consdiered. (22nd Day. WEATHER CLEAR. TEMPERATURE 62 DEGREES.)

Value of race $9,500, value to winner $5,700, second $2,090, third $1,140, fourth $570. Mutuel pool $131,572, OTB pool $180,984.

Last Raced		Horse	Eqt.	A.	Wt	PP	St	¼	½	Str	Fin	Jockey	Cl'g Pr	Odds $1
31Mar84	^{1}Aqu^{10}	Royal Duel	b	4	117	1	3	1^4	1^6	1^6	12¼	Maple E	12500	8.70
20Feb84	^{1}Aqu^8	Swiss Connection		5	117	4	8	8	8	6½	2^{nk}	McCarron G	12500	9.80
26Mar84	^{9}Aqu^2	Rasselas	b	6	117	7	5	3½	31½	2½	31¼	Davis R G	12500	1.80
31Mar84	^{9}Aqu^6	Raised Trouble	b	4	113	2	6	7½	7^{hd}	5^{hd}	4^{nk}	MacBeth D	10500	25.50
26Mar84	^{9}Aqu^5	Hawaiian Moonshine		4	112	6	1	6^{hd}	6½	7^5	5^{nk}	Ward W^5	12500	9.40
18Mar84	^{2}Aqu^7	Buck's Spirit	b	4	117	5	4	2^{hd}	4½	3^2	61¾	Murphy D J	12500	9.90
31Mar84	^{9}Aqu^1	Handsome Dancer	b	4	114	3	7	5^4	2^{hd}	4^{hd}	7^{11}	Belmonte J E^5	12500	3.40
19Mar84	^{3}Aqu^2	Nightly Battle		5	117	8	2	4^{hd}	5^2	8	8	Santagata N	12500	3.80

OFF AT 1:00 Start good, Won driving. Time, :22⅘, :46⅖, 1:13⅕ Track fast.

Official Program Numbers↘

$2 Mutuel Prices:			
1-(A)-ROYAL DUEL	19.40	9.40	5.40
4-(E)-SWISS CONNECTION		11.00	6.60
7-(H)-RASSELAS			3.20

Dk. b. or br. c, by Souboj—Louise's Riddle, by Siama's Turn. Trainer O'Connell Richard. Bred by Liddell C M (Pa).

ROYAL DUEL quickly sprinted clear, drew off around the turn and was all out to hold sway. SWISS CONNECTION, off slowly, finished full of run while racing very wide. RASSELAS finished with good energy. RAISED TROUBLE failed to seriously menace with a mild late response. HAWAIIAN MOONSHINE had no apparent excuse. BUCK'S SPIRIT saved ground to no avail. HANDSOME DANCER moved up outside horses at the turn but lacked a late response. NIGHTLY BATTLE was finished early.

We would like to make one additional point here regarding speed handicapping methodology. Part of the attraction of Royal Duel came from the exceptional pace figure he earned on March 31. Yet Handsome Dancer also ran a fast pace figure on the same day. During the winter months, changing weather conditions from one race to the next may account for uneven race variants from par during a day's card and could contribute to what appear to be exceptionally fast or slow pace or final-time figures for certain races. Since Royal Duel's performance came in the first race on March 31, and Handsome Dancer's in the ninth, it is more likely their figures for that day are legitimate rather than caused by extreme changes in weather or variable wind conditions. But only those who were present at Aqueduct on March 31, and alert to wind conditions, would know for certain.

Chapter 33

Controlling Speed on a Golden Rail

AT ENTRY TIME, the 1984 Gotham Stakes, run on April 7 at Aqueduct, appeared to be an interesting match-up between two-year-old champion Devil's Bag, seeking vindication after his first career set-back, and Secret Prince, a rising potential star, whose connections were confidently looking forward to the confrontation. The other four horses entered received little, if any, attention from the press during the days preceding the race.

On the day before the race, however, Devil's Bag was scratched—reportedly because poor track conditions during the week of the race interrupted his training schedule. And on the day of the Gotham, a powerful track bias cast the race in a completely different light.

Let's take a look at the remaining five contestants:

BEAR HUNT

With Devil's Bag in the race and contesting the pace, Bear Hunt seemed to have little chance, even with a twelve-pound pull in the weights. He could only contribute to the champion's defeat but would probably be first to back out of the picture. But with Devil's Bag scratched, Bear Hunt became "controlling speed on the rail." And the bias Gotham Day favored speed on the rail very strongly. Also making Bear Hunt appear an attractive betting proposition was the fact that his speed figure on March 18 was better than any of his rival's route figures, indeed two points higher than Secret Prince's average route figure, which had been earned while carrying moderate weights. Today, Secret Prince was being asked to shoulder 126 pounds and concede twelve pounds to Bear Hunt.

8 AQUEDUCT 1 MILE 70 YDS INNER DIRT TRACK AQUEDUCT

1 MILE 70 YARDS. (INNER-DIRT). (1.40) 32nd Running THE GOTHAM (Grade II). $150,000 Added. (Plus $50,000 Breeders' Cup Premium Awards). 3-year-olds. Weight, 126 lbs. By subscription of $300 each which should accompany the nomination; $4,000 to pass the entry box, with $150,000 added. The added money and all fees to be divided 60% to the winner, 22% to second, 12% to third and 6% to fourth. Non-winners of a race of $60,000 allowed 3 lbs. Of a race of $25,000, 5 lbs. Of two races of $15,000 in 1983–84, 8 lbs. Of such a race in 1983–84, 12 lbs. Starters to be named at the closing time of entries. Trophies will be presented to the winning owner, trainer and jockey. Nominations close Wednesday, March 14, 1984. Closed with 28 nominations.

Bear Hunt — B. c. 3, by Naskra—Ashwood Bow, by Gun Bow
Own.—Taylors Purchase Farm — Br.—Little W P (Ky) — Tr.—Laurin Roger — 114
Lifetime 6 3 0 2 $43,920 — 1984 3 1 0 1 $15,120 — 1983 3 2 0 1 $28,800 — Turf 1 0 0 0
18Mar84- 3Aqu fst 170 ⊡:48 1:13⅗ 1:43⅕ Alw 22000 2 1 14½ 11 12½ 13½ MacBeth D ◉ 117 3.30 84-24 Bear Hunt 1173½ Dixie's Island 112½ Groom'sImage1179 Drew out 7
18Feb84- 8Hia fm 1 1/16 Ⓣ 1:41⅗ Dade County 5 12 1314 1415 1423 1417¼ Maple E b 112 6.20 73-11 Dr Schwartzman 1192Klaytone112nk Calejucam113½ Wide 1st turn 14
17Jan84- 9Hia fst 1 1/16 :46⅗ 1:10⅗ 1:43⅗ Alw 16000 1 2 2hd 22½ 33 35¼ Maple E b 121 2.20 79-19 Turnberry 115hd Time for aChange1155½BearHunt1214 Weakened 8
9Dec83- 7Aqu fst 1 1/16 ⊡:49⅗ 1:14⅗ 1:46⅗ Alw 24000 7 1 1hd 11½ 11½ 12¾ Maple E b 117 2.60 79-19 Bear Hunt 1172¾ Is YourPleasure1174½Cindy'sFriend1174½ Driving 7
30Oct83- 6Aqu fst 6f :22⅗ :46⅗ 1:12⅗ Md Sp Wt 3 4 21 2½ 22 11 Cruguet J b 118 6.80 78-22 Bear Hunt 1181 Romanoletti 11810 Treanor 113½ Lugged in, driv 12
18Sep83- 4Bel fst 6f :23 :46⅗ 1:11⅗ Md Sp Wt 9 9 75½ 33 35 38 Cruguet J b 118 8.00 76-20 Basket Weave 118hd Chimes Keeper 1188 BearHunt1185 Off Slow 10
LATEST WORKOUTS Apr 3 Bel tr.t 6f fst 1:15⅕ b — Mar 28 Bel tr.t 4f fst :48⅘ b — Mar 24 Bel tr.t 4f fst :49⅘ b — Mar 16 Bel tr.t 5f fst 1:02 h

Lt. Flag * — B. c. 3, by Delta Flag—Stevens Stream, by Lt Stevens
Own.—Cedar Copse Stables — Br.—Shropshire Mrs J S (Ky) — Tr.—Amos L Douglas — 123
Lifetime 15 9 1 2 $139,577 — 1984 4 3 1 0 $105,620 — 1983 11 6 0 2 $33,957
12Feb84- 8Aqu fst 1 1/16 ⊡:47⅗ 1:12⅘ 1:46⅗ Whirlaway 4 4 44 32 2½ 1nk Velasquez J 123 *1.00 79-24 Lt Flag 123nk Wind Flyer 121½ Crude Ways 1218¾ Driving 6
28Jan84- 8Aqu fst 170 ⊡:48⅕ 1:12⅘ 1:42⅗ Count Fleet 6 2 21½ 2hd 11 12½ Velasquez J 117 6.10 88-20 Lt Flag 1172½ Empravatar 117¾ Crude Ways 1192 Bore in, clear 9
14Jan84- 6Aqu fst 170 ⊡:49⅕ 1:14⅕ 1:42⅗ Handicap 3 1 1hd 2hd 21½ 22¾ Davis R G 112 3.10 85-17 ColdAndCloudy1122¾Lt.Flg11210NorthernFortress1141½ Game try 7
7Jan84- 5Aqu fst 1 1/16 ⊡:49 1:15 1:48 Alw 22000 1 1 11½ 1½ 12 16 McHargue D G 117 6.60 72-24 Lt Flag 1176Vanlandingham1177½Cooper'sHawk1172½ Ridden out 7
5Dec83- 1Grd sly 6½f :24 :48 1:20⅗ Clm 37500 5 6 44 21½ 1½ 12½ Hosang G 114 2.80 83-29 Lt Flag 1142½ Group Of Seven 1112¼ Long Song11611 Drew clear 6
15Nov83- 1Grd my 7f :22⅗ :47⅕ 1:27⅘ Clm c-20000 3 3 22½ 21½ 11 13 Attard L 122 *1.75 78-31 Lt. Flag 1223 Nova Bluff 1112½ Michael John 1142 Handily 5
4Nov83- 1Grd my 7f :23⅗ :47⅗ 1:27⅘ Clm c-16000 3 2 31½ 32 22 12 Swatuk B 122 2.55 76-28 Lt Flag 1222 Battle Dust 1176 Winfired 114¾ Handily 8
21Oct83- 7WO fst 6½f :23⅕ :47⅗ 1:20⅗ Clm 20000 10 1 41¾ 33½ 25 35½ Attard L 122 *1.50e 65-32 Bald Admiral 1222½ Michael John 1142¾ Lt. Flag 1222½ 10
9Oct83- 1WO gd 6½f :23 :46⅘ 1:19⅘ Clm 15000 6 4 2hd 1½ 13 14½ Attard L 120 3.40e 74-23 Lt. Flag 1204½ Winfired 116¾ Praise The Prince 1142½ Handily 8
30Sep83- 6WO fst 6f :22⅘ :47 1:14 Clm 12500 4 4 1½ 2hd 1hd 11½ Attard L 119 *1.35 73-26 Lt Flag 1191½ Winfired 112¾ Prehysterical Guy 1141½ 10
LATEST WORKOUTS ●Apr 1 Bel tr.t 6f fst 1:13 h — Mar 26 Bel tr.t 5f fst 1:00⅘ h — Mar 20 Bel tr.t 6f fst 1:13 h — Mar 12 Bel tr.t 6f fst 1:14⅕ h

Devil's Bag — B. c. 3, by Halo—Ballade, by Herbager
Own.—Hickory Tree Stable — Br.—Taylor E P (Md) — Tr.—Stephens Woodford C — 126
Lifetime 7 6 0 0 $394,185 — 1984 2 1 0 0 $39,165 — 1983 5 5 0 0 $355,020
3Mar84- 11Hia fst 1⅛ :46⅗ 1:09⅗ 1:47 Flamingo 7 1 1hd 1hd 33½ 47¼ Maple E 122 *.30 90-13 Time for aChange122nkDr.Carter1226Rexson'sHope1221 Gave way 8
20Feb84- 10Hia fst 7f :23 :45⅗ 1:21⅗ Flam'go Prep 2 3 22½ 2½ 11½ 17 Maple E 122 *.05 95-16 Devil's Bag 1227 Friendly Bob 1191½ Tumbler 11511 Ridden out 4
29Oct83- 8Lrl fst 1 1/16 :46⅗ 1:11⅗ 1:42⅕ Lrl Fut'y 3 1 1hd 15 14 15½ Maple E 122 *.05 97-09 Devil's Bag 1225½ Hail Bold King 1225½ Pied A' Tierre 1228 Easily 5
15Oct83- 6Bel fst 1 :46⅕ 1:09⅘ 1:34⅕ Champagne 3 1 11½ 13 15 16 Maple E 122 *.30 94-14 Devil's Bag 1226 Dr Carter 1223¾ Our Casey's Boy 1224½ Handily 12
28Sep83- 8Bel fst 7f :22⅗ :45⅕ 1:21⅖ Cowdin 5 3 11½ 12 15 13 Maple E 115 *.50 95-19 Devil's Bag 1153 Dr Carter 1153 Exit Five B. 1153 Ridden out 9
28Aug83- 7Bel sly 6f :22 :45⅗ 1:10⅗ Alw 22000 4 3 11½ 14½ 14½ 15½ Cruguet J 122 *.50 89-16 Devil's Bag 1225½ Exit Five B. 1195 Spender 1172½ Handily 6
20Aug83- 6Sar fst 6f :22⅕ :45⅗ 1:10⅗ Md Sp Wt 6 1 12 11½ 14 17½ Maple E 118 *1.10 87-16 Devil's Bag 1187½ Chimes Keeper 1187½ FrenchFlame118nk Easily 9
LATEST WORKOUTS ●Apr 2 Aqu ⊡ 1 fst 1:38 h — ●Mar 23 Hia 6f fst 1:09⅖ h — Mar 19 Hia 1 fst 1:38⅗ b — ●Mar 15 Hia 6f fst 1:12⅖ h

On The Sauce — Ch. c. 3, by Mito or Sauce Boat—Shantung Silk, by Disciplinarian
Own.—Kimmel C P — Br.—Lussky W (Ky) — Tr.—Toner James J — 114
Lifetime 4 3 0 0 $37,800 — 1984 1 1 0 0 $12,600 — 1983 3 2 0 0 $25,200
22Mar84- 7Aqu fst 6f ⊡:22⅘ :46⅕ 1:11⅗ Alw 21000 3 3 55½ 41¾ 2½ 11½ Cordero A 117 *1.70 86-24 On The Sauce 1171½ It's Frigid 1173¾ Fighting Native117½ Driving 7
27Dec83- 8Bow fst 7f :22⅗ :44⅗ 1:21 Bow Juvenile 7 5 76½ 77 710 77 Davis R G 122 1.50 93-08 Vinny's Pride 1162 Engadine 116hd Rambler Red 1161¾ Trailed 7
10Dec83- 5Aqu fst 6f ⊡:22⅘ :46⅕ 1:11 Alw 22000 7 3 73½ 53 11½ 16 Davis R G 117 3.40 89-17 On The Sauce 1176 Tumbler 117¾RovingMinstrel1171½ Ridden out 7
19Oct83- 6Aqu sly 6f :23 :47⅗ 1:12⅗ Md Sp Wt 10 3 3½ 1hd 1½ 11 Davis R G 118 5.80 78-20 On The Sauce 1181 The Skeptic 113no Par Five 1182½ Driving 13
LATEST WORKOUTS Apr 2 Aqu ⊡ 7f fst 1:29 h — Mar 19 Aqu ⊡ 4f fst :48⅗ b — ●Mar 13 Aqu ⊡ 6f fst 1:14 h — Mar 7 Aqu ⊡ 5f fst 1:00⅗ h

Secret Prince — Dk. b. or br. c. 3, by Cornish Prince—Secret Lanvin, by Lanvin
Own.—Brodsky Elaine M — Br.—Mereworth Farm (Ky) — Tr.—Terrill William V — 126
Lifetime 8 4 2 0 $200,300 — 1984 2 2 0 0 $107,580 — 1983 6 2 2 0 $92,720
17Mar84- 8Aqu fst 6f ⊡:22⅘ :46⅘ 1:11⅕ Bay Shore 6 6 72½ 52½ 1hd 12½ Perret C 114 *1.30 88-22 SecrtPrinc1142½ThWddingGust1262½I'mARoundr114¾ Wide, easily 9
1Mar84- 7Hia fst 7f :22⅘ :45⅗ 1:22⅗ Alw 20000 1 6 35½ 22½ 1½ 12½ Perret C 115 1.90 90-20 Secret Prince 1152½ Vision 1153½ Counterfeit Money 1211 Driving 7
18Dec83- 8Hol fst 1 1/16 :45⅘ 1:10⅕ 1:41⅗ Hol Fut'y 7 7 66½ 63¾ 67½ 711¼ Vasquez J 121 32.70 76-14 Fali Time 121¾BoldT.Jay1213½Life'sMagic1183 Stumbled, checked 12
7Dec83- 8Hol fst 7f :21⅗ :44 1:22⅕ Hol Prevue 6 14 85½ 85½ 78¾ 85¾ Vasquez J 119 *1.40 80-18 So Vague115¾CountryManor115noFrenchLegionaire115hd Dull try 16
12Nov83- 8Aqu gd 1⅛ :47⅗ 1:12 1:49 Remsen 3 2 21½ 2½ 2½ 25¼ Vasquez J 117 *1.00 84-20 Dr Carter 1135¼ Secret Prince 117nkHailBoldKing1137 Held place 8
29Oct83- 6Aqu fst 1 :48 1:13⅗ 1:38⅕ Excl. Native 1 2 1hd 11 14 14¾ Vasquez J 115 2.00 75-28 SecretPrince1154¾HomecomingGme1154Spender1177 Ridden out 8
14Oct83- 4Bel gd 1 1/16 :47⅗ 1:12⅗ 1:43⅗ Md Sp Wt 5 4 2½ 13 15 12¼ Vasquez J 118 *.50 83-23 SecretPrince1182½DancingCrown1184½Rj'sAccord1181 Ridden out 7
26Sep83- 4Bel fst 1 :46 1:11 1:36⅘ Md Sp Wt 6 6 32½ 3nk 21 22¾ Vasquez J 118 5.00 78-18 Legatee 1182¾ Secret Prince 1185 MightyJoe118no Bid, weakened 12
LATEST WORKOUTS Apr 2 Aqu ⊡ 6f fst 1:12⅕ h — Mar 24 Aqu ⊡ 1 fst 1:41⅗ h — ●Mar 10 Hia 6f fst 1:12 h — Feb 25 Hia 5f fst 1:00⅘ b

Restless Meteor — B. c. 3, by Tom Rolfe—Northern Meteor, by Northern Dancer
Own.—Buckland Farm — Br.—Evans T M (Va) — Tr.—Campo John P — 114
Lifetime 4 1 1 0 $17,170 — 1984 3 1 1 0 $16,620 — 1983 1 M 0 0 $550
17Mar84- 10Tam fst 1 1/16 :46⅘ 1:11⅘ 1:44⅗ Bud Tam Dby 12 4 44½ 1315 1331 1328½ Borden D A 116 3.80 68-19 BoldSoutherner116noRexson'sHope1221½Sticklr1201½ Sp'd for 1/2 13
4Mar84- 4Aqu fst 1 1/16 ⊡:49 1:14⅘ 1:47⅗ Md Sp Wt 8 1 11½ 11½ 18 115½ Velasquez J 122 *1.90 74-21 Restless Meteor 12215½ Joey TheK.1151½AProperToff1221½ Easily 10
24Feb84- 4Aqu sly 1⅛ ⊡:48⅗ 1:13⅗ 1:52⅘ Md Sp Wt 4 1 2hd 1hd 2½ 21½ Cordero A Jr 122 *2.00 79-16 Inner Force 1221½ Restless Meteor 1222¾ Joey TheK.1225 Gamely 6
19Apr83- 3Kee fst 4½f :23⅗ :47⅗ :53⅗ Md Sp Wt 1 5 67½ 65½ 45 Espinoza J C 117 4.80 83-12 T. H. Bend 117hd Billco 1171 Loyann 1174 Checked sharply 9
LATEST WORKOUTS ●Apr 1 Bel tr.t 1 fst 1:40⅘ h — ●Mar 28 Bel tr.t 4f fst :46⅕ hg — Mar 24 Bel tr.t 6f fst 1:12⅘ h — ●Mar 15 Tam 4f fst :47 b

LT. FLAG

Winter racing in New York creates a phenomenon that many fail to fully understand. Out-of-town outfits ship their cheaper stock to New York to replace the classier outfits that go elsewhere for the colder months. When this happens, somewhat of a vacuum is created at the top, and numerous horses move up in class to fill the void. For the winter season only, though. Horses that run well in winter stakes cannot be accepted as bona fide (New York) stakes animals when the "real" horses return. Nor can most $25,000 claimers continue to compete at that level. To properly evaluate these winter horses, one need only inquire, in many cases, from whence they came. Lt. Flag is a typical example. A cheap claiming animal in Canada as a juvenile, he immediately became competitive in allowance and stakes company in New York during the winter months. Yet, despite an eight-week hiatus, he was being supported in the Gotham at the same odds as Bear Hunt, to whom he was conceding nine pounds. At the prevailing weights, he was unlikely to try to outrun Bear Hunt for the early lead in a bold attempt to secure an advantageous position on the rail. Nor would he race lapped outside his rival, out in the two-path, taking the worst from the bias. More likely, he would tuck in behind Bear Hunt, thereby conceding him an uncontested early lead.

ON THE SAUCE

This is a promising young horse, as yet untested around two turns, whose bloodlines stamp him a sprinter and whose speed figures place him several lengths behind Secret Prince and Bear Hunt.

SECRET PRINCE

There were numerous negative signs to be found in Secret Prince's past performances. The obvious one was the weight. Secret Prince had never carried anything approaching 126 pounds before—much less over a distance of ground. He won the Bay Shore while in receipt of twelve pounds from The Wedding Guest. Also, Secret Prince's bloodlines did not suggest that distance racing would be his forte. Although he had raced well at the middle distances as a juvenile, many precocious youngsters "go farther" at two than at any other time in their career. Serious students of bloodlines had to wonder whether this might become the case with Secret Prince. There was also the biased surface to consider. Unless his rider was aware of the situation, and got to the rail quickly, Secret Prince faced the possibility of being outside all the way over a track favoring inside speed. Further complicating that issue was the fact that jockeys riding "clearly the best horse" often take the overland route to keep the horse out of possible traffic jams that may develop inside—especially if the horse is carrying excess poundage. It is difficult to get a horse, especially one carrying high weight, back into gear after it has been forced to check. Secret Prince's rider was the final problem. Craig Perret, who had ridden Secret Prince in his first two starts of the year, was in Florida riding a moderate stakes horse in a relatively meaningless stakes. If Perret considered Secret Prince a serious contender for the upcoming classics, why didn't he stay in New York with the horse?

RESTLESS METEOR

A typical ambitiously placed horse from the Campo barn, Restless Meteor might contest the early pace from his outside post, but he was unlikely ever to see the rail. His figure for that impressive fifteen-length victory on March 4 was subpar.

When Secret Prince went to the post at 9–10 odds—much higher than expected—it seemed that many in the crowd had picked up on these negative signs. We may have been right, but we'll never know for certain. Bear Hunt used his inside post to advantage, quickly opening a clear lead, then widening through the stretch. Secret Prince, out in the three-path all the way, was out of contention before reaching the final turn. Later it was discovered that he suffered a minor injury during the Gotham, yet he was rushed back a few weeks later for the Derby Trial, in which he finished a distant third to Devil's Bag. After a dismal performance in the Derby itself, Secret Prince disappeared from the racing scene until the following spring. Lt. Flag, who raced second on the rail all the way, never recaptured his "winter form." He failed to win in the year following the Gotham.

EIGHTH RACE
Aqueduct
APRIL 7, 1984

1 MILE 70 YARDS.(INNER DIRT). (1.40) 32nd Running THE GOTHAM (Grade II). $150,000 Added. (Plus $50,000 Breeders' Cup Premium Awards). 3–year–olds. Weight, 126 lbs. By subscription of $300 each which should accompany the nomination; $4,000 to pass the entry box, with $150,000 added. The added money and all fees to be divided 60% to the winner, 22% to second, 12% to third and 6% to fourth. Non–winners of a race of $50,000 allowed 3 lbs. Of a race of $25,000, 5 lbs. Of two races of $15,000 in 1983–84, 8 lbs. Of such a race in 1983–84, 12 lbs. Starters to be named at the closing time of entries. Trophies will be presented to the winning owner, trainer and jockey. Nominations close Wednesday, March 14, 1984. Closed with 28 nominations. Breeders' Cup Fund Award to Bear Hunt.

Total purse $212,400. Value of race $209,400, value to winner $136,440, second $40,128, third $21,888, fourth $10,944. Nominator Award $3,000. Mutuel pool $283,523, OTB pool $221,170.

Last Raced	Horse	Eqt.	A.Wt	PP	St	¼	½	¾	Str	Fin	Jockey	Odds $1
18Mar84 3Aqu1	Bear Hunt	b	3 114	1	1	1^{2}	1^{2}	$1^{1\frac{1}{2}}$	1^{4}	$1^{4\frac{3}{4}}$	MacBeth D	4.20
12Feb84 8Aqu1	Lt. Flag		3 123	2	2	2^{1}	2^{1}	2^{3}	$2^{\frac{1}{2}}$	2^{2}	Samyn J L	4.20
22Mar84 7Aqu1	On The Sauce		3 114	3	5	$4^{1\frac{1}{2}}$	4^{4}	3^{5}	3^{16}	3^{18}	Cordero A Jr	4.30
17Mar84 8Aqu1	Secret Prince		3 126	4	4	3^{1}	$3^{\frac{1}{2}}$	4^{4}	$4^{\frac{1}{2}}$	4^{nk}	Bailey J D	.70
17Mar84 10Tam13	Restless Meteor	b	3 114	5	3	5	5	5	5	5	Miranda J	18.10

OFF AT 4:47. Start good for all but ON THE SAUCE. Won driving. Time, :23⅘, :47, 1:11⅖, 1:36⅖, 1:40⅖ Track fast.

$2 Mutuel Prices:				
	1–(A)–BEAR HUNT	10.40	5.00	9.40
	2–(B)–LT. FLAG		4.20	7.60
	3–(D)–ON THE SAUCE			6.80

B. c, by Naskra—Ashwood Bow, by Gun Bow. Trainer Laurin Roger. Bred by Little W P (Ky).

BEAR HUNT quickly sprinted clear, saved ground while making the pace to the stretch and drew away while under brisk urging until the final 40 yards. LT. FLAG prompted the pace in the stretch but was not match for the winner while lugging in slightly. ON THE SAUCE broke in the air moved up along the inside approaching the end of the backstretch, continued to save ground into the stretch but lacked a further response. SECRET PRINCE, outside horses while racing within easy striking distance until near the end of the backstretch, had nothing left. RESTLESS METEOR wide into the first turn, wasn't able to keep pace.

Chapter 34

There But for a Track Bias Went a Triple Crown

SERIOUS HANDICAPPERS HAVE BEEN aware of track biases for years and fully understand the implications of the condition. But many regular players still remain perplexed by the apparent ups and downs in a horse's form cycle that are so easily explained by good and bad trips—not to mention the casual player or fan, whose knowledge of the game is purely superficial.

Many in this third category probably still wonder how a top-class Thoroughbred like Swale could run so powerfully in the Kentucky Derby, then so dismally in the Preakness, and then so brilliantly again in the Belmont Stakes. They probably accept what they read in their local newspaper—that Swale ran his best only every other race. Nothing could be further from the truth. The real reason was perfectly evident to trip handicappers aware of track biases and race conditions that favor one horse over another on a given afternoon.

Let's take a closer look at Swale and his rivals during the 1984 Triple Crown series. During the months preceding the Kentucky Derby, the consensus was that there were four outstanding three-year-olds preparing for the classics, and that all four were campaigning in Florida. Speed figures confirmed that Devil's Bag, Dr. Carter, Time For A Change, and Swale were indeed an exceptional group, well above average. Unfortunately, illness and "injury" left only Swale to contest the Derby. Despite rumors in the New York press that the colt was suffering from tuberculosis, Swale confirmed early-season form with an authoritative victory in the only truly run race of the series. After the Derby, track biases and trips clouded the issue, giving trip handicappers the kind of situation only they can fully understand and exploit.

Pimlico, site of the Preakness, has long had a reputation for its "golden rail." Some claim that bias was never stronger than on Preakness Day 1984. The prime victims that day, Swale and Pine Circle, would end up running first and second in the Belmont three weeks later. Each raced three or four wide the entire trip in the Preakness. The two horses who exploited the Pimlico bias, Gate Dancer and Play On, failed to reproduce that form three weeks later as the second and third choices of the large New York audience.

Before taking a closer look at the Belmont field, consider the following facts about that classic event:

(1) No horse has won the Belmont off a layoff longer than the normal three-week interval between the Preakness and the Belmont in at least 25 years.
(2) The last horse to win the Belmont directly from the allowance ranks, in his stakes debut, was Stage Door Johnny in 1968. Most Belmont winners were already major stakes winners, or at very least had been competitive in Grade I stakes.
(3) Of the last nineteen Belmont winners, only five weren't "right there" in contention at the head of the stretch. Only six were regarded, prior to the Belmont, as confirmed slow-starting stretch-runners, the type whose late rush at shorter distances gives the impression that they would love the Belmont distance.

Apparently it is wise to look only at those horses with good recent stakes form and the ability to stay fairly close early if one wishes to be successful at betting the Belmont Stakes, and possibly other major stakes events at classic distances as well.

And now for the 1984 Belmont field:

PLAY ON

Overcoming an outside post, Play On had a perfect rail trip in the Preakness and raced well despite a bout of prerace jitters. Immediately after watching the Preakness, I tabbed Play On as my Belmont horse. He was a fast-developing young horse whose two recent races represented significant achievement. He was in the capable hands of Billy Turner, one of the country's outstanding young horsemen. He seemed the ideal bet—until I learned of the situation at Pimlico on the day of the Preakness and realized the conditions he would face in the Belmont.

8 BELMONT

1½ MILES. (2.24) 116th Running THE BELMONT (Grade I). $350,000 added. 3-year-olds. By subscription of $200 each to accompany the nomination; $2,500 to pass the entry box; $5,000 to start. A supplementary nomination of $7,500 may be made on Wednesday, June 6 with an additional $25,000 to start, with $350,000 added, of which 60% to the winner, 22% to second, 12% to third and 6% to fourth. Colts and Geldings, 126 lbs. Fillies, 121 lbs. Starters to be named at the closing time of entries. The winning owner will be presented with the August Belmont Memorial Cup to be retained for one year, as well as a trophy for permanent possession and trophies will be presented to the winning trainer and jockey. Closed Wednesday, February 15, 1984 with 296 nominations. Supplementary nominee: Morning Bob.

Play On
Dk. b. or br. c. 3, by Stop the Music—Little Tobago, by Impressive
Br.—Hillbrook Farm (Ky)
Tr.—Turner William H Jr
Own.—Welcome Farm
126 — Lifetime 5 2 3 0 $136,790 — 1984 4 1 3 0 $124,790 — 1983 1 1 0 0 $12,000

19May84- 8Pim fst 1⅜ :45⅘ 1:09⅕ 1:53⅗ Preakness 10 5 55 63¼ 33 21½ Samyn J L 126 8.10 100-07 Gate Dancer 1261½ Play On 1263¼ Fight Over 126¾ Best of others 10
9May84- 8Bel fst 1 :46⅘ 1:12 1:36⅘ Withers 3 4 41¾ 62¾ 2hd 11 Samyn J L 126 10.90 83-21 Play On 1261 Morning Bob 1262¼ Back Bay Barrister1261 Driving 10
18Feb84- 4Hia fst 6f :22 :44⅘ 1:09⅗ Alw 14000 9 2 41½ 1hd 1hd 2¾ Bailey J D 115 *1.00 94-11 Tonto 115¾ Play On 1153 Rupert's Wing 1152¼ Came out 11
4Feb84- 9Hia fst 7f :22⅘ :45⅗ 1:23 Alw 14000 10 2 21 3nk 1hd 2nk Bailey J D 115 2.70 88-12 Darn That Alarm 121nk Play On 115¾ Outfitter 1217 Just missed 11
8Nov83- 4Aqu fst 6f :22⅘ :46⅕ 1:12⅕ Md Sp Wt 12 8 31½ 1hd 2hd 1nk Bailey J D 118 *1.30 80-26 Play On 118nk Circle Round 1184¾ Bligh 118¾ Raced evenly, drg 14
LATEST WORKOUTS Jun 6 Bel 5f fst 1:01⅗ b ●Jun 1 Bel 7f gd 1:26⅗ b May 16 Bel 5f fst 1:01⅕ b May 8 Bel 3f fst :36 b

Coax Me Chad
B. c. 3, by L'Enjoleur—Platterland, by First Landing
Br.—Brooks L Sr (Ky)
Tr.—Warren Ronnie G
Own.—Miller E E
126 — Lifetime 16 2 2 2 $255,666 — 1984 4 0 1 0 $100,000 — 1983 12 2 1 2 $155,666

5May84- 8CD fst 1¼ :47⅗ 1:36⅘ 2:02⅖ Ky Derby 19 17 1716 76 25 23¼ McCauley W H 126 9.90f 82-19 Swale 1263¼ CoaxMeChad1262AtTheThreshold126nk Finished well 20
1Apr84- 9Lat fst 1⅛ :46 1:10⅕ 1:42⅘ Jim Beam 8 10 99 66½ 66½ 63¼ McCauley W H 121 57.10 92-18 AtThThrshold1211BoldSouthrnr1211ThWddngGust121¾ No factor 12
11Feb84- 10Hia fst 1⅛ :46⅘ 1:10 1:47 Everglades 1 11 1121 1123 1020 1020¾ St Leon G 119 84.50 76-09 Time for a Change 112½ Bello 1175 Rexson's Hope 1194 Outrun 11
7Jan84- 9Crc fst 1⅛ :47⅗ 1:12⅘ 1:46 Trp Pk Dby 8 13 1111 1117¼ 911 810 DePass R 121 20.40 79-14 Morning Bob 1211¼ ☐Rexson's Hope 1212DonRickles121¼ Outrun 15
24Dec83- 7Crc fst 170 :48⅘ 1:14 1:44⅗ What A Plesr 4 8 88¼ 710 67¼ 35¼ DePass R 120 *1.30 82-16 Papa Koo 1151½ CounterfeitMoney1134CoaxMeChad120hd Rallied 9
24Dec83-Run in two divisions 7th & 9th races
13Dec83- 7Crc fst 7f :22⅘ :46⅗ 1:26 Alw 12000 2 6 68¾ 64¼ 41¾ 2½ DePass R 116 4.00 85-22 D. White 114½ Coax Me Chad 1162 Jim Bracken 1144¼ Gamely 6
19Nov83- 8CD fst 1⅛ :48⅘ 1:12⅘ 1:46⅕ Ky Joc Club 4 7 712 611 45½ 48¼ Espinoza J C 122 7.90 69-22 BiloxiIndian1193CountryManor119nkTaylor'sSpecial1195 Bore out 7
5Nov83- 8Med fst 1⅛ :46⅕ 1:11⅗ 1:45⅕ Yng America 9 12 813 712 412 59¼ Moyers L 122 22.90 73-20 Swale 122no Disastrous Night 1193 Dr. Carter 1196 No menace 16
8Oct83- 7Kee fst 1⅛ :47⅕ 1:11⅗ 1:44 Brds Ful'y 6 7 65¾ 65¾ 53¾ 43 Espinoza J C 121 3.80e 83-14 Swale 121hd Spender 1212½ Back Bay Barrister 121½ Wide 8
4Sep83- 10RD fst 1⅛ :47⅗ 1:12⅕ 1:46⅗ Cradle 9 8 611 44½ 1hd 13½ Espinoza J C 120 2.50 76-22 Coax Me Chad1203½TallGrassWalker1201TahDah11711 Ridden out 12
27Aug83- 8AP sly 7f :22⅘ :46 1:27 Arl Wash Fty 11 17 1714 1516 65¾ 42½ Espinoza J C 122 5.40f 64-36 AllFiredUp1221½HolmeOnTop122noSmrtNSlick1221 Circled horses 17
14Aug83- 8AP fst 6f :22 :45⅗ 1:12⅕ Arch Ward 4 11 117¾ 99½ 88½ 52½ Cuffari S J 114 53.60 79-26 Bello 1141½ Biloxi Indian 114nk DHDelta Trace 124 Wide 11
30Jly83- 6CD fst 6f :22⅘ :46 1:11⅘ Alw 9340 3 5 67 66½ 44 37 Cuffari S J7 b 110 4.40 80-15 Textile 1175 Trans E. T. 1172 Coax Me Chad 110hd Mild rally 6
8Jly83- 8CD fst 5½f :22⅘ :46 1:05 Bashfd Manor 13 11 129 1313 119 89½ Cuffari S J b 115 11.30e 86-20 Betwixtn'Between1153RelShrpDncr121½BiloxiIndin118¾ No factor 13
28Jun83- 7CD gd 5½f :22⅘ :46 1:05⅘ Alw 12000 1 5 79 612 56 44 Cuffari S J5 b 110 19.10 89-20 Biloxi Indian 1173 Betwixtn'Between115½TrickyNick117½ Mild bid 8
1Jun83- 3CD fst 5f :23 :46⅘ 1:00 Md Sp Wt 5 5 64½ 66 43 12½ Cuffari S J7 b 108 3.60 89-15 Coax MeChad1082½OurMichaelSmith1181½StreetKing1184 Driving 6
LATEST WORKOUTS May 30 CD 7f fst 1:27 h ●May 23 CD 6f gd 1:14 h Apr 25 CD 7f fst 1:29⅘ b Apr 15 CD 6f fst 1:14⅗ b

Silent King *
Ch. c. 3, by Screen King—Red Damask, by Jet Action
Br.—Gaines & Johnson & Sturgill (Ky)
Tr.—Delp Grover G
Own.—Hawksworth Farm
126 — Lifetime 8 4 2 1 $121,230 — 1984 5 1 2 1 $106,110 — 1983 3 3 0 0 $15,120

5May84- 8CD fst 1¼ :47⅗ 1:36⅘ 2:02⅖ Ky Derby 11 20 2024 1915 1113 99 Shoemaker W 126 4.80 76-19 Swale 1263¼ Coax Me Chad 1262 AtTheThreshold126nk Very wide 20
26Apr84- 7Kee fst 1⅛ :47⅗ 1:12⅖ 1:52⅕ Blue Grass 2 9 921 814 35½ 23¼ Shoemaker W 121 2.80 73-31 Tylor'sSpecil1213¼SilentKing1212½ChrmedRook1215 Circled field 9
25Mar84- 11FG fst 1⅛ :46⅗ 1:10⅘ 1:49⅗ La Derby 2 7 719 715 45¾ 21 Solis A b 120 2.60 95-18 Taylor's Special 1181 Silent King 1201 Fight Over 1232½ Late bid 7
10Mar84- 10FG fst 1⅛ :47 1:11 1:43 Handicap 2 5 518 519 39 35 Mueller C 118 1.90 92-16 Taylor's Special 1213½ Fight Over 1161½ Silent King1182 Mild bid 5
18Feb84- 10FG fst 1⅛ :46⅕ 1:38⅘ 1:45⅕ Lecomte H 1 8 824 817 33¾ 11 Mueller C 115 1.20e 86-21 Silent King 1151 Taylor's Special 1225FairlyStraight1111½ Driving 8
14Dec83- 9FG fst 140 :47⅗ 1:14 1:41⅗ Alw 10200 2 6 611 55½ 11 15 Franklin R J 119 *.40 85-23 Silent King 1195 Dewan For Us 119¾HomeByTwelve11511 Handily 8
7Dec83- 10FG fst 140 :46⅗ 1:13⅘ 1:41⅗ Alw 10200 5 9 812 43 11 15½ Franklin R J 115 *.90 85-19 Silent King1155½HomeByTwelve1152MississippiMan116hd Driving 10
27Nov83- 2FG sly 1⅛ :48 1:15 1:48 Md 30000 10 12 710 54½ 12 19 Franklin R J 119 4.60 72-25 Silent King1199RebornofWater119nkOl'BlueEyes1198½ Ridden out 12
LATEST WORKOUTS Jun 7 Bel 4f fst :48 b May 31 AP 1 fst 1:39⅗ h ●May 24 AP 7f gd 1:26⅘ h ●May 19 AP 6f gd 1:13⅘ h

Gate Dancer *
B. c. 3, by Sovereign Dancer—Sun Gate, by Bull Lea
Br.—Davis W R (Fla)
Tr.—Van Berg Jack C
Own.—Opstein K
126 — Lifetime 11 4 4 2 $444,425 — 1984 7 2 2 2 $411,725 — 1983 4 2 2 0 $32,700

19May84- 8Pim fst 1⅜ :45⅘ 1:09⅕ 1:53⅗ Preakness 3 6 65½ 42 11 11½ Cordero A Jr 126 4.80 102-07 Gate Dancer 1261½ Play On 1263¼ Fight Over 126¾ Tried lug in,cl. 10
5May84- 8CD fst 1¼ :47⅗ 1:36⅘ 2:02⅖ Ky Derby 20 19 1817 97¼ 66¾ 45¼ Delahoussaye E b 126 18.90☐ 79-19 Swale1263¼CoxMeChd1262AtTheThreshold126nk Poor st., bore in 20
5May84-Disqualified and placed fifth
21Apr84- 9OP fst 1⅛ :46⅗ 1:10⅕ 1:46⅘ Arkansas Dby 6 10 74¾ 53¼ 26 37 Delahoussaye E b 118 *1.60 102-04 Althea 1217 Pine Circle 118no GateDancer118nc Forced out 1st tr 11
25Mar84- 8SA fst 1⅛ :46⅗ 1:10⅗ 1:42⅗ San Felipe H 2 6 67¾ 54¾ 41½ 2hd Delahoussaye E 117 4.40 88-17 FaliTime122hdGateDancer1173½Commemorate117½ Lugged in late 6
14Mar84- 8SA gd 1⅛ :47⅕ 1:11⅕ 1:43⅗ ☐S Catalina 5 9 97¼ 78¾ 34½ 33½ Delahoussaye E 120 4.00 79-26 Tights 1203 Prince True 117½ Gate Dancer 1201¾ Rallied 10
20Feb84- 4SA fst 1⅛ :46⅕ 1:11⅕ 1:43⅖ Alw 30000 6 5 511 45 1½ 11½ Delahoussaye E 115 *1.20 84-16 GateDancer1151½PrinceTrue1203HeavenlyPlain117¾ Lugged in str 7
5Feb84- 8BM fst 1⅛ :46⅕ 1:10⅗ 1:42⅖ El Camino 1 8 912 67½ 56 22 Cauthen S 120 4.10 85-17 FrenchLegionire1202GteDncer120½HevnlyPlin120no Lacked room 11
29Dec83- 8SA fst 6f :21⅘ :44⅕ 1:09 ☐Los Feliz 1 6 65½ 55½ 45 25 Delgadillo C b 120 10.90 88-24 Commemorate1205GteDncer120nkMightyAdversry1204 Lugged in 8
16Dec83- 6Hol fst 6f :22 :45 1:10 Alw 25000 5 3 41¾ 2½ 1hd 1¾ McCarron C J b 114 *1.00 87-22 GteDncer114¾LuckyBuccneer1143PrincBowr1142 Bore in, driving 6
16Jly83- 5Aks fst 5½f :22⅕ :45⅖ 1:06⅖ Alw 12000 2 5 41½ 31 2hd 2½ Jones K 117 *.70 77-25 Izapappa 110½ Gate Dancer 1173 Median Prince 1175 Failed 8
29Jun83- 4Aks my 5½f :23 :47⅖ 1:07⅕ Md Sp Wt 11 1 31½ 1½ 15 18 Jones K 118 6.60 74-27 Gate Dancer 1188 Wind Flyer 1182½ Dr. Log 118¾ Easily 12
LATEST WORKOUTS ●Jun 6 Bel 5f fst :58⅘ h May 31 Bel 1 sly 1:42⅗ b May 16 Pim 4f fst :47⅗ h ●May 2 CD 4f fst :48 h

*Minstrel Star
B. c. 3, by Averof—Gallant Bid, by Galivanter
Br.—Behrens W E (Eng)
Tr.—Lundy Sarah A
Own.—Ramsden Glenda B
126 — Lifetime 2 2 0 0 $19,200 — 1984 2 2 0 0 $19,200 — 1983 0 M 0 0

25May84- 7Bel fst 1 :46 1:11⅘ 1:37⅘ 3+ Alw 21000 7 4 42½ 4¾ 15 14 Bailey J D 110 11.40 77-23 Minstrel Star 1104 Le Gosse1163½CoastRange1161½ Bore in, clear 8
17Mar84- 5GP fst 7f :23⅖ :46⅗ 1:25⅕ Md Sp Wt 11 9 71½ 1hd 11 12 St Leon G 122 14.30 78-17 MinstrlStr1222IBlivInMgc122nkCommndrRbu1221 Sluggish, Clear 12
LATEST WORKOUTS Jun 3 Sar tr.t 1 fst 1:44⅖ b May 17 Del 6f fst 1:15⅕ b

Swale *
Dk. b. or br. c. 3, by Seattle Slew—Tuerta, by Forli
Br.—Claiborne Farm (Ky)
Tr.—Stephens Woodford C
Own.—Claiborne Farm
126 — Lifetime 13 8 2 2 $1,273,641 — 1984 6 3 1 1 $781,690 — 1983 7 5 1 1 $491,951

19May84- 8Pim fst 1⅜ :45⅘ 1:09⅕ 1:53⅗ Preakness 5 2 22½ 31½ 55½ 76¾ Pincay L Jr 126 *.80 95-07 Gate Dancer 1261½ Play On 1263¼ Fight Over 126¾ Bothered 10
5May84- 8CD fst 1¼ :47⅗ 1:36⅘ 2:02⅖ Ky Derby 15 3 31½ 12 15 13¼ Pincay L Jr 126 3.40 85-19 Swale 1263¼ Coax Me Chad 1262 At The Threshold126nk Drew off 20
17Apr84- 7Kee sly 1⅛ :47⅕ 1:11⅗ 1:45⅗ Lexington 2 2 32½ 25½ 25 28 Pincay L Jr 123 *.10 71-23 HeIsAGreatDel1118Swle1237½TimelyAdvocte1127½ Best of others 5
31Mar84- 10GP fst 1⅛ :46⅗ 1:10⅕ 1:47⅗ Florida Dby 7 2 2½ 2hd 1½ 1¾ Pincay L Jr 122 2.70 94-14 Swale 122¾ Dr. Carter 1227 Darn That Alarm 1221 Driving 9
17Mar84- 9GP fst 1⅛ :47⅗ 1:11⅕ 1:43 Ftn Of Youth 7 3 2½ 2hd 32 31½ Maple E 122 *.40 84-17 Darn ThatAlarm112½CounterfeitMoney1121Swale122nk Weakened 8
7Mar84- 9GP fst 7f :22⅘ :45⅗ 1:22⅕ Hutcheson 10 3 3nk 2hd 1hd 18 Maple E 122 *1.00 93-21 Swale 1228 For Halo 1141 Darn ThatAlarm1122½ Wide, ridden out 12
5Nov83- 8Med fst 1⅛ :46⅕ 1:11⅗ 1:45⅕ Yng America 7 5 47¾ 33 22 1no Maple E 122 2.30 83-20 Swale 122no Disastrous Night 1193 Dr. Carter 1196 Driving 16
8Oct83- 7Kee fst 1⅛ :47⅕ 1:11⅗ 1:44 Brds Ful'y 3 3 2hd 1hd 1hd 1hd Maple E 121 *1.10 86-14 Swale 121hd Spender 1212½ Back Bay Barrister121½ Wide, driving 8
10Sep83- 8Bel fst 7f :22⅘ :45⅗ 1:24 Futurity 4 2 1½ 1hd 2½ 1no Maple E 122 *1.60 82-15 Swale 122no Shuttle Jet 122¾ Hail Bold King 1225 Driving 5
21Aug83- 8Sar fst 6½f :21⅘ :45⅕ 1:17⅗ Hopeful 3 7 32 21½ 1hd 33½ Maple E 122 3.40 82-23 Capitol South 1222¾ Don Rickles 122½ Swale 122hd Weakened 13
1Aug83- 8Sar my 6f :22⅕ :46 1:12⅗ Sar Special 4 5 2hd 12 14 1¾ Maple E 117 2.60 77-24 Swale 117¾ Shuttle Jet 1173¾ Big Walt 117½ Driving 7
21Jly83- 4Bel fst 6f :22⅘ :45⅘ 1:11⅗ Md Sp Wt 7 2 12 16 14 11½ Maple E 118 *.60 85-20 Swale 1181½ Capitol South 1181½ Legatee 1187¾ Driving 7
7Jly83- 4Bel fst 5f :22⅘ :45⅘ :58 Md Sp Wt 2 3 1½ 11½ 1½ 22½ Maple E 118 *.70 96-19 Shuttle Jet 1182½ Swale 1186 Rowdy Yates 1181 Lugged in 8
LATEST WORKOUTS Jun 7 Bel 4f fst :48⅗ b Jun 2 Bel 7f sly 1:28⅕ b May 28 Bel 5f fst 1:01 b ●May 17 Pim 4f fst :46 h

Romantic Tradition
B. c. 3, by Sham—Romanticize, by Francis S
Br.—Harbor View Farm (Ky)
Tr.—Martin Frank
Own.—Harbor View Farm
126 — Lifetime 9 2 0 5 $42,986 — 1984 9 2 0 5 $42,986 — 1983 0 M 0 0

27May84- 8Bel fst 1⅛ :46 1:10⅘ 1:50 Peter Pan 6 6 73½ 31 2hd 33½ Bailey J D 114 11.40 74-20 BckByBrrstr1173GlintHour114nkRomnticTrdition114nk Weakened 9
9May84- 7Bel fst 1¼ :49⅘ 1:40 2:04⅕ 3+ Alw 21000 3 5 41½ 1hd 11½ 13 Bailey J D 113 3.10 77-21 RomntcTrdton1133OnForEvryon1143½WstJckson110nk Drew clear 7
30Apr84- 7Aqu fst 1⅛ :47⅘ 1:12⅕ 1:52 Alw 21000 7 4 3½ 1½ 2½ 32¾ Bailey J D b 117 *1.60 72-23 CllMRbl117hdTwntytwoBhm1102¾RomnticTrdition1172 Led wknd 7
21Apr84- 5Aqu fst 1 :47⅘ 1:13⅘ 1:39⅘ Alw 21000 3 5 31 51¾ 41 33 Cruguet J b 117 *1.60 64-30 Exattic 1171¾ West Jackson 1101½RomanticTradition1171½ Evenly 8
7Apr84- 5Aqu fst 6f ☐:22⅘ :46⅗ 1:11⅘ Alw 20000 4 5 32 21 2hd 31 Cordero A Jr b 119 2.00 84-16 Coopr'sHwk1101RunningBold119hdRomnticTrdition1194¾ Bore in 7
17Mar84- 9GP fst 1⅛ :47⅗ 1:11⅕ 1:43 Ftn Of Youth 6 7 72¾ 74¾ 68½ 67¾ Londono O J b 114 81.80 78-17 Darn That Alarm112½CounterfeitMoney1121Swale122nk No factor 8
3Mar84- 8Hia fst 7f :22⅘ :45⅗ 1:24⅖ Md Sp Wt 7 5 51½ 2½ 2hd 11 Londono O J b 120 3.00 81-13 RomntcTrdton1201Inct1201½AndrsonSprng120½ Swerved, driving 12
21Feb84- 6Hia gd 7f :22⅘ :45⅗ 1:24 Md Sp Wt 3 11 97 75½ 43½ 3nk Vasquez J b 120 *1.60 83-12 HighlyRegarded120hdSpotterBy120nkRomnticTrdition120½ Rallied 12
13Feb84- 7Hia fst 6f :22⅕ :45⅕ 1:11 Md Sp Wt 12 2 55½ 47½ 59½ 48½ Vasquez J b 120 *2.00 79-18 Chief Steward 1203 Green Cedars 120½ Romanoletti 1205 Evenly 12
LATEST WORKOUTS Jun 4 Bel tr.t 6f fst 1:12⅘ h May 22 Bel tr.t 1 fst 1:41⅗ b ●May 16 Bel tr.t 5f fst :59⅘ h ●May 7 Bel tr.t 4f fst :46⅗ h

```
Morning Bob            Gr. c. 3, by Blushing Groom—Guillotine Miss, by The Axe II        Lifetime   1984 6 3 1 0   $254,342
                       Br.—Howell G B (Ky)                                          126   13 6 2 1  1983 7 3 1 1    $55,458
  Own.—Mike-Rich Stable  Tr.—Zito Nicholas P                                               $309,800
28May84- 9Key fst 1⅛  :47   1:11⅗ 1:49⅗  Pa Derby     4 7 714 79¼ 42½ 1hd  McCarron G 122 1.60  88-17 MorningBob122hdAtThThrshold122²½[DH]BiloxiIndin122 Up in time 7
 9May84- 8Bel fst 1   :46⅘ 1:12  1:36⅘  Withers      4 10 1012 74¾ 42½ 21  Maple E    126 3.30  82-21 Play On 126¹ Morning Bob 126²½ Back Bay Barrister 126¹ Wide 10
17Mar84-10Tam fst 1 1/16 :46⅘ 1:11⅗ 1:44⅘ Bud Tam Dby 13 12 1213 68¾ 58 53½ Rivera M A 122 *1.50 93-19 Bold Southerner 116noRexson'sHope122¹½Stickler120¹½ No factor 13
 7Mar84- 8Tam fst 1 1/16 :48⅗ 1:14⅕ 1:47  S F Davis   8 6 711 42½ 2hd 13½ Rivera M A 124 *.40  84-32 Morning Bob 124³½ Sagittarian115²FourthVerse120nk Ridden out 8
     7Mar84-Run in divisions
11Feb84-10Hia fst 1⅛  :46⅗ 1:10  1:47   Everglades   11 9 815 911 58½ 510¾ Maple E   119 1.70  86-09 Time for aChange112½Bello117⁵Rexson'sHope119⁴ Sluggish, wide 11
 7Jan84- 9Crc fst 1 1/16 :47⅘ 1:12⅘ 1:46  Trp Pk Dby  7 12 1211 129¼ 1hd 11½ Maple E   121 *1.00 89-14 MorningBob121¹½[D]Rexson'sHop121²DonRickls121½ Wide, driving 15
24Dec83- 9Crc fst 170 :47⅘ 1:13⅘ 1:43⅘ What A Plesr 6 7 76½ 1hd 12½ 12½ Rivera M A 115 *2.20 93-16 Morning Bob 115²½ D. White 115¾ Plentyofsense 115²½ Driving 9
     24Dec83-Run in two divisions 7th & 9th races
28Nov83- 7Aqu my  1⅛  :49   1:13⅘ 1:51⅘  Alw 24000    3 6 44 51¾ 12 15¾  Ycaza M    117 2.90  77-30 Morning Bob 117⁵¾ Exattic 117³ IsYourPleasure117⁵½ Ridden out 7
17Nov83- 5Aqu fst 7f  :23   :47   1:25⅘  Alw 22000    6 5 77 52½ 22 21½  Maple E    117 2.00  72-29 HomecomingGme117¹½MorningBob117⁵½CutThMusic117¾ Gamely 8
 7Nov83- 7Aqu fst 6f  :22⅘  :46⅗ 1:10⅘  Alw 22000    8 7 77½ 79 611 59¾  Lovato F Jr 117 12.40 78-22 Agile Jet 117⁷¾ Tumbler 122¾ A Hard Ten 117nk No factor 8
 8Sep83- 5Bel fst 6f  :22⅘  :46⅕ 1:10⅘  Alw 22000    1 5 54 44 56 510¾  Maple E    119 9.30  78-19 Exit Five B. 119⁷¾ Aggressive Bid 117¹½ Spender 117¾ Evenly 7
12Aug83- 4Sar sly 5½f :22⅘  :47   1:05⅘  Md Sp Wt     5 4 616 43 2½ 11½  Maple E    118 *2.10 88-23 Morning Bob 118¹½ Fast Track Pat 118⁹ Saggitarius118²¼ Driving 9
 4Aug83- 4Sar fst 5½f :22⅘  :46⅘ 1:05⅘  Md Sp Wt     6 7 811 88½ 66 35  Maple E    118 *3.50 84-16 Don Rickles 118²½HailBoldKing118²¾MorningBob118½ Steadied st 12
  LATEST WORKOUTS   Jun 5 Bel 5f fst 1:01⅗ b   May 25 Bel 5f fst 1:01⅘ b   May 21 Bel 6f sly 1:16 b   May 17 Bel 5f fst 1:03⅕ b

Exattic                B. c. 3, by Exceller—Pilferer, by No Robbery                     Lifetime   1984 3 2 0 1    $28,320
                       Br.—North Ridge Farm (Ky)                                    126   13 3 2 3  1983 10 1 2 2   $31,600
  Own.—Anchel E        9-18  Tr.—LaBeccetta Frank                                          $59,920  Turf 2 0 1 0    $4,840
12May84- 6Bel fst 1 1/16 :45⅘ 1:09⅘ 1:41⅘ Alw 22000 4 5 57½ 57 35 12  Davis R G b 122 8.80 13 95-17 Exattic 122² Go Go Regal 117¾ Charmed Rook 119nk Wide, clear 7
21Apr84- 5Aqu fst 1   :47⅘ 1:13⅘ 1:39⅘  Alw 21000    2 6 51½ 41½ 1hd 11¾ Davis R G b 117 2.80 4 67-30 Exttic117¹¾WstJckson110¹½RomnticTrdton117¹½ Off slowly, clear 8
 8Apr84- 6Aqu fst 1⅛ [•]:48⅘ 1:14⅘ 1:53⅕ Alw 21000    2 3 21 2½ 2hd 3¾  Venezia M   b 117 4.20 75-21 Gold Studs 117½ Golden Immigrant 117nk Exattic 117¹½ Willingly 5
18Dec83- 7Aqu fst 1 1/16 [•]:48⅘ 1:14 1:47⅘ Alw 22000 1 8 74 63½ 44½ 45½ Migliore R b 117 2.60 70-25 IsYourPlesur117¾Coopr'sHwk117³RovingMinstrl117¹½ No menace 9
28Nov83- 7Aqu my  1⅛  :49   1:13⅘ 1:51⅘  Alw 24000    7 4 54½ 41¾ 22 25¾ Velasquez J b 117 11.00 71-30 Morning Bob 117⁵¾ Exattic 117³ Is Your Pleasure117⁵½ Game try 7
31Oct83- 6Aqu fst 1⅛  :49⅕  1:14⅘ 1:54  Md Sp Wt     8 8 73¾ 54 1½ 14½  Fell J      b 118 *2.10 65-24 Exattic 118⁴½ Par Five 118² Loyal Knight 118⁴ Steadied, clear 10
14Oct83- 4Bel gd  1 1/16 :47⅘ 1:12⅘ 1:43⅘ Md Sp Wt   1 7 610 68 414 412 Velasquez J b 118 5.60 71-23 Secret Prince 118²½ DancingCrown118⁸½Raja'sAccord118¹ Outrun 7
21Sep83- 2Bel fm  1 1/16 [T]:48⅘ 1:12 1:43⅘ Md Sp Wt  6 4 32½ 2hd 22 24  Velasquez J b 118 *1.50 80-15 Don't Be Home Late 118⁴ Exattic 118⁵FireInTheNight118⁴½ Tired 8
12Sep83- 5Bel fst 7f  :23⅕  :47   1:24   Md Sp Wt     10 3 116½ 86¾ 58½ 312½ Velasquez J b 119 9.40 70-22 Dr. Carter 118³ Country Manor 118⁹½ Exattic 119hd Wide str. 13
27Aug83- 4Bel fm  1   (T):47⅘ 1:12⅘ 1:37⅘ Md Sp Wt    2 6 118 108½ 77½ 65½ Fell J    118 2.20 72-19 Golf Ace 118¹½ Dominated 118½ Bold Jove 118¹¾ Lacked room 12
15Aug83- 6Sar fst 7f  :22⅘  :45⅘ 1:24⅕  Md Sp Wt     11 5 117½ 812 67½ 34¾ Fell J     118 14.80 76-15 Hail Bold King 118²½ Gallant Hour 118²½ Exattic 118¾ Rallied 14
30Jly83- 4Sar fst 6f  :22⅘  :46⅘ 1:12   Md Sp Wt     4 6 53½ 65 64½ 42½ Davis R G   118 12.90 78-14 Deific 118¹ Winter Guise 118no Cindy's Friend 118¹½ Rallied 9
 7Jly83- 4Bel fst 5f  :22⅘  :45⅘ :58    Md Sp Wt     4 7 810 811 511 510 Fell J      118 39.10 89-19 Shuttle Jet 118²½ Swale 118⁶ Rowdy Yates 118¹ No factor 8
  LATEST WORKOUTS   Jun 7 Aqu 4f fst :50⅘ b   Jun 2 Aqu 1 sly 1:41 h   May 27 Aqu 1⅛m fst 1:52⅘ h   May 21 Aqu 6f sly 1:13⅘ h (d)

Back Bay Barrister     B. c. 3, by Big Spruce—Cherry Lady, by Bold Lad                  Lifetime   1984 3 2 0 1    $81,780
                       Br.—Bradyleigh Farms Inc (Ky)                                126   7 4 0 2   1983 4 2 0 1    $37,442
  Own.—Cohen Myra      Tr.—Blengs Vincent                                                  $119,222
27May84- 8Bel fst 1⅛  :46   1:10⅕ 1:50   Peter Pan    4 8 86 84½ 1hd 13  MacBeth D  117 *1.80 5 77-20 BckByBrrstr117³GlintHour114nkRomnticTrdton114nk Ridden out 9
 9May84- 8Bel fst 1   :46⅘ 1:12  1:36⅘  Withers      5 8 74½ 1½ 1hd 33½  MacBeth D  126 2.00  80-21 Play On 126¹ Morning Bob126²½BackBayBarrister126¹ Weakened 10
27Apr84- 7Aqu fst 1   :45⅘ 1:10  1:36⅕  Alw 22000    6 5 48 43½ 1hd 12½  MacBeth D  117 4.90  85-21 BackBayBarrister117²½Admirl'sFlg117¹¾Cooper'sHwk117² Driving 7
 8Oct83- 7Kee fst 1 1/16 :47⅕ 1:11⅘ 1:44 Brds Fut'y  7 6 76½ 53½ 43½ 32½ Petro N J5 116 12.70 83-14 Swale 121hd Spender 121²½ Back Bay Barrister 121½ Rallied 8
24Sep83-10Suf fst 6f  :22⅕  :45⅘ 1:10⅘  Cape Cod     3 2 32 1hd 11½ 14½  Petro N J  114 5.90  89-18 BckByBrrister114⁴½DonBrtB.117⁶FillRon'sPockts119² Ridden out 9
 7Sep83- 6Suf fst 6f  :22⅘  :46⅕ 1:11⅕  Md Sp Wt     4 4 31 41½ 13 19    Petro N J5 113 *2.00 85-19 BackBayBarrister113⁹CherokeeRelic118¹½Rockier115¹ Ridden out 6
18May83- 1Suf fst 4½f :23⅕  :47⅘ :53⅘   Md Sp Wt     1 3    58½ 46½ 411½ Bush W V  118 12.80 79-10 Whist 113⁴½ Burnstein 118⁴½ Sunstyle 115²½ No factor 10
  LATEST WORKOUTS   ●Jun 6 Bel tr.t 5f fst :59⅘ h   May 25 Bel tr.t 3f fst :36 h   May 19 Suf 7f fst 1:28⅘ b   May 7 Bel tr.t 3f fst :37⅘ b

Pine Circle            Dk. b. or br. c. 3, by Cox's Ridge—Gaebele, by Gallant Man       Lifetime   1984 5 0 1 0   $120,725
                       Br.—Loblolly Stable (Ky)                                     126   12 1 3 2  1983 7 1 2 2    $26,210
  Own.—Loblolly Stable Tr.—McGaughey Claude III                                            $146,935
19May84- 8Pim fst 1 3/16 :45⅕ 1:09⅕ 1:53⅘ Preakness  6 10 913 99 89 56¾  Smith M E  126 53.80 95-07 Gate Dancer 126¹½ Play On 126³½ Fight Over 126¾ Wide 10
 5May84- 8CD  fst 1¼  :47⅘ 1:36⅘ 2:02⅘  Ky Derby     18 14 149 1211 77¾ 67½ Smith M E 126 6.00e 78-19 Swale126³½CoaxMeChd126²AtTheThreshold126nk Lacked fin. bid 20
21Apr84- 9OP  fst 1⅛  :46⅘ 1:10⅕ 1:46⅘  Arkansas Dby 7 11 117 106 68½ 27 Day P      118 24.20 102-04 Althea 121⁷ Pine Circle 118no Gate Dancer 118no Lacked room 11
16Mar84- 3SA  fst 1 1/16 :46⅕ 1:10⅕ 1:43 Alw 32000   1 6 69½ 613 617 615 Toro F     118 10.20 71-20 Fifty Six InaRow114¹M.DoubleM.115³½BoldBatterUp114hd Outrun 6
22Jan84- 7SA  fst 1 1/16 :46⅘ 1:10⅘ 1:43⅘ Alw 27000  1 4 48 612 616 515 McCarron C J 120 8.30 67-21 Tights 120²½ Bold Batter Up 114¹¾ Bedouin 117¾ No factor 6
10Dec83- 8Haw gd  1 1/16 :47⅘ 1:13⅘ 1:46⅘ Juvenile  5 9 109¾ 46 31½ 12½ Smith M E 112 *3.00[D] 66-30 [D]Pine Circle 112²½DoubleClever113¾BlushOfFame112¹½ Bore out 11
     10Dec83-Disqualified and placed second
 5Nov83- 2CD  fst 1   :47⅕ 1:12⅘ 1:39⅘  Md Sp Wt     2 9 55 52½ 2hd 12½  Day P      117 *.90  72-18 Pine Circle 117²½ Bookmark 117nk Well What Else 117¹½ Driving 12
19Oct83- 4Kee gd  1 1/16 :48⅕ 1:13⅘ 1:48 Md Sp Wt    3 8 67 56½ 32½ 2¾ Allen K K  116 *1.40 65-24 Telegraph Key 116¾ Pine Circle 116² Quick Learner 116³ Rallied 12
26Aug83- 2CD  fst 6½f :23   :46⅘ 1:18⅘  Md Sp Wt     4 6 611 67½ 48 47   Allen K K  119 5.80  79-13 Dolcie's Boy 119⁴ Coax Me Again 119² Grundoon119¹ No mishap 6
19Aug83- 1CD  fst 6f  :22   :46⅕ 1:11⅘  Md Sp Wt     6 8 67 33½ 36½ 35  Allen K K  118 2.80  82-13 Scorned Lad 118hd Coax MeAgain118⁵PineCircle118hd No mishap 8
16Jly83- 1CD  fst 5½f :23⅘  :46   1:04⅘  Md Sp Wt     4 3 65¾ 57½ 34 37¾  Allen K K  119 10.50 90-14 Blind Man's Bluff 119nk FlyingFinish119⁷¾PineCircle119³ No rally 8
24Jun83- 3CD  fst 5½f :23⅕  :46   1:05⅘  Md Sp Wt     5 6 64½ 56 56 54½   Day P      119 8.00  88-12 Taylor'sSpecial119²LouN'Maur119¾FairwayTrveler119¹ No threat 8
  LATEST WORKOUTS   ●Jun 7 Bel 4f fst :46⅘ b   Jun 3 Bel 5f sly 1:02 b   ●May 18 Pim 3f fst :35 h   May 14 CD 5f gd 1:02 bg
```

COAX ME CHAD

A surprise second in the Derby, while coming from far back early, but no race since. Not the ideal Belmont profile.

SILENT KING

This is a more consistent, if not better, horse than Coax Me Chad, but with the same two negatives.

GATE DANCER

The Preakness winner closed ground in the Derby despite starting from post 20. However, he raced on drugs in that race and the Preakness, and would have to run without them in the Belmont.

Memories of Codex, the 1980 Preakness winner who ran so poorly in the Belmont without "that little help from his friends."

MINSTREL STAR

This horse is unbeaten, but is ambitiously placed against Grade I stakes competition after only two career starts. The distance and weight further compromise his chances.

SWALE

Although the victim of the bias at Pimlico, Swale was the expected beneficiary in the Belmont. He was the lone speed in the field, with the possible exception of the outclassed Minstrel Star, and figured to control the pace of the race. Swale represented the ideal trip situation—going from victim to victor—and every trip handicapper in the Northeast was on hand to cash in. Those suspicious of the colt's fitness only had to ask themselves what two consecutive dull performances might have done to his potential syndication value, and realize that trainer Woody Stephens would do nothing to harm the colt's reputation.

ROMANTIC TRADITION

This allowance horse placed third in a weak field in the Peter Pan, the final prep for the Belmont in New York. He now had to carry 126 pounds in better company. Little chance.

MORNING BOB

This colt had been rallying nicely at the middle distances, but as a son of the great world-class miler Blushing Groom, he had to be suspect at the Belmont distance. Morning Bob had been purchased after the Pennsylvania Derby and was making his first start for his new connections. He had previously been a lesser regarded member of the Woody Stephens string. Why would Stephens sell a horse with apparent Belmont credentials before the big race? Obviously he either doubted the horse's ability to get the distance in top company or felt he had a better horse (Swale) in the barn. If nothing else, the sale of Morning Bob erased any lingering doubts about the well-being of Swale.

EXATTIC

This was everyone's dark horse for the Belmont. Although bred for the classic distances, this promising colt had yet to race in stakes company, and his most recent start came a week before the Preakness.

BACK BAY BARRISTER

This improving, lightly raced colt was also bred for the classics. However, both Play On and Morning Bob, fresh off layoffs, had passed him in the stretch run of the Withers. The field he beat for the Peter Pan was extremely weak, and so was his winning figure for that performance.

PINE CIRCLE

The other victim of the Pimlico bias, Pine Circle seemed to be the bridesmaid type, the late closer serious players prefer to bet against. However, he had edged Gate Dancer for second in the Arkansas Derby at Oaklawn Park, where drugs are not allowed. And his work blowing out for the Belmont was unusually quick for a horse with his running style, suggesting sharpness.

Speed figures added the final touch to the analysis of the 1984 Belmont. With the aid of the bias at Pimlico, Gate Dancer and Play On were only able to run back to their previous top figures. These fell five lengths behind Swale's peaks established in the Florida and Kentucky Derbies. Of the others, only Exattic had an interesting recent figure, and that had become somewhat stale, as mentioned above.

With the best speed figures and a tactical advantage over a track conducive to early speed, Swale was the logical selection. Only Play On, with continued improvement expected, posed a serious threat to upset. Of the closers, Pine Circle, with hidden form, seemed preferable to the drugless and more heavily bet Gate Dancer, the middle-distance-bred Morning Bob, or the suspiciously inactive darkhorse Exattic.

Swale controlled the pace as expected, and won easily. Pine Circle came with the strongest late run to gain the place, possibly aided by the fact that Play On threw a shoe during the running. Swale returned his many supporters just $5.00, while the exacta with Pine Circle paid $125.80.

EIGHTH RACE
Belmont
JUNE 9, 1984

1 ½ MILES. (2.24) 116th Running THE BELMONT (Grade I). $350,000 added. 3-year-olds. By subscription of $200 each to accompany the nomination; $2,500 to pass the entry box; $5,000 to start. A supplementary nomination of $7,500 may be made on Wednesday, June 6 with an additional $25,000 to start, with $350,000 added, of which 60% to the winner, 22% to second, 12% to third and 6% to fourth. Colts and Geldings, 126 lbs. Fillies, 121 lbs. Starters to be named at the closing time of entries. The winning owner will be presented with the August Belmont Memorial Cup to be retained for one year, as well as a trophy for permanent possession and trophies will be presented to the winning trainer and jockey. Closed Wednesday, February 15, 1984 with 296 nominations. Supplementary nominee: Morning Bob.

Value of race $516,700, value to winner $310,020, second $113,674, third $62,004, fourth $31,002. Mutuel pool $1,154,610, OTB pool $1,729,316. Exacta Pool $525,638. OTB Exacta Pool $1,167,879.

Last Raced	Horse	Eqt.	A.	Wt	PP	¼	½	1	1¼	Str	Fin	Jockey	Odds $1
19May84 ^{8}Pim^{7}	Swale		3	126	6	1^{1}	1^{1}	$1^{1\frac{1}{2}}$	$1^{1\frac{1}{2}}$	1^{3}	1^{4}	Pincay L Jr	1.50
19May84 ^{8}Pim^{5}	Pine Circle		3	126	11	9^{1}	7^{1}	9^{2}	5^{2}	$4^{1\frac{1}{2}}$	2^{3}	Day P	26.70
28May84 ^{9}Key^{1}	(S)Morning Bob		3	126	8	$5^{\frac{1}{2}}$	$6^{1\frac{1}{2}}$	$5^{1\frac{1}{2}}$	4^{3}	2^{1}	3^{hd}	Velasquez J	6.80
19May84 ^{8}Pim^{2}	Play On		3	126	1	2^{hd}	$3^{\frac{1}{2}}$	$2^{\frac{1}{2}}$	$2^{\frac{1}{2}}$	$3^{\frac{1}{2}}$	$4^{\frac{3}{4}}$	Samyn J L	3.70
5May84 ^{8}CD^{2}	Coax Me Chad		3	126	2	6^{hd}	11	$10^{2\frac{1}{2}}$	6^{2}	6^{8}	$5^{2\frac{3}{4}}$	McCauley W H	24.20
19May84 ^{8}Pim^{1}	Gate Dancer		3	126	4	$4^{2\frac{1}{2}}$	4^{3}	3^{1}	3^{2}	$5^{1\frac{1}{2}}$	6^{8}	Cordero A Jr	4.70
5May84 ^{8}CD^{9}	Silent King	b	3	126	3	11	10^{2}	$8^{1\frac{1}{2}}$	8^{hd}	9^{14}	7^{hd}	Brumfield D	14.60
12May84 ^{6}Bel^{1}	Exattic	b	3	126	9	$7^{\frac{1}{2}}$	5^{hd}	6^{hd}	9^{6}	8^{hd}	$8^{\frac{1}{2}}$	Davis R G	11.00
27May84 ^{8}Bel^{3}	Romantic Tradition		3	126	7	10^{1}	$9^{\frac{1}{2}}$	$7^{\frac{1}{2}}$	$7^{2\frac{1}{2}}$	$7^{\frac{1}{2}}$	9^{28}	Hernandez R	67.20
27May84 ^{8}Bel^{1}	Back Bay Barrister		3	126	10	$8^{\frac{1}{2}}$	8^{hd}	11	11	10^{3}	$10^{6\frac{3}{4}}$	MacBeth D	20.10
25May84 ^{7}Bel^{1}	Minstrel Star		3	126	5	3^{1}	2^{1}	$4^{3\frac{1}{2}}$	$10^{\frac{1}{2}}$	11	11	Bailey J D	46.90

(S) Supplementary nomination.

OFF AT 5:38. Start good. Won ridden out. Time, :24⅘, :49⅖, 1:13⅗, 1:37⅗, 2:02⅕, 2:27⅕, Track fast.

$2 Mutuel Prices:

6-(F)-SWALE	5.00	4.40	3.60
11-(K)-PINE CIRCLE		15.00	7.00
8-(H)-MORNING BOB			4.40

$2 EXACTA 6-11 PAID $125.80.

Dk. b. or br. c, by Seattle Slew—Tuerta, by Forli. Trainer Stephens Woodford C. Bred by Claiborne Farm (Ky).

SWALE took over soon after the start, remained well out from the rail while allowed to make his own pace, responded readily to turn back PLAY ON and GATE DANCER leaving the far turn and drew away under intermittent urging. PINE CIRCLE wide into the backstretch, moved to the inside at the far turn, saved ground into the stretch, came out to split horses leaving the furlong grounds and finished well to best the others. MORNING BOB, never far back, rallied along the inside leaving the far turn, continued his bid until inside the final furlong but lacked a further response. PLAY ON taken back after breaking in front, was allowed to follow the pace while saving ground to the far turn, came out between horses to go after SWALE approaching the stretch but weakened during the drive. COAX ME CHAD saved ground into the stretch, came off the rail for the drive but failed to seriously menace while moving back to the inside nearing the finish. GATE DANCER, reserved behind the leaders while racing well out in the track, rallied approaching the end of the backstretch, remained a factor to the stretch and tired. SILENT KING, wide throughout failed to be a serious factor. EXATTIC moved within easy striking distance entering the backstretch but was finished nearing the far turn. ROMANTIC TRADITION was always outrun. BACK BAY BARRISTER wasn't able to keep pace. MINSTREL STAR raced forwardly to the far turn and stopped badly.

Chapter 35

Will He Get off the Rail?

WHILE WATCHING SCRIPT OHIO charge down the middle of the track en route to victory in the 1984 Young America Stakes at the Meadowlands, I caught a glimpse of another horse moving quickly on the inside. For a brief moment, I was startled. When you have a $76.00 horse looking like a winner, even a leaf blowing across the track can cause palpitations—all the more so with this horse, because I didn't know who he was. I had each of the other logical contenders spotted, but a mystery horse had now entered the picture.

After the race I identified the horse as Tank's Prospect, a lightly raced shipper from California making his first start over a distance of ground and around two turns. I was impressed. The next day I spoke with Vic Gilardi, longtime agent for Jorge Velasquez, and found that he too had been impressed by the horse and had already secured the mount for Velasquez in the upcoming Champagne Stakes at Aqueduct on October 27. With normal improvement, the horse looked like a solid contender.

Favored at even money for the Champagne based on his victory in the Laurel Futurity was Mighty Appealing, who had passed up the $500,000 Young America in favor of New York's $250,000 purse. Since the horses that finished second and third in the Laurel race had subsequently finished behind Tank's Prospect at the Meadowlands, and since Mighty Appealing himself had made a sharp right-hand turn in deep stretch at Laurel, I had no doubt the second choice was the better animal. The other four contestants simply didn't figure.

By the time the six horses came to the paddock for the Champagne, however, my opinion had wavered. The track was muddy, and a strong track bias favoring outside speed—Mighty Appealing—was playing tricks with the day's form, making Tank's Prospect's task now seem quite formidable. Complicating matters was the fact that Mighty Appealing was sporting front bandages, normally a negative sign, especially with young stakes horses. In my mind, these confirmed suspicions, born at Laurel, that had grown when the colt failed to contest the richer Young America at the Meadowlands.

Heavy rains, either overnight or the previous day, always raise the possibility of a biased racing surface the following day, and the handicapper must be especially attuned to how the day's races are being run. Let's take a look at the results of the earlier races on October 27, looking specifically for evidence of a bias:

Videogenic, a first-starter offered at 5–1, won the first race as "second speed," from the outside.

The second race went, as expected, to the 4–5 favorite Mepache, who simply outclassed her field and elected to prove her point without racing too close to the rail.

The previously faint-hearted Very Ultimate quickly sprinted to a clear lead and won the mile third event while remaining far from the rail.

Very Ultimate — B. f. 3, by Exclusive Native—Redpath, by Indian Chief II
Br.—Harbor View Farm (Ky)
Own.—Harbor View Farm — Tr.—Martin Frank — **114**
Lifetime 8 1 1 0 $10,780 — 1984 8 1 1 0 $10,780 — 1983 0 M 0 0 — Turf 1 0 0 0 $1,260

29Sep84- 2Bel	yd	1 1/16 Ⓣ	:47	1:12⅕	1:45⅕	3+ⒻAlw 21000	7	6	41½	32½	45½	46½	Cruguet J	113	18.50	63-22	Fur Scarf 1153 Double Saucy 1133 Temple Goddess 113½	Tired	12
19Sep84- 6Med	fst	6f	:22⅗	:46⅕	1:12⅘	3+ⒻAlw 12000	7	2	56	76¾	68½	47	McCauley W H	118	8.40	71-21	Bitter Cold 1073½ Mt. Prospect 1121½ Cher Cheval 1162	Wide	8
11Sep84- 7Med	fst	6f	:22⅘	:46⅗	1:13	3+ⒻMd Sp Wt	1	3	51¾	41½	2½	11	McCauley W H	118	*.80e	77-20	Very Ultimate 1181 Tempestously 1131 My Cliche 1186½	Driving	9
1Sep84- 5Med	fst	6f	:22⅘	:46⅖	1:11⅘	3+ⒻMd Sp Wt	1	1	11½	2hd	2hd	2nk	McCauley W H	118	3.90	83-13	True Charmer 118nk Very Ultimate 1183½DamaskSky1183	Gamely	6
24Aug84- 7Mth	fst	5f	:22⅗	:45⅖	:58⅕	3+ⒻAlw 11000	8	6	88	811	79½	77	Velez R I	113	13.10	88-24	Silver Dora 1133½ Nahadeh 1112½ Puff Away 109¾	Outrun	8
6Apr84- 6Aqu	fst	6f ⊡	:23	:46⅗	1:12⅖	3+ⒻMd Sp Wt	12	1	32½	58½	611	69½	Miranda J	112	79.60	73-18	BornALady114hdMirrorOfHumanity1144TripsinLdy112¾	Fin. early	12
15Mar84- 4Aqu	fst	6f ⊡	:23	:47⅕	1:13⅕	ⒻMd Sp Wt	11	5	65	78	1319	1317	Murphy D J	121	44.50	61-25	Sterner Stuff 1212½ Satch 1141 Mirror OfHumanity1213	Fel' back	14
23Feb84- 6Aqu	fst	6f ⊡	:23	:47⅖	1:13⅘	ⒻMd Sp Wt	12	1	95¾	97¾	912	711¼	Murphy D J5	116	21.70	63-22	Cinder Lass 1213½ Evergreen Miss 1211¾ Explicit Gal 1212	Outrun	12

LATEST WORKOUTS — Oct 23 Bel tr.t 5f gd 1:02⅖ b — Oct 16 Bel tr.t 5f fst 1:02 b — Oct 9 Bel tr.t 5f fst 1:01 h — ●Sep 28 Med 3f sly :36⅕ b

Crême Fraiche, a first-starter from the Woody Stephens barn, overlooked at 20–1 from his rail post, made an explosive move around the turn once off the rail and prevailed by three and a half lengths in the fourth event despite returning to the rail in the stretch.

The fifth race went to Nickolette, the longest price in the short field, who raced outside rivals all the way, almost bolting on the final turn, in fact.

Nickolette — Gr. f. 3, by Ali Oop—Sandy Nichols, by Baffle
Br.—Dogwood Farm Inc (Fla)
Own.—Langsam E — Tr.—Barbara Robert — **112**7
Lifetime 4 0 0 0 — 1984 4 M 0 0 — 1983 0 M 0 0

17Oct84- 1Bel	fst	6f	:22⅖	:46⅕	1:12⅖	3+ⒻMd 35000	11	10	77¾	79½	916	918	Santagata N	119	9.00	62-21	Shift Key 1173 Gentle Ram 115½ Cynge 1196	Wide	11
28Jly84- 1Bel	my	1 1/16	:47⅕	1:12⅘	1:44⅗	3+ⒻMd Sp Wt	5	2	1hd	33½	715	723¼	Samyn J L	116	3.40	56-16	Austerlitz Station 11611 Kotuku 1163 Sweet Miranda 1091	Tired	8
4Jly84- 2Bel	fst	6f	:22⅖	:46	1:11	3+ⒻMd Sp Wt	5	4	64½	66	69	612	Day P	116	10.80f	75-11	Sorbet 1164 Life's Light 1163¾ Leotard 116no	Evenly	14
18Jun84- 2Bel	fst	6f	:22⅘	:46⅘	1:12	3+ⒻMd 50000	12	13	107¼	911	411	511¼	Samyn J L	114	35.20	71-20	Accostage1095LadyLitchfield114nkGentleRm1096	Off slowly, wide	13

LATEST WORKOUTS — Sep 14 Aqu 4f fst :50⅖ b

7 AQUEDUCT

TURF COURSE 1⅛ MILES AQUEDUCT

1⅛ MILES. (Turf). (1.48⅘) ALLOWANCE. Purse $25,000. 3-year-olds and upward which have never won three races other than Maiden, Claiming or Starter. Weights, 3-year-olds 119 lbs. Older 122 lbs. Non-winners of two races other than maiden or Claiming over a mile since September 15 allowed 3 lbs. Of such a race since then 5 lbs.

Coupled—Fatih and Solidified.

Desert Chief

B. g. 3, by Hula Chief—Desert Gypsy, by Tollie Jester
Br.—Valli Hi Thoroughbred (Ark)
Own.—Koester Laura J Tr.—Koester Laura J
116 Lifetime 16 3 4 5 $32,698 | 1984 15 3 4 4 $32,248 | 1983 1 M 0 1 $450 | Turf 2 0 1 1 $3,265

13Oct84- 5Kee fst 1 1/16 :48⅖ 1:12⅗ 1:44⅗ 3+ Alw 16630 1 7 78 74¾ 3½ 1¾ McKnight J 112 4.80 83-18 Desert Chief 112¾ Spartan Hope 113no Ismore 1132 Driving 7
12Sep84- 9Lat fst 1 1/16 :47⅘ 1:12⅘ 1:45⅘ 3+ Alw 10800 3 6 57½ 44½ 35 36 Romero A 117 7.50 76-33 Sorroto 115hd Flying Trophy 1156 Desert Chief 1178 Evenly 7
25Aug84- 7RD fm 1 ①:47⅘ 1:13 1:37⅘ Alw 10000 6 7 74½ 1hd 21½ 22 D'Amico A J 116 2.20 91-07 Bet Blind 1132 Desert Chief 1164 Donna Roberta 1121½ Weakened 11
18Aug84- 4RD my 170 :48 1:13⅕ 1:45 3+ Alw 8000 3 6 45½ 31 11½ 17 D'Amico A J 112 *1.50 74-25 Desert Chief 1127 Star Of State 113hd Golden Rain 1152½ Driving 6
25Jun84- 8AP fst 1 :47⅘ 1:11⅘ 1:37⅕ 3+ Alw 12000 3 7 67¾ 67¾ 57½ 48¼ Howard D L 110 18.10 67-24 Golden Tower113hdT.H.Bend1106¾BlushingHonours1132 No factor 6
13Jun84- 7AP fm 1 1/16 ①:48 1:13⅕ 1:45 3+ Alw 11500 6 11 1110 1111 33½ 31 Gallitano G 112 5.60 83-16 Bail Fixer 119nk Stress 112¾ Desert Chief 1124 Rallied 12
25May84- 7AP sly 1 :46⅘ 1:13⅘ 1:41⅘ 3+ Alw 11500 6 4 44½ 22½ 2½ 2no Tejeira J 114 2.60 53-41 WhoCouldForget119noDsrtChf1148YoungTribut1195 Just missed 7
19May84- 8Tdn my 170 :47⅘ 1:13⅖ 1:44 3+ Alw 10000 3 3 31½ 35 37 38½ Avalon W A III 113 *3.10 76-30 Mykish 1164½ Record Breaker 1164 Desert Chief 1135½ Weakened 8
14Apr84- 8Kee fst 1 1/16 :47⅘ 1:13⅘ 1:48⅗ Alw 16160 3 4 37 42 2½ 2nk Borden D A 112 11.70 63-29 Charmed Rook 120nkDesertChief1127O C Fisher1151½ Just missed 5
6Apr84- 8Kee fst 1 1/16 :47⅗ 1:13 1:48⅕ Alw 14810 9 10 813 54 42 41¾ Borden D A 115 54.10 63-22 Mining Dust 1131½ Old Broadway 115nkO.C.Fisher112nk Mild rally 10

Broadway Harry

B. c. 4, by Big Spruce—Cesica, by Raise a Native
Br.—Roach B & T (Ky)
Own.—Stonewall Farm Tr.—Jerkens H Allen
117 Lifetime 24 4 1 7 $101,195 | 1984 15 3 1 4 $79,745 | 1983 7 1 0 2 $17,880 | Turf 7 1 0 3 $30,600

20Oct84- 8Bel fst 1½ :49⅗ 2:03⅘ 2:28⅘ 3+ J C Gold Cp 4 4 45½ 518 526 532¼ Graell A b 126 25.00 44-17 Slew O Gold 1269¾HailBoldKing1211BoundingBasque1263 Outrun 5
20Oct84-Grade I
6Oct84- 6Bel fm 1 1/16 Ⓣ:46⅘ 1:11 1:43⅘ 3+ Alw 28000 5 3 34 21 32½ 33 Graell A b 117 5.20 80-23 PapalBull1172¾Lutyens119nkBroadwayHrry117hd Needed response 7
29Sep84- 1Bel gd 1¼ Ⓣ:51⅗ 1:40⅗ 2:05⅕ 3+ Clm 175000 8 2 2½ 2hd 11½ 1¾ Graell A b 112 11.10 66-22 Broadway Harry 112¾ Balitou 116hd Palace 112nk Driving 8
22Sep84- 7Bel fm 1¼ Ⓣ:48⅘ 1:37 2:01⅗ 3+ Alw 36000 6 3 43 41¾ 22½ 32½ Graell A b 117 16.20 85-10 Intensify 1191 Balitou 1151½ Broadway Harry 1172 Closed well 8
13Sep84- 9Med fst 170 :45⅗ 1:10⅘ 1:42 3+ Alw 16000 4 2 42½ 54½ 43½ 32¾ Perret C b 116 2.00 86-22 NorthernPlesure111nkJne'sDilemm1132¾BrodwyHrry1163 Mild bid 6
29Aug84- 8Bel fm 1¼ Ⓣ:50 1:37 2:00⅗ 3+ Manhattan H 8 10 119¾ 1012 109½ 119½ Velez R I 110 4.80e 81-14 Win 1142¼ Fortnightly 1122 Norwick 110½ Far back 12
29Aug84-Grade I
18Aug84- 1Sar fst 1⅛ :49 1:13⅕ 1:50⅕ 3+ Bld Reason H 6 1 2hd 43 63½ 65 Velasquez J 110 4.20 79-15 Moro 123nk Fast Gold 116nk Exattic 109hd Tired 6
3Aug84- 7Sar fm 1 1/16 ①:46 1:10⅖ 1:41⅕ 3+ Alw 28000 6 4 57 43½ 32½ 33½ Velasquez J 119 8.30 87-20 StayTheCourse1123½Ayman117noBrodwyHrry1194¼ Wide into str 6
15Jly84- 4Bel fm 1¼ Ⓣ:49 1:37 2:01⅕ 3+ Alw 25000 2 1 21½ 42 42½ 42¼ Davis R G 119 9.50 86-14 Papal Bull 117¾ Nepal 119nk Crazy Moon 1171½ Weakened 6
4Jly84- 8Key fst 1¼ :48⅖ 1:39 2:05 3+ Indepndce H 1 3 35½ 31½ 1½ 12½ Castaneda K 114 6.30 85-20 BrodwyHrry1142½LordDeL'Orn1173MonyByOrlns115nk Drew clear 6
LATEST WORKOUTS Oct 17 Bel 7f fst 1:30⅖ b | Oct 13 Bel tr.t 3f fst :36⅗ b | Sep 11 Bel 4f fst :49⅘ b | Sep 8 Bel 4f fst :49⅗ b

Fatih

B. c. 4, by Icecapade—Native Nurse, by Graustark
Br.—Pine Tree Stable (Ky)
Own.—Harbor View Farm Tr.—Martin Frank
117 Lifetime 24 5 5 2 $72,464 | 1984 13 4 3 1 $69,180 | 1983 9 1 1 1 $1,348 | Turf 22 4 5 2 $59,144

17Oct84- 7Bel fm 1 1/16 Ⓣ:48⅗ 1:12 1:42⅖ 3+ Alw 25000 7 3 32 31½ 43 44 Cruguet J 117 3.40 85-20 Spring Fever 119¾ Go Go Regal 1141¼ Bountiful II 1162 Weakened 7
7Oct84- 2Bel fm 1 ①:46 1:09⅘ 1:35⅖ 3+ Clm 95000 1 2 11 11½ 11½ 1¾ Cruguet J 120 4.50 88-17 Fatih120¾Aristocratical122noFerlessLeder114no Drifted out drvng 7
15Sep84- 3Bel sly 1 :45⅘ 1:11⅗ 1:38⅕ 3+ Alw 22000 6 2 11½ 14 15 17¼ Cruguet J 117 2.70 74-18 Fatih 1177¼ Swoon 1174¾ Steepbank 113¾ Ridden out 6
6Sep84- 7Bel gd 1 1/16 Ⓣ:50 1:14 1:44⅘ 3+ Alw 22000 6 3 3½ 2½ 22 21¾ Cruguet J 117 6.10 75-27 Ends Well 1181¾ Fatih 117½ Steepbank 1131¾ Game try 8
26Aug84- 5Sar fm 1 1/16 ①:47 1:11⅗ 1:43⅗ 3+ Alw 22000 8 7 54 54½ 42 31¼ Cruguet J 117 12.20 78-21 Roving Minstrel 113¾ Penzance 117½ Fatih 117¾ Rallied 11
19Aug84- 5Sar fm 1 Ⓣ:47 1:11⅘ 1:36⅘ 3+ Clm 90000 3 6 64½ 58 47½ 510 Guerra W A 118 5.40 82-20 Disco Count 1225½ Red Brigade 1162½ Forkali 118no Raced wide 7
28Jun84- 7Bel fm 1 1/16 ①:45⅖ 1:09⅘ 1:41⅘ 3+ Alw 22000 9 4 42 32 55½ 67½ Bailey J D 117 6.40 79-18 Nepal 117¾ Go Go Regal 1091¾ Steepbank 1142 Weakened 12
16Jun84- 6Bel fm 1⅜ Ⓣ:48⅖ 1:37⅘ 2:15⅖ 3+ Alw 22000 5 4 42 2½ 21½ 22¼ Bailey J D 117 *2.30 78-20 He's Vivacious 1192¼ Fatih 1175¼ Call Me Rebel 1091 2nd best 7
8Jun84- 6Bel fm 1 1/16 ①:45⅖ 1:09⅗ 1:42⅗ 3+ Alw 22000 1 1 1hd 3nk 52½ 68 Cordero A Jr 117 *1.70 75-14 Quick Dip 1171¾ Sir Roland 109no Go Go Regal 109½ Gave way 8
19May84- 7Bel fm 1 1/16 ①:47 1:11 1:42⅕ 3+ Alw 22000 6 2 21 2½ 23 22¼ Cruguet J 124 *.50 83-14 Onyxly 1132¼ Fatih 1243 Dr David Nathan 1212¼ Best of others 7
LATEST WORKOUTS Oct 25 Bel tr.t 4f gd :47⅕ h | Oct 15 Bel tr.t 3f fst :35⅗ h | Oct 4 Bel tr.t 4f fst :47⅖ h | Sep 23 Bel tr.t 4f fst :47⅖ h

Stormy Puddles

Dk. b. or br. c. 4, by King Pellinore—Big Puddles, by Delta Judge
Br.—Boggiano & Schwartz (NY)
Own.—Schwartz Arlene Tr.—Schwartz Scott M
117 Lifetime 21 3 4 1 $80,060 | 1984 11 2 2 0 $45,240 | 1983 10 1 2 1 $34,820 | Turf 5 1 0 1 $21,060

8Oct84- 8FL fst 1⅛ :47⅕ 1:13 1:53⅗ 3+ Wadsworth H 8 7 68 55½ 75½ 811 Reynolds R L 117 6.00 77-23 Org 121½ Broadway Buck 1122½ Wimborne's Gater 1122½ Tired 11
27Aug84- 6Sar fm 1 1/16 ①:47 1:11⅕ 1:43⅘ 3+ Alw 25000 2 6 64¾ 53½ 62½ 64 Santagata N 119 14.70 74-17 Roman Bend 117½ Haste to Finish117¾NoMan'sLand117nk Outrun 7
20Aug84- 9Sar fm 1⅛ Ⓣ:47⅖ 1:12 1:50⅘ 3+ ⓈAlw 27500 9 6 66½ 54½ 11½ 1nk Santagata N 117 25.10 86-19 Stormy Puddles 117nk Equity Kicker 112½TunedOut1122¾ Driving 12
12Jly84- 7Bel fst 1 1/16 :46⅗ 1:10⅘ 1:42⅗ 3+ ⓈAlw 27500 9 7 99 1017 1019 919¾ Murphy D J 117 22.00 69-17 SinghAmerica1124½Carey'sBoy1112¼TalentedJacques1111½ Outrun 10
20May84- 7Bel fm 2 ①:51 2:55⅗ 3:20⅘ 3+ Handicap 5 3 68½ 716 620 523¾ Murphy D J 108 46.60 74-13 Anne's Lover 1142¾ Erin Bright 1171¾ Nassipour 1202¾ Tired 10
6Apr84- 8Aqu fst 1⅛ ⊡:46⅗ 1:11⅗ 1:52 3+ ⓈAlw 27500 2 2 21½ 67½ 514 519¾ Cordero A Jr b 121 4.30 62-16 Lively Teddy 1212¾ Groom's Image 111¾ Tuned Out 1118¾ Tired 6
12Mar84- 7Aqu fst 170 ⊡:48⅖ 1:13⅗ 1:44⅖ ⓈAlw 28500 6 5 46½ 45 47½ 27 Cordero A Jr 117 2.40 72-22 SpiritOfAim1177StormyPuddles117nkLivlyTddy1191¼ Up for place 7
7Mar84- 8Aqu fst 1 1/16 ⊡:47⅗ 1:11⅘ 1:43⅗ 3+ ⓈKing Point H 1 6 53½ 814 819 720½ Santagata N 111 20.50 73-17 Jacque's Tip 118hd Startop's Ace 1078 Stiff UpperLip1113 Outrun 9
25Feb84- 2Aqu gd 1 1/16 ⊡:47⅗ 1:12 1:45⅗ ⓈAlw 28500 2 7 31½ 11½ 11½ 2½ Santagata N 117 13.30 83-12 NorthernExchnge117½StormyPuddls117nkLivlyTddy1222½ Gamely 9
9Feb84- 7Aqu fst 1 1/16 ⊡:46⅘ 1:11⅗ 1:44 Alw 24000 10 10 98¾ 96¾ 917 816¼ Santagata N 119 29.80 76-18 Seen The Glory 1171¾ Colonel Law 1221 Minabchar 117no Outrun 10
LATEST WORKOUTS ●Oct 24 Sar tr.t 4f fst :49⅘ b | ●Oct 18 Sar tr.t 3f fst :37⅖ b | ●Oct 5 Sar tr.t 4f my :49⅖ h | Sep 28 Sar tr.t 4f fst :51⅖ b

Go Go Regal

B. c. 3, by Regal And Royal—Go Go Windy, by Restless Wind
Br.—Kohr E D (Fla)
Own.—Sweet Meadow Farm Tr.—Gullo Thomas J
114 Lifetime 21 3 6 4 $76,920 | 1984 14 1 6 4 $54,120 | 1983 7 2 0 0 $22,800 | Turf 5 1 3 1 $31,680

17Oct84- 7Bel fm 1 1/16 Ⓣ:48⅗ 1:12 1:42⅖ 3+ Alw 25000 5 2 2½ 11 12 2¾ Davis R G b 114 4.00 88-20 Spring Fever 119¾ Go Go Regal 1141¼ Bountiful II 1162 Gamely 7
28Sep84- 8Bel yl 1 1/16 ①:47 1:12⅖ 1:44⅘ 3+ Alw 25000 1 2 2½ 1½ 11½ 24¼ Davis R G b 113 4.30 68-36 Lutyens 1174¼ Go Go Regal 1132¼ No Man's Land 1171½ 2nd best 8
19Sep84- 8Bel fst 1 :46⅗ 1:11⅗ 1:36⅖ 3+ Alw 25000 4 2 23 21½ 45 59¾ Davis R G b 113 11.00 73-19 Steady Beat 1152¾ Exattic 1132 Regal Humor 1135 Tired 7
12Aug84- 7Sar fm 1 1/16 Ⓣ:47 1:11 1:42⅕ 3+ Alw 22000 1 3 42 32½ 33½ 1¾ Guerra W A b 112 *2.40 94-07 Go Go Regal 112¾ Steepbank 112no One For A. B. 1122 Driving 10
5Aug84- 6Sar fst 6f :22 :44⅗ 1:09⅗ 3+ Alw 23000 1 3 32 3½ 21½ 34½ Guerra W A b 112 3.70 87-09 Majestic Venture1123¾DonRickles112¾GoGoRegal1121 Drifted out 6
28Jun84- 7Bel fm 1 1/16 ①:45⅖ 1:09⅘ 1:41⅘ 3+ Alw 22000 1 1 1½ 1hd 1½ 2¾ Guerra W A b 109 7.60 86-18 Nepal 117¾ Go Go Regal 1091¾ Steepbank 1142 Gamely 12
22Jun84- 7Bel fst 1 :45⅕ 1:10⅘ 1:37⅕ 3+ Alw 22000 5 1 2½ 1½ 2hd 32½ Davis R G b 109 5.20 76-21 Slew the Coup 1042 Potentiate 117½ Go Go Regal1091 Weakened 6
8Jun84- 6Bel fm 1 1/16 ①:45⅖ 1:09⅗ 1:42⅗ 3+ Alw 22000 3 3 3½ 1hd 2hd 31¾ Davis R G b 109 8.40 81-14 Quick Dip 1171¾ Sir Roland 109no Go Go Regal 109½ Weakened 8
30May84- 8Bel sly 6f :22 :45⅘ 1:10⅕ 3+ Alw 21000 1 2 33½ 32 35½ 38 Davis R G b 109 *1.40 83-20 Lost Canyon 1137 Exit Five B. 1101 Go Go Regal 109¾ Wide 6
20May84- 6Bel fst 1 1/16 :46⅖ 1:10⅗ 1:42⅘ 3+ Alw 22000 4 1 1hd 1½ 2hd 2no Cordero A Jr 113 *1.10 88-18 ReglHumor110noGoGoRegl1132Spitlfields1101¾ Drifted out,bmpd 7
LATEST WORKOUTS Oct 6 Bel tr.t 5f fst 1:01⅗ h | Sep 12 Bel tr.t 3f fst :36⅗ b | Sep 6 Bel tr.t 5f fst 1:02⅘ b | ●Sep 1 Bel tr.t 6f fst 1:17⅖ b

Monkey Bread

B. c. 4, by Dewan—Baobab, by Pronto
Br.—Cherry Valley Farm Inc-Marjory Corp (Ky)
Own.—Rosenberg Mrs L Tr.—Hawkins Luke X
117 Lifetime 47 5 7 3 $101,845 | 1984 19 3 2 1 $56,180 | 1983 21 2 5 1 $42,665 | Turf 26 4 4 1 $81,290

17Oct84- 7Bel fm 1 1/16 Ⓣ:48⅗ 1:12 1:42⅖ 3+ Alw 25000 6 5 52½ 65½ 66½ 65 Velasquez J 117 6.10 84-20 Spring Fever 119¾ Go Go Regal 1141¼ Bountiful II 1162 Outrun 7
23Sep84- 7Pen fm 1 1/16 ① 1:39⅗ 3+ Gov's Cup H 10 9 1013 1010 107½ 108¾ Gomez E R 111 79.10 83-15 Castelets 1142½ Tough Mickey121hdMoneyByOrleans114no Outrun 10
23Sep84-Grade III
14Sep84- 7Bel fm 1 1/16 ①:46⅕ 1:09⅘ 1:43 3+ Alw 36000 4 5 511 513 411 47½ Clayton M D 115 17.40 73-23 Who's For Dinner117¾DiscoCount110¾Hero'sHonor1226 No factor 6
14Sep84-Awarded third purse money
23Aug84- 8Sar sf 1⅝ ①:52⅗ 2:08⅖ 2:49⅗ 3+ Seneca H 9 6 66 813 815 722½ Cruguet J 109 6.80 — — Persian Tiara 112no Four Bases 1118¼ Nassipour 108¾ Tired badly 11
23Aug84-Grade III
13Aug84- 6Sar fm 1⅜ ①:49⅘ 1:13⅖ 1:56⅘ 3+ Alw 25000 3 4 54½ 53½ 31½ 21 Cruguet J 119 3.80 81-12 ChrgingThrough1171MonkeyBrd1191Nssipour1171½ Lacked room 6
19Jly84- 8Bel yl 1⅜ ①:50 1:40⅘ 2:19⅘ 3+ Alw 22000 3 6 65 22 12 13 Cruguet J 122 *1.70 63-37 MonkeyBred1223CutThMusic111nkShortAndShrp1178 Ridden out 6
5Jly84- 7Bel fm 1½ ①:49⅗ 2:02 2:30⅖ 3+ Alw 21000 3 7 76½ 1½ 11 11½ Cruguet J 117 3.50 72-23 Monkey Bread 1171½ Star Topper1167¼Sayad111hd Drifted out,Dr 7
23Jun84- 2Bel fm 1⅜ Ⓣ:49⅕ 1:38⅕ 2:15⅗ 3+ Alw 21000 6 9 410 32½ 66 68½ Miranda J 117 5.30 70-18 Chopper Charlie 117¾ Delta Deity 1174½OurLeader1171½ Bothered 10
15Jun84- 2Bel fm 1¼ Ⓣ:50 1:40⅕ 2:05⅕ Clm 45000 1 10 98¾ 43½ 12 13½ Miranda J 113 3.20 68-18 Monkey Bread 1133½ValDeLaMeuse117noBroadly1173¼ Ridden out 10
4Jun84- 8Bel fst 1 1/16 :48 1:13⅗ 1:45⅖ 3+ Alw 21000 3 4 42½ 41½ 64¾ 64¾ Miranda J 117 5.20 70-19 Print Money 1092 Coast Range 112hd Chapparel 1131½ Tired 7
LATEST WORKOUTS Oct 24 Sar tr.t 3f fst :39 b | Oct 13 Sar tr.t 1 fst 1:47⅖ h | Oct 8 Aqu tr.t 6f fst 1:18⅖ b | Oct 5 Sar tr.t 4f my :53 b

Equity Kicker

B. g. 3, by Cormorant—Silkys Angle, by Angle Light
Br.—Sonnenblick J E (NY)
Own.—Hellson Stable Tr.—Hertler John O
109⁵ Lifetime 14 4 2 1 $75,340 | 1984 12 3 2 1 $58,600 | 1983 2 1 0 0 $16,740 | Turf 2 0 1 1 $9,290

11Oct84- 5Bel fm 1 ①:45⅗ 1:09⅘ 1:35⅖ Clm 80000 3 7 67½ 63¾ 54½ 32½ Privitera R7 107 4.60 85-12 Ice Bucket 118½ Steepbank 1132 Equity Kicker 1073 Rallied 8
1Oct84- 6Bel sly 1 1/16 :47⅕ 1:12⅕ 1:44⅕ 3+ ⓈAlw 27500 6 6 52 3½ 14 12¾ Ward W A5 109 *1.70 81-24 Equity Kicker 1092¾ Tuned Out 114½ Carasco 1194 Driving 7
15Sep84- 9Bel sly 1 :45⅖ 1:11 1:36⅘ 3+ ⓈAlw 27500 5 6 75½ 32 33½ 22¾ Ward W A5 108 7.90 78-18 High Ice 1132¾ Equity Kicker 1081TalentedJacques1135 Wide str 11
20Aug84- 9Sar fm 1⅛ Ⓣ:47⅖ 1:12 1:50⅘ 3+ ⓈAlw 27500 11 9 915 76½ 21½ 2nk Cruguet J 112 15.80 86-19 StormyPuddls117nkEquityKickr112½TundOut1122¾ Best of others 12
9Aug84- 2Sar fst 7f :21⅘ :44⅗ 1:23 3+ ⓈAlw 26000 8 3 812 68½ 44 41¼ Ward W A5 107 24.70 86-14 Comic Flare 117¾ Flying Skipper 114no High Ice 114½ Wide 10
23Jly84- 2Bel fst 1 1/16 :47⅕ 1:12⅖ 1:45⅘ Clm 25000 7 8 63½ 54¼ 1½ 12 Ward W A5 112 *2.20 73-21 Equity Kicker 1122 Great Amar 113nk ⒹMr. Radius 117¾ Driving 10
12Jly84- 7Bel fst 1 1/16 :46⅗ 1:10⅘ 1:42⅗ 3+ ⓈAlw 27500 5 4 34½ 46 54½ 68 Ward W A5 106 31.00 81-17 SinghAmeric1124¼Crey'sBoy1112¼TlentedJcques1111¼ Drifted out 10
20Jun84- 7Bel fst 7f :23 :45⅗ 1:24⅗ 3+ ⓈAlw 26000 5 6 87½ 85½ 98½ 810 Murphy D J 111 51.90 69-18 Gothic Revival 1124 Loughrea 117hdTexasGentleman104nk Outrun 9
1Jun84- 7Bel fst 1 :47⅖ 1:11⅘ 1:36⅘ 3+ ⓈAlw 27500 6 6 41½ 85¾ 814 815½ Murphy D J 114 8.90 65-20 Bright Rex 117½ Talented Jacques114¾SinghAmerica1122¾ Outrun 8
20May84- 9Bel fst 1 1/16 :47⅕ 1:12⅗ 1:45⅘ 3+ ⓈAlw 26000 8 3 32½ 31 31½ 1hd Murphy D J 110 *2.30 73-18 EquityKicker110hdRpidDeploymnt1122SpiritofPgsus1105½ Driving 11
LATEST WORKOUTS Sep 25 Bel 4f fst :50 b | Sep 7 Bel tr.t 4f fst :49⅗ b

Solidified — Dk. b. or br. c. 3, by Tell—Swingin Axe, by The Axe II
Br.—Harbor View Farm (Cal)
Own.—Harbor View Farm — Tr.—Martin Frank
116 — Lifetime 7 2 2 2 $46,326 — 1984 7 2 2 2 [illegible] — 1983 0 M 0 0 — Turf 3 2 0 1 $35,106

13Oct84- 8Bel fm 1½ Ⓣ:48⅕ 2:01⅗ 2:28 Realz'tn 6 5 57½ 66½ 35 32¾ Bailey J D 114 7.10 81-21 Roving Minstrel 1232¾ Vision 123½ Solidified 114nk Wide into str. 10
13Oct84-Grade II
6Oct84- 5Bel fm 1 Ⓣ:46 1:10⅘ 1:36⅘ 3+ Alw 21000 9 9 99¼ 53½ 31½ 1¾ Cruguet J 119 *1.60 81-23 Solidified 119¾ Inrhetoric 1142½ Pigwidgeon 114no Driving 11
23Sep84- 9Bel fm 1 1/16 Ⓣ:45⅗ 1:09⅖ 1:41⅘ 3+ Md Sp Wt 7 8 310 37½ 11½ 16½ Velasquez J 118 *2.00 87-14 Solidified 1186½SpecialAgent1182¾LongestStraw1181¼ Ridden out 12
13Sep84- 7Bel fst 1 1/16 :46⅖ 1:11⅖ 1:44⅖ 3+ Md Sp Wt 1 3 43½ 32¼ 33½ 41 Ward W A5 113 2.70 79-21 MjorityLeder118½Excommunicte118hdGenerlOfficr118½ Weakened 8
5Sep84- 5Bel fst 7f :22⅗ :45⅗ 1:22⅖ 3+ Md Sp Wt 4 6 75½ 74¼ 57½ 28 Ward W A5 113 *1.50e 82-12 Sanpam 1188 Solidified 113¾ Magnetize 118nk Wide 9
19Aug84- 9Sar fst 7f :23 :46⅕ 1:23⅘ 3+ Md Sp Wt 8 2 31½ 21 3½ 33½ Guerra W A 117 *1.80 79-15 Silver Stark 1173½ MajorityLeader117noSolidified1175¾ Weakened 8
10Aug84- 2Sar fst 6f :22⅕ :45⅗ 1:10⅕ 3+ Md Sp Wt 3 7 65½ 76 35 25¾ Ward W A5 112 13.60 83-13 Loud And Clear 1175¾ Solidified 112hd Incite 1173½ Gained place 14
LATEST WORKOUTS ●Oct 22 Bel tr.t 4f fst :46 h Oct 1 Bel tr.t 4f fst :50 b ●Sep 21 Bel tr.t 3f fst :35⅖ h Sep 2 Bel tr.t 4f fst :49⅕ h

Palace — Ch. h. 7, by Golden Palace—Miss Newberry, by Killam II
Br.—Marsh Thoroughbred Farm (Va)
Own.—Davis A — Tr.—Moschera Gasper S
112⁵ — Lifetime 67 12 15 9 $220,808 — 1984 14 2 4 3 $51,190 — 1983 13 1 4 1 $33,280 — Turf 33 8 12 5 $156,190

22Oct84- 7Bel fm 1 1/16 Ⓣ:48 1:12⅖ 1:42 3+ Alw 36000 6 2 24 32 36 35¾ Ward W A5 b 110 4.30 85-18 Jump Shot 1152¾ McCann 1153 Palace 1104¾ Tired 8
14Oct84- 2Bel fm 1⅜ Ⓣ:48 1:37⅘ 2:16 3+ Clm 45000 3 6 55 54½ 53½ 54½ Cruguet J b 117 *1.70 72-18 EsyChoice113nkElFntsm1173PuttingGren113hd L'ckd lt. response 9
7Oct84- 2Bel fm 1 Ⓣ:46 1:09⅘ 1:35⅖ 3+ Clm 75000 5 6 31½ 53¾ 66½ 65½ Ward W A5 b 107 6.10 83-17 Fatih 120¾ Aristocratical 122no Fearless Leader 114hd Weakened 7
29Sep84- 1Bel gd 1¼ Ⓣ:51⅖ 1:40⅖ 2:05⅕ 3+ Clm 175000 3 6 63½ 43½ 42½ 3¾ Cruguet J b 112 6.70 67-22 Broadway Harry 112¾ Balitou 116hd Palace 112nk Rallied 8
24Sep84- 2Bel fm 1 1/16 Ⓣ:46 1:10⅗ 1:42 3+ Clm 70000 3 4 53¾ 42½ 32 1nk Samyn J L b 113 11.30 86-20 Palace 113nk Fearless Leader 1171¾ Beagle 1131 Driving 12
10Sep84- 1Bel fm 1⅜ Ⓣ:49⅕ 1:38⅗ 2:17⅕ 3+ Clm c-40000 7 9 96½ 64 53 22¼ Cordero A Jr 119 *1.80 74-20 El Fantasma 1172¼ Palace 119nk Turn To Johnny 117no Gamely 11
25Aug84- 4Sar gd 1⅜ Ⓣ:50⅗ 1:41⅖ 2:20 3+ Clm 40000 8 8 86¾ 52 1½ 1nk Cordero A Jr 117 *1.20 68-32 Palace 117nk Pumas Pride 1132¼ Turn To Johnny 1171¼ Drivng 10
11Aug84- 2Sar fm 1⅛ Ⓣ:48 1:12 1:49⅘ 3+ Clm 40000 3 4 42 54 42½ 2hd Velasquez J 117 *2.10 78-22 Freon 117hd Palace 1172¼ Esprit De Romeo 112hd Game try 11
1Aug84- 2Sar fm 1 3/16 Ⓣ:48⅕ 1:12⅕ 1:55⅕ 3+ Clm 45000 4 7 75 64½ 33½ 21¼ Velasquez J 113 6.10 89-09 Lord Calvert 1171¼ Palace 1131¾ King Neptune 117½ Wide 11
8Jly84- 2Bel fst 1¼ :48⅘ 1:37⅕ 2:01⅘ 3+ Clm 35000 5 7 44 48 312 416¼ Samyn J L 117 6.40 73-15 Startop's Ace 1179 Share The Risk 1176½ HeroicSpirit119¾ Evenly 8
LATEST WORKOUTS Sep 22 Bel tr.t 4f fst :48⅕ h

Also Eligible (Not in Post Position Order):

Regal Humor * — Dk. b. or br. c. 3, by Regal and Royal—Funny Humor, by Diplomat Way
Br.—Farnsworth Farm (Fla)
Own.—Schoninger B — Tr.—Ribaudo Robert
114 — Lifetime 19 3 2 2 $48,950 — 1984 11 2 1 2 $38,800 — 1983 8 1 1 0 $10,150 — Turf 4 0 0 0 $1,750

11Oct84- 6Bel fst 1 1/16 :47⅗ 1:11⅘ 1:44⅕ 3+ Alw 25000 1 1 12 14 11½ 21½ Guerra W A b 114 2.30 79-26 Silver Stark 1141½ Regal Humor114hdBosunMate1162½ Weakened 5
28Sep84- 8Bel yl 1 1/16 Ⓣ:47 1:12⅖ 1:44⅘ 3+ Alw 25000 7 4 45 3½ 21½ 47¾ Guerra W A 113 12.70 64-36 Lutyens 1174¼ Go Go Regal 1132¼ NoMan'sLand1171¼ Ducked out 8
19Sep84- 8Bel fst 1 :46⅗ 1:11⅖ 1:36⅖ 3+ Alw 25000 7 4 44 31½ 22 34¾ Guerra W A 113 6.30 78-19 Steady Beat 1152¾ Exattic 1132 Regal Humor 1135 Weakened 7
3Sep84- 7Bel fm 7f Ⓣ:23⅕ :45⅖ 1:21⅘ 3+ Alw 33000 7 1 42 21½ 45½ 59¼ Guerra W A 111 23.10 85-14 Disco Count 1101¾ Paris Prince 1151¼ Fearless Leader1152¾ Tired 7
27May84- 8Bel fst 1⅛ :46 1:10⅕ 1:50 Peter Pan 3 5 53¼ 41¼ 4nk 53¾ Davis R G 117 8.70 73-20 BackBayBrrister1173GlintHour114nkRomnticTrdition114nk Evenly 9
27May84-Grade I
20May84- 6Bel fst 1 1/16 :46⅖ 1:10⅗ 1:42⅘ 3+ Alw 22000 7 3 2hd 2½ 1hd 1no Davis R G 110 3.30 88-18 RegalHumor110noGoGoRegal1132Spitlfields1101¾ Bumped, drvng 7
21Apr84- 3Aqu fst 1 :47⅗ 1:13⅖ 1:39⅕ Alw 21000 9 6 1½ 16 114 118½ Davis R G 117 7.80 70-30 Regal Humor 11718½ Mansei1172RunForRiver1171¾ Strong urging 9
7Mar84- 7Aqu fst 1 1/16 ⊡:49 1:13⅘ 1:45⅕ Alw 22000 7 6 65 43 44 46¼ Murphy D J5 112 10.50 80-17 Macho Devil 1072¼ Inner Force 1223 Greyfield 1171 Rallied 8
11Feb84- 9Hia fst 6f :22 :45⅗ 1:10⅕ Alw 14000 12 1 87¼ 710 1016 1119½ Rocco J b 121 26.00 72-09 Dinner Money 1211½ Earthmover 1151 FloridaDesign1151½ Outrun 12
24Jan84- 9Hia fst 1⅛ :47⅕ 1:11⅘ 1:49⅘ Alw 14000 4 2 2½ 1hd 22½ 34½ Maple E 120 4.70 78-19 CounterfeitMony1143½Gnomncltur1141RglHumor1204½ Weakened 12
LATEST WORKOUTS Oct 22 Bel tr.t 4f fst :49⅕ b ●Oct 8 Bel tr.t 4f fst :47⅕ h Sep 17 Bel 4f fst :48⅖ h Sep 12 Bel 4f fst :47⅗ h

Highest Star, who was crunched in the late betting down to 3–1, quickly established a long lead in the sixth and hung on despite bearing out through the stretch.

If Very Ultimate raised the possibility of an outside speed bias, and Nickolette confirmed those suspicions, the result of the seventh race established the existence of the bias beyond all doubt. Take a look at the eight contestants for this "nonwinners on three" allowance event switched to the main track by the heavy rains the day before:

On paper three horses—Fatih, Go Go Regal, and (possibly) Regal Humor—figured to contest quickly-run early fractions, so one might look for a closer to take advantage of the situation. Desert Chief, on the rail, was an unknown quantity from the Midwest. Broadway Harry, near the rail, had the bloodlines best suited to the muddy conditions. His sire, Big Spruce, a son of Herbager, enjoyed his greatest success over similar "day after" muddy conditions. The New York-breds, Stormy Puddles and Equity Kicker, appeared to be outclassed in open company. And Monkey Bread was a grass specialist who had won only once in twenty-one tries on dirt.

I decided to bet Broadway Harry and hope that jockey Octavio Vergara would quickly extricate the Allan Jerkens-charge from the rail. He didn't. Instead, Regal Humor, the outside speed, blew away Fatih, then Go Go Regal, and won as he pleased. A quick look at his recent record made the power of his performance hard to believe, unless the horse had been aided by a strong bias. Regal Humor and Go Go Regal had dueled head-to-head for a full mile and a sixteenth on May 20 at Belmont. More recently, Go Go Regal had outrun Regal Humor, at least in the early stages, on both September 19 and 28.

SEVENTH RACE
Aqueduct
OCTOBER 27, 1984

1 ⅛ MILES. (1.47) ALLOWANCE. Purse $25,000. 3–year–olds and upward which have never won three races other than Maiden, Claiming or Starter. Weights, 3–year–olds 119 lbs. Older 122 lbs. Non–winners of two races other than maiden or Claiming over a mile since September 15 allowed 3 lbs. Of such a race since then 5 lbs. (Originally carded to be run on turf.)

Value of race $25,000; value to winner $15,000; second $5,500; third $3,000; fourth $1,500. Mutuel pool $144,438, OTB pool $103,747. Exacta Pool $279,691. OTB Exacta Pool $180,415.

Last Raced	Horse	Eqt.A.Wt	PP	St	¼	½	¾	Str	Fin	Jockey	Odds $1
11Oct84 ^{6}Bel^{2}	Regal Humor	b 3 114	8	2	$2^{\frac12}$	3^{2}	1^{hd}	$1^{3\frac12}$	1^{2}	Guerra W A	3.80
13Oct84 ^{5}Kee^{1}	Desert Chief	3 116	1	6	6^{2}	$5^{1\frac12}$	5^{2}	3^{1}	$2^{1\frac12}$	Velez R I	14.50
20Oct84 ^{8}Bel^{5}	Broadway Harry	b 4 117	2	4	3^{hd}	4^{4}	$4^{2\frac12}$	$2^{1\frac12}$	3^{3}	Vergara O	3.40
11Oct84 ^{5}Bel^{3}	Equity Kicker	3 111	7	1	$7^{\frac12}$	7^{hd}	6^{4}	5^{3}	$4^{1\frac34}$	Ward W A^{5}	7.00
17Oct84 ^{7}Bel^{2}	Go Go Regal	b 3 114	5	5	4^{3}	1^{hd}	$3^{1\frac12}$	4^{1}	$5^{\frac34}$	Davis R G	3.50
17Oct84 ^{7}Bel^{6}	Monkey Bread	4 117	6	8	8	8	7^{6}	$6^{\frac12}$	$6^{9\frac14}$	Velasquez J	14.70
17Oct84 ^{7}Bel^{4}	Fatih	4 117	3	3	1^{1}	$2^{\frac12}$	2^{1}	7^{14}	$7^{4\frac12}$	Cruguet J	3.10
8Oct84 ^{8}FL^{8}	Stormy Puddles	4 117	4	7	5^{hd}	$6^{\frac12}$	8	8	8	Santagata N	15.50

OFF AT 3:53, Start good, Won driving. Time, :24, :47⅖, 1:10⅘, 1:35⅗, 1:48⅘ Track muddy.

$2 Mutuel Prices:			
9–(J)–REGAL HUMOR	9.60	6.20	3.80
2–(A)–DESERT CHIEF		14.60	7.20
3–(B)–BROADWAY HARRY			4.00

$2 EXACTA 9–2 PAID $89.00.

Dk. b. or br. c, by Regal and Royal—Funny Humor, by Diplomat Way. Trainer Ribaudo Robert. Bred by Farnsworth Farm (Fla).

REGAL HUMOR, close up early, reached the front from the outside on the far turn and after drawing away was under pressure to hold sway. DESERT CHIEF moved around horses leaving the far turn, altered course to the inside of BROADWAY HARRY and finished with good energy. BROADWAY HARRY came out while moving approaching the stretch but lacked the needed late response. EQUITY KICKER failed to be a serious factor. GO GO REGAL moved through along the inside to gain a narrow advantage after going a half, raced forwardly until near the stretch and gave way. FATIH tired badly. BROADWAY HARRY raced with mud calks.

Regal Humor's record itself did not suggest soundness. After returning from a seven-week layoff with an eighteen-length "laugher" on April 21, then edging Go Go Regal a month later, Regal Humor raced in contention to the stretch call in the Peter Pan before fading, losing the place by less than a length—and then disappeared for the entire summer. After returning to the races with a promising performance at seven furlongs on September 3, Regal Humor appeared to have tried—and failed—in each of his three subsequent starts. The "ducked out" comment on September 28 seemed to confirm my suspicions of unsoundness. The surprise early speed on October 11, so often a sign of improvement, appeared counterfeit. The first half mile of that race had been run in exceptionally slow time for allowance runners, yet Regal Humor could not take advantage of a clever front-running ride from Walter Guerra.

All the evidence added up to the fact that Regal Humor was neither especially sharp nor on the improving side of his form cycle. Yet the bias made him seem to be both. Obviously the bias was strong.

How, then, to play the Champagne? I had no interest in Mighty

Appealing at 2–5 odds, especially with those front bandages, in spite of his having the bias completely in his favor. If Mighty Appealing were to be beaten, though, he would have to be challenged early, and his most likely adversary appeared to be Keepayourmouthshut, from his rail post. That would open a slot on the rail for Tank's Prospect, allowing him to save ground, and consequently lose all chance, while fighting the bias.

8 AQUEDUCT

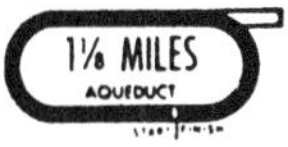

1⅛ MILES. (1.47) 113th Running THE CHAMPAGNE (Grade I). Purse $250,000 added. (Plus $50,000 Breeders' Cup Premium Awards.) 2-year-olds. Weights, 122 lbs. By subscription of $500 each, which should accompany the nomination, $4,000 to pass the entry box, with $25,000 added. The added money and all fees to be divided 60% to the winner, 22% to second, 12% to third and 6% to fourth. Starters to be named at the closing time of entries. The New York Racing Association to add The Champagne Challenge Cup, to be won three times, not necessarily consecutively, by the same owner before becoming his or her property. The owner of the winner will also receive a trophy for permanent possission and trophies will be presented to the winning trainer and jockey. Closed Wednesday, October 10, 1984 with 23 nominations.

Keepayourmouthshut — Gr. c. 2, by Silent Dignity—Marked Miss, by No Robbery — Lifetime 8 2 3 0 $21,040 — 1984 8 2 3 0 $21,040
Br.—Graves J H IV (Ky)
Own.—Schwartz B K — Tr.—Jerkens Steven T — 122

4Oct84- 6Med fst 6f :22⅘ :46⅘ 1:12⅘ Alw 12000 4 6 66¾ 43 1½ 1¼ Ward W A5 109 3.60 80-20 Kprmthsht109¼ThJk'sOnY1172½DstntOrbt1141¾ Forced out st.clr 7
11Sep84- 5Med fst 6f :22⅘ :46⅘ 1:12⅕ Md 45000 5 2 3½ 12 14 19¾ Ward W A5 111 *.80 81-20 Keepayourmouthshut1119¾LeWigg118noTigershrk1202 Ridden out 6
31Aug84- 4Bel fst 6f :23 :46⅗ 1:11 Md 50000 3 6 68½ 57¼ 45 43¾ Ward W A5 113 *1.50 83-13 Stonewhite 1091½ Scholastic 1141Jal sInTime1181½ Mild response 11
15Aug84- 4Sar fst 5f :22 :45⅘ :58⅘ Md Sp Wt 1 6 915 614 610 510 Cordero A Jr 118 2.10 87-14 Twin Rocket 118¾ Strike Up 1188 Nordance 1181½ Evenly 10
20Jun84- 8Bel fst 5½f :22⅘ :46⅗ 1:05⅘ Juvenile 7 7 109½ 913 911 79¼ Hernandez R 113 24.00 78-18 SkyCommand1152½MoonProspector1151DoItAginDn1131¾ Outrun 10
15Jun84- 4Bel fst 5½f :23⅕ :46⅗ 1:05⅘ Md c-60000 7 1 1hd 1hd 2½ 21½ Ward W A5 113 *1.00 85-18 GoldnChf1181½Kpyourmouthsht1137Kits'Nsh114no Altered course 9
30May84- 4Bel sly 5f :23 :46⅕ :58⅘ Md 50000 5 2 11½ 11½ 11½ 2¾ Migliore R 118 *1.70 92-20 Bay Guy 118¾ Keepayourmouthshut1189TopTalk1181½ Drifted out 8
26Apr84- 3Kee fst 4½f :22⅘ :46⅘ :53⅕ Md Sp Wt 10 2 2½ 21½ 21½ Bryan M W 118 18.20 87-11 Helen'sBirdie1181½Kpyourmouthshut1183StormScop118¾ Gamely 11
LATEST WORKOUTS Oct 25 Aqu 5f fst 1:00 h Oct 20 Bel 1 fst 1:45⅖ b Sep 30 Bel 7f fst 1:32 b Sep 23 Bel tr.t 6f fst 1:17 b

Tank's Prospect — B. c. 2, by Mr Prospector—Midnight Pumpkin, by Pretense — Lifetime 4 1 1 1 $69,275 — 1984 4 1 1 1 $69,275
Br.—Seltzer E A (Ky)
Own.—Klein E V — Tr.—Lukas D Wayne — 122

18Oct84- 8Med fst 1⅛ :46 1:11⅕ 1:45 Yng America 9 9 714 77¼ 56 31 MacBeth D 119 16.00 83-22 Script Ohio 119¾ Spend ABuck122nkTank'sProspect1192 Fin. well 11
18Oct84-Grade I
5Oct84- 6SA fst 6f :22⅘ :45⅘ 1:10⅘ Md Sp Wt 6 7 67¾ 66½ 32 13½ Delahoussaye E 117 4.80 85-16 Tank'sProspect1173½Chieftain'sClass1171¾QualityJet117½ Handily 9
11Jly84- 4Hol fst 6f :22⅘ :46 1:11⅕ Md Sp Wt 6 6 63¼ 43½ 43 22¼ Valenzuela P A 116 8.20 78-16 Metronomic 1162¼ Tank's Prospect 116no Royal Olympia 116¾ 9
1Jly84- 6Hol fst 5½f :22⅘ :45⅕ 1:04⅘ Md Sp Wt 3 8 76½ 68¼ 69½ 56¾ Valenzuela P A 116 13.80 81-16 Lomax 1164 Royal Olympia 116¾ Michadilla 1161½ 8
LATEST WORKOUTS Oct 13 SA 7f fst 1:29⅘ h Sep 30 SA 5f fst 1:01⅖ h Sep 25 SA 5f fst 1:01 h Sep 17 Dmr 5f sly 1:03⅘ h

Alfred — B. c. 2, by Our Liberty—Lecanto Bolina, by Southern Brook — Lifetime 4 3 0 0 $30,463 — 1984 4 3 0 0 $30,463
Br.—Abel R L (Fla)
Own.—Hinson A L — Tr.—Hinson Al W — 122

10Oct84- 9Crc fst 170 :48⅕ 1:13⅘ 1:45⅘ Alw 20800 4 5 53½ 1hd 13 113½ Molina V H b 112 *1.50 81-23 Alfred 11213½ Mr. Introienne 1121 Hopalong Justice11211 Handily 5
12Sep84- 9Crc fst 7f :22⅘ :46⅗ 1:25⅗ Foolish Plsr 3 5 31½ 31½ 44 46½ Smith A Jr 116 4.40 83-20 EmergencyCll1184½Bobbin'sKey116nkMr.Introinn1161½ Weakened 7
15Aug84- 2Crc fst 6f :22⅘ :46⅕ 1:13⅘ Alw 13400 9 3 85¼ 71¾ 3½ 11½ Smith A Jr 116 7.10 82-22 Alfred 1161½PlatinumProspect114nkHickoryHillFlyer1181½ Driving 9
8Aug84- 4Crc fst 6f :22⅘ :47⅗ 1:15⅕ Md 25000 6 11 610 66 2½ 12½ Wagers P 116 16.70 75-23 Alfred 1162½ Cherokee D'Or 1164 Prince Case 1161½ Drew clear 11
LATEST WORKOUTS Oct 18 Crc 1⅛m fst 1:58 b ●Oct 3 Crc 1 fst 1:43 h Sep 28 Crc 1 fst 1:46 b Sep 22 Crc 5f sly 1:04⅗ b

Do It Again Dan — Dk. b. or br. c. 2, by Mr Leader—Bimbo Sue, by Our Michael — Lifetime 11 3 2 3 $86,174 — 1984 11 3 2 3 $86,174
Br.—Edgehill Farm (Ky)
Own.—Edgehill Farm — Tr.—Perlsweig Mark — 122

18Oct84- 8Med fst 1⅛ :46 1:11⅕ 1:45 Yng America 1 7 814 67 711 68¾ Velasquez J 119 7.10 75-22 Script Ohio 119¾ Spend ABuck122nkTank'sProspect1192 Steadied 11
18Oct84-Grade I
6Oct84- 8Bel fst 1 :45⅗ 1:10⅗ 1:36⅗ Cowdin 8 6 65½ 38 410 419¾ Cordero A Jr b 122 10.80 62-17 Chief's Crown 1226BionicLight12212½ScriptOhio1221¼ Raced wide 8
6Oct84-Grade I
22Sep84- 6Med fst 6f :22⅘ :45⅘ 1:11 Ⓡ Comet 2 4 33 2½ 1½ 14 Velasquez J b 112 *1.00 87-18 Do It Again Dan 1124 Vindaloo 1126 I'm A Rutabaga 1125 Driving 5
8Sep84- 3Med fst 6f :22⅘ :45⅘ 1:10⅘ Alw 12000 3 1 34 21 11 11½ Velasquez J b 115 1.80 88-18 Do It Again Dan1151½FutureReality1187½Boutinierre1184½ Driving 5
26Aug84- 8Sar fst 6½f :21⅘ :44⅘ 1:16 Hopeful 6 2 75¼ 53½ 54½ 711¼ Miller D A Jr b 122 22.30 80-15 Chief's Crown 1223¾ Tiffany Ice1223¾Mugzy'sRullah122½ Brushed 9
26Aug84-Grade I
11Aug84- 9Mth fst 6f :22⅕ :45⅕ 1:10⅗ Sapling 5 4 77½ 56½ 47½ 35½ Miller D A Jr b 122 5.50 82-12 Doubly Clear 1221 Tiltalating 1194½ Do It Again Dan1221½ Rallied 10
11Aug84-Grade II
3Aug84- 8Sar fst 6f :22⅘ :46 1:10⅕ Sar Spec'l 6 1 55 42 32½ 22¾ Miller D A Jr b 117 7.30 86-19 Chief's Crown 1172¾DoItAgainDan117hdSkyCommand122¾ Rallied 6
3Aug84-Grade II
18Jly84- 9Mth sly 5f :22⅘ :45⅘ :58 Md Sp Wt 6 1 2hd 2hd 1½ 12 Miller D A Jr b 118 *.80 96-17 Do It Again Dan 1182FutureReality1138DiamondRich1181 Driving 11
20Jun84- 8Bel fst 5½f :22⅘ :46⅗ 1:05⅘ Juvenile 6 5 54½ 44 43 33½ Davis R G b 113 4.10e 83-18 SkyCommand1152½MoonProspector1151DoItAgainDan1131¾ Wide 10
8Jun84- 5Mth fst 5f :22 :45⅖ :58 Md Sp Wt 5 2 22 21½ 22 2nk Vega A b 118 *1.30e 96-19 JonIan118nkDoItAgainDan1187RunningMemories1183 Just missed 10
LATEST WORKOUTS ●Oct 17 Med 3f fst :35 h ●Oct 5 Med 3f fst :35 h

For Certain Doc — Dk. b. or br. c. 2, by Doc Sylvester—For Certain, by In Reality — Lifetime 13 2 2 1 $31,749 — 1984 13 2 2 1 $31,749 — Turf 3 1 0 1 $21,459
Br.—Parr E Q (Ky)
Own.—Chuck P — Tr.—DeBonis Thomas A — 122

20Oct84- 1Bel fm 1⅛ Ⓣ:47⅘ 1:11⅘ 1:43⅘ To Market 3 3 32 42 34½ 34¾ Davis R G b 117 5.90 79-12 Danger's Hour 1151 Quintile 1153¾ForCertainDoc1171¼ Weakened 7
20Oct84-Run in divisions
30Sep84- 7Bel fm 1 Ⓣ:45⅘ 1:10⅘ 1:36⅘ Donut King 2 3 34 34 44 43¾ Davis R G b 117 4.50 78-27 WesternChamp117½Don'tFoolWithMe1173JonIan122nk Weakened 10
20Sep84- 8Bel fm 1⅛ Ⓣ:46⅘ 1:11⅘ 1:44 Alw 21000 6 2 21 21 1½ 13½ Davis R G b 117 25.40 76-24 ForCertinDoc1173½Mgnminous122¾McAtTheTrck117hd Drew clear 6
1Sep84- 7Bel fst 6f :22⅘ :45⅘ 1:10⅕ Alw 20000 5 7 67½ 78 713 717½ Zuniga M b 117 33.60 73-13 Ziggy's Boy 1172½ Full of Spice 1175¾ DesertWar1193¼ Slow start 7
16Aug84- 3Mth fst 5½f :22⅘ :46⅗ 1:05⅘ Md 50000 2 5 43½ 3nk 12 16 Zuniga M 118 1.70e 87-16 ForCertinDoc1186RcetrckRomo118¾Tigrshrk113nk Bore out, clear 7
2Aug84- 6Mth fst 6f :22⅘ :45⅘ 1:11⅗ Clm 40000 4 9 76¾ 79 59½ 49 Zuniga M 113 7.30e 74-20 I'm ARutabaga1082½NeatSam1136FootballCoach113½ Roughed st 9
26Jly84- 6Bel fst 6f :22⅘ :46⅕ 1:11⅘ Md Sp Wt 8 6 74½ 76¾ 69½ 613 Zuniga M 118 9.40e 71-17 Salem Drive 118¾ Anconeus 1181½ Haberdasher 1184 Outrun 10
13Jly84- 4Bel fst 5½f :23⅕ :47 1:05⅘ Md 35000 4 4 21 2½ 2½ 21¼ Zuniga M 114 4.80 86-15 First One Up 1181¼ ForCertainDoc1144LiberatedMan113¾ Gamely 8
5Jly84- 4Bel fst 5½f :23⅘ :47⅘ 1:06⅘ Md 25000 3 5 3½ 2hd 2hd 2nk Zuniga M 118 9.20 81-15 HndfulOfSteel118nkForCrtinDoc1182½AwsomIssu1163½ Driftd out 7
22Jun84- 4Bel fst 5½f :22⅕ :46⅕ 1:05⅘ Md Sp Wt 10 7 77¼ 1019 1028 1035¼ Migliore R b 118 85.60 52-21 Secretary General 1181 Chief'sCrown1181½TiffanyIce1189 Outrun 10
LATEST WORKOUTS Oct 18 Bel 3f fst :35⅘ h Oct 13 Bel 5f fst 1:01 h Oct 8 Bel 1 fst 1:43 b Sep 28 Bel 4f gd :47⅕ h

Mighty Appealing — Ch. c. 2, by Valid Appeal—Patsy's Lil Girl, by Roi Dagobert — Lifetime 3 3 0 0 $180,885 — 1984 3 3 0 0 $180,885
Br.—Ocala Stud Farms Inc (Fla)
Own.—Cohen I — Tr.—Gaudet Dean — 122

6Oct84- 8Lrl fst 1⅛ :46⅘ 1:12⅘ 1:43 Laurel Fty 6 6 63½ 63 1½ 12½ Smith G P 122 *1.60 93-15 MghtyAppIng1222½CtlssRlty122hdRhmnRl12210 Drifted out, drvng 12
6Oct84-Grade I
27Sep84- 6Lrl fst 7f :23 :46⅗ 1:24⅘ Alw 10500 1 1 1½ 12½ 16 19 Smith G P 117 *.60 87-22 Mighty Appealing 1179BanjoDancing11510BeaQuality1085 Handily 5
12Sep84- 5Lrl fst 6f :23⅘ :48⅕ 1:13⅘ Md Sp Wt 8 1 1hd 13 16 116 Smith G P 118 2.30 74-31 MightyAppeling11816Jok'nJoe118nkPutOutThFir1131½ Ridden out 11
LATEST WORKOUTS Oct 21 Lrl 7f fst 1:25⅕ b ●Oct 13 Lrl 7f fst 1:26 h ●Oct 3 Lrl 4f gd :48⅖ b Sep 22 Lrl 5f fst 1:02 b

Rather than back off a horse I really liked, I cut my bet and hoped that Velasquez would be aware of the biased conditions and quickly move his horse to the outside. He wasn't. By the time he did get off the rail the field had reached the final turn, and Tank's Prospect was a tired animal, weary from his early efforts fighting the deeper conditions along the inside. He was hardly the fresh closer, ready to move, as he might have been had he been on the outside all the way.

As luck would have it, Mighty Appealing quickly grabbed a clear lead, and with it the rail. Maryland-based jockey Greg Smith, unaware of the bias, had fallen into a trap that a wiser Velasquez could have exploited. Instead, it was the unheralded Marcel Zuniga, aboard the unappealing For Certain Doc, who moved up from close contention to wear down Mighty Appealing from the outside, nipping the favorite at the wire as the 28–1 longshot of the worst Champagne field in recent history.

EIGHTH RACE
Aqueduct
OCTOBER 27, 1984

1 ⅛ MILES. (1.47) 113th Running THE CHAMPAGNE (Grade I). Purse $250,000 added. (Plus $50,000 Breeders' Cup Premium Awards.) 2-year-olds. Weights, 122 lbs. By subscription of $500 each, which should accompany the nomination, $4,000 to pass the entry box, with $25,000 added. The added money and all fees to be divided 60% to the winner 22% to second, 12% to third and 6% to fourth. Starters to be named at the closing time of entries. The New York Racing Association to add The Champagne Challenge Cup, to be won three times, not necessarily consecutively, by the same owner before becoming his or her property. The owner of the winner will also receive a trophy for permanent possission and trophies will be presented to the winning trainer and jockey. Closed Wednesday, October 10, 1984 with 23 nominations. Breeders' Cup Fund Awards to: Mighty Appealing and Tank's Prospect.

Total purse $336,000. Value of race $304,000; value to winner $171,600; second $76,420; third $38,820; fourth $17,160 $30,000 Reverts to BCFA; $2,000 Nominator Awards. Mutuel pool $187,328, Minus show pool $5,842.67, OTB pool $140,482. Exac Pl $152,569 OTB Exac Pl $138,215 OTB Minus Pl $2,020.32

Last Raced	Horse	Eqt.A.Wt	PP	St	¼	½	¾	Str	Fin	Jockey	Odds $1
20Oct84 1Bel3	For Certain Doc	b 2 122	5	2	$2^{1\frac{1}{2}}$	3^{2}	$2^{\frac{1}{2}}$	2^{4}	1no	Zuniga M	28.60
6Oct84 8Lrl1	Mighty Appealing	2 122	6	1	$1^{\frac{1}{2}}$	1^{1}	1^{1}	$1^{\frac{1}{2}}$	2^{4}	Smith G	.40
18Oct84 8Med3	Tank's Prospect	2 122	2	3	5^{1}	4^{hd}	$4^{\frac{1}{2}}$	$4^{1\frac{1}{2}}$	3^{nk}	Velasquez J	3.00
18Oct84 8Med6	Do It Again Dan	2 122	4	5	$3^{\frac{1}{2}}$	$2^{2\frac{1}{2}}$	3^{2}	3^{1}	$4^{3\frac{1}{4}}$	Davis R G	10.50
4Oct84 6Med1	Keepayourmouthshut	2 122	1	4	4^{2}	$5^{\frac{1}{2}}$	$5^{1\frac{1}{2}}$	5^{4}	$5^{4\frac{3}{4}}$	Ward W A	15.20
10Oct84 9Crc1	Alfred	b 2 122	3	6	6	6	6	6	6	Molina V H	8.90

OFF AT 4:28 Start good, Won driving. Time, :24⅖, :48⅕, 1:12⅕, 1:36⅖, 1:49⅕ Track muddy.

$2 Mutuel Prices:			
5-(E)-FOR CERTAIN DOC	59.20	8.40	2.10
6-(F)-MIGHTY APPEALING		2.60	2.10
2-(B)-TANK'S PROSPECT			2.10

$2 EXACTA 5-6 PAID $200.80.

Dk. b. or br. c, by Doc Sylvester—For Certain, by In Reality. Trainer DeBonis Thomas A. Bred by Parr E Q (Ky)

FOR CERTAIN DOC, prominent early, was eased back entering the backstretch, moved up along the inside approaching the far turn, came out between horses to go after MIGHTY APPEALING and was under pressure to be up in the final stride. MIGHTY APPEALING saved ground while making the pace, settled into the stretch with a narrow advantage and just failed to last in a stiff drive. TANK'S PROSPECT moved within striking distance midway of the far turn, came over in front of KEEPAYOURMOUTHSHUT near the final sixteenth but failed to seriously menace. DO IT AGAIN DAN moved closest to MIGHTY APPEALING from the outside entering the backstretch, raced forwardly until near the stretch and weakened. KEEPAYOURMOUTHSHUT saved ground to no avail and was steadied behind TANK'S PROSPECT nearing the final sixteenth. A foul claim against TANK'S PROSPECT by the rider of KEEPAYOURMOUTHSHUT for alleged interfernce leaving the furlong grounds, was not allowed. ALFRED was always outrun. KEEPAYOURMOUTHSHUT raced with mud caulks.

Tank's Prospect came out of the Champagne to run a strong second to champion Chief's Crown in the Breeders' Cup Juvenile, an effort that certainly would have taken the Champagne. The result of that race further emphasized the power a track bias can exert over the form of even top-class animals.

Not surprisingly, For Certain Doc came back to run absolutely last in the Remsen Stakes at Aqueduct, at 9–1 odds. Obviously few of the smart bettors at Aqueduct were unaware of the conditions that produced his surprise victory in the Champagne.

As a postscript, we quote from Mike Watchmaker's column in the January 26, 1985 *Racing Form:*

> Right now, Regal Humor is in the kind of form he figured to be in over the summer, but Ribaudo stopped on his Regal And Royal colt and freshened him instead. "I ran him in the Peter Pan last spring (in which Regal Humor was a relatively close fifth to Back Bay Barrister) and he came up empty in the race," Ribaudo recalled. "I gave him the summer and he trained very well at Saratoga. When he came back at Belmont, he made winning moves in his races, but would then veer in or out and lose interest. His mind just wasn't in it. I put the blinkers on him for that reason, and they've made a big difference mentally."

The October 27 race was at least the third time Regal Humor raced with the hood. Most certainly, the blinkers helped the horse, for he went on to win twice in his next three starts with blinkers, including a victory in the Edison Handicap at the Meadowlands, with a third-place finish in the Roamer at Aqueduct his only loss. But surely the bias didn't hurt his chances on October 27.

Many trainers (and a few jockeys, too) simply don't believe in track biases. Bobby Ribaudo, Regal Humor's trainer, is apparently among the enlightened. We quote again from the same article:

> "What happened in the Roamer was strictly my doing," Regal Humor's trainer Bobby Ribaudo admitted Friday morning. "If you remember, that day most everything was winning from off the pace. And, it was Regal Humor's first time going the distance and running with Fight Over early didn't figure to do him much good. So I told Robbie Davis to take him back. As it turns out, Fight Over also took back early and got a perfect trip, while Regal Humor was climbing early. But he came on and I thought he ran well."

Handicapping horses is a difficult proposition at best, all the more so because of the numerous human personalities that are part of the equation. When the serious player reads an article like this, he files away the useful piece of information that trainer Ribaudo is attuned to track biases, and will probably keep his riders aware of these conditions. His horses can be bet without undue fear on days when track biases are dictating the results of races.

Chapter 36

The California Connection

KNOWING WHERE ONE'S TRACK (or circuit) fits into the national scheme of things is one of the keys to the proper evaluation of shippers. Does the invader come from a stronger circuit? A weaker one? How do shippers from that circuit fare on the local scene? Has the trainer shipped in successfully in the past? These are all significant questions the successful player must and will be able to answer.

In recent years the entire country has become aware of California's predominant position on the racing scene. Shippers from Los Angeles have, on numerous occasions, sacked New York and captured its traditional fixtures. It was not always so.

During the 1970s, though, New Yorkers witnessed a springtime "California Connection" of striking proportions. Horses returning to New York from Los Angeles in late winter or early spring would win immediately in New York, no matter how awful their West Coast form. Whether it was the cool breezes off Jamaica Bay, the smog in Los Angeles, or simply softer competition in New York, California form seemed to translate at a significantly higher level to New York. This pattern repeated year after year, mostly with allowance horses, although the number of these shippers has declined in recent years now that fewer New York outfits winter on the West Coast.

The results of two sprint stakes at Aqueduct early in 1985 rekindled memories of those good old days. On February 18, Fighting Fit arrived in New York for the Sporting Plate Handicap.

The six-year-old was an accomplished stakes winner on the West Coast, with lifetime earnings in excess of $700,000. He had finished a rallying third as second choice in the Breeders' Cup

8 AQUEDUCT

6 FURLONGS INNER DIRT TRACK AQUEDUCT

6 FURLONGS. (InnerDirt). (1.08⅖) 11th Running THE SPORTING PLATE HANDICAP. $60,000 added. 3-year-olds and upward. By subscription of $100 each, which should accompany the nomination; $1,000 to pass the entry box, with $60,000 added. The added money and all fees to be divided 60% to the winner, 22% to second, 12% to third and 6% to fourth. Weights Wednesday, February 13. Starters to be named at the closing time of entries. A trophy will be presented to the winning owner. Closed with 23 nominations Wednesday, January 30, 1985.

Coupled—Entropy and Eskimo.

Muskoka Wyck *

B. h. 6, by Tentam—Lachesis, by Iron Ruler
Br.—Marydel Farm (Md)
Tr.—Greene Thomas M
Own.—Rapetti A A
117
Lifetime 38 9 14 3 $318,203 | 1985 2 1 0 1 $32,522 | 1984 12 1 5 1 $104,743 | Turf 1 0 0 0

27Jan85- 8Aqu fst 6f ⊡:22⅕ :45⅗ 1:10⅕ Coaltown 6 1 11 11 1hd 14 Ward W A b 114 5.60 93-20 DH Entropy 1234 DH Muskoka Wyck 1144 Main Stem 1173¾ Driving 6
27Jan85-Dead heat
12Jan85- 8Bow fst 6f :21⅘ :44⅕ 1:09⅘ 3+S Maryland H 8 6 32 22½ 33½ 33 Kaenel J L b 115 4.90 91-14 SalvageConsultant1111Amanti1152MuskokaWyck115no Weakened 8
23Dec84- 8Aqu fst 6f ⊡:21⅘ :44⅗ 1:09⅗ 3+Gravesend H 4 7 45½ 56 56¾ 58½ Davis R G b 116 16.70 88-17 Elegant Life 115no Tarantara 1203 Top Avenger 126½ Sluggish st 8
13Dec84- 6Med fst 6f :22⅗ :45⅖ 1:10 3+Alw 25000 1 5 3½ 3½ 43½ 42¾ Cordero A Jr b 115 1.30 89-20 Top Avenger 117¾AmericanDiabolo117Habitonia115hd Weakened 5
25Nov84- 8Aqu fst 6f :22 :45⅗ 1:10⅘ 3+Sport Pg H 12 4 1½ 1hd 1hd 2nk Bailey J D b 114 15.00 87-25 Tarantara 117nkMuskokaWyck114nkNewConnection1131½ Gamely 13
25Nov84-Grade III
6Nov84- 7Aqu fst 6f :22⅗ :45⅗ 1:10⅗ 3+Alw 33000 2 4 41½ 53¾ 33½ 41¾ Bailey J D b 117 2.30 87-20 Rollin on Over 117¾ Chas Conerly 115nk Tenifly 117¾ Weakened 7
20Oct84- 7Bel fst 7f :22⅕ :45 1:22 3+Vosburgh 1 5 32 44 711 715 Guerra W A b 126 — — 77-17 TrackBarron1233½TimelessNative1263¾Raj'sShrk1231½ Tired badly 9
20Oct84-Grade I; Raced for purse money only
23Sep84- 8Bel fst 6f :22⅕ :45⅗ 1:10⅘ 3+Fall Hiwt H 12 8 51¾ 2hd 2hd 32¾ Guerra W A b 131 24.40 88-19 Mamaison1301TimelessNative1381¾MuskokWyck1312½ Weakened 12
23Sep84-Grade II
12Sep84- 7Bel fst 7f :23 :45⅗ 1:22⅘ 3+Alw 33000 3 5 2½ 2hd 21 2¾ Guerra W A b 119 *.90 87-14 Basket Weave 111¾ Muskoka Wyck 119nk Eminency 1151 Gamely 7
2Sep84- 8Bel fst 6f :22⅗ :45⅗ 1:09⅘ 3+Boojum H 7 4 32 3½ 32 21¾ Day P b 115 *1.20 94-17 Tarantara 1111¾ Muskoka Wyck 1151½ Cannon Shell 117¾ Gamely 8
2Sep84-Grade III

LATEST WORKOUTS ●Feb 15 Aqu ⊡ 4f fst :48⅘ b ●Jan 24 Aqu ⊡ 4f fst :45⅘ h Jan 9 Bel tr.t 5f fst 1:02⅘ b ●Dec 20 Med 3f my :35 h

Main Stem

Ch. h. 7, by Clem—Whale Tail, by Knave
Br.—Willwerth G & Sandra (Va)
Tr.—Sedlacek Sue
Own.—Tresvant Stable
110
Lifetime 100 16 19 15 $480,467 | 1985 4 1 1 1 $42,228 | 1984 17 3 3 2 $92,535 | Turf 6 0 0 0 $3,931

10Feb85- 5Aqu fst 6f ⊡:22⅘ :46 1:10 Alw 36000 3 5 3½ 1½ 1½ 1nk Garrido O L5 b 112 2.30 94-18 Main Stem 112nk Eskimo 1102 Talc Power 1152¾ Driving 5
27Jan85- 8Aqu fst 6f ⊡:22⅕ :45⅗ 1:10⅕ Coaltown 3 5 53 34 35 34 Thibeau R J b 117 9.10 89-20 DH Entropy 1234 DH Muskoka Wyck1144MainStem1173¾ No threat 6
18Jan85- 8Aqu fst 6f ⊡:22⅗ :45⅘ 1:10⅗ Handicap 4 7 64½ 56 51¾ 2hd Thibeau R J b 112 9.00 91-21 Sluggard 111hd Main Stem 112½ Leroy S. 117½ Wide 7
12Jan85- 8Aqu fst 6f ⊡:22⅘ :45⅘ 1:10⅗ 3+Paumonok H 4 6 45 54½ 56½ 45¾ Thibeau R J b 109 20.30 86-24 Entropy 114¾ Don Rickles 1103 Elegant Life 1162 Even try 7
31Dec84- 5Med fst 6f :23 :46 1:10⅗ 3+Alw 25000 5 3 31½ 42½ 42 1½ Corpes M A5 b 110 4.20 89-22 Main Stem 110½ Northern Ice 1151½ Faces Up 122¾ Driving 7
13Dec84- 8Aqu fst 6f ⊡:22⅗ :45⅘ 1:10⅕ 3+Handicap 4 6 53 53½ 57 55½ Guerra W A b 110 11.10 87-19 Entropy1132¾EliteSyncopation107noGen'lPractitioner1173 Outrun 6
24Nov84- 7Key fst 7f :22⅘ :46 1:23⅘ 3+Alw 16000 5 7 55 32 22 41½ Cole M A5 b 113 3.50 88-21 Quicksilver115hdGallntGentlemn1141½Dr.Kroy115hd Tried hear out 8
13Nov84- 8Med fst 170 :46⅘ 1:13⅕ 1:44⅘ 3+Alw 25000 6 3 2½ 1hd 34 411¾ Garrido O L7 b 112 2.20 66-28 Castle Guard 1192½ Bill Wheeler 1176½ Class Hero 1153 No threat 7
25Oct84- 8Med fst 6f :22⅗ :45⅗ 1:10⅗ 3+Alw 25000 3 5 33 610 45 47 Lopez V3 b 116 2.80 83-23 Fortunate Prospect 1142 Ringside1103RockyKnave1192 No threat 6
6Oct84- 8Med fst 6f :22⅗ :45 1:09⅘ 3+Chief Penk H 6 2 55 46 47½ 47½ Lopez V b 114 19.60 85-18 Eillo 1245 Introspective 1122½ Rollin on Over 114nk Evenly 6

Don Rickles

Blk. c. 4, by Icecapade—I Got My Reasons, by Forli
Br.—Gamble Jane A (Ky)
Tr.—Parisella John
Own.—Sabarese T M
109
Lifetime 17 4 6 0 $173,870 | 1985 3 0 2 0 $23,188 | 1984 10 2 3 0 $77,098 | Turf 2 0 0 0 $5,868

27Jan85- 8Aqu fst 6f ⊡:22⅕ :45⅗ 1:10⅕ Coaltown 1 3 43 57 612 612½ Venezia M b 114 3.70 81-20 DH Entropy 1234 DH Muskoka Wyck 1144 Main Stem 1173¾ Tired 6
12Jan85- 8Aqu fst 6f ⊡:22⅕ :45⅘ 1:10⅗ 3+Paumonok H 2 1 67 43½ 33 2¾ Venezia M b 110 *2.10e 91-24 Entropy 114¾ Don Rickles 1103 Elegant Life 1162 Gamely 7
5Jan85- 7Aqu fst 6f ⊡:22⅗ :46⅗ 1:09⅘ Alw 36000 6 2 11 1hd 2hd 21½ Cordero A Jr b 117 *1.50 94-17 Hagley's Reward 1151½ Don Rickles 1175Barcelona1151½ 2nd best 8
17Dec84- 8Aqu fst 170 ⊡:47⅗ 1:12⅘ 1:42⅘ 3+Alw 40000 5 1 11 1½ 2½ 22 Davis R G b 113 3.20 87-19 King's Swan 1152 Don Rickles 1133¼ High Honors115hd Game try 7
25Nov84- 8Aqu fst 6f :22 :45⅗ 1:10⅘ 3+Sport Pg H 10 8 109 88 74½ 63 Davis R G 112 12.30 84-25 Tarantara117nkMuskokWyck114nkNewConnection1131½ No threat 13
25Nov84-Grade III
10Nov84- 7Aqu fst 6f :22⅗ :45⅘ 1:11⅘ 3+Alw 25000 2 5 45 54 31½ 11¾ Davis R G 115 *1.80 84-23 Don Rickles 1151¾ Agile Jet 115hd Huckster 112hd Riddenout 6
27Aug84- 6Sar fm 1⅟₁₆ Ⓣ:47 1:11⅘ 1:43⅘ 3+Alw 25000 5 1 1hd 1½ 1½ 41¾ Cordero A Jr 112 2.40 77-17 Roman Bend117½HastetoFinish117¾NoMan'sLand117no Weakened 7
5Aug84- 2Sar fst 6f :22 :44⅘ 1:09⅘ 3+Alw 23000 5 2 2½ 2½ 32 23¾ Cordero A Jr b 112 *1.20 88-09 MajesticVenture1123¾DonRickles112¾GoGoRegl1121 Gained place 6
3Jun84- 8Bel sf 1⅟₁₆ Ⓣ:50⅘ 1:15 1:48⅘ Hill Prince 2 2 2½ 2½ 43 48¾ Bailey J D 123 7.50 45-46 A Gift 1141½ Is Your Pleasure 1264¾ Jesse's Hope 1172¾ Tired 7
3Jun84-Grade III
28May84- 9Key fst 1⅛ :47 1:11⅘ 1:49⅘ Pa Derby 1 1 11 1hd 65½ 69 Vergara O b 122 9.70 79-17 Morning Bob 122hdAtTheThreshold122¾ DH BiloxiIndian122 Tired 7
28May84-Grade II

LATEST WORKOUTS Jan 24 Bel tr.t 4f fst :48 h Dec 31 Bel tr.t 4f fst :49⅘ b

Entropy

Ch. h. 5, by What A Pleasure—Ta Wee, by Intentionally
Br.—Tartan Farms (Fla)
Tr.—Nerud Jan H
Own.—Tartan Stable
126
Lifetime 18 8 3 1 $228,629 | 1985 2 2 0 0 $70,832 | 1984 12 3 3 1 $120,597

27Jan85- 8Aqu fst 6f ⊡:22⅕ :45⅗ 1:10⅕ Coaltown 4 6 32 21 2hd 14 Bailey J D b 123⁴ *1.50 93-20 DH Entropy 1234 DH Muskoka Wyck 1144 Main Stem1173¾ Driving 6
27Jan85-Dead heat
12Jan85- 8Aqu fst 6f ⊡:22⅕ :45⅘ 1:10⅗ 3+Paumonok H 1 7 23 2hd 13 1¾ Bailey J D b 114 2.70 92-24 Entropy 114¾ Don Rickles 1103 Elegant Life 1162 Driving 7
13Dec84- 8Aqu fst 6f ⊡:22⅗ :45⅘ 1:10⅕ 3+Handicap 3 3 2½ 2hd 12 12½ Bailey J D b 113 *2.20 93-19 Entropy1132¾EliteSyncoption107noGn'lPrctitionr1173 Ridden out 6
8Sep84- 9Crc fst 6f :22⅗ :46⅕ 1:12 3+Miami B'ch H 11 10 1010 1011 74¾ 73 Smith A Jr b 117 3.80 88-19 I Really Will 120hd Mo Exception 120¾ElKaiser1121 Lacked room 11
31Aug84- 9Crc fst 6f :22⅗ :45⅗ 1:11⅘ 3+Alw 19200 3 5 42½ 41¾ 1hd 21 St Leon G b 116 *1.80 92-19 Mo Exception 1181 Entropy 1162 Chief Steward 1141 Weakened 6
7Jly84- 9Crc fst 7f :22⅘ :45⅘ 1:23⅘ 3+Broward H 1 8 62¾ 43½ 47½ 911¾ St Leon G b 117 5.40 85-15 Opening Lead 1175½ Harry 'N Bill 110hd Mo Exception 1111 Tired 12
11Jun84- 9Crc fst 6½f :22⅕ :45⅘ 1:19 3+Alw 16000 3 8 67 45½ 2hd 22¾ St Leon G b 122 *1.20 87-19 Fort Guard 1162¾ Entropy 1224 Harry 'N Bill 1181 Best of others 8
5May84- 8Aqu fst 7f :22⅗ :44⅘ 1:21⅘ 3+Carter H 5 9 65½ 53½ 53¾ 65 Cruguet J b 115 23.80 87-16 Bet Big 115½ Cannon Shell 109no A Phenomenon 1262¾ Tired 10
5May84-Grade II
20Apr84- 8Aqu fst 6f :22⅗ :45⅘ 1:09⅘ 3+Boldruler H 1 8 75 56 44½ 45 Cruguet J b 121 9.10 87-28 Top Avenger 1213½ BelieveTheQueen1191AuPoint123¾ Went wide 10
20Apr84-Grade III
11Mar84- 8Aqu fst 6f ⊡:21⅘ :45⅘ 1:10⅗ 3+Toboggan H 3 3 2hd 1hd 2½ 42 MacBeth D b 114 *1.80 90-23 Top Avenger 1201¾ Main Stem 109½ Elegant Life116hd Weakened 9
11Mar84-Grade III

LATEST WORKOUTS Feb 7 Bel tr.t 4f fst :52⅕ bg Jan 4 Bel tr.t 4f fst :48⅘ h Dec 30 Bel tr.t 4f gd :51⅘ b (d) Dec 23 Bel tr.t 4f fst :49⅘ b

Elegant Life *

Dk. b. or br. h. 5, by Distinctive—Life, by Bold Hour
Br.—Koerner J H (NY)
Tr.—Brice Michael
Own.—Brice Irma
115
Lifetime 45 11 7 9 $397,018 | 1985 1 0 0 1 $8,328 | 1984 19 5 3 3 $211,226 | Turf 1 0 0 0

Entered 17Feb85- 8 AQU
12Jan85- 8Aqu fst 6f ⊡:22⅕ :45⅘ 1:10⅗ 3+Paumonok H 3 4 35 33 44½ 33¾ Davis R G b 116 3.50 88-24 Entropy 114¾ Don Rickles 1103 Elegant Life 1162 Even try 7
23Dec84- 8Aqu fst 6f ⊡:21⅘ :44⅗ 1:09⅗ 3+Gravesend H 8 1 33½ 34½ 3½ 1no Velasquez J b 115 2.90 97-17 Elegant Life 115no Tarantara 1203 Top Avenger 126½ Driving 8
12Dec84- 8Aqu fst 6f ⊡:22⅗ :45⅘ 1:10⅕ 3+SJoe Palmer 7 1 2hd 1hd 12 14 Velasquez J b 119 *2.10 93-20 Elegant Life 1194 Mugatea 122hd Shadowmar 1191 Ridden out 10
11Oct84- 8Bel fst 6f :22⅗ :46 1:10⅕ 3+Handicap 7 2 21 1hd 11½ 11½ Cruguet J b 112 10.60 91-26 Elegant Life 1121½ Shifty Sheik 1171½ Cannon Shell122¼ Driving 7
23Sep84- 8Bel fst 6f :22⅕ :45⅗ 1:10⅘ 3+Fall Hiwt H 1 7 119¾129¾ 97¾ 87 Velasquez J b 125 14.90 84-19 Mamison1301TimelessNtive1381¾MuskokWyck1312½ Stumbled st 12
23Sep84-Grade II
5Sep84- 8Bel fst 1⅟₁₆ :45⅘ 1:09⅘ 1:41⅘ 3+SHudson H 7 2 2½ 2hd 21½ 23½ Velasquez J b 124 *1.90 92-12 Restless Feet 1123½ Elegant Life 1241¾ MusicPrince117no Gamely 9
23Aug84- 7Sar sly 6½f :21⅘ :44⅘ 1:15⅘ 3+Alw 33000 2 2 43 42½ 44½ 47 Velasquez J b 119 *1.80 89-22 Concorde Bound 1135¾ RapidGray1191½StopCard115hd No excuse 5
29Jly84- 8Bel fst 1⅟₁₆ :45⅘ 1:09⅘ 1:42⅘ 3+SEvanShipman 1 3 2hd 2hd 2hd 2hd Velasquez J b 119 *1.40 90-15 Mugatea 119hd Elegant Life 1195 Jan's Kinsman 12310½ Sharp try 6
7Jly84- 7Bel sly 6½f :21⅘ :44⅘ 1:16 3+Alw 33000 8 5 65½ 64½ 33 1½ Velasquez J b 117 9.50 96-16 Elegant Life 117½ Chan Balum 1151½ Tarantara 1171½ Driving 9
23Jun84- 7Bel fm 6f Ⓣ:22 :45⅗ 1:09⅘ 3+Alw 33000 2 10 1212 1218 1215 1113½ Hernandez R 119 17.20 79-18 Sitzmark 1171½ Meru 1171½ Rollin on Over 117½ Outrun 12

LATEST WORKOUTS ●Feb 11 Bel tr.t 3f fst :35 h Feb 5 Bel tr.t 4f fst :49⅘ b

Fighting Fit *

Ch. h. 6, by Full Pocket—Napalm, by Nilo
Br.—Nuckols Bros (Ky)
Tr.—Frankel Robert
Own.—Moss Mr-Mrs J S
118
Lifetime 43 11 6 7 $701,970 | 1985 1 0 0 0 $2,500 | 1984 12 2 3 3 $331,250 | Turf 2 0 0 0

13Jan85- 8SA fst 7f :22⅕ :44⅘ 1:21⅘ San Carlosh 2 5 67 66 55 56½ Delahoussaye E b 118 2.70 86-13 DebonireJunior125¾TennesseeRit1122½FiftySixInRow1161½ Outrun 6
13Jan85-Grade II
30Dec84- 8SA gd 6f :22 :45⅘ 1:10⅕ Palos Vrds H 2 7 1hd 1hd 46 713½ Lipham T b 119 2.90 73-16 DebonaireJunior1204½ChargingFalls1125Premiership117¾ Stopped 7
22Dec84- 8Hol fst 1 :44⅘ 1:09⅘ 1:35⅘ 3+N Diver H 3 3 33 22¾ 22½ 2nk Delahoussaye E b 118 2.50 98-10 Lord At War 120nk Fighting Fit 118¾ Video Kid1185½ Just missed 6
22Dec84-Grade III
1Dec84- 8Hol fst 6f :22 :45⅕ 1:10 3+Sprnt Chmp 8 3 77½ 77½ 55 53¾ Delahoussaye E b 118 *.70 95-03 Lovlier Linda 1211½ Sonrie Jorge116nkFaliTime1221½ Forced wide 9
1Dec84-Grade III; Run in Divisions
24Nov84- 7Hol sly 7f :21⅘ :44⅘ 1:22⅘ 3+Alw 45000 1 6 55¾ 41½ 12 17 Delahoussaye E b 117 *.80 96-07 Fighting Fit 1177Sam'sTable1152¾Mr.PrimeMinister115hd Handily 9
10Nov84- 3Hol fst 6f :22⅘ :45⅗ 1:10⅕ 3+Br Cp Sprnt 11 9 118½ 76½ 56 31½ Delahoussaye E b 126 2.70 — — Eillo 126no Commemorate 1241½ Fighting Fit 1262½ Rallied wide 11
10Nov84-Grade I
20Oct84- 7SA fst 6f :22 :44⅘ 1:08⅘ 3+Alw 45000 5 4 72¾ 54 54½ 33½ Delahoussaye E b 122 *1.00 91-13 SharperOne119½ChargingFalls1153FightingFit1221½ Steadied 3/8's 7

10Jun84- 8Hol fst 1⅛ :47⅘ 1:11 1:47⅗ 3↑Californ'n 4 4 3^1 $3^{1½}$ $6^{6¾}$ $8^{12¼}$ McCarron C J b 120 12.80 78-17 Desert Wine 121^1 Interco $126^{2½}$ Sari's Dreamer 116no Wide,tired 8
10Jun84-Grade I

20May84- 8Hol fst 1 :45⅘ 1:09⅕ 1:34⅕ 3↑M Le Roy H 5 2 $2^½$ 2^{hd} $2^½$ 2no Delahoussaye E b 120 *1.60 95-17 Sari's Dreamer 112no Fighting Fit 120^{nk} Ancestral 115^3 Sharp 7
20May84-Grade II

14Apr84- 8SA fst 1⅛ :47 1:11 1:48 S Berndno H 4 2 2^1 2^1 $2^{2½}$ $3^{3½}$ Delahoussaye E b 121 *1.20 86-16 Journey At Sea 122^3 MyHabitony118^{nk}FightingFit121^8 Weakened 5
14Apr84-Grade II

LATEST WORKOUTS **Feb 15 Hol 5f fst 1:00⅘ h** **Feb 7 Hol 7f fst 1:29⅕ h** **Feb 1 Hol 6f fst 1:13⅘ h** **Jan 27 Hol 4f fst :48⅗ h**

Eskimo **B. h. 5, by Northern Dancer—Dr Mary Lou, by Dr Fager**
Br.—Tartan Farms (Fla)
Tr.—Nerud Jan H
Own.—Tartan Stable **110**

Lifetime 31 5 7 4 $162,221 — **1985** 3 0 1 0 **$12,065** — **1984** 13 1 2 3 **$71,596** — **Turf** 10 0 2 3 **$22,620**

10Feb85- 5Aqu fst 6f ⊡:22⅘ :46 1:10 Alw 36000 5 1 $4^{1½}$ 4^2 $2^½$ 2^{nk} Guerra A A7 110 5.40 94-18 Main Stem 112^{nk} Eskimo 110^2 Talc Power $115^{2¾}$ Game try 5

26Jan85- 8Key fst 7f :22⅘ :45⅕ 1:23 3↑Gallant Bob 1 10 $11^{8½}$ $8^{5¾}$ $5^{3½}$ $4^{2½}$ Castaneda K 117 *3.00 90-22 Rocky Knave 115^{nk} Reliable Jeff 116no Obgyn 115^2 Rallied 12

6Jan85- 7Aqu fst 1^{70} ⊡:47⅕ 1:12⅕ 1:42⅘ Alw 40000 4 5 5^8 5^4 4^2 $4^{3½}$ Santagata N 115 4.50 83-17 Last Turn $115^{1½}$ Flying Skipper 115^{hd} Harry L. 115^2 No excuse 8

2Dec84- 8Key fst 6f :22⅘ :46 1:10⅕ 3↑ⓇAl Hattab 4 5 $5^{2¾}$ 4^3 $5^{5½}$ $4^{3¾}$ Castaneda K 114 *1.20 86-23 Ringside $116^{1½}$ Obgyn 116^2 Moving Wind 112no Evenly 7

25Nov84- 8Aqu fst 6f :22 :45⅗ 1:10⅘ 3↑Sport Pg H 6 9 12^{11} 11^{12} 8^5 7^3 Venezia M 112 36.60 84-25 Trntr117^{nk}MuskokWyck114^{nk}NewConnection$113^{1½}$ Sluggish early 13
25Nov84-Grade III

3Nov84- 8Key fst 7f :22⅘ :46⅕ 1:22⅘ 3↑Quaker H 1 5 5^3 $4^{2½}$ $3^{2½}$ $1^{2¾}$ Castaneda K 114 10.50 94-19 Eskimo $114^{2¾}$ North Glade 118^{nk} Vittorioso 116no Drew clear 7

6Oct84- 8Med fst 6f :22⅘ :45 1:09⅘ 3↑Chief Penk H 5 3 $6^{5½}$ $6^{9½}$ 6^{10} $6^{9¾}$ Ward W A 110 17.80 84-18 Eillo 124^5 Introspective $112^{2½}$ Rollin on Over 114^{nk} Outrun 6

29Sep84- 4Bel gd 6f Ⓣ:22⅘ :45 1:09⅗ 3↑Alw 33000 6 4 $6^{5¾}$ 6^{11} $6^{8½}$ $5^{8½}$ Cruguet J 115 7.00 84-22 Alev $115^{1½}$ Mayanesian $112^{3½}$ Fortunate Prospect $113^½$ Wide 7

21Sep84- 7Med fst 6f :22⅘ :45⅘ 1:10⅖ 3↑Alw 20000 5 1 4^2 $4^{1¾}$ $2^{1½}$ 2^{nk} Cordero A Jr 115 3.80 90-18 Lordly Love 115^{nk} Eskimo 115^2 Private Sun $119^{¾}$ Game try 7

2Sep84- 8Bel fst 6f :22⅘ :45⅗ 1:09⅕ 3↑Boojum H 6 7 $7^{7½}$ $8^{7½}$ $5^{6½}$ $6^{7¼}$ Venezia M 109 8.80e 89-17 Tarantara $111^{1¾}$ Muskoka Wyck $115^{1½}$ Cannon Shell $117^{¾}$ Outrun 8
2Sep84-Grade III

LATEST WORKOUTS **Feb 7 Bel tr.t 3f fst :38 b** **Jan 23 Bel tr.t 4f fst :52 b** **Dec 30 Bel tr.t 4f gd :48 b (d)**

Sprint the previous season. While his most recent efforts were subpar, suggesting that a freshening might be in order, trainer Bobby Frankel instead shipped the horse across the country to tackle what he no doubt expected to be softer competition—over a softer racing surface he knew the horse preferred. Frankel, no stranger to New York, had the local scene pegged correctly. Fighting Fit challenged for the lead immediately while under wraps, then blew away his eastern rivals when asked to run. The important point, of course, was that a seemingly off-form California shipper was able to run a powerful race (his 117 figure was superb) when pitted against what proved to be softer, though in form, New York winter competition.

The seven-furlong Bay Shore Stakes for three-year-olds on March 23 highlighted a different aspect of the "California Connection."

EIGHTH RACE
Aqueduct
FEBRUARY 18, 1985

6 FURLONGS.(InnerDirt). (1.08⅘) 11th Running THE SPORTING PLATE HANDICAP. $60,000 added. 3-year-olds and upward. By subscription of $100 each, which should accompany the nomination; $1,000 to pass the entry box, with $60,000 added. The added money and all fees to be divided 60% to the winner, 22% to second, 12% to third and 6% to fourth. Weights Wednesday, February 13. Starters to be named at the closing time of entries. A trophy will be presented to the winning owner. Closed with 23 nominations Wednesday, January 30, 1985.
Value of race $69,300; value to winner $41,580; second $15,246; third $8,316; fourth $4,158. Mutuel pool $225,214, OTB pool $130,537.

Last Raced	Horse	Eqt.A.Wt	PP	St	¼	½	Str	Fin	Jockey	Odds $1
13Jan85 ⁸SA⁵	Fighting Fit	b 6 118	5	3	2^1	1^1	1^5	$1^{6¾}$	Migliore R	3.40
10Feb85 ⁵Aqu¹	Main Stem	b 7 110	2	4	$4^½$	4^1	3^1	$2^½$	Thibeau R J	7.50
27Jan85 ⁸Aqu⁶	Don Rickles	b 4 109	3	5	6	5^1	$4^½$	$3^¾$	Venezia M	8.10
27Jan85 ⁸Aqu¹	Entropy	b 5 126	4	6	3^1	$3^{1½}$	$2^{1½}$	4^2	Davis R G	a-1.20
10Feb85 ⁵Aqu²	Eskimo	5 110	6	1	$5^{1½}$	6	6	$5^¾$	Murphy D J	a-1.20
27Jan85 ⁸Aqu¹	Muskoka Wyck	b 6 117	1	2	1^{hd}	$2^½$	5^2	6	Ward W A	2.30

a-Coupled: Entropy and Eskimo.
OFF AT 4:34 Start good, Won easily. Time, :22⅘, :45⅕, 1:09⅘ Track fast.

$2 Mutuel Prices:				
	6-(F)-FIGHTING FIT	**8.80**	**4.40**	**4.00**
	3-(B)-MAIN STEM		**6.80**	**5.40**
	4-(C)-DON RICKLES			**4.60**

Ch. h, by Full Pocket—Napalm, by Nilo. Trainer Frankel Robert. Bred by Nuckols Bros (Ky).

FIGHTING FIT attending MUSKOKA WYCK under wraps, assumed lengthy advantage when given bit of rein nearing stretch and never threatened, was being taken in hand final seventy yards posting impressive victory. MAIN STEM racing well away from inner barrier, had needed response besting DON RICKLES. The latter, widest during final drive remained well clear of others. ENTROPY slow as usual leaving gate was immediately rushed into contending position, and laboring under impost final quarter mile gave way. ESKIMO was outrun. MUSKOKA WYCK discouraged when unable to draw clear early, stopped once displaced.

8 AQUEDUCT

7 FURLONGS
AQUEDUCT

7 FURLONGS. (1.20⅕) 26th Running THE BAY SHORE (Grade II). Purse $100,000 added. (Plus $25,000 Breeders' Cup Premium Awards.) 3-year-olds. Weights, 126 lbs. By subscription of $200 each, which should accompany the nomination; $3,000 to pass the entry box, with $100,000 added. The added money and all fees to be divided 60% to the winner, 22% to second, 12% to third and 6% to fourth. Non-winners of a race of $100,000 in 1985 allowed 3 lbs. Of a race of $75,000 at any time 5 lbs. Of a race of $50,000 in 1985, 7 lbs. of a race of $35,000 at any time, 9 lbs. Of two races other than Maiden or Claiming 12 lbs. Starter to be named at the closing time of entries. A trophy will be presented to the winning owner, trainer, and jockey. The New York Racing Association reserves the right to transfer this race to the inner track to be run at six furlongs. Closed Wednesday, March 6, 1985 with 31 nominations.

Spend A Buck

B. c. 3, by Buckaroo—Belle De Jour, by Speak John
Br.—Harper & Irish Hill Farm (Ky)
Tr.—Gambolati Cam
Own.—Diaz D
123
Lifetime 8 5 2 1 $667.985 — 1984 8 5 2 1 $667,985

10Nov84- 1Hol fst 1 :45 1:10 1:36⅘ Br Cp Juv 3 1 1hd 12½ 11 31½ Cordero A Jr 122 6.40 — — Chief'sCrown122¾Tnk'sProspect122¾SpndABuck122⁶½ Weakened 10
10Nov84-Grade I
18Oct84- 8Med fst 1 1/16 :46 1:11⅕ 1:45 Yng America 4 1 11½ 11 1½ 2¾ Cordero A Jr 122 *1.00 83-22 Script Ohio 119¾ Spend A Buck 122nk Tank'sProspect119² Gamely 11
18Oct84-Grade I
22Sep84- 9AP fst 1 :44⅘ 1:10 1:38 Arl Wa Fty 6 3 2¹ 2hd 1½ 1½ Hussey C 122 2.90 71-24 Spend A Buck 122½ Dusty's Darby 122²½ Viva Maxi 122¹¾ All out 7
22Sep84-Grade I
2Sep84-11RD fst 1 1/16 :47⅗ 1:12 1:45⅘ Cradle 6 2 11 14 18 115 Hussey C 120 *1.20 80-18 Spend A Buck 120¹⁵ Grand Native 120⁶ Alex's Game 120nk Easily 13
16Aug84- 7Crc fst 6f :22⅗ :46⅕ 1:12⅘ Alw 15000 1 1 11½ 14 16 19½ Hussey C 112 *.50 87-23 Spend A Buck 112⁹½ Secret Goal 112⁸½Mr.Introienne114³ Handily 5
4Aug84- 9Crc fst 5½f :22⅗ :47 1:07 Criterium 4 2 2³ 2² 22½ 22½ Hussey C 116 *.60 87-21 Smile 114²½ Spend A Buck 116hd Cherokee Fast 116⁴½ Held place 7
4Aug84-Run In Divisions
25Jly84- 8Crc fst 5½f :22⅗ :46⅗ 1:06 Alw 11000 3 1 1½ 11½ 13 14 Hussey C 113 2.40 95-20 SpendABuck113⁴Mr.Introinn116¹½PlyingPolitics114⁴½ Ridden out 8
14Jly84- 2Crc fst 5½f :23 :47 1:07⅕ Md Sp Wt 6 3 11½ 1hd 12 1nk Hussey C 116 5.50 89-19 SpendABuck116nkHickoryHillFlyer116³SuperbAnswr116³½ Driving 12
LATEST WORKOUTS ●Mar 22 Aqu 3f fst :35⅘ h ●Mar 15 Crc 6f fst 1:12⅕ h (d) ●Mar 9 Crc 5f fst 1:00⅘ h (d) ●Mar 3 Crc 4f fst :48 h (d)

Bro Stache

B. c. 3, by An Eldorado—First Evening, by First Family
Br.—Dilibero Farm (Fla)
Tr.—Fredella Dennis
Own.—Mavorah E
114
Lifetime 9 2 2 4 $31,771 — 1985 5 2 1 2 $27,626 — 1984 4 M 1 2 $4,145

10Mar85- 8Key fst 6f :22⅗ :46 1:11⅕ ⓢNorth Call 1 2 4⁴ 35½ 33½ 33½ Alligood M A 122 3.60 82-19 Overbought 117³ Sports Medicine 117nk Bro Stache 122³½ Evenly 5
16Feb85- 8Key fst 7f :21⅘ :44⅘ 1:24⅗ Sentinel 2 6 77 66 32 1nk Alligood M A 112 21.30 84-20 BroStch112nkBtMDddy122²Jck'sGoldrunnr112¹½ Bumped. driving 7
27Jan85- 3Key fst 170 :47⅗ 1:13 1:43⅗ Md Sp Wt 4 2 2hd 1hd 13½ 13 Alligood M A 120 *1.10 83-20 Bro Stache 120³ Count Upwards 120³ Approaching 120² Driving 8
12Jan85- 3Key fst 170 :46⅕ 1:11⅕ 1:41⅘ Md Sp Wt 5 3 55 53 22 23½ Alligood M A 119 *2.00 89-13 Shalom Dancer 119³½ BroStache119³Perula'sChant119¾ Drifted in 9
5Jan85- 3Key sly 6f :22⅗ :47⅘ 1:15 Md Sp Wt 6 5 79 712 57½ 36½ Alligood M A 119 7.30 59-38 Star Quality 119⁶½ Sicilian Law 119no Bro Stache 119no Fin.fast 10
26Dec84- 3Key fst 6½f :22⅗ :46 1:18⅗ Md Sp Wt 2 10 98½ 96½ 45½ 2½ Alligood M A 120 5.50 79-25 Soft Rock 120½ Bro Stache 120½ Flying Rice 120¹½ Rallied 11
12Dec84- 3Key fst 6f :22 :45⅖ 1:12⅘ Md Sp Wt 9 1 67 68½ 66 35 Lukas M 120 35.00 74-27 Rocking Chair 120³ Approaching 120² Bro Stache 120² Rallied 9
23Aug84- 6Sar sly 7f :22⅗ :46 1:24⅘ Md Sp Wt 8 4 74 59½ 1119 1124½ Murphy D J 118 29.40 55-22 Coyote Dancer 118⁴½ Haberdasher 118²¼ Foligno 118¾ Tired 14
22Jly84- 4Bel my 5½f :23 :46⅘ 1:05⅘ Md 35000 7 7 46 45 38 311 Murphy D J 114 25.60 77-21 TheRunningKind118⁷½Flippant114³½BroStache114¹ Raced greenly 8
LATEST WORKOUTS Mar 6 Key 4f fst :48⅘ h

Don't Hesitate

Dk. b. or br. c. 3, by Native Uproar—Time To Step, by Time Tested
Br.—Bettersworth J R (Ky)
Tr.—Winfree Donald
Own.—Devaney J J
117
Lifetime 4 3 0 1 $48,685 — 1985 2 1 0 1 $25,440 — 1984 2 2 0 0 $23,245

9Mar85- 8Aqu fst 6f ⊡:21⅗ :44⅘ 1:10 Swift 5 2 1½ 2hd 2hd 32 Migliore R b 117 *.80 92-16 King Babar 114² CleverChamp120hdDon'tHesitate117¹ Weakened 6
9Mar85-Grade III
2Feb85-10FG fst 6f :21⅘ :45 1:11 Handicap 5 3 13 14 15 12½ Espinoza J C b 118 *1.50 90-18 Don't Hesitate 118²½ Power Scene 113¹ Fuzzy 121¹ Won eased 9
24Jun84- 9RD fst 6f :21⅗ :44⅗ 1:09⅘ Rascal 6 3 12 12 16 110 Espinoza J C b 114 *.70 94-19 Don't Hesitate 114¹⁰TheRoyalFreeze114²½Mr.Smirnoff114³ Easily 10
6Jun84- 3CD fst 5f :22 :45⅕ :58⅘ Md Sp Wt 5 5 12 12½ 16 18 Espinoza J C b 118 2.40 97-13 Don't Hesitate 118⁸ First County Fair 118¾StepProud118⁴½ Easily 7
LATEST WORKOUTS ●Mar 17 Aqu 6f fst 1:13⅘ hg ●Mar 4 Aqu ⊡ 5f fst 1:00⅖ hg

First One Up

B. c. 3, by Johnny Appleseed—Clearly Early, by Distinctive
Br.—Weinsier R (Ky)
Tr.—Barrera Luis
Own.—Weinsier R
119
Lifetime 18 6 3 2 $158,090 — 1985 4 3 0 0 $104,460 — 1984 14 3 3 2 $53,630 — Turf 4 0 1 0 $7,140

9Mar85- 6Aqu fst 170 ⊡:47 1:12 1:41⅘ Great Power 3 2 21½ 21½ 515 521 Migliore R b 119 3.60 72-16 Nordance 115½ Haberdasher 115²½ Roo Art 122² Tired 6
9Feb85- 8Aqu fst 1 1/16 ⊡:48⅕ 1:13⅕ 1:46⅕ Whirlaway 8 2 1hd 1hd 1½ 1nk Migliore R b 123 *1.50 79-26 First One Up 123nk King Babar 117½ Trophy Hunter 117⁴½ Lasted 11
26Jan85- 7Aqu fst 170 ⊡:47⅗ 1:13⅕ 1:44 Count Fleet 7 3 32 2½ 11½ 12¼ Migliore R b 117 5.40 80-20 First One Up 117²¼ Ah So Tony 117¾ Trophy Hunter117⁶½ Driving 8
4Jan85- 7Aqu fst 170 ⊡:48⅗ 1:13⅘ 1:44⅘ Clm 100000 7 2 21 1½ 12 1nk Cordero A Jr b 122 *1.70 76-21 First One Up 122nk FeelingGallant114nkHaberdasher107hd Driving 8
22Dec84- 5Aqu fst 6f ⊡:22 :45 1:09⅘ Alw 22000 10 2 3½ 1² 12 12½ Cordero A Jr b 117 2.40 95-09 First OneUp117²¼Kilts'Nashua117hdAlongCameJones117² Driving 10
2Dec84- 2Aqu fst 7f :23⅕ :46⅕ 1:23⅘ Alw 22000 8 1 2½ 21½ 26 39½ Bailey J D b 117 9.70 72-24 BoldSmoocher119⁹TrophyHunter117½FirstOneUp117¹¼ Weakened 9
26Nov84- 5Aqu fst 1⅛ :50⅖ 1:15⅕ 1:53⅗ Alw 23000 1 1 11 1hd 21½ 34½ Ward W A⁵ b 112 1.50 62-25 Stack 122³¼ Uncle Daddy 110¹¼ First One Up 112⁵½ Weakened 6
19Nov84- 5Aqu fst 6f :23 :47⅕ 1:12⅘ Alw 22000 8 3 52¼ 31 1hd 25 Migliore R b 117 7.50 72-33 El Basco 117⁵ First One Up 117¾ He's HomeFree117hd Weakaned 9
12Nov84- 5Aqu gd 7f :23 :46 1:25 Clm 70000 7 3 31 2hd 1½ 12 Bailey J D b 113 10.00 76-25 First One Up 113² Jet Wave 117hd Kilts' Nashua 113¹½ Driving 8
25Oct84- 5Aqu gd 7f :23 :46⅗ 1:24⅕ Clm 45000 5 4 52 33 24 24¾ Guerra W A b 117 2.30e 75-21 Keep ItDown117⁴¾FirstOneUp117¹¼SavageRunner113nk No match 8
LATEST WORKOUTS Mar 21 Bel tr.t 4f fst :50⅗ b ●Mar 16 Bel tr.t 5f fst 1:01 h Mar 5 Bel tr.t 6f sly 1:20⅘ b Feb 18 Bel tr.t 5f fst 1:03⅕ b

Cutlass Reality

Ch. c. 3, by Cutlass—Landera, by In Reality
Br.—Carrion J S (Fla)
Tr.—Marks Mervin
Own.—Kruckel T V Jr
114
Lifetime 9 1 3 0 $77,489 — 1985 2 0 0 0 $150 — 1984 7 1 3 0 $77,339

13Mar85- 7Aqu fst 7f :23⅕ :46⅘ 1:25⅕ Alw 25000 3 4 52½ 53½ 611 618 Ward W A⁵ b 112 2.50 57-28 Eternal Prince 122⁶¾ Super Scope 117² Verbascum 117⁶ Dull 7
20Feb85- 7GP fst 6f :22⅗ :45⅗ 1:10⅗ Alw 15000 1 8 77 87¾ 56¾ 89¾ Perret C b 117 4.10 76-23 First Guess 122⁷½ Leakey 119nk Night Detective 117½ Outrun 9
18Oct84- 8Med fst 1 1/16 :46 1:11⅕ 1:45 Yng America 3 3 33 31½ 68½ 79¾ Perret C b 119 8.40 74-22 Script Ohio 119¾ Spend A Buck 122nk Tank's Prospect119² Tired 11
18Oct84-Grade I
6Oct84- 8Lrl fst 1 1/16 :46⅘ 1:12⅗ 1:43 Laurel Fty 11 2 2½ 11 31 22½ Perret C b 122 36.40 90-15 MightyAppealing122²½CutlssRelity122hdRhomnRule122¹⁰ Gamely 12
6Oct84-Grade I
15Sep84- 8Key sly 6f :22⅕ :46 1:11⅕ Kindergarten 3 7 64 33 23½ 24½ Perret C b 114 3.70 80-21 Doubly Clear 121⁴½ Cutlass Reality 114⁷½ Jon Ian 118¾ 2nd best 7
26Aug84- 8Sar fst 6½f :21⅘ :44⅘ 1:16 Hopeful 5 5 64¾ 74½ 65 48 Perret C b 122 58.80 84-15 Chief'sCrown122³¾TiffnyIce122³¾Mugzy'sRulin122½ Lacked room 5
26Aug84-Grade I
17Aug84- 6Mth fst 5½f :23 :46⅕ 1:04⅘ Md Sp Wt 8 1 11½ 13 12½ 14 Perret C b 118 1.70 91-17 Cutlass Reality118⁴GranOleOpry118⁶Elloree'sChoice118hd Driving 8
3Aug84- 8Crc fst 6f :23 :46⅘ 1:15⅕ Md Sp Wt 7 4 41½ 55 45 2½ Velez J A Jr b 116 7.00 74-24 DustyHotLine116½CutlassReality116³FoundationPlan116½ Gaining 9
18Jly84- 6Crc fst 6f :23 :47⅖ 1:14⅕ Md Sp Wt 11 6 3nk 2½ 43½ 55 Hernandez C 116 14.20 75-20 Playing Politics 116³½ Lautaro 116no Water Gate 116¹¼ Faltered 12
LATEST WORKOUTS Mar 9 Bel tr.t 4f gd :52⅕ b Mar 4 Bel tr.t 4f fst :48 h Feb 14 GP 3f fst :39 b Feb 10 GP 6f fst 1:19⅗ b

Eternal Prince

B. c. 3, by Majestic Prince—Eternal Queen, by Fleet Nasrullah
Br.—Kinsman Stud Farm (Fla)
Tr.—Lenzini John J Jr
Own.—Hurst B J
114
Lifetime 5 2 2 0 $36,622 — 1985 2 2 0 0 $27,000 — 1984 3 M 2 0 $9,622

13Mar85- 7Aqu fst 7f :23⅕ :46⅘ 1:25⅕ Alw 25000 6 1 1½ 11 14 16¾ Migliore R b 122 *.80 75-28 Eternal Prince 122⁶¾ Super Scope 117² Verbascum 117⁶ Easily 7
4Mar85- 6Aqu fst 6f ⊡:23 :46⅖ 1:11⅗ Md Sp Wt 5 1 11½ 12 16 18 Migliore R b 122 *1.00 87-22 Eternal Prince 122⁸ ChangeTheLock122nkAlex'sGame122no Easily 10
31Jly84- 9Mth fst 5½f :22⅕ :45 1:04 Tyro 8 9 108 710 79 413 Delgado A b 113 30.10 82-15 Doubly Clear 122³ Ziggy'sBoy116⁷Whatever'sRight122³ No threat 11
16Jly84- 6Bel fst 6f :22⅗ :46 1:11⅗ Md Sp Wt 1 1 2hd 2hd 2hd 24 Cordero A Jr b 118 14.10 81-24 Nickel Back 118⁴ Eternal Prince 118no Anconeus 118¹ No match 13
27Jun84- 4Bel fst 5½f :23 :47⅕ 1:06⅗ Md 40000 5 3 1hd 1½ 11½ 21½ Migliore R 118 2.60 81-17 BernaCgney111¹½EternlPrince118¹½WesternChmp116⁴ Weakened 9
LATEST WORKOUTS ●Mar 20 Aqu 4f fst :46⅘ h Mar 10 Aqu 4f fst :48⅗ h ●Mar 1 Aqu ⊡ 4f fst :47 hg ●Feb 23 Aqu ⊡ 5f fst 1:00⅖ h

El Basco

Ch. c. 3, by Vigors—La Basque, by Jean-Pierre
Br.—Wimpfheimer J D (Ky)
Tr.—Sedlacek Sue
Own.—Wimpfheimer J D
114
Lifetime 10 2 1 0 $36.398 — 1984 10 2 1 0 $36,398 — Turf 2 0 0 0

8Dec84- 6Aqu fst 6f ⊡:22 :45⅘ 1:10⅘ Hoist Flag 5 5 59 43½ 2½ 2hd McCarron G b 115 5.80 90-15 Clever Champ 119hd El Basco 115⁴½ Recognized 115¹ Just missed 5
19Nov84- 5Aqu fst 6f :23 :47⅕ 1:12⅘ Alw 22000 6 9 99¼ 65¼ 3½ 15 McCarron G b 117 36.10 77-33 El Basco 117⁵ First One Up 117¾ He's Home Free 117hd Handily 9
7Oct84- 5Bel fm 1 Ⓣ:46 1:10⅖ 1:37⅘ Alw 22000 6 6 33 88 89 85¼ Cordero A Jr b 117 10.80 71-17 Venidium 117¾ Lightning Leap 117²¾ Radar Alarm117nk Gave way 9
20Sep84- 8Bel fm 1 1/16 Ⓣ:46⅘ 1:11⅗ 1:44 Alw 21000 4 6 66½ 64 44½ 55¼ Velasquez J b 117 3.60 71-24 ForCertainDoc117³½Magnaminous122¾McAtTheTrck117hd Outrun 6
10Sep84- 4Bel fst 7f :22⅗ :46⅕ 1:25⅕ Md Sp Wt 4 7 56 43 2hd 1½ Velasquez J b 118 6.90 76-19 El Basco 118½ Alert Response 113⁴ Revelrout 118¹ Driving 12
18Aug84- 4Sar fst 6f :22⅗ :46⅕ 1:11⅗ Md Sp Wt 8 10 66½ 56½ 69 610 Lopez V⁵ b 113 8.40 73-15 Woltan 118³ Senator Brady 118³½ Scholastic 118hd Broke slowly 10
4Aug84- 6Sar fst 6f :22 :45⅖ 1:10⅘ Md Sp Wt 6 14 1113 911 67½ 410 Lopez V⁵ b 113⁴ 16.80f 76-13 Desert War 118³½ Herat 118⁶½ Alex'sGame118hd Off slowly,borein 14
4Aug84-Dead heat
9Jly84- 6Bel fst 5f :22⅕ :45⅗ :57⅗ Md Sp Wt 8 8 815 815 615 616¾ Lopez V⁵ 113 33.90 82-14 Ziggy's Boy 118⁶½ Varick 118³¾ Roman River 118³¾ Slow start 8
LATEST WORKOUTS ●Mar 18 Aqu 5f fst 1:02 bg Mar 1 Pay 4f fst :51⅘ b Feb 23 Pay 4f fst :54⅘ b Jan 27 Pay 4f fst :53⅖ b

Secretary General — Dk. b. or br. c. 3, by Foolish Pleasure—Sippican, by Stage Door Johnny
Br.—Ryan E B (Ky) — 114 — Lifetime 7 2 1 2 $30,372 — 1985 4 1 0 2 $15,172 — 1984 3 1 1 0 $15,200
Own.—Allen H — Tr.—Jacobs Eugene

18Feb85-10GP fst 1⅛ :46⅗ 1:11⅕ 1:43⅗ Ftn Youth 12 2 2½ 2hd 2hd 1124¾ Cruguet J 112 39.90 59-22 ProudTruth112nk Stephan'sOdyssey1224DoItAgnDn1124½ Faltered 14
18Feb85-Grade II
4Feb85-8GP fst 1⅛ :46⅗ 1:11⅗ 1:44⅖ Alw 16000 7 2 41½ 2hd 21 37½ Santos J A 117 2.90 72-18 ProudTruth1176CrowningHonors1171½SecretryGenrl117½ Faltered 10
19Jan85-6GP fst 7f :22⅖ :45⅗ 1:24⅖ Alw 14000 5 3 2hd 1½ 12 12 Cruguet J 117 *.40 82-15 SecretaryGeneral1172SittinOnHold1171½FlyerEscpe122hd Handily 10
8Jan85-9GP fst 6f :21⅖ :44⅗ 1:10⅖ Spect'lr Bid 6 6 55½ 41¾ 45½ 31½ Cruguet J 112 *1.80 85-16 Cherokee Fast 112½ Vindaloo 1121 SecretaryGeneral1121½ Rallied 11
10Nov84-1Hol fst 1 :45 1:10 1:36⅕ Br Cp Juv 2 3 41¾ 812 1018 1033¾ McCarron C J 122 12.70 — — Chief's Crown 122¾ Tank's Prospect 122¾SpendABuck1226½ Tired 10
10Nov84-Grade I
28Oct84-6Aqu gd 7f :22⅕ :45 1:22⅗ Alw 20000 2 3 1hd 2½ 2hd 2½ Velasquez J 117 2.40 87-14 Another Reef 117½ Secretary General1172¾SkipTrial117nk Gamely 7
22Jun84-4Bel fst 5½f :22⅕ :46⅕ 1:05⅗ Md Sp Wt 2 2 1½ 1hd 12 11 Velasquez J 118 3.70 87-21 Secretary General 1181 Chief'sCrown1181½TiffanyIce1189 Driving 10
LATEST WORKOUTS ●Mar 17 GP 6f fst 1:14 h — Mar 12 GP 5f fst 1:02⅖ b — Feb 16 GP 4f fst :49 b — Feb 12 GP 6f fst 1:15 b

Pancho Villa — Ch. c. 3, by Secretariat—Crimson Saint, by Crimson Satan
Br.—Gentry T (Ky) — 114 — Lifetime 3 1 1 0 $16,700 — 1985 3 1 1 0 $16,700 — 1984 0 M 0 0
Own.—French L R Jr — Tr.—Lukas D Wayne

16Mar85-4SA fst 6½f :21 :43⅗ 1:15⅘ Alw 23000 5 5 44 22 2½ 22½ McHargue D G b 120 8.40 89-18 Phone Trick 1202½ Pancho Villa 1202½ Palestine Sun 1143 6
2Mar85-6SA fst 6f :21⅘ :45 1:10⅗ Md Sp Wt 7 3 1hd 1hd 11½ 13½ McHargue D G b 118 28.40 85-18 PnchoVill1183½Alln'sProspct1181½LuckyProspct1181½ Ridden out 12
2Feb85-6SA fst 6f :21⅗ :44⅘ 1:10 Md Sp Wt 4 10 109¾ 1016 1014 1013¾ Toro F 118 19.30 74-18 Full Honor 1182½ Lone Star Bar 1186 Lord'n Ruler 118½ 12
LATEST WORKOUTS Mar 10 SA 5f fst 1:01⅕ h — ●Feb 27 SA 3f fst :35 h — Feb 10 SA 5f fst 1:01 h

Beat Me Daddy — Dk. b. or br. c. 3, by Tim The Tiger—Why Fight, by Big Brave
Br.—Lynn C L (Can) — 119 — Lifetime 9 2 1 1 $71,533 — 1985 3 1 1 0 $27,640 — 1984 6 1 0 1 $43,893
Own.—Napton Hill Farm — Tr.—Wheeler Robert E

9Mar85-8Aqu fst 6f ⊡:21⅗ :44⅖ 1:10 Swift 2 5 33½ 32 31 43 Bracciale V Jr b 120 13.00 91-16 King Babar 1142 CleverChamp120hdDon'tHesitate1171 Weakened 6
9Mar85-Grade III
16Feb85-8Key fst 7f :21⅘ :44⅖ 1:24⅗ Sentinel 3 4 1hd 1hd 11 2nk Lloyd J S b 122 2.70 84-20 BroStache112nkBetMeDddy1222Jck'sGoldrunner1121½ Just failed 7
1Jan85-8Key fst 6f :22 :45⅖ 1:11⅕ Philmont 7 2 12½ 1hd 1hd 1hd Lloyd J S b 122 8.70 85-24 BetMeDddy122hdJck'sGoldrunner1142½EstrnTrdition114no Driving 9
15Nov84-8Med fst 6f :22 :45⅗ 1:12⅗ Morven 2 5 43 43 66 54¾ Miller D A Jr b 121 7.90e 74-22 Medieval Love 113hd Clever Champ 118¾ Amorphous 1142 Tired 6
15Nov84-Grade III
4Nov84-7Lrl fst 6f :22⅖ :46 1:12 Alw 9000 1 5 1hd 21 22½ 76½ Miller D A Jr b 122 *.50 76-22 Ramten 1151 The GreatEscaper115noLittleBoldJohn1194 Stopped 8
26Aug84-8Sar fst 6½f :21⅘ :44⅘ 1:16 Hopeful 9 8 86¾ 85¾ 911 919¾ Guerra W A 122 77.60 72-15 Chief's Crown 1223¾ Tiffany Ice 1223¾ Mugzy'sRullah122½ Outrun 9
26Aug84-Grade I
3Aug84-8Sar fst 6f :22⅗ :46 1:10⅕ Sar Spec'l 1 6 43 3½ 53½ 510½ Maple E 122 5.70 82-19 Chief's Crown 1172¾ Do ItAgainDan117hdSkyCommand122¾ Tired 6
3Aug84-Grade II
8Jly84-8Bel fst 6f :22⅕ :45⅘ 1:12⅕ Tremont 1 4 47 24 1hd 14¾ Maple E 113 3.00 81-15 BtMDddy1134¾LordCrlos1171½MountRlity11315¾ Lugged in, clear 4
8Jly84-Grade III
24May84-4Bel fst 5f :22⅗ :45⅘ :57⅗ Md Sp Wt 3 4 76¾ 77½ 36 39 Nicol P A Jr 118 *1.50 90-15 Moon Prospector1183NickelBack1186BeatMeDaddy1183½ In close 8
LATEST WORKOUTS ●Mar 19 Lrl 5f fst :59⅘ h — ●Mar 1 Lrl 5f fst 1:00⅖ h — ●Feb 8 Lrl 6f fr 1:11⅘ h

I Am The Game — B. c. 3, by Lord Gaylord—Kitchen Window, by Dead Ahead
Br.—Jones W L Jr (Md) — 117 — Lifetime 5 4 0 1 $96,343 — 1985 4 3 0 1 $84,343 — 1984 1 1 0 0 $12,000
Own.—Leatherbury King T — Tr.—Leatherbury King T

9Mar85-8Lrl fst 1 :46⅕ 1:11⅘ 1:38 Ⓢ St De Naskra 2 1 2hd 1½ 13½ 13½ Delgado A 112 *.40 82-27 I Am The Game1123½JoyfullJohn112hdLittleBoldJohn1126 Driving 5
18Feb85-8Lrl fst 1 :46⅕ 1:11⅘ 1:37⅘ Gen George 6 1 3½ 2hd 2½ 36 Delgado A 119 *.40 78-20 Roo Art 1222 Joyfull John 1124 I Am The Game 1191½ Wide 8
3Feb85-8Lrl sly 7f :23⅕ :46⅗ 1:24⅕ F. Scott Key 2 1 11 12 11½ 15½ Delgado A 122 *1.20 90-28 I Am The Game 1225½ Sparrowvon 110nk JoyfullJohn112hd Driving 10
23Jan85-8Lrl fst 6f :22⅖ :45⅘ 1:10⅘ W P Burch 1 2 21½ 2hd 1hd 11 Delgado A 113 *.30 89-14 I Am The Game1131JayBryan119noAlongCameJones115nk Driving 6
30Dec84-7Aqu fst 6f ⊡:23 :46⅘ 1:11⅖ Md Sp Wt 8 4 1½ 1½ 14 14 Cordero A Jr 118 2.60 87-15 IAmThGm1184FirstConqust1131½HistoryRsponds118½ Ridden out 11
LATEST WORKOUTS Mar 20 Lrl 3f fst :36⅘ b — Mar 7 Lrl 3f fst :37⅕ b — Feb 14 Lrl 5f fr 1:00⅕ b — Feb 1 Lrl 4f sly :51⅖ b

The Bay Shore had received a good deal of prerace publicity because it was expected to feature the three-year-old debut of the speedy Spend A Buck, one of the leading juveniles of 1984. Spend A Buck had been working quite impressively over the deep Calder surface, and many experts figured the Bay Shore would be a mere formality for the colt. They overlooked several significant negative signs:

(1) Spend A Buck was making his first start since having arthroscopic surgery to remove a bone chip from his knee and might not be asked to give his all in his first race of the year.
(2) Spend A Buck was being asked to concede from four to nine pounds to his more seasoned rivals, while carrying highweight of 123 pounds.
(3) The rail at Aqueduct that day was the deepest part of the racing surface, and Spend A Buck had drawn the one-hole.
(4) Don't Hesitate, one of Spend A Buck's expected rivals for the early lead, set an exceptionally fast pace (114) in the Swift two weeks earlier. A repetition of that kind of pace would not help Spend A Buck's chances.
(5) Spend A Buck's figures as a juvenile were not overly impressive and indeed were in the same ball park as those recently posted by some of his key rivals in the Bay Shore.

At odds of 7–5, Spend A Buck did not appear to be a worthwhile betting proposition. Who was the logical alternative? During the week leading up to the Bay Shore, my interests focused on Eternal Prince, an impressive winner of his two starts at the meet, in good times, suggesting that he "could be any kind." However, he had never faced the blistering pace that Don't Hesitate and Spend A Buck were likely to throw at him, and it was impossible to tell how he would react to it. In his favor, however, was the fact that he had finished "out well" in his most recent start, after leading all the way. (See Chapter 30 for an explanation of the "out well" concept.) Yet at 7–2, his odds didn't seem sufficient to cover the risk.

Don't Hesitate, on the other hand, could conceivably improve off his first race in New York and, in the absence of his early rival from th Swift (Clever Champ), might have the speed to get clear early and dictate more reasonable fractions. His numbers for the Swift (114–107) made him a threat, especially if he could rearrange them somewhat.

El Basco, the established closer in the field, had been idle over the winter, and one had to guess that the Bay Shore would be nothing more than a conditioning race for him.

I Am The Game won three of four stakes tries in Maryland, with his lone defeat coming at the hands of Roo Art. The latter had failed to menace in his local debut two weeks earlier, as can be seen in the past performance lines of First One Up. The latter, king of the hill during the winter months, seemed to have lost his grip. And Secretary General, once considered a top prospect, appeared to have collapsed in his latest start.

So it seemed that each of Spend A Buck's rivals had his drawbacks, making each an unattractive, or risky, alternative to the favorite. All but Pancho Villa, that is, the surprise, last-minute entry from the West Coast. Ordinarily, one would not consider backing the chances of a horse still eligible for "nonwinners of a race other than" in a stakes such as the Bay Shore. At least one allowance victory, and preferably some stakes experience, would seem a logical prerequisite. Accurate West Coast speed figures, however, made Pancho Villa appear competitive with the likes of Spend A Buck, Eternal Prince, El Basco, and Don't Hesitate. His maiden victory, over a dull Santa Anita surface, rated 108. Phone Trick, the undefeated colt who beat Pancho Villa on March 16, earned a 107 for his debut victory, then a 109 when he repeated. Many observers regarded Phone Trick as the fastest three-year-old (sprinter) on the West Coast at the time.

If the California form translated east at its usual higher level, Pancho Villa certainly had to be accorded a reasonable chance in the Bay Shore. And indeed he did! The California invader stalked the early pace of Don't Hesitate, took over with a rush on the turn, then won as he pleased. He returned a stunning $30.80 to the "California dreamers" at Aqueduct that day. His 116 figure rated among the five fastest for the Bay Shore over the past thirty years.

EIGHTH RACE
Aqueduct
MARCH 23, 1985

7 FURLONGS. (1.20⅕) 26th Running THE BAY SHORE (Grade II). Purse $100,000 added. (Plus $25,000 Breeders' Cup Premium Awards.) 3-year-olds. Weights, 126 lbs. By subscription of $200 each, which should accompany the nomination; $3,000 to pass the entry box, with $100,000 added. The added money and all fees to be divided 60% to the winner, 22% to second, 12% to third and 6% to fourth. Non-winners of a race of $100,000 in 1985 allowed 3 lbs. Of a race of $75,000 at any time 5 lbs. Of a race of $50,000 in 1985, 7 lbs. of a race of $35,000 at any time, 9 lbs. Of two races other than Maiden or Claiming 12 lbs. Starter to be named at the closing time of entries. A trophy will be presented to the winning owner, trainer, and jockey. The New York Racing Association reserves the right to transfer this race to the inner track to be run at six furlongs. Closed Wednesday, March 6, 1985 with 31 nominations. Breeders' Cup FUnd Awards to: Pancho Villa and El Basco.

Total purse $164,200. Value of race $159,450; value to winner $97,020; second $37,374; third $16,704; fourth $8,352. $2,250 Nom. Awards. $2,500 Reverts to Breeders Cup. Mutuel pool $211,932, OTB pool $190,052. Exacta Pool $227,077. OTB Exacta Pool $204,516.

Last Raced	Horse	Eqt.A.Wt	PP	St	¼	½	Str	Fin	Jockey	Odds $1
16Mar85 ^{4}SA^2	Pancho Villa	b 3 114	8	4	$4^{1/2}$	1^{hd}	1^4	$1^{3 3/4}$	Lovato F Jr	14.40
8Dec84 ^{6}Aqu^2	El Basco	b 3 114	7	9	9	7^4	4^1	$2^{1 3/4}$	McCarron G	8.30
10Nov84 ^{1}Hol^3	Spend A Buck	3 123	1	6	$3^{1 1/2}$	$4^{1/2}$	3^{hd}	3^2	Cordero A Jr	1.40
9Mar85 ^{8}Aqu^3	Don't Hesitate	b 3 117	3	2	1^1	2^{hd}	$2^{1/2}$	4^{nk}	Day P	4.00
9Mar85 ^{6}Aqu^5	First One Up	b 3 119	4	5	6^4	6^1	6^2	$5^{3/4}$	Davis R G	24.60
13Mar85 ^{7}Aqu^1	Eternal Prince	b 3 114	6	1	2^{hd}	3^1	5^1	$6^{3/4}$	Migliore R	3.70
9Mar85 ^{8}Lrl^1	I Am The Game	3 117	9	3	5^{hd}	5^3	7^5	$7^{5 3/4}$	Vasquez J	5.60
13Mar85 ^{7}Aqu^6	Cutlass Reality	b 3 114	5	7	7^1	8^4	8^{10}	$8^{9 3/4}$	Skinner K	79.80
10Mar85 ^{8}Key^3	Bro Stache	3 114	2	8	$8^{1/2}$	9	9	9	Alligood M A	60.00

OFF AT 4:52. Start good, Won ridden out. Time, :22⅘, :45⅗, 1:09⅗, 1:22⅕ Track fast.

$2 Mutuel Prices:				
	8-(I)-PANCHO VILLA	**30.80**	**11.60**	**4.80**
	7-(G)-EL BASCO		**10.60**	**5.40**
	1-(A)-SPEND A BUCK			**3.00**
	$2 EXACTA 8-7 PAID $133.20.			

Ch. c, by Secretariat—Crimson Saint, by Crimson Satan. Trainer Lukas D Wayne. Bred by Gentry T (Ky).

PANCHO VILLA allowed to relax settling into stride along the backstretch, accelerated when giving rein wresting command midway of turn and ridden out, while safely in front final quarter-mile scored impressively. The winner survived claim of foul lodged by jockey G. McCarron rider of runner up EL BASCO for alleged interference leaving the gate. The latter slow getting underway, leveled off approaching stretch and splitting rivals making solid late run, emerged clearly second best. SPEND A BUCK right there racing along the rail until leaving three furlong pole, swung out lodging bid and laboring under impost while showing tendency to lug in, was unable to pose serious threat. DON'T HESITATE setting and forcing pace shortened stride soon after straightening into stretch. FIRST ONE UP was never dangerous. ETERNAL PRINCE between horses dueling early gave way. I AM THE GAME racing wide flattened out. CUTLASS BEAUTY and BRO STACHE were soundly beaten.

"Class advantages" like this, favoring shippers from one specific track to another at a particular time of the year, no doubt crop up across the country. The reader is advised to be on the alert for such developments involving his home circuit.

There is a strange twist to the "California Connection" that is worth mentioning. In many cases, the extreme "class advantage" we have been discussing lasts just the one race. I have yet to hear a logical explanation for why this is true, but it has happened too often, over too long a period of time, to pretend that it is not true.

Fighting Fit, for example, raced again three weeks after his smashing victory in the Sporting Plate and was hard pressed to edge a slightly weaker field in the Toboggan.

EIGHTH RACE
Aqueduct
MARCH 10, 1985

6 FURLONGS.(InnerDirt). (1.08⅘) 92nd running THE TOBOGGAN HANDICAP (Grade III). Purse $75,000 Added. 3-year-olds and upward. By subcription of $150 each, which should accompany the nomination; $1,200 to pass the entry box, with $75,000 added. The added money and all fees to be divided 60% to the winner, 22% to second, 12% to third and 6% to fourth. Weights Tuesday, March 5. Starters to be named at the closing time of entries. A trophy will be presented to the winning owner. Closed Wednesday, February 20, 1985 with 13 nominations. Value of race $85,350; value to winner $51,210; second $18,777; third $10,242; fourth $5,121. Mutuel pool $135,473, OTB pool $109,119. Exacta Pool 4212,456. OTB Exacta Pool $145,560.

Last Raced	Horse	Eqt.A.Wt	PP	St	¼	½	Str	Fin	Jockey	Odds $1
18Feb85 ^{8}Aqu^{1}	Fighting Fit	b 6 123	6	1	4^{hd}	2^{1}	$3^{1\frac{1}{2}}$	1^{hd}	Migliore R	.50
18Feb85 ^{8}Aqu^{4}	Entropy	b 5 123	2	4	2^{hd}	1^{hd}	1^{hd}	2no	Bailey J D	4.70
17Feb85 ^{8}Aqu^{2}	Shadowmar	6 107	1	6	$1^{\frac{1}{2}}$	3^{1}	$2^{\frac{1}{2}}$	$3^{\frac{3}{4}}$	Ward W A	17.80
6Feb85 ^{8}Aqu^{8}	Sluggard	b 5 110	4	3	6	6	4^{4}	$4^{3\frac{1}{4}}$	Davis R G	31.30
18Feb85 ^{8}Aqu^{2}	Main Stem	b 7 109	3	5	$5^{\frac{1}{2}}$	5^{hd}	5^{1}	$5^{2\frac{1}{4}}$	Thibeau R J	12.60
17Feb85 ^{8}Aqu^{1}	Elegant Life	b 5 116	5	2	3^{1}	$4^{\frac{1}{2}}$	6	6	Velasquez J	3.70

OFF AT 4:48. Start good, Won driving. Time, :22⅕, :44⅘, 1:09⅗ Track fast.

$2 Mutuel Prices:				
	7-(G)-FIGHTING FIT	3.00	2.40	2.20
	3-(C)-ENTROPY		3.40	2.40
	2-(B)-SHADOWMAR			2.80

$2 EXACTA 7-3 PAID $8.00.

Ch. h, by Full Pocket—Napalm, by Nilo. Trainer Frankel Robert. Bred by Nuckols Bros (Ky).

FIGHTING FIT forced to race six wide around turn, accelerated reaching leaders turning for home and fighting furiously in a three way duel as field straigntened away, determinedly, forced to front seventy yards out, gaining nod in a blanket finish. ENTROPY between horses entire way forcing and setting pace held ground courageously just missing. SHADOWMAR displaying more early foot than usual while saving ground throughout battled gamely to the end in a sharp effort. SLUGGARD wanting for room entering stretch finished well. MAIN STEM could not keep up. ELEGANT LIFE retired early.

Although able to win, he could no longer be regarded as a dominant force in the sprint ranks. Had the New York weather affected him? Was the New York trainer left in charge of the horse unable to maintain the razor-sharp edge Frankel had honed?

Pancho Villa also failed to follow up. He lost the Gotham on April 6 to Eternal Prince, whom he had smothered in the Bay Shore, proving once again that no matter how good a horse looks on paper, it still has to run once around the racetrack. Unlike Fighting Fit, though, Pancho Villa seemed to have a plethora of possible excuses for his defeat. A strong tail wind on the backstretch favored the front-running Eternal Prince, as such conditions usually do. Also, Pancho Villa was asked to race on a negative rail the entire trip, and that could not have helped his chances. Prior to the Gotham, and a few late scratches that reduced the size of the field, there was considerable talk about the obstacles post 1 presents in mile races run out of a backstretch chute. Horses starting from the rail MUST break alertly. Otherwise they will be forced to sit behind the early leaders and face the possibility of being boxed in as the field reaches the far turn. In this kind of race, the closers begin moving at that point, the long run down the back side giving them the chance to get into gear earlier than usual. To make things worse, if an inside horse doesn't break sharply, it faces the possibility that rivals from the outside will move into the rail to save ground—as they tend to do in this kind of race—and pinch the inside horse back even farther.

One additional fact—Pancho Villa did not look as sharp in the paddock for the Gotham as he had for the Bay Shore, information passed along to me by Paul Mellos, a truly astute paddock observer. This, of course, raised the possibility that Pancho Villa might become another in a long list of California invaders that go off form after just one sharp race in the East.

Eternal Prince's form reversal from the Bay Shore to the Gotham surprised many observers, but not the sharpest of trip handicappers. They had noticed the colt fighting for his head, resenting the rating tactics restraining him in the early stages of the Bay Shore. We quote from an article that appeared in the April 10 issue of *The Thoroughbred Record:*

> "That's my fault," volunteered owner Hurst. The youthful looking horseman is quite active in planning the careers of his horses. "I thought that he'd have a better shot at winning the Bay Shore if he were rated off a pace that was obviously going to be set by Don't Hesitate, and that is a very, very fast colt," continued Hurst. "It didn't work."

EIGHTH RACE
Aqueduct
APRIL 6, 1985

1 MILE. (1.33⅕) 33rd Running THE GOTHAM (Grade II). $150,000 Added (Plus $50,000 Breeders' Cup Premium Awards). 3-year-olds. By subscription of $300 each, which should accompany the nomination; $4,000 to pass the entry box, with $150,000 added. The added money and all fees to be divided 60% to the winner, 22% to second, 12% to third and 6% to fourth. 126 lbs. Non-winners of a race of $100,000 at a mile or over in 1985 allowed 3 lbs; of two races of $75,000 at any time, 5 lbs.; of a race of $50,000, 8 lbs.; of a race other than maiden or claiming at a mile or over, 12 lbs. Starters to be named at the closing time of entries. Trophies will be presented to the winning owner, trainer and jockey. Closed with 38 Nominations Wednesday, March 20, 1985. Breeders' Cup Fund Awards to: Eternal Prince, Pancho Villa and El Basco.
Total purse $251,400. Value of race $246,400; value to winner $147,840; second $57,808; third $28,668; fourth $12,084. Nominator Awards $5,000. Mutuel pool $239,304, OTB pool $243,817. Exacta Pool $256,008. OTB Exacta Pool $254,586.

Last Raced	Horse	Eqt.	A.	Wt	PP	St	¼	½	¾	Str	Fin	Jockey	Odds $1
23Mar85 ^{8}Aqu^{6}	Eternal Prince	b	3	114	7	1	$1^{1\frac{1}{2}}$	$1^{1\frac{1}{2}}$	$1^{1\frac{1}{2}}$	1^{2}	1^{5}	Migliore R	18.40
23Mar85 ^{8}Aqu^{1}	Pancho Villa	b	3	121	1	6	$3^{2\frac{1}{2}}$	3^{4}	3^{5}	2^{1}	$2^{\frac{1}{2}}$	Lovato F Jr	1.10
23Mar85 ^{8}Aqu^{2}	El Basco	b	3	114	4	7	7	7	4^{2}	4^{5}	$3^{1\frac{1}{4}}$	McCarron G	2.90
9Mar85 ^{6}Aqu^{1}	Nordance	b	3	118	5	3	2^{hd}	2^{1}	2^{1}	$3^{1\frac{1}{2}}$	$4^{5\frac{3}{4}}$	Skinner K	5.80
2Mar85^{11}GP^{3}	Do It Again Dan		3	114	6	2	6^{2}	5^{hd}	6^{4}	$5^{1\frac{1}{2}}$	$5^{2\frac{3}{4}}$	MacBeth D	3.20
22Mar85 ^{8}Aqu^{4}	Uene	b	3	118	3	4	4^{1}	$4^{1\frac{1}{2}}$	5^{hd}	6^{3}	6no	Santagata N	49.30
16Mar85^{10}Tam^{6}	Testimonial	b	3	114	2	5	$5^{2\frac{1}{2}}$	6^{hd}	7	7	7	Cordero A Jr	29.00

OFF AT 4:44 Start good, Won driving. Time, :22⅕, :44⅕, 1:08⅖, 1:34⅖ Track fast.

$2 Mutuel Prices:				
	8–(J)–ETERNAL PRINCE	38.80	9.80	5.60
	1–(A)–PANCHO VILLA		3.20	2.60
	5–(F)–EL BASCO			3.20

$2 EXACTA 8–1 PAID $130.40.

B. c, by Majestic Prince—Eternal Queen, by Fleet Nasrullah. Trainer Lenzini John J Jr. Bred by Kinsman Stud Farm (Fla).

ETERNAL PRINCE raced slightly out from the rail while making the pace, held a clear lead into the stretch and drew away under brisk urging. PANCHO VILLA, a factor to the stretch while saving ground, was no match for the winner. EL BASCO, off slowly, failed to seriously menace while racing wide. NORDANCE, prominent to the stretch while racing well out from the rail, tired. DO IT AGAIN DAN was always outrun. UENE, in tight quarters leaving the chute,tired. TESTIMONIAL, steadied slightly between horses leaving the chute, lacked a further response.

Some horses simply cannot be rated, and sulk when such tactics are employed, usually quitting badly after a few furlongs. Eternal Prince was such a colt. Allowed to role early in the Gotham (and subsequent Wood Memorial), he looked like a world beater. His 120 figure for the Gotham was the fastest for that fixture in at least thirty years. His 129 pace figure for the first three quarters was truly outstanding. The wind helped him win, no doubt, but has been factored into these figures.

Chapter 37

Dr. Alphabet's Back in Town

THE SUCCESSFUL HANDICAPPER of the 1980s realizes that he is playing a difficult game. He must match selections with legions of clever rivals, most of whom come armed with accurate speed figures and/or detailed trip notes, yet still overcome a 17–20 percent take. To succeed, he must have some additional weapons, information that others in the crowd don't share. One of the last frontiers in this respect is the field of trainer analysis. Is a certain trainer competent? Does he (or she) employ certain pet strategies to produce a consistent flow of winners or put across a good percentage of longshots?

The successful player must be able to answer such questions, and not only in reference to the trainers on his local circuit. He must also be familiar with the trainers who ship in from nearby circuits and know how well they have raided the local treasury in the past.

As a keen advocate of grass racing, I pay particular attention to those trainers who excel at the infield sport, indeed point their charges for careers as grass runners. In New York, this means Mack Miller, Angel Penna, Sr., Angel Penna, Jr., Jonathan Sheppard, Tom Skiffington, Adrian Maxwell, to mention just a few. During the latter part of the 1984 season, I took note of a trainer/veterinarian named J.R.S. Fisher (Dr. Alphabet, as he came to be known to the New York press), whose horses seemed to perform consistently well when shipped to New York to race on the grass. I decided to follow him closely the following spring at Belmont Park.

Fisher first hit the entries on May 31 with a maiden filly named Coda, who was scheduled for her grass debut that day. Coda had shown speed to the head of the stretch in her most recent start (at Pimlico), her first attempt at a route distance in her second start of the year. She ran second at Belmont on May 31, missing by a neck at 5–1.

Coda Ch. f. 3, by Codex—Last Line, by Kalamoun
Own.—Pillar Farm
Br.—Pillar Stud Inc (Ky)
Tr.—Fisher John R S
113
Lifetime 4 0 0 0 $570
1985 2 M 0 0 $570
1984 2 M 0 0
10Apr85- 6Pim fst 1 1/16 :47⅘ 1:13⅖ 1:46⅘ 3+ Ⓕ Md Sp Wt 6 2 2 1½ 3 1 6 7½ 7 8¾ Jones S R5 107 4.30 61-19 Full Attack 112no Lady Doughnut 1241 Savannah Girl 1122½ Tired 9
13Mar85- 6Key fst 6f :22⅘ 46⅗ 1:13 Ⓕ Md Sp Wt 4 6 8 7¾ 7 10 6 7 5 6½ Antley C W 122 15.90 69-26 Carmella Sweets 1223RiverLiffey1221½DBiueBella1221½ Squeezed 8
13Mar85-Placed fourth through disqualification
27Dec84- 6Bow fst 6f :22⅘ :46⅖ 1:13 Ⓕ Md Sp Wt 2 6 5 3¾ 6 15 7 15 5 9¾ Hutton G W 120 *1.50e 65-23 CpturedMemory1205¼Redstrte1202¼PrincssPipit1201¾ Brief speed 12
1Dec84- 5Key fst 6f :22⅗ :46⅗ 1:12⅘ Ⓕ Md Sp Wt 10 4 5 2¾ 9 10 10 23 10 32 Vigliotti M J b 120 4.20 45-27 ContessaRidge1151CarmellSweets12011CountessZero1201 Outrun 10
LATEST WORKOUTS May 21 Fai tr.t 5f fst 1:03 b ●May 15 Fai 5f fst 1:01⅕ b May 8 Fai tr.t 4f fst :49⅘ b Apr 6 Fai tr.t 4f fst :53⅕ b

Next came another maiden filly, this one named Wooki, who bid and hung a month earlier at Pimlico in her grass debut, in a race won by stablemate Dictionary. Playable off that race, Wooki ran ninth at Belmont at 8–1.

Wooki Dk. b. or br. f. 3, by Star De Naskra—Cofimvaba, by Verrieres
Own.—Willbrook Farm
Br.—Pillar Stud Inc (Ky)
Tr.—Fisher John R S
114
Lifetime 4 0 1 0 $2,215
1985 3 M 0 0 $315
1984 1 M 1 0 $1,900
Turf 1 0 0 0
30Apr85- 5Pim fm 1 Ⓣ:46⅘ 1:12⅕ 1:39⅗ 3+ Ⓕ Md Sp Wt 8 5 5 10 5 6 3 1½ 6 3¾ Hutton G W 112 *3.20e 77-14 Dictionary 1151 Go Bay Go 107nkLadyJumna114no Bid, weakened 12
6Apr85- 6Pim fst 6f :23 :46⅘ 1:13⅗ 3+ Ⓕ Md Sp Wt 2 5 5 4½ 5 6 6 9 9 12¾ Miller D A Jr b 115 3.80 65-15 AmbassadorofLove113¾LadyLuisa1141PeceKeeper1221½ Fell back 10
27Mar85- 4Key fst 6f :22⅕ :45⅘ 1:11⅗ Ⓕ Md Sp Wt 8 2 5 5 5 4½ 5 5½ 5 11¾ Terry J 122 5.60 72-14 Hail The State 1224 Resolute Lady 1224 River Liffey1222½ Evenly 10
30Dec84- 3Key fst 6f :22⅗ :47⅕ 1:14 Ⓕ Md Sp Wt 1 7 6 9 6 8 4 3½ 2 3 Antley C W 120 3.30 68-26 Pink Rice 1203 Wooki 1201¾ Rich Rose 120½ Best of others 9
LATEST WORKOUTS Jun 4 Fai tr.t 3f fst :37⅘ b ●May 23 Fai tr.t 7f fst 1:29 b May 18 Fai tr.t 4f fst :49⅘ b Apr 24 Fai 4f fst :49⅘ b

On Saturday, June 15, Fisher came to town with two horses. He won the second race with the seven-year-old Cantonero, who appeared to be moving up several notches in claiming value, at odds of 15–1.

***Cantonero** B. h. 7, by Lefty—Capricciolì, by Saint Crespin III
Own.—Watriss J B
$35,000
Br.—Haras Las Ortigas (Arg)
Tr.—Fisher John R S
117
Lifetime 21 5 5 4 $26,882
1985 3 1 0 1 $4,125
1984 6 0 0 2 $2,146
Turf 12 4 2 3 $21,649
27May85-11Pen fm 170 Ⓣ 1:38⅘ Clm 22500 8 4 5 6½ 4 3½ 3 4 3 5½ Aviles R B 115 8.10 86-17 Mydrone 1122 Gray Dude 1123½ Cantonero 115½ Rallied 9
13May85- 7Del fm *1 Ⓣ:48⅕ 1:13⅗ 1:39⅖ 3+ Clm 14000 3 2 1hd 1½ 1 1 1 1 Terry J 116 3.40 91-09 Cantonero 1161 Buddy Hasher 1165 Sportsmanship 1122½ Driving 9
1May85- 7Pim fm 5f Ⓣ:21⅘ :45⅖ :57⅘ Clm 18500 9 9 10 13 10 20 9 18 9 15½ Miller D A Jr b 115 10.20 83-05 Dr. Tipton 1194 March To Moscow 1122½SoberParson114¾ Outrun 10
15Dec84- 6Key fst 170 :48 1:13⅗ 1:44⅘ 3+ Clm 11000 7 11 9 8½ 10 11 10 15 10 16¾ Vigliotti M J 116 21.90 60-26 Singh Boldly 116hd RescueMeRoscoe1162Intheblack1161½ Outrun 12
30Nov84- 6Key fst 1 1/16 :47⅗ 1:11⅗ 1:43⅘ 3+ Clm 32000 4 6 6 11 — — — Vigliotti M J 116 13.80 — — Almeden 1141 Vagabond Sergeant1143MyGallantBoy11710½ Eased 6
23Nov84- 7Med fst 170 :48⅕ 1:12⅘ 1:43⅕ 3+ Clm 40000 6 3 1hd 4 7½ 7 11 7 13½ Rocco J 116 16.10 69-26 Mountaineer Joe114hdAnne'sRainbow1123FlightofTime1143 Tired 8
28Oct84- 6Lrl fm 1 1/16 Ⓣ:47⅖ 1:11⅗ 1:41⅖ 3+ Clm 40000 5 2 3 2½ 2 3 3 6½ 3 8½ Miller D A Jr 116 5.40 88-09 Tim Tamber 1146 Tyralno 1162½ Cantonero 116no Weakened 8
14Oct84- 7Pen fm 1 Ⓣ 1:34⅘ 3+ Alw 8600 4 5 5 7 5 7 5 6½ 3 2½ Colton R E 113 7.00 89-16 Four Lane 1161½ Reliable Jeff 1131½ Cantonero 113¾ Rallied 10
21Sep84- 7Lrl fm 1 1/16 Ⓣ:47 1:11⅗ 1:41⅗ 3+ Clm 40000 8 2 2hd 6 2¾ 7 8 8 10½ Bracciale V Jr 116 5.80 85-03 The Ripleyite 1161½ King Neptune 116½ Subarctic 1141 Faltered 8
16Oct83 ♦1Hipodromo(Arg) hy*1¼ 2:02⅕ Premio Villares(Alw) 3 14 Liceri E 126 *.35 — — Intensive 1192 Mart 11512 Cantonero 1263½ 7
LATEST WORKOUTS Apr 30 Fai tr.t 3f fst :39 b

And the fourth with the beautifully bred maiden filly Romanette, who had finished with a rush in her seasonal debut over six furlongs at Monmouth on May 27. Romanette returned $9.80 for her impressive victory at ten furlongs.

Romanette Dk. b. or br. f. 3, by Alleged—Laughing Bridge, by Hilarious
Own.—Holtsinger Christina
Br.—Holtsinger Inc (Ky)
Tr.—Fisher John R S
114
Lifetime 3 0 1 2 $4,155
1985 1 M 0 1 $1,210
1984 2 M 1 1 $2,945
27May85-10Mth fst 6f :22⅘ :47⅕ 1:13⅘ 3+ Ⓕ Md Sp Wt 2 3 4 4 6 2¾ 6 2¾ 3nk Rocco J 115 6.50 71-26 Golden Sabre 115nk Breezily 123no Romanette 115¾ Rallied 12
15Dec84- 5Key fst 6½f :22⅗ :46⅘ 1:21 Ⓕ Md Sp Wt 8 6 8 8¾ 7 8¾ 5 5 2 1¾ Vigliotti M J 120 3.10 66-26 P. R. Pakman 1201¾ Romanette 120nk ScrabbleQueen1203 Gamely 9
22Nov84- 4Key fst 6f :22⅗ :46⅗ 1:13 Ⓕ Md Sp Wt 2 7 6 3¾ 6 8½ 3 8½ 3 1½ Vigliotti M J 120 6.80 74-18 Dungarvin Princess 115½ResoluteLady1201Romanette1208 Rallied 11
LATEST WORKOUTS Jun 12 Fai tr.t 4f fst :49 b ●May 22 Fai tr.t 5f fst 1:01⅘ b May 15 Fai 5f fst 1:03⅗ bg May 7 Fai tr.t 5f fst 1:04 b

Four days later the aforementioned Dictionary shipped in, sporting three excellent performances in her three career grass outings. The New York audience, aware of what had transpired the preceding weekend, made Dictionary their 5–2 favorite, but the Elocutionist filly could do no better than sixth.

Dictionary — Dk. b. or br. f. 3, by Elocutionist—Julie's Image, by Dancer's Image
Own.—Lawribru Stables — Br.—Gelb R (Ky) — Tr.—Fisher John R S — **109**

	Lifetime				
	13 1 2 4				
	$15,637				
1985	8	1	2	3	$14,582
1984	5	M	0	1	$1,045
Turf	3	1	1	1	$9,582

11Jun85- 7Mth	fm	1 1/16	Ⓣ:48 1:12⅕ 1:44⅗	3+ⒻAlw 13000	5	9	9^{10}	$8^{6½}$	$6^{3¼}$	2½	Rocco J	111	5.30	81-16	BrooklynPrincess118½Dictionary111^{nk}Ryn'sDughter109^{nk}	In close	10
24May85- 8Mth	fst	1 1/16	:48⅗ 1:13⅕ 1:47⅕	3+ⒻAlw 13000	3	4	$4^{5½}$	4^{10}	4^{9}	4^{16}	Antley C W	111	3.00	53-25	Vital Move 119no Darbrielle 114^{4} Stats Anna 119^{12}	No threat	9
13May85- 8Del	fm	*1	Ⓣ:48⅘ 1:14 1:39⅗	3+ⒻAlw 6200	1	3	2½	2½	1hd	1½	Walford J	114	*1.20Ⓓ	90-09	ⒹDictionary 114½ Let's Go Twice 119^{3½} Wistoral 119^{nk}	Bore out	9
13May85-Disqualified and placed third																	
30Apr85- 5Pim	fm	1	Ⓣ:46⅗ 1:12⅕ 1:39⅗	3+ⒻMd Sp Wt	6	4	3^{8}	4^{3}	1½	1^{1}	Miller D A Jr	115	*3.20e	81-14	Dictionary 115^{1} Go Bay Go 107^{nk} Lady Jumna 114no	Driving	12
9Apr85- 1GS	fst	170	:46⅗ 1:11⅗ 1:41⅗	ⒻMd Sp Wt	10	3	2^{1}	$2^{1½}$	$3^{6½}$	3^{9}	Antley C W	118	8.60	— —	Rey s Joyce 118^{5} Our Aquilon 118^{4} Dictionary 118^{3½}	Weakened	10
1Apr85- 6Pim	gd	1 1/16	:47⅖ 1:13⅕ 1:47⅖	3+ⒻMd Sp Wt	5	5	$4^{5½}$	$3^{6½}$	$3^{4½}$	$3^{6½}$	Miller D A Jr	115	4.70	60-27	Ros'sEightyDys107^{4½}KntuckyMoonshin112^{2}Dictionry115^{1½}	Evenly	10
23Feb85- 5Lrl	fst	7f	:22⅘ :47 1:26⅕	ⒻMd Sp Wt	4	8	7^{7}	$5^{7½}$	6^{14}	$6^{18½}$	Hutton G W	b 120	5.90	62-24	Classy Cut 120^{4}PrincessAurora120^{no}PrincessPipit120^{1½}	No factor	9
7Feb85- 4Lrl	sly	6½f	:22⅗ :47 1:21⅘	ⒻMd 25000	5	7	$4^{3½}$	2^{4}	$2^{2½}$	2^{1}	Miller D A Jr	b 120	3.80	— —	Lenapes' Image 113^{1} Dictionary 120^{4} Gal 120^{hd}	Game try	8
28Dec84- 3Med	fst	6f	:22⅘ :46⅖ 1:12	ⒻMd 32000	3	—	—	—	—	—	Antley C W	b 118	5.40	— —	The Baker's Wife 113^{6½} Smu 118^{1½} Shame On Esther 113^{2}	Dwelt	8
6Dec84- 3Aqu	sly	6f	⊡:22⅗ :46⅕ 1:12⅕	ⒻMd 50000	4	8	$6^{3¼}$	7^{10}	5^{8}	$5^{8½}$	Guerra W A	b 117	22.10	75-12	Dream Puss 117^{5} Regal Lynco 113^{1½} SweetSound113^{1}	No mishap	9

LATEST WORKOUTS Jun 6 Fai tr.t 5f fst 1:02⅗ b Apr 24 Fai 5f fst 1:02⅗ b

The following day brought with it Carlypha, with whom Fisher had been successful twice in five tries in New York the previous fall. Despite a good performance in her seasonal debut at Monmouth on May 27—speed to the stretch call after breaking from post 10—Carlypha was allowed to start at odds of 8–1. She ran a close second, missing by a neck.

***Carlypha** — Gr. f. 4, by Bellypha—Carloir, by Val De Loir
Own.—Lawribru Stable — Br.—Gelb R (Ire) — Tr.—Fisher John R S — **117**

	Lifetime				
	10 2 0 1				
	$30,195				
1985	1	0	0	0	$840
1984	9	2	0	1	$29,355
Turf	8	2	0	0	$29,535

27May85- 5Mth	fm	1 1/16	Ⓣ:48⅕ 1:12 1:43⅕	3+ⒻAlw 14000	10	2	2½	1hd	1hd	$4^{3½}$	Perret C	119	3.70	86-08	IllustriousJonne119^{2}RueSt.Honore121½LReineRos119¾	Weakened	10
17Nov84- 9Del	fst	1 1/16	:48 1:12⅗ 1:46⅘	Ⓕ[R]N. S. Gal	7	4	$5^{5¼}$	6^{10}	$6^{9¾}$	$6^{18½}$	Nied D	122	5.70	56-28	ⒹShould Excell 122½ Pocobella 119^{11} Magic Circle 112^{2}	Tired	7
4Nov84- 5Aqu	gd	1 1/16	Ⓣ:50⅖ 1:15⅖ 1:47⅕	3+ⒻAlw 21000	6	7	$6^{2¾}$	$4^{1½}$	4¾	1½	Davis R G	115	*3.60	69-26	Carlypha 115½ [DH]Dawna 112 [DH]Halloween Queen 115^{2¾}	Driving	10
19Oct84- 7Bel	fm	1¼	[T]:48⅗ 1:38⅕ 2:02⅘	3+ⒻAlw 21000	9	5	$5^{2½}$	4^{3}	$5^{2¾}$	$4^{2½}$	Ward W A^{5}	109	10.70	77-24	BareEssence119^{2½}Mickey'sLady114^{nk}CourgeousKren116^{no}	Rallied	12
28Sep84- 1Bel	yl	1⅜	[T]:48⅘ 1:39⅘ 2:19⅕	3+ⒻAlw 21000	1	2	2hd	3^{2}	2^{2}	$4^{2¾}$	Ward W A^{5}	113	10.60	58-36	Enhanced113^{nk}QueenofZend113^{2½}OneDncingLdy115^{nk}	Weakened	8
6Sep84- 2Bel	gd	1⅜	[T]:48 1:41⅘ 2:20⅖	3+ⒻMd Sp Wt	10	6	$5^{4½}$	2hd	2hd	1nk	Ward W A^{5}	113	6.00	55-27	Crlyph113^{nk}CourgeousKrn118^{4½}JddSpirit118^{1¾}	Lugged in, driving	11
20Aug84- 4Sar	fm	1½	[T]:49⅖ 2:08 2:33⅘	3+ⒻMd Sp Wt	4	5	$6^{5½}$	$5^{2½}$	4^{2}	$4^{3½}$	MacBeth D	117	2.80	70-19	June Bride 117no Flora Scent 117^{2¾}CourageousKaren112½	Rallied	9
3Aug84- 7Mth	fm	1 1/16	Ⓣ:48⅖ 1:12⅗ 1:45 +	3+ⒻMd Sp Wt	2	6	6^{5}	$7^{4¾}$Apr	$4^{3½}$	$4^{2¾}$	Terry J	116	3.50	73-17	Minety 123^{2} Kitty Tatch 116^{nk} Rhonda Vu 111½	Boxed in	9
13Jly84- 5Mth	fm	1 1/16	Ⓣ:48 1:12⅗ 1:46	3+ⒻMd Sp Wt	3	10	$8^{8¾}$	6^{5}	6^{5}	$5^{2½}$	Terry J	115	5.40	78-16	WyetteCoughlin115¾JddSpirit115¾RhondVu110^{1}	Stded,atLbear in	11
2Jly84- 5Atl	fst	1 1/16	:47⅕ 1:12 1:46⅖	3+ⒻMd Sp Wt	7	3	3^{2}	3^{5}	$3^{6½}$	$3^{5¾}$	Terry J	114	9.00	67-20	Faithful J. A. P. 114^{5} Mayoress 114¾ Carlypha 114^{1}	Slow start	7

LATEST WORKOUTS ●Jun 15 Fai tr.t 5f fst :59⅗ b ●Jun 8 Fai tr.t 4f fst :51 b May 23 Fai tr.t 3f fst :39 bg ●May 20 Fai tr.t 5f fst 1:00 b

The evidence we have seen—two wins and two close seconds from six starters—suggests quite emphatically that Dr. Fisher was an extraordinary horseman, one capable of bringing a horse up to a peak performance—even at a classic distance—off a single prep race. Indeed, Fisher seemed to use races in New Jersey, Pennsylvania, Maryland, and Delaware to prepare his charges for winning efforts in New York, where the purse structure is the highest on the East Coast. When Fisher shipped a horse to New York, one could be certain that he thought the animal was ready for a peak effort.

The six horses we looked at were all stabled at Fair Hill, which suggests that Fisher's roots might be found in steeplechase racing. Many graduates of the steeplechase ranks have gone on to prove themselves more than competent trainers in New York, the most notable recently being Tom Skiffington. Almost to a man, the steeplechase people are outstanding horsemen. They know how to train

2 BELMONT

INNER TURF COURSE
1¼ MILES
BELMONT PARK
START • FINISH

1¼ MILES. (InnerTurf). (1.58⅘) MAIDEN SPECIAL WEIGHTS. Purse $23,000. Fillies and Mares, 3-year-old and upward. Weights, 3-year-olds, 114 lbs. Older, 122 lbs.

Graceful Power
B. f. 3, by Mullineaux—Luv U Grace, by Vested Power
Own.—Tamily Margaret
Br.—Tamily H (NY)
Tr.—Coladonato Eugene J
114
Lifetime 7 0 0 0 $1,590 | 1985 7 M 0 0 $1,590 | 1984 0 M 0 0 | Turf 1 0 0 0 $1,590

3Jun85- 2Bel fm 1¼ T :48⅕ 1:39⅘ 2:06⅘ 3+ F S Md Sp Wt 6 8 818 613 412 415 McCarron G b 114 52.50 47-28 Sister Sophie 1143 Karabar 1229 Shawanna 1223 No factor 9
9May85- 9Bel fst 1⅛ :47⅘ 1:13⅘ 1:47⅘ 3+ F Md 30000 4 9 1017 920 921 931¼ Cruguet J b 111 39.30 32-25 PrincipalAsset1122PlumIslandGirl113¾RelativeAffair1116¼ Outrun 11
3May85- 3Aqu sly 6f :23⅘ :48⅘ 1:14⅘ 3+ F Md 20000 5 12 1211 1216 814 710¾ Cruguet J b 113 31.10 57-26 Whiskey Mama 1032¼ Jintzy 111¾ Full Explanation 1206¼ Slow st 13
22Apr85- 2Aqu fst 1⅛ :49⅘ 1:15⅗ 1:55⅗ 3+ F Md 22500 7 5 43¼ 56 717 816¼ Reed R L7 b 103 59.50 41-23 Hawaii Drone 1134¼ Mind Flight 105¼ Lady In Lights 1241¾ Tired 9
10Apr85- 3Aqu fst 1⅛ :49⅘ 1:14⅘ 1:57 3+ F S Md Sp Wt 10 10 913 913 712 612¾ Thibeau R J b 112 25.30 37-29 Far N' Swift 1241 Find The Cure 1123¼ Shemadeit 124¼ Outrun 10
2Apr85- 9Aqu fst 1⅛ :50⅘ 1:15⅘ 1:56 3+ F Md 25000 6 3 51¾ 96¾ 915 67¾ Espinosa R E7 b 105 52.00 47-20 Visible Marie 1122¼ Q. Qui 107nk Lady In Lights 124nk Fell back 11
16Mar85- 4Aqu fst 1 :47⅕ 1:13⅘ 1:41 F S Md Sp Wt 3 13 1316 1325 1128 1129¾ Garrido O L5 116 20.00e 31-34 Boris The Cat 121¾ Mullie Yep 1214 Etoile Joyeux 1211¼ Outrun 13
LATEST WORKOUTS Jun 28 Bel 4f fst :50 bg Jun 24 Bel 3f fst :37 h Jun 18 Bel 4f fst :50⅘ b Jun 14 Bel 5f fst 1:04 b

Miss Marble
Dk. b. or br. f. 3, by Drone—Annely, by Nashua
Own.—Li M Y
Br.—Greely & Crutcher (Ky)
Tr.—Baillie Sally A
114
Lifetime 9 0 1 2 $10,200 | 1985 9 M 1 2 $10,200 | 1984 0 M 0 0 | Turf 3 0 0 0 $2,760

15Jun85- 4Bel fm 1¼ T :48⅕ 1:37⅕ 2:03 3+ F Md Sp Wt 4 6 67 43½ 45 47¼ Davis R G b 114 17.30 72-18 Romanette 1144¼ My Cliche 122¾ Village Jazz1142 Bid, weakened 8
7Jun85- 6Bel gd 1⅛ T :47 1:13⅘ 1:46⅘ 3+ F Md Sp Wt 5 9 85¾ 51¾ 34 47¼ Davis R G b 114 52.50 57-27 Rumor 114no One MomentPlease1146ChampagneBabe1141¼ Wide 12
11May85- 2Bel fm 1¼ T :47⅘ 1:38 2:04⅕ 3+ F Md Sp Wt 2 12 1120 910 914 912¾ MacBeth D b 113 32.20 60-17 Communictor119nkHighlnd'sBest1131¼Chrlie sAngel1243¼ Outrun 12
13Apr85- 6Aqu fst 1 :47 1:12⅕ 1:39⅘ F Md Sp Wt 1 3 22 56¼ 59¾ 510¼ Ward W A 121 5.20 58-21 Sois Sage 121¾ Also Glorious 121¾ Princess Ivory 1144 Tired bdly 6
18Mar85- 3Aqu fst 1 :49⅘ 1:15⅘ 1:42⅘ F Md Sp Wt 7 5 42¼ 23 23 33¾ Davis R G 121 13.60 50-38 Sweet Sound121¾VaguelyFoolish1213MissMarble1216¼ Weakened 8
7Mar85- 6Aqu fst 1⅟₁₆ ⊡ :49⅘ 1:15 1:49⅘ F Md Sp Wt 8 4 41¾ 53 65¾ 67¼ Samyn J L 121 4.60 53-21 Nancy English 1211 Our Aquilon 1211¾ExplosiveCandy1142¾ Tired 12
20Feb85- 6Aqu fst 6f ⊡ :23⅕ :47⅘ 1:13⅘ F Md Sp Wt 7 8 73¼ 54 55¼ 56¼ Samyn J L 121 *1.50 69-23 Talanta 121¾ Charming Luisa 1163¼ Too Sunny 121nk No threat 12
10Feb85- 2Aqu fst 6f ⊡ :23⅕ :47⅘ 1:12⅘ F Md Sp Wt 6 11 105¾ 47¼ 46¼ 36 Samyn J L 121 7.40 75-18 Sherry Mary 1212 Classy Cut 1214 Miss Marble 1213¼ Raced wide 12
25Jan85- 2Aqu fst 6f ⊡ :23⅘ :47⅘ 1:13⅘ F Md 45000 5 12 64¼ 3nk 23 2¾ Guerra A A5 112 22.10 74-23 TinaMaus111¾MissMrble1121Pellinore'sPride1215¾ Raced greenly 12
LATEST WORKOUTS Jun 13 Bel 4f fst :49 h Jun 2 Bel 6f fst 1:18⅘ b May 26 Bel 5f fst 1:04⅘ b May 20 Bel 5f fst 1:02⅘ b

Village Jazz
B. f. 3, by Stage Door Johnny—Crazy Music, by Hail To Reason
Own.—Greentree Stable
Br.—Greentree Stud Inc (Ky)
Tr.—Reinacher Robert Jr
114
Lifetime 4 0 1 2 $10,580 | 1985 4 M 1 2 $10,580 | 1984 0 M 0 0 | Turf 2 0 0 2 $5,520

15Jun85- 4Bel fm 1¼ T :48⅕ 1:37⅕ 2:03 3+ F Md Sp Wt 7 4 22¼ 31½ 33¼ 35¼ Velasquez J b 114 *1.30 74-18 Romanette 1144¼ My Cliche122¾VillageJazz1142 Needed response 8
31May85- 7Bel fm 1⅜ T :49⅘ 1:40⅘ 2:19⅕ 3+ F Md Sp Wt 3 9 910 911 511 37 Velasquez J 113 *1.80 59-28 I'm A Bell Raiser 113nk Coda 1136¾ Village Jazz 1132¼ Stride late 11
22May85- 3Bel fst 7f :22⅘ :45⅘ 1:23⅕ F Md Sp Wt 5 6 87¼ 812 613 616 Velasquez J 121 1.90 70-14 Coup De Fusil 1147 Hawaiian Tea 1211¼ MissGeneral1212¼ Outrun 8
9May85- 1Bel fst 1⅟₁₆ :47 1:12⅘ 1:46⅕ 3+ F Md Sp Wt 1 3 31 2¼ 22 21¼ Velasquez J 113 3.10 70-25 Dismasted 1131¼ Village Jazz1137Ms.Chamois1133¼ Bore in,hes.st. 7
LATEST WORKOUTS Jun 24 Bel 4f fst :50⅘ b ● Jun 9 Bel 6f gd 1:13⅘ h May 17 Bel 4f fst :48⅘ h May 7 Bel 4f fst :48 h

Winerette
Dk. b. or br. f. 3, by Sir Wimborne—Benderette, by Triple Bend
Own.—Mirrione V
Br.—Eaton & Thorne (NY)
Tr.—Mirrione Vincent
114
Lifetime 3 0 1 0 $5,830 | 1985 3 M 1 0 $5,830 | 1984 0 M 0 0 | Turf 1 0 1 0 $5,830

21Jun85- 6Bel fm 1⅟₁₆ T :46⅘ 1:11⅘ 1:44 3+ F S Md Sp Wt 9 8 912 56 34¼ 210¼ McCarron G 114 64.20 65-14 CrypticMiss11410¼Winerette1143¼CastlesofIce104¼ Best of others 12
9Jun85- 9Bel gd 7f :22⅘ :46⅘ 1:26 3+ F S Md Sp Wt 9 6 42 52¼ 816 923¼ Maple E 114 41.00 48-18 Playing Foolish 11413¼ Bro's Sissy1151¼Star'sEstrelita1141¼ Tired 12
22May85- 2Bel fst 7f :22⅘ :46⅕ 1:25⅕ 3+ F S Md Sp Wt 9 11 79¼ 88¾ 815 720¼ Santagata N 113 52.80 56-14 National Paisley 1131 Entangle 11310¾ Shawanna 124no Outrun 12
LATEST WORKOUTS May 7 Bel 5f fst 1:05 b

Caviar and Toast
Ch. f. 3, by Czaravich—Sundestine, by Clandestine
Own.—Fraser J A
Br.—Fraser J A (Ohio)
Tr.—Laurin Roger
114
Lifetime 5 0 0 2 $5,580 | 1985 1 M 0 0 | 1984 4 M 0 2 $5,580 | Turf 1 0 0 0

23Jun85- 2Bel fm 1⅟₁₆ T :46⅕ 1:10⅘ 1:42⅕ 3+ F Md Sp Wt 8 10 1111 910 815 920 Skinner K 114 7.80 65-12 My Regrets 1143 Blint 1147 Inca Rose 114¾ Outrun 11
9Nov84- 4Aqu fst 1⅛ :50 1:15⅘ 1:56⅕ F Md Sp Wt 3 2 2½ 2½ 45 47¼ Velasquez J b 117 *1.50 46-32 Glorious Grey 1171¾ Hawaiian Tea 1171¾ Rebut 1174 Weakened 8
1Nov84- 4Aqu fst 1 :47⅕ 1:12⅘ 1:39 F Md Sp Wt 5 6 63 55 46 35 Skinner K 117 9.00 66-21 Affirmance 1172¾ Perfect Point 1172¼CaviarandToast1171 Rallied 8
11Oct84- 7Bel fst 7f :23⅘ :47⅘ 1:27⅘ F Md Sp Wt 9 10 1111 86¼ 53¼ 32 Skinner K 117 33.30 62-26 Beths Song 117¾ Madame Called 1171¼CaviarandToast1172¾ Wide 12
26Sep84- 4Bel fst 6f :23⅕ :47⅘ 1:13 F Md Sp Wt 2 7 1217 1114 1014 1114 MacBeth D 117 7.50 63-25 Carrie'sDream117¾IndinRomnce112⁸¼DncingPuddles1171¼ Outrun 13
LATEST WORKOUTS Jun 29 Bel T 6f fm 1:15⅘ h Jun 7 Bel 7f fst 1:29⅘ b May 30 Bel T 6f sf 1:17⅘ b (d) May 23 Bel T 5f gd 1:04 b (d)

My Cliche
B. f. 4, by Spring Double—Kit's Charger, by Native Charger
Own.—Cove Hill Farm
Br.—Binn M (NY)
Tr.—Campo John P
122
Lifetime 17 0 1 2 $8,010 | 1985 8 M 1 0 $5,060 | 1984 9 M 0 2 $2,950 | Turf 3 0 1 0 $5,060

15Jun85- 4Bel fm 1¼ T :48⅕ 1:37⅕ 2:03 3+ F Md Sp Wt 3 1 12½ 1hd 21 24¼ Bailey J D b 122 26.20 74-18 Romanette 1144¼ My Cliche 122¾ Village Jazz 1142 No match 8
7Jun85- 6Bel gd 1⅛ T :47 1:13⅘ 1:46⅘ 3+ F Md Sp Wt 1 1 2hd 41½ 612 613½ Alvarez A5 b 117 44.10 51-27 Rumor114noOneMomentPlease1146ChmpgneBbe1141¼ Weakened 12
31May85- 7Bel fm 1⅜ T :49⅘ 1:40⅘ 2:19⅕ 3+ F Md Sp Wt 4 2 11 1hd 38¼ 610¾ Privitera R5 b 119 60.20 55-28 I'm A Bell Raiser 113nk Coda 1136¾ Village Jazz 1132¼ Tired 11
5Apr85- 2Aqu fst 6f :23⅕ :47⅘ 1:13⅘ 3+ F Md 20000 13 10 124½ 118 1211 1212½ Davis R G b 120 20.30 60-23 GllntTrtmnt120noSpringActon1056¼StrongAndLucky106nk Outrun 13
15Mar85- 5Aqu fst 1 :49⅘ 1:17 1:44⅕ F Md 20000 1 6 44¼ 57 611 614¼ Thibeau R J 118 20.00 31-40 What A Steel 1225¼ Smart Indian 113¼ I Merrily 1224 Tired 8
21Feb85- 4Aqu fst 6f ⊡ :22⅘ :46⅘ 1:13⅘ F Md 20000 3 11 1114 918 810 611¼ Thibeau R J 118 24.80 65-29 Rita'sShadow118nkNearlyFmous118⁸Story'sVeryRich120nk Outrun 11
24Jan85- 2Aqu fst 1⅛ ⊡ :48⅘ 1:14⅕ 1:55⅕ F Md 20000 5 7 714 712 711 615 Thibeau R J 118 13.50e 51-21 I'm Full Up 1133¼ I Merrily 1225¼ Derivation 118hd No factor 12
10Jan85- 6Aqu fst 6f ⊡ :22⅘ :47 1:12⅘ F Md Sp Wt 2 7 67¼ 68 59 613 Thibeau R J 122 39.50 68-22 No Mur Murs 122⁸ Just Johnson 1222¾ Jade Beach 112nk Outrun 8
9Dec84- 1Aqu fst 1⅟₁₆ ⊡ :48⅘ 1:13⅘ 1:46⅕ 3+ Md 30000 7 5 66¾ 613 726 739¼ Cordero A Jr b 113 9.70 41-19 True Turn 11610 Moonquib 12011¼ Pine Hollow 116¼ Tired 8
25Nov84- 1Aqu fst 6f :23⅘ :47⅘ 1:13⅘ 3+ F Md Sp Wt 3 6 85¼ 77½ 76 78¼ Ward W A5 b 115 21.10 65-25 Tempestously 1131¼ Affirmable 1204 Cynge 1202 Outrun 9
LATEST WORKOUTS May 23 Bel tr.t 4f fst :50 b May 17 Bel 4f fst :49⅕ hg May 2 Bel tr.t 4f gd :48⅘ h

Jolie Dam
Dk. b. or br. f. 3, by Damascus—Cyamone, by Cyane
Own.—Pen-Y-Bryn Farm
Br.—Pen-Y-Bryn Farm (Ky)
Tr.—Whiteley David A
114
Lifetime 3 0 0 0 | 1985 3 M 0 0 | 1984 0 M 0 0

20Jun85- 3Bel fst 1 :48 1:13⅘ 1:40 F Md Sp Wt 8 2 32 616 725 737¼ MacBeth D 121 5.10e 27-24 Battle Drum 12110¾ Gay Senorita 1212¼ Miss General 1213¾ Tired 8
1Jun85- 4Bel fst 6f :22⅘ :46 1:11⅘ F Md Sp Wt 5 10 12¹⁴ 1013 107¾ 74¼ Guerra W A 121 10.90 78-11 Northern Vogue 1112 Gay Senorita 121hd Stridency 121nk Outrun 12
23May85- 2Bel fst 6f :22 :45⅘ 1:11⅘ 3+ F Md Sp Wt 6 7 77 68¼ 59¼ 57 Vasquez J 113 7.80 78-20 Ruby Slippers 1132¼ Tamanaco Day 1132¼Tex'sToots113hd Outrun 9
LATEST WORKOUTS Jun 27 Bel 3f fst :36 h Jun 18 Bel 4f fst :48 h Jun 13 Bel 4f fst :49⅕ b Jun 8 Bel 4f fst :49 b

French Fizzle
Dk. b. or br. f. 3, by French Colonial—Buck's Fizz, by Barbizon
Own.—Millian J Z
Br.—Warner M L Jr (Ky)
Tr.—Smith David
114
Lifetime 4 0 0 0 | 1985 4 M 0 0 | 1984 0 M 0 0

24Jun85- 1Bel fst 7f :22⅘ :46⅕ 1:25 3+ F Md Sp Wt 4 5 78¼ 713 514 518¼ Migliore R 114 29.10 59-17 Luminosity 1142 DutyDance11410¾TopoftheRainbow104nk Outrun 7
17May85- 3Bel fst 6f :22⅘ :45⅘ 1:12 3+ F Md 70000 8 7 69¼ 512 68¼ 66 Thibeau R J 109 9.00 76-19 Obstinacy 113¾ Skyjak 1132¾ Jungle Secret 1112¼ Outrun 8
5May85- 6Aqu fst 6f :22⅘ :46⅘ 1:13⅘ 3+ F Md Sp Wt 1 2 85¼ 88¾ 58¼ 56¾ Guerra A A7 106 40.60 67-22 Letty's Pennant113¼Tex'sToots1133¼GossimerVeil113hd No factor 8
17Apr85- 6Aqu fst 6f :23 :45⅘ 1:11⅘ 3+ F Md Sp Wt 6 5 76¾ 617 521 518 Guerra A A7 105 34.50 65-30 Soli 1124¼ Rose Gayle Honey 11211 Nasty Belle 112¾ Outrun 9
LATEST WORKOUTS Jun 13 Aqu T 4f fm :51⅘ b ● May 14 Bel tr.t 3f fst :35⅘ h Apr 30 Bel 5f fst 1:01⅘ h

Dr. Gay Senk
B. f. 3, by Dickens Hill—Sayaah, by Dr Fager
Own.—Timber Bay Stable
Br.—Entenmann W (Fla)
Tr.—Boland William
104[10]
Lifetime 2 0 0 0 | 1985 2 M 0 0 | 1984 0 M 0 0

20Jun85- 3Bel fst 1 :48 1:13⅘ 1:40 F Md Sp Wt 7 6 88¼ 825 837 847¼ Cruguet J 121 30.60 — — Battle Drum 12110¾ Gay Senorita 1212¼ MissGeneral1213¾ Outrun 8
13May85- 4Bel fst 6f :22⅘ :46⅕ 1:11⅘ F Md Sp Wt 5 14 1119 1327 1336 1337¼ Guerra W A 121 33.10f 45-20 RoseGyleHoney1217¾SsidGmbl1211¼RubySlipprs1211¼ Never close 14
LATEST WORKOUTS ● Jun 27 Bel tr.t 7f fst 1:31 b Jun 12 Bel 4f fst :48⅕ hg Jun 5 Bel tr.t 5f fst 1:01⅘ h May 31 Bel tr.t 3f fst :36 h

It's Maria
Dk. b. or br. f. 3, by Gregorian—Tracey Herman, by Bold Bidder
Own.—Green Fay R
Br.—Magenta Farm (Fla)
Tr.—Gulio Thomas J
114
Lifetime 9 0 0 3 $4,080 | 1985 9 M 0 3 $4,080 | 1984 0 M 0 0

21Jun85- 2Bel fst 1⅟₁₆ :47⅘ 1:13 1:46⅘ 3+ F Md 30000 2 8 88 611 49 311¼ Santagata N b 112 6.40 57-23 Almost Royal 112¼ Stephanie Can 10311 It's Maria 112¾ Rallied 11
6Jun85- 2Bel my 1⅟₁₆ :46⅘ 1:12⅘ 1:45⅘ 3+ F Md 30000 3 8 107¼ 86¾ 810 811¼ Guerra W A b 110 4.60 64-17 Northern Rosey 1184 Stephanie Can 1143 Flyspeck 1101¼ Outrun 13
30May85- 2Bel fst 6f :23 :47 1:11⅘ 3+ F Md 30000 13 12 109 88¼ 69¼ 311¾ Guerra W A b 109 17.10 71-19 Plum Island Girl 11311 Affectable 107¾ It's Maria 109¾ Rallied 14
16May85- 2Bel fst 6f :22⅘ :47 1:13⅕ 3+ F Md 30000 12 9 118¼ 1112 68¼ 55¼ Guerra W A b 109 16.20 70-18 SpringAction104hdHeegeebee1132¾PluggedIn1032¼ No real threat 14
17Apr85- 2Aqu fst 7f :23⅘ :47⅘ 1:27⅕ 3+ F Md 32500 7 11 117¾ 88¼ 710 66¾ Guerra W A b 110 15.80 58-30 Bet The Rent 1102¾ Norsal 105¾ Plum Island Girl 1131¼ No factor 11
4Mar85- 3Aqu fst 170 ⊡ :49⅕ 1:15 1:46⅘ F Md 45000 6 7 76 78¼ 713 714 Giglio D Jr7 b 110 8.50 53-22 Distant Lullaby 1173¼ Sweet Sound 1141¼ Nazizi 1171¼ Outrun 9
18Feb85- 2Aqu fst 1⅟₁₆ ⊡ :49⅘ 1:16⅕ 1:52⅕ F Md 35000 1 7 35¼ 26 38 38 Giglio D Jr7 b 114 25.50 41-28 Rebel Love 121¾ Q. Qui 1147¾ It's Maria 114hd Weakened 12
26Jan85- 9Aqu fst 1⅟₁₆ ⊡ :48⅘ 1:15⅕ 1:49 F Md Sp Wt 11 9 88¼ 1012 1017 920¾ Giglio D Jr7 b 114 44.10 44-20 Why Did I 1214 Kicking Star 1211 Go Go Has It1212¾ Never close 11
14Jan85- 6Aqu fst 6f ⊡ :22⅘ :46⅘ 1:12⅘ F Md Sp Wt 4 12 1218 1222 1029 821¾ Giglio D Jr7 b 114 23.80 59-20 Femininity 1212¼ I'm Well Bred1217¾KickingStar1212¾ Slow start 12
LATEST WORKOUTS Jun 5 Bel tr.t 3f fst :38⅕ b May 27 Bel tr.t 3f fst :37 h May 8 Bel tr.t 5f fst 1:02⅘ b May 6 Bel tr.t 3f fst :37 b

Pudical Dk. b. or br. f. 3, by Sassafras—Puritanical, by Never Bend
Own.—Pillar Farms Br.—Pillar Stud Inc (Ky) Tr.—Fisher John R S **114**
Lifetime 3 0 1 0 $1,220 | 1985 2 M 1 0 $1,220 | 1984 1 M 0 0 | Turf 1 0 1 0 $1,220
14Jun85- 6Del fm 1 1/16 Ⓣ:47⅗ 1:12⅕ 1:44⅗ 3+ⒻMd Sp Wt 7 1 1^3 1^2 2^{hd} 2^2 Walford J b 114 4.80 79-11 Auspicate 117^2 Pudical 114^3 Northern Tale 114^4 2nd best 12
5Jan85- 5Bow sly 6½f :22⅗ :46⅘ 1:20⅘ ⒻMd Sp Wt 1 1 1^2 1^1 $2^{1/2}$ $5^{4 1/2}$ Miller D A Jr b 122 4.70 79-22 Silver Design117^2Bill'sFriend122^{nk}MadameCalled$122^{1 1/2}$ Weakened 11
15Dec84- 4Bow fst 6½f :22⅗ :46⅗ 1:20 ⒻMd Sp Wt 5 4 $4^{5 1/2}$ $5^{6 1/2}$ $6^{9 1/2}$ 6^{11} Bracciale V Jr b 120 12.90 79-17 Martins Choice $120^{9 1/2}$ Redstarte $120^{1/2}$ Baba Rebob 120no Tired 12
LATEST WORKOUTS Jun 25 Fai tr.t 4f fst :48⅘ b Jun 11 Fai tr.t 4f fst :50 b Jun 5 Fai tr.t 6f fst 1:15⅗ bg May 28 Fai tr.t 5f fst 1:03 b

One Moment Please Ch. f. 3, by Good Counsel—Cherished Moment, by Graustark
Own.—DiMauro S Br.—Galbreath D M (Ky) Tr.—DiMauro Stephen **114**
Lifetime 2 0 1 0 $5,060 | 1985 2 M 1 0 $5,060 | 1984 0 M 0 0 | Turf 1 0 1 0 $5,060
7Jun85- 6Bel gd 1 1/16 Ⓣ:47 1:13⅗ 1:46⅗ 3+ⒻMd Sp Wt 11 5 $4^{1 1/2}$ 3^{nk} 1^1 2no Migliore R 114 36.50 64-27 Rumor114^{no}OneMomentPlease114^6ChampgneBbe$114^{1 1/2}$ Game try 12
22May85- 3Bel fst 7f :22⅘ :45⅘ 1:23⅕ ⒻMd Sp Wt 2 7 $6^{5 1/2}$ $6^{9 1/2}$ 7^{14} 7^{20} Migliore R 121 45.90 66-14 Coup De Fusil 114^7 Hawaiian Tea $121^{1 1/2}$ MissGeneral$121^{2 1/2}$ Outrun 8
LATEST WORKOUTS Jun 19 Bel 5f fst 1:02 h May 30 Bel Ⓣ 1 sf 1:43⅗ b (d) May 11 Bel 6f fst 1:16 b May 6 Bel 5f fst 1:02 hg

horses and how to care for horses. They race their animals only when they are physically fit; otherwise they keep them in the barn.

On June 29, Fisher returned with Romanette and still another maiden filly, this one named Pudical, whom he had entered in a ten-furlong contest over the Inner grass course, termed good after recent rains.

Pudical showed good early lick in her seasonal debut at Delaware two weeks earlier, before weakening slightly in the final eighth mile. She appeared ready for a winning effort and was bet down late to 4–1 in a relatively weak field of eleven, several of whom do not rate even a comment here. Let's take a brief look at her more serious contenders:

VILLAGE JAZZ

Bred for grass, this Greentree filly disappointed as favorite in both her outings on turf. Although she employed a different running style on each occasion, there was no apparent improvement from one race to the next. I'll gladly bet against this kind any day, especially when the crowd likes them. In this case, the New York audience made Village Jazz their 7–2 second choice.

WINERETTE

A distant second in state-bred competition first time on the grass at 64–1. This is the real world!

MY CLICHE

Second to Romanette last time, although still a maiden after seventeen starts. More of interest, though, was her early speed, a commodity she and Pudical seemed to monopolize in this field.

JOLIE DAM

Awful dirt form, but her dam, Cyamome, was a good grass runner.

DR. GAY SENK and IT'S MARIA

Again, the dirt form is woeful, but in both cases European stallions—both top-class runners—raise the possibility of improved performance on the sod.

ONE MOMENT PLEASE

This horse was the logical favorite after her promising grass debut, in which she missed by a nose to the highly regarded Rumor, while finishing well ahead of the third-place filly. Indeed, the *Form*'s running line hardly does justice to the magnitude of her performance that day. Breaking from post 11, she was forced to race five-wide the entire trip and was never afforded the luxury of a breather. At 2–1 today, many thought she was a big overlay.

Normally I would have been enthusiastic about a filly (or colt) like One Moment Please. But in this particular case three things made me embrace Pudical instead, she being the only logical alternative to the favorite. First, there was Good Counsel, sire of One Moment Please, who seemed to sire many runners plagued with seconditis. Of lesser importance was One Moment Please's relative inactivity during the three weeks since her most recent race—just a single moderate five-furlong workout. That difficult, albeit impressive, effort on June 7 just might have taken a little out of her. And finally, there was Dr. Alphabet himself heading the opposition.

Pudical's task would not be an easy one. The less-than-firm course mitigated against her chances as a front-runner, and the presence of My Cliche further complicated that situation. Pudical's sire, Sassafrass, who pinned the first defeat on the brilliant Nijinsky in the 1970 Arc de Triomphe, had no trouble with the distance, and if I remember correctly, preferred the going soft. On the other hand, Never Bend, the broodmare sire, found ten furlongs well beyond his best trip.

To make a long story short, Pudical went as far as she could but succumbed to One Moment Please in midstretch. She easily held second, and the obvious "saver" quinella returned a generous $16.00. Then Romanette lost the fourth race, finishing a solid second despite a very tough pace-prompting trip from her outside post position.

Although neither filly won, watching Fisher handle Pudical in the paddock prior to her race only increased my respect for the man's horsemanship. Pudical apparently had trouble paddocking at

Delaware prior to her recent race there. At Belmont, Fisher saddled her under the "Saratoga trees," away from the hubbub of the usual saddling enclosure, and personally oversaw her preparation, keeping the filly remarkably calm. Since he had acquired the services of Angel Cordero, he gave the bettor every assurance that his filly was well-meant for that race. Seldom have I left the paddock with a more positive feeling about a trainer's intentions. It took unfavorable track conditions and a tough rival to foil Fisher's mission.

SECOND RACE
Belmont
JUNE 29, 1985

1 ¼ MILES.(InnerTurf). (1.58⅘) MAIDEN SPECIAL WEIGHTS. Purse $23,000. Fillies and Mares, 3-year-old and upward. Weights, 3-year-olds, 114 lbs. Older, 122 lbs.

Value of race $23,000; value to winner $13,800; second $5,060; third $2,760; fourth $1,380. Mutuel pool $120,898, OTB pool $127,017. Quinella Pool $178,737. OTB Quinella Pool $228,575.

Last Raced	Horse	Eqt.	A.Wt	PP	¼	½	¾	1	Str	Fin	Jockey	Odds $1
7Jun85 ^{6}Bel^{2}	One Moment Please		3 114	11	4^{3}	4^{5}	$3^{1\frac{1}{2}}$	$3^{2\frac{1}{2}}$	2^{3}	$1^{2\frac{3}{4}}$	Migliore R	2.00
14Jun85 ^{6}Del^{2}	Pudical	b	3 114	10	$1^{2\frac{1}{2}}$	1^{2}	1^{2}	1^{2}	$1^{1\frac{1}{2}}$	$2^{4\frac{1}{4}}$	Cordero A Jr	4.00
15Jun85 ^{4}Bel^{3}	Village Jazz	b	3 114	3	7^{2}	7^{3}	$6^{\frac{1}{2}}$	5^{hd}	$5^{1\frac{1}{2}}$	$3^{2\frac{3}{4}}$	Romero R P	3.60
15Jun85 ^{4}Bel^{2}	My Cliche	b	4 122	6	3^{2}	$3^{\frac{1}{2}}$	2^{2}	$2^{1\frac{1}{2}}$	3^{3}	$4^{1\frac{1}{4}}$	Maple E	6.90
23Jun85 ^{2}Bel^{9}	Caviar and Toast		3 114	5	$5^{2\frac{1}{2}}$	$5^{1\frac{1}{2}}$	4^{1}	$4^{1\frac{1}{2}}$	4^{1}	$5^{3\frac{1}{2}}$	Skinner K	25.40
21Jun85 ^{6}Bel^{2}	Winerette		3 114	4	6^{hd}	6^{hd}	$7^{1\frac{1}{2}}$	6^{1}	$6^{1\frac{1}{2}}$	$6^{\frac{1}{2}}$	McCarron G	17.60
15Jun85 ^{4}Bel^{4}	Miss Marble	b	3 114	2	10^{6}	$8^{\frac{1}{2}}$	8^{1}	7^{2}	7^{4}	7^{4}	Davis R G	17.00
20Jun85 ^{3}Bel^{7}	Jolie Dam		3 114	7	9^{1}	$9^{1\frac{1}{2}}$	9^{3}	8^{4}	8^{2}	$8^{2\frac{1}{4}}$	Vasquez J	9.20
21Jun85 ^{2}Bel^{3}	It's Maria	b	3 114	9	$8^{1\frac{1}{2}}$	10^{6}	$10^{1\frac{1}{2}}$	9^{2}	9^{8}	$9^{1\frac{3}{4}}$	Santagata N	18.40
3Jun85 ^{2}Bel^{4}	Graceful Power	b	3 114	1	11	11	11	10^{6}	10^{12}	10^{16}	Cruguet J	40.50
20Jun85 ^{3}Bel^{8}	Dr. Gay Senk		3 104	8	$2^{1\frac{1}{2}}$	2^{2}	5^{hd}	11	11	11	Decarlo C P[10]	50.90

OFF AT 1:30 Start good, Won driving. Time, :24, :48⅕, 1:13⅗, 1:39⅕, 2:04⅕ Course good.

$2 Mutuel Prices:			
11-(L)-ONE MOMENT PLEASE	6.00	3.20	2.60
10-(K)-PUDICAL		4.40	3.40
3-(C)-VILLAGE JAZZ			3.00

$2 QUINELLA 10-11 PAID $16.00

Ch. f, by Good Counsel—Cherished Moment, by Graustark. Trainer DiMauro Stephen. Bred by Galbreath D M (Ky).

ONE MOMENT PLEASE, reserved early, rallied leaving the far turn and drew away after catching PUDICAL. The latter saved ground while making the pace, held a clear lead into the stretch but wasn't able to withstand the winner. VILLAGE JAZZ failed to seriously menace. MY CLICHE raced forwardly to the stretch and tired. CAVIAR AND TOAST lacked a late response. JOLIE DAM was always outrun. DR. GAY SENK bore out badly at the first turn and was finished after going five furlongs.

Are we suggesting that an automatic win bet on each and every Fisher shipper is warranted? Perhaps so. It seems clear that if the good doctor feels that a horse is worth shipping to New York, he thinks it is a fit animal with a real chance of winning. His statistics for 1985 in New York through the Saratoga meeting confirm this:

NH	*NW*	*WPCT*	*NM*	*MPCT*	*$NET*
21	6	28.6%	13	61.9%	$3.20

Chapter 38

The Stranger and the Scratch

NO ONE CAN DISPUTE the fact that handicapping is a complex undertaking. To the uninitiated, opening the *Racing Form* to the past performance pages can be a traumatic experience. The wealth of information contained in those pages can serve only to confuse those who are unprepared and lacking a well-thought-out game plan. Where does one look first?

In this chapter we will discuss a couple of points of entry into the handicapping process. One deals with the use of pace figures as a means of picturing the race before it is run, thereby setting up possible trips before the horses leave the gate. Since the outcome of a race is a function of pace, a clear picture of where each horse will be in the early running, and how fast it will be traveling, can prove an indispensable handicapping aid.

We will also discuss an aspect of class handicapping that will in certain cases give the player a good idea of where (not) to look for the winner in terms of the class demands imposed by the obvious contenders in the race. In many races, one will find that several of the contestants have been competing against each other at approximately the same level. Indeed, in some cases, that these same horses have been taking turns finishing ahead of each other, with none of the group able to find the winner's circle. A situation such as this calls for a "stranger"—a horse dropping down, moving up, or shipping in—essentially a horse trying the present company for the first time of late. Chances are, if the player looked back at the past performances for recent races in that same classification, he would find that the majority of the winners could be termed "strangers." Maiden races and contests for the cheaper claimers on the grounds often fall into this category.

4 BELMONT

6 FURLONGS (BELMONT PARK)

6 FURLONGS. (1.08⅖) CLAIMING. Purse $18,000. 4-year-olds and upward. Weight, 122 lbs. Non-winners of two races since May 15, allowed 3 lbs.; of a race since then, 5 lbs. Claiming price $35,000; for each $2,500 to $30,000, 2 lbs. (Races when entered to be claimed for $25,000 or less not considered.)

Coupled—Shining Out and Lively Teddy; Just Any Time and Zephyr Cove; Tenifly, Restless John and Agile Shoebill.

Wandering Feet

B. g. 5, by Dewan—Footsie, by Cyane — $35,000 — Br.—Vanderbilt A G (MD) — Tr.—Frank Maud — Own.—Abacus Ranch — 117

Lifetime 28 3 3 1 $58,500 — 1985 8 0 0 0 $6,560 — 1984 17 3 3 0 $49,860 — Turf 2 0 0 0

Date	Race	Cond	Dist	Fractions	Class	PP St 1/4 1/2 Str Fin	Jockey	Wt	Odds	Chart / Comment	Field
3Jun85-	3Bel	fst	6f	:22⅘ :44⅘ 1:08⅘	3+Alw 25000	4 1 32 34 58½ 616	Vasquez J	117	14.70	83-13 Pancho Villa 112no Solgne 1119 Kilts' Nashua 112½ Tired	8
17May85-	1Bel	fst	7f	:23⅕ :46⅕ 1:23⅘	Clm 50000	2 2 1½ 2½ 43¼ 45¼	MacBeth D	117	5.60	80-19 AccountReceivable113noSpeedBroker1191¼HarpersBazr1134 Tired	7
11May85-	6Bel	fm	6f	ⓣ:22 :45⅗ 1:09⅘	3+Alw 36000	4 1 2hd 21½ 33 510	MacBeth D	119	15.60	83-17 Sitzmark 1195¼ Alev 121no Alchise 1193¾ Gave way	11
2May85-	7Aqu	fm	1 1/16	ⓣ:47⅘ 1:12⅘ 1:44⅘	3+Alw 40000	2 4 42 52½ 65½ 65¾	MacBeth D	119	14.80	77-17 FrayStar1191¼StormyPuddles1191¼JudgeCost1191¼ Bore out gate	10
22Apr85-	6Aqu	fst	6f	:23 :46 1:10⅘	3+Alw 23000	3 1 1½ 1hd 2½ 42¾	MacBeth D	121	*1.50	85-23 Sly Boots 1212¾ Attune 121hd Dixie's Island 121no Weakened	7
2Apr85-	5Aqu	fst	6f	:22⅘ :46 1:10⅕	3+Alw 23000	3 2 11 2hd 43 45¼	Castaneda K	121	4.30	84-20 Crimson Medal1111¼Fool'sDancer1161CallMeRebel1213¼ Faltered	4
26Jan85-	5Aqu	fst	6f	⊡:22⅘ :46⅘ 1:11⅘	Alw 23000	5 3 23 21½ 31½ 44¾	Santagata N	117	9.90	82-20 Mt. Livermore 117¾ Alamacani 1171¾ Sir Leader 1222¼ Weakened	8
13Jan85-	9Aqu	fst	6f	⊡:22 :46 1:12⅘	Clm 35000	3 7 55½ 67 44 44¼	Hernandez R	117	5.70	76-27 Charles Son 1171¼Can'tCatchjohn117noBalancingAct1173 No rally	11
29Dec84-	3Aqu	fst	6f	⊡:22 :45 1:09⅘	3+Clm 22500	3 4 11 1½ 13 13	MacBeth D	115	35.40	97-09 WanderingFeet1153RouletteWheel1153Comedion1151½ Drew clear	12
17Dec84-	9Aqu	fst	6f	⊡:22⅘ :46 1:11⅘	3+Clm 25000	8 7 62¾ 67 69½ 68½	Lovato F Jr	117	33.20	78-19 Tarpaulin 115½ Gauguin Native 112hd Royal Rollick 1175¼ Outrun	11

LATEST WORKOUTS May 27 Bel 5f fst 1:00 h — Apr 16 Bel tr.t 5f gd 1:02⅕ b

Carry It Full

Ch. h. 5, by Full Pocket—Carry It High, by Hoist the Flag — $30,000 — Br.—Labrot Barbara (Ky) — Tr.—Dunham Bob G — Own.—Uptick Stable — 113

Lifetime 13 2 1 2 $31,620 — 1985 2 0 0 0 — 1984 5 1 1 0 $16,620

Date	Race	Cond	Dist	Fractions	Class	PP St 1/4 1/2 Str Fin	Jockey	Wt	Odds	Chart / Comment	Field
3Jun85-	3Bel	fst	6f	:22⅘ :44⅘ 1:08⅘	3+Alw 25000	7 3 58½ 713 716 817¼	Venezia M	117	36.10	82-13 Pancho Villa 112no Solgne 1119 Kilts' Nashua 112½ Fin gamely	8
24May85-	7Bel	fst	7f	:22⅘ :45⅗ 1:22⅘	3+Alw 25000	2 7 78¾ 712 717 721¾	Venezia M	121	18.70	67-18 Senator Brady 1131½ Solgne1123¼RomanticTradition1212½ Trailed	7
17Mar84-	5Aqu	fst	6f	⊡:23⅘ :47⅘ 1:12⅘	Alw 21000	4 6 51½ 41 2hd 2no	MacBeth D	b 117	28.40	80-22 Sky Falcon 117no Carry It Full1172Ⓓ ForgottheRing1102 Bore out	8
4Mar84-	6Aqu	fst	170	⊡:48 1:12⅘ 1:43	Alw 24000	4 4 42¾ 77 712 718¼	Venezia M	117	17.50	67-21 Minabchar 117no Tampa Town1175¾MorningReview1222½ Stopped	7
13Feb84-	6Aqu	fst	6f	⊡:22⅘ :46⅕ 1:11	Alw 22000	1 5 64 76½ 79 67½	Venezia M	119	13.70	81-18 Bold Target 117nk Pams McAllister 1171½ Top Hat 1172½ Outrun	8
1Feb84-	6Aqu	fst	6f	⊡:23⅕ :46⅘ 1:12⅕	Alw 20000	4 4 2½ 1hd 11½ 1¾	Venezia M	117	2.70	83-18 Carry It Full 117¾ Upper Style 1171½ Coast Range 117nk Driving	10
21Jan84-	5Aqu	fst	6f	⊡:23 :47 1:13	Alw 20000	1 3 88¾ 89¾ 69 58	Venezia M	117	7.80	71-30 Mc Michael112hdFlyingGeneral1124½PrideOfSatan1102½ No factor	11
27Jun83-	7Bel	fst	6f	:22⅘ :45⅘ 1:10⅕	3+Alw 20000	10 3 86 911 712 311½	Venezia M	109	18.30	79-19 A Phenomenon 11110BigMcCoy1091½CarryItFull109¾ Rallied wide	11
18Jun83-	1Bel	fst	7f	:22⅘ :45⅗ 1:23⅘	3+Alw 20000	2 2 42 43 36½ 39½	Venezia M	109	11.30	76-18 A Real Leader 1174½ Press Badge 1045 Carry It Full 1094 Tired	8
9Jun83-	9Bel	fst	6f	:23 :46⅕ 1:11	3+Alw 20000	6 3 109 1012 1013 89½	Venezia M	109	29.20	77-17 Private Sun 1171¾ Primary Care1171½Flip'sLittleBoy110nk Outrun	10

LATEST WORKOUTS ●May 21 Aqu ⊡ 4f fst :47⅘ h — ●May 16 Aqu ⊡ 6f fst 1:14⅘ b — May 12 Aqu ⊡ 6f fst 1:15⅘ h — ●May 6 Aqu 6f fst 1:15⅖ h

Shining Out *

B. h. 5, by Full Out—All Agleam, by Gleaming — $35,000 — Br.—Greathouse D & E & J W Jr (Ky) — Tr.—Barrera Oscar S — Own.—Barrera O S — 117

Lifetime 36 6 6 3 $88,528 — 1985 11 2 2 1 $34,640 — 1984 12 2 1 1 $42,260 — Turf 9 2 2 1 $7,088

Date	Race	Cond	Dist	Fractions	Class	PP St 1/4 1/2 Str Fin	Jockey	Wt	Odds	Chart / Comment	Field
7Jun85-	2Bel	fst	7f	:22⅘ :45⅘ 1:24	Clm c-25000	13 6 41 31½ 1hd 2hd	Migliore R	b 117	4.80	82-19 Rapid Wing 119hd Shining Out 117¾ Ship Mint 117¾ Gamely	13
27May85-	2Bel	fst	6f	:22⅕ :45⅗ 1:10⅕	Clm 45000	12 10 54½ 66 76 95¾	Migliore R	b 113	7.10	85-15 Ecstatic Pride 108nk Sir Leader 1171 See for Free 113¾ Tired	12
17May85-	8Bel	fm	7f	ⓣ:22⅕ :44⅘ 1:20⅘	3+Alw 36000	6 4 43½ 66 514 613½	Migliore R	b 119	18.80	86-11 RedWingDream1191½StayTheCourse1244DiscoCount124nk Outrun	8
28Apr85-	1Aqu	fst	7f	:22⅘ :45⅘ 1:23⅘	Clm 45000	7 3 31 31 32 33½	Migliore R	b 115	*1.40	78-21 Fibak 1172½ Hueco 1171½ Shining Out 1151½ Evenly	8
19Apr85-	7Aqu	sly	7f	:22⅘ :45⅘ 1:23⅕	Clm 70000	5 2 33½ 22 22½ 22	Migliore R	b 113	*1.90	83-22 Agile Shoebill 1172 Shining Out 113¾ Faces Up 1171¾ Gamely	6
8Apr85-	2Aqu	fst	7f	:22⅘ :45 1:23⅕	Clm 50000	2 7 54½ 42½ 2hd 1¾	Migliore R	b 117	12.60	85-24 ShiningOut117¾FstAsThBrz113nkSpirtdBoy1101 Stumbd st., drvng	8
21Mar85-	7Aqu	fst	6f	:23⅕ :46⅘ 1:11⅘	Alw 24000	8 5 31 21 31½ 55	Migliore R	b 117	3.00	77-34 MorningThunder1172Dixie'sIsland112¾BoldJulius1221½ Used early	8
13Mar85-	4Aqu	fst	7f	:22⅘ :46 1:24⅘	Clm 32500	3 7 42 51¾ 1½ 11½	Migliore R	115	*1.10e	78-28 ShiningOut1151½Cn'tCtchjohn1175SkyFlcon117½ Blocked, driving	12
27Feb85-	9Aqu	fst	6f	⊡:23 :47 1:12⅘	Clm c-25000	7 1 1hd 2hd 76¾ 89	Migliore R	b 117	5.80	71-24 Canadian Currency 115nk Charismo1132Mr.Radius112nk Bothered	12

27Feb85-Placed seventh through disqualification

Date	Race	Cond	Dist	Fractions	Class	PP St 1/4 1/2 Str Fin	Jockey	Wt	Odds	Chart / Comment	Field
17Feb85-	9Aqu	fst	6f	⊡:22⅘ :46⅘ 1:12⅘	Clm 25000	11 2 61 3nk 31½ 43	Migliore R	b 117	3.30	78-25 Rapid Wing 1172¾ Mr.Radius112nkOntheContrary115hd Weakened	12

LATEST WORKOUTS Apr 15 Aqu 4f fst :48⅘ h

Big McCoy

B. h. 5, by The Real McCoy—Mary Saint, by Lord Date — $35,000 — Br.—North Star Ranch (Fla) — Tr.—Dutrow Richard E — Own.—Dutrow R E — 117

Lifetime 45 8 8 14 $164,760 — 1985 7 1 1 3 $21,560 — 1984 28 4 6 7 $90,380

Date	Race	Cond	Dist	Fractions	Class	PP St 1/4 1/2 Str Fin	Jockey	Wt	Odds	Chart / Comment	Field
22May85-	9Bel	fst	6f	:22⅕ :45 1:09⅘	Clm 35000	7 3 3½ 2½ 1hd 3½	Davis R G	117	7.00	93-14 Infinite Saga 117hd Zephyr Cove 115½ Big McCoy 1173 Weakened	11
15Apr85-	1Aqu	fst	6f	:22⅘ :45⅗ 1:11	Clm 35000	2 3 2hd 13 12½ 21¾	Vasquez J	117	*1.30	84-17 Sir Leader 1171¾ Big McCoy 117½ Deedee's Deal 1174 Weakened	7
23Mar85-	4Aqu	fst	6f	:22⅘ :46⅕ 1:10⅘	Clm 35000	1 5 41½ 44½ 45½ 34	Hernandez R	117	13.80	83-23 Ecstatic Pride 1121½ Spirited Boy 1172¾ Big McCoy 1171¾ Rallied	8
13Mar85-	4Aqu	fst	7f	:22⅘ :46 1:24⅘	Clm 35000	6 3 2hd 2hd 1013 1016	Moore D N5	112	5.40	62-28 Shining Out 1151½ Can't Catchjohn 1175 Sky Falcon117½ Stopped	12
22Feb85-	1Aqu	fst	6f	⊡:22⅘ :45⅗ 1:11⅘	Clm 45000	6 1 32 42½ 43½ 43½	Lovato F Jr	113	7.70	84-22 AgileShoebill1071½FstAsTheBrez1171¾EcstlicPrid117no Weakened	7
10Feb85-	1Aqu	fst	6f	⊡:23⅘ :47⅘ 1:12⅘	Clm c-35000	6 2 11½ 11 1½ 1nk	Davis R G	117	*1.50	82-18 Big McCoy 117nk Hereford Man 106½ Rock All Night1171 Driving	8
4Jan85-	5Aqu	fst	6f	⊡:22⅘ :45⅘ 1:10⅘	Clm 45000	1 5 11 1½ 2½ 32½	Venezia M	113	11.10	87-21 Talc Power 110no Just Any Time 1132½ BigMcCoy113¾ Weakened	6
23Dec84-	5Aqu	fst	6f	⊡:22⅘ :45⅗ 1:11	3+Clm 45000	9 1 31½ 31 65½ 74½	Davis R G	113	*2.80	84-17 Talc Power 108no Speed Broker117noDeemedDividend117hd Tired	9
5Dec84-	5Aqu	fst	6f	⊡:22⅕ :45⅗ 1:10⅕	3+Clm 70000	5 2 11½ 13 21 47½	Bailey J D	113	7.00	85-19 Huckster 1172 Tenifly 1132¾ Will Of Iron 1172¾ Tired	6
24Nov84-	5Aqu	fst	6f	:22⅘ :46⅗ 1:11⅗	3+Clm 70000	8 3 1½ 1½ 52½ 53½	Cordero A Jr	113	7.30	80-27 Fast AsTheBreeze1131½InFromDixie117nkMr.Tatt1061½ Weakened	8

LATEST WORKOUTS May 12 Aqu ⊡ 4f fst :50⅕ b — May 6 Aqu 4f fst :49 b

Just Any Time

Ch. g. 5, by Vice Regent—Overpraised, by Raise A Native — $30,000 — Br.—Dogwood Farm Inc (Ky) — Tr.—DeBonis Robert — Own.—Starlann Stable — 113

Lifetime 46 8 7 6 $109,040 — 1985 10 1 2 0 $20,060 — 1984 18 4 2 2 $51,450

Date	Race	Cond	Dist	Fractions	Class	PP St 1/4 1/2 Str Fin	Jockey	Wt	Odds	Chart / Comment	Field
5May85-	4Aqu	fst	6f	:22⅘ :45⅘ 1:11⅕	Clm 25000	7 7 41½ 31 21 1¾	Cordero A Jr	b 117	6.40	85-22 Just Any Time 117¾ Royal Rollick 117¾ Hockey Fan 1101½ Driving	9
15Apr85-	1Aqu	fst	6f	:22⅘ :45⅗ 1:11	Clm 35000	1 4 1hd 45½ 710 714	Davis R G	b 117	6.10	72-17 Sir Leader 1171¾ Big McCoy 117½ Deedee's Deal 1174 Tired	7
28Mar85-	1Aqu	fst	6f	:22 :45 1:10⅘	Clm 45000	2 7 77½ 79½ 69½ 59½	Espinosa R E7	b 106	5.40	79-25 Spirited Boy 1083¾ Hereford Man 1151½ Banjo Pete 1173½ Outrun	7
21Mar85-	7Aqu	fst	6f	:23⅕ :46⅘ 1:11⅘	Alw 24000	6 1 42½ 44½ 53 65¾	Santagata N	117	11.40	76-34 Morning Thunder 1172 Dixie's Island 112¾ Bold Julius1221½ Tired	8
9Mar85-	7Aqu	fst	6f	⊡:22 :45⅗ 1:10⅘	Alw 23000	6 4 511 67½ 68 58	Espinosa R E7	b 110	2.50	83-16 Water Skier 1172½MorningThunder1172¾ZephyrCove1171½ Outrun	6
20Feb85-	8Aqu	fst	6f	⊡:22⅘ :45⅘ 1:12⅕	Alw 25000	7 1 85½ 76½ 53 21½	Espinosa R E7	b 110	10.50	82-23 Spender 1121½ Just Any Time 110nk ⒹZephyr Cove1171¾ Bumped	8
13Feb85-	8Aqu	fst	170	⊡:47⅘ 1:12 1:42⅘	Alw 25000	1 1 1hd 32½ 513 825½	Davis R G	117	7.10	62-20 Closed Corp 1171 ClearTheBases112nkLordAshdale1222½ Stopped	8
6Feb85-	7Aqu	gd	6f	⊡:22⅘ :46⅘ 1:12⅘	Alw 23000	1 3 32½ 32 22 43	Davis R G	117	4.00	78-27 SirLeder122¾MorningThunder122nkTellTheMrines1122 Weakened	7
16Jan85-	9Aqu	fst	6f	⊡:23⅕ :46⅘ 1:12	Alw 23000	7 1 62½ 65½ 711 911½	Santagata N	117	6.40	73-27 Cooper'sHwk1172¾SteppinBttlr1173InSightOfStrs119nk No factor	11
4Jan85-	5Aqu	fst	6f	⊡:22⅘ :45⅘ 1:10⅘	Clm 45000	2 3 41½ 41 1½ 2no	Santagata N	113	4.30	90-21 Talc Power 110noJustAnyTime1132½BigMcCoy113¾ Brushed fence	6

LATEST WORKOUTS May 31 Bel tr.t 5f fst 1:00 h — May 23 Bel tr.t 5f fst 1:00⅘ h — May 14 Bel 4f fst :51⅘ b — Apr 24 Bel tr.t 5f fst 1:01⅕ h

Strike A Coin

B. g. 5, by Strike the Anvil—Roman Coin, by Bristol Bristol — $35,000 — Br.—Chibcha Farm (Fla) — Tr.—Gullo Thomas J — Own.—Middle Bay Farms — 117

Lifetime 22 6 2 2 $59,009 — 1985 5 1 0 0 $11,850 — 1984 10 3 1 2 $28,045

Date	Race	Cond	Dist	Fractions	Class	PP St 1/4 1/2 Str Fin	Jockey	Wt	Odds	Chart / Comment	Field
27May85-	2Bel	fst	6f	:22⅕ :45⅗ 1:10⅕	Clm 50000	10 4 1hd 1½ 2½ 53½	Guerra W A	117	10.70	87-15 Ecstatic Pride 108nk Sir Leader 1171 See for Free 113¾ Used up	12
15May85-	2Bel	fst	6½f	:22⅘ :45⅗ 1:16⅘	Clm 70000	4 2 2½ 2½ 68½ 710½	Pino M G	113	16.40	83-17 KnightofArmor1172½MgneticFieldII1193¾Fibk1131 Speed for half	8
19Apr85-	7Aqu	sly	7f	:22⅘ :45⅗ 1:23⅕	Clm 70000	2 3 23 44 613 613½	Guerra W A	113	14.60	72-22 Agile Shoebill 1172 Shining Out 113¾ Faces Up 1171¾ Fin. early	6
12Jan85-	4GP	fst	6f	:22⅘ :45⅘ 1:10⅕	Clm 70000	2 5 1hd 62¾ 79 814½	Solis A	118	*1.40	73-16 Right And Regal 118hd Thalassocrat 1171½ Dr. WiseGuy1175 Tired	9
1Jan85-	8Crc	fst	6f	:22 :45 1:10⅘	Clm 70000	7 3 1½ 11 11 13	Solis A	113	4.30	97-17 Strike A Coin 1133 Citius 1132 Fibak 1142¾ Driving	8
11Dec84-	7Crc	fst	6f	:22⅕ :45⅗ 1:12⅘	3+Clm 50000	6 1 12 14 12½ 2no	Solis A	116	1.90	89-22 Gallant Prelude 116no Strike A Coin 1161¾ Fibak 1143½ Bore out	6
3Nov84-	7Crc	sly	1	:48 1:13⅘ 1:42	3+Alw 20800	6 1 12 12 1½ 55½	Wilson B G	113	7.10	73-25 CommandAttention1193½GloryO.So112½SuperbMissile117½ Tirewd	7
27Oct84-	8Crc	fst	7f	:22⅕ :45⅕ 1:24⅘	3+Alw 17000	1 6 11 2hd 87¾ 810	Smith A Jr	117	6.80	84-15 JimBrcken1121BrotherLim1191½CommndAttntion119no Gave way	9
6Oct84-	7Crc	fst	6½f	:22⅕ :45⅗ 1:19⅘	3+Alw 19700	3 2 1hd 13 1½ 32¾	Wilson B G	122	1.90	84-20 NorthernOcen1222¾MyG.P.117noStrikACoin1228 Drifted out,bobb.	6
22Sep84-	7Crc	fst	6½f	:22⅘ :45 1:18⅘	3+Alw 17100	7 1 11½ 16 15 14	Wilson B G	117	5.70	93-28 Strike A Coin1174IrishPrince1192¾TheGhost1153¾ Drifted, driving	7

LATEST WORKOUTS ●May 13 Bel tr.t 3f fst :34⅘ h — Apr 13 Bel tr.t 4f fst :49 b

Castle Knight

B. g. 7, by Irish Castle—Smoke Eater, by High Drag — $35,000 — Br.—Evans J D (Ky) — Tr.—O'Connell Richard — Own.—Bicycle Stable — 112[5]

Lifetime 33 9 7 1 $215,189 — 1985 2 0 1 0 $3,960 — 1984 3 0 1 0 $8,460

Date	Race	Cond	Dist	Fractions	Class	PP St 1/4 1/2 Str Fin	Jockey	Wt	Odds	Chart / Comment	Field
1Jun85-	1Bel	fst	7f	:23⅘ :46⅘ 1:23⅕	Clm 35000	6 1 1½ 11 2½ 21½	Moore D N5	112	4.40	85-11 Bright Rex 1171½ Castle Knight 1122 Restless John 1171¾ Gamely	7
22May85-	9Bel	fst	6f	:22⅕ :45 1:09⅘	Clm 35000	5 6 86¾ 109½ 108½ 77	Moore D N5	112	16.40	87-14 Infinite Saga 117hd Zephyr Cove 115½ Big McCoy 1173 Outrun	11
24Apr84-	7Aqu	my	7f	:22⅕ :44⅘ 1:23	Clm c-75000	5 3 35 37½ 36 45¾	Velasquez J	117	*1.80	80-21 Shifty Sheik1061¾InfiniteSaga1131¾FleetReceiver1142½ Weakened	6
16Apr84-	8Aqu	gd	6f	⊡:22⅘ :45⅗ 1:10⅕	3+Alw 33000	5 1 2hd 1hd 1½ 2¾	Velasquez J	119	3.60	92-13 Wild Moment 119¾ Castle Knight 1194½ ShiftySheik1142¾ Gamely	6
5Apr84-	8Aqu	sly	6f	⊡:22⅘ :45⅘ 1:11	Alw 33000	7 3 2½ 21½ 33 54½	Velasquez J	115	4.80	85-25 Shining Out 110hd Shifty Sheik 1082 North Glade 1191 Weakened	9
27Jan83-	9GP	fst	1⅛	:48⅕ 1:12 1:50⅘	Alw 25000	7 1 11 1½ 1hd 2nk	Velasquez J	122	*1.10	78-23 Pirouette117nkCstleKnight1222BltimoreCnyon115½ Returned sore	7
4Dec82-	7Aqu	gd	1 1/16	⊡:47 1:11⅘ 1:44⅘	3+Handicap	3 1 12 1hd 1½ 1¾	Hernandez R	117	*1.90	89-15 Castle Knight 117¾ Faces Up 1132 John Casey 1121½ Driving	7
25Nov82-	8Aqu	fst	1 3/16	:48 1:12⅘ 1:58⅕	3+Queens Co H	4 1 12 11½ 22½ 23¾	Velasquez J	111	6.40	67-26 Bar Dexter 1123¾ Castle Knight 111hd NicePirate1105½ Held place	5
6Nov82-	4Lrl	fst	1 1/16	:47⅘ 1:12⅕ 1:43⅘	3+Handicap	5 1 1hd 11 2hd 22½	Maple E	118	2.30	95-11 BlackieDaw1192½CstleKnight1182½SunnyWinters118no Weakened	7
24Oct82-	6Aqu	fst	6f	:23⅘ :46⅘ 1:10⅕	3+Handicap	6 3 32 33 53½ 43½	Velasquez J	112	7.00	86-25 Triocala 1151 Contare 1111½ In From Dixie 1121 Wide, weakened	6

LATEST WORKOUTS May 10 Bel 5f fst 1:01⅘ hg — May 5 Bel tr.t 4f fst :50 b — Apr 25 Bel tr.t 3f fst :37 b

Sincere Wish
Ch. c. 4, by Princely Native—Inspire Me, by California Kid
$35,000 Br.—Harbor View Farm (NY)
Tr.—Martin Frank
Own.—Harbor View Farm
117
Lifetime 15 3 5 0 $84,972 | 1985 5 1 1 0 $22,140 | 1984 10 2 4 0 $62,832

27May85- 2Bel fst 6f :22⅕ :45⅘ 1:10⅘ Clm 50000 4 3 43½ 76½ 65½ 85 Lovato F Jr 117 17.60 86-15 Ecstatic Pride 108nk Sir Leader 1171 See for Free 113¾ Tired 12
22Mar85- 5Aqu fst 6f :22⅘ :45⅗ 1:12 [S]Alw 27000 9 2 43 23 21½ 11¾ Lovato F Jr 117 9.80 81-27 SincerWish1171¾AdirondckPrid1171½PoppChrliK.117hd Drew clear 11
15Mar85- 7Aqu fst 1 :47 1:13⅘ 1:40⅘ [S]Alw 28500 11 4 53 33 37 813½ Lovato F Jr 117 6.10 52-40 Groom'sImage1121¾PoppaCharlieK.1177ColumbiaPride117½ Tired 11
25Feb85- 9Aqu fst 6f ⊡:23⅘ :47 1:12⅘ [S]Alw 27000 2 3 2hd 1½ 1hd 22½ Lovato F Jr 117 *3.70 80-25 Oatley 1172½ Sincere Wish 117nk Rock AllNight117nk Saved place 11
27Jan85- 5Aqu fst 6f ⊡:22 :45⅗ 1:12⅘ [S]Alw 27000 6 2 66½ 913 88½ 63½ Lovato F Jr 117 10.40 79-20 Sweet Devil 1171½ Adirondack Pride 122½ Oatley 117¾ Tired 12
20Jun84- 7Bel fst 7f :23 :45⅗ 1:24⅘ 3+[S]Alw 26000 9 1 32 31 87 915 Lovato F Jr 112 6.50 64-18 GothicRevival1124Loughrea117hdTexasGentlemn104nk Wide, tired 9
24May84- 2Bel fst 7f :22⅘ :46⅖ 1:23⅕ 3+[S]Alw 26000 8 2 95½ 93¾1111 1112½ Lovato F 110 8.60 74-15 Mr. T. And Me 1133½ Restless Feet 110½ Loughrea1211 Very wide 12
5May84- 5Aqu fst 6f :22⅘ :46⅖ 1:11 3+[S]Alw 26000 5 3 32 3nk 1½ 2¾ Lovato F Jr 113 *1.20 85-16 French Tab 110¾ Sincere Wish 113¾ Bright Rex 121hd Game try 8
21Apr84- 2Aqu fst 7f :24⅖ :48⅘ 1:26⅘ 3+[S]Alw 24500 8 1 1½ 12 19 15½ Lovato F Jr 112 2.50 67-30 SincereWish1125½CommnderAlmy1212½GuyPebo121hd Ridden out 9
1Apr84- 9Aqu fst 6f ⊡:22⅕ :45⅗ 1:11⅗ 3+[S]Alw 24500 12 1 31 1hd 11 21¾ Lovato F Jr 113 *1.80 84-19 Talc Duster 1121¾ Sincere Wish 113¾ Tenancy 1211½ Gamely 12
LATEST WORKOUTS Jun 3 Bel tr.t 4f fst :47⅕ h ●May 20 Bel tr.t 6f fst 1:16⅗ b May 13 Bel tr.t 5f fst 1:02⅗ b May 7 Bel tr.t 4f fst :49 b

Running Bold
Ch. g. 4, by Nasty and Bold—Mush Mouse, by Hedevar
$35,000 Br.—Whitney T P (Ky)
Tr.—Johnson Philip G
Own.—Cobble View Stable
117
Lifetime 26 3 5 4 $54,649 | 1985 6 0 0 0 $1,200 | 1984 19 3 4 4 $49,269 | Turf 1 0 0 0

22May85- 9Bel fst 6f :22⅕ :45 1:09⅗ Clm 35000 10 9 911 99 55 53½ Samyn J L 117 31.60 90-14 Infinite Saga 117hd Zephyr Cove 115½ Big McCoy 1173 Outrun 11
12May85- 9Bel fst 7f :22⅘ :46 1:24⅕ Clm 35000 3 4 1½ 1½ 32 54¾ Samyn J L 117 8.80 76-19 SeeforFree1171¾Deedee'sDeal117hdHarpersBazar117hd Weakened 9
28Mar85- 1Aqu fst 6f :22 :45 1:10⅖ Clm 50000 4 2 41½ 45½ 37 48¾ Moore D N5 112 *.60e 80-25 Spirited Boy 1083¾ Hereford Man1151½BanjoPete1173½ No excuse 7
25Mar85- 5Aqu fst 7f :23⅕ :47⅕ 1:23⅘ Clm 75000 7 1 31 3nk 43 69½ Davis R G 117 39.70 72-35 Cooper'sHwk1132BlueQudrnt1182I'mSoMerry1081¾ Flattened out 9
18Mar85- 8Aqu fst 7f :23⅗ :47⅘ 1:25⅘ Alw 25000 6 2 2hd 31½ 65¾ 67½ Davis R G 117 37.60 64-38 Vinny's Pride 117nk Bienestar 117nk Special Care1173½ Early foot 9
26Jan85- 3Aqu fst 6f ⊡:22⅘ :46⅘ 1:11⅘ Clm 90000 9 7 73¾ 54 1014 1015½ Samyn J L 118 47.60 71-20 Magnetic Field II 1112½ Charles Son 112nk WillOfIron1121½ Tired 10
30Aug84- 7Bel fm 1116 Ⓣ:46⅕ 1:09⅘ 1:41⅘ Clm 75000 2 2 28 48½ 521 621 Ward W A 112 7.40 71-13 Mr Chromacopy1171¾RedWingDream1137StarCoral1182½ Stopped 6
19Aug84- 6Key gd 6f :22⅘ :45⅘ 1:11⅕ 3+Alw 12500 5 5 52 32¾ 22½ 26 Barrera C 117 *2.00 79-21 Towie 1166 Running Bold1172FullConfidence1111½ Best of others 5
10Aug84- 7Key fst 6f :22⅕ :45⅘ 1:11⅕ 3+Alw 12500 3 3 32½ 2½ 2hd 2hd Barrera C 117 3.00 85-20 [D]Mike'sSurpris117hdRunningBold1171Boomi'sLuck1162½ Bumped 6
10Aug84-Placed first through disqualification
29Jly84- 7Key fst 6f :22 :44⅘ 1:10⅘ Alw 11000 2 5 42 43 36 67 Barrera C 115 *2.20 83-17 RelGoldGttr1123½BoldMccn1161½DncingBrrls116nk Altered course 9
LATEST WORKOUTS Jun 7 Bel 4f fst :52 b May 31 Bel 6f fst 1:14⅖ h May 20 Bel 3f fst :37⅗ b May 5 Bel 6f fst 1:15⅗ b

Zephyr Cove
B. c. 4, by Hatchet Man—Always Lovely, by Beau Gar
$30,000 Br.—Hobeau Farm Inc (Fla)
Tr.—DeBonis Robert
Own.—Chasrigg Stable
113
Lifetime 39 2 7 6 $69,930 | 1985 13 0 2 2 $16,640 | 1984 20 2 2 3 $39,550 | Turf 7 0 3 2 $21,740

22May85- 9Bel fst 6f :22⅕ :45 1:09⅗ Clm 32500 11 10 1012 89 43 2hd Bracciale V Jr b 115 16.00 94-14 Infinite Saga 117hd Zephyr Cove 115½ Big McCoy 1173 Gamely 11
12May85- 9Bel fst 7f :22⅘ :46 1:24⅕ Clm 32500 9 1 73 3½ 22 42 Guerra W A b 115 8.40 79-19 SeeforFree1171¾Deedee'sDeal117hdHarpersBazar117hd Weakened 9
2May85- 7Aqu fm 1116 Ⓣ:47⅘ 1:12⅗ 1:44⅖ 3+Alw 40000 4 7 74½ 1012 1036 1033 Cruguet J 119 12.80 50-17 FrayStr1191½StormyPuddles1191½JudgeCost1191½ Bothered start 10
26Apr85- 9Aqu fst 7f :23⅕ :46⅗ 1:25⅕ Clm c-25000 7 9 92½ 52½ 65¾ 63½ Vasquez J b 117 *2.80 71-23 HollywoodHndrson117¾Ontt117½WhtAChrgr1151 Changed course 10
14Apr85- 1Aqu fst 6f :23⅕ :46⅖ 1:11⅕ Clm 25000 5 7 96½ 86½ 55¼ 43¾ Messina R b 117 3.90 81-22 Ecstatic Pride 114¾ Act It Out 1171¾ Fletcher 1131½ Wide str. 12
5Apr85- 1Aqu fst 7f :22⅘ :46 1:23⅗ Clm 25000 9 2 72 3nk 11 31 Messina R 117 4.50 82-23 Lddy'sLuck119¾AccountReceivble117nkZphyrCov1171¾ Weakened 10
2?Mar85- 4Aqu fst 6f :22⅘ :46⅕ 1:10⅘ Clm 30000 3 7 73¾ 54½ 58½ 45¾ Messina R b 113 8.20 81-23 EcstticPride1121½SpiritedBoy1172¾BigMcCoy1171¾ Sluggish early 8
13Mar85- 4Aqu fst 7f :22⅗ :46 1:24⅗ Clm 35000 7 5 54 4¾ 31 57½ Garrido O L5 b 112 *1.10e 71-28 Shining Out 1151½Can'tCatchjohn1175SkyFalcon117½ Raced wide 12
9Mar85- 7Aqu fst 6f ⊡:22 :45⅖ 1:10⅗ Alw 23000 5 3 411 45 35 35½ Migliore R b 117 3.00 86-16 Water Skier 1172½ Morning Thunder 1172¾ZephyrCove1171½ Wide 6
20Feb85- 8Aqu fst 6f ⊡:22⅗ :45⅘ 1:12⅕ Alw 25000 6 3 75½ 65½ 42 31½ Migliore R b 117 3.20e[D] 81-23 Spender 1121½ Just Any Time110nk[D]ZephyrCove1171¾ Came over 8
20Feb85-Disqualified and placed sixth
LATEST WORKOUTS May 9 Bel tr.t 3f fst :38 b ●Apr 22 Aqu 4f fst :48⅖ h

Sweet Devil
Ch. c. 4, by Crimson Satan—Sweet Cream, by Gallant Man
$35,000 Br.—Koerner J H (NY)
Tr.—Kelley Walter A
Own.—Murrell J R
117
Lifetime 25 3 0 5 $65,640 | 1985 5 1 0 0 $17,820 | 1984 12 1 0 4 $28,080 | Turf 1 0 0 0

17May85- 1Bel fst 7f :23⅕ :46⅕ 1:23⅗ Clm 45000 6 7 41 32 66½ 58½ Moore D N5 108 28.80 77-19 AccountReceivable113noSpeedBroker1191½HarpersBazr1134 Tired 7
7Mar85- 5Aqu fst 6f ⊡:22⅗ :45⅕ 1:10⅕ Clm 45000 8 8 66¾ 69½ 715 713¾ Santagata N 113 23.40 79-21 HerefordMan1132½FastAsTheBreeze115½EcstticPride1122 Outrun 8
18Feb85- 4Aqu fst 170 ⊡:48 1:12⅗ 1:43 Clm 70000 2 5 65½ 66½ 79 69 Thibeau R J 113 11.90 76-28 King's Swan 117½ Nice Pirate 1132 Vinny's Pride 119½ No factor 8
27Jan85- 5Aqu fst 6f ⊡:22 :45⅗ 1:12⅘ [S]Alw 27000 5 10 87¾ 68½ 36 11½ Migliore R 117 6.00 82-20 Sweet Devil 1171½ Adirondack Pride 122½ Oatley 117¾ Driving 12
5Jan85- 5Aqu gd 6f ⊡:23 :46⅘ 1:12⅘ [S]Alw 27000 7 9 84¾ 86 75½ 41½ Davis R G 117 14.80 80-17 TimeTogether110½StgeGossip1171EddieRivrsid110no Wide, rallied 9
22Dec84- 3Aqu gd 6f ⊡:22⅗ :45⅖ 1:10⅕ 3+[S]Alw 27000 3 7 76¾ 711 77½ 64½ Davis R G 115 10.60 88-09 IndividualLad112¾SpiritofPegasus117¾EddieRiverside117¾ Outrun 8
26Nov84- 9Aqu fst 7f :22⅘ :46 1:24⅖ 3+[S]Alw 27000 4 10 65 63½ 56½ 67¾ Guerra W A 115 5.80 71-25 UltraMod1202½Can'tCtchjohn1153TexsGentlemn1152½ No menace 10
29Oct84- 7Aqu my 1⅛ :47⅗ 1:12⅗ 1:50⅘ 3+[S]Alw 27500 5 4 42½ 2hd 1hd 3hd Guerra W A 114 2.50 81-18 Uncle Sal 110no Tuned Out 114hd Sweet Devil 114nk Weakened 7
13Oct84- 5Bel fst 6f :22⅗ :46⅗ 1:12⅖ 3+[S]Alw 26000 7 7 710 77½ 63½ 34½ Guerra W A 116 2.40 76-25 Fletcher 1101½ Texas Gentleman 1143 Sweet Devil 116½ Rallied 7
1Oct84- 6Bel sly 1116 :47⅕ 1:12⅕ 1:44⅕ 3+[S]Alw 27500 7 3 31 53 64¾ 67½ Cordero A Jr 119 2.20 73-24 Equity Kicker 1092¾ Tuned Out 114½ Carasco 1194 Tired 7
LATEST WORKOUTS Jun 6 Bel 5f sly 1:01⅗ b May 31 Bel tr.t 4f fst :51⅖ b May 25 Bel tr.t 4f fst :49 b May 16 Bel tr.t 3f fst :37⅘ b

Tenifly
Dk. b. or br. g. 6, by Tentam—Beach Buggy, by Francis S
$35,000 Br.—Sharp Bayard (Md)
Tr.—Moschera Gasper S
Own.—Davis A
117
Lifetime 88 12 18 15 $220,478 | 1985 16 1 3 1 $33,580 | 1984 24 6 5 5 $115,250 | Turf 6 0 2 0 $6,140

5Jun85- 3Bel sly 1116 :46⅖ 1:10⅘ 1:43⅖ Clm 35000 4 5 44 45½ 44½ 46½ Davis R b 117 4.70e 79-17 Arabian Gift 1133½ Speier's Luck 1131¾RestlessJohn1171 Even try 8
1Jun85- 1Bel fst 7f :23⅗ :46⅗ 1:23⅕ Clm 35000 2 5 42½ 54 66 68½ Samyn J L b 117 3.20e 78-11 Bright Rex 1171½ Castle Knight 1122 Restless John 1171¾ Tired 7
25May85- 1Bel fst 1 :47 1:11⅘ 1:36⅗ Clm 35000 5 5 41½ 74½ 76½ 710½ Maple E b 117 2.70e 71-11 [D]Spr'sLck113nkChrmdRook1173½RstlssJohn1172½ Spped for half 7
28Apr85- 1Aqu fst 7f :22⅘ :45⅘ 1:23⅘ Clm 45000 1 7 52½ 53¾ 56½ 44¾ Bailey J D b 113 7.70e 77-21 Fibak 1172½ Hueco 1171½ Shining Out 1151½ No factor 8
20Apr85- 4Aqu my 1 :46⅖ 1:10⅖ 1:35⅘ Clm 45000 1 4 63½ 64½ 54 64 Migliore R b 113 3.70e 83-18 I'm So Merry 106no Sky Falcon 117nk Talc Power 1131½ Fell back 8
17Apr85- 7Aqu fst 6f :22⅘ :46⅘ 1:11⅗ Clm 45000 11 8 94 63¾ 35 22½ Santagata N b 115 13.10e 80-30 Speed Broker 1172½ Tenifly 115¾ Fibak 1172½ Gamely 11
8Apr85- 2Aqu fst 7f :22⅗ :45 1:23⅕ Clm 45000 6 4 65½ 63¾ 55 63 Samyn J L b 115 7.10e 82-24 Shining Out117¾FastAsTheBreeze113nkSpiritedBoy1101 No factor 8
30Mar85- 2Aqu fst 1 :46⅘ 1:11⅘ 1:37⅘ Clm 45000 1 6 54½ 42 1½ 1hd Cordero A Jr b 113 3.80e 77-28 Tenifly 113hd I'm So Merry 1103½ Restless John 1132 Driving 9
25Mar85- 5Aqu fst 7f :23⅕ :47⅕ 1:23⅘ Clm 70000 3 8 74 61¾ 58 45¾ Samyn J L b 113 8.50e 76-35 Cooper'sHawk1132BlueQuadrnt1182I'mSoMerry1081¾ Raced wide 9
25Feb85- 7Aqu fst 1⅛ ⊡:48 1:12⅘ 1:52 Clm 45000 4 6 62½ 53 46 34 Samyn J L b 113 5.70 78-25 Blue Quadrant 1131½ Lively Teddy 1062¾ Tenifly 1136 Wide turn 7
LATEST WORKOUTS May 20 Bel 3f fst :38⅕ b May 13 Bel 3f fst :36⅕ h May 10 Bel 4f fst :50⅘ b

Infinite Saga
B. g. 7, by Accipiter—Discourse, by Speak John
$35,000 Br.—Evans T M (Va)
Tr.—Lenzini John J Jr
Own.—Dee Pee Stable
119
Lifetime 66 14 6 7 $176,770 | 1985 2 1 0 0 $10,800 | 1984 11 4 2 1 $54,010 | Turf 2 0 0 0

22May85- 9Bel fst 6f :22⅕ :45 1:09⅗ Clm 35000 8 8 41½ 31½ 32 1hd Santagata N b 117 *2.90 94-14 Infinite Saga 117hd Zephyr Cove 115½ Big McCoy 1173 Driving 11
17Apr85- 7Aqu fst 6f :22⅘ :46⅘ 1:11⅗ Clm 50000 7 5 2hd 32½ 1118 1115½ Migliore R b 117 5.70 67-30 Speed Broker 1172½ Tenifly 115¾ Fibak 1172½ Stopped 11
20Aug84- 8Mth fst 6f :22⅗ :45⅖ 1:10⅖ 3+Alw 13000 2 3 1hd 1hd 1hd 1no Bracciale V Jr b 116 2.90 88-18 Infinite Saga 116no Fuddy Dud 1084 Father Roland 1131 Driving 6
31Jly84- 8Mth fst 6f :22⅕ :44⅘ 1:09⅘ 3+Alw 14000 1 2 2hd 1hd 1hd 45¾ Delgado A b 116 *1.30 85-15 Tumbler 112¾ Fuddy Dud 1081 Shir Tel 1164 Tired 5
17Jun84- 5Bel fst 6f :22⅗ :46 1:11⅖ Clm 75000 7 5 2½ 2hd 21½ 3nk Murphy D J b 119 4.00 85-22 Hominy Hill 106no Big McCoy 113nk InfiniteSaga119hd Weakened 7
10Jun84- 7Bel fst 6f :22⅕ :45⅖ 1:10⅘ 3+Alw 23000 5 7 43½ 53 55 62¾ Murphy D J b 117 7.50 85-20 ThWddingGust112hdUnmistkn117nkI'mARoundr111no Raced wide 8
2Jun84- 8Pim yl 5f Ⓣ:22⅗ :45⅘ :58⅕ 3+Mister Diz H 3 5 46½ 510 711 710 Delgado A b 110 3.30 85-21 Knight of Armor 109¾ Big Dreams 1103½ Hear Hear 108¾ Tired 7
25May84- 5Bel fst 6f :22⅘ :46⅕ 1:10⅘ Clm 75000 4 2 11½ 1½ 12 1nk Murphy D J b 119 3.10 88-23 infinite Saga 119nk Mighty Nasty 1151½ Big McCoy 1134 Driving 6
4May84- 7Aqu sly 6f :22⅖ :45⅘ 1:10 Clm 75000 5 2 1hd 1½ 1½ 11½ Murphy D J b 117 *1.30 91-17 Infinite Saga 1171½ Fleet Receiver 1132½ Hominy Hill1174 Driving 8
24Apr84- 7Aqu my 7f :22⅕ :44⅘ 1:23 Clm 70000 6 1 11½ 15 15 21¾ Murphy D J b 113 8.50 84-21 Shifty Sheik 1061¾InfiniteSaga1131¾FleetReceiver1142½ Game try 6
LATEST WORKOUTS ●Jun 4 Aqu ⊡ 5f fst 1:01 h ●May 19 Aqu ⊡ 4f gd :47⅗ h ●May 13 Aqu ⊡ 5f fst :59⅘ h ●May 6 Aqu 5f fst 1:01 h

Can't Catchjohn
B. g. 4, by Big John Taylor—Dont Get Caught, by Watch Your Step
$32,500 Br.—Seminole Syndicate (NY)
Tr.—Galluscio Dominick
Own.—Pokoik L
115
Lifetime 20 4 3 1 $80,140 | 1985 11 1 2 0 $23,140 | 1984 9 3 1 1 $57,000

Entered 9Jun85- 7 FL
1Jun85- 1Bel fst 7f :23⅗ :46⅗ 1:23⅕ Clm 32500 7 2 32 31½ 55 57½ Cruguet J b 115 4.40 78-11 Bright Rex 1171½ Castle Knight 1122 Restless John 1171¾ Tired 7
22Apr85- 1Aqu fst 7f :23 :46 1:23 Clm 35000 2 5 11 1½ 410 613½ Vasquez J b 117 3.80 72-23 ActItOut1173½AccountReceivble117¾EcstticPrid1124½ Sluggish st. 7
19Apr85- 5Aqu sly 1 :46 1:11⅗ 1:37⅗ Clm 35000 3 1 11½ 14 11½ 43¾ Vasquez J b 117 2.50 74-22 Lddy'sLuck1172½AndrsonSprng115nkOnthContrry1171½ Weakened 8
30Mar85- 2Aqu fst 1 :46⅘ 1:11⅘ 1:37⅘ Clm 50000 3 1 1hd 21 67 711 Davis R G b 117 7.20 66-28 Tenifly 113hd I'm So Merry 1103½ Restless John 1132 Stopped 9
13Mar85- 4Aqu fst 7f :22⅗ :46 1:24⅗ Clm 35000 9 4 31 3nk 2½ 21½ Davis R G b 117 8.70 77-28 Shining Out 1151½ Can't Catchjohn 1175 Sky Falcon 117½ Gamely 12
25Feb85- 7Aqu fst 1⅛ ⊡:48 1:12⅘ 1:52 Clm 45000 3 3 31 65 721 724½ Lovato F Jr 115 4.10 57-25 Blue Quadrant 1131½ Lively Teddy 1062¾ Tenifly1136 Stumbled st. 7
17Feb85- 7Aqu fst 170 ⊡:47⅗ 1:12⅗ 1:43 Alw 40000 4 1 11½ 2hd 711 718½ Migliore R 115 8.80 67-25 I'm A Rounder 1151 Carjack 1103½ Barcelona 119hd Tired 7
6Feb85- 5Aqu gd 1⅛ ⊡:49 1:14⅘ 1:52⅗ Clm 45000 7 1 12 11 15 16 Migliore R 113 7.80 79-27 Can't Catchjohn 1136 Tenifly 1133 J. Strap 108hd Ridden out 9
30Jan85- 5Aqu fst 1116 ⊡:47⅗ 1:13 1:46⅖ Clm 45000 3 1 1½ 1½ 3½ 44½ Migliore R 113 10.80 74-25 Nice Pirate1132EquityKicker117noHollywoodHendrson1082½ Tired 11
19Jan85- 1Aqu fst 6f ⊡:22⅖ :46 1:11⅗ Clm 45000 2 3 42½ 87¾ 912 98¾ Lovato F Jr 113 13.20 78-22 Speed Broker 1173½ Talc Power 110½FastAsTheBreeze1171¾ Tired 9
LATEST WORKOUTS May 29 Aqu ⊡ 4f sly :50 b (d) May 21 Aqu ⊡ 4f fst :51⅘ b May 12 Aqu ⊡ 3f fst :36⅗ h

Also Eligible (Not in Post Position Order):

Delay of Game — Gr. g. 8, by T V Commercial—Jungle Rhythm, by Nail
Own.—Maryde Farm — $35,000 — Br.—Marydel Farm (Md) — Tr.—Odom George P — 117
Lifetime 32 5 6 8 $128,892 — 1984 1 0 0 1 $2,880 — 1983 8 1 1 2 $29,580 — Turf 3 1 0 1 $16,260

15Jun84- 1Bel	fst	6f	:22⅘ :45⅘ 1:09⅘	Clm 85000	2 2 31½ 1hd 2½ 34	Velasquez J	b 116	3.30	89-18 Meru 1123 Top Hat 1121 Delay of Game 116½	Weakened	6
23Oct83- 9Aqu	sly	6f	:22 :45 1:11	3+Alw 37000	8 1 43½ 44½ 45½ 42	Vasquez J	b 115	6.60	84-14 Semaj 115hd Agile Shoebill 1141½ Cutting Thru 113½	Wide str	9
8Oct83- 7Bel	gd	6f	Ⓣ:22⅕ :46⅗ 1:12⅗	3+Alw 37000	6 5 35½ 34 42 44½	Velasquez J	b 115	3.30	72-30 Prosper 1171½ One Never Nose 115½ Mayanesian 1122¾	Weakened	8
23Sep83- 7Bel	fst	6f	:22⅕ :45⅗ 1:10⅘	3+Alw 37000	6 3 31½ 11½ 11½ 42¾	Vasquez J	b 115	2.20	88-21 Stop Card 118¾ Jan's Kinsman 1172½ Alchise 111no	Weakened	8
8Sep83- 6Med	fm	5f	Ⓣ:22⅕ :45⅕ :57⅕	3+Alw 17000	1 5 54¼ 43 1hd 15	Vasquez J	b 117	*1.00	97-09 Delay of Game 1175 J. J. Roman 1122½ Citius 117nk	Ridden out	5
17Aug83- 1Sar	fst	6f	:22⅕ :44⅘ 1:09⅕	3+Clm 75000	1 4 21 21½ 22½ 22½	Vasquez J	b 117	*1.20	92-11 RoyalRollick1152½DelayofGme1173½SpringCommnder113½	Gamely	7
29Jly83- 1Sar	fst	6f	:21⅗ :44 1:08⅗	3+Alw 27000	6 1 53 35 36 36¾	Vasquez J	b 117	7.90	90-12 Shimatoree 1172¾ Strike Gold 1134 Delay of Game 1173	Wide str.	6
25Jun83- 6Bel	fst	6f	:23 :46 1:10⅘	Clm 75000	1 10 65 64½ 44 47½	Vasquez J	b 117	*1.90	83-22 I'mSoMrry108¾MightyNsty1175½StgGossip1131½	Slow St., Drifted	10
4Jun83- 1Bel	my	6½f	:22⅗ :45 1:16⅘	3+Alw 27000	1 3 1hd 2hd 11 31¾	Vasquez J	b 117	7.90	93-10 Will OfIron1171½SilverExpress117nkDelayofGame1171½	Weakened	5
24Oct82- 6Aqu	fst	6f	:23⅗ :46⅗ 1:10⅘	3+Handicap	3 6 42½ 43 64½ 67½	Graell A	b 111	3.70	82-25 Triocala 1151 Contare 1111½ In From Dixie 1121	Tired	6

LATEST WORKOUTS May 31 Del 5f gd 1:02⅕ b May 8 Del 4f fst :49⅘ b

Lively Teddy — Ch. g. 6, by Teddy's Courage—Lively Debate, by Wolfram
Own.—Barrera O S — $35,000 — Br.—Edwards R L (NY) — Tr.—Barrera Oscar S — 119
Lifetime 51 10 6 7 $165,240 — 1985 21 5 3 3 $82,080 — 1984 12 3 1 3 $58,470 — Turf 3 0 0 0

3Jun85- 7Bel	fst	1⅟₁₆	:46⅘ 1:11⅕ 1:42⅗	3+Alw 29000	1 1 2hd 31 1hd 1hd	Cordero A Jr	b 117	6.40	89-13 Lively Teddy117hdGoldenImmigrant117¾WildChorus117hd	Driving	7
31May85- 1Bel	fst	1⅛	:47⅕ 1:14 1:50⅘	Clm 22500	2 2 1½ 2½ 11 11½	Cordero A Jr	b 115	3.20	73-16 Lively Teddy 1151½ Pitchpipe 1151Wimborne'sGater1151½	Driving	9
27May85- 6Bel	fm	1⅟₁₆	Ⓣ:48 1:11⅘ 1:42⅕	3+Alw 29000	4 4 44 88½ 814 820½	MacBeth D	b 121	12.40	69-19 Go Go Regal 1214 Judge Costa 1212½ Harcolite 1141	Tired	8
24May85- 9Bel	fst	1⅛	:47⅕ 1:11⅗ 1:50	Clm c-17500	3 3 1hd 2hd 35½ 38½	Samyn J L	b 117	7.30	69-18 Full Concert 1178½ Pitchpipe 1172 Lively Teddy 1171¾	Tired	10
15May85- 3Bel	fst	1⅛	:47⅕ 1:11⅕ 1:49⅗	Clm 35000	7 2 1hd 43½ 611 714¾	Samyn J L	b 117	13.50	64-17 Colonel Law 1171¾ Charmed Rook 1173½ Deedee's Deal1153	Tired	10
3May85- 8Aqu	sly	1	:47⅘ 1:12⅗ 1:38⅕	3+Alw 27000	5 3 43½ 416 316 318¾	Samyn J L	b 121	2.50	56-26 Bienestar 12110¾ Broadway Harry1218LivelyTeddy1212¾	No threat	5
18Apr85- 8Aqu	fst	1⅜	:50⅕ 2:33⅗ 3:12⅘	3+Handicap	5 2 1½ 45 523 521¾	Davis R G	b 111	6.70	— — Erin Bright 118hd Eecio 10815½ Easy Choice 1181¾	Tired	6
23Mar85- 3Aqu	fst	1⅝	:49 2:07⅘ 2:46⅗	Hcp 25000s	4 3 33½ 11 13 1nk	Samyn J L	b 116	6.50	69-23 Lively Teddy 116nk Arbitor's Image 1173 Doubter 1152¾	Driving	8
16Mar85- 5Aqu	fst	1⅛	:49⅕ 1:14 1:54⅕	Clm 32500	3 1 11½ 11 1½ 1nk	Samyn J L	b 115	9.30	64-34 Lively Teddy 115nk Eecio 117½ Charmed Rook117¾	Drifted, drvng	8
11Mar85- 4Aqu	fst	1¼	⊡:50⅗ 1:40⅕ 2:06⅗	Clm c-25000	7 6 65 79 48½ 35½	Espinosa R E7	b 112	*.70e	77-18 Gene'sDream1084½Wimborne'sGater108¾LivelyTeddy1122½	Rallied	8

LATEST WORKOUTS Apr 27 Aqu 3f fst :38⅕ b Apr 15 Aqu 5f fst 1:04 b

Restless John — Ro. g. 4, by Royal John—Forbidden Wind, by Restless Wind
Own.—Davis A — $35,000 — Br.—McKee J D (WVa) — Tr.—Moschera Gasper S — 117
Lifetime 58 11 5 15 $162,093 — 1985 18 1 0 6 $31,140 — 1984 21 4 3 2 $40,130 — Turf 2 0 0 0

5Jun85- 3Bel	sly	1⅟₁₆	:46⅗ 1:10⅘ 1:43⅗	Clm 35000	7 6 65 35½ 34½ 35½	Maple E	b 117	4.70e	80-17 Arabian Gift 1133½ Speier's Luck 1131¾ Restless John1171	Rallied	8
1Jun85- 1Bel	fst	7f	:23⅗ :46⅗ 1:23⅕	Clm 35000	3 6 67½ 67 44½ 32½	Maple E	b 117	3.20e	83-11 Bright Rex 1171½ Castle Knight 1122 Restless John 1171¾	Rallied	7
25May85- 1Bel	fst	1	:47 1:11⅗ 1:36⅗	Clm 35000	3 6 52 52¾ 42½ 32½	Bailey J D	b 117	2.70e	78-11 ⒹSpeier's Luck 113nkCharmedRook1173½RestlessJohn1172½	Wide	7
22May85- 9Bel	fst	6f	:22⅕ :45 1:09⅗	Clm 35000	9 11 1117 1115 1111 108	Hernandez R	b 117	17.60	86-14 Infinite Saga 117hd Zephyr Cove 115½ Big McCoy 1173	Outrun	11
2May85- 4Aqu	fst	1	:46⅘ 1:11⅗ 1:37⅕	Clm 35000	1 10 98½ 912 914 810½	Garrido O L5	b 112	7.70	69-26 FingersIntheTill119hdEspritDeRomeo1131½SeeforFre1171½	Outrun	10
28Apr85- 1Aqu	fst	7f	:22⅗ :45⅗ 1:23⅗	Clm 45000	2 8 811 813 812 810	Garrido O L5	b 108	7.70e	72-21 Fibak 1172½ Hueco 1171½ Shining Out 1151½	Broke slowly	8
20Apr85- 4Aqu	my	1	:46⅗ 1:10⅗ 1:35⅘	Clm 45000	3 7 42½ 54 43 42	Bailey J D	b 113	3.70e	85-18 I'm So Merry 106no Sky Falcon 117nk Talc Power 1131¾	Wide	8
17Apr85- 7Aqu	fst	6f	:22⅘ :46⅘ 1:11⅗	Clm 45000	6 10 109 108¾ 79½ 45¾	Bailey J D	b 113	13.10e	77-30 Speed Broker 1172½ Tenifly 115¾ Fibak 1172½	Rallied	11
30Mar85- 2Aqu	fst	1	:46⅘ 1:11⅗ 1:37⅗	Clm 45000	5 9 76 64 43½ 32½	Samyn J L	b 113	3.80e	73-28 Tenifly 113hd I'm So Merry 1102½ Restless John 1132	Rallied	9
25Mar85- 5Aqu	fst	7f	:23⅕ :47⅕ 1:23⅗	Clm 70000	9 9 98½ 95 710 58¾	Cordero A Jr	b 113	8.50e	73-35 Cooper's Hawk1132BlueQuadrant1182I'mSoMerry1081¾	No threat	9

LATEST WORKOUTS May 21 Bel 3f fst :37 b May 16 Bel 4f fst :48⅕ h May 9 Bel 4f fst :48 h Apr 27 Bel 3f fst :36 h

Agile Shoebill — B. h. 5, by Duck Dance—Agilely, by Semi-Pro
Own.—Davis A — $35,000 — Br.—Heubeck E Jr & Harriet (Fla) — Tr.—Moschera Gasper S — 1107
Lifetime 30 10 11 6 $244,370 — 1985 7 2 3 2 $55,020 — 1984 16 3 2 3 $81,270 — Turf 1 0 0 0

11May85- 3Bel	fst	6f	:22⅕ :45⅕ 1:10⅘	Clm 85000	6 2 1½ 2hd 21 22	Bailey J D	b 116	*1.80	88-12 Magnetic Field II 1162 Agile Shoebill 1161 Faces Up112¾	Gamely	6
8May85- 6Bel	fst	7f	:22⅕ :45⅕ 1:23⅗	3+Alw 36000	3 1 12½ 14 12 32½	Garrido O L5	b 116	7.80	82-18 Spender 1192½ Tough Critic 119nk AgileShoebill1161½	Drifted out	7
19Apr85- 7Aqu	sly	7f	:22⅗ :45⅗ 1:23⅕	Clm 75000	4 1 13 12 12½ 12	Bailey J D	b 117	3.80	85-22 Agile Shoebill 1172 Shining Out 113¾ Faces Up 1171¾	Driving	6
17Mar85- 6Aqu	fst	7f	:23 :46⅘ 1:25⅕	Alw 36000	1 1 11 1hd 22 38½	Ward W A5	b 110	*.60	67-33 Jacksboro 119nk Barcelona 1228 Agile Shoebill 110nk	Weakened	6
11Mar85- 8Aqu	fst	6f	⊡:21⅗ :44 1:09⅘	Alw 36000	2 2 2hd 2hd 2½ 22½	Ward W A5	b 110	2.80	96-18 Mt. Livermore 1222½ Agile Shoebill1107Spender117nk	Best others	7
25Feb85- 8Aqu	fst	6f	⊡:23 :46⅕ 1:11	Alw 36000	3 4 2hd 1hd 2hd 21½	HendersonJC10	b 105	4.80	87-25 Mt. Livermore 1151½ Agile Shoebill 1051½Huckster1191½	Game try	6
22Feb85- 1Aqu	fst	6f	⊡:22⅗ :45⅗ 1:11⅗	Clm 50000	3 5 1hd 1hd 13 11½	HendersonJC10	b 107	3.80e	87-22 AgileShoebill1071½FstAsTheBreeze1171¾EcstticPrid117no	Driving	7
15Jun84- 1Bel	fst	6f	:22⅘ :45⅘ 1:09⅘	Clm 85000	3 1 11 2hd 1½ 44½	Cordero A Jr	b 116	*1.10	88-18 Meru 1123 Top Hat 1121 Delay of Game 116½	Gave way	6
28May84- 8Mth	sly	6f	:22⅗ :45⅗ 1:11⅕	3+Handicap	3 — — — 46 44½	Santagata N	b 113	5.30	79-19 For Halo 114¾ Count His Fleet 110hd Rocky Marriage 1224	Fog	5
12May84- 7Bel	fm	1	Ⓣ:46⅗ 1:09⅘ 1:35⅗	3+Alw 36000	1 1 2hd 33½ 56 715½	Ward W A5	b 114	9.40	72-15 Who's For Dinner 119¾ NativeRaid1212¾Reinvested1192½	Stopped	7

LATEST WORKOUTS May 27 Bel tr.t 4f fst :48⅕ h May 5 Bel 4f fst :47⅘ h ●Apr 13 Bel 5f fst :59⅗ h

In the race we are about to study, both the pace and class approaches point to the same horse, an improving dropdown who figures to have things his own way in the early stages. Here, then, are the past performances for the fourth race at Belmont on June 10, 1985.

Note that we have intentionally reproduced the past performances for the entire eighteen-horse field as originally entered. In other words, we are simulating actual working conditions faced by many handicappers, who spend a few hours at home, either the night before or the morning of the races, working in the dark, so to speak, unaware of the scratches, either early or late. One must be careful not to overlook the horses on the also-eligible list. Since many players give these horses only a cursory glance, bargains can often be found among them. And their presence in a race can completely change the picture, at least as far as pace is concerned. Indeed, so too can their absence, or the absence of any speed horse scratched, either early or late.

The race we will analyze was carded for older male $35,000 claimers, a classification two notches below the top rung on the New York claiming ladder. At least seven of the eighteen horses entered had raced for $35,000 lately, though none with any notable success. Here, then, are some comments on the field:

WANDERING FEET

This horse is a front-runner who has been tiring of late and apparently needs the drop in class. He was aided by a slow pace on May 17 when he competed at the $50,000 level, then was run off his feet by quick allowance rivals on June 3. I would have to guess that a drop back to $25,000—the scene of his most recent win—would be more appropriate.

CARRY IT FULL

First time in a claimer—possibly in his career—after showing nothing against above-average three-year-olds in his first two starts of the year. That fourteen-month layoff is a cause for concern, and the sharp class drop today suggests that this lightly raced horse is having problems. But why not start at the top of the claiming ranks to find where the horse really fits?

SHINING OUT

First time out for Oscar Barrera after a claim, and consequently a threat, yet hard to take as 2–1 favorite. Established at the $50,000 level prior to disappointing from a difficult post on May 27, one has to wonder why the previous trainer chose to cut his price in half on June 7 rather than accept that legitimate excuse at face value.

BIG McCOY

Big McCoy is another front-runner, one that has challenged at this level in his last three starts, yet failed to bring home a victory. Since his last race was his first serious exercise after a five-week freshening, one might expect some improvement today. But, as we shall soon see, the pace situation in today's race figures to be tough.

JUST ANY TIME

This horse was off for five weeks after winning for the first time in at least ten tries—clearly a suspicious situation. He appears to have needed the drop to $25,000, and there is no reason to like him in this field.

STRIKE A COIN

A hard-knocking speedball on the Florida circuit the previous season, Strike A Coin seems to be rounding to form. He has carried his speed one call farther each time out in New York, last time despite breaking from the disadvantageous 10-post going six furlongs at Belmont. He's an improving horse.

CASTLE KNIGHT

A speedball whose last in today's class looks like a big improvement but is merely an illusion created by a ridiculously slow pace for $35,000 animals.

SINCERE WISH

This is a state-bred allowance horse who was dropped into an (open) claimer first time back from a two-month layoff. The horse drops again today, but don't expect much.

RUNNING BOLD

This horse has been dropping this year, seeking his proper classification. His last two efforts at today's level suggest that he is still in over his head.

ZEPHYR COVE

A late-charger that has been unable to get the job done at this level or the one immediately below it. Zephyr Cove's lifetime record of 39–2–7–6 says it all. He is the enemy, the kind of horse intelligent handicappers love to bet against, no matter how good his form might look on paper. If every field included a horse like Zephyr Cove, starting at a mandatory 5–1, the player's lot would improve considerably. If nothing else, such a horse would negate the pari-mutuel take.

SWEET DEVIL

Good speed prep in a seven-furlong race last time, in his first start after a ten-week layoff. Drops one notch today to a new low, and may fit well here. The major question is the horse's ability to get up at six furlongs in fast company.

TENIFLY

Nothing last three at this level, although at longer distances. The preponderance of seven-furlong races in his record suggests that the gelding's connections do not consider him quick enough for the shorter six-furlong distance.

INFINITE SAGA

Dropped in for $35,000 last time, Infinite Saga responded with his first win of the season, in only his second start of the year. Indeed, the seven-year-old gelding performed a miracle of sorts, winning from off the pace for the first time in recent memory (if ever). The horse he barely held off, however, was our bridesmaid friend Zephyr Cove, taking some of the luster from Infinite Saga's performance. Another negative note—although his 1984 record shows Infinite Saga to have been a solid $75,000 runner, that his trainer apparently does not consider him to be the same horse this year and is not moving him back up in class following his recent win, as one might expect.

CAN'T CATCHJOHN

A consistent speed type at longer distances, Can't Catchjohn backed up in his last three starts, all at this level. However, his recent performances are no guarantee that the four-year-old will be able to set the pace at the shorter distance—nor that he would be able to hang on better should he get to the lead. The faster six-furlong pace may not be to the horse's liking.

DELAY OF GAME

The first of four also-eligibles, Delay Of Game is making his first start in nearly a year and only his second in twenty months. The sharp drop in class off the layoff suggests that all is not well with this horse.

LIVELY TEDDY

A router coming off consecutive wins, presumably prepping at six furlongs for future engagements, Lively Teddy is part of the favored entry but not a likely contributor.

RESTLESS JOHN

A stretch-runner coming off three consecutive third-place finishes in today's company, although not likely to be suited by the six-furlong distance.

AGILE SHOEBILL

One of the quickest gate horses on the New York circuit, Agile Shoebill is taking a very suspicious class drop following a month's hiatus. Would certainly be a factor if fit.

It doesn't take a very sophisticated player to realize that the early pace in this race will be hotly contested. Nine of the eighteen horses entered are early speed types, and six of these—Wandering Feet, Big McCoy, Strike A Coin, Castle Knight, Can't Catchjohn, and Agile Shoebill—appear to be incapable of winning unless they are able to get to the lead quickly and without undue pressure. Accurate pace figures, however, cast the pace situation in a different light. Although rating seven of the nine speedballs virtually inseparable, the figures emphatically suggest that Agile Shoebill and Strike A Coin are about two or three lengths faster than the rest of the early contenders for the first half mile, although they will probably be at each other's throats.

I had made a small wager on Strike A Coin on May 27, anticipating improvement in his form cycle, although aware that his task that day would not be easy, breaking from the outside with the start so close to the turn. I liked his effort that day, although it was compromised by the outside post and had him on my "Horses to Watch" list. I was not too thrilled, though, to find a noted speedball like Agile Shoebill standing in his way on June 10, threatening to force Strike A Coin into a suicidal speed duel.

When dealing with a race packed with early speed, one either goes with the fleetest of the fleet or selects a speed type with proven ability to come from just off the pace. The late runner is another alternative, although one that should be avoided unless the track is clearly biased against early speed or none of the speed types figure to have much chance after debating the issue early. Horses like Zephyr Cove, Sweet Devil, Tenifly, and Restless John are seldom worth backing at six furlongs, even in a race overloaded with early speed, such as the one under consideration. Their normally difficult task will be compounded by the fact that they must either go around or weave their way between all the speed horses ahead of them, many of whom will be backing up in the paths of the closers trying to get by them.

Since Strike A Coin and Agile Shoebill appeared hard to separate on pace figures, and none of the "just off the pace" types were very appealing, this race posed quite a dilemma. A smart (patient) player would pass such a race, reasoning that Strike A Coin will race again, possibly with another deceiving running line added to his record, hiding his improving form and adding a few points to his odds.

Fortunately, the scratches cleared away the clouds hanging over the crystal ball. Agile Shoebill didn't get into the race, leaving Strike A Coin the main speed in the race. Unfortunately, Zephyr Cove was another casualty, eliminating the race's primary antagonist. Also scratched were Sweet Devil, Infinite Saga, and Lively Teddy.

As now set up, the race offered a prime betting opportunity. The improving Strike A Coin figured to dominate the six other speedsters still in the race. Adding to his appeal was the fact that he was a "stranger" to these $35,000 horses, dropping into the class for the first time, with no recent history of futility against the "regulars"

FOURTH RACE
Belmont
JUNE 10, 1985

6 FURLONGS. ($1.08\frac{4}{5}$) CLAIMING. Purse $18,000. 4-year-olds and upward. Weight, 122 lbs. Non-winners of two races since May 15, allowed 3 lbs.; of a race since then, 5 lbs. Claiming price $35,000; for each $2,500 to $30,000, 2 lbs. (Races when entered to be claimed for $25,000 or less not considered.)

Value of race $18,000; value to winner $10,800; second $3,960; third $2,160; fourth $1,080. Mutuel pool $127,755, OTB pool $119,688. Ex Pool $161,145 OTB Ex Pl $125,346 Q $88,116 OTB Q $96,915

Last Raced	Horse	Eqt.	A.Wt	PP	St	¼	½	Str	Fin	Jockey	Cl'g Pr	Odds $1
27May85 2Bel5	Strike A Coin		5 117	6	6	3^{hd}	$3^{\frac{1}{2}}$	$2^{1\frac{1}{2}}$	$1^{1\frac{1}{4}}$	Guerra W A	35000	7.70
22May85 9Bel3	Big McCoy		5 117	4	2	$2^{1\frac{1}{2}}$	1^{hd}	$1^{1\frac{1}{2}}$	2^{nk}	Cordero A Jr	35000	2.50
7Jun85 2Bel2	Shining Out		5 117	3	3	$9^{\frac{1}{2}}$	$6^{\frac{1}{2}}$	3^{hd}	3^{2}	MacBeth D	35000	2.30
5May85 4Aqu1	Just Any Time	b	5 113	5	7	5^{hd}	$5^{1\frac{1}{2}}$	$4^{1\frac{1}{2}}$	4^{1}	Bailey J D	30000	22.30
3Jun85 3Bel8	Carry It Full	b	5 113	2	10	10^{5}	10^{4}	$7^{1\frac{1}{2}}$	5^{3}	Venezia M	30000	19.60
5Jun85 3Bel4	Tenifly	b	6 117	10	12	12^{5}	11^{5}	$8^{\frac{1}{2}}$	6^{nk}	Davis R G	35000	a-8.40
3Jun85 3Bel6	Wandering Feet		5 117	1	1	$4^{1\frac{1}{2}}$	$4^{1\frac{1}{2}}$	$6^{\frac{1}{2}}$	$7^{1\frac{1}{2}}$	McCarron G	35000	16.30
1Jun85 1Bel2	Castle Knight		7 112	7	8	$6^{\frac{1}{2}}$	$7^{\frac{1}{2}}$	9^{2}	$8^{\frac{1}{2}}$	Moore D N5	35000	9.90
15Jun84 1Bel3	Dēlay of Game	b	8 117	12	4	1^{hd}	$2^{1\frac{1}{2}}$	$5^{\frac{1}{2}}$	9^{nk}	Vasquez J	35000	10.70
5Jun85 3Bel3	Restless John	b	4 117	13	13	13	13	10^{2}	10^{3}	Maple E	35000	a-8.40
1Jun85 1Bel5	Can't Catchjohn	b	4 115	11	11	11^{hd}	$12^{1\frac{1}{2}}$	11^{hd}	$11^{1\frac{1}{2}}$	Ayoub L	32500	52.60
22May85 9Bel5	Running Bold		4 117	9	9	$8^{1\frac{1}{2}}$	$8^{1\frac{1}{2}}$	$12^{1\frac{1}{2}}$	$12^{1\frac{1}{2}}$	Samyn J L	35000	24.60
27May85 2Bel8	Sincere Wish		4 117	8	5	$7^{\frac{1}{2}}$	9^{hd}	13	13	Hernandez R	35000	46.10

a-Coupled: Tenifly and Restless John.

OFF AT 2:36. Start good, Won driving. Time, :22⅗, :45⅘, 1:10⅖ Track fast.

$2 Mutuel Prices:				
	7-(F)-STRIKE A COIN	17.40	8.80	4.80
	5-(D)-BIG MCCOY		4.20	2.80
	4-(C)-SHINING OUT			3.00

$2 EXACTA 7-5 PAID $91.00. $2 QUINELLA 5-7 PAID $49.00.

B. g, by Strike the Anvil—Roman Coin, by Bristol Bristol. Trainer Gullo Thomas J. Bred by Chibcha Farm (Fla).

STRIKE A COIN close up and racing outside WANDERING FEET early, moved out for the stretch run and wore down BIG MCCOY under good handling. The latter contested the pace racing just off the rail, opened a clear lead in upper stretch but weakened late and lasted for the place. SHINING OUT rallied along the inside approaching the stretch and finished with good speed outside BIG MCCOY. JUST ANY TIME never too far back, lacked needed late bid outside. CARRY IT FULL was going well at the finish from the outside. TENIFY improved his position along the inside without threatening. WANDERING FEET close up and saving ground early, tired soon after entering stretch. CASTLE KNIGHT between horses early, tired. DELAY OF GAME contested the pace outside BIG MCCOY and was weakening when squeezed back and steadied between horses in upper stretch. RESTLESS JOHN broke sluggishly. RUNNING BOLD raced outside and tired.

that cluttered this field. The "new kid on the block" figured to show his heels to his early pursuers, throttle down into second gear for a while, then draw clear when asked to run at the head of the lane, with enough in reserve to hold off potential challenges from the likes of Shining Out and Restless John.

Things didn't work out quite as expected on the front end, though. Delay Of Game flashed uncharacteristic speed, as might be expected from a horse returning from a layoff, and the freshened Big McCoy ran faster than his recent pace figures predicted. They left Strike A Coin slightly in arrears, inexplicably a couple of lengths behind where his figures predicted. But the energy he didn't call upon in the early stages was there when he needed it, as Strike A Coin reached the peak of his form cycle with a strong stretch run.

One point is worth emphasizing. It is foolish to "marry" oneself to a horse before knowing the scratches, track conditions, and biases. Psychologically, it is difficult to change horses in midstream, to back away from an animal originally thought to be one of the day's better bets. Yet one scratch, or a change in track conditions, can completely change the nature of a race, the way it sets up from the standpoint of pace. It is best to wait as long as possible—almost until post time, if conditions allow—before making a final decision about how to bet a race.

Chapter 39

Accurate Speed Figures Without Daily Variants

SPEED HANDICAPPING HAS ENJOYED enormous popularity during the past ten years despite a potentially serious flaw in its methodology. Good speed figures are all too dependent on daily variants, numbers that accurately measure the true speed of a racing surface on a given day. But there is no universally accepted formula for calculating "the" daily variant. Two highly qualified speed handicappers can easily disagree on what the variant should be on any given day.

The simple fact of the matter is that a daily variant based on the mathematical average of a small sample of deviations from par figures can produce an inaccurate assessment of track speed, unless those deviations from par form a rather homogeneous set of numbers, closely clustered about their average. When they don't, most accomplished speed handicappers add a little judgment, establishing their variant for the day perhaps a point or two above or below the average, possibly canceling the effect that one or two races on the card may have had on the average. Consequently, different handicappers can come up with different variants for the same day. The one with the better feeling for the numbers will end up with the more accurate speed figures.

In my previous two books, I described in great detail how the "class pars" approach to daily variants works. But this methodology often produces days when one or two races have deviations from par well out of line with the rest of the card simply because the fields for those races were exceptionally strong or weak for the stated classification. If used in the calculation of an average, such races can seriously distort the day's variant. Strange race deviations of this type are far less likely to arise when the player uses the

1 BELMONT

WIDENER TURF COURSE — 1 MILE — BELMONT PARK — START — FINISH

1 MILE. (Turf). (1.33) CLAIMING. Purse $7,000. 3-year-olds and upward. Weight, 3-year-olds, 118 lbs. Older, 122 lbs. Claiming price $100,000; for each $5,000 to $75,000 allowed 2 lbs.

Coupled—Freon and Meru.

Lutyens *

Ch. c. 4, by Avatar—Flying Buttress, by Exclusive Native
$75,000 Br.—Brant P M (Ky) Tr.—DeBonis Robert — 112
Own.—Masilipin Stable
Lifetime 46 8 0 6 $142,716 — 1984 15 3 0 2 $57,636 — 1983 22 5 0 3 $79,920 — Turf 17 4 0 3 $76,476

29Aug84- 5Bel fm 1 1/16 Ⓣ:48 1:11⅗ 1:42⅘ 3+Clm 75000 1 3 43 53½ 52 43 Ward W A5 112 *2.20 86-14 Red Brigade 119¾ Come To London 119¾ Beagle 1151½ Weakened 7
8Aug84- 9Mth fm 1 1/16 Ⓣ:48⅘ 1:12⅘ 1:42⅘+ 3+Alw 17000 6 3 33 51¾ 44 45 Antley C W5 110 3.00 84-13 Data Swap 115no Always Up 1153 St. Brendan 1152 Tired 6
30Jly84- 8Bel gd 1 1/16 Ⓣ:48⅘ 1:12 1:43 3+Viceregal 6 6 64½ 65½ 711 49 Guerra W A 115 18.50 77-29 Intensify 1227 Quick Dip 1151¾ Nepal 115nk Rallied 8
23Jly84- 6Bel yl 1 1/16 Ⓣ:48 1:12⅘ 1:45⅘ Clm 175000 6 7 614 58½ 44½ 33¾ Maple E 113 5.70 70-29 Quick Dip 1123½ Fray Star 114nk Lutyens 113½ Rallied 8
12Jly84- 5Bel gd 1 Ⓣ:47 1:11⅗ 1:36⅘ Clm 175000 10 5 63½ 51¾ 2½ 1no Lopez V5 107 15.60 83-24 Lutyens 107no Fray Star 114nk Quick Dip 112¾ Driving 10
1Jly84- 8Bel sly 1⅜ :46⅕ 1:37⅘ 2:18⅘ 3+Tidal H 3 2 2hd 34½ 515 529½ Lopez V 105 6.40 57-20 Win 11111 Anne's Lover 1089 Four Bases 1125½ Tired 6
20Jun84- 5Bel fm 1 1/16 Ⓣ:46 1:10⅘ 1:41⅗ Clm 70000 10 5 42½ 22 11 12 Lopez V5 108 17.10 89-17 Lutyens 1082 Meru 1171½ Freon 1131 Ridden out 12
7Jun84- 7Bel fm 1⅜ Ⓣ:49⅘ 1:38 2:14⅘ 3+Alw 25000 7 2 42 3½ 43½ 48¾ Cruguet J 117 8.60 84-13 Talakeno 1172½ Nassipour 1174 Head of the House 119½ Tired 7
20May84- 7Bel fm 2 Ⓣ:51 2:55⅗ 3:20⅘ 3+Handicap 4 5 53½ 44½ 44½ 47½ Venezia M 112 11.70 91-13 Anne's Lover1142¾ErinBright1171¾Nassipour1282½ Lacked fin. bid 10
11May84- 2Bel fm 1¼ Ⓣ:48⅘ 1:37⅘ 2:02⅘ Clm 45000 6 5 54½ 55½ 43½ 11 Lopez V5 108 17.80 82-17 Lutyens 1081 Quick Dip 117¾ Class Hero 115½ Driving 10
LATEST WORKOUTS Aug 22 Bel 3f fst :36⅘ h Jly 20 Bel tr.t 3f fst :36 h Jly 10 Bel tr.t 3f fst :37⅘ h

Red Brigade

B. g. 5, by Daryl's Joy—Red Gossip, by Hard Work
$90,000 Br.—Mufson Rhoda (Fla) Tr.—Barrera Luis — 118
Own.—Happy Valley Farm
Lifetime 41 13 10 4 $244,040 — 1984 10 4 2 0 $64,780 — 1983 13 4 3 2 $102,620 — Turf 36 12 10 4 $238,040

29Aug84- 5Bel fm 1 1/16 Ⓣ:48 1:11⅗ 1:42⅘ 3+Clm 75000 2 2 31 31 3½ 1¾ Guerra W A b 119 3.20 89-14 Red Brigade 119¾ Come To London 119¾ Beagle 1151½ Driving 7
19Aug84- 5Sar fm 1 Ⓣ:47 1:11⅘ 1:36⅘ 3+Clm 85000 7 3 32½ 36½ 25 25½ Cordero A Jr b 116 2.40 87-20 Disco Count 1225½ Red Brigade 1162½ Forkali 118no Wide 7
12Aug84- 2Sar fm 1 Ⓣ:46⅘ 1:10⅗ 1:36⅘ 3+Clm 80000 9 5 3½ 2hd 11 1hd Cordero A Jr b 114 *2.00 95-07 Red Brigade 114hd Upmost 1123½ Forkali 1171½ Driving 10
5Aug84- 5Sar fm 1⅛ Ⓣ:48⅘ 1:12⅘ 1:50 3+Clm 75000 2 2 21½ 1hd 1½ 2hd Cordero A Jr b 117 *1.00 90-13 El Fantasma 117hd RedBrigade1172½BlueEmmanuelle113½ Gamely 8
1Aug84- 5Sar fm 1 1/16 Ⓣ:47⅘ 1:11 1:54⅘ 3+Clm 50000 1 4 32½ 33 1½ 11½ Cordero A Jr b 117 4.50 95-09 Red Brigade 1171½ Come To London 117¾ Broadly 115½ Driving 10
21Jly84- 9Bel sly 1 1/16 :46 1:11 1:43⅘ Clm 70000 2 2 24 818 840 852½ Bailey J D b 113 5.90 31-21 King's Swan 1173 Beagle 1135 Jumbler 1104½ Stopped 8
12Jly84- 5Bel gd 1 Ⓣ:47 1:11⅗ 1:36⅘ Clm 180000 8 2 1hd 1hd 52½ 77 Bailey J D b 114 20.00 76-24 Lutyens 107no Fray Star 114nk Quick Dip 112¾ Gave way 10
20Jun84- 5Bel fm 1 1/16 Ⓣ:46 1:10⅘ 1:41⅗ Clm 75000 9 2 2½ 32 97½ 99½ Cordero A Jr b 117 *1.40 80-17 Lutyens 1082 Meru 1171½ Freon 1131 Gave way 12
9Jun84- 3Bel fm 1 1/16 Ⓣ:45⅘ 1:09⅘ 1:40⅘ 3+Blue Larkspr 5 4 64½ 76 78½ 79¾ Day P b 117 6.80 84-07 NativeRaid1175½RemndedII1221½Who'sForDinner117nk Early foot 9
9Jun84-Run in divisions
17May84- 7Bel fm 1 1/16 Ⓣ:46⅘ 1:10⅘ 1:41⅘ Clm 185000 3 4 2hd 21½ 1hd 12 Cordero A Jr b 116 4.80 89-16 DH Red Brigade 1162 DH Remanded II 1122 Fray Star1142½ Driving 9
17May84-Dead heat
LATEST WORKOUTS Jly 19 Bel tr.t 4f gd :53 b (d) Jly 9 Bel tr.t 4f fst :51⅘ b

*Wicked Will

B. h. 6, by Mill Reef—Green Glade, by Correspondent
$100,000 Br.—Mellon P (Eng) Tr.—Kelly Thomas J — 122
Own.—Ardboe Stable
Lifetime 51 8 9 6 $195,006 — 1984 3 0 0 0 $1,680 — 1983 9 2 1 2 $48,278 — Turf 41 6 9 3 $161,203

3Sep84- 7Bel fm 7f Ⓣ:23⅘ :45⅘ 1:21⅘ 3+Alw 33000 6 6 717 721 716 712½ Rivera M A 115 16.90 82-14 Disco Count 1101½ Paris Prince 1151½FearlessLeader1152¾ Outrun 7
23Jly84- 6Bel yl 1 1/16 Ⓣ:48 1:12⅘ 1:45⅘ Clm 175000 1 8 810 711 55½ 44½ Cruguet J 112 5.40 70-29 Quick Dip 1123½ Fray Star 114nk Lutyens 113½ Rallied 8
21Jun84- 7Bel fm 1 1/16 Ⓣ:47 1:09⅘ 1:41 Clm 175000 5 6 68½ 69½ 67½ 57¼ Samyn J L 112 10.20 88-16 Fray Star 114nk Remanded II 1122½ Prosper 1142 Outrun 7
24Sep83- 6Bel gd 1⅜ Ⓣ:49⅘ 1:38⅘ 2:03⅘ 3+Poker 1 4 32½ 58½ 511 514¾ Cruguet J 115 *1.30 63-26 Freon 1152½ Nadasdy 1132 Kentucky River 1177 Tired 5
11Sep83- 6Bel fm 1¼ Ⓣ:46⅘ 1:36⅘ 2:01⅘ 3+Alw 40000 7 7 719 56 33 2no Fell J 117 7.80 88-12 Erin's Tiger 122no Wicked Will 1173 Piling 112¾ Just missed 7
24Aug83- 8Bel fm *1 1/16 Ⓣ:45⅘ 1:08⅘ 1:38⅘ 3+B Beach H 2 12 1216 1215 1112 1111¾ Cruguet J 112 14.30 — — Bold Style 1191½ Ten Below 113nk McCann 115½ Outrun 12
12Aug83- 5Sar sly 1⅛ :47⅘ 1:11⅘ 1:51⅘ 3+Alw 37000 2 5 511 46 44 32½ Fell J 117 4.60 77-23 AccountReceivble1171¾ImperilDilmm117½WickdWill1172½ Rallied 5
27Jly83- 6Sar fm 1 1/16 Ⓣ:48 1:11⅘ 1:42⅘ 3+Alw 37000 2 7 715 79½ 58½ 42 Fell J 115 12.10 92-11 Disco Count 119½ Fray Star 1191½ Erin's Tiger 119no Rallied 7
21Mar83- 9Hia fm 1 1/16 Ⓣ 1:41⅘ 3+Royal Palm H 11 8 811 712 77½ 78¾ Rivera M A 115 7.80 82-14 Discovered1131½DReimbursement1101½Snto'sJoe109no No factor 11
21Mar83-Run in two divisions 7th & 9th races
5Feb83- 8GP yl *1 1/16 Ⓣ 1:47⅘ 3+Can Turf H 1 11 1114 107¾ 65½ 32½ Rivera M A 116 12.90 68-30 Data Swap 1151½ Northrop 1181 Wicked Will 1161 Rallied 12
5Feb83-Run in two divisions, 8th & 10th races
LATEST WORKOUTS Aug 27 Bel tr.t 5f fst 1:02⅘ b Aug 22 Sar Ⓣ 4f fm :52 b Jly 15 Bel tr.t 4f fst :50⅘ b

Freon

Dk. b. or br. g. 7, by Icecapade—Miss Summons, by Helioscope
$85,000 Br.—Walden B P (Ky) Tr.—Barrera Oscar S — 116
Own.—Silver Mate Stable
Lifetime 81 19 17 9 $318,170 — 1984 13 2 4 1 $52,960 — 1983 13 4 3 2 $102,840 — Turf 61 19 14 6 $293,390

3Sep84- 7Med fm 1 70 Ⓣ:45⅘ 1:09⅘ 1:38⅘ 3+Alw 25000 9 1 11½ 11½ 13 14 Davis R G b 115 *2.90 96-04 Freon 1154 Juanca 115nk Erin's Tiger 1151 Ridden out 9
27Aug84- 3Sar fm 1⅛ Ⓣ:47⅘ 1:11⅘ 1:50 3+Clm c-45000 1 2 21¾ 26 11 21 Velasquez J 113 3.50 89-17 Clarinet King 1191 Freon 1134½ The Ripleyite 117½ Gamely 8
15Aug84- 5Sar fm 1 1/16 Ⓣ:45⅘ 1:09⅘ 1:42⅘ 3+Clm 45000 6 4 47 32 21 2¾ Samyn J L 113 4.10 85-14 Clarinet King 119¾ Freon 1135 Oratavo 1131 Gamely 10
11Aug84- 2Sar fm 1⅛ Ⓣ:48 1:12 1:49⅘ 3+Clm 40000 9 3 31 11½ 11 1hd Samyn J L 117 3.30 78-22 Freon 117hd Palace 1172½ Esprit De Romeo 112hd Drifted, drvng 11
1Aug84- 5Sar fm 1 1/16 Ⓣ:47⅘ 1:11 1:54⅘ 3+Clm 45000 2 2 21½ 2½ 75 710 Samyn J L 113 5.20 85-09 Red Brigade 1171½ Come To London 117¾ Broadly 115½ 10
19Jly84- 6Bel fst 1⅜ :49 1:39⅘ 2:18⅘ Clm 50000 2 1 1hd 32 613 619½ Samyn J L 117 3.80 67-15 Clarinet King 1174HeroicSpirit1133½EspritDeRomeo1085 Used up 7
12Jly84- 5Bel gd 1 Ⓣ:47 1:11⅗ 1:36⅘ Clm 175000 7 9 96½ 97½ 75¾ 56 Davis R G 112 13.90 77-24 Lutyens 107no Fray Star 114nk Quick Dip 1124½ Pssd tired ones 10
30Jun84- 2Bel sly 1¼ :49⅘ 1:40⅘ 2:06⅘ Clm 70000 2 1 12 21 21 24½ Venezia M 117 7.40 60-27 Nicene 1174½ Freon 113½ Clarinet King 11311 Gamely 7
20Jun84- 5Bel fm 1 1/16 Ⓣ:46 1:10⅘ 1:41⅗ Clm 70000 6 6 74 53½ 35 33½ Bailey J D 113 5.30 85-17 Lutyens 1082 Meru 1171½ Freon 1131 Mild bid 12
11Jun84- 7Bel hd 1 1/16 Ⓣ:45⅘ 1:09⅘ 1:39⅘ Clm 75000 11 6 63 31½ 44 47½ Cordero A Jr 113 3.70 89-14 Persian Poet 122no Crown 1123½ Clarinet King 1124 Weakened 11
LATEST WORKOUTS Sep 1 Bel tr.t 3f fst :39 b Jly 30 Bel tr.t 4f fst :48 h Jly 28 Bel tr.t 4f my :48⅘ h Jly 9 Bel tr.t 4f fst :48⅘ h

Meru *

Ro. g. 6, by Dewan—Tenderly, by Native Charger
$75,000 Br.—Johnson & Taylor Susan Chatfield (Ky) Tr.—Barrera Oscar S — 112
Own.—Barrera O S
Lifetime 57 14 13 12 $209,590 — 1984 19 7 3 3 $106,880 — 1983 16 2 3 3 $30,420 — Turf 5 0 2 2 $15,235

Entered 5Sep84- 7 BEL
24Aug84- 3Sar my 7f :22⅘ :45⅘ 1:23 3+Clm 70000 4 4 21½ 2hd 21½ 1no Cordero A Jr b 115 *1.40 87-09 Meru 115no Thalassocrat 1131½ Majestic Wine 1143 Driving 8
17Aug84- 7Sar fm 1 1/16 Ⓣ:47⅘ 1:12 1:42⅘ 3+Alw 36000 6 3 31½ 41½ 64½ 67½ MacBeth D b 115 5.10 75-17 Quick Dip 1171½ Lost Canyon 114nk Roman Bend 115½ Tired 9
11Aug84- 1Sar fst 7f :22⅘ :45⅘ 1:22⅘ 3+Clm 70000 2 8 3½ 11½ 14 14¾ MacBeth D b 113 *2.30 90-15 Meru 1134¾ Speed Broker 1171½ Will Of Iron 117½ Driving 9
1Aug84- 3Sar fst 7f :22⅘ :45 1:22⅘ 3+Clm 75000 10 3 77½ 87½ 54 2¾ Lovato F Jr b 112 11.10 90-13 Pinstripe 122¾ Meru 1121½ Fleet Receiver 1122¾ Gamely 11
20Jly84- 8Bel fst 1 :45⅘ 1:09⅘ 1:35⅘ 3+Alw 36000 1 2 2½ 33 37 510 MacBeth D b 115 8.00 79-18 Verbarctic119¾ValiantLark1154½Jan'sKinsmn119¾ Fin. leaving trn 5
11Jly84- 3Bel fst 1 1/16 :46⅘ 1:10⅘ 1:42⅘ Clm 70000 5 2 21 21½ 1hd 1½ MacBeth D b 113 *2.00 89-14 Meru 113½ Sharp Destiny 1131 Irish Waters 1133 Driving 7
4Jly84- 3Bel fst 7f :22⅘ :45⅘ 1:22⅘ Clm 45000 4 4 42 1½ 11 1nk Day P b 118 *1.80 88-11 Meru 118nk Irish Waters 1133½ Mighty Nasty 1152¾ Driving 9
28Jun84- 9Bel fst 7f :22⅘ :44⅘ 1:22⅘ Clm 70000 11 2 77 99½ 88¾ 810½ MacBeth D b 115 *2.50 79-19 Pinstripe 1176¾ Space Mountain1062½HarpersBazaar113nk Outrun 11
23Jun84- 7Bel fm 6f Ⓣ:22 :45⅘ 1:09⅘ 3+Alw 33000 11 6 63½ 54½ 52½ 21½ MacBeth D b 117 8.90 91-18 Sitzmark 1171½ Meru 1171½ Rollin on Over 117½ Gamely 12
20Jun84- 5Bel fm 1 1/16 Ⓣ:46 1:10⅘ 1:41⅗ Clm 72500 12 1 1½ 12 21 22 Velasquez J b 117 5.40e 87-17 Lutyens 1082 Meru 1171½ Freon 1131 Best of others 12

Swaps Qui

Ch. c. 3, by Qui Native—Swaps Mommy, by Swaps
$80,000 Br.—Beller S (Ky) Tr.—Sanborn Charles P — 110
Own.—Beller S
Lifetime 15 4 3 2 $38,535 — 1984 13 4 3 2 $37,875 — 1983 2 M 0 0 $660 — Turf 8 3 2 2 $29,505

23Aug84- 9Mth gd 1 Ⓣ:47⅘ 1:11⅘ 1:37⅘ 3+Alw 12000 6 2 11 11 11 31½ Antley C W 113 *.50 85-15 Bev's Boy 1201 Prince Quid 120½ Swaps Qui 1136 Weakened 7
10Aug84- 9Mth fm 1 Ⓣ:48⅘ 1:11⅘ 1:36⅘ 3+Alw 12500 5 2 1hd 16 16 18 Antley C W5 108 *.70 94-14 Swaps Qui 1088 Noelito 1185 Heir To The Throne 113½ Easily 8
2Aug84- 9Mth fm 1 1/16 Ⓣ:48 1:11⅘ 1:43 + 3+Alw 12500 5 1 12 11 11½ 2hd Rujano M 114 4.80 86-22 Strike the Set 113hd Swaps Qui 1142 Noelito 118no Just failed 11
14Jly84- 6Mth fm 1 1/16 Ⓣ:46⅘ 1:10⅘ 1:42⅘+ 3+Alw 12500 4 2 11 1¾ 13 3nk Antley C W5 108 *1.70 87-11 Bev's Boy 118hd Hail To Nauset 112hdSwapsQui1083 Held gamely 10
28Jun84- 7Mth fm 1 Ⓣ:46⅘ 1:09⅘ 1:35⅘ Clm 37500 5 1 13½ 15 13 12 Antley C W5 110 *1.80 97-03 Swaps Qui 1102 Paris Blade 1163 Ski Fleet 1162 Never headed 8
11Jun84- 3Mth fst 6f :22⅘ :46⅘ 1:11⅘ Clm 40000 2 4 31½ 52 55 55½ Beans B J7 108 13.60 75-22 Rowdy Yates 1141½ Strong Mountain 1142 Kill Shot 116no Tired 7
23May84- 2Mth fst 6f :22⅘ :45 1:11⅘ Clm 50000 3 4 64½ 59 412 612 Gonzalez M A 116 6.70 70-22 Frozen Mark 111no Strong Mountain 1082 Venta 1146 No threat 7
5May84- 8GP hd 1 Ⓣ:46 1:10⅘ 1:35⅘ Alw 12000 2 3 21 1hd 22 25½ Hernandez C 117 *2.00 89-07 Purple Comet 1195½ SwapsQui1172FreeFrenchman1171½ 2nd best 8
27Apr84-10GP fm *1 1/16 Ⓣ 1:44⅘ Clm 35000 6 1 13 16 15 14¾ Fires E 117 8.40 83-17 SwapsQui1174¾LondonExchange117noMoreRiches1191 Ridden out 10
6Apr84- 8GP fm *1 Ⓣ 1:37⅘ 3+Clm 45000 2 1 2½ 2½ 3½ 76¾ Gonzalez M A 117 6.50 84-14 MoreRiches113nkLondonExchange1164LeglSttus114no Weakened 10
LATEST WORKOUTS Jly 27 Mth 5f my 1:03 b Jly 21 Mth 4f fst :49 b Jly 13 Mth 3f fst :36⅘ b Jly 7 Mth 4f gd :51⅘ b (d)

Forkali

Ch. g. 6, by Forli—Mama Kali, by Tom Rolfe
$90,000 Br.—Wooden Horse Investments (Ky) Tr.—Zito Nicholas P — 113[5]
Own.—Manhasset Stable
Lifetime 65 5 8 12 $166,013 — 1984 10 0 0 2 $10,620 — 1983 18 1 4 2 $60,518 — Turf 36 4 4 6 $115,466

24Aug84- 5Sar yl 1 1/16 Ⓣ:49⅘ 1:15 1:59⅘ 3+Clm 90000 6 2 3½ 2hd 45½ 616¾ Samyn J L 118 4.90 52-40 Come To London 1136 Lord Calvert 112¾ Upmost 1166 Tired 7
19Aug84- 5Sar fm 1 Ⓣ:47 1:11⅘ 1:36⅘ 3+Clm 90000 6 2 21½ 25 35 37¾ Davis R G 118 9.10 84-20 Disco Count 1225½ Red Brigade 1162½ Forkali 118no Weakened 7
12Aug84- 2Sar fm 1 Ⓣ:46⅘ 1:10⅗ 1:36⅘ 3+Clm 100000 5 2 2hd 43½ 43 33¼ Ward W A5 117 11.70 92-07 Red Brigade 114hd Upmost 1123½ Forkali 1171½ Weakened 10
16Jly84- 8Bel fm 7f Ⓣ:23⅘ :46⅘ 1:22 3+Alw 33000 6 3 31½ 32½ 48 411 Skinner K 117 14.40 83-15 Stay The Course 1093 Azarin 115hd Eskimo 1173 Gave way 7
7Jly84- 4Bel sly 7f :22⅘ :45⅘ 1:22⅘ Clm 90000 2 2 21 36 66½ 714½ Skinner K 118 13.90 73-16 Sky Falcon 112hd Irish Waters 1124 Huckster 1221 Tired 8
23Jun84- 7Bel fm 6f Ⓣ:22 :45⅘ 1:09⅘ 3+Alw 33000 4 2 73¾ 99 74½ 63½ Skinner K 117 29.20 89-18 Sitzmark 1171½ Meru 1171½ Rollin on Over 117½ 12
15Jun84- 8Bel fm 1 Ⓣ:45⅘ 1:09⅘ 1:35⅘ 3+Alw 36000 5 4 52½ 46½ 48½ 49¾ Davis R G 117 19.40 77-18 Geraldine'sStore1172¾DominatingDooley1173½Mr.Bdger1193 Tired 6
11Jun84- 7Bel hd 1 1/16 Ⓣ:45⅘ 1:09⅘ 1:39⅘ Clm 100000 10 3 42 64½ 1014 817½ Samyn J L 122 27.40 80-14 Persian Poet 122no Crown 1123½ Clarinet King 1124 Tired 11
27May84- 7Bel fm 1 Ⓣ:46⅘ 1:12 1:37⅘ Clm 100000 6 2 1hd 31 912 914½ Cruguet J 122 9.60 64-34 Persian Poet 1121½ Freon 112¾ Alchise 1077 Tired 9
12May84- 7Bel fm 1 Ⓣ:46⅘ 1:09⅘ 1:35⅘ 3+Alw 36000 6 3 33 65½ 68 613¾ Bailey J D 119 17.60 73-15 Who's For Dinner 119¾ Native Raid 1212¾ Reinvested 1192½ Tired 7
LATEST WORKOUTS Sep 3 Bel 4f fst :50 b Aug 5 Sar tr.t 5f fst 1:03⅘ b

Alchise — Gr. c. 4, by Al Hattab—Beat the Chief, by Chieftain — $75,000 — Br.—Carrion J S (Ky) — Tr.—Kelly Edward I Jr — 107⁵
Own.—Jayeff Stable — Lifetime 34 4 6 6 $96,504 — 1984 11 0 4 1 $21,240 — 1983 18 1 1 5 $48,381 — Turf 11 3 2 1 $34,523

29Aug84- 7Mth fm 5f ①:22⅘ :45⅘ :57⅘ 3+Alw 13000 7 5 74½ 64 53½ 23 Vega A 116 3.10 93-08 Private Sun 116³ Alchise 116½ Eversohumble 111nk Gamely 8
11Jly84- 3Bel fst 1 1/16 :46⅘ 1:10⅗ 1:42⅘ Clm 70000 7 5 56 55½ 55 55½ Ward W A5 108 2.90 84-14 Meru 113½ Sharp Destiny 113¹ Irish Waters 113³ No factor 7
28Jun84- 9Bel fst 7f :22⅘ :45⅗ 1:22⅘ Clm 70000 6 10 11 10 109½ 68 59½ Ward W A5 108 4.80 80-19 Pinstripe117⁶½SpaceMountin1062½HrpersBzr113nk Without speed 11
17Jun84- 5Bel fst 6f :22⅗ :46 1:11⅗ Clm 70000 2 6 713 711 77½ 51 Ward W A5 108 10.40 84-22 Hominy Hill 106no Big McCoy 113nk Infinite Saga 119hd Steadied 7
27May84- 7Bel fm 1 ①:46⅘ 1:12 1:37⅘ Clm 75000 9 9 95 61½ 32½ 32½ Ward W A5 107 7.10 76-34 Persian Poet 1121½ Freon 112½ Alchise 1077 Hung 9
14May84- 5Bel fst 7f :22⅘ :46⅖ 1:23 Clm 75000 1 7 710 77½ 44½ 24 Ward W A5 112 14.70 83-17 Mr. Badger 1134 Alchise 1122½ Fleet Receiver 114no Best others 8
17Apr84- 5Aqu fst 170 ⊡:47 1:11⅕ 1:41⅕ Clm 70000 2 3 58½ 49 34 26 Ward W7 106 3.30 88-15 Gauley 1136 Alchise 106½ I'm So Merry 108hd Wide 7
17Mar84- 6Aqu fst 170 ⊡:48⅕ 1:13⅗ 1:43⅗ Alw 25000 2 6 64½ 64½ 56½ 59 MacBeth D 117 8.90 73-22 Luv A Libra 117½ In the Ruff 1176½ Special Care 1172 Outrun 8
11Feb84- 4Aqu fst 170 ⊡:48⅘ 1:13⅕ 1:44⅘ Alw 27000 2 2 21 2hd 31 55 MacBeth D 117 3.90 74-20 Bold Trumpeter 112nk Ask Mikey 1123 InstantAlamode117½ Tired 7
30Jan84- 6Aqu fst 1⅛ ⊡:48⅘ 1:12⅗ 1:51⅘ Alw 27000 8 5 46 56 58½ 58½ Davis R G 117 6.50 77-25 Puntivo 1229 Bold Trumpeter 112hd Wilhelm 112½ No threat 8
LATEST WORKOUTS Aug 25 Bel 3f fst :37 b Jly 7 Bel tr.t 4f sly :50 b

***El Fantasma** — B. h. 6, by Kasteel—Espiritosa, by Immortality — $75,000 — Br.—Haras Los Cerrillos (Arg) — Tr.—Alvarez L C — 112
Own.—Singing Frog Stable — Lifetime 30 7 5 4 $44,211 — 1984 10 2 0 1 $25,950 — 1983 8 3 1 1 $5,969 — Turf 20 7 2 1 $40,693

23Aug84- 8Sar sf 1⅜ ①:52⅘ 2:08⅘ 2:49⅘ 3+Seneca H 5 3 32½ 1131 1143 1172½ Graell A 108 34.20 — — Persian Tiara 112no Four Bases 1114½ Nassipour 108½ Stopped 11
17Aug84- 3Sar fm 1 3/16 ①:46⅘ 1:10⅕ 1:55 3+Clm 75000 1 3 43 63½ 84½ 77½ Rivera M A 119 4.70 84-17 GoldenChmpII1131½CristldeLune108nkComeToLondon1131½ Tired 9
5Aug84- 5Sar fm 1⅛ Ⓣ:48⅘ 1:12⅘ 1:50 3+Clm 75000 3 4 33 42 2½ 1hd Vergara O 117 17.10 90-13 El Fantasma 117hd RedBrigade1172½BlueEmmanuelle113½ Driving 8
26Jly84- 2Bel fm 1 1/16 ①:47 1:11 1:43⅕ Clm 35000 8 4 31 1½ 1½ 11½ Cordero A Jr 117 5.00 80-17 El Fantasma 1171½ HomeSecretary117hdPumasPride1171½ Driving 12
19Jly84- 6Bel fst 1⅜ :49 1:39⅘ 2:18⅘ Clm 50000 6 5 43 64½ 714 722 Vergara O 117 12.70 65-15 Clarinet King 1174 Heroic Spirit 1133½ EspritDeRomeo1085 Tired 7
30Jun84- 2Bel sly 1¼ :49⅕ 1:40⅘ 2:06⅘ Clm 70000 1 3 44 69½ 614 618½ Cordero A Jr 113 7.70 45-27 Nicene 1174½ Freon 113½ Clarinet King 11311 Tired 7
13Jun84- 5Bel fm 1 1/16 ①:46⅘ 1:10⅘ 1:42 Clm 40000 4 5 57½ 47 47 44½ Cordero A Jr 117 6.40 81-16 Fearless Leader 117½ CannonRoyal1081FullConcert1132½ Mild bid 11
9Mar84 ♦ 10Hipodromo(Arg) fst*1¼ 2:04 Premio Figurita(Alw) 419 Fajardo J 123 1.30 — — Manguero 11911 Picarel 126nk Chapulin 1208 6
24Feb84 ♦ 10Hipodromo(Arg) hy*1¼ 2:04⅗ Clasico Labrador Hcp 619 Pezoa C 117 6.00 — — Categorico 1103 El Cantabro 1186 Brady 1313 8
1Jan84 ♦ 6SanIsidro(Arg) fm*1¼ 1:58⅘ ① Clasico Botafogo(Gr.3) 32½ Pezoa C 133 3.05 — — Maspicante 132½ Sol Dorado 1321½ El Fantasma 1335 12
LATEST WORKOUTS Jly 14 Aqu 5f fst 1:01⅘ b

Also Eligible (Not in Post Position Order):

Waitlist — Ch. h. 5, by Avatar—Renounce, by Buckpasser — $90,000 — Br.—Phipps O M (Ky) — Tr.—Penna Angel — 118
Own.—Phipps O M — Lifetime 15 4 1 1 $69,140 — 1984 7 0 0 1 $9,540 — 1983 5 3 1 0 $48,800 — Turf 1 0 0 0

1Aug84- 3Sar fst 7f :22⅘ :45 1:22⅕ 3+Clm 100000 7 8 87½ 109½ 76½ 45½ Davis R G 122 8.50 86-13 Pinstripe 122½ Meru 1121½ Fleet Receiver 1122½ Wide 11
2Jly84- 1Bel gd 1 :44⅘ 1:09⅘ 1:34⅘ 3+Alw 36000 4 3 411 414 414 514½ Bailey J D 115 8.60 79-15 Slew O' Gold 1157½ Cannon Shell 1151½ NorthernIce1083½ Outrun 5
2Jly84-Awarded fourth purse money
25Jun84- 8Bel fst 7f :23⅕ :46⅕ 1:22⅕ 3+Alw 33000 3 5 54 32 47 48½ Bailey J D 119 *1.30 82-16 Verbarctic1176½McMichel117hdTlcDuster111no Lcked furthr resp. 5
1Jun84- 8Bel fst 7f :22⅘ :45⅘ 1:22⅘ 3+Alw 33000 5 5 77 75½ 46 34½ Davis R G 117 13.30 83-20 ⒹMagnetic Field II 109nk Reinvested 1174½ Waitlist 1171½ Rallied 8
10Feb84- 8Aqu fst 170 ⊡:48⅗ 1:13⅗ 1:42⅕ Alw 33000 1 6 43 57½ 514 520 Cordero A Jr 117 8.60 70-20 Puntivo 1222½ Jacque's Tip 11710 North Glade 1175½ No threat 6
29Jan84- 8Aqu fst 1 1/16 ⊡:47⅘ 1:12⅘ 1:43⅘ 3+Aqueduct H 5 9 95 96½ 78½ 710½ Lovato F Jr 112 7.30 84-15 Moro 120½ Jacksboro 1202 Ask Muhammad 1172 No factor 9
13Jan84- 8Aqu fst 1⅛ ⊡:49⅘ 1:14⅘ 1:52⅘ Alw 38000 2 6 31 41½ 54½ 58½ Lovato F Jr 117 3.50 75-20 Lark Oscillation 1151½ Deedee's Deal1153½ToErin119hd Weakened 7
12Sep83- 8Bel fst 1⅛ :47⅘ 1:11⅘ 1:49 3+Alw 30000 5 3 3nk 1hd 14 15½ Bailey J D 119 *.70 82-22 Waitlist 1195½ Count Normandy 117hd Bashert 1135½ Ridden out 5
20Aug83- 1Sar fst 1⅛ :47⅕ 1:11 1:50 3+Alw 23000 3 3 32 33 33 11½ Bailey J D 119 *1.10e 85-16 Waitlist 1191½ Kleiglight 117no Luv A Libra 1121½ Wide str., clear 7
30Jly83- 1Sar fst 1⅛ :47⅕ 1:11 1:49⅘ 3+Alw 21000 6 3 42½ 31½ 2hd 1no Bailey J D 117 2.30 87-14 Waitlist 117no Inner Circuit 1125½ Norclin 1113½ Bumped, driving 7
LATEST WORKOUTS Sep 3 Bel 4f fst :47⅘ h ●Aug 17 Sar tr.t 5f fst 1:02 h Aug 16 Sar tr.t 3f fst :39⅕ b Aug 11 Sar tr.t 4f fst :49 b

projection method, wherein a race par is established based on the recently established form and figures of those horses that ultimately do contest the issue in the race.

There are other problems as well. The speed of a racing surface can change during the course of a day's racing. Wind conditions can make it appear to change several times during the day. The speed of one part of a course—the clubhouse turn—can make routes appear uniformly faster (or slower) than sprints on a given day. Even worse, if only one or two races are run at a particular distance (two-turn routes), or over a particular surface (grass), or after heavy rains dampened the racing surface during the middle of an afternoon, the speed handicapper often finds it difficult to decide on an accurate variant for that particular group of races.

The technique we are about to discuss allows the player to circumvent daily variants completely, yet establish a figure for a race while looking at it as an entity in itself, as if it were the only race run that day. The method is ideally suited for grass racing, where wear and tear on the racing surface allows the racing secretary to card only a limited number of races per day. The projection method, as we will explain later, is a simple extension of this approach.

The race we will use for an example was the first at Belmont on September 6, 1984, carded at one mile over the Widener turf course.

To set the scene, there were four grass races at Belmont that afternoon. The eighth race was to be run at seven furlongs over the same Widener course, while the second and seventh races were scheduled to be run over the inner turf course, the former at a mile and three eighths, the latter at the more conventional mile and a sixteenth. Four grass races—often sufficient to construct a decent grass variant—yet the speed handicapper must treat each as a separate entity, with speed and pace deviations from par in any one case bearing little relationship to those for any of the others. Consequently, this race provides a perfect example of the setting in which the approach we are about to discuss proves useful and necessary.

We start with the result chart for the race, and note two things: which horses were running well at the finish, and which were in contention at the half-mile and six-furlong pace calls.

FIRST RACE **1 MILE.(Turf). (1.33) CLAIMING. Purse $27,000. 3-year-olds and upward. Weight, 3-year-olds, 118 lbs. Older, 122 lbs. Claiming price $100,000; for each $5,000 to $75,000 allowed 2 lbs. (8th Day. WEATHER CLEAR. TEMPERATURE 64 DEGREES).**

Belmont

SEPTEMBER 6, 1984

Value of race $27,000; value to winner $16,200; second $5,940; third $3,240; fourth $1,620. Mutuel pool $110,207, OTB pool $170,230.

Last Raced	Horse	Eqt.A.Wt	PP	St	¼	½	¾	Str	Fin	Jockey	Cl'g Pr	Odds $1
29Aug84 ^{5}Bel^{1}	Red Brigade	b 5 118	2	4	$5^{1\frac{1}{2}}$	$4^{1\frac{1}{2}}$	$2^{\frac{1}{2}}$	$1^{1\frac{1}{2}}$	$1^{3\frac{1}{2}}$	Guerra W A	90000	2.90
29Aug84 ^{5}Bel^{4}	Lutyens	4 114	1	7	6^{6}	$5^{1\frac{1}{2}}$	5^{2}	$4^{1\frac{1}{2}}$	$2^{1\frac{1}{2}}$	Cordero A Jr	75000	4.80
3Sep84 ^{7}Med^{1}	Freon	b 7 116	4	3	2^{hd}	$2^{\frac{1}{2}}$	$3^{1\frac{1}{2}}$	3^{hd}	3no	Davis R G	85000	1.10
29Aug84 ^{7}Mth^{2}	Alchise	4 112	7	8	$7^{\frac{1}{2}}$	7^{2}	6^{2}	5^{2}	$4^{\frac{3}{4}}$	Cruguet Jt	75000	8.60
23Aug84 ^{9}Mth^{3}	Swaps Qui	3 110	5	5	3^{1}	1^{hd}	$1^{2\frac{1}{2}}$	$2^{1\frac{1}{2}}$	$5^{3\frac{1}{4}}$	Samyn J L	80000	11.60
3Sep84 ^{7}Bel^{7}	Wicked Will	6 122	3	6	8	8	7^{4}	6^{3}	$6^{8\frac{1}{2}}$	Rivera M A	100000	19.40
24Aug84 ^{5}Sar^{6}	Forkali	6 113	6	2	$1^{\frac{1}{2}}$	$3^{2\frac{1}{2}}$	$4^{\frac{1}{2}}$	7^{6}	$7^{1\frac{3}{4}}$	Ward W A^{5}	90000	15.00
23Aug84 ^{8}Sar^{11}	El Fantasma	6 112	8	1	4^{1}	6^{4}	8	8	8	Vergara O	75000	29.70

OFF AT 1:00. Start good, Won ridden out Time, $:23\frac{2}{5}$, :47, $1:11\frac{1}{5}$, $1:36\frac{4}{5}$ Course good.

Official Program Numbers↘

$2 Mutuel Prices:

3-(B)-RED BRIGADE	7.80	3.40	2.40
2-(A)-LUTYENS		5.00	3.00
1-(D)-FREON			2.40

B. g, by Daryl's Joy—Red Gossip, by Hard Work. Trainer Barrera Luis. Bred by Mufson Rhoda (Fla).

RED BRIGADE made a run from the outside approaching the stretch and drew away under good handling after catching SWAPS QUI. LUTYENS came out for the drive and finished well to best the others. FREON weakened from his early efforts. ALCHISE, wide into the stretch, failed to seriously menace while lugging in. SWAPS QUI sprinted away to a clear lead on the turn but gave way under pressure. FORKALI tired badly. EL FANTASMA was finished early.

We then jot down speed figures for these horses based on previous races in which they had been competitive, either at the finish, or at a pace call—whichever is relevant. Here, then, is our worksheet, with speed figures based on our own variants:

Lutyens

8/29	x	— x	— 107
7/30	x	— x	— 106
7/12	x	— x	— 107

Red Brigade

8/29	100 — 107 — 110
8/19	106 — 105 — 107
8/12	112 — 112 — 104
8/5	78 — 102 — 109
8/1	106 — 111 — 113

Freon

8/27	82 — 108 — 109
8/15	96 — 108 — 109
8/11	94 — 106 — 109
8/1	110 — 113 — 103

Forkali

8/24	104 — 107 — 96
8/19	106 — 106 — 104
8/12	112 — 109 — 101

Alchise

5/27	x — x — 106

Note that we have listed final-time speed figures only for the two closers, Lutyens and Alchise. And we have used only those races in which a particular horse reached contention at some call.

Often speed handicappers must work around gaps in their information base. Since I did not have speed and pace figures for the New Jersey tracks, I had no line whatsoever on Swaps Qui, who would lead at both pace calls, nor for Freon's September 3 race at the Meadowlands nor Lutyens's August 8 race at Monmouth. Nevertheless, I still had more than enough information to rate this race satisfactorily.

At this point, the speed handicapper attempts to fit the evidence together, creating figures for the race that will be closely aligned with figures previously earned by the horses involved. Toward this end, the consistent horse becomes the handicapper's greatest ally. In this particular race, the consistent final speed figures of both Lutyens and Freon, and the recent consistency of Freon and Forkali at the six-furlong pace call, make the rest of the job all the easier.

We start by attempting to rate the half-mile pace call for the race. If we use 106, which is Red Brigade's average over his latest four figures, as our yardstick, and add six points (twice the three lengths he trailed at the half-mile call), we establish 112 as our half-mile pace figure. This implies that Freon ran a 112 pace figure for the first half, close to his rating August 1, and Forkali just a shade above 110, his near number of August 12.

At the six-furlong pace call, we use Freon's recent pair of 108's as our guideline. Since he trailed Swaps Qui by three lengths at this point, our second-pace figure for the race becomes 111, with Red Brigade between 108 and 109 and Forkali between 106 and 107, all in line with recent evidence.

Finally, for the race figure itself, noting that Red Brigade and Lutyens nearly duplicated their relative finish of August 29, we establish a final-time figure of 110 for Red Brigade, placing Lutyens between 106 and 107, and both Freon and Alchise at 105. We note that this places Freon four points behind his recent string of 109's, but attribute this to the fast four-furlong pace. Note the similarity to his August 1 race.

Here, then, in summary, are our figures for the race itself, and for each of the five horses we have discussed:

Race	***112 — 111 — 110***
Red Brigade	106 — 109 — 110
Lutyens	102 — 106 — 107
Freon	112 — 108 — 105
Alchise	92 — 104 — 105
Forkali	110 — 107 — 93

Once again we point out that all of our "calculations" were quite subjective, with race figures selected to please our sense of "fit," chosen so that they might best explain the performances of all horses that entered contention at some point in the race.

We are finished— at least with this race. However, let us suppose for a moment that there had been three races at this distance over the Widener course that day. What then? We could use the above technique for each of the three races, establishing figures for each as if the other two had not been run. Or we could use the projection method in its full power.

Our work thus far has established the figures 112–111–110 for this race, without ever referring to the actual running times of the race. These same figures, however, also could be used to project par times for the race—indeed, they represent par figures for this field. Our par-times table for Belmont's Widener course is based upon a 100-rating ($10,000 claiming) line that reads:

100 = 46.9 111.2 136.1 142.4

We can now convert our figures into par times for the race, as follows:

46.3 110.1 134.1

Remember that pace figures are measured in tenths of seconds and that there is a special "two for one" adjustment necessary at the four-furlong pace call in routes. (See *Thoroughbred Handicapping—State of the Art* for more details.)

We could do the same for the other two races as well, establishing projected pars in the same manner. Then compare actual running times for the three races with their respective pars, establishing a "daily variant" for the course. Next, adjust our 100-figure base line accordingly, and finally assign figures to the three races. In essence, once par times have been established, we proceed as if we were using the "class pars" methodology described in either *Winning at the Races* or *Thoroughbred Handicapping—State of the Art.*

We conclude with the warning that this methodology, when applied to races in isolation, assumes the "average" and may not pick up on exceptionally fast or slow pace, or final times. On the grass, especially, races must frequently be rated solely on their own merits. It is far better, though, when the results of several races can be analyzed as a group, based on projected pars. During periods of fairly stable weather and course conditions, grass races from consecutive days can be combined in this manner. And then, exceptionally fast or slow races will stand out and can be rated accordingly.

Chapter 40

How to Use Figures for Interior Fractions in Routes

I HAVE OFTEN BEEN ASKED why I advocate a pair of pace figures for route races (for the half-mile and six-furlong points of call), but only one for sprints (at the half). Why not a second sprint pace figure to quantify the situation after the first quarter mile has been run? My answer has been that figures for such a short distance (two furlongs) tend to be relatively meaningless and do a poor job of separating classes. Cheap horses can run a quarter of a mile almost as fast as stakes horses cover the same distance.

Having two pace figures available for routes, however, affords the speed handicapper at least two distinct advantages. First, he can better interpret the "middle moves" that take place between the half-mile call and the top of the stretch, moves that are far more prevalent in routes than in sprints. Second, he can get a better line on how well a horse turning back in distance from a route to a sprint might fare.

In this chapter we will look at examples of each of the above situations. We start with the seventh race at Belmont on Saturday, June 15, 1985, a weakly conditioned classified allowance contest on the grass that was restricted to horses that hadn't won a race at a mile or longer with a winner's share of $15,000 or more during either 1984 or 1985—almost eighteen full months. Interestingly, the conditions excluded state-bred races from eligibility considerations, thereby attracting four New York-bred runners who appeared on paper to be solid contenders but really didn't rate that highly. Let's take a look at the field:

7 BELMONT

1 1/16 MILES. (Turf). (1.39⅕) ALLOWANCE. Purse $40,000. 3-year-olds and upward which have not won a rce of $15,000 at a mile or over in 1984–85. Weight, 3-year-olds, 114 lbs. Older, 122 lbs. Non-winners of two races of $12,500 at a mile or over since October 1 allowed 3 lbs. Of such a race since January 1, 5 lbs. Maiden, claiming, starter and state bred races not considered.)

Coupled—Dominating Dooley and Romantic Tradition.

Mayanesian
Ch. h. 6, by Bold Hour—Cozumel, by T V Lark
Br.—Madden Preston (Ky)
Own.—Gordonsdale Farm
Tr.—Zito Nicholas P
117
Lifetime 60 8 9 5 $227,977
1985 6 0 0 0 $2,360
1984 12 2 3 0 $68,195
Turf 8 2 3 1 $82,980

6Jun85- 8Bel gd 6f :22⅕ :44⅘ 1:10⅘ 3+Handicap 1 4 33 35 65½ 63½ Ward W A b 113 10.20 87-15 Basket Weave 114hd River Demon 1101½ Alev 115½ No excuse 7
10May85- 8Bel fst 6f :22⅕ :45⅗ 1:11 3+Alw 36000 5 6 711 716 716 716½ Falcone J10 b 114 8.10 71-20 Cozzene1241½BasketWeve124½MomentoII1192½ Rider lost control 7
25Apr85- 6GS fst 5f :22 :44⅕ :56⅕ 3+Bld Resong H 3 4 31 54¾ 48½ 59½ Ward W A b 115 8.40 92-13 Rollin on Over 1122½ Roast 1104 Burts Star 1161½ Tired 6
25Apr85-Run in divisions
27Mar85- 9Hia fst 6f :21⅗ :44⅘ 1:09 Kendall 7 1 1½ 11½ 45½ 610¾ Bailey J D b 119 20.90 85-17 FortunteProspect117nkMysticVntur1176RoxburyPrk1171 Faltered 7
19Mar85- 9Hia fst 6f :21⅘ :44⅘ 1:09 Alw 17000 5 2 12 1½ 24 57 Bailey J D b 119 6.20 89-13 TheWddingGust1194NorthrnOcn1221½[D]FrindlyBob1191 Bothered 11
19Mar85-Placed fourth through disqualification
6Mar85- 8GP fst 6f :21⅗ :44⅘ 1:09 Alw 23200 4 3 13 12½ 22 712½ Bailey J D b 115 20.00 81-20 Hrry'NBill1158½Rupert'sWing122½[D]FortunteProspct1151 Faltered 8
6Mar85-Placed sixth through disqualification
2Dec84- 8Key fst 6f :22⅗ -:46 1:10⅕ 3+[R]Al Hattab 1 4 32½ 67 712 77¼ Black A S b 120 6.30 82-23 Ringside 1161½ Obgyn 1162 Moving Wind 112no Tired 7
25Nov84- 8Aqu fst 6f :22 :45⅗ 1:10⅘ 3+Sport Pg H 5 3 64 1213 1314 1311¾ Ward W A b 114 32.30 75-25 Tarantara 117nk MuskokaWyck114nkNewConnection1131½ Outrun 13
25Nov84-Grade III
14Nov84- 7Aqu fst 6f :23 :47⅕ 1:11⅖ 3+Alw 36000 6 2 1hd 41 612 616½ Ward W A5 b 117 4.90 68-33 Tarantara 122no Birdie's Legend1172½CrudeWays1133½ Lugged in 7
LATEST WORKOUTS Jun 3 Bel 4f fst :48⅕ h ●May 30 Bel 3f fst :34⅕ h May 21 Bel 5f fst 1:01⅕ b May 6 Bel 5f fst 1:02⅖ b

Another Summer
Ch. c. 3, by Prince Dantam—Summer Sister, by Cambridge
Br.—Tringale C P (NY)
Own.—Tringale C R
Tr.—Cincotta Vincent J
109
Lifetime 10 3 3 1 $76,244
1985 10 3 3 1 $76,244
1984 0 M 0 0

30May85- 3Bel fst 6f :22⅗ :45⅘ 1:11⅖ 3+[S]Alw 29000 2 6 64¾ 47½ 34 1nk Santagata N 111 2.00 85-19 AnthrSmmr111nkAdrndckPrd1211½SlntSlndr105½ Bumped, driving 8
19May85- 4Bel fst 1⅛ :48 1:13 1:44⅗ 3+[S]Alw 30500 4 1 2hd 31½ 55½ 710½ Migliore R 112 *1.40 68-20 Black Ore 1211½ Arms Race 116nk AccordingToLuke1133 Used up 11
27Apr85- 8Aqu fst 1 :47⅗ 1:12⅗ 1:38⅕ [S]Big Apple H 7 1 21 2½ 1½ 2hd Migliore R 111 6.20 75-26 GllopRhythm111hdAnothrSummr1111¾SlntSlndr1152¾ Just missed 9
13Apr85- 9Aqu fst 1 :47 1:12 1:37⅗ 3+[S]Alw 27000 11 1 2½ 11 13 15¾ Migliore R 112 4.60 78-21 AnotherSummer1125¾AccordingToLuke109nkTkeATlc121¼ Driving 11
1Apr85- 7Aqu fst 6f :22⅕ :45⅗ 1:10 3+[S]Alw 25500 2 8 95½ 96 47 26½ Migliore R 109 12.50 85-17 GllopRhythm1126½AnthrSmmr109hdStrOfBrdx1122½ Gained place 12
14Mar85- 1Aqu fst 6f :23⅕ :47 1:12⅗ [S]Alw 25500 5 6 31 31 23 36½ McCarron G 119 8.10 72-35 ClbFghtr1172½HstoryRsponds1173¾AnothrSmmr119nk Wide, hung 7
28Feb85- 4Aqu fst 6f ⊡:23⅕ :47⅗ 1:14 [S]Md Sp Wt 5 10 84 56½ 34 1¾ McCarron G 122 *1.90 74-22 AnotherSummer122¾RootCanal1222SiempreFidelius122nk Handily 12
4Feb85- 4Aqu fst 6f ⊡:23 :47⅕ 1:11⅘ Md Sp Wt 10 5 73½ 45 48½ 512½ McCarron G 122 6.10 72-21 Aetolian 1226 It's Affirmed 1224½ Alpine Raja 122½ Weakened 10
25Jan85- 4Aqu fst 6f ⊡:22⅗ :46⅗ 1:12⅘ Md Sp Wt 10 4 54½ 42½ 1½ 2½ McCarron G 122 27.20 79-23 ReviveTheEchoes122½AnothrSummr1223½It'sAllM122½ Just failed 12
10Jan85- 9Aqu fst 6f ⊡:22⅘ :46⅗ 1:12⅘ [S]Md Sp Wt 7 10 87¾ 811 69½ 611¼ McCarron G 122 16.90 69-22 Dewan Light 122½ Glenn Brooke 1172½ Rare Diligence 1171¾ Wide 12
LATEST WORKOUTS Jun 13 Bel [T] 3f fm :37 h Jun 11 Bel 5f fst 1:00⅕ h Jun 8 Bel tr.t 5f fst 1:02 b May 28 Bel tr.t 4f fst :49⅕ b

*Without Reserve
B. c. 4, by Auction Ring—Fear Naught, by Connaught
Br.—Mount Coote Stud (Ire)
Own.—Johnstone B
Tr.—Johnston Bruce
117
Lifetime 15 2 3 2 $25,841
1985 4 0 0 0 $320
1984 5 0 2 0 $6,823
Turf 15 2 3 2 $25,841

30May85- 7Bel gd 1⅛ Ⓣ:46⅗ 1:10⅗ 1:42⅗ 3+Alw 26000 10 8 58 66½ 815 819 Cruguet J b 121 38.60 64-14 ExclusivePartner1124BarbadinReef1134½Wollston1131½ Slow start 10
20May85- 4Bel fm 1¼ [T]:47⅗ 1:36⅕ 2:01⅕ 3+Alw 26000 3 5 53 33 711 818½ Vasquez J b 121 29.00 70-15 Welcome Suitor 1212 Cold Feet II 1214½ Pigwidgeon 1211¾ Tired 11
19Apr85- 8Hia gd *1⅛ Ⓣ 1:50⅗ 3+Alw 15000 3 4 43½ 34½ 3nk 89½ Tejeira J b 117 39.10 70-29 Moulabad 117no Dissonance 1173½ Pup's Pet 1234 Tired 9
25Jan85- 9GP fm *1 Ⓣ 1:38⅕ Alw 17000 5 1 1½ 1015 1027 1026½ MacBeth D b 117 11.40 62-22 Cool 1171½ Rexson's Hope 1172 Nepal 1172 Gave way 10
8Aug84♦5PhoenixPk(Ire) gd 7f 1:17⅗ ⓉHardwicke Cup Plate 58¾ Craine S b 128 6.00 – – Committed 1321½ Atlantic Salmon 1235 Masubeni1251½ Bid, tired 7
30Jun84♦4Curragh(Ire) fm 1 1:36 ⓉHello Gorgeous Stakes 21 Crains S b 127 10.00 – – Monongelia1291 WithoutReserve1271½ Paymaster125nk Bid, hung 11
20Jun84♦1Ascot(Eng) gd 7f 1:28 ⓉJersey Stakes(Gr.3) 911 Cauthen S b 132 16.00 – – Miss Silca Key 119hd Mystery Ship1193 Roundhill1281½ Bid, tired 16
2Jun84♦4PhoenixPk(Ire) gd 1 1:40⅘ ⓉWhat A Guest Stakes 63½ Craine S b 123 7.00 – – Argosy 118½ Committed 1341 Hollywood Party1321 Bid, impeded 9
28Apr84♦5Curragh(Ire) gd 7f 1:25 ⓉTetrarch Stakes(Gr.3) 23 Craine S b 126 2.00 – – Secreto 1193 Without Reserve 1262 Deasy's Delight 1191 Rallied 7
29Oct83♦5Leopardst'n(Ire) gd 7f 1:32⅕ ⓉLarkspur Stakes(Gr.3) 32½ Kinane M J b 128 3.00 – – WestrnSymphnoy1261 [D]SignOfLif1191½ WithoutRsrv128¾ Rallied 9
29Oct83-Placed second through disqualification
LATEST WORKOUTS Jun 8 Bel 4f fst :48⅗ b May 28 Bel 4f fst :50⅗ b May 16 Bel [T] 6f fm 1:16⅕ b (d) May 2 Hia 5f fst 1:05 b

Stormy Puddles
Dk. b. or br. h. 5, by King Pellinore—Big Puddles, by Delta Judge
Br.—Beggiano & Schwartz (NY)
Own.—Nagle K
Tr.—Ferriola Peter
117
Lifetime 26 3 6 1 $99,002
1985 3 0 2 0 $18,942
1984 13 2 2 0 $45,240
Turf 7 1 1 1 $34,282

5Jun85- 2Bel sly 1⅜ :48 1:37⅗ 2:17⅘ Clm c-70000 1 4 41½ 34 26 28½ Cruguet J 113 4.60 82-17 Deedee'sDeal1138½StormyPuddles1132½LstTurn1176½ Second best 6
15May85- 8Bel fm 1⅛ Ⓣ:46 1:10 1:41⅘ 3+[S]Kingston 5 5 64½ 44 42 42 Santagata N 119 *4.20 85-16 High Ice 119nk[DH]JudgeCosta119[DH]FearlessLeader1191½ Steadied 9
2May85- 7Aqu fm 1⅛ Ⓣ:47⅘ 1:12⅗ 1:44⅖ 3+Alw 40000 6 8 84¾ 64½ 55 21½ Santagata N 119 18.40 82-17 FrayStar1191½StormyPuddles1191½JudgeCost1191¼ Sluggish early 10
11Nov84- 8Aqu fst 1⅛ :47⅘ 1:12⅗ 1:52⅗ 3+[S]Macarthur H 8 5 89¾ 88½ 819 821 Santagata N 113 19.40 52-25 Org 117¾ Talc Duster 1161½ Judge Costa 1101½ Outrun 8
27Oct84- 7Aqu my 1⅛ :47⅗ 1:10⅘ 1:48⅘ 3+Alw 25000 4 5 68 817 825 822¾ Santagata N 117 15.50 68-16 Regal Humor 1142 Desert Chief 1161½ Broadway Harry1173 Tired 8
8Oct84- 8FL fst 1⅛ :47⅕ 1:13 1:53⅗ 3+Wadsworth H 8 7 68 55½ 75½ 811 Reynolds R L 117 6.00 77-23 Org 121½ Broadway Buck 1122½ Wimborne's Gater 1122½ Tired 11
27Aug84- 6Sar fm 1⅛ Ⓣ:47 1:11⅕ 1:43⅗ 3+Alw 25000 2 6 64¾ 53½ 62½ 64 Santagata N 119 14.70 74-17 Roman Bend 117½ Haste to Finish117¾NoMan'sLand117no Outrun 7
20Aug84- 9Sar fm 1⅛ [T]:47⅗ 1:12 1:50⅘ 3+[S]Alw 27500 9 6 66½ 54½ 11½ 1nk Santagata N 117 25.10 86-19 Stormy Puddles 117nk Equity Kicker 112½TunedOut1122¾ Driving 12
12Jly84- 7Bel fst 1⅛ :46⅗ 1:10⅘ 1:42⅗ 3+[S]Alw 27500 9 7 99 1017 1019 919¾ Murphy D J 117 22.00 69-17 SinghAmerica1124½Carey'sBoy1112½TalentedJacques1111½ Outrun 10
20May84- 7Bel fm 2 Ⓣ:51 2:55⅗ 3:20⅘ 3+Handicap 5 3 68½ 716 620 523¾ Murphy D J 108 46.60 74-13 Anne's Lover 1142¾ Erin Bright 1171¾ Nassipour 1202¾ Tired 10
LATEST WORKOUTS May 29 Sar tr.t 4f fst :50⅗ b ●May 11 Sar tr.t 4f fst :49⅘ b ●Apr 29 Sar tr.t 5f fst 1:01⅘ h Apr 25 Sar tr.t 6f fst 1:18⅖ b

Dominating Dooley
Ch. h. 5, by Teddy's Courage—Frajan, by Francis S
Br.—Harbor View Farm (Fla)
Own.—Harbor View Farm
Tr.—Martin Frank
117
Lifetime 44 5 6 8 $153,007
1985 3 0 0 1 $3,600
1984 12 2 1 2 $40,381
Turf 22 3 3 7 $89,427

2Jun85- 4Bel gd 1 Ⓣ:46⅗ 1:10⅗ 1:36⅘ Clm 90000 9 2 21½ 1hd 1½ 32¾ Guerra W A 118 22.90 78-21 Fray Star1122PiedA'Tierre116¾DominatingDooley1182½ Weakened 10
19May85- 2Bel fm 1 Ⓣ:47⅕ 1:10⅗ 1:35⅕ Clm 100000 8 7 63 1012 1015 1015¼ Venezia M 122 14.30 74-12 Spring Fever1223½TrinbagoPride1072GoldenChampII1221½ Outrun 11
11May85- 6Bel fm 6f Ⓣ:22 :45⅗ 1:09⅗ 3+Alw 36000 1 6 53½ 63½ 98½ 1014½ Migliore R 119 29.90 79-17 Sitzmark 1195½ Alev 121hd Alchise 1193¾ Steadied near str 11
12Jly84- 5Bel gd 1 Ⓣ:47 1:11⅗ 1:36⅗ Clm 175000 9 8 52½ 73¾ 98¾ 912 Venezia M 112 7.70 71-24 Lutyens 107no Fray Star 114nk Quick Dip 1124½ Tired 10
21Jun84- 7Bel fm 1⅛ [T]:47 1:09⅘ 1:41 Clm 185000 7 2 2½ 2hd 31½ 45 Venezia M 116 5.30 91-16 Fray Star 114nk Remanded II 1122¾ Prosper 1142 Weakened 7
15Jun84- 8Bel fm 1 Ⓣ:45⅗ 1:09⅗ 1:35⅘ 3+Alw 36000 4 3 31 2hd 21 22¾ Venezia M 117 5.10 83-18 Gerldine'sStor1172¾DomintingDooly1173½Mr.Bdgr1193 Held place 6
2Jun84- 1Bel sly 6f :22⅕ :45⅖ 1:10⅗ 3+Alw 33000 1 5 44½ 65½ 68½ 610½ Maple E 117 9.90 80-19 Will Of Iron 1173¾ Vincennes Road 117hd RollinonOver117¾ Tired 7
14May84- 8Bel gd 1⅛ [T]:48⅘ 1:12⅗ 1:43⅗ 3+Alw 36000 6 5 32 31½ 42½ 33¾ Cruguet J 119 7.50 80-22 Intensify 1191½ Erin's Tiger 1212½ DominatingDooley119hd Evenly 6
7May84- 8Aqu gd 1⅛ Ⓣ:48 1:12⅗ 1:43⅗ 3+Ft. Marcy H 2 7 64 44½ 45½ 56¾ Cruguet J 113 5.30e 80-22 Hero's Honor 1152 Super Sunrise 1263¾ Reinvested 1131 Tired 9
7May84-Grade III
28Apr84- 7Aqu fm 1 Ⓣ:47⅘ 1:13⅘ 1:39⅗ 3+Alw 36000 9 3 43½ 42 31½ 35½ Cruguet J 119 4.60 72-21 ToughMickey1213Erin'sTiger1212½DomintingDooley119¾ Steadied 9
LATEST WORKOUTS Jun 10 Bel tr.t 4f fst :47 h ●May 27 Bel tr.t 5f fst :59⅘ h May 8 Bel tr.t 4f fst :48⅘ b Apr 28 Hia 6f fst 1:15 b

Fortnightly
B. h. 5, by Dance Spell—Out Cold, by Etonian
Br.—Bwamazon Farm (Ky)
Own.—Sabarese T M
Tr.—Parisella John
117
Lifetime 25 4 9 2 $354,058
1985 2 0 0 0
1984 6 0 3 0 $64,734
Turf 23 4 9 2 $354,058

25May85- 6Bel fm 1 Ⓣ:46 1:10⅗ 1:37 3+Alw 40000 1 5 43½ 32 41½ 55½ Migliore R b 119 2.50 74-24 Red Brigade 1191¾ High Ice 1192¾ Sondrio 119¾ Weakened 8
27Apr85- 9Pim fm 1⅛ Ⓣ:45⅘ 1:09⅘ 1:40⅗ 3+Riggs H 3 8 78¾ 56½ 813 914¼ Venezia M b 112 *1.70 94 – Onyxly 1141¾ [D]Act Away 113hd Count My Love 1133½ No factor 9
27Apr85-Grade III
22Sep84- 8Bel fm 1½ Ⓣ:48⅘ 2:01⅗ 2:25⅕ 3+Trf Classic 2 6 610 64½ 68 68½ Cordero A Jr b 126 19.80 89-10 John Henry 126nk Win1264Majesty'sPrince126hd Lacked response 6
22Sep84-Grade I
8Sep84- 8Bel fm 1⅜ [T]:47⅗ 1:36 2:14⅗ 3+Man O' War 5 5 55 11½ 3nk 42 Cruguet J b 126 14.80[D] 82-16 Majesty's Prince 126¾ Win 1261 Cozzene 126nk Came over 9
8Sep84-Grade I; Disqualified and placed ninth
29Aug84- 8Bel fm 1¼ [T]:50 1:37 2:00⅗ 3+Manhattan H 9 5 43 3½ 21½ 22¼ Cruguet J b 112 3.70 89-14 Win 1142¼ Fortnightly 1122 Norwick 110½ 2nd best 12
29Aug84-Grade I
28Jly84- 8Bel sf 1½ Ⓣ:49⅕ 2:05⅗ 2:31 3+Swd Dncer H 1 6 43½ 52½ 32 68½ Cordero A Jr b 114 5.20 63-31 Majesty's Prince 1243½ Nassipour 1091½ Four Bases 112nk Tired 11
28Jly84-Grade I
4Jly84- 9AP fm 1⅛ Ⓣ:45⅗ 1:09⅘ 1:41⅖ 3+Strs Strp H 4 13 1412 1311 64 21¼ Venezia M b 115 3.20 101-09 Tough Mickey 1191¼ Fortnightly 1151½ Jack Slade 1131½ Wide 15
4Jly84-Grade II
9Jun84- 7Mth fm 1 Ⓣ:48 1:11⅗ 1:36⅘ 3+Red Bank H 3 7 67½ 21 1½ 21¼ Perret C b 117 7.30 92-09 Tough Mickey 1181¼ Fortnightly 117no RomanBend1082 Game try 9
9Jun84-Run in divisions
15Oct83- 7Kee fst 1⅛ :47⅗ 1:11⅗ 1:48⅘ 3+Fayette H 3 5 58½ 58¾ 512 — Sellers M S b 115 13.70 – – [DH]Frost King 1232 [DH]Cad 1162 Bold Style 1202 Eased 5
LATEST WORKOUTS Jun 11 Bel tr.t 4f fst :49⅗ b Jun 7 Bel 6f fst 1:14⅕ h Jun 2 Bel tr.t 4f fst :49 b ●May 23 Bel [T] 4f gd :48⅗ h (d)

Deedee's Deal — Dk. b. or br. g. 8, by Hickory—Me Carla, by Gallant Romeo
Br.—Amlung R (Fla)
Tr.—Barrera Oscar S
Own.—Barrera O S
112⁵ — Lifetime 111 21 19 21 $440,122 — 1985 21 2 2 4 $53,520 — 1984 8 0 3 1 $26,100 — Turf 30 4 4 5 $89,860

12Jun85- 8Bel gd 1⅛ Ⓣ:46 1:11⅕ 1:43⅘ 3+Alw 40000 5 6 711 612 412 316½ Privitera R5 b 112 13.50 61-33 Roving Minstrel 1177½ Masterful 1179 Deedee's Deal1123¾ Rallied 8
5Jun85- 2Bel sly 1⅜ :48 1:37⅗ 2:17⅘ Clm 70000 4 2 1hd 11 16 18½ Cordero A Jr b 113 2.10 91-17 Deedee'sDeal1138½StormyPuddles1132¾LastTurn1176½ Ridden out 6
29May85- 4Bel fst 1¼ :48⅕ 1:37 2:03⅕ Clm 35000 2 2 31 12½ 14 12¾ Cordero A Jr b 117 2.20 82-15 Deed'sDl1172¾FlingTooMuch11711½StillChmpion1172½ Ridden out 8
25May85- 1Bel fst 1 :47 1:11⅘ 1:36⅗ Clm 30000 2 4 62½ 42½ 54 46 MacBeth D b 113 5.40 76-11 ⒹSpeier'sLuck113nkChrmdRook1173½RstlssJohn1172½ Weakened 7
20May85- 1Bel fst 1½ :48⅖ 2:04⅘ 2:31⅕ Clm 25000 9 2 1hd 1hd 21½ 27 MacBeth D b 117 *2.30 57-22 FeelingTooMuch1157Deede'sDl1172Wimborn'sGtr1157 Weakened 9
15May85- 3Bel fst 1⅛ :47⅕ 1:11⅕ 1:49⅗ Clm 32500 5 7 72¾ 33 25 35 MacBeth D b 115 4.20 74-17 ColonelLaw1171¾CharmedRook1173½Deedee'sDeal1153 Weakened 10
12May85- 9Bel fst 7f :22⅘ :46 1:24⅕ Clm 35000 5 5 41½ 53 43½ 21¾ MacBeth D b 117 4.40 79-19 See for Free 1171¾ Deedee'sDeal117hdHarpersBazaar117hd Rallied 9
2May85- 4Aqu fst 1 :46⅘ 1:11⅗ 1:37⅕ Clm 35000 4 7 85 76 55½ 53 Vasquez J b 117 *2.40e 77-26 FingersIntheTill115hdEspritDeRomeo1131½SeeforFr1171½ Late bid 10
29Apr85- 2Aqu fm 1⅛ Ⓣ:48 1:12⅖ 1:50⅖ Clm 45000 5 5 31½ 43½ 51½ 83½ Vasquez J b 113 3.20 88-15 HallOfHonor113noRedBrigde117nkBoldAmteur113nk Lckd rm. str. 11
24Apr85- 4Aqu fm 1⅛ Ⓣ:48⅕ 1:13⅘ 1:52 Clm 70000 6 2 21 21 2hd 41¾ Cordero A Jr b 113 2.50 82-12 Martie'sLight113noFrayStar1171¾SirIvor'sVerdict117hd Weakened 7

High Ice — B. c. 4, by Icecapade—Lambay, by Dewan
Br.—Kinderhill Fm Brd & Rcg Prog 80 Ser (NY)
Tr.—Carroll Del W II
Own.—Farish W S III
117 — Lifetime 24 4 3 3 $121,700 — 1985 6 1 2 0 $59,640 — 1984 18 3 1 3 $62,060 — Turf 4 1 2 0 $58,020

8Jun85- 6GS fm 1⅛ Ⓣ:46⅖ 1:10⅖ 1:42⅖ 3+Alw 25000 5 6 511 57 4nk 21 MacBeth D b 119 *1.80 — — Flight of Time 1171 High Ice 119½ Finian's Rainbow115½ Bumped 7
25May85- 6Bel fm 1 Ⓣ:46 1:10⅖ 1:37 3+Alw 40000 3 7 67½ 55 31 21¾ Davis R G b 119 5.50 78-24 Red Brigade 1191¾ High Ice 1192¾ Sondrio 119¾ Wide str. 8
15May85- 8Bel fm 1⅛ Ⓣ:46 1:10 1:41⅘ 3+ⓈKingston 9 6 54 54½ 31¾ 1nk Davis R G b 119 21.70 87-16 High Ice 119nk ⒹⒽJudge Costa119ⒹⒽFearlessLeader1191¾ Driving 9
11May85- 5Bel fst 6f :22⅕ :45⅕ 1:09⅘ 3+Alw 27000 2 4 46½ 510 58½ 47½ Davis R G b 121 15.90 86-12 Ziggy's Boy 1101¾ Main Top 1215EliteSyncopation111½ No factor 6
27Apr85- 7Aqu fst 1⅛ :46⅗ 1:11⅖ 1:50⅗ 3+Alw 40000 4 9 914 912 917 916½ Ward W A b 119 51.40 65-26 Waitlist 1212¾ Blue Quadrant 119no Jacque's Tip 119no Trailed 9
10Apr85- 7Aqu fst 1 :46 1:11 1:36⅗ 3+Alw 40000 7 9 85 84¾ 67½ 610½ Ward W A b 119 15.50e 73-29 Spender 119hd Vigumand 1144 Carjack 114½ Outrun 9
16Oct84- 6Kee fst 6f :22⅘ :45 1:10⅕ 3+Alw 17995 10 9 95¾ 97½ 79 65½ Day P b 122 2.70 86-17 HopefulWord1161GoldenTower116noHawkin'sTrick1162 No factor 11
6Oct84- 7Bel fst 6f :22⅗ :45⅘ 1:10⅗ 3+Alw 33000 8 6 63½ 68½ 89½ 88½ MacBeth D b 112 7.90 80-17 UpPopsAwinner112nkI'mARounder112noNorthrnTrdr116nk Outrun 8
15Sep84- 9Bel sly 1 :45⅖ 1:11 1:36⅘ 3+ⓈAlw 27500 10 2 2hd 1½ 12 12¾ Day P b 113 3.50 81-18 High Ice 1132¾ EquityKicker1081TalentedJacques1135 Drew clear 11
31Aug84- 5Bel fst 6f :22⅗ :45⅖ 1:09⅗ 3+ⓈAlw 26000 3 4 46 25 24½ 22½ Ward W A5 b 107 *2.10 91-13 Venelli 1122½ High Ice 1071¾ Black Ore 1121¾ Rallied 10
LATEST WORKOUTS ●Jun 1 Bel 5f gd 1:00 h May 22 Bel 5f gd 1:01 b May 7 Bel 4f fst :46⅘ h ●May 3 Bel 5f sly 1:00 h

Melthemi — Ch. h. 5, by RestlessWind—Surfboard Betty, by Bold Commander
Br.—Hutchison Emily N K (Md)
Tr.—Elder Andrew
Own.—Hutchison Emily
117 — Lifetime 27 5 1 2 $49,172 — 1985 9 2 0 0 $18,390 — 1984 4 0 0 0 — Turf 20 4 1 2 $39,782

1Jun85- 8Pim fst 5f :22⅕ :45⅖ :57⅖ 3+Mister Diz H 3 4 65 67½ 55 55½ Wright D R 108 22.10 93-17 Prince Valid 1172½ Whoop Up 116no Ryburn 1161½ Outrun 7
9May85- 8Bel fm 1⅛ Ⓣ:45⅕ 1:10⅗ 1:43 3+Alw 40000 10 2 21 42 913 915½ Maple E 119 27.30 65-13 Mr Chromacopy 1191½ Masterful 119¾ Ends Well 1214½ Tired 10
1May85- 8Pim fm 1⅛ Ⓣ:46⅕ 1:10⅗ 1:43 Alw 15000 3 1 11½ 12½ 14 12¾ Nicol P A Jr 114 8.80 96-05 Melthemi 1142¾ Rambler Red 1151¾ Stabalizer 117½ Driving 8
15Apr85- 5Pim fst 6f :23⅖ :46⅕ 1:10⅘ Alw 13500 3 2 2½ 2hd 21 21 Hunter M T b 114 10.70 91-16 ⒹCold Creation 1141 Melthemi 1146¾ Alias 1192 Gamely 5
15Apr85-Placed first through disqualification
6Apr85- 5Pim fst 6f :23 :46⅕ 1:11⅘ Alw 13500 5 2 3nk 32 32½ 44½ Bracciale V Jr b 115 4.30 82-15 Mobjack Bay 1192½ Sir Damascus 1171½ ColdDawn119¾ Gave way 6
16Mar85- 7Pim fst 6f :23⅕ :45⅘ 1:10 Alw 13500 8 3 34 37½ 49½ 717 Bracciale V Jr 115 7.80 79-15 Roast 11411 Mobjack Bay 119nk Northern Retreat 1141½ Tired 9
11Mar85- 8Aqu fst 6f ⊡:21⅗ :44 1:09⅕ Alw 36000 4 4 35 36 47 611¾ Wynter N A10 105 39.60 86-18 Mt. Livermore 1222½ Agile Shoebill 1107 Spender 117nk Faded 7
22Feb85- 8Key fst 6f :22 :45 1:09⅘ Alw 16000 2 6 4¾ 1hd 32 54½ Wynter N A10 102 32.30 88-21 King's Bluff 112nk Good Ole Master 112hd Kastanie 1122 Tired 7
15Feb85- 7Aqu fst 6f ⊡:22⅗ :46 1:11⅕ Alw 25000 4 6 55½ 67½ 713 714¾ Skinner K 117 44.10 73-26 Mt. Livermore 1191½ Whoop Up 1101½ Cooper'sHawk1191 Outrun 7
15Jun84 ♦4York(Eng) gd 7f 1:24⅖ Ⓣ SanJuan deCapistranoHcp 66¾ Hodgson K 124 5.00 — — SwingingRebel 114no El Mansour 1244 Hooligan 1221½ Prom 5f 8

Fearless Leader — B. g. 7, by Mr Leader—Salvaje II, by Hot Dust
Br.—Whitney T P (NY)
Tr.—Preger Mitchell C
Own.—Wolosoff J K
117 — Lifetime 56 9 12 9 $314,997 — 1985 1 0 1 0 $12,529 — 1984 16 2 3 4 $68,008 — Turf 21 3 6 4 $120,603

15May85- 8Bel fm 1⅛ Ⓣ:46 1:10 1:41⅘ 3+ⓈKingston 4 1 2½ 2½ 2hd 2nk Cordero A Jr b 1194 6.40 87-16 High Ice 119nk ⒹⒽJudge Costa119ⒹⒽFearlessLeader1191¾ Gamely 9
15May85-Dead heat
17Nov84- 1Aqu gd 1⅛ Ⓣ:48⅘ 1:14 1:53⅘ 3+Clm 75000 1 2 21 2hd 51¾ 63¾ MacBeth D b 117 5.20 72-25 Lutyens 117½ Steepbank 1151½ Remanded II 1131½ Gave way 9
9Nov84- 8Aqu gd 1 Ⓣ:48⅘ 1:14 1:39⅘ 3+Alw 36000 5 3 33 32 34½ 34½ Davis R G b 115 8.40 73-26 Aristocratical 1101½ Alev 1173 Fearless Leader 115½ Fair effort 8
7Oct84- 2Bel fm 1 Ⓣ:46 1:09⅘ 1:35⅖ 3+Clm 80000 7 1 21 31½ 32 3¾ MacBeth D b 114 5.30 87-17 Fatih 120¾ Aristocratical 122no Fearless Leader 114hd Weakened 7
24Sep84- 2Bel fm 1⅛ Ⓣ:46 1:10⅗ 1:42 3+Clm 75000 7 3 32 2½ 1½ 2nk MacBeth D b 117 *4.20 86-20 Palace 113nk Fearless Leader 1171¾ Beagle 1131 Just failed 12
3Sep84- 7Bel fm 7f Ⓣ:23⅕ :45⅖ 1:21⅘ 3+Alw 33000 5 3 32 32½ 33½ 33 MacBeth D b 115 10.70 92-14 Disco Count 1101¾ParisPrince1151½FearlessLeader1152¾ Even try 7
22Aug84- 8Sar fm 1⅛ Ⓣ:48⅕ 1:12⅘ 1:44⅘ 3+ⓈWest PointH 10 3 2hd 1hd 1hd 1no Davis R G b 110 11.20Ⓓ 73-20 ⒹFerlessLdr109noGothicRvivl1122MusicPrinc1181½ Bore out, drv. 11
22Aug84- Disqualified and placed second
15Aug84- 5Sar fm 1⅛ Ⓣ:45⅗ 1:09⅘ 1:42⅕ 3+Clm 50000 4 3 34 21½ 53 69¾ MacBeth D b 117 5.00 77-14 Clarinet King 119¾ Freon 1135 Oratavo 1131 Weakened 10
22Jun84- 1Bel fm 1⅛ Ⓣ:47 1:10⅘ 1:42⅗ Clm 45000 7 1 2½ 1hd 11 1nk MacBeth D b 113 *1.60 88-19 Fearless Leader 113nk Beagle 1132½ Full Deck 117¾ Driving 7
13Jun84- 5Bel fm 1⅛ Ⓣ:46⅗ 1:10⅖ 1:42 Clm 40000 1 1 1½ 1hd 1½ 1¾ MacBeth D b 117 *1.60 86-16 Fearless Leader 117¾ Cannon Royal1081FullConcert1132¾ Driving 11
LATEST WORKOUTS Jun 10 Bel tr.t 4f fst :47⅖ h Jun 5 Bel tr.t 4f fst :49 b May 27 Bel tr.t 4f fst :48⅗ h May 13 Bel tr.t 4f fst :49⅖ b

Dance Caller — Ch. h. 5, by Marshua's Dancer—All In, by Gallant Man
Br.—Morgan Nancy Penn (Ky)
Tr.—Jerkens H Allen
Own.—Hobeau Farm
117 — Lifetime 28 4 1 5 $139,096 — 1985 5 0 0 1 $2,200 — 1984 9 0 1 $24,596 — Turf 4 1 2 $22,320

17May85- 7GS my 170 :46⅕ 1:11 1:41⅕ Alw 20000 4 5 67 45½ 46½ 37½ Samyn J L 114 4.10 86-18 KingOfBridlewood1142½GallantPrelude1145D CUer114½ Rallied 7
18Apr85- 8Aqu fst 1⅞ :50⅕ 2:33⅖ 3:12⅘ 3+Handicap 2 4 67 622 637 633¾ Graell A 116 5.60 — — Erin Bright 118hd Eecio 10815½ Easy Choice 1181¾ Fell back 6
13Apr85- 8Aqu fst 1¼ :50⅗ 1:39⅖ 2:04⅕ 3+Excelsior H 7 7 75½ 812 815 816¾ Graell A 109 23.50 58-21 Morning Bob 1122½ Lord of theManor1124¾LastTurn110nk Outrun 8
13Apr85-Grade II
4Apr85- 8Aqu fst 1 :46⅗ 1:10⅘ 1:36⅕ 3+Alw 30000 4 7 714 714 713 711 Garcia G G b 121 10.40 74-19 Cooper's Hawk 117¾ Vinny's Pride 121nk Spender 1211 Outrun 7
23Mar85- 6Aqu fst 7f :23⅘ :46⅘ 1:23⅖ Alw 28000 4 6 62¾ 64 612 69¾ Skinner K b 117 12.20 74-23 Key To TheFlag114noTalcPower1122EliteSyncopation1172 Trailed 6
28Jly84- 8Bel sf 1½ Ⓣ:49⅕ 2:05⅗ 2:31 3+Swd Dncer H 9 9 99¾118 107¾109¾ Velasquez J b 111 29.60 60-31 Majesty's Prince 1243½ Nassipour 1091½ Four Bases 112nk Outrun 11
28Jly84-Grade I
21Jly84- 8Bel sly 1½ :48⅖ 2:02 2:27⅖ 3+Brooklyn H 3 3 46½ 612 616 625 Miranda J b 111 10.80 58-21 Fit to Fight 12912½ Vision 1095 Dew Line 116hd Tired 8
21Jly84-Grade I
4Jly84- 8Bel fst 1¼ :47⅖ 1:35⅕ 2:00⅗ 3+Suburban H 2 6 65½ 68½ 69 57¾ Miranda J b 111 14.30 87-11 Fit to Fight 1263¾ Canadian Factor 116no Wild Again1164 Outrun 7
4Jly84-Grade I
8Jun84- 8Bel fst 1⅛ :47⅕ 1:11⅖ 1:48⅘ 3+Nasau Cty H 7 4 63¾ 42 42½ 31 Miranda J b 113 8.10 82-19 Moro 115¾ Canadian Factor 117nk Dance Caller 113hd Rallied 8
8Jun84-Grade II
25Mar84- 8Aqu fst 170 ⊡:47⅗ 1:12 1:41⅘ 3+Westchstr H 4 6 89¾ 811 66¾ 66½ Velasquez J b 114 4.40e 85-16 Jacque'sTip114nkMinstrelGlory107½Havagreatdate1111½ No factor 8
25Mar84-Grade III
LATEST WORKOUTS Jun 12 Bel 5f fst 1:06 b Jun 7 Bel tr.t 4f fst :48⅗ h Jun 2 Bel 4f fst :48⅕ h May 25 Bel 3f fst :36 b

MAYANESIAN

In previous years, Mayanesian was a real bullet from the gate and a horse to be reckoned with in local grass sprints. Although he seems to have lost some of his zip and is certainly suspect at the distance, Mayanesian figures to cook anything that tries to keep up with him early. His presence in this race creates an unnatural situation for the other speed types. How each will cope with Mayanesian is hard to predict.

ANOTHER SUMMER

A New York-bred three-year-old making his grass debut, sporting bloodlines that say "no" to grass racing. If three strikes aren't enough, Another Summer prefers to race on or from just off the early pace in route races. How fast will Mayanesian make him run early? How will Another Summer react if he can't keep in touch with Mayanesian? We have no evidence, but can only conclude that the pace situation will probably not work in his favor.

WITHOUT RESERVE

Has shown nothing thus far in four starts in this country.

STORMY PUDDLES

A New York-bred with a low lifetime win percentage, Stormy Puddles finished within two lengths of today's favorite High Ice in the Kingston despite traffic problems. He was claimed from his last race by Peter Ferriola, and that alone could make up the difference. The fact that the horse competed in the claiming ranks recently should not, as a rule, be held against him, at least not in such a weakly conditioned classified race.

DOMINATING DOOLEY

Another horse with an alarmingly low lifetime win ratio, Dominating Dooley's most recent effort reflected considerable improvement, albeit against high-priced claimers. Impressive indeed were his pace figures on that occasion—both 115, before falling off to a final-time figure of 108. Freshened horses sporting big pace numbers often improve dramatically next time out.

FORTNIGHTLY

Although winless during 1984 and 1985, Fortnightly did finish close up in both the Manhattan Handicap and Man O'War Stakes during the fall of 1984. Both were Grade I events. Unlike his competition, Fortnightly has competed almost exclusively in top-class stakes company, bypassing easy purses in allowance or high-priced claiming contests. He would appear to outclass his rivals in this race. In addition, and more to our point, he made a move ("bid and hung") in his most recent start, his second of the year. Indeed, his move was made into the fastest part of that race, its third quarter. Figures for the race read 112–118–111. Fortnightly gained a couple of lengths at a point where race speed quickened by six lengths. That he hung in the late stages was excusable, especially in light of his relative lack of seasoning during 1985.

HIGH ICE

Race favorite at 2–1, High Ice finished ahead of Fortnightly on May 25, rallying late after the six furlong-pace had taken its toll on the early contenders. He's a sharp horse, but one whose late move—notice his usual positioning after six furlongs—can get him into trouble. Not the kind of horse worth backing as favorite.

MELTHEMI

This horse is a Maryland-based shipper who has failed on three previous excursions to New York. His early speed won't help him in this field.

FEARLESS LEADER

Another New York-bred, Fearless Leader's first start of the year was tough—the gelding seems to have fought tooth and nail the entire trip—and could conceivably set him back for a few weeks. Even if he is not plagued by muscle soreness, he'll probably be burned out early by Mayanesian.

DANCE CALLER

Winless over the past year and a half, Dance Caller woke up in allowance company at Garden State last time out. But this is New York, and the horse can't be liked based on such skimpy out-of-state evidence.

To summarize, then, our pace figures suggest that both Fortnightly and Dominating Dooley are ready for improved efforts, although the latter, and all other speed types, will probably find today's expected pace difficult to overcome. The presence of the fleet sprinter Mayanesian figures to work to the advantage of closers like Stormy Puddles, Dance Caller, the favored High Ice, and the seemingly classier Fortnightly, none of whom are easy to like because of their apparent reluctance to win and/or low odds. Fortnightly, though, did appear to be the one most likely to succeed.

Fortnightly won this race rather handily, returning $8.60 to his backers, while High Ice rallied up late for second money. Surprisingly, Mayanesian failed to enter contention at any point of the race, giving the other early speed horses a far better shot than we had accorded them. Dominating Dooley stalked the pacesetting Melthemi, then held second position until the final sixteenth of a mile. He went on to win two of his next three starts, when dropped back down into the high-priced claiming ranks, delivering the performance his outstanding pace figures of June 2 had promised.

SEVENTH RACE
Belmont
JUNE 15, 1985

1 $\frac{1}{16}$ MILES.(Turf). (1.39$\frac{1}{5}$) ALLOWANCE. Purse $40,000. 3-year-olds and upward which have not won a rce of $15,000 at a mile or over in 1984–85. Weight, 3-year-olds, 114 lbs. Older, 122 lbs. Non-winners of two races of $12,500 at a mile or over since October 1 allowed 3 lbs. Of such a race since January 1, 5 lbs. Maiden, claiming, starter and state bred races not considered.)

Value of race $40,000; value to winner $24,000; second $8,800; third $4,800; fourth $2,400. Mutuel pool $210,332, OTB pool $65,488. Exacta Pool $334,631. OTB Exacta Pool $274,745.

Last Raced	Horse	Eqt.	A.	Wt	PP	St	¼	½	¾	Str	Fin	Jockey	Odds $1
25May85 ^{6}Bel^5	Fortnightly	b	5	117	6	6	$4^{1\frac{1}{2}}$	$3^{\frac{1}{2}}$	$3^{1\frac{1}{2}}$	$1^{2\frac{1}{2}}$	1^3	Cordero A Jr	3.30
8Jun85 ^{6}GS^2	High Ice	b	4	117	7	7	$9^{1\frac{1}{2}}$	8^1	$5^{\frac{1}{2}}$	3^{hd}	2no	MacBeth D	2.40
15May85 ^{8}Bel^2	Fearless Leader	b	7	117	9	4	3^{hd}	4^1	4^3	$4^{\frac{1}{2}}$	3^1	Davis R G	5.00
17May85 ^{7}GS^3	Dance Caller		5	117	10	5	$6^{\frac{1}{2}}$	6^{hd}	6^1	5^4	$4^{2\frac{3}{4}}$	Hernandez R	24.90
2Jun85 ^{4}Bel^3	Dominating Dooley		5	117	5	2	2^2	$2^{\frac{1}{2}}$	1^{hd}	2^1	5^1	Guerra W A	11.40
6Jun85 ^{8}Bel^6	Mayanesian		6	117	1	3	8^{hd}	7^2	7^4	$6^{1\frac{1}{2}}$	6^8	Ward W A	10.70
1Jun85 ^{8}Pim^5	Melthemi		5	117	8	1	$1^{2\frac{1}{2}}$	$1^{1\frac{1}{2}}$	2^1	7^8	$7^{10\frac{1}{2}}$	Maple E	34.30
30May85 ^{3}Bel^1	Another Summer		3	110	2	8	10	$9^{\frac{1}{2}}$	8^6	8^6	$8^{6\frac{1}{4}}$	Santagata N	23.90
5Jun85 ^{2}Bel^2	Stormy Puddles		5	117	4	10	$7^{\frac{1}{2}}$	10	10	9^4	9^4	Bailey J D	3.50
30May85 ^{7}Bel^8	Without Reserve	b	4	117	3	9	$5^{\frac{1}{2}}$	5^1	9^{hd}	10	10	St Leon G	43.70

OFF AT 4:28 Start good, Won driving. Time, :22$\frac{4}{5}$, :45$\frac{2}{5}$, 1:09$\frac{2}{5}$, 1:34$\frac{1}{5}$, 1:41 Course firm.

$2 Mutuel Prices:

6–(G)–FORTNIGHTLY	8.60	4.60	3.00
7–(I)–HIGH ICE		3.40	2.20
9–(K)–FEARLESS LEADER			3.00

$2 EXACTA 6–7 PAID $31.40.

B. h, by Dance Spell—Out Cold, by Etonian. Trainer Parisella John. Bred by Bwamazon Farm (Ky).

FORTNIGHTLY, never far back, split horses to make his bid leaving the turn and proved clearly best under strong handling. HIGH ICE raced wide while moving nearing the stretch and outgamed FEARLESS LEADER for the place. The latter made a run nearing the stretch but wasn't good enough. DANCE CALLER moved to the inside after spliting horses leaving the turn but failed to sustain his rally. DOMINATING DOOLEY prompted the pace, headed MELTHEMI approaching the stretch but gave way under pressure. MAYANESIAN failed to be a serious factor. MELTHEMI was usedup making the pace. STORMY PUDDLES raced wide. WITHOUT reserve rushed up approaching the end of the backstretch but was finished soon after going a half.

Route pace figures can be interpreted as equivalent to figures for a six-furlong race. Exceptionally fast-route pace numbers often point to fit horses capable of successfully turning back in distance. However, figures alone do not convert a router into a sprinter, and the player must be certain to check whether or not such a horse is, in fact, accomplished at the sprint distances and is indeed capable of keeping in touch during the early stages of a sprint. That is why we demand "faster than par" pace figures for the route immediately preceding the turnback. Average (par) pace figures do not necessarily imply the sprint sharpness needed.

2 BELMONT

6 FURLONGS
BELMONT PARK

6 FURLONGS. (1.08⅗) CLAIMING. Purse $20,000. 3-year-old fillies. Weights, 121 lbs. Non-winners of two races since May 15 allowed 3 lbs. Of a race isnce then 5 lbs. Claiming Price $50,000; for each $2,500 to $45,000, 2 lbs. (Races when entered to be claimed for $40,000 or less not considered.)

Sweet Ridge — B. f. 3, by Riva Ridge—Run Royal Run, by Might
$50,000 Br.—Kubat & Smith & Viking Farms Ltd (Ky)
Own.—Chasrigg Stable — Tr.—DeBonis Robert
1097 — Lifetime 16 5 1 2 $61,990 — 1985 8 3 0 0 $42,660 — 1984 8 2 1 2 $19,330

1Jun85- 9GS fst 6f :22⅘ :46 1:11 3↑ ⒻAlw 14000 4 5 31 22½ 45 511¼ Marquez C H Jr7 106 2.90 76-12 Hail The State 114nk Confirmed Affair 1102 Oaxaca 1134 Tired 6
20Apr85- 1Aqu my 7f :22⅘ :46 1:24⅕ ⒻClm 70000 1 3 1½ 1hd 2hd 43¼ Migliore R 112 *.90 77-18 Highland Singh 1162¼TooSunny107½BrutishBeast116nk Weakened 7
11Mar85- 5Aqu fst 6f ⊡:22⅘ :46⅕ 1:11⅘ ⒻAlw 22000 6 1 2hd 1½ 14 11 Migliore R 116 2.60 85-18 Sweet Ridge 1161FlyingHeat116¾SaraThompson1065 Bled. driving 6
2Mar85- 6Aqu fst 6f ⊡:22⅘ :47 1:13 ⒻAlw 22000 8 2 3½ 2½ 31 46½ Davis R G 116 4.60 72-19 Halo Country 1182¾ Dream Puss 1163 K.'s Solution 116¾ Faltered 11
13Feb85- 7Aqu fst 1⅟₁₆ ⊡:48 1:13⅘ 1:48⅗ ⒻAlw 24000 8 1 11 2½ 46½ 517¾ Davis R G 116 *.80e 49-20 Lady on the Run 1166½ Waltha 1096 Adda Girl 1161½ Tired 8
2Feb85- 1Aqu my 1⅟₁₆ ⊡:48⅕ 1:14⅕ 1:48⅗ ⒻClm 60000 3 1 12 1hd 13 12½ Davis R G 112 *2.10 68-28 Sweet Ridge 1122½ Adda Girl112¾StrategicAsset1122 Ridden out 7
24Jan85- 9Aqu fst 6f ⊡:22⅘ :45⅘ 1:11⅘ ⒻClm 45000 4 4 1½ 11 11 13 Davis R G 112 22.10 85-21 Sweet Ridge 1123 Regal Lynco 1072½ Right Girl 112hd Driving 12
10Jan85- 3Aqu fst 6f ⊡:22⅘ :46⅗ 1:12⅗ ⒻClm 45000 4 3 41½ 41½ 62½ 62¾ Garrido O L5 107 17.80 78-22 Flying Hope 1161 Dawn's Answer 105hd Regal Lynco 109no Tired 9
19Dec84- 6Med fst 6f :22⅘ :46⅖ 1:13 ⒻAlw 12000 7 1 2hd 1½ 2½ 36 Antley C W 114 *2.40 71-23 Lu Lu's Girl 1206 My Marisa 108hd Sweet Ridge 1142 Tired 7
6Dec84- 5Aqu sly 6f ⊡:22 :45⅘ 1:11⅘ ⒻClm 62500 1 5 3nk 3½ 88 815¾ MacBeth D b 114 3.30 69-12 Nell Diamond 116½ Carnegie Hill 1052½ Singing Praise112nk Tired 8
LATEST WORKOUTS Jun 13 GS 3f fst :38⅗ b May 26 Bel 4f fst :47⅘ h May 18 Bel tr.t 5f gd 1:05 b May 10 Bel 4f fst :48 h

Too Sunny — B. f. 3, by Tudor Grey—Sun For All, by One For All
$50,000 Br.—Wilson C T (Ky)
Own.—Wilson C T Jr — Tr.—Hernandez Ramon M
1115 — Lifetime 9 1 3 1 $21,880 — 1985 7 1 2 1 $19,680 — 1984 2 M 1 0 $2,200

6Jun85- 9Bel gd 6½f :22⅘ :45⅗ 1:18⅕ ⒻClm 50000 3 6 46 47½ 26 25½ Moore D N5 111 13.80 80-15 Proximal1165½TooSunny1114½FncyMissNncy112hd Best of others 8
6May85- 1Aqu fst 1 :46⅗ 1:11⅗ 1:37⅗ 3↑ ⒻAlw 23000 1 3 22½ 36 615 625 Ramirez M R5 105 8.90 54-23 Self Image 11012 Screen Landing 1211½ Floating 1162½ Tired 6
20Apr85- 1Aqu my 7f :22⅘ :46 1:24⅕ ⒻClm 70000 7 2 53 3½ 1hd 22½ Ramirez M R5 107 10.70 77-18 Highland Singh 1162½ Too Sunny107½BrutishBeast116nk Game try 7
11Apr85- 3Aqu fst 6f :23⅗ :47⅗ 1:13 3↑ ⒻMd 50000 7 4 42½ 3nk 11½ 12½ Ramirez M R5 107 2.80 76-24 Too Sunny 1072½ Flurried 1122¾ Regal Squaw 120hd Ridden out 7
18Mar85- 3Aqu fst 1 :49⅗ 1:15⅗ 1:42⅗ ⒻMd Sp Wt 4 3 74½ 715 816 821¼ Lovato F Jr 121 5.80 33-38 Sweet Sound121¾VaguelyFoolish1213MissMarble1216½ Dull effort 8
11Mar85- 6Aqu fst 6f ⊡:22⅘ :46⅕ 1:13 ⒻMd Sp Wt 5 11 77¾ 77 85½ 56 Lovato F Jr 121 3.10 73-18 Daraly 1141¾ Redolent 121¾ Northern Gannet 1211½ Began slowly 12
20Feb85- 6Aqu fst 6f ⊡:23⅕ :47⅖ 1:13⅘ ⒻMd Sp Wt 12 2 52 43 34 34 Lovato F Jr 121 6.20 71-23 Talanta 121¾ Charming Luisa 1163½ Too Sunny 121nk Evenly late 12
10Nov84- 4Aqu fst 7f :23⅕ :46⅘ 1:26⅗ ⒻMd Sp Wt 3 6 72½ 74¾ 69½ 68 Lovato F Jr 117 5.90 61-23 Dawn'sCurtsey117nkBoldButLovely117noNstyBelle1171½ No factor 7
2Nov84- 1Aqu fst 6f :23 :47⅗ 1:14 ⒻMd 50000 4 6 75 52¾ 3nk 21 Lovato F Jr 117 16.00 70-35 RedyMid1131TooSunny117¾SuddenShower117¾ Broke awkwardly 7
LATEST WORKOUTS May 27 Bel 5f fst 1:02⅕ h ●May 1 Bel tr.t 4f fst :47⅗ h

Regal Lynco — B. f. 3, by Screen King—Lynco Jo, by Fearless Knight
$50,000 Br.—Flying Zee Stable (Ky)
Own.—Flying Zee Stable — Tr.—O'Connell Richard
1115 — Lifetime 12 3 3 3 $51,300 — 1985 8 3 2 2 $46,860 — 1984 4 M 1 1 $4,440

15May85- 5Bel fst 6f :22⅘ :46⅗ 1:11⅘ 3↑ ⒻAlw 25000 1 3 62¾ 74 65 67¼ Moore D N5 1056 5.10 76-17 Crrie'sDrem110nkFindHppiness1101¾ScreenLnding1212 No factor 8
15May85-Dead heat
5May85- 3Aqu fst 6f :22⅕ :45⅗ 1:11⅗ ⒻClm 85000 1 5 21 43 23 22¾ Moore D N5 110 2.30 80-22 Notice Me 1152¾ Regal Lynco 1101¾ Test Shot 115no Second best 6
26Apr85- 5Aqu fst 6f :23⅗ :47 1:11⅘ ⒻAlw 23000 1 4 31 31 21 11¾ Moore D N5 111 14.30 82-23 Regal Lynco 1111¾ FoxcroftValue1211½VideoTalc1163 Going away 8
13Apr85- 4Aqu fst 6f :22⅘ :46 1:12 ⒻClm 50000 4 4 3½ 11 1½ 1hd Moore D N5 111 9.00 81-21 Regal Lynco 111hd Proximal 1162 Baby Chris 1121¾ Driving 8
1Mar85- 4Aqu fst 6f ⊡:22⅗ :45⅘ 1:12⅕ ⒻClm 45000 6 5 41½ 42 33 34¾ Ward W A5 107 4.40 78-25 Flying Hope 116½ Baby Chris 1124½ Regal Lynco 107nk Rallied 12
24Jan85- 9Aqu fst 6f ⊡:22⅘ :45⅘ 1:11⅘ ⒻClm 45000 10 3 2½ 21 21 23 Ward W A5 107 6.00 82-21 Sweet Ridge 1123 Regal Lynco 1072½ RightGirl112hd Second best 12
10Jan85- 3Aqu fst 6f ⊡:22⅘ :46⅗ 1:12⅗ ⒻClm 45000 6 1 2hd 2hd 1hd 31 Ward W A5 109 5.10 80-22 Flying Hope 1161Dawn'sAnswer105hdRegalLynco109no Weakened 9
1Jan85- 4Aqu fst 6f ⊡:22⅘ :44⅗ 1:11⅗ ⒻMd 47500 7 3 21 11 12 1hd Ward W A5 114 *1.40e 86-13 Regal Lynco 114hd Classi Flag 1121½ Sweet Sound 1171 Driving 10
21Dec84- 6Aqu fst 6f ⊡:23⅗ :47⅗ 1:13⅗ ⒻMd 70000 3 9 62½ 53 3½ 3¾ Ward W A5 108 2.20e 74-22 Brutish Beast 117nk Gaylord'sAmber108½RegalLynco1082½ Rallied 12
6Dec84- 3Aqu sly 6f ⊡:22⅘ :46⅕ 1:12⅕ ⒻMd 45000 9 1 1hd 12 2½ 25 Samyn J L 113 *1.70e 78-12 Dream Puss 1175 Regal Lynco1131¾SweetSound1131 Second best 9
LATEST WORKOUTS Jun 3 Bel tr.t 4f fst :48⅗ h

Nile Flirt — B. f. 3, by Upper Nile—Brazen Flirt, by Brazen Brother
$45,000 Br.—McLean & Miller Jr (Ky)
Own.—Paulson A — Tr.—Nickerson Victor J
1075 — Lifetime 14 2 3 1 $30,980 — 1985 7 1 2 1 $19,940 — 1984 7 1 1 0 $11,040 — Turf 1 0 0 0

19May85- 5Bel fst 1 :47⅕ 1:12⅘ 1:38⅗ ⒻClm 45000 7 2 2hd 1½ 22 35¼ Moore D N5 b 107 3.10 67-20 Carnegie Hill 1125 Nasty Belle 116nk Nile Flirt 1073¼ Weakened 7
28Apr85- 2Aqu fst 7f :22⅘ :45⅘ 1:24⅘ ⒻClm 30000 3 9 33 32 25 24¾ Moore D N5 b 107 9.10 72-21 Baby Chris 1164¾ Nile Flirt 1075 Madame Mystique1072¾ 2nd best 10
4Apr85- 5Aqu fst 7f :22⅘ :46 1:24⅗ ⒻClm 25000 8 1 11 1½ 13 15¾ Moore D N5 b 111 3.70 78-19 Nile Flirt 1115¾ Majennique 118nk Cousin Bette 114no Ridden out 8
25Mar85- 4Aqu fst 6f :23⅗ :48 1:14⅕ ⒻClm 25000 2 6 2hd 32 41¾ 22¼ Moore D N5 b 111 6.20 67-35 Majennique 1142¼ Nile Flirt 1112¼ Luke's Girl 1161¾ Best others 12
15Feb85- 4Aqu fst 6f ⊡:23 :47⅗ 1:14⅕ ⒻClm 30000 6 4 3½ 31½ 52 67¼ Santagata N b 112 15.00 66-26 K.'sSolton1161¾ToonInTomorrow1091¾MdyMndy112nk No mishap 10
9Feb85- 3Aqu fst 6f ⊡:23⅗ :49 1:15⅖ ⒻClm 45000 1 2 11 1½ 41½ 45½ Venezia M 112 13.10 61-26 Carnegie Hill 105nk Baby Chris 111nk Effigy 1125 Weakened 8
24Jan85- 9Aqu fst 6f ⊡:22⅘ :45⅘ 1:11⅘ ⒻClm 45000 12 1 31 32½ — — Venezia M b 112 44.20 — — Sweet Ridge 1123 Regal Lynco 1072½ Right Girl 112hd Pulled up 12
10Oct84- 7Bel sly 1 :46⅕ 1:11⅗ 1:39 ⒻAlw 21000 4 3 46 516 518 525 Venezia M b 116 16.40 45-24 Golden Silence 1163 Endear 116hd Winters' Love 11610½ Tired 6
10Sep84- 3Bel fst 6f :23 :46⅘ 1:12⅘ ⒻMd 50000 1 4 21 21½ 22½ 12¾ Venezia M b 117 *2.60 80-19 Nile Flirt 1172¾ Ever Pleasant 1178 Young Sister 1102 Driving 7
31Aug84- 6Bel gd 1 Ⓣ:48⅘ 1:13 1:39⅗ ⒻMd Sp Wt 6 4 31½ 44 56½ 65½ Venezia M b 117 6.50 61-31 Adieu Babette 117hd I'm A Bell Raiser117nkBoardGame117¾ Tired 11
LATEST WORKOUTS ●Jun 7 Aqu ⊡ 4f fst :46⅘ h ●May 14 Aqu ⊡ 3f fst :35⅘ h ●Apr 21 Aqu 3f fst :36 h

Rough Miss — B. f. 3, by Poison Ivory—Gem In The Rough, by Mr Prospector
$45,000 Br.—Aisco Stable (Fla)
Own.—Our Winter Stable — Tr.—Sallusto Justin
1075 — Lifetime 6 1 1 1 $8,260 — 1985 3 0 0 1 $2,640 — 1984 3 1 1 0 $5,620

6Mar85- 7Aqu fst 1⅟₁₆ ⊡:48⅘ 1:14⅘ 1:48⅘ ⒻAlw 23000 7 2 2hd 79 719 725¾ Privitera R5 b 111 13.50 40-26 StrtegicAsst116¾HighlndSingh116¾ToonInTomorrow111½ Stopped 7
2Mar85- 6Aqu fst 6f ⊡:22⅘ :47 1:13 ⒻAlw 22000 3 11 61¾119¼1013 1014¾ Thibeau R J 116 8.80 64-19 Halo Country 1182¾ Dream Puss 1163 K.'s Solution 116¾ Outrun 11
18Feb85- 6Aqu fst 6f ⊡:22⅘ :47 1:12⅗ ⒻAlw 22000 5 4 42 42 49 39½ Thibeau R J 116 5.20e 71-28 Koluctoo's Power 1168¾ Sherry Mary121¾RoughMiss1163½ Rallied 7
21Nov84- 8Med fst 6f :22⅗ :46⅖ 1:12 ⒻHolly 2 1 811 812 712 716½ Ayarza I 112 50.60 66-28 Willowy Mood 1182½ Shanaleen1181½PlasticLady1127 Bore out st. 8
3Nov84- 9Del fst 6f :22⅗ :46 1:12⅕ ⒻⓇSensational 4 5 2hd 23½ 25½ 27 Winnett B G Jr 112 8.00 73-27 Plastic Lady 1127 Rough Miss 1122NellDiamond1145 Second best 6
5Jly84- 4Atl fst 4½f :23 :47 :53⅗ ⒻMd Sp Wt 2 2 2hd 2½ 12 Terry J 117 5.20 92-08 Rough Miss 1172 Gay Happiness 1174SunEmpress1172 Drew clear 10
LATEST WORKOUTS ●Jun 12 Aqu ⊡ 5f fst 1:01⅗ h May 23 Aqu Ⓣ 5f sf 1:04⅘ b (d)

Inherently — Ch. f. 3, by Princely Native—Frozen Account, by Sham
$50,000 Br.—Harbor View Farm (Ky)
Own.—Harbor View Farm — Tr.—Martin Frank
116 — Lifetime 11 1 2 4 $27,700 — 1985 8 0 1 3 $13,620 — 1984 3 1 1 1 $14,080

8Jun85- 9Bel my 1⅟₁₆ :45⅕ 1:10⅗ 1:44 ⒻAlw 25000 6 5 77½ 914 921 923¾ Lovato F Jr 116 10.90 58-12 Sois Sage 1163 Great Lady 1162½ Dawn's Curtsey 1163 Fell back 9
20May85- 5Bel fst 1 :46⅕ 1:10⅘ 1:36⅖ ⒻAlw 25000 8 8 75 36 38 310½ Cruguet J 116 26.20 72-22 FvorbleReview1166½TlentLin1164Inhrntly1163½ Wide lacked resp 8
5May85- 7Aqu fst 7f :23 :46⅕ 1:25⅗ ⒻAlw 22000 6 1 3½ 2hd 55 58 Lovato F Jr 116 12.50 65-22 Medan 111nk Bare Assets 1164 Toon In Tomorrow 1113 Tired 7
26Apr85- 5Aqu fst 6f :23⅗ :47 1:11⅘ ⒻAlw 23000 6 2 53½ 54½ 511 612¾ Cruguet J 116 12.40 69-23 Regal Lynco 1111¾ Foxcroft Value 1211½VideoTalc1163 No factor 8
2Mar85- 2GP fst 7f :22⅕ :45⅗ 1:23⅗ ⒻAlw 16800 6 8 54 108½ 913 916¾ Santos J A 118 *1.70 69-15 Denver Express 1218 Wigwam's AreOut121½PureFire116nk Outrun 11
3Feb85- 7Aqu sly 170 ⊡:48 1:14⅕ 1:46⅖ ⒻAlw 23000 4 3 22 22 26 28¾ Ward W A5 111 *.90 59-30 Plenteous 1168¾ Inherently 1112¾ Got The Edge 1143 2nd best 6
25Jan85- 9Aqu fst 1⅟₁₆ ⊡:47⅘ 1:13⅕ 1:47⅘ ⒻAlw 23000 4 3 31 1hd 3nk 32 Lovato F Jr 116 3.80 71-23 ElineHemmings116¾SuchANut1161½Inherntly116½ Lacked late bid 11
7Jan85- 8Aqu fst 6f ⊡:22⅘ :47 1:12⅗ ⒻAlw 22000 1 2 62½ 77½ 66½ 34½ Lovato F Jr 116 3.60 76-27 Private Iron 1211½ Street Savy 1213½ Inherently 116no Checked 9
20Dec84- 7Aqu fst 6f ⊡:22⅗ :46⅘ 1:13⅕ ⒻAlw 22000 4 2 41½ 31½ 21½ 2¾ Lovato F Jr 118 9.40 77-19 Find Happiness 118¾Inherently1182½SuchANut116hd Wide, rallied 8
9Dec84- 5Aqu fst 6f ⊡:22⅘ :45⅘ 1:11⅖ ⒻAlw 22000 7 1 31½ 31½ 35 38½ Lovato F Jr 121 5.20 78-19 Run WithStyle116noFate'sReward118½Inherently121hd Lugged in 7
LATEST WORKOUTS May 21 Bel tr.t 4f fst :52 b ●May 13 Bel tr.t 5f fst 1:01 h May 11 Bel tr.t 4f fst :53⅗ b May 6 Bel tr.t 3f fst :39 b

Carnegie Hill — B. f. 3, by Be A Native—Dove Flight, by Blue Prince
$45,000 Br.—Grandon E L (Cal)
Own.—Spiegel R — Tr.—Schaeffer Stephen
114 — Lifetime 18 3 1 1 $42,940 — 1985 11 2 0 1 $30,000 — 1984 7 1 1 0 $12,940 — Turf 1 0 0 0

26May85- 2Bel fst 7f :22⅗ :46 1:23⅕ 3↑ ⒻAlw 24000 2 5 54½ 53½ 59½ 616½ Santagata N b 111 7.70 70-13 RoseGayleHoney1139½Letty'sPennant113¾SherryMary1103 Outrun 6
19May85- 5Bel fst 1 :47⅕ 1:12⅘ 1:38⅗ ⒻClm 45000 5 4 31½ 31 12 15 Cordero A Jr b 112 3.00 72-20 Carnegie Hill 1125 Nasty Belle 116nk Nile Flirt 1073¼ Drew off 7
4May85- 4Aqu fst 1 :45⅗ 1:10⅖ 1:37 ⒻClm 45000 2 3 2hd 22 25 36¾ Privitera R5 b 107 2.90 74-15 Irish Point 1166 Etoile Joyeux 118¾ Carnegie Hill1071¾ Weakened 6
27Apr85- 5Aqu fm 1⅛ Ⓣ:48⅕ 1:13 1:50⅗ 3↑ ⒻAlw 23000 2 7 95½ 72¾ 816 822 Privitera R5 104 17.80 69-09 Forever Command 1123½ RoyalCousin1214½EasyWay1091¾ Outrun 11
13Apr85- 4Aqu fst 6f :22⅘ :46 1:12 ⒻClm 45000 8 7 63¾ 57 47 43¾ Privitera R5 107 17.00 77-21 Regal Lynco 111hd Proximal 1162 Baby Chris 1121¾ Wide 8
8Mar85- 5Aqu fst 6f ⊡:22⅗ :48 1:11⅘ ⒻClm 35000 3 11 117¾ 86¾ 55 45¾ Privitera R5 b 113 16.30 79-18 Moody Monday 116nk Quiescence1185½BernaCagney116hd Rallied 11
1Mar85- 4Aqu fst 6f ⊡:22⅗ :45⅘ 1:12⅕ ⒻClm 47500 5 12 119½ 1117 1115 1112½ Privitera R7 b 109 30.70 70-25 Flying Hope 116½ Baby Chris 1124½ Regal Lynco 107nk Outrun 12
9Feb85- 3Aqu fst 6f ⊡:23⅗ :49 1:15⅖ ⒻClm 45000 4 6 66 43½ 31 1nk Privitera R7 b 105 25.20 67-26 Carnegie Hill 105nk Baby Chris 111nk Effigy 1125 Driving 8
2Feb85- 1Aqu my 1⅟₁₆ ⊡:48⅕ 1:14⅕ 1:48⅖ ⒻClm 60000 4 3 32½ 44½ 516 621¾ Privitera R7 b 105 6.50 46-28 Sweet Ridge 1122½AddaGirl112¾StrategicAsset1122 Retired early 7
16Jan85- 1Aqu fst 6f ⊡:23⅕ :47⅘ 1:14⅖ ⒻClm 60000 4 6 76 69½ 57½ 66¾ Privitera R7 b 105 6.60 65-27 Jeremiah Bullfrog 116¾ Dream Puss 1163½ Right Girl 112½ Outrun 7
LATEST WORKOUTS Jun 3 Bel tr.t 4f fst :47⅗ h May 12 Bel tr.t 4f fst :48⅘ b Apr 21 Bel tr.t 4f fst :47⅘ h

Dance Hall Miss B. f. 3, by Bold Forbes—Ten Cents A Kiss, by Key To The Mint

Own.—Davis A $45,000 Br.—Peters L J (Ky) Tr.—Meschera Gasper S **112**

Lifetime								
8 1 0 1	1985	7	0	0	1	$6,752
$18,752	1984	1	1	0	0	$12,000
	Turf	1	0	0	0	$1,200

6Jun85-	9Bel	gd	6½f	:22⅖	:45⅗	1:18⅕	ⒻClm 45000	1	5	2^{2}	3^{7}	4^{10}	5^{11}	Maple E	112	7.20	74-15	Proximal 116$^{5\frac12}$ Too Sunny111$^{4\frac34}$FancyMissNancy112^{hd}	Early foot	8
23May85-	5Bel	fm	1	Ⓣ:47	1:13	1:41⅕	ⒻClm c-35000	3	2	2^{2}	$3^{1\frac12}$	4^{2}	$4^{5\frac34}$	Moore D N5	111	*3.40	53-31	Jilladella 116^{nk} Visible Marie 116$^{3\frac12}$ Rebel Love 116^{2}	Weakened	12
16May85-	3Bel	fst	6f	:22⅗	:46⅕	1:11⅕	ⒻAlw 24000	6	4	3^{1}	$7^{5\frac34}$	$7^{8\frac14}$	$6^{13\frac12}$	Moore D N	b 116	24.40	73-18	Quitman 116^{6} Great Lady 116^{1} Brown Crown 116^{2}	Fin. early	8
23Feb85-	8Lrl	fst	7f	:22⅘	:46⅗	1:25⅘	ⒻⓇContessa	8	6	2^{hd}	$3^{\frac12}$	4^{4}	$4^{7\frac12}$	Pino M G	b 114	4.70	74-24	LaunchingShot116^{2}UnderFire113^{2}ContessaRidge115$^{3\frac12}$	Sp'd. tired	8
16Feb85-	6Aqu	fst	6f	⊡:22⅕	:45⅗	1:12⅖	ⒻBandala	4	5	4^{4}	5^{7}	6^{10}	$5^{8\frac34}$	Migliore R	b 114	22.60	73-29	Shanaleen 121$^{5\frac34}$ Carrie's Dream 114$^{\frac12}$ Top Issue 114$^{\frac34}$	Outrun	6
28Jan85-	7Aqu	fst	6f	⊡:22⅖	:46⅗	1:12⅖	ⒻAlw 23000	1	5	1^{3}	1^{3}	$1^{1\frac12}$	$3^{3\frac12}$	Ward W A5	b 111	4.20	78-25	Carrie'sDream116$^{\frac34}$FlyingHeat116$^{2\frac34}$DnceHllMiss111^{3}	Used in pace	6
7Jan85-	8Aqu	fst	6f	⊡:22⅘	:47	1:12⅗	ⒻAlw 22000	2	6	3^{1}	5^{5}	$5^{3\frac12}$	$4^{4\frac12}$	Ward W A5	113	3.50	76-27	Private Iron 121$^{1\frac12}$ Street Savy 121$^{3\frac12}$ Inherently 116no	Weakened	9
10Dec84-	6Aqu	fst	6f	⊡:23	:46⅗	1:12⅘	ⒻMd Sp Wt	8	6	$6^{3\frac12}$	$5^{6\frac12}$	$3^{2\frac12}$	1no	Ward W A5	112	11.00	80-21	DnceHllMiss112^{no}GrndCrtion117$^{\frac12}$I'mWllBrd117$^{4\frac34}$	Bore in, driving	10

LATEST WORKOUTS May 31 Bel 5f fst 1:00⅗ h May 30 Bel 3f fst :34⅗ h May 10 Bel 4f fst :46⅘ h May 1 Bel 4f fst :48⅘ h

Nasty Belle B. f. 3, by Nasty And Bold—Le Belle M'selle, by Semillant

Own.—Meadowhill $45,000 Br.—Meadowhill (Ky) Tr.—Johnson Philip G **107**^{5}

Lifetime						
8 1 4 3	1985	4	1	2	1	$20,980
$33,600	1984	4	M	2	2	$12,620

19May85-	5Bel	fst	1	:47⅕	1:12⅖	1:38⅗	ⒻClm 50000	1	1	1^{hd}	$2^{\frac12}$	$3^{2\frac12}$	2^{5}	Samyn J L	b 116	*1.50	67-20	Carnegie Hill 112^{5} Nasty Belle 116^{nk} Nile Flirt107$^{3\frac12}$	Gained place	7
1May85-	6Aqu	fst	6f	:22⅘	:46⅕	1:12⅗	3+ⒻMd 75000	2	6	$3^{3\frac12}$	$3^{3\frac12}$	2^{2}	1^{2}	Samyn J L	b 113	*1.20	78-24	Nasty Belle 113^{2} Skyjak 113$^{5\frac12}$ Miss Otani 113$^{2\frac34}$	Driving	6
17Apr85-	6Aqu	fst	6f	:23	:45⅘	1:11⅗	3+ⒻMd Sp Wt	8	8	$8^{8\frac14}$	4^{16}	4^{19}	$3^{15\frac14}$	Vasquez J	112	3.60	68-30	Soli 112$^{4\frac14}$ Rose Gayle Honey 112^{11} Nasty Belle 112$^{\frac34}$	Rallied	9
9Apr85-	6Aqu	fst	6f	:23⅕	:47⅕	1:12⅕	ⒻMd Sp Wt	12	7	5^{3}	$2^{1\frac12}$	2^{4}	2^{3}	Samyn J L	121	*2.50e	77-25	Foxcroft Value 121^{3} Nasty Belle 121^{3} HawaiianTea116$^{\frac34}$	Game try	13
13Dec84-	4Aqu	fst	170	⊡:49⅗	1:14⅘	1:45⅘	ⒻMd Sp Wt	9	5	$5^{2\frac12}$	2^{3}	2^{5}	2^{7}	Samyn J L	117	*2.10	64-19	Plenteous 117^{7} Nasty Belle 117$^{\frac34}$ Strategic Asset 117$^{\frac34}$	Gamely	10
1Dec84-	4Aqu	fst	7f	:23⅗	:47⅗	1:27⅖	ⒻMd Sp Wt	3	8	$6^{1\frac34}$	$6^{2\frac12}$	4^{2}	$2^{\frac34}$	Samyn J L	117	*2.20	63-28	Elaine Hemmings 117$^{\frac34}$ Nasty Belle 117^{hd} Rey's Joyce 117^{4}	Wide	9
10Nov84-	4Aqu	fst	7f	:23⅕	:46⅘	1:26⅖	ⒻMd Sp Wt	5	7	$6^{2\frac14}$	$6^{1\frac34}$	$3^{2\frac12}$	3^{nk}	Samyn J L	117	4.60	69-23	Dwn'sCurtsey117^{nk}BoldButLovely117^{no}NstyBelle117$^{1\frac12}$	Lugged in	7
27Oct84-	1Aqu	my	6f	:23⅕	:46⅗	1:10⅘	ⒻMd 45000	2	8	1^{hd}	2^{hd}	$2^{3\frac12}$	$3^{7\frac12}$	Samyn J L	113	5.90	80-16	Videogenic 117^{5} Imitate 112$^{2\frac12}$ Nasty Belle 113$^{2\frac34}$	Slw st.,spd,tired	8

LATEST WORKOUTS Jun 11 Bel tr.t 4f fst :48 h May 31 Bel 3f fst :35⅘ b May 13 Bel 4f fst :47⅖ h Apr 25 Bel tr.t 3f fst :36⅕ h

A Hot Number Ch. f. 3, by Spellcaster—Princess Rain, by Rainy Lake

Own.—Tresvant Stable $45,000 Br.—Appleton A I (Fla) Tr.—Sedlacek Sue **105**^{7}

Lifetime						
17 3 4 3	1985	10	1	3	2	$21,120
$36,860	1984	7	2	1	1	$15,740

6Jun85-	4GS	fst	1	:47	1:12⅘	1:40⅕	ⒻClm c-25000	8	5	5^{4}	4^{1}	3^{2}	$4^{2\frac12}$	Lovato F	b 115	*1.70	71-19	Gold Kiss 115$^{1\frac34}$ Mama Caba 115^{nk}MomentarilyRich115$^{\frac12}$	Steadied	9
30May85-	7GS	fst	6f	:22⅕	:45⅖	1:10⅗	3+ⒻClm 25000	3	5	6^{3}	$6^{4\frac12}$	$4^{4\frac12}$	3^{3}	Lovato F	b 115	5.10	86-16	Swanlinbar115^{1}Babyneedsnewshoes118^{2}AHotNumber115^{5}	Rallied	7
23May85-	6GS	my	170	:46	1:11⅖	1:43⅖	3+ⒻAlw 15000	3	6	$5^{7\frac34}$	$5^{8\frac12}$	5^{9}	$5^{9\frac14}$	Lovato F	b 110	13.70	73-21	One Double 119^{nk} White Linen 119^{4} Ruthie'sMove115^{2}	No factor	7
6May85-	6GS	fst	$1\frac{1}{16}$	:46⅘	1:10⅘	1:44⅕	3+ⒻAlw 16000	6	5	6^{10}	5^{11}	6^{13}	$7^{20\frac14}$	Lovato F	b 110	6.10	67-13	Power Proof 118$^{1\frac12}$ One Double 118$^{9\frac12}$ RueSt.Honore122$^{6\frac12}$	Outrun	7
24Apr85-	6GS	fst	170	:46⅘	1:12	1:42⅗	ⒻAlw 16000	6	3	3^{3}	$3^{3\frac12}$	$2^{2\frac12}$	2^{2}	Lovato F	b 114	4.00	84-13	PrincessRebu114^{2}AHotNumbr114$^{4\frac14}$MskdScout117^{no}	Second best	6
17Apr85-	8GS	fst	$1\frac{1}{16}$	:46⅘	1:11⅗	1:43⅖	3+ⒻAlw 16000	4	1	1^{2}	1^{hd}	2^{4}	3^{9}	Lovato F	b 110	*2.90	— —	GoNotA'Rmblin112^{5}Mry'sDouble113^{4}AHotNumber110^{1}	Weakened	7
2Mar85-	8Key	fst	170	:47⅕	1:12⅗	1:43⅕	ⒻBryn Mawr	5	5	$4^{3\frac12}$	4^{4}	$5^{5\frac14}$	$5^{11\frac12}$	Lovato F	b 115	11.00	72-23	Lamsey Dotes 122$^{2\frac12}$ Plenteous 119^{2} Confirmed Affair 112^{4}	Tired	7
17Feb85-	8Key	fst	170	:46⅘	1:12⅗	1:43⅖	ⒻⓇMornngHgh	4	2	1^{hd}	2^{hd}	3^{2}	2^{6}	HampshireJFJr	b 117	3.50	77-23	LmseyDotes122^{6}AHotNumbr117$^{\frac12}$NorthEstonMiss122^{7}	Held place	5
11Feb85-	8Key	fst	170	:47⅗	1:14⅖	1:48	ⒻAlw 11500	3	2	$2^{\frac12}$	1^{4}	1^{7}	1^{9}	Lovato F	b 120	*1.40	60-26	AHotNumber120^{9}TurfGoddess120^{3}DungarvinPrincess117^{8}	Driving	7
8Jan85-	7Key	fst	170	:47⅘	1:14	1:45	ⒻAlw 11500	7	1	1^{1}	$1^{2\frac12}$	$1^{1\frac12}$	2^{3}	Lovato F	b 115	8.40	72-31	NorthEstonMiss115^{3}AHotNumber115^{10}TurfGoddess115$^{\frac34}$	2nd best	10

LATEST WORKOUTS May 21 GS 4f fst :48⅘ h May 15 GS 4f fst :48⅘ b May 2 GS 4f fst :51 b Apr 16 GS 3f fst :38⅖ b

Let's turn to the second race at Belmont on Sunday, June 16, 1985, for an example.

TOO SUNNY

Second in similar company in her only two sprint starts since leaving the maiden ranks, Too Sunny has to be respected, even though her latest rider, D. N. Moore, chose the favored Regal Lynco after being named on both fillies.

REGAL LYNCO

The 9–5 favorite is somewhat suspect in that she has not raced for a full month, with just one workout during that time, and is now dropping down below her established performance level. An uncharacteristically poor race just prior to that layoff adds to the confusion. But if jockey Moore chose Regal Lynco after that poor effort, obviously neither he nor his agent was too concerned about it, or didn't especially like Too Sunny. Note that Regal Lynco had finished in the money nine consecutive times prior to that race. Her speed figures for her three most recent good races place her in front of this field by two or three lengths if she can run back to them.

NILE FLIRT

One of three fillies coming out of the fifth race at Belmont on May 19, a mile contest for $50,000 fillies. In that race Nile Flirt raced head-to-head with Nasty Belle, outside her rival, through exceptionally fast (106–107) fractions, only to weaken slightly, and expectedly, in the stretch.

CARNEGIE HILL

This is the filly that exploited the Nile Flirt-Nasty Belle speed duel on May 19, sitting behind the dueling leaders in the early stages, then running by them when they tired. Hers was an easy trip that day. Carnegie Hill has since run far out of the money behind boom winner Rose Gayle Honey in allowance company, doing nothing in that race except to confirm that she belongs in the claiming ranks.

DANCE HALL MISS

A recent Moschera claim that failed miserably when moved up in company to today's level, Dance Hall Miss appears to have gone downhill since her recent three-month freshening.

NASTY BELLE

The second half of the May 19 speed duel, is in her first start outside the maiden ranks. However, her record hints of "seconditis"—she has never been out of the money but shows only one win in eight lifetime starts.

A HOT NUMBER

Moving well up in class after being claimed for $25,000 at Garden State, this filly appears to be a router prepping for future engagements.

The betting action for this race was quite interesting, especially as it relates to the three fillies coming out of the May 19 race. Nasty Belle received the most support, with the June 16 audience establishing her as their 3–1 second choice. Carnegie Hill started at 5–1, and Nile Flirt at almost 9–1. Considering that neither Nasty Belle nor Carnegie Hill had the early speed to make them reliable win bets at six furlongs, and that Nile Flirt had the more difficult outside trip on May 19 when she was narrowly edged by Nasty Belle, the odds easily could have gone the other way. Indeed, Nile Flirt had to be regarded as the "horse to watch" coming out of the May 19 race.

Despite her outside trip, she was ahead of Nasty Belle for more than seven furlongs that day.

One could react to the betting action on June 16 by concluding that "someone really likes Nasty Belle today," or fearing that "the stable doesn't like Nile Flirt." Or by seizing the occasion to make a good bet on a horse that seems to be a huge overlay. Inexplicable betting patterns like this occur regularly, and the player must have the courage of his own convictions to exploit them.

We conclude our analysis on a confusing note. The predictability of the June 16 race is clouded by uncertainty regarding the pace of the race. Coming out of a route, Nile Flirt's early speed might be dulled somewhat. Nor can we count on either Regal Lynco or Dance Hall Miss to set the pace, their overall form being suspect. When the identity of the early leaders is unknown, the serious player is best advised to be cautious—and to play a horse with at least a modicum of early speed, such as Nile Flirt. The pace situation in the June 16 race really did not favor closers such as Nasty Belle and Carnegie Hill. It is difficult to make up a lot of ground in the stretch when the front-runners are not tiring.

Nile Flirt did in fact rally from midpack to win this race, returning $19.80 to her scattered backers.

SECOND RACE
Belmont
JUNE 16, 1985

6 FURLONGS. (1.08⅘) CLAIMING. Purse $20,000. 3-year-old fillies. Weights, 121 lbs. Non-winners of two races since May 15 allowed 3 lbs. Of a race since then 5 lbs. Claiming Price $50,000; for each $2,500 to $45,000, 2 lbs. (Races when entered to be claimed for $40,000 or less not considered.)

Value of race $20,000; value to winner $12,000; second $4,400; third $2,400; fourth $1,200. Mutuel pool $101,201, OTB pool $93,077. Quinella Pool $150,764. OTB Quinella Pool $165,275.

Last Raced	Horse	Eqt.	A.	Wt	PP	St	¼	½	Str	Fin	Jockey	Cl'g Pr	Odds $1
19May85 ^{5}Bel^3	Nile Flirt	b	3	112	3	6	4½	5½	5^1	1¾	Alvarado R Jr†	45000	8.90
6Jun85 ^{9}Bel^5	Dance Hall Miss		3	112	5	1	3^4	3^1	2½	2^{nk}	Maple E	45000	11.20
15May85 ^{5}Bel^6	Regal Lynco		3	111	2	4	1^{hd}	1^2	1^3	3½	Moore D N^5	50000	1.90
6Jun85 ^{4}GS^4	A Hot Number		3	105	7	3	6^{1½}	4½	3½	4^{nk}	Espinosa R E^7	45000	10.80
19May85 ^{5}Bel^2	Nasty Belle	b	3	107	6	7	7	6^2	6^4	5^{4¼}	Privitera R^5	45000	3.20
6Jun85 ^{9}Bel^2	Too Sunny		3	111	1	2	2^{2½}	2^2	4^{hd}	6^{3¾}	Alvarez A^5	50000	4.00
26May85 ^{2}Bel^6	Carnegie Hill	b	3	114	4	5	5^{hd}	7	7	7	Cordero A Jr	45000	4.90

OFF AT 1:32 Start good, Won driving. Time, :22⅗, :46, 1:11⅘ Track sloppy.

$2 Mutuel Prices:				
	3-(D)-NILE FLIRT	19.80	10.00	4.80
	7-(H)-DANCE HALL MISS		12.60	5.20
	2-(C)-REGAL LYNCO			3.20

$2 QUINELLA 3-7 PAID $119.00.

B. f, by Upper Nile—Brazen Flirt, by Brazen Brother. Trainer Nickerson Victor J. Bred by McLean & Miller Jr (Ky).

NILE FLIRT rallied along the inside after entering the stretch, came out between horses to continue her bid and outfinished DANCE HALL MISS. The latter, never far back while racing well out in the track, continued on with good courage. RGAL LYNCO showed good early foot, shook off TOO SUNNY approaching the stretch but weakened during the drive. A HOT NUMBER, wide into the stretch, failed to seriously menace with a mild late response. NASTY BELLE hesitated at the start, split horses leaving the turn but failed to be a serious factor while making up ground late. TOO SUNNY, a factor to the stretch, drifted out while tiring. CARNEGIE HILL was always outrun.

Chapter 41

Toward More Comprehensive Speed Figures

MOST OF THE INTERESTING new handicapping ideas I've come across in the past couple of years have had something to do with pace and its relationship to final time. We will begin this chapter by discussing just three of these ideas.

At Handicapping Expo '84, Howard Sartin spoke of his theory of incremental velocity and energy distribution. He described how individual horses tended to distribute their energy between the pace and stretch portions of a race consistently from race to race. And how the racing surface itself, on any given day, places certain demands on energy distribution that a horse must meet, or face an uphill climb to the winner's circle. Unfortunately, I have had neither the time nor the data base to test Sartin's theories myself. However, I do find them quite fascinating and would recommend that the interested reader take a closer look.

At the same conference, Andy Beyer expressed an interest in having a formula that combined pace and final time into one all-encompassing number rating a horse's performance. Prior to the conference, I had developed a categorical approach to such a formula. Upon closer study, though, I found that it tended to leak at its seams, where the various categories overlapped. Subsequent research, however, has led to the development of the formula that will be discussed later in this chapter.

More recently, the performance of Spend A Buck in the 1985 Jersey Derby raised some controversy related to the effect of pace on final time. Speed handicappers decried his slow final time. Pace advocates, on the other hand, looked at the race differently, crediting Spend A Buck for much more than gameness under fire. To them, quick pace figures compensated for, even predicted, the colt's final time for the race.

We will begin our discussion of pace with Spend A Buck and his figures for the Jersey Derby and his two races immediately preceding that contest:

Spend A Buck B. c. 3, by Buckaroo—Belle De Jour, by Speak John
Own.—Hunter Farm Br.—Harper & Irish Hill Farm (Ky) Tr.—Gambolati Cam
127 Lifetime 13 9 2 2 $3,998,509 1985 5 4 0 1 $3,330,524 1984 8 5 2 1 $667,985

27May85- 9GS fst 1¼ :45⅗ 1:35 2:02⅘ Jersey Dby 5 1 1hd 1½ 1½ 1nk Pincay L Jr 126 *.05 — — Spend A Buck 126nk Creme Fraiche 126hd El Basco 1264¾ Driving 9
27May85-Grade III
4May85- 8CD fst 1¼ :45⅘ 1:34⅘ 2:00⅕ Ky Derby 10 1 16 16 15 15¼ Cordero A Jr 126 4.10 96-08 SpendABuck1265¼Stephn'sOdyssey126½Chif'sCrown126nk Driving 13
4May85-Grade I
20Apr85- 8GS fst 1⅛ :45⅗ 1:09⅘ 1:45⅘ Garden State 2 1 13½ 13 16 19½ Cordero A Jr 122 *.40 — — SpendABuck1229½IAmTheGme1175½DoItAginDn115nk Ridden out 9
6Apr85- 8GS fst 1 :45⅗ 1:10 1:35⅘ Chrry Hill H 7 1 12½ 12 16 110½ Cordero A Jr 122 1.70 — — Spend ABuck12210½IAmTheGame115¾KingBabar1161¼ Ridden out 14
23Mar85- 8Aqu fst 7f :22⅘ :45⅗ 1:22⅕ Bay Shore 1 6 31 41¼ 34½ 35½ Cordero A Jr 123 *1.40 84-23 PnchoVill1143¾ElBsco1141¾SpendABuck1232 Wknd under impost 9
23Mar85-Grade II
10Nov84- 1Hol fst 1 :45 1:10 1:36⅕ Br Cp Juv 3 1 1hd 12½ 11 31½ Cordero A Jr 122 6.40 — — Chief'sCrown122¾Tnk'sProspect122¾SpndABuck122¾ Weakened 10
10Nov84-Grade I
18Oct84- 8Med fst 1 1/16 :46 1:11⅕ 1:45 Yng America 4 1 11½ 11 1½ 2¾ Cordero A Jr 122 *1.00 83-22 Script Ohio 119¾ Spend A Buck 122nk Tank'sProspect1192 Gamely 11
18Oct84-Grade I
22Sep84- 9AF fst 1 :44⅘ 1:10 1:38 Arl Was Fut 6 3 21 2hd 1½ 1½ Hussey C 122 2.90 71-24 Spend A Buck 122½ Dusty's Darby 1222½ Viva Maxi 1221¾ All out 7
22Sep84-Grade I; Grade I
2Sep84-11RD fst 1 1/16 :47⅘ 1:12 1:45⅕ M H Cradle 6 2 11 14 18 115 Hussey C 120 *1.20 80-18 Spend A Buck 12015 Grand Native 1206 Alex's Game 120nk Easily 13
16Aug84- 7Crc fst 6f :22⅘ :46⅕ 1:12⅘ Alw 15000 1 1 11½ 14 16 19½ Hussey C 112 *.50 87-23 Spend A Buck 1129½ Secret Goal 1129½Mr.Introienne1143 Handily 5
LATEST WORKOUTS ●Jly 25 Mth 3f fst :34 b Jly 16 Mth 7f fst 1:22 b ●Jly 9 Mth 5f fst :58 h Jly 2 Mth 4f fst :48⅘ b

	Half Mile	*3/4 Mile*	*Final*	*Total*
Jersey Derby	126	123	112	361
Kentucky Derby	123	136	123	382
Garden State	126	128	125	379

There is a popular term making the rounds these days, called the "tiring linear constant," or TLC for short. As I understand the concept, it has nothing to do with the (false) notion that horses tire, or decelerate, at a linear rate (especially during the stretch run). Rather, the TLC is telling us that an incremental change in pace velocity (either faster or slower than normal) will have a predictable linear effect on final time. If a horse runs faster than it is accustomed to early, its final time will probably suffer as a result, and by a predictable amount linearly related to the difference in pace. This fact manifests itself quite simply through the type of speed and pace figures advocated in *Thoroughbred Handicapping—State of the Art.* Theoretically, it predicts that the sum of a horse's speed and pace figures should remain constant from race to race, everything else being equal. In fact, reality closely approximates the theory. Based on a considerable number of case studies (see Chapter 10 of *Thoroughbred Handicapping*), I found that this total varies with a small standard deviation of three points for sprints and between four and five points for routes (with two pace figures contributing to the totals). The small differences could easily be explained by "everything else not being equal."

One can easily see, then, that Spend A Buck's races in the Garden State and the Kentucky Derby were quite close, reflecting the same level of fitness and performance, but that the horse fell off dramatically in the Jersey Derby. Why? Clearly his pace figures in the Jersey Derby were no faster (actually, they were slower) than they were for his previous two races. Why, then, did his final time figure drop off so much?

The answer is quite simple. The pace in the Jersey Derby was contested, while in both the Garden State and Kentucky Derby, Spend A Buck galloped along on an unchallenged early lead. The early pressure obviously had an effect on the horse's final time in the Jersey Derby, and this is something handicappers must keep in mind. Early fractions alone do not tell the entire story. Competition for the early lead is also a vital part of the equation, albeit one that is difficult to quantify.

When the speed handicapper establishes a rating for a front runner, he must make sure that figure is based (whenever possible) on races in which the horse faced a pace situation similar to what it will encounter today. If the expected pace figures to be fast, how has the horse functioned in the past when faced with severe early pressure? If the pace projects slow, or uncontested, what kind of figure is the horse capable of producing when allowed to relax early?

Pace—or energy distribution—can provide speed handicappers with some needed insight when calculating their daily variants. For example, suppose a day's racing resulted in the following deviations from par figures for a set of five sprint races:

FAST	3
FAST	4
SLOW	2
FAST	3
FAST	2

How does the player handle these numbers? Does he simply strike a numerical average, ignoring the fact that one of the five is "different"? Four of the five races suggest quite convincingly that the track was FAST 3. However, if the one out-of-line race is included in the calculations, the average becomes FAST 2, distorting the player's figures for the day by a full length. Let's look at how pace might bring this picture into sharper focus. Here are the same five sprint races, this time with pace deviations from par included:

Pace	Final Time
FAST 2	FAST 3
FAST 1	FAST 4
FAST 6	SLOW 2
EVEN	FAST 3
FAST 1	FAST 2

Now we can see that the exceptionally slow final time for the third race resulted from an especially fast pace for that day. But note that the sum of the pace and final-time deviations from par for this race total FAST 4, which just happens to match the day's average. Under closer scrutiny, therefore, we have determined track speed, modulo energy distribution. Clearly the running times for the third race agree with the speed of the racetrack that day, yet must be ignored when calculating the day's variant because of the unusual energy distribution in that race. Consequently, we can estimate that the day was FAST 3 for final times, and FAST 1 for the half-mile pace call. With base figures established using these guidelines, ratings for the third race will reflect the exceptionally fast pace and slow final time for the race.

And now, to address the possibility of a "magic formula" that combines pace and final-time figures into one number that rates a horse's overall performance. One's first inclination would be to add a horse's pace and speed figures, but this approach unfairly penalizes come-from-behind types whose pace figures as a rule come up relatively weak. What we would like instead is a formula that relates a horse's running style to the "shape of the race," something that would give a speed horse more credit for battling an exceptionally fast pace and a stretch-runner more points for overcoming a particularly slow pace. Indeed, a formula that will make use of a horse's stretch "figure" as well as its early speed and final time.

Although what follows might seem rather complex to some readers, it is actually a relatively simple process to implement on a programmable calculator or microcomputer. The main formula (for sprints) is a short one:

RATING = WT1 * PA + WT2 * SR + WT3 * STR

being the total of the horse's pace, final time, and stretch figures, each weighted differently. How do we calculate the components of the formula? We start with the pace and speed figures for the race itself, call them PACE and SPEED, respectively, and then calculate:

$$\text{DELTA} = \text{PACE} - \text{SPEED}$$

and

$$\text{LQTR} = \text{PAR} - \text{DELTA}$$

where PAR is the race's par time figure, LQTR rates the stretch run of the race, and DELTA very crudely describes the "shape of the race." For any horse in that race, we can calculate:

$$\begin{aligned} \text{PA} &= \text{PACE} - \text{BLF}/2 \\ \text{SR} &= \text{SPEED} - \text{BLR}/2 \\ \text{STR} &= \text{LQTR} + (\text{BLF}-\text{BLR})/2 \end{aligned}$$

where BLF represents the number of lengths behind at the half, and BLR the number of lengths beaten in the race. Therefore, BLF—BLR is just the "stretch gain" or "stretch loss," as the case may be.

The three weights are defined as follows, supporting the tremendous significance of early speed on the outcome of races:

$$\begin{aligned} \text{WT1} &= 4.0 + \text{DELTA}/10 \\ \text{WT2} &= 1.0 - \text{DELTA}/20 \\ \text{WT3} &= 1.0 - \text{DELTA}/20 \end{aligned}$$

Note that as things worked out, the second and third weights turned out to be equal.

By way of example, suppose that we have a "FAST–SLOW" race shape with:

$$\begin{aligned} \text{PAR} &= 106 \\ \text{PACE} &= 108 \\ \text{SPEED} &= 104 \end{aligned}$$

We then calculate:

$$\begin{aligned} \text{DELTA} &= 108 - 104 = 4 \\ \text{LQTR} &= 106 - 4 = 102 \end{aligned}$$

with the last number being relatively low compared to the race par, suggesting that the last quarter was run rather slowly.

Our weights then become:

$$\begin{aligned} \text{WT1} &= 4.0 + 4/10 = 4.4 \\ \text{WT2} &= 1.0 - 4/20 = 0.8 \\ \text{WT3} &= 1.0 - 4/20 = 0.8 \end{aligned}$$

suggesting that in such a race (shape), early speed is more significant than usual, and a strong stretch run may be an optical illusion.

If we take a horse that was four lengths behind at the (half mile) pace call, then only two lengths behind at the finish, we calculate:

$$\begin{aligned} PA &= 108 - 4/2 = 106 \\ SR &= 104 - 2/2 = 103 \\ STR &= 102 + (4-2)/2 = 103 \end{aligned}$$

and then rate the horse:

$$RATING = 4.4 * 106 + 0.8 * 103 + 0.8 * 103 = 631.2$$

On the other hand, a horse that led at the pace call, only to fade six lengths in the stretch, would have figures:

$$\begin{aligned} PA &= 108 - 0/2 = 108 \\ SR &= 104 - 6/2 = 101 \\ STR &= 102 + (0-6)/2 = 99 \end{aligned}$$

and be rated

$$RATING = 4.4 * 108 + 0.8 * 101 + 0.8 * 99 = 635.2$$

Note that in this race, the horse that faded in the stretch rated higher than the one with the apparent stretch kick—and that this is reasonable, indeed desirable, considering the shape of the race. We emphasize that our formula was constructed to intelligently measure a horse's performance against the shape of the race in which it competed.

Does the formula work? At the moment, it is just a theory being proposed. I have no data base that contains accurate pace and speed figures on which to run a test. The concept sounds good—great care was taken to find a formula that did the right thing at the right time, from a handicapping point of view. How it performs in actual practice, only time will tell.

How the ratings should be used is an open question. Should a horse's final number be based on the average of (say) its last three ratings? Can a projected pace figure for today's race somehow be factored in, adjusting each horse's final rating to the race shape it is expected to encounter? How should route races be handled? Should the two pace figures be combined, as above, into one pace number, which can then be combined, again as above, with the final-time figure into one number rating the horse's overall performance in the race? Obviously we have only touched the surface in this chapter.

In the final analysis, though, one must ask whether one number is better than the two or three it summarizes. Or do the components together offer more, painting a picture of how a race was run that can be more valuable than one rather unsuggestive number rating a performance?